P_0 Put value at date 0

P Price of security

P_i Probability of state i

rf Continuously compound risk-free rate

RF Discrete compound risk-free rate

r_{ij} Correlation coefficient between security i and j

R_t Return in period t

$\overline{R}$ Arithmetic average return

ROE Return on Equity

RP_M Risk premium on the Market Portfolio

S_0 Spot asset value at date 0

σ^2 Variance of security returns

σ Standard deviation of returns

S_p Sharpe performance measure

$S_t^{d/f}$ Spot exchange rate domestic per foreign at date t

T_p Treynor performance measure

UV_T Unit value at date T

X Option exercise price

X_i Percentage invested in security i

INVESTMENT

CONCEPTS

ANALYSIS

STRATEGY

Fifth Edition

Robert C. Radcliffe

University of Florida

 **ADDISON-WESLEY**

An imprint of Addison Wesley Longman, Inc.

Reading, Massachusetts • Menlo Park, California • New York • Harlow, England
Don Mills, Ontario • Sydney • Mexico City • Madrid • Amsterdam

Acquisitions Editor: *Joan Cannon*
Director of Development: *Arlene Bessenoff*
Developmental Editor: *Rebecca Kohn*
Supplements Editor: *Julie Zasloff*
Text Design and Project Management: *Interactive Composition Corporation*
Cover Design: *Kay Petronio*
Cover Photograph: *Photodisk, Inc.*
Art Studio: *Interactive Composition Corporation*
Electronic Production Manager: *Eric Jorgensen*
Manufacturing Manager: *Hilda Koparanian*
Electronic Page Makeup: *Interactive Composition Corporation*
Printer and Binder: *RR Donnelley & Sons Company*
Cover Printer: *The Lehigh Press, Inc.*

For permission to use copyrighted material, grateful acknowledgment is made to the copyright holders on p. 905-906, which are hereby made part of this copyright page.

Library of Congress Cataloging-in-Publication Data

Radcliffe, Robert C.
    Investment: Concepts, Analysis, Strategy/Robert C. Radcliffe. –5th ed.
        p.   cm.
    Includes bibliographical references and index.
    ISBN 0-673-99988-2
    1. Investments.   2. Investment analysis.   3. Securities.
4. Speculation.   I. Title.
HG4521.R26   1996
332.63'2—dc20   96-569
                                                         CIP

ISBN 0-673-99988-2

45678910—DOC—020100

TO THE GRANDCHILDREN: PRESENT AND FUTURE

BRIEF CONTENTS

CONTENTS

Part 1 Introduction   1

1

2

Investment Decisions 28

3

Investment Types 71

4

Investment Markets 118

Part 2 Investment Concepts   161

5

Basic Investment Concepts 163

6

7

Capital Asset Pricing Model 256

8

Capital Asset Pricing Extensions 292

9

Efficient Market Theory 331

Part 3 Security Analyses   371

10

Valuation of Fixed Income Securities 373

11

Management of Fixed Income Securities 417

12

Valuation of Equity Securities 469

13

Management of Equity Securities 506

14

Commingled Investment Portfolios 557

15

Global Investment 599

16

Financial Futures 643

17

Options 689

Part 4 Strategy   739

18

The Process of Investment Management 741

19

Asset Allocation 775

20

Manager Selection and Taxes 810

21

Performance Monitoring 846

PREFACE

Instructors and students who seek moderately advanced coverage of investments, yet highly interactive pedagogy and presentation, will no doubt appreciate the fifth edition of *Investment: Concepts • Analysis • Strategy*. This edition continues to reflect the educational objectives of preceding editions. Principal among these goals are:

• To integrate practical applications with theoretical concepts,

• To stress the economic rationale and intuition for important investment concepts, and

• To cultivate the reader's appreciation for well-functioning security markets in today's world.

This book is aimed primarily at graduate and undergraduate students who are considering a professional career in finance. This text, however, is also used extensively in courses geared to individual investors who wish to make better personal investment decisions. A major goal of this revision has been to improve the learning experience of both types of readers. In particular, I increased coverage of investment situations and problems faced by individual investors.

Another goal of this revision has been to provide a more user-friendly presentation by reducing the amount of mathematics and expanding discussion of the economic intuition underlying investment concepts. Even the best students can get so caught up in mathematical details that they miss the more important economic principles.

Common Themes with Prior Editions

Each of the editions of *Investment* has had a number of common themes that both professors and students find useful. These include:

• *Asset Allocation.* The fifth edition continues to stress the importance of asset allocation. Principles are presented earlier in this edition in a new Chapter 2. A realistic asset allocation study is conducted in Chapter 6. Part 4 of the text is devoted to many practical issues associated with developing and implementing an asset allocation strategy. Software support and extensive databases are available to help students conduct professional asset allocation studies, investment manager searches, and tests of historical manager performance.

• *Practical Applications.* This edition continues to integrate practical issues with theoretical concepts. This is done by presenting realistic investment scenarios, using actual market data to illustrate concepts in both chapter examples and end-of-chapter problems, and expanding the use of the CFA exam questions at the end of each chapter. Many of the investment scenarios and examples used in the book come from actual consulting studies which I have conducted for various defined contribution and defined benefit pension plans.

Major Content Changes in the Fifth Edition

I focused on the following significant improvements for this edition:

- *Balanced coverage of individual and institutional investing.* While previous editions of this text were oriented towards professional institutional investors, this edition presents a more balanced discussion. Differences in the investment situations faced by institutional and individual investors are discussed along with many topics presented from the viewpoint of both types of investor.

- *International component.* Previously titled *International Investing,* the new Chapter 15, *Global Investment,* simplifies the discussion of international parity relationships, shows how the different parity conditions are interrelated, and includes a new section on emerging markets.

- *Reorganization.* I reorganized the content to merge similar topics in one section and to avoid unnecessary repetition. The material in the former Chapter 9, *Derivative Securities,* has been integrated into the futures and options chapters. Coverage of security market indexes, previously in Chapter 4, has been tightened up and the resulting space devoted to other more important topics.

- *Expanded coverage of mortgage markets.* A new appendix to Chapter 11 examines the way in which mortgage-backed securities are formed and traded. In addition, coverage of mortgage-backed securities in Chapter 3 has been expanded.

- *NEW! Chapter 2 - Investment Decisions.* This chapter presents an up-front review of the major decisions that all investors, individual or institutional, must make. These include: "How should assets be allocated?" "How should assets be managed?" and "Who should manage assets?" This is done from the perspective of three different investors: a young individual investor, a large pension fund, and a newly formed mutual fund.

- *Expanded coverage of securities.* Chapter 3, *Security Types,* and Chapter 4, *Security Markets,* examine types of asset classes available to investors as well as how transactions in the primary and secondary markets are conducted. Coverage of mortgage-backed securities, mutual funds, and international investing has been expanded. The explanation of margin trading has been totally rewritten and expanded using a balance sheet approach. A section on transaction costs has been added. This section includes bid-ask spreads, typical full-service and discount commission costs, and price impacts of large trades and the tax consequences of trading.

- *NEW! Chapter 14 - Commingled Investment Portfolios.* Due to the growing importance of commingled portfolios, I have added this new chapter to the Fifth Edition. It covers mutual funds and closed-end funds and provides a general overview of other products provided by professional investment management firms.

- A new appendix has been added to Chapter 6 showing that the longer the investment horizon, the greater the need for diversification.

- *NEW! Chapter 20 - Manager Selection and Taxes.* Historically, manager searches have been a very important issue to institutional investors, particularly pension trustees who employ multiple managers to invest fund assets. The principles that underlie institutional manager searches, however, also apply to individual investors who need to select managers within their defined contribution pension plans, make investments in mutual funds, or participate in a broker's wrap program. Taxation is also covered in this chapter because it is closely intertwined with the decision to manage a portfolio personally or to hire an external manager.

- *Investor interviews*. The Fourth Edition included a number of interviews with professional investors that were so positively received, we decided to include one in every chapter for this edition. Some interviews show how a chapter concept applies in actual investment situations, others provide insights about careers in investment management, and yet others simply offer an insider's view on a particular investing issue.

  In developing the list of individuals to be interviewed, we aimed at creating a diverse set of interviews. We sought diversity in the career paths investors followed, in the stages in their careers, and in their preferred analytic techniques. Each interviewee is highly respected in his or her field. These contributors deserve special recognition because each person interviewed did so solely with the desire to increase students' understanding of how investment markets operate and which career paths are available.

  Anne C. Christ, CFA, was in charge of arranging and conducting the interviews. Anne's broad knowledge of all aspects of the professional investment community greatly enhanced our efforts to bring some "real life" into an academic text. I thank the following individuals for providing interviews.

Individual Interviewed	Professional Organization
Steve Cusimano, CFA	Florida State Board of Administration
Gautam Dhingra, CFA	Hewitt Associates, LLC
Dan DiBartolomeo	Northfield Information Services
Todd Doersch	BARRA, Inc.
Ann Dominic, CFA	MCI Communications Corporation
Ron Frashure, CFA	Acadian Asset Management
Warren Isabelle, CFA	Pioneering Management Corporation
Dennis Johnson, CFA	Peachtree Asset Management
David Kushner, CFA	ICC Capital Management, Inc.
Mark Kritzman, CFA	Windham Capital Management
John Markese	American Association of Individual Investors
Adolfo Marzol	Fannie Mae
Patricia McQueen	Association for Investment Management and Research
Tom Murphy	MJ Meehan & Company
Robert Penter, CFA	Hewitt Associates LLC
Robert C. Puff, Jr., CFA	Twentieth Century Companies
Alex Saitta	Salomon Brothers Inc.
John Schiavetta, CFA	Fitch Investor Services
Charles Smithson	CIBC Wood Gundy
Donna Terry, CFA	Barnett Capital Advisors
Janet Tussing	Albanese, Hemsley & Tussing

Charles Tschampion, CFA   GM Investment Corp.
Eric Wetlaufer, CFA   Cadence Capital Management

Text Organization

The general organization of the book remains the same as in the previous edition. Chapter content within each section, however, is somewhat different.

PART 1 - INTRODUCTION

The chapters in Part 1 provide an overview of how the security markets are structured and the economic benefits provided by these markets (Chapter 1); the decisions that all investors, individual or institutional, must make (Chapter 2); the types of securities traded in world markets (Chapter 3); and how market transactions are conducted (Chapter 4).

PART 2 - INVESTMENT CONCEPTS

Major investment concepts that underlie security selection and valuation are presented in Part 2. Chapter 5, *Investment Concepts,* discusses the determinants of the nominal risk-free rate and provides an overview of the standard deviation of portfolio returns. For this edition, I have added a discussion of the relationship between portfolio risk and the investment horizon. This chapter demonstrates that portfolio risk clearly increases with the investment horizon, a statement that contradicts the widely-held belief that risk decreases as the investment horizon increases. The chapter concludes with a discussion of how the investment horizon might influence the investor's asset allocation.

Chapters 6 through 8 continue the discussion of portfolio theory, the capital asset pricing model (CAPM), and extensions to CAPM such as arbitrage pricing theory and multi-beta models. A new appendix to Chapter 6 shows that the longer the investment horizon, the greater the need for diversification. A new discussion in Chapter 7 examines the market capitalization of the U.S. equity market and how well indexes such as the S&P 500, the Wilshire 5000, and the Russell 3000 capture this market. Part 2 concludes with an updated chapter on efficient markets theory. The major change in this chapter is a critique of Shiller's hypothesis that equity market prices are too volatile.

PART 3 - ANALYSES

The eight chapters in Part 3 discuss each security type in detail. Fixed income securities and equities are covered in the first two chapters, with one chapter devoted to valuation and the other devoted to management of the security from both an individual investor's and an institutional investor's viewpoint. Equity valuation is presented in Chapter 12. Most of Chapter 13 is devoted to fundamental security analysis; however, that chapter now has separate sections that cover the unique issues facing individual investors versus institutional investors. A new checklist of a top-down fundamental security analysis is presented and discussed in detail. I have also added a fundamental analysis illustrating the recent history of IBM. The new Chapter 14, *Commingled Investment Portfolios,* reviews the professional management business and the various ways in which individual investors can employ professional managers to run a part, or all, of their portfolios. Chapter 15 on global investment simplifies the discussion of international parity relationships and shows how the different parity conditions are interrelated. A new section on emerging markets has been added. The last two chapters in this part provide a complete discussion of financial futures and options integrating material from the last edition's chapter on derivative securities.

PART 4 - STRATEGY

Part 4 concludes the book with four chapters devoted to the practical aspects of developing an investment strategy. Chapter 18 discusses the portfolio investment process as well as the formal statement of investment policy. A variety of realistic case examples are presented. Chapter 19 includes updated coverage of strategic and tactical asset allocation. Chapter 20, *Manager Selection and Taxes,* is a new chapter that covers the principles underlying manager searches, provides an overview of security taxation, and devotes a section to tax deferral. The last chapter, *Performance Monitoring,* begins with detailed coverage of the *Performance Presentation Standards* of the Association for Investment Management and Research. This chapter includes a variety of very practical topics such as the use of cash versus accrual accounting and how management fees should be handled. A discussion of the variety of ways to evaluate performance follows. Finally, the chapter reviews empirical evidence on timing and selection, and recent research on the persistence of fund performance.

Assignments and Supplements to the Fifth Edition

Chartered Financial Analyst Exam Questions

Chartered Financial Analyst Exam Questions appear at the end of virtually every chapter. Questions are marked by an icon for quick reference. Formatted like those found in the CFA certification examination, these give students extra practice for sitting for the exam.

Datafile Analyses

When students themselves analyze actual market data, they can more readily connect investment concepts to realistic applications and can promote these analytical skills in the job market. In these Datafile Analysis assignments, students use personal computers to examine various datasets of historical security market information. Such analysis provides several pedagogical advantages over the typical end-of-chapter problems. Abstract investment ideas take shape and meaning in the real world. Students increase their awareness of types and uses of data available and enrich their knowledge of the techniques used by professional investment managers and consultants. Datafile Analyses, found at the end of each chapter, include the following:

- risk management using both naive stock diversification and asset allocation

- calculation of mean-variance efficient frontiers

- examination of the January Effect on large and small stocks

- test of the predictability of future security returns using past returns

- cross-country return correlations and global diversification

- financial statement analysis

- selection of actively managed U.S. equity mutual funds

- CAPM-based performance of U.S. equity mutual funds.

Important note: Many of these analyses are abbreviated versions of actual studies conducted by investment consultants for institutional and individual investors. Instructors can use each Datafile Analysis as a separate homework assignment, as part of an extensive term project, or as an in-class demonstration if the classroom is equipped with a computer, a liquid crystal display, and an overhead projector.

ASSETALL

CREATED BY ROBERT C. RADCLIFFE, UNIVERSITY OF FLORIDA

The ASSETALL computer package calculates mean-variance efficient frontiers for up to 50 securities based on their expected returns, standard deviations of returns, and correlation coefficients. The menu-driven program allows for three basic options. Students can: (a) create or revise an input file, (b) calculate an efficient frontier where short sales are *not* allowed, and (c) calculate an efficient frontier where short sales *are* permissible. The program automatically saves the output efficient frontiers according to the dataset name specified by the user. Students can print output files through the program itself or through the DOS print command. Although the menu commands should be sufficient, as most students can figure out how to run the program on their own, a user's manual is stored in ASCII format on the program disks for students to print and use as a reference.

A number of preprogrammed spreadsheet packages are provided that allow the student to perform a number of complex investment calculations. These include Black-Scholes option valuations (with continuous or discrete dividends), portfolio expected returns, and standard deviations for a large number of securities and forecasts of percentile terminal wealth distributions for periods of between two and sixty years.

Important note on software: Instructors should ask their Addison-Wesley representative for the IBM-compatible master disks containing the datasets and ASSETALL, *both of which are free only to adopters for students to copy and use.*

INSTRUCTOR'S MANUAL WITH TEST BANK

PREPARED BY ROBERT C. RADCLIFFE, UNIVERSITY OF FLORIDA, AND MARIANNE HITE, UNIVERSITY OF COLORADO, DENVER

To save instructors valuable lecture preparation time, the new Instructor's Manual includes a thoroughly revised Test Bank with over 200 all-new questions, documentation for dataset and ASSETALL software, supplemental handouts, and detailed solutions to end-of-chapter questions and problems. Instructors who need the Test Bank in electronic form should contact their publisher's representative for more information.

STUDY GUIDE

CREATED BY MARIANNE HITE, UNIVERSITY OF COLORADO, DENVER

More accessible to students, this guide features a section on the CFA designation and on how to use a financial calculator. To build student confidence, each chapter features the following sections: Overview, Chapter Outline, Summary of Key Concepts, Summary of Key Equations, Review Questions, Review Problems, and Test Bank, an objective item test bank for student self testing. Answers and solutions appear either at the end of the chapter or in appendices.

Acknowledgments

Truly engaging educational products are never far removed from either the classroom or the investments business. Users of previous editions, professional and academic colleagues, manuscript reviewers, supplements authors, and students have all contributed to my writing and teaching efforts in the field of investments.

In addition I would like to acknowledge the following for their helpful advice:

Gilbert Bickum, University of Western Kentucky

Eugene F. Brigham, University of Florida

Robert Brooks, University of Alabama

Young Hoon Byun, Myong Ji University

Alyce Campbell, University of Oregon

Anne Christ, BenchMark Portfolios, Inc.

Ronald Christener, Loyola University

Maureen Connors, Dimensional Fund Advisors, Inc.

Vinay Datar, Seattle University

Gautam Dhingra, Hewitt Associates, Inc.

David Distad, University of California, Berkeley

Dale Domian, Michigan State University

Frank Elston, Eastern New Mexico University

Thomas Eyssell, University of Missouri, St. Louis

James Feller, Middle Tennessee State University

John Gallo, University of Nevada, Reno

Louis C. Gapenski, University of Florida

Jerry Gramig, PI Analytics, Inc.

R. Stevenson Hawkey, Golden Gate University

Shalom Hochman, University of Houston

Joel Houston, University of Florida

Roger Huang, Vanderbilt University

Bill Jerkovsky, California State University, Northridge

Jeffrey Jewell, University of Florida

Karen Krawczyk, Arizona State University

Richard LaNear, Missouri Southern State University

Miles Livingston, University of Florida

Christopher Ma, Texas Tech University

Steven Mann, University of South Carolina

Timothy Manuel, University of Montana

Adolfo Marzol, Fannie Mae

Lalatendu Misra, University of Texas, San Antonio

Andy Naranjo, University of Florida

M. P. Narayanan, University of Michigan

M. Nimalandran, University of Florida

David Nye, University of Florida

Thomas O'Brien, University of Connecticut

Richard Ogden, PI Analytics, Inc.

Robert Pari, Bentley College

Robert Penter, Hewitt Associates, Inc.

John Pickett, Principal/EGT Inc.

Robert Ross, Drexel University

Michael Ryngaert, University of Florida

Anthony Sanders, The Ohio State University

Ed Saunders, Northeastern University
Louis Scott, University of Illinois at
    Urbana-Champaign
John Settle, Portland State University
Pat Smith, University of New Hampshire
Paul Swanson, University of Cincinnati
Janet Thatcher, University of Wisconsin-
    Whitewater
Andrew Szakmary, Southern Illinois
    University

Brian Thompson, Principal/EGT Inc.
Weston Tompkins, Hewitt Associates, Inc.
Robert Webb, University of Virginia
Robert Wood, Bridgewater College
Robert Wood, Pension Consultant
Soushan Wu, National Chiao-Tung
    University, Taiwan
Thomas Zwirlein, University of Colorado,
    Colorado Springs

Special thanks are due Lydia Moss, who helped with the typing of the manuscript, and Rebecca Kohn, who aided in reviewing and editing. A number of other individuals added significant value to the book, especially Marianne Hite, who increased the quality and utility of the supplements package, and Anne Christ, who succeeded in bringing some "real-life" into this text through the interviews of professional investors. To the investors who provided interviews I would like to thank each one of you. Your contributions will add significantly to the knowledge of students who read this text. The book team at Addison-Wesley deserves a nod for its efforts on this project: my sponsor, Joan Cannon; Arlene Bessenoff and Hun Ohm in development; and Eric Jorgensen, Lisa Kinne, and Anne Hahn in production. Finally, the person who deserves my deepest thanks is my wife, Irene. Without her patience and support, this revision could not have been completed.

R.C.R.

PART 1

Introduction

"What security-selection strategy should I follow in order to achieve the highest possible returns without bearing unacceptable risk?" This is the fundamental question faced by all investors.

The goal of any investment text should be to help the reader develop a clear idea of the pros and cons of potential selection strategies. But such strategies can be clearly understood only after one has a solid foundation in the basic concepts and analytic techniques that apply to all securities. Consequently, this text is divided into three broad areas—concepts, analysis, and strategies.

Concepts are discussed in Part 2. The major concepts include (1) why risk-free interest rates change over time, (2) what security risk is and how it can be measured, and (3) how expected security returns are related to their risks. In Part 3, we analyze the critical features of specific security instruments, including (1) bonds, (2) stocks, (3) futures, (4) options, (5) commingled portfolios and (6) global investments. Finally, Part 4 examines various strategies of portfolio management.

But before we can begin to address any of this material, there are certain fundamental issues and institutional characteristics that need to be reviewed. That is the purpose of Part 1.

In **Chapter 1,** we examine how security markets are structured and the benefits which they provide to a society. In **Chapter 2,** the three basic decisions which all investors must make are reviewed. A clear understanding of these decisions will help the reader understand the importance of materials presented in later chapters. In **Chapter 3,** the legal and economic characteristics of major types of security instruments are summarized. Finally, the ways in which security transactions take place in major U.S. markets are discussed in **Chapter 4.**

1

INTRODUCTION

*After reading this chapter you should
have an understanding of the function
and benefits created by primary
markets, secondary markets, and
professional management.*

Security markets hold a particular fascination for many people. A folklore has developed around past investors such as J.P. Morgan as well as contemporary investors such as Warren Buffet.[1] Market traders have developed their own unique language (*index arbitrage, market neutral positions, technical corrections,* etc.) Many people believe that with a little knowledge and good luck, they too can earn substantial returns.

But for all the pleasures and possible monetary rewards that investors receive from security trading, the game is played in earnest. The future welfare of individuals and institutions depends on the strategies they use to select securities.

General Overview

This book deals with investment. **We can think of an investment as the sacrifice of (certain) current wealth for (possibly uncertain) future wealth.** Since most investments have uncertain future values, investors in such assets will require positive expected future

---

[1] For example, John Pierpont Morgan is credited with personally reversing a major stock market collapse in the early 1900s by calling representatives of a number of large investment banks into his office and demanding that they become active buyers of stock. Warren Buffet started from scratch in 1956 to amass a portfolio now worth $12 billion, simply by trading stocks. If you had invested $10,000 with Warren Buffet when he began in 1956, its value today would be $95 million.

returns. Estimating the risk of an investment and determining an appropriate return to expect are major themes we discuss throughout the book.

When we define investment so broadly, then time spent studying, the purchase of land on which to grow crops, and the purchase of bonds to provide income during retirement are all forms of investment. Study represents an investment in **human capital,** purchasing land is an investment in **real assets,** and buying bonds is an investment in **financial assets.** Although the text deals almost exclusively with investment in financial assets (securities), you should recognize that the nature of a person's human capital and ownership of real assets can certainly influence his or her security investment decisions.

We explore three broad areas of security investment:

1. **Investment Concepts.** Concepts deal with issues such as (a) how should investment risk be defined and measured, (b) how can investment risk be managed, (c) what is the relationship between risk and expected returns, (d) what factors determine a security's market price, and (e) can we predict future prices.
2. **Investment Analysis.** Analysis consists of examining the economic characteristics that make a security unique and applying appropriate procedures to determine whether a security is fairly priced. We examine in detail four broad types of securities: (a) debt instruments, (b) equities, (c) derivatives, and (d) commingled portfolios.
3. **Investment Strategy.** Strategy deals with portfolio management issues. These issues include (a) how should the portfolio be invested across the various security classes that are available, (b) will the portfolio be actively managed in search of speculative profits or passively managed in expectation of earning returns solely for bearing risk, and (c) evaluating portfolio performance.

We begin with a general overview to investing in Chapters 1 through 4. Chapter 1 examines the types of existing investment markets and the economic benefits they provide. In Chapter 2, we identify and explain the importance of three decisions all investors must make if they are to have a properly planned portfolio strategy. Chapters 3 and 4 discuss the types of securities traded in world markets and the ways in which security transactions are handled.

In Chapters 5 through 9, we discuss **concepts** that provide the foundation for all analytic techniques and strategy decisions. **Analyses** of individual security classes are treated in Chapters 10 through 17. To make intelligent strategy decisions, investors must have a clear understanding of the alternatives available. Finally, building on our knowledge of concepts and security classes, we examine the issues involved in developing portfolio **strategy** for various types of investors in Chapters 18 through 21.

This chapter provides a brief overview of the structure of security markets and the economic benefits they provide. We start by identifying the types of investors who trade, the types of security markets in which they trade, and the types of investments available for trade. Then we analyze why people save and the economic benefits provided by security markets. A review of major investment management issues of the 1990s concludes the chapter.

Types of Security Investors

Any legal economic unit may transact in securities trading, including individuals, profit-oriented corporations, governmental bodies, investment companies, charitable organizations, and investment clubs. However, it is useful to identify two principal types of investors: individual investors and institutional investors. The fundamental difference between the two is the size of the portfolios involved.

Individuals usually invest in securities to develop wealth to meet their future consumption needs. Typical of these needs are a down payment on a house, funding for a child's college expenses, and retirement income. While the market value of portfolios created to meet these needs might seem large to the individual investor, they are small when compared to portfolios managed by institutional investors. For example, a $100 million portfolio would not be uncommon for an institutional investor. Organizations that control portfolios of this size typically consist of pension funds, charitable foundations, and professionally managed portfolios such as mutual funds. Some institutional portfolios are owned by very wealthy individuals, but they represent a very small fraction of the value of all securities.

In theory, both individual investors and institutional investors should use the same process of portfolio management. We review this process of portfolio management in Chapter 2 and discuss it at length in Part IV.

In practice, however, the portfolio holdings of an individual investor might differ considerably from the securities held by an institutional investor. The reasons for such differences are easy to understand. First, institutional portfolios are much larger than most individual investor portfolios; managers can afford to conduct a variety of sophisticated analyses that small investors can not afford. Second, the investment needs of the two groups might differ considerably, calling for quite different investment strategies. Finally, individual investors must consider the tax consequences of their security decisions whereas most institutional investors pay little, if any, tax.

Prior to the early 1960s, virtually all security trading was conducted by individual investors. They remain an important force in security markets today. But the role of institutional investors has grown dramatically over the past few decades. At the end of 1994, institutional investors owned about 58% of the market value of U.S. equities with individual investors owning the remaining 42%.

Who Are Institutional Investors?   When we speak of institutional investors, we have three types of organizations in mind. One consists of the portfolios managed by pension funds. These represent the retirement savings of employees of a given firm. Individuals receive significant tax advantages if they save for retirement by participating in a retirement program "sponsored" by their employer. Thus, most retirement savings are placed into employer pension funds. In the mid-1990s, about $3.0 trillion were invested in U.S. pension plans.

Another important type of institutional investor, albeit smaller than pension funds in terms of the total value of assets managed, are foundations. These are legal entities created to conduct specified philanthropic objectives. Examples include foundations created to support:

- education at a particular college or university,

- medical research for cures of various forms of cancer,

◼ book acquisitions at a local library, and

◼ activities of an organization such as the Girl Scouts of America.

Finally, professionally managed portfolios are also referred to as institutional investors. An example is the mutual fund industry. Mutual funds represent large pools of money that are managed by professional investors for shareholders of the fund. Shares of a mutual fund may be owned by both individual investors and by other institutional investors (such as a pension fund).

Does It Matter?   It is important for you to distinguish between these two investor types because the security markets are structured to meet the needs of one party or the other. Large trading networks exist to service each class of investor. For example, consider the security brokerage community at firms such as Merrill Lynch or Dean Witter. For individual investors, security brokers are often an important source of information and ideas. For institutions, security brokers are used almost exclusively to provide efficient trade execution and rarely used as a source of information.

While you may have more interest in one type of investor over another, most students of finance need to develop a broad knowledge of both.

Types of Security Markets

Figure 1-1 illustrates the general structure of the security markets. By the late 1980s, security markets had developed to the point that it was quite common for a security issuer in, say, the European Union to sell bonds denominated in U.S. dollars to anyone who wished to purchase them. Similarly, it was common for institutional investors to actively trade on security exchanges throughout the world. Transactions in today's security markets have few political borders and security market structure should be viewed from a global perspective.

The far left box in Figure 1-1 represents the actual **suppliers of capital** to financial securities markets.[2] Funds are provided by individual investors, institutional investors, and (to a smaller extent) business firms. These organizations and people pay cash in return for the ownership of a security. The securities they acquire come from one of three sources:

◼ newly issued securities,

◼ existing securities traded in public markets, and

◼ ownership claims to professionally managed security portfolios.

The far right box represents the eventual **users of capital.** These are mainly governmental bodies such as the U.S. Treasury, business firms raising capital for expansion, and households whose major borrowing is to purchase housing.

---

[2] Figure 1-1 illustrates only one facet of the overall financial market system, the security markets. There are many other equally important elements of the system of financial intermediaries. Among these are the commercial banking and insurance system.

FIGURE 1-1 STRUCTURE OF THE SECURITY MARKET

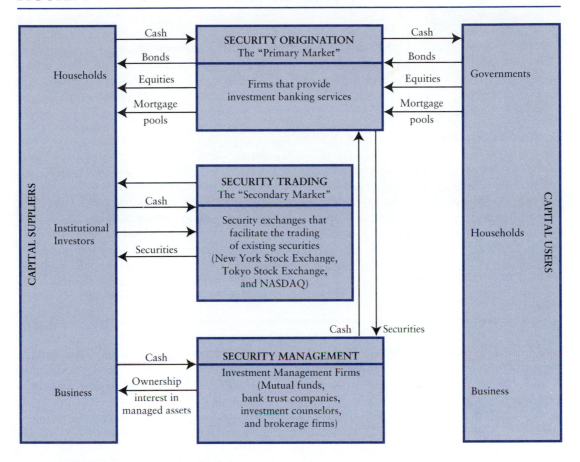

The Primary Market. The three boxes in the middle of Figure 1-1 represent three functions provided by security market financial intermediaries. The top box represents the origination of new securities in what is called the **primary market.** A variety of financial firms help those who need to obtain capital decide what type of security they should issue and identify capital suppliers who might wish to purchase the new securities. People who provide these services are called **investment bankers.** Investment banking services are provided by a wide variety of organizations including brokerage firms, mortgage bankers, and banks. Outside the United States, banks are major players in this market. Within the United States, commercial banks are just returning to this market after being excluded since the 1930s by federal regulation. Notice the arrows showing that investment bankers collect cash and deliver new securities to two types of parties: (1) the end suppliers of capital, and (2) professional portfolio managers.

The Secondary Market. The middle box represents the security trading market in which existing securities are bought and sold. This market is known as the **secondary**

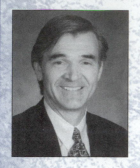

John Markese, Ph.D.

President
American Association of Individual Investors
University of Illinois, Ph.D.
University of Illinois, M.S.
University of Illinois, B.S.

The American Association of Individual Investors is an independent not-for-profit corporation formed in 1978 for the purpose of assisting individuals in becoming effective managers of their own assets through programs of education, information, and research. As a senior in high school, Mr. Markese was elected president of the investment club. Because of a new hot sports car, the Studebaker Avanti, the club invested in the automobile manufacturer. Studebaker was soon defunct. So started a lifelong interest in the study of investing and investor behavior. Before becoming president of the AAII, Mr. Markese was a finance professor and remarks that only the average age of his audience has changed.

Q: What is the most common question or problem individual investors have?

A: The primary question is how to judge an investment and how to decide among the universe of investment opportunities. In other words, they need to develop a framework of knowledge to make those decisions. The framework goes from dealing with professionals like brokers to individuals managing their own portfolios. While selecting individual investments is challenging, the most difficult part of the decision process is putting together a cohesive, meaningful, rational portfolio that makes sense in terms of an individual's long-term financial goals and also makes sense on an investment basis. Questions about this process are probably the most frequently asked. People might feel comfortable making decisions on a particular security but they might not feel comfortable with the final structure of their portfolio.

Q: So the asset allocation decision really becomes an obstacle?

A: Yes, there's the question of whether the portfolio is appropriate for their investment goals. Do these assets make sense? Every decision shouldn't be about the risk of individual assets but rather about the portfolio and how that portfolio behaves. These questions are important decisions to make. You have to develop an intuitive understanding of the markets and a framework for analysis. That's really the bottom line.

Q: For people that aren't in the investment business everyday, do you attempt to give them as much knowledge as you can so they can make the same educated decision a professional would make?

A: Exactly, but they don't need quite the detail or the quantitative models to do so. But they certainly need to put together a reasonable program to make judgments or realize when they have to hand it over to a professional. The AAII gives no investment advice; we try to build a structure and a framework. Markets are so dynamic that we have to teach basic structure because new investments are coming down the pike so quickly. The derivative issue is a good example. If investors have a firm understanding about the markets, while they might not understand a lot of the intricacies of derivatives, they should be able to grasp that they add substantial risk.

Q: But often derivatives are used to moderate risk. How do you explain that in the wake of the Orange County, California, crisis?

A: That's a very difficult question. The AAII went through that. If invested in derivatives, it's the investor's responsibility to take the time to understand what a derivative is and understand what it can do in terms of enhancing and reducing risk. In our membership only a few portfolios were using derivatives to reduce risk. On the other hand, some members would say their portfolio was fine but on closer inspection they were in mortgage investments. The investor says they're not derivatives, they're mortgages. Well, in a lot of ways they act like derivatives and embedded in a CMO might be a derivative. Securities can be labeled very innocuously. In mutual funds, for example, it's very hard to pick up a prospectus and actually understand what a fund is doing because they have a lot of latitude of action. Sensitizing investors to the issues of risk is extremely important. Everyone has an idea about return, but risk is an intangible, difficult concept to grasp. Investors don't have to know standard deviation or beta but they have to be aware of what drives a portfolio both from the asset types in the portfolio and from a market sense. Once they grasp that, they're on the road.

Q: When should a person start investing?

A: It's interesting; most people don't have the financial wherewithal or find it important until later in life. You should start investing as soon as you can. Probably the greatest mistake individual investors make is that they don't start investing early enough. It's not that they make terrible decisions; it's that they wait too long. For example, dollar cost averaging won't make you rich but it will get you going and help prevent you from putting all your money in the market at a terrible time and getting discouraged. Everyone makes bad investments but that's why we have the first rule of investing—diversification. The more education about investing people have, the more likely they are to start early, come up with a reasonable plan, and be successful in the long term. Part of the game is simply being in it.

market and consists of the various security exchanges around the world. These exchanges are of two basic types: those where all security trades take place at a specific location and those that link buyers and sellers via a computer network. An example of the former is the Tokyo Stock Exchange and of the latter is the NASDAQ (naz-dak), a computerized trading system of U.S. security dealers.

Security Management. The bottom box represents professional security management, a type of financial intermediary that has become quite important in recent years. Investment management firms offer their knowledge of different types of securities to the end suppliers of capital. For example, in the mid-1990s the California Public Employees Retirement System (known in the investment business as CalPERS) had more than $80 billion of assets invested in securities around the world in order to pay retirement benefits to employees of the state of California. Trustees of institutional portfolios such as CalPERS must decide whether the assets should be managed internally, by employees of the state, or externally, by firms that act as an agent for CalPERS. Historically, CalPERS has used both approaches.

When using external managers, the funds placed with the management firm can be **commingled** with funds of other people to purchase a jointly owned portfolio or maintained in a **separate account.**[3] The decision to commingle or not commingle funds is generally driven by cost and legal factors. Professional security management firms offer their services to both individual investors and institutional investors through products that are legally different but economically very similar. The most well-known example of professionally managed commingled portfolios are shares of mutual funds.

Types of Securities Traded

Securities traded in modern markets are of two broad types: **direct claim** and **indirect claim** instruments.

Direct Claim Instruments. Direct claim instruments provide a direct claim to the future cash flows of a "real" asset that underlies the security. These are sometimes referred to as "spot securities" and consist of debt and equity claims.

Debt claims promise (do not guarantee) to pay a rate of interest on the amount borrowed plus the return of the amount borrowed (principal). An equity claim has ownership rights to a real asset (if all promised debt claims on the asset are repaid) plus claims to all profits on the real asset (after debt interest has been paid). These securities are the basic forms of legal instruments issued by organizations in order to obtain capital.

Why are there two types of instruments issued and purchased as opposed to a single form of security? Simply because investors have different investment goals and tolerances for risk. Security issuers find that the rates of return required by capital suppliers can be minimized if they offer claims to business assets which appeal to a variety of different investor types. In fact, investment bankers have been quite facile at creating new forms of securities that appeal to different types of investors. For example, some investors wish to have both protection of principal (the amount they invest) and the opportunity to share in

---

[3] Commingled portfolios are discussed extensively in Chapter 14.

the good fortunes of the company in which they invest. A debt security with rights to buy shares at a prespecified price fits the desires of such an investor.

Debt claims are usually thought of as securities that provide a predictable series of future cash flows, periodic interest payments plus a principal payment when the debt claims mature. However, a major new form of debt claim became popular during the 1980s: the mortgage-backed security. **Mortgage backs** represent pools of individual mortgages that have low risk of default. When people in a given pool repay the interest and principal they owe, these cash flows are immediately "passed through" to owners of the mortgage pool. But even though the default risk is small, future cash flows of a mortgage-backed security can be more uncertain than other forms of debt because of uncertainty about when the end borrower will repay the principal on the loan.

Mortgage backs are a prime example of how new securities are developed to meet a societal need. In this case, mortgages had historically been held by depository institutions (banks, and savings and loans). These institutions were unable to handle the interest rate risk inherent in owning long-term debt instruments. During the volatile interest rate period of the 1970s and 1980s, the solution was to "securitize" the mortgages by placing them into large pools and selling the pools to investors in the security market. This resulted in a better match of the needs of both the capital supplier and the capital user.

Indirect Claim Instruments. The second type of financial security traded in modern markets provides an indirect claim to future cash flows of a "real" asset. This indirect claim arises because these securities have a claim to a specified spot debt or equity instrument (or a specified portfolio of debt or equity claims). These securities are referred to as "derivatives" because their value derives from the value of the direct claim security that underlies the derivative.

Futures contracts are agreements entered into today that *obligate* the buyer (seller) to purchase (sell) a specified direct claim security at a stated price on a stated future date. **Option contracts** are agreements made today that *allow but do not obligate* the option owner to buy (a call option) or sell (a put option) a specified direct claim security.

Organized markets in derivative securities were developed during the 1970s and 1980s and have become an important tool in portfolio risk management.[4]

Direct security claims (bonds and stocks) have a different economic role from derivatives (futures and options). When a debt or equity instrument is issued in the primary market, the issuer receives capital that is invested in new productive real assets. Direct claim instruments exist in order to allocate capital between those who need it and those who have it. In contrast, the trading of a derivative does not transfer capital from one party to another at the time the derivative is traded. The economic benefits created by the presence of the derivatives market comes from their use in portfolio risk management since, by trading in the derivative, one obtains an indirect position in the underlying spot security.

Assume you are a trustee for CalPERS and believe the fund's ownership position of U.S. stocks should be decreased from 40% of portfolio assets to 35% with the difference going into short-term low-risk debt. For a portfolio the size of CalPERS, equity and debt funds are usually managed by a number of different investment management firms. To

---

[4] Option and futures markets on commodities such as corn and wheat have existed for many years. In this book, we restrict our discussion to options and futures on financial assets.

FIGURE 1-2 ESTIMATES OF GLOBAL SECURITY VALUES

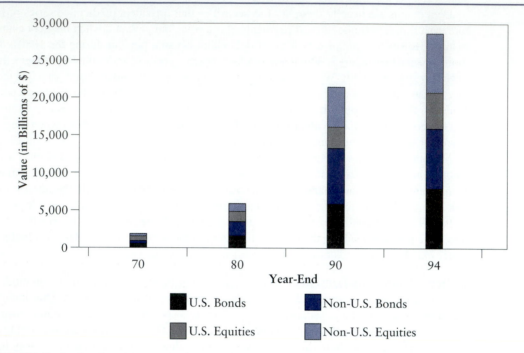

SOURCES: Equity data from Morgan Stanley Capital International Perspectives and bond data from Salomon Brothers International Bond Analysis.

accomplish the desired portfolio rebalancing you could either (1) trade in the spot securities by taking funds from equity managers and giving them to short-term bond managers, or (2) trade in stock derivatives by selling an appropriate number of stock futures contracts. The first alternative would probably be time consuming and costly. It certainly would not be favored by the managers from whom you intend to take funds. The second alternative could be accomplished at a small cost and within 30 minutes.

How Big Is the World Security Market?

During the past 25 years, the value of securities traded in world markets has increased from $1.9 trillion to more than $28.0 trillion. In this section, we develop a general overview of the global security market.

Estimates of the value of global debt and equity markets are shown in Table 1-1 and Figure 1-2 for the period 1970 through 1994. The word *estimates* must be stressed, since security values are available only for economically well-developed countries and data collection procedures have improved in recent years.[5]

---

[5] Notice that no value has been placed on derivative markets because the sum of all security value owned and all security value owed would be zero. No net real asset is created in a derivative trade. In contrast, the value placed on debt and equity securities can be thought of as the public's perception of the value of the security's underlying real assets.

TABLE 1-1   ESTIMATES OF GLOBAL SECURITY VALUES (IN BILLIONS OF U.S. DOLLARS)

	1970	1980	1990	1994
By Security Types:				
Debt Value Estimates				
U.S.	$553.8	$1,627.4	$5,927.8	$ 8,023.1
Non-U.S.	390.4	1,906.5	7,494.3	8,052.1
Total	$944.2	$3,533.9	$13,422.1	$16,075.2
Equity Value Estimates				
U.S.	$700.9	$1,380.6	$2,890.0	$ 4,898.1
Non-U.S.	309.2	1,049.3	5,367.5	8,013.5
Total	$1,010.1	$2,429.9	$8,257.5	$12,911.6
Grand Total	$1,954.3	$5,963.8	$21,679.6	$28,986.8
By Country of Origin:				
United States				
Debt	$553.8	$1,627.4	$5,927.8	$ 8,023.1
Equity	700.9	1,380.6	2,890.0	4,898.1
Total	$1,254.7	$3,008.0	$8,817.8	$12,921.2
Non-U.S.				
Debt	$390.4	$1,906.5	$7,494.3	$ 8,052.1
Equity	309.2	1,049.3	5,367.5	8,013.5
Total	$699.6	$2,955.8	$12,861.8	$16,065.6
Grand Total	$1,954.3	$5,963.8	$21,679.6	$28,986.8

SOURCES: Equity data from *Morgan Stanley Capital International Perspectives*, as well as from Roger Ibbotson and Lawrence Seigal, "The World Wealth Portfolio," *The Journal of Portfolio Management*, Winter 1983. Bond data from Salomon Brothers, *International Fixed Income Research*.

All values are shown in units of U.S. dollars. Thus, they are affected by changes in the value of the U.S. dollar relative to other currencies. For example, assume the exchange rates between U.S. dollars and U.K. pounds is 0.5 pounds per $1 at the start of the year and 0.4 pounds per $1 at the end of the year. Then a 100-pound debt obligation would be valued at $200 at the start of the year and $250 at year-end.

A review of Figure 1-2 and Table 1-1 shows the following:

◾ At the end of 1994, the estimated aggregate value of all world securities was $28,986.8 billion with the value of debt slightly greater than for equities.

◾ The value of total U.S. securities was about 45% of the world total.

▪ The aggregate value of the debt markets has grown somewhat faster than the equity markets.

But the most striking aspect is the dramatic growth that has taken place over the past 25 years. Some of this apparent growth is fictitious, since it is influenced by more reliable estimates over time as well as the decline of the U.S. dollar's value relative to other currencies. But much of the growth is real, created by both positive security returns (on average) and new security formation.

Growth of the debt market in the United States has been largely a result of the U.S. Treasury financing large federal deficits as well as the creation of the mortgage-backed security market. Security formation outside the United States came from the creation of securities used to finance the rapid growth of the international economy. The world security markets will likely continue to experience rapid growth, particularly as the economies in countries such as those in Latin and South America, Africa, the Pacific Rim, and China develop. The U.S. markets will continue to be an important global participant, but only one of many.

Why Save?

Why do people save? On first thought, this might appear to be a trivial question. Don't people save simply to increase their future wealth? While true in general terms, this answer is not precise enough to convey the true motives for saving. The economic benefits of saving are twofold: consumption smoothing and speculative opportunities.

Consumption Smoothing

First, we save in order to achieve future consumption levels higher than would be available if we were not to save. For example, a salesperson whose income is erratic from year to year will save in years of above average income in order to obtain a desired consumption level in years of depressed earnings. Similarly, we all save during our working years in order to have resources to consume in our retirement years. This motive for saving is often referred to as the *consumption smoothing motive*.

Retirement Savings. Consider the case of Claire, a recent college graduate who has just obtained a job with CDX Corp. She is presently 25 years old and will initially have a yearly after-tax income of $17,500. Although Claire will probably retire at age 65 and live until about 85, she is presently more interested in making a down payment on a new car than in her future retirement. But management at CDX realizes it is best if employees save for retirement throughout their working careers. Therefore, CDX makes yearly contributions to a pension plan for each of its employees.

The **goal** of the CDX pension plan is **to provide a yearly retirement benefit equal to an employee's career average annual after-tax income.**

The **basic question** management must answer is, **what fraction of Claire's after-tax yearly income should be invested in order to meet its investment goal?**

Naturally, the answer depends on assumptions made. The following assumptions appeared to be reasonable in Claire's case:

> All projections will be made in today's dollars; inflation will not be considered.
> Yearly real (before inflation) salary growth will be 2%.
> Real investment returns of 6% per year during employment.
> Real investment returns after-tax of 2% per year during retirement. (Claire would probably take small investment risk during retirement and, thus, would earn a lower return.)
> Retirement will start after age 65.
> Death is expected at age 85.

It is a relatively simple task to use a computer spreadsheet package to find an answer to the question facing CDX management.

"11.55% of after-tax salary must be saved every year in order to provide the desired retirement benefit."

In Figure 1-3, various elements of this savings plan are shown. Yearly after-tax income, consumption, and savings are shown in the top panel. Notice that savings become negative during retirement. This represents the withdrawal of funds from Claire's retirement portfolio required to provide her yearly consumption once she is retired. In the bottom panel, the expected value of her portfolio is shown from age 25 to age 85. At the end of age 25, this value is simply the savings made during that year. In future years until retirement is reached, the portfolio grows due to 6% interest earnings on the prior year's value plus any new savings made during the year. Beginning at age 66, the portfolio is assumed to earn a return of 2% on its beginning value each year after which it is reduced by withdrawals for consumption.

Everything in this model is assumed to occur at year-end; there is no uncertainty built into the model. While these conditions are not realistic, the example provides a reasonable start at evaluating Claire's savings needs.

What can we learn from this example? Notice that, even though the savings plan starts at the relatively young age of 25 years, more than 11% of Claire's yearly after-tax income is needed to accomplish the retirement benefit goal. If the savings plan is started at a later date, either the savings rate or the expected investment return would have to be increased.

Notice also that a large part of the investment portfolio comes from investment earnings. In the bottom panel of Figure 1-3, the accumulated savings before any interest earnings is shown as the curve that ends at age 65. By age 65, a total of $126,500 would have been invested. But with investment earnings, the portfolio value at age 65 is about $436,000.

Finally, notice that Claire, who does not have aspirations to unusually large yearly incomes during her life, will still be faced with managing a fairly large portfolio by the time she retires.[6] The management of a $436,000 portfolio should be taken very seriously.

---

[6] This is probably an overstatement. Some of her retirement income will probably come from social security. But regardless of the source, she will need assets worth about $436,000 at age 65 to provide the desired retirement income level. It should also be noted that this example does not include effects of inflation on her retirement income.

FIGURE 1-3 RETIREMENT PLANNING

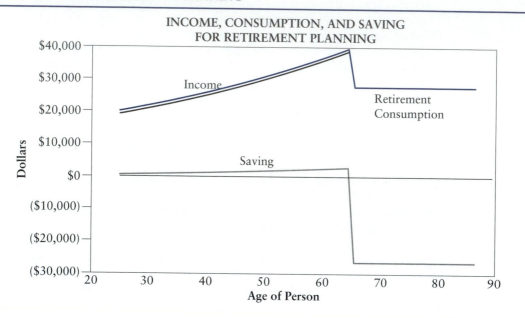

INCOME, CONSUMPTION, AND SAVING
FOR RETIREMENT PLANNING

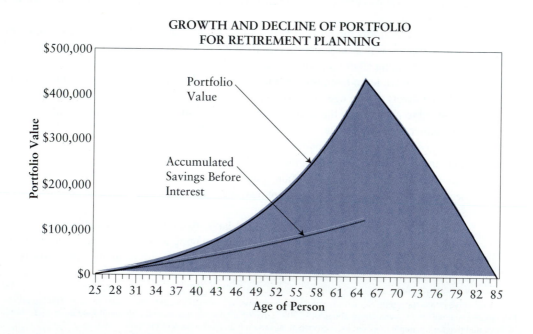

GROWTH AND DECLINE OF PORTFOLIO
FOR RETIREMENT PLANNING

Speculative Opportunities

Let's return to the question of why people save. In addition to consumption smoothing, people save in order to take advantage of potential speculative opportunities. In this book, the term *speculation* does not refer to the amount of risk taken. In fact, a speculation could have very little risk or considerable risk. A **speculation** is a situation in which the expected security return is different from the expected returns on other securities having similar risk.

To illustrate, assume you have just finished an analysis of short-term debt issues of two municipal government debt issues, say a one-year maturity Boston issue and a similar Pittsburgh issue. You conclude they have identical degrees of risk. But they are priced such that the Boston issue is expected to provide an 8% return during the next year and the Pittsburgh issue is expected to provide a 12% return. What should you do? Clearly you should buy the Pittsburgh issue (assuming you trust your facts).

In fact, you might wish to engage in a fancier transaction called an arbitrage. The strict definition of an **arbitrage** is a trade that requires zero net capital, has no risk, and produces a certain profit. Most arbitrages consist of buying and selling an equal dollar amount of two economically similar (but legally different) securities when their prices are not the same.

It is easy to recognize that you could purchase either security. What many students do not recognize is that certain individuals and organizations are able to sell a security they do not own and use the sale proceeds to purchase other securities. The sale of a security that is not owned is referred to as a **short sale**.[7] If you were to sell $1,000 of the Boston issue, purchase $1,000 of the Pittsburgh issue, and maintain the position until the securities mature in one year, your cash flows would look like this:

Transaction	Cash Today	Cash in One Year
Today:		
Sell $1,000 Boston	+$1,000	
Buy $1,000 Pittsburgh	−$1,000	
In One Year:		
Repay on the Boston		−$1,080
Collect on the Pittsburgh		+1,120
Net Proceeds	$0.00	+$40

Looks pretty good, doesn't it? But your suspicions are correct. Something as easy as this is very unlikely to exist in real security markets. A "yield spread" of 400 basis points between two equivalent issues is not going to arise. In fact, it is the presence of a large number of arbitrage traders who simply won't allow a situation like the one in this example to occur.

Security market prices are created by the trading decisions of a large number of people. And each person who decides to buy or sell does so based on information and beliefs he or she has about the security. As such, a security's price is a reflection of the information

---

[7] Short sales are discussed in more detail in Chapter 4. Not everyone who short-sells a security may use the proceeds to buy another security.

people have about the security. If you believe the security is mispriced, you are actually claiming to have different information about the security from other market participants. **In short, a speculative trade is an information-based trade.**

If you decide to engage in a speculative trade, it could be your information is, in fact, better than the information currently reflected in existing security prices. But it is always worth asking, "do I really know more about this security than other market participants?"

Consider a second speculation example. In this case you have just completed an analysis of the Mexican stock market and the stock market in Brazil. You believe a portfolio of Mexican stocks has the same risk as a portfolio of Brazilian stocks. However, it is your opinion that Mexican stocks will have greater rates of return during the next year than those of Brazil. The speculation would consist of buying Mexican stocks (and maybe short-selling Brazilian). But it would be very difficult to construct an arbitrage between the two markets. Thus, whatever trade you make would have substantial risk. Your information about these two markets could be something not presently factored into their current price levels. If so, you would earn a speculative profit. But it is also possible you are simply wrong; that there is information of which you are unaware.

Efficiently Priced Security Markets

The only way investors can earn speculative profits is to have better information about security prices than other market participants. Thus, competition for information is intense.

Many investment professionals believe that in well-functioning security markets, competition for information is so extensive that all information which can presently be known about a security will be appropriately reflected in the security's price. If this is the case, the market is said to be *efficiently priced.* In such a market, if you believed a security is presently mispriced given the information you have about the security, you are simply lacking some information which is known to other market participants.

If a security market is efficiently priced, then it is impossible to earn profits consistently from speculative trading. Some attempts at price speculations will result in profits; others, losses. And some people who actively speculate may incur what appears to be a long string of speculative profits. But in an efficiently priced market, such apparent profits arise solely by chance. In an efficiently priced market, speculators with a long string of profits are not truly skilled at what they do. They are simply lucky.

The concept of efficiently priced markets was first investigated in the late 1960s. Since then it has become one of the most controversial but influential investment concepts. Because of its importance, we return to the notion of efficiently priced markets throughout the book.

Why Do Security Markets Exist?

Financial markets play a vital role in modern societies. They increase investment opportunities and standards of living, provide diversification opportunities, and allow opportunities to shift one's investment risk level. In this section we examine the role and benefits provided by (1) primary markets, (2) secondary markets, and (3) professional security management.

Primary Market Benefits

Recall that the primary market refers to trades in which a user of capital issues a security to a capital supplier in return for cash. The security issuer then uses the cash to acquire (hopefully) profitable real assets. Benefits provided by primary markets are twofold: (1) wealth of a society is increased, (2) consumption and investment flexibility is increased.

Wealth of Society. Consider individuals such as Thomas Edison, Henry Ford, and William Gates. During their careers, these people created new industries that led to significant employment and increased standards of living. Each had a unique idea that resulted in a value to society. But none had (initially) enough personal capital to implement his idea. By selling financial securities, these people were able to obtain the capital needed to implement their ideas. Society benefited by improved productivity, these entrepreneurs benefited by increased wealth, and purchasers of the securities also benefited from increases in the value of securities they bought.

The story of these individuals is an obvious extreme. But the point that financial markets help increase the future wealth of society also relates to everyday life. For example, how many college readers of this text would be able to personally afford their education costs if they had to rely solely on personal assets? Students who borrow to help finance their education costs are using the financial markets to make an investment in their personal human capital. The ability to borrow improves their future wealth as well as their value to society.

Consumption and Investment Flexibility. The presence of financial markets also increases consumption and investment flexibility. If a primary market (issue a financial claim in return for cash) did not exist, people could consume no more than the market value of any real assets that they owned. Automobiles and houses could not be purchased until people had sufficient real assets to do so. But with the presence of a primary market, individuals can borrow and spend today using a promise to repay with future income.

From the investment perspective, without the existence of securities created in a primary market, people accumulating savings would be forced to save by acquiring real assets (which they might not have the skill and time to manage or are more risky than they desire). The presence of financial securities created in the primary market provide such savers with an easy and inexpensive way to accumulate wealth through financial investment.

In short, primary markets *increase the wealth of society* and provide an ***improvement in consumption and investment flexibility.***

Securities created in the primary market can either be held by the security buyer or traded in secondary markets. Securities that are held by the buyer are referred to as **private placements.** A loan made by a bank to a business or individual is an example of a private placement. The bank intends to hold the security for the full life of the security with no intention of selling it to another party. Securities that are to be traded in secondary markets are referred to as **public placements.** A mortgage loan made by a bank becomes part of a public placement when it is pooled with other mortgage loans and sold in secondary markets as a mortgage-backed debt obligation.

Secondary Market Benefits

Recall that the term *secondary market* refers to trades between a buyer and seller after the original security issue. Consider these benefits created by the existence of a secondary market: (1) Price discovery, (2) Reduced transaction costs, (3) Diversification improvements, and (4) Liquidity.

Price Discovery. By knowing the market price at which market participants are willing to currently trade the security, we can infer the rate of return that investors who own a given security require. For example, the rate of return that investors require on a bond issue of AT&T can be calculated by knowledge of the bond's maturity, promised interest payments, and current market price. Similarly, knowledge of AT&T's current stock price helps in estimating the required return on the firm's common stock. Knowledge of current capital costs helps financial managers decide whether new projects are likely to cover the required financing costs. This is of considerable value to society, since it allocates resources to business ventures that are expected to create wealth for society.

Reduced Transaction Costs. Significant economies of scale are possible from creating a network that brings together potential buyers and sellers. For example, having a central location at which a large number of different stocks can be traded makes it much less costly for buyers and sellers to find each other. Many developments in the way in which securities are traded have occurred simply in an effort to reduce trading costs. Examples include methods by which large quantities of stock are traded, the growth of discount brokerage houses, and the recent growth of 'on-line' computer trading. To a large extent, the existence and form of secondary markets is driven by desire to minimize trading costs.

Diversification Improvements. Diversification consists of owning a large number of different securities. It is a principal way in which portfolio risk can be minimized. Although diversification can be achieved via primary market purchases, small investors find it much easier to achieve a reasonable level of diversification by trading in secondary markets, simply because a smaller quantity of securities may be traded.

For example, a $100 million portfolio conceivably could obtain sufficient diversification by purchasing a large number of new issues in primary market transactions. But an individual with only $25,000 to invest would find such an approach almost impossible.[8]

Liquidity. A commonly cited reason for the existence of secondary markets is the improved liquidity they provide. A perfectly liquid security could be sold immediately and at no cost (commissions, taxes, effects on price, etc.). To the extent that time and costs arise in a trade, liquidity decreases.

---

[8] This would not be true if the individual is purchasing a new issue of a commingled portfolio such as a mutual fund. As we note later, diversification benefits are a major reason for the existence of ownership interests in professionally managed portfolios.

The benefits of having liquid markets are obvious; they allow one to trade when there is a need for cash or when excess cash is available. As an example, consider the shares of Fictitious Corp. Assume that when you purchase a share of this firm's common stock you have the rights to any dividends the company will pay in the future. But you are not allowed to ever sell the shares (perhaps because there is no secondary market available).[9] Would you be willing to purchase the shares? Probably, if the share price was low enough! Now let's say that a market is created in which you are allowed to trade the shares at low cost and rapidly at any time you wish. Would you be willing to purchase the shares at a higher price than without the secondary market? Certainly. The *option to trade has a value* that is created by secondary markets.

While no secondary market is perfectly liquid, most markets provide relatively rapid and low-cost opportunities to trade.[10]

Professional Security Management Benefits

Ownership interests in professionally managed security portfolios have become such an important element of security market transactions that they must be considered a vital component of the overall security market structure. In fact, individual and institutional investors could conduct all of their investment activities through such security management firms, never having to go directly to either the primary or secondary markets.

Many variants of professionally managed portfolios exist, each appealing to the needs of a group of investors. For example, in the case of mutual funds, investors place cash into the portfolio and in return receive an ownership claim equal to the proportion their investment represents of total assets. So, if the market value of a portfolio was $9 million at the close of trading on a particular day and a college foundation contributed $1 million to the portfolio at that time, the foundation would receive a 10% ownership claim. Mutual funds are professionally managed investment companies and are discussed in Chapter 14.

Professionally managed portfolios provide three potential advantages: (1) Diversification, (2) Lower cost of portfolio management, and (3) Professional management.

Diversification. By pooling their capital, individual investors are able to purchase a larger number of different securities than if they had simply invested on their own. This is an important advantage for individual investors with small amounts to be invested.

Lower Cost of Portfolio Management. The percentage cost of managing a portfolio is inversely related to the dollar amount being managed. For example, the manager of a large portfolio can negotiate trading commissions with brokers to levels not available to smaller investors. And accounting costs can be spread over all investors in the portfolio. In addition, there is the cost associated with selecting securities to be held in the portfolio. For a given research effort, security analysis costs are the same whether the portfolio has

---

[9] It might appear implausible that one could never sell an asset. But this is exactly what many foundations face when they are donated land under the condition that it never be sold.

[10] There are exceptions, of course. For example, secondary exchanges in developing countries are often costly and time consuming. Even in the United States, liquidity virtually disappeared on "Black Monday." We say more about these exceptions in later chapters.

$10,000 in assets, $100 million in assets, or $1 billion. Notice the words "for a given research effort." It is likely that greater research efforts would go into a $100 million portfolio than for a $10,000 portfolio. But even then, economies of scale result in lower selection cost per $1 of managed asset.

Professional Management. Many investment companies claim that an advantage of using their services is the portfolio will be managed by a full-time experienced portfolio management group. The extent to which professional investors are able to "add-value" from active speculative trading is a topic we take up in later chapters. Although the answer is not clear, by turning the management of a security portfolio over to professionals, investors might be less likely to make poor decisions about the types of securities purchased.

Investment Management In the 1990s

The types of securities traded as well as the way in which they are traded are constantly evolving as technology, society's needs, and political conditions change. The pace of change seems to be accelerating, driven both by increasing numbers of investors and competition. Most professionals agree that the major areas of change are in (1) globalization, (2) securitization, (3) derivatives, and (4) technology.

Globalization

Perhaps the most significant long-term development of recent years has been the creation of a truly global security market. Users of capital compete around the world for sources of money, and investors recognize the diversification and return advantages of investing beyond their own political borders. Security firms that had previously conducted business solely within their local country have created alliances with firms in other countries which give both a global presence.

Global investing has become the "thing to do." One significant reason is the growth of free market capitalism and democratic institutions. For example, Pacific Rim countries (known as the Pac-Rim) have experienced dramatic growth in both real economies and financial markets. In some of these countries, equity returns of 500% in a year are common. (It goes both ways; large negative returns also occur.) Eastern Europe is seeing a rebirth in real asset growth and the financial markets needed to supply the capital and liquidity to support such growth. And the growth potential of China is almost unimaginable.

Even in well-developed economies, international competition has forced a reduction in the regulation of security market transactions and led to significant growth of trading. In England, for example, fixed commission rates were eliminated during the 1980s and created a growth in trading and repositioning of securities firms, referred to as the "big bang."

Advances in technology have made global integration physically possible. Satellite communications allow markets to be continuously linked so prices in foreign markets can be accurately monitored and orders can be executed within minutes on the major world exchanges.

The growth of institutional investors has also spurred the movement to global investing. Institutions were among the first to recognize the value of global investment and they had a large enough asset base to motivate investment firms to make any changes necessary to allow them to do so. For example, without pressure from pension funds and endowment funds, banks (which hold custody of the international securities owned) would probably not have improved their international custodial services as rapidly as they did.

The history of financial markets has entered a new era; which brings with it both opportunities and risks. Serious investment students must become more aware of differences in world cultures, be attentive to potential political risks, and learn about currency risk. Global markets are discussed throughout the book.

Securitization

The term **securitization** refers to taking a pool of loans and using them as collateral for a bond issue that is sold in the primary market and later traded in secondary markets. Securitized issues are often called "asset backs" because they are backed by a specific pool of loans. Another term applied to them is "pass-throughs," since both principal and interest is passed-through to the security holder when paid.

The most common form of asset-backed security is the mortgage-backed obligation. The mortgage-backed market is principally in the United States. During the past 25 years, the mortgage pass-through market has grown from virtually zero to almost 20% of the value of all U.S. bond issues. A smaller market also exists in securities backed by credit card and automobile loans.

We noted earlier in the chapter that the growth of the asset-backed market is an illustration of how financial markets react to a societal need. In this case, banks did not wish to hold long-term mortgage obligations during periods of rapidly changing interest rates. Securitization of the mortgages allowed them to be held by security market participants who were more willing to accept their interest rate risk.

But managing the risks of these securities requires new investment concepts and tools. Among these are new forms of financial derivatives.

Derivatives

Although active markets in options and futures were created earlier, it is in the decade of the 1990s that they came to their maturity. They are now widely used by sophisticated investors to manage various forms of investment risk. For example, during the period when a bank is putting together a mortgage pass-through that will be sold in the primary market, the bank has an investment in loans which bears interest rate risk. To offset this risk, the bank can take an appropriate position in mortgage futures.

Although futures and options represent useful risk management tools, *they should not be used unless one has a full understanding of them*. Like a powerful medicine, unless they are used properly, **they can cause serious harm.**

For an overview of derivatives see Chapter 3. More complete reviews of options and futures are presented in Chapters 16 and 17.

Technology

Recent advances in technology have had profound affects on the types of information available, the way in which securities are traded, and the techniques used to select securities.

A few decades ago information about individual stocks and bonds was usually obtained from paper documents that were often updated only once a year. For example, if you wished to obtain information on a common stock, you would write the company for a copy of its annual report, copy security registration documents filed with governmental bodies such as the Securities and Exchange Commission, and examine investment information manuals printed by firms such as Moody's and Standard & Poor's. Information about stock prices was available on only current prices via a phone call to one's broker.

Today a wealth of information is available via computer-based products. Computer networks, such as the Bloomberg System, provide extensive data on virtually all actively traded securities in the United States plus analytic programs that aid in evaluating a particular trading strategy. Standard & Poor's provides a CD-ROM that has 20 years of financial statement data as well as past prices and dividends on virtually all actively traded stocks in the world. Morningstar has a CD-ROM that furnishes past returns and portfolio holdings on more that 4,000 investment company portfolios. Compact Disclosure supplies full copies of recent corporate annual reports. The list continues to grow.

The way in which securities are traded has also been permanently changed by new technologies. Numerous computer-based networks link security traders so they can find current prices at which they can buy or sell and actually execute orders. Many discount brokerage houses now provide individual investors with the ability to buy and sell securities without ever contacting a broker. Even the Internet provides ways of buying and selling securities (as well as extensive databases such as access to corporate documents filed with the Security Exchange Commission).[11]

Finally, analytic techniques used in security selection have changed significantly with advances in computer use. This has led to the creation of new approaches such as "quantitative investing," "high-tech investing," "factor model selection," and so on. We examine a number of these approaches to security selection in later chapters.

SUMMARY

This chapter provided an overview of the structure of security markets and the benefits they provide. Here are the key concepts:

- There are two basic types of investors: individual investors and institutional investors. Institutional investors consist of pension funds, endowment funds, mutual funds, and other large investors.

- Major components of the securities markets are the primary market, the secondary market, and portfolio management firms.

- Securities traded are of two general types: those providing a direct claim to cash flows on an underlying real asset (debt and equity instruments), and those providing an indirect claim by having a claim on a debt or equity instrument (derivatives).

---

[11] See Appendix 3A for review of current computer-based sources of information and trading systems.

◾ A rapid growth occurred in the value of security markets over the past 25 years caused by both positive returns on existing securities plus the creation of new securities to supply capital to business firms and governments.

◾ In the mid-1990s, the market value of U.S. securities represented about 45% of the world value of traded securities.

◾ There are two reasons to save: (1) to smooth consumption over one's lifetime, and (2) to take advantage of speculative opportunities.

◾ Speculative profits represent returns earned above the returns on securities of similar risk. Many professional investors question whether speculative profits are possible in highly competitive markets. The issue is very controversial and not resolved.

◾ Primary markets provide two benefits to a society: the ability to increase standards of living, and increased flexibility in consumption and investment.

◾ Secondary markets offer four major benefits to market participants: (1) price discovery, (2) reduced transaction costs, (3) diversification opportunities, and (4) liquidity.

◾ Professional security management provides three potential benefits to market participants: (1) improved diversification, (2) reduced costs of portfolio management, and (3) experienced professionals making investment decisions.

QUESTIONS AND PROBLEMS

1. Briefly discuss the main difference(s) between individual investors and institutional investors. What are the implications of these differences on the sources of information, the types of analyses, and investment markets each group will use? (At detailed answer is neither desired nor possible at this stage of your learning. A very general response is all that is desired. But the implication of this answer is important to your understanding.)
2. What are the economic differences among debt claims, equity claims, and derivatives?
3. Briefly discuss the two major reasons for the growth of market value of the world security markets. What implications should be drawn from this?
4. What are the two economic motives for saving?
5. Develop your own example of a speculative security trade. Try not to simply repeat the text examples. What aspect of this example makes you say it is a speculative trade?
6. U.S. Treasury bills (T-bills) are short-term debt instruments of the U.S. Treasury. They offer no default risk. For a particular issue you pay a price today and in return receive, say, $1 million in a specified number of days from now, the maturity date. Different T-bill issues have different maturity dates. T-bills are bought or sold from many banks in the United States. If you were to short-sell a T-bill, assume you would be able to use the proceeds to purchase something else.

   Given this information, create an example of an arbitrage in T-bills. Hint: You need to be very specific about the maturity dates of securities in your example. Why?

7. You are in a class of 1,000 investment students (poor you). Your instructor has decided to play a game. At the start of each week, each student will toss a penny. If "heads" come up, the student uses this as a prediction that returns on U.S. T-bills will be greater than returns on U.S. common stocks. The game is played for a total of ten weeks.

   a. After the first week, how many students do you expect will have predicted the investment with the greater return?

   b. After two weeks, how many students do you expect will have predicted the security with the best return in both weeks?

   c. After the full ten weeks, how many students do you expect will have predicted the security with the best return in each of the ten weeks?

   d. After the ten-week experiment, there is one student whose prediction was correct every week. Did this student own a coin that truly was able to predict security returns?

8. You are considering investing in a mutual fund. The salesperson for one fund states that management of their fund is very skilled at predicting whether U.S. stocks or Treasury bills will provide the greater return during a given year. As proof the salesperson says, "Of the 3,000 mutual funds that have been in existence during the past five years, we have been one of only 90 funds which have been successful in predicting whether stocks or T-bills would provide the greater return in each year." Comment on this claim.

9. What is meant by the term *efficiently priced security market?*

10. What economic advantages are created by the existence of:

    a. Primary markets

    b. Secondary markets

    c. Portfolio management firms

DATAFILE ANALYSIS

In this chapter we examined Claire's retirement savings program. The spreadsheet data-file called "Claire.wk1" contains the data and calculations used in this example. Use a spreadsheet program to open the datafile and review the way in which calculations are made.

The objective in Claire's problem is to find the level percentage of after-tax income that must be saved if Claire can expect to have a portfolio which will allow her to consume an amount in her retirement equal to her average income in years prior to retirement. There are many ways to perform this calculation. This datafile does it in the simplest way. After all input assumptions are made, the analyst tries various percentages in the cell noted on the spreadsheet to do so. Most entries will provide savings either too large or too small. In that case, the cell below the percentage savings rate will say either TOO HIGH or TOO LOW. After some trial and error you will find the correct value of 0.11546.

After you become familiar with the model's structure, address the following questions:

1. How might different salary growth rates affect the required savings rate? Change the assumed real salary growth rate to 0.00 and 0.05 (0% and 5%) and find the new required savings rate. Explain why these results occur.

2. Let's look at sensitivity of the savings rate to changes in expected returns. Reset the real salary growth to 0.02 and try returns during employment of 0.00, 0.06, and 0.08. Explain your results.

3. Continue to play with the model and try to explain results that arise.

S E L E C T E D   R E F E R E N C E S

Individual investors will find a number of publications prepared by the American Association of Individual Investors (AAII) to be very helpful. The AAII is located at 625 North Michigan Ave., Chicago, IL, 60611. Examples include:

AAII Journal, American Association of Individual Investors, published ten times per year.

COMPUTERIZED INVESTING, American Association of Individual Investors, published bimonthly.

The Individual Investor's Guide to COMPUTERIZED INVESTING, 11th edition, American Association of Individual Investors, Chicago, IL, 1994.

Two institutional trade publications provide interesting stories about current events and developments:

Institutional Investor, Institutional Investor Inc., published monthly.

Pensions & Investments, published biweekly by Craine Communications, Inc., 965 E. Jefferson Ave., Detroit, MI 48207.

INVESTMENT DECISIONS

After reading this chapter you should have an understanding of the major decisions that all investors must make and the importance of investment planning.

Introduction

It was like everyone had won a lottery! Procter & Gamble Co. had just sold its pulp plant and suddenly 1,000 of the plant's employees found more than $50 million of cash in their hands, their pension plan funds that P&G paid to them when the plant was sold. Some employees received more than $100,000. Most of these employees continued at work for the new owner of the pulp plant and failed to understand the need to invest this perceived windfall for their retirement. They bought boats, houses, trailers, and fishing gear. Some even took trips to Las Vegas. Local new-vehicle registrations jumped 45% over the previous year.[1]

When the funds were with P&G, the company had invested it so it would grow to a future value sufficient to provide reasonable retirement income to each employee. After this pension money had been transferred to the employees (in what is called a "lump sum" distribution), they should have "rolled it over" into new investment plans because, of course, once consumed, it would not be available at retirement. The moral to this story is obvious. Too often, people do not understand the need to save and invest but would rather spend

---

[1] This is a true story as reported in the *Wall Street Journal* on July 31, 1995.

whatever they have. Pressing problems of the moment are more important than saving. The decision to invest instead of to consume is important.

In this chapter, we assume the decision to invest has been made and the investor now faces the problem of how to do so. Consider the dilemma of a P&G employee who has just received $50,000 and recognizes the need to invest the money. What steps should the employee take? For someone with no investment training or experience, this can be a formidable task. Even knowing where to begin to look for advice and information can be perplexing.[2]

But before an investor begins an actual investment program, a number of important investment decisions must be made. These are the subject of this chapter. **What decisions must an investor make in order to have a well-thought-out investment plan?**

These decisions are not as simple as finding a security broker and asking, "What stocks and bonds do you recommend I buy?" or finding a highly rated mutual fund in a magazine. Instead, there are more basic decisions which all investors should give serious thought to before they seek a broker or fund manager.

Future returns and risks of a security portfolio are determined in large part by the following investment decisions:

1. To what extent will *speculative strategies* be used? In the parlance of modern investment management, will the portfolio be "actively or passively managed"?
2. What should be the portfolio's *asset allocation?* What asset classes should be held in the portfolio and in what proportions?
3. How will *security selection* be accomplished? Should the selection decisions be made by the owner of the portfolio (internally) or should an external professional be employed?

There is no single answer to any of these decisions. Considerations such as the purpose of the portfolio, the investor's knowledge, tax consequences, and, most importantly, the investor's ability to tolerate risk all influence the best decision for a given case. By the end of the chapter, you should have a clear understanding of what each of these decisions entail as well as why investors do not all choose similar investment policies.

Developing an understanding of these decisions and deciding what would be best given the investor's objective and constraints results in a logical investment plan, a road map to how the investment portfolio will be managed.

Planning Is Important

An analogy can be made between planning an investment strategy with planning an extended vacation to other countries. Most of us would readily agree that planning for such a vacation is vital if one is to get the most out of the trip. In fact, planning the trip is a lot of fun in itself! The same is true for planning an investment strategy. It is vital to the success of the investment and can be fun in itself.

---

[2] The references at the end of this chapter provide a diverse list of readings and other resources that should be helpful to both new and experienced investors.

If you were making plans for an extended vacation, you would have to answer the following questions: (1) Should I visit the standard attractions of each country or should I seek out lesser known areas that might give me more enjoyment? (2) What countries should I visit and how long should I stay in each? (3) Should I make the arrangements myself or should I use a travel agent? These questions are quite similar to the questions that investors should make before they actually commit money to specific investments.

Deciding whether to visit the standard attractions of a country or to seek out unusual locations is similar to the speculative investment decision. An active approach might result in a more adventurous trip. But it could also take you to places that fall far short of expectations. A passive approach of visiting the standard attractions at least has the benefit of knowing better what to expect. One thing you do know for certain. The active approach will be more costly.

Deciding which countries to visit and how long to stay in each is similar to the asset allocation decision faced by an investor. There are two important considerations to both, the risk you decide to take and the diversification you use to reduce risk. For example, assume you are a Danish citizen. A trip to Norway or Germany would have much less uncertainty than a trip to countries with considerably different languages and cultures. Yet the more uncertain choices probably offer greater adventure. To reduce the risk that you might not enjoy your trip, it would be wise to visit a number of different countries. After all, an unpleasant stay in one country can be offset by better than expected visits to other countries.

Finally, the decision to make all travel arrangements oneself, rather than hiring a travel agent, is similar to the investor's security selection decision. Making travel arrangements yourself might be a lot of fun and you would certainly learn a lot. But hiring someone else to do so has the benefits of using a professional who can probably find the lowest cost itinerary and has knowledge of the danger areas in international travel. And it frees up time for you to do other things.

Just as proper planning is important to a successful trip, it is vital to a successful investment strategy. This plan consists of making informed decisions regarding (1) speculative policies, (2) asset allocation, and (3) security selection.

What Is Being Planned: Future Returns

These three decisions are the keys to future returns and risk of a portfolio. While risk measurement is a topic best left to future chapters, we discuss rate of return calculations here, since they are easy to understand, and we refer to returns throughout the chapter.[3]

Consider the market prices and dividends paid by Microsoft and IBM during 1994. Prices shown are at the end of each calendar quarter. While dividends were paid just before the end of each quarter, for now it is best to assume they are received at quarter-end.

---

[3] Technically, there is a difference between a "rate of return" and a "return," in that rate of return refers to the growth rate of a security whereas return refers to the ending value of an initial investment of 1.0 unit of value. Formally, the rate of return is equal to the return minus 1.0. For example, if you invest $1.00 at the beginning of a period and have $1.20 at the end, the return is 1.2 and the rate of return is 20%.

	Dec 31, 1993	Mar 30, 1994	Jun 30, 1994	Sep 30, 1994	Dec 31, 1994
Stock Prices					
IBM	$56.500	$54.625	$58.750	$69.625	$73.500
Microsoft	$40.312	$42.375	$51.625	$56.125	$61.125
Dividends Per Share					
IBM		$0.25	$0.25	$0.25	$0.25
Microsoft		$0.00	$0.00	$0.00	$0.00

The return an investor receives comes from two sources: (1) a dividend payment (or interest if the security is a bond) which the security pays, and (2) changes in the value of the security. The first is called a **dividend yield** and the second **price appreciation.** Symbolically, if R_t refers to the rate of return during period t, D_t refers to the dividend paid at the end of period t, and P_t refers to the price at the end of period t, then:

	Dividend Yield		Price Appreciation	
Security Rate of Return During Period t	R_t	$= D_t \div P_{t-1}$	$+$	$(P_t - P_{t-1}) \div P_{t-1}$	**(2-1)**

For example, during the first quarter of 1994, the returns on IBM and Microsoft would be:

IBM:
$$R_{IBM} = \$0.25 \div \$56.50 + (\$54.625 - \$56.50) \div \$56.50$$
$$-0.0288 = 0.0044 - 0.0332$$

Microsoft:
$$R_{MSFT} = \$0.00 \div \$40.312 + (\$42.375 - \$40.312) \div \$40.312$$
$$+0.0512 = 0.0000 + 0.0512$$

During the first quarter of 1994, investors who bought IBM at the start of the quarter would have paid $56.50 per share. In return, they would have received $0.25 in dividends (a 0.44% dividend yield) and a loss in share value of $1.875 (a price appreciation of a negative 3.32%). Microsoft investors would have received all their return from price changes, since Microsoft paid no dividends.

Rates of return for each of the four quarters of 1994 were as follows:

	1st Quarter	2nd Quarter	3rd Quarter	4th Quarter
IBM	−2.88%	8.00%	18.94%	5.92%
Microsoft	5.12%	21.83%	8.72%	8.91%

To calculate rates of return over a number of periods, the single period returns are compounded. For example, the rate of return on IBM and Microsoft during the full year of 1994 would be calculated as follows:

IBM 1994: $0.321 = (1 - 0.0288)(1 + 0.08)(1 + 0.1894)(1 + 0.0592) - 1$

Microsoft 1994: $0.516 = (1.0512)(1.2183)(1.0872)(1.0891) - 1$

Rates of return of 32.1% and 51.6% are unusually good. See Chapters 5 and 21 for further details on return calculations.

The Cases of Three Investors

To illustrate why investors reach differing conclusions when they evaluate these decisions, we focus on the situations facing three hypothetical investors. While these investors are fictitious, the investment problems they must address are common to actual situations.

You should not consider the decisions our hypothetical investors are assumed to make as the best decision each individual should make. Instead, their decisions are intended to illustrate a range of decisions that reasonable people reach in actual situations as well as the logic underlying each decision.

To make informed investment decisions, begin with a clear understanding of the purpose of the investment portfolio as well as any special characteristics of the investor. Understanding why the investment is being made provides insights that point toward an appropriate investment strategy, such as the length of the investment horizon and whether inflation is a concern. Understanding special characteristics of the investor such as investment knowledge, tax status, need for liquidity, and risk tolerance are also critical factors in setting a reasonable strategy.

Let's take a close look at each of our investors.

Claire

We first met Claire in Chapter 1. She is now 45 years old and happily married to Chuck. They have raised two children who are both financially independent of their parents. (Time flies!) The company for which Claire has been working for the past 20 years was recently acquired by a competitor. Although Claire will continue to work for the new employer, she must decide what to do with the pension assets to which the first employer says she has a claim.

The present market value of Claire's pension assets is slightly more than $100,000. She has been told that the money could be either transferred to an individual retirement account (IRA) or placed in her new employer's pension plan. If she decides to roll the money over into an IRA, she will have to establish one at her local bank, through a brokerage firm, or even with a mutual fund company. She would be free to decide how the money is to be invested, and all earnings on the funds would be tax exempt until she retires and begins to make withdrawals. The firm at which she sets up the IRA would serve as a custodian of any securities owned (and report to tax authorities any premature withdrawals).

The alternative is to transfer the money to the new employer's pension plan. Since this can be done with little effort, Claire has decided to use this approach.

Claire is able to make this type of transfer because the new employer offers a retirement savings program called a **defined contribution** plan. One advantage of this particular plan is that any future contributions she makes are matched by her employer (with limits and not including the initial $100,000). Once the money is invested, it belongs to her. If she leaves her current employer, she may take any accumulated funds to her new employer's defined contribution plan.[4] This feature is called *portability* and is one advantage of defined contribution plans that has made them increasingly popular in recent years. These plans are so called because the employer's legal liability consists of a precisely defined contribution. Once the employer makes this (yearly) contribution, the employer has no further liability; *all investment risk is borne by the employee.*

The fact that employees who are members of a defined contribution pension plan bear all investment risk suggests that each employee should have major control over the risks of the securities held for them. This is usually the case. Employers typically offer a variety of investment options that differ in risk and allow each employee to decide how his or her portion of pension assets are to be invested. We assume that Claire's employer gives her complete freedom to invest across any or all investment vehicles offered by the firm.

Within legal limits, any contributions made by the employee and employer, as well as all profits and losses, are not taxed. The only requirement is that the money be left in a retirement plan until retirement.[5] Not only will the tax savings increase the expected market value of her portfolio at retirement, but saving via a tax sheltered program simplifies the tax issues associated with her investment strategy.

Finally, although Claire finds the idea of owning and managing a security porfolio both exciting and interesting, she is not trained in investments and wishes to spend minimal time in managing the portfolio in the future. She does not want investing to become a hobby.

Hilbert Pension Trust (HPT)

Hilbert's is a well-known grocery chain with more than 100 stores located in North Carolina and Virginia. The firm provides a **defined benefit** pension plan for its employees. Under this plan Hilbert's promises to pay a specified pension benefit to each of its retired employees. In the Hilbert plan, the yearly retirement benefit is equal to "2% times the number of years the employee worked for Hilbert's times the employee's final salary." For example, an employee who had worked for 25 years would receive 50% of final salary during each year of retirement. This type of pension plan is called a defined benefit plan, since benefits (as opposed to contributions) are legally defined. To assure that funds will be available to meet its retirement promises to employees, Hilbert's makes yearly contributions to its pension portfolio. The size of the yearly contribution is estimated by an actuary using information about the number of employees and their ages, current and projected salaries, the market value of the current investment portfolio, and assumed future investment returns. If future portfolio returns turn out to be greater than the actuary had expected, the actuary will reduce future yearly contributions. If returns are lower than

---

[4] If the new employer does not have a defined contribution plan, she should establish an individual retirement account.

[5] Withdrawals from the portfolio during Claire's retirement will be fully taxed as ordinary income (early withdrawals are subject to tax penalties). Notice, however, that she benefits by the time value of money associated with delaying taxes and, possibly, from a lower tax rate during retirement.

expected, the contribution requirement will be increased. Thus, in the case of defined benefit plans, *all investment risk is borne by the employer.*

Hilbert's board of directors has appointed a group of pension trustees who are charged with developing investment strategies and monitoring the pension portfolio's performance. Dan Hilbert is a senior trustee. Although Dan grew up in the grocery business and has been a significant force in the growth and profitability of Hilbert's, he has developed a special interest in managing of the HPT portfolio. Dan spends much of his time trying to find ways that would increase the fund's diversification and rates of return. Together with the other trustees, he provides active and ongoing oversight of pension assets.

The market value of portfolio assets is presently about $400 million. Because of Hilbert's rapid growth during the past, most of these assets are being held to meet the retirement needs of current employees who are typically many years away from retirement. The number of past employees who are now drawing retirement benefits are few. In fact, the actuary has estimated that company contributions going into the portfolio will exceed retirement benefit payments coming out of the portfolio for at least 20 years.

Comparison of HPT with Claire. Even though Claire is a small individual investor and HPT is a large institutional investor, they have a number of common characteristics. Both investors have a relatively long investment horizon. Both wish to provide a source of retirement income. Both face no taxation of any income generated from portfolio securities. And both will have cash outflows during retirement that are positively related to inflation prior to retirement. For Claire, inflation rates higher than she expects before retirement will increase the amount of money she needs during retirement in order to maintain her desired standard of living. For HPT, retirement benefit payments are directly tied to final employee salaries, which, of course, are positively related to inflation.

But there are also important differences between Claire and HPT that affect their investment strategies. Because HPT's asset base is much larger than Claire's, HPT can afford to pay for investment services that are beyond Claire's reach. In addition, there is a clear difference in the amount of attention each portfolio will be given. Claire wants something that will require minimal attention on her part. Dan and the trustees intend to spend time fine-tuning whatever investment strategies they select. There are clear differences in the knowledge and interest of these investors.

Trust Company of the East (TCE)

Trust Company of the East is a subsidiary of a major regional bank with headquarters in Boston. Prior to the 1970s TCE's principal business was the investment management of personal trusts. Most of these trusts were set up to provide income to an individual's heirs at death. However, with the growth of pension fund assets in the 1970s and 1980s, the mix of assets managed by TCE shifted heavily toward pension fund assets. By the early 1990s, virtually all marketing resources were aimed at bringing in new pension business. In fact, TCE had become well known as a succesful "large cap" manager, meaning it managed companies with large total market value.

In the early 1990s, federal requlations were relaxed to allow bank trust companies the opportunity to create mutual funds to be sold to customers of the bank. TCE's marketing philosophy was to create "one-stop shopping" that would enable customers to conduct all their financial transactions with them. The first mutual fund created by TCE was called the

Core U.S. Equity Fund and was managed in much the same fashion as TCE had recently been managing pension fund assets.

However, TCE management believed they needed to develop alternative investment products in order to attract additional customers. As a start, they decided to develop two new mutual funds. One portfolio would invest in stocks of other developed nations and would be called the Core Non-U.S. Equity Fund. By owning both "Core" funds, investors would obtain broad diversification across the major world equity markets.

The other new fund would invest in Latin American stocks. In the words of TCE's president, "This fund will offer some adventure, some thrills, some sizzle for those with the willingness to accept the risks of investing in an emerging regional stock market: Latin America." The manager of this portfolio would be a newly hired portfolio manager at TCE, Maria Perez.

In the ten years since she graduated from college with a business degree, Maria had worked for a major investment counsel firm in Atlanta known as The A Group. She began as a security analyst of companies in Latin America. During this time she successfully identified a number of Latin American stocks that eventually proved to yield large returns. This, together with her passing all parts of the Chartered Financial Analyst exam, led to her promotion as a co-portfolio manager of stocks which clients of The A Group had in Latin America.

Based on her successful record, TCE hired her to manage their new TCE Latin America Fund. The purpose of this mutual fund, as stated in registration documents with the Securities and Exchange Commisssion, is as follows:

> The TCE Latin America Fund will invest principally in stocks of companies domiciled in Mexico, Brazil and Argentina. Stocks of companies in other Latin American countries will occasionally be held. The portfolio will be actively managed in an attempt to provide the greatest returns available. Because stocks in these countries might become overvalued or undervalued, management of the Fund will actively manage the percentage of portfolio assets held in cash equivalents and equities. All investments in cash equivalents will be in U.S. Treasury Bills. Investments in Latin American securities bear considerably greater risks than those of the United States. These risks include market volatility risk, exchange rate risk and political risk.

Investors in the fund will pay a management fee to TCE equal to 1% of the average market value of fund assets in a given year. Thus, it is in TCE's and Maria's interest to earn high rates of return that will attract a large number of investors to the fund.

Comparison of TCE with HPT and Claire. There is only one similarity among the portfolios of our three investors: taxes. Any income generated by the portfolios will not be taxed as long as it is kept in the portfolio. Distributions to Claire after she retires, benefits paid to employees of Hilbert's in their retirement, and dividends paid by TCE's Latin America Fund to shareholders of the fund will be taxed. But as long as income is retained in each portfolio, it is not taxed. In most other respects, the nature of the portfolio that Maria will manage is different. HBT and Claire are interested in long-run portfolio payoffs. In contrast, Maria will focus on good portfolio performance in the near term in order to attract a large number of investors to the fund. She has no particular interest in hedging against inflation risk. Rather, she faces the risk that the values of the currencies of the countries in which she invests will deteriorate. Finally, registration documents of the Latin America Fund state that the fund will be actively managed in an attempt to earn speculative profits.

FIGURE 2-1   THE IMPORTANT INVESTMENT DECISIONS

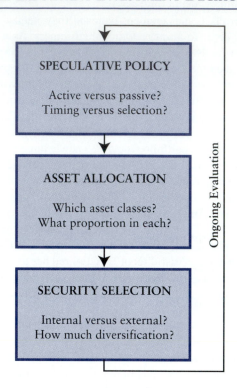

A Review of the Decisions and Investors

Figure 2-1 diagrams the three fundamental investment decisions these people face. The first decision involves determining the speculative strategy that will be used. For many investors, the best strategy will be to attempt no speculation. This policy is known as **passive management.** An investor who uses a passive strategy expects to earn reasonable future returns. But these expected returns are due to the risk inherent in owning the portfolio. In contrast, an investor who searches for incorrectly priced securities is following an **active management** strategy. The returns from active management come from both the bearing of investment risk and any speculative profits. The two broad categories of speculation, called **timing** and **selection,** are discussed later.

The second decision requires determining an appropriate asset allocation for the portfolio. Probably the most important decision the investor will make, it involves deciding what asset classes will be held in the portfolio and in what proportions.

The third decision involves actual security selection. Will the investor personally decide which securities to own or will a professional manager be employed to make these decisions? And how much diversification is needed in each asset class?

Claire, Dan Hilbert of HPT, and Maria Perez of TCE must make these decisions based on their individual objectives and special characteristics. These are summarized in Table 2-1.

TABLE 2-1   PURPOSE AND CHARACTERISTICS OF THREE ILLUSTRATIVE INVESTORS

Investor	Purpose of Portfolio	Special Considerations
Claire	Retirement income	Young investor with long horizon Desires inflation hedge Little investment knowledge Desires a simple but effective approach No tax concerns
HPT	Retirement income	Long investment horizon Desires inflation hedge Sophisticated investor Willing to learn and try new things No tax concerns

TCE	For bank:
	Income from
	   assets being managed
		Focus on short-term returns
		Active management
		Emerging market investment:
		   Currency risk concerns
		   Very volatile returns
		   Possible liquidity problems
		No tax concerns

	For fund buyers: Diversification Professional management Good returns at low cost	

Decision 1: Speculative Policy

Many beginning investors are unaware they have a choice between active and passive management strategies. Too often their opinions about investing have been formed by the media, which sensationalizes aspects of active trading and gives little attention to passive strategies. However, both approaches are widely used by institutional as well as individual investors. You should not dismiss either approach without studying them closely. Each investor is different. Some should follow a 100% passive strategy. Others should mix active and passive strategies. And others will chose an active approach for all aspects of portfolio management. The recent trend has been toward passive investing, but the vast majority of all investment money is still actively managed.

What Do We Mean by Active and Passive?

The terms *passive* and *active* apply to only one aspect of investment management, the search for speculative profits. A passive strategy seeks profits solely from bearing investment risk.

An active strategy also attempts to profit from identifying mispriced securities. Speculative strategies are commonly classified as either timing or selection.

Timing.   All investors must determine a portfolio asset allocation that provides them with the best mix of risk and return. Passive investors make this decision in the belief that the expected returns on different asset classes are fair given the risk of each asset class. Active investors will attempt to identify periods when, say, stocks are overvalued or undervalued relative to other asset classes. When they believe an asset class is overvalued, they **underweight** (hold less than they would normally) the asset class in their portfolios. When they believe an asset class is undervalued, they **overweight** (hold more than they would normally) the asset class. This type of active management has historically been called **market timing.** More recently it has gained the fancier title of **tactical asset allocation.**

There are many ways of defining an asset class. The following is a list of asset classes that most professionals would find satisfactory:[6]

Money market securities: Securities with a repayment date of one year or less that have little risk of default.

Intermediate and long-term bonds: Securities with repayment dates greater than one year. Default risk varies. So a number of subclasses are often used to differentiate default risk. Subclasses for various maturity dates are also used.

Common stock: Securities that represent ownership claims in a company. Subclasses are often based on firm size and earnings growth rates.

Selection.   The securities that a passive investor owns within a given asset class will probably differ from those held by an active investor. For example, say we have defined one asset class to be those common stocks traded in the United States that are in the bottom 20% of all U.S. stocks in terms of market capitalization.[7] Call this asset class "U.S. Small Cap." Passive investors who wish to place such securities in their portfolios would attempt to obtain the broadest possible diversification within the asset class. In concept, this would be done by owning all securities in the asset class and weighting each according to their individual market capitalization. If stock of Firm A represents 2% of the total value of the U.S. Small Cap class, then 2% of any money committed to this class should be invested in Firm A. Since most investors do not have a portfolio large enough to actually do this, special commingled portfolios called **index funds** have been created. Although the index fund may not own every stock in the defined index in exact market capitalization weights, they do hold a large sample of stocks which has returns that closely track returns on the index. Many types of index funds are available. They range from funds that track aggregate U.S. bond returns to funds that track stock returns in specific regions of the world.

---

[6] It is common to have at least two asset classes for each of these, one representing securities denominated in the investor's local currency and the other representing foreign currencies.

[7] Recall that capitalization refers to the total market value of a firm's common stock and is calculated by multiplying the stock price by the number of outstanding shares.

While the passive investor's goal within a given asset class is diversification, the active investor's goal is to find securities that are undervalued or overvalued. As with asset allocation, the active investor will overweight or underweight the individual securities in the class. This is referred to as **security picking** or **security selection.**[8] Active security picking within an asset class usually results in a portfolio that is less diversified than a passive index fund.

Passive Is Active.   A passive management strategy is passive in the sense that no attempts are made to find mispriced securities. In all other respects a passive strategy is active, requiring the active involvement of the investor in designing the portfolio and monitoring it over time. For example, consider the situation of Hilbert's pension trust. If the trustees decide to follow a passive strategy across the total portfolio, they will still have to answer many questions such as these:

1. What should be the portfolio's asset allocation?
2. Which passive managers can provide the greatest diversification within each asset class at the lowest cost?
3. Should derivatives be used to manage asset allocation?
4. How should we monitor derivative trades to assure they do not create unnecessary risk?
5. Should we take positions in new asset classes such as emerging international markets?
6. Should we attempt to hedge currency risk of our foreign holdings?

Each of these decisions are intellectually interesting and can require considerable analysis. Passive investing does not have to be boring.

Why Be Passive?

There are a number of reasons why a passive strategy can turn out to be more successful than an active approach. These include:

- ◤ **Costs of active investment.** Active investors who wish to make personal security selections must consider the time they spend in deciding which securities to buy and sell as well as the costs associated with obtaining data needed to make their trading decisions. One way to reduce these costs is to employ an active professional investment manager. But active professionally managed portfolios are still more costly than passive professionally managed portfolios, since they incur research, data collection, and trading costs that are not incurred by passively managed portfolios.[9] The costs of an actively managed professional portfolio typically range between 0.25% to 2.50% per year more than passively managed professional portfolios.

---

[8] It is unfortunate that the term security selection is used to refer to two very different ideas. Security selection by an active manager means something very different from the security selection decision that all investors must make. The former refers to the search for mispriced securities. The latter refers to whether the investor will personally decide which securities to own or whether a professional manager will be hired to make these decisions.

[9] There are also costs associated with deciding which active portfolio managers should be employed and monitoring the performance of these managers.

- **Less diversification.** Actively managed portfolios are usually less diversified than passively managed portfolios. For example, consider holdings of stocks in, say, Latin America. The goal of a passive management firm would be to obtain the greatest diversification possible across Latin American stocks. In contrast, an active manager would invest in a much smaller sample of Latin stocks and, thus, provide less diversification. In fact, it might be necessary to own a number of active Latin America managers in order to achieve the diversification provided by a single passive portfolio.

- **Active investment might not work.** Even before the costs of active investment are considered, many people question whether active investment strategies are able to "beat" passive strategies. This issue is discussed next and remains an important topic throughout the book.

Why Be Active?

The obvious reason to choose an active management approach is in the hopes of earning greater returns than equivalent-risk passive management would provide. As we have noted before, there is a heated debate among practitioners and scholars about whether this is possible in well-developed security markets. But there are often cases where an active management policy is required. These include:

- **Tax management issues.** Many investors are forced to pay taxes on certain profits that the security portfolio generates. For example, personal savings not placed in an IRA or part of an employer-sponsored pension plan are subject to taxation. In that case, it often makes sense to manage the portfolio actively in an attempt to maximize after-tax returns.

- **Nature of the investment.** Certain types of investments require an active management policy in order to minimize risk exposure. Examples include real estate, emerging markets in developing economies, and securities in industries subject to unique risks. The less price efficient the security market, the more active the investment strategy.

Market Efficiency

The decision to pursue an active or passive strategy depends largely on your opinion about market efficiency.

The efficient markets hypothesis (EMH) was originally developed in the late 1960s. It states that market prices should reflect all information known about a security. Clearly, the notion of an efficiently priced market is an extreme concept. Scholars and practitioners have been investigating the extent to which EMH applies to real-world markets for more than 35 years. We know they can not be perfectly efficient. If they were, there would be no incentives to attract financial analysts to watch for or develop new information.

Most research has been addressed to well-developed markets such as those in the United States, United Kingdom, Europe, and Japan. Some inefficiencies have been found, and a number of so-called market anomalies have been discovered that we do not yet understand very well. But most tests show these well-developed markets are more effi-cient than many people believe.

Empirical tests of market efficiency have examined three issues:

1. Are returns predictable? Tests of return predictability are referred to as tests of **weak form** market efficiency.
2. How do prices react to new information? This is referred to as **semi-strong form** market efficiency.
3. Do some investors have private information? This is referred to as **strong form** market efficiency.

In Chapter 9, we examine tests of each form of market efficiency in depth. But a brief review here is useful, since it will help you develop a perspective on whether investors should use active or passive management. Of course, the markets are not perfectly effi-cient. But they are more efficient than many people believe.

Are Returns Predictable?   Wouldn't it be nice if you could find a simple rule that would predict future security returns? You could become the guru of the investment world. In Chapter 9, we explore this question in some depth. However, our purpose here is to develop a general understanding of the issues involved so you can develop an informed opinion about active versus passive management.

There are two generations of research into the predictability of security returns. During the 1960s and 1970s most studies focused on trading strategies used by individuals called **technicians.** Starting in the mid-1980s, researchers began to examine whether **fundamen-tal variables,** such as a firm's size, are related to future returns.

Technicians use past data on variables such as stock prices and trading volume in an at-tempt to identify predictable patterns. A large number of different techniques are used by technicians. In fact, most technicians try to find a personal trading rule or procedure that works better than others.

One approach used by technicians, "support and resistance levels," conveys the basic idea underlying **technical analysis.** Consider the information plotted in Figure 2-2. In this figure, the month-end price of a stock is plotted over the past 60 months. Notice the price has varied a lot, but always within a band of $18 to $28. Whenever the stock increases to near $28, it has always declined in value. A technician would call this stock price a **resis-tance level.** Similarly, every time the stock falls to near $18, it has always increased in value. This stock price is called a **support level.** A technician would reason as follows:

For the past five years, the stock's price has tested the $28 and $18 levels many times and been unable to break through either. So a good strategy would be to buy near $18 and sell near $28. Also, if the stock is able to break through the support (resistance) level on high volume, the importance of the news will be great enough to cause further price decreases (increases). When this happens, I should sell (buy) fast before further price adjustments occur.

On first thought, this rule seems reasonable. There does appear to be a pattern in this stock's past prices. But if such a simple idea actually did work, then so many people would

FIGURE 2-2   ILLUSTRATION OF SUPPORT AND RESISTANCE LEVELS

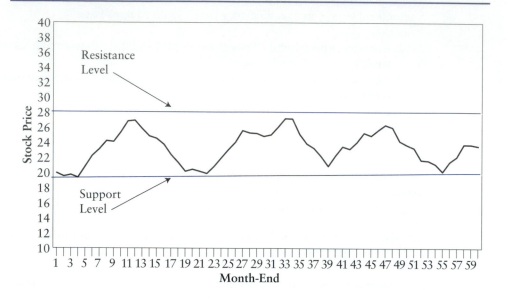

begin to use it that any possible usefulness in the rule would disappear. For example, if everyone began to buy shares of the stock as its price fell toward $18 and sell as its price rose toward $28, then a single new equilibrium price at around $23 would arise. At prices below $23, a large number of people would try to buy, but no one would be willing to sell. At prices above $23, exactly the opposite would occur. Thus, the shares would trade only at $23, until new information about the stocks value becomes available to the public! Notice that the attempt of many people trying to take advantage of a presumed market inefficiency has the effect of creating an efficient market! This also suggests that the apparent price pattern in Figure 2-2 was exactly that, apparent. At each date, the stock price should represent the market's assessment of its equilibrium value.

There is a more fundamental problem with rules such as "support and resistance": the potential for **data mining.** If you test a large number of rules on past data, you are bound to find rules that seem able to predict future prices.

For example, consider a class of 50 finance students, each armed with a coin. At the start of each week, each student tosses the coin and if "heads" come up the student predicts stock prices will rise during the next week. If "tails" come up, the prediction is that stock prices will fall. If this game is played for five weeks the probability of successfully predicting all five weekly price movements is 3.125% (0.5 raised to the fifth power), pretty small.[10] But in a class of 50 students, we would expect at least one student's coin would be successful in predicting all five price moves. Is this student's coin a good market predictor or were the results simply due to chance?

---

[10] This example assumes the probability of a weekly increase in stock prices is 0.5. In reality, the probability is slightly higher, since, on average, stocks increase in value over time.

A principle that underlies most technical selection strategies is that security prices tend to move in trends, and price movements are likely to continue in the same direction as they have recently been moving. This belief leads to statements such as, "This is a bad time to be in the stock market, since prices have taken a real beating lately." This opinion has been the subject of innumerable studies. With minor exceptions, no significant relationship can be found between past and future returns.

To illustrate this point, consider the data plotted in Panel A of Figure 2-3. Data used in the figure consists of monthly rates of return on an index of 500 large U.S. stocks called the S&P 500. The returns cover a period extending from the late 1920s through the mid-1990s. Each point in the figure shows the return in one month (call this month t) and the return in the subsequent month (month $t + 1$). If stock returns in month t can be used to predict returns in month $t + 1$, we would expect to see a clear relationship between the two. This clearly was not the case. The lack of any predictive content in past returns can also be seen in Panel B of the figure. In Panel B, all monthly returns greater than $+20\%$ or less than -20% have been excluded so we can zoom in on details of the dark mass in Panel A. Again, there is no predictive content observable. The returns from period to period appear to be random. In fact, this observation underlies a theory called the **random walk theory.** According to the random walk theory, returns from one period to another are random, they can not be predicted.

More recent studies of return predictability have focused on fundamental stock variables as predictors of future returns. Fundamental variables refer to stock characteristics such as the stock's ratio of stock price to earnings, the stock's ratio of dividends to stock price, and the stock's market capitalization (often called size). The results from these studies have been more positive than earlier tests of technical trading.

Consider the information depicted in Figure 2-4. The data is based on all stocks traded on the New York Stock Exchange and the American Stock Exchange during the years 1963 to 1991. At the start of each year, the market capitalization of each stock is calculated (stock price times shares outstanding) and placed into one of ten groups. These groups are based on market capitalization with group 1 consisting of the smallest stocks and group 10 the largest. The rate of return during the next year is then calculated for each group. This exercise is then repeated for each year between 1963 and 1991.

The vertical axis shows the average annual rate of return for each group. Notice that returns were the greatest for small capitalization stocks and the smallest for large capitalization stocks. This fact is referred to as the **small firm effect.**

A number of other fundamental variables that are statistically related to average future returns has also been found. Based on these studies, many professional investors are managing portfolios consisting of the types of stocks that historically had the greatest average returns. But investors should use information like this with caution because we simply do not know why these relationships existed in the past or whether they will continue in the future. It could be that these findings are actually market inefficiencies. But it is also possible that these fundamental variables are proxies for security risk.

How Do Prices React to New Information?   The efficient markets hypothesis predicts that market prices will adjust immediately to new information and that there will be no consistent overreaction or underreaction. Again, we leave a detailed review of this issue to Chapter 9. However, the following story is instructive.

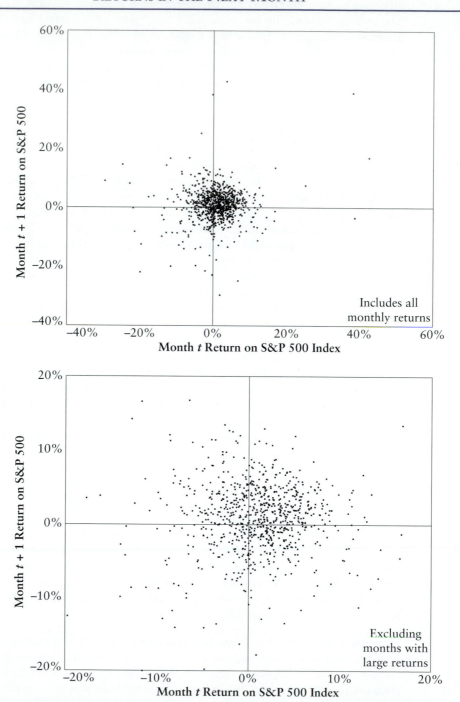

FIGURE 2-4   AVERAGE ANNUAL RETURNS ON STOCK WITH DIFFERENT CAPITALIZATION

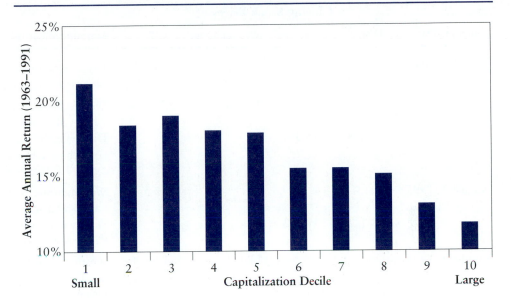

Within a two-day period in the summer of 1995, two announcements were made that were to have profound effects on the entertainment and television industries. On Monday July 31, Walt Disney Company announced that an agreement had been reached with Capital Cities/ABC to combine the firms. The announcement was unexpected and became the hot news of the day. For each share of Capital Cities/ABC, Disney would pay $65 in cash plus one share of Disney. On Tuesday, Westinghouse announced an agreement with the management of CBS, Inc. in which Westinghouse would purchase all shares of CBS, Inc. at a price of $81 per share. While this announcement was important, it was not unexpected. The financial press had published numerous articles about negotiations between Westinghouse and CBS during the previous few weeks.

Details of these announcements and closing stock prices for each firm are shown in Table 2-2 for the week of the announcements. On the prior Friday (July 28), none of the firms made any announcements that were reported in the Monday *Wall Street Journal*. On Monday, information about the Westinghouse-CBS deal suggested that Westinghouse was expected to offer $5 billion for CBS shares. In reaction to this information, CBS shares closed "2 points" ($2) higher than Friday's close. But the totally unexpected news of Monday was the Disney-Capital Cities/ABC disclosure. Based on Disney's agreement to pay $65 in cash plus one share of Disney for each share of Capital Cities/ABC, the closing price of Capital Cities/ABC shares rose from 96 1/8 on Friday to 116 1/4 on Monday, a 21% increase in a single day.[11] Market prices of CBS shares didn't respond much to the Westinghouse

---

[11] If Capital Cities/ABC shares had fully reflected the value that Disney had offered, they would have closed at 123 5/8 on Monday. The fact that they closed at 116 1/4 can be explained by uncertainty over whether the deal might actually take place.

TABLE 2-2 ANNOUNCEMENT DETAILS OF TWO MERGERS

Calendar Date	Closing Stock Prices of				Announcement Information(1)
	Disney	ABC	Westinghouse	CBS	
July 28, 1995			13 7/8	75 7/8	No information reported
	57 3/8	96 1/8			No information reported
July 31, 1995			13 5/8	77 3/4	Westinghouse expected to buy CBS for $5 billion
	58 5/8	116 1/4			Disney agreed to purchase ABC for $65 plus 1.0 Disney share
August 1, 1995			15	77 3/4	Westinghouse will buy CBS for $81 a share
	61 1/2	119 1/2			Disney and Capital Cities/ABC will push ahead
August 2, 1995			14 1/4	78 1/4	Westinghouse will cut costs at CBS
	60 5/8	119			Disney is considering . . . not related to ABC
August 3, 1995			14	78 1/2	No information reported
	59 3/8	117 3/8			Disney will program ABC Saturday mornings
August 4, 1995			14 1/8	78 5/8	No information reported
	58	115 1/2			No information reported

SOURCE: From the *Wall Street Journal* published the day after the closing prices shown. For example, the announcement shown for July 31 was in the August 1 *Wall Street Journal*. But the public announcement occurred on July 31 before the close of stock trading.

announcement because it contained little new information. In contrast, the Disney announcement contained significant new information and share prices reacted appropriately.

On Tuesday, Westinghouse made a formal announcement that it intended to pay $81 per share for CBS. Since this information had already been "discounted" in the price of CBS shares, the announcement had no effect on share prices of CBS.

This is a single example of how rapidly share prices react to information that is truly new. In Chapter 9, we examine evidence which suggests to some scholars that investors overreact to certain types of information. But this evidence is the subject of wide debate. On the whole, most academic studies have found that prices adjust rapidly to new information and there does not appear to be a consistent bias towards over- or underreaction.

Do Some Investors Have Private Information? The EMH implies that no investors have information that allows them consistently to earn higher returns than a passive strategy of equivalent risk.

Some investors might believe they have unique information that is not reflected in existing market prices and trade accordingly. Strong form EMH states that such investors will be lucky one-half the time and earn greater returns than a passive strategy. But they will also be unlucky the other one-half the time and earn lower returns than the passive strategy.

Most academic studies looking for private information have focused on two groups: corporate insiders (such as officers and directors) and professional portfolio managers. The results have been mixed. Trading activities of corporate insiders do appear to earn significantly larger returns than a passive strategy of equivalent risk. Most people consider this to be a clear violation of EMH. Studies of the returns earned by professional portfolio managers, however, are less clear. Early studies suggested that such managers had no private information and that one would be as well off, or better off, by owning a passive portfolio. More recent studies suggest that some portfolio managers have private information sufficient to cover the management fee which they charge for managing a portfolio. But no studies of active portfolio managers have found that active management returns dominate passive returns of the same risk.

The Decision to Be Active or Passive

The decision to follow an active or passive strategy should be based on two criteria: (1) the type of the investment, and (2) the investor's knowledge. Securities that are actively traded in major financial markets are most likely efficiently priced. Unless the investor has special skills, a passive approach to managing such securities is the most cost effective. However, other securities, such as those traded in emerging markets or real estate claims, might not be properly priced and require an active management approach.

The investor's personal knowledge is also important. People with little knowledge should probably follow a passive strategy whereas someone with special training and rapid access to information could use an active strategy.

Both of these ideas are displayed visually in Figure 2-5. Let's see how they apply to the decisions that Claire, Dan Hilbert, and Maria Perez make.[12]

Claire has decided to invest only in securities traded in active markets and realizes she has little investment knowledge. Thus, she has decided to follow a totally passive strategy. Her major decision is what asset allocation to select. Once this decision has been made, she intends to purchase an index fund for each asset class.

Dan Hilbert and the other trustees of HPT have decided to follow a mixed active-passive approach. After deciding on the portfolio's asset allocation, they intend to maintain this mix for a number of years as opposed to engaging in "timing" their investment in each asset class. However, because they have the time and resources, they have decided to follow an active strategy within each asset class. They have hired an investment consultant who will help them find a number of investment managers who will actively manage securities within a given asset class.

Maria Perez intends to pursue a very active approach in managing her mutual fund's investments in Latin America. She will actively manage the percentage of the portfolio committed to Latin American countries in total, to individual countries, and to individual securities. In addition, she intends to actively manage the portfolio's exposure to currency exchange rate risks. But even Maria intends to use a passive approach to one segment of

---

[12] As noted earlier, there are no single best choices to be made for each investor. The choices suggested here are offered only as reasonable alternatives, the types of decisions made by actual investors.

FIGURE 2-5 WHAT SPECULATIVE STRATEGY IS APPROPRIATE

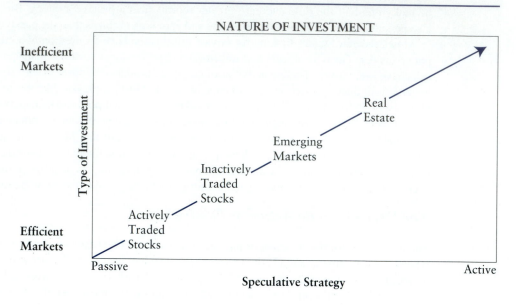

NATURE OF INVESTMENT

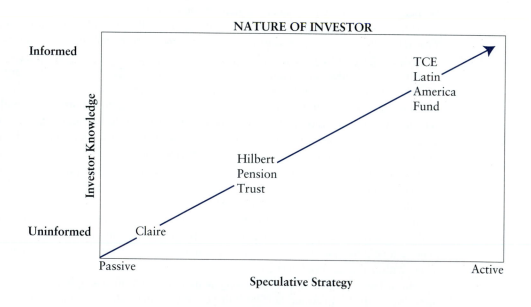

NATURE OF INVESTOR

Patricia D. McQueen

Director, Advocacy Programs

Association for Investment Management and Research (AIMR)

College of Saint Elizabeth, B.A.

New York University, M.B.A.

New York University, Ph.D.

AIMR's Advocacy Programs represent the views of AIMR members to regulatory authorities, legislative bodies, proessional associations, the investment industry, and the general public in both the U.S. and aborad. The various advocacy committees together with AIMR staff monitor legislative and regulatory activities to identify issues of interest to AIMR members of the investing public. Patricia McQueen manages these programs.

In March 1995, pursuant to the Securities Act of 1933 and the Securities Exchange Act of 1934, the U.S. Securities and Exchange Commission (SEC) solicited the opinions of investment professionals regarding the potential abbreviation of financial statements issued by publicly traded companies. The following is a partial presentation of the comments by the Financial Accounting Policy Committee (FAPC) and the Corporate Information Committee (CIC) of the Association for Investment Management and Research (AIMR) regarding the rule proposal.

Q: The footnotes that are included with financial statements contain a great deal of detailed information. In order to conduct a thorough analysis of a company's financial condition and future prospects, are these "notes" mandatory?

A: Although there is continuing debate on the degree to which market efficiency actually exists, there is general agreement that financial information does affect security prices. The corollary is that markets could not possibly be efficient if financial statements were not available. Information is the lifeblood of all markets. In *Financial Reporting in the 1990's and Beyond,* we point out many ways in which the myriad of detailed information contained in the annual report is used by financial analysts and other knowledgeable investors, thus contributing to the efficiency of the capital markets.

Q: Generally, are the proposed abbreviated financial statements appropriate and useful for both investors and issuers?

A: No. We disagree in principle with the concept of abbreviated financial statements. Investors, professional or otherwise, must all receive the same information on an equal and timely basis so that the nonprofessional is not disadvantaged. We also believe that the observed increase in note disclosures, which forms the basis of this rule proposal, is the result of (1) a more complex business environment (e.g., growth of derivative securities, environmental obligations) than existed 20 years ago, and (2) decisions by the FASB to favor footnote disclosures of these complexities rather than measurement and recognition in the financial statements. Complex matters (e.g., pensions, other post-employment benefits, income taxes, leases, and stock option costs) are not fairly presented on the face of the financial statements. These topics are covered *only* in the footnotes that the Commission proposes to omit. We believe that the affairs of giant enterprises operating in a complex world cannot be explained in short, succinct financial statements. To pretend otherwise by reducing the information delivered to shareholders is naive and unfair to the inexperienced shareholder and investor. Despite our opposition to the use of abbreviated financial statements, we recognize the need to make financial statement disclosures readable and understandable by the average investor.

Q: If the proposed rule is approved, what are a few suggestions you would make in order to protect the investor?

A: (1) The delivery of full financial statements in the annual report to shareholders is a shareholder right—not a privilege. Therefore, we suggest that investors be given the opportunity to "opt out" of receiving the full financial statements rather than being forced to "opt in." We suggest that registrants be required to provide a toll-free number in order to encourage and facilitate requests for Form 10-K containing full financial statements. In addition, registrants must be required to maintain a standing list of all interested parties, not limited to shareholders, who wish to receive the full financial statements or Form 10-K on an annual basis. We also believe as long as companies are prepared to provide Form 10-K, they should be able to provide Forms 10-Q, 8-K, etc., through the same mechanism.

(2) Registrants should provide full financial statements in their entirety in Part II of the registration statement. Since so much of the burden of information acquisition is shifted to the investor by this rule proposal, investors should be able to request one comprehensive document to get the information they need. We must emphasize again that our concern is primarily for nonprofessional investors and the role they play in making markets efficient. Investment professionals are accustomed to retrieving and using information from a variety of sources in analyzing financial information and making investment decisions. Nonprofessionals may not have the time to acquire, or easy access to, additional data and should not be further disadvantaged by having to retrieve from multiple sources the information which they have been accustomed to receiving in one package.

(3) Unless they provide primary financial statements in accordance with U.S. GAAP, foreign private issuers should not be eligible to provide abbreviated financial statements.

(4) We recommend that the abbreviated financial statements include a prominent warning that the shareholder has not received a complete set of financial statements and an investment decision with respect to the securities of the company should not be made until the investor has received and conducted a thorough review of the full financial statements.

(5) We ask the Commission to identify the enforcement mechanisms that will be put in place to ensure that companies respond promptly to requests for full financial statements. We recommend that failure to comply with the delivery provision result in loss of eligibility to use abbreviated financial statements.

In 1995, the SEC retreated from its desire to abbreviate financial statements. The efforts of the advocacy groups that McQueen directs, among others, were instrumental in illuminating the value of readily accessible, fully disclosed documentation by public companies.

the portfolio. Specifically, any funds not invested in Latin America will be placed in short-term U.S. Treasury bills. Although she might be able to obtain slightly higher returns on such funds if she were to buy short-term debt securities having a little default risk, she does not have the time or knowledge needed to evaluate them properly.

In short, the decision to use an active versus a passive approach to managing an investment portfolio depends on the types of securities to be owned and the investor's knowledge.

Decision 2: Asset Allocation

Asset allocation refers to the types of asset classes held in a portfolio and the percentage weights assigned to each class. There is no single way of defining an asset class. One person might consider all stocks traded in the United States to be a single class, while another might wish to divide U.S. stocks into a number of asset classes based on variables such as market capitalization, dividend growth, and risk.

Regardless of how one choses to define asset classes, there is little doubt that **asset allocation is the major determinant of the risk and future returns of diversified portfolios.** The asset allocation of a diversified portfolio is considerably more important than the individual securities held.

To illustrate this fact, consider the data shown in the top half of Table 2-3. This data represents yearly rates of return earned by nine different portfolio managers during the first five years of the 1990s. These are actual returns on well-diversified, actively managed portfolios. The asset classes in which the portfolios invested were as follows:

2 invested in short-term U.S. fixed income securities
2 invested in long-term U.S. fixed income securities
2 invested in U.S. stocks
2 invested in stocks of non-U.S. well-developed countries
1 invested in Latin American stocks

TABLE 2-3   WHICH PORTFOLIOS ARE IN THE SAME ASSET CLASS?

Percentage Annual Return on Each Fund
Randomized Fund Listing

Year	A	B	C	D	E	F	G	H	I
1990	9	87	9	7	−3	8	−6	−1	−14
1991	11	88	9	16	28	15	11	22	13
1992	4	29	5	9	8	6	−6	8	−5
1993	4	56	4	11	18	10	32	14	34
1994	3	−20	3	−5	−3	−4	−2	0	−7

Ordered Fund Listing by Asset Class

	Short-Term Bond Funds		Long-Term Bond Funds		U.S. Stock Funds		Non-U.S. Stock Funds		Emerging Market Fund
Year	A	C	D	F	E	H	G	I	B
1990	9	9	7	8	−3	−1	−6	−14	87
1991	11	9	16	15	28	22	11	13	88
1992	4	5	9	6	8	8	−6	−5	29
1993	4	4	11	10	18	14	32	34	56
1994	3	3	−5	−4	−3	0	−2	−7	−20

Most professional managers who use active management strategies specialize either in timing across asset classes or in security selection within an asset class. None of these portfolio managers engaged in timing. Instead, they chose to specialize in a particular asset class. They did so because it is virtually impossible to be well informed about the securities in more than one asset class. But any two managers investing in the same asset class held different securities in their individual portfolios. Thus, the returns on each of these nine managers will differ for two reasons: (1) they invested in different asset classes, and (2) they held different securities within an asset class.

In the top half of Table 2-3 the order of the funds is not the same as the listing here. Instead the funds are displayed in a random manner. Can you determine which funds belong to the same asset class? Try it! While there are a lot of numbers, you will be surprised how easy it is to classify them.

The proper classification is shown in the bottom half of the table. Funds A and C clearly belong together, since they have the least volatile returns; these are the two short-term fixed income funds. Funds D and F have very similar returns; these are the two long-term U.S. bond funds. Funds E and H are the U.S. stock funds and Funds G and I are the "international" stock funds.[13] Finally, Fund B is the Latin America fund.

---

[13] In the United States, an *international fund* refers to one which owns securities in countries other than the United States. The term *global* refers to securities in both the United States and other countries.

This informal analysis illustrates what many more rigorous studies have shown. Most of the returns and risks of a portfolio are determined by the asset classes held in the portfolio, not by the individual securities held. In fact, many studies have shown that the asset allocation of a diversified portfolio usually accounts for 90% or more of a portfolio's rates of return.

Principles of Investment Risk

Security investment is risky. Some asset classes have relatively little risk (such as funds A and C in the preceeding example), while others have considerable risk (such as fund B). A major objective here to help you develop a clear understanding of investment risk and how it can be managed. In Chapters 5 through 8, various measures of investment risk are discussed in detail. In this chapter, we focus on five basic principles of investment risk.

Principle 1: Investment risk is best defined as uncertainty about the value of a portfolio when it is expected to be liquidated. Remember Claire? She has decided to begin a new investment program that will pay for an extended trip around the world, which she wants to take in five years from now. She is considering three investment alternatives:

1. Alternative 1 consists of buying a sequence of one-year certificates of deposit (CDs). When each CD matures, Claire would roll the maturing value over into a new one-year CD. The current one-year rate on these certificates is 5%. She does not know the interest rates that CDs will pay in future years.
2. Alternative 2 consists of buying a five-year CD. For each $1.00 she invests today, the five-year CD will pay $1.276 at the end of five years. This represents an annualized rate of return equal to 5%. The only date at which this CD provides a cash flow is at the end of five years; no intermediate cash flows will be received. If Claire wishes to cash the CD in before the end of year 5, she will receive cash equal to the market value of the CD at that time. Its market value can fluctuate considerably as interest rates change over time. But the $1.276 at the end of year 5 is certain.
3. Alternative 3 consists of buying an index mutual fund that invests in U.S. stocks. The value of this fund can fluctuate considerably from year to year and there is considerable uncertainty about the fund's value five years from now.

Which of these three alternatives is the least risky, given Claire's wish to liquidate the portfolio in exactly five years?

Clearly, alternative 3 is the most risky. But alternative 1 is also risky to Claire, since she does not know today what one-year CD rates will be in years 2 through 5. Even though the current one-year CD rate is known with certainty, a sequence of one-year CDs is risky. Only investors who intend to liquidate their portfolio in one year would consider alternative 1 to be risk free.

Given Claire's objective of liquidating this portfolio in five years, the five-year CD is least risky. During the time she owns the five-year CD, its market value might fluctuate considerably. But she should be unconcerned about this volatility if she is confident she will need to liquidate the portfolio only at the end of year 5.

This example illustrates that the risk of an investment should be viewed in the context of when the portfolio is to be liquidated. To keep our analyses simple, we usually assume a single future liquidation date. The time between the initial investment and the single liquidation date is called the **investment horizon.**

Principle 2: With a few exceptions, the longer the investment horizon, the greater the uncertainty about the future value of the portfolio.[14] The relationship between investment risk and the length of the investment horizon is widely misunderstood. Many people believe that time provides a form of diversification such that long-term investors face less risk than do shorter term investors. They reason that "good years offset bad years." Unfortunately, this belief is wrong. Bearing investment risk for ten years is more risky than bearing investment risk for one year. Stated differently, there is more uncertainty about the value of an investment portfolio in ten years from today than there is about its value in one year.

Principle 3: Different asset classes have different amounts of investment risk. Since this principle is well known, there is no need to discuss it at length here. In later chapters, when we quantify investment risk, we will be able to measure how much riskier one investment is than another.

Principles 2 and 3 are illustrated graphically in the three panels of Figure 2-6. In each panel the real growth of a $1 investment is traced for various past time spans. (Real growth means that inflation has been subtracted.) When we examine real growth of an investment, we are focusing on the growth of consumption power. If $1 grows to $2, the ability to consume has doubled.

Each panel contains seven lines. One line traces the real growth of a $1 investment made at the start of 1930 through each of the next ten years ending at December 31, 1939. Another line starts at 1940 and goes through 1949. The same is true for 1950–1959, 1960–1969, 1970–1979, and 1980–1989. The last line extends from 1990 to 1994. Thus, we are looking at seven different investment outcomes, each independent of the others.

Each panel presents data for a different asset class. In the top panel, the real growth of a $1 investment in U.S. Treasury bills is shown. In the middle panel, the investment is in U.S. Treasury bonds. In the bottom panel, the investment is in the Standard & Poor's 500 (S&P 500), an index of stock returns on a portfolio of 500 large U.S. companies.

A visual comparison of the panels confirms the following:

◾ Principle 2. The longer the investment horizon, the greater the uncertainty about the value of the portfolio. For example, consider the panel that shows outcomes from investments in the S&P 500. The dispersion of investment values for a ten-year investor is considerably larger than for a one-year investor.

◾ Principle 3. Different asset classes have different amounts of investment risk. Regardless, of the investment horizon, the dispersion of outcomes from Treasury bills was the smallest and the dispersion of S&P 500 outcomes the greatest.

---

[14] The major exception to this principle is the illustration here in which a long-term, default-free fixed income security is available that provides a single cash inflow at a known future date.

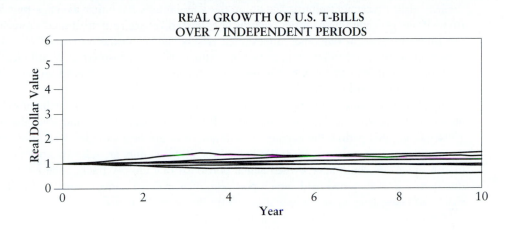

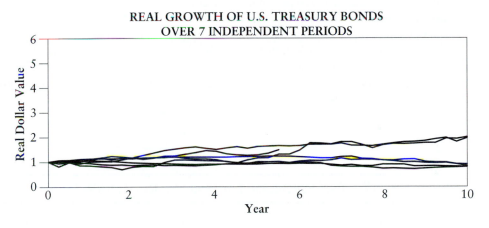

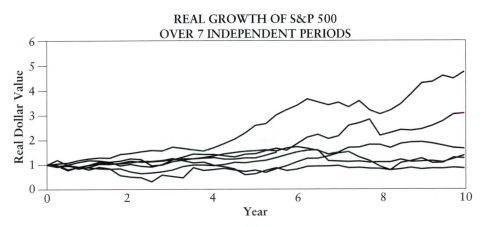

Principle 4: Investment risk can be reduced by diversification across securities in an asset class and across asset classes. Consider the information shown in Figure 2-7, a standard graph depicting the relationship between investment returns and security risk. Investment returns shown on the vertical axis are either **average past returns** if one is examining historical returns or **expected future returns** if one is forecasting future investment outcomes. Investment risk is shown on the horizontal axis. For now, you do not need to understand how investment risk is measured. It is sufficient to recognize that if investment X has 30 units of risk and investment Y has 15 units of risk, then X is twice as risky as Y.

Figure 2-7 contains two boxes and one curve. The box positioned at 16 units of risk is based on the yearly rates of return on the S&P 500 Index over the period 1969 through 1994. During this period, the average annual rate of return on this index was 11.3% and the number of risk units was 15.8. While the S&P 500 is simply an index of stock performance, investors could have owned actual portfolios that closely tracked the returns on this portfolio. If they had held such a portfolio, their average annual return and units of risk would have been identical to that shown for the S&P 500 index.

The other box, shown above 30 risk units, represents the average outcomes from investing in a single stock that was part of the S&P 500 Index. Think of it in this way. There is a large box in which one share of each company in the S&P 500 Index is placed. Investor number 1 steps up to the box and draws one of these shares at random. This single stock then represents the investor's portfolio over the period 1969 to 1994. In order to give each successive investor the same chances at drawing similar stocks, a new share of the first stock drawn is placed in the box. Investors 2, 3, 4 until 1,000 repeat the exercise of investor 1, drawing a single share which represents their portfolio over the 1969 to 1994 period.

What will be the average annual return these 1,000 investors earn? Clearly, it will be the same as the average return on the aggregate index of 11.3%. Some investors will incur

FIGURE 2-7   THE POWER OF DIVERSIFICATION (1969–1994)

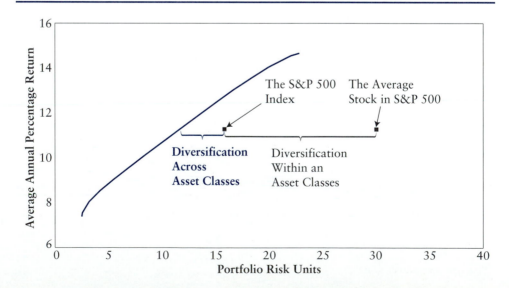

a larger average annual return and some lower. But across all 1,000 investors they will have an average of 11.3%.

But the average risk these investors in a single stock portfolio incur will be considerably greater than the risk of a portfolio of all the stocks. In fact, the number of risk units that the average investor in these single stock portfolios face would have been about 30.

By diversifying across a large number of securities within an asset class, investment risk can be reduced. In the example just cited, diversification cut the risk of stock ownership in half!

The curve in Figure 2-7 represents the *lowest risk that could have been achieved during this time period for various levels of average annual returns.* This curve is known as the **efficient frontier.** It plays an important role in investment risk management. In Chapter 6, we discuss how efficient frontiers are calculated. The efficient frontier shown in Figure 2-7 consists of investments in the following asset classes: U.S. Treasury bills, U.S. Treasury bonds, the S&P 500, an index of small U.S. stocks not contained in the S&P 500, and an index of stock returns in well-developed countries other than the United States.

The bottom left of this efficient frontier represents a portfolio that had the lowest risk between 1969 and 1994. It consists of an investment of 92% in T-bills, 4% in Treasury bonds and 4% in international stocks. The top right of the efficient frontier represents the portfolio that had the highest annual rate of return between 1969 and 1994.[15] It also had the greatest units of risk and consisted of a 100% investment in international stocks.

Between the lowest and highest risk portfolios are an infinite number of possible choices. But let's consider the portfolio that had the same rate of return as did the S&P 500 (11.3%). This portfolio consisted of the following:

Asset Class	Optimal Percentage to Invest in to Achieve the Same Return as S&P 500	Portfolio Information
Treasury bills	21.8%	Average annual Rate of return
Treasury bonds	26.7%	(1969–1994) = 11.3%
S&P 500 Index	0.8%	
Small U.S. stocks	10.8%	
International stocks	39.9%	Units of Risk = 11.8
Total	100.0%	

By diversifying across each of these asset classes, an average return identical to that of the S&P 500 could have been earned, but at lower risk. Risk units in the S&P 500 were 15.8. Risk units on this efficient frontier portfolio were 11.8, a 25% percent reduction. The moral of the story should be clear: *Thou shalt diversify,* both within an asset class and across asset classes.

Principle 5: Investment risk can be managed by changing the asset allocation of the portfolio. Once the investor has calculated (or been given) an efficient frontier of

---

[15] The period 1969 through 1994 was selected simply because trustworthy rates of return on international stocks are not available for years before 1969.

portfolios, the risk that is incurred can be adjusted by selecting different portfolios on the efficient frontier. For example, consider Figure 2-8. In the figure the same efficient frontier is shown as in Figure 2-7. Details of four portfolios on this efficient frontier are shown directly below each portfolio. The least risky portfolio consisted of investing 92% in Treasury bills, 4% in Treasury bonds, and 4% in international stocks. It might seem strange that the least risky portfolio includes an investment in international equities, but they provide a diversification advantage that lowers the risk of investing solely in Treasury bills.

Increased average returns are available only by accepting greater risk. For example, the second and third portfolios have reduced exposure to Treasury bills and increased exposure to more risky asset classes. The most risky portfolio consisted of a 100% allocation to international equities.

Selecting an Asset Allocation

The following factors should be considered when selecting a particular asset allocation:

1. Investment time horizon   5. Tax considerations
2. Real vs. nominal needs   6. Regulations
3. Knowledge   7. Unique needs
4. Liquidity needs   8. Risk tolerance

The ordering of the list does not reflect their relative importance. In fact, the most important consideration, risk tolerance, is listed last so it can be highlighted.

Investment Horizon. It is widely believed that long-term investors should invest in more risky portfolios. This is probably true, but not for the reason many people believe.

The reason commonly offered for long-term investors to seek greater risk is best described as "diversification over time." As we noted earlier in the chapter, this logic suggests that "good years will offset bad years," resulting in lower risk for long-term investors. This simply is not true. When portfolio risk is defined as *uncertainty about the value of a portfolio at the date when it is to be liquidated,* it is clear that uncertainty about portfolio value is positively related to the length of the investment horizon. For example, uncertainty about the value of $1 invested in the S&P 500 Index is greater for a ten-year horizon than it is for a one-year horizon.[16]

However, there are valid reasons for longer-term investors to bear greater risk. First, long-term investors have **options** that are not available to short-term investors. Consider two people who are investing for retirement income. One investor, Claire, has 20 years until retirement and the other, Neal, is aged 75 and already retired. If Claire suffers a number of losses in portfolio values, she has the option to work at increasing her labor income. Neal does not have such an option.

Second, consider the wealth of each of these two investors. Much of Claire's wealth consists of the present value of future job income, an asset that might not be particularly risky. The percentage of Claire's wealth held in marketable securities might be relatively small relative to her job income wealth. Thus, Claire might be willing to accept greater risk in the part of her wealth invested in financial assets. In contrast, Neal has no present value of future job income; all of his wealth is invested in financial assets. Thus, Neal might wish to have less risk in his security portfolio than when he was younger.

Real vs. Nominal Needs. Most investors save in order to provide future consumption and, thus, have a need for real (after inflation) portfolio growth. However, there are some investors who do not need to worry about inflation. An example would be a life insurance

FIGURE 2-8 RISK MANAGEMENT WITH ASSET ALLOCATION (1969–1994)

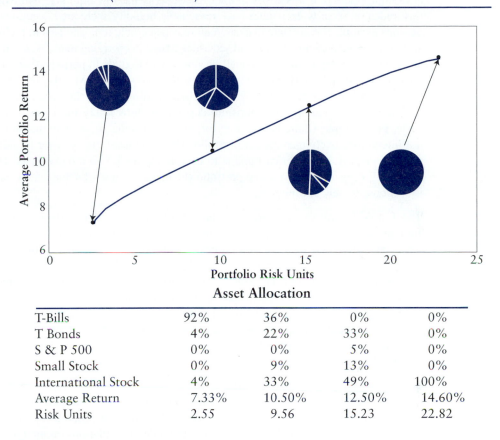

Asset Allocation

T-Bills	92%	36%	0%	0%
T Bonds	4%	22%	33%	0%
S & P 500	0%	0%	5%	0%
Small Stock	0%	9%	13%	0%
International Stock	4%	33%	49%	100%
Average Return	7.33%	10.50%	12.50%	14.60%
Risk Units	2.55	9.56	15.23	22.82

company that promises to pay a fixed dollar amount at the death of an insured. Since the payment is not tied to inflation, the insurance company does not need an inflation hedge. The question as to how well different investment strategies act as inflation hedges is beyond the scope of this chapter.

Knowledge. This very important consideration is not sufficiently appreciated. Before an investment is made in any asset class, investors should have a clear understanding of the risks of the investment. Otherwise, they are likely to do something foolish. For example, during 1973 and 1974, an investment in the S&P 500 lost 53% of its real value. Many investors bailed out of stocks to invest in what they believed to be more sure things (like diamonds and gold). But in the subsequent two years, the real value of the S&P 500 rose 55%! Know the risks of the investment before investing.

---

[16] We will see in later chapters that the confusion which has arisen over this issue grows out of how one defines risk. Proponents of time diversification look at the volatility of annualized rates of return. Uncertainty about annualized returns does decrease as the investment horizon increases, but solely due to the way in which annualized returns are calculated. The apparent reduction in risk is due to mathematics of the calculation. When risk is more properly focused on portfolio values, it becomes clear that risk increases in time.

Liquidity Needs. If a security can be traded rapidly and at little cost, then it has high liquidity. But if some time (an hour, a day, or more) is needed to find someone willing to trade at existing prices or if it is costly to trade, the security has low liquidity. While most securities traded on security exchanges have reasonable liquidity, there are exceptions. The most obvious example is real estate that can require considerable time and cost to trade. Other examples include municipal bonds and securities traded in emerging markets. Even stocks that are usually very liquid can occasionally become hard to trade in periods of dramatic market moves. For example, during the stock market gyrations of Black Monday in 1987, trading in all stocks on the New York Stock Exchange became difficult and time consuming.[17]

The need for liquidity in a portfolio depends on how likely the investor will wish to trade. For example, Claire is investing for retirement some 20 years in the future and does not intend to actively manage her portfolio. Thus, she has little need for liquidity. In contrast, the TCE Latin America Fund is to be actively traded on a daily basis. Thus, Maria Perez will keep a large part of the portfolio she manages in stocks that can be easily traded in response to new information.

Tax Considerations. In concept, future returns and risks of a portfolio should be evaluated on an after-tax basis. In practice, this is often difficult to do, since each investor's tax situation differs and changes over time. In addition, the complexity of tax codes and changes in them over time make it difficult to develop well-defined tax strategies. However, the tax consequences of alternative investment strategies deserve some attention. For example, Claire and Hilbert Pension Trust do not pay taxes on any income of their investment portfolios. Thus, they should not purchase securities that provide tax shelters such as municipal bonds. Other investors who are taxed might find the after-tax returns on municipal bonds to be greater than after-tax returns on other bonds of similar risk. We discuss taxes in further detail in Chapter 19.

Regulations. Many investment portfolios are subject to various regulations. For example, until recently, the pension fund for employees of the city of Atlanta was restricted by a city ordinance to own only fixed income securities. And insurance companies, as well as banks, are subject to a wide variety of state and federal regulations on the types of securities they may own.

Unique Needs. Aside from governmental regulations, the investor might wish to place personal constraints on the types of securities to be owned. Common restrictions relate to social concerns such as human rights policies, environmental concerns, and concerns about the type of product a company sells. If such constraints are to be imposed, care should be taken to assure that the portfolio remains sufficiently diversified.

Risk Tolerance. For most investors, the asset allocation they choose will be determined largely by their risk tolerance. All investors prefer higher expected portfolio returns to lower. But at some point, higher expected returns come with unacceptable risks.

Measuring an investor's risk tolerance is difficult, if not impossible. However, we can provide information to investors about the risks inherent in portfolios on an efficient frontier in a manner they can understand and help them make informed decisions. This information could be stated in terms of "risk units" as shown in Figure 2-8. But unless the investor is well

---

[17] Black Monday refers to October 19, 1987, when the Dow Jones industrial average fell by 508 points—down almost 23% in a single day.

trained in investment theory, it is doubtful he or she will be able to understand what, say, ten risk units (in later chapters, ten standard deviations) means. There are other ways, however, of displaying investment risk in a manner that unsophisticated investors can understand. Our theories of investment management remain unchanged. But the manner in which the results are communicated should be designed with the knowledge of the investor in mind.

One very effective device is to show the investor past yearly returns which each portfolio would have earned such as in Table 2-4. Other approaches are shown in later chapters.

TABLE 2-4   PAST YEARLY RETURNS ON FOUR EFFICIENT PORTFOLIOS

Portfolio Composition	A	B	C	D
T-bills	0.92	0.36	0.00	0.00
T bonds	0.04	0.22	0.33	0.00
S&P 500	0.00	0.00	0.05	0.00
Small stocks	0.00	0.09	0.13	0.00
International stocks	0.04	0.33	0.49	1.00

Percentage Annual Rates of Return, 1969–1994

6	−1	−5	3
6	0	−3	−11
6	16	23	31
5	15	21	38
6	−6	−13	−14
7	−6	−14	−22
7	22	32	37
5	11	15	4
5	11	12	19
8	16	20	34
10	9	9	6
11	15	18	24
14	5	−0	−1
11	15	18	−1
9	15	19	25
10	9	8	8
11	31	43	57
9	31	44	70
6	9	10	25
7	16	21	29
9	11	14	11
7	−5	−12	−23
6	14	20	−12
3	2	1	12
5	18	25	33
3	3	3	8

TABLE 2-5 DETERMINANTS OF ASSET ALLOCATION

Considerations When Selecting an Asset Allocation	Implications for		
	Claire	Hilbert Pension Trust	TCE Latin America Fund
Investment Time Horizon	Initially long term. Begin with moderate risk and reduce risk as retirement approaches.	Long term for many years. Maintain moderate to above average risk exposure until employee work force matures.	Not applicable to a portfolio such as this.
Real *vs.* Nominal Needs	Nominal. Seek inflation hedges, do not overweight long-term bonds.	Nominal. Seek inflation hedges, do not overweight long-term bonds.	Not applicable to a portfolio such as this.
Knowledge	Little. Do not invest in asset classes she has little knowledge about. Suggests small commitment to international.	Considerable. Seek out new asset classes in attempt to broaden portfolio diversification.	Considerable in the asset class being managed.
Liquidity Needs	Initially little but will increase as she approaches retirement.	Little. There is little need to demand liquidity from investments.	Considerable. Needs to be able to trade rapidly in response to new information. Stocks held should be very liquid.
Tax Considerations	None. Do not buy tax-sheltered securities.	None. Do not buy tax-sheltered securities.	None.
Regulations	None.	Highly regulated but no regulations on investment strategy.	Must follow registration with SEC that states types of allowable investments.
Unique Needs	None.	None.	None.
Risk Tolerance	Moderate.	Moderate to high.	High.

Asset Allocation of the Three Investors

Table 2-5 summarizes of the asset allocation considerations for our three investors. Claire would probably select a moderate risk portfolio due to her long-time horizon and relatively little investment knowledge. HPT would probably select a more risky portfolio due to their greater knowledge and willingness to actively monitor the portfolio. The TCE Latin America fund would have large risk by definition of the securities to be held in the portfolio.

Decision 3: Security Selection

Of the three key investment decisions discussed in this chapter, security selection is probably the most straightforward and easiest. Should the investor decide which individual securities will be held in the portfolio or employ one or more professional managers to do so? This is not an "either or" decision; certain portions of the portfolio might be personally managed and other portions placed in the hands of management companies.

There is a close tie between a decision to use passive management strategies and how securities are selected, since the most cost-effective way to implement a passive strategy is to employ passive index funds. Typically these index funds specialize in a single asset class such as U.S. stocks, stocks traded in well-developed countries other than the U.S., and stocks traded in emerging markets. Thus, an index fund is usually bought for each asset class.

Our discussion of security selection is aimed mainly at investors who choose an active investment strategy. What are the advantages to personally selecting the securities to be held versus employing managers to do so?

Advantages of Personal Selection

First, it can be fun. Many people find the analysis and selection of securities intellectually stimulating. In addition, investors are able to select securities that best meet their particular investment situation. This is especially true for managing the tax consequences of investment decisions. For example, consider two stocks bought at a cost of $50 two years ago. One is now priced at $75 and the other at $25. Proper tax strategy would call for selling the $25 stock in order to realize a taxable loss and holding on to the $75 stock in order to delay taxes on its gains. But if the investor believes the $75 stock is overvalued and will soon fall in value, both stocks could be sold for a zero net taxable profit. If the investor had employed a professional manager such as a mutual fund, the manager would not consider the investor's tax situation when deciding which securities to trade. The ability to obtain tax savings from personal management is an important value that is largely given up if professional managers are employed.[18]

Advantages of Professional Selection. As we noted in Chapter 1, there are three potential advantages to using professional managers: cost, diversification, and manager expertise. Because these managers run large sums of money, they are able to achieve economies of scale not available to small investors. Costs of obtaining information are spread across many investors and they are able to negotiate rock bottom trading costs.

---

[18] In recent years, a few mutual fund companies have created new tax-managed funds that follow strategies designed to minimize U.S. income taxes.

Greater diversification is obtained by pooling investor funds into commingled portfolios. And, although the "value added" by professional active managers is the subject of much debate, professional managers are less likely to overreact to unexpected events than less knowledgeable individual investors.

Statement of Investment Policy

Once decisions have been made regarding active/passive management, asset allocation, and security selection, the decisions should be documented in a written statement of investment policy. This is not a nicety that only large portfolios need—it is a necessity for all portfolios.

There is no single best organization for this document. Use an organization that will be best understood by the investor. However, it is common to have three sections: (1) investment objective, (2) investment constraints, and (3) investment policies.

The investment objective is usually a return objective related to the asset allocation that has been chosen. For example, "The portfolio objective is to earn a rate of return over the next five years that is greater than available from owning a passive index fund in each of the asset classes held in the portfolio." Investment constraints can include factors such as liquidity constraints, tax requirements, and any other relevant constraints. But the most important constraint is the asset allocation which will be used and how adjustments will be made to it as time passes. Investment policies represent the strategies that are to be used. Will active or passive management be used? Will timing across asset classes be allowed? Who will perform the security selection?

A sample statement of investment policy (SIP) is shown for Claire in Table 2-6. Given Claire's situation, her SIP is very basic.

TABLE 2-6   STATEMENT OF INVESTMENT POLICY FOR CLAIRE

General Considerations

The purpose of this portfolio is to supplement my retirement income. Since my retirement will be in about 20 years, I am willing to accept more investment risk today than I will as my retirement approaches. This also means I do not have special needs for liquidity in portfolio investments. This investment portfolio is being maintained through my employer's defined contribution plan; thus, there are no taxes on portfolio income. A major risk I face is future inflation. Thus, I should attempt to hedge inflation by underweighting long-term bonds and overweighting common stocks.

A large portion of my wealth is invested in my home and the land on which it is built. Thus, I need little further investment in real estate other than to provide diversification against the fall in local real estate values. Finally, I am not very knowledgeable in security investment. Thus, I will follow a passive strategy and employ index funds in each asset class I own.

Asset Allocation

The initial asset allocation of my portfolio will be as follows:

Type of Index Mutual Fund	Percentage of Portfolio	Passive Benchmark Index
Money Market Funds	20%	U.S. Treasury Bills
U.S. Bond Funds	5%	Lehman Aggregate Bond Index
International Bond Funds	0%	Not Applicable
Large Capitalization		
U.S. Stock Funds	40%	S&P 500 Index
International Stock Funds	20%	EAFE Index
Small Capitalization		
U.S. Stock Funds	5%	DFA Mutual Fund
International Stock Funds	0%	Not Applicable
Real Estate Funds	10%	Consumer Price Index
	100%	

Investment Objective

Since the funds are to be invested in passive index funds, my objective is to earn a return on each equal to the passive benchmark index less 25 basis points per year to cover operating costs of the funds.

Constraints

1. At the start of each year, the portfolio's asset allocation will be rebalanced to the percentages shown above.
2. Every two years, I will reevaluate the asset allocation of the portfolio with the intent of reducing investment risk as I approach retirement.
3. No tax-sheltered investments will be made.

Policies

1. I will not personally engage in active trading strategies or employ anyone to do so.

SUMMARY

In this chapter, we reviewed the three basic decisions all investors must make to have a well-thought-out investment plan: (1) will an active or passive investment strategy be used, (2) what should be the portfolio's asset allocation, and (3) who should select the securities—the investor or a professional manager? Here are the key concepts:

- Planning the investment strategy is much more important than selecting individual securities to be held.

- ◼ A "passive" investment strategy seeks returns from bearing risk. An "active" investment strategy also seeks returns from identifying mispriced securities.

- ◼ There are two broad approaches to active strategies. One attempts to "time" the percentage owned of various asset classes by overweighting those expected to have high returns in the near future and underweighting those expected to have low returns. The other approach examines securities within an asset class and overweights securities that are expected to have the best short-term returns.

- ◼ The advantages of passive investing relative to active investing include lower cost, increased diversification, and the fact that active management might not work in well-functioning markets.

- ◼ The concept known as the efficient markets hypothesis implies that passive management should be used. There are three levels of the EMH. "Weak form" EMH says that future returns can not be predicted using past and current information. "Semi-strong form" EMH says that prices adjust immediately to new information. "Strong form" EMH says there are no groups that have private access to information.

- ◼ The asset allocation of a well-diversified portfolio is the most important determinant of the portfolio's future risk and returns.

- ◼ Investment risk represents the uncertainty of a portfolio's value at the future date when it is to be liquidated. The longer the investment horizon, the greater the uncertainty.

- ◼ Much investment risk can be reduced by diversification.

- ◼ The asset allocation an investor selects should depend in large part on the investor's risk tolerance, investment horizon, and knowledge.

- ◼ Finally, investors must decide whether they will select the securities to be held or employ a professional manager to do so. Advantages of personal selection include the enjoyment of selecting securities and tax minimization. However, professionally managed portfolios have cost advantages, the potential for greater diversification, and are less likely to overreact to unexpected events.

- ◼ After the decisions discussed in this chapter have been made, they should be documented in a written statement of investment policy (SIP).

REVIEW PROBLEM

Quarter-end market prices and dividends paid during the quarter (DPS) are given for two securities. IBM is International Business Machines and American Mutual Fund is a mutual fund that invests in stocks—primarily U.S. stocks but some international stocks are also held.

Quarter	IBM Price	IBM DPS	AMF Price	AMF DPS	Quarter	IBM Price	IBM DPS	AMF Price	AMF DPS
90Q4	105.375		18.67		93Q1	54.375	0.54	21.62	0.00
91Q1	113.875	1.21	20.18	0.00	93Q2	49.375	0.54	22.56	0.21
91Q2	97.250	1.21	20.29	0.22	93Q3	42.000	0.25	23.29	0.21
91Q3	103.625	1.21	20.91	0.22	93Q4	56.500	0.25	21.77	1.53
91Q4	89.000	1.21	21.05	1.10	94Q1	54.625	0.25	21.07	0.21
92Q1	83.500	1.21	20.75	0.42	94Q2	58.750	0.25	21.11	0.21
92Q2	97.875	1.21	21.34	0.22	94Q3	67.625	0.25	21.60	0.21
92Q3	86.625	1.21	21.39	0.22	94Q4	73.500	0.25	20.11	1.08
92Q4	50.375	1.21	20.79	1.51					

a. Calculate the quarterly rates of return on each security.

b. Calculate the annual rates of return on each security.

c. Although this topic was not discussed at length in the chapter, why might the rates of return on AMF be less variable than those of IBM?

Solution

a. Quarterly rates of return:

Quarter	IBM	AMF	Quarter	IBM	AMF
			93Q1	9.012%	3.992%
91Q1	9.215%	8.088%	93Q2	−8.202%	5.319%
91Q2	−13.537%	1.635%	93Q3	−14.430%	4.167%
91Q3	7.799%	4.140%	93Q4	35.119%	0.043%
91Q4	−12.946%	5.93%	94Q1	−2.876%	−2.251%
92Q1	−4.820%	0.570%	94Q2	8.009%	1.187%
92Q2	18.665%	3.904%	94Q3	18.936%	3.316%
92Q3	−10.258%	1.265%	94Q4	5.925%	−1.898%
92Q4	−40.450%	4.254%			

b. Annual rates of return:

	1991	1992	1993	1994
IBM	−11.383%	−39.641%	15.703%	32.159%
AMF	21.188%	10.320%	14.136%	0.249%

c. AMF has less volatile returns than IBM because AMF is a diversified portfolio of many stocks.

QUESTIONS AND PROBLEMS

1. In this chapter, we examined three basic decisions that all investors, individual or institutional, should carefully evaluate: (1) the speculative strategy to be used, (2) the asset allocation to be selected, and (3) who will select the securities to be held.

    a. What determines whether the investor should choose an active or passive management strategy?

    b. What determines the type of asset allocation to be held?

    c. What determines whether the investor will personally select securities for the portfolio or turn security selection over to a professional manager?

2. In a job interview with an investment counseling firm, you are sent to talk with Donna, one of the firm's partners who manages "large cap" U.S. stocks. In the course of the interview, Donna says, "I have skills at selecting large capitalization stocks in the U.S. market, sort of a feeling that certain stocks in this group are able to outperform others. Over the past five years, I have been fairly good at it—beating the S&P 500 by 2% per year. I have one way of running money. And I would stick to it regardless of who the investor is, mutual fund, endowment, pension fund, or even a retired individual investor."

    a. Given that Donna has been able to beat the S&P 500 by 2% per year for the past five years, does this mean that strong form efficient markets theory is wrong?

    b. What do you think about her statement that she would manage moneys assigned to her in the same way, regardless of who the investor is? (There are two different but valid answers to this. Be able to explain each.)

3. Your uncle has recently taken early retirement from MidTelCo. His normal retirement would have been at age 65 but, in an attempt to cut staff, MidTelCo offered him a bonus of $100,000 if he would retire at age 62. He will receive monthly retirement benefits from the company's defined benefit pension plan that are sufficient for his wife and him to live a comfortable life. But he wants to know what he should do with the $100,000 to add a little extra income for vacations and extra pleasures. He has been reading about a new mutual fund that invests in Latin American stocks and has seen the double-digit returns such stocks generated in the 1990s. This sounds very attractive. But a golfing buddy is also an account executive (broker) with a well-known investment company. This person said last Saturday, "Stop by my office and we will look at your situation. I know of a number of municipal bond funds on which you would not have to pay any taxes."

Your uncle wants your advice. Tell him what he must consider before taking any actions. If there are further details you need to know more about, identify them.

4. Assume your uncle eventually decides to buy a number of mutual funds that are actively managed. Each fund invests in a different asset class, so he obtains increased diversification from this.

    a. What does your uncle lose by employing active professional investment managers?

    b. What does your uncle gain by employing active professional investment managers?

5. Why might your uncle decide to follow an active investment approach? Why might your uncle decide to follow a passive investment approach?

6. In what ways is the decision to follow an active versus passive management approach related to the decision to personally select securities versus employing a manager to do so?

7. Passive management is active. Explain.

8. Define the following terms: (1) defined benefit plan, (2) defined contribution plan, and (3) IRA.

9. Jon is aged 30 and starting an investment plan. Jon's parents are aged 70 and have a sizable investment portfolio. Why might Jon be willing to accept greater risk in his security portfolio than his parents?

10. If the efficient markets theory is correct, what are its implications for each of the three investment decisions discussed in this chapter?

11. What does data mining refer to in the context of investment trading rules?

12. List the five principles of investment risk discussed in the chapter. Explain each, using examples to illustrate your points.

13. The following data provides an estimate of the total market value of stocks traded in European countries at a recent date (all stated in terms of billions of U.S. dollars):

Austria	30	Italy	177
Belgium	84	Netherlands	224
Denmark	46	Norway	36
Finland	36	Spain	151
France	444	Sweden	118
Germany	476	Switzerland	284
Ireland	19	United Kingdom	1145

Total capitalization equals $3,270

You work for G.T. Capital Management, a global investment management firm. The firm is thinking about creating a passive equity portfolio of stocks traded in these 14 countries.

a. If $100 million of capital is to be raised, how much of it should be invested in each country? Explain.

b. G. T. already manages considerable funds for U.S. residents that are invested in Europe using active investment strategies. In what different ways could the firm engage in active speculative trading of European stocks?

c. One of the active European equity managers states, "I am not sure this passive index fund you are creating is a good idea. The U.K. market is somewhat overvalued and all of the Scandinavian counties are significantly overvalued. Our active portfolios are underweighted in the United Kingdom and own nothing in Denmark, Finland, Sweden, and Norway." If you are to make the case for a passive investment that would include these countries at "neutral weightings," what would be your response?

d. Further research indicates that the total market value of traded stocks in Germany is 28.5% of Germany's gross domestic product (GDP). However, in the United Kingdom, the value of traded stocks is 163% of GDP. Average price to earnings ratios are 27:1 in Germany versus 21:1 in the United Kingdom and both countries are suffering mild recessions. Why might stocks represent 28.5% of GDP in Germany but 168% of GDP in the United Kingdom?

CFA 14. John Smalle, an associate in your firm, has asked you to help him establish a financial plan for his family's future. John is 27 years old and has been with your firm for two years. Anne, his 26-year-old wife, is employed as a psychologist for the local school district. They are childless now, but may have children in a few years. John and Anne have accumulated $10,000 in savings and recently inherited $50,000 in cash. They believe they can save at least $5,000 yearly. They are currently in a 25% income tax bracket and both have excellent career opportunities. They are eager to develop a financial plan and understand it will need to be adjusted periodically as their circumstances change. You tell John you would be happy to meet with him and Anne to discuss their financial plan.

a. Identify and describe an appropriate investment objective and constraints for the Smalles and prepare a comprehensive investment policy statement that is based on that objective and constraints.

b. State and explain your asset allocation recommendations for the Smalles based on the policy statement you developed in part a.

CFA 15. "Random walk" occurs when:

a. Past information is used in predicting future prices.

b. Future price changes are uncorrelated with past price changes.

c. Stock prices respond slowly to both new and old information.

d. Stock price changes are random but predictable.

CFA 16. Which one of the following would provide evidence against the semistrong form of efficient market theory?

    a. Low P/E stocks tend to have positive abnormal returns.

    b. Trend analysis is fruitless in determining stock prices.

    c. All investors have learned to exploit signals about future performance.

    d. In any year, approximately 50% of pension funds outperform the market.

DATAFILE ANALYSIS

Access the datafile called "INDEXES.WK3" and review the contents. Do the following for the S&P 500 Index returns. Go to the page that provides monthly returns and calculate the minimum and maximum monthly return for the period January 1926 to December 1994. Repeat this for the page that has quarterly returns as well as the page with yearly returns. What are the investment implications of your results? (The longer the investment horizon, the greater the investment uncertainty.)

SELECTED REFERENCES

The references provided here are intended for new investors who simply want to know where to start and what they are facing. Unfortunately, there are not a lot of resources available.

1. One place to start is with how security investing fits into the broader issue of financial planning. Here a book such as the following is useful: Terry Savage, *Terry Savage's New Money Strategies for the 1990's,* New York: HarperBusiness, 1994.

2. Individual investors will find considerable help in various publications and seminars offered by the American Association of Individual Investors (AAII) (see References, Chapter 1). Some of the resources available from AAII are:

   Maria Crawford Scott, *Investing Basics,* Chicago: American Association of Individual Investors, 1994.

   Maria Crawford Scott, "The Basic Process Used in Fundamental Analysis: Part 1 of a New Series," *AAII Journal,* January 1994.

Investment Education Seminars are also given throughout each year in major cities in the United States. Topics include portfolio management, how to be your own financial planner, fundamentals of investing, and mutual funds.

3. Investors interested in mutual funds will find the commentary discussions provided in Morningstar Mutual Funds to be an unbiased and useful guide to selecting mutual funds. The Morningstar service is available at most libraries. Information about subscriptions are available at 800-876-5005.

4. Two very different philosophies toward investing are presented in the following three books:

   Lowensein, Roger. *Buffet: The Making of an American Capitalist,* New York: Random House, 1994.

   Lynch, Peter. *One Up on Wall Street,* New York: Simon & Schuster, 1989.

   Bogle, John. *Bogle on Mutual Funds: New Perspectives for the Intelligent Investor,* New York, Irwin Professional Publishing, 1994.

5. An insightful and very enjoyable book about market efficiency is Burton G. Malkiel, *A Random Walk Down Wall Street,* New York: W.W. Norton, 1990.

6. A thorough but nontechnical book about historical security returns on many asset classes in many countries is Roger G. Ibbotson and Gary P. Brinson, *Investment Markets: Gaining the Performance Advantage,* New York: McGraw-Hill, 1987.

INVESTMENT TYPES

After reading this chapter you should have an understanding of the major types of securities traded in world markets.

In Chapter 2, we discussed how allocating portfolio investments across various asset classes is a major determinant of the investment portfolio's future returns and risk. In this chapter, we review the major types of securities traded in world markets.

Although no two securities are exactly alike, it is useful to categorize them into various classes based on their type and amount of investment risk. Direct security claims are assigned to one of three asset classes: (1) debt securities with a maturity of less than one year referred to as **money market** instruments, (2) debt securities with a maturity of more than three years referred to as **capital market** fixed income securities, and (3) **equity** securities. Indirect claims are classified as either **derivatives** or **commingled portfolios**. An estimate of the 1994 U.S. dollar value of direct security claims is shown here:

ESTIMATED 1994 MARKET VALUE

Security Type	($ in Trillions)		
	U.S.	Non-U.S.	Total
Debt Securities			
Money Market	$ 2.0	NA	$ 2.0
Fixed Income	8.0	8.1	16.1
Total	10.0	8.1	18.1
Equity	4.9	8.0	12.9
Total	$14.9	$16.1	$31.0

To help understand how these security classes differ from one another, consider the information displayed in Figure 3-1. Percentage annual rates of return are shown on the vertical axis of each panel. These are real returns (after subtracting the Consumer Price Index) to U.S. investors. In order to make visual interpretations easier, the scaling used on the vertical axis is the same across all four panels. Returns are shown for a recent 25-year period.

In all but one of the panels, rates of return are shown for three different security indexes that belong to the asset class being examined. For example, data for U.S. money market securities include Treasury bills, commercial paper, and certificates of deposit. (The only panel with a single security index is the one that displays returns on international common stocks.)

Two things are visually obvious. First, while the securities plotted within any one of the panels have similar returns, there are significant differences in return volatility across the panels. These are truly different asset classes. Second, rates of return in any given year are different between the asset classes. Returns on an asset class within any year are **not highly correlated** with returns on the other asset classes. This is why there is an advantage to diversifying across asset classes.

Money Market Securities

Money market securities are debt obligations that usually have low risk of default, short maturities (one year or less), and are actively traded in financial markets. Estimates of the market value of U.S. money market securities at the end of 1994 are shown in Table 3-1. The total value of $2.0 trillion represented about 20% of the value of all publicly traded debt securities in the United States.

Organizations with temporary needs for cash sell money market securities to individuals and organizations with temporary excess cash. Transactions are large ($100

TABLE 3-1   ESTIMATES OF THE MARKET VALUE OF U.S. MONEY MARKET SECURITIES END OF 1994 IN $ BILLIONS

Security Type	Estimated Value of Securities Outstanding
Treasury bills	$733.8
Commercial paper	595.4
Negotiable certificates of deposit	362.0
Repurchase agreements	275.2
Bankers acceptances	29.8
Short-term municipals	NA
Eurodollars	NA
Total	$1,996.2

SOURCE: "Estimates of the Market Value of United States Money Market Securities," derived from the Federal Reserve Bulletin June 1995.

FIGURE 3-1 PAST ANNUAL REAL RETURNS

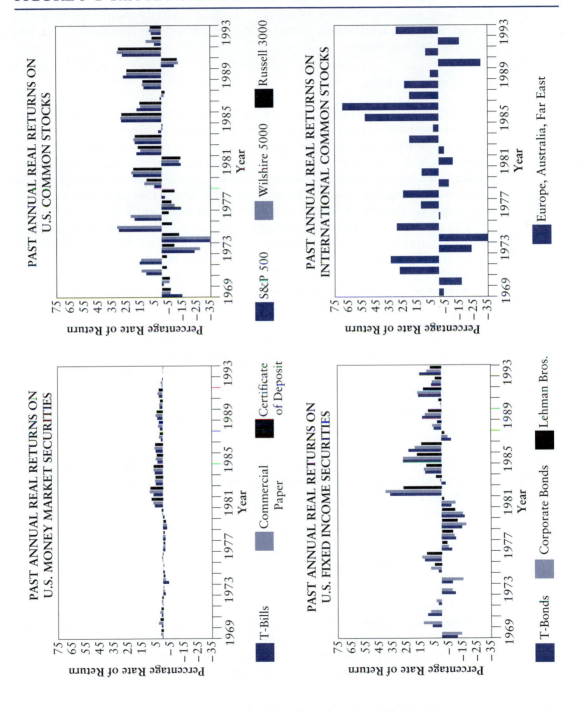

million is not uncommon) and span short intervals (overnight to one year). Large organizations participate in the money market by direct ownership of instruments. Individuals with smaller sums of money to invest typically participate indirectly through **money market funds,** mutual funds that pool shareholder resources to buy money market instruments.

U.S. Treasury Bills

At the end of 1994, U.S. Treasury bills (or T-bills) had a market value of about $730 billion. This represented about one-third the value of all money market securities in the United States. T-bills are obligations sold by the U.S. Treasury to help finance federal expenditures. At the time of the initial sale, an auction procedure is used in which money market banks, dealers, and other institutional investors submit competitive bids for a given dollar amount. Prices are quoted as a percentage of the T-bill's face value. For example, a bank might submit a bid of 98.275 on a $100 million issue, which, if accepted, means $98.275 million will be paid for bills having a face value of $100 million. Noncompetitive bids may also be made. When the new issue is awarded, the total face value of all noncompetitive bids is subtracted from the face value amount of bills being sold, and the remainder is distributed to competitive bidders offering the highest prices. Competitive bidders pay the price they bid, and noncompetitive bidders pay a price equal to the weighted average price of the competitive sales.

T-bills are referred to as **pure discount bonds** because they do not pay a coupon; the return to the owner comes totally from any price appreciation. As noted earlier, T-bill prices and discounts are stated as a percentage of face value. Discounts and percentage prices are determined using a procedure known as the **bank discount method,** assuming there are 360 days per year, according to the following formula:

Bank Discount Method

$$D = Fd(t \div 360)$$

$$P = F - D$$

(3.1)

where D equals the dollar discount on a $100 face value, F equals the $100 face value, d equals the quoted yearly discount, t equals the number of days to maturity, and P equals the price per $100 of face value.

For example, if a new three-month (91-day) T-bill is bought at a quoted discount of 8.55%, the price paid would be 97.83875% of face value.[1]

$$D = \$100 \ (0.0855)(91 \div 360) = \$2.16125$$

$$P = \$100 - \$2.16125 = \$97.83875$$

It is important to recognize that the quoted discount on a T-bill is not the true yield to the owner. This discount represents a percentage below face value, whereas the true yield represents the percentage return on the price paid.

There are two general ways of expressing the annual rate of return on a T-bill. The first is based on **simple interest** and the second is based on **compound interest.** To convert

---

[1] Minimum T-bill face values are $10,000. We use $100 in text examples for simplicity.

from quoted discounts to effective simple interest annual returns, the following formula is often used:[2]

Simple Interest Annualized $$r = \frac{365 \times d}{360 - dt}$$ (3.2)
T-Bill Rate of Return

Here the symbol r refers to the simple interest annualized T-bill rate of return.

Using the formula, an 8.55% discount on a 91-day T-bill results in an annualized simple interest return of 8.86%:

$$r = \frac{365 \times 0.0855}{360 - (0.0855 * 91)}$$

$$= 0.0886$$

To understand more clearly what this annualized simple interest yield of 8.86% is, consider the following. First, the bill is purchased for $97.83875 and pays back $100 ninety-one days later. This represents a 2.209% 91-day return:

$$91\text{-day return} = \frac{\$100 - \$97.83875}{\$97.83875}$$

$$= 0.02209$$

To annualize this 91-day return, it is multiplied by the number of 91-day periods there are in a 365-day year. The result is 8.86%, identical to that obtained with Equation (3.2):

$$0.0886 = 0.02209 \, (365 \div 91)$$

To calculate the compound interest annualized rate of return, Equation (3.3) would be used where r' represents the compound annualized return:

Compound Interest Annualized $$r' = (F \div P)^{365 \div t} - 1.0$$ (3.3)
T-Bill Rate of Return

Using the data here, the compound interest annualized T-bill return would be:

$$r' = (\$100 \div \$97.83875)^{365 \div 91} - 1.0$$

$$= (1.02209)^{4.011} - 1.0$$

$$= 0.09159$$

The reason the two annualized yields vary is easy to see. During the 91-day holding period, the rate of return is clearly 2.209%. To annualize this 91-day return, the simple interest approach multiplies by 4.01 (the number of 91-day periods in a year), whereas the compound interest approach compounds this return for 4.01 periods. But which approach is the better one to use? If this is a onetime purchase, the simple interest approach is a realistic estimate

---

2 The simple interest approach is referred to in practice by two names: the **Annual Percentage Rate (APR)** and the **Bond Equivalent Yield.**

of the equivalent annual return. However, if a policy of "rolling over" a sequence of such 91-day bills is expected to be used, then the compound interest approach should be used.

Buying T-Bills.   Individual investors can buy new T-bills directly from the U.S. Treasury, thus not incurring any brokerage commissions. Every Monday, the U.S. Treasury offers new 26-week T-bills. Small investors who wish to invest in these may go to their local bank and fill out a form called a **Tender for 26-Week Treasury Bills.** Each T-bill has a par value of $10,000, which the investor pays when the tender is submitted. Once the discount on this new T-bill is determined in the following Monday's auction, the Treasury will remit the discount to the investor. For example, assume you submitted a tender for two T-bills. You would pay $20,000 at the time of the tender. After the auction is completed on Monday, the average competitive discount accepted is, say, 6.00% of par, or $1,200 on $20,000 of par. The Treasury will then refund this $1,200 to you. Net of this refund, you would have paid $18,800 for a security that will repay $20,000 in 26 weeks.

Previously issued T-bills that are now traded in secondary markets must be bought from or sold to banks and brokers who are qualified to act as **government security dealers.** Government security dealers provide an active secondary market in all U.S. government securities. Prices at which they are willing to buy or sell are quoted daily in the financial press.

An illustration of how T-bill quotes appear in the financial press is shown next. The quotes are for the afternoon of July 31, 1995.

SAMPLE T-BILL QUOTATIONS FOR JULY 31, 1995

| Maturity | Days to Maturity | Discount | | Ask Yield | |
		Bid	Ask		
Aug 17, '95	15	5.40	5.30	5.39	
Sep 28, '95	57	5.38	5.34	5.48	
Nov 2, '95	92	5.42	5.40	5.57	Reviewed below
Jul 25, '96	358	5.35	5.33	5.64	

As we discussed earlier, quotes are stated in terms of discounts. The **bid discount** is the highest price at which a dealer was willing to buy. The **asked discount** is the lowest price at which a dealer would sell. Notice that the quotes are from the dealer's viewpoint.

The number of days to maturity are two less than the actual number of calendar days. This allows for a two-day period between the date of a trade and the actual date at which cash is paid out and the security registered with the new owner. This is referred to as skip day delivery.[3] For example, the T-bill maturing on November 2, 1995, was quoted to have 92 days to maturity whereas there were actually 94 days between July 31 and November 2. This T-bill could have been bought from a dealer at 98.62% of par or sold to a dealer at 98.6149% of par.

Dealer's selling price: $= 100 - 0.0540 \,(100) \times (92/360)$

$= 98.62$

---

[3] Most T-bill trades are actually settled the following day (i.e., have a one-day delivery). Prices quoted in the financial press, however, are assumed to have a two-day delivery. This skip day delivery assumption is used because individuals view the quote in the financial press one day after the quote occurred.

Dealer's buying price: $= 100 - 0.0542\,(100) \times (92/360)$

$= 98.6149$

The spread between the dealer's selling price and their buying price represents a profit to the dealer. In this example, the profit would be $0.0051 per $100 par (98.62 − 98.6149). On a $1 million par this **bid-ask spread** represents $51.

The yield shown in the price quotation is based on simple interest techniques. The only complication in this example is that the year subsequent to July 31, 1995 was a leap year and, thus, consisted of 366 days. Using Equation (3.2), it would be calculated as:

Simple Interest
Annual Return $$0.0557 = \frac{366 * 0.054}{360 - 0.054\,(92)}$$

The other way to find this simple interest annual return is to find the 92-day rate of return and then multiply that return by the number of 92-day periods in a 366-day year. This is shown below:

$$0.0557 = [(100.00 - 98.62) \div 100.00](366 \div 92)$$

$$= [0.013993](3.9783)$$

To calculate the effective compound interest yield, Equation 3.3 would be used (with 366 days in a year):

Compound Interest $0.0568 = (100.00 \div 98.62\,)^{(366 \div 92)} - 1.0$
Annual Return $= (1.013993)^{(3.9783)} - 1.0$

U.S. T-bills have par values as small as $10,000. State and local taxes are not paid on T-bill income. Owners are registered in Federal Reserve Board computers.

Commercial Paper

Commercial paper is an **unsecured promissory note** issued by financially strong finance companies and manufacturing firms. In recent years, it has been the second largest type of money market instrument outstanding in the United States. Commercial paper issuers use this form of financing as an alternative to short-term bank loans.

Commercial paper is generally issued on a discount basis with maturities of 270 days or less. To reduce the risk of default, commercial paper is backed with lines of credit from banks that guarantee the issuer will have the cash necessary at maturity. Commercial paper is initially sold both directly by the issuer and through commercial paper dealers. Denominations are in amounts of $100,000 and up. While a relatively active trading market exists, many purchasers hold the paper until maturity. Commercial paper rates are close to those available on certificates of deposit and bankers' acceptances with similar maturity. Income is not exempt from state and local tax, and the securities have more default risk and less liquidity than T-bills.

Certificates of Deposit

At the end of 1994, negotiable certificates of deposit available in the United States had a market value of about $360 billion. **Negotiable certificates of deposit** (CDs) are large deposits ($100,000 or more) placed in commercial banks at a stated rate of interest. Unlike other bank CDs, negotiable CDs may be bought and sold in the open market. They qualify as money market instruments because they have short maturities, low default risk (although they are insured in part by the Federal Deposit Insurance Corporation, their risk features depend on the issuing bank), and are reasonably marketable because of their salability in the open market. Their yields are slightly higher than those of equivalent maturity T-bills (25 to 100 basis points) because of their greater risk and poorer marketability.

Repurchase Agreements

Repurchase agreements (repos, or RPs) are not physical securities issued by one party to another. Instead, they are **contractual agreements** between two parties to buy and sell U.S. government securities at particular points in time. Consider the hypothetical example of First Income Securities Corporation, a dealer in U.S. government obligations. First Income Securities generates profits in three ways: by acting as a wholesaler of government securities (standing ready to buy at bid and sell at asked prices), by speculating on future changes in interest rates (buying bonds when rates are expected to fall and selling when rates are expected to rise), and by a variety of arbitrage transactions. In the course of business, the firm is likely to own government securities in amounts considerably in excess of the company's equity capital. The firm can finance this security inventory using either a bank loan or a repurchase agreement. Since repos are often cheaper, they are extensively used.

To enter into a repurchase agreement, First Income will sell a portion of the firm's government securities to, say, a city government that has temporary excess cash and will agree to repurchase the securities at a stated price on a stated date. Although the repo is written in a way suggesting that securities are actually sold and are later to be repurchased, in substance the municipality has given the dealer a short-term loan collateralized by U.S. government securities. The effective interest rate on the loan (return to the repo buyer) is simply the percentage difference between the sale price and the purchase price. Such a trade is often profitable to the repo seller (First Income Securities), since the interest rate paid to the repo buyer is often less than the yield on the government securities owned. For example, 181-day T-bills yielding 8.50% might be RP'd for three months at 8.40% and RP'd again for another three months at 8.40%. The repo seller would take the 10 basis-point "carry" as profit. The repo buyer would be willing to accept such a low yield because alternative investments with similar risk and scheduled maturity are unavailable. This is especially true for "overnight repos"—situations in which the lender wishes to invest for one day but can find no alternatives available other than a repurchase agreement. Dealers can thus finance large holdings of U.S. governments by continuously reentering into a sequence of many overnight repos.

The term **reverse RP,** which refers to the mirror image of an RP in which securities are acquired with a simultaneous agreement to resell, is sometimes used.

Bankers' Acceptances

A bankers' acceptance is a time draft that the accepting bank has agreed to pay at a specified future date. Historically, most bankers' acceptances have arisen in the course of international trade. For example, a U.S. firm might wish to import shoes from a Japanese exporter. The U.S. firm will have its U.S. banker write a **letter of credit** to the Japanese exporter guaranteeing the goods will be paid for. After receiving the letter of credit, the exporter will ship the goods and simultaneously prepare a draft on the domestic bank. This draft is taken to a Japanese bank together with supporting documentation, such as the letter of credit and shipping documents, and the Japanese bank pays the exporter. The draft is then sent to the U.S. bank, where it is "accepted." At this point, a **bankers' acceptance** has been created, which may be returned to the Japanese bank (if it wishes to hold the acceptance as an investment), kept by the domestic bank (if the Japanese bank wants immediate cash and the domestic bank wishes to hold it as an investment), or sold in the open market.

In effect, a bankers' acceptance is a **promissory note** that stipulates a payment amount and a date at which it will be paid. Final payment is made by the U.S. importer or by the accepting bank if the importer defaults. Acceptances are traded on a discount basis with the return to the owner consisting of the difference between the price paid and the acceptance's face value. Denominations of $100,000 or more are normal. Since both the importer and the accepting bank have agreed to pay, default risk is minimal. This low risk and a fairly active trading market allow bankers' acceptances to trade at yields only 25 to 100 basis points greater than those for T-bills with similar maturity.

Bankers' acceptances are used by borrowers who are either too small or too risky to use commercial paper. As a result, the rates are slightly above commercial paper rates. In recent years acceptances have been increasingly used to finance domestic as well as international transactions.

Eurodollars

Eurodollars are simply **deposits in foreign banks denominated in U.S. dollars.** The market initially developed in Europe, hence the term **Eurodollars.** Today the name is a misnomer, since U.S. dollar-denominated deposits can be made in almost any country. Deposits are usually made for a stated time interval (six months or less) and pay a stated rate of interest. Banks receiving Eurodollar deposits use them to make loans also denominated in dollars. The Eurodollar market is a relatively recent phenomenon, growing to major international importance since the early 1960s. Today it represents a major source of financing and investment to large international organizations. Eurodollar deposits are relatively free of default risk, can be easily bought or sold, and are not subject to many of the regulations imposed by the U.S. government on deposits made in domestic U.S. banks. Because of the activities of domestic banks in the market, interest rates tend to track very closely the rates charged on domestic Federal funds.

Federal Funds

The only traders in the Federal (or Fed) funds market are commercial banks that are members of the Federal Reserve System. These banks are required to maintain a specified portion of their total deposits in cash, either as cash in their vaults or as cash deposited with the Federal Reserve System. Since rates of return are not paid on any required reserves maintained with the Federal Reserve, member banks attempt to maintain the smallest possible reserve position. However, since deposit increases and withdrawals cannot be predicted with complete accuracy, some banks find themselves with temporary excess reserves while others are temporarily deficient. As a result, a market has arisen that allows banks with excess reserves to lend to those with deficiencies. This market is known as the Fed funds market.

The Fed funds market is extremely active and deals with huge sums of money. Most borrowing and lending is done on an overnight (one-day) basis, although some term Fed funds are traded. Many banks rely on brokers to bring together buyers and sellers, although some banks rely on correspondent banks or personal knowledge. While the market is not available to nonbank borrowers or lenders, many traders believe the overnight Fed funds rate is the base on which other money market rates rest.

Historical Default Spreads on Money Market Instruments

The yields on short-term U.S. T-bills represent the floor for yields on alternative money market instruments. The extent to which they provide greater yields depends on each security's default risk as well as general market concern about potential default. For example, the annualized spreads between 30-day certificates of deposit and 30-day T-bills are shown in Figure 3-2 for the period 1972 to 1995. The sharp spikes in the mid-1970s were due to concerns over the economic impacts of the Arab oil embargo. During the 1980s, concerns over a new oil embargo were compounded by the bankruptcy of a number of large banks. You can even see the uncertainty caused by the stock market crash in October 1987. More recently, economic concerns have abated and yield spreads have narrowed.

FIGURE 3-2   ANNUALIZED CD AND T-BILL SPREADS

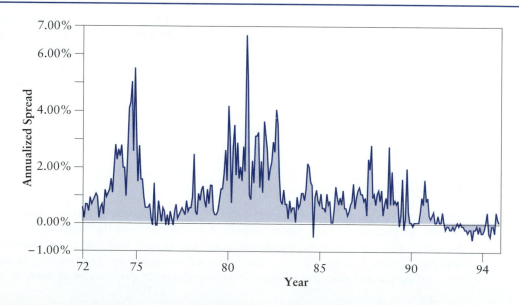

Fixed Income Capital Market

Capital market securities differ from money market securities in one or more of the following ways: (1) their maturity is greater than one year, (2) their default risk is greater, and (3) their marketability is poorer. However, a clear distinction between capital market and money market instruments doesn't always exist. For example, Treasury notes and bonds that are about to mature might well be considered money market securities. The distinction between these two markets is made to add some (slightly artificial) clarity and organization to what is indeed a complex realm of securities.

We examine only publicly traded fixed income securities. It is important to realize, however, that substantial amounts of debt are privately owned. This private debt market ranges from World Bank loans to countries to credit card loans to individuals.

The international debt markets consist of the following four types of securities:

1. **Debt obligations issued and traded in the issuer's home country.** Examples include U.S. Treasury bonds that are issued and traded in the United States and U. K. government bonds (known as Gilts) that are issued and traded in the United Kingdom. These debt issues are denominated in the currency of the home country.
2. **Debt obligations issued and traded in a country other than the issuer's home country.** Examples include bonds sold in the United States by corporations domiciled in Japan and bonds sold in Switzerland by corporations domiciled in the United States. These debt issues are denominated in the currency of the country in which they are sold. They often have colorful names such as **Yankee bonds** (for issues sold in the United States), **Samurai bonds** (for issues sold in Japan), and **Bulldog bonds** (for issues sold in the United Kingdom).
3. **Debt obligations sold in what is called the Eurobond market.** This is an unregulated international bond market in which bond securities can be denominated in most any currency the issuer wishes. The most common currencies used are U.S. dollars, German marks, Japanese yen, and U.K. pounds.
4. **Debt obligations of supranational organizations such as the World Bank.** These obligations are denominated in the currency of the country in which they are sold.

Estimates of the market value of debt securities traded in each of these market are shown in Table 3-2. Because the U.S. debt market is the largest by far, we focus mainly on U.S. debt obligations. Similar securities are traded in other countries.

U.S. Treasury Issues

The U.S. Treasury offers two types of fixed income securities with maturities greater than one year: Treasury notes and Treasury bonds. These are essentially identical except that **notes** have an initial maturity of ten years or less, whereas **bonds** have a maturity in excess of ten years. Both pay coupons semiannually. They are initially offered by the Treasury in competitive auctions similar to T-bill auctions except that bidders submit desired yields to maturity, as opposed to discounts, for bills. The average winning bid is

TABLE 3-2   MARKET VALUE OF PUBLICLY TRADED FIXED INCOME SECURITIES (END OF 1994 IN $ BILLIONS)

Security Type	Estimated Value of Securities Outstanding		
	United States	Non-U.S.	Total
I. Obligations Traded in Issuer's Home Country			
Central Government			
Treasury	$2,422.1	$5,152.0	$7,574.1
Agencies	727.3	539.4	1,266.7
Total	$3,149.4	$5,691.4	$8,840.8
Mortgage Backed	$1,703.4	NA	$1,703.4
State and Local Governments	$ 904.2	$ 317.0	$1,221.2
Corporate	$1,509.0	$ 790.2	$2,299.2
Total	$7,266.0	$6,798.6	$14,064.6
II. Obligations Traded in Country Other Than Issuer's			
Total	$ 137.5	$ 692.5	$ 830.0
III. Eurobonds	$ 619.6	$ 561.0	$ 1,180.6
IV. Supranationals	NA	NA	NA

SOURCE: Rosario Benavides, *International Bond Market Analysis,* August 1995, Salomon Brothers, New York.

then used to determine the issue's coupon (stated in eighths of a dollar) so the securities can be sold at close to total face value.

Once issued by the Treasury, notes and bonds can be bought or sold in the same manner as T-bills, through government security dealers. Buyers pay the dealer an asked price and sellers receive the bid price. An illustration of how note and bond quotes appear in the financial pages is shown here.

SAMPLE T-BOND AND NOTE QUOTATIONS FOR THE CLOSE OF TRADING ON JULY 31, 1995

Coupon Rate	Maturity	Bid	Ask	Ask Yield	
6 1/8	July 96n	100:12	100:14	5.67	
5 7/8	July 97n	100:00	100:02	5.84	
10 3/4	Aug 05	130:20	130:24	6.53	
11 3/4	Nov 09–14	144:31	145:03	6.77	
7 5/8	Feb 25	109:20	109:22	6.86	Reviewed below

The coupon rate represents the annual coupon paid on the bond, although coupons are actually paid semiannually. For example, the 7 5/8's pay $38.125 each six months (in August and February in this case) for a $1,000 face value. Maturities with the symbol "n" refer to Treasury notes. All others are Treasury bonds. Bid and ask prices are shown with a colon. For example, the 7 5/8 coupon bond due in February 2025 has a quoted bid price of 109:20. The :20 means 20/32. This issue could have been sold to a representative government bond dealer at a price equal to 109.625% of par.

Many Treasuries are callable prior to maturity, which means the Treasury can repurchase such bonds at a date before the scheduled maturity. These issues are those with two maturity dates. For example, the 11 3/4 issue can be retired any time between November 2009 and November 2014.

The ask yield to maturity column represents the **yield to maturity** if one were to buy from a government bond dealer at 109.6875% of par. Basically, the yield to maturity is the best estimate of the annual rate of return available to people who intend to hold the bond to its scheduled maturity. (When callable bonds are selling at prices above face value—above 100—the yield shown is the yield to first call date.)

The 7 5/8 issue due in February 2025 has an expected yield to maturity of 6.86% per annum. This particular issue has a 30-year maturity. At any point in time, there will always be a thirty-year Treasury bond outstanding, representing the most recent Treasury bond issue. It is often referred to as the **bellwether Treasury bond.**

Treasury notes and bonds have the lowest default risk and greatest marketability possible on securities of their maturity. As such, they represent the foundation on which yields of other bonds having similar maturity but different risk and marketability are based.

STRIPS.   In 1985, the U.S. Treasury announced the **Separate Trading of Registered Interest and Principal of Securities,** STRIPS. Under the STRIPS program, selected Treasury securities may be maintained in the book entry system operated by the Federal Reserve banks in a manner that permits separate trading and ownership of the interest and principal payments. The Treasury does not actually auction zero-coupon bonds. All sales of new bonds are conducted exactly as they have been in the past, with coupon-bearing bonds. However, once the bond is outstanding, the Federal Reserve facilitates the purchase or sale of specified coupons or principal cash flows. Many of the new Treasury bonds are noncallable. Thus, a truly long-term default-free and noncallable zero-coupon bond is available.

Illustrative quoted prices for U.S. Treasury STRIPS are shown here. As with Treasury bonds, all quotes are in 1/32nds.

SAMPLE U.S. TREASURY STRIPS QUOTATIONS FOR THE CLOSE OF TRADING ON JULY 3, 1995

Maturity	Type	Bid	Ask	Ask Yield	
Aug 97	ci	88:30	89:00	5.81	
Aug 97	np	88:25	88:27	5.89	
Aug 98	np	83:11	83:14	6.06	
Feb 25	bp	13:26	13:30	6.79	Reviewed below

Consider the STRIPS issue due February 2025. The "bp" symbol means this represents cash "stripped" from the principal of the bond issue due in February 2025, the bellwether 30-year bond previously discussed. (The term "ci" stands for stripped coupon interest and "np" stands for note principal.) This February 2025 STRIPS could have been bought for 13 26/32% of par. No cash flows would have been received until February 2025 when par value would be paid. The annualized rate of return on this issue if held to maturity is the ask yield of 6.79%.

Notice that the two STRIPS with a maturity date of August 1997 were trading at different yields to maturity. The reason why this occurs is not fully understood, but seems to be related to differing liquidity between individual STRIPS.

U.S. Agency Issues

Agency issues are not direct obligations of the Treasury. Instead, they are sold by various governmental agencies to support their financial activities. A few are backed by the full faith and credit of the United States, and many are guaranteed or supported by the Treasury. But even though agency issues don't have a direct guarantee of payment, they are considered to have top investment quality because governmental backing is implied. Due to the moderately greater risk inherent in agency obligations and their lower liquidity, they provide slightly greater promised yields than equivalent maturity Treasuries. Examples of federal agencies that issue publicly traded debt are the Federal Home Loan Bank, the Farm Credit Assistance Corporation, Federal Land Bank, Student Loan Marketing, and the Resolution Trust Corporation. The Resolution Funding Corporation is the government agency responsible for resolving liabilities of savings and loan firms that went bankrupt in the late 1980s and early 1990s.

State and Local Government Obligations

Municipal issues are bonds sold by states, counties, cities, and other political corporations. The most important feature of municipal bonds is their special tax treatment. Coupon income is totally excluded from federal income tax and from state income tax in the bond's state of origin. For example, an investor residing in Ohio would pay no income tax on coupon income received from Ohio Turnpike Authority bonds and would pay only state income tax on West Virginia Turnpike Authority bonds. Capital gains on municipal obligations are fully taxed at appropriate capital gains tax rates.

Municipal bonds are of two basic types: general obligations and revenue obligations. **General obligations** (GOs) are backed by the full faith and credit of the issuer and repaid from taxes received by the issuing body. **Revenue obligations** are sold to finance a particular project and are repaid from the income earned on the project. Revenue issues do not have a claim to the tax receipts of the issuer, but instead are repaid from the revenue generated by the particular project. For example, municipal electric systems, turnpike and airport authorities, and sewage systems all issue revenue bonds.

Risk, maturity, and marketability of municipal obligations vary considerably. Usually, GOs are less risky than revenues, but risks vary widely among different issuers. Maturities range from the very short-term tax anticipation notes mentioned earlier to 25-year debentures. Typically, long-term municipal issues are sold as serial bonds, as opposed to term bonds. **Serial bonds** have a predetermined series of bonds maturing each year until final maturity. **Term bonds** are repaid in full at one terminal maturity date. For example, if the city of San Francisco sells a 20-year, $50 million serial issue, it might retire $2.5 million of specified bonds each year during the next 20 years. As a result, the average life of this 20-year obligation is about 10 years.

Serial bonds are used for two reasons. First, when a portion of principal is retired each year, the default risk might be lower. The municipality is forced to have capital available each year instead of waiting until maturity to come up with a large lump sum. Second, major buyers of municipals are financial institutions that like to stagger the maturity distribution of their bond portfolios over a number of years. When marketing the issue, the municipality can sell a piece of the issue with a given maturity to an institution that needs more bonds of that particular maturity. Thus, the issuer hopes serialization will aid in the initial marketing of the bonds.

Corporate Issues

Long-term corporate debt obligations are usually term bonds with maturities of five years or more. The financial obligations of the corporate issuer are set forth in a security agreement known as an **indenture.** Indenture agreements usually specify the bond's repayment schedule, restrictions on dividend payments and liquidity, types of collateral, and so on. It is the job of the trustee (usually a commercial bank) to ascertain that all indenture covenants are compiled with. Types of information provided in the indenture include the following:

1. **Call provisions.** A call provision allows the issuer to redeem the bond by purchasing it from the holder at a specified price. Most corporate bonds are sold with a deferred call provision. Deferred call bars the issuer from calling the bond for a stipulated period (commonly five to ten years), after which time the bond is callable at stipulated prices. Call prices are initially set above face value and decline, in steps, to face value prior to maturity. Initial **call premiums** (the difference between the call price and the face value) are normally equal to one year's coupon payment. In Chapter 10 we see that a call provision increases an investor's uncertainty about future realized yields, since the investor has no way of knowing whether or when the issue will be called. As a result, promised yields on callable bonds exceed those on noncallable issues.
2. **Sinking funds.** Sinking funds are annual payments made to a trustee to ensure eventual repayment of the bonds. Sinking funds may be left to accumulate as a deposit with the trustee or used to immediately retire a portion of the outstanding issue through purchase in the open market.
3. **Collateral provisions.** Bonds that have a legal claim to specific assets of the firm in the event of liquidation or reorganization are secured bonds. A **mortgage bond** is secured by a lien on real property, such as plants and buildings. Typically, mortgage bonds will be backed by a lien on a specified set of real assets, but occasionally a blanket mortgage is used that provides a lien on all assets of the firm. First, second, third, and so on, mortgages can be placed on property with respective claims to assets during liquidation. Mortgage bonds may also be open end, limited open end, or closed end. Open-end mortgages

allow the issuer to sell additional bonds having equal claim to the mortgaged assets. Such open-end agreements will usually include an after-acquired property clause requiring all future real assets purchased be added to the initial mortgage. Limited open-end mortgages allow new bond sales to have a lien on the same property up to a limit. This limit is normally stated as a percentage of the mortgaged debt to property cost, say 30%. Finally, a closed-end mortgage prohibits future debt sales with equivalent claim to the assets.

Unsecured bonds are known as **debentures.** Debenture holders are general creditors of the firm and have no legal claim to specified assets. In the event of liquidation they will be paid only after all mortgage bondholders have been reimbursed. Holders of **subordinated debentures** have a lower claim to assets than do general creditors, such as trade creditors (accounts payable).

Income bonds are repaid from the income earned on asset investments. Unlike other bonds, for which the issuer is contractually obligated to repay principal and interest regardless of current income, an income bond has no contractual commitment to pay interest and principal unless income is sufficient to do so. Revenue bonds sold by municipalities are income bonds.

Corporate bonds are often given special features that act as inducements to potential purchasers as well as cost-saving devices to the corporation in arranging future financing. Examples of such inducements are convertibility and warrants. **A convertible bond** is a debt obligation that allows the owner to tender the bond to the corporation and convert it into a given number of shares of stock. The attraction of convertibility to the bondholder is the guaranteed fixed income plus the ability to share in rapid stock price rises if they should occur. Cost savings to the issuing corporation are largely in lower yields required by investors because of the convertibility.

Bonds are often sold with **warrants** attached. Like a convertible provision, a bond with a warrant provides the owner with a fixed income plus the ability to share in future stock price increases. The issuing corporation hopes to save through lower required bond yields and automatic future equity sales at the exercise date. A warrant is a legal claim that allows the owner to buy a certain number of common shares at a specified **exercise price** any time before a specified **exercise date.** Exercise prices are initially set at levels that are expected to give the owner an eventual price break in buying the stock. For example, assume a firm will need new equity capital two years hence. Management expects its stock price to be $70 at that time but cannot be sure of this. The firm could issue warrants with an exercise price of $60 and a maximum exercise date of two years. The $60 exercise price is set lower than the expected stock price to allow for management's uncertainty about the $70 value and to provide a potential inducement to exercise the warrant in two years. If the stock does sell for more than $60 two years hence, all warrants will be exercised. Warrant owners will get a favorable stock price and management will get the new equity financing needed.

Corporate bonds can have a **fixed interest rate** or a **floating rate.** A fixed rate is exactly what its name implies, the interest rate is fixed at a specified level throughout the bond's life. A floating rate is a rate indexed to another interest rate such as U.S. T-bill rates or **LIBOR** rates. LIBOR stands for the London Interbank Offer Rate, the rate of interest which large London banks are willing to pay on new deposits. For example, assume a new floating rate issue is indexed against the three-month LIBOR rate plus 2%. If the three-month LIBOR rate is 5% (annualized) when the issue is sold, the bond will pay 7%. Three months later, the bond's interest rate will be readjusted to the prevailing three-month LIBOR rate plus 2%.

A floating rate bond is a long-term bond with short-term interest rates. The advantage of a long-term floating rate bond to the issuer is reduced costs. Instead of incurring the refinancing costs of rolling over a sequence of short-term loans, the issuer pays a single transaction fee when the bond is issued.

Asset-Backed Securities and Pass-throughs

One of the more interesting phenomena of the 1980s was the increased *securitization* of the financial markets. Securitization refers to publicly traded security issues that are collateralized by a collection of many small loans to consumers. For example, credit card purchases of a large number of individuals are collected into a total pool and used as collateral for an *asset-backed* bond issue.

The most common form of an asset-backed security are those collateralized by home mortgages. For example, the Federal National Mortgage Association issues both short- and long-term bonds referred to as **FNMA** issues (pronounced Fannie Mae). Proceeds are used to purchase mortgages held by savings and loans, mortgage companies, banks, and so on. In addition, the Government National Mortgage Association guarantees pools of qualified mortgages that act as collateral for **GNMA** (Ginnie Mae) issues. GNMA issues were the first major type of pass-through securities. As payments of interest and principal are made by mortgagees, they are "passed through" to the GNMA owner. Whereas most other fixed income securities receive all principal payments at the bond's stated maturity, GNMA issues receive both principal and interest throughout the bond's stated life. As such, the average life of a Ginnie Mae pass-through is much shorter than its stated maturity.

Fannie Mae and Ginnie Mae issues have become popular enough with the investing public that private investment firms have started to offer their own version of mortgage-backed securities. These are referred to as **Collateralized Mortgage Obligations,** or CMOs. CMOs are also backed by a pool of mortgages but they differ from GNMA and FNMA obligations in that investors purchase the cash flow associated with a given date. This is done by breaking the CMO into various **tranches** (or repayment periods). Owners of the earliest tranche receive all payments made by the mortgage pool until they are fully repaid. After the first tranche is fully repaid, investors in the second tranche begin to receive payments until they are fully repaid. The process continues until all tranches are repaid.

Mortgage-backed securities have relatively little default risk, since they are backed by mortgages on people's homes, and all mortgages placed into a given mortgage pool must meet rigorous default criteria. But the sensitivity of their prices to interest rate changes can make them very risky. The prices of all bonds are sensitive to interest rate changes, but mortgage obligations have a special type of risk, the risk that mortgagees will prepay their mortgage obligation when interest rates decline.

This risk of early prepayment is referred to as "call" risk. Mortgagees have the right to repay the mortgage whenever they wish to do so. Technically speaking, mortgagees own a "call option" that allows them to buy back their debt prior to its stated maturity. If interest rates drop to a level where it would be profitable to refinance an old mortgage with a new one, mortgagees will pay off the old mortgage with the proceeds from a new mortgage. To the owner of a mortgage-backed obligation, early prepayment is a concern, since interest payments that had been expected over the anticipated life of the mortgage will be shortened.

Investors in any callable bond face the risk of an early repayment. But call risk is a particular problem for certain types of collateralized mortgage obligations. To illustrate, consider the following **hypothetical** example. Assume a mortgage pool has been broken up into a number of tranches. You have invested in the tranche which will receive all interest payments made between years 6 through 8. Comfortable with the low default risk of your investment, you are proud of yourself and sleep calmly at night. Suddenly, interest rates drop and all mortgages in the pool are paid off with none left to pay interest in years 6 through 8. The value of your investment would fall to zero.

This example is hypothetical. No investors (or at least few) would invest in something with such call risk. But many collateralized mortgage obligations contain significant call risk. In fact, the bankruptcy of Kidder, Peabody and Company, a large and well-known investment banking firm, was due in large part to the call risk inherent in the CMOs they owned.

Regardless of the interest rate risk inherent in certain types of mortgage obligations, the securitization of the mortgage markets has been a major success story. Consider Figure 3-3 in which the market value of the mortgage-backed market is shown from 1980 through 1994. In 1980 their market value was about $70 billion. By the end of 1994, it had grown to $1.2 trillion. This represented about 30% of all debt issues traded in the United States.

FIGURE 3-3 MARKET VALUE OF MORTGAGE-BACKED SECURITIES TRADED IN THE UNITED STATES

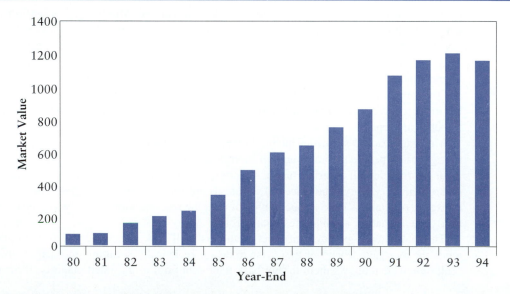

SOURCE: Various issues of Lehman Indices, Fixed Income Research, Lehman Brother.

Yankee Bonds

Yankee bonds are sold in the United States by organizations domiciled outside the United States. These provide a convenient way for U.S. investors who wish to purchase bonds of organizations located outside the United States but receive all payments in U.S. dollars. Similar but smaller markets exist in the United Kingdom (called Bulldog bonds) and Japan (called Samurai bonds).

Guaranteed Investment Contracts

Referred to as GICs, guaranteed investment contracts are intermediate maturity obligations sold by insurance firms primarily to pension funds, endowment plans, and foundations. Their principal benefit is an above average "guaranteed" (actually only promised) rate of return. Returns are either guaranteed for the next calendar year or for a fixed number of years (typically five years or less). GICs are not marketable, and the investor can withdraw funds from the insurance company prior to maturity only at substantial penalties. Their attraction is an above average fixed interest return. (Some people believe another attraction is the unknown GIC market value. Owners report their values based on an accrued cost accounting basis, which is less variable than actual market values.) The guarantee underlying a GIC is only as good as the assets of the insurance issuer. High GIC rates can be offered to purchasers only if the insurance company uses the proceeds to purchase other securities that provide high returns. Higher returns come with greater risk of loss.

Eurobonds

Eurobonds are bond issues sold in Europe (typically London) that are denominated in a currency other than that of the issuer's domicile country. Eurodollar bonds (denominated in U.S. dollars) are most common, although Euro-yen (Japanese currency), Euro-deutschemark (German currency), and Euro-sterling (U.K. currency) bonds are also issued. The motives for issuing a Eurodollar bond are two. First, since they do not have to be registered with the U.S. Securities and Exchange Commission, they can be sold quickly and at a lower cost than if issued in the United States. Second, they are denominated in U.S. dollars and require future payments of U.S. dollars by the issuer. This is exactly what issuers would wish if they have an immediate need for U.S. dollars (to purchase U.S. products) and will have future profits denominated in U.S. dollars.

Eurobonds are traded around the clock among financial institutions located throughout the world. Dealers in Eurobonds have formed the **Association of International Bond Dealers** (AIBD). Eurobond offerings often have quite exotic terms. Consider these examples:

- Bonds whose coupons and principal are indexed to the price of gold, energy costs, a stock market index, or any other index.

- Fixed coupon bonds that are exchangeable for floating rate bonds at the option of either the borrower or bond owner.

- Bonds issued in one currency but convertible into stock of another currency.

Floating rate bonds whose interest payment for a given period (say six months) is determined at the end of the period are common.

Equity Securities

Equity securities provide a residual claim on asset returns once all fixed income claims have been paid. There are two forms of equities. In the United States, they are called **preferred** and **common stock**. Outside the United States, they are typically called preference and ordinary shares.

Accurate estimates of the aggregate value of preferred stock are not available. However, trends in the global value of equity securities are available and they tell a dramatic story. Consider the data displayed in Figure 3-4. Between 1960 and 1994, the value of world equity markets grew from $0.5 trillion to $13 trillion. This represents a compound annual growth rate of almost 10%. The greatest share of this growth occurred between 1980 and 1990. While equity value growth occurred throughout the financially developed world, Japanese equity values grew the fastest. Clearly, equity investment strategies need to be made with a global perspective.

Preferred (or Preference) Stock

Preferred stock is actually a hybrid security with features of both a fixed income obligation and a pure equity security. Similar to income bonds, preferred stocks pay a stipulated yearly cash payment only if corporate income is sufficient to do so. Preferred dividends are usually expressed as a percentage of the preferred's par value. For example, a $100 par, 6% preferred issue would pay a $6 dividend each year. If the issue is *cumulative*, any unpaid past dividends (dividends in arrears) accumulate and must eventually be paid before any dividends can be distributed to owners of common stock. Unpaid dividends on *noncumulative* preferred shares do not have to be paid. Some preferred issues are *participating*, which allows the preferred dividend to increase in a stipulated fashion as common stock dividends increase. Owners of preferred stock are usually given the right to vote for directors of the firm (and thus exert some true equity control) only if dividends have not been paid for a year or more. Preferreds also receive preferential ("preferred") treatment if the firm's assets must be liquidated, in that they have a par value claim to assets before any liquidating dividends are distributed to owners of common stock.

These features are not unique to preferred stock. They are also available on many income bonds. While an indenture agreement does not secure the preferred stock issue, such issues commonly have callability, convertibility, sinking fund, and other features found on income bonds. Because of this, many people consider preferred stock to be the economic equivalent of income bonds.

Common (or Ordinary) Stock

The common stockholders of a corporation represent the firm's ownership. Shares of common stock sold to investors give their owners a claim to any asset returns after all debt and preferred stock obligations are fully satisfied. Common stockholders have a nonguaranteed,

FIGURE 3-4 GROWTH OF INTERNATIONAL EQUITY VALUES (IN BILLIONS OF U.S. DOLLARS)

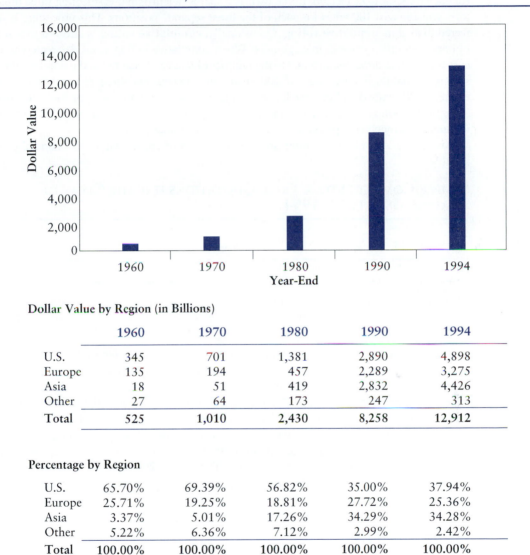

Dollar Value by Region (in Billions)

	1960	1970	1980	1990	1994
U.S.	345	701	1,381	2,890	4,898
Europe	135	194	457	2,289	3,275
Asia	18	51	419	2,832	4,426
Other	27	64	173	247	313
Total	525	1,010	2,430	8,258	12,912

Percentage by Region

	1960	1970	1980	1990	1994
U.S.	65.70%	69.39%	56.82%	35.00%	37.94%
Europe	25.71%	19.25%	18.81%	27.72%	25.36%
Asia	3.37%	5.01%	17.26%	34.29%	34.28%
Other	5.22%	6.36%	7.12%	2.99%	2.42%
Total	100.00%	100.00%	100.00%	100.00%	100.00%

residual claim to asset returns. If the firm is successful, common stockholders will share in its success, and debt holders receive only their promised fixed returns. If the firm should fail, common stockholders receive liquidating dividends only after all debt holders and preferred holders have been repaid the face value of their securities.

Because of the ownership risk position that common shareholders bear, they are given two basic rights: the right to managerial control and the right to retain an initial percentage ownership. The **right to control** is provided by allowing common shareholders to vote for members of the board of directors. Normally, ownership of one share will allow one vote for each director to be elected. If you own 100 shares in a firm that is selecting three directors, you can cast 100 votes for each of the three separate positions. This procedure is referred to as **noncumulative voting.** Occasionally, **cumulative voting** is allowed to assure minority groups a voice in management. When cumulative voting is used, a vote can be cast for any one directorship equal to the number of shares owned times the number of positions available. For example, if 100 shares are owned and three directors are to be elected, 300 votes could be cast for one director's position and none for the other two. Shareholder voting occurs at annual meetings of the corporation. If a shareholder is unable to attend this meeting, a **proxy** vote can be given to another party.

An illustration of how common stock price quotations are shown in the financial press is shown here.

SAMPLE COMMON STOCK PRICE QUOTATIONS FOR THE CLOSE OF TRADING ON JULY 31, 1994

52 Week					Yield				Net		
Hi	Lo	Stock	Sym	Div	%	PE	100's	Hi	Lo	Close	Chng
111¼	61½	IBM	IBM	1.00	0.9	13	26352	111¼	108½	108⅞	−1¾
109¼	51½	Microsoft	MSFT	...		39	63397	93½	90	90½	−2⅛

The first quote is for shares of International Business Machines whose **ticker symbol** (a short abbreviation used by the brokerage community to identify a stock) is IBM. During the previous 52 weeks, IBM had sold for as high as $111.25 and as low as $61.50. The dollar dividend shown is an annual approximation based on the last dividend declaration. The dividend yield percentage is simply the dollar dividend divided by the current stock price. The price-to-earnings ratio (PE) is equal to the stock's current price divided by earnings over the most recent four quarters. It is a measure of the true cost of one share. Volume represents the number of shares traded in units of 100 shares. Thus, 2,635,200 shares of IBM were traded on July 31. The final set of numbers refer to prices on the day of the quote. At the close of trading, a share of IBM was worth $108.875. (Notice that stocks trade in units of 1/8.)

International Equity

The Amsterdam Bourse is considered to be the oldest stock exchange in the world, created in the early seventeenth century. In fact, the first stock to trade on the exchange was the famous East India Trading Company. Most stock exchanges began their lifes in informal and humble conditions. The Amsterdam exchange began in what was referred to as the Old Church and later moved to the New Church. In Paris, a stock market began on a bridge. In London, stock trading began in a tavern. And, in New York, trading began in a coffeehouse.

Today the largest equity market is in the United States. At the end of 1994, the total value of U.S. traded stocks was $4.9 trillion. This was followed by Japan ($3.6 trillion), the United Kingdom ($1.1 trillion), Germany ($0.5), and France ($0.4 trillion). Virtually

TABLE 3-3   1993 MARKET VALUE OF EQUITY SECURITIES AS A PERCENTAGE OF GROSS DOMESTIC PRODUCT

Country	Equity Value as Percentage of GDP
United Kingdom	163%
United States	71%
Japan	70%
Canada	60%
Denmark	39%
France	36%
Germany	28%
Israel	15%
Italy	15%

all countries of the world now have at least one stock exchange. Like the first markets in Amsterdam, London, and New York, some of these are very small with only a few securities being traded.

An interesting statistic to compare between countries is the ratio of total equity value in a country to that country's gross domestic product. This ratio is shown for a sample of countries in Table 3-3. The ratios range from 163% for the United Kingdom to 15% in Italy and Israel. These differences reflect the extent to which companies rely on public versus private equity markets to raise equity capital. For example, in the United States, heavy reliance is given to public markets. In part, this is due to historical regulations that forbid banks from providing equity money to corporations (the Glass-Stegall Act). In other countries, such as Italy, France, and Germany, tradition calls for maintaining a private ownership of equity capital as much as possible. In addition, some of the largest companies in countries such as France and Italy are nationalized.

Many companies **dual list** their shares, meaning their shares are traded on stock exchanges of two or more countries. This gives them a more diversified shareholder base and makes the firm's name better known in the foreign country. Better name recognition can improve sales as well as make it easier to borrow in the foreign country. For example, shares of Royal Dutch Shell are traded on numerous exchanges. The procedures for dual listing vary across countries. Dually listing on U.S. exchanges is among the most difficult, since the firm must first register the issue with both a stock exchange and the Securities and Exchange Commission and then provide yearly updates in English. Dual listing on the London exchange is comparatively easy.

How to Buy an International Stock. There are a number of ways to purchase stocks domiciled in another country. By far the easiest and cheapest way is to buy shares of a company that is dually listed on a local stock exchange. For example, in the mid-1990s about 250 foreign companies traded in the U.S. market called NASDAQ (see Chapter 4).

Warren J. Isabelle, C.F.A.

Vice President, Director of Research

Pioneering Management Corp.

Lowell Technological Institute, B.S.

University of Massachusetts, M.S.

Wharton Graduate School, M.B.A.

Pioneer was founded in 1928 and now manages 24 open-end mutual funds for more than 950,000 investors. Total assets under management worldwide exceed $13 billion. Mr. Isabelle is portfolio manager of Pioneer Capital Growth Fund and Pioneer Small Company Fund. Mr. Isabelle's interest in the investment marketplace began when as a teenager, he went to a Merrill Lynch investment seminar and picked up a booklet on how to read financial statements.

Q: How important is all the math and statistics that often accompanies discussions about the market?

A: You have to put investing in mathematical terms because money is a quantity. If you can't quantify what it is you're looking at, you can't make a judgment on a stock. You need that to determine value.

Q: What's the first thing to do when deciding to invest?

A: You have to have an objective. There's no reason to invest unless you have a financial objective. You have to sort that out and determine whether it's short term, long term and also what level of risk you're willing to take. Some people can afford to take risk and have no qualms about it. But for most of us, risk needs to be moderated. If you're younger you can afford to add some risk to increase reward. You need to assess your income stream and what you want to accomplish from your investment.

Q: Mutual funds are often thought of as good investments for the uninformed and risk-averse. Are mutual funds appropriate in these cases?

A: It is one approach to achieving diversification and having a professional manage your money, two ways to decrease your risk. But it is not the only approach. For example, many doctors do well because they invest in things they are familiar with and are knowledgeable about by virtue of their practices. While it may go against conventional wisdom, not having a mutual fund doesn't necessarily mean you're skewing your risk. There are many types of risk. You should never invest in anything you're unfamiliar with; the fastest way to get into trouble is to invest on a whim or a tip or in something you haven't done your homework on.

Q: So while doctors may not be adequately diversified against market risk they may have an acceptable level of investment risk because they have an increased knowledge about a product or service?

A: I think you minimize the risk by increasing the knowledge about a security but you can only take this so far. I'm not suggesting you should only buy one stock but you can address the diversification issue by looking at the long term and making sure your judgments are sound.

Q: Why would anybody buy a mutual fund that has a load fee?

A: The argument for buying no-load mutual funds is that you have no investment cost, but I believe no- or low-load funds have large amounts of advertising and administrative costs that may not be borne by the load funds and have to be accounted for in some way. Eventually the customer pays one way or another. In addition you may trust the judgment of the person selling you the fund and his or her time and effort is worth something. If you're not a high volume trader and you have a long-term horizon, the extra dollar you put into the load or commission is not that great. Some people want to have guidance in making investment decisions. Their lifestyles dictate that they don't have the time or interest to make the decisions on their own. If you find someone

knowledgeable and trustworthy it pays for itself.

Q: How do a college students with a small amount of money increase their knowledge and get started investing?

A: First, decide your objective; then make use of what's around you. Go to the local library for information like Value Line, Morningstar, and the S&P Stock Guide. You can call the SEC for lists of documents companies produce. They will tell you what the documents are and what they're used for. The American Association of Individual Investors charges a small annual fee and provides lots of objective information. You can make use of the Internet; for example, the SEC and NASD have home pages. As a professional I have a lot of tools, such as proprietary databases, at my disposal to make information gathering easier.

Q: Is this one of the reasons to hire a professional money manager?

A: Yes, although the speed and breadth with which portfolio managers are accustomed to getting data is now available to many people at an increasingly inexpensive rate. The advantage will be gone before we know it.

A similar approach is to buy **American Depository Receipts** (ADRs) on shares of the company. An ADR represents a claim to shares of a foreign stock that are held by a domestic U.S. bank. To avoid strange prices, a single ADR might provide a claim to a multiple of the foreign shares. For example, since a Japanese stock might trade for a few yen per share, the ADR would be on 100 shares.

If the stock is not dually listed or available via ADRs, it is possible a brokerage firm in the local country carries an inventory of the stock and would be willing to sell it. Finally, an investor could have a broker arrange to trade the security directly in a foreign market, either in the London market or the country of origin. This last alternative is difficult and potentially costly for individual investors. However, for large institutions, it is often the best approach, since they will be trading sizable quantities and need the liquidity the foreign market can provide.

Probably the best way for small investors to obtain ownership of foreign stocks is to purchase a professionally managed commingled portfolio. This provides immediate diversification and eliminates problems of stock commissions, foreign taxes, and security custody.

Commingled Portfolios

The securities just discussed all provide a **direct claim** on the assets of an organization. In contrast, commingled portfolios provide an **indirect claim** to the assets.

A commingled portfolio is a group of securities owned in common by a large number of investors. For example, the Prudential Retirement Income Separate Account (PRISA) portfolio consists of geographically diversified commercial properties in the United States that are managed by an investment team working for Prudential Life Insurance. Owners of the PRISA portfolio are numerous pension funds, endowments, and foundations. They all own the same set of assets.

Commingled portfolios provide three potential advantages: (1) portfolio management costs are reduced due to the economies present in large portfolios, (2) greater diversification can be achieved when investors pool their capital to acquire a single portfolio, and (3) the portfolio is professionally managed. Commingled portfolios are offered by bank trust companies, insurance companies, and investment counsel firms.

Open-End Investment Trusts

Open-end investment trusts are commingled portfolios that can be bought by the general public. In the United States, they are called **mutual funds.** In many other countries, they are called **unit trusts.** Before ownership interests in the portfolio (shares) can be offered to the public, detailed information about the portfolio's objective, types of securities to be traded and investment strategies that will be used must be filed with various governmental authorities (the Securities and Exchange Commission in the United States). The purpose of this information is to ensure that potential buyers receive full disclosure about the nature of the fund and its risks. In the United States, this information is presented in a document known as the **prospectus.** This is an important source of information that all potential buyers should read carefully.

Ownership of mutual funds has grown dramatically over the past 20 years. Today more mutual funds are available to investors in the United States than there are stocks listed on the New York Stock Exchange. And in the United Kingdom, investment companies own about 80% of the value of all U. K. stocks. Thus, we devote more discussion to them than other securities discussed in this chapter.

New mutual funds are usually started by an investment company as a way of increasing the company's total revenue. Mutual funds, however, are only one of many ways investment companies provide their investment services. The investment company invites a number of qualified people to act as an independent board of directors of the fund and then negotiates with the directors to act as the **investment adviser** to the fund. In return for providing investment management services to the fund, the investment adviser receives a yearly fee. This fee is usually a specified percentage of assets managed (0.25% to 1.5% are common fees), although some fees are based on meeting specified performance targets.

Most securities are bought and sold in secondary security markets such as the New York Stock Exchange. Shares of mutual funds, however, are bought and sold directly with the mutual fund. If someone purchases 200 shares, then the fund's outstanding shares increase by 200. If someone wishes to sell 300 shares, then outstanding shares decline by 300. This is why these investment portfolios are called open-end companies. Further details about share purchases and sales are discussed next.

With the exception of balanced funds, most mutual funds identify a single asset class in which the portfolio investments will be made. For example, consider the mutual funds offered by a well-known investment advisory firm as shown in Table 3-4. Included in the list are money market funds, tax exempt municipal bond funds, fixed income funds, actively managed U.S. and international equity funds, and a variety of passive index funds. Each of these commingled portfolios is concentrated on one of the asset classes discussed in this chapter. Managers of the funds specialize. They do so for two reasons. It is difficult for a portfolio manager to closely follow more than one type of asset class. In addition, this allows each investor in the funds the opportunity to pick and choose a combination of the funds that best meet his or her personal needs.

The exception to asset class specialization are balanced funds. **A balanced fund** owns a number of asset classes, typically about one-half fixed income and one-half equities.

Mutual funds are not an asset class. They are a vehicle for investing in an asset class. In Chapter 2, we said one of the decisions an investor must make is the security selection decision: Who will decide which securities are to be held, the investor or a professional

TABLE 3-4   TYPES OF MUTUAL FUNDS OFFERED BY THE VANGUARD GROUP

Fixed Income Funds	Balanced Funds	Actively Managed Equity Funds	Index Funds
Money Market Funds	Asset Allocation Fund	Growth and Income Fund	U.S. Bond Index Funds
Tax Exempt Money Market Funds	Life Strategy Fund	Convertible Fund	U.S. Tax Managed Equity Fund
Fixed Income Funds			U.S. Equity Index Funds
Tax Exempt Fixed Income Funds		Growth Funds	
		Aggressive Growth Funds	International Equity Index Funds
		International Funds	International Equity Emerging Markets Fund

manager? Mutual funds provide the way for small investors to employ professionals to manage part, or all, of their investment portfolio.

Sources of Mutual Fund Returns.   As with any security, investors in mutual funds receive returns in the form of dividends and capital appreciation (or depreciation). Understanding the sources of these dividends and price changes improves our understanding of how mutual funds operate.

Money provided by fund shareholders is invested in a portfolio of many securities. For example, on June 30, 1995, the portfolio of American Mutual Fund (AMF) consisted of the following:

American Mutual Fund Summary of Portfolio Holdings as of June 30, 1995	Dollar Value (in $ Millions)
Money market securities	$1,202
Fixed income securities	496
U.S. stocks	4,188
International stock	157
Total	$6,043

A fund is not taxed on any dividend and interest income the fund receives on securities owned by the fund if the income is distributed to fund shareholders in the year in which received. Such distributions to shareholders are referred to as **income dividends.** Shareholders pay taxes on any such income dividends. But the fund does not. For example, during the first six months of 1995, AMF had received (net of fund expenses) $0.42 per share of dividend and interest income, which was distributed as income dividends on each share of the fund.

Changes in the value of securities owned by the fund are referred to as capital gains or losses. When a fund sells a security in which it has a capital gain and buys a new security, the capital gain on the security that was sold is said to be a **realized gain.** When securities are sold at a loss, the realized loss is netted against realized gains. Typically, all realized capital gains are also distributed to shareholders so the fund does not have to pay taxes on its net realized gains. Distributions of realized capital gains to shareholders are referred to as **capital gain dividends.** As with income dividends, shareholders pay taxes on any capital gain dividends. But the fund does not. In the case of AMF, no capital gain distributions had been made during the first six months of 1995, since managers of AMF were unsure how trading during the second six months of 1995 would affect realized gains for the full year. Capital gain dividends are typically paid in one payment late in the year.

Changes in the value of securities that have not yet been sold are referred to as **unrealized capital gains**. From one year to the next (after realized capital gains have been distributed), changes in unrealized gains are the principal cause for changes in a fund's net asset value.

Net Asset Value.   The net asset value (NAV) of a mutual fund is calculated as follows:

Net
Asset $$NAV = \frac{(\text{Market Value of Portfolio Assets}) - (\text{Fund Liabilities})}{\text{Number of Shares Outstanding}} \qquad (3.4)$$
Value

TABLE 3-5 **BALANCE SHEET OF VANGUARD INDEX TRUST 500 PORTFOLIO AT JUNE 30, 1995**

ASSETS	(In 000's)	Liabilities and Equity	(In 000's)
U.S. Treasury Bills	$ 8,885	Short-Term Liabilities	$ 180,551
Repurchase Agreements	191,338		
Total Cash	200,223	Equity (250,784,765 shares)	
Investments		Paid in Capital	9,958,881
Miscellaneous Assets	163,525	Undistributed Net	
		Investment Income	51,542
		Accumulated Net	
		Realized Gains	4,278
		Unrealized Appreciation	
		of Investments	2,814,059
Common Stocks	12,645,563	Total Equity	12,828,769
Total Assets	$13,009,311	Total Financing	$13,009,311

Net Asset Value per Share = $12,828,760 ÷ 250,784.765 = $51.15

As an example, consider the balance sheet information of a mutual fund called Vanguard Index Trust 500 shown in Table 3-5. This is one of the oldest and largest U.S. equity index funds. As its name suggests, the fund attempts to index the S&P 500 Index. The fund maintained a small investment in cash equivalents (money market securities) and had a small amount of nonsecurity assets (shown as miscellaneous assets). But the vast majority of this fund's assets were investments in stocks that were components of the S&P 500 Index. The total market value of a mutual fund's investments is calculated at the end of each day. At the close of trading on June 30, 1995, the market value of the Vanguard portfolio was $13,009,311,000—yes, $13 billion. On the same day, the fund had various short-term liabilities worth $180,551,000. And before processing any requests to buy or sell shares of the fund that had been received during the day, the fund had 250,784,765 shares outstanding. Thus, its net asset value per share was equal to $51.15.

$$\$51.15 = \frac{\$13,009,311,000 - \$180,551,000}{250,784,765}$$

After a fund's NAV has been calculated at the end of a day's trading, requests received during the day to buy or sell shares are transacted at the newly established NAV. This assures that buyers and sellers trade at fair values. In the Vanguard example, a request to buy $10,000 of the fund would represent 195.5034 new shares ($10,000 ÷ $51.15). And a request to sell 300 shares would provide cash to the seller of $15,345.00 (300 * $51.15). Sales of mutual fund shares are referred to as **redemptions.**

FIGURE 3-5   HYPOTHETICAL MUTUAL FUND TRANSACTIONS

TRANSACTION	FUND NAV	FUND SHAREHOLDER
1. Fund is formed and shareholder buys a single share of the fund.	10.00 ←	−10.00
2. Fund takes cash received from shareholder and buys stocks.	10.00	
3. Fund receives $1 in dividends from stocks owned by fund.	11.00	
4. Market value of securities increases by $3.	14.00	
5. Fund pays a $1 income dividend to shareholder.	13.00 →	1.00
6. Fund "realizes" a $2 capital gain when it sells some stock and buys other stock.	13.00	
7. Fund distributes "realized" capital gain by paying a $2 dividend to shareholder.	11.00 →	2.00
Final Share Value		11.00

		DIVIDEND YIELD	plus	CAPITAL APPRECIATION
Total Return	equals	3/10	+	1/10
0.40	=	0.30	+	0.10

What causes the NAV of a mutual fund to change? Consider the hypothetical transactions shown in Figure 3-5.

- ◼ On date 1, an investor purchases one share of a fund at an NAV of $10. At the time of receipt, this $10 is placed into the cash account of the mutual fund. This purchase has no effect on the fund's NAV, since shares are traded at their net asset value.

- ◼ On date 2, the cash is used to buy $10 of stocks. This also has no effect on NAV, since it simply represents a transfer of $10 in cash to $10 in stocks.

◼ On date 3, the fund receives a dividend on its investments in stocks that are worth $1 per share. This increases fund NAV by $1 per share to $11.[4]

◼ On date 4, the value of securities owned by the mutual fund increases by $3 causing the NAV to grow to $14.

◼ On date 5, the fund pays an income dividend of $1 on each share of the fund. This reduces the NAV by $1 because assets equal to $1 per share have been transferred from the fund to investors in the fund.

◼ On date 6, the fund realizes $2 of its $3 capital gain by selling securities in which it has the $2 gain. This has no effect on NAV (at that time) because the asset value is retained within the firm.

◼ On date 7, the fund pays a capital gain dividend of $2 on each share of the fund. This reduces the NAV by $2 because assets equal to $2 per share have been transferred from the fund to investors in the fund. The final NAV is $11.

Why and How to Buy Mutual Funds.   In Chapter 1, we discussed why people might wish to own shares of one or more mutual funds. They provide individual investors with a way of obtaining broad diversification. The costs of personal portfolio management are almost always greater than the annual costs incurred by a mutual fund. And the portfolio is managed by a professional. Active professional management may, or may not, provide better returns than passive management. This is an issue that is not resolved. But having the portfolio managed by a professional (active or passive) is less likely to result in irrational, spur of the moment decisions.

There are two ways to buy a mutual fund, through a security broker or directly from the fund. If a security broker is used, the broker receives a commission referred to as the **load.** Load fees currently range between 3% to 6% and are typically paid when the shares are purchased; a **front-end** load. For example, the front-end load fee to buy shares of AMF is 5.75%. If you give your broker $10,000 to purchase AMF shares when its NAV is $20, the broker would take $575 as a commission ($10,000 ∗ 0.0575) and invest the remaining $9,425 in 471.25 shares ($9,425 ÷ $20).

If shares in the fund are bought directly from the fund, a load fee is not paid. Libraries have extensive information about no-load funds that give addresses and telephone numbers. But even no-load funds will often impose what is called a redemption fee if the investor sells the shares before a specified period, typically a year or two.

The references at the end of this chapter identify a number of the main sources of information about mutual funds.

Closed-End Investment Companies.   Closed-end investment companies are similar to mutual funds (open-end companies) in a number of respects. Both tend to

---

[4] We are assuming the dividend of $1 does not decrease the market value of the securities that paid the dividends. In reality, the value of stocks that pay a dividend will fall by an amount approximately equal to the dividend. The assumption is made to keep the analysis simple, to avoid straying into more complex issues.

specialize in a particular asset class. Both provide broad diversification at relatively low cost. And both pay no taxes on dividends, interest, and realized income that is passed on to shareholders.

The major difference in the form of the securities comes from how they are purchased and sold. Shares of mutual funds are bought and sold directly with the fund. Closed-end companies, however, are traded like other securities, in secondary security markets in which public buyers trade with public sellers using brokers as the intermediary. Unlike mutual funds, they do not have to trade at a fund's underlying NAV. And they don't.

This is the mystery of closed-end investment companies, why they sell at sizable premia or discounts from their net asset values. Consider the data plotted in Figure 3-6. The vertical axis shows the percentage by which each fund traded above net asset value (premia) or the percentage below net asset value (discounts). The funds were chosen more or less at random. One fund invests in U.S. fixed income securities, another in U.S. equities, and the third in U.S. convertible bonds. Many explanations have been put forth for why investors trade these securities at prices very different from their true underlying economic values. In Chapter 20, we examine these possible explanations. But no consensus opinion has yet emerged. Discounts and premiums on these funds remain a mystery!

Prior to the 1940s, the number of closed-end funds dominated open-end funds. But after World War II, the number of closed-end funds in the United States declined dramatically as they either liquidated assets and went out of business or converted to open-end funds. By the late 1970s, few closed-end funds existed. However, recent years have seen a

FIGURE 3-6   CLOSED END FUND DISCOUNTS AND PREMIA

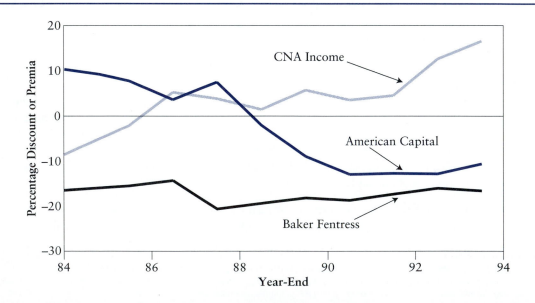

resurgence in closed-end investment companies and they now number in the hundreds.[5] Many of these new U.S. closed-end funds are designed to minimize income taxes by investing in municipal bonds of a specified state or are designed to provide international exposure by investing in the securities of specified foreign countries. The latter type of fund is known as a **country fund.**

Relative to mutual funds, closed-end funds have both advantages and disadvantages. The main advantage is that there might not be an equivalent open-end fund that invests in similar securities. For example, some closed-end funds invest in countries that have constraints on the withdrawal of capital. Such constraints would cause problems for mutual funds that might have to sell securities in order to pay shareholders who wish to redeem their shares in the mutual fund. But closed-end funds do not have to worry about share redemptions and can invest in such countries. The main disadvantages of owning a closed-end fund are liquidity and the presence of uncertain discounts and premia. Closed-end shares do not trade as actively as most publicly traded stocks. Thus, institutional investors, who trade in large quantities, stay away from closed-end funds. Even individual investors will find the market in closed-end shares to be less liquid than for most publicly traded shares. The existence of discounts and premia on closed-end shares adds an additional element of risk to the uncertainty inherent in the value of the securities held by a closed-end fund.

Derivative Securities

Derivative securities also do not have a direct claim on a real asset. Instead, they have a claim on another security such as a common stock or a bond. As implied by their name, their market value is derived from the market value of an underlying direct security. The two broad types of derivative securities are (1) futures, and (2) options. Many types of futures and option securities are traded in world markets. We examine such instruments on financial securities in Chapters 16 and 17. For now, however, it is best to focus on how these securities differ from the underlying assets to which they have a claim.

Our example is based on the common stock of ABC Corporation. These shares have a market value today, but we are mainly interested in their market value at some specified future date T. This is because futures and options give claims to the underlying asset only at a specified future date. For example, a **futures** will require the owner to buy a security in 180 days and an **option** will allow the owner to buy in 180 days.

Think of a graph. In our example, the horizontal axis of this graph will always be the market value of one share of ABC stock at future date T. This market value could be as low as $0.00. However, we will examine cases when the stock is worth $50, $100, and $150. On the vertical axis, we will plot the value of some security at date T (whose value depends on the stock price at that time). Four asset positions will be plotted on the vertical axis: (1) own the stock, (2) own a futures contract on the stock, (3) own a call

---

[5] In countries other than the United States, such as the United Kingdom, closed-end investment companies did not decline in number during the post–World War II era and have always been important vehicles by which investors could obtain broad diversification and professional management at low cost.

option on the stock, and (4) own a put option on the stock. The derivatives are defined as follows:

- **Futures.** The **owner is obligated to purchase** the underlying asset from the seller at an agreed on price at a specified future date. The **seller is obligated to deliver the good** to the owner at date T.[6]

- **Call Options.** The **owner has the right to purchase** the underlying asset from the call seller at an agreed on price at a specified future date T. If the call owner exercises this right, the seller of the call must deliver the good.

- **Put Options.** The **owner has the right to sell** the underlying asset to the put seller at an agreed on price at a specified future date T. If the put owner exercises this right, the seller of the put option must buy the asset.

We will use $100 as the date T price at which the futures owner must buy, the call owner may buy, and the put owner may sell.

Consider A through D panels in Figure 3-7. Panel A is the easiest, since it reflects a direct ownership of the stock. If the stock is worth $100 at T, the position is also worth $100.

The long futures position in Panel B (*long* means ownership, *short* means you owe) moves in the same direction as the direct stock ownership but is always $100 lower. This $100 spread between the stock ownership and the futures ownership is due to the obligation to pay $100 at date T. If the stock is worth $150, the futures is worth $50. If the stock is worth $50, the futures is worth $-$50. At date T, the futures contract is the same as underlying stock minus the obligated purchase price. This simple fact is the basis on which all futures contracts are valued at dates prior to T.

The ownership of the call at date T is shown in panel C and will have a positive value if the stock is worth more than the stated purchase price at which the owner has a right to buy. If the stock is worth $150, the call is worth $50. It is important, though, to realize the call owner has a right to buy but not an obligation. Thus, if the stock is worth $50, the call's value is $0.0, not -$50.

The ownership of the put at date T is shown in panel D and will have a positive value if the stock is worth less than the $100 stated price at which the owner may sell. If the stock is worth $50 at date T, then the right to sell at $100 (the put) is worth $50. Because the put provides a right and not an obligation, its value will never be negative.

Notice that the lines in each panel move across the page at 45-degree angles. The importance of this is that one of the securities can be emulated by combinations of the others. For example, what is the date T outcome if you owned both one future and one put? Since the put pays off when the futures have a loss, the net of this combination is the same as a call option. This observation is the key to how derivative securities are priced in financial markets.

---

[6] Futures contracts are traded on futures exchanges. Their counterpart, called a forward contract, is traded in the over-the-counter market. The terms of a forward contract can be negotiated whereas the terms of a futures contract are set by the exchange.

FIGURE 3-7 ANALYSIS OF DERIVATIVES

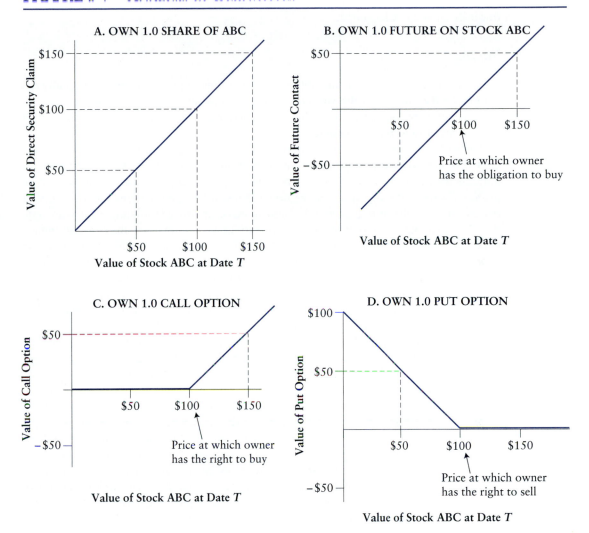

Why do complex securities such as these derivatives exist? The answer is simple; they provide cost-efficient means of hedging security price risk. For example, assume you now own a share of ABC stock and intend to sell it in 180 days, since you need cash at that time. By selling a 100-day future on the share, you have guaranteed the price you will receive. Alternatively, if you wish to continue to own the share but want to limit your losses if its value should decline, you could buy a long put. This put would guarantee a minimum selling price over the life of the put.

One difference between futures and options is that the futures is a legal obligation whereas the option is a legal right. There is another important difference between them.

Future buyers pay nothing to a futures seller until a stated future date. Call option and put option buyers, however, pay a price to the seller when the trade takes place. The reason for this is discussed in Chapter 17.

Swaps

Swaps are exactly what the name implies, a swap of one thing for another. Originally developed in the late 1970s, the swap market has become an important element of modern financial markets. Typically, a swap involves an exchange of interest payments on the debt obligations of two **counterparties.**

The earliest form of swaps were **currency swaps.** Assume a company domiciled in the United States wishes to build a new production plant in Germany. Cash payments for building the plant as well as payments for inventories and ongoing labor costs will all be made in German marks. Cash receipts from sales will also be in German marks. Thus, it makes sense for the firm to borrow in German marks in order to minimize exchange rate risk. For example, if the borrowing was done in the United States in the form of dollars, the firm would face exchange rate risks during two time periods. During the time period the plant is being constructed, dollars will have to be converted to German marks in order to pay for services and materials in Germany. Once the plant is operational and generating income, the income will have to be exchanged into dollars in order to pay interest and principal on the U.S. borrowings. Since the U.S. firm will not know the future rates of exchange between dollars and marks, it incurs an exchange rate risk.

Assume a company in Germany wishes to do exactly the opposite, build a new plant in the United States from which sales denominated in U.S. dollars will be generated. These firms face identical but opposite risks. As such, they could eliminate exchange rate risks to each firm if they simply swapped liabilities. The U.S. firm would sell a debt obligation in the United States and the German firm would sell an equivalent (similar default risk and maturity) in Germany. Then the firms would enter into a swap agreement in which the U.S. firm would agree to pay all of the German firm's obligations in Germany and the German firm would agree to pay all the U.S. firm's obligations in the United States.

This currency swap is an illustration of how financial arrangements can be created that are of a clear benefit to all participants. But why doesn't the U.S. firm simply sell a debt issue denominated in marks in Germany and the German company sell a dollar-denominated issue in the United States? If security markets between the two countries were perfectly efficient, they would. But international markets are not perfectly efficient. The credit risk of each firm is likely to be better known in its home country. Thus, a new debt issue placed within each firm's local country would require less credit analysis and a lower interest rate. For example, if both companies could sell similar bond issues at an interest cost of 8% in their home countries but be required to pay 9% in the foreign country, then a currency swap could save each firm 100 basis points a year. (A basis point is $1/100$ of 1%.)

There have been many other types of swap arrangements developed since the late 1970s. These include the following:

- ◾ **Interest rate swaps,** in which the counterparties exchange fixed rate debt for floating rate debt. For example, a company might have a five-year bond issue outstanding on which the interest rate is set equal to the LIBOR rate plus 2%. If the firm is concerned that short-term interest rates will increase during the next five years, an interest rate swap with a bank could be arranged in which the firm pays a fixed rate to the bank (for five years) and the bank assumes the firm's future floating rate interest payments.

■ **Basis rate swaps,** in which both parties have floating rate interest payments, but the rates are tied to different indexes (such as the LIBOR rate versus 30-day T-bills).

■ **Timing swaps,** in which one counterparty pays interest semiannually and the other annually.

Initially, swap arrangements were made between two parties and tailored closely to the needs of each. More recently, banks have offered standardized swap contracts. These standardized contracts save transaction costs and provide an element of liquidity, since they can be traded in secondary security markets.

S U M M A R Y

This chapter has provided an overview of the types of investments traded in world security markets. Here are the key concepts:

■ The principal difference between different asset classes is risk. Some securities such as short-term governmental obligations have little risk. Other securities such as small stocks and stocks of companies in emerging markets provide rates of return that are very volatile.

■ Debt securities are classified as money market instruments if they have maturities of one year or less. Capital market instruments have maturities greater than a year.

■ Treasury bills are priced using a technique known as the bank discount method. The simple interest and compound interest annual rates of return are larger than the quoted discount.

■ Capital market debt securities are of four types: (1) obligations issued and traded in the issuer's home country, (2) obligations sold and traded in a country different from the issuer's home country, (3) obligations sold in the Eurobond market, and (4) obligations of supranationals that are denominated in a variety of currencies.

■ In U.S. debt markets, obligations of the federal government and its agencies represented about 48% of the value of all U.S. debt issues in the mid-1990s, and mortgage-backed securities represented almost 30%.

■ Open-end investment companies (called mutual funds in the United States) provide an inexpensive way for investors to obtain well-diversified positions in different asset classes.

R E V I E W   P R O B L E M

You are given the following price quotations on a T-bill for the close of trading on May 31 and June 30. (Note that as of June 30, this T-bill has a 90-day remaining life.)

T-BILL INFORMATION

	On May 31		On June 30	
Maturity	Bid	Asked	Bid	Asked
Sept 28	9.10%	9.00%	9.30%	9.25%

a. On May 31, the T-bill had a 120-day remaining life. On that day, what percentage of par value would you pay to purchase the T-bill?
b. On that day, what were the simple interest and compound interest annualized rate of return?
c. Assume you purchased the T-bill on May 31 and later sold it on June 30. What rate of return did you earn during this one-month period? If you were to express this return on an annualized basis, what would the return be?

Solution

a. $P = 100 - 100\,(0.090)\,(120 \div 360) = 97.00$
b. Simple interest $= r = [(100 - 97) \div 97]\,(365 \div 120) = 0.09407$
   Compound interest $= r' = [(100 \div 97)^{365 \div 120} - 1.0 = 0.09707$
c. Purchase price from above equals 97.00
   Selling price $= 100 - 100\,(0.093)\,(90 \div 360) = 97.675$
   One-month gain $= (97.675 - 97.00) \div 97.00 = 0.00696 = 0.696\%$
   Annualized simple interest $= 0.00696\,(365 \div 30) = 0.08468$
   Annualized compound interest $= 1.00696^{365 \div 30} - 1.0 = 0.08805$

Q U E S T I O N S   A N D   P R O B L E M S

1. Sample quotes on U.S. T-bills are shown here for two dates, January 1 and January 15. Assume the quotes represent end-of-day transactions and that trades could actually be made at these prices.

Maturity	Discount		
	Bid	Ask	Yield
As of January 1 (close)			
Jan 15	9.00	8.70	8.851
Feb 15	9.10	8.75	8.970
Mar 15	9.12	8.79	–
As of January 15 (close)			
Feb 15	8.80	8.70	–
Mar 15	8.85	8.75	9.000

a. As of January 1, at what price (percentage of par value) could you buy the January 15 T-bill (assume a full 14-day period)? At what price could you sell?
b. As of January 1, at what price could you buy the March 15 T-bill? Sell?
c. Find the missing yield values.

d. What would your dollar profit be if you buy $10 million face value of the March T-bill on January 1 and sell it on January 15?

e. Assume that on January 1 you buy $100 million of February T-bills at the 8.75% discount. This amount considerably exceeds the equity capital of your firm, and you must finance the inventory in some way. Explain how financing might be arranged and why the financing cost might be less than the 8.75% discount. (Hint: Think about repurchase agreements.)

2. Two competitive bidders submit bids on $1 million of 91-day bills being offered by the U.S. Treasury. The bids differ by 1 basis point. What is the total dollar difference between each bid?

3. You are given the following T-bill quotations as of the close of trading on June 1 and June 10:

	Discount	
Maturity	Bid	Ask
As of June 1 (close)		
June 30	9.00	8.80
As of June 10 (close)		
June 30	9.50	9.45

a. At the end of June 1, how much would you have to pay to purchase $1 million in par value of the T-bills?

b. Note that only discount quotations are shown. What would be the price quotations for June 1 as they would appear in the financial press?

c. If you purchased some T-bills on June 1, what would be the simple interest and compound interest annualized yields? Why do they differ?

d. Assume you purchased the T-bill on June 1 and later sold it on June 10. What was your nine-day profit (or loss) in percentage terms? What was the cause of this profit (or loss)? What is the annualized equivalent yield?

4. The U.S. Treasury offers $2 billion in 91-day new T-bills and receives the following bids. What yield will the noncompetitive bidders receive?

Discount	Competitive Bids
8.50%	$200 million
8.55	400 million
8.56	600 million
8.58	1,000 million
8.59	1,500 million
8.60	1,000 million
Discount	Noncompetitive Bids
NA	$500 million

5. An importer must finance various planned purchases of goods. Commercial paper rates are now 7.53%, and bankers' acceptance rates are 7.68%. Why might the importer utilize the bankers' acceptance instead of commercial paper?

6. Price quotations on two mutual funds are shown here:

Fund	Net Asset Value	Front-End Load
Fidelity Magellan	33.37	3.0%
Price New Horizon	12.88	No Load

    a. If you invest $1,000 in each fund, how many shares would you receive of each?

    b. Interpret what NAV means.

7. You are given the following information on First Street Growth Fund, a mutual fund that invests mainly in high-growth stocks.

Total market value of assets	= $500 million
Liabilities	= 10 million
Number of shares outstanding	= 7 million

    a. What is the net asset value per share?

    b. If this is a no-load fund, how many shares could be acquired with $10,000?

8. What would happen to the net asset value per share of First Street Growth Fund above if:

    a. You invest $10,000 in the fund?

    b. Another investor who owns 1,000 shares sells them back to the fund(redeems them?)

    c. The market value of securities held increase by $20 million (prior to parts a or b above)?

    d. The fund pays a $5 income dividend on each share of the fund(prior to parts a - c)?

9. Assume that a municipal bond and a corporate bond have identical marketability, default risk, and maturity. The municipal is selling at a 5% yield to maturity; the corporate is selling for an 8% yield to maturity.

    a. Should a person in a 30% tax bracket buy the municipal or the corporate security? (Assume the full 8% yield on the corporate is taxable at 30%)

    b. What is the break-even tax bracket at which an investor is indiffenet between the two issues?

10. Define Eurobond bond and a Yankee bond. Why would someone wish to issue such securities?

11. What is meant by the LIBOR rate?

12. What is a STRIPS? If you wished to create a market in a new type of STRIPS that represent claims to coupons or principal values of bonds isued by corporations, what kind of problems might investors in your STRIPS be concerned about?

13. Investors in mortgage-backed securities face relatively little default risk. But there can be considerable risk to investing in these securities. What is this risk?

14. What is a commingled portfolio?

15. What are the potential advantages of purchasing a commingled portfolio?

16. Futures and options are available on shares of XYZ common stock. The futures require that buyers pay $50 per share in exactly one year. In return, they will receive one share of XYZ. Call options allow buyers to purchase the shares for $50 in one year and put options allow buyers to sell at $50 in one year. Parts a through e of this question require graphs. In each case, the horizontal axis will represent the value of XYZ shares in one year. Its scale should have a minimum value of $0.0 and a maximum value of $75.

    a. On the vertical axis, plot the value in one year of owning one futures contract on XYZ shares.

    b. On the vertical axis, plot the value in one year of owning one call on XYZ shares.

    c. On the vertical axis, plot the value in one year of owning one put on XYZ shares.

    d. How does the ownership of one future on XYZ shares differ from the ownership of one XYZ share (in a year from now)?

    e. Assume you purchase one future on XYZ and one put. Plot the one year payoff of this position.

17. A futures contract exists that allows traders to purchase (or sell) bushels of corn at $3 per bushel in exactly one year. Why might people wish to trade this contract today? Focus on how trades could reduce future uncertainty, not on speculative motives.

18. In what fundamental ways do options and futures differ?

CFA   19. Investment dealer A purchases 91-day U.S. T-bills from Investment dealer B. At the same time, A agrees to sell the bills back to B for delivery three weeks later at a predetermined price. Investment Dealer A is transacting a:
a. repurchase agreement.
b. reverse repurchase agreement.
c. call loan.
d. put loan.

CFA   20. A revenue bond is distinguished from a general obligation bond in that revenue bonds:
a. are issued by counties, special districts, cities, towns, and state-controlled authorities, whereas general obligation bonds are only issued by the states themselves.
b. are typically secured by limited taxing power, whereas general obligation bonds are secured by unlimited taxing power.
c. are issued to finance specific projects and are secured by the revenues of the project being financed.
d. have first claim to any revenue increase of the tax authority issuing the bonds.

CFA   21. Yankee dollar bonds are U.S.-pay bonds that are:
a. issued by foreign-domiciled issuers who register with the SEC.
b. traded principally in London, but to a growing degree in New York as well.
c. free of withholding tax to non-U.S. investors.
d. all of the above.

CFA   22. Income bonds differ from ordinary bonds in that the income bond's coupon:
a. can vary up or down according to changes in the net income of the issuer.
b. varies, but can only move up according to changes in the income of the issuer.
c. is fixed, but payment of interest may be deferred.
d. is fixed, but payment of interest is contingent on the income of the issuer being sufficient for that purpose.

CFA   23. The dollar value of a U.S. T-bond quoted at 92.24 is:
a. $922.75
b. $922.40
c. $927.50
d. Cannot be determined

CFA   24. Eurodollar bonds are:
I. denominated in U.S. dollars.
II. underwritten by an international syndicate.
III. sold at issue to U.S. investors.
a. I, II, and III
b. I and II only
c. II only
d. III only

CFA   25. Serial obligation bonds differ from *most* other bonds because:
a. they are secured by the assets and taxing power of the issuer.
b. their par value is usually well below $1,000.
c. their term to maturity is usually very long (30 years or more).
d. they possess multiple maturity dates.

26. On January 1, you buy a mutual fund for $12. Two dollars of the fund's NAV represents price gains on securities the fund has not yet realized. Explain how the following affect the NAV of this fund.
a. On date 1 the fund receives $1 per share in interest payments, which it keeps as cash. The market value of the securities owned do not change.
b. On date 2 the fund uses the $1 in cash per share to buy bonds.
c. On date 3 the value of securities held rise by $1.50 per share.

   d. On date 4 a new investor buys shares at $14.50.

   e. On date 5 the fund trades securities, which result in realized gains of $3.50 per share.

   f. On date 6 the fund pays an income dividend of $1 per share and a capital gain dividend of $3.50 per share.

D A T A F I L E   A N A L Y S E S

The purpose of the datafile analyses in this chapter are to review historical changes in annualized promised yields on a variety of U.S. money market instruments as well as yield spreads between these securities.

1. Money Market Rates. Access the datafile called INDEXES.WK3' and locate the annual rates of return commercial paper, bankers' acceptances, negotiable certificates of deposit, and U.S. T-bills.
Plot these returns with time on the horizontal axis. Examine their levels and changes in levels over time. Why they change is an important topic in Chapter 5. As a student of finance, you should be knowledgeable of the level and variability past yields, particularly the high levels of the late 1970s and early 1980s.
2. Yield Spreads. Calculate yield spreads between each money market instrument and three-month U.S. T-bills. The yield spread is the difference between an instrument's annualized yield and that of the three-month U.S. T-bill. Explain why these yield spreads exist.

R E F E R E N C E S

A thorough examination of money market instruments can be found in the following:

Cook, Timothy Q. and Timothy D. Rowe, *Instruments of the Money Market,* Richmond, VA: Federal Reserve Bank of Richmond, 1986.

Kidwell, David S., M. Wayne Mann, and G. Rodney Thompson, "Eurodollar Bonds: Alternative Financing for U.S. Companies," *Financial Management,* Winter 1985.

Stigum, Marcia. *The Money Market,* Homewood, IL: Dow Jones-Irwin, 1983.

A detailed discussion of U.S. federal debt issues is *Handbook of Securities of the United States Government and Federal Agencies,* Boston: First Boston Corporation, published biannually.

Detailed statistics of security offerings can be found in these sources:

United States Federal Reserve Bulletins, published monthly.

Treasury Bulletin, Department of Treasury, Washington, DC, published monthly.

Mutual Fund Fact Book, Investment Company Institute, Washington, DC, published annually.

Nasdaq Fact Book & Company Directory, National Association of Security Dealers, Washington, DC, published annually.

Extensive Mutual Fund data is available in the following:

Investment Companies, New York: CDA/Weisenberger, published annually.

Morningstar Mutual Funds, Chicago, IL: Morningstar, Inc.

Survey articles of recent developments in security markets include:

Goldberg, Craig J. and Karen Rogers, "An Introduction to Asset Backed Securities, "*Journal of Applied Corporate Finance,* Fall, 1988 pp. 20–31.

Miller, Martin A. "Financial Innovation: The Last Twenty Years and the Next," *Journal of Financial and Quantitative Management,* December 1986, pp. 459–471.

Ocampo, Juan M. and James A. Rosenthal, "The Future of Securitization and the Financial Services Industry," *Journal of Applied Corporate Finance*, Fall, 1988 pp. 90–101.

Detailed analyses of option and futures instruments can be found in:

Goss, B. A. and B. S. Yamey, eds., *The Economics of Future Trading*, London: Macmillan, 1976.

Stoll, Hans R. and Robert E. Whaley, *Futures and Options: Theory and Applications* Cincinnati, OH: Southwestern, 1993.

APPENDIX 3A

SOURCES OF BASIC FINANCIAL INFORMATION

This appendix lists and briefly describes the major sources of security information the *nonprofessional investor or speculator* might find useful. In addition to the listings shown, most brokerage houses distribute market letters and recommendations to customers that can be quite informative. The listing does not include sources of information that professionals would use (such as computerized databases and academic journals). The outline first lists major newspapers, journals, and periodicals. After this, guides to industry and company data are listed. Finally, sources for particular types of securities are shown.

I. The General Financial Press

A. Newspapers

1. *The Wall Street Journal:* daily; reviews articles on current business topics and extensive market price data.
2. *The European Wall Street Journal:* similar to *WSJ* in the United States but covers European markets.
3. *The Asian Wall Street Journal:* similar to *WSJ* in the United States but covers Asian markets.
4. *Financial Times* (London, Paris, Frankfurt, New York, Tokyo): daily; extensive coverage of international news and security markets.
5. *The New York Times* daily; reviews articles on current business topics and extensive market price data.
6. *Commercial and Financial Chronicle:* weekly; contains daily prices on New York, American, and Toronto exchanges plus weekly prices on regional exchanges and the OTC market.
7. *Barron's:* weekly; articles on investment topics and extensive weekly price data.
8. *M/G Financial Weekly:* weekly; prices, charts, and basic financial information on most actively traded securities.
9. *Wall Street Transcript:* twice weekly; reproduces selected brokerage house reports and interviews with security analysts on a specific industry.

B. Journals and Periodicals

1. *Business Week:* weekly; articles on a variety of general business topics.
2. *Financial World:* biweekly; articles on investment topics.
3. *Forbes:* biweekly; articles on investment topics and opinions.
4. *Finance:* monthly; reviews articles on current events in the financial market.
5. *Financial Executive:* monthly; news of the Financial Executives Institute.
6. *Fortune:* biweekly; articles on general business trends for corporate managers.
7. *Institutional Investor:* monthly; articles of interest to managers of large institutional portfolios.
8. *Financial Analysts Journal:* bimonthly; articles of interest to practicing financial analysts.
9. *OTC Review:* monthly; analysis and discussion of stocks traded in the over-the-counter market, plus financial data.

10. *Journal of Portfolio Management:* quarterly; articles of interest to the professional portfolio manager.

II. Industry and Company Information

A. Industry Data: General Statistics

1. *Statistical Abstract of the U.S.:* industrial, social, political, and economic statistics.
2. *Business Statistics:* historical data for the United States updated monthly by the *Survey of Current Business*.
3. *Standard & Poor's Statistical Service:* statistics in nine major industrial groups, plus stock price averages.
4. *Basebook:* historical data by Standard Industrial Classification (SIC) number.
5. *Predicasts:* forecasts by SIC number.
6. *U.S. Industrial Outlook:* brief analysis of 200 industries.
7. *F & S Index to Corporations and Industries:* list of articles dealing with industries classified by SIC code.
8. *American Statistics Index:* guide to statistical publications of the U.S. government.
9. U.S. government publications:

Census of Mineral Industries
Census of Selected Services
Census of Construction Industry
Census of Transportation
Census of Retail Trade
Census of Wholesale Trade
Annual Survey of Manufacturers

B. Industry Data: General Information

1. *Dun & Bradstreet Key Business Ratios:* financial ratios for 125 industries.
2. *Robert Morris Associates Annual Studies:* ratios for a variety of industries.
3. *Standard & Poor's:* reports including the *Investment Advisory Service, Industry Surveys,* and *Outlook*, which provide summaries of financial data and current events.
4. *Value Line Investment Surveys:* summaries of financial data and current events.
5. *Moody's Manuals:* basic industry information and financial data.

C. Company Data

1. Corporate reports: quarterly and annual reports to shareholders by corporate management.
2. Security Prospectus: registration statement filed with the Securities and Exchange Commission (SEC) on any new security offering.
3. Required SEC Reports: monthly statement 8-K, semiannual statement 9-K, and annual statement 10-K provide information that is often more current or thorough than that reported to shareholders.
4. *Standard & Poor's Corporation Record:* historical and financial data.
5. *Standard & Poor's Analysts Handbook:* basic financial information.
6. *Standard & Poor's Stock Reports:* short reviews of financial data and forecasts.
7. *Standard & Poor's Stock Guide:* compact summary of financial information on actively traded stocks.

8. *Moody's Manuals:* historical and financial data; separate volumes deal with industrial, OTC industrial, utility, transportation, and bank-finance stocks.

9. *Value Line Investment Service:* basic financial data and projections on over 1,700 actively traded stocks.

III. Information by Type of Security

A. Money Market Instruments and Bonds

1. *Money Manager:* weekly events occurring in the short- and long-term bond markets.
2. *Weekly Bond Buyer:* weekly events occurring in the short- and long-term bond markets.
3. *Bankers Trust Credit and Capital Markets:* survey of current trends in interest rates.
4. *Moody's Bond Survey:* weekly review of events and financial data.
5. *Value Line Options and Convertibles:* financial data on convertible bonds.
6. *Moody's Bond Record:* financial data on major corporate bonds outstanding.
7. *Moody's Municipal and Government Manual:* data on U.S. government and municipal obligations.
8. *Standard & Poor's Bond Guide:* compact review of major financial data.
9. *Standard & Poor's Convertible Bond Reports:* basic information about actively traded convertible bonds.

B. Stocks: see information listed in parts IA, IB, and IIC.

C. Other Instruments

1. *Value Line Options and Convertibles:* basic information about options.
2. *Vickers Guide to Investment Company Portfolios:* general information on investment companies.
3. *CDA/Weisenberger Investment Companies:* annual background, management policy, and financial records for all U.S. and Canadian investment companies.
4. *Investment Dealers Digest Mutual Fund Directory:* semiannual statistics for mutual funds.
5. *Johnson Investment Company Charts:* data on market and various types of funds.
6. Investment Company Institute's *Mutual Fund Fact Book:* basic statistics for the industry.
7. *Commodity Yearbook:* production, prices, and so on, for 100 commodities.
8. *Guide to World Commodity Markets:* information and statistics on commodity markets.
9. *Morningstar Mutual Fund:* detailed information on mutual funds.

A P P E N D I X   3 B

PERSONAL COMPUTER DATA SOURCES

This appendix lists and briefly describes the major sources of security information available for personal computer users. Computer data used by academic researchers is not listed due to its cost and the need for mainframe computer facilities.

1. *Dow Jones News/Retrieval*. On-line service connecting to more than 40 databases providing current business and general news, company and industry information, stock quotations, and other business and financial services. U.S. prices only.

2. *Compact Disclosure*. Database containing financial and management information extracted from SEC filings and annual reports for more than 12,000 U.S. public companies. Includes five years of annual financial data.

3. *CIRR Index*. Computer index with abstracts of U.S. brokerage house reports.

4. *Compustat PC Plus*. Financial data on more than 2,000 U.S. corporations stored on CD-ROM. Program allows search for firms per user-defined criteria.

5. *Value Screen*. Financial data on firms covered in *Value Line*. Program allows search for firms with user-defined criteria.

6. *Morningstar Mutual Funds OnDisc*. Financial information and returns on 1,500 U.S. mutual funds. CD-ROM.

4

INVESTMENT MARKETS

*After reading this chapter you should
have an understanding of how new
securities are issued in the primary
market and the procedures used in
trading securities in secondary markets.*

In this chapter, we review the procedures used to trade equities and fixed income obligations in major world markets. After reading the chapter you will have a good understanding of:

- how securities are issued in the primary markets,

- how trades occur in secondary markets on listed exchanges (such as the New York Stock Exchange) and over-the-counter markets,

- details of trade executions such as trading costs, margin, and short selling,

- how security markets are regulated, and

- trading on the London and Tokyo stock exchanges.

Security transactions occur in either the **primary market** or the **secondary market.** In a primary market transaction, a buyer gives the original issuer of the security cash in exchange for ownership of the security. For example, weekly T-bill offerings by the U.S. Treasury, municipal bond sales by the state of Ohio, and stock sales by British Airways are all primary market transactions. The key to a primary market transaction is that the original security issuer receives cash, and the public then holds a security that previously didn't exist. Subsequent to the primary offering, the security is traded between members of the public in what are referred to as secondary markets. These secondary markets include both formal exchange markets (such as the New York Stock Exchange and London Stock Exchange) and less formal markets referred to as over-the-counter (OTC) markets. The issuer of a security is unaffected by secondary market transactions.[1] The sale of a T-bill by a dealer in bills to a commercial bank, the sale of a municipal bond by a New York bond house to a California savings and loan association, and the sale of British Airways ordinary shares by Ms. A to Mr. B are all secondary market transactions.

Primary Market

The Investment Banker

As we just noted, a primary market transaction represents the initial sale of a security by an issuer to the public. The issuer receives cash to invest in productive assets or realign its capital structure, and the public receives securities.

Figure 4-1 illustrates various decisions a security issuer faces. First, the legal character of the issue must be determined. Second, issuers must decide whether they are willing to assume the risks of price declines during the distribution period or would rather shift these risks to some other party. Third, a formal marketing strategy must be developed. At any stage of the security offering, the issuer may decide to rely on internal expertise or call on the services of an investment banking firm. Investment bankers, organizations that specialize in the creation and placement of securities in the primary market, provide three basic services: (1) advice, (2) underwriting, and (3) distribution.

Advice. Many security issuers do not have the internal expertise or knowledge of market conditions necessary to put together a security issue. In such cases, investment bankers can provide advice about the following:

1. **Type of security offering.** Given the issuer's financial structure and security market conditions, the investment banker can advise the issuer on what type of security—equity or debt—should be sold.
2. **Timing of the offering.** Given current and expected market conditions, the investment banker can suggest whether the offering should be sold immediately or delayed in hopes of a better price.
3. **Legal characteristics of the issue.** For example, if a debt issue is contemplated, the investment banker can provide advice about coupon rate, maturity, protective covenants, convertibility, call prices, and so on.
4. **Price of the security.** Given suggestions about each of the above, the investment banker will suggest a price at which the security can be sold.

---

[1] Secondary market transactions can have an indirect effect on the original security issuer, however, because of information provided by secondary market prices. For example, the price of IBM common stock and debt can be used by IBM management to evaluate their past performance and determine the financing costs necessary to float new issues.

FIGURE 4-1   CREATION AND SALE OF A NEW SECURITY ISSUE

Issuers may elect to use only the advice services of investment bankers without using their underwriting and distribution services. In such cases, a consulting fee is paid. Many issuers, of course, have the internal financial expertise to make all necessary decisions. For example, national treasuries and many large corporations do not use investment bankers for their advice services.

Underwriting. Once the type of security, date of issue, and security price have been decided on, the issuer can proceed to sell to the public. However, if the price at which the markets would be willing to absorb the issue is set too high or if the market as a whole declines, the issuer might not receive the total dollar amount desired. For example, assume Georgia-Pacific wishes to raise $100 million in a common stock offering to support new product expansion. Based on a secondary market price of $27 for their existing common stock and discussions with their investment banker, management decides to sell 4 million shares at $25 per share. (The $2 price difference is used as an inducement to attract buyers and encourage fast sale.) Unfortunately, soon after the securities are offered, the price at which they are able to sell the shares actually falls to $22. This could occur either because management misjudged the price inducement necessary to attract large numbers of buyers or because all stock prices fell as a result of bad economic news. Regardless of the reason, Georgia-Pacific would receive only $88 million of the desired $100 million in cash.

Investment bankers stand ready to absorb any part of the price risk an issuer would rather not accept. This is referred to as **underwriting** an issue. Three basic degrees of underwriting are used:

1. In a **firm commitment,** the banker purchases the full amount of the issue from the seller at an agreed-upon price. All market risk is shifted from the issuer to

the investment banker. The banker will reoffer the securities to the general public at a higher price than that paid to the issuer. In the Georgia-Pacific example, the issue might be underwritten at $24 (for 4.17 million shares to assure $100 million in cash) and reoffered at $25 to the general public. The $1 difference between what the issuer receives and what the public pays is known as the **underwriter spread** and represents the underwriter's compensation for assuming market risks, searching for buyers, and providing financial advice.

2. In a **stand-by agreement,** the underwriter agrees to help sell the new issue for some stated time interval (usually 30 days) but will not "position the security at risk." Once the interval is passed, the underwriter purchases any unsold securities at a predetermined price. Stand-by agreements are commonly used for stock sales that are being distributed through a rights offering.

3. In a **best-efforts** basis sale, the investment banker has no obligation to purchase any of the security issue. The banker acts solely as a broker and returns any unsold securities to the issuer. A best-efforts sale is used for two types of issuers. In the first case, the issuing firm demands a best-efforts sale because it is confident the securities will be fully sold (because of the firm's size, the risk, and the market's interest in the new securities). In the second case, the investment banker requires a best-efforts sale because the issuing firm is small, unestablished, and risky.

When a firm commitment is used, a **purchase group** of many investment bankers will be formed. The **lead underwriter** (or managing underwriter) conducts all negotiations with the issuer, oversees registration with appropriate regulatory bodies (such as the Securities and Exchange Commission, SEC, in the United States), maintains accounting records, and selects other members of the purchase group. However, all members of the purchase group purchase (or "position") a part of the issue. By positioning a portion of many new issues, as opposed to positioning all of one issue, the underwriter obtains greater diversification and lower risk.

Distribution. Some issuers have the ability to market new issues directly to the general public and don't need the distribution services of an investment banker. The largest direct issuer is, of course, the U.S. government, which uses periodic competitive bid sales for Treasury and agency obligations. In addition, common stock sales using rights offerings to existing shareholders have been used increasingly by large corporations that prefer to by-pass investment bankers.[2] However, most issuers don't have the extensive contacts with potential buyers that investment bankers are able to develop.

In fact, the buying syndicate itself may not have any direct contact with potential buyers. Security firms have found it profitable to specialize over the years. Some firms have concentrated on providing financial advice and underwriting services to issuers; others have concentrated on developing large networks of retail offices. As a result, members of the purchase group often do not have direct contact with potential buyers. To develop an

---

[2] One interesting technique of selling shares by utilities occurred during the 1920s. They had meter readers sell to households on their rounds.

effective distribution team, a **selling group** is usually created that consists of members of both the purchase group and selected retail brokerage houses.

Once the underwriting syndicate has been formed, market conditions seem favorable, and all legal requirements have been met, the securities can be actively sold to the public. Prior to that time, potential buyers will have investigated the issue and perhaps even expressed interest to members of the selling group. However, actual purchase orders can't be taken until a formal "opening of the books." Some issues will have an active demand and be sold out within hours, or may even be oversubscribed. Other issues require a longer time to be distributed. During this interval, the managing underwriter is allowed to stabilize the market by placing orders to buy the security at a fixed price. This is the only form of security price manipulation legally allowed in the United States. Underwriters claim that market stabilization is necessary to ensure an orderly sale and offset temporary price declines. They claim the use of price stabilizing reduces their risk exposure and thus reduces the costs to issuing firms.

Negotiated vs. Competitive Selection. When the selling efforts of an investment banker are used, the issuer must decide whether the banker is to be selected on a **competitive** or a **negotiated basis.** In a competitive underwriting, all details of the security offering (type, timing, and legal characteristics) except price are specified, and the investment banker offering the best bid price is selected. A specific time and place are set at which competitive bids are opened. Competitive bid offerings are common in municipal bond sales as well as in debt and equity sales by regulated companies. Competitive bid offerings provide the issuer the potential advantage of receiving the highest possible price because of active competition for the issue. They have the disadvantage of inflexibility because the investment banker is obligated to a firm price and is exposed to considerable market risk.

In a negotiated underwriting, the issuer selects the underwriter it believes is best able to provide the unique advice, underwriting, and selling efforts necessary to the success of the particular offering. The investment banker's compensation is negotiated, as opposed to being set in a formal competitive bid. Statistical tests conducted to date suggest that competitive offerings do provide some cost advantages over negotiated underwritings. However, the cost of issuing a security is difficult to measure, and these results might well be due to inadequate cost data.[3]

Private vs. Public Placement

Private Placement. A privately placed security is one that is sold to fewer than 25 buyers and, as a result, needn't be registered with the SEC. While some stock issues are privately placed (often with venture capital firms), bond issues are the more predominant. In recent years, more than 25% of all bond issues have been privately placed.

The major advantages of private placements stem from the fact that such issues aren't registered with the SEC. As a result, a new issue can be placed quickly and without

---

[3] Negotiated fees include compensation for underwriter advice whereas competitive fees do not include similar compensation.

incurring the large costs of preparing a registration statement. Investment bankers might be used to find buyers, for which they are paid a finder's fee of 1 1/4% to 1 1/2% of the issue. But their underwriting services aren't required, thus eliminating any compensation for these services. In addition, loan covenants on privately placed bonds can be less restrictive than if the issue were sold to the general public. The issuer and buyer can "tailor fit" any required covenants, whereas a public sale might require a large number of additional covenants to attract a sufficient number of buyers.

The major disadvantage of a private placement is its lack of marketability. Because the issue is not registered with the SEC, buyers are limited in their ability to subsequently sell the issue, resulting in greater required yields.

Public Placement. With the few exemptions we note in a moment, any new security issue sold to more than 25 buyers must be registered with the SEC. The purpose of a registration statement is to ensure that investors receive full and accurate disclosure of any information relevant to the issue. While statutes set a 20-day waiting period between the time the registration statement is filed and the time securities may be sold to the public, in practice the SEC can shorten or lengthen the period as necessary to enable the SEC staff to review the statement for any omissions or apparent misrepresentations of fact. During periods of heavy activity, six months or more may pass before the registration is acceptable to the SEC staff. Table 4-1 provides a partial listing of the types of information required.

Before individuals are allowed to purchase a new issue, they must be given a **prospectus.** The prospectus is essentially the same as the registration statement, with certain

---

TABLE 4-1 TYPICAL INFORMATION REQUIRED IN AN SEC REGISTRATION STATEMENT

1. General information on the issuer location, products, and so forth
2. Purposes of issue
3. Price at which offered to the public
4. Price at which offered to any special group
5. Promoters' fees
6. Underwriting fees
7. Net proceeds to the company
8. Remuneration of any officers receiving over $25,000 annually
9. Disclosure of any unusual contracts, such as managerial profit sharing
10. Detailed capitalization statement
11. Detailed balance sheet
12. Detailed earnings statement for three preceding years
13. Names and addresses of officers, directors, and underwriters
14. Names and addresses of stockholders owning more than 10% of any class of stock
15. Pending litigation
16. Copy of underwriting agreement
17. Copy of legal opinions
18. Copy of articles of incorporation or association
19. Copies of indentures affecting new issues

FIGURE 4-2 ILLUSTRATION OF A PROSPECTUS

PROSPECTUS
INSTITUTIONAL CLASS
December 28, 1994

PIMCO Advisors Institutional Funds (the "Trust"), formerly PFAMCo Funds, is a no-load, open-end management investment company which currently offers its Institutional Class in eighteen separate diversified investment portfolios (the "Funds"), each with its own investment objective and policies. **The Institutional Class** (formerly the Institutional Shares) of the Trust is primarily designed to provide pension and profit sharing plans, employee benefit trusts, endowments, foundations, corporations, other institutions, and high net worth individuals with access to the professional investment management services offered by PIMCO Advisors L.P. ("PIMCO Advisors"), and its investment management affiliates.

The following Funds of the Trust are described in this Prospectus:

Money Market Fund*	**Cadence Small Cap Growth Fund****
PIMCO Managed Bond and Income Fund	**Columbus Circle Investors Core Equity Fund**
Utility Stock Fund	**Columbus Circle Investors Mid Cap Equity Fund**
NFJ Equity Income Fund	**Columbus Circle Investors Small Cap Equity Fund**
NFJ Diversified Low P/E Fund	**Parametric Enhanced Equity Fund**
NFJ Small Cap Value Fund	**Parametric International Equity Fund**
Cadence Capital Appreciation Fund	**Blairlogie Emerging Markets Fund**
Cadence Mid Cap Growth Fund	**Blairlogie International Active Fund**
Cadence Micro Cap Growth Fund	**Balanced Fund**

* Investment in the Money Market Fund (or in any other Fund) is neither insured nor guaranteed by the U.S. Government. There can be no assurance that the Money Market Fund will be able to maintain a stable net asset value of $1.00 per share.

** Not currently available for investment.

Information about the investment objective and policies of each Fund, along with a description of the types of securities in which each Fund may invest, are set forth in this Prospectus. There can be no assurance that the investment objective for any Fund will be achieved.

The Trust is no-load, which means there is no sales charge when you buy or redeem shares.

The Trust offers two classes of shares - the Institutional Class and the Administrative Class. **This Prospectus sets forth concisely the information a prospective investor should know before investing in the Institutional Class of the Trust.** Please retain it for future reference. A Statement of Additional Information, dated December 28, 1994, containing additional and more detailed information about the Trust has been filed with the Securities and Exchange Commission and is hereby incorporated by reference into this Prospectus. It is available without charge and may be obtained by writing or calling:

PIMCO Advisors Institutional Funds
840 Newport Center Drive
Newport Beach, California 92660
Telephone: (800) 800-7674

THESE SECURITIES HAVE NOT BEEN APPROVED OR DISAPPROVED BY THE SECURITIES AND EXCHANGE COMMISSION OR ANY STATE SECURITIES COMMISSION, NOR HAS THE SECURITIES AND EXCHANGE COMMISSION OR ANY STATE SECURITIES COMMISSION PASSED UPON THE ACCURACY OR ADEQUACY OF THIS PROSPECTUS. ANY REPRESENTATION TO THE CONTRARY IS A CRIMINAL OFFENSE.

technical information deleted.[4] SEC approval of the registration statement and prospectus does not constitute an opinion about the risks or investment merits of the security. Approval by the SEC simply means the issuer has disclosed all facts required by law. Certain securities are exempt from registration. Major types include (1) U.S. government obligations, (2) municipal obligations, (3) commercial bank and savings and loan issues, (4) issues sold intrastate, and (5) issues sold to 25 or fewer buyers. Figure 4-2 shows the cover page of a prospectus.

Shelf Registration

In 1982, the Securities and Exchange Commission (SEC) instituted Rule 415, which has had profound implications for the way transactions take place in the primary market. Rule 415 allows issuers to preregister a security sale. The issuing firm announces its intention to sell a security, files necessary information with the SEC, and accepts competitive bids from investment bankers for the issue. Once the issue is approved by the SEC, the firm can either accept the best competitive bid or delay sale indefinitely. Generally, the registration will be delayed until the issuer truly needs capital or prices are viewed to be favorable. When the sale does take place, there is no delay associated with SEC filing and approval. Thus, the sale can be executed rapidly.

Issuing Costs

The costs of issuing securities consist of three components:

1. **Out-of-pocket** costs associated with internal clerical costs, management time spent putting the issue together, payments to legal counsel, payments to certified public accountants, and so on.
2. The **underwriter spread,** which is the difference between the price received by the issuer and the price at which the underwriter offers it to the public.
3. A **price concession,** which is an inducement offered to the first buyers. The price concession is theoretically equal to the difference between the equilibrium price of the security and the price at which the security is offered to the public.

For example, assume ABC Corp. sells 100,000 new common shares at a time when its currently outstanding shares are selling in the secondary market for $50. To attract a large number of buyers for the new issue and to encourage quick distribution, the underwriter suggests an offering price of $48. In addition, the underwriter sets a $2 underwriter spread to compensate for the market risks of positioning the issue, to cover the costs of finding buyers, and to provide a fair profit. Net of the underwriting spread, ABC Corp. receives $46 per share. Finally, total out-of-pocket costs associated with the sale are $100,000.

---

[4] Prior to approval by the SEC, a tentative version of the prospectus, known as a "red herring," is distributed. The red herring differs from a prospectus in two ways. First, stamped on the front page in red is a statement indicating the prospectus and registration documents have not yet received SEC approval. Second, the issue price is not shown.

Issuing costs would be as follows:

Nature of Cost	Cost per Share	Details
Out-of-Pocket Costs	$1	$100,000 ÷ 100,000 shares
Underwriter Spread	$2	Specified
Price Concession	$2	$50 equilibrium − $48 offer
Total	$5	

Little is known about the size of out-of-pocket costs, since accurate data have never been compiled. Underwriter spreads range anywhere from $1/2\%$ to 15% or more of the issue's offering price. The size of such spreads depends on the risks and distribution efforts faced by underwriters. For example, firm commitments on large municipal bond issues require spreads of only 1% or so during normal market conditions, since underwriters are exposed to little market risk and there is an easy-to-identify and active buying market for such issues. However, small preferred stock issues from high-risk corporations can require spreads of 15% or more. Such a large spread would be due to the potential difficulty in finding buyers, the small size of the issue (most authorities believe there are clear economies of scale to underwriting), and the large price risks incurred while the securities remain in the underwriter's inventory. The split of the underwriter spread varies, but a typical split of a $2 spread on a $50 common stock would be $0.40 to the managing underwriter, $0.40 to each member of the purchase group, and the remaining $1.20 to the broker of the stock.

The costs of price concessions are difficult to measure, since equilibrium security prices are difficult to estimate. These equilibrium prices represent the price at which the security would sell (under current market conditions) if it were not part of a new offering.

There do appear to be clear price concessions on *new* common stock offerings. These new offerings are referred to as *initial public offerings,* or IPOs. Ibbotson found an average return of 11.4% could have been earned in the month following a new IPO if (1) investors had purchased a broad sample of new offerings between 1960 and 1969, (2) the stocks were acquired at the offering price, and (3) the stocks were sold at the bid price at the end of the month. This 11.4% was statistically significant and represents a rather healthy one-month return. Individual security results were quite variable, however. Some IPOs provided a 70% monthly gain; others yielded a 60% loss. To receive the 11.4% average return, investors would have had to participate in virtually every new offering.

Ibbotson's results confirm statistically what has been called the "new issues fad." Requests to buy into new stock offerings often exceeded the size of the offerings by a multiple of 5 to 1.[5] And Ibbotson's results have been confirmed by many other research studies. The true economic causes for price concessions on IPOs are not yet fully understood.

Secondary Markets

Secondary markets refer to the locations or means by which individuals and institutional investors trade securities that were previously issued in the primary market. We start the discussion with the largest stock exchange in the world.

---

[5] Oversubscribed issues are often allocated by brokers to favored customers. Clearly, it pays to be on a broker's favored list. But to be so may require payments of larger than competitive brokerage fees.

The New York Stock Exchange

The New York Stock Exchange (NYSE) is the largest and oldest organized security market in the United States. Formed in 1792 by a group of merchants to trade federal notes and bonds, the exchange has seen its volume grow from a few bond trades over morning coffee to more than 200 million common stock shares per day in the 1990s. Interestingly, this supposed bastion of free enterprise was formed under a constitution that had all the characteristics of a cartel. Members of the NYSE agreed to trade only among themselves and to charge identical commission rates. These two agreements remained virtually unchanged for more than 150 years and were the fundamental cause of many changes in trading practices during the 1970s and 1980s.

Membership. The NYSE is a corporate association of about 1,500 members, each of whom has bought a **seat** (membership) and has been approved by other members. The cost of a seat is determined by the prevailing demand and supply of memberships, which are in turn a function of the future prospects for the NYSE. In the post–World War II era, seats have sold for as much as $515,000 and for as little as $35,000. Membership prices during the past 20 years dropped dramatically below the "go-go" days of the 1960s as the NYSE encountered increased competition from other markets and the likely elimination of many monopolistic rates. In addition to regular members who own a seat on the exchange, the NYSE allows various firms access to the trading floor by paying an annual fee.

Members are assigned particular roles, as follows.[6]

1. **Commission brokers** are partners in a brokerage firm and execute orders for their firm's clients on the floor of the exchange. Large brokerage houses will have more than one commission broker on the floor to ensure that customers' orders are rapidly executed.
2. **Floor brokers** are freelance commission brokers. They do not have direct contact with the public, but handle order overflows the commission brokers are unable to handle. A portion of the commission broker's fee is paid to the floor broker.
3. **Registered traders** buy and sell solely for their own account. They do not handle public orders. Often called floor traders, they are speculators who attempt to buy securities experiencing a temporary influx of sell orders (which are forcing prices down) and sell securities experiencing a temporary influx of buy orders (which are forcing prices up). As a result, floor-trading operations are said to reduce price volatility and add to the market's liquidity. In recent years, floor-trading memberships have been few and their trading activity negligible.
4. **Specialists** stand in the middle of every trade, both figuratively and literally. We discuss their vital role in completing a transaction later.

Listing Requirements. Only listed securities may be traded on the NYSE floor, and until recently, members were not allowed to trade listed stocks in any market other than

---

[6] In the recent past some members acted as dealers in odd-lot transactions (trades of less than 100 shares). Today, odd-lot transactions are handled within the large brokerage firms trading at current market prices with the inventory of the brokerage house.

TABLE 4-2   New York Stock Exchange Listing Requirements

To be listed on the New York Stock Exchange, a firm must have:
1. Earnings before taxes of at least $2.5 million in the most recent year
2. Earnings before taxes of at least $2.0 million during the two preceding years
3. Net tangible assets of at least $18 million
4. Total market value of common stock of at least $18 million
5. At least 1.1 million shares publicly held
6. More than 2,000 holders of 100 shares or more

---

the NYSE.[7] In the mid-1990s, approximately 2,300 stocks and 3,000 bonds were listed, which represented a major portion of publicly traded U.S. corporate securities. The original issuer of the security makes the decision to list or not. The major advantage claimed for listing is an improvement in security marketability. Minimum initial listing requirements must be satisfied, and, to remain listed, the firm must fill various continued listing requirements. In selecting securities to be listed, exchange officials seek firms that are national in scope and have a major standing in a growing industry. The more important listing requirements are shown in Table 4-2.

Specialist Operations. About 25% of all NYSE members act as specialists. Usually, they form partnerships or corporations with other specialists to diversify risk exposure and spread administrative costs. These organizations are referred to as **specialist units,** and each unit is assigned a number of stocks in which it acts as specialist. For illustrative purposes, however, it is easiest to think in terms of one specialist assigned to one stock. Specialists perform two functions. First, they act as **brokers** by maintaining the **limit book.** Second, they act as **dealers** by selling and buying shares in which they are specialists.

A **limit order** is a request to buy or sell a security at a given price or better. For example, a limit order to buy XYZ Corp. at $75 must be transacted at $75 or less. Since limit orders are usually placed at prices "away from the market" (different from current price levels), the commission broker will leave limit orders with the specialist. The specialist records limit orders in a limit book similar to that shown in Figure 4-3.[8] The figure shows a variety of orders to buy at prices of $30.375 or less and offers to sell at prices of $30.625 or more.[9] Requests to buy are referred to as **bid prices,** and offers to sell are called **asked prices.** None of these limit orders will trade now, since the actual market price lies somewhere between the highest bid and the lowest ask. Over time, however, the price of the stock will undoubtedly increase or decrease as favorable or unfavorable news is reported. And when a price change occurs, the specialist will execute any limit orders at that price. For this service, the specialist is given a commission by the limit trader's broker.

The more complex and important role of the specialist is to serve as a dealer in the stock. The NYSE uses the specialist's dealer function in an attempt to provide continuous

---

[7] Rule 390 prevented member firms from trading listed stocks in a market other than the NYSE.

[8] In the past, the limit book was physically a book. Today a computer screen displays all limit orders. Access to view the limit orders on this screen is available to all members on the NYSE floor.

[9] Recall that stocks trade in units of 1/8 dollar, 12.5 cents.

FIGURE 4-3   SAMPLE ENTRIES IN A SPECIALIST BOOK

LOT	BUY	PRICE	SELL	LOT
3	Escher	30		
6 1	Zohail Andress	1/8		
4	Williams	1/4		
5	Jacobson	3/8		
		1/2		
		5/8	Nelson Myers	3 4
		3/4	Chance	4
		7/8	Brown Goedel Bach	8 2 1

and liquid markets. To fully understand how the specialist can provide these services, a short digression is helpful.

There are any number of ways to mechanically structure security trading activity. One method is known as a **call auction,** in which the name of each security is periodically called off (say, twice a day). At such times, buyers and sellers state the price and number of shares at which they are willing to trade. The resulting trade price is that which allows the greatest number of trades. A system similar to this was used in the early history of the NYSE and is still used on various foreign exchanges. Today's procedures on the NYSE, however, are closer to what we might term a **continuous auction.** Buyers and sellers continuously place orders on the exchange and seek to buy at the lowest price and sell at the highest price.

Return to Figure 4-3 and assume two commission brokers arrive simultaneously at the specialist's post. Commission broker A has a customer order to buy 300 shares at the best price then possible, and commission broker B has an order to sell 300 shares. They ask the specialist, "How's the market?" If the specialist decides not to trade for his own account, he will reply, "30 3/8 to 5/8." This means the best price to sell (the bid price) is $30.375, and the best price to buy (the asked price) is $30.625. Commission brokers A and B will recognize they can better these prices for their customers if they trade with each other, so A will offer to buy 300 at $30.50 and B will agree to sell. But this favorable result occurred simply because the brokers were lucky enough to arrive at the specialist's post at the same moment with identical-size orders. If broker A had arrived moments earlier, the customer would have had to buy at $30.625 and broker B's customer would have had to sell at $30.375. It is exactly such situations that the specialist is designed to aid.

Acting as a **dealer** in the stock, the specialist trades at prices between the limit book's high bid and low offer. **In this role, the specialist will absorb temporary imbalances in buy and sell orders.** As compensation, the specialist hopes to earn a profit over time by selling at prices higher, on average, than paid.

If specialists perform their duties as the exchange desires, the public gains in three ways. First, average bid-ask spreads are narrowed by the specialist's quoting prices between the limit book prices. Second, market participants can be assured that prices will not swing erratically over short time periods, as would be the case if all orders were matched against the limit book. Finally, market participants can expect only small price changes for larger than normal orders, since the specialist is supposed to stand ready to take on or dispose of larger amounts of stock. (In fact, specialists will occasionally short sell—a term discussed later—to meet buy orders.)

To properly fulfill their duties of providing continuous and liquid markets, specialists will often have to "go against the market" for extended periods, and their profits can be quite variable over time. The specialist has no idea whether a particular order is motivated by someone's need for (or excess of) liquidity or by special information. Against the liquidity trader, specialists profit. Against the information trader, they lose. In fact, specialist partnerships are formed in an attempt to diversify away some of the risk of dealing in single stocks. To ensure that specialists are able to provide sufficient depth of liquidity, the NYSE places minimum capital requirements on specialist units. As the volume of trading has increased over time, the minimum capital requirements have also increased.

But specialist operations have received considerable criticism. For example, a special study by the SEC suggested the gross income per average dollar invested for an average specialist unit was about 100% per year.[10] While the NYSE has no rules barring competition between specialist units for the same stock, until the late 1970s it was a standard practice to assign only one unit per stock. The exchange rationalized the practice by stating that assigning more than one unit would fragment trading activity and cause a decline in liquidity. However, this policy was reversed in the late 1970s, and units were allowed to compete with one another. As a result, a few units did begin to compete.

But even though NYSE specialists have little direct competition on the floor of the exchange, they do face considerable competition from specialists trading similar stocks on other exchanges. As a result, in 1984 NYSE specialists substantially reduced their fees, to approximately $1.50 per round lot. More alarming, however, was the near breakdown of

---

[10] United States House Committee on Interstate and Foreign Commerce, Subcommittee on Commerce and Finance, *Securities Industry Study: Reports and Hearings,* 92nd Congress, 1st and 2nd sessions, Chapter 12.

the specialist system and the potential bankruptcy of many specialist units that occurred in the stock market crash of October 19, 1987—Black Monday.

How did the specialist system respond to the massive price drops of Black Monday? (During that day, the value of stocks on the NYSE fell by almost 25%!) The answer is "mixed." Some units did attempt to provide price stability by purchasing securities in response to massive public desires to sell. But by the end of the day, they had bought large amounts of securities whose value had dropped dramatically. Banks, which usually finance specialist inventories, threatened to not do so because of the large losses these specialists had suffered. For "doing their duty," these specialists were threatened with bankruptcy. The normal system of trading securities almost fell apart. But under Federal Reserve System pressure, bank credit was provided. The story for many other specialist units was less sanguine. About 30% of all specialists were net sellers during the day.

Recent Automation of NYSE Trading

To handle the volume of trading activity on the NYSE efficiently, the exchange has computerized much of the trading process. It refers to this process as SuperDOT (designated order turnaround). In 1991, SuperDOT had the capacity to handle 600 million share trades on a given day. At that time, average daily volume was approximately 100 million shares. At the opening of each day, SuperDOT accepts up to 30,099 market orders from a given member firm, pairs requests to buy or sell, and notifies the specialist of the net imbalance. This assists the specialist in deciding at what price a stock should open. After trading begins, SuperDOT accepts market orders of up to 2,099 shares and typically executes them within one minute. Limit orders as large as 99,999 shares are recorded in the specialist's electronic book and stored until canceled or executed. The specialist's electronic book is a computer display terminal that replaces the old hand-held specialist's book of limit orders. Computerization of limit orders has reduced human errors associated with maintenance of paper records and improved the ability to trace the cause for any errors that do occur.

Other Exchanges

The American Stock Exchange. The American Stock Exchange (AMEX) is often referred to as the "Curb Exchange" because its earliest brokers traded outdoors on the curb of Wall and Broad streets in New York City. Clerks would accept requests to trade by telephone and lean outside the office window to pass the order information on to the broker, who was standing on the street. Brokers wore bright multicolored hats so they could be recognized by the clerk, and trade information was passed by means of complex hand signals.

The AMEX moved indoors in 1921 and adopted its present name in 1953. The hats are gone, but the hand signals remain. For many years there were no formal listing requirements, but today all securities traded must meet certain financial tests (similar to, but less stringent than, NYSE listing requirements).

Regional Exchanges. A number of regional exchanges exist that provide two basic services. First, they list securities of smaller companies of only regional interest. Second, they dually list popular NYSE stocks and charge lower commissions. This second factor was a major impetus to their growth. Brokers who could not afford a seat on the NYSE

Thomas J. Murphy Jr.

Specialist
M.J. Meehan & Company
Allegheny College, B.S. economics

Tom Murphy's early experiences with the world of finance and investments included working as a caddie for various Wall Street people and then, during summers as a college student, for a $2 broker. Before becoming a specialist, he was a backup clerk, then a clerk.

Q: A specialist's job is to maintain a fair and orderly market. What exactly does that mean?

A: We act as agents trying to coordinate the buyers and sellers and bring them together at fairly steady prices. If you think about a specialist as a whole, we have to become the other side of the market. For example, if there is fabulous news out on General Motors and everybody, whether they are small investors, large investors, institutional investors, would love to buy GM as it's going up, our job is to make sure it goes up in steady increments. We make sure the appreciation is not too varied or too unruly. If necessary, we are there to provide our own capital to stabilize that move up.

Q: If you're selling when people are buying how does a specialist make money?

A: If we are sellers when they're lifting the stock up or conversely if we're buying when there are only sellers around, then that's a day when we get crushed. But because I know the stock, and know my own parameters, I know that when the stock hits a certain level it usually holds there. On some days the sellers still may be thinking the stock is not going to hold this level. So if I buy stock to make the market stabilize and then all of a sudden it holds that level or goes up, then we make money. If it gets to a certain level, what we call *hitting its head*, and I sell stock short and it comes down, then we make money there. Our primary function is making sure the buyers and sellers are brought together. Only secondary is our function as a principal, where we trade for our own account.

Q: How many stocks can a specialist effectively trade?

A: Right now I have seven stocks. But I have just one major trader, United Healthcare. It's somewhat subjective.

When things get very hairy it's hard to have more than one major trader. A specialist has to have a good memory and be able to handle crowds well. Memory is very important because it helps you execute trades. In bigger stocks, buyers and sellers are already aware of what's going on. But in the thinner stocks, which do very little trading, memory is extremely important. For example, I'll remember that two months ago at this price level that a broker had a major seller. They might not have been in the stock for two months and all of a sudden I catch a buyer. So I call the broker and do the trade. Both sides are content even though I did nothing as a principal in that situation. I'm just an agent bringing buyers and sellers together.

Q: What do clerks do?

A: Clerks are assistants to specialists. They are right there in the arena. Even though they are not making decisions, they are learning and getting used to being under the gun. That's important because when clerks make the transition out they need to be unflappable and calm. Clerks realize that if they're calm when everyone else is screaming, then cooler heads will prevail and they'll get more business done. I learned from guys that were very calm and very good.

Q: Does your experience as a clerk help determine your stock assignments as a specialist?

A: When you come out as a new specialist, you usually get slow-trading stocks. It's a learning process. You don't want to be knocked off your feet. I was fortunate; I clerked for about eight years in very high-profile stocks, WalMart and General Motors. Because of that exposure, I was used to having to be quick. A regular crowd may have four people but I've been in General Motors when there are thirty people, screaming, yelling, pinning you up against the post; it is wild.

Q: Where do you work?

A: I work at Post 10 in the main room of the New York Stock Exchange. There are seventeen different posts. It's an outrageous place to be. When you go in the main room you know it—the atmosphere is crazy. I may not go to lunch or the bathroom on any given day. When the bell rings in the afternoon I might not leave. Or in the summer when things are slower I might get to enjoy dinner on the beach with my wife and kids.

Q: What kind of education do you need to be a clerk or a specialist?

A: I've seen people with two years of high school education from the streets of Brooklyn working on the floor. But without a college education it's harder to get your foot in the door and harder to move up. Generally speaking, firms hire people who have strong educational backgrounds and who understand concepts like regression analysis. On the floor it is different though. You can't really teach someone in grad school about the feel of your belly or how to handle themselves when they're getting their doors blown off.

could purchase a less expensive seat on a regional exchange and be able to trade the more popular NYSE stocks. Without the regional exchanges, such brokers would have had to feed their orders to NYSE member firms and give up a portion of their commissions. In addition, institutions wishing to trade large blocks of stock could trade at lower commission rates on regional exchanges than on the NYSE.

The Over-the-Counter Market. Transactions not handled on one of the organized exchanges are called over-the-counter (OTC) transactions. The OTC has no central location at which all trading occurs. Instead, it is a diffuse network of brokers and dealers connected by either telephone or computer terminals. The term *over-the-counter* refers to the trading practices in the 1800s, when buyers and sellers of unlisted stocks would physically present cash or securities at a commercial bank. The bank and trader would actually trade over the counter. With the advent of telephones, the market became a telephone network between brokers and dealers. The OTC market now links participants by a computer network. The market is among the most technologically advanced in the country, and many experts believe the modern OTC market is a picture of what the future will bring to most markets.

Securities traded in the OTC market differ considerably in size of issuer, legal nature, risk, marketability, and so on. Most bank and finance stocks, corporate bonds, and U.S. government and municipal obligations are traded OTC. In addition, securities that are too small or unprofitable to meet the listing requirements of an organized exchange are traded OTC. (Many firms that could be listed choose not to be.) The true size of the market is hard to determine, since any corporate issue is a candidate. All that is needed is a brokerage firm willing to act as the **market maker** in a security.

The market maker plays essentially the same dealer role for an OTC stock that the specialist does for an exchange-listed stock. The market maker carries a trading inventory of a particular security and is willing to buy and sell with members of the general public. Market makers serve a useful purpose, since the public buyer needn't spend time trying to find a public seller. The market maker is known and continuously stands ready to buy or sell. In return for this service, a bid-ask spread is required. Buyers acquire securities at the higher asked price, and sellers dispose of securities at the lower bid price. Actively traded OTC securities will have as many as 15 to 20 market makers competing for public orders. Investment bankers often make a market in the securities they underwrite, and regional brokerage houses typically make markets in local securities. However, many of the large brokerage firms enter the business simply to increase the services available to customers and increase their profits.

Brokers and dealers in OTC securities have formed a self-regulating body known as the National Association of Security Dealers (NASD), which licenses brokers and oversees trading practices. In 1971, the NASD instituted a computerized trading network known as the **NASD Automated Quotation System (NASDAQ;** pronounced naz-dak). To be included in the NASDAQ, a security must have at least two market makers, a minimum number of publicly held shares, and meet certain asset and equity capital requirements. NASDAQ is simply a "real time" information system. Current bid and ask quotations of all market makers on a security are continuously maintained through a telecommunication network. Prior to NASDAQ, a broker could obtain bid-ask quotes only by calling various dealers who made a market in the security. The best bid or ask price could take so long to find that the quote could change before the broker had time to place an order. In fact, there was no guarantee the best quote had been found, since the broker often wouldn't call all market makers. So the advantages of NASDAQ are twofold: (1) it provides current quotations, and (2) it brings together quotes from all important market makers. At present about 5,400 stocks are carried on NASDAQ. In the mid-1990s there were more than 500 market makers for NASDAQ stocks with an average of about ten market makers for each stock.

There are three levels of NASDAQ services. At Level I, the broker can view on a computer terminal the highest bid and the lowest ask that market makers are currently offering on each NASDAQ stock. At Level II, all bid and ask quotations currently offered are shown with an identification of the market maker providing each quote. At Level III, the user has the ability to actually enter bid and ask quotes into the NASDAQ system. When a bid or ask quote has been entered into the system it is shown to all users of Levels II and III, and the dealer must be willing to trade at least one round lot (100 shares) at these prices until the dealer changes the quotations. It is important to point out, however, that NASDAQ is currently only a reporting system. Actual trades are not made through the NASDAQ computer system but by direct contact between dealers and brokers. However, the system could be easily modified to allow for the actual "crosses" between two parties directly on the system.

OTC stocks with relatively active trading volume are designated by the NASD as **National Market Issues.** All transactions in NASDAQ National Market Issues are immediately reported on the NASDAQ system. For less active issues, dealers report only total transactions at the end of a day.

In addition to OTC stocks traditionally carried on NASDAQ, there are thousands of small, thinly traded stocks whose prices had been reported only once a day on what are referred to as Pink Sheets. The Pink Sheets include 11,000 or more inactively traded stocks, including many "penny" stocks and stocks having only a narrow geographic interest. Beginning in 1988, the current quotes for such stocks were also made available on NASDAQ through what is called the OTC Bulletin Board. Because of the extreme thinness of trading in such stocks, prices shown on the OTC Bulletin Board should be viewed with caution.

Prior to the 1980s, trading volume in the OTC market had historically been much smaller than that on formal exchange markets such as the NYSE, AMEX, or regionals. During the 1980s, however, NASDAQ made trading of OTC stocks so much easier that OTC trading volume has increased dramatically. In recent years, shares traded on NASDAQ have been approximately the same as or greater than the volume of shares traded on the NYSE.

Third and Fourth Markets. The **third market** refers to an OTC transaction in a security that is also traded on an organized exchange. The growth of the third market in the 1960s and early 1970s was due to two factors: the growth of institutional trading in large blocks of stock, and minimum commission fees charged at the time by exchange members.

Throughout the 1960s large financial institutions (trust companies, pension funds, mutual funds, insurance firms, etc.) managed increasingly larger amounts of marketable securities and tended to trade more actively than they had previously. Large-block trades (transactions of 10,000 shares or more) became quite common. In the 1960s and early

1970s, all members of the NYSE had to transact any NYSE-listed stock on the exchange floor at a minimum commission. But the marginal cost of putting a block together is substantially lower than the minimum commission that was charged, so nonexchange members started to act as block traders. They could perform the same services as member firms but were not bound by exchange rules to charge abnormally high commissions. Exchange member firms attempted to overcome the excessive commissions by offering other services below cost, taking losses on the prices of securities positioned, and so on. But all of these attempts were burdensome at the least and often unsuccessful. As a result, the third market flourished. By 1972, third-market trading represented about 8 1/2% of the volume of all NYSE transactions. Since then, activity in the third market has declined significantly because the SEC decided to eliminate fixed commissions. Between 1971 and 1975, negotiated fees were slowly phased in on large-block transactions. Since May 1, 1975 (**May Day**), all commissions have been negotiated and open to full competition.

The **fourth market** refers to transactions made directly between a buyer and a seller of a large block. Brokers and dealers are totally eliminated. The **Instinet** system is a wire network somewhat similar to NASDAQ that provides current information on the number of shares subscribers are willing to buy or sell at specified prices (much like entering limit orders into a computerized specialist book). Institutions willing to trade at a quoted price can indicate their willingness through the network. The network will then record the trade and initiate clearing procedures. Another fourth-market system is called the Portfolio System for Institutional Trading (**POSIT**). Transactions in the fourth market are negligible at present.

Security Orders

Types of Orders. The standard unit of trading in stocks is a **round lot,** or 100 shares. Any fraction of 100 shares is referred to as an **odd lot.** Because odd-lot transactions require special servicing (assembly of many odd lots into round lots is performed either by one's broker or by the specialist), they require a larger commission per share than do round lots. The most common type of order is a **market order,** in which a customer instructs a broker to trade at the best price then available. The exact transaction price will not be known with complete certainty when the order is placed, although the eventual trade price will be quite close to prices at the moment the order is placed. The advantage of a market order is there is no doubt it will be executed.

A **limit order** is a request to buy or sell at a specified price or better. For example, a limit order to sell at $40 obligates the broker to sell at a price of $40 or more. As we noted earlier, most limit orders are placed at prices somewhat away from prevailing market prices and will be left with the specialist to be entered in the limit book. The disadvantage of a limit order is that the investor is not sure the security will indeed be bought or sold. For example, assume Lois Lane believes the prospects of SMI Corp. are strong. The stock is selling at $30 per share, but, in an attempt to pick up a point or two, she places a limit order to buy at $29. If the shares of SMI Corp. immediately soar to $50, Lois will never have bought.

Finally, a **stop order** is an order specifying a given price at which point it becomes a market order. For example, a stop order to sell at $70 will become a market order to sell the moment the stock trades at $70. There is no assurance the stop order will be filled at the stop price, but it is likely to be transacted at a price reasonably close. Stop orders to sell are commonly used to protect profits or minimize losses when an investor owns the related stock. Stop orders to buy are used to protect profits or minimize losses when the investor has previously sold the stock short (discussed later). For example, assume Lois Lane had initially placed a market order to buy a round lot of SMI and had been able to buy at $30. If the stock subsequently increased to $50, she would have an unrealized paper profit of $20. To guard this profit, she could place a **stop-loss order** (an order to sell) at, say, $47. If the stock falls below $47, she automatically sells at about $47 and takes a realized profit of $17. If the stock continues to rise or stays at $50, the stop order is not executed.

Unless stated otherwise, all orders are assumed to be **day orders.** They must be transacted that day or they are terminated. Since market orders are almost always executed on the same day the order is placed, specification of a time period during which the order is valid is used mainly with limit and stop orders. A **good-till-canceled** (GTC) order is, of course, valid until the trader cancels it.

Execution and Clearing. At this point in our discussion, it might be useful to trace through the various steps of a normal stock trade. Any number of execution and clearing paths are possible. We will follow a fairly common one.

Early Monday morning Clara Voigent calls her broker, Sam Lynch, and indicates she wants to place a market order for five round lots of SMI Corp. common stock. The stock has recently been selling for about $30, and, based on an article she read in the Sunday financial press about a new patent received by SMI, Clara believes the stock is undervalued and should soon increase in value. Broker Sam will first obtain current price quotes on SMI Corp. by using a computer terminal that is tied into various exchange markets. Assume the best quotes are available on the NYSE and are $32 bid and $32 1/4 ask. (Obviously, Clara wasn't the only one who read the favorable news about SMI.) This means the highest price at which an investor could sell is $32 (the specialist's or limit book's highest bid) and the lowest price at which an investor could buy is $32 1/4 (the specialist's or limit book's lowest ask). Since the best prices are available on the NYSE, Sam decides to route the order to that exchange.

Next Sam needs to decide whether the order will be routed to the NYSE through the exchange's SuperDOT system or through the brokerage firm's commission broker on the floor of the exchange.

Assume Sam chooses the second alternative, since it allows us to look more closely at the basic mechanics of a trade. Broker Sam prepares a trade ticket describing the details of the trade and transmits the ticket to his firm's trading department. The trading department then communicates the order to the floor of the exchange, where the commission broker is notified. The commission broker walks to the specialist's post where SMI is traded and asks, "How's the market?" The specialist replies, "32 to 1/4." Seeing no other brokers in the crowd, the commission broker indicates to the specialist "500 bought," and they exchange cards with information about the trade. The specialist's card is optically scanned by machines at the NYSE, and notice of the trade is printed on a ticker tape throughout the country. The commission broker's information card is returned to employees of the firm's trading department. They notify broker Sam and send Clara a **confirmation** of the trade in the mail. Sam calls Clara to notify her personally and everyone is happy (at least for a while).

Since Clara didn't indicate otherwise, this was a **regular way** trade, meaning the **settlement date will be three business days after the trade date.** On the settlement date, the brokerage firm and the customer exchange cash and securities, and the customer becomes the legal owner of the securities (or no longer the owner if securities had been sold). If Clara had desired, she could have requested a **cash contract,** which requires settlement and passing of title on the trade date. Another form of contract is a **seller's option,** which allows the seller to choose the settlement date.[11] Nonetheless, on the following Thursday Clara is required to **deliver** to the brokerage firm $16,125 (500 times $32.25) plus commissions and, in return, be the legal owner of the stock. That same Thursday, the brokerage firm will settle with the other side of the trade—in this case, the specialist.

In any trade there is a buyer who promises to deliver cash for securities and a seller who promises to deliver securities for cash. Clearing refers to how this process actually takes place.

Clearing consists of two steps. First, brokers to each side of the trade agree on the number of shares traded and the price. If a disagreement occurs, it must be reconciled. Second, cash and securities are delivered to the respective sellers and buyers on the settlement date.

Clearing between firms is accomplished in one of four ways. First, the securities and cash can be physically delivered between the two firms representing the buyer and the seller. This is a time-consuming, costly, and error-prone procedure, although it is sometimes used between firms in the same city. Second, small firms can use the services of larger brokerage houses to net out their purchases and sales and deliver only the required net cash and securities. Carried one step further, the services of the **National Securities Clearing Corporation** can be used. This organization handles trades made on the NYSE, AMEX, and OTC. Each member delivers only the net amount of securities or cash necessary to settle its accounts with the clearing corporation. Finally, the **Depository Trust Company** (DTC) has been organized, at which brokers and dealers may deposit large quantities of "street name" certificates on most actively traded securities. **Street name** refers to securities registered in the name of a brokerage firm. Customer orders are cleared simply by computer debits and credits to each firm's accounts at DTC. This reduces to a minimum the flow of paperwork required to physically move stock certificates.

The stock certificates evidencing Clara's ownership of 500 shares of SMI may be physically transferred to her name and either delivered to her or maintained by the brokerage firm in **safekeeping.** Alternatively, Clara may allow the firm to keep the securities for her in street name. In that case, her evidence of ownership is a monthly statement from the broker indicating she owns the shares. Clara will probably not want to be bothered with physical possession of the securities and will keep them in safekeeping or in street name. Because of the large clerical costs associated with keeping customer certificates in safekeeping, most brokerage firms request that the certificates be held in street name. This allows the broker, for example, to maintain only one certificate in the amount of 30,000 shares for 30 customers who each own 1,000 shares. Each customer's ownership is reflected in the accounting records of the brokerage firm.[12]

In recent years, there has been a movement to eliminate all certificates of stock ownership. Computer records and periodic statements would provide evidence of ownership. In fact, a certificateless market is virtually the case in the United States, since institutions rely

---

[11] Cash contracts and seller options are normally used for tax purposes when title must be passed on a particular date.

[12] Dividends, proxy statements, and any other literature distributed by a corporation on securities registered in street name are sent to the brokerage firm. The broker will then forward them to the actual owner.

solely on computer-registered ownership. Many individuals, however, wish to possess a physical document. As a result, stock certificates are likely to still be available but less common.

Institutional investors are typically managing money for another party. For example, mutual fund assets are managed for the shareholders of the fund. Similarly, investment counsel firms manage the assets of pension plans and wealth of individuals. To protect the true asset owner from possible theft, all securities owned by the institutional investor will be held in **custody.** Securities will still be registered in the institution's name, but their physical control and all accounting is performed by a security custodian (typically, a commercial bank).

Recent Developments in Trade Execution

Technology has enabled brokers to automate many of the traditional procedures of executing trades. Today a standard trade can be executed within a minute. A customer's order is viewed by the broker as part of an overall order flow. It is matched with other orders and routed to a specific market or market maker through a predetermined algorithm developed by the brokerage firm. Large brokerage firms cross their trades internally and only send net balances to buy or sell to an exchange. Some firms send all orders in certain stocks to affiliated specialists or market makers (members of the same corporation). Some brokers even send orders to market makers who pay a fee to the broker for doing so. We used the illustration of Clara's trade here in order to show all the players in the system. In actual practice, retail brokers (those executing individual investor orders) believe it is too expensive and inefficient to make trade routing decisions on a trade by trade basis.

Program Trading and Large Blocks

About one-half of all shares traded on the NYSE and OTC are for institutional investors. Although institutions often trade securities in the same fashion as do individual investors, they also rely on program trades and block trades.

Program Trading. A program trade is a trade of many stocks at a single time. Complete portfolios can be bought or sold. Program trading initially developed as part of index arbitrage "programs." In these arbitrage transactions, a portfolio of stocks is traded simultaneously with a futures or option contract. (Index arbitrages are discussed in Chapters 16 and 17.) Today, program trades often are not parts of an arbitrage transaction but simply the purchase or sale of a large number of stocks. Program trades are facilitated by the SuperDot system on the NYSE. A list of stocks is faxed to the NYSE, which places the list into the electronic SuperDot System. The trades are immediately routed to the specialist post where they are executed immediately. Individual orders are also placed into the SuperDot system, but they represent a small fraction of orders when compared with program trades.

Block Trades. A block trade is a trade in a large quantity of a single stock. Trades of 10,000 shares or more are often considered as block trades. Realizing that trading at the specialist post would be unable to absorb the block without unacceptable price impacts, the party who initiates the block calls a trader in a block trading firm to help. These people are called **block traders** and work in what is called the **upstairs market.** The block trader will call other investors who might wish to participate in the transaction, but will be careful not to disclose whether the initiating party wishes to buy or sell. Eventually, the size of the block might be larger than the initiator wanted to trade, since many buyers and sellers can become part of the block. Prior to Black Monday, the block trader often took a position in the block in order to have total buys equal total sales. After significant losses on Black Monday, block traders prefer not to take positions.

While the block is being assembled, the trader might "work off" some of the block by placing small orders at the specialist post. But this runs the danger of disclosing the originating party's desire to buy or sell. When a price has been agreed to by all parties, the transaction is placed on one of the exchanges. Commonly this will be done by **crossing** on the NYSE by informing the specialist of the transaction. For technical reasons, some blocks are executed in the OTC or on regional exchanges.

Margin Trades

When an account is opened at a brokerage house, it will be specified as either a **cash** or a **margin** account. In a cash account, the customer must pay fully for all securities bought. In a margin account, a portion of the securities bought may be paid for with a loan obtained from either the broker or the investor's bank.

The word *margin* refers to the percentage of the market value of securities owned that is financed by the investor. Required margin refers to the minimum percentage the investor must finance. Actual margin refers to the actual percentage the investor is financing. For example, assume the actual margin is 50% and the market value of a portfolio of securities is $10,000. Then the balance sheet of the investor would look as follows:

$$\text{Asset Value} = \$10,000 \qquad \text{Debt} = \$5,000$$
$$\text{Equity} = \$5,000$$

We discuss next what happens when the actual and required margins differ.

There are two levels of required margin: (1) **initial margin,** which applies when a new security is purchased, and (2) **maintenance margin,** which applies to the value of the portfolio at dates after the initial purchase. By law, the Federal Reserve System specifies the initial margin. The Federal Reserve uses the initial margin minimum as one of its policy tools for controlling economic expansions and recessions. Initial margin is usually higher for stocks than for corporate bonds. Since initial margin requirements were first set in 1934, rates have ranged between 40% and 100% for common stocks. The current initial margin on stocks is 50%. Initial margin requirements on bonds are typically 10%. Exchanges and brokerage firms may specify more rigid initial margin requirements. In fact, some brokerage firms allow cash accounts only. Maintenance margins are set by individual exchanges. But, as with initial margins, individual brokerage firms may set higher maintenance margins.

Investors may borrow to partially finance the purchase of securities from either a bank or their brokerage firm. The more convenient approach is typically the brokerage firm. To set up a margin account at a brokerage firm, the investor will be asked to sign a **hypothecation**

agreement. This grants the brokerage firm the legal right to use the securities bought as collateral on a bank loan given to the broker. To finance customer borrowings, the broker obtains money from a bank at a rate of interest called the **broker's call money rate** and lends it to the customer at the same rate plus a service fee of about 1% per year. The broker's loan is collateralized by the customer's securities. In addition, the broker will require that securities bought on margin be registered not in the name of the customer, but in street name form. Registering in street name makes it easier for the broker to use the securities as collateral on bank loans.

Advantages and Disadvantages of Using Margin. The advantage provided by a margin account is clearly the increased opportunity for profit. For a given dollar equity capital, a larger quantity of securities can be bought. But, although the use of financial leverage increases the investor's expected return, it also increases the investor's risk.

Consider the following example. The current market price of Entron shares is $50 and you wish to purchase 100 shares. Assume the required initial margin is 50% and the broker charges an annual interest rate of 8%. Let's examine three margin levels: (1) you pay the full cost of the securities, (2) you put up 75% margin, and (3) you decide to pay the minimum required margin of 50%. After the trade occurs, the three possible balance sheets would be as follows:

Balance Sheets at Date of Initial Trade

100% Margin	75% Margin		50% Margin	
Asset Value	Asset Value	Debt = $1,250	Asset Value	Debt = $2,500
= $5,000 Equity = $5,000	= $5,000	Equity = $3,750	= $5,000	Equity = $2,500

Now let's see what the situation would be after one year for each scenario with two different stock prices: $60 and $40—a price change of plus and minus $10 from the initial trade price. The value of assets is simply 100 shares times the assumed stock price. The value of the initial loan increases by 8% to allow for interest the broker charges. Finally, the equity value is simply the difference between the value of assets and the debt value.

Balance Sheets in One Year at a Stock Price of $60

100 % Margin	75% Margin		50% Margin	
Asset Value	Asset Value	Debt = $1,350	Asset Value	Debt = $2,700
= $6,000 Equity = $6,000	= $6,000	Equity = $4,650	= $6,000	Equity = $3,300
Return on Equity = 20%	Return on Equity = 24%		Return on Equity = 32%	

Balance Sheets in One Year at a Stock Price of $40

100% Margin	75% Margin 50%		Margin	
Asset Value	Asset Value	Debt = $1,350	Asset Value	Debt = $2,700
= $4,000 Equity = $4,000	= $4,000	Equity = $2,650	= $4,000	Equity = $1,300
Return on Equity = −20%	Return on Equity = −29%		Return on Equity = −48%	

The important line to look at in each case is the one showing the return on equity, which is simply the change in the value of equity during the year divided by beginning equity. For example, when 100% margin is used and the stock price increases to $60, the return on equity is 20% = ($6,000 − $5,000) ÷ $5,000.

The use of debt financing magnifies any positive or negative returns on portfolio assets. When no debt financing is used, the return on equity is identical to the return on portfolio assets. But when debt financing is used there are two effects. First, interest must be paid. So if the asset value remains unchanged, the return on equity is negative because interest must be paid. Second, even if the interest rate were zero, the use of debt financing exposes the equity holder to greater risk. For example, when 50% margin is used, each dollar of equity money is exposed to the risk of $2 of assets.

The effect of margin on the variability of return on equity is displayed in Figure 4-4. The data used in the figure is the same as in our previous example. The vertical axis shows the return on equity during the next year and the horizontal axis shows various stock prices. The solid dark line represent the use of zero debt financing. When the stock price remains at $50, the return on equity is 0%. The other lines reflect outcomes for 75% margin and 50% margin. When the stock price remains at $50, the returns on equity for these positions are negative due to the interest expense. But the real story displayed in the figure is the slope of the lines that represent how sensitive equity returns are to underlying portfolio asset returns. The greater the use of debt financing, the greater the risk exposure.

In short, if the expected return on portfolio assets is greater than the interest cost of debt financing, the use of debt financing increases the expected return on equity. But debt financing also increases equity risk.

FIGURE 4-4   EFFECT OF MARGIN ON RETURN ON EQUITY

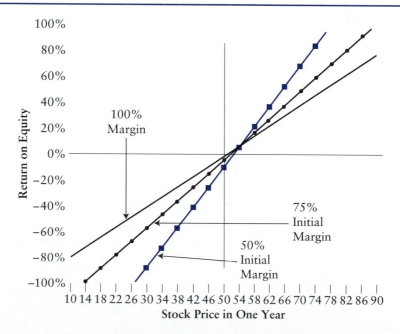

Margin Calls. After the initial trade date, the actual margin of an account will change from day to day as the value of portfolio assets change. The actual margin is simply equal to the value of equity at that time divided by the value of assets:

$$\text{Actual Margin} = \frac{\text{Equity}}{\text{Asset Value}}$$

$$= \frac{\text{Asset Value} - \text{Debt Value}}{\text{Asset Value}}$$

At the end of each day, the brokerage firm will calculate the actual margin of the account and compare it with the required maintenance margin. (This is called **mark-to-market.**) We will discuss cases in which actual margin exceeds the maintenance margin later. For now, let's concentrate on situations that require a margin call. A **margin call** occurs when actual margin is less than the required maintenance margin. In such cases the broker calls on the investor to take an action that will restore the account to the required maintenance margin. If the customer does not respond, the broker may sell securities held in the account in order to bring the actual margin in compliance with required maintenance margin.

Consider the previous example data in which 100 shares of Entron stock are bought for $50 per share. If the brokerage firm has a maintenance margin requirement of 30%, what stock prices would force a margin call for the two cases of initial margin equal to 75% and 50%?

When a single stock is owned, the actual margin of an account is equal to:

$$\text{Actual Margin} = \frac{(\text{Number of Shares})\,(\text{Share Price}) \text{ minus } (\text{Debt Value})}{(\text{Number of Shares})\,(\text{Share Price})}$$

For simplicity, we will neglect the effect of interest cost on the debt value. When 75% initial margin is used, the price that will force a margin call is found by solving the following equation.

$$0.30 = \frac{(100)\,(\text{Share Price}) \text{ minus } (\$1{,}250)}{(100)\,(\text{Share Price})}$$

$$\text{Share Price} = \$17.86$$

When 50% initial margin is used, the price that will force a margin call is found in the same way, but using the initial debt of $2,500 instead of $1,250.

$$0.30 = \frac{(100)\,(\text{Share Price}) \text{ minus } (\$2{,}500)}{(100)\,(\text{Share Price})}$$

$$\text{Share Price} = \$35.71$$

If an account falls below the maintenance margin requirement, the broker will request the investor do something to bring the account up the required margin. To avoid a large number of margin calls, it is best to maintain a comfortable balance in the account above the maintenance margin. However, if a margin call is received, there are a number of ways to bring the account into balance. For example, the investor could (1) add new cash to the account and leave it in the form of cash, (2) add new cash to the account and use it to repay some of the loan, or (3) sell shares and repay a portion of the loan. Examples of each are shown next.

Assume 100 Entron shares were bought at $50 a share using 50% initial margin. The stock drops rapidly on bad news about a product line and is now selling at $30, below the value of $35.71 that would trigger a margin call. At that time, the investor's balance sheet would appear as follows:[13]

Balance Sheet Prior to Margin Call

	Debt = $2,500
Stock = $3,000	Equity = $ 500

If new cash is to be placed into the account and kept in the form of cash, then the following formula would be solved for the value of cash:

$$0.30 = \frac{(\text{Cash} + \$3,000) - \$2,500}{(\text{Cash} + \$3,000)}$$

The solution is $571.43 of new cash. If this amount is placed into the account, the actual margin would equal the maintenance margin of 30% and the balance sheet would look as follows:

Balance Sheet After Adding Cash to Assets

Cash = $ 571.43	Debt = $2,500
Stock = $3,000	Equity = $1,071.43

If new cash is to be placed into the account and used to repay some of the loan, then the following formula would be solved for the value of cash:

$$0.30 = \frac{\$3,000 - (\$2,500 - \text{Cash})}{\$3,000}$$

The solution is $400 in cash. When the loan is $2,100, the actual margin is 0.3 and the balance sheet would look as follows:

Balance Sheet After Loan Reduction

	Debt = $2,100
Stock = $3,000	Equity = $ 900

If shares are sold and the proceeds are used to repay a portion of the loan, the following formula would be solved for shares sold (SS):

$$0.30 = \frac{[\$3,000 - SS(\$30)] - [\ \$2,500 - SS(\$30)]}{[\$3,000 - SS(\$30)]}$$

---

[13] This example neglects any interest that might be due on the debt. In reality, any unpaid interest would be considered part of the debt balance.

The solution is 45 shares, which would raise $1,350 to repay a portion of the loan. In this case, the balance sheet would look as follows:

Balance Sheet After Share Sale

	Debt = $1,150
Stock = $1,650	Equity = $ 500

Restricted Accounts. Generally share prices will not fall sufficiently to require a margin call. However, whenever the actual margin is between the maintenance and initial margin, the account is restricted. If an account is restricted, no transactions are allowed that would further reduce the actual margin. For example, if an account is restricted, cash could not be withdrawn from the account. However, cash could be used to purchase other securities, since this would not reduce the actual margin.

Pyramiding. If the stock rises in price causing the actual margin to be greater than the required initial margin, the account is **overmargined** or **unrestricted.** The investor could then withdraw cash from the account as long as actual margin does not fall below the initial margin requirement. Alternatively, the excess funds could be used to purchase additional securities. This is called **pyramiding.**

For example, assume the market value of all assets is $10,000 and debt to the broker is $3,000. Then the actual margin is 70%. If the excess asset value is used to buy new securities on margin and result in a new actual margin of 50%, then the following formula would be solved for $New:

$$0.50 = \frac{(\$10{,}000 + \$New) - (\$7{,}000 + \$New)}{(\$10{,}000 + \$New)}$$

The solution is that $4,000 of new securities could be bought without having to place further cash into the account.

Short Sales

When people buy securities, it is referred to as going **long,** and they do so in the hopes of future price increases. When people sell securities they own, it is referred to as going **short,** and they do so with the expectation prices will soon drop. When people sell a security they don't own, it is referred to as **short selling,** and they do so in the hopes of buying the stock in the future at a lower price.

The mechanical process of short selling, which is actually quite simple, is displayed in Figure 4-5. Initially, the short seller places an order to short sell, say, 100 shares of a stock he or she believes is overvalued. The broker will find a willing buyer at, say, $30 per share and execute the sale. Three business days later, the broker will have to borrow shares from a **lender of shares** in order to deliver to the buyer. The lender of shares may be anyone willing to do so, but often the broker will act as the lender by delivering securities held in street name for customers. The buyer receives the 100 shares, pays the $3,000 purchase price, and goes merrily on his or her way. The lender, however, will demand collateral for the shares lent, the most likely collateral being the $3,000 cash received from the

FIGURE 4-5   SHORT SELLING

A. ORIGINATION OF SHORT SALE

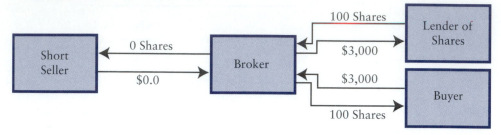

B. COVERING OF SHORT SALE

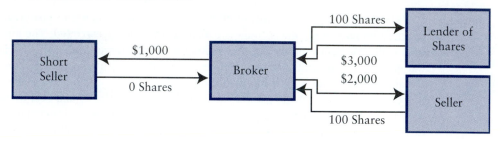

buyer. Typically, the cash collateral is provided "flat," that is, without any interest fee paid to the short seller. If this is the case, it's quite easy to see why many investors are willing to lend shares. They still have an ownership claim to the shares (through the short seller) but now have additional cash that can be invested to provide a short-term risk-free return. The share loan is a "call" loan, cancelable at any time by either party. If the lender wants the shares returned, the short seller can either find another lender or buy in the open market.

Continuing with this example, assume the share's price actually does fall to, say, $20. The short seller will cover the short by asking the broker to buy 100 shares. The new seller will receive $2,000 and give up 100 shares, which are returned to the lender of shares. In turn, the lender gives the $3,000 collateral value back to the broker, who returns a $1,000 profit to the short seller.

With that basic review of short selling, we can mention a few intricacies. First, SEC rules require all short sale transactions to be specified as such. Each month the volume of short sales in various stocks is compiled and reported in the financial press. Second, the SEC requires that a short sale be made on either an "up tick" or a "zero tick" if the previously different stock price was lower. For example, assume the sequence of market transactions in a stock is 20, 18, 18 1/8, 18 1/8, 18 1/4, 17 7/8.

The first move from 20 to 18 is a down tick. The next move from 18 to 18 1/8 is an up tick, and the next two moves are zero ticks. A short sale could have been transacted at 18 1/8 or 18 1/4. The up-tick rule was created because of a concern that short sellers might start a price decline which the public would continue to feed. As the public continued to sell and further depress prices, the short sellers would cover at artificially low prices.[14]

Next, what happens to cash dividend payments? The new buyer will be carried as a shareholder of record on the corporation's books and receive payments directly from the corporation. The lender of shares (who is also an owner of the stock and deserves dividends) will be paid the dividends by the short seller. The short seller is indifferent to the dividend payment, since the dividend payment loss is offset by the profit obtained by share price declines when dividends are paid. In addition, short sellers must post margin in the same amount as if they had gone long. In the previous example, if the initial margin had been 50%, the short seller would have had to place equity values with the broker totaling $1,500. This is probably not a burden to the short seller because any unrestricted long securities can be used as margin. Finally, since the shares will be registered in the new buyer's name, he or she will receive all voting rights. The lender of shares will not retain any voting rights.

Short sales are a tool for sophisticated traders who know how to place stop orders to reduce risks and are able to closely follow changes in market conditions.

Costs of Trading

Trading costs depend on what you are trading. For example, if a new U. S. Treasury security is purchased directly from the Federal Reserve there is no commission paid to a broker. In contrast, the costs of buying a small quantity of a low-priced stock in the United States can easily represent 10% or more of the transaction value.

In this section we review the types of costs that can be incurred when a security is bought or sold and illustrate the size of these costs with data pertaining to U.S. stocks. Before we begin, keep two facts in mind. First, the average annual real (after inflation) return on U. S. stocks since the mid-1920s has been about 9%. Thus, transaction costs do not have to be very large before they wipe out any investment gains. Second, most securities incur transaction costs at both the purchase and sale. If a commission of 1% is required to trade, the full commission cost of investing in the security is actually 2%.

There are four types of trading costs: (1) bid-ask spreads, (2) commissions, (3) price impacts, and (4) tax effects.

Bid-Ask Spreads. *Bid* refers to the price at which a market maker will buy a security. *Ask* refers to the price at which the market maker will sell. Of course, the bid price will always be less than the ask price at any point in time. Market makers have conflicting interests when setting a given bid-ask spread. If they set a large spread, each round-trip trade results in greater revenue. But small spreads increase the number of trades placed with the market maker. In practice, the bid-ask spread that arises in the markets is set by competition between market makers and is sufficient to cover the costs and risk of being a market maker.

The most important determinant of bid-ask spreads is order flow. For securities with a large volume of trading, small spreads provide sufficient compensation to market makers.

---

[14] Such an operation is known as a bear raid. In contrast, a bull raid involves creating an initial heavy buying demand to force prices up. As the general public sees the buying activity, it steps in and also buys, thus forcing prices even higher as the bull raiders begin to sell their positions. Bear and bull raids are impossible in an efficient market. However, during the 1800s and early 1900s, they were accepted as fact. Whether they are possible today in actively traded securities is doubtful.

TABLE 4-3   PERCENTAGE BID-ASK SPREADS

	NYSE and AMEX Percentage Bid-Ask Spread Estimates			OTC Percentage Bid-Ask Quotes		
Portfolio	Average Market Value (in $ million)	Average Volume (in thousands)	Percentage Bid-Ask Spread	Average Market Value (in $ million)	Average Volume (in thousands)	Percentage Bid-Ask Spread
1	7.1	NA	3.26%	25.1	29.1	5.22%
2	23.9	NA	2.04			
3	63.6	NA	1.32	67.9	38.7	3.13
4	185.3	NA	0.96			
5	1447.4	NA	0.70	384.6	85.2	1.63

SOURCE: Adapted from T. J. George, G. Kaul, and M. Nimalendran, "Estimation of the Bid-Ask Spread and Its Components: A New Approach," *The Review of Financial Studies, 4* (4), 1991.

For stocks with small trading volume, larger spreads are necessary. Consider Table 4-3. In the table, bid-ask spreads are shown as a percentage of the market price of the security. Two sets of percentage spreads are shown. One set represents estimates of percentage spreads for stocks traded on the NYSE and AMEX.[15] The other set represents actual percentage spreads for stocks traded in the OTC market. Both sets are grouped by the total market value of the stocks examined and by firm size. Firm size and trading volume are closely related. So you can also think of the percentage bid-ask spreads as being grouped by trading volume.

Notice that the percentage spreads were indeed inversely related to trading volume and firm size. In addition, the sizes of these percentage spreads are not trivial. To put this into perspective, assume you are trading a stock in the OTC that was in the group labeled Portfolio 1. Also assume the equilibrium price of the stock is $10.00. Given the percentage spread of 5.22% in the table, the average spread on such a stock is $0.522. Assume the spread on the $10.00 stock is actually $0.50. That means the dealer will buy (public sells) at $9.75 and sell (public buys) at $10.25. So, if you bought 100 shares you would pay $1,025. And if you sold the 100 shares immediately (not a smart thing to do, of course) you would receive $975; a loss of almost 5%.

Commissions. When the NYSE was formed in 1792, the founders agreed to trade at fixed minimum commissions. In the early 1970s, the SEC decided all commissions should be negotiated between the broker and the customer—that is, they were to be subject to competition. Between 1971 and 1975 negotiated fees were slowly phased in on large-block transactions. And since May Day in 1975, all security commissions have been nego-tiated rates. In practice, most brokerage firms try to set firmwide rates that apply to partic-ular types of transactions and customers. Thus, the customer and the broker might not

---

[15] Estimates had to be used, since historical bid-ask spreads for stocks on the NYSE and AMEX are not available.

actually negotiate a commission every time a trade is made. This is particularly true for a small trade. Commissions for large-block trades, however, are actively negotiated, and the customer who engages in a large block will actively shop around for the cheapest rate.

Three levels of commission rates exist: (1) full-service rates, (2) discount broker rates, and (3) rates for very large block trades. Because commissions are negotiated, there is no single set of rates to compare. Commissions depend on the following:

- The liquidity of the security. Stocks with low prices tend to have less active markets and require greater efforts by the broker to find the opposite side with which to trade.

- Size of the order also increases costs because larger orders are less liquid.

- Other services the broker is requested to provide such as research advice, price quotations, security delivery (it is cheaper to keep securities in street name than require delivery), and maintenance of IRA accounts.

- The amount of trading the investor does over a full year. Customers who are going to be active will pay far lower rates than someone who intends to trade only a few times during the year.

The best advice is to shop around for the best charges available, given what you intend to do. The data in Table 4-4, however, should provide you with a basic understanding of the size of brokerage commissions. The table includes one typical full service brokerage firm and ten representative discount brokers. To put the data in perspective, large trades by mutual funds and advisers to pension funds are commonly executed at 6 cents a share. But some are executed for only 25 basis points, that is, 1/4 of one cent!

Commissions charged by a representative full service brokerage firm are shown in the first row. A trade of 100 shares of a $50 stock would cost $103 (or 103 cents per share) and represent 2.06% of the value of the transaction. Allowing for both purchase and sale, the round-trip cost of transacting in the security is greater than 4% of the security's value.

Discount broker fees are shown in the other rows. A discount broker provides only a few of the services provided by full service brokers and, in some cases, they provide trade execution only. Because each discount brokerage firm offers their own menu of services, their fees vary considerably from firm to firm. On the whole, however, fees paid to a dicount broker will be about one-half the fees of a full service broker. And even though they are labeled discount, their commissions are still not trivial. For example, using the average across the ten discount brokers, 100 shares of a $50 stock would cost $46 (or 46 cents per share) and represent slightly less than 1% of the trade value. Allowing for both purchase and sale, the round-trip cost to buy and sell would be almost 2%.

Price Impacts.   Price impacts represent effects on prices due to the size of an order. For example, the "inside" bid-ask prices might be 40 1/4 and 40 3/8. But these quotes could well be for only 100 shares. If an order is not too large, the market maker would probably fill it at one of these prices. But if the trade is, say, a request to sell 2,000 shares of an inactively traded stock, then the bid price at which the order would be filled would be lower than 40 1/4.

TABLE 4-4   TYPICAL FULL-SERVICE AND DISCOUNT BROKER COMMISSIONS

Commissions

	100 Shares at $50/Share Total: $5,000			500 Shares at $50/Share Total: $25,000			1,000 Shares at $5/Share Total: $5,000			
Firm	$	% of Trade	Cents Per Share	$	% of Trade	Cents Per Share	$	% of Trade	Cents Per Share	Min. $
Full Service	103	2.06	103	411.2	1.64	82	216.3	4.3	21.6	NA

Discount Brokers

1	55	1.10	55	155	0.62	31	90	1.80	9	39
2	54	1.08	54	154.5	0.62	31	88.5	1.77	8.8	38
3	45	0.90	45	140	0.56	28	90	1.80	9	40
4	46.2	0.92	46	135.5	0.54	27	67.77	1.36	6.8	37
5	115	2.30	115	325	1.30	65	115	2.30	11.5	50
6	40	0.80	40	100	0.40	20	52.5	1.05	5.3	20
7	49	0.98	49	119.5	0.48	24	60.5	1.21	6.1	37.5
8	75	1.50	75	155	0.62	31	110	2.2	11	35
9	48	0.96	48	145	0.58	29	85	1.70	8.5	38
10	35	0.70	35	111.7	0.45	22	54.72	1.09	5.5	35
Avg	46	0.92	46	106.1	0.42	21	71.73	1.43	7.2	
Max	115	2.30	115	325	1.30	65	132.5	2.65	13.3	
Min	25	0.50	25	25	0.10	5	32	0.64	3.2	

Note: Each of the discount brokerage firms included in the table provide the following services:
1. Insurance with Security Investors Protection Corporation.
2. Investment of free cash in a money market mutual fund.
3. Ability to invest in no-load mutual funds (some require a payment by investor).
4. IRA accounts.

SOURCE: Adapted from "Spot the Bargains Using the 1994 Discount Broker Survey," *AAII Journal*, January 1994.

Although price impacts do exist, their size is difficult to judge. There is little a small individual investor can do about potential price impacts other than to use a well-qualified broker. Usually, trades by individual investors are small enough that price impacts are minimal or nonexistent. Price impacts present a larger problem to institutional investors that often trade in massive quantities. As a result, the manner in which institutions trade is often different than for "retail" (individuals) customers of a brokerage firm.

Tax Effects. A neglected cost of trading is the increased tax burden associated with paying taxes immediately instead of delaying the realization of capital gains. Assume you sell

100 shares of a stock for $50 per share. The stock had been bought at $25 per share and your capital gains tax rate is 30%. Thus, taxes would be $750.

Sales Value	$5,000
Cost Value	2,500
Capital Gain	2,500
times Tax Rate	0.30
Taxes	$ 750

If you had delayed the sale for one year and the stock price had remained at $50, the taxes due at that time would also be $750. But you would be better off to delay the payment for one year due to the time value of money. The size of this benefit depends on your opportunity cost of money. For illustration, let's use a 10% yearly opportunity cost. In that case the present value of a payment of $750 in exactly one year is $681.82 ($750 ÷ 1.10). In present value terms, delaying the tax for one year saves you $68.18 ($750 − $681.82). This represents 1.6% of the after-tax cash value from immediate sale ($68.18 ÷ $4,250). Similar figures for waiting five and ten years before recognizing the gain are shown here.

Pay in:	Present Value of Tax	PV $ Loss	$ Loss as % of $4,250
5 years	$465.69	$284.31	6.69%
10 years	$289.16	$460.84	10.84%

Of course, if you are worried the security's price might decline soon, you might wish to realize the gain and pay the tax early.

Security Market Regulation

The main authority for regulating security markets in the United States is the SEC. The Securities Act of 1933 requires most new security offerings to be registered with the federal government in documents that disclose all relevant information about the issue and issuer. The Securities Exchange Act of 1934 extended the SEC's mandate to cover trading in secondary markets. Oversight and regulatory responsibilities of the SEC include the following:

- All national stock exchanges.

- Self-regulatory securities organizations (SROs) such as the NASD.

- Investment companies, mutual funds, and closed-end funds.

- Investment advisers such as portfolio managers and brokers who provide advice.

- Insider trading.

- Proxy voting by shareholders.

The SEC delegates some of its powers to the various exchanges by allowing them to develop rules of trading practices (which the SEC usually informally agrees to beforehand).

The principal regulator for trading in futures and options markets is the **Commodity Futures Trading Commission** (CFTC), not the SEC. With growth in derivatives trading and the close tie between prices in "spot" securities markets and derivatives markets, there have been questions about the efficiency of two regulatory bodies overseeing two such closely linked markets.

An important piece of legislation that became law in 1970 created an organization called the **Security Investors Protection Corporation** (SIPC). The SIPC protects up to $500,000 of securities that investors have left with a brokerage firm in street name if the firm should go bankrupt. To provide this insurance, the SIPC charges each brokerage firm an annual insurance premium.

Perspective on Global Markets

Trading in securities take place virtually 24 hours a day across various world markets. And trading in a given market will represent shares of firms located in that country as well as shares issued in other countries. In Figure 4-6, the trading hours of major world equity

FIGURE 4-6   TRADING HOURS OF MAJOR WORLD EQUITY MARKETS

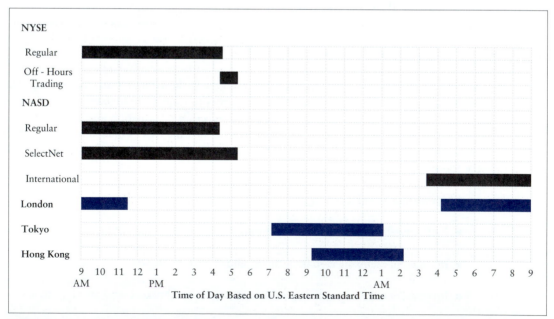

SOURCE: Adapted from *1994 NASDAQ Fact Book & Company Directory* (Washington, DC: National Association of Securities Dealers, 1995).

markets are shown. There are three U.S. markets not previously discussed: the NYSE OHT (off-hours trading), the NASD SelectNet, and the NASD International. SelectNet allows NASDAQ market makers to trade directly over computer terminals. The other two represent attempts by the exchanges to increase their trading hours, thus making U.S. markets even more attractive for foreign investors. In addition, trades occur off exchanges in a 24-hour world over-the-counter telephone market.

In Figure 4-7, dollar volume of equity trading is shown for various markets across the world. At present, the major world financial centers are in the United States, Japan, and the United Kingdom. Not only do they have the three largest security markets but they are geographically positioned to provide virtually 24-hour trading of financial assets. Because of their importance, we now review the London and Tokyo exchanges.

British Security Market

The London Stock Exchange (LSE) was incorporated in 1773. Like the NYSE, it was a product of an informal market developed around the coffeehouses in the city of London. Although the London exchange was overwhelmingly the largest in the United Kingdom (it was the world's largest until World War I), local share markets were also established. These local markets peaked at 30 but now include only 6 exchange floors. The British exchanges were merged in 1973 into the London Stock Exchange.

Securities traded on the LSE include ordinary shares (common stocks), preference shares (preferred stock), regional government issues, treasury (gilt-edge) bonds, and shares of investment management firms. A large number of non-U. K. securities are traded on the LSE. Over 58% of all "cross-border" trading takes place on the LSE. An equivalent to the U.S. over-the-counter market does not exist.

FIGURE 4-7   DOLLAR VALUE OF EQUITY TRADING IN MAJOR WORLD MARKETS: 1994

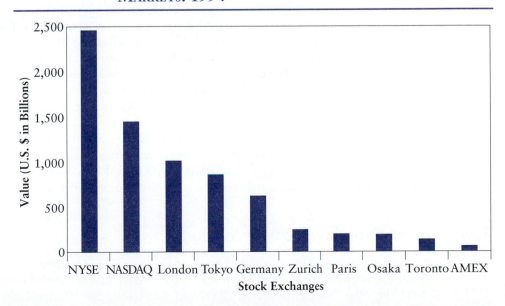

Security trading on the LSE is fully computerized under the Stock Exchange Automated Quotations (SEAQ) system. Competitive market makers place bid and ask prices into the computer system against which market orders are matched.

Prior to 1986, two features of the U. K. markets made them fundamentally different from the U.S. market. First, security firms engaged in only one of two activities. They either acted as an agent (broker) for individuals and organizations or as a dealer (market maker in the United States and jobber in the United Kingdom). Second, fixed minimum commission rates were charged. Following a court decision on fixed commissions, major changes were triggered by an agreement between the British government and the stock exchange. Fixed commissions were abolished. Security firms were allowed to act as both security agent and dealer. And foreign companies could own British security firms. This event was so dramatic it has come to be known as the **Big Bang.**

In the mid-1990s, only about 20% of stocks traded on the LSE were owned by individuals. The remaining 80% consisted of:

1. 65% owned by pension funds, insurance companies, and investment trusts.
2. 15% owned by charities, banks, commercial companies, the public sector, and overseas holders.

The Tokyo Stock Exchange

At the end of 1989, the Tokyo Stock Exchange (TSE) was the world's largest equity market in terms of the value of shares listed on the exchange. But after a 40% decline in its value in 1990 followed by a 25% decline in early 1992, it returned to second place.

Although there are stock exchanges in eight cities, Tokyo accounts for over 80% of total trading. Osaka and Nagoga handle about 13% and 1%, respectively. Stock exchanges in Japan were first established in 1878, but the structure of the markets today is a product of legislation following World War II. The Securities Exchange Law is patterned on the U.S. Securities Act of 1933 and the Securities and Exchange Act of 1934.

There are three defined sections on the Japanese exchanges. The **First Section** consists of larger companies and represents about 96% of total market capitalization. The **Second Section** handles younger, newly quoted firms that would otherwise be traded in the over-the-counter market. The **Third Section** is the over-the-counter market. Trading in First Section securities is handled on the exchange floor through Saitori members, who are similar to U.S. specialists. Second Section trades are handled by computers, similarly to the U.S. NASDAQ and British SEAQ systems.

Interest in the stock market is a public pastime, evidenced by the fact that 70% of all trades are for 5,000 shares or less. However, institutional ownership accounts for about 78% of all shares. Much of this institutional ownership is in **tokkin** accounts. These are share trading accounts of Japanese corporations, whose main business activity is not share trading.

Trends in an Evolving Security Market

In January 1994, the SEC released a lengthy study that reported its opinions about likely future developments in financial markets as well as areas it thought needed further regulation. The report was titled *Market 2000: An Examination of Current Equity Market*

Developments. The report made clear the dramatic evolutionary changes that had taken place in the prior 30 years and the forces at work which would cause future changes. The following is taken from the SEC report.[16]

The *Division believes that four trends will continue to drive this evolution.*

First, Institutional investors will continue to account for a majority of trading volume. As is the case today, it is difficult for established markets to accommodate the variety of institutional and retail investors. Alternative markets are likely to continue to emerge to serve institutions' specialized needs. In addition, the increasing dominance of equity trading by institutional investors and large intermediaries will strain the market's ability to handle liquidity demands. This could increase systemic risk.

Second, global trading will continue to grow. Capital will move more easily around the world, benefitting the providers and users of capital. At the same time, the United States will face stronger competition as the leading international marketplace. Foreign markets may compete by setting differing regulatory standards that offer U. S. Market participants the opportunity to avoid U. S. regulatory requirements. The competitive pressure from different foreign regulatory standards will affect the Commission's regulatory program. If the Commission is to maintain strong regulatory standards, U.S. market participants will have to be convinced of the attractiveness and benefits such standard bring to U. S. Markets.

Third, the derivatives markets will continue to grow. . . .

Fourth, technology will continue to drive the evolution of the equity markets. The Division believes that, at a minimum, technological advances will make it possible for public investors to obtain access to markets and other market participants directly. Technology now allows institutional investors to transact with one another without professional intermediation. This will increase in the future. . . .

SUMMARY

This chapter provided an overview of the structures of security markets. Here are the key concepts:

◾ Transactions in the securities markets can arise in either the primary market, when an issue is first sold to the general public, or in the secondary markets, where members of the public trade between themselves.

◾ The major participant in placing securities in the primary market is the investment banker. Investment bankers specialize in primary offerings and are able to provide advice, underwriting, and placement services to security issuers. A consulting fee is paid when the investment banker provides only advice. But when underwriting and distribution services are also provided, the investment banker's return comes in the form of an underwriter spread.

◾ Securities may be privately or publicly placed. Private placement can be cheaper and quicker, but public placement offers increased marketability. Most publicly

---

[16] *Market 2000: An Examination of Current Equity Market Developments,* Division of Market Regulation, United States Securities and Exchange Commission, Washington, DC: U.S. Government Printing Office, January 1994.

placed issues must be registered with the Securities and Exchange Commission (SEC) to ensure full disclosure of information about the issue.

▪ Secondary market transactions can occur on formal, organized exchanges or in the over-the-counter market.

▪ By far the dominant formal exchange market is the New York Stock Exchange (NYSE). It lists the largest and most actively traded stocks in the United States, and their market values exceed the market values of all stocks traded OTC or on other exchanges. Transactions on the NYSE are handled on the exchange floor by a commission broker who contacts the specialist in a stock to determine existing bid-ask prices.

▪ The specialist maintains a book of limit orders (from which a commission is earned if a limit order is traded), but, more importantly, acts as a dealer in the stock. As a dealer, the specialist absorbs temporary imbalances in the flow of buy and sell orders with the objective of providing continuity in prices over time and depth of liquidity. In the process, the specialist earns a profit from buying at lower bid prices and selling at higher asked prices. Market makers perform an equivalent role in the OTC market.

▪ The costs of trading can be significant. These consist of (1) bid-ask spreads, (2) commissions, (3) potential price impacts, and (4) paying taxes perhaps earlier than necessary.

R E V I E W   P R O B L E M

On Monday, July 3, you ask your broker to buy 200 shares of IBM at market, using the 50% allowed initial margin. The broker charges a commission of 2% and the brokerage firm has a 30% mainte-nance margin. The broker later calls you and says the trade was executed at $70 per share. (Note that July 4 is not a business day.)

  a. Why might you use a market order as opposed to a limit or stop order?
  b. On what date must you pay the brokerage firm? How much must be paid?
  c. Since the stock was bought on margin, below what stock price will a margin call be required?
  d. If the stock falls to $40 and you intend to deposit more cash into the account to bring it back to the maintenance margin by repaying part of the loan, how much cash must you deposit?
  e. If the stock falls to $40 and you intend to sell stock to repay some of the debt to bring it back to the maintenance margin, how many shares must you sell?

Solution

  a. A market order assures that a trade takes place at the existing best price. A limit order would be transacted only if prices are at the limit price or better. A stop order specifies a price at which the trade becomes a market order.
  b. The settlement day on which cash is paid and securities received is three *business* days after the trade date. Since July 4 is a business holiday, settlement will take place on

Friday, July 7. At that time you will pay:

Value of securities bought		
200 times $70	=	$14,000
Plus commission		
$14,000 times 0.02	=	280
Total	=	$14,280
Less margin loan		
0.50 times $14,000	=	7,000
Net due	=	$ 7,280

c. Maintenance margin = (Security Value − Loan) ÷ Security Value

$$0.30 = ((P \times 200) - \$7,000) \div \text{Security Value}$$

$$P = \$50$$

d. $$0.30 = ((\$40 \times 200) - (\$7,000 - Cash)) \div (\$40 \times 200)$$

$$Cash = \$1,400$$

e. $$0.30 = [(\$40 \times (200 - N)) - (\$7,000 - (\$40 \times N))] \div (\$40 \times (200 - N))$$

$$N = 116.23 \text{ shares (117 actually)}$$

QUESTIONS AND PROBLEMS

1. What are the relative advantages and disadvantages associated with negotiated and competitive underwritings?
2. How does the specialist make a profit?
3. What is an ADR?
4. Discuss the advantages and disadvantages of:
   a. Market orders
   b. Limit orders
   c. Stop orders
5. Carolina Carpets has just sold 50,000 new common shares to the public at an offering price of $70 per share. The underwriter's spread was $2.50, and management has estimated the internal management costs of selling the issue were $37,500. Immediately after the issue, the price of the stock rose in the secondary markets to $72, where it has remained for the last week.
   a. Identify the various costs involved in this sale.
   b. These are costs to Carolina Carpets. Who are the recipients?
   c. If management had forced the underwriter to offer the issue at $71 per share, what would the underwriter's response likely have been?
   d. If management had used a competitive bid selection instead of a negotiated selection, would its cost have been lower?
6. Short sellers can theoretically lose an infinite amount of money but, at most, earn 100%.
   a. True or false? Explain.
   b. How might stop orders be used to reduce the risks of short selling?
7. Lawrence Carver has just opened a margin account with a local brokerage firm. The firm has a policy of 60% initial margin and 40% maintenance margin. Mr. Carver initially buys 500 shares of a stock at $40 per share on margin.

   a. What are his initial equity and loan balances?
   b. To what price may the security decline before a margin call is required?
   c. If the stock suddenly falls to $20 per share and the broker requires that the maintenance requirement be restored, how much cash must Lawrence add to his position if it is used to repay a portion of the loan?
   d. If the stock suddenly falls to $20 per share while Lawrence is on an annual vacation to the Himalayas, how many shares must be sold to restore the maintenance margin?
8. Various studies have shown that the market prices of new security offerings rise more in the month or two after initial public sale than would be expected given the security's risk. What does this suggest about the original selling price set by underwriters and the underwriters' ability to stabilize prices?
9. Jennifer and Jason both purchased 100 shares of Little Mint Inc. at the start of the year at a price equal to $50 per share. Jennifer paid the full cost of $5,000 and Jason used 50% margin. His borrowings had an interest rate of 8% per annum.
   a. Calculate that rate of return to each investor if shares of Little Mint Inc. are $69 at year-end and a $1 dividend is received at that time.
   b. Repeat part a but assume the end-of-year share price is $39.
   c. What conclusion should you draw from this example about the use of margin in acquiring a stock position?
10. Gerry sold short 100 shares of Little Mint Inc. and borrowed the shares from her broker.
   a. Why would the broker be willing to lend her the shares?
   b. During the year, Little Mint Inc. pays a $1 dividend per share to registered owners of the stock. At that time, Gerry must also pay her broker (the lender of shares) $1 per share. Why would she not be losing any money when she pays the broker these dividends?
11. Identify the various types of costs investors incur in trading stocks.
   a. Discuss how these relate to trades by individual investors.
   b. Discuss how these relate to trades by institutional investors.
12. During the late 1980s, memberships on the NYSE were trading at prices in excess of $500,000. Why would a brokerage firm pay such a large price?

13. You wish to sell short 100 shares of XYZ common stock. If the last two transactions were at 34 1/8 followed by 34 1/4, you can sell short on the next transaction only at the price of:
   a. 34 1/8 or higher.
   b. 34 1/4 or higher.
   c. 34 1/4 or lower.
   d. 34 1/8 or lower.

DATAFILE ANALYSIS

The purpose of this exercise is to compare the returns of stocks on large corporations in the United States, United Kingdom, and Japan since 1970. Knowledge of past international returns is crucial to developing a global perspective of investing. We will use this type of data in future chapters to help you calculate optimal portfolio investment strategies.

Review the INDEXES.WK3 datafile and locate the annual return series for the S&P 500, U. K. Financial Times (in dollars), and Japan Large Company (in dollars). These returns represent portfolio returns that U.S. investors would have earned if they had held portfolios of the largest corporations in each country. Calculate the average annual returns, minimums, and maximums of each return series. Why do you believe they differ?

S E L E C T E D   R E F E R E N C E S

A thorough discussion of current markets in the United States is *Market 2000: An Examination of Current Equity Market Developments,* Division of Market Regulation, United States Securities Exchange Commission, Washington DC: U.S. Government Printing Office, January 1994.

An overview of world security markets is presented in Bruno Solnik, *International Investments,* Reading, MA: Addison-Wesley, 1988.

G. T. Guide to World Equity Markets, London: Euromoney Publications; updated annually.

Surveys of current investment banking issues are presented in the following:

Ibbotson, Roger G. and Jody L. Sindelar, "Initial Public Offerings," *Journal of Applied Corporate Finance, 1,* (2), 1988.

Silber, William L. "Discounts on Restricted Stock: The Impact of Illiquidity on Stock Prices," *Financial Analysts Journal,* July–August 1991.

Smith, Clifford W. "Investment Banking and the Capital Acquisition Process," *Journal of Financial Economics,* January–February 1986.

Wagner, Wayne H. *The Complete Guide to Securities Transactions,* New York: Wiley, 1989.

Review articles of the events surrounding Black Monday include:

Malkiel, Burton. "The Brady Commission Report: A Critique," *Journal of Portfolio Management,* Summer 1988.

Roll, Richard. "The International Crash of 1987," *Financial Analysts Journal,* September–October 1988.

Rubinstein, Mark. "Portfolio Insurance and the Market Crash," *Financial Analysts Journal,* January–February 1988.

PART 2

Investment Concepts

In Part 2 we examine the major concepts that are the foundation of modern investment management. We start in Chapter 5 by first developing a theory of the risk-free nominal interest rate and then discussing the principal measure used to evaluate investment risk, the standard deviation of portfolio returns.

Principles of portfolio theory are presented in Chapter 6. The most important of these is the value of broad diversification. After demonstrating the benefits of diversification, we develop a model of "efficient diversification," which shows how to minimize the risk of a portfolio for a specified expected portfolio return. Professor Harry Markowitz received the Nobel Prize in economics for his original work in developing this model of efficient diversification. It is widely used today by investment advisers.

Chapters 7 and 8 explore two conceptual models that extended the work of Markowitz in an attempt to explain overall market equilibrium relationships between investment risk and required investment returns. These models are known as the capital asset pricing model (CAPM) and the arbitrage pricing theory (APT). One of the most important concepts of both models is the notion of nondiversifiable security risk. In the CAPM, a security has a single type of nondiversifiable risk, which is measured by a variable called beta. In the APT, a number of different nondiversifiable risks exist. There are proponents for and opponents to both models. And competing models will surely be developed in the future as our understanding of investment risk and security markets grows. But the CAPM and APT are widely used in investment management today. Professor William Sharpe received a Nobel Prize in economics for his contributions to the development of the CAPM.

Chapter 9, the final chapter in Part 2, reviews the theory of efficient markets. We discuss what the theory implies about security prices, the conditions that would lead to efficient markets, and major empirical tests of the theory. If the efficient market hypothesis is correct, passive investment management is the best approach to portfolio management. If market inefficiencies can be found, they should be the basis of an active management strategy.

5

BASIC INVESTMENT CONCEPTS

After reading this chapter you should have an understanding of the economic forces which create the risk-free interest rate and how portfolio risk is measured.

During the twentieth century, there have been two major stock market crashes. The first occurred during 1929 when the U.S. stock market lost more than one-third of its value between October and the end of December. The second occurred more recently, during October and November 1987, when stocks fell in value by almost one-third again. Both events had traumatic effects on investors and strained all aspects of the financial system. These events are two of the most dramatic examples of the risk that stock investors incur.[1]

But with risk comes reward. For example, investors who bought stocks in the S&P 500 Index at the end of 1929 and held them through the end of 1987 would have earned an average annual return equal to 11.4%. In comparison, the annual average return on T-bills during the same period was 3.5%.

This is the first in a sequence of five chapters that explore the trade-off between expected investment returns and investment risk. After you have completed this chapter, you will understand:

1. the market forces that create prevailing risk-free rates of return,
2. how two types of investment returns are calculated,

---

[1] Speak to anyone invested in bonds during the 1970s and it will be clear that bond investors also face considerable risk.

3. how to interpret the statistic that is typically used as a measure of investment risk, the standard deviation of portfolio returns,
4. how past average returns and standard deviations vary across major asset classes, and
5. how the investment horizon affects investment risk and investment strategy.

In short, the objective of this chapter is to help you develop a basic understanding of investment returns and investment risk. Investors are willing to commit their capital to an investment only if they expect future returns that fairly compensate them for the risk they incur. Investment risk and expected returns on the investment are clearly related. This is a principle about which few people would disagree.

But what is investment risk? And what should be the relationship between expected returns and investment risk? These are the central issues that have driven investment research for more than three decades. Out of this research, two theoretical models have emerged: the capital asset pricing model (CAPM) and arbitrage pricing theory (APT). The CAPM is discussed in Chapter 7 and APT is discussed in Chapter 8. Both models imply that the expected return on a security (or portfolio of securities) consists of a risk-free return plus a risk premium. That is:

The Required Rate-of-Return for a Security	equals	**A Nominal Risk-Free Return**	plus	**Risk Premium(s) Given the Risk(s) of the Security**

CAPM and APT differ in their underlying economic assumptions. As a result, they differ in their investment implications. CAPM implies that investors should diversify broadly across all risky assets by purchasing a portfolio of risky assets called the "market" portfolio. According to the CAPM, the risk premium on any security (or security portfolio) is related to a single type of risk known as market risk. APT also suggests that investors diversify broadly. But APT suggests a number of different types of risk influence the return that investors require.

The validity of both theories is presently the subject of considerable debate among scholars.[2] There is no consensus of opinion today as to which model of expected returns is the better, whether refinements in our understanding of each model are needed, or whether a totally new theoretical model of investment risk is required. However, most researchers and practitioners would agree that (1) the concept of a nominal risk-free return underlies all expected returns, and (2) the standard deviation of possible future portfolio value is a good proxy for investment risk.

We discuss four general topics in this chapter:

◪ The economic forces that create prevailing nominal **risk-free interest** rates.

◪ Various ways of measuring **realized security returns.**

◪ How **portfolio risk** is measured as the standard deviation of potential holding period returns.

---

[2] We review much of this debate in Chapters 7 and 8.

■ How the **investment horizon** affects portfolio risk.

An understanding of these topics is the foundation to our study of both the CAPM and APT.

Risk-Free Interest

Among many past societies, the taking of interest was considered to be unnatural. The ancient Greeks referred to interest as offspring, which led Aristotle to object that the charging of interest was unnatural, since money cannot have offspring. Jewish Mosaic laws forbade interest between fellow Jews. Romans were forbidden to charge interest to other Romans, and the Christian religion strongly discouraged interest taking throughout the Middle Ages. Saint Thomas Aquinas stated that interest constituted a payment for time, which he felt should more properly be considered a free gift of the Creator. Even in more recent times, many people considered interest to be an inherent evil, the extortion of income from the have-nots by the haves.

But in spite of such opinions, interest plays a fundamental economic role in all societies. Basic economic theory shows how prices are set on various goods so that society can efficiently allocate scarce resources. For example, an ounce of gold costs more than an ounce of sand because the supply of gold is less than sand and the demand for gold is greater. The risk-free interest rate is also a price, the price of time. The level of interest rates influences people's decision to consume today versus investing for consumption tomorrow.

Natural Real Rates

Economists call the rate of interest that prevails in a society, before any considerations are given to inflation or risk, the **natural real risk-free rate.** Also called the **pure rate,** we denote it by the letters *pr*.

To provide a graphic presentation of the determinants of a natural real risk-free rate of interest, consider a world in which there are only two dates, Date 0 and Date 1. Also assume there is no risk. Everything is known.

Consider panel A in Figure 5-1. At Date 0, society is endowed with total resources equal to R_0. These resources may be fully consumed at Date 0 or a portion could be invested in real assets (land, tractors, buildings, and education are examples of real asset investments). If some portion of Date 0 resources is invested in real assets, a known productive return will be earned (this is a risk-free world). For example, the first bushel of corn seeded on productive soil at Date 0 might yield 2 bushels at Date 1. The curve between R_0 and R_1 represents all possible consumption levels at Dates 0 and 1. The slope of this curve at any point represents the increase in Date 1 consumption available if one additional unit of Date 0 resources is invested in real assets. Notice that the slope of the **consumption possibility curve** decreases as real investment at Date 0 is increased. This reflects a declining marginal return on real asset investment as the amount of investment increases. (The second bushel of corn must be thrown on less productive soil.) In panel B of Figure 5-1, this marginal return is shown as the line *DD*.

Now consider the dotted curves in panel A, called **utility indifference curves.** Any point on a given curve provides the same level of economic utility to society. The higher a curve, the greater the level of economic utility. The slope of an indifference curve at any point represents the increase in Date 1 consumption necessary to provide the same level of

FIGURE 5-1   SOCIETY'S INVESTMENT CONSUMPTION CHOICE

A. CONSUMPTION OPPORTUNITIES AND UTILITY INDIFFERENCE CURVES

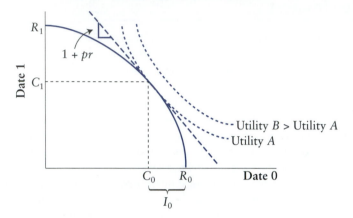

B. AVAILABLE MARGINAL INVESTMENT YIELDS

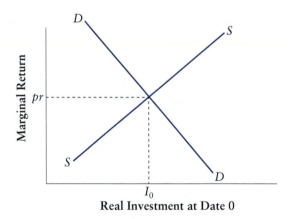

current utility if one unit of Date 0 consumption is given up. The fact that the slope of the indifference curves increases as additional consumption at Date 0 decreases means that higher rates of return are demanded. In panel B, this required return is shown as line *SS*.

So how much real investment will be undertaken at Date 0 and what rate of return will be earned? The answer is clearly at a point *when the marginal return available on investment is equal to the marginal required return.* In panel A, an amount C_0 will be consumed, and R_0 minus C_0 will be invested in real assets. And the equilibrium risk-free interest rate will be the pure rate of interest shown in the figure as *pr*.

Note the following:

1. Interest is indeed a natural phenomenon. It is the economic force that determines the extent to which real resources will be invested or immediately consumed.

2. The equilibrium real rate of interest is determined by an interaction between (a) the consumption time preferences (thriftiness) of society, and (b) the productivity of available resources.
3. In a world of complete certainty, this equilibrium interest rate is set at a level such that investors' *required returns are exactly equal to the productive yields generated* from their investments. Investors will receive the return they require.

While it is impossible to directly observe the pure rate of interest on riskless real assets, indirect estimates can be obtained by examining financial asset prices. Because risk-free investment in a financial asset is a perfect substitute for a risk-free investment in real assets, financial asset returns must be identical to real asset returns. If they differed, an arbitrage opportunity would exist.

Nominal Risk-Free Rates

When we examine the returns available on securities that have little or no risk of default, two things are obvious. First, they vary considerably over time. Second, at any point in time, they vary considerably from country to country. The principal explanation for these phenomena was first developed by Irving Fisher.

The Fisher Equation. Irving Fisher was one of the most insightful of all classical economists. In 1895, at the request of the American Economic Association, Fisher undertook a detailed examination of the effect of inflation on the rate of interest. These studies were summarized in his text, *The Theory of Interest*. In spite of its age, Fisher's book is still one of the best discussions of why interest rates exist and what their inherent determinants are.

Fisher's analysis of interest rates is as straightforward and simple as it is important in explaining why interest rates change over time. Fisher begins with the assumption that individuals who lend money realize that what is being lent is not so much pieces of paper (cash) but control of real goods. The rate of return that lenders demand from a loan of capital represents not so much a return on money as it does an increase in their command of real goods. When a sum of money is lent, the lender wishes to receive an increase in purchasing power equal to the equilibrium pure rate. If lenders expect an inflation in commodity prices, they will demand a rate of return that provides compensation for both a required real rate of return and the inflation that is expected.

Suppose both the borrower and lender know with perfect certainty that inflation during the next year will be 5%. If a real rate of 3% is required on a loan, the lender will charge a nominal rate of 8.15%. For each $1 lent today, $1.05 must be returned at the end of the year to keep the lender's purchasing power intact. If the lender requires a 3% increase in next year's purchasing power, he or she will demand a $1.0815 ($1.05 × 1.03) payment.

The relationship between real and nominal risk-free rates can be expressed symbolically. If *pr* represents the pure rate of interest per annum and $E(I_t)$ represents the annual average inflation expected over the next *t* years, then the nominal risk-free rate of interest on a security maturing in year $t(RF_t)$ would look like this:

Fisher Equation for the Nominal Risk-Free Rate

Nominal Risk-Free Rate	equals	1.0 plus Risk-Free Pure Rate	times	1.0 plus Expected Inflation	minus	1.0

$$RF_t = [1 + pr][1 + E(I_t)] - 1.0 \qquad\qquad (5.1)$$

Assume Shawn Smith is the manager of a mutual fund that invests in U.S. Treasury bonds and is attempting to determine what might be an appropriate return to expect on the purchase of bonds of various maturities. He believes a real return of 2% per year is reasonable and has received the following inflation forecasts:

Year-End	1	2	3	4	5
Average Yearly Inflation	4%	5%	4%	3%	3%

Given these forecasts and using Equation 5.1, Shawn should expect the following nominal rates before investing in Treasuries:

Bond Maturity	1 yr	2 yr	3 yr	4 yr	5 yr
Expected Return Requirement	6.08%	7.1%	6.08%	5.06%	5.06%

Notice that, if inflation rates are expected to change over time, then the required nominal return will depend on a bond's maturity. In our example, the bond maturing in year 2 has the highest required nominal return because two-year inflation rates are the highest. Anticipated changes in inflation rates over time is a reasonable explanation for the shape of a Treasury bond yield curve. A **yield curve** is a plot of the promised nominal return on a bond versus the bond's maturity. The yield curve shown in Figure 5-2 reflects the nominal returns that Shawn will require.

FIGURE 5-2   ILLUSTRATION OF A YIELD CURVE

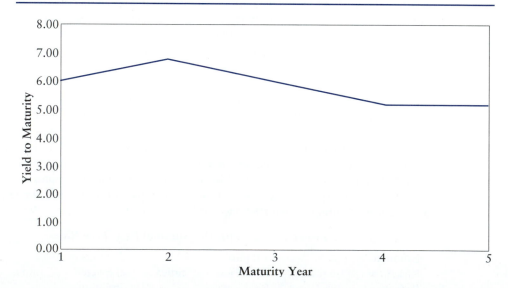

Alternatively, Shawn could use prevailing nominal returns on risk-free Treasury yields to forecast the market's consensus of future inflation. For example, assume he believes other investors require a pure rate of 2%. If prevailing yields on Treasury obligations with different maturities are as shown here, he could calculate an estimate of the marketwide consensus of inflation:

Maturity Year	Yield on Treasury Bond Maturing in Year	Pure Rate	Implied Average Yearly Inflation
1	7%	2%	4.90%
2	9%	2%	6.86%
3	6%	2%	3.92%
4	5%	2%	2.94%
5	5%	2%	2.94%

Notice that Equation (5.1) involves a compounding of the pure rate and the expected inflation rate. While this compounding is logically necessary, not much accuracy is lost if we simply add the expected inflation rates to the pure real rate. We refer to this relationship as the **approximate Fisher equation.**

Approximate Fisher Equation

Nominal Risk-free Rate	equals	Real Risk-free Rate	plus	Expected Inflation

$$RF_t = pr + E(I_t) \tag{5.2}$$

The International Fisher Equation. The relationship between nominal and real interest rates should exist in all countries. If we denote the domestic country by the letter D and a foreign country by the letter F, then the following relationships should be true:

$$(1.0 + RF_D) = [1 + pr_D][1 + E(I_D)]$$

$$(1.0 + RF_F) = [1 + pr_F][1 + E(I_F)]$$

Recognizing these relationships, economists are able to explain interest rate differences between countries by an international version of the Fisher equation.

International Fisher Equation

$$\frac{(1 + RF_D)}{(1 + RF_F)} = \frac{[1 + pr_D]}{[1 + pr_F]} \times \frac{[1 + E(I_D)]}{[1 + E(I_F)]} \tag{5.3}$$

For example, assume one-year T-bill interest rates are 6% in the United States and 8% in the United Kingdom. Then the difference of two percentage points would be attributed to differences in pure rates and inflation expectations in the two countries.

Assume that good estimates of one-year inflation rates can be made and that these are 3% in the United States and 4% in the United Kingdom. This implies the pure rate is 2.91% in the United States and 3.85% in the United Kingdom.

$$0.0291 = (1.06 \div 1.03) - 1.0$$

$$0.0385 = (1.08 \div 1.04) - 1.0$$

Where would you invest?[3] Assuming the inflation forecasts are correct, an investment in the United Kingdom would clearly provide the greater return. But you certainly would not be the only person to notice the difference in the pure rates available. Many investors would sell their holdings of U.S. T-bills and purchase U.K. T-bills. As they do so, the differential in the pure rates would narrow until the pure rates are identical between both countries.

If investors are able to conduct arbitrages like the one here at no cost, then pure rates of interest would be identical in all countries and the sole reason for differences in nominal interest rates would be due to differences in expected inflation.

Do the Fisher Relationships Work?   How well do the Fisher equations explain actual rates of return on securities with no risk? There is little doubt that interest rates on securities such as U.S. T-bills are sensitive to potential future inflation. When monetary and governmental authorities set policies that market participants believe will affect inflation, interest rates move exactly as the Fisher equation (5.1) suggests. And when interest rates across countries are examined, they are directly related to inflationary conditions in the local economies. Even though accurate tests of the relationship are not possible because market inflation forecasts cannot be observed, there appears to be a strong tie between potential inflation and the level of interest rates.

In addition to changes in inflation expectations, nominal interest rates are also affected by policy actions of monetary authorities. For example, during the 1930s and 1940s, the U.S. Federal Reserve Board pegged interest rates at artificially low levels in order to spur economic expansion and reduce government borrowing costs. (This policy was discontinued with the Federal Reserve Accord of 1953.) In addition, many countries place controls on capital movements into or out of their country, which make arbitrage transactions difficult.

Measuring Realized Returns

The purpose of all investment is to earn future returns. In this section we examine various return definitions and learn how security returns are calculated.

Basic Definitions

The term *return* can be used in a variety of contexts. To help avoid confusion, let's review four common uses here:

◾ **Required return** represents the minimum rate of return that investors require before they would invest in a given security.

◾ **Expected return** represents the actual return investors expect from investing in a security. If their required return is equal to or less than the expected return, they would purchase the security.

---

[3] When investing in a foreign country, investors incur exchange rate risk. In this example, however, exchange rate risk can be eliminated by trading in derivative securities. We discuss hedging exchange rate risk in Chapter 15.

■ **Promised return** represents the return that investors would earn if the issuer of the security makes all promised future cash payments. Promised returns apply only to debt obligations.

■ **Realized return** represents the actual return that investors earn on the investment.

Consider a commercial paper issue of Magna International Ltd. that promises to pay a single future cash flow equal to $100, exactly one year from today. After considering Magna's default risk, the liquidity of the issue, and returns available on other commercial paper issues, you come to two conclusions. First, even though Magna has promised to repay $100, you believe there is a significant chance of default on some amount of the repayment and your best expectation of the final repayment is $98. Second, to induce you to purchase the security you would require a 12% return. Given this **required return** and expected future cash flows, you would be willing to pay $87.50 ($98 divided by 1.12).[4]

It turns out that other investors are more optimistic about the issue than you, and Magna is able to receive an initial issue price equal to $90. If you were to purchase the security for $90 and expect a future inflow of $98, your **expected return** is 8.9% ($98 divided by $90 minus 1.0). Since your 12% required return is larger than your 8.9% expected return, you should not purchase the issue.

The **promised return** is the interest rate that discounts promised cash flows back to the security's current price. In this case, Magna International is promising an 11.1% return ($100 divided by $90 minus 1.0).

A year passes and you read in the financial press that Magna International has, in fact, declared bankruptcy and will only be able to repay $80 instead of the promised $100. Thus the **realized return** (earned by investors who initially paid $90) is a negative 11.1%. The realized return is the interest rate that discounts actual future cash flows back to the original price paid.

Throughout the rest of this chapter, we limit our discussion to realized returns and expected returns. Chapters 7 and 8 discuss models of required returns. Promised returns are discussed in Chapter 10.

Return Calculations

The return on an investment represents the increase in investment value over a given period of time. For example, a 20% return means a $1.00 investment grew in value to $1.20 by the end of the period. The period could be any length of time we wish to use.

A difference can exist between the return an investor actually earns and the return on the underlying securities owned. This happens when the investor either adds cash to or withdraws cash from an investment during the period over which the return is being measured. For example, assume that at the start of a month Jennifer owns 100 American Depository Receipts (ADRs) of Zeneca Group worth $50 each. During the month, the value of the ADRs grows to $75. Believing this to be a favorable sign, she purchases an additional 100 ADRs at $75 on January 8. Unfortunately, by the end of the month, the ADRs fall back to the original value of $50.

---

[4] The required return is the interest rate used to discount expected future cash flows in order to determine the present value of the investment to you.

The return during January on Zeneca Group ADRs was clearly zero. This return is called a **time weighted return,** the return on the underlying securities owned. But the return Jennifer earned was negative. This return is called a **dollar weighted return,** the return earned by the owner of the securities.

The cause of this return difference comes from the fact that Jennifer effectively had two investments in Zeneca Group. The value of her ADR position at the start of the month did not change by month's end. Thus it had a zero return (identical to the time weighted return on Zeneca Group ADRs during January). But the return on the additional cash she used to purchase ADRs at $75 was negative because these ADRs fell in value to $50 by month-end.

Unless dramatic changes are made in the holdings of a portfolio, time weighted returns and dollar weighted returns are usually very similar for short time periods. But, over long time periods, they can be quite different.

Time Weighted Returns. In Chapter 2, we showed that the rate of return during a given time period comes from both a cash yield and price changes during the period. The single period return equation was given as follows:

Return in Period t equals   Cash Yield   plus   Percentage Price Change

Security Return During Period t

$$R_t = D_t \div P_{t-1} + (P_t - P_{t-1}) \div P_{t-1} \tag{5.4}$$

Here D represents the dividends received during the period and P represents the security's price at different dates.[5]

For example, assume you buy a stock for $20 on January 1. During the month, you receive $0.80 in dividends, and the stock is worth $22 on January 30. According to Equation 5.4, your return during January was 14%:

$$0.14 = \$0.80 \div \$20 + (\$22 - \$20) \div \$20$$

Equation (5.4) assumes that all cash inflows from interest or dividends are received at the end of the period. If such cash inflows are received before then, an explicit adjustment must be made for their reinvestment. Usually it is assumed that interest and dividends are reinvested in the security paying the cash.

To calculate the **time weighted return** (TWR) for a given period, the period is divided into subperiods. Each subperiod ends when a cash flow occurs, and the return during the subperiod is calculated using Equation (5.4). The various subperiod returns are then compounded in order to calculate the total period return. The procedure used is shown next.

Time Weighted Returns

$$TWR_t = (1.0 + S_1)(1.0 + S_2) \ldots (1.0 + S_N) - 1.0 \tag{5.5}$$

Each subperiod return, S, represents the return earned from the date of the last cash flow to the date of the next cash flow using Equation (5.4).

---

[5] For investments in debt securities, coupon interest payments are substituted for dividend payments.

To illustrate this procedure for calculating TWRs, assume the $0.80 dividend was paid on January 20 and the stock price was $21.50 immediately after the dividend payment. The January TWR would be 14.09% and be calculated as follows:

$$\sum[(beg + earnings) \div beg][end \div beg] - 1$$

$$R_{Jan} = [(\$21.50 + \$0.80) \div \$20][\$22 \div \$21.50] - 1.0$$

$$= [1.1150][1.0233] - 1.0$$

$$= 0.1409$$

The value of the investment is $20 at the start of the month. When the $0.80 dividend is paid, the stock's value is $21.50. Thus, the $20 has accumulated to a value equal to $22.30 ($21.50 + $0.80). The subperiod return during this 20-day interval was 11.5%. After the dividend payment, the stock price increases from $21.50 to $22, representing a subperiod return of 2.33%. When the two subperiod returns are compounded, the full month TWR is 14.09%.

As another example, consider the case of Jennifer's investment in Zeneca Group ADRs. Calculation of the TWR on these ADRs could be viewed from, two perspectives: the management of Zeneca Group or Jennifer's. From the managements perspective, the return is simple to calculate. Since no cash dividends were paid, the January TWR is simply 0.00%:

$$0.0000 = (\$50 - \$50) \div \$50$$

From Jennifer's perspective we need to calculate subperiod returns, since she made an incremental cash investment in the security during January. The first subperiod return covers the time interval from the start of the month until she places cash into the investment:

$$S_1 = 0.5000 = (\$75 - \$50) \div \$50$$

The second subperiod covers the time interval after the cash investment until the end of the month:

$$S_2 = -0.3333 = (\$50 - \$75) \div \$75$$

The full-month TWR from Jennifer's perspective can now be calculated using Equation 5.5:

$$TWR = (1.50)(0.6666) - 1.0$$

$$= 0.0000$$

Notice that, regardless of whose perspective is used, the TWR was the same. This makes perfect sense when we recall what the time weighted return represents: the return on the underlying securities.

Dollar Weighted Returns. Dollar weighted returns represent the return the owner of an investment portfolio actually receives. Think of the portfolio as a box that holds all securities. If the investor does not add cash to the box or take cash out, TWRs and DWRs will be identical. But if cash is invested or withdrawn, then TWRs and DWRs will be different.[6]

---

[6] Any cash flows received from dividends and interest that are reinvested in the portfolio (stay in the box) do not have to be considered in DWR calculations. Since such cash is reinvested, the net cash flow to the investor is zero.

The DWR is actually an internal rate of return (IRR) calculation, which is familiar to students of finance. It is found by solving for DWR in the following equation:

Dollar Weighted Return

$$MVE = MVB\,(1 + DWR) + \sum F_i\,(1 + DWR)^{w(i)} \qquad (5.6)$$

Here MVE equals the portfolio's market value at the end of the period, MVB is the portfolio's market value at the beginning of the period, the F values are cash flows into (F is positive) or out of (F is negative) of the portfolio, and $w(i)$ is the fraction of the period a given cash flow was in or out of the portfolio.

Consider the following example. The value of a portfolio is $10,000 at the start of the month. On the tenth of the month an additional investment of $1,000 is made. On the twentieth of the month a withdrawal of $2,000 in cash is taken. Finally, at month-end (day 30) the portfolio has a market value equal to $9,800.67. The DWR would be calculated as follows:

$$\$9{,}800.67 = \$10{,}000\,(1 + DWR) + \$1{,}000\,(1 + DWR)^{2/3} - \$2{,}000\,(1 + DWR)^{1/3}$$

A calculator or desktop computer can be used to find the value of DWR here. It turns out to be 8%.

What would be the DWR in the Zeneca Group example used in the beginning of this section? The beginning market value is $5,000 (100 times $50). The ending value is $10,000 (200 times $50). And the cash inflow on January 8 is $7,500 (100 times $75). Given that there are 31 days in January, Equation (5.6) would be set up as follows:

$$\$10{,}000 = \$5{,}000\,(1 + DWR) + \$7{,}500\,(1 + DWR)^{23/31}$$

Using a calculator, we find the DWR turns out to be negative 23.2%.

Which Return Measure Should Be Used? The answer to this question depends on what we are trying to measure. If you are interested in the returns on a security or portfolio of securities, the time weighted return should be used. If you are interested in the return the owner of a security or portfolio of securities has actually earned, the dollar weighted return should be used.

The returns discussed in the rest of the chapter should be thought of as TWRs.

Unit Value Series. Given that you have a series of TWRs, it is often useful to create what is known as a **unit value** series. To do so, assign some base number (say, 1.0) to the date preceding the first return. This base number is then compounded by each period's return:

Unit Value Series

$$UV_T = 1.0\,(1 + R_1)(1 + R_2)\,(1 + R_3) \ldots (1 + R_T) \qquad (5.7)$$

For example, assume the following TWRs were earned in years 1 through 5:

Year	1	2	3	4	5
Return	10%	15%	−20%	0%	5%

Then the unit value at the end of year 5 would be

$$UV_5 = 1.0\,(1.10)\,(1.15)\,(0.80)\,(1.0)\,(1.05)$$

$$= 1.0626$$

Later in this chapter, we examine unit value series on a number of security classes.

Arithmetic vs. Geometric Averages. What was the typical yearly return on an investment in, say, the S&P 500 between 1990 and 1994? Yearly returns are shown next.

Year	1990	1991	1992	1993	1994
Nominal S&P 500 Time Weighted Returns	− 3.17%	30.55%	7.67%	9.99%	1.32%

The answer depends on whether we want to know the **arithmetic average** yearly return or the **geometric average** yearly return. The arithmetic average is calculated by adding all single period returns and dividing the sum by the number of periods. The geometric average is calculated by compounding the series of single period returns in order to find the terminal value of initially investing $1.00 and then finding the single rate of return that would have resulted in the same terminal value.

The arithmetic average was 9.27% and is calculated as follows:

Arithmetic Average Return

$$= (\text{Sum of all returns}) \div \text{Number of years}$$

$$\overline{R} = \left(\sum_{t=1}^{N} R_t \right) \div N \tag{5.8}$$

$$9.27\% = (-3.17 + 30.55 + 7.67 + 9.99 + 1.32) \div 5$$

Over this time period, the typical investor who bought a portfolio equivalent to the S&P 500 at the start of a year and sold it at the end of the year would have had an average return of 9.27%. The one-year holding is a critical assumption.

Most investment strategies, however, involve holding periods greater than one year. In that case, the investor is subject to a compounding of the sequence of returns. If there is any variability in the return series, the arithmetic average will not be the same as the average compound return, which is referred to as the geometric mean. We denote the geometric mean as $\overline{G}$.

The geometric mean return is calculated as follows:

Geometric Mean Return

$$= \text{Add } 1.0 \text{ to each return; multiply the series;}$$

$$\text{take the } N \text{th root; subtract } 1.0$$

$$\overline{G} = \left[\prod_{t=1}^{N} (1 + R_t) \right]^{1 \div N} - 1.0 \tag{5.9}$$

$$= [UV_T]^{1 \div N} - 1.0$$

$$0.0869 = [(1 - 0.0317)(1 + 0.3055)(1.0767)(1.0999)(1.0132)]^{1 \div 5} - 1.0$$

To see why arithmetic means differ from geometric means, consider the following example. You invest $100 at the start of year 1. During year 1, you experience a positive 20% return. During year 2, you experience a negative 20% return. As shown next, your $100 initial value declines to $96 at the end of year 2:

	Year 1	Year 2
Return	+20%	−20%
Value of the $100	$120	$96

The arithmetic average return is 0% and suggests you didn't win or lose. But you know the initial $100 is now worth $96; you know you lost! In contrast, the geometric mean return associated with an investment of $100 becoming $96 two periods later is a negative 2.02%:

$$-0.0202 = [(1.2)(0.8)]^{1 \div 2} - 1.0$$

Why was the geometric mean smaller than the arithmetic mean in this example? Simply because a given percentage decline in value cannot be offset by an identical percentage increase in value. This is why geometric means will always be smaller than arithmetic means if returns are not constant. The arithmetic mean treats an X% decline as identical in impact to an X% increase. But in fact the two do not have an equal effect on portfolio values.

When return variability exists, the arithmetic average will always be larger than the geometric mean and this difference grows as return variability increases.

Use of the Unit Value Series. Unit value series are particularly useful in calculating geometric mean returns for various time periods. Recall that the unit value at any point in time is the compound growth of 1.00 from the base period to that point in time. If the unit value at date T is divided by the unit value at, say, date $T - 2$, the result is the growth of 1.0 from $T - 2$ to T.

For example, assume you are given the following end-of-year unit values:

	Unit Value at End of Year		
	0	10	20
Unit Value	1.0000	2.3674	8.0623

The geometric mean returns over various subperiods are:

Year 0–20: $(8.0623 \div 1.0000)^{1 \div 20} - 1.0 = 0.11$ or 11%

Year 0–10: $(2.3674 \div 1.0000)^{1 \div 10} - 1.0 = 0.09$ or 9%

Year 10–20: $(8.0623 \div 2.3764)^{1 \div 10} - 1.0 = 0.13$ or 13%

Janet N. Tussing, C.F.P.

Vice President
Albanese, Hemsley & Tussing, LTD
University of Iowa, B.A.

Janet Tussing is a principal in her own financial planning and advisory firm. She became interested in financial planning when her work as a paralegal convinced her that many women were not adequately involved in or informed about their financial situations. Today, her company is committed to helping everyone make better financial choices.

Q: What sort of background and training are necessary to become a certified financial planner?

A: The College of Financial Planning offers a program of five courses necessary to become a certified financial planner (CFP). The program has been in existence for about 25 years. Unfortunately, it's not as practical as I would like for it to be. After completing the five-course program and the two-day testing, there still is no requirement for you to write a financial plan. The program is more academic in nature and while I wish there was more emphasis on practicality, I don't want to minimize the importance of the program; it's invaluable. There are also continuing education requirements that are more practical in nature. These programs encourage you to interact with other professionals in a group which might consist of an insurance person, an accountant, and an investment planner. Bringing all these different disciplines together is what I think makes financial planning so valuable and helps financial planners get a better perspective.

Q: Where is the most likely place a newly minted CFP will find a job?

A: Banks and brokerage firms are the major employers. Banks have sponsored many people through the program and have asked that courses be taught on site. Some banks have even set up departments for people with these credentials. In addition, people with other relevant experience and possibly a client base have set up their own businesses. A lot of CPAs find the background helpful for what they do.

Q: How did your business get started?

A: I was a paralegal in the 1970s and felt there were a lot of financial issues women should know that they did not. So a friend and I started teaching classes and there was a huge demand. As this progressed, people asked for more and more advice. I was seeking additional education and became involved with the CFP program. Once I was certified I felt more comfortable giving advice. It was sort of unusual to have this existing client base but it really helped get my business started.

Q: How do you assess a client's needs?

A: The whole process is very goal oriented. People don't call unless they have a need or are really uncomfortable about something. I get people talking about the investments they own. If they haven't done any more than go to a local bank, that tells me a lot. If they own a mutual fund, I'll get the Value Line or Morningstar report and do some research on the fund and also see how knowledgeable the client is about his or her investments. Really, the determination of what a person needs comes directly from the client.

Q: What sort of advice does a planner provide?

A: Financial planners have a more comprehensive perspective. If someone comes in to talk about a lump sum retirement payment, I'm very prepared to talk about the tax consequences as well as the investment potential. We are also very good at the "what-if" questions. We have the background to ask important critical questions and provide a rational, objective perspective on the tough process of determining reasonable long- and short-term financial goals.

My most important job is to provide sound and comprehensive advice. I want to get clients thinking about the implications of the money they are spending, taking into consideration their taxes, savings plans, insurance, etc., and to be very goal oriented.

Q: How do you keep informed?

A: I attend continuing education seminars to keep current with the tax and investment regulations and outlooks. I do a lot of reading on topical subjects. One of the most important but overlooked information sources is the clients themselves. After being in the business 10 to 15 years you learn a lot from the clients, whether it's from their mistakes, good fortunes, or working through their problems and situations.

Q: Do you use software and computer modeling?

A: Yes, but mostly I took the notes from the many courses I taught and turned them into the text for my planning. I use Morningstar to take multiple mutual fund information and put it together in a portfolio and analyze it for asset and industry class allocation. Morningstar will also run hypothetical models for potential savings and investments, but I tend to use it more to analyze where a client is right now.

Q: How is your practice different from the advice a broker might give?

A: Brokers are approaching the problem solely from the side of the investment. I try to look at it from the side of the person. I want to know as much as I possibly can about my clients. If I know the people, then I know what their needs are, what their expectations are, what they're going to feel comfortable with. I don't want them to lose any sleep and I don't want to either.

By using a unit value series in this way, geometric mean returns can be calculated for any intermediate period.

Risk Measurement

The concept of investment risk is easy to understand intuitively. You know how much money you put into financial securities today. There is an uncertainty about how much you will take out at the end of your planned investment horizon. All quantitative measures of risk as well as strategies to control risk are based on this intuitive notion: *Investment risk is uncertainty about the value of the portfolio when it is expected to be liquidated.*

We have three goals in this section:

- The first is to introduce a widely used measure of investment risk: the **standard deviation.** While it is important to have a technical understanding of how standard deviations are calculated, it is more important that you are able to interpret what the term means and apply it to assessing risk. (We can have an intellectual understanding of how an automobile is put together, but unless we can drive it, knowing how it is made is of little use.)

- Our second goal is to examine **historical returns** on a variety of security classes. We do this because it is instructive to understand the levels of risk to which investors have been historically exposed.

- Finally, we introduce two basic ways in which **investment risk can be controlled:** by changes in the portfolio's asset allocation and by broad diversification.

If there is uncertainty today about the value of the portfolio at the date when it is to be liquidated, then this uncertainty can be visually displayed in a probability distribution of portfolio holding period returns. In the next section, we examine a simple type of probability distribution called a discrete distribution.

Discrete Distributions of Future Investment Values

The word *discrete* in the heading here means there are a finite number (a discrete number) of possible outcomes. To help illustrate the use of discrete probability distributions, we employ the following plausible scenario.

The Scenario. Suppose you are a financial planner, the person who provides advice to families on how they might reduce taxes, obtain cost-effective insurance, and invest in financial securities. Roger and Ying, who have savings they wish to invest for one year, will be meeting with you in an hour to discuss alternative investment strategies. They intend to liquidate the investment portfolio after the year has passed and make a down payment on a house. Their total savings are sufficient today to make the minimum required down payment but no more. They have chosen to delay purchase for one year in order to establish themselves in new jobs.

TABLE 5-1   RETURN ESTIMATES FOR THREE ASSET CLASSES

Investment Return If State Occurs

State of Economy	Probability of Occurrence	Money Market	Government Bonds	S&P 500 Stocks
Deep Recession	0.05	6.0%	10.0%	−27.0%
Mild Recession	0.20	3.0%	6.0%	−5.0%
Typical Economy	0.50	2.0%	4.0%	9.0%
Mild Boom	0.20	1.0%	2.0%	23.0%
Strong Boom	0.05	−2.0%	−2.0%	45.0%
	1.00			
Expected Rate of Return		2.0%	4.0%	9.0%
Variance of Return		2.0%	5.2%	208.0%
Standard Deviation		1.4%	2.3%	14.4%

Roger and Ying have asked you to discuss three investment possibilities: (1) a mutual fund that purchases money market securities, (2) a mutual fund that owns long-term government bonds, and (3) a mutual fund that invests in stocks similar to the S&P 500 Index.

You decide any rate of return you show to Roger and Ying should be stated in real return form (after inflation).[7] You also decide that returns on each type of asset will depend on the state of the economy in a year from now. Your best guesses for these returns are shown in Table 5-1.

As a proxy for money market mutual fund returns, you decide to use the one-year return on T-bills. Current nominal returns on one-year U.S. T-bills can be found in the financial press. Assume a 6.0% nominal return is available with no uncertainty. If someone bought $1.00 worth of such securities, they would pay off $1.06 in one year. After inflation is subtracted from the nominal return, however, the real return on T-bills is uncertain. If economic conditions are typical over the next year, inflation will be 4.0%. Thus, you assign a 2.0% (6.0% minus 4.0%) real return on money market securities to the economic state defined as "typical economy." If recessionary conditions arise, the decline in economic activity could cause rates of inflation to decrease, resulting in greater real returns on securities such as T-bills. In contrast, if economic activity accelerated, inflation would increase and real returns on money market securities would be lower.

To proxy a one-year return on government bond mutual funds, you estimate potential one-year returns on long-term Treasury bonds. Promised yields on long-term Treasuries can also be found in the financial press. Assume the present yield to maturity on U.S. Treasury bonds that are not callable for 15 years is 8.0%. Inflation during the next year will affect real returns on these securities in the same manner as with money market se-

---

[7] Since house prices are related to inflation rates, the required down payment will also be tied to inflation. Thus, they will be interested in real rates of return.

curities. In addition, the market values of long-term Treasuries in a year from now will depend on interest rate levels which prevail at that time. As a result, the one-year return that investors in such securities will realize depends on future interest rates. The government bond data in Table 5-1 assumes interest rates will decline if economic activity declines. Decreases in interest rates would cause price increases in long-term bonds, leading to greater realized one-year returns. The opposite results would occur if economic activity accelerates.

Real stock returns are also affected by inflation and changes in interest rates. In addition, stock prices are sensitive to public perceptions of the future profitability of corporations. The one-year stock return data in Table 5-1 assumes stock prices will decline if economic conditions deteriorate. Conversely, if the economy accelerates, stock prices and one-year returns are assumed to be greater than otherwise.

A **probability distribution** is defined as a set of possible outcomes, with a probability assigned to each outcome. The probability distributions shown in Table 5-1 are referred to as **discrete** distributions, meaning there are a finite number of possible outcomes.

The discrete probability distributions in Table 5-1 are displayed graphically in Figure 5-3. Potential returns are shown on the horizontal axis. The probability of a given return is shown on the vertical axis. Notice that the dispersion of returns on stocks is the greatest. It is this dispersion of possible returns that is used as a measure of risk.

Expected Return. If we multiply the probability of a given economic state by the return in that state and then sum these products, we have the weighted average return outcome. This is called the expected rate of return or, symbolically, $E(R)$.

$$\text{Expected Return} = \text{Probability of a State times Return in the State}$$
$$\text{Summed over All States}$$

$$E(R) = \sum_{i=0}^{N} P_i R_i \tag{5.10}$$

Here P_i is the probability of state i, R_i is the return in state i, and there are N possible states. For example, the expected real return on the S&P 500 in our example is equal to 9.0%:

$$E(R) = (0.05)(-27.0) + (0.20)(-5.0) + (0.50)(9.0)$$
$$+ (0.20)(23.0) + (0.05)(45.0)$$
$$= 0.09$$

Variance and Standard Deviation. The expected return is one measure of the midpoint of a return probability distribution. The statistical measures of variance and standard deviation are measures of the dispersion of potential returns.

To calculate the variance of a discrete probability distribution, we use the following procedure:

1. The expected return is subtracted from each possible return outcome. This difference is then squared.

FIGURE 5-3   DISCRETE PROBABILITY DISTRIBUTIONS

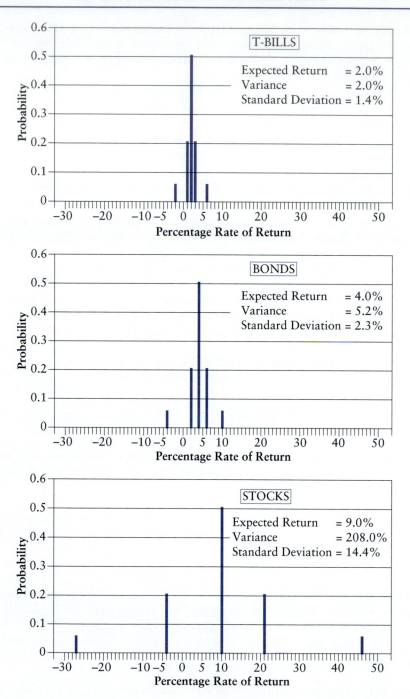

2. Each squared difference is multiplied by the probability of the return outcome.

3. These weighted squared differences are then added.

The variance is simply the weighted average squared deviation from the expected outcome calculated by the following formula:

Variance of Discrete Distribution = Weighted Average Squared Deviation of

Returns from the Expected Return

$$\sigma^2 = \sum_{i=1}^{N} [R_i - E(R)]^2 P_i \tag{5.11}$$

Using the data in Table 5-1 for the S&P 500, its variance is calculated as follows:

$$208.0\% = (-27.0 - 9.0)^2 \, 0.05$$
$$+ (-5.0 - 9.0)^2 \, 0.20$$
$$+ (9.0 - 9.0)^2 \, 0.50$$
$$+ (23.0 - 9.0)^2 \, 0.20$$
$$+ (45.0 - 9.0)^2 \, 0.05$$

The measure of variance is stated in the same units as the expected return (in our example, as a percentage). It is a useful statistic that we refer to often in later chapters. But because it is expressed as a squared average deviation from the mean, people have a difficult time mentally interpreting it. Few people are accustomed to thinking in units of squared returns. To express return dispersion in more easily understood units, the square root of variance is calculated. This is known as the **standard deviation.** The term *standard* can be thought of as standardizing squared return deviations back to a nonsquared value. The standard deviation of a discrete probability return distribution is calculated as follows:

Standard Deviation = Square Root of Variance

$$\sigma = [\sigma^2]^{1 \div 2} \tag{5.12}$$

Thus, the standard deviation of the S&P 500 returns shown in Table 5-1 would be 14.4%:

$$14.4\% = [208.0\%]^{1 \div 2}$$

Back to the Scenario. There are three important aspects to the investment situation facing Roger and Ying: (1) a short investment horizon, (2) the need for a real dollar return, and (3) the fact that their current savings are able to meet a minimum down payment but no more. Each of these distinguishes their investment situation from those of other people and will affect the investment decision they finally make.

In reviewing Table 5-1 and Figure 5-3, Roger and Ying discover their suspicions are correct. Higher expected returns come at the cost of greater uncertainty. In reviewing the information with them, you interpret the data in a variety of ways. For example:

	Mutual Fund Type		
	Money Market	Govt. Bond	S&P 500 Stock
Probability of negative real returns	0.05	0.05	0.25
Probability of a real return equal to or greater than 10%	0.00	0.05	0.25
There is a one-in-four chance that the real return will be this or less	1.0%	2.0%	−5.0%
Expected return	2.0%	4.0%	9.0%
Standard deviation	1.4%	2.3%	14.4%

After some discussion, they exclude the S&P 500 alternative as being too risky. They also exclude the money market alternative as having insufficient expected return. They feel comfortable with the government bond alternative risk and expected return. As they leave your office they say, "You have been very helpful, but we never did understand that standard deviation thing." You reply, "That's okay. It is used mainly by professionals like myself and is more helpful when we deal with continuous return distributions."

Continuous Return Distributions

The scenario just outlined dealt with a discrete probability distribution with only five possible outcomes. In reality, there are an infinite number of possible return outcomes. To reflect this fact, we use continuous distributions.

A special type of continuous distribution is shown in Figure 5-4. It is known as a **standardized normal distribution.** An understanding of how it is interpreted is critical to understanding investment risk.

All normal distributions are symmetric and centered around a mean. In the case of the standardized normal distribution, the mean is zero. In addition, standard normal distributions always have a standard deviation equal to 1.0.

The fact that these distributions are what statisticians call normal distributions means we can find the area between any two points. Unlike a discrete probability distribution, a specific probability is not attached to specific outcomes. (Given the large number of possible returns, the probability of a return equal to a specific value is infinitely small.) Instead, we find the probability of an outcome occurring between two points. This probability represents the area under the standardized normal distribution between the two points.

Consider the standard normal distribution in Figure 5-4. It has a mean of zero and a standard deviation equal to 1.0. The probability of an outcome below the mean is 0.5. Similarly, the probability of an outcome above the mean is also 0.5. The shaded area in the figure represents the area covered by a point one standard deviation below the zero mean and a point one standard deviation above the mean. This area represents about 68% of the total area of the curve.

The number of standard deviations that a point is from the mean of the normal distribution is commonly referred to as a **z-score.** The labels on the horizontal axis of Figure 5-4

FIGURE 5-4 STANDARD NORMAL DISTRIBUTION

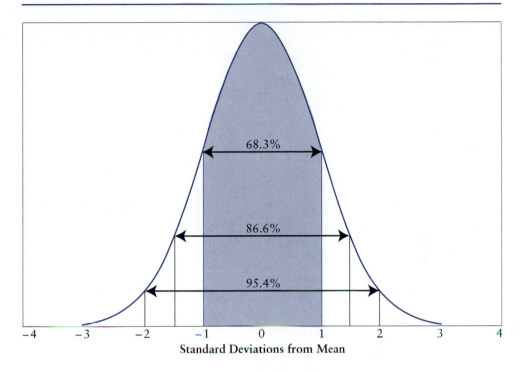

Standard Deviations from Mean

are z-scores. For example, the -2 represents a z-score two standard deviations below the mean of zero and the $+2$ is a z-score two standard deviations above the mean.

When using a normal distribution that does not have a zero mean and standard deviation equal to 1.0, the z-score associated with a particular return is calculated as follows:

$$z\text{-score} = \text{Number of Standard Deviations Away from the Mean}$$

$$= \frac{\text{Return Being Evaluated minus Mean Return}}{\text{Standard Deviation}} \qquad \textbf{(5.13)}$$

The information in Figure 5-5 illustrates another way of interpreting the standard normal distribution. In this case, we focus on the probability of being below a given z-score. In practice, professionals usually concentrate on the probabilities shown below and refer to the analysis as a **percentile distribution.**

PERCENTILE DISTRIBUTION INFORMATION

Probability of an Outcome Below	0.05	0.10	0.25	0.50	0.75	0.90	0.95
Associated Z-score	-1.64	-1.28	-0.67	0.00	$+0.67$	$+1.28$	$+1.64$

FIGURE 5-5 STANDARD NORMAL DISTRIBUTION

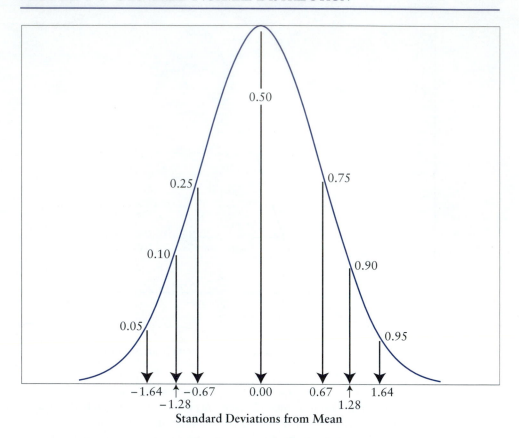

Assume you are evaluating a portfolio that has an expected return of 10% and a standard deviation of yearly returns of 15%. To calculate a percentile distribution of one-year returns for this portfolio you would take the z-score associated with a given percentile and multiply it by the standard deviation of 15%. This would then be added to the expected return of 10%.

For example, if you are interested in the return for which there is a 5% chance of being below, the calculation would be as follows:

$$-1.64\,(15\%) + 10\% = -14.6\%$$

The full percentile distribution given the 10% mean and 15% standard deviation is shown next.

PERCENTILE DISTRIBUTION INFORMATION

Probability of an Outcome Below	0.05	0.10	0.25	0.50	0.75	0.90	0.95
Associated Return	−14.6%	9.2%	−0.05%	10.0%	20.05%	29.2%	34.6%

The data would be interpreted as follows. There is a 5% chance the return during the next year will be lower than negative 14.6%. On the positive side, there is also a 5% chance the return will be greater than 34.6%.

Estimates for Continuous Return Distributions. There are a number of ways in which expected return and standard deviation estimates of a continuous return distribution might be developed. For example, a scenario analysis used to develop a discrete probability distribution could provide estimates of the continuous distribution's expected return and standard deviation. However, historical returns are more commonly used to develop initial estimates. These historical estimates are then subjectively adjusted by the analyst to reflect current market conditions. For example, the analyst might not believe the volatility of bond returns during the 1970s and 1980s will be repeated and thus use a smaller standard deviation than the historical value.

Consider the following hypothetical annual returns:

Year	1	2	3	4
Return	10%	-15%	40%	5%

The arithmetic average return is calculated by adding the returns and the dividing by the number of observations.

Average Return
$$\overline{R} = \left(\sum_{t=1}^{N} R_t \right) \div N \tag{5.14}$$

Applied to this data, the average was 10%:

$$10\% = (10\% - 15\% + 40\% + 5\%) \div 4$$

The variance of the return series is again a weighted average squared deviation from the mean. But now each squared deviation is given an equal weight. To calculate the variance of historical returns, we use the following procedure:

1. The average return is subtracted from each single period return. This difference is then squared.
2. The squared differences are summed.
3. This sum is divided by the number of periods.

Variance of Past Returns = Average Squared Return Deviation

$$\sigma^2 = \left[\sum_{t=1}^{N} (R_t - \overline{R})^2 \right] \div (N) \tag{5.15a}$$

Equation (5.15a) assumes we have no uncertainty about the true mean return; that the true population mean is actually the average return we calculate. In reality, of course, we actually do not know the true mean. Therefore, we actually face two uncertainties: (1) volatility risk and (2) uncertainty about the true mean return.

To account for uncertainty about the mean return, statisticians have shown that Equation (5.15a) should be multiplied by N divided by $(N - 1)$. The net effect of doing so is that the sum in the numerator is divided by N minus 1 instead of by N.

Variance of Past Returns

Adjusted for Uncertain Mean
$$\sigma^2 = \left[\sum (R_t - R)^2 \right] \div (N - 1) \qquad \textbf{(5.15b)}$$

Unless stated otherwise, we use Equation (5.15b) when calculating the variance of past returns. Using our hypothetical return data, the variance is

$$[(10 - 10)^2 + (-15 - 10)^2 + (40 - 10)^2 + (5 - 10)^2] \div (4 - 1) = 517\%$$

As we saw earlier, squared deviations are difficult to interpret. So the square root of variance is calculated, which represents the standard deviation:

$$\sigma = [\sigma^2]^{1 \div 2}$$

$$22.7\% = [517\%]^{1 \div 2}$$

Applied to Past Real S&P 500 Returns. Between 1926 and 1994, the average annual real return on the S&P 500 Index was about 9.0% and the standard deviation was about 20%. The information depicted in Figure 5-6 reflects a continuous distribution based on this data. The shaded area reflects the probability of having a return below 0.0% given the average return of 9.0%. It is found by calculating the number of z-scores that 0.0% is

FIGURE 5-6 CONTINUOUS DISTRIBUTION OF ANNUAL S&P 500 INDEX RETURNS

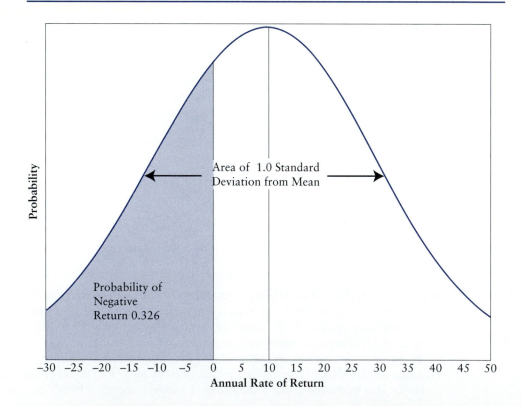

away from the mean and then referring to Appendix A to find the probability associated with such a z-score. The z-score, or number of standard deviations away from the mean, is a negative 0.45 in this example:

$$-0.45 = \frac{0.0\% - 9.0\%}{20\%}$$

The probability associated with a negative 0.45 is 0.3264. This means that, in about one out of every three years investors in the S&P 500 would incur negative real returns.

A Review of Past Returns

Unit values for a variety of security classes are shown in Table 5-2. Returns for the EAFE Index are available only since 1969. A unit value series is also shown for the U.S. Consumer Price Index so that real returns can be calculated. All returns are stated in U.S. dollars. Non-U.S. citizens would have experienced different returns due to changes in currency exchange rates. Finally, these unit values assume that all cash received in the form of interest or dividends was reinvested at no cost.

Looking at Table 5-2, a number of points are immediately obvious. For example, U.S. equities had much larger returns than the U.S. bonds. A dollar invested in T-bills at the start of 1926 and constantly reinvested in new T-bills would have grown to $12.05 by the end of 1994. A similar investment in the S&P 500 would have grown to $811. Notice also that the unit value of the CPI at the end of 1994 was 8.36. A typical good that cost $1.00 at the end of 1925 cost $8.36 by the end of 1994. So the T-bill investor with $12.05 in pocket at the end of 1994 didn't truly fare very well. Such an investor earned an average annual geometric return over this 69-year period of 0.53%.

$$0.0053 = (12.0498 \div 8.3604)^{1 \div 69} - 1.0$$

But stock investors happy with their $811 experienced some trying times during this 69-year period. For example, look at the declines in S&P 500 unit values between 1927 through 1932, 1936 through 1937, and 1972 through 1974.

In Figure 5-7, continuous distributions are shown for real returns on (1) U.S. T-bills, (2) U.S. T-bonds, and (3) the S&P 500. Each distribution is based on the arithmetic average annual real returns and standard deviations over the 1926 through 1994 period. These distributions show visual proof of the historical trade-off between average returns and return volatility.

Assuming that past average real returns and standard deviations can be used to describe the continuous distribution of real security returns, percentile distributions of one-year real returns would be as shown in Table 5-3. During the 1926 through 1994 period, there was a 10% chance that real T-bill returns would be less than a negative 3.7% or greater than positive 4.7%. For the S&P 500 Index, the equivalent values were negative 16.9% and positive 34.8%.

Risk Management

There are two ways of controlling the risk of an investment portfolio: diversification and asset allocation. Diversification works because the return outcomes on different securities are not perfectly correlated. Unexpected good returns on some securities offset unexpected bad

TABLE 5-2   UNIT VALUE SERIES

YEAR	CPI 1.0000	30-day T-Bills 1.0000	L.T. T-Bonds 1.0000	S&P 500 Index 1.0000	Small Company 1.0000	EAFE
1926	0.9851	1.0327	1.0777	1.1161	0.9422	
1927	0.9645	1.0650	1.1740	1.5344	1.1816	
1928	0.9553	1.0994	1.1750	2.2036	1.8124	
1929	0.9573	1.1515	1.2152	2.0183	0.8641	
1930	0.8995	1.1795	1.2717	1.5157	0.4685	
1931	0.8139	1.1924	1.2040	0.8586	0.2260	
1932	0.7301	1.2037	1.4068	0.7882	0.2179	
1933	0.7338	1.2073	1.4058	1.2137	0.5697	
1934	0.7487	1.2095	1.5467	1.1963	0.7479	
1935	0.7711	1.2112	1.6240	1.7665	1.2665	
1936	0.7805	1.2135	1.7458	2.3656	2.1677	
1937	0.8047	1.2170	1.7496	1.5372	0.9945	
1938	0.7823	1.2165	1.8460	2.0159	1.1906	
1939	0.7785	1.2166	1.9559	2.0074	1.1068	
1940	0.7860	1.2164	2.0750	1.8111	0.9692	
1941	0.8624	1.2169	2.0943	1.6014	0.8566	
1942	0.9426	1.2203	2.1617	1.9269	1.2785	
1943	0.9726	1.2246	2.2065	2.4262	2.5680	
1944	0.9932	1.2286	2.2687	2.9049	4.1052	
1945	1.0156	1.2325	2.5121	3.9625	7.4932	
1946	1.2000	1.2370	2.5099	3.6427	6.5319	
1947	1.3081	1.2432	2.4438	3.8504	6.3640	
1948	1.3436	1.2532	2.5264	4.0625	5.9478	
1949	1.3193	1.2673	2.6892	4.8259	7.2087	
1950	1.3956	1.2827	2.6905	6.3576	10.6033	
1951	1.4776	1.3018	2.5845	7.8847	11.5523	
1952	1.4907	1.3233	2.6145	9.3316	12.0606	
1953	1.5003	1.3475	2.7094	9.2401	11.4395	
1954	1.4927	1.3591	2.9039	14.1023	18.7196	
1955	1.4981	1.3805	2.8667	18.5501	22.9165	
1956	1.5410	1.4146	2.7068	19.7670	23.6659	
1957	1.5875	1.4591	2.9090	17.6341	20.3219	
1958	1.6156	1.4814	2.7312	25.2821	34.5228	
1959	1.6400	1.5254	2.6690	28.3108	40.9889	
1960	1.6643	1.5662	3.0370	28.4411	39.2387	
1961	1.6754	1.5994	3.0662	36.0889	51.2261	
1962	1.6957	1.6429	3.2771	32.9383	42.3281	
1963	1.7238	1.6940	3.3168	40.4417	47.9959	
1964	1.7447	1.7538	3.4332	47.1186	57.1823	
1965	1.7784	1.8225	3.4572	52.9849	78.7286	
1966	1.8380	1.9091	3.5831	47.6599	72.5877	
1967	1.8938	1.9893	3.2538	59.0935	145.6763	

TABLE 5-2 (*Continued*)

YEAR	CPI 1.0000	30-day T-Bills 1.0000	L.T. T-Bonds 1.0000	S&P 500 Index 1.0000	Small Company 1.0000	EAFE
1968	1.9832	2.0931	3.2453	65.6410	218.7330	1.0000
1969	2.1042	2.2306	3.0808	60.0681	149.6352	1.0279
1970	2.2195	2.3760	3.4536	62.4889	126.1874	0.9081
1971	2.2941	2.4804	3.9108	71.4373	149.4437	1.1766
1972	2.3725	2.5756	4.1326	84.9961	149.0253	1.6044
1973	2.5808	2.7541	4.0871	72.5271	90.9650	1.3650
1974	2.8957	2.9747	4.2649	53.3365	64.9036	1.0490
1975	3.0987	3.1472	4.6568	73.1830	107.5517	1.4203
1976	3.2480	3.3071	5.4373	90.6371	162.4568	1.4563
1977	3.4679	3.4768	5.4020	84.1293	205.9952	1.7192
1978	3.7811	3.7271	5.3382	89.6566	259.1420	2.2800
1979	4.2847	4.1140	5.2736	106.1714	371.0654	2.3885
1980	4.8165	4.5772	5.0648	140.5815	526.3934	2.9277
1981	5.2471	5.2509	5.1590	133.6790	512.2335	2.8608
1982	5.4501	5.8039	7.2417	162.2997	655.7101	2.8077
1983	5.6572	6.3146	7.2917	198.8333	915.8302	3.4729
1984	5.8847	6.9322	8.4248	211.3002	854.7444	3.7301
1985	6.1065	7.4680	11.0331	279.2754	1065.5243	5.8246
1986	6.1749	7.9273	13.7307	330.8576	1138.5127	9.8688
1987	6.4373	8.3602	13.3600	348.1615	1032.6310	12.2982
1988	6.7206	8.8919	14.6532	406.6874	1268.7938	15.7740
1989	7.0317	9.6370	17.3054	534.7533	1398.0839	17.4367
1990	7.4614	10.4253	18.3784	517.8016	1096.6570	13.3482
1991	7.6897	11.0091	21.9181	675.9900	1586.0950	14.9954
1992	7.9135	11.3757	24.0886	727.8384	1955.1793	13.1693
1993	8.1430	11.7056	28.4812	800.5473	2365.3368	17.4570
1994	8.3604	12.0498	27.5185	811.1145	2438.8988	18.8169

Summary Information for the Period 1929–1994

	CPI	30-day T-Bills	L.T. T-Bonds	S&P 500 Index	Small Company	EAFE
Arithmetic Mean	3.23%	3.72%	5.25%	12.16%	18.29%	
Geometric Mean	3.13%	3.67%	4.92%	10.19%	11.97%	
Standard Deviation	4.57%	3.28%	8.62%	20.20%	38.74%	

Summary Information for the Period 1969–1994

	CPI	30-day T-Bills	L.T. T-Bonds	S&P 500 Index	Small Company	EAFE
Arithmetic Mean	5.74%	7.00%	9.13%	11.34%	13.14%	14.15%
Geometric Mean	5.69%	6.96%	8.57%	10.15%	9.72%	11.95%
Standard Deviation	3.18%	2.74%	11.32%	15.78%	26.73%	22.50%

FIGURE 5-7 CONTINUOUS DISTRIBUTIONS OF ANNUAL SECURITY RETURNS

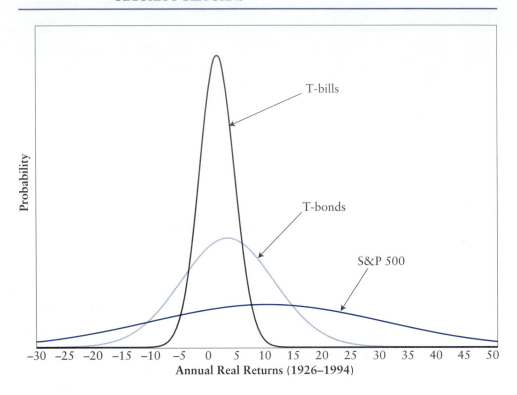

Annual Real Returns (1926–1994)

TABLE 5-3 PERCENTILE REAL RETURN DISTRIBUTIONS BASED ON PAST ANNUAL REAL RETURNS

	Percentile: Probability of This Return or Less				
	0.10	0.25	0.50	0.75	0.90
U.S. T-Bills	−3.7%	−1.7%	0.49%	2.7%	4.7%
Long-Term Treasuries	−9.0%	−3.8%	2.0%	7.8%	13.1%
S&P 500 Index	−16.9%	−4.6%	8.9%	22.5%	34.8%

returns on other securities. Consider the following experiment. You have a basket containing 500 sheets of paper. On each sheet is the name of one company in the S&P 500 Index. The average return and standard deviation on each stock are different. But assume the grand average of the stock's average yearly return is 9.0% and the grand average of their yearly return standard deviation is 40%. You are asked to select one sheet at random. Before you select, what average return and standard deviation do you expect to draw? Clearly, 9% and 40%! And if many people had their own baskets and selected one sheet, the average result across all individuals would be an average return equal to 9% and a standard deviation equal to 40%.

These numbers of 9% and 40% are close to the average annual real return and standard deviation for individual stocks in the S&P 500 Index. But we know from work in this chapter that the equivalent data for the aggregate S&P 500 Index between 1926 and 1994 were 9% and 20%. The risk of a single stock was about double the risk of the aggregate portfolio!

The concept of diversification is displayed graphically in panel A of Figure 5-8. Notice, however, that diversification across securities cannot totally eliminate investment risk.

FIGURE 5-8 CONTROLLING INVESTMENT RISK

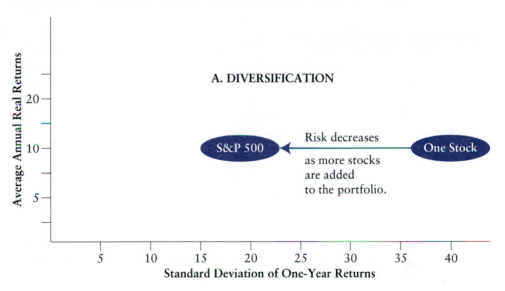

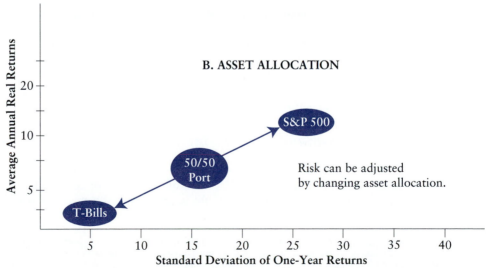

This nondiversifiable risk is referred to as **systematic risk** and it plays an important role in asset pricing models such as the capital asset pricing model (CAPM).

Now consider panel B of Figure 5-8. This panel illustrates how risk can be altered by changing a portfolio's asset allocation. The standard deviation and average of yearly real returns are shown for two asset classes: the S&P 500 and U.S. T-bills. If the S&P is too risky for an investor but the average returns on T-bills too low, a compromise can be achieved by holding some combination of the two. For example, the 50/50 portfolio shown consists of 50% invested in T-bills and 50% invested in the S&P 500. This 50/50 portfolio would have a risk and average return halfway between T-bills and the S&P 500.

> One of the most important principles of investing is that diversification and asset allocation drive the risk and average returns of the portfolio.

The Investment Horizon

We turn now to a discussion of how investment risk and investment strategy are affected by the length of an investor's time horizon. These are important issues to investors, too often misunderstood. Unless students of investment have a good grasp of how longer investment horizons affect potential portfolio payoffs and investment strategy, they are likely to give poor advice to future employers.

Up to this point we have considered investment returns and risk mainly over annual holding periods. But most investments are made with a longer horizon in mind. For example, in the mid-1990s about 30% of the value of U.S. equities was owned by pension funds that typically have investment horizons of more than 20 years. In addition, a large portion of the money invested in mutual funds represents personal retirement savings as well as retirement savings through employer-defined contribution pension plans.[8] In fact, many investment professionals believe no money should be invested in equities unless the investment horizon associated with the investment objective is long term in nature.

In this section, we focus on the following two topics:

◼ how the investment horizon affects portfolio uncertainty, and

◼ how the investment horizon affects the asset allocation an investor chooses.

Our objective is to develop an intuitive understanding of both issues and the investment implications that arise. Appendix 5A presents details of the mathematical procedures used in developing multiperiod percentile return distributions.

Portfolio Uncertainty and the Investment Horizon

Investment risk is uncertainty about the value of a portfolio when it is to be liquidated. Although most investment programs consist of a sequence of contributions to a portfolio followed by a sequence of withdrawals, the issues discussed in this section are easier to un-

---

[8] Much of the money invested into employer-sponsored defined contribution plans is given to investment advisers who manage a "family" of mutual funds. The advantages of using mutual fund families consist of low cost, the ability to diversify across a number of funds, and ease of transacting. In addition, the investor can follow the progress of the fund by looking at mutual fund quotes in the financial press.

derstand if we assume a single initial investment followed by a single liquidation date some number of periods later. A period of time is denoted by the letter t. For example, $t = 2$ refers to period 2. The initial investment is made at the start of period $t = 1$ and the liquidation occurs at the end of period $t = T$. For clarity of interpretation, the length of each period of time is assumed to be a year. Thus, *investment risk is uncertainty about the value of a portfolio when it is to be liquidated in T years from today.*

Let's begin by considering the multiperiod risk of an investment that will have either a positive return of 33 1/3% or a negative return of 25% in any given year. Assume returns in any year are independent of prior year returns. Which investor faces the greater uncertainty in owning this investment, an investor with a one-year investment horizon or an investor with a three-year investment horizon? Given that investment risk represents uncertainty about the value of the portfolio when it is to be liquidated, the three-year investor clearly faces the greater uncertainty.

Possible outcomes on this investment are shown in Figure 5-9. The one-year investor faces terminal wealth outcomes that range from $0.75 to $1.33. In contrast, the three-period investor's terminal wealth outcomes range from $0.42 to $2.37.

This demonstrates that **increases in the investment horizon result in increased uncertainty.**

Holding Period Returns. A **holding period return** (HPR) represents the increase in the value of a portfolio over a specified holding period, usually expressed as a certain

FIGURE 5-9   MULTIPERIOD OUTCOMES ON AN INVESTMENT THAT CAN RETURN +33 1/3% OR −25% IN A PERIOD

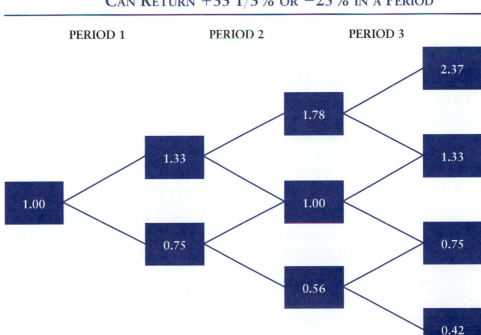

number of years. For example, if you made a single investment of $1.00 ten years ago and it is presently worth $2.37, then your ten-year HPR is 137%. Earlier in the chapter, we discussed unit value series that represent the future value of an initial investment of $1.00. Holding period returns are simply the unit value minus 1.0 (the initial investment). If a unit value is equal to 2.37, the HPR is 1.37 or 137%.

People are not accustomed to thinking in terms of returns over, say, a 10-year or 20-year period. As a result, HPRs (over periods longer than a year) are usually annualized. This is done by calculating the annual geometric mean return associated with the holding period return. We illustrate such calculations later. But a possible misinterpretation of how investment risk is related to the investment horizon arises if we use geometric returns to express the outcomes of a given investment portfolio. This misinterpretation does not occur when holding period returns are used. Thus, we focus on the risk of holding period returns.

Simple intuition suggests that investment risk should increase as the intended holding period increases.[9] *If investing for one period of time involves risk, then investing for N periods should have N times as much risk.* In fact, when returns are uncorrelated over time, the variance of an N-period holding period return is equal to N times the variance of a one-period return. Denoting $\sigma^2(N)$ as the variance of the N-period return and $\sigma^2(1)$ as the variance of the 1-period return, then the following relationships are true:[10]

Variance of N-Period Return $\sigma^2(N) = N \, \sigma^2(1)$ **(5.16a)**

Standard Deviation of N-Period Return $\sigma(N) = \sqrt{N} \, \sigma(1)$ **(5.16b)**

For example, assume you believe the variance of annual returns on a portfolio consisting of large U.S. stocks (as proxied by the S&P 500 Index) is 0.04 (a standard deviation of 20%). Then the variance and standard deviation of an investment held in this portfolio for holding periods of 10 or 20 years would be as follows:

	Holding Period Return	
Investment Horizon	Variance	Standard Deviation
10 years	10 times 0.04 = 0.40	$\sqrt{10}$ times 0.20 = 0.6324
20 years	20 times 0.04 = 0.80	$\sqrt{20}$ times 0.20 = 0.8944

Holding Period Returns for T-Bills and Stocks. To illustrate the effect of the length of the holding period on the distribution of holding period returns, let's consider two portfolios that differ considerably in one-year risk. Two logical choices are U.S. T-bills and U.S. stocks as proxied by the S&P 500 Index.

In Figure 5-10, continuous distributions of T-bills and the S&P 500 Index are shown for three different holding periods. Each panel shows real (after inflation) HPRs based on annual returns between 1926 and 1994. In the top panel, the holding period is assumed to be one year. The middle panel assumes a 10-year holding period, and the bottom panel

---

[9] The key assumption in the analysis presented here is that returns from period to period are independent. If returns are positively correlated, risk grows faster than discussed in the text. If returns are negatively correlated, risk grows slower. The case of negative correlation is discussed later.

[10] Technical details are discussed in Appendix A.

FIGURE 5-10a DISTRIBUTIONS OF ONE-YEAR RETURNS ON T-BILLS AND THE S&P 500

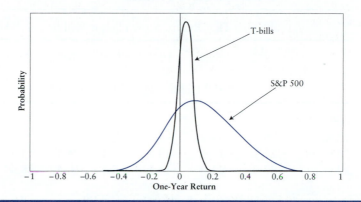

FIGURE 5-10b DISTRIBUTIONS OF TEN-YEAR RETURNS ON T-BILLS AND THE S&P 500

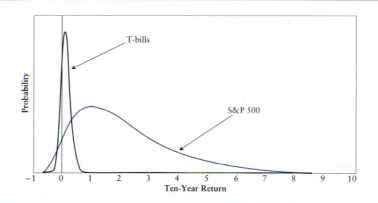

FIGURE 5-10c DISTRIBUTIONS OF TWENTY-YEAR RETURNS ON T-BILLS AND THE S&P 500

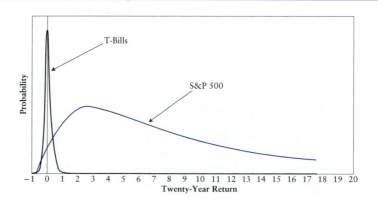

TABLE 5-4 PERCENTILE DISTRIBUTIONS FOR VARIOUS INVESTMENT HORIZONS

Probability That Return Shown Below Will Be Less Than the Return

	1%	5%	10%	25%	50%	75%	90%	95%	99%
T-Bill Holding Period Returns (in Percentages)									
Holding Period									
1 year	−9.5	−6.7	−5.2	−2.6	0.4	3.5	6.3	8.0	11.4
10 years	−25.1	−17.5	−13.1	−5.4	4.1	14.4	24.7	31.2	44.5
20 years	−32.0	−22.0	−16.1	−5.3	10.5	28.4	39.8	50.3	72.3
S&P 500 Index Holding Period Returns (in Percentages)									
Holding Period									
1 year	−32.1	−22.0	−16.0	−5.0	8.9	24.9	41.3	52.1	74.8
10 years	−47.3	−18.2	3.3	52.6	135	262	435	576	950
20 years	−33	24.3	72.8	200	453	920	1,671	2,363	4,488

assumes a 20-year holding period. In Table 5-4, percentile distributions are shown for the same data.

A long look at both the figure and table is well worth the time. Notice the following:.

■ **Uncertainty about the value of a portfolio increases as the investment horizon increases.** Ninety-eight percent of the S&P one-year return distribution is between negative 32% and positive 75%. In contrast, 98% of the 20-year HPR distribution is between a negative 33% to more than 4,000%!

■ **The distributions of holding period returns are skewed to the right.** This fact is actually the result of an assumption in the forecasting model that portfolio values can not be lower than zero (holding period returns can not exceed a negative 100%). The assumption makes perfect economic sense. While each of the distributions shown in Figure 5-10 and Table 5-4 have positive skewness, the effect of this skewness is most dominant in long holding periods for the more risky S&P 500 Index. Investors who have long investment horizons should be aware of this skewness. There is a small chance of winning very big.

■ **The probability of a loss decreases as the investment horizon increases.** In Figure 5-10, the probability of a loss is the area of a given distribution that is to the left of a zero HPR. Although the variability of holding period returns increases as the holding period increases, so too does the expected holding period return.

FIGURE 5-11 SHORTFALL RISK: T-BILLS VS. U.S. STOCKS

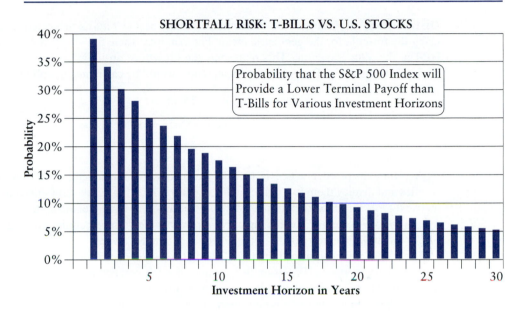

SHORTFALL RISK: T-BILLS VS. U.S. STOCKS

Probability that the S&P 500 Index will Provide a Lower Terminal Payoff than T-Bills for Various Investment Horizons

Investment Horizon in Years

■ **The probability that the more risky portfolio will have a lower rate of return than the less risky portfolio decreases as the investment horizon increases.** The chance that a more risky portfolio will have a lower holding period return than the less risky portfolio is called **shortfall risk.**

The extent of shortfall risk in this example is displayed in Figure 5-11.[11] If the investment horizon is one year, there is about a 39% chance the S&P 500 will have a worse holding period return than T-bills. If the investment horizon is 20 years, the probability of a shortfall in the S&P 500 drops to less than 10%.

But even though shortfall risk declines as the holding period increases, this does not necessarily mean long-term investors should favor the more risky portfolio. Although the probability of a loss decreases with time, the size of the possible loss also increases with time.

Thus far we have carefully avoided an observation about the data in Figure 5-10 and Table 5-4, which may be the first thing you noticed. The more risky portfolio appears to dominate the less risky portfolio over long investment horizons. In the panel that displays one-year returns, the S&P 500 Index seems to provide a little more return for a lot more possible variability. But in the long-horizon panels, the risk of the S&P 500 Index appears to be "good" uncertainty in that the S&P 500 generally has higher holding period returns than T-bills. Is it true that long-term investors should favor the more risky alternative whereas short-term investors should favor the less risky portfolio? This is a

---

[11] Figure 5-11 is based on the same assumptions underlying Figure 5-10 and Table 5-4 plus an assumption about the correlation between S&P 500 and T-bill annual returns. The assumption was a zero correlation. Shortfall risk is clearly a function of the assumptions one makes.

topic best left for our discussion of how the investment horizon influences the asset allocation decision.

Distribution of Geometric Returns. Holding period returns are often annualized using the formula for the geometric mean. For example, Table 5-4 shows a 453% 20-year HPR at the 50th percentile. This represents the growth of an initial $1.00 investment to $5.53 (1.0 plus 4.53). The geometric mean return would be calculated as follows:

$$\$1.00 \, (1.0 + G)^{20} = \$5.53$$

$$G = (\$5.53 \div \$1.00)^{1 \div 20} - 1.0$$

$$= 0.0893$$

A commonly used practice is to calculate geometric mean returns for various percentiles and display them in a figure such as Figure 5-12. This figure shows percentile geometric returns for the S&P 500 Index data used earlier. For example, the bottom curve represents the 5th percentile and the top curve represents the 95th percentile. The heavy black line in the middle represents the 50th percentile geometric means.

The visual implication of Figure 5-12 is that investment risk decreases as the investment horizon increases. For example, consider the 5th percentile curve at the bottom of the figure. There is a 5% chance that a one-year investor would incur a return less than a negative 22%. For a 20-year investor there is a 5% chance of incurring an annualized geometric return of less than a positive 1%.

Exhibits such as Figure 5-11 certainly make it look like long-term investors face less risk than do short-term investors. And there is a fairly compelling story that is told to

FIGURE 5-12 Geometric Return Percentiles: S&P 500 Index

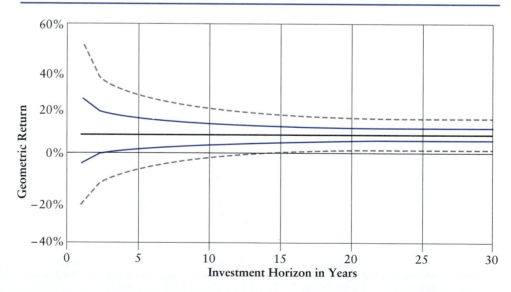

explain why the distribution of geometric returns narrows as the investment horizon lengthens: time diversification. The belief is that good years offset bad years, resulting in less variable **average** returns.

This is true. For example, assume you have a sequence of 50 past annual rates of return on a stock index. The series would have considerable volatility from year to year. Using this series you create a new series. The first observation in the new series is the arithmetic average return from year 1 through year 5. The second is the arithmetic average from year 2 through year 6. In other words, the new series of returns is a moving average of returns over the most recent five-year period. Would the moving average series show less variability than the series of annual returns? Certainly. Does this mean long-term investors face less risk than short-term investors? No.

The problem with using either geometric or arithmetic average return distributions to assess investment risk is that both variables are simply the result of a mathematical calculation. You can not purchase goods with a geometric return. Goods are purchased with cash. Portfolio risk is the uncertainty about the **value** of a portfolio when it is to be liquidated. And this uncertainty increases as the investment horizon increases.

Asset Allocation and the Investment Horizon

In this section, we explore the relationship between the length of the investment horizon and the investor's asset allocation decision.

Assume you have $10,000 to invest today and the investment horizon is one year.[12] At the end of the year, the investment will be liquidated and the proceeds used to make a down payment on a house. (A down payment of about $10,000 will be barely sufficient to purchase the type of house you wish.) Look back at the one-year holding period distributions shown in Figure 5-10 and Table 5-4. Would you place the investment in T-bills, the S&P 500 Index, or some combination of the two? Call this decision asset allocation 1.

A year passes and you are settled in your new house. Unexpectedly, you receive a job bonus of $10,000 and decide to invest this second $10,000 for future retirement income that will be 20 or more years into the future. Look at the 20-year holding period distributions shown in Figure 5-10 and Table 5-4. Would you place the investment in T-bills, the S&P 500 Index, or some combination of the two? Call this decision asset allocation 2.

The question we address in this section is whether asset allocation 1 will be identical to asset allocation 2 and, if not, why.

There is a popular belief that long-term investors should bear more investment risk than short-term investors. While there may be a lot of truth to this belief, the popular rationale is that long-term investors face less investment risk than do short-term investors. As shown here, this is not true. If there is a relationship between the investment horizon and asset allocation, it must be due to something else.

---

[12] This $10,000 represents your total savings.

The asset allocation decision could be related to the length of the investment horizon for either of two principal reasons:

1. differences in the distributions of investment payoffs faced by short-term and long-term investors, and
2. differences in the willingness of short-term and long-term investors to accept risk.

Differences in Payoff Distributions. A comparison of the T-bill and S&P 500 distributions shown in Figure 5-10 suggests that the relationship between the two distributions changes considerably as the investment horizon lengthens. Specifically, the 20-year S&P 500 distribution appears to dominate the 20-year T-bill distribution. In large part this is caused by the increased positive skewness of the riskier portfolio.

Some investors will undoubtedly find the larger positive skewness associated with long-term payoffs from risky investment attractive and will invest more in risky assets than they would if they had a shorter investment horizon. But this will not be true for everyone. Some investors will be so risk-averse that changes in their investment horizon will have no effect on the asset allocation they choose.

While changes in the nature of the distributions that occur as the investment horizon changes might cause some investors to tie their asset allocation to their investment horizon, we should not generalize this to all investors.

What we can say, however, is that investors should be given full information about the HPR distributions of portfolios of varying risks. One-year return distributions do not provide sufficient information to investors with considerably longer investment horizons.

Differences in Willingness to Accept Risk. In general, the longer the investment horizon, the greater the ability and willingness to accept risk. There are two basic reasons for this:

◄ **Long-term investors have opportunities not available to short-term investors.** For example, young individuals saving for retirement have the opportunity to work longer hours if their investment portfolio does poorly. Individuals in retirement do not have this opportunity. Institutions such as pension funds can accept risk because they have many years to increase contributions to the portfolio if returns are below expectations. Institutions such as an endowment fund created to pay for a new medical building will take little risk, since a specified amount of money is needed in a short period of time.

We began this section with the question about why asset allocation 1 (for a down payment on a house) and asset allocation 2 (retirement savings) might differ. The most likely reason is the difference in the ability to offset the investment risk with other actions. Long-term investors are able to be more risk tolerant.

◄ **The portion of one's wealth that is held in securities is usually smaller for long-term investors.** When people are young, a large fraction of their wealth represents the present value of future income. Wealth held in securities is usually a smaller fraction. Assuming the risk inherent in future income is less than the risk of equities, then they might be willing to accept large risk in their security portfolio. However, when people enter retirement, the fraction of wealth held in securities is usually quite large; a security risk that was acceptable when they were younger is no longer appropriate.

Even if a person's risk tolerance is not related to his or her investment horizon, the components of the person's wealth changes over time. This can result in levels of security risk that are directly related to the length of the investment horizon.

The key point here is that there are valid reasons for long-term investors to bear more investment risk than short-term investors. But the notion that investment risk decreases as the investment horizon increases is not one of these reasons. In fact, it is wrong.

Effects of Return Correlation. The discussion here is based on a fundamental assumption that returns are uncorrelated from year to year. Because of this assumption, the variance of holding period returns is equal to the number of periods, N, times the variance of a single period, $\sigma^2(1)$. Risk grows linearly with the investment horizon.

Some asset classes, however, have positively correlated returns. T-bills are a prime example. A large part of the return on T-bills is compensation for expected inflation. High inflation rates tend to be followed by high rates and low inflation rates tend to be followed by low rates. This causes Treasury bill returns to have positive correlation from period to period. If returns are positively correlated, investment risk grows more rapidly than suggested in the chapter. Thus, the risk of long horizon investment in T-bills shown in Figure 5-10 is biased downward.

Recent research has suggested that three- to five-year holding period returns on stocks might be negatively correlated. If stock returns are negatively correlated over long investment horizons, then the long-term risk of owning stock would be less than suggested in this chapter. It would also provide another reason for there to be a direct tie between the investment horizon and a portfolio's asset allocation. Care should be given to this issue, however, since there has been little research over time periods of ten years or more.

S U M M A R Y

This chapter provided an introduction to basic investment principles. Here are the key concepts:

- The risk-free interest rate that prevails in financial markets is determined by economic forces in the real goods market. In theory, the risk-free rate of interest is determined by the marginal thriftiness of a society and the marginal productivity of real investment. We defined this as the pure rate of interest.

- Returns on most financial securities are directly tied to future inflation. Thus, investors will adjust the price they are willing to pay for a security to compensate for expected future inflation. The relationship that should exist between nominal interest rates, pure rates, and inflation expectations is known as the Fisher equation. It states that the nominal interest rate is equal to the pure real rate compounded by expected inflation. The Fisher equation is useful in explaining why fixed-income securities trade at different yields to maturity.

◼ We then examined the differences between geometric return averages and arithmetic return averages. For long-term investors, geometric averages communicate better the realized returns they might expect. Arithmetic averages are more appropriate for shorter term investors. The concept of a unit value series was shown to be a convenient way to display historical security returns.

◼ Investment risk involves the uncertainty of future portfolio values. This uncertainty can be captured by the statistical measures of variance and standard deviation. Variance is the weighted average squared deviation from the mean, and standard deviation is the square root of variance.

◼ Assuming a continuous return distribution can be described as a continuous normal distribution, the mean and standard deviation can be used to calculate the probability that a return will occur within a given return interval. This fact can be used to create percentile return distributions, which are useful devices in explaining the degree of investment risk to people who do not understand standard deviation.

◼ Investment risk can be controlled through diversification and asset allocation. These are major topics in the next few chapters.

◼ We concluded the chapter with a discussion of how the length of the investment horizon affects investment risk. Contrary to popular belief, investment risk is positively tied to the investment horizon. However, there are various reasons why long-term investors would be willing to accept greater risks than would short-term investors.

R E V I E W   P R O B L E M

You are given the following set of returns:

Year	1	2	3	4
Return	25%	10%	−30%	15%

a. Find the average, variance, and standard deviation. (Round to the nearest percentage.)
b. Use these as estimates for a continuous normal distribution to calculate the probability of a return below negative 10%, 0%, and 5%.

Solution

a. Average = $(25 + 10 - 30 + 15) \div 4$
   = 5%

   Variance = $[(25 - 5)^2 + (10 - 5)^2 + (-30 - 5)^2 + (15 - 5)^2] \div (4 - 1)$
   = 583%

   Standard Deviation = $[583]^{1 \div 2}$
   = 24%

b. Refer to Appendix for values of z-scores:

Return	z-scores	Probability of being below
−10%	$(-10 - 5) \div 24$ $= -0.62$	0.2676
−0%	$(0 - -5) \div 24$ $= -0.21$	0.4168
5%	zero	0.50

Q U E S T I O N S   A N D   P R O B L E M S

1. What are the economic determinants of the real risk-free rate of interest?

2. You wish to earn a real return of 3% per year on various investments. These investments are in default-free zero-coupon Treasury bonds that pay $100 at their maturities. Maturities range from end-of-year 1 through end-of-year 4. Your inflation forecast for the next four years are as follows:

Year	1	2	3	4
Inflation	4%	6%	8%	5%

   a. Using the Fisher equation, what nominal (annualized) return would you require on each of the four issues?
   b. Using the approximate Fisher equation, what nominal (annualized) return would you require on each of the four issues?
   c. Using the answer to part a, what price would you pay for each investment?

3. Why might fixed income securities that are identical, except in maturity, trade at different promised returns?

4. You purchase a one-year T-bill at 90% of par. During the year the inflation rate is 5%. What is your real rate of return?

5. In August 1995, representative yields to maturity on government bonds of different countries were as follows:

Country	Yield to Maturity	Country	Yield to Maturity
Australia	9.07%	Netherlands	6.70%
Germany	6.66%	Sweden	10.18%
Italy	11.2%	U.K.	8.00%
Japan	3.07%	U.S.	6.93%

   a. Assuming the pure rate of interest is 2%, what should be the expected inflation in Italy and Japan?
   b. You strongly believe inflation in the United States and United Kingdom will average 4.83% and 3.85%, respectively. In which country would you earn the better return?

6. What are the differences between required returns, expected returns, promised returns, and realized returns?

7. On June 1 you purchased 100 shares of a mutual fund at a net asset value (NAV) of $20 per share. On June 10, a $1.00 dividend per share was paid by the fund (after which its NAV was $25). You reinvested your $100 into four new shares of the fund. On June 20, you buy an additional 100 shares at a NAV of $27 per share. On June 30, the shares are worth $22.

    a. What was the time weighted return of the fund during June?
    b. What was your dollar weighted return?
    c. Explain why the two return numbers differ.
    d. Which rate of return number is the correct one?

8. You are an analyst for Global Equity Mutual Fund. During the past five years, returns on the fund have been as follows:

Year	1	2	3	4	5
Return	−20%	30%	5%	15%	−4%

    a. What was the arithmetic average yearly return?
    b. What was the geometric average yearly return?
    c. Why do the two differ?
    d. Create a unit value series starting at 1.0.
    e. Use this unit value series to calculate the geometric average return between the end of year 2 to the end of year 5.
    f. Calculate the variance and standard deviations of annual returns.

9. You plan to invest for only one year. What types of risks do you face from the following security types:
    a. One-year maturity T-bills?
    b. One-year maturity commercial paper?
    c. Twenty-year maturity Treasury bonds?
    d. Common stocks?

10. Why might future inflation not be a concern to some investors?

11. Sandi Weston is a financial planner. To aid her clients in their investment selections, she has developed the following scenario analysis for returns on various security classes based on potential economic states:

Economic State in One Year	Probability	Real Investment Return If State Occurs		
		T-Bills	Corporate Bonds	S&P 500 Stocks
Poor	0.2	5.0%	8.0%	−15.0%
Normal	0.6	3.0%	5.0%	10.0%
Good	0.2	1.0%	0.0%	35.0%

Calculate the expected return, variance, and standard deviation for each investment.

12. Between 1926 and 1994, the average annual nominal return on an index of small capitalization stocks was about 20%. The standard deviation was about 40%. Using these values as the mean and standard deviation of a continuous distribution, prepare the following percentile distribution:

Percentile							
Return	0.05	0.10	0.25	0.50	0.75	0.90	0.95

CFA

13. Johanne Smythe, CFA, is reviewing an article about the relationship between holding period and standard deviation of return. Smythe knows the standard deviation of total holding period return, as a proxy for risk, should *increase* as the length of the holding period increases. However, a table in the article (shown here) suggests that standard deviation of average annual return decreases as the number of annual holding periods increases. In the article, this table was used to support the claim that, as the number of annual holding

periods increases, the standard deviation of the stock returns decreases to about the same standard deviation of annualized return as Treasury bills. Therefore, the article concluded, the longer the time period, the less risky stocks become.

STANDARD DEVIATION OF AVERAGE ANNUALIZED RETURNS

Horizon in Year	Standard Deviation
1	21.75
2	14.47
3	11.55
4	9.43
5	6.72
10	4.61

In terms of total holding period return, explain why the article is incorrect when it concludes that risk decreases over time.

14. An analyst estimates that a stock has the following probabilities of return depending on the state of the economy.

State of Economy	Probability	Return
Good	0.10	15%
Normal	0.60	13
Poor	0.30	7

The expected return of the stock is:
a. 7.8%
b. 11.4%
c. 11.7%
d. 13.0%

15. A portfolio realized a 10% return in year 1 and a −10% return in year 2. The geometric mean return over the two-year period is:
a. −0.50%
b. 0.00%
c. 0.99%
d. 0.995%

16. The population variance for the data, 1, 3, 5, 7, is:
a. 2.0
b. 2.2
c. 5.0
d. 5.3

17. Given a data series that is normally distributed with a mean of 100 and a standard deviation of 10, about 95% of the numbers in the series will fall within:
a. 60 to 140
b. 70 to 130
c. 80 to 120
d. 90 to 110

DATAFILE ANALYSIS

In this analysis, you should use the index return series (monthly, quarterly, or annual) in the data set called INDEXES.WK3.

1. **Diversification Across Asset Classes.** Access one of the index return files and identify the return series for the S&P 500 and the EAFE index. EAFE returns begin in 1969. In a blank column of the worksheet, calculate the periodic returns available from a portfolio in which 25% is invested in the EAFE index at the start of each period and 75% is invested in the S&P 500. Find the average and standard deviation of this return series. Repeat this exercise for portfolio mixes of 100/0, 50/50, 25/75, and 0/100. What important investment principles do the results document?

2. **Risk and Asset Allocation.** Repeat the analysis above, but this time assume portfolios consist of combinations of U.S. T-bills and the S&P 500. What important investment principle do the results document?

3. **Unit Value and Geometric Means.** Use the U.S. T-bill and S&P 500 return data to calculate unit value series (using a base value of 1.00) starting in 1926 and ending in 1994. Interpret the results (notice how much larger the S&P 500 unit value is in 1994 than is true for T-bills). Calculate the arithmetic and geometric average returns. Why do they differ substantially for the S&P 500 but not as dramatically for T-bills?

4. **Risk and the Time Horizon.** Find the annual return series on the S&P 500 Index. Calculate the standard deviation of these annual returns. (Hint: Use the spreadsheet function for the standard deviation.) Next, starting in 1930, find the average yearly return for the years 1926 through 1930. Copy this calculation to 1931 through 1994. Find the standard deviation of the five-year average return series. Notice the moving average series has the smaller standard deviation. Does this prove that investment risk decreases as the investment horizon increases?

REFERENCES

The definitive guide to calculating (and reporting) investment returns is *Performance Presentation Standards*, Association for Investment Management and Research, Charlottesville, VA, 1993.

A classic work on the relationship between expected inflation and nominal interest rates is Irving Fisher, *The Theory of Interest: As Determined by Impatience to Spend Income and Opportunity to Invest It*, New York: Augustus M. Kelley, 1965 (published originally in 1930).

More recent discussion of interest rates include the following:

Fama, Eugene. "Short-Term Interest Rates as Predictors of Inflation," *American Economic Review*, June 1975.

Feldstein, Martin and Otto Eckstein, "The Fundamental Determinants of the Interest Rate," *The Review of Economics and Statistics*, November 1970.

Rose, A. "Is the Real Interest Rate Stable?" *Journal of Finance*, December 1988.

Interesting studies of the power of diversification include the following:

Brennan, Michael J. "The Optimal Number of Securities in a Risky Asset Portfolio Where There Are Fixed Costs of Transacting: Theory and Some Empirical Results," *Journal of Financial and Quantitative Analysis*, September 1975.

Evans, John L. and Stephen H. Archer, "Diversification and the Reduction of Dispersion: An Empirical Analysis," *Journal of Finance*, March 1978.

Statman, Meir. "How Many Stocks Make a Diversified Portfolio?" *Journal of Financial and Quantitative Analysis*, September 1987.

A P P E N D I X   5 A

EXTRAPOLATING INVESTMENT RISK

The situation we address is the following. An initial investment of $1.00 is made at the beginning of year 1. This investment is placed in a portfolio that has a constant risk and expected return. For example, if the portfolio consists of 60% invested in equities and 40% invested in T-bills, then the mix is always maintained at 60/40. If the stocks earn a higher return than the T-bills in a given period, then some of the stock is sold and transferred to T-bills in order to keep a constant risk exposure. (This, of course, assumes the risk of equities and T-bills does not change over time.)

In each future year, a return is earned on the portfolio that depends on the portfolio's expected return and standard deviation. We assume that returns drawn in one year are unrelated to any future returns. This is an assumption that could be dropped, but it makes calculations easier and is often characteristic of actual return outcomes.

The question we examine is, *If all profits are reinvested, what is the distribution of terminal wealth after N years?*

To answer this question, we need to use a slightly different measure of return than discussed previously, a continuous compound return. The rate of return we have used in this chapter implicitly assumes all compounding occurs at the end of the period in which the return is measured. In contrast, the continuous compound return assumes earnings are compounded continuously.

We need to use continuous compound returns for two reasons:

1. If we use end-of-period compounding and assume such returns are normally distributed, there is the possibility that negative future terminal wealth will be forecast. This, of course, is not possible in reality. The smallest a portfolio value can be is zero. When continuous compound returns are used, terminal wealth can never be below zero.

   When we assume continuous compound returns are normally distributed, we are also assuming terminal wealth is log normally distributed. This simply means that terminal wealth is bounded by a lower value of zero but not bounded on the upside.

2. The use of continuous returns actually makes it easier to calculate terminal wealth percentile distributions for investment horizons longer than a single period.

   Define R_t as the end of period compound return in period t and r_t as the continuous compound return in t. Also define TW_T as the terminal wealth after T periods (years perhaps) from investing $1 at date 0. The following mathematical relationships exist between these variables:

$$r_t = \ln (1 + R_t) \tag{5A.1}$$

$$(1 + R_t) = \exp(r_t) \tag{5A.2}$$

$$TW_T = (1 + R_1)(1 + R_2) \ldots (1 + R_T) \tag{5A.3}$$

$$= \exp(r_1 + r_2 + \ldots + r_T) = \exp(\textstyle\sum r) \tag{5A.4}$$

Exp(x.) refers to the transcendental number e (2.718) raised to the power of (x.). For example, consider the sequence of end of period compound yearly returns of 10%, -20%, and 30%. Then:

$$r_1 = \ln(1.10) = 0.09531$$

$$r_2 = \ln(0.80) = -0.22314$$

$$r_3 = \ln(1.30) = 0.26236$$

And terminal wealth after these three returns are earned can be found in two ways:

$$TW_3 = (1.10)(0.80)(1.30) = 1.144$$

$$TW_3 = \exp(0.09531 - 0.22314 + 0.26236) = 1.144$$

The key to forecasting percentile distributions of future terminal wealth lies in the summation of the r_t values. One uses the assumptions of how individual r_t returns are distributed to infer the distribution of their summation over N years. Once the distribution of the summation of r values is known, use Equation 5A.4 to calculate the distribution of terminal wealth.

Assuming that each r_t is distributed with a constant mean of r, a standard deviation of s, and is uncorrelated with prior returns, then the distribution of the summation of r_t over N periods is normal, with an expected value and standard deviation of:

$$E\left(\sum r_t\right) = Nr$$

$$s\left(\sum r_t\right) = s\sqrt{N}$$

For example, if the expected yearly continuous return is 10% and its standard deviation is 20%, then the expected summation and standard deviation of the summation of r_t values over a 10-year investment horizon would be:

$$E\left(\sum r_t\right) = 10(0.10) = 1.00$$

$$s\left(\sum r_t\right) = 0.20\sqrt{10} = 0.6325$$

To calculate the distribution of terminal wealth in year 10, we first need to calculate the distribution of the year-10 summation of r_t values. This summation will be normally distributed, since it is based on the addition of variables that are normally distributed. Using the standard normal density z-scores presented in the chapter, the cumulative distribution of r_t is shown next.

Cumulative Percentile	0.10	0.25	0.50	0.75	0.90
Z-score from average	-1.28	-0.67	0.00	$+0.67$	$+1.28$
Summation of r_t	0.19	0.57	1.00	1.42	1.81

Finally, the terminal wealth for each percentile is found as follows:

Cumulative Percentile	0.10	0.25	0.50	0.75	0.90
Terminal Wealth equals	exp(0.19) $1.21	exp(0.57) $1.77	exp(1.00) $2.71	exp(1.42) $4.14	exp(1.81) $6.11

6

PORTFOLIO THEORY

After reading this chapter you should
have an understanding of the benefits
of portfolio diversification and how
the risk of an individual security
is measured.

Without doubt, risk is one of the most striking characteristics of the security markets. An ability to understand, measure, and properly manage investment risk is fundamental to effective investment management.

Until the mid-1960s the nature of security risk was poorly understood. Investment texts were only able to loosely define types of risk and to note that required returns should be commensurate with the risk of a security. Since then a major revolution has occurred in our understanding of investment risk. Today, reasonable approaches to risk measurement and management exist. While major questions remain unanswered, many of the concepts and techniques have gained widespread acceptance in the financial markets.

Our discussion of investment risk extends over three chapters. In this chapter, we examine the theory of portfolio risk management from the perspective of a single investor. This investor could be an individual investor or an institutional investor. In Chapters 7 and 8, we examine how decisions made by a large number of single investors result in a marketwide relationship between a security's risk and its expected return.

The world is complex. It does not operate according to the strict rules of some mechanical model. Throughout the next three chapters, however, we attempt to impose some order on the complexities. This often requires that we make what appear to be extreme assumptions at various stages. For example, during most of the discussion we deal with a world in which all investors have identical one-period investment horizons. This is clearly

211

not true to reality. But the models that result from this and other assumptions provide some profound investment implications.

After reading this chapter you will understand:

1. What makes a person risk-averse.
2. Why the risk of a portfolio can be reduced by diversification.
3. How the risk of a portfolio that cannot be reduced by diversification can be managed by asset allocation changes.
4. Why the risk of a single security should not be calculated in the same way as the risk of the total portfolio.

Investment Risk Aversion

At lunch one day your security broker, Sam, offers to play the following game with you. Broker Sam will toss a coin in the air and, if heads comes up, he will give you $1. However, if tails comes up you will have to pay him $1. He says the game will be played only once. Would you play? Probably. The game is a reasonable way to pass time, offers a little adventure, and, besides, what is $1 worth these days anyway? But what if Sam offers to replay the game (only once, he says) with stakes of $5,000? Would you play? If you are like most people, you wouldn't. Why?

Although this simple game might seem rather trivial when compared with the complex decisions that investors must address, it really isn't. The beauty of Sam's game and the questions—"Would you play?" and "Why?"—is their simplicity. They reduce to simple terms the nature of the problem faced by all investors. If we can understand why people are willing to invest in risky securities, we are well on our way to understanding and managing investment risk.

Wealth and Utility of Wealth

To explain why people make a given investment decision, financial economists rely on the theory of utility maximization. Utility theory is a way of describing the relative preferences of an individual for different wealth levels. For example, if the utility of wealth level 2 is greater than the utility of wealth level 1, we can say that wealth level 2 is preferred to wealth level 1. Utility is often described in terms of the psychological satisfaction or pleasure a person receives from a given wealth level. And economists often talk as if they can somehow calibrate the absolute level of someone's utility as consisting of so many utils. But thinking of utility in terms of a number of utils of pleasure and happiness is simply a convenient mental device. We cannot actually measure utility and say wealth level 2 provides twice as many utils as level 1. All we can say is that wealth level 2 is preferred to wealth level 1. In fact, we shouldn't even assign words such as happiness, satisfaction, or pleasure to the concept of utility. We can say only that one wealth level is preferred to another wealth level. **Utility analysis is simply a way of describing the relative preferences that an individual has for different wealth levels.**

In theory, people seek to maximize the expected utility of a stream of unknown future consumption levels over their life. Symbolically, this can be expressed as:

Utility of Lifetime Consumption

$$\text{Maximize: Expected Utility of } (C_0, C_1, C_3, \ldots, C_E) \qquad (6.1)$$

Here $C_0, C_1, C_3, \ldots, C_E$ represents a stream of consumption from period 1 through the person's lifetime. The term C_E reflects the value placed on any estate which is left.

It is at this point that we must make our first assumption to keep the analysis tractable: **A single-period world exists.** Decisions are made today that have an uncertain outcome one period hence. This removes the multiperiod terms (C_2, C_3, etc.) from Equation (6.1). In this situation, the individual wishes to maximize expected utility of consumption at the end of period 1. Since C_1 will be equal to the person's wealth at that time (W_1), the investor's goal can be stated symbolically as Equation (6.1a).

Utility of Expected Terminal Wealth

$$\text{Maximize: } E[\text{Utility of } (C_1)] \qquad (6.1a)$$

$$= E[\text{Utility of } (W_1)]$$

There are any number of ways in which differing wealth levels might be preferred, but most economists assume more wealth is preferred to less. As one's wealth level increases, so does the utility attached to it. Figure 6-1 illustrates three wealth preference orderings that all show increasing utility with wealth.

FIGURE 6-1 WEALTH AND UTILITY

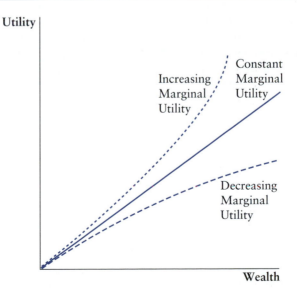

The solid line represents a constant, or linear, relationship between wealth and the utility attached to it. If wealth doubles, so does utility. For each unit change in wealth, the change in utility remains constant. An incremental $1,000 provides the same amount of additional utility at an initial wealth level of $10,000 as it does at an initial wealth level of $100,000. In the parlance of economics, the solid line depicts a case of **constant marginal utility** of wealth.

The dashed curve also shows an increase in utility as wealth increases but illustrates the case of **decreasing marginal utility**. An incremental $1,000 provides less utility to a person with an initial wealth of $100,000 than it would if the same person's initial wealth was $10,000.

Finally, the dotted curve illustrates the case of **increasing marginal utility**. An incremental $1,000 provides more utility to a person with an initial wealth level of $100,000 than it would if the same person's initial wealth was $10,000.[1]

The manner in which people order wealth preferences (the shape of the utility of wealth curve) has important implications about investment risk measurement. People who can be characterized as having constant marginal utility curves are completely indifferent to risk. People with increasing marginal utility curves are risk seekers. And people with decreasing marginal utility curves are risk-averse.

Uncertain Outcomes and Expected Returns

Figure 6-2 plots the utility of wealth curve for Sue Antony. Like most other people, Sue prefers more wealth to less but can be characterized as having decreasing marginal utility. An extra $1 would increase her utility, but not by as much as a $1 loss would decrease her utility. Sue is a fairly well-off person with a current wealth (W_0) of $100,000, which provides a corresponding current utility of wealth (U_0).

One day Sue meets with you and your broker for lunch and Sam immediately offers to play his usual coin-tossing game. If heads comes up, Sam will pay Sue $5,000. If tails comes up, Sue will pay Sam $5,000. Sue immediately inspects the coin and says: "Nope— this is a fair coin. The odds of winning or losing are identical. Why should I expose myself to a risk without a corresponding return? My expected utility of wealth if I decide to play the game is lower than my expected utility if I don't play."

To see the truth and insight of Sue's statement, refer again to Figure 6-2. Sue has two choices: to play the game or not play the game. If she elects not to play the game, her wealth remains the same and her utility remains at U_0. If she plays the game, her wealth will be either $95,000 or $105,000, with respective utilities of U_L and U_W. Thus, if she decides to play the game with a fair coin, her expected utility would be:

$$E(U \text{ given the gamble}) = (0.5 \ U_L + 0.5 \ U_W) \text{ which is less than } U_0$$

Her expected utility from playing the game is less than her current utility, so she won't play.

---

[1] There is no reason for these three curves to be the only possibilites. For example, a person with a very low wealth level might display risk-seeking behaviour, but if the person's wealth increases he or she might then become risk-averse.

FIGURE 6-2 UTILITY THEORY AND RISK AVERSION

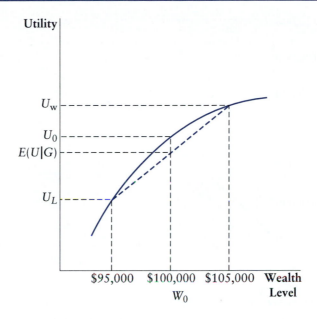

Sue faces a fair gamble. The chances of winning or losing are the same. And the amount she would win or lose is the same. But Sue would not be willing to play the game because she has a decreasing marginal utility of wealth. The increased utility obtained by a $5,000 increase in her wealth is more than offset by the decreased utility associated with a $5,000 loss. Individuals with decreasing marginal utility are risk-averse.[2]

People are averse to investment risk because they value a dollar increase in their wealth less than a dollar decrease in wealth. The only way to induce risk-averse investors, such as Sue, to accept risk is to offer them an expected positive return. Thus, investment risk aversion depends on the investor's utility of wealth.

Quadratic Utility

There are many ways of mathematically expressing an individual's utility of wealth. The most widely used approach to date is known as quadratic utility. In this case, the utility assigned to a given wealth level is expressed as in Equation (6.2).

Quadratic Utility of Wealth

$$U(W) = a(\text{Wealth}) - b(\text{Wealth})^2 \tag{6.2}$$

---

[2] Increasing marginal utility of wealth implies the person is a risk seeker, and constant marginal utility implies risk indifference.

FIGURE 6-3 A QUADRATIC UTILITY CURVE

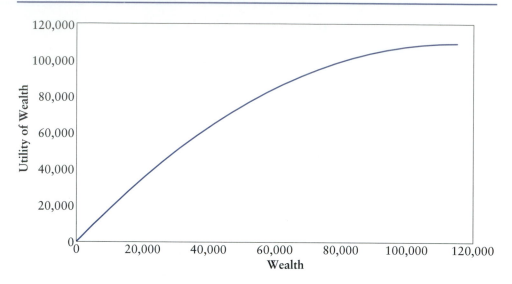

Increased wealth leads to increased utility through the "*a*" times wealth term. But as wealth becomes larger, utility is dampened by the "*b*" times "wealth squared" term. Increases in wealth result in greater utility but the rate of change decreases.

An illustration of a quadratic utility curve is shown in Figure 6-3. This particular curve is based on the following equation:

$$U(W) = 2(W) - 0.000009(W^2)$$

Quadratic utility functions have important portfolio theory implications. Specifically, investors who have quadratic utility of wealth functions will make their portfolio selection based solely on two variables: (1) the expected end-of-period wealth, and (2) the standard deviation of end-of-period wealth. If a portfolio's rate of return is defined as end-of-period wealth divided by beginning wealth, then the same can be said about portfolio returns! **Quadratic utility functions imply that investors will base their portfolio selection decisions on the portfolio's expected return and standard deviation of return.** This is the economic justification for using return standard deviations as the risk proxy.

Measuring Portfolio Risk

When analyzing investment risks, we must start with the investor's **total portfolio.** While risks and returns on individual securities are clearly important, it is the individual's wealth level, or portfolio of all holdings, that is of primary concern. For example, assume you own stock in two beer companies. If one firm improves its market share and earnings at the expense of the other, your total portfolio value might not change. The stock price increase in one firm is exactly offset by the stock price decline in the other. On net, the market value of your portfolio might remain the same.

This is a crucial point. The investor's major concern is with the risk to his or her total wealth. Individual stocks must be considered in relationship to other stocks in the portfolio and are risky only to the extent to which they add risk to the total portfolio. **It is from the viewpoint of the portfolio that individual stocks are judged risky.** Thus, we start our review of risk at the portfolio level.

Alternative Risk Measures

For illustrative purposes, let us assume we are interested in the risk of a portfolio patterned after the S&P 500. It might or might not be the best portfolio to own, and, in practice, people have a variety of portfolios that differ in relative degrees from the S&P 500 Index. But because it is well known and often emulated, we use it as an illustration. Past yearly real (after inflation) rates of return on the S&P 500 are shown in Table 6-1. We use real returns as opposed to nominal returns, since they are a better measure of changes in people's true wealth levels.

Numerous statistical measures can be used to assess the dispersion of return outcomes and, thus, proxy risk. These include the following:

1. **Range:** the high outcome less the low outcome. If the maximum possible return on a portfolio is 25% and the lowest possible return is -10%, the range would be 35%. The difficulties of using range as a risk proxy are that it doesn't consider returns between the extremes and gives no weight to the likelihood of one outcome versus another. The range of returns on the S&P 500 as shown in Table 6-1 was 68.86% and occurred between 1974 and 1975.

TABLE 6-1   HISTORICAL REAL RETURNS ON THE S&P 500 INDEX: 1965–1994

Year	Real Return	Year	Real Return
1965	10.52	1980	20.00
1966	−13.40	1981	−13.85
1967	20.95	1982	17.54
1968	6.36	1983	18.71
1969	−14.59	1984	2.25
1970	−1.45	1985	28.40
1971	10.96	1986	17.35
1972	15.56	1987	0.98
1973	−23.45	1988	12.41
1974	−38.66	1989	26.86
1975	30.20	1990	−9.28
1976	19.03	1991	27.49
1977	−13.95	1992	4.76
1978	−2.46	1993	7.09
1979	5.10	1994	−1.35

2. **Mean absolute deviation:** the average absolute difference between the possible returns on a portfolio and its expected return. Although this might be a reasonable proxy for a portfolio's risk, it is statistically quite difficult to use. In particular, there is no way of easily capturing the effects of correlation among security returns. The mean absolute deviation of S&P 500 returns was 13.25%.

3. **Probability of negative return:** the percentage of the time that returns are less than zero. While intuitively pleasing, this measure doesn't fully address all aspects of risk. For example, returns between 0 and the expected return are neglected. In addition, uncertain returns greater than the expected returns are still uncertain and should be accounted for. Finally, it is difficult to capture the effects of correlations among security returns. Of the 30 years reported in Table 6-1, there were 10 years with less than a zero return. Thus, in 33% of all years, returns on this portfolio were negative.

4. **Semivariance:** the statistical measure of variance of returns below the expected return. Semivariance does not consider uncertainty of returns larger than the expected return and also makes it difficult to capture the effects of correlations between security returns. Semivariance measures involve complex equations and, since we will not be using them, we will not illustrate them.

5. **Standard deviation:** the most common measure of portfolio risk. As we discussed in Chapter 5, the standard deviation is the square root of variance. Variance is the weighted average squared deviation from the mean. The continuous return distributions for two portfolios, A and B, are shown in Figure 6-4. Both have the same expected return, but the return standard deviation of B is larger and thus B is more risky. Also, because A has the same expected return as B but less risk, portfolio A is said to **dominate** portfolio B.

As shown in Chapter 5, the average returns, variances, and standard deviations of past returns are calculated as follows:

Average Return

$$\overline{R} = \left(\sum_{t=1}^{N} R_t \right) \div N \qquad (6.3)$$

Variance of Returns

$$\sigma^2 = \left[\sum_{t=1}^{N} (R_t - \overline{R})^2 \right] \div (N - 1) \qquad (6.4)$$

Standard Deviation

$$\sigma = [\sigma^2]^{1 \div 2} \qquad (6.5)$$

where R_t is the return in period t and there are N periods. When applied to the returns in Table 6-1, these values are calculated as follows:

$$\overline{R} = (10.52 - 13.40 + \cdots - 1.35) \div 30$$

$$= 5.70\%$$

FIGURE 6-4 PORTFOLIO RETURN DISTRIBUTIONS

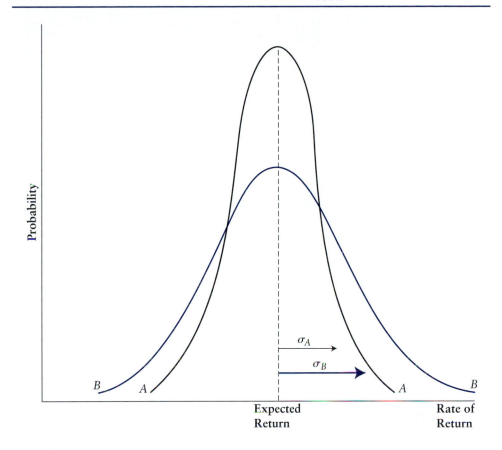

$$\sigma^2 = [(10.52 - 5.70)^2 + (-13.40 - 5.70)^2 + \cdots + (-1.35 - 5.70)^2] \div (30 - 1)$$

$$= 278.73\%$$

$$\sigma = (278.73)^{1\div 2}$$

$$= 16.7\%$$

Criticisms of Standard Deviation

Criticisms of the standard deviation as an appropriate measure of risk have been numerous. Some people question whether portfolio standard deviations by themselves are adequate measures of risk. They believe that if rates of return are distributed in a skewed fashion, more statistical information is needed. A skewed distribution is one that is not symmetric; more observations lie in one tail of the distribution than in the other. For example, in Figure 6-5 distribution A is positively skewed, distribution B is symmetric, and distribution C is negatively skewed. Assuming the expected returns and standard deviations of each distribution

FIGURE 6-5 ILLUSTRATION OF SKEWED RETURN DISTRIBUTIONS

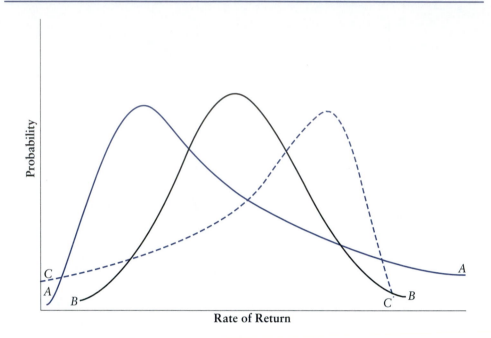

are equal, our theory so far says the investor would be indifferent among the three. However, if skewness does matter, then all other things being equal, positive skewness would be preferred.

The importance of skewness remains unresolved. For example, various studies have shown that statistical measures of skewness are quite sensitive to the time period over which data are collected. However, some empirical evidence suggests that investors prefer positive skewness. In fact, we saw clearly in Chapter 5 that future wealth must be positively skewed, since wealth cannot fall below zero, but the potential for increase in one's wealth is unlimited.

A reasonable argument can be made that retains the fundamental importance of standard deviations, even if the investor faces a long investment horizon and thus significantly skewed terminal portfolio values. If people were forced to hold a single portfolio to some anticipated horizon date, then positive skewness would be large and probably important in the investment decision. But if individuals have the ability to **continuously rebalance** their portfolio holdings, then standard deviations dominate any short-term skewness that might exist.

This argument is based on the ability to continuously rebalance. If prices move dramatically before a rebalancing trade is possible (such as Black Monday in 1987) or if it takes time before the individual can actually decide whether to rebalance, then skewness may be important.

It is time to make our second major assumption: **The standard deviation of portfolio returns is the proper measure of portfolio risk.**

Diversification

Diversification is the key to effective risk management. Through proper diversification, risk exposure can be minimized without affecting expected portfolio returns. Diversification can be thought of in two ways: **naive diversification** and **efficient diversification.** Naive diversification is appropriate only if we are unable to distinguish between the expected returns and risks of various securities. This is probably not true in reality. Yet, the extent to which risk can be reduced by such a simple rule speaks to the power of diversification.

Naive Diversification

Naive diversification is random diversification, the purchase of a large number of securities without regard to firm size, industry classification, expected returns, or standard deviations of potential returns. To illustrate the concept of naive diversification, assume you have a list of all stocks contained in the S&P 500 and attach the list to a dartboard. One way to select a naively diversified portfolio would be to throw darts at the listing (assuming you are a poor dart player so that selection is indeed random). If you desire a portfolio of 20 stocks, you would throw 20 darts and invest an equal dollar amount in each (unless you're a really bad dart player and some of your tosses totally miss the board).

Figure 6-6 displays the results when such a strategy is applied to stocks contained in the S&P 500. The horizontal axis shows the number of stocks in the randomly selected portfolio, and the vertical axis shows the average standard deviation (of annualized return) that results from a portfolio of a given size. When only one stock is held, the portfolio standard deviation is identical to the standard deviation of the average stock that was reported above. However, as additional stocks are held, the standard deviation of the portfolio falls substantially. Reductions in portfolio risk caused by adding the first few stocks to the portfolio are dramatic, whereas the marginal risk reduction of adding a new stock to a larger portfolio appears to be small. Although the marginal reduction in risk decreases as the portfolio size increases, adding one more stock to any portfolio will (on average) continue to reduce the portfolio risk.

Some care should be given to the interpretation of Figure 6-6. The reductions in risk that are shown to result from randomly increasing the number of securities are the **average results** over many computer simulations. The results are never exactly as shown. The variability is greatest when few securities are held, whereas the outcomes for large portfolios (those with more than 50 stocks) are relatively close to the curve shown. In sum, for the average person the results will be as shown in Figure 6.6, but any single person may experience little or no risk reduction until a large number of stocks are held.

Systematic and Unsystematic Risk. Before we move into the mathematics of why diversification works, it is a good time to point out two concepts that will be important throughout the rest of the book and can be seen in the results of naive diversification.

1. Some risk cannot be eliminated by diversification. There is an underlying volatility of returns that is **systematic** to all risky securities. Diversification cannot eliminate this **systematic risk.** It can only eliminate return uncertainties that are unique to individual securities—**unsystematic risk.**
2. Individual securities have differing amounts of this nondiversifiable, systematic risk.

FIGURE 6-6 RISK AND NAIVE DIVERSIFICATION USING REAL S&P 500 RETURNS

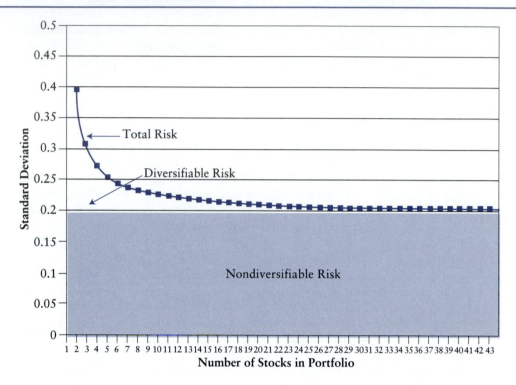

Systematic risk is often referred to as **market risk** or nondiversifiable risk—uncertainties about returns that affect all securities. It is created by the sensitivity of a security's return to broad economic forces such as inflation, economic growth, changes in interest rates, and world political conditions. Systematic risk is commonly measured by beta, a variable we discuss later in the chapter.

Unsystematic risk is often referred to as **firm-unique risk,** uncertainties about returns on one firm that can be offset by holding securities of other firms in the portfolio. For example, a labor strike at one firm might reduce its profits but lead to higher profits at other firms.

When and Why Diversification Reduces Risk

Why does diversification work? Does it always reduce risk? What effect does it have on expected portfolio returns? To answer these questions, we need to understand how individual securities held in a portfolio determine the expected return and standard deviation of the total portfolio. To minimize needless mathematics so we can focus on the economic intuition, we deal with two securities. Call these stocks A and B.

Assume that X_A and X_B are the percentages invested in stocks A and B. Since these are the only investments held, X_A plus X_B equals 1.0.

The expected return for the total portfolio is equal to the **weighted average** of the expected returns of the securities held in a portfolio. The weight applied to each security is simply the percentage of the portfolio invested in the security.

Expected Portfolio Return = Weighted Average of Expected Returns on Securities Held in the Portfolio

Expected Portfolio Return

$$E(R_P) = X_A E(R_A) + X_B E(R_B) \tag{6.6}$$

Now suppose the standard deviation was also a weighted average of the individual stock standard deviations. **It is not!** But this assumption gets to the heart of the diversification issue. If this was true, then:

Portfolio Standard Deviation $\sigma_p = X_A \sigma_A + X_B \sigma_B$

and

Portfolio Variance $\sigma_P^2 = (X_A \sigma_A + X_B \sigma_B)^2$

$$= X_A^2 \sigma_A^2 + X_B^2 \sigma_B^2 + 2 X_A X_B \sigma_A \sigma_B$$

Except in a very special case, these equations are **not true.** The error lies in the far right portion of the variance equation where σ_A and σ_B are multiplied. This term is intended to reflect the return interaction between the securities. But to do this correctly, the σ_A and σ_B must be multiplied by the extent to which the security returns are correlated. This is known as the **correlation coefficient.**

Defining r_{AB} as the correlation coefficient for stocks A and B, the correct equations for portfolio variance and standard deviation are as follows:

Variance = Weighted Variances + Weighted Covariances

Two- Security Portfolio Variance

$$\sigma_p^2 = [X_A^2 \sigma_A^2 + X_B^2 \sigma_B^2] + 2 X_A X_B \sigma_A \sigma_B r_{AB} \tag{6.7a}$$

Portfolio Standard Deviation

$$\sigma_p = [\sigma_p^2]^{1 \div 2} \tag{6.7b}$$

The $\sigma_A \sigma_B r_{AB}$ term in Equation (6.7a) is known as the **covariance** between stock A and B. Notice that it is determined in part by the correlation coefficient. The maximum that two securities can be correlated is $+1.0$ (perfect positive correlation) and the minimum is -1.0 (perfect negative correlation). Portfolio variance and standard deviation are the greatest when $r = +1.0$. Also notice that if $r = +1.0$, the portfolio standard deviation is a weighted average of the individual security standard deviations.

Real securities, however, rarely have returns that are perfectly correlated. **Whenever the correlation coefficient is less than $+1.0$, the portfolio standard deviation is less**

than the weighted average of the security standard deviations. Individual security risks are offsetting.

The three panels in Figure 6-7 illustrate various degrees of correlation. In panel A, returns on stocks i and j always move in the same direction. Stock i is twice as volatile as stock j and thus has the larger standard deviation. Nonetheless, returns on the stocks are perfectly correlated, $r = +1.0$. In panel B, a relationship between the returns on i and j doesn't exist. Returns on each are totally uncorrelated, $r = 0.0$. In panel C, the returns consistently move counter to each other. They are perfectly inversely correlated, $r = -1.0$.

FIGURE 6-7 ILLUSTRATIONS OF VARIOUS CORRELATION COEFFICIENTS

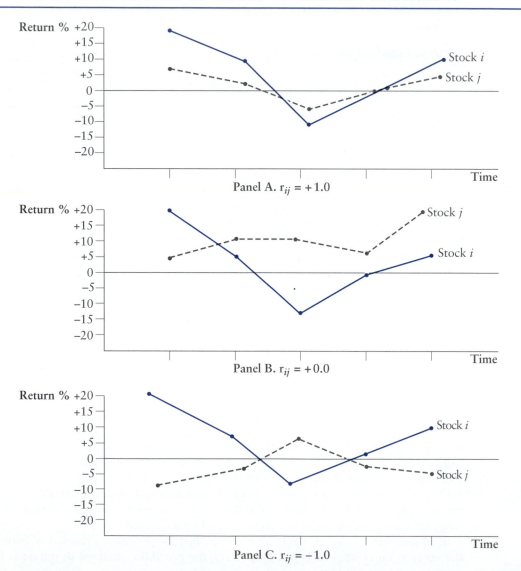

A Simple Example. Assume two stocks have identical expected returns of 12% and standard deviations of 40%. The portfolio risk of a combination of the two would depend on the percentage invested in each and their return correlation. For example, the data shown in Table 6-2 is based on a correlation coefficient equal to 0.0 and varying combinations of the stocks. The expected portfolio return, of course, is unaffected by the combination chosen. In contrast, portfolio risk is reduced when some amount of both stocks are held. Given the data in this example (zero correlation and identical standard deviations), the minimum risk portfolio consists of an equal investment in each stock.

The minimum risk portfolio given this data is a 50/50 portfolio of the two stocks. Let's examine the minimum portfolio risk for various correlation coefficients. This is shown in panel A of Figure 6-8. As the correlation coefficient declines, so too does the portfolio risk. In fact, **portfolio risk can be eliminated by holding only two assets if their returns are perfectly negatively correlated.** Unfortunately, this simply does not happen with actual securities.

But even if portfolio risk cannot be eliminated by finding two securities that have perfect negative correlation, it can be reduced by judicious diversification. In fact, panel A in Figure 6-8 understates the potential for diversification because it deals only with two stocks. What if we had a large number of securities with expected returns and standard deviations identical to stocks A and B? If we invested an equal amount in each security, portfolio risk would move toward the points shown in panel B of Figure 6-8. (The points shown are minimum risk limits as the number of securities increases.)

As before, if security returns are all perfectly correlated, diversification does not reduce risk. Notice, however, that risk can theoretically be eliminated if security return correlations are equal to zero. Like a -1.0 correlation, this is not the case for most stocks. Returns on actual stocks typically have correlation coefficients between 0.3 and 0.5.

Another Example. Assume now that the expected returns and standard deviations on stocks A and B differ. Specifically $E(R_A) = 15\%$, $E(R_B) = 10\%$, $\sigma_A = 40\%$, and $\sigma_B = 30\%$. Figure 6-9 shows the risk/return combinations for various correlation coefficients. As the correlation coefficient declines, a lower level of risk is incurred for a given expected return; the risk/return line bends to the left.

TABLE 6-2   TWO-STOCK PORTFOLIO RISK WITH CORRELATION COEFFICIENT EQUAL TO ZERO

Percentage Invested in		Portfolio	
A	B	Return	Deviation
100	0	12%	40.0%
80	20	12%	33.0
60	40	12%	28.8
50	50	12%	28.3
40	60	12%	28.8
20	80	12%	33.0
0	100	12%	40.0

FIGURE 6-8 EFFECTS OF CORRELATION ON PORTFOLIO RISK

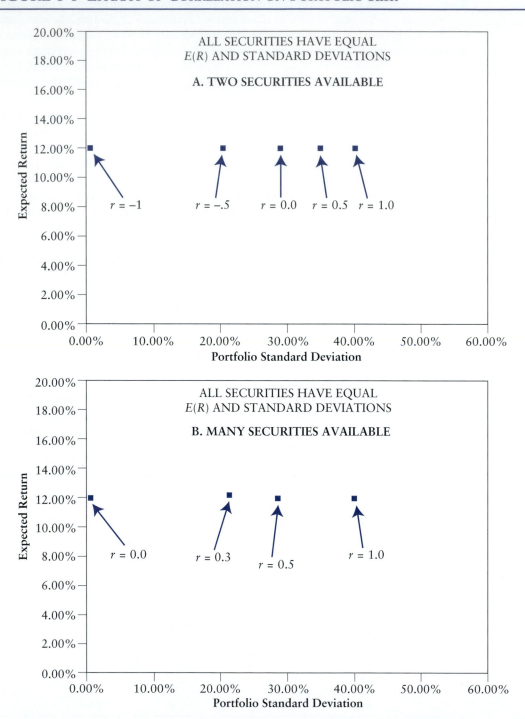

FIGURE 6-9 EFFECTS OF CORRELATION ON PORTFOLIO RISK WITH DIFFERENT EXPECTED RETURNS AND STANDARD DEVIATIONS

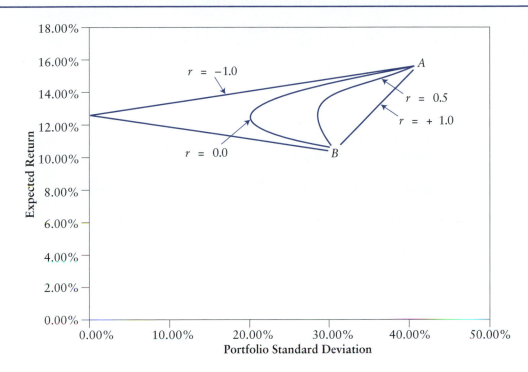

Two concepts are illustrated in Figure 6.9. First, to reduce the risk of a portfolio, you should try to identify securities whose returns have a low correlation with the current portfolio. This concept is the motivation for why many investors diversify beyond their traditional holdings of U.S. stocks and bonds into holdings of real estate, non-U.S. stocks, and non-U.S. bonds. Second, as you diversify across additional assets, the expected return might change. For example, assume you start with 100% invested in stock A. As you diversify into B, the expected portfolio return falls. We will see how you can retain the expected return on stock A but still reduce risk by diversifying into B later in the chapter when we add a risk-free security to the portfolio.

The Minimum Risk Portfolio. When only two securities are being considered, the following formula can be used to find the percentage to invest in the first security, X_A, and the second, X_B, which results in the least risk:

Minimum Risk Portfolio

$$X_A = \frac{\sigma_B^2 - \sigma_A \sigma_B r_{AB}}{\sigma_A^2 + \sigma_B^2 - 2(\sigma_A \sigma_B r_{AB})} \tag{6.8}$$

$$X_B = 1.0 - X_A$$

For example, if we use the expected returns and standard deviations on stocks A and B here and assume the correlation coefficient is 0.5, then the percentage investment in each that will result in minimum risk is calculated as follows:

$$X_A = \frac{[(0.3)(0.3) - (0.3)(0.4)(0.50)}{(0.4)(0.4) + (0.3)(0.3) - 2(0.4)(0.30)(0.5)}$$

$$= 0.23$$

$$X_B = 1.0 - 0.23 = 0.77$$

Calculating Correlation Coefficients. Because security correlation determines the extent to which diversification works, it is important that we understand how correlation coefficients are calculated. The basic formula is as follows:

$$\text{Correlation Between } i \text{ and } j = \frac{\text{Covariance between } i \text{ and } j}{\text{Standard Deviation of } i \text{ times Standard Deviation of } j}$$

Correlation coefficients are calculated for two different situations:

1. **Ex ante correlations** are based on probabilities of future economic states and returns in each state.
2. **Ex post correlations** are based on a time series of past returns.

To calculate an ex ante correlation coefficient, Equation (6.9) is used:

Ex Ante Correlation Coefficients

$$r_{ij} = \left[\sum_{s=1}^{S} P_s (R_{is} - \overline{R}_i)(R_{js} - \overline{R}_j) \right] \div [\sigma_i \sigma_j] \qquad (6.9)$$

Here P_s represents the probability of state s, R_{is} is the return on security i in state s, and $\overline{R}_i$ is the expected return on security i.

An example is shown in Table 6-3. Expected returns, variances, and standard deviations are calculated using the procedures discussed in Chapter 5. In this example, the correlation coefficient is a negative 0.8064.

When calculating an ex post correlation coefficient, use past time series of returns and Equation (6.10).

Ex Post Correlation Coefficient

$$r_{ij} = \frac{\left[\sum_{t=j}^{N} (R_{it} - \overline{R}_i)(R_{jt} - \overline{R}_j) \right] \div N}{\sigma_i \sigma_j} \qquad (6.10)$$

Recall from Chapter 5 that there are two ways of calculating the time series standard deviation. The way in which we usually calculate σ is to account for uncertainty about the true mean return by dividing the sum of squared return differences by N minus 1. The other way assumes the true mean is the average return of the time series. This second approach is commonly used in Equation (6.10). Both the covariance term in the numerator and the standard deviations in the denominator are calculated using N and not $(N - 1)$.

TABLE 6-3   RETURN ESTIMATES FOR TWO PORTFOLIOS

State of Economy	Probability of Occurrence	Investment Return If State Occurs	
		Portfolio A	Portfolio B
Recession	0.25	3.0%	−20.0%
Good	0.50	2.0%	8.0%
Boom	0.25	0.0%	15.0%
	1.00		
Expected Rate of Return		1.75%	2.75%
Variance of Return		1.1875	180.6875
Standard Deviation		1.09	13.4420

Calculation of Covariance:

$$
\begin{aligned}
\text{Covariance } (A, B) &= 0.25[(3.0 - 1.75)\,(-20.0 - 2.75)] \\
&\quad + 0.50[(2.0 - 1.75)(8.0 - 2.75)] \\
&\quad + 0.25[(0.0 - 1.75)(15.0 - 2.75) \\
&= -11.8125
\end{aligned}
$$

Calculation of Correlation Coefficient:

$$
\begin{aligned}
\text{Correlation } (A, B) &= \text{Covariance } (A, B) \div (\sigma_A \sigma_B) \\
r_{AB} &= -11.8125 \div (1.09 \times 13.442) \\
&= -0.8064
\end{aligned}
$$

In Table 6-4, an example is shown of how the ex post correlation coefficient is calculated. The data consists of actual returns on the S&P 500 Index and T-bills between 1990 and 1994. During this period the correlation coefficient was a negative 0.46.

Efficient Diversification

Naive diversification involves the random selection of securities. If N securities are bought, then $1/N$ of the portfolio is invested in each security. **Naive diversification is appropriate only if the investor is unable to distinguish between security expected returns, standard deviations, or correlation coefficients.** This, of course, is rarely the case. For example, it is quite easy to characterize securities by stock versus bond, industry, size of firm, dividend yield, domestic versus foreign, and so on. So instead of blindly choosing N securities from all that exist, most investors attempt to balance portfolio holdings across various security categories.

Efficient diversification improves the process even further by identifying the minimum risk portfolio for any feasible expected return.

TABLE 6-4 CALCULATING AN EX POST CORRELATION COEFFICIENT

Security	ID	1990	1991	1992	1993	1994
T-Bills	T	6.11	3.06	2.91	2.90	2.67
S&P 500	S	−3.17	30.55	7.67	9.99	1.32

Step 1: Find the Average Returns:

$$\overline{R}_T = (6.11 + 3.06 + \cdots + 2.67) \div 5 = 3.53$$
$$\overline{R}_s = (-3.17 + 30.55 + \cdots + 1.32) \div 5 = 9.27$$

Step 2: Find the Ex Post Standard Deviations:

$$\sigma_T = \{[(6.11-3.53)^2 + (3.06 - 3.53)^2 + \cdots + (2.67 - 3.53)^2] \div 5\}^{1 \div 2}$$
$$= 1.296$$
$$\sigma_S = \{[(-3.17 - 9.27)^2 + (30.55 - 9.27)^2 + \cdots + (1.32 - 9.27)^2] \div 5\}^{1 \div 2}$$
$$= 11.609$$

Step 3: Find the Covariance Term:

$$\text{Covariance} = [(6.11 - 3.53)(-3.17 - 9.27) + (3.06 - 3.53)(30.55 - 9.27)$$
$$+ \cdots + (2.67 - 3.53)(1.32 - 9.27)] \div 5$$
$$= -6.9442$$

Step 4: Find the Correlation Coefficient:

$$r_{ij} = -6.9442 \div (1.296)(11.609) = -0.4615$$

The Markowitz Model. The concept of efficient diversification was originally developed by Harry Markowitz in the late 1950s. His insights into defining and managing risk are milestones in the investment literature, and he is often referred to as the father of modern portfolio theory. In fact, the acronym MPT (for modern portfolio theory) is widely used among professional investors. Markowitz received the 1990 Nobel Prize in economics for his contributions.

Markowitz showed that if an analyst can develop estimates of expected security returns, standard deviations, and correlation coefficients, then the following equations can be solved by a computer program:

Minimize Portfolio Risk

$$\sigma_p = \left[\sum_{i=1}^{N} X_i^2 \sigma_i^2 + \sum_{i=1}^{N} \sum_{\substack{j=1 \\ j \neq i}}^{N} X_i X_j \sigma_i \sigma_j r_{ij} \right]^{1 \div 2} \tag{6.11a}$$

Subject to

A Minimum Stated Expected $$R^* \leq E(R_p) = \sum X_i E(R_i) \tag{6.11b}$$

Return Full Investment $$1.0 = \sum X_i \tag{6.11c}$$

The concept of an **efficient frontier** is shown graphically in panel A of Figure 6-10. The line between stock A and stock B represents the risk/return combinations for the securities in our previous example (assuming $r_{AB} = 0.5$). The other dots in the figure represent standard deviations and expected returns on other securities. The heavy curve represents the minimum risk portfolio for a given level of expected return considering all securities. This is known as the efficient frontier.

An infinite number of portfolios lie on the efficient frontier, simply because there are an infinite number of ways to combine any two portfolios. The portfolio that an investor selects will depend on his or her risk tolerance (see panel B). The dashed curves represent an investor's indifference curves. All points along any one curve provide a given level of utility; the higher the curve, the greater the utility. The slope represents the change in expected return that is required for a small increase in risk. The investor will select the portfolio that is tangent to the highest possible indifference curve. At that point, the risk/return trade-off provided by the indifference portfolio is equal to the trade-off the investor demands. For an individual with the dashed utility curves, this is shown as portfolio X. The dotted curve represents an indifference curve for a more risk-averse investor. We can tell this investor is more risk-averse because the slope of the curve is steeper than for the other investor. This less-risk-tolerant investor selects portfolio W.

Efficient Asset Class Diversification. When Markowitz first developed the concept of efficient diversification, he expected it would be applied to the selection of individual securities. However, when this is done, the number of required data inputs are extremely large. As a practical tool, the model is rarely applied to the selection of individual securities. However, it is widely used by sophisticated investors when they are deciding what aggregate asset classes to own and in what proportions. In this section, we review how this is done.

The process starts by identifying various asset classes to be considered. We use the five classes shown in Table 6-5. These consist of three U.S. security indexes, the Europe, Australia, and Far East Index, and a U.S. commercial real estate index known as PRISA (Prudential Real Estate Income Separate Account). Also shown in Table 6-5 are average annual real returns, standard deviations, and correlation coefficients for each asset class. Although some investors would be interested in nominal returns, most are more concerned about real increases in their wealth. Thus, only real returns are analyzed here. The returns are those that a U.S. investor would have earned. Non-U.S. investors would have experienced different returns due to different currency exchange rates.

Average annual real returns ranged from as low as 0.50% on U.S. T-bills to 9.25% for the EAFE index. Of course, greater average yearly returns came at the cost of increased yearly return volatility. For example, the standard deviation of yearly real T-bill returns was only 4.40%, whereas the EAFE index had a standard deviation of almost 25%. Correlation coefficients ranged from negative 0.14 to positive 0.64.

The next step is to develop expectations of what you believe these variables will be in the future. Historical relationships provide a reasonable basis for such forecasts but often require subjective adjustments. For example, the small real return on T-bills is due in large part to a Federal Reserve policy during the Depression and World War II of "pegging" the interest rate at artificially low levels as well as large unexpected inflation in the United States during the 1970s. Due to economic events such as these, reasonable expectations of future relationships can differ from past results. Table 6-6 shows the assumptions used in this exercise.

FIGURE 6-10 THE EFFICIENT FRONTIER OF RISKY ASSETS

A. EFFICIENT PORTFOLIOS

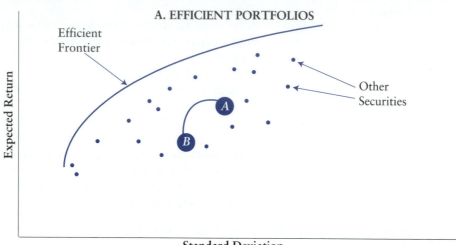

B. PORTFOLIO SELECTION

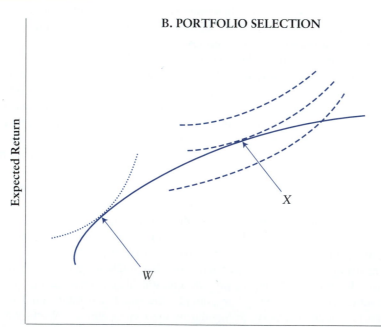

TABLE 6-5   ILLUSTRATION OF ASSET CLASS SELECTION: HISTORICAL
            REAL RETURN INFORMATION

	T-Bills	U.S. Govt.	S&P 500	EAFE	PRISA
1926–1994:					
Average Real Return	0.50%	2.02%	8.93%	NA	NA
Standard Deviation	4.40	10.42	20.94	NA	NA
1969–1994:					
Average Real Return	1.26%	3.39%	5.60%	9.25%	1.26%
Standard Deviation	2.88	13.52	17.28	24.37	7.09
Correlation Coefficients (1969–1994):					
T-Bills	1.00				
U.S. Govt.	0.64	1.00			
S&P 500	0.41	0.56	1.00		
EAFE	0.26	0.37	0.63	1.00	
PRISA	0.24	−0.14	0.22	0.31	1.00

TABLE 6-6   ASSUMED FUTURE ASSET CLASS RELATIONSHIPS

	T-Bills	U.S. Govt.	S&P 500	EAFE	PRISA
Average Real Return	1.00%	2.00%	7.50%	10.00%	4.00%
Standard Deviation	4.00	8.00	18.00	25.00	12.00
Correlation Coefficients (1969–1994):					
T-Bills	1.00				
U.S. Govt.	0.50	1.00			
S&P 500	0.20	0.40	1.00		
EAFE	0.30	0.30	0.70	1.00	
PRISA	0.50	0.10	0.15	0.20	1.00

A variety of computer programs are available that can use the data in Table 6-6 to calculate
an efficient frontier. Usually this allows for various constraints on the portfolio. For example,
many institutional portfolios are not allowed to short-sell securities. Some investors such as
endowment funds might have a minimum desired portfolio dividend yield. And other investors might wish to exclude so-called sin stocks, for example, stocks of firms that manufac-
ture or distribute alcohol or tobacco products. In this example, we do not allow short sales.

The efficient frontier generated from the data of Table 6-6 is shown in Figure 6-11.
Optimal percentages to invest in each asset class for a given expected return and risk are
shown in Table 6-7. Notice that the lowest risk portfolio does not consist solely of the lowest-
risk class but is a combination of both T-bills and a small amount of the S&P 500. This is due
to the advantages of diversification.

FIGURE 6-11 ILLUSTRATION OF EFFICIENT DIVERSIFICATION ACROSS ASSET CLASSES

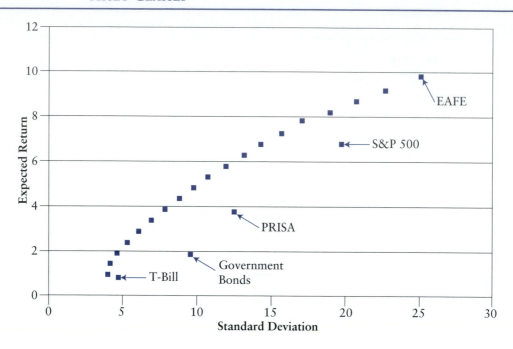

TABLE 6-7 COMPOSITION OF SELECTED OPTIMAL PORTFOLIOS

Portfolio	Expected Return	Standard Deviation	Percentage Invested in Asset Classes				
			T-Bills	U.S. Govt.	S&P 500	EAFE	PRISA
1	1.03%	4.00%	99.49	—	0.51	—	—
2	2.00	4.69	77.86	3.52	11.21	0.23	7.18
3	3.00	6.11	52.94	9.51	15.40	3.99	18.16
4	4.00	7.82	28.02	15.50	19.58	7.75	29.15
5	5.00	9.67	3.10	21.48	23.77	11.52	40.13
5.5	5.50	10.64	—	15.28	27.40	14.11	43.21
6	6.00	11.68	—	6.03	31.55	16.94	45.58
7	7.00	14.08	—	—	34.94	29.62	35.44
8	8.00	17.18	—	—	35.95	45.69	18.35
9	9.00	20.38	—	—	36.97	61.77	1.26
10	10.00	25.00	—	—	—	100.00	—

TABLE 6-8   PERCENTILE RETURN DISTRIBUTIONS

Cumulative Percentile	z-Score	Portfolio 2	Portfolio 5	Portfolio 8
Expected Return		2.00%	5.00%	8.00%
Standard Deviation		4.69%	9.67%	17.18%
0.05	−1.64	−5.69	−10.86	−20.18
0.10	−1.28	−4.00	−7.38	−13.99
0.25	−0.67	−1.14	−1.48	−3.51
0.50	0	2.00	5.00	8.00
0.75	0.67	5.14	11.48	19.51
0.90	1.28	8.00	17.38	29.99
0.95	1.64	9.69	20.86	36.18

Clearly, a major problem in creating an efficient frontier is developing reasonable input assumptions. Such a problem, however, is not unique to efficient portfolio selection. Virtually all major decisions that individuals and organizations make require uncertain inputs. As you gain an understanding of investment concepts and experience with security return distributions, assumptions such as those in Table 6-6 will become less difficult to make.

An equally difficult problem is deciding which portfolio on the efficient frontier should be selected. In theory, the answer is easy: Select the portfolio that maximizes expected utility. In real life, investors do not specify their utility function or calculate maximum expected utility. Instead, their judgments are more subjective. A device that can help to express potential returns on various portfolios is the percentile distribution. An example, using three portfolios from Table 6-7, is shown in Table 6-8.

Impacts of a Risk-Free Return

The previous discussion was concerned solely with portfolios consisting of risky securities. No risk-free securities were considered. We now expand the set of available securities to include such a risk-free asset. When this is done:

1. No longer is there an infinite number of efficient risky portfolios from which one is selected based on individual risk-return preferences. Instead, a single risky portfolio will dominate all others and will be selected regardless of individual risk-return preferences.
2. The individual achieves a personally suitable combination of risk and return by adjusting the percentage of the portfolio that is invested in risk-free securities.

As a practical matter, many investors do not have access to risk-free securities, since they desire real dollar returns. Although nominal risk-free securities are available, their returns after subtracting inflation are uncertain.

Mark Kritzman, C.F.A.

Managing Partner
Windham Capital Management
St. John's University, B.A.
New York University, M.B.A.

Windham Capital Management, located in Boston, specializes in asset allocation and currency management. Mark Kritzman serves on the Prize Committee of the Institute for Quantitative Research in Finance and on the review board of the Institute of Chartered Financial Analysts' Research Foundation. He is the author of several books and numerous articles in academic and professional journals.

Q: How important is it that investors understand the meanings of risk measures like standard deviation, beta, correlation, and covariance?

A: It is a very good idea for institutional investors to understand these concepts because they help determine risk exposure and prevent surprises caused by unexpected portfolio results. My impression is that most investors have a pretty good idea that standard deviation is a measure of dispersion and that beta is a measure of relative volatility. However, some investors think beta relates only to the market. Often investors are not sufficiently comfortable with the idea that they can transfer what they understand about stocks to other types of assets. Additionally, there seems to be some confusion about the difference between beta and correlation. Investors understand that they both refer to measures of association, but they are not often clear about the specific relationship. For example,

you can have a beta of close to one and a correlation of nearly zero. Also, people often use covariance and correlation interchangeably without understanding what they both mean.

It, too, is important for individuals to have a thorough understanding in order to make the best investment choices and to avoid getting suboptimal results. It is commonly known among professionals that two-thirds to three-fourths of all active managers underperform the S&P 500 because of transaction costs and management fees. However, most individuals are not in index funds; they are in actively managed funds. So two-thirds of those investors are going to do worse than they otherwise could. They are going to end up with less money than if they understood a variety of risk measures.

Q: Do you have to know the mechanics of how investment models are built in order to understand the end results?

A: Clearly, investors don't need to be able to reconstruct a model in order to understand the results. But they need to have a good conceptual understanding, or they won't know how much confidence to place in the reports they get. For example, in order to make the proper inferences from regression coefficients, the user needs to understand the difference between a cross-sectional regression and a time-series regression and that the correlations are much higher from time-series regressions than from cross-sectional regressions.

Q: Do assumptions like no transaction costs force many models to be too theoretical for practical use?

A: Basically, it comes down to the notion that the real world is very complex and in order to address certain issues you have to set aside some of these complexities. If the purpose is to help us understand relationships, it is not a problem to make extreme assumptions. Originally academicians made these assumptions for convenience and tractability and the reader was asked to suspend belief in order to follow the argument. As time has passed it has gotten to the point that the researchers say, "we make all the usual assumptions." As a result of these assumptions being made over and over, people subconsciously start believing them or at least disregarding the fact that they aren't realistic. It has had some influence on the way we go about investing. Probably, too little emphasis is placed on the assumptions made. It really is an empirical question about how bad it is.

Q: What are some of the major issues left unanswered by the current risk models?

A: There are a lot of issues but two which are at the forefront. One has to do with the assumption that returns are normally distributed, which allows us to use measures like beta and standard deviation and do mean-variance optimization. There is a group of people arguing that many types of assets have asymmetric returns and that certain investment strategies generate asymmetric return distributions. These returns are skewed one way or the other, or they have fat tails, making variance a poor measure of risk. They suggest looking at downside risk measures such as semivariance or some notion of skewness. That's one issue that needs to be addressed. The other area I think is of interest is the idea that investors don't have the types of utility functions that academicians have long assumed. There is a lot of evidence that investors have utility functions based on two or more definitions of risk. Investors, both individual and institutional, care about absolute risk—making money, and relative risk—whether or not they are losing to the competition. Virtually all previous approaches to risk management (this pertains to diversification as well as hedging strategies) dealt with just one kind of risk at a time by utilizing mean-variance analysis *or* mean tracking error analysis. Recently it has been proposed to do optimization and develop hedging strategies that address different definitions of risk simultaneously. Instead of generating

> the traditional efficient frontier with expected return and standard deviation, an efficient surface is derived with expected return, standard deviation, and tracking error. While most approaches haven't dealt with the simultaneous occurrence of losing to two different objectives, we've now moved into multidimensional risk management.

As before, the expected return on a portfolio that combines risk-free and risky securities is simply the weighted average of the expected returns on all securities. Assume you plan to invest 80% of your capital in the S&P 500 and 20% in the risk-free security. If the expected return on the S&P is 12% and the expected return on the risk-free security is 7%, then the expected portfolio return is 11.0%:

$$(0.20)\,7\% + (0.80)\,12\% = 11\%$$

In general, if $E(R_c)$ represents returns on the combined portfolio of risky and risk-free securities, $E(R_p)$ refers to the risky security group, and X percent is invested in the risk-free security, then:

Expected Return on Risk-Free and Risky Portfolio

$$E(R_c) = (X)RF + (1 - X)E(R_p) \tag{6.12}$$

The standard deviation of a combined portfolio is simply the percentage invested in risky securities multiplied by the standard deviation of the risky securities. By definition, the variance of returns on RF is zero, and all terms in the standard deviation equation that apply to RF disappear. Using σ_p to represent the risky portfolio's standard deviation, the combined portfolio's risk is:

Standard Deviation of Risk-Free and Risky Portfolio

$$\sigma_c = (1 - X)\sigma_p \tag{6.13}$$

For example, an 80/20 risky versus risk-free security mix would result in a 16% combined portfolio standard deviation if the risky securities had a 20% standard deviation:

$$0.8\,(20\%) = 16\%$$

When Equations (6.12) and (6.13) are combined, an interesting result occurs. The relationship between risk and return is linear and equal to:

Linear Risk/Return with Risk-Free Securities

$$E(R_c) = RF + \sigma_c \frac{E(R_p) - RF}{\sigma_p} \tag{6.14}$$

Returns expected on portfolios that combine a risk-free security with risky securities come from two sources. First, a risk-free rate is expected to be earned on both the risk-free security and the risky set of securities. In addition, a return is earned for bearing risk—a return equal to $[E(R_p)—RF] \div \sigma_p$ for each unit of σ_c. The number of units of σ_c risk incurred depends, of course, on the proportion of funds in the risky securities.

There is no guarantee that the expected return for bearing risk will be positive. That depends totally on the one or more risky securities being evaluated. In a moment we return to this "risk premium" and see how it might be maximized, but first consider some examples using the following information, which is also plotted in Figure 6-12:

Security	Expected Return	σ
IBM Stock	14%	25%
Risk-Free Security	9%	0

When a 100% investment is made in IBM, the portfolio return is 14%. This 14% comes from two sources: (1) a risk-free return of 9%, and (2) a return for bearing risk of 14% − 9% = 5%.

When a 50% investment is made in IBM, risk is half of the 100% investment level and, thus, the return for bearing risk is also half (2.5%):

$$E(R_c) = RF + \sigma_c \frac{E(Rp) - RF}{\sigma_p}$$

$$= 9.0\% + (0.5 \times 25\%)(0.20)$$

$$= 9.0\% + 2.5\% = 11.5\%$$

Portfolios that include some amount of the risk-free security are referred to as **lending portfolios** because a portion of one's money is "lent" to borrowers at the risk-free rate. But in the same way that lending portfolios can be created that reduce expected returns and risk,

---

FIGURE 6-12 PORTFOLIO COMBINATIONS OF THE RISK-FREE SECURITY WITH A RISKY SECURITY

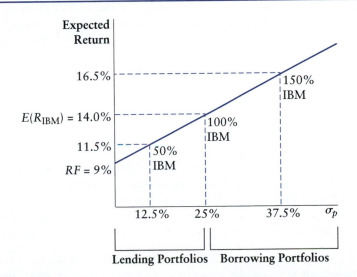

borrowing portfolios can be created that increase risk and expected returns. Borrowing portfolios essentially use margin to increase the number of shares an individual's personal equity can control.

To illustrate, assume you have $10,000 to invest and would prefer a higher return than is expected on IBM in Figure 6-12. You're also willing to accept the higher risk. Consider what would happen if you borrowed $5,000 at the risk-free rate of 9% and used the borrowing plus your personal equity to purchase $15,000 of IBM. Your expected dollar return on IBM shares would be $2,100 ($15,000 × 0.14), and after you pay $450 in interest ($5,000 × 0.09) your net dollar profit would be $1,650. On a $10,000 equity, this is a 16.5% expected return.

The same result can be obtained by using Equation (6.14), if we recognize that borrowing is simply **negative lending:**

$$E(R_c) = RF + \sigma_c \frac{E(R_p) - RF}{\sigma_p}$$

$$= 9\% + 1.5\,(25\%)[0.2]$$

$$= 9\% + 7.5\% = 16.5\%$$

On your personal equity, you earn a risk-free 9%. The borrowing also earns 9%, but you must pay that to the people from whom you borrowed, so it is a wash. However, by placing $0.50 in borrowed money into the risky security for each $1.00 of your personal equity, you have magnified your risk exposure by 50%. Thus, the expected risk premium increases from 5% to 7.5%. The new expected return is therefore 16.5%. But it comes only with an increase in portfolio standard deviation from 25% to 37.5% (1.5 × 25%).

The Portfolio Separation Theorem. One can combine borrowing and lending with any individual security or portfolio of securities, as displayed in Figure 6-13. In this figure, three lines are shown. The two dashed lines represent risk-return combinations on *RF* combined with IBM and on a portfolio called *O*, which lies on the efficient frontier we developed earlier in this chapter. Note that the slope of each line represents the return expected to be earned per unit of risk. Clearly, combinations with portfolio *O* are better than combinations with IBM, since the slope of the line is greater. However, a single portfolio on the efficient frontier will maximize the return earned for bearing risk. This is portfolio **p***, which lies on the solid line extending from *RF*.

Given the presence of a risk-free rate, two very important implications emerge:

1. **There is a single optimal portfolio of risky securities to own—regardless of the individual's risk preferences.** Different people might disagree on exactly what that optimal portfolio consists of. But for any one individual, there is only one risky portfolio that should be held.
2. **The individual can obtain a desired risk/return profile by combining this optimal risky portfolio with borrowing or lending at *RF*.** If the risky security portfolio contains more risk than desired, the risk can be reduced by placing a portion of the resources in risk-free securities. If the expected return is too low, the investor should borrow and invest the borrowing in the ideal risky portfolio.

A **separation** now exists between an identification of the ideal risky security portfolio (implication 1) and the selection of an appropriate risk level (implication 2). This

FIGURE 6-13 ALTERNATIVE COMBINATIONS OF RISKY SECURITIES WITH A RISK-FREE SECURITY

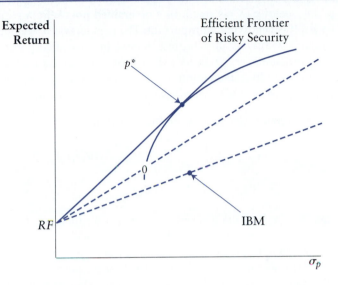

is commonly called the **portfolio separation theorem.** The investment decision is now a two-step process: (1) identify the optimal risky security, and (2) move along the borrowing-lending line to a personally acceptable risk level.

Measuring the Risk of a Security

Risk and expected return on the **total portfolio** are the two most important features of any investment program. Recognizing this, we have focused almost exclusively on the aggregate portfolio, with no mention of how individual security risk should be defined and measured. Given the benefits of broad diversification, we assume that the portfolio in which the security is held is well diversified.

Total Security Risk

The risk of the portfolio can be thought of as a weighted average of the risks of the individual securities in the portfolio. The weights applied to each security are the percentages the security represents of the total portfolio. Using variance as the measure of risk, this can be stated symbolically as follows:

Portfolio Variance

$$\sigma_p^2 = \sum_{i=1}^{N} X_i \quad [\text{Total Risk of Security } i \text{ in Portfolio Now Held}]$$

$$= \sum_{i=1}^{N} X_i \left[X_i \, \sigma_i^2 + \sum_{\substack{j=1 \\ i \neq j}}^{N} X_j \; \text{Covariance } (i, j) \right] \qquad \textbf{(6.15)}$$

where the term covariance (i, j) is equal to $(\sigma_i\sigma_j r_{ij})$.

Look at the terms in brackets. These represent the **total risk** of security i in the portfolio. In a well-diversified portfolio, the first term will be very small, since the fraction held of any security (X_i) is small. **In a diversified portfolio, a security's standard deviation by itself is relatively unimportant.** The next term is a weighted sum of the security's covariance with other investment holdings. In diversified portfolios, this term is not small, since the sum over $j = 1$ to N (where j can not be equal to i) will be almost 1.0.

In a well-diversified portfolio, the major risk a security adds to the portfolio is the covariance that the security has with the rest of the portfolio.

Total Security Risk in a Diversified Portfolio

$$= \sum_{\substack{j=1 \\ i \neq j}}^{N} X_j \, (\sigma_i\sigma_j r_{ij}) \qquad\qquad (6.16)$$

$$= \sigma_i \sigma'_p r_{ip}$$

Here σ'_p represents the standard deviation of a portfolio that does not have the security in it and r_{ij} is the correlation of the security with the portfolio of all other securities which are owned.

For example, assume the standard deviation of General Motors (GM) annual returns is 30%. Also assume the standard deviation of the portfolio of all other securities you own is 20% and the correlation coefficient between GM returns and this portfolio of other stocks is 0.25. Then the total risk of GM (in the context of the other securities owned) would be its covariance with the other securities of 150%:

$$150\% = (30)(20)(0.25)$$

Although GM has a standard deviation 50% greater than the portfolio of other securities, only one-quarter (the correlation of 0.25) of GM's standard deviation matters in this diversified portfolio, since it represents the risk of GM that is not eliminated by diversification.

Also notice that investors who have different portfolios should evaluate the risk of GM differently. For one investor, GM might add significantly to portfolio risk if it were highly correlated with existing portfolio holdings. To another investor, GM might be virtually riskless if it were uncorrelated with existing portfolio holdings. There is no one measure of total security risk that can be used by all investors; it depends on the particular portfolio held. Only when everyone holds the same portfolio will the risk of a given security be identical for everyone.

Relative Security Risk

The measure of total security risk in Equation (6.16) is difficult to interpret. For example, is GM's total security risk of 150% large or small? To overcome this problem, security risks are often expressed in terms of the risk of the security relative to the total risk of other securities held in the portfolio. Relative security risk is found by dividing total security risk by total portfolio risk:

Relative Risk of Security i

$$= \frac{\text{Total Risk of Security } i}{\text{Total Risk of the Portfolio}} \qquad\qquad (6.17)$$

$$= \frac{\sigma_i \sigma_p r_{ip}}{\sigma_p^2}$$

$$= \frac{\sigma_i r_{ip}}{\sigma_p}$$

In a broadly diversified portfolio, the relative risk of a single security is equal to (1) the standard deviation of its returns, (2) divided by the portfolio standard deviation, (3) multiplied by the security's correlation with portfolio returns. This measure of relative security risk is typically referred to as **beta.** Beta is usually denoted by the Greek capital letter for beta: β.

For example, the beta risk of General Motors would be 0.375:

$$B_{\text{GM}} = \frac{30(0.25)}{20} = 0.375$$

The concept of beta plays an important role in the capital asset pricing model discussed in the next chapter.[3]

SUMMARY

Here are the key concepts of this chapter:

- Individuals are said to be risk-averse if the pleasure they gain from a $1 increase in wealth is less than the pleasure they lose from a $1 reduction in wealth.

- Risk inherent in the total portfolio is of more direct concern to the investor than the risks of individual securities. While individual security risks do combine with one another to determine a portfolio's risk level, it is the total portfolio risk that is most crucial.

- The standard deviation of portfolio returns is not simply a weighted average of the standard deviations of the individual securities comprising the portfolio. The effects of differing levels of correlation between security returns must be accounted for.

- If security returns are perfectly negatively correlated (correlation coefficient = −1.0), diversification with only two securities can totally eliminate portfolio risk. If a large number of uncorrelated securities (correlation coefficient = 0.0) are available, broad diversification can virtually eliminate portfolio risk.

- If security returns are perfectly positively correlated (correlation coefficient = +1.0), diversification will provide no risk reduction advantages.

- Since security returns generally have a correlation coefficient between 0.0 and +1.0, there are significant advantages to diversification. But in the real world, portfolio risk

---

[3] Beta as calculated in Equation (6.17) depends on the portfolio of securites now held and will change as the portfolio changes. For example, a beta of GM when compared against the S&P 500 Index will be different than a beta when GM is compared against the Dow Jones Industrial Average.

cannot be totally eliminated. To some extent all security returns are affected by similar events, and this common component of security returns cannot be diversified away.

■ In a broadly diversified portfolio, the risk of any single security depends on the standard deviation of the security's returns and the correlation of the security's returns with the returns of the portfolio. Typically, a security's risk **relative** to the risk of the diversified portfolio to which it is added is measured by beta.

■ Relative risk, or beta, depends on the portfolio of securities held. As a result, investors holding different portfolios will evaluate the relative risk of a given stock differently.

■ Perhaps the best advice this chapter offers to both investors and speculators is to diversify. Risk reduction advantages inherent in diversification are significant. That portion of a security's risk that is diversifiable is known as unsystematic risk, whereas systematic risk refers to the nondiversifiable portion of security risk. Contrasted with naive diversification, efficient diversification models exist that allow investors to find a set of different portfolios that minimize portfolio risks for differing levels of expected returns.

R E V I E W   P R O B L E M

Percentage annual returns for International Business Machines Inc. (IBM) and Microsoft Corp. (MSFT) are shown here:

Year	1990	1991	1992	1993	1994
IBM	+25.45	−17.52	−39.99	+15.59	+32.16
MSFT	−13.50	+47.84	−23.25	−5.56	+38.54

a. Find the average annual return for each.

b. Find the variance of return for each **not adjusted** for uncertain mean (divide by N).

c. Find the standard deviation for each **not adjusted** for uncertain mean (divide by N).

d. Find the variance of return for each **adjusted for** uncertain mean (divide by $N - 1$).

e. Find the standard deviation for each **adjusted for** uncertain mean (divide by $N - 1$).

f. Find the covariance of returns between the two.

g. Find the correlation coefficient.

h. Assume you create a portfolio consisting of a 50% investment in each. At the start of each year the portfolio is rebalanced to this 50/50 mix. Calculate the following:

　　■ Average yearly return.

　　■ Standard deviation of annual return

i. Fill in the following table.

Percentage Invested in					
IBM	100	75	50	25	0
MSFT	0	25	50	75	100
Average Return					
Standard Deviation					

Solutions

a. Average return of IBM:

$(+25.45 - 17.52 - 39.99 + 15.59 + 32.16) \div 5 = 3.138\%$

Average return for MSFT:

$(-13.50 + 47.84 - 23.25 - 5.56 + 38.54) \div 5 = 8.814\%$

b. IBM variance not adjusted for mean uncertainty:

$[(25.45 - 3.138)^2 + (-17.52 - 3.138)^2 + \cdots + (32.16 - 3.138)^2] \div 5 = 756.39$

MSFT variance not adjusted for mean uncertainty:

$[(-13.5 - 8.814)^2 + (47.84 - 8.814)^2 + \cdots + (38.54 - 8.814)^2] \div 5 = 827.86$

c. IBM standard deviation not adjusted for mean uncertainty:

$(756.39)^{1 \div 2} = 27.50\%$

MSFT standard deviation not adjusted for mean uncertainty:

$(827.86)^{1 \div 2} = 28.77\%$

d. IBM variance adjusted for mean uncertainty:

$[(25.45 - 3.138)^2 + (-17.52 - 3.138)^2 + \cdots + (32.16 - 3.138)^2] \div (5 - 1) = 945.48$

MSFT variance adjusted for mean uncertainty:

$[(-13.5 - 8.814)^2 + (47.84 - 8.814)^2 + \cdots + (38.54 - 8.814)^2] \div (5 - 1) = 1{,}034.82$

e. IBM standard deviation adjusted for mean uncertainty:

$(945.48)^{1 \div 2} = 30.75\%$

MSFT standard deviation adjusted for mean uncertainty:

$(1{,}034.82)^{1 \div 2} = 32.17\%$

When variance and standard deviation are not adjusted for uncertainty about the true mean, they are smaller in value than when mean uncertainty is considered. In calculating the covariance and correlation between two securities, the unadjusted numbers are used.

f. Covariance between IBM and MSFT:

$[(25.45 - 3.138)(-13.51 - 8.814) + (-17.52 - 3.138)(47.84 - 8.814)$
$+ \cdots + (32.16 - 3.138)(38.54 - 8.814)] \div 5 = 152.502$

g. Correlation coefficient:

$152.502 \div (27.50 \times 28.77) = 0.1927$

h. Average yearly return:

$0.50(3.138\%) + 0.50(8.814\%) = 5.976\%$

Standard deviation:

$[(0.50)^2 (30.75)^2 + (0.50)^2 (32.17)^2 + 2(0.50)(0.50)(30.75)(32.17)(0.1927)]^{1 \div 2}$
$= 24.30\%$

Percentage Invested in

IBM	100	75	50	25	0
MSFT	0	25	50	75	100
Average Return	3.14	4.56	5.98	7.40	8.81
Standard Deviation	30.75	25.85	24.30	26.70	32.17

QUESTIONS AND PROBLEMS

1. Why are people risk-averse? How does utility theory suggest we measure risk?
2. This chapter deals with naive and efficient diversification.
   a. How does efficient diversification compare with naive diversification?
   b. What inputs are necessary for efficient diversification?

3. You are evaluating various combinations of Portfolio A and Portfolio B. Relevant information about each is shown here:

	Portfolio A	Portfolio B
Expected return	8%	14%
Standard deviation	10%	20%
Correlation coefficient	0.50	

Prepare a graph of various combinations of these security portfolios in which the expected return is shown on the vertical axis and standard deviation is shown on the horizontal axis. (This is easiest to do using a computer spreadsheet package.)

4. The exhibit you prepare in response to this question is widely used in the investment community to display the benefits of international investment to U.S. investors. The following information relates to the years 1969 through 1994:

	S&P 500	EAFE Index
Average annual real return	5.60%	9.25%
Standard deviation of annual real returns	17.28%	24.37%
Correlation coefficient	0.63	

Prepare a graph of various combinations of these security portfolios in which the expected return is shown on the vertical axis and standard deviation is shown on the horizontal axis. (This is easiest to do using a computer spreadsheet package.)

5. Stock 1 has an expected return of 20% and a standard deviation of 40%, Stock 2 has an expected return of 25% and a standard deviation of 50%. Their correlation is 0.00. What percentage investment in each would lead to a minimum risk portfolio?

6. The nominal returns on three international asset classes are shown here for a recent five-year period.

Year	S&P 500	Small U.S. Stocks	EAFE
1990	−3.17%	−21.56%	−23.20%
1991	30.55	44.63	12.49
1992	7.67	23.27	−11.84
1993	9.99	20.98	32.94
1994	1.32	3.11	7.79

a. Calculate the average return and standard deviation for each.
b. Calculate the correlation coefficient between each.
c. What would be the standard deviation of a portfolio that consisted of one-third invested in each (at the start of each year)?
d. Why is this portfolio standard deviation not equal to the standard deviation of each asset class added together and the sum divided by 3?

7. Assume you are considering N stocks. Unfortunately, you are unable to distinguish between them. Your expected return on each is the same. Your standard deviation on each is the same. And you assign the same correlation coefficient for each security pair. What is the optimal percentage to invest in each?

8. Assume you going to invest in stocks traded in the Pacific Rim. There are N different countries in which you will invest. Your estimates of expected returns and standard deviations for each country are identical. You also believe a correlation of 0.40 should be

applied to all pairs of the N countries. However, you know the present U.S. dollar value of stocks traded in each country differs as follows:

Country	Dollar Value of Stocks Traded
1	$100.0 billion
2	$200.0 billion
3	$300.0 billion
4	$250.0 billion
5	$250.0 billion

What percentage investment in each country would minimize your risk? Explain.

9. Anne Kaboda is evaluating the possible returns from investing during the next year in the Hong Kong and Tokyo stock markets. To help in the analysis, she has developed the following possible scenarios:

Probability	Return in Hong Kong	Tokyo	Scenario
0.25	−25%	−10%	Poor economy in both markets. Hong Kong also has problems in unification with People's Republic of China (PRC).
0.25	−5	−10	Poor economy in both markets. Unification of Hong Kong with PRC goes more smoothly than expected.
0.25	0	+25	Good economy in both markets. Hong Kong has problems in unification with PRC.
0.25	+30	+25	Good economy in both markets. Unification of Hong Kong with PRC goes more smoothly than expected.

Calculate the expected return and standard deviation from the following investment strategies:
a. 100% in Tokyo.
b. 100% in Hong Kong
c. 50% in both markets.

10. Quarterly returns are shown here for three mutual funds. The first fund invests in U.S. government bonds. The second invests in U.S. stocks. And the third invests in international (meaning non-U.S. equities). These are returns on actual mutual funds.

Quarter	U.S. Govt.	U.S. Stocks	Non-U.S. Stocks
1	1.72%	3.43%	−14.08%
2	3.75	8.67	10.59
3	4.08	9.75	5.96
4	−0.85	8.44	2.90
5	2.73	−4.99	18.23
6	2.89	3.90	0.55
7	−0.42	16.03	−0.78
8	1.91	9.62	7.26
9	0.85	16.03	4.86
10	1.04	9.62	25.58

In developing the answer to this problem, you may wish to use a computer spreadsheet package because of the number of calculations involved. If you do so, try not to use the built-in functions of the spreadsheet. Instead, go through all the calculation details.

a. For each fund, calculate the following:

■ average return

■ variance of return (use the formula for the variance that does not adjust for uncertain mean returns)

■ standard deviation of return

■ correlation with other funds

b. Why does the U.S. bond fund have returns that are not highly correlated with the U.S. equity fund?

c. Why does the U.S. stock fund have returns that are not highly correlated with the non-U.S. equity fund?

d. What would have been the standard deviation of the following portfolios?

■ 50% in the U.S. bond fund and 50% in the U.S equity fund

■ 50% in the U.S. equity fund and 50% in the non-U.S. equity fund

■ a one-third investment in each fund

11. Information on three securities follows:

Security	Expected Return	Standard Deviation	Correlation with A	B	C
A	8%	10%	1.0		
B	8%	10%	−1.0	1.0	
C	15%	20%	0.0	0.0	1.0

Calculate the efficient frontier.

12. The one-year return on a risk-free portfolio is 6.0%. A risky portfolio is available that is expected to return 11% during the next year with a standard deviation of 20%.

a. How could you combine these two portfolios to obtain an expected return of 8.5%?

b. How could you combine these portfolios to obtain a standard deviation of 10%?

c. How could you combine these portfolios to obtain an expected return of 16%?

d. How could you combine these portfolios to obtain a standard deviation of 30%?

13. What does the portfolio separation theorem imply about proper investment policy?

14. The risk of a given security is not the same for all investors if they own different security portfolios. Why?

15. Portfolio risk can be measured by the standard deviation of the portfolio's returns. Why should the risk of an individual security not be measured in the same way?

16. You presently own a well-diversified portfolio of securities that has a standard deviation of yearly returns equal to 10%. You are considering the addition of another security. This security has a standard deviation of yearly returns equal to 30%. Its correlation with the current portfolio is 0.5. What is the risk of this new security relative to the risk of your current portfolio? Explain why this relative risk is not three times the current portfolio's risk.

17. Portfolio theory as described by Markowitz is most concerned with:

a. the elimination of systematic risk.

b. the effect of diversification on portfolio risk.

c. the identification of unsystematic risk.

d. active portfolio management to enhance returns.

CFA   18. The measure of risk in a Markowitz efficient frontier is:
     a. specific risk.
     b. standard deviation of returns.
     c. reinvestment risk.
     d. beta.

CFA   19. Which one of the following statements about portfolio diversification is correct?
     a. The risk-reducing benefits of diversification do not occur meaningfully until at least 30 to 35 individual securities have been purchased.
     b. Typically, as more securities are added to a portfolio, beta would be expected to rise at a decreasing rate.
     c. Because diversification reduces a portfolio's total risk, it necessarily reduces the portfolio's expected return.
     d. Proper diversification can reduce or eliminate nonsystematic risk.

CFA   20. Standard deviation and beta both measure risk, but they are different in that beta measures:
     a. only systematic risk, while standard deviation measures only unsystematic risk.
     b. only systematic risk, while standard deviation is a measure of total risk.
     c. only unsystematic risk, while standard deviation is a measure of total risk.
     d. both systematic and unsystematic risk, while standard deviation measures only systematic risk.

CFA   21. Statistics for three stocks are shown in the tables here:

Standard Deviations of Returns

Stock	A	B	C
	0.40	0.20	0.40

Correlations of Returns

	A	B	C
A	1.00		
B	0.90	1.0	
C	0.50	0.10	1.00

    Based only on the information provided in the tables, and given a chance between a portfolio made up of equal amounts of stocks A and B or a portfolio made up of equal amounts of stocks B and C, state which portfolio you would recommend. Justify your choice.

CFA   22. Assume the return on an asset added to a portfolio is less than perfectly positively correlated with the returns of the other assets in the portfolio, but has the same standard deviation. What effect will adding the new asset have on the standard deviation of the portfolio's return? The standard deviation:
     a. will decrease.
     b. will increase.
     c. may increase or decrease depending on the individual securities mix in the portfolio.
     d. may increase or decrease depending on the asset allocation model.

CFA   23. Assume a risk-averse investor owning stock in Miller Corporation decides to add the stock of either Mac or Green Corporation to her portfolio. All three stocks offer the same expected return and total risk. The covariance between Miller and Mac is -0.05 and between Miller and Green is $+0.05$. Portfolio risk is expected to:
     a. decline more by buying Mac.
     b. decline more by buying Green.
     c. increase by buying either Mac or Green.

d. decline or increase, depending on other factors.

24. Which one of the following portfolios can not lie on the efficient frontier as described by Markowitz?

	Portfolio	Expected Return	Standard Deviation
a.	W	15%	36%
b.	X	12%	15%
c.	Z	5%	7%
d.	Y	9%	21%

DATAFILE ANALYSIS

In this analysis, you will develop a historical efficient frontier using yearly returns in the data set called INDEXES.WK3 and the efficient frontier programs called ASSETALL. Clearly, historical efficient frontiers (based on past realized returns) might not be good estimates of current efficient frontiers that you would develop (based on expectations of future returns). But historical data is easy to obtain, and the results are educational. This is not simply a textbook example, however. What you will do in the analysis is the same that professional investment consultants do for pension funds and endowments when they are trying to determine how millions of dollars will be invested.

1. **Averages and Standard Deviation.** Select five security classes from the RTNSYRLY datafile that you believe differ in average returns and standard deviations. For a period during which they all have returns available, calculate the yearly "real returns" by subtracting CPI (Consumer Pricing Index) returns. Calculate the average and standard deviation of each real return series. This can be done using the average and standard deviation functions of the spreadsheet package.

2. **Correlation Coefficients.** To calculate correlation coefficients between each series, it is easiest to use the CORREL function of the spreadsheet package. The data will be used as input to the efficient frontier program. Write it on a sheet of paper. It is best to express the averages and standard deviations in percentage form (5% should be 5.0 and not 0.05).

3. **Assetall.** The efficient frontier program is invoked by typing ASSETALL (for asset allocation). Follow the menu instructions. (A manual for ASSETALL is on the program diskette. It is in ASCII form.) You should first create an input data file of the averages, standard deviations, and correlation coefficients. In running the efficient frontier, you should use the option that does not allow short sales because it is easiest to interpret.

4. **Efficient Portfolios.** Finally, print the output data set created by ASSETALL and interpret the results. When historical efficient frontiers such as this are calculated, one usually finds an asset class in which no investment is ever optimal. Why might this be the case? If security markets are efficient, does it make sense that no investment in a security class would be optimal?

REFERENCES

The classic and first articles dealing with what we now call modern portfolio theory are as follows:

Markowitz, Harry M. "Portfolio Selection," *Journal of Finance,* March 1952.

Markowitz, Harry M. *Portfolio Selection: Efficient Diversification of Investment.* Cowles Foundation Monograph 16. New Haven: Yale University Press, 1959.

Sharpe, William F. *Portfolio Theory and Capital Markets,* New York: McGraw-Hill, 1970.

Here are two finance textbooks that provide a good review of utility theory as applied to investment decision making:

Elton, Edwin J. and Martin J. Gruber, *Modern Portfolio Theory and Investment Analysis,* New York: John Wiley, 1987.

Haley, Charles W. and Lawrence D. Schall, *The Theory of Financial Decisions,* New York: McGraw-Hill, 1979.

A few more recent articles that expand on the principles of portfolio theory include the following:

Brealey, Richard A. "Portfolio Theory versus Portfolio Practice," *The Journal of Portfolio Management,* Summer 1990.

Chopra, Vijay K. and William T. Ziemba, "The Effect of Errors in Means, Variances, and Covariances on Optimal Portfolio Choice," *The Journal of Portfolio Management,* Winter 1993.

Ezra, D. Don. "Asset Allocation by Surplus Optimization," *Financial Analysts Journal,* January–February 1991.

Lee, Wayne Y. "Diversification and Time: Do Investment Horizons Matter?" *The Journal of Portfolio Management,* Spring 1990.

Sharpe, William F. and Lawrence G. Tint, "Liabilities—A New Approach," *The Journal of Portfolio Management,* Winter 1990.

APPENDIX 6A

NAIVE DIVERSIFICATION AND THE INVESTMENT HORIZON

We have two objectives in this appendix:

1. to take a more analytical look at naive diversification, and
2. to consider how the length of the investment horizon affects the number of securities that should be held in a portfolio.

Recall that naive diversification consists of randomly selecting N securities and investing $1/N$ in each. No investment professionals ever suggest that investors actually select portfolios using a naive diversification strategy. The concept of naive diversification is simply a useful way of illustrating why diversification works and how rapidly it works.

An Analytic Look at Naive Diversification

The variance of a portfolio consisting of N securities is calculated as follows:

Portfolio Variance
$$\sigma_p^2 = \sum_{i=1}^{N} X_i^2 \sigma_i^2 + \sum_{\substack{i=1 \\ i \neq j}}^{N} \sum_{j=1}^{N} X_i X_j \ \text{cov}(ij) \tag{6A.1}$$

Here cov(ij) refers to the covariance between security i and security j. In the chapter, we expressed this term as $(\sigma_i \sigma_j r_{ij})$.

Now assume that $1/N$ is invested in each security held in the portfolio. In addition, define the following terms:

$\overline{\sigma}^2 =$ The average variance of all securities that might be owned. This is not the average variance of securities actually owned. Instead it is the average across all securities in the universe from which a random selection is made.

$\overline{\text{Cov}} =$ The average covariance of all securities that might be owned. As above, this is the average across all securities in the universe from which a random selection is made.

The **expected** portfolio variance of an N security portfolio in which $1/N$ is invested in each security is:

Expected Variance When X_i Is $1/N$
$$E(\sigma_p^2) = \frac{\overline{\sigma}^2}{N} + \frac{(N-1)\ \overline{\text{cov}}}{N} \tag{6A.2}$$

The **expected** variance is equal to:

- ■ the average variance (in the universe from which you are selecting) divided by N,

- ■ plus the average covariance (in the universe) times (N minus 1) and divided by N.

Consider the two terms on the right side of Equation (6A.2).

As N increases, the average **variance** term becomes smaller. For large values of N, the term approaches zero. **In well-diversified portfolios, the variance of returns on an individual security is relatively unimportant.**

In contrast, the average **covariance** term becomes increasingly important. For large values of N, the term approaches the average covariance between securities in the universe from which securities are selected. **In well-diversified portfolios, the risk of the portfolio is determined by the covariance in security returns.**

To explicitly see the role the correlation coefficient plays in diversification, the average covariance term in Equation (6A.1) can be expressed as:

Average Covariance
$$\overline{cov} = \overline{\sigma}^2 \overline{r} \tag{6A.3}$$

This says the average covariance in the universe from which you are selecting is equal to the average variance times the average correlation coefficient. Using this relationship, Equation 6A.2 can be reexpressed as follows:

Expected Variance When X_i Is $1/N$
$$E(\sigma_p^2) = \frac{\overline{\sigma}^2}{N} + \frac{(N-1)\overline{\sigma}^2 \overline{r}}{N} \tag{6A.4}$$

Table 6A-1 and Figure 6A-1 show how the expected portfolio standard deviation decreases as the number of randomly selected securities (N) increases.[4] Data in the table and figure is based on an average standard deviation of 50%. Results are shown for three different average correlation coefficients. When the correlation is equal to 0.0, all risk can (conceptually) be eliminated if a large number of securities are held. When the correlation coefficient is above 0.0, there is an underlying systematic risk that can not be removed by diversification. This systematic risk is directly related to the level of the average correlation between securities.

Notice that, by the time 10 to 20 securities are held, virtually all the diversifiable risk in the expected standard deviation is eliminated. This is a common finding in all empirical studies of naive diversification. And this finding is often offered as an illustration of the power of diversification.

However, this fact should also be viewed with some suspicion, since few knowledgeable investors believe a 20-security portfolio is sufficiently diversified. Three explanations argue for a much larger portfolio:

1. The data and equations we have examined relate to the expected variance and standard deviation, sort of what would happen on average. But some investors would have N stock portfolios with much larger risks then suggested here. To provide a margin of safety, a portfolio should be more diversified than Table 6A-1 implies.
2. The only form of risk considered in this analysis is volatility risk, variability around a known average return. But if there is also an uncertainty about the expected return, greater diversification is required.
3. The investment horizon displayed in Figure 6A-1 and Table 6A-1 was not specified. But a standard deviation of 50% is close to what a one-year investor would face in common stocks. Longer horizon investors face greater risks, both diversifiable and nondiversifiable. Give the increased risk for longer horizons, long-term investors should hold a larger number of securities than short-term investors.

---

[4] The standard deviations shown are equal to the square root of Equation 6A.4.

TABLE 6A-1   EXPECTED PORTFOLIO STANDARD DEVIATIONS

	Correlation Coefficient			Risk as a Percentage of Owning a Single Security		
N	0.0	0.3	0.6	r = 0.0	r = 0.3	r = 0.6
1	50.00	50.00	50.00	100.0	100.0	100.0
5	22.36	33.17	41.23	44.72	66.34	82.46
10	15.81	30.41	40.00	31.64	60.82	80.00
20	11.18	28.93	39.37	22.36	57.86	78.74
30	9.13	28.43	39.16	18.26	56.86	78.32
40	7.90	28.17	39.05	15.80	56.34	78.10
50	7.07	28.02	38.98	14.14	56.04	77.96
Minimum Possible	0.00	27.38	38.73	0.00	54.76	77.46

FIGURE 6A-1   NAIVE DIVERSIFICATION ONE PERIOD INVESTMENT HORIZON

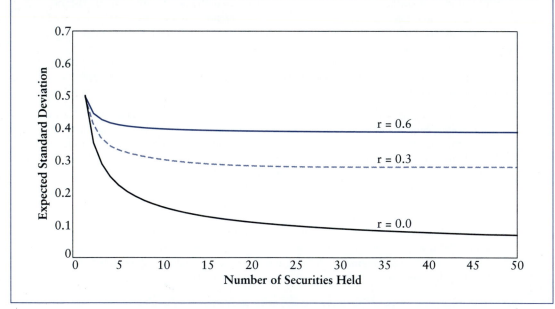

FIGURE 6A-2 NAIVE DIVERSIFICATION AND THE INVESTMENT HORIZON

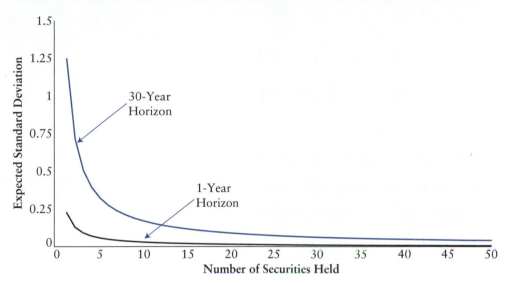

Diversifiable Risk and the Investment Horizon

In Chapter 5 we saw that investment risk increases with the time horizon. Specifically, the standard deviation of a T period investment is equal to the standard deviation of a single period investment times the square root of T.[5] Using this concept, we can examine the diversifiable and nondiversifiable risk for various investment horizons.

Consider Figure 6A-2, which plots data for the case when average security correlation is 0.30. The vertical axis in Figure 6A.2 displays the **diversifiable risk** facing both a 1-year investor and a 30-year investor. For example, in Figure 6A-1 a 1-year investor in a single stock faced an expected standard deviation of 50%. This 50% consists of a nondiversifiable risk of about 28% and a diversifiable risk of 22%. **It is the 22% diversifiable risk that is plotted in Figure 6A-2.**

The diversifiable risk facing long-term investors is considerably greater than short-term investors incur. For a 30-year horizon, this risk is about 5.5 times greater than for a 1-year horizon:

$$5.477 = 30^{1 \div 2}$$

This suggests that long-term investors should diversify more broadly than short-term investors.

---

[5] Uncertainty about the expected return also causes risk to increase with time. In fact, under reasonable assumptions, the standard deviation of the uncertain expected return creates a standard deviation of a T period holding period return that is T times the standard deviation of a single period standard deviation. This, of course, implies that long-term investors require greater diversification than do short-term investors. Uncertain mean return risk is not modeled in this section.

7

CAPITAL ASSET
PRICING MODEL

After reading this chapter you should have an understanding of the major theory relating expected security returns to the risk of a security. This security risk is called beta risk.

In the previous chapter, we concentrated on how individual investors and speculators can determine the single portfolio of risky securities that is optimal to them and how this portfolio can be combined with lending at the risk-free rate or borrowing in order to achieve a preferred risk/return trade-off. In this chapter we extend the discussion to the market in general and examine the following question:

> If all investors pursued optimal portfolio selection, how would this affect equilibrium security prices and expected returns?

Knowledge of how equilibrium market prices and expected returns are created would be invaluable to both issuers of securities and investors in securities. Security issuers would be able to make better estimates of the financial costs of raising new capital. And security investors would use this knowledge to better manage the risks and returns of their portfolios.

The equilibrium model discussed in this chapter is known as the **capital asset pricing model** (CAPM). Embodied in this model are two fundamental relationships. Since there is often confusion between the two, we state each immediately.

The first relationship, known as the **capital market line,** specifies the return an investor will expect to receive on an **efficient portfolio** (one with the lowest possible risk for a given expected return). The capital market line is written symbolically as:

Capital Market Line $E(R_p) = RF + \sigma_p(RP_M \div \sigma_M)$ **(7.1)**

The return expected on an efficient portfolio consists of a risk-free rate (earned for delaying consumption) plus a risk premium (earned for bearing risk inherent in the portfolio). The size of the risk premium is determined by the standard deviation of the portfolio and the prevailing market risk premium per unit of market risk. The market risk premium is the difference between the expected return on a portfolio called the **market portfolio** and the risk-free interest rate.

The second relationship, known as the **security market line,** is broader and able to treat individual securities as well as portfolios. It expresses the return that should be expected in terms of a risk-free rate and the **relative risk** of the security (or portfolio). The security market line is written symbolically as:

Security Market Line $E(R_i) = RF + B_i(RP_M)$ **(7.2)**

As with the capital market line, there is a risk-free and a risk component. But the security market line expresses the risk of a security in relative terms through beta whereas the capital market line treats total portfolio risk. In addition, the security market line treats any security, while the capital market line treats efficient portfolios only. As we would expect, the security market line is the more widely used because of its greater generality.

In the standard CAPM developed in this chapter, a single portfolio of risky securities emerges that all investors should hold in combination with borrowing or lending. This portfolio is referred to as the **market portfolio** and consists of all risky securities in existence, with relative holdings of each dependent on each security's total market value. The implication that such a market portfolio is the optimal risky asset portfolio is the central conclusion of this theory. From the optimality of the market portfolio comes both the capital market line and security market line. From it also come a variety of investment and speculative implications that have had major impacts on portfolio strategies within the last decade.

The implication that the market portfolio is the best portfolio of risky assets to hold is simply a logical consequence of the various assumptions made in developing CAPM. After reviewing its development, you might sit back and say, *of course, it makes perfect sense—if the assumptions are correct*. These assumptions are treated as abstractions of reality that are needed in order to develop a simple relationship between equilibrium risk and return. Although none of them is strictly true, we wait until Chapter 8 to examine the empirical accuracy of the model and the effects of lifting each assumption.

The Capital Market Line

In this chapter we develop a model that explains security prices when the security market is at **equilibrium.** Equilibrium exists when prices are at levels that provide no incentive for speculative trading. At equilibrium, the quantity of shares desired for sale by investors is equal to the quantity desired for purchase.

If the price of a given security is lower than its equilibrium level, an excess demand will arise and speculators will bid up prices until the excess demand is removed. Similarly, if prices are greater than equilibrium, speculators will create an excess supply and force prices down by their selling. The point at which price levels attract no information trading is what we consider equilibrium.

If prices are set at equilibrium, trades between buyers and sellers will continue to occur. Individuals and institutional investors who have excess cash and wish to invest come to the market with bids to buy; individuals and institutional investors who need cash come to the market with offers to sell. However, at equilibrium, no one is offering to buy or sell out of a belief that existing prices are wrong: No one trades with an information motive. For the market to be truly in equilibrium, all buyers and sellers must have the same information. If they don't, then by definition the market cannot yet be at equilibrium.

Equilibrium prices will change with the passage of time, as world events occur and provide new information about the prospects of the firms that originally issued the securities. If events are dramatic, equilibrium price changes will also be dramatic. Hence, there is nothing particularly inconsistent about having significant gyrations in security prices over time and a market that is always at equilibrium. The large price movements might simply reflect continuous and occasionally large adjustments to equilibrium levels necessary as new information unfolds. In contrast, many people would argue that actual market prices are never at equilibrium but, instead, are constantly chasing (but never finding) the changing equilibrium levels. Which theory is correct really doesn't matter here. We are interested only in equilibrium pricing, not actual prices. To begin to understand what creates an actual price we must first understand the forces that create an equilibrium price. Only then can we look for differences between actual and equilibrium prices.

Assumptions

At this point we can summarize and state our first assumption:

1. **Homogeneous expectations.** Equilibrium prices exist only when information trading is zero. This implies that all market participants have identical information—they have homogeneous expectations about the future.

This assumption of homogeneous expectations is often stated another way: *All participants have equal and costless access to information.* If new information is released to a select few people, or even released to different groups at different times, prices would be set by the speculative trades of the people or groups who first receive the information. But, again, an equilibrium exists only when all investors have common information.

Next, we will assume there are no impediments to achieving exactly the portfolio that one wishes. In other words, the *markets are frictionless.* Among the principal impediments that might exist are the following:

2. **Transaction costs.** Brokerage fees and bid-ask spread fees are assumed to be zero, so all purchases and sales desired will be transacted.
3. **Security indivisibility.** We assume all securities are infinitely divisible. Investors can take any position they wish. If an individual's optimal decision is to own 115.37 shares of AT&T, it is assumed possible.

4. **Taxes.** We assume taxes are zero.
5. **Trading price impacts.** We assume the trading actions of the individual investor do not affect price levels. Your decision, or that of another investor, to trade does not, in isolation from all other trades, affect prices. Only the aggregate of all trades causes prices to move to equilibrium.

Finally, we carry forward the assumptions of Chapter 6 regarding how the individual chooses an optimal security portfolio:

6. **Time horizon.** A one-period world exists for all investors.
7. **Utility maximizers.** Investors seek to maximize the expected utility of end-of-period wealth, and this utility is determined by expected returns and the standard deviation of returns.
8. **Risk-free interest.** People may borrow or lend any amount at a constant risk-free interest rate.

While these assumptions do not reflect actual security market conditions, they are helpful in developing a simple model of market equilibrium. In Chapter 8, we review some models that remove various assumptions.

Market Equilibrium

Given these assumptions, what would a state of market equilibrium imply about the trade-off between portfolio risk and expected return? The analysis is quite easy to understand and is depicted in Figure 7-1.

Consider the situation faced by the individual shown in the figure. The individual first evaluates the expected returns and risks available on various portfolio combinations and, from this, is able to identify the efficient frontier of risky portfolios. Next, the optimal risky portfolio is found by determining which portfolio will provide the largest risk premium when it is held in combination with the risk-free security. This optimal risky portfolio is denoted as **portfolio M.**

Now consider the situation faced by another individual. It is identical. Since investors have homogeneous expectations, each will arrive at the same conclusion: Portfolio M is the optimal risky portfolio. People will differ in the amount of risk they wish their portfolios to contain, but risk can be adjusted by altering the amount of lending and borrowing. Portfolio M is never changed. It is the only portfolio of risky securities that people wish to hold.

Well, what if some security exists that is not in M? It won't be owned—not by anyone. Instead, it will be used as wallpaper in family dens or displayed in investment classes to illustrate a great story. Conversely, any security that exists and is held in a portfolio is in M. Portfolio M consists of all owned securities.

Portfolio M is called the market portfolio, and its existence as the optimal efficient portfolio for all investors is the single most important implication of this standard version of the CAPM. Not surprisingly, this implication has come under attack from academicians and practitioners alike. Much of Chapter 8 is devoted to such criticisms. But, for now, we accept this result and see what develops from it.

FIGURE 7-1   Efficient Frontier and Borrowing-Lending Line Available to All Market Participants

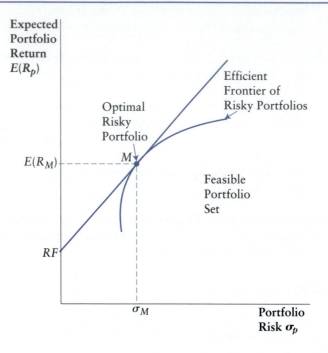

Optimal Security Holdings. The investment process consists of two steps: (1) identifying the optimal risky portfolio (the percentage to invest in each available risky security, and (2) borrowing or lending to achieve the desired risk/return trade-off. The CAPM states that the market portfolio is the optimal risky portfolio. And since all investors wish to hold this same portfolio, it should be no surprise that the percentage of a risky portfolio held in security i is equal to the total market value of security i as a percentage of the total market value of all risky securities. The following formula states formally what we mean by the optimal percentage to invest in any security i:

Proportion of Risky Portfolio Held in i $X_i^* = \dfrac{P_i N_i}{\sum\limits_{i=1}^{T} P_i N_i}$ (7.3)

where: X_i^* = optimal percentage of the risky portfolio (i.e., excluding borrowing or lending) held in security i

P_i = market price of security i

N_i = quantity of security i outstanding

T = total number of risky securities outstanding

For example, assume there are only three risky securities available:

Security	Price	Units Outstanding	Total Value	Percentage of Total
1	$ 30	200	$ 6,000	30%
2	50	200	10,000	50
3	1,000	4	4,000	20
			$20,000	100%

The total market value of these securities is $20,000. Since the securities are held by various market participants, the total wealth of these participants devoted to risky securities is also $20,000. But since they all wish to have the same percentage holdings of each, the percentage any one person will invest in a given security must be equal to the security's percentage of the total value of all risky securities. Thus, everyone will place 30% of their risky portfolio in security 1, 50% in security 2, and 20% in security 3. If this were not the case, the markets would not clear. One or more investors would remain wanting to buy or sell a specific holding.

Why the Market Portfolio? Given our assumptions, it is perfectly reasonable that the market portfolio is optimal. Portfolios differ only in expected returns and standard deviations of returns. As we saw in Chapter 6, diversification by itself has no effect on expected portfolio returns. For example, if the addition of another security reduces expected returns below the desired level, an investor can borrow to achieve the desired return but still obtain the risk reduction advantages of the increased diversification. **The market portfolio is in essence the most diversified portfolio available.** Once it is held, there is no way to further diversify away risk.

Figure 7-2 schematically shows all risky securities in the world within a large circle. A few of the individual securities are illustrated by the small boxes. Gains or losses in value incurred by particular securities are depicted by arrows showing where the gain or loss came from and went to. Security 1, for example, incurs two losses of value, one that is passed to security 2 and one that is not passed to another asset but simply leaves the system. Gains and losses to individual securities that are passed on to other securities and remain within the system can be diversified away by holding a portfolio of all securities. These are unsystematic risks. Gains or losses to the total system are nondiversifiable systematic risks.

Simply stated, the market portfolio is the most broadly diversified portfolio available. Any portfolio with fewer securities or a dissimilar percentage of investments in each security is not adequately diversified.

If the market portfolio is the optimal portfolio of risky assets to hold, then what will be the relationship between the risk of a mean-variance efficient portfolio and the expected return on the portfolio? This is the issue we examine next.

The CML Equation. The **capital market line** (CML) states the equilibrium relationship that exists between the returns that should be expected on efficient portfolios of securities and the risks of such portfolios. For reference, look back to Figure 7-1. The CML is the borrowing-lending line extending from RF through portfolio M.

In equilibrium, the return expected on a portfolio of securities must be at least equal to Equation (7.4a) or the portfolio is inefficient and will not be held. As you might expect, in

FIGURE 7-2 THE MARKET PORTFOLIO OF ALL RISKY ASSETS

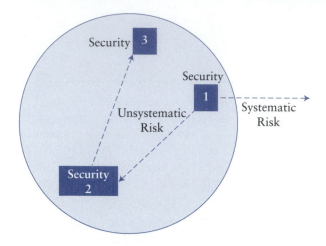

equilibrium, the only portfolios that meet the criterion are combinations of *RF* and the market portfolio.

Capital Market Line $$E(R_p) = RF + \sigma_p \left[\frac{E(R_M - RF)}{\sigma_M} \right] \tag{7.4a}$$

where: $E(R_M)$ = expected return on the market portfolio.
         σ_M = standard deviation of the market portfolio's return.

First, we should expect a risk-free return simply for delaying the consumption of the portfolio's worth. Second, a risk premium should be expected that is determined by two things: (1) the total risk of the portfolio, and (2) the best risk-related return per unit of standard deviation available in the market. Since the market portfolio dominates all other risky portfolios in equilibrium, it provides the best risk-related return per unit of standard deviation.

In Equation (7.4a), the term $[E(R_M) - RF]$ is a measure of the risk premium expected to be earned above the risk-free rate for bearing the market portfolio's risk. We refer to it as RP_M. If the expected return on the market equals 16% and the risk-free rate is 10%, then the market risk premium is 6%. You should recognize, however, that it is the market risk premium which, together with the risk-free rate, creates the expected return on the market portfolio. As such the CML is often expressed as follows:

Capital Market Line $$E(R_p) = RF + \sigma_p [RP_M \div \sigma_M] \tag{7.4b}$$

In Figure 7-3, a plot of the CML is shown.

For illustration, assume the risk-free rate is 10%, the market risk premium is 6%, and the standard deviation of the market portfolio's returns is 20%. Then the return on a portfolio

FIGURE 7-3   THE CAPITAL MARKET LINE (CML)

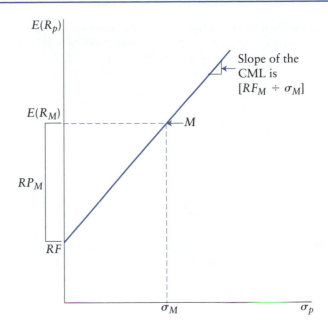

that is half as risky as the market portfolio (has a standard deviation of 10%) should provide an expected return of 13%:

$$E(R_p) = 10\% + 10\%[6\% \div 20\%]$$

$$= 13\%$$

A combination of 50% in the market portfolio and 50% in the risk-free security would provide exactly this 13% expected return.

Determinants of the Market Risk Premium. Recall from Chapter 5 that the risk-free rate of interest is determined by market participants themselves as a function of their time preferences for consumption and the marginal productivity of capital.

The risk premium is also determined in the marketplace and is a function of society's risk aversion and the marginal returns available from risky assets. To illustrate the process, consider the three panels of Figure 7-4. In panel A, the risk-free rate is removed. The dashed lines are societal indifference curves reflecting the marginal increases in expected returns for the marginal change in risk that is necessary to maintain a given utility. (Think of these indifference curves as an average across all members of society.) The ideal portfolio is denoted as M. Now move to panel B, in which a risk-free rate is introduced. Suddenly, M no longer is efficient and M(2) is held in its place. To achieve its desired risk/return level, society will attempt to borrow at RF and will place both equity and borrowings in M(2) in

FIGURE 7-4 DETERMINATION OF THE RISK PREMIUM

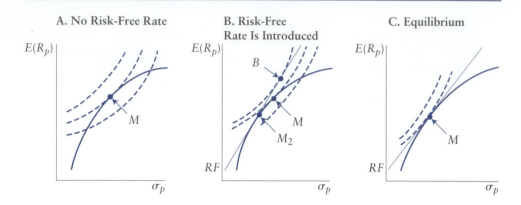

order to be at the optimal point B. But society cannot borrow from itself. The sum of all individual borrowing and individual lending must be zero. It is impossible for society to be at point B. However, attempts to purchase $M(2)$ will force the prices of $M(2)$ up and its expected return down. Similarly, lack of demand for M will cause its expected returns to rise as its prices fall. Equilibrium will finally result when the optimal risky portfolio M is consistent with zero net borrowing and lending, as shown in panel C.

There are two important points to recognize in this illustration. First, the risk premium is not forced on society by risks and expected returns associated with risky assets. Instead, it is the interaction of available risk/return trade-offs with society's risk preferences that determines the risk premium. Second, any such equilibrium must also be consistent with zero net lending and borrowing.

The Market Portfolio

In theory, the market portfolio consists of all risky assets. These would include all risky assets in the world: equities, bonds, real estate, commodities, paintings, and so on. In practice, the market portfolio cannot actually be held or even identified. And market frictions make trading with certain countries impossible and with others very costly. But the crude data available suggests some interesting implications.

Table **7-1** provides a recent estimate of what the market portfolio might consist. In the far right column, the value of non-U.S. assets is estimated to be 64% of the world total. It should be clear that a large part of portfolio M consists of non-U.S. assets, that international diversification is necessary to obtain the broadest diversification possible. Next, consider only the information shown on domestic U.S. assets. Real estate dominates holdings of either equity or debt. To diversify broadly over only U.S. assets, an individual's portfolio should contain about 33% of its value in real estate.[1]

---

[1] In fact, a large part of most people's wealth consists of the equity they have in their homes and land. If the value of these are highly correlated with other real estate assets, this equity ownership in homes and land probably achieves much of the diversification suggested in real estate.

TABLE 7-1   ESTIMATED MARKET VALUE OF VARIOUS ASSET CLASSES (1994)

	Market Value (U.S. $ Trillions)	Percentage U.S. Total	Percentage World Total
Domestic U.S. Equities	$4.9	25.5%	
Debt	8.0	41.7	
Real Estate	6.3	32.8	
Total U.S.	19.2	100.0%	37.3%
Non-U.S. Equities	8.0		
Debt	8.0		
Real Estate	16.3		
Total Non-U.S.	32.3		63.7
Total	51.5		100.0%

The data in Table 7-1 are very imprecise. But they do suggest the important roles that international securities and real estate should play in the creation of a well-diversified portfolio. In fact, increased attention has recently been focused on exactly these two asset categories, and most investment portfolios have substantially increased investments in each.

The Security Market Line

The CML specifies the equilibrium relationship between expected return and risk for efficient portfolios. It cannot be used to evaluate the equilibrium expected return on a single security because the standard deviation of a security's return is not a proper measure of a security's true risk. As we saw in Chapter 6, the risk of a security depends on the portfolio to which it is added and must reflect the covariability of the security's returns with other assets in the portfolio.

In this section, we examine how the nondiversifiable risk of a security should be measured when the markets are in equilibrium. The analysis is similar to that in Chapter 6, where we evaluated the risk of a single security to one individual. The principal difference here is that we know what the optimal risky asset portfolio is, the market portfolio. The model that is developed is known as the security market line (SML).

Beta: A Security's Nondiversifiable Risk

Three important principles we developed in Chapter 6 are as follows:

1. the risk of a security depends on the portfolio to which it is added,
2. in diversified portfolios, the dominant risk of a security is the covariance of its returns with other securities held in the portfolio, and
3. the risk of a security relative to the risks of other securities held in the portfolio can be calculated by dividing the covariance of the security's returns with other

securities held by the variance of returns on other securities held. This relative risk is called beta.

The CAPM implies that the only portfolio of risky assets which investors should own is the market portfolio. If this is true, then security betas should be calculated using the market portfolio as the reference portfolio.

The CAPM implies that the beta of a security should be calculated as follows:

Beta of Security i $$B_i = \frac{\sigma_i r_{iM}}{\sigma_M} \qquad (7.5)$$

Dividing the standard deviation of the security by the standard deviation of the market portfolio provides a measure of how volatile the security is in relation to the volatility of the market portfolio. Multiplying by the correlation coefficient determines how much of this relative volatility should be counted. If the security is perfectly correlated with the market portfolio, then all of the relative volatility counts. None of it can be eliminated by diversifying across the market portfolio. If the correlation is zero, then none of the volatility counts. All of it can be eliminated by diversification when the security is combined with the market portfolio. In actual situations, however, individual securities have correlations with proxies of the market portfolio of about 0.3.

Betas of the Market Portfolio and the Risk-Free Security. The risk of the market portfolio relative to itself is, of course, 1.0:

Market Portfolio Beta $$B_M = \frac{\sigma_M r_{iM}}{\sigma_M} = 1.0 \qquad (7.6)$$

Any security with a beta equal to 1.0 has the same amount of nondiversifiable risk as in the market portfolio. So the return that should be expected on a security with a beta of 1.0 should be the same as the expected return on the market portfolio.

The risk of the risk-free rate is by definition equal to zero and it will have a beta of zero:

Risk-Free Security Beta $$B_{RF} = \frac{0.0(0.00)}{\sigma_M} = 0.0 \qquad (7.7)$$

Any security that has a beta of 0.0 should be priced to provide an expected return equal to the risk-free rate. That does not mean zero-beta securities will have a realized return equal to the risk-free rate. They may not if they have a positive standard deviation of returns. But as long as returns on the security are uncorrelated with the market portfolio's returns, all such volatility can be diversified away. And if such uncertainty can be eliminated by diversification, the expected return should be equal to the risk-free rate.

Expected Return on Individual Securities (SML)

Recall from Equation (7.4b) that the capital market line expresses the expected return on an efficient portfolio in terms of the standard deviation of the portfolio:

Capital Market Line $$E(R_p) = RF + \sigma_p[RP_M \div \sigma_M]$$

The security market line expresses the expected return on any security or portfolio in terms of the nondiversifiable risk of the asset, beta.

Security Market Line $E(R_i) = RF + B_i[RP_M]$ (7.8)

$$= RF + B_i[E(R_M) - RF]$$

The expected return on any security consists of a risk-free return plus a risk premium. This risk premium is equal to the security's nondiversifiable risk (relative to the market portfolio) times the risk premium required on the market portfolio. The security market line is depicted graphically in Figure 7-5.

Betas of a Portfolio

There are two ways of calculating the beta of a portfolio: (1) at the portfolio level, or (2) at the component security level. At the portfolio level, the beta is simply:

Portfolio Beta $$B_p = \frac{\sigma_p r_{pM}}{\sigma_M}$$ (7.9)

The standard deviation of portfolio returns is divided by the standard deviation of the market portfolio to find the amount of uncertainty in the portfolio relative to the market portfolio's uncertainty. This value is then multiplied by the correlation between the portfolio

---

FIGURE 7-5 THE SECURITY MARKET LINE

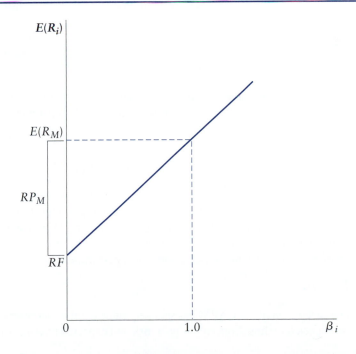

and the market portfolio to determine what portion of the relative uncertainty will not be diversified away when the portfolio is held. If the correlation coefficient and standard deviations are ex ante measures, this is a proper way of measuring the portfolio beta. Such an ex ante beta measures subjective beliefs about the portfolio's relative nondiversifiable risk.

However, ex post measures are commonly used as proxies for ex ante data, in which case standard deviations and correlation coefficients of the portfolio's historical returns are used to estimate beta. There are two possible biases in such beta estimates:

1. The past can be a poor predictor of the future. Estimates will depend to a large degree on the time period chosen, and such estimates are often inaccurate predictors.
2. If the composition of the portfolio has changed over time, the beta associated with current holdings will not be the beta calculated from the past returns of different holdings. The beta measured will not be the beta for the current portfolio.

The beta of a portfolio can also be calculated as a weighted average of the betas on the securities that make up the portfolio:

Portfolio Beta
$$B_p = \sum_i^N = B_i X_i \qquad (7.10)$$

For example, the beta of a portfolio consisting of the following securities is 1.0:

Security	X_i	B_i	Product
A	0.25	1.5	0.375
B	0.25	1.0	0.250
C	0.25	1.2	0.300
D	0.25	0.3	0.075
			1.000

In short, the bias in a beta estimate that may arise if a portfolio's composition has changed over time can be easily reduced if the beta on each constituent security is estimated and then averaged.

Potential Uses of the Capital Asset Pricing Model

The theory we have been discussing is the classic version of what is known as the theory of capital asset pricing, or the capital asset pricing model (CAPM). In this section we review some of its implications and see how they might be used in practice. We examine three major topics: (1) analysis of security pricing, (2) development of an ideal investment strategy, and (3) evaluation of a portfolio's performance.

Pricing

Our discussion of the CAPM has said very little so far about prices. Rather, we have focused on expected returns. Concentrating on risk and expected return is simply a convenient way to

Gautam Dhingra, C.F.A.

Principal

Hewitt Associates LLC

University of Florida, Ph.D.

Hewitt Associates is a consulting firm specializing in financial and human resource functions. Mr. Dhingra is the Manager of Investment Services consulting with plan sponsors on developing investment policies and objectives, investment manager selection, and performance attribution.

Q: The topic of this chapter is the Capital Asset Pricing Model. Does your firm use this model in its consulting work?

A: We do not use the Capital Asset Pricing Model (CAPM) to any significant extent. Theoretically, CAPM can be used for performance evaluation as well as asset allocation. However, in practice, it has several limitations which reduce its usefulness. For example, performance evaluation models based on beta as the only measure of relevant risk have failed to explain stock performance. It appears that other factors such as industry effect, price-to-book ratio, size, etc. explain investment performance better. In addition, there is also the problem that beta is not a stable measurement of risk.

In considering a portfolio's asset allocation, CAPM has been useful in that it pointed out that the market portfolio might be mean-variance efficient. However, our pension fund clients consider many other factors besides mean-variance efficiency of the portfolio. In particular, our clients need to consider the magnitude, timing and interest rate sensitivity of their pension liabilities in making their asset allocation decisions.

Q: Is CAPM not useful at all in making investment decisions?

A: No, I would not go that far. As I mentioned, CAPM pointed out that the market portfolio is probably very efficient. This observation was in part responsible for the big move towards passive management of equity assets that we observed in the 1980s. The move towards passive management acknowledges that some markets are efficient so paying high fees for active management is not necessary. However, it appears to us that not all markets are efficient. Our observation is that the large capitalization, U.S. stock market is quite efficient but other markets such as small capitalization U.S. stocks, real estate, etc. are not efficient. This gives a competent investor the chance to add value via active management.

Let me stress, however, that mean-variance models such as CAPM are very useful in pointing out the importance of covariance in assessing the attractiveness of various asset classes and stocks. This realization has led to better investment decision making because pension plan sponsors now often evaluate whether their portfolio is efficient in the mean-variance framework. While interesting, our clients look beyond mean-variance to make appropriate asset allocation decisions for their pension funds.

Q: How exactly do you help your pension fund clients make asset allocation decisions?

A: It is very important for our clients to analyze their future pension liabilities to determine their investment time horizon and also to determine the interest rate sensitivity of the liabilities. We project assets and liabilities under all possible economic scenarios using a Monte Carlo simulation technique. We then evaluate the impact of various portfolios on pension costs and funded status of the pension fund under each scenario. The client evaluates the risk-return tradeoff by comparing the expected pension cost and funded status associated with various portfolios. Risk and return, in this context, can be defined in a manner customized to each client. The portfolio that best meets those goals can be selected. This approach has at least three advantages over the approaches based on mean-variance models: (1) risk can be defined in a manner most relevant to each client instead of the client being forced to use standard deviation or beta as the measure of risk; (2) this approach is a multi-period approach and is not constrained by the single-period framework of CAPM or mean-variance models; (3) the model allows us to incorporate relevant information such as interest rate sensitivity of assets and liabilities directly into the decision making process.

approach the problem, but it is a security's price that is transacted in the markets and determines whether speculative opportunities exist.

The equilibrium price should provide no opportunity for speculative profits. It should be set at such a level that expected returns from buying the security are identical to those available on an efficient portfolio of equivalent nondiversifiable risk. For example, if the risk-free rate is 10%, the market risk premium is 6%, and the beta of a stock is 0.7, then the stock should be priced to provide an expected return of 14.2%:

$$E(R_i) = RF + B_i(RP_M)$$

$$14.2\% = 10.0\% + 0.7(6.0\%)$$

If this security is trading at a price lower than equilibrium, then a speculative profit is possible and excess demand will exist until the price is forced up to equilibrium. If the security is trading at a higher than equilibrium price, speculators will sell (short-sell if there are no restrictions on doing so) until the price is at equilibrium. In short, the expected return from owning a security should be:

Equilibrium Required Return

$$E(R_i) = RF + B_i(RP_M) \tag{7.11}$$

The return that will actually be earned consists of any increases (or decreases) in the security's price plus any cash payoff, such as dividends on a stock or coupons on a bond. In the case of a stock:

Actual Security Return

$$R_{i1} = \frac{P_{i1} - P_{i0} + D_{i1}}{P_{i0}} \tag{7.12}$$

where: P_{i1} = price of security i at the end of period 1
P_{i0} = price of security i at the end of period 0
D_{i1} = dividends received at the end of period 1

For the security to be priced at equilibrium, the expected outcome of Equation (7.12) should be equal to the fair return expressed in Equation (7.11):

Equilibrium Required Return = Expected Security Return

$$RF + B_i(RP_M) = \frac{E(P_{i1}) - P_{i0} + E(D_{i1})}{P_{i0}} \tag{7.13}$$

Rearranging this quite logical statement and letting P_{i0}^* represent the equilibrium price of security i, we see this equilibrium price is simply the present value of the expected end-of-period price and dividend discounted at a return appropriate for its level of nondiversifiable risk:

Equilibrium Security Price

$$P_{i0}^* = \frac{E(P_{i1}) + E(D_{i1})}{1.0 + RF + B_i(RP_M)} \tag{7.14}$$

For example, let's compute the equilibrium price of a stock given the following data:

$$RF = 5.0\% \qquad\qquad E(D_{i1}) = \$4.00$$
$$RP_M = 6.0\% \qquad B_i = 0.5 \qquad E(P_{i1}) = \$100$$

According to the SML, we should expect a 8.0% return on an investment in this stock:

$$8.0\% = 5.0\% + 0.5\,(6.0\%)$$

Since the expected price at the end of the period (say, one year) is $100 and the expected dividend is $4, the equilibrium price today would be $96.30:

$$\$96.30 = \frac{\$100.00 + \$4.00}{1.08}$$

The equilibrium pricing formula stated in Equation (7.14) strictly applies to a single-period world that meets all the assumptions we made at the start of the chapter. There is no warranty on its validity when it is used in other situations. In practice, however, the principal features of the model are used widely. Security analysts forecast expected future dividends and prices on a stock and discount them to the present using a discount rate generated from the SML. A detailed illustration of how this is done is delayed to Chapter 13, where we have the opportunity to explore the process of security analysis in some depth.

Strategy

The implications for portfolio strategy that arise from the CAPM are quite profound. At the center of this theory is the market portfolio. In order to obtain the broadest possible diversification, investors who choose to own risky assets should own the market portfolio. If they wish a portfolio risk level different from the risk of the market portfolio, this can be accomplished by combining holdings of risk-free securities with the market portfolio.

The difficulty of implementing this policy is that we do not know precisely the contents of the market portfolio. But even if the market portfolio cannot actually be held, we should not discard the principle of broad **diversification.** Diversification provides balance to a portfolio. Broad diversification leaves only systematic, nondiversifiable risks in a portfolio. An easy and cheap way of diversifying across a large number of securities traded in world markets is to purchase index funds. Index funds are currently available for virtually all classes of securities traded in world markets.

The CAPM implies that the optimal percentage to invest in a security depends on the market value of that security relative to the market value of all securities. While we surely have difficulty in defining this portfolio with any precision, it certainly includes stocks traded in world stock markets. For illustrative purposes, consider stocks traded in the United States.

Table 7-2 shows the equity value of the largest eight stocks traded in the United States (in early 1995). These are obviously very large companies. In fact, the total equity value of these eight companies represented 10% of the value of all traded U.S. stocks at that time!

TABLE 7-2   LARGEST U.S. EQUITY VALUES: MARCH 31, 1995

Company Name	Equity Value (in $ billlions)	Percentage of Total U.S. Equity Value
Philip Morris	55.328	0.97%
Wal-Mart Stores	58.869	1.03%
Hewlett-Packard	61.573	1.08%
Royal Dutch Petro NY shares	64.328	1.13%
Coca-Cola Co.	71.529	1.26%
AT&T Corp.	81.836	1.44%
Exxon Corp.	82.763	1.46%
General Electric	91.469	1.61%
Total	567.695	9.98%

The theory of CAPM implies that 10% of an investor's investment in U.S. stocks should be placed in these securities.

After a portfolio is diversified broadly, the investor can adjust the borrowing-lending mix to achieve a preferred risk/return level. Lending portfolios can be created by purchasing U.S. Treasury securities, and borrowing portfolios can be created by using margin. As we see in Chapters 16 and 17, options and financial futures also provide a number of ways to alter a portfolio's risk level and move along the borrowing-lending line.

Finally, we should always remember a basic point of CAPM: Greater expected returns come only with greater uncertainty.

Performance Evaluation

Concepts of the CAPM are widely used by individual and institutional investors to evaluate the performance of professional investment managers. Several important techniques used include the following:

1. The average return earned above the risk-free rate divided by the standard deviation of returns, the *Sharpe performance measure*.
2. The average return earned above the risk-free rate divided by the beta of the security returns, the *Treynor performance measure*.
3. The average return earned above the risk-free rate given the investment's beta and past market returns, the *Jensen's alpha*.

In Chapter 21, we take a close look at each of these performance measures. At this point, you should simply appreciate that the principles of the CAPM are widely used today to judge the performance of professionally managed portfolios.

Estimating a Security's Beta

In theory, beta represents the nondiversifiable, systematic risk of an individual security or portfolio of securities. It reflects a risk for which a return should be expected. Theory treats it as a *subjective estimate* made by each individual of what the future might hold. It is, indeed, an ex ante opinion of likely systematic risk during the next period of time.

In practice, it is rare that subjective estimates of beta are made. Instead, estimates based on historical returns are used. In this section, we examine how these historical estimates of the true beta are prepared. Since the techniques provide only estimates of the true beta, we must be careful to differentiate between the two. Theoretical beta will continue to be represented by a capital B in the term for beta. Estimates of the true beta will be shown with a lowercase b.

When we move from the theoretical concept of beta to a real-world beta estimate, we encounter a variety of serious problems. For example, the world does not consist of one period. Should beta be estimated over a time period that consists of the past month, the past five years, or the past twenty years? Should beta be estimated using daily, weekly, monthly, quarterly, or annual returns? How should changes in the product line of a firm be factored in? How does one estimate the beta of a bond whose life is continually changing and thus will be less sensitive to systematic economic shocks? The list of problems associated with estimating beta is long and many of these problems remain unresolved. Yet beta estimates are commonplace today and the techniques used to develop them should be understood. The procedure used to estimate beta is known as the market model.

The Market Model

The market model (MM) is an equation that relates the return on security i during time period t to the return on a proxy for the market portfolio during the same time period. The MM is written as follows:

Market Model

$$\tilde{R}_{it} = A_i + b_i(\tilde{R}_{Mt}) + \tilde{e}_{it} \tag{7.15}$$

The term R_{it} represents the volatile return on security i during period t. It is equal to the sum of three components. First, a constant return is earned in each period regardless of the return on the market portfolio. This term is often referred to as alpha. Next, the security is said to have a sensitivity to the market portfolio return denoted by the b_i term. When this beta sensitivity is multiplied by the market return, R_{Mt}, we have the security return caused by its market risk exposure. Finally, there is a difference between what the actual return on security i is and what the first two terms suggest the return should have been. This difference is known as the **residual error** term e_{it}.

Due to variability in the nominal risk-free rate of interest, the MM is often estimated in **excess return form**. This simply means that an estimate of the nominal risk-free return in period t is subtracted from both the security's return in period t as well as the return on the market portfolio as follows:

Excess Return Market Model

$$(\tilde{R}_{it} - \tilde{RF_t}) = a_i + b_i(\tilde{R}_{Mt} - RF_t) + \tilde{e}_{it} \tag{7.16}$$

In this form, the constant alpha term represents the constant security return in excess of the risk-free rate of interest.

Figure 7-6 is a graphical representation of the excess return MM. When the market portfolio proxy has a zero return, the excess security return is expected to have a return of a_i. As the market portfolio has a positive or negative excess return, the extent to which security i tends to share in this return depends on the slope of the line b_i. During any time period, however, the security's excess return might not be exactly equal to $a_i + b_i(R_{Mt} - RF_t)$. Events that have no effect on the aggregate market portfolio might have an effect on security i. These errors are the e_{it} terms.

For example, assume you are given the following excess return market model data for a mutual fund called AMF:

$$a_{AMF} = 2.0\% \qquad (R_{AMFt} - RF_t) = 12.0\%$$

$$b_{AMF} = 0.7 \qquad (R_{Mt} - RF_t) = 10.0\%$$

The data are displayed in Figure 7-7. If the excess market portfolio return had been 0.0%, the expected excess return on AMF would have been 2.0%. However, the market portfolio's excess return was 10.0%. The 0.70 beta of AMF indicates that AMF would be expected to have a return equal to 7.0% above the alpha of 2.0%.

FIGURE 7-6 THE MARKET MODEL

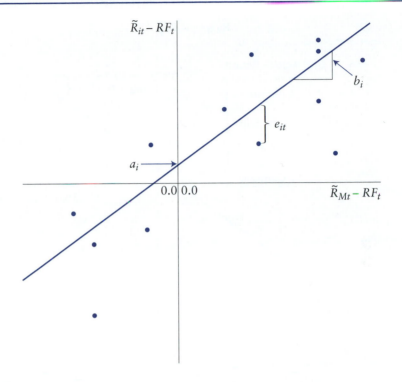

In short, given the 10.0% excess market return, the expected return on AMF would be 9.0%. However, AMF's actual return was 12.0%. The difference of a positive 3.0% is AMF's residual error during this time period. On average, these error terms will be zero because of the way in which the alpha and beta terms are statistically estimated.

The Market Model vs. the SML. The excess return version of the market model and the security market line (Equation 7.8) are shown next:

Excess Return Market Model

$$(\tilde{R}_{ti} - \tilde{R}F_t) = a_i + b_i(\tilde{R}_{Mt} - \tilde{R}F_t) + \tilde{e}_{it}$$

$$\tilde{R}_{it} = \tilde{R}F_t + a_i + b_i(\tilde{R}_{Mt} - \tilde{R}F_t) + \tilde{e}_{it}$$

Security Market Line

$$E(R_i) = RF + B_i[RP_M]$$

$$= RF + B_i[E(R_M) - RF]$$

They look suspiciously similar. Obviously, this is not a coincidence, since beta is intended to be an estimate of the true beta. But are they the same? The answer is, maybe. There are two principal differences between them: (1) alpha in the MM, and (2) a possible difference between the true market portfolio in the SML and the market proxy in the MM.

FIGURE 7-7 SAMPLE MARKET MODEL FOR IBM

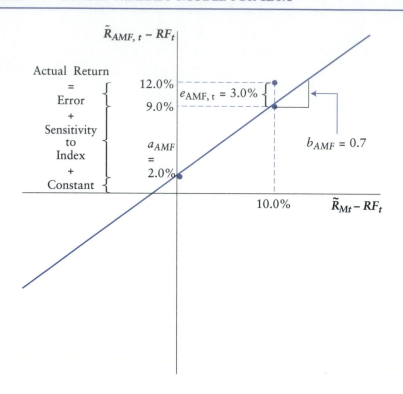

For the MM to be a good representation of the SML, the average alpha term should be zero. If this is not true: (1) the market might be in a state of disequilibrium, (2) the market proxy used in the MM might be substantially biased, or (3) the SML might simply be a poor description of real security markets.

Beta Estimates. The alpha and beta parameters in the MM are calculated by regressing a security's historical returns against the returns on a reasonable market portfolio proxy. To illustrate the results of this process, quarterly excess returns (returns in excess of 90-day U.S. T-bills) of two securities were regressed against excess returns on the S&P 500 Index. The period included the five years 1991 through 1994. The securities were IBM stock and shares of American Mutual Fund (AMF). Regression results are shown here:

Market Model Regression for IBM:

$$(\tilde{R}_{IBMt} - \tilde{R}F_t) = -0.95\% + 0.16 \, (\tilde{R}_{SPt} - \tilde{R}F_t)$$

$$(1.10) \qquad\qquad R^2 = 0.18$$

Market Model Regression for AMF:

$$(\tilde{R}_{AMFt} - \tilde{R}F_t) = +0.76\% + 0.51 \, (\tilde{R}_{SPt} - \tilde{R}F_t)$$

$$(0.10) \qquad\qquad R^2 = 0.62$$

The left-hand-side variables are referred to as the **dependent variables** and the right-hand-side variables are referred to as **independent variables.** Alpha estimates are a negative 0.95% and a positive 0.76%, respectively. The beta estimates are 0.16 and 0.51. Numbers shown in parentheses below the beta estimates are standard deviation estimates of the beta parameters.

The R^2 value measures the proportion of volatility in the dependent variable explained by volatility in the independent variable. R^2 can range from 0.0, in which case there is no relationship between the variables, to 1.0, in which case the variables are perfectly correlated.

Notice that the R^2 value for the mutual fund AMF is much larger than for IBM. This is due to the fact that AMF consists of a broadly diversified portfolio of stocks. In contrast, the R^2 for IBM is only 0.18.

Usually, beta estimates for IBM are closer to 1.0. The much smaller beta during this time period reflects the fact that the major events affecting IBM during this time interval were unique to IBM. Broad market events affecting all stocks had little effects on IBM share values. This illustrates the dangers of relying on past betas as estimates of the theoretical beta.

The Characteristic Line. Figure 7-8 shows the results for AMF graphically. The line drawn through the scatter diagram represents the regression equation shown earlier. It is commonly known as the **characteristic line.**

The slope of the characteristic line is our beta estimate and the intercept on the vertical axis is the alpha estimate. The regression procedure used to calculate beta uses an equation

FIGURE 7-8   CHARACTERISTIC LINE FOR AMF

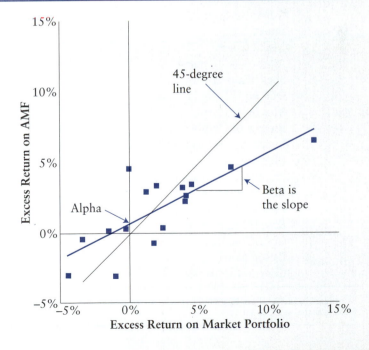

similar to Equation (7.9) that defines the true beta value for a security. The only difference is that beta values are based on past returns and a proxy for the market portfolio.

Beta estimates such as these are available from any number of sources. The major brokerage houses, banks, and investment advisory firms are all very willing to sell their beta values. To calculate the regression equation, all investors need is access to historical returns and a regression computer package. The beta values obtained from each source will be somewhat different, since each beta supplier has its own unique way of calculating the characteristic line. For example, different indexes are used. Some use daily returns and others use monthly returns. And many provide adjusted beta values (discussed in Appendix 7A). Most of the estimates, however, are reasonably similar.

To illustrate, Table 7-3 presents beta values created by the author for many of the largest companies traded in the United States. The index used to generate these beta values was the S&P 500. We discuss later various indexes that might be used.

Diversifiable vs. Nondiversifiable Risk. The returns plotted in Figure 7-8 can be used to illustrate again the difference between diversifiable and nondiversifiable risk. Notice that rarely does the return plot exactly on the characteristic line; an error almost always exists. It is these error terms that are diversified away. As long as the error term on one security is uncorrelated

TABLE 7-3   ILLUSTRATIVE BETAS

Company	Beta Estimate
GTE Corp.	0.88
General Motors Corp.	0.72
American International Group	1.22
Intel Corp.	1.42
Mobil Corp.	0.64
Johnson & Johnson	1.23
Shell Trans & Trade	0.65
DuPont (EI) De Nemours	1.04
Microsoft Corp.	1.04
Procter & Gamble Co.	1.02
International Business Machines	0.54
Merck & Co.	1.10
Philip Morris Cos Inc.	1.16
Wal-Mart Stores	1.22
Hewlett-Packard Co.	1.63
Royal Dutch Petro	0.69
Coca-Cola Co.	1.15
Exxon Corp.	0.48
General Electric Co.	1.26

Developed by author using 60 monthly returns for the period ended December 1993. The market portfolio proxy was the S&P 500 Index.

with the error term on all other securities, the errors will go to zero when all stocks are combined. If the error terms are correlated, either we have a poor index proxy for the market portfolio or the CAPM is wrong. These are points we examine more closely in the next chapter.

The total variance of a security's returns consists of two parts. The first reflects variability due to sensitivity to market portfolio returns. The second is due to unsystematic risk. The precise relationship is shown here:

$$\text{Total Risk} \quad \text{equals} \quad \text{Systematic Risk} \quad \text{plus} \quad \text{Unsystematic Risk}$$

$$\sigma_i^2 \quad = \quad B_i^2 \sigma_M^2 \quad + \quad \sigma_{ei}^2 \qquad \text{(7.17)}$$

where σ_{ei}^2 represents the variance of the error term in Equation (7.16).

Indexes Used to Proxy the Market Portfolio

In actual applications, the CAPM is used mainly with common stocks, and stock betas are calculated using various indexes of stock returns.

Stock return indexes differ from one another in two principal ways: (1) the number and types of stocks included in the index, and (2) the manner in which stock returns are weighted.

Stock Coverage. Most return indexes include a large number of stocks so they properly reflect overall stock market returns as opposed to a narrow segment of market returns. An exception to this are the widely publicized Dow Jones indexes. For example, the Dow Jones Industrial Average contains only 30 U.S. stocks.[2]

The most widely used stock return indexes include the following:

- **CRSP.** This stands for the Center for Research in Security Prices, maintained by the University of Chicago. These indexes are widely used by scholars in their studies of security markets. Because they are published with a considerable time lag, they are not widely used by investment practitioners. But they are important stock return indexes because of their extensive use in scholarly studies.

- **Standard & Poor's.** S&P creates a large number of indexes designed to measure stock market returns in the United States. The best known is the S&P 500 Index. This includes 500 of the larger firms traded in U.S. markets. The firms covered in the S&P 500 represent about 70% of the market value of U.S. stocks. The S&P 500 Index is currently the most widely used index by investment professionals.

- **Wilshire Indexes.** Wilshire Associates is an investment consulting firm. It calculates numerous U.S. stock return indexes. The most widely used is the Wilshire 5000. This is an index of the returns on the largest 5,000 companies in the United States. These 5,000 companies comprise virtually all the value of publicly traded U.S. stocks.

---

[2] Dow Jones recently created return indexes that include a larger number of stocks of both U.S. and non-U.S. firms. These indexes are called the Dow Jones equity indexes. They are considerable improvements over the widely quoted Dow Jones industrial, utility, transportation, and composite indexes.

■ **Russell Indexes.** Frank Russell is also an investment consulting firm that provides a variety of U.S. stock return indexes. The Russell 1000 includes the largest 1,000 firms. The Russell 2000 includes the next 2,000 largest firms. The Russell 3000 consists of both groups.

■ **MSCI Indexes.** Morgan Stanley Capital International calculates stock return indexes for various countries across the world. Its most quoted index is the EAFE (pronounced "eefa") Index. This index represents the return to a U.S. dollar investor on stocks traded in Europe, Australia, and the Far East.

In Figure 7-9 the cumulative market value of U.S. domiciled, publicly traded stocks is shown. The graph starts with the smallest companies on the far left and includes increasingly larger companies as the plot moves toward the right. The plot uses data as of March 1995. Approximately 7,200 firms were included with a total market capitalization of about $5.3 trillion.

Also shown in Figure 7-9 is the coverage of the Wilshire, Russell, and S&P 500 indexes.[3] Clearly, a large fraction of the total market value comes from a small fraction of the number of companies. The S&P 500 and Russell 1000 indexes are measures of the returns on large stocks. The Russell 3000 and Wilshire 5000 cover virtually all the value of publicly traded stocks in the United States.

FIGURE 7-9   U.S. STOCK MARKET VALUE MARCH 1995

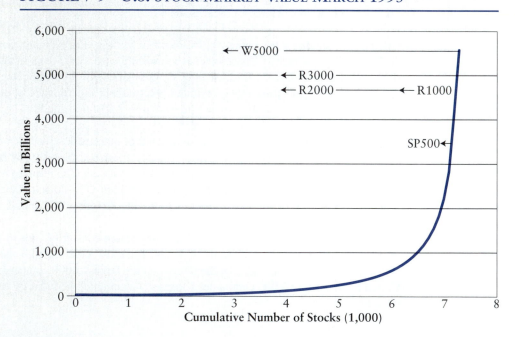

---

[3] The S&P 500 coverage is approximate because the 500 stocks included in the index are not necessarily the largest 500 companies at any moment in time.

Figure 7-10 presents another view of the value of publicly traded stocks in the United States.[4] Each block in the figure represents 10% of the total market value of all stocks traded in the United States. Companies with the smallest market capitalization represent the bottom block. Companies with the largest market capitalization represent the top block. Shown within each block are the number of firms that comprise the market value decile as well as the minimum market capitalization of a company within the block. For example, the largest market value decile consists of only seven firms, each having a market capitalization of $55.3 billion or more.

What should we make of the data in Figure 7-10? Consider the following:

- About 1,200 firms (17%) of publicly traded firms represent 90% of total market value. As we already noted, the Wilshire 5000 and Russell 3000 indexes cover virtually all of the market value of traded stocks in the United States.

FIGURE 7-10 CAPITALIZATION DECILES OF THE U.S. STOCK MARKET (MARCH 1995)

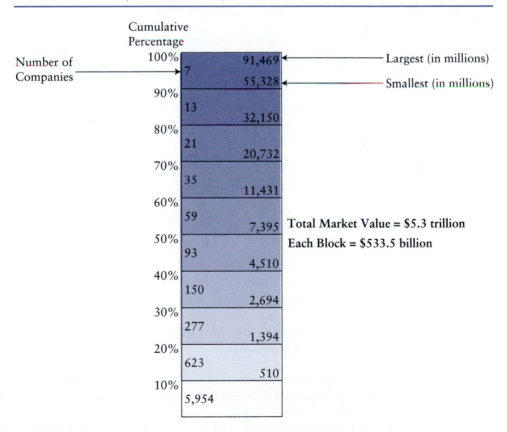

■ The 20 largest firms represent 20% of the total value, and 135 firms account for 50% of the total value. The U.S. stock market is dominated by large firms.

■ More than 80% of all firms account for only 10% of the total market value (the 5,954 firms shown in the bottom decile). If you were to strictly follow the implications of CAPM, then 10% of your investment in U.S. stocks should be spread across about 6,000 companies. The conclusion is obvious.

Security Weighting

Security weighting refers to how much weight is given to a given security return. For example, assume an index consists of only two securities and the following is known about them:

Security	Return in Period t	Market Value of Security	Percentage of Total Value
A	10%	$100	10%
B	20%	900	90%

If we were to weight each security's return equally, the average return would be 15%. This is known as an **equally weighted** index return. If we were to weight each return by the percentage the security represents of total value, the return would be 19%:

$$19\% = 0.1\,(10\%) + 0.9\,(20\%)$$

This approach is known as a **market value weighted** index return.

Both approaches are used in practice (as well as other weighting procedures). But market value weighting is the most consistent with the CAPM. Security indexes used to proxy the (stock) market portfolio when calculating beta values should be market value weighted indexes. Each of the indexes discussed here are based on market value weightings.

S U M M A R Y

This chapter examined how securities would be priced under equilibrium risk/return conditions. Here are the key concepts:

■ To develop a manageable model of equilibrium, a variety of assumptions had to be made, including the following:

1. a **one-period world** in which risk-averse individuals could determine the expected end-of-period utility by knowing the expected return and standard deviation of portfolio returns,
2. a **frictionless market,** in which brokerage fees and taxes would not impede trading,

3. all investors have equal and **costless access to information,** and
4. all individuals can borrow or lend at a **risk-free rate.**

■ The model that results from these assumptions is known as the **capital asset pricing model** (CAPM). Embodied in this model are two fundamental economic relationships: (1) the **capital market line** (CML), which specifies what the expected return on an efficient portfolio should be in terms of the portfolio's standard deviation, and (2) the **security market line** (SML), which specifies what the expected return on any security or portfolio should be in terms of its nondiversifiable risk.

■ The single efficient portfolio of risky assets that drives the CML and the SML is the **market portfolio,** a portfolio consisting of all risky assets available, with each held in proportion to its total market value.

■ In the SML, a security's risk is referred to as **beta.** Beta estimates are usually based on the **market model** in which historical returns on a security in excess of a risk-free rate are regressed against excess returns on a proxy for the market portfolio.

R E V I E W   P R O B L E M

As a financial consultant to a pension fund, you are preparing a presentation on the various aspects of the theory of risk and expected return discussed in this chapter. The following questions review certain major features of this theory:

a. What is meant by market equilibrium and what assumptions are used in its development?
b. Assume there are three major classes of risky securities available, as follows:

| Security Class | Market Value | σ | Correlation with | | | Total |
			RE	E	D	
Real Estate	$10,000	20%	1.0			0.65
Equity	6,000	30%	0.3	1.0		0.60
Debt	4,000	15%	0.3	0.3	1.0	0.30

What is the market portfolio? How much of its risky assets should the pension invest in each security type? What is the standard deviation of such a portfolio?
c. If the risk-free rate is 8.0% and the market risk premium is 5.0%, what are the CML and SML equations?
d. One member of the pension fund's board of trustees has stated that their investment portfolio should have a long-run expected annual return of 12%. In theory, how would this be obtained?
e. An assistant believes the beta of Textron common stock is 1.2. What should Textron stock be expected to earn to qualify for a purchase?
f. The local representative of a common stock mutual fund has been pressing the pension fund's trustees to invest the equity investments solely in the mutual fund he represents. One reason the representative offers is that the beta of his mutual fund is 1.0 and thus is the same as the market portfolio's beta. Comment.

Solution

a. The security market is in equilibrium if prices are at levels that attract no speculative trading. In this case, people have common beliefs about the future. Assumptions used in the model are the following:

(1) We live in a one-period world.

(2) Expected return and standard deviation of the portfolio are all that matter.

(3) Everyone may borrow or lend at the risk-free rate.

(4) All investors have homogeneous expectations.

(5) Markets are frictionless.

b. Given these assumptions, and for the markets to clear, the optimal market portfolio is:

Security	Percentage
Real Estate	50%
Equity	30%
Debt	20%

$$\sigma_p = [(0.25)(400) + (0.09)(900) + (.04)(225) \qquad \text{variance terms}$$

$$+2(0.5)(0.3)(20)(30)(0.3) \qquad \text{covariance (1,2)}$$

$$+2(0.3)(0.2)(30)(15)(0.3) \qquad \text{covariance (2,3)}$$

$$+2(0.5)(0.2)(20)(15)(0.3)]^{1 \div 2} \qquad \text{covariance (1,3)}$$

$$= 16.7\%$$

c. CML equation:

$$E(R_p) = 8.0\% + \sigma_p (5.0\% \div 16.7\%)$$

SML equation:

$$E(R_i) = 8.0\% + B_i (5.0\%)$$

d. For each unit of a portfolio's standard deviation, a return of 0.3% is earned $(5.0 \div 16.7)$ above the risk-free rate of 8.0%. Thus, to earn an expected return of 12%, the standard deviation must be $(12 - 8) \div 0.3$, or 13.33%.

$$8.0\% + 13.33\% (0.30) = 12.0\%$$

e.

$$E(R) = 8.0\% + 1.2 (5.0\%)$$

$$= 14.0\%$$

f. The mutual fund's beta may be 1.0, but this only says the fund has nondiversifiable risk identical to the market portfolio. Unless the mutual fund owns securities identical to the market portfolio, it has diversifiable risks the pension might not wish to incur.

QUESTIONS AND PROBLEMS

1. If the correlation coefficient between the returns on a portfolio and the market portfolio is 1.0, this is an efficient portfolio. True or false? Why?

2. A broadly diversified portfolio of commodities (corn, tin, gold, comic books, etc.) has a zero correlation with the market portfolio. It will therefore provide both an expected and realized return equal to the risk-free rate. True or false? Why?

3. In equilibrium, all investors have homogeneous expectations. What does this mean and why is it a necessary condition for equilibrium?

4. How would an index fund help an investor purchase the market portfolio?

5. After a thorough analysis of both the aggregate stock market and the stock of XYZ, Inc., you develop the following opinions:

	Likely Returns		
Economic Conditions	Market	Stock XYZ	Probability
Good	16%	20%	0.4
Fair	12%	13%	0.4
Poor	3%	−5%	0.2

At the present time, the risk-free rate is equal to 7%. Would an investment in XYZ be wise?

6. Assume the risk-free rate of interest is 8%, the market has an estimated risk premium of 6%, and the market's standard deviation of returns is 10%. Calculate the variance (or standard deviation) of returns for each portfolio:

Portfolio 1: 30% risk-free bonds, 70% the market

Portfolio 2: diversified portfolio with beta equal to 1.5

7. The policy committee of Investor's Diversified Corporation recently used reports from various security analysts to develop the following efficient portfolios:

Portfolio	Expected Return	Standard Deviation
1	8%	3%
2	10%	6%
3	13%	8%
4	17%	13%
5	20%	18%

a. If the prevailing risk-free rate is 6%, which portfolio is best?

b. Assume the policy committee would like to earn an expected return of 10% with a standard deviation of 4%. Is this possible?

c. If a standard deviation of 12% was acceptable, what would the expected portfolio return be and how could it be achieved?

8. Consider the following information on three securities. Which has the greatest systematic risk? Which has the smallest?

Security	σ_i	r_{iM}
1	σ_1	r_{1M}
2	$\sigma_2 = \sigma_1$	$r_{2M} > r_{1M}$
3	$\sigma_3 > \sigma_1$	$r_{3M} = r_{1M}$

9. You expect the stock of Firm X to sell for $70 a year from now and to pay a $4 dividend. If the stock's correlation with the market portfolio is -0.3, its standard deviation of returns is 40%. The market portfolio's standard deviation is 20% and has a required risk premium of 5%. The current risk-free rate is 5%. At what price should the stock trade?

10. Using the market model and five years of excess monthly returns, the following regression statistics were generated using a proxy index for the market portfolio:

Security	alpha	Standard Deviation	Correlation with Market Proxy
Mesa Petro	−0.21	14.7%	0.48
Anheuser Busch	0.15	6.3%	0.25
Teledyne	0.01	11.3%	0.51
XYZ Mutual Fund	0.20	5.2%	0.95
Market Proxy	0.00	4.3%	1.00

a. Calculate an estimate of beta for each.

b. Do you think the market model betas will be the same, higher, or lower during the next five years? (This is discussed explicitly in Appendix 7A. Simple logic, however, can suggest the proper answer.)

c. Assume the market proxy is a reasonable one. You believe the market risk premium is 7% and observe a current risk-free rate of 5%. Calculate the required return on each security.

d. Calculate the beta of a portfolio consisting of an equal holding of Mesa, Anheuser, and Teledyne.

11. You are given the following information about two stocks:

$$(\tilde{R}_{1t} - \tilde{RF}_t) = 1\% + 1.5\,(\tilde{R}_{SP_t} - \tilde{RF}_t)$$

$$(\tilde{R}_{2t} - \tilde{RF}_t) = 4\% + 1.0\,(\tilde{R}_{SP_t} - \tilde{RF}_t)$$

$$\text{Standard deviation of } (\tilde{R}_{1t} - \tilde{RF}_t) = 20\%$$

$$\text{Standard deviation of } (\tilde{R}_{2t} - \tilde{RF}_t) = 10\%$$

a. One-year T-bills are now yielding 5%. If the market portfolio is expected to return 11% during the year, what is the expected return on each stock during the next year?

b. The year goes by and the market portfolio actually provides a 10% return during the year. Given this, what is your expectation of the return earned on each stock during the year?

c. If stock 1 actually returned 15% and stock 2 returned 11%, what was the residual error for each stock?

d. Why might a residual error term arise? What is its role in diversification?

e. If the standard deviation of stock 1's residual error term is 10%, what is your best estimate of the standard deviation of excess returns on the market portfolio?

12. Management of a mutual fund is considering three alternative strategies:

Plan	Percentage Investment		Beta of Investment		
	T-Bonds	Stocks	T-Bonds	Stocks	Portfolio
1	0	100	0	1.0	?
2	20	80	0	1.0	?
3	30	70	0	1.0	?

a. Which is the most risky strategy?
b. If the risk-free rate is 7% and the expected return under plan 1 is 14%, what is the market risk premium?
c. Management believes this risk premium is too low and the market will soon adjust it upward. Given this, which plan might management wish to pursue?

13. Suppose you have gathered quarterly returns on four mutual funds and used them in the following excess return market model:

$$(\tilde{R}_{pt} - \tilde{RF}_t) = a_p + b_p (\tilde{R}_{Mt} - \tilde{RF}_t) + \tilde{e}_{pt}$$

Results are shown here:

Fund	a Coefficient	a Std. Dev.	b Coefficient	b Std. Dev.	R^2	Std. Dev. e
1	0.98%	1.00%	0.80	0.05	95%	12%
2	2.18%	1.50%	1.30	0.15	80%	23%
3	2.18%	0.75%	1.20	0.12	90%	18%
4	−0.04%	0.50%	1.02	0.08	97%	14.4%

a. Which fund's returns were the most closely correlated to market returns?
b. Which fund had the most market risk?
c. Which fund had the most total risk?
d. Restate the alpha values in terms of their annualized equivalents.

14. According to the capital asset pricing model (CAPM), the risk premium an investor expects to receive on any stock or portfolio increases:
a. directly with alpha.
b. inversely with alpha.
c. directly with beta.
d. inversely with beta.

15. The capital asset pricing model (CAPM) uses _____ as a measure of risk.
a. beta
b. standard deviation of returns
c. variance of returns
d. alpha

16. Capital asset pricing theory asserts that portfolio returns are best explained by:
a. economic factors.
b. specific risk.
c. systematic risk.
d. diversification.

17. The capital asset pricing model (CAPM) leads to all of the following conclusions except:
a. investors will not be paid for risk that can be diversified away.
b. the most important measure of stock risk is beta.
c. a well-diversified 30/40 stock portfolio has mostly systematic risk.
d. borrowing and lending do not affect portfolio results.

18. Which one of the following is not a criticism of beta?
a. Different calculation methods yield differing beta numbers.
b. Estimated betas on individual stocks are unstable.
c. In some periods, low beta stocks outperform high beta stocks.
d. Wide-scale usage has reduced the effectiveness of the beta measure.

DATAFILE ANALYSES

In this analysis, you will calculate the market model (MM) beta of a variety of mutual funds and individual common stocks.

1. Open the data set called OEFUNDS. This data set contains historical quarterly returns on many U.S. open-end mutual funds. Both bond funds and equity funds are provided. Select a few stock funds and regress their returns against the S&P 500 Index. T-bill returns are also given so the regression can be conducted in excess return form if you wish.
2. Open the data set called STCKRTNS. This data set contains historical monthly returns on many U.S. companies. Repeat the market model regression on a few stocks of your choice.

Compare the R-square values obtained in numbers 1 and 2. Why are the R-square values larger for the mutual funds? Why are the mutual fund R-square values not equal to 1.0?

REFERENCES

The capital asset pricing model (CAPM) is occasionally referred to as the Sharpe-Linter-Mossin model after the following breakthrough articles:

Lintner, John. "The Valuation of Risky Assets and the Selection of Risky Investments in Stock Portfolios and Capital Budgets," *Review of Economics and Statistics*, February 1965.

Mossin, Jan. "Equilibrium in a Capital Asset Market," *Econometrica*, October 1966.

Sharpe, William F. "Capital Asset Prices: A Theory of Market Equilibrium," *Journal of Finance*, September 1964.

A nonmathematical overview of the CAPM and its potential use in security analysis can be found in:

Modigliani, Franco and Gordon Pogue. "An Introduction to Risk and Return: Concepts and Evidence," *Financial Analysts Journal*, March–April and May–June 1974.

Articles that examine the estimation of security betas include the following:

Blume, Marshal. "Betas and Their Regression Tendencies: Some Further Evidence," *Journal of Finance*, March 1979.

Hamada, Robert S. "The Effect of the Firm's Capital Structure on the Systematic Risk of Common Stocks," *Journal of Finance*, May 1971.

Rosenberg, Barr and James Guy. "Predictions of Beta from Investment Fundamentals," *Financial Analysts Journal*, May–June and July–August 1976.

Vasicek, Oldrich. "A Note on Using Cross-Sectional Information in Bayesian Estimation of Security Betas," *Journal of Finance*, December 1973.

A P P E N D I X   7 A

ACCURACY OF BETA ESTIMATES

The market model provides estimates of historical beta values. How good are these at forecasting future beta values? Evidence developed to date suggests two major conclusions:

1. Beta estimates of single stocks are poor predictors of future beta values. Predictability improves if beta is estimated for a portfolio, and this predictability increases as the number of securities held in the portfolio increases.
2. Beta estimates tend to move toward 1.0. If beta is found to be less than 1.0 during a given time interval, chances are it will increase in the next time period. Conversely, if beta is greater than 1.0, chances are it will fall.

Predictability

A classic study of how well a past beta predicts the future beta was conducted by Blume. He used the market model on monthly returns for nonoverlapping seven-year intervals to calculate beta on portfolios consisting of from 1 stock to 50 stocks. Then for each portfolio size, he examined the correlation between an initial period's beta and the subsequent period's beta.

Blume's results are shown in Table 7A.1. For single securities, beta is a poor predictor. Only 36% of the subsequent period's variability in beta is explained by the variability in the initial period. For portfolios, however, the predictability improves markedly. For a 10-stock portfolio, R^2 is 85%, and by the time 50 stocks are held, R^2 is 96%. This is because estimation errors on single-stock beta values are uncorrelated with each other and thus disappear in portfolios. The conclusion is obvious. The market model beta for a single stock is a highly questionable estimate of the stock's true systematic risk. Beta estimates of portfolios are more trustworthy.

TABLE 7A-1   PREDICTABILITY OF BETA VALUES

Number of Securities in Portfolio	R^2
1	36%
2	53%
4	71%
7	77%
10	85%
20	95%
50	96%

R^2 equals the percentage of variability of beta in a subsequent period explained by the variability of beta in the initial period.

SOURCE: M. Blume, "Betas and Their Regression Tendencies," *Journal of Finance,* June 1975. pp. 758–796.

TABLE 7A-2   BETA ESTIMATES MOVE TO 1.0

| Portfolio | Portfolio Beta Estimate | |
	Initial Period	Subsequent Period
1	0.39	0.62
2	0.61	0.71
3	0.81	0.86
4	0.99	0.91
5	1.14	1.00
6	1.34	1.17

SOURCE: M. Blume, "On the Assessment of Risk," *Journal of Finance,* March 1971, pp. 1–10.

Betas Tend to Move to 1.0

Studies have also shown that betas estimated in one period tend to be closer to 1.0 in the subsequent period. Again using some of Blume's results, Table 7A-2 shows the estimated betas on six portfolios for two time periods. The portfolios are arranged from the smallest beta to the largest. Note that there is a definite trend for low betas in the initial period to have higher betas in the subsequent period, and for high beta portfolios in the initial period to have a smaller beta in the subsequent period.

The reason why beta estimates tend to more toward 1.0 is not fully understood. Most likely, it is due to measurement errors in the initial period's beta estimate. For example, if the initial beta is greater than 1.0, the chance that beta has been overestimated is greater than the chance that it has been underestimated.

Adjustments to Market Model Betas

Given the small predictive content of market model (MM) betas for individual stocks, a variety of methods have been suggested to improve forecasting accuracy. Three of the more popular methods include the following:

- Arbitrarily adjusting toward 1.0.
- Adjusting on the basis of Bayesian statistics.
- Relating betas to fundamental characteristics of the individual stocks.

Recognizing that MM beta estimates in one time interval tend to move toward 1.0 in the next time interval, many organizations adjust calculated market model betas toward 1.0. A variety of methods are used that vary in sophistication. For example, we could use the relatively naive procedure of saying the predicted beta will be some fraction, say halfway, between the market model estimate and 1.0. For example, an MM estimate of 1.8 would be stated as a predicted beta of 1.4, and an estimate of 0.5 would be predicted as 0.75. In his original study, Blume used a more sophisticated approach and found his MM betas in a second time period were related to those in a prior time period as follows:

$$b_{i2} = 0.343 + 0.677 \ (b_{i1})$$

There is no guarantee, however, that such relationships remain stable over time.

Another approach, first suggested by Vasicek, is based on **Bayesian** statistics. First, MM estimates are calculated for a large number of stocks. Among the output will be the following statistics:

$$b_i = \text{estimate of beta for stock } i$$

$$\sigma(b_i) = \text{standard deviation of stock } i\text{'s beta}$$

$$b = \text{average of all betas calculated}$$

$$\sigma_{\text{all}} = \text{standard deviation of the betas calculated}$$

Vasichek suggested that a revised beta, b_i^*, be calculated for each stock as follows:

Bayesian Beta Estimation

$$b_i^* = b_i \, \frac{\sigma_{\text{all}}^2}{\sigma_{\text{all}}^2 + \sigma^2(b_i)} + b \, \frac{\sigma^2(b_i)}{\sigma_{\text{all}}^2 + \sigma^2(b_i)} \tag{7A.1}$$

Other researchers have suggested that we try to explain future betas not only in terms of past beta estimates but also in terms of fundamental characteristics of the stocks. Such betas, which have come to be known as **fundamental betas,** are widely used. To illustrate, assume we have calculated market model betas on a large number of stocks in periods 1 and 2. In addition, we have information about certain fundamental characteristics of the stocks. Our data consist of the following for each stock:

$$b_{it,} \, b_{it-1} = \text{beta estimate for stock } i \text{ in periods } t \text{ and } t - 1$$

$$\text{IND}_i = \text{a measure of the firm's industry}$$

$$\text{SIZE}_i = \text{a measure of the firm's size}$$

$$\text{LEV}_i = \text{a measure of the firm's leverage}$$

Then the following regression could be run in order to determine the importance of each variable in predicting beta:

$$b_{it} = a_0 + a_1(b_{it-1}) + a_2(\text{IND}_i) + a_3(\text{SIZE}_i) + a_4(\text{LEV}_i) + e_i$$

The estimated regression parameters could then be used to predict betas on stocks not in our sample or to predict future betas, given past betas and fundamental characteristics of the stock.

8

CAPITAL ASSET PRICING EXTENSIONS

After reading this chapter you should have an understanding of the arbitrage pricing model, multi-beta models, and empirical research conducted to date on various asset pricing models.

The capital asset pricing model (CAPM) has two major attractions: (1) its simplicity, and (2) its implications. The CAPM is not strictly true, of course. It cannot be, given its assumptions. But the extent to which both its simplicity and its implications should be rejected is largely an empirical question. If the model predicts actual security returns in a reasonable fashion, it should not be rejected until a better predictive model is developed. Recent empirical evidence does raise serious questions, however, about the model's validity. As a result, practitioners and scholars are actively studying alternative ways of explaining the determinants of a security's expected and realized return. The principal competition to the CAPM at present is a model based on arbitrage theory. Unlike the CAPM, in which a single variable (beta) determines the expected return on a stock, arbitrage pricing theory (APT) allows for a multiple number of sources of risk. Unfortunately, this theory does not clearly identify what these multiple risks might be.

We begin the chapter with an overview of APT, which leads into a discussion of multi-factor CAPM models. Finally, we review some of the more important empirical studies testing variants of each theory.

Arbitrage Pricing Theory

In the early 1970s, Stephen Ross offered a model of security pricing known as **arbitrage pricing theory (APT).** In this section we develop the basic APT theory and implications. A word of warning is necessary before we begin, however. The final APT model can look deceptively similar to the CAPM. In fact, the two theories **can** lead to the same investment implications. But the theories are based on completely different logical developments and **do not necessarily** result in the same investment implications. As we develop the logic of APT, you will probably understand it better if you put the CAPM out of your thoughts for a while and focus solely on what APT suggests. After this new theory is fully developed, you can then recall your knowledge of CAPM and directly compare the two models. APT is a theory that competes with CAPM—it is not an extension. It is another way to view the world.

Theory of Arbitrage

The Law of One Price. A basic principle of economics is that two goods that are perfect substitutes for each other must be priced identically. If not, arbitrage transactions will occur until the prices of the goods are identical. For example, consider two grocery stores located next to each other and the price of grade A eggs in each. What would happen if store 1 was to sell the eggs for $1.00 a dozen and store 2 was to sell them for $2.00 a dozen? Some enterprising person would stand outside store 2 and take orders to sell eggs for (say) $1.50. Then, each time she received an order, she would immediately buy eggs for $1.00 from store 1. On each order, she would earn a $0.50 arbitrage profit. Of course, the arbitrage would continue until the price of eggs in each store was identical. At that point the arbitrageur would look for other price discrepancies.

We defined arbitrage back in Chapter 1, but it is useful to review the definition in the context of the egg example. First, note that our arbitrageur made no investment. She bought eggs only when she made a sale. True arbitrage involves no capital commitment. Second, note that the arbitrageur had no risk. The purchase and sale prices were known. True arbitrage involves no risk. In short, an arbitrage transaction results in a risk-free profit with no capital commitment. It is the potential for such arbitrage profits between securities that drives the arbitrage pricing theory.

The formal arbitrage pricing theory is a development of the 1970s, but arbitrage transactions have existed since humans developed the most primitive economies. Today arbitrage in the security markets is extensive. A large number of people earn a living by selling gold in one country and simultaneously buying it in another, by purchasing T-bills from one bank and simultaneously selling them to another (remember bid-ask spreads), by purchasing shares of IBM on one stock exchange and simultaneously selling them on another, and so on. Arbitrage operations are possible as long as prices of perfect substitutes are different. As we see in Chapters 16 and 17, the potential for arbitrage profits is also the force responsible for market prices of security options and futures contracts.

The end result of arbitrage is that two perfect substitutes must sell for the same price. This is known as the **law of one price.** Without calling it such, we have, in fact, made use of this principle when developing the standard CAPM. For example, the expected return on securities with the same betas must be identical in equilibrium.

Determinants of Security Returns.   Proponents of APT state that returns on securities are due to a variety of events that cause investors to assess what the value of a security should be. For example, inflation rates, food production, and population growth affect the investment worth of all securities to varying degrees. Other events, such as labor strikes in the airline industry or clothing fads, affect a subset of all securities. Finally, certain events have an effect on only a single security. APT expresses this belief as follows:

APT Realized Returns

$$\tilde{R}_{it} = a_{0t} + b_{i1}\tilde{F}_{1t} + b_{i2}\tilde{F}_{2t} + b_{i3}\tilde{F}_{3t} \ldots b_{iN}\tilde{F}_{Nt} + \tilde{e}_{it} \tag{8.1}$$

$$= a_{0t} + \sum_{K=1}^{N} b_{iK}\tilde{F}_{kt} + \tilde{e}_{it}$$

The $\tilde{F}_{Kt}$ terms are referred to as **factors**—events in one period that affect all securities or subsets of securities. For example, $\tilde{F}_{1t}$ might represent real growth of GNP in the United States during year t and thus take on a value of, say, 4.0%. The notion that these factors can influence the returns on either all securities or only particular subsets of securities is important and something we have more to say about later. The b_{iK} terms represent the return sensitivity of security i to the level of factor K. The a_{0t} term is the return that is expected in period t on all securities when the value of all factors is zero. Finally, the e_{it} term represents the return that is unique to security i in period t.

Two of these variables have symbols similar to CAPM variables (b_{iK} and e_{it}), and to a degree they measure somewhat similar forces. But they should not be confused with CAPM betas or residual errors. One of the b_{iK} APT variables might represent the sensitivity of a security's returns to returns on the market portfolio, but then again it might not. APT is silent as to what the factors are. The factors might be found via statistical tests, but knowledge of the factors is unimportant in the development of this theory. In addition, in APT $\tilde{e}_{it}$ reflects returns unique to security i, whereas in CAPM it is simply a return that is uncorrelated with the market portfolio.

Note that Equation (8.1) is a *linear* equation. None of the terms is raised to an exponent (other than 1.0), and their cumulative effects are summed. This is not done for simplicity—it is a logical consequence of the theory and a major empirical implication. We show why this is so soon.

Equation (8.1) can be used to state the expected return on a security as follows:

APT Expected Returns

$$E(R_{it}) = a_{0t} + b_{i1}\overline{F}_{1t} + b_{i2}\overline{F}_{2t} + \cdots + b_{iN}\overline{F}_{N}$$

$$= a_{0t} + \sum_{K=1}^{N} b_{iK}\overline{F}_{Kt} \tag{8.2}$$

where $\overline{F}_{Kt}$ denotes the expected value of factor K in period t. This relationship is then used to reexpress the actual realized return in period t as follows:

APT Realized Returns

$$\tilde{R}_{it} = a_{0t} + b_{i1}(\overline{F}_{1t} + \tilde{f}_{1t}) + b_{i2}(\overline{F}_{2t} + \tilde{f}_{2t}) \ldots$$

$$+ b_{iN}(\overline{F}_{Nt} + \tilde{f}_{Nt}) + e_{it}$$

$$= a_{0t} + b_{i1}\overline{F}_{1t} + b_{i2}\overline{F}_{2t} \cdots + b_{iN}\overline{F}_{nt} \tag{8.3}$$

$$+ b_{i1}\tilde{f}_{1t} + b_{i2}\tilde{f}_{2t} \cdots + b_{iN}\tilde{f}_{Nt} + \tilde{e}_{it}$$

$$= E(R_{it}) + (b_{i1}\tilde{f}_{1t} + b_{i2}\tilde{f}_{2t} \cdots + b_{iN}\tilde{f}_{Nt}) + \tilde{e}_{it}$$

where the $\tilde{f}_{Kt}$ terms represent the **unexpected outcome** of a given factor in period t. For example, assume factor 1 reflects real growth in U.S. GNP. If expected GNP growth is 4.0% but actual growth turns out to be 3.5%, then $\tilde{f}_{1t}$ would be -0.5%.

The last line of Equation (8.3) says the realized return is composed of two parts: the return that is expected and an unexpected return. The unexpected return is also composed of two parts: return sensitivity to unexpected factor outcomes and to unexpected security-unique events.

Effects of Arbitrage

According to APT, Equation (8.3) is not simply a convenient way to approximate the process by which security returns are generated. The theory of arbitrage pricing implies that Equation (8.3) must be true! If disequilibriums in security market prices are fully arbitraged, then security returns will be generated by exactly such a linear model.

To ensure that all possible arbitrages are in fact conducted, APT makes the following three assumptions:

1. Short selling is unrestricted and short sellers have full use of cash proceeds. If limits are placed on the amount investors could short-sell or if the cash inflow from short sales cannot be used to finance an offsetting purchase, then complete arbitrage of mispriced securities might not be possible.
2. There are no costs to trading. If transaction costs such as brokerage fees must be paid, the arbitrage of a mispriced security is limited.
3. There are a sufficient number of securities available such that security-unique risk (the uncertainty about e_{it}) can be eliminated by holding a well-diversified portfolio. If the "idiosyncratic" risk can be eliminated, then the only uncertainties that must be dealt with are uncertainties about factor outcomes.

Given these assumptions, Equations (8.1) through (8.3) must be true.

This is best illustrated if we consider a one-factor world. In such a world, APT states that expected and realized returns should be generated by the following relationship:

One-Factor Expected Return

$$E(R_{it}) = a_{0t} + b_{i1}\overline{F}_{1t} \tag{8.4a}$$

One-Factor Realized Return

$$\tilde{R}_{it} = E(R_{it}) + b_{i1}\tilde{f}_{1t} + \tilde{e}_{it} \tag{8.4b}$$

Let's begin the analysis of why this should be so by first assuming it is not. Consider the three securities shown in Figure 8-1. Clearly their expected returns are not linearly related to their factor sensitivities.

FIGURE 8-1   ILLUSTRATION OF ONE-FACTOR EXPECTED RETURNS

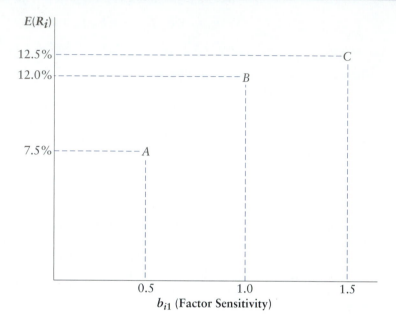

Consistent with APT assumptions, we will assume each security is actually a well-diversified portfolio such that all firm-unique risk is zero. That is, the variance of each $\tilde{e}_{it}$ term is zero.

An arbitrage consists of a transaction guaranteeing a risk-free profit with no capital commitment. Given the data shown in Figure 8-1, there is a clear arbitrage available. This consists of buying portfolio B and financing the purchase by short-selling a combination of A and C having a factor sensitivity identical to that of B.

Portfolio B has a factor sensitivity of 1.0 and an expected return of 12%. If we were to invest 50% in A and 50% in C, the net factor sensitivity would also be 1.0, but the expected return would only be 10%. In terms of factor pricing we could think of the relationships as follows:

For Portfolios A and C:

$$E(R_{it}) = 5\% + b_{i1}\,(5\%)$$

For Portfolio B:

$$E(R_{it}) = 7\% + b_{i1}\,(5\%)$$

It is this extra 2% constant return that will provide the arbitrage profit.

To illustrate the arbitrage, assume we decided to buy $100,000 of portfolio B. To finance the purchase, portfolios A and B would be short-sold in an aggregate amount of $100,000. Since we want the factor risk of the A and C portfolios to exactly offset the 1.0 factor risk of B, 50% of the $100,000 would be obtained from A and the remaining 50% from C. Potential outcomes of this transaction are shown in Table 8-1. Three possible unexpected factor outcomes are shown in order to prove that a known profit is indeed guaranteed. The

TABLE 8-1   ONE-FACTOR ARBITRAGE OUTCOME

	Today		End of Period		
	$	Factor Risk	Low $(f_{1t} = -5\%)$	Expected $(f_{1t} = 0)$	High $(f_{1t} = 5\%)$
Buy Portfolio B	−100,000	+1.0	+107,000	+112,000	+117,000
Sell Portfolio A, C					
Portfolio A	+50,000	−0.25	−52,500	−53,750	−55,000
Portfolio C	+50,000	−0.75	−52,500	−56,250	−60,000
Net	0.0	0.0	2,000	2,000	2,000

Low Calculations:

$$100,000 + 100,000\,[12\% + 1.0\,(-5\%)] \quad = 107,000$$
$$50,000 + 50,000\,[7.5\% + 0.5\,(-5\%)] \quad = 52,500$$
$$50,000 + 50,000\,[12.5\% + 1.5\,(-5\%)] = 60,000$$

High Calculations:

$$100,000 + 100,000\,[12\% + 1.0\,(5\%)] \quad = 117,000$$
$$50,000 + 50,000\,[7.5\% + 0.5\,(5\%)] \quad = 55,000$$
$$50,000 + 50,000\,[12.5\% + 1.5\,(5\%)] = 60,000$$

profit of $2,000 represents the 2.0% greater constant return available on portfolio B. Of course, anyone seeing the situation depicted in Figure 8-1 would jump at such an arbitrage. As a result of many such trades, the prices of the securities would adjust until the relationship between each security's expected return and its sensitivity to the factor is linear.

This notion is reinforced in Figure 8-2, where expected returns on securities are related to the single common factor by a wavy curve. Clearly, there are a large number of potential arbitrages available depicted in the curve. The important point, however, is that these arbitrage transactions will finally result in a linear relationship between expected returns and factor sensitivities such as that shown by the dashed line.

Factor Portfolios. Let's now consider a world in which there are two factors that affect the returns on all securities. In this case, APT states that expected and realized returns would be generated by the following relationships:

Two-Factor Expected Return

$$E(R_{it}) = a_{0t} + b_{i1}\tilde{F}_{1t} + b_{i2}\tilde{F}_{2t} \tag{8.5a}$$

Two-Factor Realized Return

$$\tilde{R}_{it} = E(R_{it}) + b_{i1}\tilde{f}_{1t} + b_{i2}\tilde{f}_{2t} + \tilde{e}_{it} \tag{8.5b}$$

FIGURE 8-2   GENERAL ILLUSTRATION OF ONE-FACTOR EXPECTED RETURNS

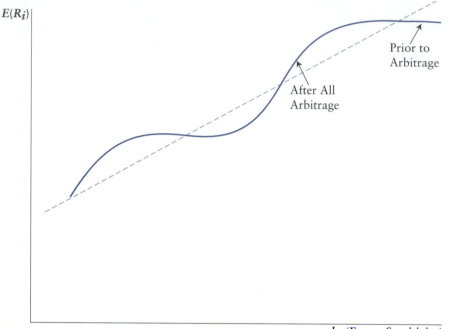

In this case, expected returns are related to expected factor outcomes by a hyperplane such as that shown in Figure 8-3. In this case, of course, the expected return on a security (such as X shown in the figure) will depend on the security's sensitivity to both factors.

If there are two factors, any arbitrage must result in zero factor sensitivity for both factor 1 and factor 2. This can be done by selecting proper percentage holdings of the various portfolios available. For example, assume that four well-diversified portfolios have factor sensitivities as shown here:

Factor Sensitivities

Security Portfolio	b_{i1}	b_{i2}	Expected Return
W	0.80	0.40	7.6%
X	0.40	0.80	7.2%
Y	1.20	0.00	8.0%
Z	0.00	1.20	8.0%

If expected returns on either factor are not linearly related to factor sensitivity, then an arbitrage is possible. Let's consider factor 1 first. We do this by eliminating all factor 2 risk. Notice that portfolios W and X could be combined in a manner that would result in zero factor 2 sensitivity. This would consist of either:

FIGURE 8-3   RELATIONSHIP OF EXPECTED RETURNS TO EXPECTED FACTOR OUTCOMES

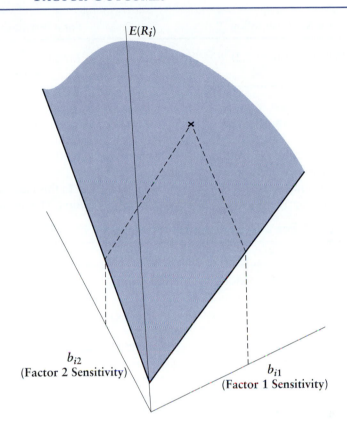

For a Net Cash Inflow:	For a Net Cash Outflow:
Purchase $1 of X	Sell $1 of X
Sell-Short $2 of W	Buy $2 of W

Letting X_i refer to the percentage of your net investment in security i, the resulting factor 1 and factor 2 sensitivities would be:

$$b_{pK} = (X_X \times b_{XK}) + (X_W \times b_{WK})$$

Factor	For a Net Cash Inflow:	For a Net Cash Outflow:
1	$b_{p1} = (1.0 \times 0.40) + (-2.0 \times 0.80)$ $= -1.2$	$b_{p1} = (-1.0 \times 0.40) + (2.0 \times 0.80)$ $= +1.2$
2	$b_{p2} = (1.0 \times 0.80) + (-2.0 \times 0.40)$ $= 0.0$	$b_{p2} = (-1.0 \times 0.8) + (2.0 \times 0.40)$ $= 0.0$

And the resulting expected returns would be:

$$E(R_{pt}) = X_X \times E(R_{Xt}) + X_W \times E(R_{Wt})$$

For a Net Cash Inflow	For a Net Cash Outflow
$E(R_{pt}) = (1.0 \times 7.2) + (-2.0 \times 7.6)$ $\quad = -8.0\%$	$E(R_{pt}) = (-1.0 \times 7.2) + (2.0 \times 7.6)$ $\quad = +8.0\%$

In short, when W and X are combined to have zero factor 2 sensitivity, they provide an expected return of either $+8.0\%$ or -8.0%, depending on whether there is an initial cash outflow or inflow. Similarly, factor 1 sensitivity of this portfolio is either $+1.2$ or -1.2. Since the expected return and factor sensitivity of portfolio Y are also $+8.0\%$ and $+1.2$, it is clear there is no arbitrage available on factor 1.

In contrast, an arbitrage is available on factor 2. In this case, factor 1 risk is eliminated by trading $2 of X and $1 of W in an opposite position. The results are summarized here:

For a Net Cash Inflow:			For a Net Cash Outflow:		
Sell $2 X	Plus	Buy $1 W	Buy $2 X	Plus	Sell $1 W
$b_{p1} = (-2 \times 0.4)$ $\quad = 0.0$	$+$	(1×0.8)	$b_{p1} = (2 \times 0.4)$ $\quad = 0.0$	$+$	$(-1 \times .8)$
$b_{p2} = (-2 \times 0.8)$ $\quad = -1.2$	$+$	(1×0.4)	$b_{p2} = (2 \times 0.8)$ $\quad = +1.2$	$+$	$(-1 \times .4)$
$E(R_{pt}) = (-2 \times 7.2)$ $\quad = -6.8$	$+$	(1×7.6)	$E(R_{pt}) = (2 \times 7.2)$ $\quad = +6.8$	$+$	(-1×7.6)

Since portfolio Z has identical factor 2 risk but a greater expected return, the arbitrage would consist of:

	Cash	Factor 2 Sensitivity
Buy $1 Portfolio Z	$-\$1$	$+1.2$
Sell Portfolio of W and X	$+1$	-1.2
Net	$\$0$	0.0

This example serves to point out three important ideas.

1. Arbitrageurs can create portfolios that focus on individual factors, portfolios which are insensitive to all other factor outcomes. Therefore, they can arbitrage mispricing within each possible factor and ensure that a linear relationship exists between expected returns and the various factors.
2. Investors can create portfolios that have factor sensitivities which meet their unique needs. For example, assume an oil factor exists and you are investing pension assets for an oil firm. By proper selection, a portfolio could be created that hedges (to various degrees) the risk to employees of a decline in the oil business.
3. Finally, this example points out the relationship between the factor sensitivity of a total portfolio and the sensitivities of the securities held. The sensitivity of the

total portfolio to a given factor is simply a weighted average of the factor sensitivity of each security held. Symbolically:

Portfolio Sensitivity M to Factor K

$$b_{pK} = \sum_{t=1}^{M} X_i b_{iK} \tag{8.6}$$

where X_i = the percentage invested in security i and b_{iK} = the sensitivity of security i to factor K.

Priced Factors. The proponents of arbitrage pricing theory believe that expected returns on a security are determined by a constant return associated with all securities plus sensitivities to various economic events, or factors. Earlier we expressed this in Equation (8.2) as follows:

APT Expected Returns

$$E(R_{it}) = a_{0t} + b_{i1}\overline{F}_{1t} + b_{i2}\overline{F}_{2t} + \cdots + b_{iN}\overline{F}_{Nt}$$

The relationship must be linear and must hold for all securities and portfolios, or arbitrage profits will be available.

Note that the expected return consists of a risk-free return plus a number of terms that could be thought of as risk premiums. A risk-free rate is available, since it is (theoretically) possible to create a portfolio that has no net exposure to factor uncertainties and no residual security risk. The risk-free rate might change over time. But within any single period, a known risk-free rate will apply to all securities. The more interesting terms are the factors and security sensitivities.

In our earlier discussion we thought of F_{1t} as being, say, the expected real growth of GNP. The F_{1t} could take on a value of, say, 4%, and b_{i1} might be 3.0. Similarly, F_{2t} might reflect changes in the level of employment with $F_{2t} = 200,000$ and $b_{i2} = 0.00003$. If these are the only two factors used in determining what the expected return on a security should be, they are referred to as priced factors. A **priced factor** is an uncertain economic event that affects the expected return investors will require.

Earlier we classified the types of events that could affect a security's return into three groups:

1. Events affecting all securities
2. Events affecting a subset of all securities
3. Events affecting only a single security

Clearly, events that affect only a single security can essentially be diversified away. Thus, they will not be priced factors—investors will not require compensation for bearing such uncertainties. Similarly, it is clear that events affecting the returns of all securities will be priced—investors will demand compensation for bearing their uncertainties. The difficulty arises with events that affect subsets of all securities. APT is mute on whether such factors will be priced. The conceptual answer is probably that it depends on whether such uncertainties can be diversified away. Economic events whose uncertainties can be eliminated through reasonable diversification should not be factors that investors price.

The pragmatic answer given by proponents of APT is that they don't know—that only empirical studies can determine what factors are in fact priced.

Let's assume two factors are priced and we know the following:

	Factor 1	Factor 2
Type of event	GNP Growth	Employment Change
Expected F_{Kt}	4.0%	200,000
Security A's b_{iK}	3.0	0.00003
Current risk-free rate of interest = 4%		

In this case the expected return on security A would be 22%:

$$= 4.0\% + 3.0(4.0\%) + 0.00003(200,000)$$

$$= 4.0\% + 12.0\% + 6.0\%$$

$$= 22.0\%$$

The two values of 12% and 6% associated with the priced factors are thought of as risk premiums. When this is done, the factor sensitivity terms are standardized in a way that makes the average sensitivity = 1.0. The b_{iK} values we have discussed are divided by the average b_{iK} values across all securities.

Assume the average b_{iK} values in the example are:

$$b_{i1} \text{ average} = 2.0$$

$$b_{i2} \text{ average} = 0.00004$$

Then the expected return on security A could be expressed as:

$$E(R_{At}) = 4.0\% + \frac{3.0}{2.0}(4.0\% \times 2.0) + \frac{0.00003}{0.00004}(200,000 \times 0.00004)$$

$$= 4.0\% + 1.5(8\%) + 0.75(8\%)$$

$$= 22.0\%$$

After this standardization, APT is usually expressed as:

APT Expected Returns

$$E(R_{it}) = a_{0t} + b_{i1}\lambda_{1t} + b_{i2}\lambda_{2t} \cdot \cdot \cdot + b_{iN}\lambda_{Nt} \tag{8.7}$$

where the average b_{iK} term is now 1.0 and the λ_{Kt} terms are thought of as the risk premium associated with each priced factor.

APT and the CAPM

You should now recall your knowledge of the CAPM so we can compare and contrast the two theories.

The theories are similar in a number of respects. Both express the expected return on a security as the sum of a risk-free rate plus a risk premium. Both imply broad diversification.

And if there is only one priced factor, b_{i1} of APT is the same as beta of the CAPM, and λ_{1t} is the same as the risk premium on the market portfolio.

They differ, however, in their fundamental assumptions. Whereas the CAPM is based on utility theory, APT is based on the economic principle of arbitrage. Although a one-factor model might look suspiciously like the CAPM's security market line, or multifactor models like multibeta CAPM models, they are in fact different species. APT does not assume that investors care only about expected returns and standard deviations of returns. **The theory also says nothing about the optimality of the market portfolio.**

Multifactor CAPM Models

The standard version of the CAPM presented in Chapter 7 implies that (1) the market portfolio is an efficient portfolio, and (2) expected returns on any security are directly related to the security's beta in the following risk/return relationship:

$$E(R_i) = RF + B_i [RP_M]$$

This model says there is a single variable (or factor) that captures the relevant risk of any security. This result, of course, is a logical consequence of the assumptions on which the model is based. Under differing assumptions, asset pricing theories that have multiple sources of risk can be developed. These are known as multifactor CAPM models. The following is a brief summary of a few of the CAPM-based models that have been developed:

- ◼ **Zero-beta model.** One obvious weakness of the basic CAPM is the assumption of a risk-free rate. Although a nominal risk-free rate is available from the purchase of default free, zero-coupon Treasury issues, a risk-free real return is not available. Fischer Black has shown that when a risk-free security does not exist, the lowest risk security is one that has a zero beta. We need not go into this model in any depth here. It is sufficient to note that in this model there are two sources of uncertainty: the market portfolio return and the zero-beta portfolio return. This model is commonly called the two-factor CAPM.

- ◼ **Tax models.** If the same tax rate is applied to both capital gains (price changes) and ordinary income (dividends and interest), the existence of taxes does not remove the optimality of the market portfolio or create other sources of risk. But if the capital gains rate is different from the ordinary tax rate, a security's expected return will be affected by both its beta and its dividend yield. If ordinary tax rates are greater than capital gains rates, securities with larger dividend yields will have to provide larger pretax expected returns.

- ◼ **Investor expectations.** The basic CAPM requires that all investors have the same knowledge. From this assumption, it follows logically that they will all wish to own the same portfolio of risky securities. But if there are segments of market participants that have different opinions (say, professional institutional investors versus individual investors), each segment will identify a different optimal risky portfolio. This can result in more than one source of risk affecting security returns. For example, institutional investors might restrict their holdings only to stocks of firms with large market capitalization. This could in turn create a "size effect"—different returns on large capitalization stocks than small capitalization stocks.

- ◾ **Nonmarketable assets.** Not all assets can be publicly traded. The obvious example is human capital, or our personal abilities. Models that account for this fact show that a security's covariability with returns on both the security market portfolio and human capital returns are important in determining a fair expected return.

- ◾ **Multiperiod models.** The CAPM developed in Chapter 7 was built on a single investment horizon. When consumption over a series of periods is considered, there are a number of risks faced by investors that are not captured by the standard CAPM beta.

For example, assume the market portfolio return in a year is positive 10%. This return will be viewed very differently if:

1. Inflation is 12% versus 2%,
2. You are unemployed versus employed, or
3. Interest rates are low versus high.

In addition to knowing what a security's CAPM beta is, you probably would like to know how the security's returns covary with events such as these. That is, when there are future investment periods beyond, say, the next year, you would like to know how a security's returns covary with changes in the set of investment opportunities and changes in your personal situation.

In short, asset pricing models based on investors maximizing their personal utility functions can result in equilibrium models in which there is more than one source of risk. The benefit to such utility-based models is that one knows the sources of risk—they can be defined. The disadvantage to utility-based models is that they can always be criticized for certain assumptions that are required to make the model mathematically tractable.

The situation for arbitrage-based models is exactly the opposite. Assumptions used to develop the APT are subject to less criticism. But the number of factors and the nature of the factor risks (i.e., inflation, industrial growth, etc.) are not defined by APT theory.

Using Multifactor Models

The Problem. The basic CAPM is a single-factor model that implies the realized return on a security in excess of the risk-free rate can be expressed as follows:

$$\tilde{R}_{it} - \tilde{RF}_t = a_i + B_i(\tilde{R}_{Mt} - \tilde{RF}_t) + \tilde{e}_{it} \tag{8.8}$$

The return on security i in period $t(R_{it})$ in excess of the risk-free return (RF_t) is composed of a constant return (a_i) plus the security's beta (B_i) times the excess return on the market portfolio $(R_{Mt} - RF_t)$ plus a residual error (e_{it}).

This residual error term is important, since it represents the risk of owning the security that can be eliminated by diversification. But for this to actually be the case in practice, the error term on any security must be uncorrelated with the error term on all other secu-

TABLE 8-2 RESULTS OF THE KING STUDY

| | Proportion of Return Variability Due to | | | | | |
| | 1952–1960 | | | 1927–1952 | | |
	Market Effects	Industry Effects	Stock Effects	Market Effects	Industry Effects	Stock Effects
Tobacco Industry	9%	17%	74%	36%	15%	49%
Oil Industry	37	20	43	54	19	27
Metals Industry	46	8	46	63	9	28
Railroad Industry	47	8	45	63	11	26
Utilities Industry	23	14	63	47	13	40
Retail Trade	23	23	8	69	48	11
Overall	31	12	51	52	13	35

SOURCE: Adapted from B. King, "Market and Industry Factors in Stock Price Behavior," *Journal of Business,* January 1966, pp. 139–190. Reprinted by permission of The University of Chicago Press.

rities. Although the basic CAPM implies the error terms will be uncorrelated, considerable evidence shows this is not true in the real world. For example, as early as 1966 we knew that stock returns were affected not only by broad market movements but also by industry-related events. For example, the results of a study conducted by King are shown in Table 8-2, suggesting that as much as 20% of a stock's return variability can be traced to industry-related events.

So what does this mean? Well, if the error terms are uncorrelated across securities, we would be safe in saying:

When error terms are uncorrelated

Expected Excess Stock Return

$$E(R_i - RF) = a_i + b_i E[R_M - RF] \tag{8.9}$$

Stock Variance of Excess Return

$$\sigma_i^2 = B_i^2 \sigma_M^2 + \sigma^2(e_i) \tag{8.10}$$

Expected Excess Portfolio Return

$$E(R_p - RF) = \sum_{i=1}^{N} X_i a_i + \sum_{i=1}^{N} X_i B_i E(R_M - RF] \tag{8.11}$$

Portfolio Variance of Excess Return

$$\sigma_p^2 = \sum_{i=1}^{N} X_i B_i^2 \sigma_M^2 + \sum_{i=1}^{N} X_i^2 \sigma^2(e_i) \tag{8.12}$$

For example, assume we have estimated the single-factor variables for two stocks as shown in Table 8-3. Then the expected excess return, variance, and standard deviation of each stock would be:

Expected Excess Return

$$A = 1.0\% + 1.2[10\% - 3\%]$$
$$= 9.4\%$$
$$B = 0.0\% + 0.8[10\% - 3\%]$$
$$= 5.6\%$$

Variance of Excess Return

$$A = (1.2)^2(15\%)^2 + (20\%)^2$$
$$= 724\%$$
$$B = (0.8)^2(15\%)^2 + (30\%)^2$$
$$= 1044\%$$

Standard Deviation of Excess Return

$$A = (724\%) = 26.9\%$$
$$B = (1044\%) = 32.3\%$$

And if an equal investment were made in each stock, the same variables for the portfolio would be:

Portfolio Expected Excess Return

$$= [0.5(1.0\%) + 0.5(0.0\%)] + [0.5(1.2) + 0.5(0.8)][10\% - 3\%]$$
$$= 0.5\% + [1.0][7\%]$$
$$= 7.5\%$$

TABLE 8-3   SINGLE-FACTOR ESTIMATE

	a_i Constant	b_i Beta Estimate	$\sigma(e_i)$ Standard Deviation of Error
Stock A	1.0%	1.2	20%
Stock B	0.0%	0.8	30%

Expected Market Portfolio Returns = 10%
Risk-Free Rate of Interest = 3%
Standard Deviation of Market Portfolio Excess Return = 15%

Portfolio Variance of Excess Return

$$= [0.5(1.2) + 0.5(0.8)]^2(15\%)^2$$
$$+ (0.5)^2(20\%)^2 + (0.5)^2(30\%)^2$$
$$= 225 + 325$$
$$= 550\%$$

Portfolio Standard Deviation of Excess Return

$$= [550\%]$$
$$= 23.4\%$$

But when security error terms are in fact correlated, calculations based on Equations (8.9) through (8.12) would be wrong. The size of the error made when these equations are used is still being researched. But many practitioners have developed multifactor models that they believe work better than the single-factor model implied by the standard CAPM.

An Illustration. Assume you believe a two-factor model is necessary to better explain security returns. You believe the first factor is the usual return on some broadly based stock index during period t (R_{Mt}) and the second is the rate of inflation in period t (I_t). Specifically, you hypothesize:

$$\tilde{R}_{it} - \tilde{RF}_t = a_i + B_{i1}(\tilde{R}_{Mt} - \tilde{RF}_t) + B_{i2}(\tilde{I}_t) + \tilde{e}_{it}$$

To estimate the a_i, B_{i1}, and B_{i2} terms, analysts usually rely on multiple regression procedures applied to historical data. For example, assume you have done such a regression analysis for stocks A and B and found the result shown in Table 8-4. In this multifactor model, the expected return and variance of stock i would be calculated as follows:[1]

$$E(R_{it} - RF) = a_i + B_{i1}E(R_{Mt} - RF_t) + B_{i2}E(I_t)$$

TABLE 8-4   MULTIFACTOR VARIABLE ESTIMATES

Stock	a_i	B_{i1}	B_{i2}	$\sigma(e_i)$
A	1.0%	1.2	0.5	19.4%
B	0.0%	0.8	−1.2	27.5%

Expected Market Portfolio Return = 10%.
Expected Inflation Rate = 2%.
Risk-Free Rate of Interest = 3%.

Standard Deviation of Market Portfolio Excess Return = 15%.
Inflation = 10%.

---

[1] This assumes excess market returns and inflation are uncorrelated.

$$\sigma_i^2 = (B_{i1})^2 \sigma_M^2 + (B_{i2})^2 \sigma_I^2 + \sigma^2(e_i)$$

When the data in Table 8-4 is applied to stocks A and B,

Expected Stock Excess Return

$$A = 1.0\% + 1.2(10\% - 3\%) + 0.5(2\%)$$

$$= 10.4\%$$

$$B = 0.0 + 0.8(10\% - 3\%) - 1.2(2\%)$$

$$= 3.2\%$$

Variance of Stock Excess Return

$$A = (1.2)^2(15\%)^2 + (0.5)^2(10\%)^2 + (19.4\%)^2$$

$$= 725\%$$

$$B = (0.8)^2(15\%)^2 + (-1.2)^2(10\%)^2 + (27.5\%)^2$$

$$= 1044\%$$

Standard Deviation of Stock Excess Return

$$A = (725\%) = 26.9\%$$

$$B = (1044\%) = 32.3\%$$

Notice that when this version of a multifactor model is used, the total individual stock standard deviation does not change, but the expected individual stock returns do change.

Multifactor models such as this are used for timing and performance evaluation. Consider its use in timing. If you have no special knowledge about returns on a market portfolio of stocks but you believe inflation will be much greater than other people believe, then you might create a portfolio with a B_1 value equal to 1.0 and a B_2 value that is as low as possible. Quantitative portfolio managers actively run portfolios based on such bets.

When used in performance evaluation, analysts are able to attribute the return earned on a portfolio to each of the factors they have decided to examine. For example, BARRA is a quantitative investment consulting firm that uses 13 fundamental stock factors plus 55 industry factors in their multifactor models. These BARRA factors are widely used by portfolio managers to evaluate the source of their portfolio returns. The data shown in Table 8-5 is extracted from a paper that appeared in the *Journal of Portfolio Management*. This paper explained how the manager uses BARRA factors to understand why his portfolio had good returns. As displayed in the table, the manager's portfolio did well due to the size, earning, price ratio, and price/book ratio factors of the stocks selected. The manager performed poorly in terms of the LOCAP and variability in market factors.

TABLE 8-5   DETERMINANTS OF PORTFOLIO RETURNS

Five Factors Contributing to Best Results

Factor	Cumulative 91-Month Total	Annual*
Size	23.3%	3.07%
Price/Earnings	7.3	0.96
Price/Book	7.2	0.95
Specific Asset Selection	1.5	0.20
		6.12%

Five Factors Contributing to Worst Results

Factor	Cumulative 91-Month Total	Annual*
LOCAP	(7.2)%	(0.95)%
Variability in Market	(7.0)	(0.92)
Drugs, Medicine	(2.3)	(0.30)
Telephone, Telegraph	(1.2)	(0.16)
Transport by Water	(1.1)	(0.15)
		(2.48)%

*Not compounded; cumulative divided by 7.58 years (91 months/12).

SOURCE: H. Russell Fogler, "Common Stock Management in the 1990s," *Journal of Portfolio Management*, Winter 1990.

Empirical Tests of CAPM

The Nature of the Tests

Clearly, the CAPM rests on a number of assumptions that are not strictly true in the real world. This does not mean, however, that the model is totally without merit. Its validity can be assessed only by examining how well it predicts real-world phenomena. This is an empirical question.

The CAPM is an ex ante model. Individuals develop subjective judgments about (1) the risk-free rate, (2) the beta of a security, and (3) the appropriate market risk premium. While people may not go through such an explicit mental process, perhaps they act as if they do. Tests of the CAPM are always tests of the SML:

Security Market Line

$$E(R_i) = RF + B_i[RP_M] \qquad\qquad (8.13)$$

This is an ex ante relationship. People develop (common) beliefs about what the systematic risk of security i will be in the future and are faced with a future expected risk premium.

Unfortunately, in testing the model we can't look into investors' minds to see whether this is the relationship they use to determine equilibrium expected returns. For example, investors might be totally blind to the importance of security covariance and price a security's standard deviation instead of its covariance to the market. But it is doubtful that serious tests of ex ante pricing could be performed; at least none have been conducted to date. Instead, we rely on history. Do past security returns tell a story that is consistent with the CAPM? In particular, is the average historical return earned on security i equal to (1) the average historical risk-free rate (RF) plus (2) a risk premium equal to the security's estimated historical beta (b_i) multiplied by the average historical risk premium earned on the market (RP_M)?

The Historical Test

$$\overline{R}_i = \overline{RF} + b_i[\overline{RP}_M] \tag{8.14}$$

Compare this statement of how securities should have behaved in the past (if the CAPM is valid) with the ex ante SML in Equation (8.13). They have very similar terms, but the SML terms are expectations of the future, whereas the statistical tests rely on averages of the past.

Equation (8.14) is justified as the historical equivalent of the SML based on simple logic. Over long intervals, expectations will be equal to average outcomes. People are rational enough to recognize when they are consistently over- or underestimating returns or betas. If they find such a bias, they will adjust their expectations until observed outcomes average what they expect them to. If this is true:

1. average historical returns will reflect past expectations of returns,
2. average historical systematic risk will reflect past expectations of systematic risk, and
3. average historical risk premiums will reflect past expectations of risk premiums.

The difficulty of using Equation (8.14) to test the SML is not in its logic; the difficulty lies instead in its implementation. In particular, how should the beta values be estimated and what index should be used to measure the market portfolio? Empirical tests that attempt to determine whether Equation (8.14) supports the CAPM are actually testing whether:

■ The b values are true estimates of historical betas.

■ The index used to measure historical risk premiums is the market portfolio.

■ The CAPM is correct.

If any of these fails, the test as a whole will fail.

Empirical tests of the SML examine the following regression equation equivalent of Equation (8.14):

Regression Test of SML

$$R_i = a_0 + a_1 b_i \tag{8.15}$$

where the known quantities are:

$\bar{R}_i$ = the average single-period return on security i during some past time interval

b_i = the estimated historical beta for security i

and the statistically estimated values should be:

a_0 = the average risk-free rate that prevailed during the testing period, $\overline{RF}$

a_1 = the market risk premium earned during the testing period, $\bar{R}_M - \overline{RF}$

Regardless of the means of testing the CAPM, there are a number of implications of the theory that statistical tests should support or question:

1. The intercept term in Equation (8.15) should not be significantly different from the average risk-free rate during the testing period. Occasionally, empirical tests are performed on excess returns, where the risk-free rate that prevailed during a particular period is subtracted from both the left- and right-hand sides of Equation (8.15). In this case, a_0 should not be statistically different from zero.
2. The relationship between $\tilde{R}_i$ and b_i should be linear.
3. The term a_1 should be positive and equal to $(\bar{R}_M - \overline{RF})$, the earned risk premium. Beta should be the only factor related to average historic returns. Variables such as a security's diversifiable risk should be statistically insignificant.

Tests on Individual Stocks

Douglas examined the relationship between average security returns and various risk measures on a sample of more than 600 stocks for various time intervals between 1926 and 1960. Using different five-year intervals, he calculated (1) each stock's average quarterly rate of return, (2) the variance of each stock's quarterly rate of return, and (3) the covariance of the stock's return with the quarterly returns of an index of all 600 stocks. Using these values, he then estimated the following regression equation for each five-year period:

Douglas Single-Stock Test

$$(1 + \bar{R}_i) = a_0 + a_1(\sigma_i^2) + a_2(\sigma_{ij}) + e_i \tag{8.16}$$

where $\bar{R}_i$ = the average quarterly return on stock i during the five-year period, σ_i^2 = the variance of i's quarterly return, σ_{ij} the covariance between i's return and the index of all the 600 stocks during the five-year period, and e_i = random estimation errors.

His results for each five-year period are displayed in Table 8-6. The a_o regression coefficient should reflect one plus the quarterly risk-free rate. While his estimates were perhaps slightly higher than quarterly values of $1 + RF$, they weren't the major concern raised by his results. His estimates of a_1 reflect the impact of a security's total risk on average returns. Per the CAPM, a_1 values should be zero. But most are positive and statistically significant, with 95% confidence or better, contrary to the CAPM. Estimates of a_2, on the other hand, should reflect the earned price of risk: $(R_M - RF) \div \sigma_m$. Yet most of these values are statistically insignificant. In a related study of individual stock returns and betas, Lintner found similar results.

But both the Douglas and Lintner studies appear to suffer from various statistical weaknesses that might explain their anomalous results. In a subsequent study, Miller and Scholes reviewed these statistical problems and concluded the empirical relationship between average security returns and unsystematic risk could be due to (1) measurement errors incurred

TABLE 8-6   DOUGLAS TEST OF CAPM

$$(1 + \bar{R_i}) = \alpha_0 + \alpha_1(\sigma_i^2) + \alpha_2(\sigma_{ij})$$

| | σ_0 | α_1 | | α_2 | |
Period	Coefficient	Coefficient	T-Value	Coefficient	T-Value
1926–31	0.99	0.15	2.14	0.63	0.72
1931–36	1.03	0.18	6.00	0.17	0.81
1936–41	0.99	0.39	2.60	−0.30	−0.54
1941–46	1.04	0.69	4.93	1.19	1.43
1946–51	1.01	0.08	0.38	0.66	0.53
1951–56	1.02	−0.21	−0.68	−3.51	−1.99
1956–60	1.03	1.13	4.18	−3.21	−2.08

SOURCE: G. Douglas, "Risk in the Equity Markets: An Empirical Appraisal of Market Efficiency," *Yale Economic Essays*, 9, (1) 1969.

in estimating individual stock betas, (2) the fact that estimated betas and unsystematic risks are highly correlated, and (3) a skewness that was present in the distribution of observed stock returns. While Miller and Scholes don't reject the implications of the Douglas and Lintner studies, they suggest the statistical problems encountered when individual stocks are used might be the reason for the discouraging results.

Tests on Portfolios

Because of these statistical problems, most tests since then have concentrated on portfolios of securities.

The Black, Jensen, and Scholes Study. Black, Jensen, and Scholes used all NYSE stocks for the period 1931 to 1965 to form 10 portfolios of different beta levels. Then average monthly "excess returns" on each portfolio were regressed against the portfolio's beta. For example, let's say we have identified 10 different portfolios for each month between 1931 and 1965. During a given month, the return on each portfolio is calculated and the 30-day risk-free rate (which existed at the start of the month) is subtracted. This results in a monthly series of excess returns for each portfolio. The average of each series is then calculated, and this average is regressed against the portfolio betas.

Results of the Black, Jensen, and Scholes study are displayed in Figure 8-4 and shown here:

Monthly Average − Excess Return = $\alpha_0 + \alpha_1$ (portfolio beta)

$$(\bar{R_p} - \overline{RF}) = 0.359\% + 1.08\% \ (b_p)$$

(T-value)   (6.53)   (20.77)

These results conform with the CAPM in that a clear linear relationship exists between average excess returns and beta. They do not conform with the version of the traditional CAPM in which a known risk-free rate exists. Recall that the portfolio returns are excess returns. If

FIGURE 8-4 BLACK, JENSEN, AND SCHOLES STUDY

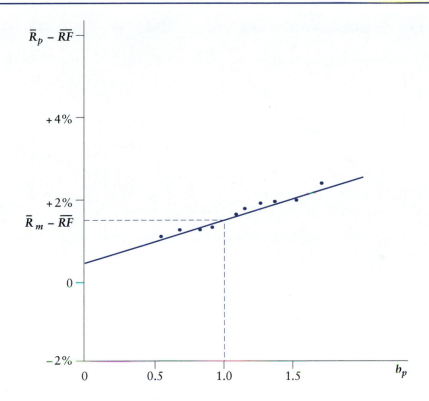

the 30-day T-bill rate had been the risk-free rate, the intercept term should have been zero. However, the intercept term of 0.359% implies the return on a portfolio with zero systematic risk is not RF but something larger. This evidence is contrary to the traditional CAPM. As a result, Black developed a zero-beta CAPM theory, which we discussed earlier.

Black, Jensen, and Scholes also examined the same regression for various time intervals. Results are shown in Figure 8-5. Again, a linear relationship exists, but the intercept term is usually greater than zero and changes in each period. The slope isn't always positive, implying there are lengthy time intervals during which beta and average returns are negatively related.

Roll's Critique of CAPM Studies

Many other studies of the CAPM have been conducted. But all have been brought into serious doubt due to a critique presented by Richard Roll.

In theory, the market portfolio M consists of all risky assets. Since these include stocks, bonds, futures contracts, real estate, human capital, and so on, portfolio M is impossible to identify. Typically, people have compromised by assuming the returns on the broad stock market indexes are highly correlated with returns on the true portfolio M. The appropriateness of this compromise and, in fact, the testability of any version of the CAPM have come under sharp attack, however, in a breakthrough article by Roll. The results of Roll's critique of the CAPM are summarized as follows:

FIGURE 8-5 BLACK, JENSEN, AND SCHOLES RESULTS

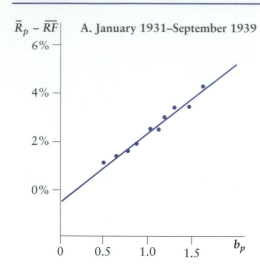

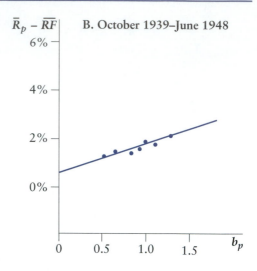

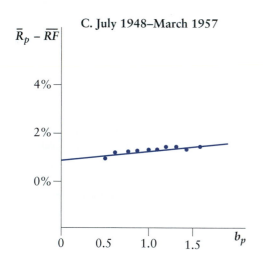

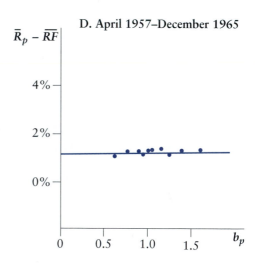

1. Tests of the CAPM are in reality tests of the market portfolio's mean-variance efficiency.
2. The market portfolio consists of all risky assets, which can never be totally observed. Thus, the CAPM (that is, the efficiency of M) is untestable.
3. As long as the proxy used for M is mean-variance efficient (sits on the efficient frontier) ex post, then the betas calculated against this proxy and average security returns will mathematically be linearly related to the proxy portfolio's risk and return. The linearity observed in most of the empirical research between security betas and average returns is a mathematical tautology. Its only economic meaning is that the proxy portfolio was mean-variance efficient. But this efficiency of the proxy does not prove the efficiency of the market portfolio or the validity of the CAPM.

4. If the proxy used for M is not ex post mean-variance efficient, the empirical results have no meaning whatsoever, and any form of relationship might be found between average security returns and beta (approximately linear, curvilinear, residual error risk found to be significant, etc.).
5. Models that attempt to evaluate investment performance via the CAPM are inappropriate.

Roll's critique of the CAPM elegantly expressed what many people had previously stated more informally but without such force and economic rigor. Because of the potential significance of these arguments to existing financial theory, modern investment management techniques, and performance evaluation, we must examine the ideas more thoroughly. The fact that the mean-variance efficiency of the market portfolio is the single testable hypothesis of the CAPM is easy to understand intuitively. For example, in a world in which a risk-free security exists, the CAPM is based on all individuals electing to hold only one portfolio of risky assets. This portfolio must be M—the market portfolio of all risky assets. Tests of CAPM are inherently tests of portfolio M's mean-variance efficiency. But it is clear that researchers will never be able to completely identify of what portfolio M consists. As a result, the CAPM is untestable. Roll's third and fourth conclusions are more difficult to understand, and their mathematical proof lies beyond the scope of this book. Nonetheless, we must understand the meaning of the conclusion to appreciate the true status of empirical tests of the CAPM. Assume there are an unidentifiably large number of risky assets available. To proxy these assets, we examine the historical returns on, say, 1,000 observable common stocks. In calculating individual stock betas, we measure a stock's ex post standard deviation (σ_i), the standard deviation of ex post returns on some portfolio (r_{ip}), and the ex post correlation coefficient between the stock's and the portfolio's return (r_{ip}). Beta is then measured as beta $= (\sigma_i \cdot r_{ip})/s_p$. An infinite number of reference portfolios could be created using the 1,000 stocks. Of such possible reference portfolios, some will be ex post efficient (in that they provide the lowest variance of returns for a given mean return) and others will not be efficient. If we happen to use any of the ex post efficient portfolios, then the following precise mathematical relationship will exist:

Estimated SML

$$\bar{R}_i = RF + B_i[\bar{R}_p - RF] \qquad (8.17)$$

While this is the empirical version of the CAPM tested, Roll showed the relationship is purely mathematical. There is no economic content to it. Studies that have found a linear relationship offer no proof at all that the CAPM is correct. If an empirical test finds a linear relationship, it simply means the researcher was fortunate enough to have chosen an ex post mean-variance efficient portfolio as a market proxy. If the researcher does not find a linear relationship between historical beta and mean security returns, nothing can be concluded at all. Either the researcher used an inefficient portfolio as the market proxy, or the CAPM is invalid. But it is impossible to distinguish between the explanations.

Roll's fifth conclusion can be illustrated with the use of Figure 8-6. Assume the CAPM is true. The dashed lines represent the actual efficient set of risky real assets and the true capital asset pricing line. However, individuals wishing to evaluate investment performance use a market portfolio proxy, say, the Standard & Poor's Composite Index. If the researchers are lucky, the S&P Composite will represent one of the many available efficient portfolios. Since the composite index is assumed to be efficient, a linear relationship will exist between return and beta risk, shown as the solid SML line.

With this as background, what is to be concluded about the performance of mutual funds A and B? While A appeared to outperform the market, all it really did was outperform combinations of borrowing and lending portfolios of the S&P. Its apparent good performance is meaningless. Roll's observation is intuitively quite simple. If the market portfolio is the best set of risky assets to hold, no other portfolio can ever beat it. If some investment or speculative strategies seem to "beat the market," then either the CAPM is wrong (in which case, it shouldn't be used to evaluate performance), or a poor market proxy was used (in which case, again, it shouldn't be used). In conclusion, Roll's observations have raised fundamental questions about the CAPM's truth, testability, and use in evaluating investment performance.

Recent Evidence

In recent years, tests of the CAPM have investigated whether there is a statistically significant relationship between average stock returns and a number of variables including an estimate of a stock's betas. These tests are referred to as cross-sectional regression tests. One of the first cross-sectional regression tests was published by Fama and French in 1992. The procedure which they used consisted of the following:

FIGURE 8-6 EFFECTS OF ROLL'S COMMENTS ON PERFORMANCE EVALUATION

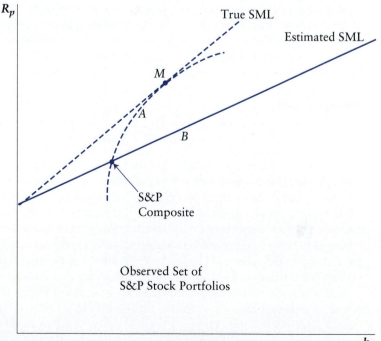

■ A time period is chosen during which information on all variables to be tested is available. Fama and French selected the period between July 1963 and December 1990, since July 1963 was the first date at which they were able to develop accurate estimate of all stock variables they wished to study.

■ Starting with the month of July 1963, a number of cross-sectional regressions were run such as the following:

$$R_i = a + M_1 \text{(beta}_i) + M_2(\ln(\text{Market Cap}_i)) + M_3(\ln(\text{Book to Market}_i))$$

In this regression, R_i represents the return on security i during the month of July 1963. The variable beta is an estimate of stock i's true beta at the start of the month. Market Cap represents stock i's market capitalization (price times shares outstanding) at the start of the month. And Book to Market represents the ratio of accounting book value of equity divided by the market price of the stock.[2]

The various M terms are regression parameters that capture how a security's return is related to each variable.

■ The cross-sectional regression was then run again for each month included in their testing period. This resulted in a total of 330 separate cross-sectional regression estimates of each M term.

■ Finally, the average value of the 330 estimates of each M term was calculated. To test whether the average was statistically different from zero, the average was divided by the time-series standard deviation of the 330 estimates of the M.

The results of five different cross-sectional regressions found by Fama and French are shown in Table 8-7. The first regression model tested whether stock returns were related to their beta estimates. While the average cross-sectional regression parameter of 0.15 was positive, the t-statistic of 0.46 indicates it is not statistically different from zero.

The second model tested whether stock returns were related to a stock's market capitalization and found, as have so many other studies, a strong negative relationship. In the third model, both beta and market capitalization are included. Again beta was not statistically significant and market capitalization was highly significant.

Fama and French claim, however, that the most important variable appears to be the ratio of a firm's accounting book value to its stock price. Models 4 and 5 in the table show quite large t-statistics for the book to market variable.

What Does It Mean? Fama and French suggest that no evidence in their study supports the theory that average stock returns are directly related to beta estimates. If we believe that, on average, investors price securities so they will get what they expect, this evidence suggests no relationship between beta estimates and expected returns. There is, however, a strong relationship between a stock's average return and its market capitalization as well as its book to market ratio. These variables could be proxies for two (unknown) APT factors. But do not declare the CAPM dead quite yet! Many researchers believe the Fama-French results are due to poor beta estimates, others believe the results are due to inappropriate

---

[2] The Fama-French study examined a number of other stock variables. Our discussion is limited to beta and two other variables they believed to be most important.

TABLE 8-7 FAMA-FRENCH CROSS-SECTIONAL REGRESSION RESULTS

Regression Model	Beta	Natural Log of Market Cap	Natural Log of Book to Market
Number 1	0.15 (0.46)		
Number 2		−0.15 (−2.58)	
Number 3	−0.37 (−1.21)	−0.17 (−3.41)	
Number 4			0.50 (5.71)
Number 5		−0.11 (−1.99)	0.35 (4.44)

SOURCE: Adapted from: Eugene F. Fama and Kenneth R. French, "The Cross-Section of Expected Stock Returns," *The Journal of Finance*, June 1992.

methodology, and others believe the time periods used in such tests are much too small to capture a relationship between expected returns and true betas. The following is a quote from Fischer Black on the Fama-French study:

> Estimating expected return is hard. Daily data hardly helps. We need decades of data for accurate estimates of average expected return. We need such a long period to estimate the average that we have little hope of seeing changes in expected return.[3]

In short, while there is little empirical evidence in support of the CAPM, it might not be feasible to test the theory accurately.

Empirical Tests of APT

Because of Roll's suggestion that the CAPM is logically untestable, most recent empirical research has explored the validity of APT. These tests can be classified into two types:

1. tests in which the researcher does not hypothesize any specific type or number of factors but, instead, extracts statistically significant factors from historical returns, and
2. tests of whether explicitly defined potential factors are related to security returns.

We refer to the first class of tests as unspecified factor tests and the second class as specified factor tests.

---

[3] This quote comes from Fischer Black, "Estimating Expected Return," *Financial Analysts Journal*, September–October 1993.

Todd D. Doersch

Director, Marketing and Sales
BARRA
Stanford University, B.A.
Harvard Business School, M.B.A.

BARRA provides innovative analytical models, software, and services that enable its more than 900 clients worldwide to make superior investment and trading decisions. When Todd Doersch was in college he risked his living expense money to start a small company. The business was a success and the experience taught him one key lesson: to bundle service with the product. He embodies this idea in his position with BARRA.

Q: The name BARRA has become ubiquitous with risk and return modeling. Tell me about the BARRA model.

A: The underlying theory is that a portion of a portfolio's total risk is explainable by commonalties which span individual stocks, the most intuitive of which might be industries. There are other commonalties like size and price-to-earnings ratio. Breaking down total risk into different categories can be very helpful in numerous investment management applications. One way is to use it as a forecasting tool to emphasize certain characteristics in a portfolio which you think are going to go up and de-emphasize the characteristics that you think will suffer negative performance. As a fine-tuning tool it can be very helpful in forward-looking portfolio construction. Another way to use the same construct is to focus on the past and do historical performance attribution. Here the return experienced for a given time period is divided into the same categories that were defined by the factors of the model. Rearview mirror performance attribution is insightful when assessing portfolio strengths or weaknesses for an investment management organization that is trying to fine-tune its strategy or conduct back testing. Pension sponsors could use the same technology to investigate strengths and weaknesses of investment managers they have hired or are considering hiring.

Q: Who is the most typical user?

A: There are three types of historical users: pension sponsors, pension consultants, and large master trust banks. The very largest pension sponsors use the model quite heavily. They have the same portfolio problem that the manager does. They have a portfolio of managers, or a portfolio of portfolios, just as an investment manager has a portfolio of assets. Pension consultants use it as a communication device as do the custodial banks. They take the performance of a manager and present to the sponsor diagrams, graphs, and reports that outline not only how much return the manager generated by overemphasizing a particular industry but also how much risk the manager took in a particular category. These results are presented as a tree diagram where the base of the tree is the total return with the corresponding total risk. Total return and total risk are broken down into branches where each is again branched into more and more detailed categories. At the end point of each branch one can compare two numbers—a risk number and a return number. You can see not only at the total level but down at the detailed tactical level whether or not a particular investment decision paid off in a risk-adjusted way. That is the power of historical attribution.

Q: How is the model used as a forecasting tool?

A: It can be used in several ways. There are active managers who attempt to forecast the behavior of the factor characteristics themselves. For instance, people will try to time when growth will outperform value or value will outperform growth. Independently from BARRA these managers generate their own proprietary forecasts that they would like to translate into a portfolio of stocks containing this intentional bias. Using the risk model to break out what is a common influence versus what is idiosyncratic to an individual

name permits the manager to blend return forecasts from multiple sources. That, I think, is a powerful and important trend in investment management. Managers are getting better at blending independent, non-overlapping sources of information together as part of their return forecasts. More bottom-up managers who have already decided on their list of attractive stocks would use the BARRA model primarily as a rebalancing tool, to help ascertain appropriate weights of the individual assets that they already know they like.

There are managers who mistakenly believe they could simply equally weight their stock picks in order to get the most desirable portfolio. But, in fact, the equal weighting decision overlooks rather significant correlations across that manager's favorite picks. So a more enlightened approach would be to adjust the individual assets weightings to take into account that correlation. The end result is a superior portfolio on a risk-adjusted basis even though the constituents of the portfolio, the individual assets, would be the same as under the equally weighted alternative.

Q: The model has been out quite some time and you're very familiar with it. What continues to make your job interesting?

A: The multiple factor modeling approach has been around for about 20 years. However, the BARRA model is actually quite a misrepresentation because BARRA has many models and continues to research and improve existing models. Part of what makes my job interesting is keeping abreast of marketing development. As emerging markets become transparent and liquid enough for institutional investment, we try to apply the same multiple factor apparatus to those markets. When structural changes happen in a developed market, we try to research the development of those changes and reflect those in our models. Even an existing model that has repeatedly demonstrated its value and is used by hundreds of managers controlling hundreds of billions of dollars constantly evolves and improves. I also find it enriching to maintain my dialogue with existing clients discussing with them things like trends in valuation techniques. I enjoy the variety.

Unspecified Factor Tests

In these tests, the researcher begins the study with no preconceived idea as to how many priced factors exist or what any such factors might represent. Instead, a statistical procedure known as factor analysis is used to extract whatever statistically significant factors might be present in a sample of security returns.

Factor analysis is a complex statistical procedure that was developed much before and independent of the development of APT. It takes observations on a large number of variables and tries to identify one or more statistically significant underlying forces that could have created the variables observed. For example, assume you collect the following observations on a sample of people: height, weight, age, hair color, and hair length. If factor analysis is used, a single important factor related to height, weight, and hair length would emerge. Age and hair color would be unrelated to the factor and unexplained by the model. The factor analysis procedure would not be able to identify what the single factor is a proxy for—even though you could logically deduce that it is a gender factor.

When applied to security returns, a time series of returns on a sample of securities is used. Factor analysis then finds various underlying factors that best explain the covariance of returns within the sample. The number of factors found depends on the statistical significance desired by the researcher and the particular version of factor analysis employed. (There are many.)

In essence, the procedure uses a large number of return observations on many securities to determine whether the returns can be explained by a few common forces. If all security returns are what we have called firm-unique returns, then no common factors would be found. If the CAPM is correct, a number of common factors might be found, but only one priced factor.

After a set of common factors is found, a factor sensitivity is found for each stock and each factor. We will define these as:

$$\hat{b}_{iK} = \text{the sensitivity of security } i \text{ to common factor } K$$

Although these $\hat{b}_{iK}$ values are statistical estimates of our earlier b_{iK} terms, their units can differ considerably.

To examine which of the factors are priced by investors, a cross-sectional regression similar to the following is performed:

Factor Regression

$$\overline{R}_i + a_0 + a_1 \hat{b}_{i1} + a_2 \hat{b}_{i2} + \cdots + a_N \hat{b}_{iN} + e_i \qquad (8.18)$$

where $\overline{R}_i$ = the average return on security i, $\hat{b}_{iK}$ = the estimated factor sensitivities, and e_i = an unexplained error term. The regression parameters that are estimated include the constant return term a_0 and the slope coefficients a_1 through a_N.

If a particular factor is priced by investors, the slope term associated with the factor should be statistically significant. For example, if factor 1 is a priced factor, a_1 will be statistically different from 0.0. Alternatively, if a factor is found for which investors do not require compensation in the form of higher (or lower) expected returns, the a_K regression estimate will not be statistically different from zero.

In the earliest version of this test, Roll and Ross used a sample of daily returns on 42 portfolios of 30 stocks each. They suggested that at least three but no more than six common priced factors appeared to exist in their sample. Other studies have found similar results. But these studies are not without critics, as we discuss later.

Specified Factor Tests

One of the principal difficulties with the approach just outlined is that the procedure does not suggest what the priced factors represent. Therefore, a number of researchers have hypothesized a variety of possible factors that might be priced and have developed tests to see whether they are. For example, Fogler, John, and Tipton tested a model in which they claim that three factors (returns on a stock market proxy, changes in interest rates, and changes in bond default rates) are related to individual stock returns. In addition, Oldfield and Rogalski investigated aggregate stock returns and T-bill returns as common factors.

The most complete test of a specified factor model to date was conducted by Chen, Roll, and Ross. They suggested that a large portion of the covariances between securities can be explained by unanticipated changes in four variables:

- The difference between long-term and short-term Treasury yields to maturity

- Inflation rates

- The difference between yields to maturity of BB-rated bonds and Treasuries

- Growth of industrial production

But Is APT Testable?

Serious questions remain, however, whether APT can ever be empirically tested. Studies by Dhrymes, Friend, and Gultekin provided evidence that the number of common factors found in an unspecified factor test increased as (1) the number of securities in the sample increased, and (2) the length of the time period sampled increased. Roll and Ross responded that this would be expected. As additional securities or returns are collected, additional common factors might emerge. For example, as the sample size increases, firms from a number of new industries might be included that share a common factor. Roll and Ross point out that it is the number of priced factors which is important, not the total number of factors.

FIGURE 8-7   ESTIMATED MONTHLY STANDARD DEVIATIONS OF THE S&P 500

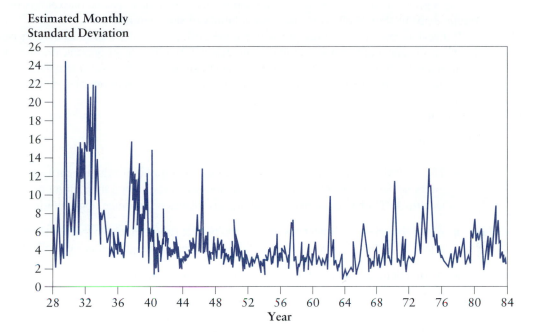

Estimated Monthly Standard Deviation

Perhaps the most telling criticism of APT was made by Shanken. His argument goes as follows. Assume that APT does apply to the underlying economic structure of the economy. There are certain basic economic industries, each of which is sensitive to various factors that are priced by investors. Individual firms then create portfolios of these basic industries. When firms create such asset portfolios, they alter the level of factor risk inherent in their securities. For example, assume two underlying priced factors exist. Firm A might invest in the underlying economic industries in a way that eliminates all of factor 2. Thus, if APT researchers sample firms similar to firm A, they will conclude that factor 2 doesn't exist. The returns that are examined on securities can mask or exacerbate the underlying factor risks in the economy.

This could be a particular problem if firms are constantly changing the nature of their asset portfolios, as in the case of mutual funds. No one would suggest obtaining empirical estimates of common priced factors from mutual fund returns, since the security holdings of the funds are constantly changing. The problem is less severe at the individual stock level, since firms do not shift asset mixes as rapidly as mutual funds do. Nonetheless, the problem remains.

Stationarity of Risk Premiums

Underlying all of the CAPM and APT tests was an unstated assumption: the return-generating process is stationary. By this we mean the covariances between the returns of any two securities don't change and the market risk premium doesn't change.

Research into this stationarity assumption is in its infancy, but a number of studies suggest it is a problem. For example, consider Figure 8-7, in which estimates of monthly standard deviations of the S&P 500 are shown. There is considerable variability in this risk proxy—enough to suggest that investors might change whatever risk premiums they require.

A recent study by French, Schwert, and Stambaugh indicates this may be the case. When changes in estimates of stock price volatility were related to returns on the S&P 500 during a given month, these researchers found evidence that the expected market risk premium is positively related to the predicted volatility of stock returns.

If investors' perceptions of risk and their required risk premiums are continuously changing over time, tests of various asset pricing models will be difficult. At present, we must be open-minded and continue to explore. We do seem to know two things: (1) return variability and required returns are directly related, and (2) diversification reduces return variability.

SUMMARY

Here are the key concepts we discussed in this chapter:

- The CAPM and APT present two ways of viewing how equilibrium security prices might be determined. CAPM is based on investors maximizing their utility of wealth. APT is based on investors taking advantages of arbitrage opportunities.

- APT is based on the **law of one price;** two perfect substitutes must trade at identical prices. If perfect substitutes trade at different prices, arbitrage profits are available.

- A strict definition of arbitrage is the ability to earn risk-free profits at no investment.

- The APT is appealing in that it says nothing about the optimality of some elusive market portfolio. Its weakness is that the sources of risk are not defined by the theory; they must be empirically identified.

- The basic CAPM presented in Chapter 7 implies there is a single source of risk for which investors must be compensated. This risk is the return uncertainty associated with holding the market portfolio of all risky assets. When various assumptions on which the basic CAPM theory is based are lifted, the models that arise often have multiple sources of risk.

- Empirical tests of either theory are difficult to construct, since they are based on investor expectations whereas the data available to researchers are realized security returns. In fact, some economists believe it is conceptually impossible to test either theory empirically using historical data.

- In the case of the CAPM, we don't know whether the market portfolio proxy being tested is not the true market portfolio.

- In the case of the APT, it is difficult to determine, say, whether factor 2 found in one period of time is not the same factor 2 found in another period.

It is also important to realize that tests of these theories are actually joint tests of two hypotheses: (1) that the model being tested fairly describes how equilibrium prices are determined, and (2) that security prices are at a state of equilibrium according to the model.

Neither pricing theory has yet stood up to rigorous empirical testing. But that does not mean the models are deceiving ways of thinking about how security prices might be determined. There is much to be learned from the models about portfolio risk management.

R E V I E W   P R O B L E M

David and Sue are portfolio managers for a defined benefit pension fund that has $20 billion invested in U. S. stocks. A large portion of these funds are passively invested to match the returns of the Wilshire 5000 index. Recently, top administrators of the pension plan have asked David and Sue to develop an active investment strategy that will initially be used on a small portion of the $20 billion. If the active strategy they develop is successful, it will be used on a larger percentage of the $20 billion.

David and Sue have decide to use the concept of arbitrage pricing theory (APT) in developing their active investment strategy.

a. What does APT state?
b. David and Sue recognize that to use the concepts of APT, they must identify a number of "common factors" which influence the returns on all stocks in the United States. What common factors would you consider if you were in their place?
c. They decide their initial APT model will include the following three common factors:

$$N = \text{percentage change in consumer nondurable good purchases}$$

$$D = \text{percentage change in consumer durable good purchases}$$

$$I = \text{percentage change in consumer price inflation}$$

Following the standard way of symbolically expressing the APT, they write the following equation:

$$\tilde{R}_{it} = a_{0t} + b_{iN}(\tilde{N}_t) + b_{iD}(\tilde{D}_t) + b_{iI}(\tilde{I}_t) + e_{it}$$

Define what the following terms mean: $a_{0t}, b_{iN}, \tilde{N}_t$.
d. After considerable statistical analysis, they develop the following factor estimates for stock 1:

$$b_{1N} = 1.0 \ b_{1D} = 1.5 \ b_{1I} = -0.5$$

They believe a_{01} should be the one-year risk-free rate of 4%. In addition, they believe the security markets expect N, D, and I to be the following during the next year:

Factor	Expected Value
N	2.0%
D	3.0%
I	1.5%

If these assessments are correct, what expected return does the market expect on stock 1 during the next year?

e. David and Sue agree with the expected value of N and I. But they believe the percentage growth of durable consumer purchases (common factor D) during the next year will be 5.0%. How should they use this opinion in developing their active management strategy?

f. What is the role of the e_{it} term in the equation?

g. What difficulties do you see in using APT to develop an active management strategy?

Solution

a. Arbitrage pricing theory states that realized security returns are created by certain events. Some of these events affect many, or all, stocks and are called common factors. The returns on individual stocks have differing sensitivities to these factors. The expected return on a given stock is determined by the stock's sensitivity to each common factor and the expected outcome of each factor.

b. Any economic event that would affect the return on more than a single stock.

c. a_{0t} is the constant rate of return on all stocks in period t (the return expected for a security whose b_{ik} values are all zero)

b_{iN} is the sensitivity of stock i to percentage changes in nondurable consumer purchases (the average value across all stocks is 1.0)

N_t is the uncertain percentage change in nondurable goods purchases in period t

d. $E(R_1) = 4.0\% + 1.0(2.0\%) + 01.5(3.0\%) - 0.5(1.5\%)$
$= 9.75\%$

e. Given that they expect common factor D to have a larger payoff than expected by other investors, their portfolio should have a sensitivity to factor D larger than normal. Usually this means the portfolio will have a factor sensitivity in excess of 1.0.

f. The term e_{it} is the stock unique return during period t. To minimize the impacts of stock unique returns on portfolio returns, the portfolio should be broadly diversified.

g. Probably the most difficult aspect of using APT as a tool for active management is the identification of common factors. If this can be done, there is then the difficulties of creating a model that will successfully predict the common factor outcomes. (For example, how should David and Sue develop their opinion that factor D would be greater than expected by others?)

QUESTIONS AND PROBLEMS

1. In the CAPM, the market portfolio is a mean-standard deviation efficient portfolio. True, false, or uncertain, and why?

2. In the chapter, we examined expected excess returns, variance of excess returns, and standard deviation of excess returns for stocks A and B (refer to pages 306–307). This was done in the context of both a one-factor and a two-factor model. Consider an equal investment in stock A and stock B.

   a. According to the two-factor model, what would be this portfolio's expected return, variance of return, and standard deviation?

   b. Why are the results in part a different from those found in the chapter when this portfolio was viewed solely from the context of a one-factor model?

3. Briefly, what are the conceptual advantages (disadvantages) of the CAPM and the APT?

4. The SML states that $E(R_i) = RF + B_i[RP_M]$

   Empirical tests of this relationship examine a regression of historical average returns on a beta estimate:

$$\overline{R}_i = -a_0 + a_1 b_i$$

  a. What is the logic in using the empirical equation as a test of the theory?
  b. How are b_i values obtained? Do you see any potential problems in determining appropriate b_i values?
  c. If the theory is supported, what should a_0 and a_1 turn out to be?

5. A number of researchers have tested non-CAPM versions of historical returns on single stocks, such as:

$$\overline{R}_i = a_0 + a_1(\sigma_i^2) + a_2(b_i)$$

If a_1 turns out to be positive and statistically significant, is this contrary to CAPM? How might the test, when applied to single stocks, be biased? How does a test using portfolios of securities overcome some of these biases?

6. What were the major conclusions of the Black, Jensen, and Scholes study of CAPM?

7. What are the major implications of Roll's critique of the CAPM?

8. Stocks 1 and 2 are affected by three factors, as shown here. Factors 2 and 3 are unique to each stock. Expected values of each are $E(F_1) = 3.0\%$, $E(F_2) = 0.0\%$, and $E(F_3) = 0.0\%$. Neither stock pays a dividend, and they are now selling at prices $P_1 = \$40$ and $P_2 = \$10$. You expect their prices in a year to be $E(P_1) = \$45$ and $E(P_2) = \$10.70$.

$$\tilde{R}_1 = 6.0(\tilde{F}_1) + 0.3(\tilde{F}_2) + 0.0(\tilde{F}_3)$$
$$\tilde{R}_2 = 1.5(\tilde{F}_1) + 0.0(\tilde{F}_2) + 0.4(\tilde{F}_3)$$

  a. What do factors 2 and 3 reflect? In the context of a broadly diversified portfolio, should the 0.3 and 0.4 be positive, as they are shown?
  b. Neglecting F_2 and F_3, create a riskless arbitrage.
  c. Relate the return equations to the CAPM.

9. In what ways is APT different from the CAPM?

10. Stocks X and Y are affected by three factors, as indicated here:

$$\tilde{R}_X = 3(\tilde{\phi}_1) - 1.0(\tilde{\phi}_2) + 0.0(\tilde{\phi}_3)$$
$$\tilde{R}_Y = 1.5(\tilde{\phi}_1) + 0.0(\tilde{\phi}_2) + 0.3(\tilde{\phi}_3)$$

The factors ϕ_2 and ϕ_3 are security-unique factors, and ϕ_1 is a common factor. Stock X is now selling for \$50 and stock Y is selling for \$25. Neither pays a dividend. You (and other arbitrageurs) expect that stock X will be selling for \$58 in one year and stock Y will be selling for \$26. Expected ϕ_1 is 4.0.
  a. Create a riskless arbitrage between the two.
  b. Logically, why are ϕ_2 and ϕ_3 unimportant?
  c. What price levels of X and Y would no longer provide an arbitrage profit?
  d. If actual ϕ_1 is 6.0, ϕ_2 is 2.0, and ϕ_3 is 4.0, what is the realized return on each?

11. You are given the factor sensitivities on four well-diversified stock portfolios. Both factors 1 and 2 are priced factors.

Portfolio	b_{i1}	b_{i2}	$E(R_i)$
A	0.4	0.6	7.8%
B	0.6	0.4	8.2%
C	1.0	0.0	9.0%

D	0.0	1.0	8.0%

a. What is meant by a "priced" factor?
b. Find the percentage to invest in A and B such that the combination has zero factor 1 risk. Repeat for zero factor 2 risk.
c. Is portfolio C correctly valued?
d. What is the relationship between factor 1 and expected returns in the following:

$$E(R_i) = a_0 + b_{i1}\overline{F}_{1t}$$

e. Is portfolio D correctly valued?
f. What is your best estimate of the following relationship:

$$E(R_i) = a_0 + b_{i1}\overline{F}_{1t} + b_{i2}\overline{F}_{2t}$$

g. Create an arbitrage using A, B, and D in which $100,000 of D is traded. Show the end-of-period value of this arbitrage for the following actual outcomes of factor 2:

Low:	$F_2 = 0$
Expected:	$F_2 = 3$
High:	$F_2 = 6$

h. Why is a risk-free rate available in this model?
i. Why must a fully arbitraged APT model be linear?

12. What are the difficulties associated with testing APT?
13. What is the difference between a specified factor model and an unspecified factor model?
14. Research on the CAPM and beta has concluded that:

   a. short-term results may contradict the CAPM.
   b. estimated betas change over time.
   c. estimated beta depends on the choice of the market index.
   d. all of the above.

15. Compared to CAPM, in the APT:

   a. beta is eliminated as a pricing factor.
   b. inflation is eliminated as a pricing factor.
   c. the risk-free rate loses its significance.
   d. multiple factors are present in the return generation process.

16. The feature of APT that offers the greatest potential advantage over the CAPM is the:

   a. use of several factors instead of a single market index to explain the risk/return relationship.
   b. identification of anticipated changes in production, inflation, and term structure as key factors explaining the risk/return relationship.
   c. superior measurement of the risk-free rate of return over historical time periods.
   d. variability of coefficients of sensitivity to the APT factors for a given asset over time.

17. As the manager of a large broadly diversified portfolio of stocks and bonds, you realize changes in certain macroeconomic variables may directly affect the performance of your portfolio. You are considering using an APT approach to strategic portfolio planning, and want to analyze the possible impacts of the following four factors:

   ✖ industrial production;
   ✖ inflation;

■ risk premia or quality spreads; and

■ yield curve shifts.

a. Indicate how each of these four factors influences the cash flows and/or the discount rates in the traditional discounted cash flow valuation model. Explain how unanticipated changes in each of these four factors could affect portfolio returns.

b. You now use a constant-proportion portfolio allocation strategy of 60% stocks and 40% bonds, which you rebalance monthly.

c. Compare and contrast an active portfolio approach that incorporates macroeconomic factors, such as the four factors listed here, to the constant-proportion strategy currently in use.

18. You are an investment officer at Pegasus Securities and are preparing for the next meeting of the investment committee. Several committee members are interested in reviewing two asset pricing models—the CAPM and the APT—and their use in portfolio management and stock selection.

a. Describe both the CAPM and APT, and identify the factor(s) that determines returns in each.

b. "The APT model is more general than the CAPM." Explain how this observation has meaning in the stock selection process.

19. In contrast to the capital asset pricing model, arbitrage pricing theory:

a. Requires that markets be in equilibrium.

b. Uses risk premiums based on micro variables.

c. Specifies the number and identifies specific factors that determine expected returns.

d. Does not require the restrictive assumption of the market portfolio.

D A T A F I L E   A N A L Y S E S

In these analyses, you will examine changes in the volatility of historical monthly returns on two asset classes. The issue is whether investment risk changes over time.

1. **Bond Volatility.** Access the monthly return series in the INDEXES datafile. Identify the return series for 20-year U.S. corporate bonds. Find the standard deviation of monthly returns during the 36-month period 2601 to 2812 (January 1926 to December 1928). Copy this cell formula to all future months for which returns on this bond series are available. This will give you a series of standard deviations based on returns during the previous 36 months.

2. **Stock Volatility.** Repeat this exercise for monthly returns on the S&P 500.

3. **Does Risk Change.** Plot the two standard deviation series as a line graph. The Y-axis should consist of the two standard deviation series (i.e., have two lines plotted). The X-axis should be each month-end. Interpret the results. What implications does this have on tests of asset pricing models?

R E F E R E N C E S

Classic empirical tests of the CAPM include the following:

Black, Fischer and Michael C. Jensen and Myron Scholes. "The Capital Asset Pricing Model: Some Empirical Tests." In Michael C. Jensen (ed.), *Studies in the Theory of Capital Markets,* New York: Praeger, 1972.

Dhrymes, Phoebus, Irwin Friend and Bulent Gultekin, "A Critical Reexamination of the Empirical Evidence on the Arbitrage Pricing Theory," *The Journal of Finance,* June 1984.

Fama, Eugene F. and James MacBeth, "Tests of Multiperiod Two-Parameter Model," *Journal of Political Economy,* May 1974.

Fogler, H. Russell, Kose John, and James Tipton, Three Factors, Interest Rate Differntials and Stock Groups," *The Journal of Finance,* May 1981.

Levy, Haim. "The Capital Asset Pricing Model: Theory and Empiricism," *Economic Journal,* March 1983.

Oldfield, George and Richard Rogalski, "Treasury Bill Factors and Common Stock Returns," *The Journal of Finance,* May, 1981.

Roll, Richard. "A Critique of the Asset Pricing Theory's Tests: Part I on the Past and Potential Testability of the Theory," *Journal of Financial Economics,* March 1977.

Recent empirical tests of the CAPM include:

Fama, Eugene F. and Kenneth R. French, "The Cross-Section of Expected Stock Returns," *Journal of Finance,* June 1992.

Kothari, S. P. and Jay Shanken and Richard Sloan, "Another Look at the Cross-Section of Expected Stock Returns," *Journal of Finance,* March 1995.

Chan, Louis K. C. and Josef Lakonishok, "Are the Reports of Beta's Death Premature?" *The Journal of Portfolio Management,* Summer 1993.

Extensions to the standard CAPM include:

Breeden, Douglas T. "An Intertemporal Asset Pricing Model with Stochastic Consumption and Investment Opportunities," *Journal of Financial Economics,* June 1979.

Mayers, David. "Nonmarketable Assets and the Determination of Capital Asset Prices in the Absence of a Riskless Asset," *Journal of Business,* April 1973.

Merton, Robert. "A Simple Model of Capital Market Equilibrium with Incomplete Information," *Journal of Finance,* July 1987.

One of the original articles to develop the APT is Stephen A. Ross, *"The Arbitrage Theory of Capital Assest Pricing,"* Journal pf Economic Theory, December 1976.

APT tests and reviews include:

Chen, Nai-Fu, Richard Roll and Stephen Ross, *"Economic Forces and the Stock Market,"* Journal of Business, July 1986

Roll, Richard and Stephen Ross, *"An Empirical Investgation of the Arbitrage Pricing Theory,"* Journal of Finance, December 1980.

Shanken, Jay. *"The Arbitrage Pricing Theory: Is It Testible?"* Journal of Finance, December 1982.

An illustration of how portfolio managers use multifactor models is discussed in H. Russel Fogler, *"Common Stock Management in the 1990's,"* Journal if Portfolio Management, Winter 1990.

Recent tests of asset pricing models include the following:

Fama, Eugene F. and Kenneth R. French, *"The Cross-section if Expected Stock Returns,"* Journal of Finamce, June 1992.

French, Kenneth, William Schwert, and Robert Stambaugh, *"Expected Stock Returns and Volitility,"* Journal of Financial Economics, *19,* 1987.

9

EFFICIENT MARKET THEORY

After reading this chapter you should have an understanding of the three major types of market efficiency tests: return prediction, price adjustment to new information and tests for privately held information.

Few ideas are more controversial or hold more profound trading implications than the concept of an efficient securities market. No longer is it taken for granted that active security trading can result in higher long-run rates of return than those available from a passive investment strategy.

In its strictest interpretation, efficient market theory (EMT) states that security prices will always fully reflect all known information. If a firm announces unexpected positive information about earnings, the investing public rushes to buy the security at previous prices—only to find they must trade at a higher new price that fully reflects the announcement. When investors buy at the new price, they can expect only a fair return given the security's risk.

Expressed somewhat differently, EMT states the security market is a fair game: The odds of having a future return greater than should be expected, given a security's present risk, are the same odds of having a lower return than should be expected—50%. There is no way to use the information available at a given point in time to earn abnormal returns. Positive returns will be expected, of course, because securities contain risk for which a premium is expected to be earned. However, long-run abnormal returns will be zero.

Although the EMT has caused a major revolution in investment management, it is highly controversial. While active security selection can be intellectually challenging and emotionally exciting, the "game" is played in deadly earnest. People's careers and savings are at stake. To many technicians and fundamentalists, persons who espouse the efficient market theory are ignorant of the facts of life. They believe such investment strategies are likely to prevent people from earning all they might from their investments (as well as cause many technicians and fundamentalists to lose their jobs). To many proponents of an efficient market, technicians and fundamentalists are either charlatans or naive optimists whose policies would needlessly drain investors' savings. Because of this controversy and its profound implications, we review a broad range of empirical studies.

Empirical studies of efficient markets can be thought of as belonging to one of two eras. During the 1960s and 1970s, virtually all tests of EMT were supportive. To the extent that potential inefficiencies were present in the tests, they were not pursued. The concept of an efficient market was a logical and clearly important new theory. And most empirical evidence suggested it was, indeed, a powerful theory. Beginning in the 1980s, a number of studies began to appear that indicated either security markets were not as efficient as scholars previously believed or our understanding of asset pricing models and market efficiency had to be considerably broadened. We present empirical tests from both eras here to give you a complete taste of the development of EMT.

Three Approaches to Security Selection

Three distinct schools of thought claim to offer the ideal way to select securities: technical selection, fundamental selection, and selection based on the efficient market hypothesis. Both technical and fundamental approaches advocate active trading in the hopes of earning excess risk-adjusted returns. Efficient market strategies call for a passive management approach in order to minimize transaction costs. Because tests of EMT are closely tied to the approaches used by technicians and fundamentalists, it is helpful to review each.

Technical Analysis

Technicians believe an examination of historical price and volume movements can identify price patterns from which future prices can be forecast. Because of their reliance on price charting, technicians are also referred to as **chartists.** A pure technician pays no attention to a company's earnings prospects, financial condition, product risk, patent protection, and so forth, believing historical price movements tell the whole story.

Dow Theory.   The classic technical tool is Dow theory. Originally developed by Charles H. Dow, editor of the *Wall Street Journal* from 1889 to 1902, as a means of describing historical market movements, it was expanded upon by William Hamilton, who suggested it could be used to predict market moves. Dow theorists believe price movements consist of three types, all of which are occurring at any moment in time. Primary moves consist of major trends that usually last between one and four years. Primary moves up are referred to as **bull markets** (aggressive and charging). Primary moves down are referred to as **bear markets** (defensive and retreating). Within each primary move are a number of intermediate or secondary moves that interrupt the primary move and retrace a substantial portion of the change in prices since the last intermediate move. Intermediate moves are said to be technical corrections that drain the energy of speculative excesses which might have developed. These corrections usually last less than two months. Finally, minor price changes or ripples will occur more or less randomly around the basic primary and secondary moves. Dow theorists often describe these price movements in terms of the movement of the ocean. Primary moves are akin to tidal flows, intermediate moves are similar to waves, and minor moves represent ripples.

Figure 9-1 provides hypothetical price and volume data on the Dow Jones Industrial Average (DJIA) and Dow Jones Transportation Average (DJTA). From date 0 to date 2 the market has been at a trough and not moving in any particular direction. Starting around date 2, "smart money" begins to realize that economic conditions are likely to improve and result in higher stock values. A period of "stock accumulation" begins in which shares are acquired by "strong hands" from "weak hands" (by leaders from followers). Slowly, trading volume picks up and prices rise until date 3. On date 3, a technical correction begins as individuals who had bought shares at depressed prices sell in order to take their profits. However, prices don't fall far because the smart money continues to buy. Soon prices resume their upward direction in the bull market. Trading volume and prices continue to increase as additional demand for shares is created by the "followers" who had previously been pessimistic but are now changing their opinion in the face of substantially higher prices. A second intermediate move occurs at date 5, but again prices recover and rise above the date 5 peak. The bull market continues. Eventually, trading volume reaches an all-time high as extreme optimism and speculation prevail. It is at this time of speculative excess that smart money begins to sell and cause a price decline at date 7. Although prices rebound, the new peak at date 8 is lower than the prior peak. Although this suggests a bear market has developed, it must be "confirmed" by the transportation index. By date 9 the transportation index also has an abortive recovery and confirms that a bear market indeed is in process. (Unfortunately, by then prices of the industrials have continued to fall.) The scenario of a bear market is the opposite of a bull market.

Head and Shoulders. Consider another example of charting. Figure 9-2 illustrates a hypothetical bar chart. Technicians will search such a chart for a "pattern" that can be used to predict future price moves. As drawn in Figure 9-2, the bar chart illustrates what technicians label a "head and shoulders" pattern. The left shoulder is supposed to build on a strong rally (good volume and price rises). Profit taking on high volume causes prices to fall temporarily and completes the left shoulder. A similar pattern of price increase (rising above the left shoulder) followed by profit taking follows, but this time on more moderate volume. Finally, the right shoulder is formed on light volume, indicating a growing technical weakness (inability of buying support to sustain the general upward trend of the left shoulder and head). At this point it is important to identify the "neckline," which is a straight line connecting low points in the last two technical corrections. If the price on the right should "break through" the neckline on high volume, the technician considers this to be a sell signal. Inverted head-and-shoulder movements are upside-down patterns with a declining neckline.

Support and Resistance Levels. A support level is a price level at which prices are unlikely to fall through; or if they do, the fall will come only on high volume and considerable bad news about the firm. Resistance levels are price levels that are unlikely to be exceeded; but if they are, the rise will come on high volume and considerable good news about the firm. Breakthroughs of support and resistance levels on low volume will soon be

FIGURE 9-1 DOW THEORY ILLUSTRATION

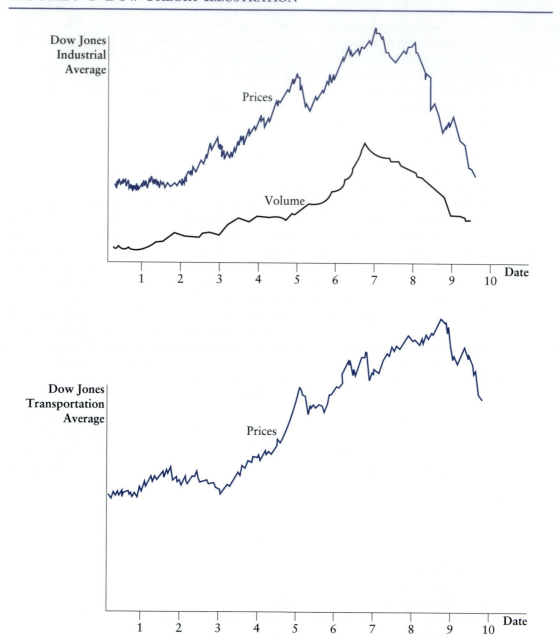

FIGURE 9-2 HYPOTHETICAL HEAD AND SHOULDER MOVE

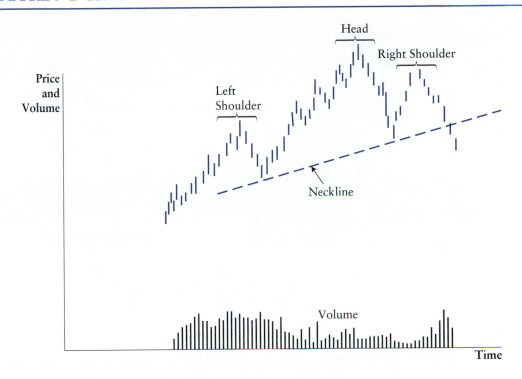

reversed. The explanation given for support and resistance levels relates to a perceived market psychology. Most people will know the price band in which the stock has been traded and observe it hasn't recently broken through the support or resistance levels. Therefore, they stand ready to buy when prices hit the support level (prices are more likely to rise than fall) and sell at the resistance level (prices are more likely to fall than rise).

Figure 9-3 illustrates a hypothetical price band and a break through the resistance level on high volume. The breakthrough would be considered a bullish sign, and some technicians believe what had been the former resistance level will now be the new support level. The opposite is believed about a breakthrough of the support level.

Other Technical Tools. There could easily be as many ways of employing technical selection techniques as there are technicians. A widely publicized statistic is the **advance-decline line.** Each day the number of stocks that decline are subtracted from the number of advances and the net accumulated over time. It is intended to be an indicator of the "breadth" of price rises or declines. It is often considered a leading indicator of price movements in DJIA or S&P 500 stocks. **Moving average** price lines represent the average price for, say, the past 200 days. There is no one single trading rule based on moving averages, but they are all based on the level of current prices relative to it. Trading rules are also based on statistics such as the amount of odd-lot trading, the quantity of short sales, and the average mutual fund cash position.

FIGURE 9-3 HYPOTHETICAL SUPPORT AND RESISTANCE LEVELS

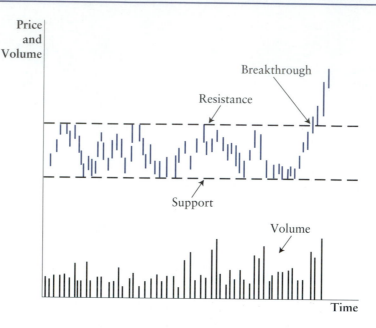

Does It Work? Whether a technical analyst is able to identify securities that will provide future returns in excess of what they should, given their risk, is an empirical issue. But logically, should such procedures work in a competitive security market in which a large number of people are seeking a road to wealth? If a pattern that continually repeats itself can be identified by one investor, it is likely the same pattern will be identified by many investors. Soon, their trading activities will alter prices so the pattern no longer exists.

For example, consider the widely cited "summer rally" in which stock prices are supposed to rise during the early summer months (as the weather improves and vacation season arrives). If you observe that prices rise every June more than in May, what would you do? Buy in May and sell after June! Naturally you won't be alone, and soon the June rally will move to May, then April, until there is no single month in which returns are greater, on average, than any other month. For technical selection to work, it takes either an inattentive market or an individual with an uncanny ability to uncover trends.

If security markets are efficiently priced, then technical selection rules will not work. Technicians will, on average, earn positive returns but only because they invest in risky securities. But any patterns that might have existed in past prices will currently be reflected in current prices. Past prices are a part of current information.

Fundamental Selection

Proponents of the second approach are known as **fundamentalists.** It has been said that a technician is to a fundamentalist as an astrologer is to an astronomer. Fundamental analysts examine basic economic forces affecting a company in an attempt to forecast future earnings, dividends, and security risks. Given projections of potential returns and risks, fundamental analysts estimate what they believe to be the fair market value of a security. This so-called **intrinsic value** is then compared with the security's current market price and a buy, sell, or hold recommendation is made. Simply put, fundamentalists believe that thorough financial analysis of a security can identify mispriced securities.

The job of a good fundamentalist is complex, requiring unique analytic skills and training. The **Association for Investment Management and Research,** a professional association of financial analysts and portfolio managers, has developed a certification program similar to the certified public accountant designation. A sequence of three day-long tests is taken over a minimum three-year period. Upon successful completion, the participant is granted the designation of **Chartered Financial Analyst (CFA).** Only individuals involved in investment management may take the exams. The purpose of the CFA designation is to ensure high standards of professional training and ethical conduct. While the CFA designation is not a formal requirement for individuals wishing to engage in investment management, it is widely respected and informally required for advancement in many firms.

The goal of a fundamental analyst is to find information about a security that is not yet reflected in its market price. In a highly competitive market, developing such information from sources other than illegal insider sources is difficult and costly. Analysts must be trained to understand a company's financial statements, have a knowledge of the risks and potentials of a firm's product offering, and spend the time necessary to examine many securities. The time and out-of-pocket cost of only sitting for the CFA exam, for example, is not trivial.

Efficient Market Selection

The efficient market theory states that fundamental analysts are so good at their jobs that all mispriced securities have been identified. Therefore, mispriced securities won't exist. The market price of a security will equal its fair intrinsic value. If this were not the case, well-informed and sophisticated fundamentalists would immediately recognize the potential profits and, through buying and selling, instantly drive the market price into equilibrium.

If the notion of an efficient market is correct, security selection turns out to be quite simple. First, define the level of risk acceptable for a given portfolio. Then create a combination of broadly diversified holdings of stocks and bonds which provides that risk level. Finally, never trade simply because you believe prices are too high or too low; they aren't—they are always fair. Trade only if you have excess cash, need cash, or want tax advantages.

The Concept of an Efficient Market

Why?

Security prices are determined by expectations of future economic profits, risks, and interest rates. In developing such expectations, individuals assess any information available at that time. For example, when deciding whether IBM common stock is fairly priced, you would review international economic conditions, competition, the state of computer technology,

Dan DiBartolomeo

President
Northfield Information Services, Inc.
Cornell University, B.S. Applied Physics

Northfield is a consulting firm that develops mathematical models of financial markets. Models are implemented by investment professionals in the form of customized software and databases. While DiBartolomeo has very little formal training in these areas and is basically self-taught, he does a lot of teaching and publishing on the subject matter.

Q: Many investors are looking for more rigorous and quantitative investment approaches. What are some general problems in utilizing these techniques?

A: Investment decision models that have produced excellent results in back tests and simulations may achieve very poor results when implemented. Four general areas of possible causation are (1) the conflict between theoretical and professional environments, (2) failure to clearly identify the objective function, (3) the inherent limitations of back testing and simulated trading, and (4) failure to consider estimation error in applying the results of models. Many of the limitations are conceptual and apply irrespective of the level of statistical and experimental rigor.

Q: What are the practical complications of implementing a theoretical model?

A: The building of quantitative models often involves usage of advanced mathematics, statistics, and computer methods of which only a minority of the investment community have a functional working knowledge. Another major roadblock is business risk to people in the investment management business. For example, in a typical U.S. pension fund, asset allocation policy is set by the fund sponsor while active management of portfolios is contracted to outside investment management firms. The level of risk taken by active managers is often below that which would be consistent with the aggressiveness inherent in the sponsor's asset allocation policy. To make matters worse, large funds often have multiple active managers for each asset class, adding diversification across managers. As such, the need for diversification within each manager's portfolio is reduced. The typical result is an active management posture within an asset class, which is an order of magnitude more timid than is consistent with the asset class benchmark.

Q: Aside from the assumption that investors would prefer more return and less risk, what other specifics should be considered when developing a relevant objective function?

A: Let us suppose we are developing a valuation model for equity portfolio management. Is it our goal to find a model that produces the highest return in the long run (maximize the geometric mean return), the highest return to variability ratio (mean-variance efficient), or is our goal to find the model which maximizes return while keeping the probability of underperforming some stated goal below an acceptable level (the Telser criteria)? Depending on what your portfolio management process is actually trying to accomplish, the effectiveness of any model will be judged differently. An insidious problem is that many quantitative models are judged using measurement criteria which depend on the assumed utility function of the investor, without recognition of the form of that utility function. For example, two common measurements of investment performance, the Treynor ratio and Jensen's alpha, are applications of the classic capital asset pricing model. One of the assumptions that underlies the standard CAPM is that all investors make their investment decisions on the basis of a mean-variance utility function. However, only a small minority of the professional investment community can describe the nature of a mean-variance utility function.

Q: What makes the skepticism about the accuracy and reliability of simulations and back testing data warranted?

A: We assume a neat world of normal distributions and linear effects. As such we find only those empirical results that can be found under those constraints. The most profound problem is that no matter how rigorously they are performed, there is the final, overriding assumption that the world of tomorrow will behave like the world of today or yesterday.

Among the myriad of flaws of statistical procedure that can beset a back-test or simulation are look-ahead bias, survival bias, data cleansing, reliance on databases which are subject to revision, a phenomena called "data mining," which often arises in poorly designed experiments, and models based on a set of data that are tested only on the data from which they were derived. This "in-sample" testing is a self-fulfilling prophecy and always works well. Given the reasons cited here for potentially misleading results, the practitioner is advised to proceed carefully with claims for discovery of powerful indicators of future investment performance.

Q: Why is the error component so important?

A: In building quantitative models, one of the most obvious and yet overlooked aspect of the process is to take estimation error into account. If our quantitative model is to weigh a variety of predicted factors correctly, each with a different level of certainty to the prediction, we must try to adjust our estimates of future events to incorporate the level of our prediction accuracy. Once we admit that estimation error exists, the formation of efficient frontiers and similar constructs of portfolio theory becomes considerably more complex. Results can be improved through the usage of nonparametric statistics and other techniques not requiring assumptions of linearity, symmetry, or normality.

patents, market saturation, management expertise, antitrust legislation, inflation, and so forth. While the list of relevant information is almost endless, the point is that such information is crucial to making a pricing decision. It is in this sense that we can say that security prices might fully reflect all relevant information. **A securities market in which market prices fully reflect all known information is called efficient.**

Paradoxically, security markets can be efficient only if a large number of people disagree with the EMT and attempt to find ways of earning speculative profits. To make a speculative profit, an individual must hold unique information about a security that other market participants are unaware of. As soon as new information is obtained, speculators who have the information will immediately trade. If the speculators discover favorable information, they will attempt to purchase the security before others become aware of it and bid the price up. If speculators discover unfavorable information, they will immediately sell. As a result, profit-maximizing speculators will attempt to obtain information before other market participants. This results in a race for new information and, at the extreme, all information will be reflected in security prices as soon as it becomes available.

The term *price efficient* is used to indicate that security markets are efficient in processing information.[1] Prices will not adjust to new information with a lag but, instead, instantaneously. Four conditions will create an efficiently priced market:

1. Information is costless and available to all market participants at the same point in time. Thus, investors have **homogeneous expectations.**
2. There are no transaction costs, taxes, or other barriers to trading. The markets are **frictionless.**
3. Prices are not affected by the trading of a single person or institution. People are **price takers.**
4. All individuals are rational **maximizers of expected utility.**

Clearly, all four conditions are not strictly true. Information is provided to some individuals (corporate directors) before others, and some individuals (security analysts) might be more adept at creating new information by interrelating a complex set of previously available information. But if this is true, amateur investors (who tend to receive information last and are least able to analyze it) would hire well-informed professionals to provide them with the information and to manage their portfolios. In this way amateur investors would be capable of indirectly trading on information as soon as it becomes known. The second condition is clearly untrue, since transaction costs, taxes, and legal investment restrictions do exist. Yet transaction costs are relatively minor and wouldn't lead to the major price distortions that many fundamentalists and technicians believe exist. The effects of taxes and legal restrictions on trading activities (such as margin requirements) are less clear.

Because these criteria aren't strictly true in the "real" world, a distinction is made between a perfectly efficient and an economically efficient market. **A perfectly efficient market** is one in which prices always reflect all known information, prices adjust instantaneously to new information, and speculative profits are simply a matter of luck. In an **economically efficient**

---

[1] A price-efficient market is different from an institutionally efficient market. The latter refers to the ease, speed, and cost of trading.

market, prices might not adjust instantaneously to information, but, over the long run, speculative profits can't be earned after transaction costs such as brokerage commissions and taxes are paid.

This point has been elegantly examined in a paper by Grossman and Stiglitz titled "On the Impossibility of Informationally Efficient Markets." In a world in which information is costly to obtain, security prices must offer a profit incentive to compensate individuals for their costs incurred in searching for new information. If prices are always "correct," no one will have a profit incentive to search for new information. This would, of course, quickly lead to a situation in which new information is not discovered and reflected in prices. In the Grossman and Stiglitz analysis, actual security prices reflect the information of informed traders plus a random "noise term." This noise term is, on average, zero—so security prices do, on average, fully reflect the information held by informed traders. However, there is variability in the noise term, meaning that individual securities might be over- or undervalued. The size of such price distortions depends on a number of factors, including the number of informed traders. Their number will increase until the marginal profits available from being an informed trader are equal to the training and search costs required to become informed. Thus, security price inefficiencies will be large enough to support a profession of informed traders, but informed trader profits should be only large enough to offset their costs of being informed. Again, the security market might not be perfectly efficient but, instead, economically efficient.

So What?

From a philosophic standpoint, an efficient capital market is a crucial component of any capitalistic society. With an efficient capital market, security prices provide accurate signals for capital allocation. Security prices of high-risk industries will be set so that high rates of returns will be both demanded and expected. Security prices of low-profit industries will be low and discourage further investment. Conversely, industries that fulfill an important public need will have potentially high profits, resulting in high security prices and an influx of needed capital. Thus, an efficiently priced security market properly assesses the future of particular industries and allocates capital as needed. When firms sell securities, they expect to receive fair prices. When investors purchase securities, they expect to pay fair prices.

Second, in an efficient security market, speculative profits are, **on average,** nonexistent.[2] Because security prices reflect all known information, mispriced securities are impossible to find. Speculators who believe they have identified such a mispriced security are actually missing a crucial bit of information. Over time speculative trading does nothing but reduce the speculator's wealth as transaction costs and taxes are incurred that are not offset by speculative profits. Occasionally, some speculators will luck out and earn substantial profits. But this is not due to any permanent insight or ability on their part. Instead, such profits are due solely to chance and would be available to passive investors as well. For every lucky speculator there is an equally unlucky speculator. Speculation is a zero sum game.

---

[2] The term *speculation* is often applied to what we have defined as active management strategies. And the term *investment* is applied to a passive investment strategy.

FIGURE 9-4 DEMAND AND SUPPLY OF SHARES GIVEN HOMOGENEOUS EXPECTATIONS

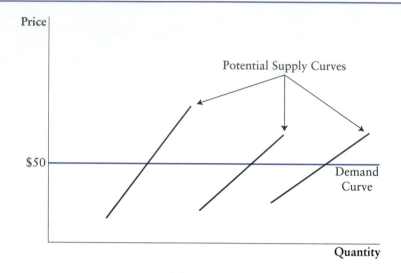

An additional implication of an efficient market is that the demand curve for a security should be perfectly elastic (see Figure 9-4.)[3] Since all investors hold the same information in an efficient market, they will all agree on the same fair market price. Investors are said to have homogeneous expectations. In Figure 9-4 the fair market price of the security (given available information) is $50. At prices above $50 an infinite number of shares would be offered, and at prices below $50 no shares would be offered. Thus, $50 would be the only market price in existence until new information entered the market. Since investors have common beliefs, shifts in the supply curve would have no impact on prices. For example, if a corporation decided to issue additional common shares, stock prices should not be affected. Any additional shares would be absorbed at existing prices. In addition, large block purchases and sales of stock by financial institutions should have no effect on share prices.

Empirical Implications

Empirical tests of EMT can be assigned to three categories:

1. **Return predictability.** Can past data be used to predict future returns? Original studies that examined this question addressed the value of technical analysis and were referred to as **weak-form** tests of efficient markets. However, recent tests have gone beyond technical rules to include predictive powers of fundamental economic variables such as dividend yield, interest rates, and

---

[3] *Elasticity* is an economic term relating the sensitivity of changes in one variable to changes in another. Typically, it relates the percentage change in quantity (demanded or supplied) to the percentage change in price.

earnings yield levels. These tests also examine whether speculative bubbles arise in security prices.

2. **Event studies.** How rapidly do security prices adjust to unexpected new events? Original studies of this issue were referred to as **semistrong-form** tests of EMT. The issues examined by these tests have not changed. But the power of the methodology has become so important to the study of finance that the studies are now commonly referred to by the name of methodology used. These studies examine the market price reaction to events such as earnings and dividend announcements, stock splits, management forecasts, and so forth.

3. **Private information.** Are there individuals with private information that they use to earn excess risk-adjusted returns? For example, do security analysts, portfolio managers, or corporate insiders have privileged information on which excess returns are earned? Original tests in this area were called **strong-form** tests of EMT.

Each category tests a level to which prices might fully reflect information. Return prediction tests examine **past information.** Event studies examine **new information.** And private information tests examine the value of **nonpublic information.**

While the concept of price efficiency applies to fixed-income securities and derivatives, the bulk of past research has focused on common stocks in the United States. In order to provide a fundamental understanding of the issues, our discussion is limited to studies of the U.S. stock market.

EMT and Asset Pricing Models

The end result of both the capital asset pricing model (CAPM) and arbitrage pricing theory (APT) is a price-efficient securities market—a market in which expected returns are directly related to the risks inherent in a security that cannot be eliminated by diversification. For both the CAPM and APT to be true, security prices must be efficient prices. But the reverse is not necessary. An efficient market could exist without the CAPM or APT as the model underlying security prices. The relationship between the CAPM and EMT (or APT and EMT) runs one way. Both the CAPM and APT imply an efficient market, but an efficient market does not imply either the CAPM or APT.

Empirical tests of EMT often require estimates of expected security returns in order to see whether a particular trading rule or group of investors can consistently earn returns in excess of an expected fair return. For example, are the returns earned by corporate insiders consistently higher than should be expected—that is, are they higher more than 50% of the time? If one were to buy stocks that rise 5% above a previous low price and sell stocks that fall 5% below a previous high price, would the returns be consistently higher than should be expected? If one buys a market index portfolio on Monday and sells it on Friday, would the returns earned be consistently higher than should be expected? There are innumerable questions such as these that require an estimate of expected security returns. In such cases the CAPM is often used. But it has been used because it was the best model of expected returns available at the time. Its use does not mean an efficiently priced market is also a market in which the CAPM prevails. Arbitrage pricing theory, in fact, has been increasingly used to test various implications of EMT.

Finally, it is important to recognize that whenever the CAPM or APT is used to test for market efficiency, the test is actually a joint test—a test of market efficiency and a test of the pricing model used. In many situations where market inefficiencies are presumably found, it is difficult to tell whether such inefficiencies really exist or whether the risk/return model used is incorrect.

Are Returns Predictable?

The first tests of market efficiency were actually done before finance scholars had even coined the term *efficient markets*. In fact, the theory of efficient markets arose not only as a logical consequence of having a highly competitive security market but also as a convenient explanation for the empirical results that had been found.

The conclusion reached in virtually all of the original tests of return predictability was that "**security prices have no memory,**" meaning that future prices are unrelated to past prices. And along with this conclusion came the opinion that technical analysis is of no use in identifying the direction of future prices. Most scholars continue to believe technical analysis does not provide abnormal return. But there is a growing evidence that past and future returns are somehow related. Precisely what this relationship is and why it would occur is hotly debated. Currently, there are two general schools of thought. The first believes security prices depart from their true fundamental values for lengthy but indeterminable periods of time. Proponents argue this can be seen in stock prices that are more volatile than they should be as well as in negative return correlations over long intervals. The other school says that market prices are always efficient, or rational. Proponents argue that both the apparent excess volatility and the observed negative correlation are simply the results of changing risks and required returns.

Early Tests

The first tests of market efficiency were conducted prior to the 1980s. Most of these tests were of two basic types: random walk and filter trading rule tests.

Random Walk Tests. If security markets are efficient, prices will reflect all known information. As a result, prices will change only as new information arrives. But, by definition, new information must be random. If information flows followed an identifiable trend, this trend would become known and thus be reflected in current prices. Thus, **"new" information must be random.** And since new information enters randomly and prices react instantaneously to the information, changes in stock prices will be random.

In an efficient market, security prices follow what is referred to as a **random walk.** By this we mean that price changes over time are random. A price rise on day 0 doesn't increase or decrease the odds of a price rise or fall on day 1, day 2, and so forth. Price changes on any particular day are uncorrelated with historical price changes. If security prices do, indeed, follow a random walk, technical trading rules are useless.

When researchers speak of randomness in security prices, they actually mean **randomness in percentage price changes.** The price level of a stock is correlated from one day to the next. In addition, dollar price changes are also correlated with previous dollar price changes. The question is whether relative (or percentage) price changes are related over time. The correlation that exists between price levels or dollar price changes exists solely because of the level of a stock's price and is economically meaningless.

The first known test of the random walk hypothesis was performed by a French mathematician, Bachelier, about 1900. Although he successfully showed that stock prices could be characterized as following a random walk, his work lay dormant for more than 50 years. In 1953, Kendall examined the correlation of weekly changes in 19 British security price indices as well as spot prices for cotton and wheat. In his analysis of the data, Kendall (rather dramatically) suggested, "The series looks like a wandering one, almost as if once a week the Demon of chance drew a random number from a symmetrical population of fixed dispersion and added it to the current price to determine the next week's price."

Since Kendall, a large number of tests of the random walk hypothesis have been performed. One of the best known was conducted by Fama. Like others, Fama was interesting in the extent to which the return on a stock in a given time period is correlated with its return in a subsequent time period. This type of correlation is referred to as either autocorrelation or serial correlation. If the autocorrelation is sufficiently large enough, then analysts can make trading decisions based on past returns. For example, if a time series of daily returns has a negative autocorrelation equal to, say negative 0.8, then investors should buy at the start of a day all stocks that had low return the previous day. For example, consider panel A of Figure 9-5. This is a visual example of what a return series with autocorrelation equal to negative 0.8 would look like. Returns on day t are represented by the horizontal axis, and returns on day $t + 1$ are represented on the vertical axis. Clearly, investors could take advantage of such a return pattern.

Fama examined daily returns for each of the 30 stocks in the DJIA between the years 1957 and 1962. Returns on day t were correlated with the returns on day $t - 1$, day $t - 2$, through day $t - 10$. He found the autocorrelation was very small but usually positive. This, of course, is not surprising because stocks are risky and, thus, will on average have positive returns. However, the average autocorrelation was very close to zero. For a one-day log, the average was 0.026, and 11 out of the 30 stocks were statistically significant. Panel B in Figure 9-5 shows what a return series looks like if it has an autocorrelation of 0.026. It is unlikely that speculative trading profits could be made using such a series.

In addition to the daily return correlations, Fama calculated correlations for returns using time intervals greater than a day. Returns were calculated over 4-day, 9-day, and 16-day intervals and then correlated with prior 4-day, 9-day, and 16-day returns. Again, few correlations were statistically different from zero and, in such cases, the correlation was small enough to be of no probable use to traders who rely on clear trends.

Many other studies similar to Fama's were conducted during the 1960s and 1970s. On the whole, these studies indicated the following:

1. Short-term security returns are generally unrelated to prior returns. This is true not only for the United States but also for many other countries.
2. In those cases where a significant correlation does exist between past and present returns, the size of the correlation is so slight, it is doubtful that profitable trading rules could be developed.
3. A minor tendency seems to exist toward positive correlation. But this can be explained by realizing that stocks contain risk and will, on average, yield

FIGURE 9-5 ILLUSTRATIVE AUTOCORRELATIONS

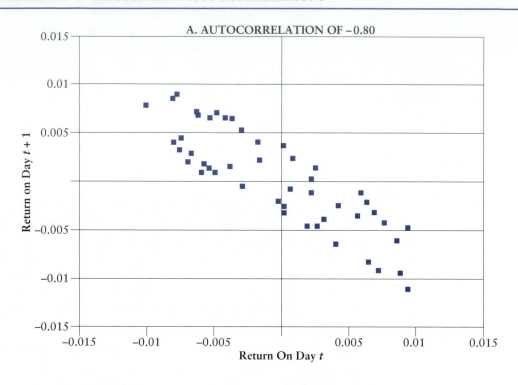

A. AUTOCORRELATION OF −0.80

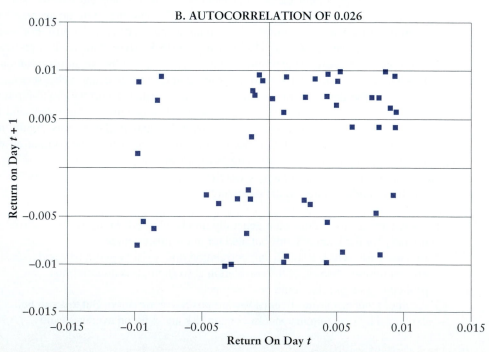

B. AUTOCORRELATION OF 0.026

positive returns. The slight positive correlation in returns simply reflects long-run positive returns on stocks. When returns are adjusted for such a risk impact, they show no correlation.

4. A "large return" day tends to be followed by another "large return" day. But there is no relationship with the direction of the subsequent return. That is, given a large price drop on day 0, the price change on day 1 is also likely to be large but the direction unknown.

5. Tests on T-bill and futures prices suggest they, too, follow a random walk.

Filter Trading Rule Tests. A **trading rule** is exactly what its name implies: a rule that specifies when a given security will be bought or sold. In practice, a large number of trading rules have been developed, and many are widely used today. A great deal of research has gone into testing the usefulness of such rules. On the whole, this research suggests that trading rules practitioners have used in the past do not work. However, many of the studies performed during the past decade have uncovered price anomalies that might provide excess trading-rule profits. Some of these are discussed later.

There are four criteria that any trading rule must meet before it can be declared a winner:

1. It must be based only on information known at the date the rule is implemented.
2. Returns must be calculated after all transaction costs and taxes.
3. Returns must be compared against an equivalent-risk passive buy-hold strategy.
4. Excess risk-adjusted returns must be earned consistently over a long time period.

One **filter trading rule** consists of the following decision criteria:

If the security price moves up by X percent above a prior low, buy and hold until the price falls by Y percent below a previous high, at which time simultaneously sell and go short.

Such a rule is close to the spirit of many chartist policies and is easily testable. Alexander, as well as Fama and Blume, has examined the profitability of such a rule. In a 1961 study, Alexander concluded, "In fact, at this point I should advise any reader who is interested only in practical results, and who is not a floor trader and so must pay commissions, to turn to other sources on how to beat buy and hold."

Since the Fama and Blume study included several features not present in Alexander's study, we concentrate on their results. They tested the profitability of 24 potential filters ranging in size from 0.5% to 50% on each of the 30 Dow Jones industrials. Average results for each of these filters are shown in Table 9-1. Note the following:

- Average security returns before commissions (column 1) varied, depending on the filter. The most profitable filter appears to be the smallest (0.5%). Thus, it seems that some slight positive correlation within security returns did exist which an extremely small filter could capture to yield positive returns. (Recall the slight positive correlation noted in the early Fama study.)

- Average security returns after commissions were usually negative or quite small. This is consistent with the belief that security markets are not perfectly efficient but are economically efficient.

TABLE 9-1   ANNUAL RETURNS FOR VARIOUS FILTERS

Average Return Before Commissions

Filter	Before Commissions (1)	After Commissions (2)	Long (3)	Short (4)	Number of Profitable Securities per Filter (5)	Total Transactions
0.005	0.1152	−1.0359	0.21	0.01	27/30	12,514
0.025	−0.02	−0.37	0.07	−0.14	13/30	3,750
0.05	−0.02	−0.17	0.06	−0.16	13/30	1,484
0.10	0.03	−0.01	0.08	−0.10	19/30	435
0.25	0.03	0.02	0.07	−0.20	15/29	73
0.50	−0.21	−0.23	−0.04	−0.16	0/4	4

SOURCE: Adapted from E. Fama and M. Blume, "Filter Rules and Stock-Market Trading," *Journal of Business, Special Supplement,* January 1966, pp. 226–241.

◾ Columns 3 and 4 decompose the before-commission returns into respective long and short positions. Clearly, someone who wishes to use a filter trading rule should think twice about short selling. Returns on short positions were disastrous.

In sum, the slight positive correlation that may exist in short-term security returns did not lead to a profitable filter trading rule. The extremely low filter necessary to capture such correlations required extremely large commission fees. Given this evidence, Fama and Blume saw no point in examining the consistency of nonexistent profits or adjusting for equivalent risk levels. The only people who might be enriched by using filtering techniques of this sort would be brokers. Speculators would quickly go bankrupt.

Although filter rules are close in spirit to the principles suggested by technicians, they are not widely used in practice. However, the use of moving averages is broadly acclaimed. The moving average rule reads as follows:

If the stock's price moves above its moving average by X percent, buy it and hold until the price moves Y percent below its moving average and then sell short.

Often 5% filters and a 200-day moving average are suggested by technicians. Such a rule has been tested by various researchers—with mixed but essentially unfavorable news for technicians. For example, in one study by Seelenfreund, Parker, and Van Horne, daily prices were obtained for 30 randomly selected NYSE stocks. Initially, $1,000 was assumed either to be invested via a buy-hold strategy in each of the 30 stocks or to be speculated with by following a moving average rule. Various filters and moving averages were used.

Rarely did a moving average filter yield larger profits than the buy-hold strategy—before or after commission fees. In fairness to the moving average rule, however, a number of adjustments in the methodology might have yielded better results. First, there is no guarantee that risks inherent in the buy-hold strategy are equivalent to those in the trading strategy. Using the moving average strategy, one is periodically "out of the market" and, thus, will incur no market risk. Using the buy-hold strategy, one is constantly invested in the market and exposed to market risk. Conceptually, buy-hold returns should have been higher because of risk exposure. Second, when the moving average strategy requires that one be out of the market, cash is assumed to be held. Superior results might be available if, on such occasions, a diversified portfolio of stocks were held instead of cash. In fact, other studies have suggested moving averages may yield better results. The question remains unresolved, but no one has presented results that are clearly in favor of a moving average rule.

Recent Findings

Early tests of random walk had three common characteristics: (1) they examined individual stocks as opposed to portfolios, (2) they looked at returns over relatively short time horizons (daily and weekly), and (3) they assumed stationarity of risk and expected returns. Each of these could bias the results against finding statistically significant autocorrelations. For example, the large standard deviation associated with individual stocks could mask any autocorrelation that might be present. However, if portfolios of many stocks are formed, much of the single-stock volatility is diversified away and it might be easier to see any autocorrelation. Also, by looking at short time intervals, we are unable to observe any long-term mispricing that might be present. Finally, if expected returns and risks are constantly changing over time, what might appear to be a random series over, say, a five-year period, could be an orderly one within various subsets of the period. Recent studies have taken up such issues.

Random Walk Revised. Recent research shows that future returns are more predictable than early studies suggested. The first serious challenge to random walk was a study by Lo and McKinley. Forming portfolios of stocks based on firm capitalization (shares outstanding times price per share), they found that weekly returns were positively autocorrelated, particularly for the smallest capitalization stock portfolios.

The fact that the smallest capitalization portfolio has the greatest autocorrelation suggested to many researchers a possible bias in the Lo and McKinley study that is referred to as nonsynchronous trading. This simply means that not all stocks in a portfolio trade on the date at which a return is calculated. When this occurs, there is an artificial autocorrelation present in the return series. To resolve the matter, Conrad and Kaul formed a size-based portfolios of stocks that traded at the end of a return period and showed the Lo and McKinley result was not seriously biased. Conrad and Kaul found autocorrelations of weekly returns of the large capitalization portfolios on the order of 9%. Smaller capitalization portfolios had autocorrelations close to 30%!

But can you profit from such autocorrelation? A recent study by Jegadeesh suggests it might be possible. Jegadeesh formed ten portfolios at the end of each month between 1934 and 1987 based on the predicted return of a stock. Predicted returns were based on autocorrelation coefficients developed from monthly returns over the previous five years. The market model we discussed in Chapter 7 was used to measure abnormal returns. Surprisingly, the average monthly abnormal return for the portfolio predicted to do the best was a positive 1.87%, and the equivalent for the portfolio predicted to do the worst was a negative 0.33%. These are CAPM risk-adjusted excess monthly returns.

Long Horizon Results. Even if returns over daily, weekly, or monthly intervals were uncorrelated, this does not mean the EMT is correct. For example, suppose the fundamental value of a security is constant over time but its market price departs from the fundamental value for years, such as Figure 9-6 shows. Researchers who examine daily returns over longer intervals are clearly negatively autocorrelated. Differences between market prices and fundamental values are called **bubbles.**

In 1981, Shiller published a paper that caused considerable excitement. The telling part of Shiller's study is captured in Figure 9-7. The line labeled P* is the detrended value of the S&P 500 if investors had perfectly forecast future real dividend payments of the S&P 500. Each P* is the present value of actual future real (adjusted for inflation) dividends. (Since dividends beyond 1979 were unknown, Shiller made a future growth assumption based on past growth rates.) The variable denoted P represents the detrended value of the actual security index (also adjusted for inflation). From the figure, it appears that actual stock prices are much more volatile than they should have been.

Shiller's basic point can be summarized as follows. A major source of uncertainty to investors is uncertainty about future dividends.[4] But, when we observe the actual path of past dividends, the path does not exhibit dramatic variability from year to year. There is little variability in dividends around their long-run growth rate. Since dividends have shown so little variability around their long-run growth rate, why are stock prices so volatile?

At first look, the evidence Schiller presents in favor of excess stock price volatility appears quite compelling. Stock prices have indeed been more volatile than the series of past dividend payments. But the major uncertainty that investors face regarding future dividends is not variability from one year to the next around a long-run growth rate. The major uncertainty is about what the long-run growth rate will be! The long-run sequence of dividends that Shiller examined represents a single realized long-run growth rate. Many other growth rates could have been realized.

In short, the excess price volatility Shiller suggests is probably due to his using an inappropriate dividend risk measure.

Debondt and Thaler investigated the notion of bubbles as applied to individual stocks. Research in experimental psychology indicates that most people tend to overreact to unexpected and dramatic news events. Debondt and Thaler created portfolios of past "winner" and "loser" stocks, that is, stocks that had recently had large returns or small returns. Examining the subsequent returns on these portfolios, they found the "loser" portfolio outperformed the previous "winner" portfolio. Their results are shown in Figure 9-8. The vertical axis is a measure of the accumulation of excess returns. Loser portfolios outperformed the equity market by 19.6% 36 months after formation. Winner portfolios underperformed the market by 5%.

Many people believe this is not actually evidence of market bubbles and overreaction. Instead, it could be due to the well-known January effect associated with small capitalization stocks. Notice that most of the loser portfolio returns arise in January. Loser stocks are likely, by definition, to have small capitalizations.

---

[4] In fact, it can be demonstrated that the standard deviation of potential future dividends should be greater then the standard deviation of future prices.

FIGURE 9-6 ILLUSTRATION OF PRICE BUBBLES

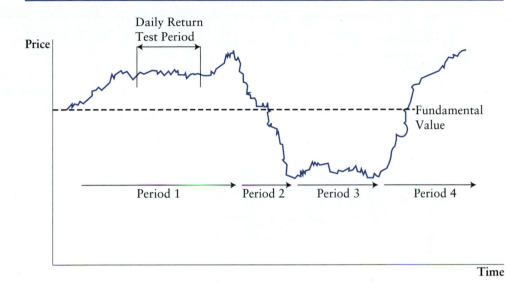

FIGURE 9-6 ILLUSTRATION OF PRICE BUBBLES

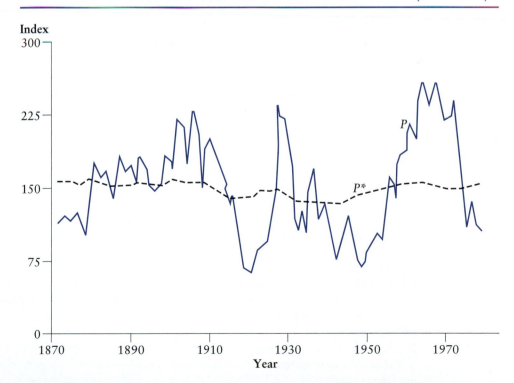

FIGURE 9-7 SHILLER'S DETRENDED ESTIMATES OF A PERFECT
FORESIGHT STOCK INDEX VS. ACTUAL INDEX (S&P 500)

FIGURE 9-8 THE PERFORMANCE OF PAST WINNER AND LOSER PORTFOLIOS

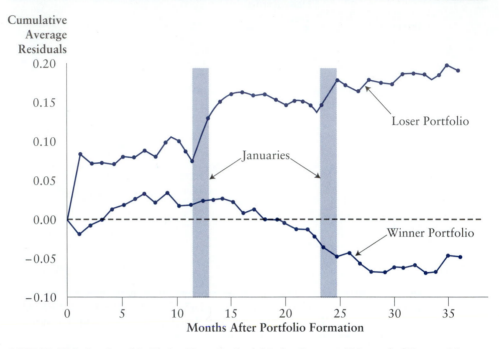

SOURCE: W. DeBondt and R. Thaler, "Does the Stock Market Overreact?" *Journal of Finance*, July

Return Patterns. If the random walk hypothesis is valid, there should not be any consistent patterns in security returns. While early tests of random walk did not detect any strong evidence that return patterns exist, more recent studies have found persuasive evidence of systematic patterns in stock returns. These patterns are referred to as follows:

1. The January effect
2. The monthly effect
3. The weekly effect
4. The daily effect

The **January effect** refers to the fact that stock returns in January are greater than returns in other months. This is particularly true for stocks of relatively small firms. In a study conducted by Keim, portfolios of small firms always had January returns greater than portfolios of large firms during the period 1963 to 1979. Previous to the Keim study, it was well known that portfolios of small stocks tended to have greater yearly returns than portfolios of large stocks, even when adjusted for estimated CAPM betas or APT factors. But the startling evidence of Keim showed that nearly 50% of this excess return comes in the first five days of January!

Figure 9-9 is based on the Keim study. Months of the year are shown on the horizontal axis. The vertical axis represents the average difference between excess returns on a portfolio of the smallest 10% of NYSE and AMEX stocks and excess returns on a portfolio of

FIGURE 9-9 THE JANUARY EFFECT, 1963–1979

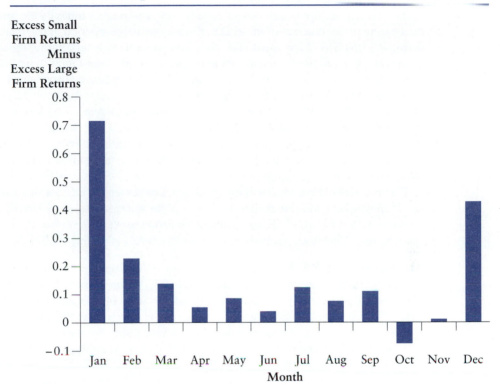

SOURCE: Adapted from D. Kiem, "Size-Related Anomalies and Stock Return Seasonality: Some Further Evidence," *Journal of Financial Economics*, June 1983.

the largest 10% of NYSE and AMEX stocks. During January the average difference was positive l0.714%. The average difference for all months excluding January was positive 0.102%. When annualized, these figures translate to yearly returns of about 8.9% and 1.2%, respectively.

Clearly something unusual is happening to small stocks in January. What this might be is still unknown. The major explanation offered to date is known as the tax selling hypothesis.

The folklore underlying the tax selling hypothesis is that, late in the year, individuals sell stocks that have declined in value during the year in order to realize a capital loss for tax purposes. Proceeds from the sales are then reinvested in early January, and the buying pressure causes the prices of such stocks to rise. Since stocks with small capitalization are likely to be heavily weighted in the small stock portfolios, returns on such portfolios would tend to exhibit the greatest returns in January. While some empirical evidence supports this view, much does not. For example, in Keim's study, small firms that hadn't experienced price declines in the previous year still incurred large positive returns in January. In addition, the January effect is worldwide, observed even in countries in which there are no capital gains taxes and countries in which the taxable year does not end in December. Also, why should people who sell low-priced securities in order to realize a capital loss wait until January of the next year to reinvest?

A difference has also been found in the pattern of returns during any month, which is referred to as the **monthly effect.** Ariel found that during the period 1963 to 1981, returns in the first half of any month (on an equally weighted market index) were much greater than during the second half of the month. During this 19-year period, the annualized return during the first half of any month was 51.1% versus a 0.0% return during the second half of the month. Even when January returns were removed, Ariel found statistically significant average returns in each half of the month. Why this occurs is unexplained.

The **weekly effect** refers to the unusual behavior of stock returns on Monday versus other days of the week. Evidence shows that Monday stock returns are lower, on average, than those on other days of the week. Logic would suggest that, if daily stock returns are positive over long sampling periods and if stock returns arise from a continuous accumulation of new information, the Monday returns should be three times as large as on other trading days. This simply isn't the case.

Finally, a **daily effect** has also been found: Stock prices tend to increase dramatically in the last 15 minutes of trading, regardless of the day of the week. In a study by Harris, which used transactions data for all NYSE stocks during the period between December 1981 and January 1983, he found that stock prices rose in the last 15 minutes of trading 90% of the time.

The Small-Firm P/E Effect. Prior to the late 1970s a number of studies had suggested that stocks with a low price-to-earnings ratio (P/E) outperformed those with high P/Es. However, a rigorous study of this possibility in the context of the CAPM was not conducted until 1977 when Basu used a standard market model approach to the question. Basu sampled an average of 500 stocks over the years 1956 to 1969. For each year, the stock's P/E was calculated and then placed in one of five P/E groups. Monthly returns were then calculated on each group (portfolio) assuming an equal investment in each stock in the group. This was done using a buy-hold strategy for the next 12 months. Market model estimates were then obtained for each group's monthly returns over the full 14-year period.

The results are summarized in Table 9-2. Portfolio A was the highest P/E group and portfolio E the lowest. Average annual returns were lowest for the high P/E firms and

TABLE 9-2   PORTFOLIO PERFORMANCE BY P/E GROUP

	Price-to-Earnings Group					
	A	A*	B	C	D	E
Median P/E	35.8	30.5	19.1	15.0	12.8	9.8
Average Annual Rate of Return	9.34%	9.55%	9.28%	11.65%	13.55%	16.30%
Estimated Beta	1.11	1.05	1.04	0.97	0.94	0.99

A* contains the highest P/E quintile stocks in A but excludes those with negative earnings.

SOURCE: Adapted from S. Basu, "Investment Performance of Common Stocks in Relation to Price-Earnings Ratios, A Test of the Efficient Markets Hypothesis," *Journal of Finance,* June 1979.

greatest for the low P/E firms. P/E and average returns were inversely related. This could make sense, of course, if the low P/E stocks had the greatest systematic risk. But the table shows this was not the case. Low P/E stocks had the lowest estimated betas. Strange . . .

In 1981, Reinganum confirmed Basu's finding but suggested perhaps it really wasn't a low P/E causing the excess returns but instead a "small-firm effect." When Reinganum compared excess daily returns on portfolios of stocks having different total market capitalization (price per share times shares outstanding), he found results similar to Basu's. Low-capitalization stocks outperformed high-capitalization stocks.

Event Studies

In a perfectly efficient security market, prices adjust instantaneously to new information. For example, if Texas Instruments announces it has a patent on a new transistor that is both cheaper to produce and longer lived than existing transistors, the price of its stock should increase immediately to a new equilibrium level. If its price adjusts with a lag or overadjusts, speculative profits would be available. This is illustrated in Figure 9-10, where price is plotted against time. Period 1 represents the date of a favorable announcement by the firm. Prior to date 1, investors believe the company's long-run dividend growth will be a constant 6% per year and that a return on equity of 13% would be fair. Given these beliefs, together with last period's dividend payment of $4.62 per share, the stock sells for $70 per share [$70 = ($4.62 × 1.06) ÷ (0.13 − 0.06)]. At date 1 the firm announces a new product line that should increase its long-run growth in dividends to 7% per year without adversely affecting the firm's risk. If the EMT is correct, the stock price should increase to $82.40 at date 1 (immediately after the announcement) and remain there until further new information arrives. The path of EMT prices is shown by the solid line. However, if market participants do not immediately recognize the importance of the

FIGURE 9-10 IMMEDIATE VS. LAGGED PRICE ADJUSTMENT

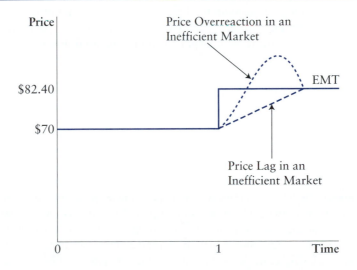

firm's announcement, a lag in price adjustment will occur, as illustrated by the dashed line. Clearly, if a lagged response to new information exists, speculative profits would be available and equal to $82.40 − $70.00. Alternatively, prices might consistently overreact to the announcement, as shown by the dotted curve that initially rises above the equilibrium price. In this case speculators could also earn profits on any overreaction.

The Methodology as Applied to Stock Splits

A **stock split** is simply an increase (or a decrease for a reverse split) in the number of shares that a corporation has outstanding. In a 2-for-1 split, shareholders would receive two new shares for each old share. Stock dividends are small stock splits, typically cases where one-quarter or fewer new shares are received for each initial share held. Because a split has no effect on a firm's investments or financial structure, it should also have no effect on the firm's total market value. Individual share prices would decline, of course, but total firm value would remain unchanged. Stock splits represent a fairly easy event on which to test the semistrong-form EMT because the announcement of data can be reasonably determined and because we know what the effect of the announcement should be. Moreover, they provide a good introduction to how one might conduct a semistrong-form test.

In the best known test of stock splits, Fama, Fisher, Jensen, and Roll (FFJR) examined 940 splits on the NYSE between 1927 and 1959. Virtually all splits greater than 5 for 4 were examined. FFJR hypothesized that splits themselves provide no new information about a firm. Price movements to levels other than those suggested by the split should be related to more fundamental information, such as cash dividend announcements. For example, an $80 stock that undergoes a 2-for-1 split should provide the investor with a zero return on the split date and have a postsplit price of $40.

If a positive (or negative) return was consistently found on the split date that was not associated with more fundamental company news, then security prices would be reacting to the split, and evidence of market inefficiency would be found.

According to the CAPM, stock returns are affected by both aggregate-market and company-unique information. Thus, if one is attempting to identify the impact of a firm-unique event, the market-related part of returns must be controlled for. Unadjusted, raw stock returns at the date of a split should not be used. For example, if a security's return on a split date was a positive 5.0%, this could be due to favorable market information affecting all stocks, favorable company information, or both. In an attempt to isolate that part of a security's return which was unique to company events alone, FFJR examined residual errors from the market model, that is:

Raw Return on Day t = Alpha + Return Due to Market Moves + Return Due to Firm News

$$\tilde{R}_t = a \ + \ b(\tilde{R}_M) + \tilde{e}_t \tag{9.1}$$

where R_t equals the return on a stock in period t, the letter a is the constant average return (alpha), the letter b represents the beta estimate of the stock, R_M represents the return on the aggregate market portfolio during period t, and e_t is the residual error in period t (the portion of the raw return due to firm-unique events). Estimates of a and b can be developed using a regression equation relating a stock's historical returns to historical market returns. Using regression estimates of the a's and b's, FFJR calculated the e_t values for each stock split during the 29 months prior to and 30 months following each split.

Two additional steps were taken before the data were analyzed. First, an average firm-unique return (AR) was found for each month surrounding the split, as follows:

Average Market Model Residual in Month *t*

$$AR_t = \frac{\sum\limits_{t=1}^{N} e_{i,t}}{N} \tag{9.2}$$

where AR_t equals the average firm-unique return for month t (any of the 29 months before or 30 months after the split), $e_{i,t}$ equals firm-unique return on stock i during month t, and N equals the number of splits examined in a given month.

Second, a cumulative average firm-unique return (CAR) was found for each month by summing all average firm-unique returns through a particular month. Mathematically:

Cumulative Market Model Residual in Month *r*

$$CAR_t = \sum\limits_{t=-29}^{N} AR_k \tag{9.3}$$

To evaluate the price impact of a split empirically, either the AR or the CAR values may be examined. Conventionally, the cumulative average return is discussed the most.

Figure 9-11 presents a plot of CAR for each of the 60 months surrounding a split. Month 0 represents the month in which the split occurred. An examination of the figure suggests the following:

- Stocks that split appear to have had a dramatic increase in price during the 29 months prior to the split. This is reflected in the substantial growth in CAR prior to the split date. However, these price increases cannot be attributed to the eventual split, since rarely was a split announced more than four months prior to the effective date of the split.

- After the split date, the CAR is remarkably stable. This implies that from the split date forward, firm-unique returns were zero. The split had no immediate or long-run impact on security prices.

Results displayed in Figure 9-11 suggest the market is efficient in that splits, by themselves, had no observable effect on security prices. In addition, FFJR examined how more fundamental economic news provided at the date of the split would affect stock prices. To do this, they segregated the split stocks into two groups: one in which cash dividends were reduced and the other in which cash dividends were increased. They hypothesized that a change in cash dividend payments would provide indirect information about the firm's future prospects and that market prices would adjust rapidly to the new information.

Results for each of these groups are displayed in Figure 9-12. When CARs are grouped according to this more fundamental economic news, the series behaves differently. Companies

FIGURE 9-11 STOCK PRICE MOVEMENT AROUND STOCK SPLITS

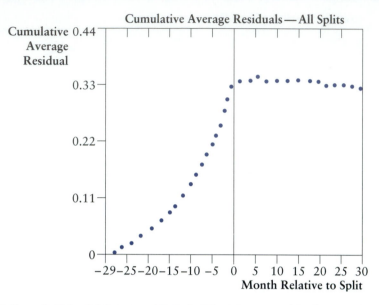

SOURCE: E. Fama, L. Fisher, M. Jensen, and R. Roll, "The Adjustment of Stock Prices to New Information," *International Economic Review,* February 1969. Copyright © 1969.

that increased cash dividends had a positive growth in CAR after the split (prices continued to rise with the favorable news). For stocks in the "decreases" group, security prices fell. In sum, splits by themselves appear to have had no impact on stock prices. But when real information is provided coincident with the split, prices adjust in the direction expected.

The FFJR study was the first in a series of studies that relied on a methodology suggested by the CAPM. Refinements have been made to the procedure, but the basic methodology remains unchanged. Even if you believe that empirical tests of the CAPM and Roll's comments have cast doubts on the model's validity, there is little disagreement that aggregate market returns must be controlled when firm-unique events are being examined. For example, a market factor can play a dominant role in the arbitrage pricing model (APM), the major alternative to the CAPM. Examination of average and cumulative firm-unique returns derived from a market model similar to Equation (9.2) is one of the best techniques we have at present to evaluate the price effects that are firm unique.

Earnings Announcements

Early studies examining the behavior of stock prices during the weeks surrounding an earnings announcement all indicated that the announcements possessed informational content and the value of the information was rapidly reflected in share prices. The real question, however, is not whether earnings announcements do or don't have an informational value but, instead, what are **the impacts of expected versus unexpected** earnings announcements on stock prices. Corporate earnings announcements may or may not represent new

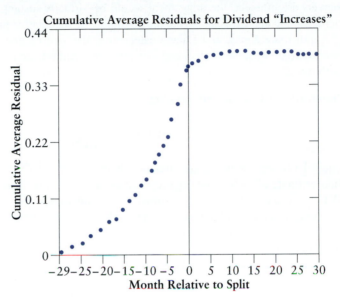

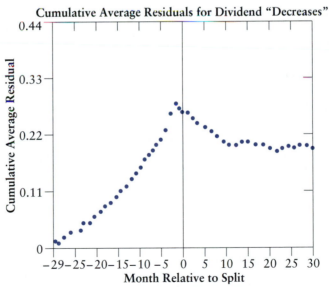

SOURCE: E. Fama, L. Fisher, M. Jensen, and R. Roll, "The Adjustment of Stock Prices to New
Information," *International Economic Review,* February 1969. Copyright © 1969.

information to investors. To the extent that announced earnings are what investors expect, stock prices should have already discounted the announced earnings level. However, to the extent that announced earnings are unexpected, a price adjustment would be necessary. If markets are efficient, the adjustment would be virtually instantaneous. If they are ineffi-cient, a lag would exist and signal the possibility of speculative profits.

Rendleman, Jones, and Latane categorized the size of unexpected earnings into ten groups. To do this, they calculated a measure of standardized unexpected earnings (SUE), as follows:

Standardized Unexpected Earnings

$$SUE = \frac{EPS - E(EPS)}{SEE} \qquad (9.4)$$

where **EPS** represents the earnings per share announced for a given quarter, **E(EPS)** is their estimate of EPS based on a regression analysis of the firm's historical earnings, and **SEE** is the standard error of the estimate (the standard deviation of the error term in the re-gression). Data were obtained from quarterly earnings announcements made by approxi-mately 1,000 firms during the period 1972 to 1980. SUE was calculated for each firm for a given quarter and, based on its value, the firm was placed into one of ten groups. This was done for all quarters. Finally, CAR was calculated for each group starting 20 days before the announcement through 90 days after the announcement.

Average results are shown in Figure 9-13. Note that immediately prior to the announce-ment day, security returns moved exactly in the direction we would expect. Firms with positive values of SUE had positive returns in excess of what the market model would suggest, and firms with negative values of SUE had returns lower than expected. This is consistent with the rapid price adjustment that EMT implies. The results are not consistent with EMT, however, if the announcement was "leaked" to some individuals, as the slight preannouncement moves in CAR tend to suggest. More important, however, are the con-tinued movements in CAR over the 90 days after the announcement. For EMT to be strictly true, all price adjustments should occur at the date of the announcement. Yet the CAR values after the announcement date are large enough to cover transaction costs and leave a tidy speculative profit. Either the market model did not adequately capture the ex-pected returns on these securities or we have a violation of semistrong-form efficiency.

In sum, prices do appear to adjust to unexpected announcements. But the speed of this adjustment process is questionable. There is evidence of a lag that might provide specula-tive profits—particularly if the speculator doesn't have to pay large brokerage fees.

Initial Public Offerings

According to the efficient market theory (EMT), the prices at which new security offerings are sold to the public should, on average, be equal to their equilibrium levels. There should not be a persistent undervaluing of new shares, since corporate issuers will insist their under-writers obtain the best price possible. Similarly, a persistent overvaluation shouldn't exist, as buyers wish to pay the lowest price possible. If investors have homogeneous beliefs, new issue prices should be equal to their equilibrium values. Ibbotson has investigated the histor-ical price behavior of new issues during the first 60 months of a new issue's life and found

FIGURE 9-13 EVIDENCE ON UNEXPECTED EARNINGS

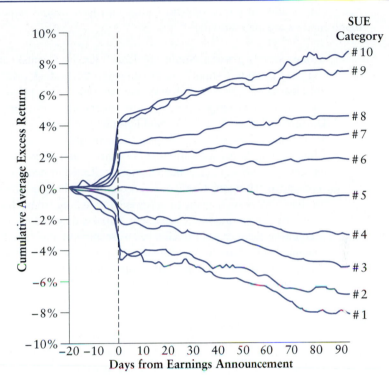

SOURCE: R. Rendleman, C. Jones, and H. Latane, "Empirical Anomalies on Unexpected Earnings and Importance of the Risk Adjustment," *Journal of Financial Economics*, November 1982.

mixed results. Based on Ibbotson's data, initial purchasers of new issues appear to receive approximately an 11% to 12% abnormal return during the first month the security is held. However, by the third month new issue prices appear to have reached equilibrium levels.

The statistically significant abnormal returns during the first couple of months of a new issue's life have to be disturbing to strict proponents of the EMT. Initial purchasers appear to be given a price inducement to accept the new offering. Yet when viewed from the perspective of a technician or of many fundamentalists, who believe that gross inequities remain in the markets for lengthy periods of time, the results must be even more disturbing. From their viewpoint, the apparent inefficiency found by Ibbotson isn't nearly as large as other inefficiencies they believe are commonplace, and it is eliminated within a couple of months. We should also note that Ibbotson's results were based on the CAPM and might not adequately reflect the total risk taken on by first-time purchasers of new issues. In fact, Ibbotson's results suggest continuing decreases in beta risk during the first 60 months of an issue's life. There may well have been a large, unmeasurable risk associated with the first couple of months that could reasonably explain the apparent 11% to 12% abnormal performance. But until we gain a better understanding of such risks, the results are contrary to semistrong-form efficiency.

Other Studies

Many other studies of semistrong-form efficiency have been conducted. Some of the more representative are the following:

1. **Money supply growth.** Studies by Rozeff and by Rogalski and Vinso all suggest that money supply growth directly affects stock prices. However, anticipated changes in the growth rates are reflected in prices before the change, and unexpected changes are almost instantaneously reflected in prices.
2. **Dividend change.** Both Watts and Pettit have modeled dividend changes and shown that prices tend to anticipate such changes.
3. **Management forecasts.** Various studies have found the unexpected forecasts of earnings by a firm's management are fully reflected in stock prices within two days.
4. **Accounting changes.** Changes in accounting techniques that have a real effect on share values such as the tax effects of switching from FIFO to LIFO inventory accounting have immediate impacts on stock prices. Cosmetic accounting changes refer to changes in accounting policies that change financial statements of a firm but have no effect on future cash flows of a firm. Cosmetic changes do not seem to cause share prices to change.

Tests for Private Information

Efficient market theory states that all information is reflected in security prices. This means no individual has private information that would influence prices if revealed. Tests for the value of private information have focused on three groups: (1) corporate insiders, (2) security analysts, and (3) portfolio managers.

The results have been mixed. The value of insider information is well documented. Insiders have private information on which they earn abnormal returns. But outsiders are unable to profit from insider trading once the information is made available to the general public. Some security analysts also seem to be able to develop information about security values that is not reflected in prices until released to the public. But the ability of active portfolio managers to earn abnormal returns remains an open question. Studies of mutual fund performance have yielded both positive and negative conclusions, depending on the indices against which the fund managers are evaluated.

Corporate Insiders

Corporate insiders are defined as directors, officers, and major shareholders. If anyone has access to privileged information, it should be such insiders. Studies by Jaffee, Seyhun, and Givoly-Palmon all show that corporate insiders do earn abnormal profits from their trading. Jaffee's study showed that two months after a period of intensive insider trading in a state, cumulative average excess returns on the stock were 2.09%.

In an attempt to provide full public disclosure, the Securities and Exchange Commission (SEC) reports insider trades in its **Official Summary of Insider Trading.** Once published, the information is available to the general public. Could public investors use this data, which is typically available two months after an insider trade, to earn speculative profits? Jaffee's study found that abnormal public returns of about 2.5% were possible after transaction costs. But in a follow-up study, Seyhan showed that most of this return was due to the performance of small capitalization stocks—that is, the small firm effect.

Security Analysts

Security analysts are the epitome of market professionals. Trained in sophisticated analytic techniques and devoting full-time efforts to evaluating the investment worth of a narrow list of stocks, they should be capable of identifying mispriced securities. However, this doesn't always seem to be the case.

Diefenbach examined the usefulness of research recommendations made by security analysts to institutional clients. (Generally, such reports are not available to the public at large.) His results showed that buy recommendations outnumbered sell recommendations by a 26 to 1 margin. On average, the buy recommendations fell in price by -3.0%, and only 47% of the recommendations had a price rise greater than the S&P industrials. Clearly, an analyst's buy recommendations did not, on aggregate, beat a passive strategy of buy-hold. A few analysts were able to considerably outperform the S&P Index. But when Diefenbach examined the consistency with which such analysts were able to provide superior performance, he concluded that chance alone could have done as well. There was no obvious consistency in superior performance.

Sell recommendations yielded a different story. While there were very few sell recommendations, they were more accurate. In total, 74% of the sell recommendations fell in price by more than the S&P industrials. Only one analyst suffered the indignity of having the majority of his sell recommendations outperform the S&P during the next year.

A large number of studies have examined the stock recommendations of Value Line. The *Value Line Investment Survey* publishes rankings on approximately 1,700 stocks. A ranking of 1 represents a strong buy recommendation. A ranking of 5 is the most negative recommendation. Numerous studies have shown that stocks ranked 1 statistically outperformed those with a 5 ranking over the next year. When a stock's ranking was changed, market prices of the stock reflected the change within a few days.

But some of these results may be unique to a specific time period and not available to a real portfolio strategy. For example, in a review of recent EMT studies, Fama stated,

> Over the 6.5 years from 1984 to mid-1990, group 1 stocks earned 16.9% per year compared with 15.2% for the Wilshire 5000 Index. During the same period, Value Line's Centurion Fund, which specializes in group 1 stocks, earned 12.7% per year— live testimony to the fact that there can be large gaps between simulated profits from private information and what is available in practice.[5]

---

[5] Eugene Fama, "Efficient Capital Markets: II," *Journal of Finance,* December 1991. This paper is an excellent overview of empirical studies of efficient market theory.

Portfolio Managers

The ability of portfolio managers to earn excess risk-adjusted returns has been studied extensively, but no firm conclusions have emerged. The basic problem is that we are unable to measure portfolio risk properly. For example, if risk is proxied by a portfolio's beta, three problems are encountered. First, what index should be used as a proxy for the market portfolio? The abnormal performance of equity mutual funds can (and does) depend on the index used. Second, the betas of many funds are constantly changing as portfolio managers actively trade securities. Time-series portfolio betas, such as market model betas, are single estimates of the portfolio's average beta. Finally, we know that small capitalization and low price-to-earnings stocks provide returns that are not explained by market model betas. If the CAPM is used to evaluate manager performance, managers who hold such stocks will appear to perform better than other managers.

A good example of these concerns can be seen in a recent study of equity mutual fund performance. Ippolito examined a 20-year return history for 143 funds (1965–1985). Fund returns were measured after all mutual fund expenses but before any load fees. Using the following market model regression equation, he found that the average fund had an alpha of positive 0.83% per year:

Market Model Regression

$$R_{Ft} - RF_t = \text{alpha}_F + \text{beta}_F\,(R_{SP500,\,t} - RF_t) + e_{Ft}$$

Given that the average fund outperformed passive combinations of T-bills and the S&P 500 after expenses, Ippolito concluded that before-expense returns had to be even higher; that is, the managers were truly informed traders.

In a follow-up study, Elton, Gruber, Das, and Hklarka (EGD&H) examined the effect of relying on one-year T-bills and the S&P 500 Index as proxies of the passive risk-free and risky security portfolios. Many funds own debt instruments other than T-bills as well as stocks not in the S&P 500 Index. EGD&H replaced T-bills with a return series of government and corporate bonds. They also added a third passive portfolio consisting of returns on non–S&P 500 stocks. When these three passive portfolios are used to evaluate manager performance, the average excess return dropped to a negative 1.1% per year.

Much research remains to be done on the value of actively managed portfolios. Because we have been unable to develop reliable risk benchmarks, we cannot say whether active management does or does not provide greater risk-adjusted returns than does passive management.

Strategy in an Efficient Market

The evidence presented in this chapter indicates that the markets are certainly not perfectly efficient. However, for many people with little knowledge, high search costs, and large transaction costs, the markets are probably close to being economically efficient. Such people might be wise to consider themselves as operating in an efficient market and to follow reasonable investment strategies. If they wish to speculate, it should be with a limited portion of their portfolio.

Reasonable trading strategies in an efficient market include the following:

1. **Diversify.** Purchase shares in a number of no-load stock and bond mutual funds that have a policy of minimal trading activity. Consider holding some amount of international and real estate funds. An ideal fund would be a passive index fund.
2. **Select a suitable asset allocation.** Examine the historical volatility of the aggregate security indices to determine subjectively an acceptable asset allocation.
3. **Don't try to time security price moves.** Simply buy and hold. Rebalance asset allocation as security prices rise and fall to the desired allocation. Trade when cash is needed or available. Don't try to find mispriced securities or asset classes.
4. **Keep tax considerations in mind.** For example, zero-tax pension funds should be placed in high-coupon bonds because such bonds have higher before-tax yields. Although the stock evidence is less clear, it does seem that high-dividend-yield stocks also sell at high before-tax expected yields. Some care should be taken, however, that these tax considerations don't reduce portfolio diversification.
5. **Consider marketability.** The portfolio should provide the degree of marketability that might be needed to meet unexpected cash needs.

S U M M A R Y

An efficient securities market is the consequence of intense competition for information. Individuals seeking speculative profits will search out any information that will aid in identifying mispriced securities. And, at the extreme, all such information will be reflected in existing prices.

- A perfectly efficient market is one in which market prices are exactly equal to current intrinsic values. The conditions necessary for a perfectly efficient market are the following:

  1. information must be provided freely and instantaneously to all market participants,
  2. there must be no costs associated with trading,
  3. actions taken by a single individual cannot affect prices, and
  4. people maximize expected utility

- Since the first two requirements are not strictly true, we differentiate between a perfectly efficient market and an economically efficient market. In an economically efficient market, prices may vary from true intrinsic worth, but long-run speculative profits are not available after transaction costs. In such a market, a passive strategy of investing will yield larger long-run returns than will a speculative strategy.

- The extent to which security markets can be characterized as being economically efficient can be tested only by examining empirical data. To date, such empirical evidence indicates the following:

  1. Short-term returns do not follow a pure random walk. However, the autocorrelation in returns of individual stocks is quite small. Trading rules that rely on historical price charts are useless after transaction costs are paid.

  2. Long-term returns may be negatively correlated. This could be due to market inefficiencies (bubbles) or changes in market risk premiums over time.

3. A number of "anomalies" have been found that remain unexplained. These include the small firm (or price-to-earnings) and January effects.

4. New information is reflected in security prices with little time lag. In fact, market prices often adjust before an actual announcement. There is some evidence, however, that the postannouncement price adjustment can extend over a month or more and that speculative profits may be available if one pays small transaction costs.

5. Some individuals appear to have private information that is not reflected in prices until after they trade. Corporate insiders clearly gain from their trading activities. Security analysts might also be able to develop information about a stock's value that is not reflected in its price. But the value of such private information is usually quite small, and it is difficult for the public to gain from the information after transaction costs.

6. Professional equity managers provide returns that are very close to the returns of passive portfolios. We are unable to determine whether active management beats passive management because proper risk benchmarks have not been developed.

It appears that markets are not strictly efficient. But for all practical purposes, it is wiser to approach security selection from the viewpoint of EMT than to assume that gross mispricing exists.

R E V I E W   P R O B L E M

In this problem you will use market model estimates of residual returns on two stocks to determine whether the announcement of an unexpected cash dividend had any impact on security values and whether a lag occurred in any such adjustment.

Market returns are shown here for 12 periods before the announcement ($T = -12$ to -1), the date of the announcement ($T = 0$), and 12 periods after the announcement ($T = 1$ to 12).

Before Announcement				After Announcement			
			Rates of Return				
T	Stock 1	Stock 2	Market	T	Stock 1	Stock 2	Market
−12	3	5	2	0	−11.776	−21.120	−15
−11	2	4	2	1	6.410	10.338	6
−10	14	15	11	2	2.080	2.848	1
−9	−20	−35	−24	3	6.410	10.338	6
−8	9	16	10	4	−2.250	−4.642	−4
−7	6	9	6	5	−5.714	10.634	−8
−6	5	11	6	6	0.714	1.050	0
−5	0	6	3	7	−1.884	−3.444	−3
−4	10	14	8	8	5.044	8.540	5
−3	17	32	21	9	−6.214	−10.934	−8
−2	0	−4	−1	10	−1.884	−3.444	−3
−1	5	13	5	11	11.106	19.026	12
				12	11.972	20.524	13

a. Estimate the following market model regressions for each stock using the returns for $T = -12$ to $T = -1$:

$$\tilde{R}_t = a + b(\tilde{R}_{Mt}) + \tilde{e}_t$$

b. The results of step a should yield the following:

$$R_{1t} = 0.714 + 0.866(R_{Mt})$$

$$R_{2t} = 1.050 + 1.498(R_{Mt})$$

Use these two models to estimate residual errors for days $T = 0$ to $T = +12$.

c. Compute the average residual for each day in the postannouncement period as well as the cumulative average residual.

d. Comment on whether these results are consistent with EMT.

Solution

a. The market model regressions are shown in step b.

b. through d.

T	Stock 1	Stock 2	AR	CAR
0	0.5	0.3	0.4	0.4
1	0.5	0.3	0.4	0.8
2	0.5	0.3	0.4	1.2
3	0.5	0.3	0.4	1.6
4	0.5	0.3	0.4	2.0
5	0.5	0.3	0.4	2.4
6	0	0	0	2.4
7	0	0	0	2.4
8	0	0	0	2.4
9	0	0	0	2.4
10	0	0	0	2.4
11	0	0	0	2.4
12	0	0	0	2.4

This is inconsistent with EMT in that a lag occurs in the adjustment of stock prices. By the end of day $T = 5$, a 2.4% cumulative excess return is earned.

QUESTIONS AND PROBLEMS

1. What are the four conditions that would lead to a perfectly efficient market?
2. What is the difference between a perfectly efficient and economically efficient security market?
3. If the security markets are in fact efficient, should anyone decide to become a security analyst or active portfolio manager? What would the impact of such a decision be on efficiency?
4. "For the CAPM to be correct, the security markets must be efficient." "For the security markets to be efficient, the CAPM must be correct." Evaluate these statements.
5. "The concept of a random walk in stock prices is bizarre and implies totally irrational behavior by the investing public. Nothing could be further from the truth than random walk. Prices are related to fundamental economic worth." Comment.
6. Technicians often say that trading conditions change in the market such that a rule which works during one period might not work during another period. They believe trading rules

shouldn't be inflexible but, instead, should be adjusted as new market conditions arise. Comment.

7. a. "Speculation is a zero-sum game across the market at any point in time as well as for any single speculator over time." How is this statement related to EMT?

 b. For the markets to be efficient, speculators must trade on any price disequilibriums. If speculators earn profits from doing so, is this inconsistent with market efficiency?

8. Consider the following situations and indicate in each case whether the concept of market efficiency is violated:

 a. A friend tells you that the concept of market efficiency is clearly invalid, offering as proof the fact that during the past three years she has considerably beaten the market averages. Returns on her portfolio in each year were 15%, 18%, and 25%, whereas the market returns were only 12%, 15%, and 18%.

 b. A financial consulting firm has just announced a newly designed complex computer program that would have generated consistent (risk-adjusted) excess returns after all transaction costs and taxes if it had been used during the last ten years.

 c. Ten years ago a financial consulting firm began to use a complex computer program to analyze financial reports. Since the introduction of this technique, the firm has consistently earned (risk-adjusted) excess returns after all transaction costs and taxes.

 d. During the past five years most people have earned positive average returns. However, some people have earned considerably more than others.

 e. You have correlated the percentage change in gold prices during day t with the percentage change in the NYSE Composite Index during day t. You find a statistically significant correlation coefficient of negative 0.45.

 f. A research study finds that firms switching from expensing R&D expenditures to capitalizing them have positive and statistically significant CAR levels that increase steadily for five months. Beyond five months the CAR steadily returns to zero.

 g. Trading activity by corporate insiders results in permanent and statistically significant CAR levels.

9. A large portion of the empirical studies rely on a methodology suggested by the capital asset pricing model. Do you find any logical inconsistency in using the CAPM to test for inefficiencies in the market? How is this concern at least partially resolved by the arbitrage pricing model?

10. Recent empirical tests of the EMT have uncovered a number of results suggesting that inefficiencies may exist.

 a. List and briefly discuss those presented in the chapter.

 b. Assume you wish to defend EMT in light of these apparent inconsistencies. How would you do so?

11. Recent empirical evidence suggests that expected stock returns change over time—that risk premiums are inversely related to the business cycle.

 a. Why might risk premiums change in such a manner?

 b. How does this partly explain the larger than expected volatility in aggregate stock prices (such as the S&P Composite) that Shiller found?

 c. If market risk premiums do change over time, should an investor's asset allocation (where the assets are on, say, the CAPM borrowing-lending line) be constant?

12. Suppose you have found that returns on the S&P 500 Index are negative on Mondays more than 70% of the time. What trading strategy would you pursue? Would you tell others? As others find the same fact, what will happen?

13. What is the January effect? What trading strategy does it suggest?

14. In a recent year, stock prices in Taiwan increased 500%. What implication might this have on the efficient market hypothesis? Take both the pro and con side.

15. On October 19, 1987 (Black Monday), stock prices fell by 22%, erasing more than $500 billion in investor wealth. What implication does this have on the efficient market theory (EMT)?

16. Shiller has suggested that stock prices might depart from their fundamental values causing bubbles in prices. Explain Shiller's charge that stock prices are too volatile. Do you agree with this opinion? Explain.

17. The efficient market theory (EMT) has major implications for the practice of portfolio management. One obvious implication is the determination of superior analysts. Another is how to carry out the management of portfolios, assuming no access to superior analysts. Assume that none of the analysts to whom you have access is superior. List and discuss five of the specific investment practices you should implement for your clients.

18. In recent years several major financial institutions have developed index funds and offered these to pension accounts and others.
   a. Give the justification used for investing in these index funds, which simply attempt to replicate the market?
   b. Indicate whether this justification is consistent with the EMT.

19. As vice president for quantitative research for a large investment firm, your recent studies have provided strong empirical evidence of the following:

   ◾ The stocks of small capitalization firms tend to outperform the stocks of large capitalization firms over the long term.

   ◾ The stocks with a low price-to-earnings ratio tend to outperform the stocks of large capitalization firms over the long term.

   ◾ The companies that had the largest unexpected year-to-year increases in earnings also provided the best same-year price appreciation.

   a. Comment on the practical limitations of managing a portfolio based on these findings.
   b. Comment on the adjustments that would be appropriate in an equity portfolio that incorporates the findings above given an anticipated change from a bear market to a bull market environment.

20. In an efficient market:
   a. security prices react quickly to new information.
   b. security prices are seldom far above or below their justified levels.
   c. security analysis will not enable investors to realize consistently superior returns on their investments.
   d. all of the above.

21. The weak form of the efficient market hypothesis asserts that:
   a. stock prices do not rapidly adjust to new information.
   b. future changes in stock prices cannot be predicted from past prices.
   c. Corporate insiders shold have no better investment performance than other investors do.
   d. arbitrage between futures and cash markets should not produce extraordinary profits.

DATAFILE ANALYSIS

1. **Autocorrelation of Stock Returns.** One implication of the efficient market theory is that past returns will be uncorrelated with future returns. Here, you will analyze whetehr this is true for returns on the S&P 500. Access the INDEXES datafile and find the yearly returns on the S&P 500 Index. Insert a blank column next to the S&P 500 returns. In this new column, copy the S&P 500, but offset by one year. That means the return in 1926 in one column will be next to the return in 1927, and so forth. Calculate the correlation between returns in year t with the returns in year t-1. (Hint: Use the Correl function.) Is this correlation coefficient large enough to suggest that EMH is incorrect? (No statistical test is necessary.)

2. **The January Effect.** Using the datafile INDEXES, find the monthly returns on the DFA 9-10 index. This is a series of returns on the ninth and tenth market capitalization deciles of stocks traded on the NYSE (the smallest 20% of firms traded). Next, eliminte all returns between 1926 and 1949. Using the remaining returns (1950–1994) small firm returns), calculate the average return earned by month. Notice that the average return in January is much larger than the average for other months. Repeat this exercise using monthly S&P 500 returns over the same time interval. Contrast the results.

R E F E R E N C E S

Two classic reviews of the notion of efficient markets and empirical tests of the theory were written by Fama:

Fama, Eugene F. "Efficient Capital Markets: A Review of Theory and Empirical Work," *Journal of Finance,* May 1970.

Fama, Eugene F. "Efficient Capital Markets: II," *Journal of Finance,* December 1991.

Other parties cited in the chapter that are not referenced in tables or figure are as follows:

Diefenbach, R. "How Good Is Institutional Research?" *Financial Analysts Journal,* January–February 1972.

Fama, Eugene F. "The Behavior of Stock Prices," *Journal of Business,* January 1965.

Grossman, Stanley and Joseph Stiglitz. "On the Impossibility of Informationally Efficient Markets," *American Economic Review,* June 1980.

Jaffe, Jeffrey. "Special Information and Insider Trading," *Journal of Business,* July 1974.

Lo, Andrew W. and A. Craig McKinley. "Stock Prices Do Not Follow Random Walks: Evidence from a Simple Specification Text," *Review of Financial Studies,* Spring 1988.

Rozeff, Michael. "Money and Stock Prices: Market Efficiency and the Lag Effect of Monetary Policy," *Journal of Financial Economics,* September 1974.

An interesting recent article on security market efficiency is Brown, Keith C., W. V. Harlow, and Seha M. Tinic, "How Rational Investors Deal with Uncertainty (or, Reports of the Death of Efficient Market Theory Are Greatly Exaggerated)," *Journal of Applied Corporate Finance,* Fall 1989.

To help explain security price movement in general and the market crash of 1987 in particular, some people advocate the concept of "chaos theory." A well-written book that surveys chaos theory is Peters, Edgar, *Chaos and Order in the Capital Markets: A New View of Cycles, Prices, and Market Volatility,* New York: Wiley, 1991.

PART 3

Security Analyses

Our purpose in Part 3 is to analyze in depth each major type of security class. We begin with two chapters on fixed income securities. The first examines important bond valuation principles and the second examines the management of the fixed income portion of a portfolio. These are followed by two chapters on equity securities. Similar to the discussion of bonds, a full chapter is devoted to equity valuation and another chapter discusses the management of the equity portion of a portfolio. The next four chapters examine commingled portfolios, global investment, financial futures and options.

Our discussion of security analyses in this part of the text comes between general investment concepts of Part 2 and portfolio strategy in Part 4. This organization was not idly chosen. The organization is, in fact, quite natural. It is virtually impossible to develop a good understanding of how various security types should be valued and managed without a reasonable grasp of investment concepts such as diversification, determinants of required returns, portfolio theory, and security pricing. In the same fashion, it is equally difficult to develop effective portfolio strategies without a solid knowledge of each major type of security class.

10

VALUATION OF FIXED INCOME SECURITIES

After reading this chapter you should have an understanding of the determinants of a bond's market value.

The international bond markets are large, representing about one-half of the value of all publicly traded financial securities in the world. The variety of instruments is diverse, ranging from default-free U.S. government bonds to high-risk corporate obligations having various imbedded options.

Estimates of the value of securities traded in major bond markets are shown in Table 10-1. (The table does not include money market instruments.) Three conclusions are clearly apparent. The value of securities traded in world bond markets underwent dramatic growth over the past decade and a half. As an example, the total market value of U.S. bonds increased at a compound annual growth rate of more than 13%! In addition, more than 60% of all bonds traded in the United States are obligations of governmental units or mortgage-backed securities. Finally, the U.S. bond market is clearly the largest fixed income market in the world.

Chapter 3 discussed various institutional features of bonds. Here, and in the next chapter, we develop a more complete analysis of bond investment and speculation. In this chapter, we discuss bond valuation. In the next chapter, we discuss the management of fixed income portfolios.

The price at which a bond trades is the present value of future promised cash flows discounted at a required rate of return. This required return is called the bond's **yield to maturity** (YTM). The YTM of any bond consists of four elements:

1. A nominal return required to induce people to save (commonly measured as the YTM on a U.S. T-bond).

TABLE 10-1   ESTIMATES OF WORLD BOND VALUES

Bond Category (a)	1994 U.S. Dollar Value of Publicly Traded Bonds (In $ Trillion)				
	U.S.	Japan	Germany	Other	Total
Central Government	$2.4	$2.0	$0.7	$2.6	$7.7
State and Local	0.9	0.09	0.07	0.14	1.2
Mortgage-Backed	1.7	NA	NA	NA	1.7
Subtotal	$5.0	$2.0	$0.8	$2.74	$10.5
Corporate	1.5	0.4	0	0.3	2.2
Other (b)	1.4	1.3	1.1	2.0	5.8
Total	$8.0	$3.7	$1.9	$5.0	$18.5
1981 Estimate	$1.5	$0.6	$0.3	NA	$2.4

(a) Money market securities are not included.
(b) Foreign bonds and Eurobonds.
SOURCES: Various issues of *Lehman Brothers Bond Market Reports* and *Salomon Brothers International Bond Market Analysis, 1995.*

2. Compensation for default risk.
3. Compensation for various options imbedded in the bond such as the right to call the bond prior to its stated maturity.
4. Tax and liquidity features.

Bond prices are inversely related with required yields to maturity. If YTMs increase, the market value of bonds fall; if YTMs decline, bond market values rise. And these price changes can be dramatic! In 1982, the return on long-term U.S. T-bonds was 40%—twice that year's return on U.S. common stocks. And this bond return was due solely to the fact that the YTMs on these bonds had declined from 13.4% at the start of the year to 10.5% by year-end. Clearly, a good understanding of YTMs is necessary for proper bond selection and management.

Basic Concepts

Yields to Maturity on Coupon Bonds

The yield to maturity (YTM) on a coupon bond is that interest rate which will discount future cash flows to the bond's current price. Since YTMs might be different for various maturities, we associate each yield with a given maturity as follows:

$$YTM_M = \text{yield to maturity on a bond having a maturity of } M \text{ years}$$

For a bond that pays coupons at the end of each year, the YTM_M is found by solving the following equation:

Definition of Yield to Maturity

$$P_0 = \frac{C}{(1 + YTM_M)^1} + \frac{C}{(1 + YTM_M)^2} + \cdots + \frac{C}{(1 + YTM_M)^M} + \frac{F}{(1 + YTM_M)^M} \qquad (10.1)$$

where P_0 = the current market price of the bond, C = the coupon payment received at each year-end, M = the number of years to maturity, and F = the par value of the bond.

To illustrate the formula's use, consider a five-year noncallable bond that pays a 9% coupon at the end of each year and has a $1,000 face value. If the bond is currently selling at a price of $962.10, its YTM is 10%:

$$\$962.10 = \frac{\$90}{(1 + YTM_5)^1} + \frac{\$90}{(1 + YTM_5)^2} + \frac{\$90}{(1 + YTM_5)^3} + \frac{\$90}{(1 + YTM_5)^4}$$

$$+ \frac{\$1,090}{(1 + YTM_5)^5}$$

$$= \frac{\$90}{1.1^1} + \frac{\$90}{1.1^2} + \frac{\$90}{1.1^3} + \frac{\$90}{1.1^4} + \frac{\$1,090}{1.1^5}$$

$$= \$81.82 + \$74.38 + \$67.62 + \$61.47 + \$676.81$$

Many of you will recognize the YTM as the same concept as the internal rate of return used in capital budgeting. It is a useful measure to help evaluate both historical rates of return and promised rates of return.

Bond-Pricing Theorems

Equation 10.1 specifies the relationship between bond price, coupon rate, maturity, and YTM from which the following five bond theorems have been developed. To illustrate each theorem, we examine the price of both 8% coupon bonds and 6% coupon bonds having one of three possible maturity dates: one year, five years, and ten years. Results are displayed in Figure 10-1.

1. **When the annual coupon rate and YTM are identical, a bond will always sell at par.** In Figure 10-1, this is shown as the solid horizontal lines at the par and market values of $1,000. For example, the 8% coupon rate pays $80 each year on $1,000 face value. If investors demand an annual yield of 8%, they would be willing to pay $1,000, since the $80 coupon then represents exactly what they require.

2. **Bond prices move inversely to changes in YTM.** Note in Figure 10-1 that when yields to maturity are greater than the coupon rate, the bonds sell at less than par (at a discount).[1] In such cases investors expect to receive the YTM

---

[1] **Discount bonds** are bonds that sell for less than par value (usually $1,000). **Premium bonds** are those that sell for more than par value. **Deep discount bonds** are bonds selling at sizable discounts, say, for $500 to $600.

FIGURE 10-1   RELATIONSHIP BETWEEN BOND PRICE, MATURITY, YTM AND COUPON RATE

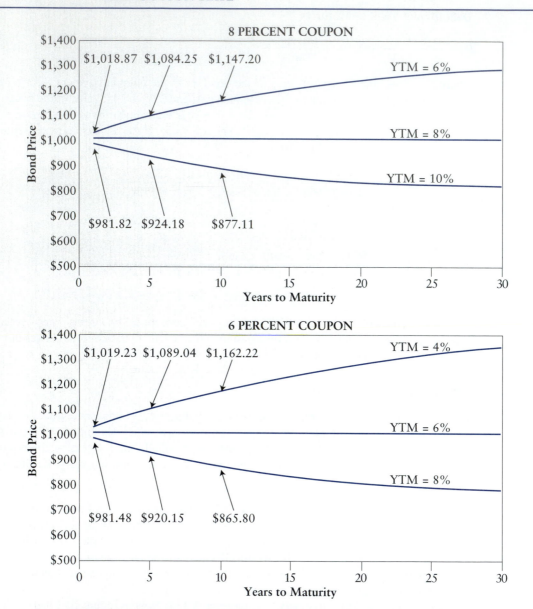

from both an annual coupon and an annual price appreciation. When the YTM is less than the coupon rate, prices will be greater than par (at a premium). Investors are then expecting a yearly return equal to the coupon payment minus an annual price depreciation.

3. **Long-term bonds are more price sensitive to a given change in the YTM than are shorter term bonds.** Note in panel A (the 8% coupon issue) that a

change in the YTM from 8% to 6% causes the one-year bond to increase in value from $1,000 to $1,018.87. The five-year bond increases from $1,000 to $1,084.25.

4. **While the price sensitivity of a bond increases with its maturity (theorem 3), this sensitivity increases at a decreasing rate.** Again refer to panel A and the shift in YTMs from 8% to 6%. Note that the one-year bond increases by $18.87, or 1.89%, whereas the five-year bond increases by $84.25, or 8.42%. The longer term bond increased by 653 basis points more (842 − 189) than the shorter term bond. However, the basis-point change is less between the ten-year and five-year issues. While the ten-year obligation increases by $147.20, or 14.72%, this is only a 630 basis-point improvement (1,472 − 842) over the five-year bond. The longer a bond's maturity, the greater its price sensitivity. But this sensitivity increases at a decreasing rate.

5. **High-coupon bonds are less price sensitive to a given YTM change than are lower coupon bonds.** To see this, examine both panels A (8% coupon) and B (6% coupon) for bonds with a ten-year maturity. If YTMs are initially 6%, the 8% coupon issue sells at a premium ($1,147.20), and the 6% issue sells at par. Now assume the YTM rises to 8%. The high coupon bond falls in price by $147.20, or 12.83%. The price of the lower coupon bond falls by $134.2, or 13.42%. The percentage price movement is greater on the low-coupon bond. (In Chapter 11, we see this coupon effect is related to the effective maturity of the bond, i.e., its duration.)

These five bond theorems play an important role in the development of the various yield curve theories as well as the management of fixed income securities.

Semiannual Interest

Most coupon bonds quote the coupon payments as if they were paid once a year, but interest is actually paid semiannually. For example, a 7% coupon, four-year bond that pays interest semiannually will provide a sequence of eight coupon payments of $35 each six months plus $1,000 at the end of four years. To value such a bond, we must think in terms of six-month periods instead of yearly periods. If the stated annual YTM is 8%, the bond's present worth would be $966.33:

$$\$966.33 = \frac{\$35}{1.04} + \frac{\$35}{1.04^2} + \frac{\$35}{1.04^3} + \cdots + \frac{\$35}{1.04^8} + \frac{\$1,000}{1.04^8}$$

When semiannual coupon payments are made, (1) the number of periods to maturity is doubled, (2) the coupon payment is half the quoted annual rate, and (3) the discount rate is half the stated annual YTM. If quarterly (or even more frequent) payments are made, adjustments similar to those involved with semiannual interest should be made.

Notice that while a stated annual YTM of 8% is used, the effective YTM is higher. The investor starts out with, say, a $1 investment on which 4 cents is earned at the end of six months. This balance of $1.04 then earns an additional 4% during the second six months. So by year-end, $1.0816 is available for each $1 invested. The effective yield is 8.16%, even though the market-quoted yield is 8%.

Value at Noninterest Dates

Equation (10.1) assumes we are finding a bond's value immediately after an interest payment date and that a full period (six months or one year, depending on coupon payment dates) remains until the next cash receipt. Bond trades, of course, are only rarely made at a coupon payment date. When trades occur at other times, accrued interest must be accounted for.

Assume you purchase a $1,000 par bond that pays $40 in coupons each six months. You buy the issue when it is first issued to the public in the primary market at a price of $1,000. Thus, your annualized YTM is 8%. Assuming interest rates do not change, the price of the bond *as quoted in the financial press* will remain $1,000. This is shown as the horizontal line in Figure 10-2.

Three months pass and you decide to sell the bond. Would you be willing to sell it for the quoted market price of $1,000? No. You owned the bond for three months and deserve to earn $20 of interest for this period of ownership. The new purchaser will pay an invoice price of $1,020. The invoice is equal to the quoted market price plus any accrued interest. In Figure 10-2, the invoice price is the jagged line, which grows to $1,040 just prior to an interest payment and falls back to $1,000 immediately after an interest payment.

Invoice prices and market quoted prices are calculated as follows:

1. Calculate the value of the bond at the next interest payment date, assuming interest has just been paid.
2. Add the next interest payment to this amount. The sum will represent the bond's value immediately prior to the next interest payment.
3. Find the present worth of this amount. This will be the invoice price.

FIGURE 10-2   INVOICE PRICE OF A COUPON BOND VERSUS MARKET QUOTE

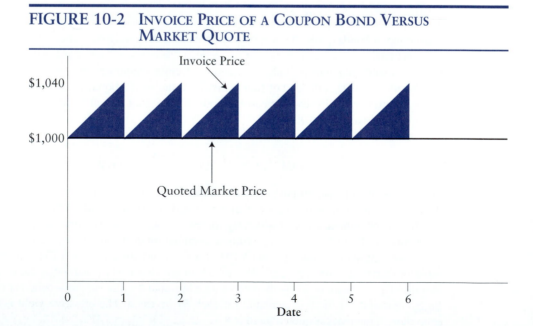

4. Subtract the interest that has accrued on the bond since the last interest payment date. This will be the quoted market price.

Consider a 10% coupon issue that matures in 10 years and 2 months. Interest is paid semiannually and investors require a quoted 8% annual *YTM*.

1. As of the next interest date, the bond will have 10 years of life remaining and should sell at $1,135.92:

$$\$1,135.92 = \sum_{t=1}^{20} \frac{\$50}{1.04^t} + \frac{\$1,000}{1.04^{20}}$$

2. Adding the $50 interest payment to be received at that time, the total value of the cash plus the security value will be $1,185.92.
3. Two months prior to this date, this sum will be worth $1,170.52. This is the invoice price.

$$\$1,170.52 = \frac{\$1,185.92}{1.04^{2/6}}$$

4. To calculate the quoted market price, accrued interest of $33.33 ($50 \times 4/6$) is subtracted from the invoice price. This results in a quoted price of $1,137.19.

Yields on Pure Discount Bonds

A pure discount bond does not pay any coupons but pays a single lump sum at its maturity. Since the only source of return on such bonds is price appreciation, they always trade at discounts from the lump sum to be received at maturity. For example, assume bond 1 and bond 2 are both pure discount bonds and mature in exactly one year and two years, respectively. If the bonds have $1,000 par values and investors desire a 5% return during the next year and a 7.5% annualized return during the next two years, the bonds will trade at the following prices:

$$\text{Bond 1 Price } \$952.38 = \frac{\$1,000}{1.05}$$

$$\text{Bond 2 Price } \$865.33 = \frac{\$1,000}{1.075^2}$$

Pure discount bonds will be of particular use in this chapter, since we will be able to use their market values to calculate a structure of underlying forward rates.

We refer to the *YTM* on a pure discount bond as I_M. It is calculated by solving the following equation:

Yield to Maturity on a Pure Discount Bond

$$P_0 = \frac{F}{(1 + I_M)^M} \tag{10.2a}$$

or

$$I_M = \left(\frac{F}{P_0}\right)^{1 \div M} - 1.0 \tag{10.2b}$$

where P_0 = the current market price of the pure discount bond, F = the bond's par value, and M = the number of years to the bond's maturity.

For example, assume we could observe the market prices of bonds 1 and 2 to be $952.38 and $865.33, respectively, but that we did not yet know their respective YTMs. Using Equation 10.2b, these yields would be calculated as follows:

$$\text{Bond 1:} \quad I_1 = \left(\frac{\$1,000}{\$952.38}\right)^{1 \div 1} - 1.0 = 0.05, \text{ or } 5\%$$

$$\text{Bond 2:} \quad I_2 = \left(\frac{\$1,000}{\$865.33}\right)^{1 \div 2} - 1.0 = 0.075, \text{ or } 7.5\%$$

YTMs calculated for coupon bonds (YTM_M) will be equal to yields to maturity of discount bonds only if the yield curve is flat. This rarely (if ever) occurs. More commonly, both yield structures tend to increase as bond maturities increase. In this case, YTM_M will be somewhat lower than I_M.

Forward Rates

At a given point in time, a set of (pure discount) yields to maturity exist for securities that are identical in all respects but maturity. We have defined this as the **term structure of interest.**

Basically, each I_M reflects the rate of return that buyers are promised if they buy the bond at current prices. The term structure depicts current, or spot, rates of interest for a given maturity. Underlying any set of yields to maturity, however, is a set of other interest rates that are referred to as implied forward rates. These forward rates play an important role in yield curve theory and in advanced investment and speculative strategies. Symbolically, we denote the forward rate as follows:

f_{Mt} = the forward rate of interest that will have an M period maturity in t years from today

For simplicity, we think of periods as being years even though periods could conceivably be of any length. Therefore:

$f_{1,0}$ = the forward rate on one-year investments as of today, that is, today's actual one-year spot rate

$f_{1,1}$ = the forward rate on one-year investments as of one year from now (start of year 2)

$f_{1,2}$ = the forward rate on one-year investments as of two years from now (start of year 3)

$f_{5,10}$ = the forward rate on five-year investments as of ten years from now (start of year 11)

Forward rates are calculated using pure discount bond yields to maturity with the following equation:

Forward Rate

$$f_{Mt} = \left[\frac{(1 + I_{t+M})^{t+M}}{(1 + I_t)^t} \right]^{1 \div M} - 1.0 \tag{10.3}$$

For example, assume that YTMs are now $I_1 = 8\%$ and $I_2 = 9\%$. This implies a forward rate on one-year investments of 10% in exactly one year from now:

$$f_{1,1} = \frac{1.09^2}{1.08^1} - 1.0 = 0.10$$

Thus, an $I_2 = 9\%$ and an $I_1 = 8\%$ imply that a one-year forward rate of return equal to 10% can be locked in (assured) today by trading in the one-year and two-year pure discount bonds.

To illustrate how an investor could lock in this 10% forward return, consider the market values of discount bonds with one- and two-year maturities. Call these bond A and bond B.

$$\text{Price of A} = \frac{\$1,000}{1.08^1} = \$925.93$$

$$\text{Price of B} = \frac{\$1,000}{1.09^2} = \$841.68$$

To lock in a one-year forward rate starting at the beginning of year 2, investors would short-sell the one-year bond and buy some multiple of the two-year bond. They will buy an amount of the two-year bond such that their initial investment in the two-year issue is identical to the cash received on the short sale of the one-year bond.

Details of the trade are shown in Table 10-2 and we can explain them as follows:

- At the start of period 1 short-sell 1.0 of bond A. This provides immediate cash inflow of $925.93, which is used to purchase 1.1 of bond B. The net cash flow at the start of period 1 will be zero.

- At the end of period 1 the short sale of bond A will have to be covered. This requires a $1,000 cash outflow. The long position of 1.1 of bond B is left untouched, so the net cash flow at the end of period 1 will be negative $1,000.

TABLE 10-2 LOCKING IN FORWARD RATES

	Cash Flows Received (Disbursed) at End of Period		
	0	1	2
1.0 Bond A	$925.93	($1,000)	—
1.1 Bond B	(925.93)	—	$1,100
Net Cash Flows	$0	(1,000)	$1,100
Return in Period 2 =	$\dfrac{\$1,100 - \$1,000}{\$1,000} = 10\%$		

■ At the end of period 2 the 1.1 of bond B will mature and provide $1,000 cash for each full bond. A net cash inflow of $1,100 will be received.

Effectively, this process allows one to be uninvested during period 1 but assured an investment during period 2 on which a 10% yield is locked in.

These examples serve to emphasize two important points. First, when thinking about interest rates we should consider existing yields as displayed in current yield curves as well as implied forward rates. *Interest rates consist of explicitly known spot rates as well as implied forward rates of interest.*

Second, *the yield to maturity on a pure discount security can be regarded as an average of many shorter term implied forward rates.* In our example, the 9.0% yield to maturity on the two-year bond B is actually an average of an immediate one-year rate of 8.0% and a forward one-year rate of 10.0%. This "average" is not an arithmetic average. Instead it is a geometric average similar to the geometric average discussed in Chapter 5.

Discount Bond Yield

$$I_M = [(1 + f_{1,0})(1 + f_{1,1})(1 + f_{1,2}) \ldots (1 + f_{1,M-1})]^{1 \div M} - 1.0 \qquad \textbf{(10.4)}$$

Using the data for the two-year bond in our example:

$$9.0\% = [(1.08)(1.10)]^{1 \div 2} - 1.0$$

Equation (10.4) is the key to understanding the three yield curve theories.

Expected Spot Rates

Earlier we defined the spot rate of interest to be the rate of return promised on a bond if an investment is made in the bond now. Spot rates are the YTM_M and I_M yields to maturity. In addition to current spot rates of interest, speculators will develop estimates of expected future spot rates. We define the expected spot rate of interest as follows:

$E(I_{Mt})$ = today's expectation of what the spot rate will be on pure discount bonds that will have an M period maturity in t years from now.

Whenever forward rates implied by the existing yield curve differ from a person's expectation of future spot rates, a speculative trade is called for. Only when forward rates are identical to expected spot rates [f_{Mt} is equal to $E(I_{Mt})$] will there be no speculative trading. We will see later that this is the basis of one yield curve theory known as the unbiased expectations theory (UET).

Yield Curve Theories

The relationship between YTMs and the maturity of a bond is known as the term structure of interest rates. Examples of the term structure (or yield curve) for U.S. Treasury securities is shown in Figure 10-3 for three different dates. Due to their low default risk, the U.S. Treasury yield curve is commonly thought of as the base on which the YTMs on other

FIGURE 10-3 Illustration of Three U.S. Treasury Yield Curves

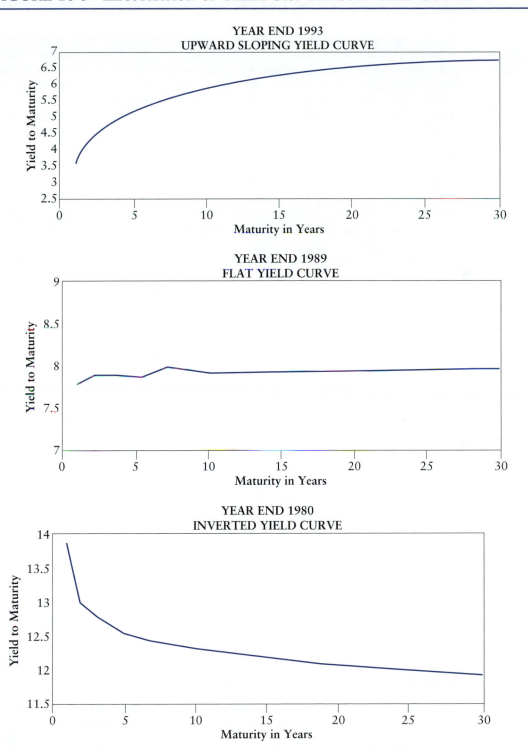

securities are founded. The curve can be an "eyeballed" best fit line or estimated using a variety of quantitative techniques.

Ideally, yield curves should be plotted for securities that are alike in all respects other than maturity. As a practical matter this is extremely difficult. All any yield curve really controls for is default risk. But securities that have similar risks of default are often substantially different in other respects—for example, in coupon rates, marketability, and callability. Such differences often cause outliers on a given yield curve.

Bonds with coupon rates below current rates of interest sell at a discount. Purchasers of such low-coupon bonds expect to earn the current rate of interest by receiving both a yearly coupon payment and a yearly price appreciation as the bond approaches face value at maturity. When this text was last revised, tax rates on ordinary income (coupons) and capital gains (price changes) were equal. For much of U.S. history and in many other countries, however, the capital gains tax rate is lower. When this is the case, the effective tax rate on low-coupon bonds is lower than the tax rate on high-coupon bonds. As a result, before-tax yields on low-coupon bonds can be lower than those on high-coupon bonds and still provide an equivalent after-tax yield.

As you can see in Figure 10-3, yield curves vary considerably over time in level and shape. Typically, they are low and upward sloping during periods of slack economic activity. During rapid business growth and full employment, they tend to be high and somewhat downward sloping. Understanding what might cause the yield curve to have a particular shape and why yield curves change over time is the purpose of this section.

Three basic theories have been used to explain the yield curve:

1. **Market segmentation theory (MST)** proponents argue that people have strong preferences about the maturity structure of their financial borrowing and lending. These preferences tend to create financial asset demand and supply conditions that are unique to each maturity segment of the yield curve. Interest rates within each segment are determined largely by current demand and supply within that segment.
2. **Unbiased expectations theory (UET)** proponents argue that arbitrageurs will seek to profit from any yield distortions between maturity segments. They will buy instruments whose yields are currently high and simultaneously sell instruments whose yields are currently low. Their trading will cause the yield on securities of differing maturities to be related. According to UET, interest rates will be determined by current as well as expected future supply and demand conditions across all maturities.
3. **Liquidity preference theory (LPT)** proponents largely accept the conclusions reached by UET but also believe that yields on long-term securities will typically be higher than yields on shorter term securities. LPT proponents argue that securities with a longer term to maturity are exposed to greater amounts of interest rate risk for which lenders will demand a compensation known as a "liquidity premium."

Market Segmentation Theory

Market segmentation theory (MST) states that economic units which demand or supply financial resources have maturity preferences (referred to as preferred habitats) that effectively create a number of somewhat independent market segments. Conventionally, these segments are referred to as short-term (less than one year), intermediate-term (one through five years), and long-term (greater than five years). For example, on the supply side, commercial banks prefer to lend short-term, savings and loans prefer intermediate-term lending, and life insurance companies prefer long-term investments. On the demand side, consumer finance firms prefer to borrow short-term, retailers finance cyclical inventory and receivable growth with intermediate-term borrowing, and plant expansion is typically financed with long-term security sales. MST states that the shape and movement of the yield curve are determined by levels of current financial supply and demand within each market segment.

Maturity Preferences. Why do economic units have preferred habitats? The answer is simple—to minimize risk. To minimize risk exposure, the average maturities of investments and financing should be equal. In Chapter 11, this statement is modified slightly when we discuss the concept of **duration,** which is simply the average date at which cash flows are received. By matching the duration of assets and liabilities investors can minimize interest rate risk.

Strictly applied, MST suggests that this creates a level of financial supply and demand unique to each particular investment maturity range. Maturity preferences are so strong that participants in any one segment are unlikely to leave that segment for better yields within other market segments. Thus, the yield curve would be determined solely by current demand and supply conditions within each market segment.

Few believers in MST apply the concept in such a strict manner. While market participants may have clear maturity preferences, a certain flexibility exists that allows trading between adjacent segments. In addition, a large number of individuals who are indifferent to maturity will arbitrage rates between markets. The operations of these arbitrageurs are discussed later. Rates between various segments will thus be related to some extent. Nonetheless, proponents of MST argue that the dominant force which shifts the yield curve is a change in financial demand and supply within imprecisely defined maturity ranges. But even in this less strict version yield curves are essentially *created by current demand and supply conditions.*

To illustrate the reasoning underlying MST, we will trace its logic in explaining shifts in the yield curve during a period of economic recovery and expansion. Figure 10-4 shows yield curves for three stages of business activity. Starting with the trough of a business recession, the yield curve is reasonably flat for all but the shortest maturity instruments. Such short-term instruments are what firms rely on to provide liquidity needs. The low level of economic activity will cause businesses to accumulate large liquidity reserves instead of reinvesting operating fund flows in unneeded inventory, receivables, and plant. The desire for increased liquidity is reinforced by businesses' attempts to guard against short-term insolvency problems that might be brought on by the recession. The net result will be a large supply of funds to the money market, causing very low short-term rates. As business activity begins to pick up, excess liquidity is spent on working capital and plant additions. In addition, total demand for credit increases across all maturity segments. This causes short-term money market rates to rise substantially while there are less dramatic rate increases across all maturity segments. Finally, as business activity moves toward the peak of the economic recovery, rates are the highest in the

FIGURE 10-4   MST AND THE BUSINESS CYCLE

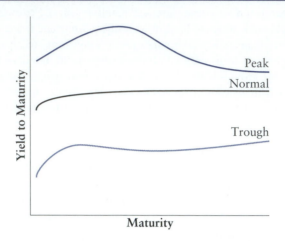

intermediate-maturity range in response to large demands for credit needed to support the cyclical expansion in receivable and inventory balances. According to MST, each shift in the yield curve is caused by a change in the current supply and demand for credit within a given maturity segment.

Unbiased Expectations Theory

Arbitrage in a Segmented Market. In a segmented market, yields to maturity are effectively created by current supply and demand conditions within each segment. If one is able to forecast changes in future supply and demand, considerable opportunity for arbitrage may exist. In a market setting such as that of MST, this shouldn't be too difficult. Consider the movement of the yield curve over the course of a business cycle. If one believes in a segmented market, a repeated pattern of yield curves will exist coincident with normal business expansion and retraction. If this is so, bonds should be bought at the peak of the economic activity (to obtain large capital gains as yields eventually fall) and sold short at the trough of a recession (to gain from price declines incurred as interest rates rise and the economy expands).

To understand the possibilities for arbitrage, consider the following example. Three pure discount bonds of different maturities exist: one year, two years, and three years. We are now at date 1, a period of normal business activity. Yields to maturity on each of three bonds can be observed as prevailing market rates at date 1. These known I_M's are shown in Figure 10-5 as the solid line. Date 2 is expected to be the peak of the economic expansion, with rather high interest rates, particularly on bonds that mature two years after the start of date 2. Date 3 represents the trough of a recession with commensurately low interest rates. I_M's expected at dates 2 and 3 are shown in Figure 10-5 as the dashed lines. To complete the example, two added facts are helpful. First, we assume the various bonds are discount bonds; that is, they pay no intermediate coupons.

FIGURE 10-5 YIELD CURVES TO BE ARBITRAGED

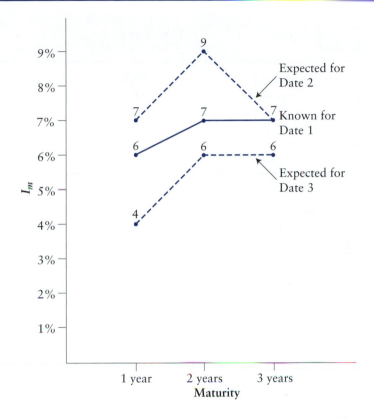

The purchaser's sole return will come from capital appreciation. Second, the arbitrageurs are willing to make up to a three-year commitment at date 1. They will not consider the purchase of three-year bonds at date 2 or two-year bonds at date 3. Both of these assumptions ease the analysis considerably but do not change the essence of the conclusions.

If arbitrageurs are willing to place their money at risk for three years, they could follow any one of a number of plans. For example, they could simply buy one three-year bond at date 1. Alternatively, they could mix a sequence of three one-year bonds or a two-year bond plus a subsequent one-year bond, and so forth. Being indifferent to bond maturity, the arbitrageurs will select a policy that is expected to maximize their total three-year return. Table 10-3 lists the various possible strategies together with the third-year expected wealth of placing $1 into a given strategy at date 1. Clearly, a strategy of buying a one-year bond at date 1 followed by a two-year bond at date 2 will yield the largest expected profit. The lowest expected total return would be received if a sequence of three one-year bonds were purchased.

Earlier in the chapter we examined how arbitrageurs might lock in a future interest rate. This concept applies directly to this example. Note that of the four strategies in Table 10-3,

TABLE 10-3 Arbitrage Strategies and Profits

Strategy	Year 3 Expected Wealth per $1 Investment at Date 1	Rank	Details of Calculation
A. One 3-year bond	$1.225	2	$1.07 \times 1.07 \times 1.07$
B. Three 1-year bonds	$1.180	4	$1.06 \times 1.07 \times 1.04$
C. One 2-year bond followed by a 1-year bond	$1.190	3	$1.07 \times 1.07 \times 1.04$
D. One 1-year bond followed by a 2-year bond	$1.259	1	$1.06 \times 1.09 \times 1.09$

those that involve purchase of a one-year bond at date 3 are ranked lowest. Arbitrageurs are capable of making larger profits in year 3 than the expected 4% one-year spot yield for that period. For example, the strategy of buying 1.07 three-year bonds at date 1 and short-selling 1.0 two-year bond at date 1 will yield a 7% locked-in return during year 3. Details of this calculation are as follows:

Market Value at Start of Year 1

2-year bond	$1,000 \div 1.07^2 = \$873.44$
3-year bond	$1,000 \div 1.07^3 = \$816.29$

Arbitrage Cash Flows at Year-End

Strategy	0	1	2	3
Short-sell 1.0 2-year bond	$873.44	—	($1,000)	—
Buy 1.07 3-year bonds	($873.44)	—		$1,070
Net cash flows	0	0	($1,000)	$1,070
				7% yield in year 3

There are a host of ways in which people can arbitrage in a segmented market. But the techniques are less important at this point in our discussion than is the idea. As long as the yield curve is determined by current demand and supply conditions, considerable arbitrage profits are available simply by making reasonable estimates of future demand and supply conditions.

Effects of a Fully Arbitraged Market. What would happen to interest rates if arbitrage was extensive? First, attempts by arbitrageurs to obtain speculative profits would eliminate all such profits. Bonds that provided large yields would be actively bought, driving their prices up and yields down. Bonds that provided insufficient yields would be actively sold, driving their prices down and yields up. Soon all possible profit opportunities would disappear. Second, long-term interest rates would be a geometric average of the current short-term spot rate and the market's consensus estimate of expected future spot rates. This theory of a fully arbitraged market, referred to earlier as the unbiased expectations theory (UET), was initially discussed by Irving Fisher and later developed by Friedrich Lutz.

According to proponents of UET, the relationship between long- and short-term rates can be written as follows:

Future Value of $1

$$[1 + I_M]^M = [1 + I_1] [1 + E(I_{11})] [1 + E(I_{12})] \ldots [1 + E(I_{1M-1})] \qquad \textbf{(10.5)}$$

where I_M equals the yield to maturity on a pure discount bond maturing in M years, and $E(I_{1t})$ equals the market's consensus forecast of expected one-year spot rates t years from today. This means, for example, that the terminal wealth expected from purchasing a 10-year pure discount bond should be the same as the expected terminal wealth on a sequence of 10 one-year bonds.

Expected Terminal Wealth on a 10-Year Bond	Expected Terminal Wealth on a Sequence of 10 One-Year Bonds
$[1 + I_{10}]^{10}$	$= [1 + I_1] [1 + E(I_{11})] [1 + E(I_{12})] \ldots [1 + E(I_{19})]$

In addition, there is no particular reason to restrict the explanation to one-year forward rates. For example, the terminal wealth expected on a 10-year bond should be equal to the terminal wealth expected from first buying a six-year bond and then buying a four-year bond.

Expected Terminal Wealth on a 10-Year Bond	Expected Terminal Wealth on a 6-Year Bond Followed by a 4-Year Bond	
	6-Year Bond	4-Year Bond
$[1 + I_{10}]^{10} =$	$\dfrac{[1 + I_6]^6}{[1 + I_1] [1 + E(I_{11})] \ldots [1 + E(I_{15})]}$	$\times \dfrac{[1 + E(I_{4,6})]^4}{[1 + E(I_{16})] \ldots [1 + E(I_{19})]}$

Consider the following numerical example. Today, the start of year 1, the yield to maturity on a one-year bond is known to be 6.0%. Somehow a market consensus is developed that the expected one-year spot rate at the start of year 2 will be 6.5% and the one-year spot rate at the start of year 3 will be 7.0%:

Start of Year	Expected 1-Year Bond Rate at Start of Year	
1	6.0%	Known—today's 1-year rate
2	6.5% ⎫	
3	7.0% ⎭	Expected spot rates

By investing \$1 at the start of year 1 in a one-year bond, \$1.06 would be received at the end of the year. Reinvesting this \$1.06 at the start of year 2 would yield \$1.129 by the end of year 2 (1.06 × 1.065). By the end of year 3, \$1.208 would be available (1.129 × 1.07). The terminal wealth on a three-year bond would have to equal exactly \$1.208 per dollar invested or arbitrage profits would be available. Thus, $(1 + I_3)^3 = 1.208$. The annual yield to maturity on the three-year bond would be the geometric average of the three yearly returns:

$$[1.208]^{1 \div 3} - 1.0 = 6.5\%$$

Using the same data:

- ◼ the YTM of a two-year bond today would be 6.25% $([(1.06)(1.065)]^{1 \div 2} - 1.0)$.

- ◼ the expected YTM of a two-year bond starting at the beginning of year 2 would be 6.75% $([(1.065)(1.07)]^{1 \div 2} - 1.0$.

- ◼ the expected YTM of a one-year bond starting at the beginning of year 3 would be 7.0% (by definition).

Determinants of Discount Bond Yield to Maturity

$$I_M = \{[1 + I_{0\,1}][1 + E(I_{11})][1 + E(I_{12})] \ldots [1 + E(I_{1,\,M-1})]\}^{1 \div M} - 1 \qquad (10.6)$$

The YTM on a bond maturing at the end of period M is equal to the geometric mean of expected yields on a sequence of shorter term bonds with equal maturity.[2]

A major implication of UET is that the forward rates implied in the yield curve are the same as the market's consensus forecast of expected future spot rates; that is, UET states:

Forward Rates = Expected Spot Rates

$$f_{Mt} = E(I_{Mt}) \qquad (10.7)$$

For example, if a five-year bond is currently yielding 9% to maturity and a four-year bond has an 8.7% YTM, then the implied one-year expected spot rate per UET at the start of year 5 would be 10.21%:

$$0.1021 = \frac{1.09^5}{1.087^4} - 1.0 = \frac{1.5386}{1.3961} - 1.0$$

Implications of UET. If UET is strictly correct, any speculative profits that might have existed under MST will have been fully arbitraged away. Returns on the next speculative transaction will be zero. If UET is not strictly correct, some speculative profits will be available for the first group of speculators who act on new information. But they must act

---

[2] Again, this equation is strictly true only for pure discount bonds. It is approximate for coupon obligations.

quickly, before their information is incorporated into existing interest rates. The unbiased expectations theory is the same as the efficient market theory, but it is EMT applied to only a narrow set of securities: debt instruments.

In addition, the return *expected* for a given holding period does not depend on the maturity of the instrument purchased. For example, if you intend to invest for a one-year period, the return you can expect will be identical whether you (1) buy a sequence of one-month instruments, (2) buy a one-year instrument, (3) buy a 20-year instrument and sell it a year from now, or (4) choose some other approach. This is true for any desired holding period.

Finally, all that is known about the likely course of future interest rates is already incorporated into present yield curves. The best predictor of future interest rates is today's yield curve. Individuals using sophisticated econometric models or simple intuition will be unable to predict future interest rates any better than individuals who use today's yield curve. This doesn't mean the yield curve is an accurate predictor of future interest rates. It only means that nothing better is available. Forward rates of interest implicit in the yield curve are unbiased estimates of expected future spot rates.[3]

Expected Inflation and Nominal Risk-Free Rates. According to a strict version of the unbiased expectations theory, a major determinant of a yield curve's shape is expectations of future inflation. For example, assume a real rate of 2% is deemed to be fair during all future years. Knowing this together with expected annual future rates of inflation, we can estimate both expected spot rates and yields to maturity on bonds of varying maturities. For example, assume you have developed the following data:

Start of Year	Desired Real Rate	+	Expected Inflation During Year	=	Expected Spot Rate	Implying a Current *IM* of
1	2%		5%		7%	7.00%
2	2%		8%		10%	8.49%
3	2%		6%		8%	8.33%
4	2%		4%		6%	7.74%

You may recognize that this relationship is simply Irving Fisher's theory about the determinants of nominal risk-free rates:[4]

Nominal Risk-Free Rate

$$RF_t = r^* + E(I_t) \tag{10.8}$$

RF_t stands for the nominal yield to maturity on a risk-free bond that matures in t years.

---

[3] Cox, Ingersoll, and Ross have demonstrated that if the risk-free rate is stochastic (uncertain over time), logical inconsistencies exist in UET. In particular, they show it is impossible for expected holding period returns for various maturities to be identical at the same time that forward rates are unbiased estimates of expected future spot rates. We bypass a discussion of their argument because of its highly technical nature and because any errors that arise in UET appear to be slight.

[4] Equation (10.8) is modified version of Equation (5.1). The interaction term between the future inflation rate and the real rate is dropped, since its size is negligible.

Market segmentation theory explains changes in the level and shape of the yield curve during the course of a business cycle as the result of changes in current demand and supply conditions within various market segments. According to UET, the overall level of the yield curve shifts as a result of two forces: (1) changes in the expectations of future demand and supply conditions across all market segments, and (2) changes in expected rates of inflation. During a business upswing, the yield curve will rise if market participants revise their expectations about future demand for and supply of funds or revise their expectations about future inflation.

Liquidity Premiums

In some respects, liquidity preference theory (LPT) is a refined version of the market segmentation theory. In its most general form, LPT states that borrowers and lenders have preferred maturity habitats but can be induced to trade in other maturity segments if offered an inducement to do so in the form of a higher rate of return. This yield inducement is referred to as a liquidity premium.

When LPT was originally developed, its proponents stated that lenders of funds (who are typically households) prefer to lend short term, whereas borrowers (who are typically corporations) prefer to borrow long term. As a result, the original proponents of liquidity preference believed lenders would demand a premium to be enticed to invest their funds long term. Investors in long term obligations would earn a higher yield than would investors who insisted on short-term securities. Borrowers would have to pay a higher interest rate to borrow long term than if they borrowed short term.

Proponents of liquidity preference argue that the implied forward rate is actually composed of the expected spot rate plus a liquidity premium. Symbolically:

Implied Forward Rate

$$f_{Mt} = E(I_{Mt}) + l_{Mt} \tag{10.9}$$

where f_{Mt} = the implied forward rate on a pure discount bond with a maturity of M years in t years from now, $E(I_{Mt})$ = the expected spot rate on a bond with a maturity of M years in t years from now, and l_{Mt} = the liquidity premium associated with a bond with a maturity of M years in t years from now.

The only difference between the LPT and UET models is whether a liquidity premium exists. For example, assume the yields to maturity on (pure discount) bonds maturing at the end of years 5 and 6 are 8.7% and 9.0%, respectively. The implied one-year forward rate at the beginning of year 6 would be 10.5%:

$$\frac{1.09^6}{1.087^5} - 1.0 = 10.5\%$$

According to UET, the expected one-year spot rate for year 6 is 10.5%. However, LPT would say that the expected spot rate is slightly lower than 10.5% by the amount of the liquidity premium.

The early developers of liquidity preference believed lenders preferred to lend short term whereas borrowers preferred to borrow long term. As a result, all liquidity premiums

FIGURE 10-6   EFFECTS OF LIQUIDITY PREMIUM ON IMPLIED FORWARD RATES

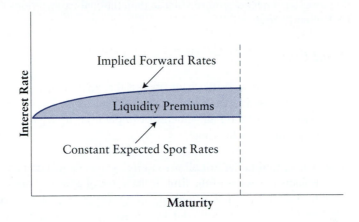

would be positive and the yield curve would provide upwardly biased estimates of expected spot rates. Figure 10-6 depicts the difference between the two models for the case of constant expected spot rates. Liquidity premiums are all positive, causing implied forward rates to be greater than expected spot rates. As a result, the actual yield curve observed in the financial press will be upward sloping even though spot rates are not expected to change.

Volatility of Long-Term Interest Rates

Both UET and LPT state that the long-term interest rate is an average of current and rationally expected future short-term rates (plus liquidity premiums in LPT). This has an important empirical implication. Since long-term rates are averages of short-term rates, the series of long-term interest rates that we observe as time passes should be less volatile than the time series of short-term rates. Long moving averages tend to smooth out the series averaged. Thus, if we were to plot the historical time series of short-term and long-term rates, the long-term rates should be much less volatile.

This simply is not the case. Although long-term rates have been somewhat less volatile than short-term rates, long-term rates have been more volatile than naive versions of either theory would imply.

Three explanations have been offered: (1) changes in desired real returns as time passes, (2) varying liquidity premiums as time passes, and (3) investor overreaction to changes in short-term rates. The first two explanations could conceivably explain the large volatility of long-term rates in the context of either UET or LPT models. In fact, even a casual observation of short-term interest rates suggests that desired real returns do change. There have been many periods in which the expected real returns on T-bills have been zero or negative. Similarly, there have been many periods in which large positive real returns could have been easily forecast on T-bills. Changing liquidity premiums are more difficult to measure. But if the large volatility in long-term rates is to be explained by changes in desired real returns and liquidity premiums, the changes in these variables must be much larger than most scholars have thought was true in the past. It is possible that long-term rates are more volatile than rational expectations models such as UET and LPT would allow.

Bond Options

Most fixed income securities have options that allow either the issuer or the owner to alter the series of cash flow payments over the bond's life. These options are either explicitly stated in bond indenture agreements or implicit in the legal system. The more important options include the following:

■ The **option to default** allows equity owners to declare bankruptcy and give debt holders the assets of the firm. If the value of a firm's assets is less then what has been promised to debt holders, equity owners may default on part or all of the cash flows they have promised debt holders. This is an implicit option created by our legal system. Under our legal system, equity owners of a firm can lose 100% of their investment in a firm. But they are not required to invest additional capital in order to guarantee payments to bond owners.

■ The **option to call** allows the borrower to repay bond principal before its scheduled maturity. This is an explicit option. Terms of the call are specified in the contract between the bond issuer and bond holders (the indenture). Most bonds are callable.

■ The **option to convert** allows owners of the bond to exchange the bond for other securities of the firm (usually common stock). This is also an explicit option with terms specified in the indenture agreement. Relatively few bonds are convertible.

The rest of the chapter discusses the effects of each of these options on bond values.

The Option to Default

Two Ways of Viewing Risky Debt

Default risk is the possibility that promised coupon and par values of a bond will not be paid. For example, in the early 1980s, the Washington Public Power Supply System defaulted on $2.5 billion of bonds that had been sold to finance nuclear power plants in the state of Washington. Although each WPPSS (as in whoops) bond had promised very specific payments to owners, it was clear investors had to expect much less. When the potential for default exists, one's expected return will be less than the bond's promised yield to maturity.

Default risk is best understood from the viewpoint of option theory. For example, consider the following simple example, which is depicted graphically in Figure 10-7. The equity owners form a corporation financed in part by the sale of risky debt. The debt

FIGURE 10-7 RISKY DEBT VIEWED FROM OPTION THEORY AT MATURITY

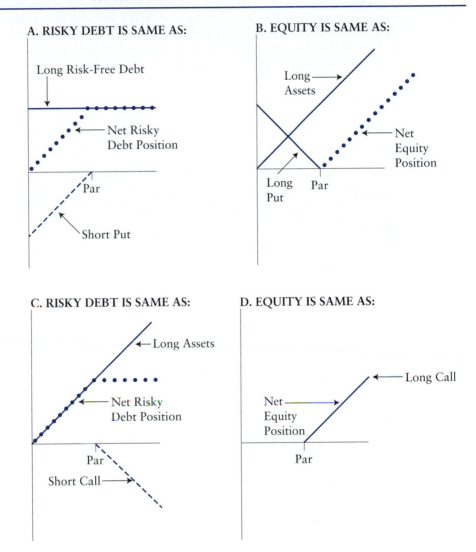

holders are promised a single future payment (the debt's par value). When this par value is due to be paid, the equity owners have an option. They can either pay the par value to debt holders, or they can turn the assets over to the debt holders and declare bankruptcy.

Essentially the equity position in the firm represents the ownership of two things: the assets of the firm and a put option that allows the equity owners the ability to sell the assets to debt holders at par. This way of viewing default risk is shown in panels A and B of the figure. In panel A, risky debt represents a portfolio of a long position in risk-free debt and a short put (which has been sold to equity owners). Equity has a long asset and a long put position.

Panels C and D provide an alternative way of viewing risky debt. In panel C, the debt owner has a portfolio consisting of long assets and a short call on the assets (sold to equity owners). Equity owners shown in panel D have a long call position on the assets of the firm.

Considering debt that faces the possibility of default from the view of option theory is more than an interesting intellectual exercise. *Option theory is the key to valuation of risky debt.*

Suppose debt having a par value of $50 is due in 1 year. The (continuously compound) risk-free interest rate is 10% per annum. The current value of the assets are $70, and the standard deviation of annualized returns on the assets is 70%. If the debt were risk free, it would be worth $45.45:

$$\$45.45 = \$50 \div 1.1$$

The $70 asset value today will be shared between the equity and debt holders. Since the equity position is the same as a 1-year call on the firm's assets, we can use option valuation models to value the equity and then back into the value of the debt![5] Based on the data in this example, the call's value would be $28. Thus, the bond's value 1 year before maturity would be $42 ($70 − $28). Notice that this is $3.45 lower than the value of a 1-year risk-free security. Also observe that the yield to maturity on the risky debt is 19%.

$$0.19 = (\$50 \div \$42) - 1$$

Thus, the default risk premium in this example is 9 percentage points.

Rating Agencies

The default risks of most actively traded bonds are rated by various independent organizations. Standard & Poor's and Moody's are the largest of these rating agencies, concentrating on corporate and municipal issues. Fitch's is a smaller organization that concentrates on institutional issues. These ratings reflect each agency's opinion about an issue's potential default, not its relative investment merits. Table 10-4 presents a summary of the ratings used by Moody's and S&P.

Not only do the ratings provide an opinion about the default risk of an issue, but they are often used to define allowable bond purchases for some investors. For example, the Comptroller of the Currency has stated that bank investments must be **investment grade.** Historically, the comptroller has defined investment grade to include bonds rated in the top four rankings (BBB or better). In addition, legal lists of approved bonds are used in some states to identify bonds that regulated savings banks, trust companies, and insurance

---

[5] Option valuation is discussed in Chapter 17. The equity option value of $28 in this example is based on the Black-Scholes option pricing model. In actual practice, it is difficult to use option theory to price bond default risk because of the complexities of real-world bonds that include coupon payments, sinking funds, and call provisions.

TABLE 10-4   CORPORATE BOND RATINGS

Standard & Poor's	Moody's	
AAA	Aaa	highest quality
AA+	Aa1	high quality
AA	Aa2	
AA−	Aa3	
A+	A1	upper medium quality
A	A2	
A−	A3	
BBB+	Baa1	medium quality
BBB	Baa2	
BBB−	Baa3	
BB+	Ba1	speculative
BB	Ba2	
BB−	Ba3	
B+	B1	very speculative
B	B2	
B−	B3	
CCC	Caa	poor quality; may be in default
CC	Ca	highly speculative
C	C	poorest quality
D		in default

companies may purchase. These legal lists rely on ratings by Moody's and Standard & Poor's. Rating designations in addition to those shown in Table 10-4 are sometimes used to more accurately reflect an agency's opinion. For example, Standard & Poor's will occasionally indicate a (+) or (−) on ratings between AA and BB. Moody's will apply A1 and Baa1 to the better quality municipals within the A and Baa categories. Nonrated issues are designated NR.

To evaluate a bond's potential for default, rating agencies rely on a committee analysis of the issuer's ability to repay, willingness to repay, and protective provisions for an issue. Ratings given by Moody's and S&P for a particular issue will usually be identical. When a difference does exist, it will be no larger than one grade and reflect the relative strength or weakness of each agency's opinion.

Issuers of bonds pay the rating agencies a fee to rate their issues.

The Historical Accuracy of Ratings

With a few important exceptions, the ratings assigned by S&P and Moody's have closely followed actual historical default rates. In a thorough study of corporate bonds issued

John L. Schiavetta, C.F.A

Senior Director
Fitch Investors Service
Bates College, B.A.

As senior director of the managed fund ratings group, John Schiavetta is responsible for all aspects of the fund ratings group, including rating criteria, portfolio risk models, individual ratings, and business development. Prior to joining Fitch in 1992, Schiavetta spent eight years with the mutual fund and pension services division of CDA Technologies, Inc., a performance evaluation firm. He began his career with the Dreyfus Corporation, working with institutional cash management products.

Q: What is a "nationally recognized statistical rating organization," and what does it do?

A: The role of rating agencies in the capital markets is to provide accurate and widely accessible assessments of investment risk. By providing these services, rating agencies bring liquidity to the markets, help to level the playing field for investors with varying amounts of resources to devote to research, and lower the cost of capital to issuers. Traditionally, these risk assessments have been limited to credit risks. Developments in structured finance and financial engineering call for rating agencies to broaden their scope. For example, several incidents during 1994 illustrate that many institutions, especially smaller government investors, did not have the resources to analyze certain of the volatile but high-credit quality issues they purchased. The clients assumed that the high-credit quality of the government-backed securities in the portfolio implied low risk.

Q: What changes have occurred in the fixed income markets to cause increasing concerns about risks?

A: The composition of the fixed income markets has shifted dramatically during the past two decades. Corporate bonds declined as a percentage of the market at the same time that mortgage-backed and other asset-backed securities were introduced as new security types. These structured financings now represent a significant portion of the total fixed income market. More recently, issuers and investors have been introduced to structured notes that provide cash flows derived from various indexes, reference rates, or asset prices. These notes are structured to meet investor preferences and reduce funding costs to issuers.

Securities like collateralized mortgage obligations (CMOs) and structured notes are two examples of derivative securities that essentially are traditional fixed income securities with embedded derivative features. Because of their structured cash flows, some of these securities respond with greater sensitivity to changes in interest rates, repayment speeds, or other factors, resulting in increased price volatility relative to traditional securities. Some instruments that incorporate significant amounts of leverage, such as mortgages, or municipal inverse floaters, are more price volatile and subject to higher levels of market risk than the underlying securities on which they are based. Their increased optionality requires portfolio managers and analysts to use new tools to evaluate possible/probable results. The inclusion of these types of securities in investment portfolios, such as bond mutual funds, can alter the portfolios' performance and risk profile dramatically.

Q: What strategies are rating agencies employing to keep up with the changing fixed income environment?

A: All of these innovations in bond structures do present a challenge to rating agencies. The majority of structured securities either are issued by "AAA"-rated or government agencies or are structured with credit enhancements to achieve high ratings. For example, the majority of CMOs and structured notes are issued by U.S. government agencies. In some cases, the optionality of the cash flows becomes the major risk consideration, yet this is wholly unaddressed by credit ratings alone. Indeed, less informed investors may

misconstrue a high credit rating as applying generally to all risks. Increasingly, rating agencies are asked for their independent view of the noncredit-related risks of securities and investment portfolios. The experience of 1994 also demonstrates that rating agencies must intensify their analysis of market risks, both for individual securities and for investment portfolios, when conducting their traditional municipal and corporate bond rating functions. Exposure to market risks through excessive leverage, derivative and illiquid securities, and liquidity mismatches can exert significant pressure on a government entity's overall credit quality. Traditionally, most mutual fund evaluation services have relied on historical performance rankings and historical volatilities, while perhaps also examining risk-adjusted performance. Unfortunately, favorable market trends often mask dormant risks. In response, Fitch developed "market risk" ratings. Each CMO tranche is evaluated using two risk measures—price volatility and cash flow volatility. A tranche's price volatility score is determined by examining the bond's price behavior across several simulated interest rate paths. The price volatility score captures the degree to which a tranche exhibits risk characteristics, such as negative convexity and leverage coupon risk, as well as the tranche's modified duration. The tranche's cash flow volatility score is calculated based on the variability of the tranche's weighted average life under severe stress scenarios. The cash flow volatility score captures the degree to which the prepayment risk of the underlying mortgage collateral has been leveraged or mitigated in tranche backed by that collateral.

Market risk rankings, like credit ratings, help inform all types of investors. They also can facilitate the marketing of particular securities to investors and the marketing of investment management services, lowering the cost of raising capital or of gathering assets. Like any quantitative measure, it is our goal that the market risk ratings be easily understood by the average investor and also be used to facilitate comparison of relative risk across funds.

between 1900 and 1943, Hickman examined by rating category the proportion of bonds that defaulted. Nine rating categories were used, with the following results:

Rating Category	Comparable S & P Rating	Percentage of Par Value Defaulting Prior to Maturity
I	AAA	6%
II	AA	6
III	A	13
IV	BBB	19
V–IX	Below BBB	42

SOURCE: W. B. Hickman, *Corporate Bond Quality and Investor Experience* (Princeton, NJ: Princeton University Press, 1958).

The two highest rated categories experienced similar and relatively low default rates. As the ratings decreased, the default rate increased.

Hickman also examined the actual realized YTMs on bonds of each rating and compared them with promised yields. If investors properly assess future rates of default, the difference between promised and realized yields should reflect the expected default rates. For each bond he calculated a realized annual return based on buying the bond at its issue price, receiving the sequence of coupons actually paid, and obtaining the terminal value of the bond when it reached maturity, defaulted, or was called. Results of this analysis are shown in Table 10-5. Surprisingly, Hickman found that realized YTMs exceeded promised YTMs. This occurred because during the period he studied, interest rates fell, resulting in a large number of bonds being called as issuers took advantage of lower rates. When the original issues were called, investors received a call premium above par and thus a higher realized return than promised. Consequently, Hickman's realized yields were unduly influenced by interest rate movements during his study period.

To correct for this, Fraine and Mills substituted promised yields for realized yields whenever realized yields were larger. Their results are shown in the far right column of Table 10-5. When modified by Fraine and Mills, promised yields exceeded realized yields, and the difference increased for the lower default ratings.

TABLE 10-5   REALIZED YTM BY RATING

Rating Category	Average Promised YTM	Realized YTM	
		Hickman	Fraine/Mills
I	4.5%	5.1%	4.3
II	4.6	5.0	4.3
III	4.9	5.0	4.3
IV	5.4	5.7	4.5
V–IX	9.5	8.6	NA

SOURCES: W. B. Hickman, *Corporate Bond Quality and Investor Experience* (Princeton, NJ: Princeton University Press, 1958); H. Fraine and R. Mills, "The Effect of Defaults and Credit Deterioration on Yields of Corporate Bonds," *Journal of Finance*, 16, (3), September 1961.

Junk Bonds

A **junk bond** is a high-default risk, high-yield bond. There are two ways a bond can become a junk bond. Many were financially sound when originally issued but became high risk over time as the financial condition of the issuer deteriorated (fallen angels). Other bonds were quite risky at the time of issue. These bonds are almost always uncollateralized and subordinated to other debt that a firm has outstanding. Junk bonds of this type became popular in the mid-1980s when Drexel Burnham Lambert used them to help finance leveraged buyouts and mergers.

Junk bonds have always played a role in bond trading but became much more common in the 1980s. For example, the average market value of newly issued bonds rated B or CCC during the 1970s was $322 million. This contrasts with total new issue value (B or CCC grade) in 1986 of $25.9 billion! In the mid-1990s, junk bonds represented about 15% of the value of publicly traded corporate bonds in the United States.

The attraction of junk bonds was the large promised return. Many studies have attempted to determine whether promised yields on junk bonds are larger than necessary given the actual default experience of the bonds. Researchers have faced two problems. Many of the bonds have not been outstanding long enough to develop a reliable estimate of their default experience. In addition, these bonds are inactively traded, so reliable prices are difficult to develop. A study by Cornell and Green suggests that returns on mutual funds which specialize in low-grade corporate bonds are approximately equal to the returns on an index of high-grade bonds. They also found that low-grade bond fund returns are sensitive to stock returns. In short, realized yields on diversified portfolios of low-grade bonds are similar to those of investment-grade securities in that they do not provide excess returns.

Yield Spreads

Yield spreads are often calculated for bonds of equivalent maturity. For example, if two bonds with ten-year maturities are selling at promised YTMs of 8% and 9.5%, respectively, the yield spread between the two is 150 basis points.

FIGURE 10-8   ILLUSTRATION OF PAST YIELD SPREADS

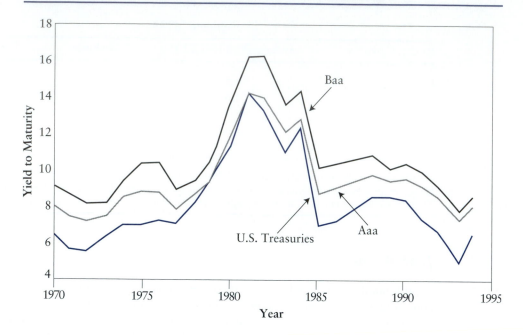

Yield spreads are typically plotted over some historical time period for bonds of similar maturity but differing default risk. For example, promised yields to maturity are shown in Figure 10-8 for U.S. Treasury bonds as well as Aaa grade and Baa grade corporate bonds. During bad economic times, there is a tendency for yield spreads to widen, more so for Baa than Aaa issues.

The Option to Call

Call Impacts on Yields

Virtually all corporate bonds and a large percentage of municipal bonds may be retired prior to formal maturity by exercise of a call provision. Issuers will call an issue if the present value of future coupon savings associated with refunding the issue offsets the costs of doing so. To the investor the effects of a call are twofold. First, the realized return during the time span for which the bond has been held will be larger than promised because principal repayment occurs earlier than anticipated and because a call premium is typically received. Second, when the bond is called, reinvestment of the call proceeds must be made at a lower rate of return than available on the original issue. On net, the second effect offsets the first, and the realized return over the horizon is lower than if the issue had not been called.

Assume you bought a ten-year, AAA, 10% coupon bond in 1995 at a promised and expected YTM of 10% (no default risk). You anticipate holding the bond for the full ten years and do not expect a change in the yield curve from 10%. Since coupons are expected to be reinvested at 10%, a 10% realized return is expected. For five years you are correct, but at the start of year 6 the yield curve drops dramatically, and the issuer calls each bond at a price of $1,050. At that date the best yield available on five-year bonds of equivalent risk is 6%.

Your realized return on the initial issue for the five years it was held will be a fine 10.67%:

$$0.1067 = \sqrt[5]{\frac{\$1,660.51}{\$1,000}} - 1.0$$

where:

Year 5 Investment Value	=	Call Price	+	Total Coupons Received	+	Interest on Interest
$1,660.51		$1,050		$500		$110.51

However, if the yield curve does not change from 6%, your realized return between years 6 and 10 will be 6%. During the full ten years, your average annual realized return will be about 8.31%:

$$8.31\% = \sqrt[10]{(1.1067^5)(1.06^5)} - 1.0$$

The low investment rate available after the call causes your ten-year realized yield to be less than promised. Naturally, investors do not like the call privilege and will request larger promised yields if call is likely.

The fact that realized yields are often less than promised yields on callable bonds does not mean such bonds are poor investments. As with their view of default risk, investors recognize that realized yields may be less than promised, and they adjust prices downward so they expect to receive a fair return. To date, research on callable bonds suggests the following:

✖ Callable bonds sell at higher promised yields than noncallable issues.

✖ Immediately callable bonds sell at higher promised yields than bonds that have a deferred call.

✖ The yield spread between callable and noncallable bonds widens during periods of high interest rates.

✖ The yield spread between callable and noncallable bonds increases with the bonds' maturities.

When people buy a callable bond, they are in effect placing a bet with the issuer. The issuer will develop expectations of future interest rate decreases and be willing to pay a higher call premium as long as the future interest savings associated with a call are expected to offset the call expense. Investors, on the other hand, are betting that the call premiums are more than adequate to offset a possible call resulting in a reinvestment at a low interest rate. Who's won the game in the past? We don't know.

When buying a callable bond, investors should examine the level to which interest rates must fall before the issue would be called. For example, assume Cadiz Pedro, Inc., sells a 20-year, 9% coupon bond at par. The issue is first callable at the end of five years at a price of $1,100. If Cadiz does call the bond at the end of year 5, it will incur a cash outflow of $1,100 per bond and save $90 per year for 15 years plus $1,000 15 years hence (in year 20). The internal rate of return on this call would be 7.84%:

$$\frac{\$90}{1.0784} + \frac{\$90}{1.0784^2} + \cdots + \frac{\$90}{1.0784^{15}} + \frac{\$1,000}{1.0784^{15}} = 1,100$$

If interest rates are expected to be 7.84% or lower by the end of year 5, the issue might well be called.

The effects of potential call on the price of this bond are shown in Figure 10-9. At interest rates considerably larger than 7.84%, the potential for call is small and the bond sells at a price close to what it would if it were noncallable. As interest rates fall toward 7.84%, the price of the bond increases (due to declining interest rates) but not as much as it would if it were noncallable. And at interest rates less than 7.84%, the bond's price is essentially capped by the call price of $1,100.[6]

FIGURE 10-9   THE PRICE EFFECT OF POTENTIAL CALL ON A BOND'S PRICE

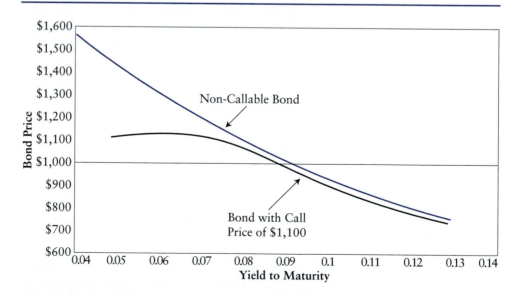

---

[6] The price might rise somewhat above $1,100 if investors believe the issuer will not immediately call the bond.

One way to control against call risk would be to purchase low-coupon, deep discount bonds. Even though interest rates may decline, prices of these issues are unlikely to rise to their stated call prices. However, before-tax yields on deep discount bonds are often lower than equivalent-risk, high-coupon bonds. This is caused by the different ways in which returns on low- and high-coupon bonds are taxed.

Mortgage-Backed Securities

Uncertainty about the timing of principal repayment on mortgages that collateralize a mortgage-backed security represents the major risk of owning such securities. Mortgage-backed securities differ from standard corporate bonds in two ways. First, principal repayments on mortgages are made monthly whereas corporate bond principal is usually scheduled to be repaid at a single future date. Second, mortgage borrowers do not pay a call premium when they pay off their mortgage early whereas corporate borrowers must pay a call premium. We discuss uncertainty about mortgage repayment in detail in the next chapter.

The Option to Convert

A convertible security is a bond (or preferred stock) that may be converted at the owner's discretion into a prescribed number of the firm's common shares. Investors purchase convertibles because they provide a fixed rate of income plus the opportunity to gain from stock price increases if the issuing firm does well in the future. The issuer chooses to sell a convertible because the rate of interest is lower than would have to be paid on a straight bond issuer.

Owning a convertible is similar to owning both the straight debt of a company plus call options on the firm's common stock. Thus, the convertible's price is greater than the straight debt's price by an amount equal to the value of the call option. There is a difference, however, between owning a convertible bond versus owning a straight bond plus call options on the stock. The convertible is exercised by turning the bond back to the company in return for shares. Call options are exercised by paying a stated cash amount, not by retiring the bonds.

The **conversion ratio** indicates the number of shares obtained when each bond is tendered for conversion. For example, a conversion ratio of 20 to 1 means that 20 shares of common stock will be received for each bond converted. The **conversion price** of a security is the bond's par value divided by the conversion ratio. For example, a conversion price of $50 on a $1,000 par bond implies a conversion ratio of 20 to 1.

Three identifiable values can be attached to convertible bonds:

- The convertible's **market value** is the price at which the convertible trades in the open markets.

- The convertible's **straight debt value** represents the value of the bond if it were not convertible into common shares. This is equal to the present value of future coupon payments and par value discounted at an interest rate appropriate for the maturity and default risk of the bond.

FIGURE 10-10   CONVERTIBLE BOND MARKET VALUES

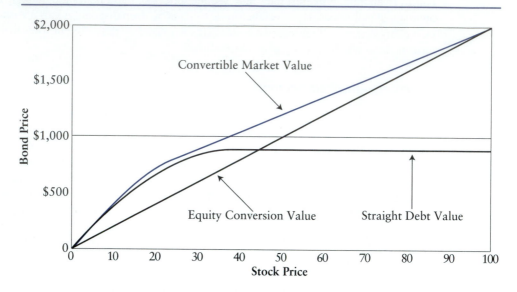

■ The convertible's **conversion value** represents the value of the bond if it were to be converted into stock. This is equal to a bond's conversion ratio times the current stock price.

An illustration of how these values are related is shown in Figure 10-10. The illustration is based on a $1,000 par value convertible bond that has a $50 conversion price (conversion ratio of 20 to 1). The bond's conversion value is, of course, directly related to the stock's price. If the stock is worth $40, the conversion value is $800 ($40 times 20). If the stock is worth $60, the conversion value is $1,200. The straight debt value is determined by the level of interest rates and the default risk on the bond. At low stock prices, the straight debt value is also small, reflecting the possibility of default. As the stock price increases, the possibility of default decreases and the convertible's straight debt value also increases. However, after a certain point, the straight debt value levels off and changes only with changes in the general level of interest rates. In the figure, the maximum straight debt value is assumed to be less than $1,000. This could be the result of an increase in interest rates since the date at which the convertible was initially issued. But even if interest rates do not change, the maximum straight debt value will generally be lower than the bond's $1,000 par value. This is because convertible bonds are initially sold to the public with coupon rates that are lower than other bonds with similar default risk.

The actual market value of the convertible bond is usually larger than either its straight debt value or its conversion value. When stock prices are low, the convertible will trade at close to its straight debt value. But the convertible's price will always be somewhat higher than the straight debt value due to the chance that the stock price will increase substantially before the maturity of the convertible. As the stock price increases, the convertible bond begins to trade based on its stock conversion value. For example, if the conversion ratio is 20 to 1 and the stock is worth $60 per share, the convertible bond will trade at a price of $1,200 plus a premium.

The size of this premium depends on bond investors' expectations of when the convertible bonds will be called. Investors rarely convert their bonds into stock voluntarily.[7] Instead, exercise is usually forced by management calling the bonds. For example, assume you own a convertible bond that has a par value of $1,000 and a conversion ratio of 20 to 1. The stock is presently trading for $60 so the conversion value of the bond is $1,200. Realizing the bond's value will increase if the stock increases but the bond has a "floor value" equal to its straight debt value, you wish to continue to hold the bond. Now, assume management is able to call the bond at a price of $1,100 and wishes to have the bond value on the firm's balance sheet transferred to equity. Management could force you to convert by announcing the bonds will soon be called. Faced with receiving $1,100 in cash from the call or $1,200 in stock value if you convert prior to the call, you will elect to convert the bonds to common shares.

Consider the two convertible bonds shown in Table 10-6. The Browning Ferris bond had a default rating of A- and would have sold at a YTM of 7.7% if it had not been convertible. Based on a coupon rate of 6 1/4% and a maturity of 17 years, the straight debt value of this bond was about $862. The price of Browning Ferris common stock was

TABLE 10-6   ILLUSTRATIVE CONVERTIBLE BOND DATA

	Browning Ferris	Boise Cascade
Straight Debt Information		
Default Rating	A−	BB−
YTM on Equivalent Risk Debt	7.7%	10.0%
Coupon	6.25%	7.00%
Maturity	17 years	21 years
Straight Debt Value	$862	$737
Stock Information		
Price per Share	$ 33.625	$ 42.875
Conversion Value	$820.11	$978.84
Convertible Bond Information		
Conversion Ratio	24.39	22.83
Convertible Market Value	$1,007.5	$1,045.0

---

[7] We show in Chapter 17 that it is usually best to not exercise an option until forced to do so.

$33.625. Multiplying this stock price times the conversion ratio of 24.39 provides the bond's conversion value of $820.11. Since the actual market value of this convertible was $1,007.5, the value placed on the conversion option on the bond was about $188 over the conversion value. The other issue shown in the table is a convertible of Boise Cascade. This issue had a much smaller conversion option value as evidenced by its market value of $1,045 and conversion value of $978.84.

Tax and Liquidity

Tax Impacts on Yields

Coupon income on corporate bonds is taxed at the investor's ordinary tax rate. Long-term capital gains and losses are often taxed at lower capital gains rates. To understand the effects that differences in ordinary and long-term capital gains rates can have on before-tax bond yields, consider the following scenario. Investors are attempting to value two bonds of identical risk.

Bond L matures in five years and pays a $30 yearly coupon. Bond H matures in five years and pays a $100 yearly coupon. Given the risks of the bond, investors wish to receive an after-tax return of 5% on each. Their tax rates on ordinary income and capital gains are 50% and 25%, respectively.

To price each bond, future after-tax cash flows should be discounted at the demanded after-tax return of 5%. Prices of bonds L and H would be:

$$P_L = \sum_{t=1}^{5} \frac{30(1 - 0.5)}{1.05^t} + \frac{1,000 - (1,000 - P_L)(0.25)}{1.05^5}$$

$$= \$811.53z$$

$$P_H = \sum_{t=1}^{5} \frac{100(1 - 0.5)}{1.05^5} + \frac{1,000 - (1,000 - P_H)(0.25)}{1.05^5}$$

$$= \$1,000$$

The price of L would, of course, be lower, since its coupons are lower.

Given these prices, what is the before-tax YTM on each? Using before-tax flows, we would find the before-tax YTM on L to be 7.68% and on H to be 10%. The low-coupon issue will sell at a lower before-tax YTM, since its effective tax rate is lower.

To determine whether a person should be in low- or high-coupon bonds that are otherwise identical, the after-tax return on each should be calculated. For example, using the preceding data, individuals with marginal tax rates higher than 50% would prefer the low-coupon bond, and individuals with lower tax rates (or even zero rates, such as endowment funds and charities) would select the higher coupon issue.

State and Local Bonds. Bond issues of state and local governments in the United States provide certain tax exemptions from federal income taxes. Thus, their pretax yields to maturity are usually lower than pretax yields of equivalent-risk government and corporate bonds.

Specifically, *interest income paid by municipal issues is not subject to federal taxes* (and usually not subject to local taxes in the state of issue). Income due to realized capital gains or losses (the price at which one sells minus the purchase price) is subject to federal taxes.

For state and local bonds trading at close to par value (hence zero expected capital gains or losses), the relationship between after-tax and before-tax yields is shown in Equation 10.10:

$$\text{After-tax YTM} = (\text{Before-tax YTM}) \text{ times } (1 \text{ minus tax rate}) \qquad \textbf{(10.10)}$$

For example, if municipals currently provide a YTM of 6.4% and one's federal tax rate is 30%, then the before-tax yield required on corporates of equivalent default risk and maturity would be 9.14%.

$$0.0914 = 0.064 \div (1 - 0.30)$$

If corporate bonds provided a YTM lower than 9.14%, equivalent municipals would be preferred.

Bond Liquidity

There have been relatively few formal studies of the liquidity of different types of bonds and the relationship between bond liquidity and required YTMs. But the research that has been done confirms informal opinions of professional bond traders. Specifically:

- Liquidity of individual bonds varies considerably. U.S. T-bills and Treasury notes are among the most liquid securities in the world. In contrast, public issues of small corporations and most municipal bonds trade in illiquid markets. While trade execution in such illiquid bonds can usually be conducted in a short time interval, the trade will generally be made with a firm that makes a market in the security (a market maker) at bid-ask spreads which are much larger than spreads of U.S. Treasuries.

- The liquidity of a bond can be judged by both the total market value of the issue outstanding as well as by the bond's bid-ask spread. In early academic studies of bonds, a significant inverse relationship was found between the market value of the issue oustanding and a bond's yield spread above equivalent maturity U.S. Treasury bonds. More recent studies have focused on bid-ask spreads and find a direct relationship between the size of the spread and the yield spread above otherwise equivalent U.S. Treasuries. Investors clearly require higher YTMs for less liquid bonds.

But this does not mean that less liquid bonds provide a greater return than more liquid bonds, since the transaction costs of trading illiquid bonds are larger.

Amihud and Mendelson argue that an investor's time horizon plays an important role in the types of bonds which should be held. A short investment horizon calls for investment in bonds that have good liquidity (in order to reduce transaction costs). A long investment horizon calls for investment in less liquid bonds (in order to benefit from the greater YTMs).

SUMMARY

Here are the key concepts:

■ The value of a bond is equal to the present worth of promised future cash flows when discounted at an appropriate yield to maturity (YTM). The YTM depends on four basic characteristics of the bond: (1) required yields on default-free bonds of similar maturity, (2) default risk inherent in the bond, (3) the ability to call the bond prior to scheduled maturity, and (4) any special tax advantages associated with the bond.

■ The term structure of interest rates (or yield curve) relates the maturity of a bond to its YTM. Three term structure theories have been developed: market segmentation theory (MST), unbiased expectations theory (UET), and liquidity preference theory (LPT).

■ Market segmentation theory states that the term structure of interest is dominated by individuals and institutions who attempt to hedge their investment risks. A hedge is created by matching the maturity of an investment with the financing maturity. Such hedging creates desires to buy or sell securities within only a narrow maturity range. As a result, the yield curve is said to be created by current levels of demand and supply in various maturity segments.

■ The unbiased expectations theory states that if MST is correct, then significant arbitrage profits would be available by forecasting future demand and supply conditions. Believers in UET suggest such arbitrage will continue until profits from additional arbitrage no longer exist. At this point the yield curve will not reflect current demand and supply conditions within particular maturity segments but, instead, will reflect expectations about future demand and supply over all maturity segments. The shape of the yield curve would reflect expectations about future interest rates.

■ Liquidity preference theory builds on UET by adding a liquidity premium to bonds of longer maturity. Since long-term bonds are quite price sensitive to interest rate changes, they have a principal risk that short-term lenders would prefer not to accept. To induce lenders to buy maturities that have such a risk, borrowers will have to offer a yield inducement—a liquidity premium.

■ The value of most bonds is affected by various options on the bonds. These include (1) the option to default, (2) the option to call, and (3) the option to convert.

■ Owners of bonds that have default risk effectively have a position in two securities. The first is default-free debt. The second is a short put position that provides equity owners the option of either repaying the debt in cash or selling the firm's assets to debt holders at the debt's par value.

■ Owners of callable bonds have the following investment position: ownership of the bond and a short call that allows the issuer to buy back the bond prior to its scheduled maturity.

◼ Owners of convertible bonds have the following investment postion: ownership of the bond and ownership of a call on the firm's common stock. The call is exercised by returning the bonds to the issuer in exchange for common shares.

◼ Yields to maturity are also affected by how the bond's income is taxed and the relative liquidity of the issue.

R E V I E W   P R O B L E M S

1. You are given the following (incomplete) data on U.S. Treasury securities. Assume a $1,000 par value for each and a coupon payment at year-end.

Security	Maturity	Coupon Rate	Price	YTM
A	2 years	10%	$982.87	—
B	4 years	10%	—	12%
C	4 years	12%	—	12%

a. Without performing any calculations, what will be the price of C?
b. Without performing any calculations, will the price of B be greater or less than that of C?
c. Calculate the missing data.
d. If interest rates rise, in what direction will the bond prices move? Which will move more, A or B? Which will move more, B or C?

2. Throughout this problem, assume we are dealing with zero-coupon bonds. YTMs on bonds having three different maturities are as follows:

Bond	Maturity	YTM
A	1 year	11.0%
B	2 years	12.0%
C	3 years	11.5%

a. Calculate the implied one-year forward rates for the starts of years 2 and 3.
b. Prepare a forecast of what the yield curve is expected to be at the start of year 2 according to UET.
c. Calculate the implied forward rate on two-year bonds for the start of year 2.
d. Assume you believe that spot rates on one-year bonds will be 8% at the start of year 3. Illustrate the arbitrage you would enter into to take advantage of this.
e. Assume UET is correct and that a real risk-free rate of 3% per annum is required. What inflation forecasts are implicit in the yield curve?
f. Assume UET is correct. What return would you expect during the next year if you:

◼ Buy the one-year bond?

◼ Buy the three-year bond and sell in a year?

S o l u t i o n s

1. a. Bond C will sell for $1,000. Bond theorem 1 states that when the annual coupon rate and YTM are identical, a bond will always sell at par.
   b. Bond B will have a lower price than C because B has a lower coupon.

c. The YTM of bond A is found by trial and error or with a calculator to be 11%:

$$\frac{100}{1.11} + \frac{1,100}{1.11^2} = 982.87$$

The price of bond B will be $939.25:

$$\frac{100}{1.12} + \frac{100}{1.12^2} + \frac{100}{1.12^3} + \frac{1,100}{1.12^4} = \$939.25$$

The price of bond C was stated to be $1,000 in part a.

d. Bond prices will move down—this is bond theorem 2. Bond B will fall more than bond A, according to bond theorem 3. And bond B will fall more than bond C, per bond theorem 5.

2. a. $f_{1,1} = \dfrac{1.12^2}{1.11} - 1$

$= \dfrac{\text{Accumulated wealth of \$1 invested in two-year bond at end of year 2}}{\text{Accumulated wealth of \$1 invested in one-year bond at end of year 1}} - 1$

$= 0.13$, or 13%

$f_{1,2} = \dfrac{1.115^3}{1.12^2} - 1$

$= 0.1051$, or 10.51%

b. In one year, the expected one-year rate is 13%, according to part a. To find the expected two-year rate, we would use Equation 10.4:

$$I_2 = [(1.13)\,(1.1051)]^{1/2} - 1$$

$$= 0.1175, \text{ or } 11.75\%$$

c. Investing $1 in a three-year bond will produce a value of $1.115^3 = \$1.3862$ at the end of year 3. Investing $1 in a one-year bond will produce a value of $1.11 at the end of year 1. For $1.11 to grow to $1.3862 two years later, the average compound return (remember G?) would be

$$\left[\frac{1.3862}{1.11}\right]^{1/2} - 1 = 0.1175, \text{ or } 11.75\%$$

d. Since the implied forward rate for year 3 is 10.51% (from part a), you would want to lock in that rate instead of eventually receiving the expected spot of 8% in year 3.

End-of-Period Cash In (Out)

Transaction	0	1	2	3
Buy 1.0 three-year bond 1,000/1.115³	(721.40)	—	—	1,000
Short-Sell 0.9049 two-year bond at				
a price of 797.19 = 1,000/1.12²	721.40	—	(940.90)	
	0	0	(940.90)	1,000
		Net Return = 10.51%		

e.

	Nominal	—	Real	=	Average Yearly Inflation
1 year	11.0%	—	3.0%	=	8.0%
2 year	12.0%	—	3.0%	=	9.0%
3 year	11.5%	—	3.0%	=	8.5%

(Note that this calculation does not allow for the interaction term in the Fisher equation—Equation (5.1)—in Chapter 5. This is often done because of its small numerical value.)

f. The one-year return from buying a three-year bond and selling in a year is not known with certainty but is expected to be 11.0%. Note that this 11% return expected during the next year on the current three-year bond is identical to the known return on current one-year bonds.

	Today	Year 1
Buy at $1,000/(1.115^3)$	(721.40)	
Sell at $1,000/(1.1175^2)$		800.76
Return = 11.00%		

The 11.75% expected yield on two-year bonds at the start of year 2 comes from part c.

QUESTIONS AND PROBLEMS

1. High-coupon bonds are less price sensitive to interest rate moves than are lower coupon bonds. Why is this so?
2. National Aviation has three bond issues of similar risk outstanding:

Issue	Par	Maturity	Coupon	Current Price
A	$1,000	5 years	7%	$ 922.30
B	1,000	10 years	10%	1,210.40
C	1,000	10 years	4%	788.96

a. What is the YTM on each of these issues?
b. Note that the YTMs for bonds B and C are equal. Is this likely to be the case if capital gains tax rates are lower than ordinary tax rates?
c. Without calculating prices, which of these three bonds will experience the greatest percentage price appreciation if YTMs fall by 100 basis points on each? Why?
d. Between bonds B and C, which will experience the greatest percentage price appreciation if YTMs on each fall by 100 basis points? Why?
e. Assume yields do drop by 100 basis points. Find the new market price of each bond.
3. Describe the rationale suggested by believers in MST for changes in the level and shape of the yield curve over the course of a classic business cycle.
4. What is an implied forward rate of interest? How can a forward rate be locked in by using existing yields on bonds of various maturities?
5. How does Fisher's theory of nominal interest rates fit into the UET approach to yield curves?
6. The YTM on a pure discount five-year bond is 8.7%. The YTM on a six-year bond (of equal risk) is 9.0%. Calculate the implied one-year forward rate for the start of year 6.

7. The YTM on a five-year bond is currently 8%, the YTM on a six-year bond is 9%, and the YTM on a seven-year bond is 9.5%.
   a. Calculate the implied forward rate on a one-year bond at the start of year 6.
   b. Calculate the implied forward rate on a two-year bond at the start of year 6.

8. If 20-year riskless bonds (say, pure discount U.S. T-bonds) are currently yielding 8% to maturity and similar five-year bonds are now yielding 8.5% to maturity, what is the expected rate on a 15-year bond that will start at the end of year 5? How might a speculator lock in this rate? Prove with calculations.

9. Assume two pure discount bonds are available. Bond X is selling at $926 and matures in one year. Bond Y is selling at $873 and matures in two years.
   a. Outline a strategy to lock in a forward rate for year 2.
   b. What return is locked in by this strategy?
   c. If you expect that in a year from now one-year rates will be 8%, should you proceed with this transaction? If not, what should be done?
   d. What does UET say about the transaction in part c—that is, is it valid or not? Why?

10. National Products, Inc., has just issued a 10-year bond at par that pays an annual coupon of 12%. The issue is first callable at $1,120 per bond any time after the first four years of the bond's life. In answering the following questions, assume neither you nor NPI will incur any transaction costs in future bond transactions.
    a. If NPI does call the bond at the start of year 5, what is the internal rate of return earned by the firm?
    b. If you expect that YTMs on six-year bonds will be 8% at the start of year 5, do you expect NPI to call the issue?
    c. Assume the yield curve is flat and remains constant at 12% during years 1, 2, 3, and 4. At the start of year 5, however, the yield curve drops to 8%. NPI calls the bond issue, and you use the proceeds to reinvest in a new six-year bond at par. Subsequently, yields remain at 8%. What is your ten-year return?

11. Interest rates on Aa corporate bonds with a ten-year maturity presently trade at an 8% yield to maturity. Similar municipal bonds have a 6% yield to maturity. Both bonds are trading at par of $1,000.
    a. John Stern's marginal tax bracket is 30%. Should he purchase the corporate or municipal bond?
    b. At what tax bracket would a person be indifferent between the two security types?
    c. Institutions such as endowments and pension funds do not pay taxes. Should they ever purchase municipal bonds?

12. Describe carefully the immediate effects on the money and capital markets of each of the following events. Consider each of the events independently.
    a. An increase in policy loans by life insurance companies.
    b. Revision of federal income tax laws to permit issuers to deduct dividends on preferred stocks in arriving at corporate taxable income. The 85% dividend income exclusion available to corporate investors will be unchanged.
    Note: Answer this question from the viewpoint of both MST and UET.

13. a. Draw a series of yield curves that should be in evidence on each of the following dates:
       Date 1: Relatively stable prices and money supply
       Date 2: Rapidly rising rates of inflation
       Date 3: The bottom of an economic downturn
       Date 4: The top of an expansionary cycle
    b. As an aggressive portfolio manager of a moderate-sized, taxable fund comprised solely of fixed income securities, discuss the strategies you would employ to optimize rates of return. Assume that quality guidelines must be maintained and you expect interest rates will either decline, or rise.

CFA   14. The following are the average yields on U.S. T-bonds at two different points in time:

	Yield to Maturity	
Term to Maturity	January 15, 19XX	May 15, 19XX
1 year	7.25%	8.05%
2 years	7.50%	7.90%
5 years	7.90%	7.70%
10 years	8.30%	7.45%
15 years	8.45%	7.30%
20 years	8.55%	7.20%
25 years	8.60%	7.10%

a. Assuming a pure expectations hypothesis, define a forward rate. Describe how you would calculate the forward rate for a three-year U.S. T-bond two years from May 15, 19XX, using the actual term structure here.

b. Discuss how each of the three major term structure hypotheses could explain the January 15, 19XX, term structure shown here.

c. Discuss what happened to the term structure over the time period and the effect of this change on U.S. T-bonds of 2 years and 10 years.

d. Assume you invest solely on the basis of yield spreads, and in January 19XX acted on the expectation that the yield spread between 1-year and 25-year U.S. Treasuries would return to a more typical spread of 170 basis points. Explain what you would have done on January 15, 19XX, and describe the result of this action based on what happened between January 15, 19XX and May 15, 19XX.

CFA   15. The investment committee of the money management firm of Gentry, Inc. has typically been very conservative and has avoided investing in high-yield (junk) bonds, although they have had major positions in investment-grade corporate bonds. Recently, Pete Squire, a member of the committee, suggested they should review their policy regarding junk bonds because they currently constitute over 25% of the total corporate bond market.

As a part of this policy review, you are asked to respond to the following questions.

a. Briefly discuss the liquidity and pricing characteristics of junk bonds relative to each of the following types of fixed income securities:

■ Treasuries;

■ high-grade corporate bonds;

■ corporate loans; and

■ private placements.

Briefly discuss the implications of these differences for Gentry's bond portfolio managers.

The committee has learned that the correlation of rates of return between Treasuries and high-grade corporate bonds is approximately 0.98; the correlation between Treasury/high-grade corporate bonds and junk bonds is approximately 0.45.

b. Briefly explain the reason for this difference in correlations, and discuss its implications for bond portfolios.

DATAFILE ANALYSIS

Review the yield curve information that is provided in the INDEXES datafile. Plot the yield curves for the end of 1971, 1981, 1991, and the current curve. You will have to refer to the financial section of a newspaper to obtain data about the current yield curve. Explain why these yield curves have been so variable.

REFERENCES

Textbooks that treat yields to maturity in detail include the following:

Livingston, Miles. *Money and Capital Markets,* Miami: Kolb, 1993.

Van Horne, James C. *Financial Market Rates and Flows,* Englewood Cliffs, NJ: Prentice-Hall, 1984.

Default risk studies include the following:

Fischer, Lawrence. "Determinants of Risk Premiums on Corporate Bonds," *Journal of Political Economy,* June 1959.

Fraine, H. G. and R. Mills. "Effects of Defaults and Credit Deterioration on Yields of Corporate Bonds," *Journal of Finance,* September 1961.

A mathematically difficult but seminal paper on yield curve theory is Cox, John, Jonathan Ingersoll, and Stephen Ross, "A Reexamination of Traditional Hypotheses About the Term Structure of Interest Rates," *Journal of Finance,* September 1981.

Here are two of the numerous studies of the junk bond market:

Altman, Edward I. "Setting the Record Straight on Junk Bonds: A Review of the Research on Default Rates and Returns," *Journal of Applied Corporate Finance,* Summer 1990.

Cornell, Bradford and Kevin Green. "The Investment Performance of Low-Grade Bond Funds," *Journal of Finance,* March 1991.

11

MANAGEMENT OF FIXED INCOME SECURITIES

After reading this chapter you should have an understanding of how bond duration and immunization are used in both active and passive management of fixed income portfolios.

During the past few decades bond interest rates have been quite volatile, many new types of fixed income securities have been created, and our understanding of how to value the options given to bond holders has improved. These events have spurred a revolution in the way bond portfolios are managed such that the management of fixed income securities today is quite sophisticated. We discuss the more important techniques used by bond managers in this chapter.

The chapter is organized into three major sections:

- **Management of Interest Rate Risk.** The major risk faced by bond owners during the past 20 years has been interest rate risk, uncertainty about future portfolio values created by volatile interest rates. As a result, considerable attention has been given to the management of a portfolio's exposure to interest rate risk. We see in this chapter that interest rate risk can be eliminated (in many cases) if the duration of portfolio investments is equal to the duration of liabilities. Duration is defined later.

- **Passive Bond Management Strategies.** In this section, we examine various aspects of passively managing a bond portfolio. This includes a discussion of the value of bond diversification, asset allocation considerations, the management of call risk, and issues associated with owning international bonds.

▪ **Active Bond Management Strategies.** In this section, we review various techniques used by active bond managers. These include timing yield curve shifts, bond swaps, and immunization strategies.

Appendix 11A discusses mortgage pass-throughs and instruments created from them called REMICs.

Management of Interest Rate Risk

Yield to maturity (YTM) is a promised rate of return that will actually be earned only under very restricted assumptions. In this section we examine why realized bond returns can be different from promised YTMs. The principal reason is uncertainty about future bond prices and coupon reinvestment rates caused by uncertainty about future interest rates.

The Horizon Date and Realized Returns

Securities are bought to be sold. When an investor purchases a security, it is with the hopes of earning a fair rate of return up to some terminal investment **horizon date,** at which time the security will be sold to provide cash for current consumption. For example, recent college graduates may need cash in a few years to support graduate education or to make a down payment on a house. A husband and wife may be investing to provide cash during retirement ten to twenty years away. And insurance firms will invest to provide cash to service expected future insurance claims. All of these investors have a horizon date in mind at which time they expect to sell their securities.[1] The concept of an investment horizon date (*HD*) is crucial to an understanding of bond yields, risks, and trading strategies.

Consider the situation of Continental Casualty Corporation, a medium-sized casualty insurance firm. CCC has just begun to offer a new type of insurance policy that is expected to require cash to meet insured losses three years after each new policy is signed. Thus, *HD* equals three years. All insurance premiums are paid when the policy is signed and these proceeds are invested in bonds.

In a sense, CCC is indifferent to intermediate yearly returns on its bond investments. The important consideration is the amount of net profit available in year 3 after all insurance losses are paid. For example, assume each policy provides CCC with a $1,000 premium at the start of year 1 that may be invested for three years, at which time the investments will have to be sold to pay expected insurance losses of, say, $1,225. If the investment of $1,000 grows to a value greater than $1,225 by the end of year 3, the firm will have earned a profit. If the $1,000 investment grows to only $1,225 (or less), the firm will just break even (or incur losses). The sequence of yearly rates of return on CCC's bond investments is of little importance. Instead, the firm is interested in the terminal worth of its investments at the end of year 3—the horizon date.

---

[1] Clearly, most individuals will have a number of horizon dates in mind. For example, a retired couple may intend to sell a portion of their security portfolio at the start of each year to meet that year's consumption needs. For simplicity's sake, however, we restrict our discussion to a single date.

Consider the following three alternative sequences of yearly returns:

Series	Return During Year		
	1	2	3
A	6.10%	5.00%	10.00%
B	20.00%	−10.00%	13.40%
C	9.00%	4.00%	8.07%

In each case a $1,000 investment grows to exactly $1,225 by the end of year 3:

Series	Horizon Date Value		Details
A	$1,225	=	$1,000 (1.061 × 1.05 × 1.1)
B	1,225	=	1,000 (1.20 × 0.9 × 1.134)
C	1,225	=	1,000 (1.09 × 1.04 × 1.0807)

Even though each series has a different sequence of yearly returns, CCC should be indifferent among them. Each provides the same terminal wealth. Expressed in the form of an annual rate of return, each series provides the same average **annual realized return.** The annual realized return on a bond investment is denoted as **ARR** and represents the constant annual discount rate that will discount the horizon date value of a bond investment back to the initial dollar investment made.[2] Mathematically:

$$\text{Initial Investment Value} = \frac{\text{Horizon Date Investment Value}}{(1 + ARR)^{HD}} \qquad \textbf{(11.1a)}$$

or

Annual Realized Return

$$ARR = \left[\frac{\text{Horizon Date Investment Value}}{\text{Initial Investment Value}}\right]^{1 \div HD} - 1.0 \qquad \textbf{(11.1b)}$$

where *HD* represents the number of years to the horizon date. In the CCC example the *ARR* would be 7.0% regardless of which series of yearly returns is earned:

$$0.07 = [\$1,225 \div \$1,000]^{1 \div 3} - 1.0$$

Determinants of ARR

The annual realized return on a bond investment is determined by the size of the investment's horizon date dollar value. Anything that can change the *HD* value will change the *ARR*. Factors that can change this *HD* value include the following:

1. Changes in the general level of interest rates that affect (a) The bond's horizon date market value, and (b) Earnings on the reinvestment of coupons.

---

[2] The annual realized return is, in concept, identical to the geometric mean return we discussed in Chapter 5.

2. Characteristics of the individual bond investment, including (a) The bond's potential default, and (b) The bond's potential call.

As an illustration, assume a 9% noncallable, four-year, default-free bond could be bought today for $1,000. Since the bond is selling at par, its promised YTM is equal to 9%—the coupon rate. Also assume the yield curve is flat, the bond is held for three years, and the level of interest rates remains unchanged at 9%. What will the *ARR* be?

To determine this, we need to know what the year 3 *HD* value will be. This value consists of the following components: the market value of the bond, the receipt of all coupons, and the receipt of interest earned on reinvestment of coupons.

The market value of the bond will be $1,000 at the end of year 3, since interest rates don't change. In total, $270 in coupons will have been received (three years times $90 per year). Finally, $25 in interest earned on interest will have been received: two years' interest on the first $90 coupon payment ($90 × 1.09^2 − $90) plus one year's interest on the second coupon ($90 × 1.09 − $90). Thus, the investment value at the end of year 3 will sum to $1,295:

Component	*HD* Value
Market Value of Bond	$1,000
Receipt of Coupons	270
Interest on Interest	25
Total	$1,295

The *ARR* will equal 9.0%:

$$0.09 = [\$1,295 \div \$1,000]^{1 \div 3} - 1.0$$

In this case the *ARR* does equal the promised YTM. But this occurs only because the following conditions are met: (1) interest rates in the economy don't change from 9%, resulting in a constant market value of $1,000 and reinvestment of coupons at a rate equal to the promised YTM; (2) the bond does not default; and (3) the bond isn't called.

Now let's change one assumption—the level of interest rates. Assume that immediately after the bond is bought at par, the level of interest rates increases to 10% and remains there. At the end of year 3 the $1,000 investment will be worth $1,288.81:

Component	*HD* Value	Details
Market Value of Bond	$990.91	($1,090 ÷ 1.1)
Receipt of Coupons	270.00	($90 × 3)
Interest on Interest	27.90	[$90($1.10^2$) − $90] + [$90(1.10) − $90]
Total	$1,288.81	

Now the *ARR* will be 8.82%:

$$0.0882 = [\$1,288.81 \div \$1,000]^{1 \div 3} - 1.0$$

Determinants of Bond Risk

Anything that influences the distribution of realized horizon date returns also affects bond risk.

Default Risk. If the issuer of a bond is unable to make all coupon and principal payments as promised, realized yields will be less than promised. The greater the uncertainty about default, the greater the uncertainty about realized returns that might be available at some horizon date.

Call Risk. As we discussed in Chapter 10, issuers are often allowed to retire a bond issue prior to scheduled maturity. This results in an uncertainty about future cash flows on the investment.

Interest Rate Risk. Interest rate risk represents uncertainty about future portfolio values created by uncertain future interest rates. There are two ways in which interest rate risk can affect portfolio values: (1) by changing the rate of return at which future cash flows are reinvested, and (2) by changing the market value of the bond. The first is called reinvestment rate risk. The second is called price risk.

1. **Reinvestment Rate Risk.** Uncertainty about possible shifts in the yield curve creates an uncertainty about future returns from coupon reinvestment. If future reinvestment rates are different from a bond's promised YTM, its realized YTM will not equal its promised yield. The same is true for yields to horizon dates. If reinvestment rates between now and a future horizon date are uncertain, realized returns as of that horizon date will also be uncertain.
2. **Price Risk.** Bond prices are inversely related to required rates of return. If required returns increase, bond prices fall, and vice versa. The only date at which a bond's price is certain is at maturity (barring default or call). As a result, price risk exists whenever an individual's horizon date and a bond's maturity differ.

Default and call risks cannot be eliminated, and required bond yields must be adjusted for the relative degrees of each. However, interest rate risks can often be eliminated by selecting appropriate bond lives.

How to Reduce Interest Rate Risk

Reinvestment rate risk and price risk both arise from uncertainty about future interest rates. But note that changes in interest rates work in opposite directions on reinvestment and price risks. If interest rates increase, reinvestment income increases whereas bond prices decline. Conversely, a reduction in interest rates causes reinvestment income to decline and bond prices to increase. Since the two forces move in opposite directions, it is possible for the favorable impacts of one to exactly offset the unfavorable impacts of the other.[3] This is the basic concept behind strategies that **immunize** a portfolio against interest rate risk. (The term *immunize* means to eliminate in the context of bond management.)

---

[3] Recall from Chapter 6 that when two securities (cash flow streams) have a correlation coefficient equal to -1.0, all risk can be eliminated by some combination of the two.

Consider the following situation. You are the investment adviser for AHI, an insurance company. The treasurer of AHI has just come to you with $100,000, which she wishes to invest for exactly 4.24 years. She states that the investment must be in default-free, non-callable bonds. The treasurer will pay you a commission based on how close her realized horizon date return is to what you initially promise. After a quick survey you believe the following default-free and call-free investment opportunities are available:

Bond	Coupon	Maturity	Promised YTM	Current Price
A	0%	4.24 years	9%	$ 693.92
B	9	2.00	9	1,000.00
C	9	20.00	9	1,000.00
D	9	5.00	9	1,000.00

In addition, the yield curve is now flat and is expected to stay flat.

If interest rates don't change between now and 4.24 years from now, you really don't have a problem; each of the four bonds would provide a 9% realized return. But since interest rates may well change, you are somewhat uncertain about each bond's realized return over the 4.24-year period. Indeed, you foresee the possibility that immediately after the $100,000 is invested, interest rates may rise to 11% or fall to 7%. What should you do?

Bond A is a zero-coupon bond maturing in exactly 4.24 years. Since all of its yield comes in the form of price appreciation, it is not exposed to price or reinvestment rate risk. Its realized return will be 9%, regardless of future shifts in the yield curve.[4] Bonds B, C, and D will each be exposed to varying degrees of price and reinvestment rate risk. Bond B has a maturity much shorter than the 4.24-year horizon date and will be exposed to considerable reinvestment rate risk. When bond B matures in two years, a new bond will have to be bought at a YTM that is currently uncertain. Bond C matures after the horizon date and will be exposed to considerable price risk, since its market value in 4.24 years will depend on interest rates at that date, which are currently uncertain. Bond D matures slightly after the horizon date and will be exposed equal but opposite reinvestment rate and price risks.

Each of these points can be seen in Table 11-1, where HD cash values are calculated for each bond and for each possible shift in the yield curve. Realized yields for bonds B and C are clearly uncertain. If the yield curve falls to 7%, realized yields on B will be less than 9% because of lower investment rates, and they will be higher than 9% for C, since its price increases more than enough to offset lower reinvestment rates. If the yield curve increases to 11%, the opposite will occur. Bond B will have a return greater than 9% because of improved reinvestment rates, and C will have a lower return because its price decline more than offsets larger interest on interest.

Notice the curious results for bond D. Regardless of shifts in the yield curve, it provides a 9% realized yield. Why? The answer lies in the fact that D's reinvestment rate and price risks exactly offset each other. The coupon rate and maturity of bond D were selected so the "average date" of its cash flows is exactly 4.24 years hence. While D repays principal of $1,000 at the end of five years, cash is received in the form of $90 coupons at

---

[4] Year 4.24 investment value = $100,000 times ($1,000 ÷ $693.92) = $144,108.83
ARR = [$144,108.83 ÷ $100,000]$^{1 \div 4.24}$ − 1.0 = 0.09.

TABLE 11-1   BOND VALUES IN 4.24 YEARS CONSIDERING REINVESTMENT AND PRICE RISKS

Interest Rate	Price at Horizon Date*	+	Total† Coupons	+	Interest on Intermediate Cash Flows	=	Horizon Date Cash Value	Realized Returns
Bond B:								
7%	$1,016	+	$320	+	$44	=	1,380	7.89%
9%	1,021	+	360	+	60	=	1,441	9.00%
11%	1,025	+	400	+	78	=	1,503	10.09%
Bond C:								
7%	1,208	+	360	+	46	=	1,614	11.95%
9%	1,021	+	360	+	60	=	1,441	9.00%
11%	874	+	360	+	75	=	1,309	6.56%
Bond D:								
7%	1,035	+	360	+	46	=	1,441	9.00%
9%	1,021	+	360	+	60	=	1,441	9.00%
11%	1,006	+	360	+	75	=	1,441	9.00%

*Includes interest accrued in year 5.
†Coupons are paid annually.

each year-end. The average date at which a dollar of cash is received on bond D is 4.24 years. *Economically, bond D is equivalent to a 4.24-year, zero-coupon bond.*

Duration

Frederick Macaulay was the first to term the "average date" at which cash is received on a bond as duration. His estimate of a bond's duration is appropriately called **Macaulay duration.** It is calculated as follows:

Macaulay Duration Equation

$$D = \frac{PV(C_1) \times 1}{P} + \frac{PV(C_2) \times 2}{P} + \cdots \frac{PV(C_M) \times M}{P} = \sum_{t=1}^{M} \frac{PV(C_t) \times t}{P} \qquad (11.2)$$

where D = the Macaulay duration of a bond, t = a given year number, M = the number of years to maturity, $PV(C_t)$ = the present value of cash flows received in year t, and P = the present value of all cash flows (the bond's price). The calculation of bond D's duration is shown below. First, the present value of each year's cash flows is found using the bond's promised YTM as the discount rate. These are then stated as a percentage of the bond's market value (the total present value). Finally, these percentages are multiplied by the year number in which the cash flow is received and the resulting products summed.[5]

---

[5] Macaulay duration is based on the assumption the yield curve is flat and that all shifts in the yield curve are parallel shifts.

Year	Cash Flow	Present Value	Percentage of Total	Year Number	Product
1	$ 90	$ 82.57	8.257%	1	0.0826
2	90	75.75	7.575	2	0.1515
3	90	69.50	6.950	3	0.2085
4	90	63.76	6.376	4	0.2550
5	1,090	708.42	70.842	5	3.5421
		$1,000.00			$D = 4.2397$ years

Understanding the Calculation of D. The calculation of D in Equation (11.2) may appear quite imposing. But the logic behind it is really very simple. To illustrate this, consider again the cash flow data on the five-year, 9% coupon bond discussed above. This bond promises to pay $90 at each year-end plus $1,090 at its maturity in five years. Now, consider this to be not one bond, but a portfolio of five distinctly different bonds. The first bond in this portfolio matures in one year and pays $90. The second bond matures in two years and has one cash payment equal to $90 at its maturity, and so forth. Finally, the last bond matures in five years and pays a single cash flow of $1,090 at its maturity. In short, our original bond is now considered to be a portfolio of five different zero-coupon bonds.

What is the duration of each of these zero-coupon bonds? Since each provides cash at one date only (its maturity), the duration of each is identical to its maturity. The duration of the one-year $90 bond is one year, the duration of the two-year $90 bond is two years, and so forth. We are just about ready to calculate the duration of this portfolio of five bonds. But to do so we must know that the duration of a portfolio is equal to the weighted average duration of the bonds held in the portfolio; that is:

Duration of a Portfolio
$$D_P = \sum_{i=1}^{N} X_i D_i \tag{11.3}$$

where D_P represents the portfolio's duration, D_i represents the duration of i, and X_i is the percentage of the portfolio invested in bond i.

Look again at the duration calculation for the original five-year, 9% coupon bond that we are now considering to be a portfolio of five zero-coupon bonds. The dollar investment made in the one-year zero-coupon bond is $82.57—the present value of $90 received in one year. The dollar investment made in the two-year zero-coupon bond is $75.75—the present value of its $90 maturity cash payment in two years, and so forth. The total value of this portfolio is $1,000. Thus, X_1 (the percentage invested in the 1-year bond) is equal to 8.26%, X_2 is equal to 7.58%, . . . , and X_5 is equal to 70.84%. We can now use Equation (11.3) to calculate the portfolio's duration:

$$Dp = X_1 D_1 + X_2 D_2 + X_3 D_3 + X_4 D_4 + X_5 D_5$$

$$= 0.08257(1) + 0.07575(2) + 0.06950(3) + 0.06376(4) + 0.70842(5)$$

$$= 4.2397 \text{ years}$$

The number and types of calculations we have just used to find the bond's duration are identical to those in Equation (11.2). But we have employed a convenient mental device that allows us to calculate a bond's duration without having to memorize Equation (11.2). All we have to do is consider a coupon bond to be a portfolio of many zero-coupon securities and recognize that the duration of a portfolio is the weighted average of the duration of the securities held in the portfolio.

A Simple Formula for Duration. Equation (11.2) requires us to perform a number of discount calculations. A formula for duration that does not require discounting is shown next. This formula is often useful in computer spreadsheet applications.

Duration of Coupon Bond

$$D = \frac{1 + Y}{Y} - \frac{(1 + Y) + T(C - Y)}{C[(1 + Y)^T - 1] + Y} \tag{11.4}$$

where Y represents the bond yield earned within the period between coupon receipts, C is the periodic coupon, and T is the total number of periods left on the bond.

For example, consider a ten-year bond with a stated coupon rate of 8% when its annual yield to maturity is 10%. If the bond pays coupons semiannually, then T equals 20, C equals 0.04, and Y equals 0.05. The bond's duration (in number of six-month periods) would be 13.6807:

$$13.6807 = \frac{1.05}{0.05} - \frac{1.05 + 20(0.04 - 0.05)}{0.04[1.05^{20} - 1] + 0.05}$$

Translating this to years results in a duration of 6.8404 years:

$$13.6807 \text{ six-month periods} = 6.8404 \text{ years}$$

What if the bond paid interest only at year-end dates? In that case, the duration would be slightly longer (7.0439 years) because of the delay in each year's coupon receipt.

$$7.0439 = \frac{1.10}{0.10} - \frac{1.10 + 10(0.08 - 0.10)}{0.08[1.10^{10} - 1] + 0.10}$$

Immunizing Against Interest Rate Risk. Figure 11-1 illustrates the relationships among a bond portfolio's duration, the investment horizon of the portfolio (HD), and net interest rate risk.

Inherent default and call risks are unaffected by duration or the investor's HD. However, reinvestment and price risks are. Whenever a bond's duration is shorter than the HD, uncertainty about future reinvestment rates dominates price risks and a net reinvestment rate risk exists. Whenever a bond's duration is longer than the HD, uncertainty about future price levels dominates reinvestment risks and a net price risk exists. However, these two risks exactly offset each other when the duration equals the HD.

A bond portfolio that has a duration equal to the investment horizon date faces no interest rate risk and is said to be immunized.

FIGURE 11-1   DURATION, HORIZON DATE, AND BOND RISKS

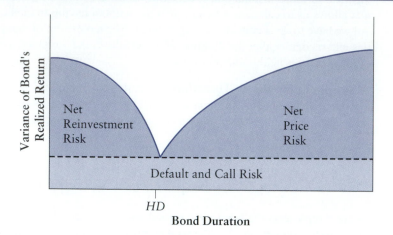

Consider the following example. The trustees of a pension fund know with certainty that $5.0 million will have to be paid to retired employees in exactly one year.[6] The duration of the liability is one year. Assume the yield curve is flat and that current interest rates on default and call-free bonds are 6.0%. Thus, the amount of money needed today to be able to pay the $5.0 million is $4,716,981 ($5,000,000 ÷ 1.06). If the $4,716,981 was invested in bonds with a duration greater than one year, trustees would face net price risk. If the money was invested in bonds with a duration less than one year, trustees would face net reinvestment rate risk. However, if a one year duration portfolio is held, interest rate risk would be zero. The easiest way of accomplishing this would be to purchase a U.S. Treasury zero-coupon bond that has a maturity and a duration of one year.

Our example focused on uncertainty in payoffs at the end of a year from today. Often people focus on the present value of both liabilities and assets. In this example the present value of the liability is $4,716,981. If this amount of money is invested in assets it is expected to cover the year-end liability of $5.0 million, if interest rates do not change.

Consider the data shown in Table 11-2. At an interest rate of 6%, the present value of the liability is the $4.717 million shown earlier. However, if interest rates fall to 4%, the present value of the liability rises to $4.808 million. And, if interest rate rise to 8%, the present value of the liability falls to $4.630 million. Thus, the present value of the liability is sensitive to interest rates. What one would like to do is invest in assets having the same sensitivity. This, of course, is accomplished by purchasing assets with the same duration as the liability duration.

This can be seen in the three columns in Table 11-2, which display asset market values for bonds with different durations. When interest rates are at 6%, the market value of each

---

[6] In this example, we neglect cash flows beyond year 1. They are considered later in the chapter.

TABLE 11-2   PRESENT VALUES OF LIABILITIES AND ASSETS AT DIFFERENT INTEREST RATES

Level of Interest Rates	Market Value of Liability	Asset Market Values for Various Durations		
		Duration of 1 Year	Duration of 0.5 Years	Duration of 2 Years
0.04	4.808	4.808	4.762	4.900
0.06	4.717	4.717	4.717	4.717
0.08	4.630	4.630	4.673	4.544

investment portfolio is $4.717, equal to the liability's present value. But when interest rates move away from 6%, the only portfolio that exactly tracks the present value of the liability is the portfolio with a duration equal to the duration of the liability (one year).

While this is a relatively naive example, it points out an important principle. In practice, sponsors of defined benefit pension plans often immunize their liabilities to retired employees. For example, assume the trustees in our example had not properly matched asset duration with liability duration but, instead, invested in the portfolio with a 2-year duration. If interest rates rose to 8%, the market value of assets would be $0.086 million less than the market value of the liability ($4.544 minus $4.630). This asset deficiency would have to be made up by addition contributions of money to the pension plan.

THE BANKRUPTCY OF ORANGE COUNTY, CALIFORNIA

There is a long history of the problems that can arise if the duration of asset investments is significantly different from the duration of liabilities. One of the more dramatic stories is that of Orange County, California. In 1994, the 2.6 million population of Orange County made it the third most populous county in the United States. Cities in the county include Anaheim, Laguna Beach, Irvine, Newport Beach, and Santa Ana.

Like most municipal governments, Orange County maintained an operating account of cash from which operating expenses were paid. Operating expenses include payments for employee salaries, ongoing road repairs, telephone charges, and purchase of supplies. Although such operating funds are continually replenished as taxes are collected, the balance of the fund at any point in time is usually spent within a year. (The liability the fund is to meet has a duration of less than a year.)

And like most municipal governments, Orange County decided to invest funds in this operating account in order to earn a return on the funds as opposed to letting them sit idle. But the investment strategies followed by the fund's investment manager (the county treasurer) were very different than typically employed. They exposed the portfolio to considerable interest rate risk.

Most municipal operating accounts are invested in securities with a duration of a year or less (often in repurchase agreements with durations of one day). But during the 1980s and early 1990s, interest rates in the United States had been falling. Seeing the larger returns being earned on longer term investments, the treasurer of Orange County decided to invest the funds in longer term fixed income securities.

For a number of years, this strategy worked marvelously. As interest rates continued to decline, returns on the fund were considerably larger than returns being earned on other local municipal operating accounts. Betwen 1991 and 1993, the county enjoyed more than a 8.5% return on investments when other bond investment funds were earning about 7.0%. In fact, profits from portfolio investments became an important source of revenue to the county, representing an incredible 22% of the county's budget in 1991.

As word got out about the performance of the fund, many other local governmental bodies asked to have their operating accounts pooled with those of Orange County in order to benefit from investment strategies used by the fund manager. By the end of 1993, more than $7.6 billion in funds were being managed, up from $3.0 billion in 1991.

The strategy of investing in securities with a duration longer than the duration of liabilities worked so well during the early 1990s (as interest rates fell) that the county decided to leverage its position. In 1994, the fund borrowed $1.2 billion, which it invested in long-term bonds and derivative securities whose values were very sensitive to interest rates. A strategy of borrowing and then investing the borrowings in derivative securities is extremely risky. Although it may be appropriate for investors with the ability to handle the large losses that are possible, it is totally inappropriate for the investment of governmental operating funds. As long as interest rates continued to fall, the strategy would continue to provide greater returns than from investing shorter term. But if interest rates were to rise, the county would be in for disaster.

Unfortunately, interest rates did rise. On November 15, 1994, the Federal Reserve Board raised the discount rate at which banks could borrow from the Fed by 0.75% in order to cool an expanding economy and reduce the potential for increased inflation. This led to an increase in interest rates throughout the United States and resulted in a large decrease in the value of the county's investments. During late November and early December, the fund was drained of cash due to demands by members of the investment pool to return funds they had invested and to provide additional margin to lenders to the fund. On December 6, 1994, Orange County filed for federal bankruptcy protection under Chapter 9 of the federal bankruptcy code.

Losses of the fund were about $1.7 billion. These losses and the ensuing bankruptcy led to significant cutbacks in services. The county had difficulty meeting payrolls. Planned expenditures on road improvements were curtailed. There was a 40% cut in health and welfare benefits. School employees were laid off. Contracts made by the county had to be renegotiated. And repayments of nearly $1.0 billion of debt obligations were postponed for nearly one year.

What lessons can we learn from this debacle?

For one, the Orange County situation is a prime example of the interest rate risk incurred when the duration of asset investments is not equal to the duration of fund needs. The manager of the fund was counting on continued decreases in interest rates that would lead to increased values of fund investments. But the manager was no better at predicting changes in interest rates than the flip of a coin.

In addition, better ways of disclosing the risks of a portfolio need to be developed and provided to the public. For example, few people knew of the extreme risk position in which the operating fund had been placed. Investors in bond issues of the county had no idea the county was pursuing investment strategies which were so risky that the strategies could cause a default on the securities they owned.

Immunization Does Not Guarantee Real Returns. A portfolio that is immunized against interest rate risk guarantees a nominal rate of return over the portfolio's investment horizon. The real return to the portfolio, however, is uncertain. For example, if you wish to purchase a home in one year, then one-year T-bills provide a certain nominal dollar value in a year. But since home prices are affected by inflation during the year, the ownership of one-year T-bills does not guarantee you will have enough money to purchase a home.

Before you decide to immunize a portfolio from interest rate risk, be clear about the purpose of the investment portfolio: Are real or nominal returns desired? If the answer is nominal returns, then it is possible to immunize interest rate risk. If the answer is real returns, then it is not possible to immunize the portfolio.

Bond Price Changes. Duration represents the weighted average date at which cash flows on a bond (or a bond portfolio) are received. As such, it is a measure of how sensitive a bond's price is to interest rates. The greater the duration, the greater the sensitivity. While not exact, the following relationship exists among percentage bond price changes, duration, and changes in a bond's YTM:

Duration Approximation of Price Return

$$R_{it} \approx -D_i\,[(YTM_t - YTM_{t-1}) \div (1 + YTM_{t-1})] \tag{11.5}$$

In this equation, R_{it} represents the (price) return on bond i during period t, D_i is the duration of bond i, and YTM stands for the yield to maturity. The negative sign is required in the equation to reflect the fact that bond prices and interest rate are inversely related.

For example, assume the YTM on a bond is now 11% but it is expected to decline to 10% in the near future. If the bond has a four-year duration, the expected price increase is (about) 3.6%:

$$0.036 \approx -4.0[(0.10 - 0.11) \div (1.11)]$$

Investors needn't examine maturity and coupon effects separately, since both are included in the duration measure. If interest rates are expected to fall across all maturities, one should buy bonds with a long duration. If yields are expected to change by different amounts in each duration range, one should buy bonds with a duration that will provide the largest return, per Equation (11.5).

Duration Principles. Because of the importance of duration in bond management, we review a number of the more important principles of duration. Many of these are visually illustrated in Figure 11-2. Principle 1 relates to zero-coupon bonds. All other principles relate to bonds that pay coupons and have no options (to convert, call, or default).

1. *The duration of a zero-coupon bond is equal to its time to maturity.* This is displayed in Figure 11-2 as the 45-degree line.
2. *Holding other factors constant, a bond's duration is directly related to the bond's maturity.*[7] This can be seen in Figure 11-2 by the fact that the slope of each curve is positive.
3. *Holding other factors constant, a bond's duration is inversely related to its coupon rate.* This can also be seen in Figure 11-2. The bottom curve shows the duration profile for a 10% coupon bond when the YTM is also 10%. The curve immediately above it shows the duration profile for bonds with a 5% coupon when YTMs are 10%. The fact that the lower coupon bond has the greater duration is due, of course, to the fact that a larger fraction of such a bond's cash flows are longer term cash flows.
4. *Holding other factors constant, a bond's duration is inversely related to yields to maturity.* Examine the two bonds in Figure 11-2 that have a 10% coupon. When prevailing YTMs are 6%, such bonds have a greater duration than when they have a YTM of 10%. This is due to the fact that, at higher interest rates, long-term cash flows represent a smaller fraction of a bond's total market value.

Modified Duration. Recall Equation (11.5) in which the (price) return on a bond was shown to be related to a bond's Macaulay duration as follows:

$$R_{it} \approx -D_i[(YTM_t - YTM_{t-1}) \div (1 + YTM_{t-1})]$$

It is often more convenient to modify the Macaulay duration number by dividing it by "one plus the beginning yield to maturity" $(1 + YTM_{t-1})$. This duration number is called **modified duration.**

Modified Macaulay Duration

$$D^* = D \div (1 + YTM_{t-1}) \tag{11.6}$$

For example, if interest rates are now 11% and the duration of a bond is four years, then the bond's modified duration is 3.6036 years $(4 \div 1.11)$. The convenience in doing this is that the percentage change in a bond's price is easier to calculate for a given modified duration than it is for a given Macaulay duration. Using the modified duration number, the approximate percentage change in a bond's price for a small change in interest rates is equal to the bond's modified duration multiplied by the change in interest rates.

Modified Duration Approximation of Bond Price Return

$$R_{it} \approx -D_i^* (YTM_t - YTM_{t-1}) \tag{11.7}$$

---

[7] There is an exception to this principle. The duration of low-coupon bonds initially increases as maturity increases. But, after some point, the duration of a low-coupon bond actually falls as maturity increases.

FIGURE 11-2   DURATION VERSUS MATURITY

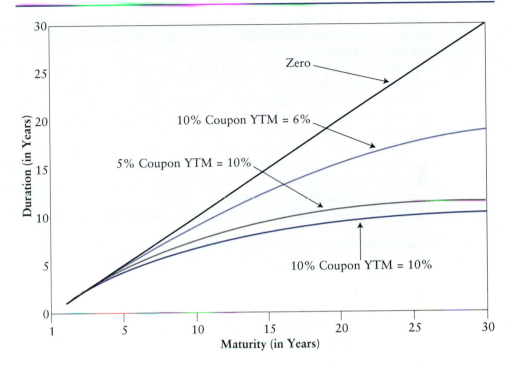

For example, if a bond's modified duration is 3.6036 years and interest rates move from 11% to 10%, then the price of the bond is expected to rise by 3.6%:

$$0.036 = -3.6036(0.10 - 0.11)$$

The interpretation of modified duration is as follows: *A bond's modified duration represents the (approximate) percentage change in the bond's price for a 1% move in interest rates.* If a bond has a 3.6 year modified duration, a 1% move in interest rates will cause a 3.6% price change; a 2% move in interest rates will cause a 7.2% price change, and so forth.

Equations (11.5) and (11.7) are only approximations. For very small changes in interest rates, the equations provide fairly accurate estimates. But for large changes in interest rates, actual bond returns can differ from the approximations considerably. The reason why these equations are approximations can be seen in duration principle 4: *Holding other factors constant, a bond's duration is inversely related to yields to maturity.* As interest rates decline, a bond's duration increases, causing its price to be even more sensitive to interest rates. As interest rates rise, a bond's duration becomes decline, causing its price to be less sensitive to interest rates. This change in bond duration is referred to as **convexity.**

Convexity. The concept of convexity is shown in Figure 11-3. The colored curve in the figure represents the market value of a 10% coupon bond with a 30-year life at various interest rates. The solid black line that is tangent with the colored curve at 10% interest represents the bond values predicted by each duration measure if interest rates start at 10% and either increase or decrease.

Notice that the price levels implied by duration are linear whereas the actual market prices are curved. The shaded area in the figure represents the differences between actual market prices at various interest rates and duration predictions. For small changes in interest rates, the actual market price will be very close to the duration prediction. But for larger changes in interest rates, sizable differences will arise.

The degree to which the relationship between bond prices and interest rates is curved is called the convexity of the bond. Various approximations of convexity are used by professional bond traders together with duration in order to more accurately predict price changes for various interest rate changes.

The colored curve in Figure 11-3 has what we call **positive convexity.**

■ As interest rates fall, bond prices rise. In addition, a bond's duration increases. This increase in duration as interest rates fall causes the bond's price to increase at an increasing rate.

■ As interest rates increase, bond prices fall. In addition, a bond's duration decreases. This decrease in duration as interest rates rise causes the bond's price to fall at a decreasing rate.

FIGURE 11-3   BOND PRICE CONVEXITY

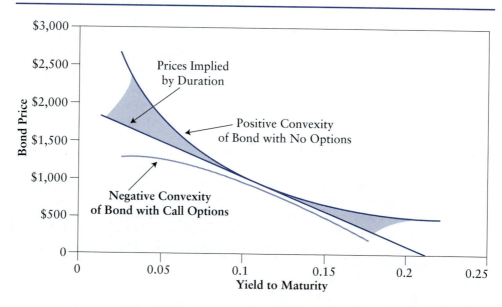

Because duration moves in the direction that investors would wish (increased duration as interest rates fall and decreased duration as interest rates raise), we call this form of convexity "positive." *Bonds with no probability of default, call, or convertibility will have positive convexity.*

If there are options associated with a bond, it is possible that a **negative convexity** relationship will exist. An example of negative convexity is shown in Figure 11-3 as the bottom curve. If a bond has negative convexity, then a decrease in interest rates will lead to a decrease in duration. Therefore, the price of a bond with negative convexity will not increase as much in response to a decline in interest rates as will the price of a bond with positive convexity.

The most common reason for negative convexity is the presence of an option to call the bond. If the issuer of the bond has an option to retire the bond at a specified call price, the call price will act as a barrier above which the bond's price will not trade.

Negative convexity is a particular problem with mortgage-backed securities, since mortgage borrowers have the option to pay off their mortgage loans without a penalty charge. When interest rates fall, mortgage loans are repaid more rapidly than expected as borrowers choose to refinance at lower rates. Although all principal is repaid, the expected amount of interest on the mortgage-backed instrument declines. As a result, the market value of the mortgage-backed security does not increase in reaction to interest rate declines as much as do straight bonds (those with no options).

In short, if the interest rate risk position of a portfolio is to be effectively managed, both duration and convexity must be managed. As an example, consider the information shown in Figure 11-4. This is a picture of a computer display that is available on the Bloomberg system. Bloomberg is a computer network that provides market prices on virtually all traded securities together with computer programs which allow traders to examine the risks associated with various trades.[8] Figure 11-4 shows the effect of a long position in 10,000 units of a 5 5/8% coupon U.S. Treasury that matures in June 1997 together with a short position of 1,273 units in a 7 5/8% coupon U.S. Treasury that matures in February 2025. The net modified duration of such a position is zero, but the net convexity is negative 0.33.

Figure 11-5 is another Bloomberg display that shows the profit or loss from such a position for various changes in interest rates. The display makes it visually clear that this is a poor position to undertake, since a loss will be incurred for any change in interest rates. It is possible, however, that options or futures contracts could be added to the position and result in a profit for any change in interest rates.

Bullet Immunization Versus Cash-Dedicated Portfolios. Assume you are the administrator of a pension fund. The fund will have payment obligations of two types: (1) future benefit payments to current employees, and (2) current and future benefit payments to retired employees ("retired lives"). Immunized portfolios are widely used to fund the pension's retired-life portion but are less used for active employees. This is because retired-life benefit payments can be projected more accurately and because

---

[8] Real-time access to market prices and computer programs that allow one to analyze the risks of various combinations of securities are vital to investment professionals who trade actively.

FIGURE 11-4

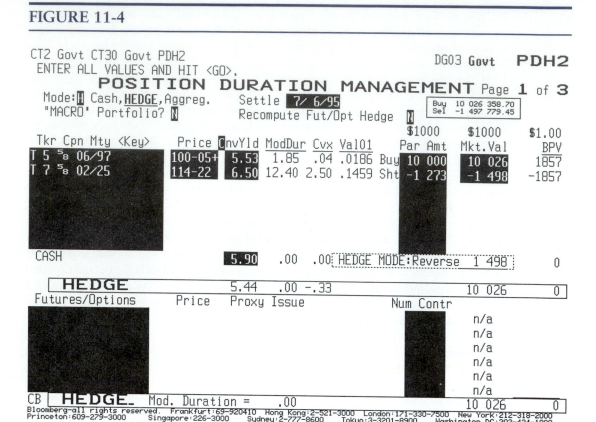

Courtesy of: Bloomberg Financial Markets Commodities News

benefits to current employees are real-dollar liabilities (tied to inflation through salary growth). Real-dollar liabilities cannot be immunized.

Table 11-3 gives hypothetical actuarial projections of the total benefits that will be paid to retired lives. Instead of a single horizon date to be immunized, a series of many horizon dates exists. Each could be immunized separately, of course, but it would be easier and cheaper if they could all be immunized at one time. This is really very simple to do. Instead of using the series of many horizon dates, a single weighted average horizon date is calculated in exactly the same way that a bond's duration is calculated.

For example, let's assume interest rates are 10% for all maturities. In order to fund the $5 million due at the end of year 1, $4,545,454.54 in zero-coupon, one-year duration bonds would have to be bought ($5 million ÷ 1.10). Similarly, to fund the $5 million due at the end of year 2, $4,132,231.41 would have to be bought ($5 million ÷ 1.10^2). Continuing with the other liabilities, a total investment of $21.47 million would be required. The duration of these liabilities is calculated here in the same fashion that the duration of a bond is calculated:

FIGURE 11-5

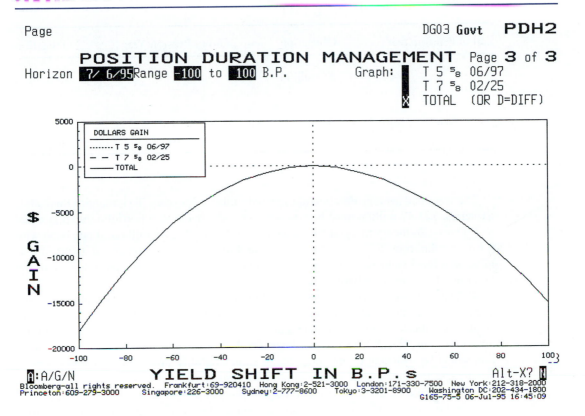

Page   DG03 **Govt**   **PDH2**

POSITION DURATION MANAGEMENT Page **3** of **3**
Horizon **7/ 6/95** Range **-100** to **100** B.P.   Graph: █ T 5 ⁵₈ 06/97
                                                                T 7 ⁵₈ 02/25
                                                          X TOTAL (OR D=DIFF)

DOLLARS GAIN
········· T 5 ⁵₈ 06/97
─ ─ T 7 ⁵₈ 02/25
───── TOTAL

A:A/G/N   **YIELD SHIFT IN B.P.s**   Alt-X? **N**

Courtesy of: Bloomberg Financial Markets Commodities News

Year	Current Funding Requirement	Percentage of Total	Weighted Average Liability
Duration			
1	$ 4.54 million	21.15%	0.2115
2	4.13	19.24	0.3847
3	3.01	14.02	0.4206
4	2.73	12.72	0.5086
5	2.48	11.55	0.5776
6	1.69	7.87	0.4723
7	1.54	7.17	0.5021
8	0.93	4.33	0.3465
9	0.42	1.96	0.1761
10	0.00	—	—
Total	$21.47 million	100.00%	3.6000 years

TABLE 11-3   HYPOTHETICAL PENSION FUND—TOTAL BENEFITS PAID TO RETIRED LIVE

End of Pension Year	Obligation	End of Pension Year	Obligation
1	$5 million	6	$3 million
2	5	7	3
3	4	8	2
4	4	9	1
5	4	10	0

The weighted average duration of these liabilities is 3.6 years. To immunize this liability series, $21.47 million must be invested in bonds that have a portfolio duration equal to 3.6 years. In theory this could be done by purchasing $21.47 million of one bond with a 3.6-year duration. This is an example of **bullet immunization.** In general, bullet immunization refers to situations in which the average duration of the bond portfolio equals the duration of the portfolio liability stream.

A **cash-dedicated** bond investment portfolio is one that will provide coupon payments and maturing principal amounts exactly when required to meet liabilities (desired cash receipts). A dedicated portfolio is an immunized portfolio, but a very special type of immunization occurs. Recall from our pension example that a single bond with a 3.6-year duration would be sufficient to immunize the pension's liability stream. If an investor wished to purchase two bonds, one with a three-year duration and one with a four-year duration, then 40% would be invested in the three-year bond and 60% in the four-year bond. This combination also results in a portfolio duration of 3.6 years. Many other combinations resulting in a 3.6-year duration are possible, of course. A cash-dedicated portfolio simply carries these possible combinations to the limit. In a cash-dedicated portfolio, rebalancing is theoretically unnecessary. Scheduled coupons and maturing principal amounts exactly match the cash needs.

Dedicated portfolios have a number of advantages over more classic immunization techniques. First, they are easier to understand. Exact cash matching as a means of immunization against interest rate risk is a much easier concept to follow than the reinvestment and price risk offsets associated with normal immunization. Second, a rebalancing is not necessary every time interest rates change, as is necessary with normal immunization. In addition, if a good cash match is in fact possible, a more accurate forecast of future returns is possible. One need not worry about the assumption used in the calculation of duration of a flat yield curve. Finally, the procedure can result in a larger number of bonds being held and thus a greater amount of diversification than might be obtained by standard immunization.

Cash-dedicated portfolios do have their costs, however. Most of these relate to reduced flexibility. In particular, many bond managers desire to trade bonds in an attempt to pick up abnormal profits through quality swaps and other speculative trades. In a dedicated portfolio, the bond manager faces more constraints on available trading opportunities.

Passive Bond Investment

By our definition of investment versus speculation, investors accept security prices as fair—that is, priced so the expected return is commensurate with the risk. Investors rely on active trading by speculators to seek out and trade in mispriced securities in order to ensure that gross distortions among security prices will not exist. While some speculative profits might exist, they are small and not worth the cost to the investor of finding them.

A passive strategy does not mean there are no decisions to be made. Passive investors must continually monitor the bond portfolio to ensure it has an appropriate default risk exposure, will not suffer from bond calls, and has the desired duration.

Asset Allocation

Bonds can expand portfolio risk return opportunities. By including bonds in a portfolio, the investor can gain in two ways. First, bond returns are less than perfectly correlated with other security classes. Thus, when mixed with other asset classes, the increased diversification causes investment risk to decline. In addition, by altering the portfolio's allocation between bonds and other security classes, total portfolio risk can be easily managed.

The risk of owning a diversified set of bonds depends on (1) whether real returns or nominal returns are desired, and (2) the bond investment strategy chosen.

Consider the following case. An insurance company has a five-year investment horizon and is not concerned about future rates of inflation. The company is considering the risks and expected returns for various equity and bond combinations. Different bond investment strategies are being considered, as follows:

1. Buy and hold a five-year duration zero-coupon government bond.
2. Purchase a one-year government bond and roll its maturity value into a sequence of new one-year government bonds.
3. Buy ten-year duration government bonds and rebalance the duration at the start of each year to maintain a constant ten-year duration.

The five-year expected returns and risks of these strategies are shown in Figure 11-6. Clearly, the first strategy is the best, since it is based on a zero-risk (default, call, and interest rate) portfolio. The second has risk associated with future reinvestment income. The third has uncertainty about the value of ten-year duration bonds in five years from now.

Notice in our example that short-term instruments such as T-bills are not risk free. Also notice that the risk-free security is a buy-hold bond portfolio with an initial duration of five years. It is not an actively managed portfolio. For example, if a constant five-year duration portfolio were evaluated it would also have risk attached to the year 5 value. In short, bond risk depends on the bond strategy chosen.

Now consider another example. Janet and Charles are saving to purchase a second home in five years. Since housing prices are expected to move perfectly with inflation, their objective is expressed in terms of a real rate of return. They are also considering the same three bond strategies as the insurance company did.

FIGURE 11-6   EFFICIENT FRONTIER FOR VARIOUS BOND STRATEGIES OBJECTIVE: NOMINAL 5-YEAR VALUE

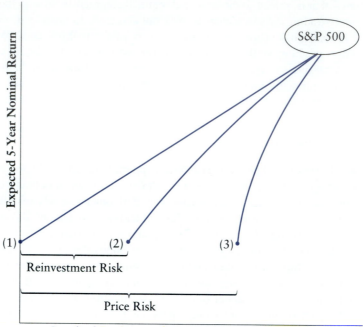

Illustrative efficient frontiers facing Janet and Charles are shown in Figure 11-7. Notice that bonds are no longer risk free; inflation risk is present. Notice also that strategies 1 and 2 are reversed. This is because unexpected inflation has a greater impact on a five-year duration bond than it does on one-year bonds. The yields on the short-term bonds are adjusted at the start of each year for any revised inflation forecasts.

Bond Diversification. Whenever the returns on securities are not perfectly correlated, diversification across the securities will reduce portfolio risk. To illustrate the potential advantages inherent in corporate bond diversification, McEnally and Boardman collected monthly rates of return for 515 corporate bonds rated Baa or better from December 1972 through June 1976. They then simulated the results that would have been obtained by holding portfolios with different numbers of bonds. Each portfolio's risk was measured by the variance of that portfolio's monthly return during the full time period examined. Portfolios were constrained to consist of only one quality rating (Aaa, Aa, a, or Baa), and the number of bonds allowed in each portfolio ranged from 1 to 40. Their results are displayed in Figure 11-8.

The reduction in bond portfolio risk made possible by increasing the number of bonds held was dramatic and achieved quite rapidly. While McEnally and Boardman showed

FIGURE 11-7   EFFICIENT FRONTIER FOR VARIOUS BOND STRATEGIES
OBJECTIVE: NOMINAL 5-YEAR VALUE

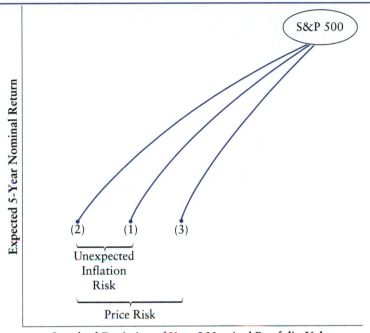

Standard Deviation of Year 5 Nominal Portfolio Value

that the benefits associated with common stock diversification are even greater, the reduction in bond risk is still substantial.[9]

Since many bonds have par value of $1,000, it is difficult for small investors to diversify by direct ownership. A realistic alternative is to purchase shares in a commingled mutual fund. During the 1980s and early 1990s, the number of bond mutual funds grew dramatically. By 1995, the aggregate value of bond mutual funds in the United States was greater than the aggregate value of stock funds. Even large investors such as pension and endowment funds invest indirectly in bonds. Often they purchase mutual fund shares. More typically, however, they employ professional investment managers to invest in bonds.

Index bond funds attempt to provide returns that emulate a specific bond index such as the Lehman Brothers Government/Corporate or Salomon Brothers World Bond Index. Many mutual funds and bond managers, however, specialize in particular bond types and particular bond durations. For example, a short-term investment fund (a STIF) will allow high-grade corporates and governments with maturities ranging from one to three years.

---

[9] Notice that the lowest risk portfolio appears to be in the highest default risk group. This is most likely due to the fact that higher default-risk bonds have shorter maturities. Thus, they would have the lower price sensitivity to shifts in the yield curve.

FIGURE 11-8   NAIVE BOND DIVERSIFICATION

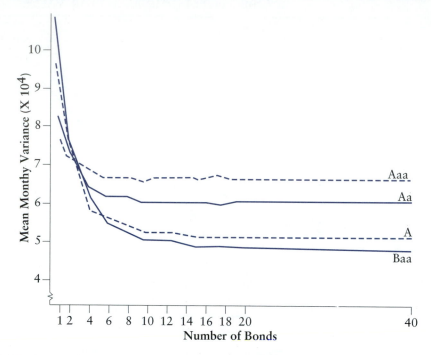

SOURCE: "Aspects of Corporate Bond Portfolio Diversification," by R. McEnally and C. Boardman from *The Journal of Financial Research,* Spring 1979. Reprinted by permission.

When purchasing bond mutual funds that specialize in a particular segment of the bond market, it is best to diversify across a number of fund types.

Effects of Calls

In the mid-1980s, investors became increasingly convinced that inflation had been licked for some years into the future. Federal Reserve monetary policies had been steadily reducing inflation over the prior four years and, in early 1986, oil prices fell dramatically as world demand for oil declined and OPEC unraveled. The result was a dramatic decrease in interest rates across all maturities. By mid-1986, 30-day T-bills were selling at a YTM of less than 6.0% and 30-year T-bonds were selling at a YTM of 7.2%. Just six months earlier these yields had been 8.5% and 11.5%, respectively. The resulting increases in bond prices were equally dramatic. Many long-term bonds experienced returns during the year prior to March 31, 1986, of 45% or more. But not all was rosy—particularly for people who owned callable bonds.

   Many people bought long-term bonds in the early 1980s with the belief that they would be getting high coupon earnings for many years to come. Unfortunately, they had paid too little attention to their bonds' call provisions. As interest rates plummeted, large numbers of call announcements appeared in the financial press. One advisory firm estimated there were more than 330 calls by taxable corporations during 1986. And potential municipal bond calls were impossible to estimate, owing to the large number of bond issues outstanding (about 53,000 different issues in 1986).

As a result, most of the price increases in bonds came in the U.S. Treasury market, because T-bonds are not callable until five years before maturity. Investment portfolios with large holdings of Treasuries increased substantially in value. But portfolios of corporate and municipal bonds had their returns limited by the call provisions on these bonds.

Besides affecting the returns on actively managed bond portfolios, these calls were an embarrassment to many professionals who had supposedly created fully immunized bond portfolios. When bonds held in such portfolios were called, all aspects of immunization were lost. It was foolhardy to try to immunize using callable bonds.

When a bond is likely to be called by the issuer prior to maturity, the YTM can be a misleading figure. In such cases the investor should calculate an expected yield to call date. Because considerable uncertainty exists about the expected call date, most bond houses calculate and publish a yield to first call return. Instead of using an expected date of call, the first possible call date is used.

Yield to Call

$$P_0 = \sum_{t=1} \frac{COUPON}{(1 + YTM_C)^t} + \frac{CALL}{(1 + YTM_C)^C} \tag{11.8}$$

where CALL is the dollar payment that would be made at the first call date, C is the number of periods until call, and YTM_c is the yield to first call.

International Bond Investment

Communication and trading procedures between countries have developed to the point that investors should consider placing a portion of their portfolio assets in fixed income securities issued in foreign countries. While non-U.S. citizens have invested heavily in U.S. bonds (particularly U.S. Treasury issues) for many years, extensive international bond investment by U.S. citizens is more recent.

Two benefits are gained from foreign bond investment. First, foreign bond returns are less than perfectly correlated with U.S. security returns. Thus, they provide an opportunity to further diversify a portfolio.

Second, there are often periods when the YTMs available on foreign bonds are greater than available for equivalent risk issues in one's domestic economy. In Chapter 15, we discuss the concept of interest rate parity. **Interest rate parity** states that in equilibrium, the real rate of interest must be the same in every country. If real rates (after expected inflation) differ across countries, then arbitrage profits are available from borrowing in the low-interest country and lending in the high-interest country. There are, in fact, extended periods during which interest rates between countries are not in equilibrium.

When one invests in a foreign country, a risk is incurred that is not present in domestic investing—this is called **exchange rate risk.** For example, assume you invest in German money market securities that will return 9% at year-end. Although the return in Germany is certain, the rate at which German marks can be converted into U.S. dollars in a year is unknown today.

Adolfo Marzol

Senior Vice President: Capital Markets,
Fannie Mae
University of Florida, M.A.
University of Florida, B.B.A., with highest honors

When this interview was given, Adolfo Marzol was the Chief Financial Officer for Chase Manhattan Mortgage Corporation, a full service mortgage bank that originates mortgage loans, securitizes and services loans for others and invests in mortgage assets. Adolofo states that, when he started in mortgage banking, he didn't know much about the business. He joined his first employer because the top three officers were very bright and enthusiastic about the business.

Q: What does the chief financial officer of a mortgage company do? How is it similar to CFOs in other industries and how is it different?

A: I have the traditional CFO responsibilities of financial and strategic planning, corporate accounting, and regulatory and audit compliance. I also have some nontraditional CFO responsibilities involving interest rate risk management. It is customary when we originate a mortgage to a borrower to commit an interest rate to that borrower prior to closing that loan. I'm responsible for the group that sets the pricing for our mortgage products and protects that value. Then I take that mortgage and aggregate it with thousands of other mortgages and issue a security in the capital markets. I have the responsibility for the group that does the pricing, the hedging, and the securitization for all of the mortgages that we do not keep in the investment portfolio of the bank.

Q: How does your bank/mortgage company go about issuing a security in the capital markets?

A: The single most common way is that we issue mortgages eligible for the programs offered by FNMA, FHLMC, and GNMA, which are government-sponsored entities whose role it is to provide liquidity in the capital markets. They guarantee to investors the timely payment of principal and interest. We take a basket of $1 million FNMA eligible loans we originated and deliver the loans to FNMA. They wave their magic wand over it and say this is now a FNMA security which an investor can buy in the markets.

Q: Is it the responsibility of the mortgage originator to attempt to write mortgages that will meet, for example, FNMA guidelines?

A: Yes, we must follow their guidelines, interpret them correctly, make credit decisions, obtain appraisals to verify the property value, and verify you have the financial resources for the down payment. All that legwork is the responsibility of the lender. There's very little work done by FNMA other than, at the end of the process, to put their seal of approval on and say this group of loans is now an FNMA-insured security, which gives that security an unquestioned credit quality. That creates liquidity and strong investor interest because investors don't have to worry about whether each loan was prudently underwritten or whether the lender is going to perform its responsibility in passing the money through. The structure of most mortgage-backed securities is that the investor gets paid whether or not the individual borrower pays because the credit risk is the responsibility of the FNMA.

Q: Who bears the interest rate risk?

A: Investors that own these securities need to be cognizant of prepayment risk. Since mortgagors get a free option to prepay their loans, as interest rates decline, prepayments speed up dramatically. If you buy a seven-year Treasury, you're going to get your coupon for seven years. Your duration is known. If you buy a CMO, your duration is affected by prepayment risk. When rates fall you start experiencing dramatic prepayment and the duration may shorten from, say, seven to three years. The enjoyment you would have had from falling interest rates because you invested at higher rates gets called away. This risk is compensated for in CMOs with higher interest rates. Certain tranches of CMOs have more of the prepayment risk concentrated into them and they have even more variability in their average life and duration. An investor in mortgages is always trying to decide, is the extra interest going to be adequate to get me to take this option risk because the mortgage may be shorter or longer lived than I thought?

Q: Does Chase care about prepayment risk?

A: We are also big investors in mortgages and a mortgage servicer, so we worry quite a bit about prepayment risk. Mortgage servicers sell the loan and retain the right to service that loan. As a servicer, Chase's principal source of compensation is to share in the interest revenue from the borrower. Consequently, I want to retain as many mortgages as possible. The more people that prepay, the less fee income I get for servicing. One reason mortgage originators are also mortgage servicers is so the risks of those businesses offset each other. To protect ourselves, we do rigorous modeling around prepayment risk, and our first line of defense is to employ financial instruments which will appreciate when rates decline. We utilize long futures, long cash Treasury instruments, swaps where we get paid a fixed rate and we pay a floating rate which is basically like owing a bond, and we buy interest rate floors in order to actively manage prepayment risk.

To hedge this risk, most international bond managers trade in futures or forward contracts. For example, assume $1 million is exchanged into German marks at an exchange rate of $0.60 per mark and invested in a one-year German government T-bill paying a return of 9%. At the end of the year, 1,816,660 marks will be available for return to the United States (1,666,666 × 1.09). To eliminate uncertainty about the exchange rate, forward contracts or futures could be traded. In this example, the ideal contract would require that 1,816,666 marks be delivered for a specific number of dollars. Let's assume the forward or futures rate is $0.59 per mark. Thus, $1,071,833 would be "locked up" for return to the United States in one year (1,816,666 × 0.59). Accounting for the change in the exchange rate, the net U.S. dollar return would be 7.18%.

Small investors wishing to acquire exchange-rate-hedged positions in foreign bonds should consider mutual funds that specialize in international bonds.

Active Bond Management

There are numerous ways to speculate in bonds. But regardless of the techniques used, certain keys to successful bond speculation include the following:

■ *Fast access to new information.* Speculators must have early access to economic and political news so they can trade before bond prices change in reaction to the new information.

■ *Liquidity.* Because speculators must be able to trade quickly on new information without affecting market prices, they prefer to trade in bonds with large active markets.

■ *Interest rate sensitivity.* Most bond speculation revolves around forecasts of future interest rates. For this reason, speculators prefer to trade largely in instruments whose prices are influenced by changes in the general level of interest rates, as opposed to those for which default and call risks are important. Most speculation is done in high-quality corporate and municipal bonds or U.S. government issues.

One way to order the process of bond speculation is shown in Figure 11-9. Initially, a set of investment objectives are specified that are used to determine the ideal bond investment portfolio. We use Leibowitz's term for this ideal investment portfolio and refer to it as the baseline portfolio. The baseline portfolio will be fully immunized, having a portfolio duration equal to the planned horizon date. In addition, the baseline portfolio should consist of bonds having appropriate default risk, call protection, tax characteristics, marketability, and other features necessary to fulfill the portfolio's stated objectives. After the baseline portfolio has been determined (but not yet bought), the manager of the portfolio will forecast future levels of the yield curve and alter the portfolio's duration in hopes of improving on the next period's return. If interest rates are expected to rise, duration will be shortened in order to reduce expected price losses and improve reinvestment income. If interest rates are expected to fall, duration will be lengthened in order to reduce expected losses from lower reinvestment income and improve expected price gains. The portfolio is not fully immunized and thus is subject to interest rate risk. But the manager might judge

FIGURE 11-9   THE PROCESS OF BOND SPECULATION

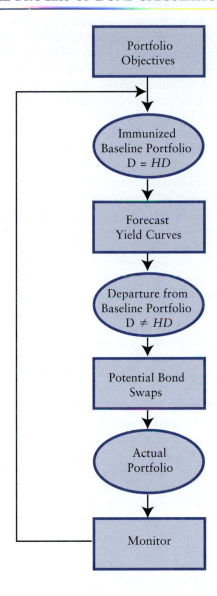

the risks well worth taking for the extra returns expected. After the portfolio's duration is set, the manager will examine individual bonds and purchase those offering the greatest yields but still meeting the portfolio's long-run objectives. (Later in the chapter we discuss how this is done when we examine bond swaps.) Finally, the manager will constantly monitor the portfolio's performance, new economic and political news, and prices of bonds that might be substituted (swapped) for those now held.

We now consider two important steps in analyzing future yield curves and potential bond swaps.

Trading on Yield Curve Shifts

Theoretically, if a fully immunized bond portfolio is maintained, the *ARR* between the time at which the portfolio is acquired and the *HD* at which the portfolio is sold should be equal to the portfolio's promised YTM when initially bought. For example, panel A in Figure 11-10 plots as the solid line a hypothetical yield curve for pure discount bonds that have no call or default risks. If the horizon date is ten years and a portfolio of bonds with a ten-year duration is initially bought, then the expected *ARR* over the next ten years is 10%. However, as we just saw, the expected returns during any single year are expected to be different from this geometric average *ARR*. For example, during year 1 the expected return would be 8% if the yield curve shifts through time as the unbiased expectations theory suggests it should. This first-year expected return is plotted as the solid line in panel B. The one-year return is shown on the vertical axis, and the difference between the duration of the portfolio selected and the horizon date is shown on the horizontal axis. When duration is equal to the horizon date ($D - HD = 0$), the portfolio is fully immunized against interest rate risks. When duration is less than the *HD*, the portfolio is exposed to net interest rate reinvestment risk. When duration is greater than the *HD*, the portfolio is exposed to net interest rate price risk.

Assuming the *HD* is ten years, the baseline portfolio should have a duration of ten years. However, the speculator will forecast future levels of the yield curve and temporarily change the portfolio's duration in an attempt to pick up yearly returns greater than expected from the immunized baseline portfolio. For example, if the dotted curve in panel A of Figure 11-10 reflects the speculator's estimate of the yield curve level in exactly one year, this would result in the one-year rates of return as shown in panel B by the dotted curve.

If the baseline portfolio is held, the speculator expects a 10% one-year return. However, by shortening the portfolio's duration, the speculator can expect a return as high as 21%. Of course, when the portfolio's duration is set below (or above) that of the baseline portfolio, interest rate risk is incurred. The portfolio manager must decide whether the added expected return is worth the risk.

An actual example of an analysis of single-period returns possible from expected changes in the yield curve is shown in Figure 11-11. This is a picture of a computer display obtained from the Bloomberg system. The initial yield curve is dated June 6, 1995, and the next yield curve for one month later. These are the two curves at the bottom of the display. The top curve represents the one-month rate of return that would be earned by owning securities of a given maturity if the yield curve changes as predicted.

Bond managers who alter a portfolio's duration based on a forecast of future interest rates are called bond timers or, more formally, interest rate anticipators. There is little empirical evidence that active bond timing works, although this does not mean all bond timing doesn't work. There will be many periods in which the interest rate forecast is correct. But studies conducted to date suggest that active bond timing decisions are about as successful as the flip of a coin would be.

Bond portfolio duration can be changed by (1) trading in "spot" bonds, or (2) trading in bond derivatives. For example, assume a bond manager wants to reduce her portfolio duration from seven years to four years. She could do so by actually selling long-duration bonds and buying bonds with shorter durations. Alternatively, she could leave the spot bond positions alone and reduce duration by selling a futures contract on U.S. T-bonds. Detailed calculations of the quantity to trade are complex enough to delay to Chapter 16. But derivative positions are often fast and cheap alternatives to trading in spot assets.

FIGURE 11-10 YIELDS ON DISCOUNT BONDS WITH NO DEFAULT OR CALL RISK

A. YIELD CURVE

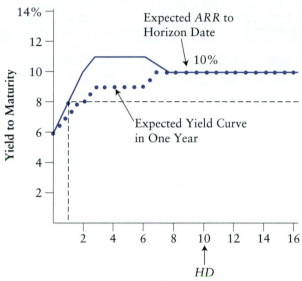

Expected *ARR* to Horizon Date

↓ 10%

Expected Yield Curve in One Year

HD

Maturity and Duration (years)

Yield to Maturity

B. EXPECTED FIRST YEAR RETURN

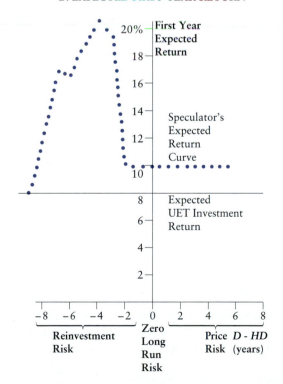

First Year Expected Return

20%

Speculator's Expected Return Curve

Expected UET Investment Return

Reinvestment Risk

Zero Long Run Risk

Price *D* - *HD* Risk (years)

FIGURE 11-11

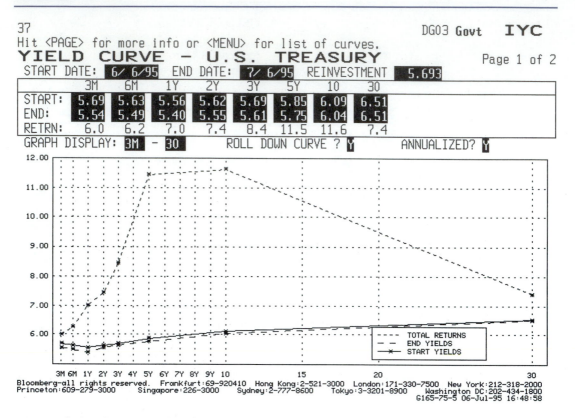

Courtesy of: Bloomberg Financial Markets Commodities News

Bond Swaps

Once a weighted portfolio duration has been determined, the speculator can begin to select particular bonds. Although our discussion has been worded to imply that this is the first time the bond portfolio has been set up, in practice speculators make modifications to existing portfolios. For this reason, the techniques used to decide which bonds to purchase or sell are known as **bond swaps.** We review a few of these bond swaps using the data shown in Table 11-4. The table shows two types of bonds—bonds now owned and potential replacements. Bonds that are now owned are designated by a single letter (Q, R, S, etc.), and potential replacements are designated by double letters (QQ, RR, SS, etc.).

Rate Anticipation Swap. If a speculator believes interest rates will soon fall (and that this has not yet been fully recognized in current prices), bonds should be bought in hopes of capital gains. To maximize price appreciation, long-term, low-coupon issues should be

TABLE 11-4 BOND SWAP DATA

Promised Bonds	Default Rating	Years to Maturity	Annual Coupon	Years to Duration*	Current Price	YTM
Now Owned						
Q	AA	10	12%	6.33	$1,000.00	12.0%
R	AA	15	12	7.63	1,000.00	12.0
S	AA	4	10	3.49	1,000.00	10.0
T	BBB	10	13	6.13	1,000.00	13.0
U	BBB	10	13	6.13	1,000.00	13.0
V	AA	10	5	7.57	646.65	11.0
W	AA	5	6	4.41	848.35	10.0
Potential Replacement						
QQ	AA	15	7%	8.48	$ 659.46	12.0%
RR	AA	13	5	8.61	550.35	12.0
SS	AA	4	10	3.49	996.83	10.1
TT	AA	10	14.25%	6.13	1,127.07	12.0
UU	AAA	10	11	6.54	1,000.00	11.0
VV	AA	14.67	12	7.57	1,000.00	12.0
WW	AA	5	6	4.41	848.35	10.0

*Calculated as Di.

acquired. Stated differently, bonds with short durations should be replaced by equivalent-risk, long-duration bonds. For example, consider bond Q, which is now owned, and bond QQ, which might be used to replace it. If promised YTMs on both bonds are expected to fall reasonably soon from 12% to 10%, the approximate percentage price increase in each would be as follows:

Bond	Actual Percentage Price Increase	$\approx$	$-D$	$\left[\dfrac{\text{Percentage}}{\text{Increase in } (1 + \text{YTM})}\right]$
Q	12.29	$\approx$		$-6.33\,(-0.0179) = 11.33$
QQ	17.04	$\approx$		$-8.48\,(-0.0179) = 15.18$

Now consider bonds R and RR. Bond R has a longer maturity but a higher coupon than RR. What should be done in this case if rates are expected to decline? Select RR, since its lower coupon offsets its shorter maturity, resulting in a longer duration than R has. If one expects rates to rise but is forced to hold some bond investments, holding bonds with short durations will minimize expected price losses.

Yield Pickup Swaps. Occasionally two identical bonds will sell at temporarily different prices and YTMs. For example, bonds S and SS are identical in all respects except that S is now selling at $1,000 to yield 10.0% to maturity, while SS is selling at $996.83 to yield 10.1% to maturity. A yield pickup swap could involve selling S and buying SS. Price imbalances like this could be due to temporary abnormal buying or selling in one of the issues. Care should be taken, however, that the two securities are indeed perfect substitutes. Minor yield differences could be due to slight default-risk differentials, differences in call features, or differences in marketability.

Quality Swaps. If the economy is currently at a peak of business expansion and headed into a recession, one might well expect both a decline in all interest rates and a widening in yield spreads between bonds of differing default risk. The trading strategy in this case would be to buy long-duration, high-quality bonds, since yields on these issues would decline the most. Yields on lower quality issues would also fall in sympathy with all rates. But increased default-risk spreads would partially offset such declines. For example, bonds T and TT have similar long durations, but TT is of better quality. If rates are expected to decline and yield spreads to widen, bond TT would be preferable.

Quality swaps are possible even if one doesn't expect overall rates to move dramatically. For example, bonds U and UU have a 2% yield spread that reflects default-quality differences between the two. If the trader believes this spread will widen, bond U should be short-sold and UU bought. Although the speculator might not know which of the two bond prices will adjust, being short in U and long in UU will cover any possible outcome. In fact, if the short and long positions are based on each bond's duration, there should be only minimal risk in the transaction. Many bond traders evaluate the appropriateness of current yield spreads by examining trends in historic averages.

Tax Swaps. A variety of tax swaps exist; we discuss two. The first of these involves trading based on coupon rates. Consider bonds V and VV, which are identical except for coupons. (Their maturities differ, but they have equal durations.) Notice that the YTM of V is lower than that of the equivalent-duration, higher-coupon issue, VV. This simply reflects the fact that effective tax rates on low-coupon bonds are lower than on higher coupon issues; thus their before-tax yields may be lower. Assume, for simplicity, that you are in a 50% tax bracket. Should you swap VV for V? The answer, of course, depends on the after-tax yield to maturity on each. In fact, the after-tax yield is 6.85% on V and 6.00% on VV. Clearly, V should be held.

A second type of tax swap involves selling a bond now owned at a taxable loss to obtain an immediate tax advantage and reinvesting both the sale proceeds and the tax savings. Assume you had originally bought bond W at $1,000. Since its current price is $848.35, you could sell it with a realized tax loss of $151.65. If your capital gains rate is 30%, taking this loss will allow you to reduce taxes by $45.50 (0.30 times $151.65). You could immediately reinvest the sale proceeds of $848.35 in bond WW and be in the same situation except you now have $45.50 in tax savings that can also be reinvested. Of course, you will pay $45.50 in capital gains when bond WW matures, but in the meantime, you have had free use of $45.50 to invest for larger total returns. To be allowed this form of tax swap, bonds W and WW must be legally different issues. For example, bond V couldn't be sold to realize a taxable loss and then immediately repurchased. The IRS considers a sale and repurchase of the same security to be a "wash sale" and will disallow the taxable loss.

Contingent Immunization

Contingent immunization is really a very simple notion. The owner of a bond portfolio and the manager agree to a minimum return that will be earned or exceeded over some future time period (commonly five years). The manager is then free to actively speculate with the portfolio until enough of its value has been lost that the only way to guarantee the minimum return is immediate immunization. Contingent immunization provides downside risk protection on the bond portfolio's return.

As an example, assume that contingent immunization is to be used to manage $10 million starting on January 1, 1995. At that date, the portfolio's owner and the manager agree to two basic objectives:

1. The minimum compound annual return will be 9.55%.
2. This 9.55% will be calculated over the next five years.

Note that the return in any one year could be much less than 9.55% because the agreement calls for an average compound return of 9.55% over the next five years. Both parties realize that the minimum portfolio value after five years will be $15.78 million ($10 million $\times 1.0955^5$).

Also assume that on January 1, 1995, the annual return available on default and call-free government bonds with a five-year duration is 11.3%. The difference between the 11.3% that could be earned if the $10 million were to be fully immunized and the 9.55% guarantee is a margin of safety given to the portfolio manager to induce active trading. The portfolio owner is willing to accept the 175 basis-point difference in the hope that the manager's active management will result in a compound return greater than the 11.3% return of a passive immunized strategy.

The portfolio manager could conceptually approach active trading in one of two ways. In the first case, he or she could take a portion of the $10 million and immunize it so it will be worth the guaranteed $15.78 million in five years. In total, $9.24 million would be necessary:

$$\frac{\$10,000,000(1.0955^5)}{1.113^5} = \$9,238,173$$

The remaining $761,827 could then be actively managed and, perhaps, even totally lost. It is unlikely that this procedure would be used, but it does point out again the margin of safety given to the manager.

Alternatively, the manager could begin to actively trade the portfolio. At the end of each day, the new fully immunized return which is then available would be calculated and compared with the portfolio's value at that time. If the portfolio's value compounded at that return is greater than the guaranteed $15.78 million promised for December 31, 1999, the manager continues to have a margin of safety. For example, assume that one year later the return available from immunizing four-year-duration government bonds has risen to 12%. If the portfolio has a value in excess of $10.03 million, a margin of safety still exists:

$$\frac{\$10,000,000(1.0955^5)}{1.12^4} = \$10,027,437$$

If the portfolio has a value equal to $10.03 million, it must be immediately immunized. (If its value is less than $10.03 million, it is time to fire the manager and the firm's computer programmers.)

Contingent immunization is a risk reduction technique. It places bounds on the risks accepted in an active bond management program. Given the volatility of interest rates in the 1970s and 1980s and the risks associated with an unencumbered active management strategy, it was a valuable risk reduction tool. However, no magic underlies its procedures. There is no reason to expect contingent immunization to result in greater returns than those available from a truly immunized strategy unless bond managers are, indeed, able to predict future bond prices. And, if they are able to do so, why limit their abilities to generating excess returns? Contingent immunization is a strategy that lies between passive bond selection and unencumbered active bond management.

S U M M A R Y

This chapter illustrated how the fundamental concepts of bond pricing and returns as discussed in Chapter 10 can be applied to both active and passive bond management. Crucial to both approaches is the concept of duration and the matching of a portfolio's duration with a planned horizon date to minimize interest rate risk exposure. While immunization might not completely eliminate interest rate risk, it can reduce it substantially.

Here are the key concepts:

◼ A major reason to have a portion of a portfolio invested in bonds is for the diversification they provide.

◼ Passive investment in bonds should (1) contain bonds of an appropriate default risk, (2) be immunized against interest rate risk, (3) be reasonably well protected against unforeseen calls, (4) have good marketability, and (5) include instruments that will increase after-tax yields.

◼ Bond speculation can be thought of as taking place at two levels.

◼ At the first level, yield curves forecast for some future date are used to calculate potential single-period returns on bonds of different durations. These are then evaluated to see whether the returns expected by departing from a fully immunized portfolio are worth the risks incurred.

◼ At the second level, individual bonds are examined to see whether a bond swap would be profitable. Swaps examined in this chapter included (1) rate anticipation swaps, (2) yield pickup swaps, (3) quality swaps, and (4) tax swaps.

▪ Contingent immunization is an approach to integrating a passive immunization strategy with a more active strategy. It sets limits on the amount of downside risk associated with an actively managed bond portfolio.

REVIEW PROBLEM

The yield curve on U.S. Treasury obligations is shown here:

Maturity	YTM	Maturity	YTM
1 year	10%	5 year	11%
2 year	10	6 year	10
3 year	11	7 year	10
4 year	12	8 year	10

1. a. Under what conditions would the maturity of various T-bonds be identical to their duration?
   b. Assume that each is a zero-coupon bond. Forecast next year's yield curve based on UET.
   c. You are the financial vice president for a casualty insurance firm and have estimated the firm will have to pay $7 million in damage claims in exactly one year and $10 million in exactly two years. How could you immunize these liabilities today?
   d. Explain the concept of convexity.
   e. If you were to place some of your money in one-year and three-year bonds today, what percentage should each represent in order to be immunized? And for one-year and two-year bonds?

   Your economic staff has forecast the following yield curve for one year hence (other years are not needed):

Maturity in One Year	YTM
1	12%
2	5%

   f. According to your economic staff, which strategy provides the greatest expected returns during the next year?

   ▪ Immunize over one-year and two-year bonds
   ▪ Immunize over one-year and three-year bonds

Solution

1. a. Maturity and duration would be identical if each security pays no cash prior to its maturity date, that is, if all are zero-coupon bonds.

b. One year from now each YTM will be what it is today less the contribution of today's one-year spot rate. YTMs for one year hence are as follows:

Maturity in One Year	YTM
1	$(1.10^2 \div 1.1) \quad - 1.0 = 10.00\%$
2	$(1.11^3 \div 1.1)^{1/2} - 1.0 = 11.50$
3	$(1.12^4 \div 1.1)^{1/3} - 1.0 = 12.67$
4	$(1.11^5 \div 1.1)^{1/4} - 1.0 = 11.25$
5	$(1.10^6 \div 1.1)^{1/5} - 1.0 = 10.00$
6	$(1.10^7 \div 1.1)^{1/6} - 1.0 = 10.00$
7	$(1.10^8 \div 1.1)^{1/7} - 1.0 = 10.00$

c.

End of Year	Liability	Present Value at 10%	Percentage of Total	Weighted Duration
1	$7.00 million	$6,363,636	43.50%	0.4350
2	10.00	8,264,463	56.50	1.1300
		$14,628,099	100.00%	1.5650

An investment of $14.63 million will have to be made in a bond portfolio having a duration of 1.565 years. This could be a single bond, multiple bonds, or even a perfect cash-matched dedicated portfolio.

d. Convexity represents the changes that occur in a bond's duration as interest rates change. The duration of a straight bond (a bond with no options) that pays coupons increases as interest rates fall and decreases as interest rates rise. This form of convexity is called positive convexity. Options associated with a bond can change its convexity. For example, the option to call the bond when interest rates decline can lead to negative convexity. Negative convexity refers to cases in which a bond's duration falls as interest rates fall and rises as interest rates increase.

e. From part c, duration must be 1.565 years. Let X_i be the percentage to invest in bonds with duration (maturity in this question) equal to i.
For X_1 and X_3:

$$1.565 = X_1(1.0) + (1 - X_1)(3.0)$$
$$X_1 = 71.75\% \text{ and } X_3 = 28.25\%$$

For X_1 and X_2:

$$1.565 = X_1(1.0) + (1 - X_1)(2.0)$$
$$X_1 = 43.5\% \text{ and } X_2 = 56.5\%$$

f. The yield curve that your staff projects is different from what UET implied in part b. Using the forecasts of your staff, the returns on each duration strategy would be:
Strategy $X_1 = 43.5\%$ and $X_2 = 56.54\%$
Return in the next year on a current two-year bond:

$$P_0 = \$1,000 \div 1.10^2 = \$826.45$$
$$E(P_1) = \$1,000 \div 1.12 = \$892.86$$

$$E(R) = \frac{892.86}{826.45} - 1.0 = 8.04\%$$

$$E(R_p) = 0.435\,(10\%) + 0.5654\,(8.04\%)$$

$$= 8.89\%$$

Strategy $X_1 = 71.75\%$ and $X_3 = 28.25\%$
Return in the next year on a current three-year bond:

$$P_0 = \$1{,}000 \div 1.11^3 = \$731.19$$

$$E(P_1) = \$1{,}000 \div 1.05^2 = \$907.03$$

$$E(R) = \frac{907.03}{731.19} - 1.0 = 24.05\%$$

$$E(R_p) = 0.7175\,(10\%) + 0.2825\,(24.05\%)$$

$$= 13.97\%$$

The strategy of immunizing over the one-year and three-year bonds provides the greatest expected return.

Q U E S T I O N S   A N D   P R O B L E M S

1. Laurie Marcus is employed as a corporate bond arbitrageur for a large broker-dealer firm. On September 1, she notices two bonds that are quite similar in nature but are selling at different promised yields to maturity. Each bond has identical call terms, default risk, and maturity. Bond A is a 10-year, 8% coupon (paid $40 each August 30 and February 30), selling at a promised YTM of 8%. Bond B is a 10-year, 8% coupon (also with the same semiannual dates), selling at a promised YTM of 7.8%.
   a. What is the market price of each bond?
   b. Which of the two bonds might she buy, and why? Might she wish to short-sell one of the bonds and go long on some of the other? Why?

2. What is the Macaulay duration for a four-year bond that pays a $40 coupon each six months? Assume YTM is a 10% stated annual rate (the effective semiannual rate is 5%). Interpret what this measure means.

3. The Macaulay duration of a bond portfolio is 7.3 years and the average YTM of bonds held is 12%.
   a. What is the bond's modified duration? Interpret what this measure means.
   b. Estimate the percentage increase in the portfolio's value if YTMs fall to 11%.

4. The bond investment officer of Pacific Insurance Corp. is evaluating the firm's current portfolio holdings and finds the following:

Bond Category	Total Market Value	Macaulay Duration	Yields to Maturity	
			Current	Expected
A	$ 50 million	1 year	9%	10%
B	$100	3 years	9	10
C	$ 50	5 years	9	10
D	$100	7 years	9	10
E	$200	12 years	9	10

    a. What is the bond portfolio's Macaulay duration? Modified duration?

    b. If the expected YTMs are estimates for one month hence, what is the approximate percentage gain or loss in the portfolio's market value during the next month?

    c. If the firm has specified a horizon date of 7.4 years, should the bond manager be worried about the expected price losses and shift into the shorter duration bonds?

    d. Assume the manager elects to maintain this immunized position. How does convexity affect the value of the portfolio?

5. The yield curve for A-quality bonds is flat at a promised YTM of 10%. You buy a 10-year, 9% annual coupon issue. Immediately the yield curve falls to 8% and remains there until you sell at the end of three years. Assuming all coupon receipts are reinvested, what is your *ARR*? Why is it not equal to the 10% promised YTM? What type of risk was most important in this situation?

6. The yield curve for A-quality bonds is flat at a promised YTM of 10%. You decide to buy a sequence of three one-year bonds (selecting bonds selling at par—that is, with coupon rates equal to the then-existing promised YTM). Immediately after you buy the first one-year bond, the yield curve falls to 8% and remains there. By the end of year 3, what is your ARR? Why is it not equal to 10%? What type of risk was most important in this situation?

7. What happens to the duration of a coupon-paying bond if YTMs rise? If they fall?

8. What happens to the duration of a zero-coupon bond if YTMs rise? If they fall? Why is this answer different from the answer in question 7?

9. You are the manager of a $50 million fixed income portfolio that is run under a strategy of contingent immunization. The plan calls for a four-year horizon and a minimum return of 10%. Currently, immunized returns available on four-year-duration bonds are 11.5%.

    a. How much could you lose on the first day and still be able to provide the 10% minimum return?

    b. A year goes by and the value of the portfolio is now $60 million. At that time, immunized returns on three-year-duration bonds are 11.0%. Do you need to immunize?

    c. If interest rates rise, this could be favorable or unfavorable to you. Explain why.

    d. At the end of four years the value of the portfolio has grown from $50 million to $87 million. Have you provided any value to the portfolio?

    e. Why do people use contingent immunization instead of simply allowing fixed income managers full discretion over the portfolio they manage?

10. A friend of yours is the administrator of a college endowment fund that is designed to pay the expenses of a unique program at the college. Expenses of the program will be $1 million each year for seven years. After seven years the program will have been outmoded by new technology and will be disbanded. Interest rates on default- and call-free bonds are 12% for all maturities. Present various immunization strategies ranging from the purchase of one bond to the creation of a dedicated portfolio. Provide calculations and a discussion of the pros and cons of each approach.

11. You are given the following current yield curve on U.S. Treasuries. Assume for all calculations that all are pure discount bonds.

Maturity	YTM	Maturity	YTM
1 year	8.0%	6 years	8.5%
2	9.0	7	8.0
3	9.5	8	7.0
4	9.0	9	7.0
5	8.5	10	7.0

a. What is the duration of each of these pure discount bonds?

b. Assume your *HD* is four years and you want to buy only bonds with maturity in years 1 and 6. What percentage investment should be made in each to assure a fully immunized portfolio?

c. Using the notion of UET, calculate next year's expected yield curve.

d. If you bought the five-year bonds and held them to maturity, what is your expected *ARR*? (Assume you believe in UET.)

e. If you bought the five-year bonds and sold them in exactly one year, what is your expected return? Why is this different from the *ARR* found in part d? (Again, assume UET.)

12. Consider the following bond data:

Bond	Default Rating	Years to Maturity	Annual Coupon	Current D	Promised Price	YTM
1	Aa	10	13%	—	$1,000.00	13.0%
2	Baa	13	4	—	415.80	14.0
3	A	8	9	7.3	—	13.2
4	Aa	5	10	4.5	—	13.0
11	Baa	10	10	—	791.31	14.0
12	Baa	15	8	—	631.47	14.0
13	A	10	11	7.1	—	13.2
14	B	7	10	4.5	—	14.5

a. Is the duration of bond 11 shorter or longer than the duration of bond 12?

b. Assume you believe the yield spread between Aa and Baa bonds should be 75 basis points (0.75%), as opposed to the 100 basis points shown between bonds 1 and 2. Develop an arbitrage strategy between the two.

c. You are considering the addition of either bond 2 or bond 12 to the portfolio of a high-tax-bracket client whose investment characteristics include a desire for moderate-to-low default risk and moderate duration. Select either 2 or 12 and justify your choice.

d. The yield curve is now flat and is expected to drop as we begin to enter a recession. Between bonds 3 and 13, which would a speculator buy?

e. The yield curve is now flat and you expect it to drop as we enter a recession. However, yields on high-default-risk bonds won't drop as dramatically as low-default-risk bonds because of an increase in risk premiums. Between bonds 4 and 14, which might you buy?

f. Consider only bond 14. If the YTM on this bond was to move downward to 12.0% (tomorrow morning), by about what percentage would its price be expected to rise?

13. Suppose you are advising someone who is planning on investing in either a long-term bond or investing in a sequence of investments in short-term bonds (i.e., rolling over the proceeds of one bond into another short-term bond). The bonds have no default or call risk.

a. The investor is saving to fund a college education. Which of the two strategies would you undertake? Defend your answer.

b. Now suppose you are told the long-term bond has a higher YTM than the short-term bond. How does this affect your choice? Again, defend your answer.

14. You are an active interest rate anticipator and believe that interest rates are more likely to rise during the next year than they are likely to fall. Your current portfolio duration is seven years. What change in duration might you make? What type of convexity would you wish to have—that is, positive or negative and large or small?

CFA 15. Convexity is more important when rates are:

    a. high.

    b. low.

    c. expected to change very little.

    d. depends on whether the note is selling at a premium or a discount.

CFA 16. Positive convexity implies:

    a. that price increases at a faster rate as yields drop, than price decreases as yields rise.

    b. that price changes are equal for increases in yields and decreases in yields.

    c. that price increases at a slower rate as yields drop, then price decreases as yields rise.

    d. nothing with respect to future price changes.

CFA 17. Most U.S. Treasury notes have the following degree of convexity:

    a. negative

    b. positive

    c. zero

    d. additional information is required

CFA 18. The ability to immunize is very desirable for bond portfolio managers in some instances.

    a. Discuss the components of interest rate risk—that is, assuming a change in interest rates over time, explain the two risks faced by the holder of a bond.

    b. Define immunization and discuss why a bond manager would immunize his or her portfolio.

    c. Explain why a duration-matching strategy is a superior technique to a maturity-matching strategy for the minimization of interest rate risk.

    d. Explain in specific terms how you would use a zero-coupon bond to immunize a bond portfolio. Discuss why a zero-coupon bond is an ideal instrument in this regard.

    e. Explain how contingent immunization, another bond portfolio management technique, differs from classical immunization. Discuss why a bond portfolio manager would engage in contingent immunization.

CFA 19. a. Assume a $10,000 par value zero-coupon bond with a term to maturity at issue of 10 years and a market yield of 8%.

    (1) Determine the duration of the bond.

    (2) Calculate the initial issue price of the bond at a market yield of 8%, assuming semiannual compounding.

    (3) Twelve months after issue, this bond is selling to yield 12%. Calculate its then-current market price. Calculate your pretax rate of return, assuming you owned this bond during the 12-month period.

    b. Assume a 10% coupon bond with a duration (D) of eight years, semiannual payments, and a market rate of 8%.

    (1) Determine the duration of the bond.

    (2) Calculate the percentage change in price for the bond, assuming market rates decline by 2 percentage points (200 basis points).

CFA 20. The trustees of the Farnsworth Pension Fund, which is expected to have a long-term positive net cash flow, are considering the purchase of one of two noncallable bonds. As indicated here, these bonds are identical in every aspect except coupon (and resulting price).

	Bond A	Bond B
Par	$1,000.00	$1,000.00
Coupon	10.00%	5.00%
Market price	100	$68^{7/8}$
Length to maturity	10 years	10 years
Yield to maturity	10.00%	10.00%
Current yield	10.00%	7.26%
Present value of $1,000 in 10 years	$ 377.00	$ 377.00
Present value of 20 semiannual coupons	$ 623.00	$ 311.00
Present value of bond	$1,000.00	$ 688.00

a. Discuss the two bonds in terms of the certainty of achieving a specific realized compound yield.
b. Discuss how your answer to part a would be affected if you expect interest rates to rise.
c. Discuss how your answer to part a would be affected if you expect interest rates to fall.

D A T A F I L E   A N A L Y S I S

Using a computer spreadsheet program, calculate the market values of the following three bonds at yields to maturity ranging from 0% to 20%:

Bond	Annual Coupon	Maturity
A	10%	30 years
B	10%	5 years
C	5%	30 years

Plot the results with the bond price on the vertical axis and the yield to maturity on the horizontal axis.

a. Explain why the curves have different shapes.
b. Use the concept of duration to explain why the curves display positive convexity.
c. After printing the graph, draw freehand the price-yield relationship of a bond with negative convexity. What causes negative convexity?

R E F E R E N C E S

Excellent discussions of bond duration can be found in the following articles:

Babcock, G. "Duration as a Link Between Yield and Value," *Journal of Portfolio Management,* Summer 1984 and Fall 1984.

Bierwag, Gerald O., and George Kaufman, "Coping with the Risk of Interest Rate Fluctuations: A Note," *Journal of Business,* July 1977.

McEnally, Richard. "Duration as a Practical Tool in Bond Management," *Journal of Portfolio Management,* Summer 1977.

Trainer, Francis, Jesse Yawitz, and William Marshall, "Holding Period Is the Key to Risk Threshold," *Journal of Portfolio Management,* Winter 1979.

The following are helpful reviews of bond management techniques:

Homer, Sydney, and Martin L. Liebowitz, *Inside the Yield Book: New Tools for Bond Management.* Englewood Cliffs, NJ: Prentice-Hall, 1972.

Liebowitz, Martin L. "Horizon Analysis: A New Analytic Framework for Managed Bond Portfolios," *Journal of Portfolio Management,* Spring 1975.

Tuttle, Donald L., ed., *The Revolution in Techniques for Managing Bond Portfolios.* Charlottesville, VA: Institute of Chartered Financial Analysts, 1983.

Interesting papers in recent practitioner journals include the following:

Bierwag, Gerald O., Charles J. Corrado, and George C. Kaufman, "Computing Durations for Bond Portfolios," *Journal of Portfolio Management,* Fall 1990.

Langetieg, Terrence C., Martin L. Leibowitz, and Stanley Kogelman, "Duration Targeting and the Management of Multiperiod Returns," *The Financial Analysts Journal,* September–October 1990.

Leibowitz, Martin L., William S. Krasker, and Ardavan Nozari, "Spread Duration: A New Tool for Bond Portfolio Management," *Journal of Portfolio Management,* Spring 1990.

Messmore, Thomas E. "The Duration of Surplus," *Journal of Portfolio Management,* Winter 1990.

For overviews of mortgage-backed securities consult these references:

Bartlett, Willim W. *Mortgage-Backed Securities: Products, Analysis, Trading.* New York: NYIF Corp., 1989.

REMICS and Mortgage-Backed Securities, A Guide to Understanding the Risk and Return, Washington, DC: Fannie Mae.

A P P E N D I X   1 1 A

MORTGAGE-BACKED SECURITIES

During the 1970s a new type of security was created in the United States: the mortgage-backed security (MBS). Due to dramatic increases in interest rates at that time, traditional owners of mortgages (mainly banks as well as savings and loan institutions) were unable to tolerate the interest rate risks of long-term fixed interest rate mortgages. To help provide investment capital to the mortgage market three federally sponsored corporations were created:

- **Ginnie Mae.** This abbreviation stands for the Government National Mortgage Association, a government-owned corporation within the Department of Housing and Urban Development.

- **Fannie Mae.** This abbreviation stands for the Federal National Mortgage Association, a shareholder-owned corporation chartered by the U.S. Congress.

- **Freddie Mac.** This term refers to the Federal Home Loan Mortgage Corporation, a shareholder-owned corporation chartered by the U.S. Congress.

These organizations insure that the principal due on a pool of mortgages will be paid. With this guarantee, the pool can then be used as collateral for an MBS.

An MBS begins when a mortgage loan is made by a financial institution to a borrower. Terms on such loans differ in two basic respects: (1) maturity, and (2) whether interest is fixed over the life of the loan or is an adjustable rate. However, all mortgage loans require monthly payments that include both principal and interest on the mortgage. Unlike most bond issues that are repaid in a single balloon payment at maturity, the principal balance of a mortgage loan is reduced monthly.

The financial institution that creates the mortgage pools it with a large number of other mortgages and then sells the pool to Ginnie Mae, Fannie Mae, or Freddie Mac who, in turn, sell a new mortgage-backed security in the secondary market.[10] Since Ginnie Mae is an agency of the U.S. government, issues that it sells are backed by the full faith and credit of the federal government. Fannie Mae issues carry a guarantee of principal and interest payment but are not backed by the full faith and credit of the U.S. government. Freddie Mac issues guarantee simply the timely repayment of principal and interest.

As borrowers within a given pool repay their interest and principal each month, the money is transferred through the banking system to owners of the MBS. Given the credit quality of loans that are placed in the pools and the repayment insurance of the various issuers, MBS have small risk of default. But there can be considerable interest rate risks. This risk arises from the uncertainty about future principal repayments. For example, if

---

[10] MBS are also issued under "private labels," in which case they do not carry insurance of principal repayment by any of these three government agencies.

interest rates fall dramatically (as they did in the early 1990s), mortgage borrowers will refinance their existing mortgages with lower cost new mortgages. This harms the owner of the MBS in that the total amount of interest they receive on the security declines, and prepayments must be invested at lower interest rates.

To make ownership of mortgage securities more attractive, the cash flows on MBS are often restructured into various classes (called tranches) that have claims to specified cash flows. These classes are then bought and sold in secondary markets. This allows investors who wish to have little prepayment risk to buy classes with little such risk. Investors willing to accept greater prepayment risk (in return for a higher expected return) can purchase tranches with more prepayment risk.

R E M I C s

In the early 1980s, securities that restructured the cash flows on MBS were first offered. These were called **collateralized mortgage obligations** (CMOs). A **REMIC** (real estate mortgage investment conduit) is a form of CMO and was first introduced in 1987 as a result of the Tax Reform Act of 1986. The following is a quote from a publication of Fannie Mae:

> The REMIC expanded the appeal and availability of the CMO structure to a wider investor base and achieved preferred tax treatment for issuers and investors. The REMIC has replaced the CMO, and, today, all CMOs are issued in the form of REMICs; however, the terms often are used interchangeably.[11]

REMICs may include any number of **regular classes** plus a single **residual class.** The regular classes, or tranches, are identified by capital letters such as A class, B class, and C class. Each class is assigned specified coupons (fixed, floating, or zero) and terms of payment. The residual class is called the Z class and receives payments only after all other classes have been repaid. As such, the Z class is like a zero-coupon bond.

Tranche Types

Sequential Pay Classes. Sequential pay classes are the most basic form of a REMIC. Assume a new $100 million par value REMIC is issued with four classes: A, B, C, and Z. For illustration, assume the principal due on the issue is split between the classes as follows:

Tranche Class	A	B	C	Z
Principal Claim (in millions)	$33	$26	$26	$15

- **A Class.** Owners of A class securities receive all principal payments made on the $100 par portfolio plus interest on any outstanding balance due on their $33 million of par. Any interest paid on the $15 par Z class securities is also paid to A class owners and treated as a reduction of A class principal.

- **B Class.** Owners of B class securities receive interest on any outstanding principal on their $26 million of par. They receive no principal payments until the $33 million of principal due

---

[11] From *REMICS and Mortgage-Backed Securities*, Washington, DC: Fannie Mae, 1994.

to A class owners is fully repaid. After A class principal is paid, B class owners receive principal payments made on the remaining $67 million par. During the period when principal is being repaid to B class owners, any interest paid on the $15 par Z class securities is paid to B class owners and treated as a reduction of B class principal.

◼ **C Class.** Cash flows to class C follow the general rules of class B securities except class C owners begin to receive principal payments only after all B class principal is repaid.

◼ **Z Class.** Owners of Z class receive no cash until all principal has been repaid on classes A, B, and C. After that, any further cash received on the mortgage pool goes to owners of the Z class.

An illustration of such a sequential pay distribution is shown in Figure 11A-1.

Consider first the cash flows to A class owners. They immediately begin to receive both principal and interest payments. The amount of interest received decreases over time as their claims to principal are repaid. Notice that the amount of cash paid to class A owners increases during the first few years. This is due to a natural increase in the amount of mortgage prepayments that incur during the first few years of a mortgage pool's life. It is expected that some mortgage borrowers will pay off their mortgage prior to scheduled maturity. (These prepayments occur for three reasons: (1) to take advantage of interest rate decreases, (2) because the underlying property is sold, or (3) simply because borrowers pay more principal than required.)

Now consider the cash flows to class B owners. During the time period when class A is receiving principal payments, class B owners receive only interest on their $26 million par value. After class A owners have been fully repaid, all principal receipts are allocated to class B. In addition, interest payments on the Z class principal is also allocated to class B principal repayment.

After class B has been repaid, all principal receipts are allocated to class C until it is also fully repaid. Once class C is repaid, all future cash flows go to Z class owners.

Risks in Sequential Pay. What are the uncertainties inherent in the cash flows shown in Figure 11A-1? While there is no uncertainty about the amount of principal that will be repaid, there is an *uncertainty about the time period over which principal will be received* by any class. For example, class B owners can only estimate the date at which class A owners will be fully repaid. Similarly, class B owners can only estimate the length of time during which they will be receiving principal. In addition, there is an *uncertainty about the amount of interest* that will be received. For example, if mortgage borrowers repay faster than expected, the amount of interest paid will be less than expected.

Both risks affect the required return on each tranche as well as the market value of the tranche. For example, claims to Z class cash flows have the greatest risk, since they receive no cash until all other classes are fully repaid, and the amount of cash they will receive is difficult to predict. Thus, Z class owners will require a larger expected return than owners of other classes. Changes in market values of Z class claims are also the most difficult to assess. For example, if prepayments occur more rapidly than expected, this shortens the life of the Z class principal and reduces the amount of interest they will receive. The first effect causes an increase in market values whereas the second effect causes a decrease in value.

Clearly the major risk of owning a MBS is uncertainty about principal prepayments. Investors realize this and develop expectations of the prepayment pattern. The standard prepayment pattern used in practice was developed by the Public Securities Association and is referred to as the PSA standard prepayment model. The PSA prepayment rate starts at 0.2% per year in the first month that a new pool is outstanding, increases at 0.2% each month until month 30, after which it remains at 6% per year for all succeeding months.

Securities firms publish yield tables and calculate market values for newly issued REMICs based on this PSA benchmark. For example, a new issue that consists of mortgages which are

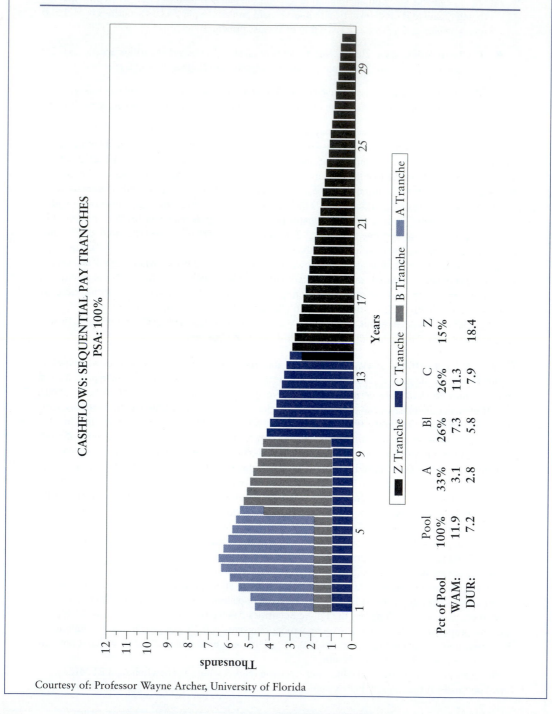

CASHFLOWS: SEQUENTIAL PAY TRANCHES
PSA: 100%

	Pool	A	Bl	C	Z
Pct of Pool	100%	33%	26%	26%	15%
WAM:	11.9	3.1	7.3	11.3	18.4
DUR:	7.2	2.8	5.8	7.9	

Years

Thousands
0 1 2 3 4 5 6 7 8 9 10 11 12

1 5 9 13 17 21 25 29

Z Tranche   C Tranche   B Tranche   A Tranche

Courtesy of: Professor Wayne Archer, University of Florida

expected to prepay more rapidly might be priced based on, say, 125% of PSA.

Figure 11A-2 shows the cash flows that would be received in our example if the PSA is actually 400%, meaning much more rapid repayment than 100% PSA. While each class receives full repayment of principal, the principal is repaid early and total interest is lower than with 100% PSA.

When interest rates fall, the faster repayment of principal and reduced interest on a pool of mortgages creates negative convexity across the pool as a whole. In a sequential pay series of tranches, most of this negative convexity is carried by owners of the Z class securities.

IOs and POs

Another type of REMIC consists of a structure in which all interest payments go to owners of claims to interest only (*IO*) and all payments of principal go to owners of claims to principal only (*PO*). Figures 11A-3 and 11A-4 illustrate the cash flows associated with each of these claims.

In Figure 11A-3, the gray bars reflect expected payments to owners of the PO if interest rates remain the same as when the mortgage pool was created. The blue shaded bars reflect expected payments to owners of the IO, again assuming interest rates do not change.

Figure 11A-4 shows the PO and IO cash flows if interest rates fall by 1%. Notice that cash flows to PO owners occur much more rapidly than expected, thus increasing the market value of the PO instruments. In contrast, cash flows to holders of the IO instruments fall dramatically, causing a significant drop in the market value of the IO.

IOs and POs are so sensitive to interest rate changes that they (as well as most REMICs) are referred to as **mortgage derivatives.** Even though they are technically not options, their values relative to interest rate changes move similar to interest rate options. For example, assume that interest rates fall and mortgage borrowers pay off their principal faster than expected. Then owners of POs receive cash faster than expected (which increases the value of the PO) and owners of IOs receive less interest than expected (which decreases the value of the IO).

The purchase of an IO or PO is essentially a bet on future changes in the level of interest rates. If you believe interest rates will increase, purchase an IO. If you believe interest rates will fall, purchase a PO.

Other Tranche Types

In an attempt to attract investors to the mortgage markets, many other cash distribution procedures have been developed. Among these are **planned amortization classes (PACs).** PACs are designed to provide less risk to certain classes. This is done by creating other classes called companion classes. Regular class owners are scheduled to receive a specified series of interest and principal based on an assumed prepayment schedule. Owners of the companion classes act as a buffer. If prepayments are faster than expected, the unexpected principal payments are assigned to the companion classes. In this case, the companion classes receive more cash than expected and much earlier than expected. As such, the value of the companion class claims increases. If prepayments are slower than expected, then cash flows expected on the companion classes in the early years of the mortgage pool are delayed to later years. This delay in cash flow causes a decrease in the value of the companion class.

Ownership of companion class claims are, like IOs and POs, bets on the direction of future interest rates.

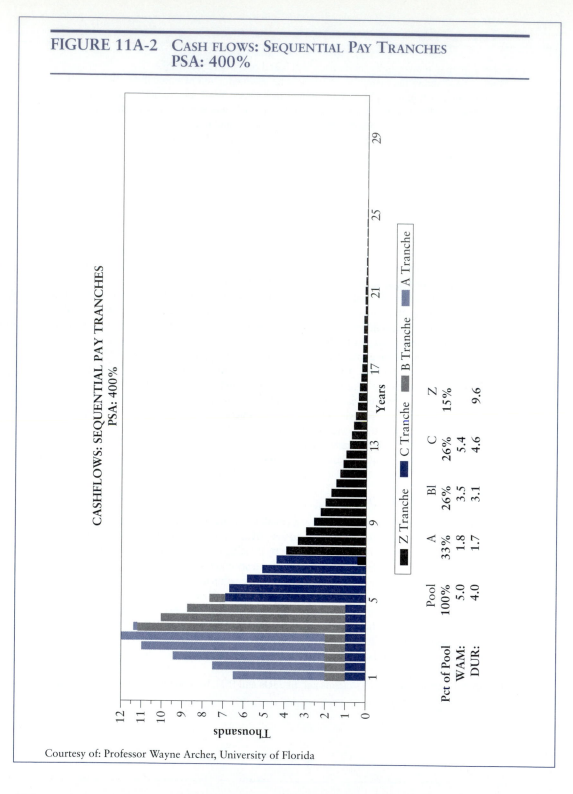

FIGURE 11A-2 CASH FLOWS: SEQUENTIAL PAY TRANCHES
PSA: 400%

CASHFLOWS: SEQUENTIAL PAY TRANCHES
PSA: 400%

	Pool	A	Bl	C	Z
Pct of Pool	100%	33%	26%	26%	15%
WAM:	5.0	1.8	3.5	5.4	
DUR:	4.0	1.7	3.1	4.6	9.6

■ Z Tranche ■ C Tranche ■ B Tranche ■ A Tranche

Courtesy of: Professor Wayne Archer, University of Florida

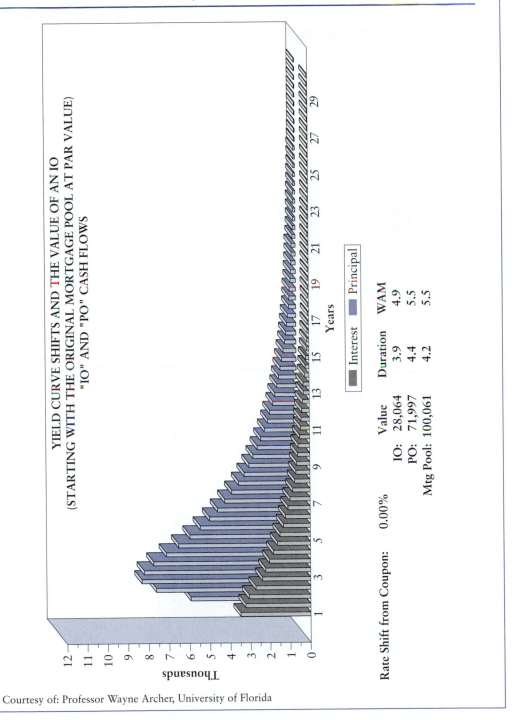

FIGURE 11A-3   YIELD CURVE SHIFTS AND THE VALUE OF AN IO
(STARTING WITH THE ORIGINAL MORTGAGE POOL AT
PAR VALUE) IO AND PO CASH FLOWS

Courtesy of: Professor Wayne Archer, University of Florida

467

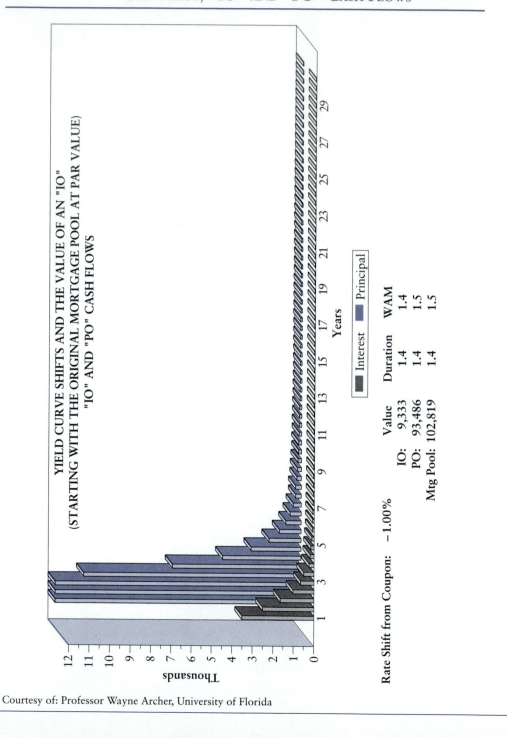

Courtesy of: Professor Wayne Archer, University of Florida

12

VALUATION OF
EQUITY SECURITIES

After reading this chapter you should have an understanding of stock valuation using the dividend discount model as well as three alternative valuation models.

The analysis and valuation of equity securities can be an exciting process. It requires a blending of many interesting disciplines including economic theory, business strategy, developments in technology, international competition, and so forth. The equity analyst must look into the heart of a business venture to assess the profit potential of the firm as well as the major nondiversifiable risks of the firm. In this chapter we examine various equity valuation models. In Chapter 13, we illustrate how an active equity analysis as well as passive equity strategies might be conducted.

Most of this chapter is devoted to a discussion of the **dividend valuation model** in which per share equity value is said to be the present value of expected future dividends per share. Since this model is based on expected future dividends, we examine how future dividend growth can be estimated. We also examine what this model says about the economic determinants of two widely used ratios of investment value: price-to-earnings and price-to-book value ratios.

There are other reasonable models that can be used to value a stock. Among these are models that focus on the earnings of a firm, the cash flow of a firm, and the investment opportunities of a firm. After presenting each model, we will see that each is a variant of the basic dividend discount model. By focusing on different aspects of stock valuation, however, they provide another way of looking at the problem.

But before any of these valuation models can be examined, we should clarify the differences in required, expected, and actual equity returns.

Equity Returns

When bond selection was discussed in Chapters 10 and 11, we made a clear distinction between expected returns, promised returns (yields to maturity), and actual realized returns. The same ideas apply to common stock selection, although the conventional terminology is somewhat different, and common stocks are usually evaluated over a single period (one month, one year, etc.), as opposed to over a planned horizon date.[1] Individuals will purchase a stock if their required return is less than (or equal to) their expected return on the stock. Conversely, they will sell a stock if their required return exceeds the stock's expected return. Once the buy or sell decision is made, a single-period actual return is realized that may be different from that expected or required.

The required rate of return should fairly compensate investors for both delaying immediate consumption and accepting the risk inherent in the security. In terms of the traditional capital asset pricing model (CAPM), this can be expressed as:

Security Market Line (SML) $RR_i = RF + \beta_i(RP_M)$ **(12.1)**

where RR_i refers to the required single-period return on stock i, RF is the current risk-free rate of interest (compensation for delaying consumption), β_i is the amount of nondiversifiable risk in stock i relative to the aggregate market portfolio, and RP_M is the risk premium required on a stock of average risk. Assume you have completed an analysis of Achilles Corporation and believe the stock has 20% more nondiversifiable risk than the average stock (implying a beta of 1.2). If the risk-free rate is now 8% and you believe a 5% risk premium on an average stock is fair, your required yearly return will be 14% [8% + 1.2(5%)]. This is shown in Figure 12-1 as point A.

Single-period expected returns on a stock are composed of an expected dividend yield plus an expected capital gains yield. Mathematically:

Single-Period Expected Return

$$E(R_t) = \frac{D_t}{P_{t-1}} + \frac{P_t - P_{t-1}}{P_{t-1}}$$ **(12.2)**

where $E(R_t)$ refers to the expected return during period t, D_t is the expected dividend to be paid at the end of period t, and P_t (or P_{t-1}) is the price of the stock at the end of period t $(t - 1)$. For example, assume that Achilles Corporation is now selling on the NYSE at $40. You expect that a year from now a $2 dividend will be paid and the stock will be selling for $46. As a result, your expected return is composed of a 5% dividend yield plus a 15% capital gain yield, a total expected return of 20%:

$$\frac{\$2}{\$40} + \frac{\$46 - \$40}{\$40} = 0.2$$

This is plotted in Figure 12-1 as point B.

Any difference between expected and required returns is referred to as an expected excess return. Excess returns represent pure profit, a profit earned above that required to

---

[1] Theoretically, the single period can be thought of as the time interval between now and the horizon date. If, for example, the horizon date is 20 years away, 20 years would be used as the single period. In practice, however, stock returns are usually evaluated over time intervals shorter than typical horizon dates.

FIGURE 12-1   REQUIRED VERSUS EXPECTED RETURNS

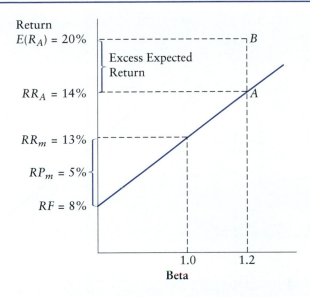

compensate for the stock's risk. According to the efficient market theory, excess returns will not exist. Individuals will buy or sell the stock until its price is set so that expected returns equal required returns. However, if the markets are not perfectly efficient, excess returns such as the difference between points A and B in Figure 12.1 might be possible.

Actual returns are calculated in the same manner as expected returns, except that actual dividends and prices are used instead of expected values. For example, if Achilles actually pays a dividend of $2.10 and sells for $43 at year-end, the actual return would be 12.75%.

$$\frac{\$2.10}{\$40} + \frac{\$43 - \$40}{\$40} = 0.1275$$

Throughout this chapter and the next we examine various aspects of common stock selection. As with the two bond chapters, this chapter concentrates on fundamental valuation concepts, and the next chapter focuses more directly upon stock trading. Two broad topics are discussed in this chapter: (1) stock valuation using the dividend discount model and (2) alternative valuation models.

Market Clearing Prices

The market price of a stock, like that of all other economic goods, is a function of supply and demand. At a given point in time, the available supply of the stock is fixed and equal to the quantity sold by the issuer. This is illustrated by the vertical line S in Figure 12-2. Total demand to own the stock depends on the price at which it could be bought. At high prices only the most optimistic individuals would be willing to hold the security in their portfolios, and demand would be small. At low prices demand would increase. Any time

FIGURE 12-2   SECURITY PRICE DETERMINATION

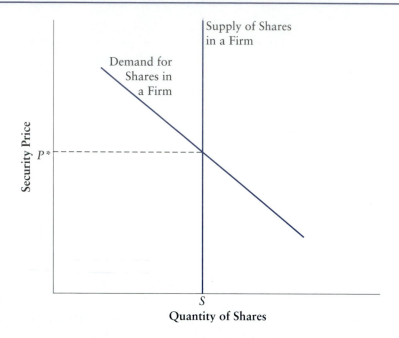

there are differences of opinion about any stock's (or any security's) future prospects, a downward-sloping demand curve, such as that shown in Figure 12-2, would result.

As shown in Figure 12-2, the equilibrium price of the stock is P^*. At P^*, total desire to own the stock equals the outstanding supply. At higher prices investors desire to hold fewer shares than are actually available, and attempts by investors and speculators to sell shares will drive prices down to P^*. At prices lower than P^* attempts to buy shares will drive prices up.

Figure 12-2 is useful in making four points:

1. Investors need not all agree about the proper value of a security. Forecasts of future prospects will differ among investors when they hold different information about the security. This is important to recognize, since the discussion of market value in this chapter is addressed largely to the single investor's assessment of a stock's value within his or her portfolio. Our aim is not so much to establish P^* as it is to determine the price a particular investor would be willing to pay. We refer to this price as its intrinsic or fair value.
2. The current market price is not a market consensus about the intrinsic value of the security. Instead, it reflects the opinion of the marginal investor. This individual would not wish to own the security if its price was slightly higher.
3. The slope of the demand curve is determined by the extent to which investors have similar beliefs about a security's prospects. When a diversity of opinions exists, the demand curve will be downward sloping, and changes in supply will affect prices. When there is complete agreement, the demand curve is horizontal;

regardless of supply, only one price will prevail.[2] The extent to which individuals assign similar values to a security depends on the information they hold. If all investors hold the same information, the demand curve is horizontal. If information is not costless and not available to everyone, a downward-sloping demand curve would result.

4. Equilibrium prices, and thus market trading prices, will change only when
   (a) new information enters the market to cause a shift in the demand curve, or
   (b) the quantity supplied changes (assuming investors have diverse opinions).

As we noted, our focus in this section is on how an individual investor might assign a value to a given stock. This value estimate may differ from existing trading prices if the investor holds either more or less information about the security than does the market average. Wise investors will attempt to determine why their value estimates differ from market prices. Is it because they have better information or poorer information?

Alternative Valuation Techniques

General Approaches to Valuation

Historically, six approaches to assessing the value of a security have been used:

1. Par value
2. Book value
3. Liquidation value
4. Replacement value
5. Substitution value
6. Present value

To help illustrate the meaning and usefulness of each approach, a hypothetical balance sheet of Busch, Inc., is shown in Table 12-1.

Par Value. The par value (or stated value) of stock is specified in the firm's corporate charter. Par value is simply a legal definition that has no economic impact on the firm. The fact that Busch common stock had a $1 par value is useful to know only because it occasionally aids in calculating the number of common shares outstanding. Dividing Busch's common stock dollar balance of $295.3 million by the $1 par shows the firm had 295.3 million shares outstanding. Many firms issue stock without designating a par or stated value.

Book Value. The total book value of a security is the dollar amount recorded on the firm's balance sheet. For example, the book value of Busch's common equity was $2,313.7 million. To find book value per share, total book value is simply divided by the

---

TABLE 12-1 BUSCH INC., CONSOLIDATED BALANCE SHEET, DECEMBER 31, 1995

Assets	(Millions)	Liabilities and Equity	(Millions)
Cash and Marketable Securities	$ 69.4	Accounts Payable	$ 491.7
Accounts Receivable	373.0	Wage and Salaries	180.0
Inventories	427.8	Other Current Liabilities	343.9
Other Current Assets	150.4		
Total	1,020.6	Long-Term Debt	1,126.8
Gross Plant and Equipment	6,099.3	Deferred Taxes	1,090.8
Accumulated Depreciation	1,671.7	Convertible Preferred	289.9
Net Plant	4,427.6	Shareholder Equity	
Other Assets	385.6	Common Stock ($1 Par)	295.3
		Capital in Excess of Par	6.1
		Retained Earnings	2,472.2
		Foreign Currency Adj.	0.9
		Treasury Stock	(460.8)
		Total	2,313.7
	5,833.8		5,833.8

number of shares outstanding. Busch had 295.3 million common shares outstanding and thus had a book value per share of $7.84 ($2,313.7/295.3).

As a general rule, book value is a poor indicator of the value of a stock for at least three reasons. First, it is historical in nature rather than future oriented. In the case of Busch, a large percentage of its land, plant, and equipment are recorded in historical, original-cost dollars and may bear little relationship to current, inflated prices. The replacement value of its assets is surely larger than recorded book values. Second, comparability of reported book values between companies is a significant problem. Two companies may be identical in all respects except for their accounting procedures. For example, LIFO versus FIFO inventory valuation, straight-line versus declining balance depreciation, capitalizing versus expensing R&D, and so forth, are all generally accepted accounting principles that can lead to significantly different book values among firms. Finally, book value reflects solely the original dollar investment made by a security holder. If this investment earns a return higher (or lower) than investors currently require, the current intrinsic worth should be higher (or lower) than the initial investment.

Liquidation Value. The liquidation value of a security represents the cash a security holder would receive if the firm discontinued operations, sold its assets, and distributed the net proceeds to security holders in order of legal priority. Liquidation is, by definition, the last action a firm would ever take, and thus liquidation value represents the *minimum* value of a security. Because corporate liquidations are rare and asset liquidation values are difficult to assess, liquidation value is typically not calculated. Even if a security's liquidation value were known, the assets of a firm are generally worth more as a going concern than in liquidation. If they are not, the firm should be liquidated.

Replacement Value. Replacement value represents a security's claim to the current re-production value of the firm's assets. It differs from liquidation value in that liquidation value applies to the net selling value of assets, whereas replacement value applies to the cost required to reproduce existing asset productivity at today's prices. If there were no transaction costs associated with liquidating a firm (attorney fees, selling commissions, disassembly costs, etc.), liquidation and replacement values should be equal. However, such costs do exist, and replacement value exceeds liquidation value.

The problem with using replacement value as a measure of a stock's worth is twofold and is similar to that of using liquidation value. First, replacement value is difficult to determine. Second, a stock bears an economic value to the extent that future cash flows are expected. These cash flows might be totally unrelated to the asset's replacement value.

Substitution Value. Substitution value reflects the value of a security when compared with that of substitute securities. An example will best illustrate this procedure. Assume we wish to assign a value to the common stock of ABC Corporation. The company's product line is shown here:

Product	Total Dollar Earnings
A	$10 million
B	7 million
C	3 million
	$20 million

If we could find three different firms each of which, respectively, sells only product A, B, or C, then we should be able to create a portfolio of the three that would exactly duplicate ABC Corporation. The total market value of the portfolio of the three firms would equal the substitution value of ABC Corporation. Assume we find three such firms, and observe:

Firm	Traded Market Value	÷	Total Dollar Earnings	=	Market Value Per $ Earnings
AAA Corp.	$500 million	÷	$50 million	=	$10
BBB Corp.	$600 million	÷	$40 million	=	$15
CCC Corp.	$ 8 million	÷	$ 1 million	=	$ 8

Knowing this, we could estimate a substitution value for ABC Corporation as follows:

Product	Market Value Per $ Earnings	×	ABC Corp. Total Dollar Earnings	=	Substitution Value
A	$10	×	$10 million	=	$100 million
B	$15	×	7 million	=	$105 million
C	$ 8	×	3 million	=	$ 24 million
					$229 million

The substitution value of ABC would equal $229 million.

There are two problems with using substitution value. First, it neglects any economies (or diseconomies) of scale that might arise when products A and B are produced together as opposed to separately. Second, and more important, is the practical problem of identifying comparable firms. Management talent, patents and copyrights, geographic areas, and so forth, all cause considerable differences in firms even though their product lines appear identical. Substitution value estimates are imperfect at best.

Present Value. The basis of the present-value approach was discussed in Chapter 10 when we presented the bond valuation model. According to the present-value model, the current worth of a security is equal to the present value of the future economic benefits that the security holder expects to receive. A variety of present-value models exist. We concentrate on the most commonly used version, known as the **dividend valuation model.**

To illustrate the dividend valuation model, we calculate the equity value of Midwest Machinery, Inc. Midwest's current financial statements are shown in Table 12-2.

TABLE 12-2   MIDWEST MACHINERY FINANCIAL STATEMENTS, END OF YEAR 0

Assets	(millions)	Liabilities and Equity		(millions)
Current Assets	$ 20	Current Liabilities	(8%)	$10
		Long-Term Debt	(8%)	30
		Total Debt		$40
Gross Plant	$150	Common Stock ($1 Par)		2
Accumulated Depreciation	(70)	Paid-in Surplus		10
Net Plant	$80	Retained Profits		48
Total Assets	$ 100	Total Equity		$ 60
		Total Liabilities and Equity		$100

	(millions)
Sales	$ 200.0
Cost of Goods Sold	120.0
Gross Profit	$ 80.0
Selling, General, and Administration	50.0
Depreciation	10.0
Net Operating Income	20.0
Interest	3.2
Net Income Before Tax	16.8
Taxes (50%)	8.4
Net Income	$ 8.4
Total Dividends Paid	$ 8.4

The Dividend Valuation Model

The most commonly used approach to valuing common stock is to find the present value of expected future dividends per share. After an analysis of the future prospects and risks of a firm, the analyst estimates the dividends per share expected to be paid in each future year as well as an appropriate rate of return to be earned in each future year. If we define D_t as the dividend per share expected to be received at the end of year t, N as the number of years during which dividends will be paid, and K_t as the required return for year t, then the value of the stock would be as follows:

General Dividend Valuation Model

$$P_0 = \frac{D_1}{1 + K_1} + \frac{D_2}{(1 + K_1)(1 + K_2)} + \cdots + \frac{D_N}{(1 + K_1)(1 + K_2) \cdots (1 + K_N)} \qquad \textbf{(12.3)}$$

Since common stock has an infinite legal life, N could be infinity. However, if investors expect that the firm's assets will be liquidated, N would be equal to the number of periods until expected liquidation.

To demonstrate the application of Equation (12.3), assume a business venture is formed to harvest timber from a large tract of land. Timber cutting is expected to last three years and to provide dividends per share of $2, $3, and $25 at the end of years 1, 2, and 3, respectively. At the end of year 3 the land is to be sold and the corporation dissolved. After an analysis of expected risk-free rates and risks associated with the project, the investor determines that a return of 9%, 10%, and 12% in each respective year would be necessary. Given this information, the value of each share would be $22.95:

$$\$22.95 = \frac{\$2}{1.09} + \frac{\$3}{(1.09)(1.10)} + \frac{\$25}{(1.09)(1.10)(1.12)}$$

Clearly, the dividend model is analogous to bond valuation models. The difference lies solely in the difficulties of specifying the inputs—the uncertainty about future dividends and the appropriate discount rate. Reasonable estimates of the level and timing of future dividends can be made only after the analyst has developed well-informed opinions about future national and international economic events, determinants of industry growth, probable firm market share, cost control, financing policies, and so forth. Developing such opinions can be a major task.

Required returns are also difficult to specify. If the assumptions of the CAPM are reasonably valid, it could be used. On that basis, the required return in year t would be equal to:

$$K_{et} = RF_t + \beta_t(RP_{Mt})$$

where K_{et} is the required equity return in year t, RF_t is the risk-free rate available in year t, β_t is the beta of the stock expected for year t, and RP_{Mt} is the market risk premium during year t. Differences in any of these return determinants from year to year would cause differences in individual K_{et}'s. Again, these variables are difficult to estimate with any reasonable confidence.

In practice, professional analysts generally apply a single discount rate to all cash flows rather than a rate unique to each year. In this case the dividend model becomes:

Dividend Valuation with a Single Discount Rate

$$P_0 = \frac{D_1}{1 + K_e} + \frac{D_2}{(1 + K_e)^2} + \cdots + \frac{D_N}{(1 + K_e)^N} \tag{12.4}$$

$$= \sum_{t=1}^{N} \frac{D_t}{(1 + K_e)^t}$$

The demanded return K is estimated from the security market line as follows:

Security Market Line $K_e = RF + \beta_e(RP_M)$ (12.5)

Conceptually the risk-free rate used is the expected yield to maturity on a risk-free security maturing in year N. As a practical matter, yields on long-term governments not subject to default or call risks are used. We use long-term nominal returns because they best reflect the inflation expectations over the life of the stock. Beta and the market risk premiums are assumed to be constant over time. The subscript e is used to designate an equity variable. K_e represents the cost of equity capital, and β_e represents the beta of equity capital (as opposed to the cost and beta of firm assets).

Capital Gains Versus Dividends

If the average stockholder was asked why a particular stock had been purchased, the answer would most likely be, "For its return—for the dividends and capital gains I expect to receive," and (neglecting risk) the answer is correct. But if capital gains are part of the returns that an investor values, why don't they appear in Equation (12.4)? They do, although not explicitly.

Consider the situation in which a shareholder expects to sell shares at the end of year 2. The value of the stock at the end of period 0 would be equal to the present value of any dividends expected during years 1 and 2 plus the present value of the expected stock price at the end of year 2:

$$P_0 = \frac{D_1}{1 + K_e} + \frac{D_2}{(1 + K_e)^2} + \frac{P_2}{(1 + K_e)^2}$$

Yet the expected price at the end of year 2 should be equal to the present value (at the end of year 2) of dividends expected to be paid after year 2:

$$P_2 = \frac{D_3}{(1 + K_e)} + \frac{D_4}{(1 + K_e)^2} + \cdots$$

Thus, P_0 is determined by both future dividends and future selling prices. But since all future selling prices must reflect future expected dividends, the base determinant of existing stock prices is expected future dividends.

Constant Growth Model

If the dividends paid by a firm are expected to grow at a constant growth rate to infinity, Equation (12.4) can be considerably simplified. Defining G as this expected constant growth rate, Equation (12.4) reduces to:

Constant Growth Model $\qquad P_0 = \dfrac{D_1}{K_e - G} = \dfrac{D_0\,(1 + G)}{K_e - G}$ $\qquad$ **(12.6)**

For example, consider the data on Midwest Machinery. Assume that after a thorough analysis of Midwest, an analyst concludes the following:

1. $RF = 8\%$
2. $RP_m = 5\%$
3. Beta of Midwest $= 1.2$
4. Long-run growth in dividends per share $= 5.6\%$
5. Expected dividend next year $= \$2.52$

Given these data, a required return of 14% is necessary [8% + 1.2(5%)], and the analyst would assess the value of Midwest to be $30 per share:

$$\$30 = \frac{\$2.52}{0.14 - 0.056}$$

Firms expected to pay dividends that will grow at a constant rate to infinity clearly do not exist. Yet some firms do have reasonably stable dividend growths over relatively long time periods. In such cases Equation (12.6) provides a good approximation of the security's worth. It is instructive to examine the composition of a stock's expected returns when the constant growth model is valid. Investors develop estimations of G and K_e and then determine a market price, P_0, so that the required return is expected to be earned. By rearranging Equation (12.6) we can see that, during each year, this expected return comes in two forms: an expected dividend yield and a growth in stock price. If the investor's required return equals the expected return, then:

Required Yearly Return		**Expected Dividend Yield**		**Expected Growth in Stock Price**	
	$=$		$+$		
K_e	$=$	$\dfrac{D_1}{P_0}$	$+$	G	**(12.7)**

For example, a stock which is selling for $25 and last paid a $0.92 dividend that is expected to grow over the long run at a constant rate of 9% per year is providing an expected return of 13%:

$$0.13 = \frac{\$0.92\,(1.09)}{\$25} + 0.09$$

Whether the 13% is an appropriate return to expect on such an investment depends on one's perceptions of the risk-free rate, the stock's beta, and the market risk premium.

In the case of Midwest Machinery, if its shares were now trading at $50, the analyst would not recommend a purchase. At a market price of $50 the expected return is 10.64% when a 14% return should be required:

$$\textbf{Expected Return} = 0.1064 = \frac{D_1}{P_0} + G = \frac{\$2.52}{\$50} + 0.056$$

As initially presented in Equation (12.6), G was defined as the dividend growth rate, but G also indicates the rate of growth in the stock's price. When a stock is priced via Equation (12.6), the best estimates of what K_e and G will be in the future are current estimates. Certainly they will change. But the best estimates of both, say five years hence, are the estimates made now, at period 0. Thus, the best estimation of the denominator in future years is today's denominator. The only term for which an expected change can be forecast is next period's dividend. Each year the numerator is expected to grow at a rate G. As a result, stock price is also expected to grow at rate G.

Consider another example. Assume that an analyst believes dividends paid on the Dow-Jones Industrial Average (DJIA) will grow at a fairly constant rate over the long run. The analyst also believes the Dows are properly valued today at a current market price of $4,800. If the long-term, risk-free rate is 8%, the market risk premium is 6%, the beta of the DJIA is 1.0, and next year's expected dividend yield on the DJIA is 5%, what is the estimated value of the DJIA one year hence? First, a required rate of return of 14% is necessary (14% = 8% plus 1.0 times 6%). Next, since the constant growth model applies, 5% of this required return will come in the form of an expected dividend yield, with the remaining 9% coming from yearly price growth. Thus, the DJIA is expected to be 9% higher, or $5,232 one year hence.

The constant growth model is appropriate whenever G is assumed constant to infinity, regardless of whether G is greater than zero, less than zero, or equal to zero. When G is exactly zero, Equation (12.6) reduces to an equation that is used to value a perpetuity:

Value with Zero Growth $$P_0 = \frac{D}{K_e}$$ (12.8)

When growth is negative, large dividend yields will be required to offset yearly price losses in order to earn required returns.

Nonconstant Growth. Few stocks can reasonably meet the assumption of constant dividend growth. Young, developing firms are likely to pay no dividends early in their lives as all profits are retained in the business to support necessary asset expansion. (An example is Microsoft during early years of rapid growth in desktop computer software.) Once such firms are well established and can institute dividend payments, the payments are likely to grow at a faster yearly rate than the firm is capable of sustaining over the long run. Finally, even mature firms are likely to have erratic dividend growth rates as the profits of the firm respond to normal business cycles.

For most of these situations, a **nonconstant growth model** would be appropriate. When using the nonconstant growth model, a future date is expected to eventually arrive beyond which the constant growth model can be used but before which dividends are expected to grow at yearly rates different from this longer-run constant rate. Working through an example will help make this clearer. Consider the stock of a department store in a city that is experiencing rapid population growth. Last year's dividend was equal to $1. During the next three years this dividend is expected to grow at 12% per year owing to a combination of population growth and lack of competition. Subsequently, growth will equal the population growth of 7% a year for another five years as competition from scheduled new store openings takes hold. Finally, as population growth slows, a long-run constant dividend growth of 3% per year is expected. What is the intrinsic value of this security if the required return is 15%?

The solution is shown in Table 12-3. First, expected yearly dividends are calculated for each of the next eight years (the years of abnormal growth). These are then discounted at a 15% required return to find their respective present values. In total, the present value of the first eight years' dividends is equal to $6.57. Beyond year 8 the constant growth model can be used. The value of a share at the end of year 8 would be equal to year 9's dividend divided by K_e minus G. This year 8 share value is $16.91. To express this future price in terms of its present value, the $16.91 is discounted at the 15% required return for eight periods to get $5.53. The value today of all dividends expected beyond year 8 is $5.53. Summing the present value of dividends between now and the end of year 8 ($6.57) with the present value of dividends beyond year 8 ($5.53), the value of the share is $12.10.

Here is the general formula applied to nonconstant growth firms:

Nonconstant Dividend Growth Valuation

$$P_0 = \sum_{t=1}^{T} \frac{D_0 (1 + G_1) (1 + G_2) \cdots (1 + G_t)}{(1 + K_e)^t} \qquad (12.9)$$

$$+ \frac{D_T (1 + G)}{(K_e - G)} \times \frac{1}{(1 + K_e)^T}$$

TABLE 12-3   ILLUSTRATION OF NONCONSTANT GROWTH MODEL

Future Year	Yearly Growth	Expected Dividend	Present Value at 15%
1	12%	$1.12	$0.97
2	12	1.25	.95
3	12	1.40	.92
4	7	1.50	.86
5	7	1.61	.80
6	7	1.72	.74
7	7	1.84	.69
8	7	1.97	.64
Total of Years 1–8			$6.57

Plus present value of price at end of year 8:

a. Price at end of year 8: $P_8 = \dfrac{D_8 (1 + G)}{K - G}$

$$= \frac{\$1.97 (1.03)}{0.15 - 0.03}$$

$$= \$16.91$$

b. Present value at period 0:

$$= \frac{\$16.91}{1.15^8} \qquad\qquad \$5.53$$

Total Value at Period 0 $12.10

where G_t represents the growth rate in any year of abnormal growth t, T is the last date of abnormal growth, and G is the long-run constant growth rate after year T.

Determinants of G. Sustainable growth in dividends per share, whether constant or not, is directly related to two fundamental factors: the rate of return on equity investments and the percentage of earnings retained in the business. Symbolically:

Sustainable Internal Growth $G = ROE \times b$ **(12.10)**

where b is the retention ratio (percentage of net income retained in the business) and ROE is the return on equity invested in the firm.

To illustrate this relationship, consider Midwest Machinery again. Assume that with the existing assets and capital structure, the firm could continue to earn net income equal to $8.4 million. Additions to plant needed to replace deteriorating equipment would be exactly covered by yearly depreciation provisions, and all income would be paid as dividends. Now assume the board of directors suddenly decides to start retaining 40% of future earnings on which a 14% rate of return can be earned. If this policy is implemented immediately, the $8.4 million net income will be apportioned between $3.36 million in retained equity (0.4 retention times $8.4 income) and $5.04 million in dividends. Since 2 million shares are outstanding, present dividends per share will be $2.52 ($5.04 divided by 2). Total equity will increase by the $3.36 million to $63.36 million. At a return on equity of 14%, next year's net income will be $8.87 million (0.14 times $63.36 million), and dividends per share will be $2.66 [$8.87 times 0.6 divided by 2.0]. As a result of this retention policy, dividends will grow from $2.52 this year to $2.66 next year, a growth rate of 5.6%:

$$G = ROE \times b$$

$$5.6\% = 14\% \times 0.4$$

The return on equity can also be separated into its individual components.[3] Analytically, ROE is a function of three factors:

1. **Asset efficiency**—the extent to which management can generate sales from a given asset base. Asset efficiency is measured by the asset-turnover ratio: sales divided by assets.
2. **Expense control**—the extent to which management can obtain income after taxes from a given sales base. Expense control is measured by the after-tax profit margin: net income divided by sales.
3. **Debt utilization**—the extent to which management relies on debt financing to support a given level of assets. Debt utilization is measured by the following ratio: total assets divided by total equity.

When these terms are multiplied, individual terms cancel to yield the return on equity:

---

[3] ROE is the accounting rate of return on the book value of equity. It is not the market rate of return that the shareholder receives. Although market returns and accounting returns are related, many factors influence market returns that do not affect accounting returns. For example, changes in the risk-free rate, a firm's beta, and the market risk premium all affect stock prices and thus market returns but have no direct effect on ROE.

Return on Equity

$$ROE = \frac{\text{Asset}}{\text{Efficiency}} \quad \text{times} \quad \frac{\text{Expense}}{\text{Control}} \quad \text{times} \quad \frac{\text{Debt}}{\text{Utilization}} \tag{12.11}$$

$$\frac{\text{Net Income}}{\text{Equity}} = \frac{\text{Sales}}{\text{Assets}} \times \frac{\text{Net Income}}{\text{Sales}} \times \frac{\text{Assets}}{\text{Equity}}$$

A decomposition similar to this one is often helpful when analyzing historical or potential changes in equity returns. In the case of Midwest Machinery, the 14% *ROE* is composed of an asset efficiency ratio of 2.0 ($2 in sales generated for each dollar of assets), an expense control ratio of 4.2% ($0.042 of profits per $1 of sales), and a debt utilization measure of 1.67 ($1.67 in assets for each $1 of equity).

Calculating Historical Growth Rates. Past dividend growth rates of individual stocks are often poor predictors of future dividend growth. But past growth is important to know, if for no other reason than to explain why such growth occurred. In contrast, dividend growth rates of aggregate security indices such as the S&P 500 are more predictable.

Two general approaches can be used to calculate the growth rate inherent in any variable (dividends in our case). We call this growth rate the **compound annual growth rate** (CAGR). The easier approach is simply an application of the geometric mean (discussed in Chapter 5). In this approach we find the annual rate of growth associated with a beginning and terminal value as follows:

Compound Annual Growth Rate

$$V_T = V_0(1 + \text{CAGR})^T \tag{12.12a}$$

$$\text{CAGR} = (V_T \div V_0)^{1 \div T} - 1.0 \tag{12.12b}$$

where V_T is the terminal value and V_0 is the beginning value. For example, the dividends per share on the S&P 500 were $0.69 in 1926 and $12.58 in 1993. This represents a CAGR over this 67-year period of 4.43%:

$$0.0443 = [12.58 \div 0.69]^{1/67} - 1.0$$

The problem with this approach is that it neglects all values between the beginning and terminal values. This can be overcome by using a CAGR calculated from a log-least-squares regression equation. In this case, the log-natural of yearly dividends per share (DPS) is calculated and regressed against a year identifier as follows:

CAGR By Log Least Squares

$$\ln(\text{DPS}_t) = a + b\,(\text{Year}_t) + e_t \tag{12.13}$$

Here $\ln(\text{DPS})$ is the random dependent variable and Year_t could be 1926, 1927, . . . 1993 or 1, 2, 3, . . . , 67. As long as successive values of Year are incremented by 1.0, the absolute scale of Year affects only the intercept term a, which is unimportant. The e_t values are random error terms. The b term is the estimated compound annual growth rate using all years of data.

In Figure 12-3, the natural logs of nominal S&P 500 dividends per share are shown on the vertical axis relative to the associated year on the horizontal axis. Actual values are

FIGURE 12-3 GROWTH OF S&P 500 DIVIDENDS (1926–1993)

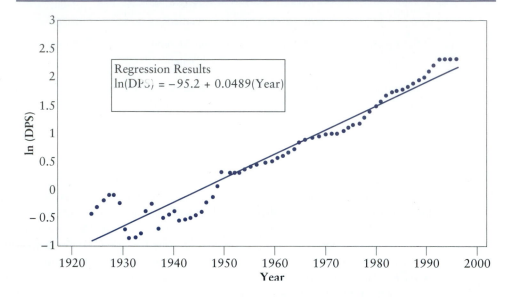

shown as dots. Predicted values obtained from regression Equation (12.3) are shown by the solid line. The slope of this line represents the CAGR based on log-least-squares methodology and the *b* coefficient in the following regression equation:

$$\ln(\text{DPS}_t) = -95.2 + 0.0489\,(\text{Year}_t)\quad R^2 = 93.4\%$$

The constant term of minus 95.2 represents the natural log of dividends when the year number is equal to 0. In a regression of this sort, the term is meaningless. The more important term is the slope of coefficient *b*. This slope represents the unit change in the natural log of dividends for each 1.0 unit change in time-one year. Because one full unit change in the natural log of dividends (or any number) is 100%, the 0.0489 value is interpreted as an average annual compound growth rate of 4.89%. The R^2 term is the percentage of variation in the dependent variable (natural log of DPS) associated with variation in the independent variables (time). *R*-squared in a regression with a single independent variable is the correlation coefficient between the dependent variables squared. It can range from 0% to 100%, where 0% indicates no correlation and 100% indicates perfect correlation. The high *R*-squared in the DPS model indicated that the annual growth rates of nominal dividends per share on the S&P 500 were fairly stable between 1926 and 1993. In Table 12-4, CAGRs based on log-least-squares regressions are shown for a variety of periods. Except for the 1920s and early 1930s, nominal growth in S&P 500 dividends has been relatively stable. Compared with the 67-year nominal CAGR of 4.89%, the post–World War II dividend growth has been 5.54%.

Growth Stocks

To most laypeople the term *growth stock* simply means a stock whose price is expected to increase at a faster rate than the average. For many years this definition was also common

Eric M. Wetlaufer, C.F.A.

Managing Director
Cadence Capital Management
Wesleyan University, B.A. earth science

Eric Wetlaufer is both a portfolio manager and stock analyst at Cadence. He has managed money market funds and junk bond portfolios and has been an investment consultant. He says he currently is happy to be managing common stocks where beating the market and other managers is his daily challenge.

Q: What kind of money management firm is Cadence Capital Management?

A: Cadence is a disciplined equity manager with $2.4 billion in assets under management for institutional clients including pension funds, endowments, foundations, and mutual funds. Utilizing a "bottom-up" stock selection process, Cadence creates portfolios focused on those issues offering a combination of improving fundamentals and favorable valuations.

Q: What screening mechanisms do you use to narrow the universe of stocks?

A: There are just too many publicly traded companies to analyze them all individually in detail. We use quantitative tools to exclude from consideration all stocks that don't exhibit good profit growth and reasonable relative valuations. The tools score stocks on a combination of factors with a focus on expected future performance using Wall Street analysts' estimates of earnings.

Q: Do you have a style objective in mind when evaluating a stock?

A: Yes, growth. We invest in stocks to make money—other asset classes are better for the preservation of capital. So, given that we are in it for strong returns, we have found the best combination of characteristics for a stock are rapid fundamental improvements in the underlying company: revenue, margin and balance sheet improvements, and relative stock valuations that don't yet reflect the company's better prospects. If we've really found sustainable growth, we know we can make a lot of money in the stock.

Q: There are many sources of stock information. Which are the most useful to you?

A: We read published financials and brokerage reports which we can immediately access on line. We talk to analysts and company executives on the phone, in our offices, and at industry conferences around the country. We speak to customers, competitors, and suppliers to get more perspective on the fundamentals of each of our investments. Collecting the right data and getting questions answered quickly is critically important to our success.

Q: What techniques do you employ to help determine whether you will purchase or sell a stock?

A: Once a stock has passed our quantitative screens, we need to understand why earnings will continue to grow in the future as well as the risks to the outlook for the company. We investigate the causes of revenue growth, margin improvement, and changes in the balance sheet to provide a framework for understanding the dynamics of a company. If we can believe that the improvements we see are sustainable over a reasonable investment horizon, we will buy the stock.

Although selling a stock successfully is a great challenge, doing it well is equally important to performance as buying good stocks. We use several disciplines to ensure that if a company's outlook is deteriorating, we are out of the stock, or on the way out at the very least.

Q: How do you monitor the performance of a stock?

A: We monitor performance of stocks hourly, daily, weekly, monthly, quarterly, and annually. But performance can be elusive. While a company successfully executes its strategy, dramatically improving its earnings, the market may be focused elsewhere on top-down concerns of a slowing economy or a faltering currency, or rising interest rates. Near-term performance can suffer, but as long as these exogenous factors don't negatively impact the company's outlook, the stock can become like a spring—ever more compressed until in a short burst, the market comes to recognize the company's fundamentals as more important than broader economic or industry risks. We will be patient with a lagging stock, so long as the reasons we initially took a position are still intact.

TABLE 12-4 LOG-LEAST-SQUARES COMPOUND ANNUAL GROWTH RATES OF S&P 500 DIVIDENDS

Period	CAGR	R^2
1926–1993	4.89%	93.4%
1926–1946	−0.96%	6.5%
1946–1993	5.54%	98.2%
1973–1993	6.89%	98.4%

within the professional analyst community. However, as understanding of the determinants of stock values has developed, a more precise definition has arisen. Today a true growth stock is one for which the available returns on investments are greater than investors' required returns.

A true growth situation has major implications for the value of the firm. Assume the return on current and future equity investments made by the firm is equal to the required equity return plus some constant difference. If we use the letter d to refer to this difference, then the return on equity investments can be expressed symbolically as:

Return on Equity Investments $ROE = K_e + d$ **(12.14)**

It can be shown that the constant growth model can be written in terms of the firm's book value per share (total equity divided by number of outstanding shares) as follows:

Market Value Versus Book Value

$$P_0 = BV_0 \frac{(K_e + d)(1 - b)}{Ke(1 - b) - db}$$ **(12.15)**

For example, if the return on equity investment is equal to the demanded equity return, the market price will equal the per share book value:

$$P_0 = BV_0 \frac{(K_e + 0)(1 - b)}{Ke(1 - b) - 0b} = BV_0$$

In cases when d is positive, the market price will be larger than book value. And in cases when the d is negative, the stock will be worth less than book value. Firms with positive d values are considered to be true growth stocks. A dollar of equity invested in the firm is able to earn a larger return than demanded by equity owners and, as a result, each dollar invested turns into a market value larger than one dollar.

These relationships are illustrated in Table 12-5 for three firms. Firm NRML represents a normal firm in which competitive pressures have forced ROE to equal K_e. Note that regardless of the retention rate, the stock price of NRML is the same as the stock's book value. Firm GRTH represents a typical growth situation in which ROE exceeds K_e. In this case the stock price increases as the retention rate increases. Finally, Firm NGRT is a negative-growth situation with K_e greater than ROE. As NGRT retains larger portions of income, its price falls.

Market Value Added. The concept just discussed has gained considerable attention in recent years under the name of **market value added (MVA).** Assume you create a new

TABLE 12-5 RELATIONSHIP BETWEEN P_0, K_e, ROE, AND b

				Price at Various Retention Rates		
Firm	Book Value per Share	K_e	ROE	$b = 0.3$	$b = 0.5$	$b = 0.8$
NRML	$50	12%	12%	$50.00	$50.00	$ 50.00
GRTH	50	12	14	62.82	70.00	175.00
NGRT	50	12	10	38.89	35.71	25.00

firm by investing $100 in various assets. To keep the example simple, assume the assets are acquired solely with equity investment (no debt is used to buy assets). Given the risks of the assets, you believe a fair rate of return on this investment would be 10%. However, once the assets are acquired, they are able to generate a yearly cash flow (after all expenses) of $20 forever. Discounting the $20 perpetuity by the 10% required return results in a present value of the cash flows equal to $200.

$$\$200 = \frac{\$20}{0.10}$$

If you were to sell your ownership of these assets to another party, you would demand a price of (at least) $200 and the other party would be willing to pay (no more than) $200. The difference between the cost of the assets and the market value of the assets represents the market value added.

A positive market value added is created when the firm has acquired assets that have positive net present values (NPV). You probably recall from a basic finance course that NPV represents the difference between the present value of expected future cash flows on an asset and the cost of the asset. Whenever the expected rate of return on an asset exceeds the required return (given the asset's risk), there will be a positive NPV.

Table 12-6 shows MVA calculations for our hypothetical company, Midwest Machinery, and two real companies, International Business Machines and General Electric. Let's examine the details of General Electric's data. The firm's 1994 balance sheet showed an equity book value of $26.387 billion. *This means that, at various times in the past, equity owners had contributed $26.387 billion in cash to the company.* A total of $1.782 billion was contributed through the issuance of new shares of stock. An additional $24.605 was contributed by shareholders through the retention of profits. The market price of General Electric shares was $51 at the end of 1994. Multiplying the per share price by the number of shares outstanding results in a total market capitalization of $91.469 billion. Management had taken $26 billion in equity investments and used the

TABLE 12-6 ANALYSIS OF MARKET VALUE ADDED

	Midwest Machinery (in millions)	IBM (in billions)	GE (in billions)
Common Stock and Paid in Surplus	$12	$7.342	$1.782
Retained Profits	48	14.990	24.605
Book Value of Equity	$60	$22.332	$26.387
Market Price per Share	$30.00	$73.50	$51.00
Shares Outstanding	2	0.6488	1.794
Market Capitalization	$60	$47.687	$91.469
Market Value Added	$0	$25.355	$65.082
Market-to-Book Ratio	1.0	2.14	3.47

Note: Data for International Business Machines and General Electric are for December 31, 1994.

funds to create a market value of $91 billion. Management had created a market value added of $65 billion.

The relationship between book values and market values can also be examined in ratio form as either the "market-to-book ratio" or the "book-to-market ratio." In Table 12-6, the market-to-book ratio is shown. The 3.47 ratio for General Electric means that investors value the equity of the firm as being worth 3.47 times the value of past investments in the firm.

Why is the MVA of Midwest Machinery zero and the market-to-book ratio 1.0? Simply because we have assumed that the demanded return of 14% is identical to the 14% return on equity.

The Price-to-Earnings (P/E) Ratio

The P E ratio of a stock is equal to the stock's current market price divided by some measure of earnings per share; that is:

Price-to-Earnings Ratio $P/E = \dfrac{\text{Market Price per Share}}{\text{Earnings per Share}}$

As such, the P E ratio indicates the dollar price being paid for each $1 of a firm's earnings. P E ratios are widely used by professional analysts as a measure of the relative prices of different stocks.

The stock's current market price is easy to determine, since it is probably reported in the financial press. Earnings per share (EPS), however, are more difficult to determine. The easiest earnings figure to use would be the latest EPS as shown on the company's financial statements. In fact, P E ratios reported in the financial press are typically calculated using such latest reported EPS numbers. However, people buy a stock not for its past earnings but, instead, for its expected future earnings. As a result, many security analysts will report P/E ratios based on next year's expected EPS. Even then a problem can arise when comparing P/E ratios among firms if some of the firms are expected to have abnormally high EPS next year whereas others are expected to have an abnormally poor year. To correct for such an unusual situation, many analysts calculate the P/E ratio based on an estimate of normalized earnings per share. Normalized EPS can be estimated either by a purely subjective guess or by using sophisticated statistical models. Regardless of how normalized earnings are calculated, they are meant to reflect the normal level of the firm's earnings exclusive of any temporary effects caused by the state of the business cycle, seasonal conditions in the industry, or unusual events affecting the firm.

Conceptually, the P/E ratio is determined by three factors: (1) investors' required returns, (2) expected earnings retention rate, and (3) expected returns on equity. Again, the easiest way to demonstrate this is to use the constant dividend growth model:

$$P_0 = \frac{D_1}{K_e - G}$$

When we divide both sides of this equation by next year's earnings per share (E_1), the P/E ratio is determined by the following relationship:

Determinants of the P/E Ratio $P_0/E_1 = \dfrac{1 - b}{K_e - G}$ (12.16)

Equation 12.16 states that if dividends are expected to grow at a constant growth rate, the P/E ratio is theoretically equal to the stock's expected dividend payout ratio (1 minus b) divided by the difference between the required return and the expected growth rate. In the case of Midwest Machinery, we have been assuming an expected payout ratio of 60%, a required return of 14%, and an expected constant growth rate of 5.6%. This would imply a theoretical P/E ratio of 7.14:

$$7.1429 = \frac{0.60}{0.14 - 0.056}$$

In other words, we should be willing to pay $7.14 for each $1 of Midwest's earnings per share expected next year. Since we had earlier assumed an earnings per share next year of $4.20 ($8.4 million net income divided by 2.0 million shares), this implies a stock price of $30.00.

Figure 12-4 shows the P/E levels for the Standard & Poor's Composite Index. Price/earnings ratios are shown for each year-end from 1926 through 1993. To measure earnings per share, Standard & Poor's used reported earnings during the year for which a P/E ratio is shown (E_0 instead of E_1). As can be seen, aggregate market P/E ratios have been quite volatile. Unfortunately, many people simply look at today's P/E ratio, compare it with historical values, and then conclude that the market (or a single stock) is either overvalued or undervalued. For example, at the end of 1979 P/E ratios were at their lowest point for a number of years, and this persuaded many people that the market was undervalued. The market may, or may not, have been undervalued in late 1979, but a simple comparison of historical averages to current P/E ratios isn't adequate information on which to make such a decision. P/E ratios should change over time in response to changes in expected payout ratios, expected corporate returns on equity, and required returns.

FIGURE 12-4 PRICE TO EARNINGS RATIO S&P 500 (1926–1993)

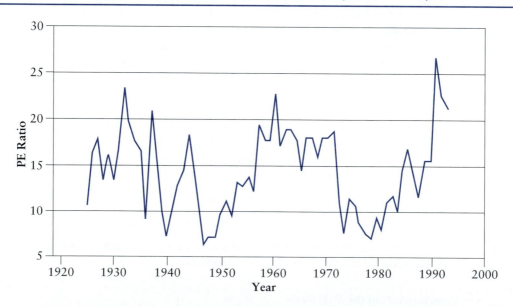

David Kushner, C.F.A.

Senior Vice President
Portfolio Manager, Equities
ICC Capital Management, Inc.
University of Florida, B.S.B.A.

David Kushner's investment career began when he interned in the "securities cage" of a bank trust department. He enjoyed all aspects of securities markets and decided his career would be in equity management. After graduation, Kushner continued to work in the trust department where he developed his fundamental investment skills. Within a few years, he was hired by a large state pension to help develop quantitative approaches to active equity management. He is presently the senior equity portfolio manager for ICC Capital Management, Inc.

Q: David, you trade equities. How many trades do you make in a given day?

A: It is easier to say how many I make in a year. My typical portfolio would have 50 to 60 names. My turnover runs about 25%, which means I sell 15 names and buy 15 in any year. So that is roughly 30 transactions in different securities per year. The number of trades needed to change these positions depends on how liquid a stock is. My turnover is much lower than most active equity managers.

Q: Do you ever have problems with liquidity, selling something rapidly with no market impact?

A: Every time you go to the market there is a question about liquidity, and sometimes it can be a serious problem. For example, there are times where I may go out to buy 100,000 shares of a stock which trades only six to eight thousand shares a day. When that occurs, you never show your full hand to Wall Street and you take your time. You do not have to be in or out of a stock in a day or a week if it effects the security's price. That is not in the best interests of your client.

Q: When you trade, is there a standard commission paid to the broker?

A: The cents per share on each trade are negotiated between the institution and the broker. They range from 1 or 2 cents per share up to full retail commission rates. As a rule of thumb, large institutional investors can do about everything at 5 to 6 cents a share. But if a Wall Street firm puts their own capital at risk to facilitate a trade for us, we might pay them 7 or 8 cents per share. You are not in the business to put Wall Street out of business. When they help us out, we must help them.

Q: David, would you describe what a "soft-dollar" payment is?

A: Sure. Every time you trade a stock, you generate commissions for a brokerage firm. These commissions cover the costs of the broker executing the trade. But commissions are often larger than the broker's costs of execution. The excess covers a wide variety of things. For example, it can provide access to analysts who work for the brokerage firm and their research reports. But the excess can also be used to pay for other services which the portfolio manager receives or the manager's client receives.

Q: Let's say you, as a manager, would like to buy the Standard & Poor's PC Plus stock data. Can you do that with soft dollars?

A: I have two choices. I can write a check to Standard & Poor's or I could trade through S&P Securities, which is a division of Standard & Poor's, to offset my cost of buying their data. Generally, I would pay two commission dollars for each dollar I would have to pay out of pocket. By the way, the money I pay out of pocket is referred to as a "hard dollar." The payment which comes from a brokerage commission is called a "soft dollar."

Q: Is there any potential for abuse of soft-dollar payments?

A: Most definitely. The use of soft dollars by a manager to purchase research is governed by SEC Rule 28E. But the definition of research is rather fluid. Some managers have used them to pay for three-week trips to the Bahamas to check out an oil refinery. Soft dollars are also used to compensate pension consultants of brokerage firms. These consultants evaluate managers of the pension funds. This creates the potential for the consultant to provide a poor evaluation of managers who do not provide sufficient commissions to the broker's firm. We should not put a consultant in a position where he or she may feel a bias against a manager because that manager did not generate sufficient commission dollars to pay the consultant's fee.

Other Valuation Approaches

The preceding discussion was based on a model that says a share of stock is worth the present value of future dividends expected to be paid on the share. This makes perfect sense. A common stock is not like a painting, a record, or a book. It isn't bought for the enjoyment gained from looking at it, listening to it, or reading it on a rainy evening. A stock is bought for the future consumption opportunities it provides. Without the potential for future dividends, a stock is worth nothing.

Other valuation models exist in which dividends are not explicitly seen in an equation. We examine three of these:

1. Earnings valuation,
2. Cash flow valuation, and
3. Investment opportunities valuation.

However, all of these approaches are simply rearrangements of the basic dividend model. The role of dividends as the source of stock value never disappears.

Earnings Valuation

Underlying any ongoing stream of dividends are the earnings of the firm. These earnings, by definition, belong to the equity shareholders, so why can't we simply express the value of a share of common stock in terms of the earnings per share that the firm is expected to generate? We can. But in doing so an important point must be recognized: Any earnings that are retained within the firm (not paid as dividends) are additional investments made by shareholders in the firm and should also be valued.

For example, let's return to the Midwest Machinery example. To review, we are at the start of year 1. During year 0, Midwest earned $8.4 million on 2 million shares, or $4.20 per share. Since none of these earnings were retained in year 0, earnings per share will also be $4.20 in year 1. However, during year 1 Midwest intends to begin retaining 40% of all profits in the firm. This would result in retained profits of $1.68 per share and dividends per share of $2.52 in year 1. Beyond year 1 the retained profits will generate an expected *ROE* of 14% and result in a sustainable growth rate of 5.6%. Finally, investors require a return of 14%. Placing this information into the constant dividend growth model, each share of Midwest is worth $30:

$$P_0 = \frac{D_1}{K_e - G} = \frac{\$2.52}{0.14 - 0.056} = \$30$$

Now consider the valuation of the expected earnings that each share has a claim to. In particular, consider the $4.20 earnings per share (EPS) for year 1. All of this $4.20 belongs to the shareholder even though the firm will retain some of it. So why not simply find its present value? It does belong to the shareholder, so why not value it? And looking beyond year 1, all subsequent EPS also belong to the shareholder. So why not find their present values and say the stock is worth the sum of the present values of all future EPS?

The answer is very simple. When a firm's management retains a portion of a shareholder's EPS, it is the same as the shareholder's being paid all EPS in dividends and then reinvesting the earnings retained. When Midwest Machinery pays dividends per share of $2.52 on earnings per share of $4.20, it is the same as paying the full $4.20 in dividends and having the shareholder immediately reinvest $1.68 in the firm. Retention of profits represents new investment by the equity owners. It is perfectly correct to value the earnings per share of a stock as long as the reinvestment of earnings is also valued. The worth of a share of common stock is equal to the present value of all future expected earnings per share less the present value of all future investments per share:

Earnings Valuation Model $$P_0 = \sum_{t=1}^{N} \frac{\text{EPS}_t - IP_t}{(1 + K_e)^t}$$ (12.17) where EPS_t is the expected earnings per share in year t and IPS_t is the expected investment per share in year t.

This equation values the expected future earnings-per-share stream that legally belongs to the shareholder. But it also values expected future investments made by the shareholder in order to generate the EPS stream.

Constant Growth Earnings Valuation. The general earnings valuation model shown in Equation (12.17) can be simplified considerably if future growth is expected to be constant. Again using G as this expected constant growth rate, Equation (12.17) reduces to:

Constant Growth Earnings Valuation

$$P_0 = \frac{EPS_1 - IPS_1}{K_e - G}$$

(12.18)

Applied to the Midwest Machinery example:

$$\$30 = \frac{\$4.20 - \$1.68}{0.14 - 0.056}$$

Note that the dividend valuation model and the earnings valuation model are identical. The dividend model focuses on net cash flows received by the investor (dividends), whereas the earnings model explicitly accounts for both the legal ownership of EPS and the incremental future reinvestment of earnings.

A Special Case. If the return that investors require (K_e) is identical to the return earned on owners' investments in the firm (ROE), the worth of a stock is simply the capitalized value of next year's earnings per share:

Value When K_e Equals ROE $$P_0 = \frac{EPS_1}{K_e}$$

(12.19)

In fact, that is exactly the case for Midwest Machinery. Investors require a return of 14% and the firm is expected to generate a 14% ROE on any equity investment made in the firm. Thus, Equation (12.19) can be used to value the shares of Midwest:

$$\$30 = \frac{\$4.20}{0.14}$$

When $ROE = K_e$, the retention of profits will have no impact on a stock's value. For example, if Midwest retains \$1.00 at period 0, the dollar will grow to \$1.14 one year later. But when this \$1.14 is discounted back to its period 0 present value at 14%, it is worth exactly \$1.00. When $ROE = K_e$, retained earnings are invested in assets that have a zero net present value. Equation (12.19) would usually apply to firms in highly competitive, mature industries, such as food distribution, paper products, and public utilities. It would not apply to developing industries, such as computer technology, or industries in decline, such as typewriter manufacturing.

Cash Flow Valuation

In principle, the worth of any asset is the present value of all future cash flows generated from the asset. In the calculation of earnings per share a number of expenses are no more than accounting entries. Depreciation, amortization of patents, goodwill, bad debt allowances, and many other "accounting expenses" involve no cash outflow during the year in which they are reported. Shouldn't they be added back to reported earnings per share in order to more fairly represent the cash flows generated from business operations?

Many analysts, in fact, do add such noncash expenses to earnings per share and compute the value of cash flows per share generated by the firm. This is referred to as a cash flow valuation model. First, expected cash flows from operations for year t (CF_t) are calculated as follows:

Cash Flow Per Share $\qquad CF_t = EPS_t + NCE_t \div N_t$ $\qquad\qquad$ (12.20)

where NCE_t refers to total noncash expenses expected in year t and N_t refers to the number of shares expected to be outstanding in year t. In addition, the investment per share (IPS_t) used in the earnings valuation model must be adjusted from a net investment to a gross investment. It was implicit in the earnings model that depreciation (and other noncash expenses) would be reinvested in the firm. However, if we wish to treat such items explicitly as cash available to equity holders, we must also explicitly recognize that such cash flows are in fact reinvested. The expected gross investment per share for year t (GPS_t) is calculated as:

Gross Investment Per Share $\quad GPS_t = IPS_t + NCE_t \div N_t$ $\qquad\qquad$ (12.21)

Using these two adjustments, the cash flow valuation model is:

Cash Flow Valuation Model $\qquad P_0 = \sum_{t=1}^{N} \frac{CF_t - GPS_t}{(1 + K_e)^t}$ $\qquad\qquad$ (12.22)

As you might imagine, a constant growth equivalent model can also be applied to this cash flow approach. We will not formally define it, since it should be obvious given the two previous constant growth models. But let's illustrate its application to Midwest Machinery. First, expected cash flow for year 1 is found to be $9.20:

$$CF_1 = EPS_1 + (NCE_1 \div N_1)$$

$$\$9.20 = \$4.20 + (\$10.0 \div 2.0)$$

Second, expected gross reinvestment is $6.68:

$$GPS_1 = IPS_1 + (NCE_1 \div N_1)$$

$$\$6.68 = \$1.68 + (\$10.0 \div 2.0) = \$6.68$$

Thus, the stock is worth $30 using the cash flow valuation model:

$$\$30 = \frac{\$9.20 - \$6.68}{0.14 - 0.056}$$

The dividend and cash flow models yield the same price, of course, because they both show the net cash that is received by shareholders—dividends. The only difference is cosmetic, in that the cash flow version explicitly shows cash flows available from operations and cash flows reinvested in the firm.

Investment Opportunities Valuation

The investment opportunities model separates the value of a share into two components: (1) the value of the existing assets, and (2) the value of future investment opportunities. As an example, let's consider a competitor of Midwest Machinery—Western Machinery Corporation—that is identical to Midwest in all respects except in the return its equity holders require. Assume the value of K_e for Western Machinery is 12%. As a result, the per share value of the stock will be:

$$\$39.375 = \frac{D_1}{K_e - G} = \frac{\$2.52}{0.12 - 0.056}$$

Let's take a close look at why the stock is selling for $39.375. First, the earnings per share of the firm are $4.20. To help make the example less complex, we assume that accounting depreciation is equal to the actual economic depreciation of the firm's assets. Thus, management could pay all earnings of the firm as dividends to shareholders and not deplete the economic productivity of the assets. The existing assets are capable of providing a perpetual stream of dividends equal to current earnings per share. The present value of this perpetual dividend flow available from existing assets is $35:

$$\$35 = \frac{\text{EPS}}{K_e} = \frac{\$4.20}{0.12}$$

Without retaining any profits, the existing assets can generate cash flows that have a current worth of $35 per share.

However, the management of Western Machinery does intend to make future investments in the firm. For example, at the end of the current year each shareholder will be asked to invest an incremental $1.68 (the retained profits per share). When this $1.68 is invested at 14%, it will yield an expected perpetual cash flow of $0.2352 ($1.68 times 0.14). Discounted at 12%, this perpetual cash flow stream will be worth $1.96 (0.2352 divided by 0.12) at the end of the year. But the shareholder has been asked to pay $1.68 for the new assets, so the end-of-year expected net present values of these new investments will be $0.28 ($1.96 minus $1.68).

The same type of analysis could be applied to all future years. Management will ask shareholders to invest in new assets that generate positive net present values. These net present values won't be forthcoming until future years, but there is no reason why their current present values should not be added to the stock's price. When the company is expected to maintain a constant retention of profits (B) and be able to invest at a constant return on new investment (ROE^*), the stock can be valued as follows:

Constant Growth Investment Opportunities Valuation

$$P_0 = \frac{\text{EPS}_0}{K_e} + \frac{b(\text{EPS}_0)}{K_e - G} \times \frac{ROE^* - K_e}{K_e} \qquad \textbf{(12.23)}$$

When applied to Western Machinery:

$$\$39.375 = \frac{\$4.20}{0.12} + \frac{0.4\,(\$4.20)}{0.12 - 0.056} \times \frac{0.14 - 0.12}{0.12}$$

The current stock value of $39.375 consists of a $35.00 value placed on existing assets plus a $4.375 value associated with today's worth of the expected future profitability of new investments.

Equation (12.23) is the constant growth version of the investment opportunities model. When ROE^* and b values are expected to change over time, the more general model shown below should be used.

General Investment Opportunities Valuation

$$P_0 = \frac{EPS_0}{K_e} + \sum_{t=1}^{\infty} \frac{b_t\,EPS_t(ROE^* - K_e)}{K_e} \,[1 \div (1 + K_e)^t] \qquad \textbf{(12.24)}$$

Again, the results obtained under each valuation model will be identical. They all value expected dividend flows. However, each focuses on a different approach to dividend valuation, and each approach can provide useful insights. For example, the investment opportunities model separates the value of existing assets from the value of future investment opportunities. If a large part of a stock's worth is associated with future opportunities, the security analyst would certainly wish to place an emphasis on technological developments and potential competition within the industry.

The Option Value of Leveraged Equity

Whenever equity holders borrow, they have the option to either pay all promised cash flows to debt holders or to declare bankruptcy and turn the firm's assets over to debt holders. The equity owner's position in this case is the same as owning the assets plus a right to sell the assets to bond holders. This right to sell is clearly a put option with an exercise price equal to the promised payments to debt owners.

Owning Equity   is the same as   **Owning Firm Assets**   plus   **Owning a Put Option on Firm Assets**

An alternative way to view the option position of equity holders is as a call option on firm assets. When promised cash flows are due to debt holders, equity holders will make the payments if the value of assets is greater than the promised payment. The exercise price of this call is clearly the promised payment to the debt holder.

Owning Equity   is the same as   **Owning a Call Option on Firm Assets**

The option position of equity holders provides a direct explanation for how shareholders might be able to "extract wealth" from debt holders. Think of the value of a firm's assets as being the present value of future cash flows from the assets (A). This value will be apportioned between the value of debt (D) and the value of equity (E). That is, $A = D + E$. If equity holders take actions that cause the value of D to fall without affecting asset value, then what is lost in *D* is gained in *E*. Since *E* is the value of a call option on *A*, anything that increases the value of an equity call option will decrease *D*.

One of the most important determinants of a call option's value in the Black-Scholes option pricing model is the standard deviation of the underlying asset's return. The greater the standard deviation of the asset's returns, the greater the value of the call. This presents equity owners with a motive to increase the riskiness of firm assets. Doing so increases bond default risk. And the reduction in bond values is simply transferred to equity holders.

Potential bond owners, of course, recognize this threat and will not purchase debt unless they are promised very high returns (e.g., junk or high-yield bonds) or are protected. Equity holders offer a variety of protections: loan covenants, collateralization with specific low-risk assets, yearly financial statement audits, dividend restrictions, and so forth.

Few (if any) security analysts actually apply option theory to the valuation of stocks. Current option models are unable to deal with the complexities of real-world financial arrangements. Yet option theory is a useful device to explain the actions of highly leveraged firms in which equity owners have little to lose but the potential for sizable gains. The limited liability aspect of equity is an important part of the value for highly leveraged firms.

Price and Earnings Growth

Growth of corporate earnings and stock prices are intimately related. Over the long run there is a close correspondence between the two. For example, in Figure 12-5 the level of

FIGURE 12-5 PRICE LEVEL AND EARNINGS OF THE S&P 500 INDEX

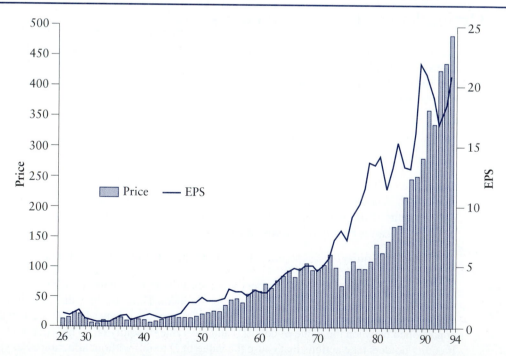

the S&P Composite Index is plotted together with its earnings per share between 1927 and 1993. Clearly, over the long run, market price levels increase with earnings. And in the short run, unexpected changes in earnings can have dramatic effects on stock prices. Stocks with unexpected favorable earnings announcements show significant price growth. Stocks with unexpected unfavorable announcements decrease in value. Unexpected earnings changes do affect stock prices. Most of a stock's price adjustment occurs before the announcement date. In order to capture possible gains, you must be able to predict unexpected earnings announcements earlier than the average person.

However, earnings and growth rate predictions are more difficult to develop than one might believe. For example, historical growth rates are very poor predictors of future growth. A large body of research suggests that historical growth rates are only slightly related to future growth. This was first noted in an article appropriately titled "Higgledy Piggledy Growth." The author of this research paper reported that successive changes in earnings per share of British firms were statistically uncorrelated. Numerous studies flowed from "Higgledy Piggledy," most confirming the results.

How have security analysts fared in their earnings predictions? The answer is debatable, but some evidence suggests not so well. The best known study of security analysts' forecasts was conducted by Cragg and Malkiel. Their study was based on earnings forecasts for 185 corporations made by five financial institutions. They found that over half the variation in forecasted growth was associated with historical growth. Even though historical growth is an extremely poor predictor of the future, a large part of the analysts' forecasts relied on this past growth.

S U M M A R Y

In this chapter we examined a variety of ways in which the value of an equity security can be estimated. Here are the key concepts:

- The most widely used stock valuation model is known as the dividend valuation model, in which the intrinsic worth of a stock is estimated by discounting all future expected dividends per share at a return that depends on the stock's risk.

- If dividends are expected to grow at a constant rate for an indefinite period of time, the general dividend model reduces to the constant dividend growth model. This model states that the intrinsic worth of a stock (P_0) is:

$$\text{Price Today} = \frac{\text{Expected Dividends per Share Next Year}}{\text{Required Return} - \text{Expected Growth Rate}}$$

- A nonconstant growth variant of this basic model allows for a number of years during which dividends per share grow at different rates but assumes that, after some point in the future, the best estimate of dividend growth is a constant rate.

- A true growth stock is a stock for which the shareholders' required return is less than the return a company is actually able to provide. Whenever a firm is able to earn a larger rate of return on shareholder investments than shareholders require, shareholders will prefer the firm to retain a larger portion (perhaps all) of the firm's earnings, since this will increase the expected future dividend stream as well as the stock's intrinsic worth. Alternatively, if required returns are equal to the marginal returns the firm is able to earn on new shareholder investment, shareholders will be indifferent to the level of profit retention in the firm.

■ Valuation models that focus on characteristics other than dividends have been developed. For example, models may be based on earnings per share, cash flow per share, or a firm's investment opportunities. Each of these, however, is no more than a variant of the basic dividend model. Without the prospect of future dividends, a stock is worth nothing.

REVIEW PROBLEM

Here is some financial and stock market information about a hypothetical firm called Data Control.

DATA CONTROL, INC.
FINANCIAL STATEMENTS FOR THE YEAR ENDED DECEMBER 1997

Assets	(millions)	Liabilities and Equity	(millions)
Current Assets	$1,300	Debt	$1,200
Net Plant	1,500	Equity	1,600
Total Assets	$2,800	**Total** Liabilities and Equity	$2,800

	(millions)
Sales	$4,800
Cash Expenses	4,110
Depreciation	150
Net Operating Income	540
Interest	100
New Income Pretax	440
Tax	(200)
Net Income	$ 240
Dividends Paid	$ 144

Market Information as of December 1997

Common Shares Outstanding	40 million
Price Per Share	$47.70
Risk-Free Rate	9%
Expected Return on the Market	14%
Estimated Beta	1.20

a. Calculate what the required return on Data Control should be using the security market line.
b. Calculate the sustainable growth rate (G) that would exist if the financial relationships shown in the balance sheet and income statements were to remain constant over time.
c. What is the fair market price of Data Control? (Use the dividend valuation model.)

d. Use the constant earnings and cash flow models to determine the stock's fair value.

e. Would you buy this stock? Why or why not?

f. What would a firm believer in efficient market theory say about your decision in part e?

g. Assume that Data Control's beta is really 1.0. Now what should the stock sell for?

Solution

a. $K_e = RF + B(RP_m)$
   $= 9\% + 1.2(14\% - 9\%) = 15\%$

b. $G = b\ (ROE) = 0.4(15\%) = 6\%$
   $b = (240 - 144) \div 240$
   $ROE = (240 \div 1600)$

c. The constant growth model can be used here, since the retention rate and ROE are expected to remain constant:
   $P_0 = [D_0\ (1 + G)] \div (K - G) = [3.60(1.06)] \div (0.15 - 0.06) = 42.40$

d. Constant earnings valuation model:
   $P_0 = [(EPS_0 - IPS_0)(1 + G)] \div (K - G)$
   $= [(6.00 - 2.40)(1.06)] \div (0.15 - 0.06)$
   $= 42.40$

   Constant cash flow valuation model:
   $P_0 = [(CF_0 - GPS_0)(1 + G)] \div (K - G)$
   $= [(9.75 - 6.15)(1.06)] \div (0.15 - 0.06)$
   $= 42.40$

   $CF_0 = 6.00 + (150$ depreciation $\div 40$ shares outstanding$)$

e. Given this information, the stock is worth $42.40. Since it is selling for $47.70, it is overpriced and you should not purchase it. In fact, if you really believe the $42.40 price, you might short-sell it.

f. "You must have missed some important information. The market price of $47.70 totally reflects all information available to the markets on the stock."

g. The required return would be 14%:
   $14\% = 9\% + 1.0(14\% - 9\%)$
   And the fair price would be $47.70:
   $47.70 = [3.60(1.06)] \div (0.14 - 0.06)$
   If the true beta is 1.0, the stock is fairly priced in the markets.

QUESTIONS AND PROBLEMS

1. Discuss the relative pros and cons of using the following approaches to estimate a security's value:
   a. Par value
   b. Book value
   c. Liquidation value
   d. Replacement value
   e. Substitution value
   f. Present value

2. Why is it wrong to say that the worth of a stock is the present value of expected future earnings per share on that stock?

3. A friend of yours has just completed a computer program that estimates the total dividends which a firm is expected to pay and finds the present value of these at the discount rate of your choosing. The friend calls the result "Total Equity Value" and divides this by the

number of shares now outstanding to calculate today's per share value. Where is your friend's grand effort in error?

4. Dividends per share of Jacques's Jackets (JJ) were $2.54 ten years ago. The latest dividend (just paid) was $5.00. The stock has a beta of 1.5. The risk-free rate is 6%, and the market risk premium is 4%.

   a. If future dividend growth is expected to be identical to historical growth, what should the market value of JJ stock be?

   b. If JJ stock is selling at the price found in part a, what are next year's expected dividend yield and capital appreciation yield?

5. Historically, WDR Corporation has retained 60% of its profits in the business. This is expected to continue. Future asset returns (ROA) are expected to be 10%, and the debt-to-equity ratio will remain constant at 25%. The risk-free rate is 8%, RP_M can be taken as 5%, and beta is about 1.3. The present dividend (just paid) was $2.50, and the stock is selling at $45. Should you buy or sell the stock?

6. You have been requested to estimate a fair market price for a new stock offering. Long-run growth will be constant, and the following data apply.

Last Year's Dividend per Share	$3
Last Year's Earnings per Share	$4
After-Tax Profit Margin	2%
Debt-to-Equity Ratio	100%
Asset Turnover	4 times
Risk-Free Rate	8%
Market Risk Premium	6%
Stock Beta	1.5

   a. Estimate the firm's return on equity.

   b. Estimate the firm's expected dividend growth.

   c. Estimate the fair value of the stock.

7. First Arizona Bancgroup dividends are expected to grow with population, personal income, and inflation at about 8% (forever). The stock is selling at $40 and beta is 0.90. RF is 8% and RP_M is 5%. What is the implied growth rate in the stock's price if next year's dividend will be $2.00? Would you buy or sell the stock?

8. The common shares of GEB Resources are currently being traded on the OTC at $35 per share. A dividend of $2.00 was just paid. You expect this dividend per share to grow at a constant rate of 6%. What must your required return be if you believe the $35 price is reasonable?

9. Hulu Huup, Inc., has introduced a new line of huups to be used only by consenting adults. In evaluating the company, you believe earnings and dividends will grow at a rate of 20% for the next three years, after which the growth rate will fall to a negative 5%. If the beta of HH is 2.0, the risk-free rate is 6%, and the market risk premium is 6%:

   a. Calculate the current fair value of the stock today if the last dividend (D_0) was $3.

   b. Calculate the value of the stock at the end of year 3 and at the end of year 4.

   c. If your projections hold true, what will the dividend yield be during year 3? Why is it so large compared with the required return?

10. Use the constant growth dividend valuation model to explain the economic forces that determine the P/E ratio of a broad stock market index. Obtain estimates of each of these as of the date you work this problem and compare the resulting P/E ratio with the actual P/E of the S&P 500.

11. A ratio that is widely used to gauge the level of the stock market is known as the price-to-book ratio (P/B ratio). It is calculated by dividing the market price of an individual stock (or a market index) by the accounting book value of the stock (or the index).

   a. Use the constant growth model to show what economic forces determine the P/B ratio.

b. Under what conditions will the ratio be greater than 1.0?

12. Under what conditions will a stock's market value be the same as its accounting book value? Explain why.

13. Consider the following information about stocks A and B:

	Stock A	Stock B
Expected Dividends Next Year	$1.00	$2.33
Expected Constant ROE	20%	20%
Expected Retention Rate	70%	30%
Required Return on Securities of Equivalent Risk	20%	20%

a. Which stock is more sensitive to changes in risk premiums and growth expectations?

b. Is either a true growth stock?

14. Many portfolio managers claim to be growth-stock managers. When asked what this means, they often respond, "We purchase stocks that are expected to have greater than average price growth over the coming decade."

a. Is this a fair definition of a true growth stock? Why?

b. Would you expect true growth-stock managers to have larger portfolio returns than managers who purchase more income-oriented stocks?

c. Would you expect true growth-stock managers to have better risk/return performance than managers who purchase more income-oriented stocks?

15. A past issue of Value Line published the following estimates for a company:

Beta = 1.15

Dividend per share at date zero = $3.10

Expected dividend per share in three years from zero = $4.00

Retention rate in three years from zero = 60%

ROE in three years from now = 15%

a. The stock was selling for $49. Estimate the expected returns from purchasing at $49 and receiving the dividend stream projected by Value Line.

b. The risk-free rate (long-term Treasuries) on this date was 11.5%. Using a market risk premium of 6%, what do you conclude about the purchase of the company's shares?

c. What would a staunch believer in EMT say about your conclusion in part b?

16. South Central Bank Corporation is a Florida bank holding company with loans and deposits of $500 million that are expected to grow at close to the local population estimates of 4% per year. Because of the continued emphasis the bank wishes to place on both wholesale (business) banking and its traditional retail business, its yield spread is expected to remain around 4%. Last year this yield spread (return on loans less cost of funds) provided a net interest income of $20 million. Expenses and taxes are expected to be 70% of net interest income. Earnings are now $6 million, or $5.00 per share. Dividend payout is, and will remain, about 50%. A fair return on South Central's stock would be 13.5%.

a. What is a share of South Central worth today?

b. If the stock is selling at $30, would you suggest it to either a retired couple or a young surgeon? (Select only one.)

17. You have made a very preliminary analysis of three common stocks with the information set forth below. All three stocks have the same investment grade or quality. Assume that the same important numerical financial ratios and relationships that currently exist (such as P/E ratio, payout ratio, dividend yield, etc.) will extend into the future, with small cyclical variations, for as far as you can see. For the investments being considered, you require a rate of return of 10% a year. Based solely on the information given in this problem:

a. Which, if any, of the stocks meet your requirements? Show your calculations.

b. Which one of the three stocks is most attractive for purchase?

CFA

	Stock		
	A	B	C
Return on Total Assets	10%	8%	12%
Return on Stockholders' Equity	14%	12%	15%
Estimated Earnings per Share in Current Year	$2.00	$1.65	$1.45
Estimated Dividend per Share in Current Year	$1.00	$1.00	$1.00
Current Market Price	27	25	23

18. Estimate the sustainable earnings growth rate given the following information:

$$\text{Return on Equity} = 20\%$$

$$\text{Dividend Payout Ratio} = 30\%$$

    a. 6%

    b. 10%

    c. 14%

    d. 20%

19. The constant growth dividend discount model can be used both for the valuation of companies and for the estimation of the long-term total return of a stock.

Assume: $20 = the price of a stock today

$$8\% = \text{the expected growth rate of dividends}$$

$$\$.60 = \text{the annual dividend one year forward}$$

    a. Using only the data provided, compute the expected long-term total return on the stock using the constant growth dividend discount model. Show calculations.

    b. Briefly discuss three disadvantages of the constant growth dividend discount model in its application to investment analysis.

    c. Identify three alternative methods to the dividend discount model for the valuation of companies.

20. A firm's earnings per share increased from $10 to $12, its dividends per share increased from $4 to $4.80, and its share price increased from $80 to $90. Given this information, it follows that:

    a. the stock experienced a drop in its P/E ratio.

    b. the company had a decrease in its dividend payout ratio.

    c. the firm increased its number of common shares outstanding.

    d. the required rate of return decreased.

21. Assuming all other factors are constant, which one of the following will reduce the P/E ratio?

    a. The dividend payout ratio decreases.

    b. Inflation expectations decline, resulting in a reduction in the nominal risk-free rate.

    c. The beta of the stock declines.

    d. The market risk premium decreases.

DATAFILE ANALYSIS

    1. **Nominal Growth Rates.** Access the INDEXES data set and find the page on which earnings per share and dividends per share are shown for various stock indexes. In new columns next to the following variables, calculate the natural log of the variable: Earnings Per Share: SP 500 and DJIA

Dividends Per Share: SP 500 and DJIA
Regress these four new variables against year for the period 1929 to 1994. (There will be four regressions.) Compare the various CAGRs and discuss why the values might differ.

2. **Real Growth Rates**. Divide the earnings per share and dividends per share by a unit value series of the Consumer Price Index. Calculate the CAGRs of these constant dollar values. Compare these constant dollar growth rates with nominal CAGRs. Notice, for example, the lower R-squares.

3. **S&P 500 Prices and Earnings.** Perform a regrression analysis in which the index price level of the S&P 500 (1926–1994) is the dependent variable and the earnings level of the S&P 500 index is the independent variable. Interpret the results.

R E F E R E N C E S

The classic text treating fundamental security selection was originally written by Graham and Dodd. Its most recent edition is:

Cottle, Sidney, Roger F. Murray, and Frank E. Block, *Graham and Dodd's Security Analysis,* 5th ed., New York: McGraw-Hill, 1988.

Interesting recent articles dealing with stock valuation include the following:

Brinson, Gary P., Brian D. Singer, and Gilbert L. Beebower, "Determinants of Portfolio Performance II: An Update," *Financial Analysis Journal,* May–June 1992.

Cutler, David M., James M. Porterba, and Lawrence H. Summers, "What Moves Stock Prices," *Journal of Portfolio Management,* Spring 1989.

Edwards, Mark and Wayne H. Wagner, "The Five W's and an H," *Journal of Portfolio Management,* Fall 1991.

Ferson, Wayne E. and Campbell R. Harvey, "Sources of Predictability in Portfolio Returns," *Financial Analysts Journal,* May–June 1991.

Fogler, H. Russell. "Common Stock Management in the 1990s," *Journal of Portfolio Management,* Winter 1990.

Leibowitz, Martin L. and Stanley Kogelman, "Inside the P/E Ratio: The Franchise Factor," *Financial Analysts Journal,* November–December 1990.

Silber, William L. "Discounts on Restricted Stock: The Impact of Illiquidity on Stock Prices," *Financial Analysts Journal,* July–August 1991.

Vander, Weide James H. and Willard T. Carleton, "Investor Growth Expectations: Analysts vs. History," *Journal of Portfolio Management,* Spring 1988.

13

MANAGEMENT OF EQUITY SECURITIES

After reading this chapter you should
have an understanding of how
passively managed equity portfolios are
created as well as the basics of a
fundamental stock analysis

The management of an equity security portfolio can be an exciting venture. Analysis of individual stocks involves a blending of economics, marketing, science, technology, international competition, and international politics. And creating the proper combination of stocks to hold in the portfolio requires a clear understanding of the nature of each stock's risk and how such risks might be diversifiable in the context of the total portfolio.

In this chapter, we examine the issues involved in management of an equity portfolio. The chapter is organized into three major sections:

◾ **Passive Equity Management.** We discuss how individuals and institutional investors can create and manage a passive equity position that is adequately diversified.

◾ **Active Equity Management.** We examine approaches to active equity management used by individual investors and institutional investors. This includes a discussion of classic fundamental security analysis.

◾ **Fundamental Analysis of IBM.** We illustrate the process of fundamental security analysis as applied to International Business Machines (IBM). The story of IBM is quite instructive in that it highlights the importance of risks of changes in technology and retrenched management, risks which can be largely eliminated through proper diversification.

Passive Equity Management

The extent to which people should rely on passive or active management of their common stock portfolios depends on two factors: (1) their *opinions* about how efficiently the stock market is priced, and (2) their own personal *knowledge*.

Individuals who believe market prices can deviate substantially from a stock's intrinsic value will often choose to actively manage their equity holdings. But more important than one's opinion about the concept of market efficiency is one's knowledge. Without appropriate training or unique skills, identifying stocks that are mispriced is a difficult task. Without unique knowledge and skills, investors should always trade as if they did believe in market efficiency (i.e., passively).

The major objective of a passively managed portfolio is diversification. The ways of achieving this objective differ for individual investors and institutional investors. The individual investor generally must work with less money to invest, less time to manage the investment, and less knowledge of sophisticated techniques of indexing. This does not mean that individual investors will have less diversified portfolios than institutional investors. After all, the individual can simply purchase shares in a passively managed institutional portfolio via an indexed mutual fund. But the procedures used to create a passive equity position will be different for these two types of investors.

Passive Management for Individual Investors

As already noted, the principal objective of a passively managed portfolio is to obtain broad diversification. As an example, consider the recent history of IBM. Throughout the 1960s, 1970s, and early 1980s, IBM was the premier computer company in the world. The firm had a lead in research and product design of mainframe computers that provided it with an effective monopoly position. This allowed the company to price its products at levels that resulted in consistent annual returns on equity (*ROE*) of 20% or more. IBM was one of the most profitable large companies in the world with every indication of an equally bright future. As a result, investors bid IBM's stock price up from $37 in 1971 to $155 in 1985. But when computer technology took a "right turn" toward desktop computers, creating a massive demand for computer hardware and software, IBM management did not react rapidly enough. Profits fell and soon became losses. The price of IBM stock fell to $50 in 1992.

It is important to understand why shares of IBM sold at a high of $155 in 1985. The high stock price reflected investor optimism about future dividends and only moderate concern about business risks facing the company.[1] But, as confident as investors were about IBM's future, they would have been seriously harmed if they had not diversified

---

[1] The investor optimism of 1985 should not be considered "overoptimism." Given the information available at that time, the optimism investors displayed was very rational. No one (at least very few people) could foresee the dramatic technological changes that arose with the introduction of the desktop computer and advances in computer chips.

across a large number of other stocks. By 1992, investors' attitudes had changed to the point that there was a serious concern IBM would go bankrupt. But if the shares an investor owned of IBM in 1985 were part of a portfolio of all traded stocks in the United States (with market value weightings), most of the risk of owning IBM would have been diversified away. Losses on IBM shares would have been largely offset by gains on firms such as Microsoft, Compaq Computer, Hewlett-Packard, and Sun Microsystems.

How Much Diversification Is Needed? The moral to the story, of course, is that to eliminate the diversifiable risk of an equity portfolio an investor needs broad diversification. How much diversification is enough? There is no single answer. But the amount of diversification an individual investor should seek is greater than most people believe.

Many investors mistakenly believe that owning 20 to 30 stocks will eliminate virtually all the diversifiable risk present in common stocks. For investors with a relatively short investment horizon (say, a few years), this is a reasonable position. But for investors who have a long investment horizon, greater amounts of diversification are necessary to reduce diversifiable investment risk.[2]

Consider two investors. Ms. Neary intends to invest in stocks for 1 year. Mr. Long intends to invest in stocks for a minimum of 20 years. Each investor faces two different types of risks: (1) volatility of yearly returns around a future average return, and (2) uncertainty about the future average yearly return. For Ms. Neary, volatility risk is the more important. For Mr. Long, volatility risk is dominated by uncertainty about the future average yearly return.

As a practical matter, almost all volatility risk can be eliminated by holding 20 to 30 randomly selected stocks. Thus, Ms. Neary could probably obtain virtually all the benefits of equity diversification that are available to her by owning 30 stocks (or a single diversified equity mutual fund). But a much larger number of stocks are needed to eliminate the diversifiable portion of uncertainty about future average security returns. Therefore, Mr. Long would have to diversify more extensively in order to reduce the diversifiable risk to which he is exposed.

Think about this issue in the context of the following market model equation:

Market Model Equation $R_{it} = a_i + B_i(R_{Mt}) + e_{it}$ **(13.1)**

where R_{it} is the return on stock i in year t, R_{Mt} is the return on the stock market proxy in year t, a_i and B_i are the market model alpha and beta values for stock i, and e_{it} is the residual return on stock i in year t.

If stocks are selected at random, volatility risk arises from uncertainty about the betas that will be drawn plus uncertainty inherent in the yearly residual returns. This type of risk is rapidly diversified. In fact, many empirical studies have shown that 20 to 30 randomly selected stocks will (on average) eliminate virtually all the diversifiable portion of volatility risk.

But diversification does not work as rapidly in reducing the uncertainty inherent in different stock alphas. Although the uncertainty inherent in annualized alpha values might appear small, when compounded over a longer investment horizon, the differences become significant. For example, consider a $1.00 investment for 40 years. If the geometric average annual return is 12%, the terminal value will be $93.05. But, if the

---

[2] A detailed explanation of why the investment horizon affects the extent to which a portfolio should be diversified is presented in Chapter 20. Only the general conclusions are presented here.

average annual return is only two percentage points lower, the terminal value will only be $45.30!

Large institutional investors such as pension funds seem to recognize the fact that long-term investors require greater diversification than do shorter term investors. This is evidenced by the fact that most pension funds invest in large numbers of different stocks.

How Individual Investors Can Diversify. Individual investors can create a diversified passive equity portfolio in any of the following ways:

1. **Purchase an equity index mutual fund.** There are many mutual funds whose goal is to earn a return that closely tracks an equity index such as the S&P 500 or the Wilshire 5000. These funds are easy to buy, guarantee the broadest equity diversification possible, and ownership costs are the lowest of all managed portfolios (often 25 basis points a year). Purchasing an index fund that tracks U.S stocks, plus a fund that tracks the Europe, Australia, and Far East index, provides worldwide diversification. Since these funds do not trade securities very often, the investor's tax liability is less than if an active manager is selected.

2. **Purchase a number of actively managed mutual funds.** This is not a pure passive strategy but one that many individuals follow. Ownership costs are higher relative to index funds (50 to 200 basis points a year is normal), and taxes are higher because the portfolios are actively traded.

   If this approach is used, a number of funds (each holding different types of stocks) should be bought in order to provide broad diversification. Mutual fund managers who follow an active investment strategy believe they have a comparative advantage in some aspect of investing that results in their holding stocks of a particular type. Some managers own only very large companies whereas others seek small companies. Some managers seek high-profit growth stocks whereas others buy only stocks with low P/E ratios. The type of securities that a mutual fund invests is called its **style**.

   There are many ways in which equity investment styles are defined. One approach followed by Morningstar Mutual Funds is illustrated in Figure 13-1. Funds are grouped on the vertical axis by the market capitalization of the companies in which they invest and on the horizontal axis by the price-to-earnings and price-to-book ratios of their holdings. The shaded box denotes a fund that buys large capitalization stocks with low P/E and P/B ratios. Individual investors should use information such as this to assure that the types of funds in which they invest are different.

3. **Make personal selection of the stocks.** This is the most costly and difficult way for an individual investor to passively manage an equity portfolio. Because of the cost and diversification advantages of commingling investments with other people in a mutual fund, the major justification for personally developing a passive equity position is to control taxes.

FIGURE 13-1   ILLUSTRATION OF STYLE BOXES

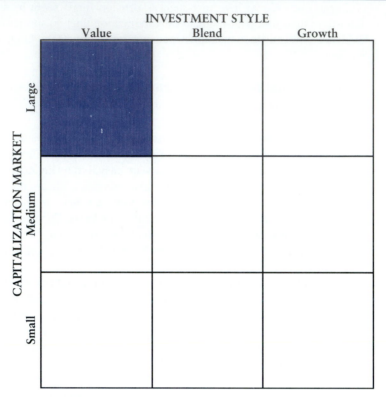

Small capitalization has firms with capitalization less than $1 billion. Medium has capitalization between $1 and $5 billion. Large capitalization funds own stocks whose capitalization exceedes $5 billion.

Value Funds have a low Price-to-Earnings and Price to Book ratios. Growth funds have a high Price-to-Earnings and Price to Book ratios.

Tax Factors. Returns on common stocks arise from both yearly dividend yields, which are taxed at ordinary tax rates, and capital gains, which are often taxed at the lower capital gains rate. When the capital gains tax rate is lower than the ordinary tax rate, many practitioners tailor a stock portfolio's mix of dividend yield and growth components to the tax characteristics of its owner.

For example, consider stocks A and B, which have identical risk. Assume stock A has the greater expected dividend yield and stock B has the greater expected price growth. If all investors paid the same tax rate on both dividend income and capital gains, both stocks would be priced to provide identical before-tax and after-tax expected returns. However, if some investors pay greater taxes on dividend income than they do on capital gains, they would prefer stock B. By owning stock B, they could minimize expected taxes by delaying recognition of capital gains until they need to sell the stock. If such investors were to buy stock A, they would have to pay taxes each year as dividends are received.

As high-taxed shareholders purchase stock B and shy away from stock A, prices of the stocks would adjust such that stock A would provide the greater before-tax expected return. As a result, investors who pay no taxes (or below average rates) would find that stock A provides the greater before-tax and after-tax expected return.[3]

While stock portfolios can be designed with an eye to reducing tax liabilities, considerable care should be taken to ensure that this doesn't leave the portfolio with large amounts of potentially diversifiable risk.

Year-end tax swaps can be used in the investment portfolio to delay tax payments in the same way they are used in bond portfolios. For example, assume you own a portfolio of stocks that is diversified by having one stock from each of the various S&P industry categories. Perhaps one of these stocks is shares in Dow Chemical that were bought at $35 but are now selling at $25. You could sell Dow for a realized taxable loss of $10 and immediately reinvest the $25 proceeds in a close substitute for Dow—say, Union Carbide. This swap leaves you with a $25 investment in the chemical industry but allows you to take an immediate tax savings on the $10 realized loss. If your capital gains tax bracket is 25%, you save $2.50 in taxes, which can be invested. When Union Carbide shares are sold, this $2.50 tax refund will have to be repaid to the government. But, in the meantime, you receive the interest earnings on the $2.50.

Passive Management by Institutional Investors

Institutional investors create passive equity positions in three basic ways:

1. **Hold all securities in the index.** Although this approach is conceptually the easiest, it is the most difficult to implement. In concept, every security in the index that is to be tracked is bought. The percentage invested in a security should be identical to the fraction that the company's market value represents of the aggregate index value. If General Electric represents 10% of the index value, then 10% of the portfolio should be in General Electric. If PECO Energy represents 0.543% of the index value, then 0.543% should be invested in PECO.

   A number of factors make this approach difficult. For example, positions in each security must match the index weighting exactly. Dividends that are received have to be allocated across all securities in proper weights. And there will always be a small cash position needed to cover unexpected withdrawals from the fund. Nonetheless, some very large index funds manage passive positions in exactly this way.

2. **Create a well-defined sample of the index.** Let's say the passive index you wish to track is the Russell 3000. Because it is difficult to create a portfolio of all 3,000 stocks with proper investment weights, it might be easier to emulate the index with a sample of stocks. We discuss how these samples are constructed later.

3. **Trade in derivatives on the index.** In Chapters 16 and 17 we see how the use of futures and options can provide a rate of return over the life of the derivative that is identical to the index return. The only source of tracking error comes from (relatively small) trading costs. The difficulties with this approach are two: (a) a

---

[3] To economists who have studied this problem, the impact of taxes on before-tax and after-tax returns is not quite so clear. While a number of studies have examined the relationships between expected stock price growth and pretax expected returns, the results have been conflicting. While some studies have found evidence favoring the belief that low-dividend-yield stocks sell at lower before-tax expected returns, other studies suggest no such relationship.

derivative may not exist on the index you wish to emulate, and (b) trading volume in the derivative may be too small to provide liquidity to large institutional trades.

Creating a Well-Defined Sample Portfolio. The most common approach to equity indexing is the creation of a sample portfolio which is expected to have returns that closely match the aggregate index. The sampling portfolio is called the **replicating portfolio.** Two principal approaches are used in creating replicating portfolios: (1) capitalization-based samples, and (2) stratified samples.

Capitalization-based samples focus on the largest capitalization stocks in an index. For example, on March 31, 1995, the Russell 3000 index was (approximately) composed of the following:

Percentage of the Index Market Value	Number of Stocks
60%	Largest 228 stocks
40%	Smallest 2,772 stocks

A capitalization-based sample could be created by purchasing 228 of the largest firms and weighting each according to the fraction they represent of the aggregate 3000 index. For example, if the aggregate value of the Russell 3000 index is $5,000 billion and IBM's market capitalization is $47.7 billion, then 0.95% would be invested in IBM ($47.7 ÷ $5,000). Once this is done 60% of the indexed fund's market value will be invested in 228 stocks with each weighted identical to the 3000 index. The remaining 40% of the index fund's assets would then be spread across a sample of the remaining 2,772 stocks. For example, one might decide to select 100 stocks at random from the remaining 2,772 stocks and invest equal amounts in each. Thus, the replicating portfolio would consist of a sample of 328 stocks from an index that consists of 3,000 stocks.

FIGURE 13-2   ILLUSTRATION OF STRATIFIED SAMPLING IN CREATING AN INDEX FUND

P/E Decile	INDUSTRY CLASSIFICATION							Total
	1	2	3	4	5	6	7	
1	3%	2%	1%	5%	3%	3%	2%	19%
2	5%	1%	2%	6%	1%	4%	4%	23%
3	5%	3%	3%	8%	2%	8%	3%	32%
4	5%	2%	7%	2%	1%	5%	4%	26%
Total	18%	8%	13%	21%	7%	20%	13%	100%

Stratified samples group the stocks in an index on the basis of one or more variables and allocate funds across the groups. This is illustrated in Figure 13-2. Stocks in the index are assigned to one of seven industry groups and four decile groups based on a stock's price-to-earnings ratio. The numbers shown in each of the 28 cells reflect the percentage of the aggregate index market value which stocks in that cell represent. Assets of the replicating portfolio are then invested in a manner that the replicating portfolio has a similar mix. However, not all stocks in the index are purchased. For example, while the index might have 150 stocks in the "decile 1, industry 1" group, the portfolio manager might own only 10 stocks in that group. But the stocks that are owned in that group will represent 3% of the replicating portfolio's value.

Factor models based on arbitrage pricing theory are widely used in creating stratified samples. One well-known and widely used model has been developed by an investment consulting firm called BARRA. The BARRA model uses 22 factors that include variables such as industry classification, market capitalization, price-to-earnings ratio, price-to-book ratio, and debt-to-equity ratio. Conceptually a replicating portfolio is created that has factor weightings close to those of the index being replicated.

Tracking Error. Because the actual index can not be perfectly replicated, there will be a difference between the return on the index and the return on the replicating portfolio during a given time period. This difference is called the tracking error.

Tracking Error Return	equals	Index Portfolio Return	minus	Replicating Portfolio Return

Tracking errors are caused by differences in the percentage composition of the portfolios and by costs borne by the replicating portfolio that are not in the index return. Errors due to differences in composition will, on average, be close to zero if the sample is unbiased. But in any given month or year, composition tracking errors can be as large as 100 basis points. Errors due to replicating portfolio costs arise from the need to maintain some cash balances and trading costs.[4]

Figure 13-3 shows estimates of tracking errors of the well-known Vanguard 500 Trust that replicates returns on the S&P 500 index. Tracking errors are shown on the vertical axis and represent the return on the Vanguard 500 Trust minus the return on the S&P 500 index (stated in percentage form). Notice that, on average, the tracking errors were negative, due in part to the costs of running the portfolio. There were two years when the replicating portfolio had a return of 50 basis points (or more) below the index return. But in most years the tracking error was plus or minus 20 basis points from the index return.

Variations on Pure Indexing. Organizations that create and manage indexed portfolios have not totally given up attempts at earning profits from active management. They do so by offering services called **enhanced indexing** and by taking bets on certain factor risks called **tilts.** In an enhanced indexing strategy, the manager of an indexed portfolio also trades futures and option contracts when the value of the derivatives are not what they should be given the value of the index. This is called *index arbitrage* and is discussed in Chapters 16 and 17. The returns from enhanced indexing are not large, at most an extra 25 to 75 basis points per year. Nonetheless, if the enhanced strategies prove successful, the

---

[4] Trading costs include commission payments and spreads between market maker bid and ask prices.

FIGURE 13-3   YEARLY TRACKING ERROR FOR VANGUARD 500

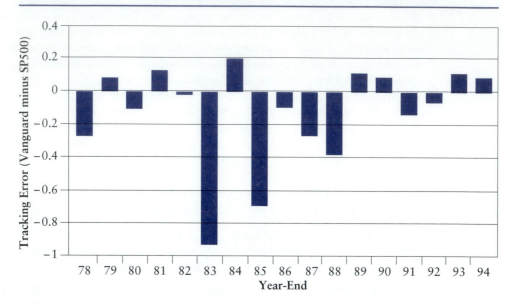

portfolio owner picks up a little extra return without much additional (if any) risk. Tilts refer to overweighting or underweighting the portfolio in certain fundamental stock characteristics (such as price-to-earnings ratios, price-to-book ratios, and market capitalization).

Active Equity Management

The purpose of active management is to add value to a portfolio. *Adding value* is the term practitioners commonly use to refer to earning higher returns from active trading than available from equivalent-risk passive portfolios.

A wide variety of approaches are used in active equity management, each drawing on skills at which the active investor believes he or she has a comparative advantage relative to other investors. For example, active investors with strong statistical knowledge apply sophisticated pricing models to security selection. Active investors with strong backgrounds in science and engineering might restrict the stocks they follow to those in the technology sector. And active investors with special language skills might focus on stocks traded in countries in which that language is spoken. In short, each active investor decides what he or she is able to do better than other investors and then applies these skills to the active management of equities.

In this section, we examine three principal issues: (1) active management of equities by individuals, (2) active management by institutions, and (3) the procedures used in a "top-down" fundamental analysis. After reading this section, you should have a good understanding of the many ways in which investors approach active equity management.

Active Management by Individual Investors

Individual investors engage in active equity management by trading stock issues of individual companies, by trading equity mutual funds, or by a combination of the two.

Dennis A. Johnson, C.F.A.

President,
Chief Investment Officer
Peachtree Asset Management
Virginia Military Institute, B.A.
Virginia Commonwealth University, M.S.

Peachtree Asset Management is an institutional investment management firm and a division of Smith Barney, Inc. located in Atlanta, Georgia.

Q: You've taken a huge entrepreneurial step and started your own investment firm. How did you go about doing it?

A: The reasons had a lot to do with timing. First, I had the opportunity to start a business with my partner, Lamond Godwin. I've known him for many years and have the utmost respect for him both personally and professionally. He's an outstanding marketer as well as an outstanding investment professional. So right off the bat, I felt I had the best partner I could ever have or run across. Secondly, I've been in the business for 14 years and during that entire time I've worked in the investment department or subsidiary of very large financial institutions. I see the pros and cons clearly but thought we could put together a vehicle that would allow us to do the best job in two important things. One is to perform on a consistent basis and the other is to be able to meet the specific needs of each individual client as opposed to a group of clients. We are very committed to that. We then approached Smith Barney with our concepts and prospects and sought initial capitalization. Smith Barney has seven investment management companies; we're the newest one and the only one that started from scratch.

Q: Since April 1994 you've been Peachtree Asset Management. How's it going?

A: The business is doing extremely well. In the course of that period of time we have just under $300 million in assets under management and a dozen clients, the likes of IBM, BellSouth, United Negro College Fund, and the National Football League. They are all outstanding names and outstanding clients and fortunately our performance has been superior as well.

Q: What style of money do you run?

A: We run large cap equity using a combination of growth and value disciplines. More often than not, the categorization attached to us is that of a large cap growth manager.

Q: Are you comfortable with that?

A: I don't want anyone to ignore the importance of value in our decision-making process and I strive to communicate that. Necessity often dictates putting managers in particular boxes. Sometimes that box isn't as clear in terms of defining our investment style as I would like for it to be. But if we're educating people on exactly what it is we do and they categorize us in a slightly different fashion then we really have no choice but to go with it.

Q: Track records are paramount in marketing investment businesses. Since you're a new firm how did you present a track record?

A: I had a seven-year track record prior to launching Peachtree. However, I'm a Chartered Financial Analyst (CFA) and therefore bound by the guidelines of the Association of Investment Management and Research (AIMR). AIMR has outlined performance presentation standards including an appendix on the transportability of prior track records. We had our attorney write a disclosure statement that deals with transportability of performance numbers so we could approach people we had managed money for before and new institutions about our ability and present the historical track record and the disclosure statement. The track record is not even a discussion anymore because we've put together good numbers over the past year and a half and people have been able to watch us closely manage money, handle relationships, and build a business. I definitely sense that they are increasingly confident in our ability to do that.

Q: How important is the pension consultant relationship to a new investment firm?

A: Because we manage institutional money it is very important. The consultants represent a target market for us because they have clients. We also market directly to institutional investors, and consultants act as a check for them when researching our firm. We appreciate the advice of the consultants and feel it's been constructive.

Q: How does the investment process work at Peachtree?

A: We do quantitative and fundamental analysis. We start out with our quantitative rankings where I put a large cap universe into rank order based on specific quantitative variables that we use. Then based on what I see in the ranking I validate that with other quantitative measures I get from another source. If I can get a confirmation of our own quant work, I will then pass the stock name on to our research staff to do the fundamental analysis. I also do analysis myself. As a result of the analytical feedback I make the decision of whether this is a stock that we want to buy or continue to own if we already have it in a portfolio.

Q: In addition to being recognized as a large cap growth manager, you have a specific investment process. Will you deviate from either to attract clients?

A: No. We have passed on some opportunities to run money where the client had an interest in us but their need was slightly different, and we didn't deviate from what we do best. We currently have 12 clients and 6 investment professionals. While we still have plenty of room to grow it will be growth based on this style, which we do well and are successful at. As we grow we will need additional personnel but, again, they will not be individuals that will lead us down a different path. They will be people that complement what we're doing at present.

Because the considerations and data used in stock selection often varies from fund selection, we discuss each in turn.

Selection of Stock Issues.   The process that an individual investor might use in managing a portfolio of individual stocks consists of the following:

- Identify a candidate stock for purchase.

- Investigate the stock's history and future potential.

- Develop rules for purchase and eventual sale.

Perhaps one of the best ways for individual investors to spot a stock with great future potential is to pay attention to the products they buy in their daily life. Individual investors are often able to spot a product and company with bright prospects before larger institutional investors because they are purchasers of the product. In fact, the well-known investor Peter Lynch has stated the following as one of his Peter's Principles: *If you like the store, chances are you'll love the stock.* This idea would have led many investors into new firms and products (such as Wal-Mart and desktop computers) early in their development. Similar ways to develop new ideas consist of using the knowledge one has of his or her own business (carpenters might be able to identify valuable new technology) and giving attention to the interests of children (the demand for video games). Financial newspapers, investor magazines, and full-service brokers are also potential sources for ideas.

A number of inexpensive sources of data should be examined. If you are working with a broker, start by asking for any information the brokerage firm has about the company and its competition. Be sure to obtain a copy of the firm's most recent annual report. For all but very small firms, the annual report can be obtained directly from the company by calling the company's 800 number and asking for "shareholder services." Corporations are pleased to provide information to potential shareholders. Read the management's discussion of recent events and plans for the future. In addition, examine the balance sheet, income statement, and statement of cash flows using the procedures discussed later.

A number of independent firms, such as Moody's, Value Line, and Standard & Poor's, collect and summarize information about companies. Such reports can be bought directly from the information provider or obtained from local libraries.

- The S&P *Stock Guide* is published monthly and provides summary data on all actively traded common stocks, convertible preferred stocks, preferred stocks, closed-end investment companies, and mutual funds.[5] An illustration is shown in Figure 13-4.

---

[5] Standard & Poor's provides a similar document for U.S. bond instruments called the *Bond Guide*.

FIGURE 13-4 ILLUSTRATION OF S&P STOCK GUIDE

104 INT-INT Standard & Poor's

¶ S&P 500 # MidCap 400 ✣ SmallCap 600 • Options

Index	Ticker	Name of Issue (Call Price of Pfd. Stocks)	Market	Com. Rank. & Pfd. Rating	Inst. Hold Cos	Inst. Hold Shs. (000)	Principal Business	Price Range 1971-93 High	1971-93 Low	1994 High	1994 Low	1995 High	1995 Low	Jun. Sales in 100s	June, 1995 Last Sale Or Bid High	Low	Last	%Div Yield	P-E Ratio	Total Return % Annualized 12 Mo	36 Mo	60 Mo
1	IHF	✔Integrated Healthcare[51]Fac	NY	NR	3		Builder of medical facilities	252	3¾	6	¼	⅝	⅛	2672	3/16	⅛	⅛	...	d	−95.8	−82.7	−71.6
2	ISSI	✔Integrated Silicon Solution	NNM	NR	49	4147	Mfrs integrated circuits	....	....	....	....	58¼	13	65946	58¼	40⅞	52¼	...	..	...	...	...
3	INTS	✔Integrated Systems Inc	NNM	B−	44	3209	Dvlp CAE/CASE software prod	17¼	5¼	19⅝	8⅜	28½	17¾	11262	28½	20	25¼	...	40	189	42.4	12.3
¶4•[1]	INTC	✔Intel Corp	NNM	B	1529	624669	Semiconductor memory circts	37⅛	1/16	36¾	28	66⅜	31½	5075940	66⅜	54¾	63¼	0.3	15	117	65.0	40.4
5•[2]	ITR	✔IntelCom Group	AS,Ch,Vc	NR	100	12158	Telecommunications services	25⅝	2½	25¼	9½	14⅛	6⅝	38992	9⅛	7½	8⅞	...	d	−20.6	14.6	...
6	ICL	✔Intellicall Inc	NY,Ph	NR	29	1451	Mfr/mkt pay telephones	18½	3	9⅝	3¾	6⅞	3	5998	6⅞	3⅞	6½	...	d	33.3	12.0	−15.1
7	ITC.EC	Intelligent Controls	ECM	NR	..	...	Mfr ind'l monitoring,ctrl eqp	....	....	....	....	6½	3⅛	307	5⅛	4⅜	4⅜	...	49	...	...	...
#8•[3]	INEL	✔Intelligent Electronics	NNM	NR	138	22807	Franchise:computer stores	30⅜	1¼	27⅝	7½	13⅞	8	54369	13⅞	11¾	13⅝	2.9	10	−6.9	28.5	10.4
9	INS	✔Intelligent Systems	AS,P	C	5	539	Personal computer enhanc'mt	32¾	⅞	2½	1¾	2¼	1⅜	536	1 15/16	1 9/16	1¾	...	d	−15.1	8.4	...
10	IPR	✔Inter-City Products	AS,To	NR	19	5855	Mfr heat/cooling equip,pipe	8¼	2¼	3⅞	2⅛	2¾	1⅜	12651	2¾	1 11/16	2½	...	d	−4.8	−28.6	−16.7
✣11	IFG	✔Inter-Regional Fin. Gr.	NY,B,Ch	B−	55	1965	Brokerage/investm't bkg svcs	34	1 5/16	32⅝	20	29¾	22¼	1552	29¾	26⅞	29½	2.2	12	36.0	28.5	34.1
12	INTL	✔Inter-Tel Inc	NNM	B	37	4472	Mfr electronic telecommun eqp	25¾	11/16	12⅛	6	16⅛	6⅞	8713	16⅛	13	15⅛	...	24	65.8	71.5	61.5
13	ICAR	✔Intercargo Corp	NNM	B+	28	3638	Underwriters specialized insur	17	3¼	12¼	7¼	11¾	8	3912	11¾	9¾	11	1.6	14	7.2	4.2	15.6
14	ISB	✔Interchange Finl Svcs	AS	A−	21	839	Commercial banking,New Jersey	21¾	1⅞	16¾	14	20⅛	14⅝	804	20	17⅞	19¼	3.7	9	22.8	16.0	23.8
15	ISS	✔INTERCO Inc	NY,Ph	NR	74	48478	Mfr residential furniture	54	6⅝	15¾	6⅛	7¼	5⅝	11190	6⅛	5⅝	5⅞	...	10	...	...	...
16•[4]	IDC	✔Interdigital Communications	AS,Ph	C	47	5636	Wireless digital communic prd	20⅝	2⅜	7⅞	2	12⅞	4¾	78629	7⅝	5¼	7	...	28	120	7.6	3.6
✣17	IFSIA	✔Interface Inc'A'	NNM	A−	78	11301	Mfr carpet/tile	19¾	3¼	17	9¾	15⅛	11⅝	14894	14¼	11⅞	12½	1.9	14	13.2	−3.0	−5.8
18	INTF	✔Interface Systems	NNM	B	22	1177	Document mgmt sys/com prod	11	⅝	10	3⅞	9¼	5⅜	7026	6¼	5⅝	5¾	2.8	8	18.1	...	...
¶19•[5]	INGR	✔Intergraph Corp	NNM	C	220	20323	Computer graphics systems	40½	3⅞	11¼	7⅜	14⅜	8⅛	65317	13⅝	11	11⅛	...	..	14.1	−5.4	−8.1
20•[6]	INTM	✔Interim Services	NNM	NR	121	9721	Temprary help services	....	....	28¼	20	31⅜	22⅞	18319	25¾	22⅞	25	...	19	8.1	...	...
21	IK	✔Interlake Corp	NY,B,Ch,P	NR	33	7834	Diversified ind'l mfg co	61¾	2⅜	3¾	1½	3¼	1¾	21313	3	2⅜	2⅞	...	d	21.1	−12.2	−19.0
22	IRC.EC	✔Interline Resources	ECM	NR	9	597	Natl gas gathering/oil prod'n	9¼	6¾	9½	3⅞	4⅝	2½	7714	4⅛	3½	3¾	...	d	−23.1	...	...
23	INLQ	✔INTERLINQ Software	NNM	NR	17	2009	Dvlp mtge lending software	9¼	6	9	3⅜	4⅜	2⅞	3746	4⅛	3½	3½	...	d	−36.4	...	...
✣24•[7]	IMG	✔Intermagnetics Genl	AS	B−	26	1411	Mfr superconductive mtls	17¼	2¼	19¾	9½	15⅞	10	11809	15⅞	13⅝	14¼	...	65	8.2	44.3	27.8
✣25	INMT	✔Intermet Corp	NNM	C	51	11166	Iron foundry-auto indus	19	3⅝	10½	4¾	9¾	6¼	13927	9¾	8¼	9½	...	d	24.6	−0.2	6.9
26	IMET	✔Intermetrics Inc[57]	NNM	B	16	543	Computer software prod & svc	20¾	2¼	6½	4¼	6¾	4	727	6¾	6¼	6¼B	...	16	24.8	18.8	18.4
27	ICM	Internacional De Ceramica ADS[59]	NY	NR	7	478	Mfr glazed ceramic tile-Mexico	....	....	21¾	20	21½	7⅛	809	7⅞	7⅛	7⅞	...	d	...	...	...
28	IAL	✔Intl Aluminum	NY,B,Ch,P	B+	47	1829	Mfr & sale aluminum prod	30¾	1	31¼	23⅜	36¾	29⅜	356	34½	31½	31¾	3.1	10	36.3	22.1	8.5
¶29•[8]	IBM	✔Intl Bus. Machines	.[9]NY,B,C,Ch,P,Ph,Mo	B−	1379	291469	Lgst mfr business machines	175⅞	37⅝	76⅜	51⅜	99⅜	70¼	669339	99⅜	88⅜	96	1.0	10	65.6	2.2	−0.4

↑

Common and Convertible Preferred Stocks **INT-INT 105**

Index	Splits ◆ Cash Divs. Ea.Yr. Since	Dividends Latest Payment Period $	Date	Ex. Div.	Total $ So Far 1995	Ind. Rate	Paid 1994	Financial Position Mil-$ Cash& Equiv.	Curr. Assets	Curr. Liab.	Balance Sheet Date	Capitalization Lg Trm Debt Mil-$	Shs. 000 Pfd.	Com.	Earnings $ Per Shr. Years End	1991	1992	1993	1994	1995	Last 12 Mos.	Interim Earnings Period	$ per Shr. 1994	1995	Index
1◆	....	0.72	6-9-89	5-26	...	Nil	....	1.68	8.01	8.64	3-31-94	10.2	909	712	Dc	Δd1.56	Δd19.08	Δd4.32	....	....	d2.52	3 Mo MarΔ	d3.00	d1.20	1
2	....	None Since Public			...	Nil	....	41.6	62.8	18.0	3-31-95	2.87	...	★16593	Sp	...	...	...	p0.34	....	....	6 Mo Mar	n/a	0.53	2
3	....	None Since Public			...	Nil	....	13.6	31.7	15.0	2-28-95	....	...	9533	Fb	d0.85	0.37	0.44	0.60	....	0.64	3 Mo May	0.07	0.11	3
4◆	1992	Q0.04	6-16-95	6-19	0.10	0.16	[52]0.11¼	2510	6824	3276	4-01-95	404	...	828200	Dc	0.98	1.24	2.60	2.62	E4.20	2.94	3 Mo Mar	0.70	1.02	4
5◆	....	None Paid			...	Nil	....	8.86	56.0	56.8	3-31-95	114	★1600	★24344	Sp	d0.65	d0.40	d0.39	d1.56	....	d1.96	6 Mo Mar	d0.61	d1.01	5
6	....	None Since Public			...	Nil	....	2.22	44.7	12.4	3-31-95	25.3	...	7668	Dc	d0.70	d3.71	d0.17	d1.91	....	d1.63	3 Mo Mar	d0.31	d0.03	6
7	....	None Since Public			...	Nil	....	0.69	4.04	1.80	3-31-95	0.26	...	3199	Dc	*0.02	*0.03	□0.15	0.09	....	0.09	3 Mo Mar	0.02	0.02	7
8◆	1993	Q0.10	6-1-95	5-9	0.20	0.40	0.36	78.2	529	503	4-29-95	....	...	31473	Ja	[53]1.11	□0.06	1.18	0.23	E1.35	0.03	3 Mo Apr	0.36	0.16	8
9	....	0.10	9-19-89	8-25	...	Nil	....	0.41	7.50	4.26	3-31-95	0.05	...	5440	Dc	d0.27	d0.56	d0.07	d1.30	....	d1.35	3 Mo Mar	d0.12	d0.17	9
10	....	None Since Public			...	Nil	....	2.85	298	90.7	6-30-94	221	2440	p38039	Dc	d1.13	d0.40	d1.32	Pd0.29	....	d0.29				10
11	1992	Q0.16	5-30-95	5-10	0.32	0.64	0.56	Equity per shr $24.68			3-31-95	45.3	...	8105	Dc	*Δ2.50	4.03	5.67	3.04	....	2.51	3 Mo Mar	1.20	0.67	11
12	....	None Since Public			...	Nil	....	12.6	52.3	14.7	3-31-95	....	...	10409	Dc	d0.53	0.37	0.45	0.58	....	0.63	3 Mo Mar	0.11	0.16	12
13◆	1992	S0.09	3-15-95	3-3	0.09	0.18	0.18	Equity per shr $5.50			3-31-95	9.43	...	7641	Dc	0.77	0.88	0.30	0.65	....	0.81	3 Mo Mar	0.11	0.27	13
14	1981	Q0.18	7-20-95	6-16	0.53½	0.72	0.70	Book Value $11.70			3-31-95	3.75	32	2697	Dc	1.26	1.79	□1.80	2.05	....	2.14	3 Mo Mar	0.42	0.51	14
15◆	....	h[54]....	11-18-94	11-21	...	Nil h[54]	....	32.1	421	115	3-31-95	399	...	50112	Dc	...	...	0.88	0.74	....	0.59	3 Mo Mar	0.30	0.15	15
16	....	None Since Public			...	Nil	....	42.9	68.5	26.5	3-31-95	0.53	106	44061	Dc	d0.39	d0.95	d1.11	d0.38	....	0.25	3 Mo Mar	d0.20	0.43	16
17	1977	Q0.06	5-26-95	5-8	0.12	0.24	0.24	1.78	299	106	4-02-95	325	250	±18250	Dc	±0.52	±0.71	±0.75	±0.82	....	0.88	3 Mo Mar	±0.14	±0.20	17
18	1994	Q0.04	8-14-95	7-13	0.12	0.16	0.16	3.74	25.2	12.0	3-31-95	0.31	...	4201	Sp	0.16	0.35	0.41	□0.71	....	0.69	6 Mo Mar	□0.35	0.33	18
19	....	None Since Public			...	Nil	....	62.2	525	257	3-31-95	25.7	...	45823	Dc	1.47	0.18	Δd2.56	d1.56	E0.05	d1.74	3 Mo Mar	d0.31	d0.49	19
20	....	None Since Public			...	Nil	....	1.36	146	85.6	3-31-95	....	...	11506	Dc	...	p0.77	[55]1.14	1.24	....	1.30	3 Mo Mar	0.22	0.28	20
21◆	....	[56]45.00	9-28-89	9-29	...	Nil	....	22.5	239	168	4-02-95	417	39	22816	Dc	d1.31	□d0.84	d1.18	□d1.84	....	d1.71	14 Wk Apr	d0.11	0.02	21
22	....	None Since Public			...	Nil	....	0.87	3.04	2.90	3-31-95	2.50	...	13772	Dc	0.01	0.01	Δ0.01	d0.05	....	d0.05	3 Mo Mar	Nil	Nil	22
23	....	None Since Public			...	Nil	....	14.8	17.2	3.68	3-31-95	....	...	5967	Je	0.06	*0.27	*0.47	□0.46	....	d0.09	9 Mo Mar	□0.43	d0.12	23
24◆	....	3%Stk	6-15-95	5-24	3%Stk	Stk	....	11.3	61.2	9.95	2-26-95	39.8	...	11064	My	0.29	0.43	0.32	Δ0.10	....	0.22	9 Mo Feb	Δ0.06	0.18	24
25	1985	0.04	8-19-93	7-30	...	Nil	....	12.7	134	101	4-02-95	79.6	...	24671	Dc	0.42	□d0.06	d0.83	d0.45	....	d0.26	3 Mo Mar	0.07	0.26	25
26	1990	0.04	2-13-95	1-30	0.04	[58]Nil	0.16	10.4	25.9	9.79	2-28-95	....	...	3993	Fb	0.63	0.37	0.68	0.35	....	0.39	3 Mo May	0.08	0.12	26
27	....	None Since Public			...	Nil	....	23.7	81.7	66.4	12-31-94	71.9	...	87856	Dc	p±0.90	p*±1.61	p*±0.82	d3.40	....	d3.40				27
28	1966	Q0.25	7-10-95	6-16	0.75	1.00	1.00	8.44	89.5	19.5	3-31-95	0.54	...	4252	Je	1.46	0.21	0.85	Δ1.74	....	3.15	9 Mo Mar	Δ1.00	2.41	28
29	1916	Q0.25	6-10-95	5-4	0.50	1.00	1.00	10490	41031	27890	3-31-95	12519	2625	580664	Dc	□d0.99	Δd12.03	□d14.02	5.02	E9.20	6.50	3 Mo Mar	0.64	2.12	29

SOURCE: *Stock Guide*, July 1995, New York: Standard & Poor's Publishers.

Two pages of data are shown for each firm. In Figure 13-4, the first page is shown in the top of the figure and the second page at the bottom of the figure.

Data on IBM is shown on line 29 (the last line shown for each page). The first page of data shows (among many other things) that at the end of 1995, IBM closed trading at $96, had a dividend yield of 1%, and a price-to-earnings ratio of 10. The second page shows that the firm has paid dividends since 1926 and the last dividend was for $0.25 paid on June 10, 1995.

The S&P *Stock Guide* is an invaluable source of data to individual investors. Within a pocket-sized pamphlet, basic information is available on virtually all traded equities in the United States.

■ *Moody's Stock Record* contains a full page of information on a given stock. An illustration, again using IBM, is shown in Figure 13-5. Basic operating statistics and a plot of past stock prices are provided. Of particular interest to individual investors is the discussion of the company's background, recent developments, and prospects (according to Moody's analysts).

In looking at Figure 13-5, it is apparent from the plot of IBM's share prices that the company has had significant problems. Based on past prices, these problems first became apparent to shareholders in 1987 and worsened in 1991. However, after mid-1993, the stock price had turned around. At the end of 1994, it was trading for $73.50. The discussion of company prospects tells why the stock had begun to increase.

■ The *Value Line* report for IBM is shown in Figure 13-6. Although Value Line does not cover as many companies as the two sources just cited, it provides two specific investment recommendations as well as forecasts of various financial data. Value Line's first recommendation is called "timeliness" and stands for the chance that the stock's price is likely to rise in the near future. The second recommendation is called "safety" and reflects the extent that the stock would decline if the aggregate market declined.

Notice the three columns of data at the far right of the tabular data. These represent Value Line's projections for various financial data for the next two years plus an average of four to six years ahead. This information is often useful in developing growth rates of dividends from which stock values can be estimated.

There are a number of ways in which the Value Line data can be used to estimate today's share value. For example, the far right column provides Value Line's estimate of the firm's earnings per share and price-to-earnings ratio for the period 1998 to 2000 of $15.50 and 13 times, respectively. Let's interpret this to represent 1999 data and say that 1999 is 4.5 years away from the date of the forecast. The forecast also calls for an increase in dividends to $1.50 in 1995 ($0.75 to be received, since the forecast was in the middle of 1995), $2.00 in 1996, and $2.50 by the end of 1999. The forecast also calls for a price in (about) 1999 of $201.50 ($15.50 times 13).

If we assume equity holders of IBM require a return of 16% per year, then the discounted present value of expected dividends through 1999 plus the estimated stock value in 1999 would be $109.77, very close to IBM's market price in mid-1995:

Year-End:	1995	1996	1997	1998	1999
Number of Periods:	0.5	1.5	2.5	3.5	4.5
					(Growing at 7.72%)
Dividend:	$0.75	$2.00	$2.15	$2.32	$2.50
Price:					$201.50
Present Value at 16%:	$0.70	$1.60	$1.48	$1.38	$104.61
Total Present Value = $109.77					

FIGURE 13-5 MOODY'S STOCK RECORD

INTERNATIONAL BUSINESS MACHINES CORPORATION

LISTED	SYM.	LTPS♦	STPS♦	IND. DIV.	REC. PRICE	RANGE (52-WKS.)	YLD.	'94 YR-END PR.
NYSE	IBM	58.2	114.7	$1.00*	72⅛	78 - 51⅜	1.4%	73½

INVESTMENT GRADE. THE ACQUISITION OF LOTUS DEVELOPMENT GIVES IBM A FOOTHOLD IN THE PROMISING GROUPWARE MARKET.

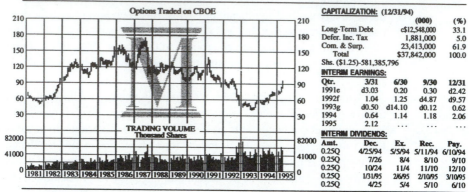

CAPITALIZATION: (12/31/94)

	(000)	(%)
Long-Term Debt	c$12,548,000	33.1
Defer. Inc. Tax	1,881,000	5.0
Com. & Surp.	23,413,000	61.9
Total	$37,842,000	100.0

Shs. ($1.25)-581,385,796

INTERIM EARNINGS:

Qtr.	3/31	6/30	9/30	12/31
1991e	d3.03	0.20	0.30	d2.42
1992f	1.04	1.25	d4.87	d9.57
1993g	d0.50	d14.10	d0.12	0.62
1994	0.64	1.14	1.18	2.06
1995	2.12	...	...	...

INTERIM DIVIDENDS:

Amt.	Dec.	Ex.	Rec.	Pay.
0.25Q	4/25/94	5/5/94	5/11/94	6/10/94
0.25Q	7/26	8/4	8/10	9/10
0.25Q	10/24	11/4	11/10	12/10
0.25Q	1/31/95	2/6/95	2/10/95	3/10/95
0.25Q	4/25	5/4	5/10	6/10

BACKGROUND:

IBM is the world's largest manufacturer of information processing equipment and systems. Application Business and Solutions Systems manufactures processors and related software and develops solutions for a broad range of industries. Enterprise Systems offers general purpose processors, operating systems and supercomputers. Networking and Pennant Systems provides products to manage networks as well as printers and printing solutions. Personal Systems and Storage products develops personal computers, workstations, tape drives and optical storage devices. Technology Products and Programming Systems manufactures logic and memory chips and develops software.

RECENT DEVELOPMENTS:

For the three months ended 3/31/95, net earnings more than tripled to $1.29 billion from $336.0 million in the equivalent period of 1994. Solid increases in all business segments except rentals and financing spurred total revenues up by 18% to $15.74 billion from $13.37 billion in the prior-year quarter. Personal computers, storage systems and mainframes all experienced strong demand as hardwae sales were $7.72 billion 23% higher than the prior-year quarter. IBM's most improved division was services, which increased its revenues by 33% to $2.45 billion versus $1.84 billion in the prior-year quarter. On 6/12/95, IBM reached an agreement with Lotus Development Corp. to acquire the software maker for an estimated $3.52 billion.

PROSPECTS:

The amiable conclusion to IBM's hostile bid for Lotus almost insures that the software company's core product team, those resposible for Lotus Notes, will remain. In concert with IBM's hardware and consulting operations the acquisition will be a good fit. Although bottom-line influence is most likely some time away. IBM will continue to slash costs company-wide, and expects to meet its goal of $8.00 billion in cost reductions by mid-1996.

STATISTICS:

YEAR	GROSS REVS. ($mill.)	OPER. PROFIT MARGIN %	RET. ON EQUITY %	NET INCOME ($mill.)	WORK CAP. ($mill.)	SENIOR CAPITAL ($mill.)	SHARES (000)	EARN. PER SH.$	DIV. PER SH.$	DIV. PAY. %	PRICE RANGE	P/E RATIO	AVG. YIELD %
85	50,056	22.4	20.5	6,555	14,637	3,955	615,418	10.67	4.40	41	158½ - 117⅜	12.9	3.2
86	51,250	15.3	13.9	4,789	15,006	4,169	605,923	7.81	4.40	56	161⅞ - 119¼	18.0	3.1
87	54,217	14.3	13.7	5,258	17,643	3,858	597,052	8.72	4.40	50	175⅞ - 102	15.9	3.2
88	59,681	14.7	13.9	a5,491	17,956	8,518	589,741	a9.27	4.40	47	129½ - 104½	12.6	3.8
89	62,710	11.0	9.8	b3,758	14,175	10,825	574,700	b6.47	4.73	73	130⅞ - 93⅜	17.3	4.2
90	69,018	16.0	14.1	6,020	13,644	11,943	571,391	10.51	4.84	46	123⅛ - 94½	10.4	4.4
91	64,792	1.5	d	cd2,827	7,345	13,231	571,018	cd4.95	4.84	N.M.	139¾ - 83½	N.M.	4.3
92	64,523	d	d	fd6,865	2,955	12,853	571,436	fd12.03	4.84	—	100⅜ - 48¾	—	6.5
93	62,716	d	d	gd7,987	6,052	15,245	581,386	gd14.02	1.58	—	59⅞ - 40⅝	—	3.1
94	64,052	8.0	12.9	3,021	12,112	12,548	588,180	5.02	1.00	20	76⅜ - 51⅜	12.7	1.6

♦Long-Term Price Score — Short-Term Price Score; See page 4a. STATISTICS ARE AS ORIGINALLY REPORTED. a-Excludes $315 million ($0.53 per share) credit for an accounting change. b-Includes $2.4 billion ($4.16 a share) charge for restructuring. c-Includes debentures convertible into common stock. e-Includes an acctg. chg. of $2.3 billion ($3.96 a sh.) and a restructuring charge of $3.4 billion. f-Incl. a pre-tax restruct. chg. of $11.6 bill. and excl. an acctg cr of $1.9 bill. g-Incl. restruct. chg. of $8.9 bill; excl. acctg. chg. of $114 mill.

INCORPORATED:
June 16, 1911 — NY

PRINCIPAL OFFICE:
Old Orchard Road
Armonk, NY 10504
Tel.: (914) 765-7777

ANNUAL MEETING:
Last Mon. in April

NUMBER OF STOCKHOLDERS:
713,060

TRANSFER AGENT(S):
First Chicago Trust Co. of N.Y.
New York, NY

REGISTRAR(S):
First Chicago Trust Co. of N.Y.
New York, NY

INSTITUTIONAL HOLDINGS:
No. of Institutions: 1262
Shares Held: 283,610,425

OFFICERS:
Chairman & C.E.O.
L. V. Gerstner, Jr.
Vice Chairman
P. J. Rizzo
Sr. V.P. & C.F.O.
J. B. York
V.P. & Treasurer
F. W. Zuckerman
V.P. & Controller
L. A. Zimmerman

FIGURE 13-6　ILLUSTRATION OF VALUE LINE INVESTMENT SURVEY

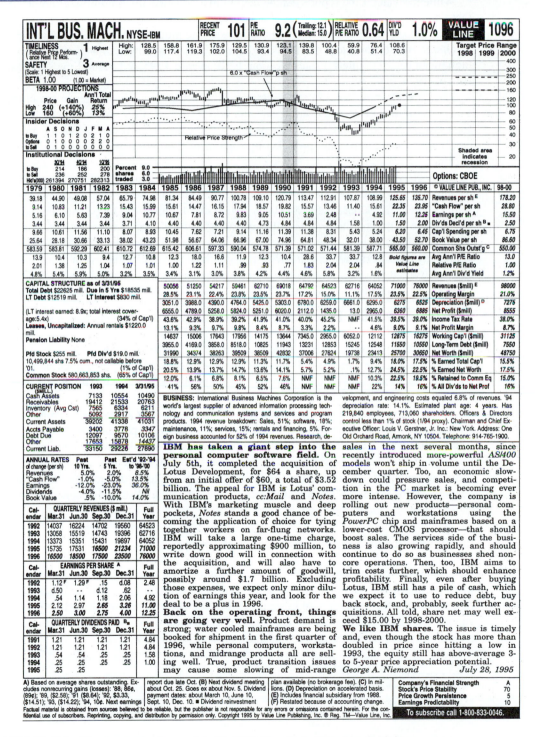

While the Value Line reports can be helpful in estimating the present worth of a stock, there are two problems with this particular example. First, implicit in the 1999 price-to-earnings ratio of 13 is a long-run dividend growth rate much larger than IBM would likely be able to sustain for many years. Second, the 16% demanded return is also probably too high given risk-free interest rates of about 6.5% in mid-1995 and Value Line's estimated beta of 1.0.

The IBM example was chosen to be consistent with the analysis later in the chapter. But a useful insight comes from it; one can not always trust the internal consistency of forecasts published by data providers such as Value Line. Even if occasional inconsistencies arise, however, the data provided by such firms can be invaluable to individual investors.

Many active investors, individual and institutional, say the biggest dilemma they face is deciding when to sell. After a security has increased in value, how does one know when to sell? Or after a stock has declined in value, when should losses be stopped and the security sold? There is no good answer to either question. If there were, a lot of people would be much wealthier. Various rules of thumb, such as a predetermined price rise or decline, are commonly used. Perhaps the best advice is to continue to evaluate the worth of the security and sell when the market price departs from this value to a significant degree. In addition, many active investors use stop loss orders (discussed in Chapter 4) to protect any gains.[6]

Selection of Mutual Funds. Many active individual investors choose to use mutual funds instead of individual stocks. The clear advantage is they obtain the broad diversification that most funds offer. Active investment in mutual funds is done in two ways: (1) buy one or more mutual funds that engage in active trading and then hold the fund(s), and (2) trade among the mutual funds in an attempt to select (time) the funds that will do better than others.

As you would expect, the first thing that most mutual fund investors examine is past performance, hoping to find a fund which has done well in the past relative to other funds of a similar type. Unfortunately, there is little evidence that past performance will be of use in predicting future performance. While some fund managers have earned rates of return considerably larger than other fund managers, this could be due to either better management skills or random chance. Researchers are not able to distinguish between the two as the cause of good mutual fund performance.[7]

Active Management by Institutional Investors

Two types of organizations are referred to as institutional investors. The first is the **owners of large portfolios** such as pension and endowment funds. The second is organizations that are hired to be **managers of large portfolios** such as investment counseling firms, insurance firms, and bank trust companies. Our discussion of active institutional management in this section is restricted to managers of large portfolios.

---

[6] The difficulty of using stop loss orders is that they can incur large tax liabilities. This happens when the stop loss price is set so close to the prevailing stock price that minor price declines trigger sales and realized capital gains.

[7] In Chapter 14 we discuss mutual funds in more depth, and in Chapter 20 we examine the investment manager decision.

Active institutional managers use a wide variety of approaches. The following listing illustrates the general approaches used:

- **Top-Down Managers.** Managers who follow a top-down approach begin with an evaluation of the aggregate economy, move next to an analysis of the industry in which a company does business, and finally examine the individual company.

- **Bottom-Up Managers.** Managers who follow a bottom-up approach begin with an evaluation of individual companies. These analyses are then aggregated to form an opinion of the prospects of a given industry. Finally, the industry analyses are aggregated into an opinion about the stock market as a whole.

- **Quantitative Managers.** With the explosion of computer technology and computerized databases, a new type of investment manager has emerged over the past 20 years, the "Quant." Managers who claim they use a quantitative discipline employ a wide variety of approaches. Some approaches are as simple as sorting a stock database by price-to-earnings ratios and price-to-book value ratios, and then buying all stocks that are in, say, the bottom decile of both sorts. Other approaches use sophisticated asset pricing models (such as variants of arbitrage pricing theory) and underweight or overweight various factors in their models.

- **Concept Managers.** Some managers simply look for a good story such as (1) a promising new technology, (2) a novel way of marketing an existing product, or (3) a theme such as changes in population demographics.

- **Value Managers.** A value manager aims at finding stocks that are trading at prices below their liquidation or economic worth. Usually this means buying stocks with low price-to-earnings and price-to-book value ratios.

- **Growth Managers.** A growth manager focuses on stocks with above average prospects for earnings growth. Usually this means buying stocks with high price-to-earnings and price-to-book value ratios.

- **Large Cap Versus Small Cap Managers.** Other managers define the market capitalization of the stocks they will trade.[8]

Each manager ultimately must decide which strategy to use based on his or her comparative advantage.

To varying degrees, each of the approaches just described is based on a fundamental analysis of the secuities they select. To gain a better understanding of active security selection, we review the procedures involved in classic fundamental analysis.

---

[8] Recall that a stock's market capitalization is equal to its market price per share times the number of shares outstanding.

Classic Fundamental Analysis

The goal of fundamental stock analysis is to develop a reasonable estimate of a stock's intrinsic value. **Intrinsic value** is the present value of expected future dividends per share discounted at a return that reflects the risk of the potential future dividend stream. If the stock's intrinsic value is above its current market price, it should be overweighted in the portfolio. If the intrinsic value is lower than the current market value, it should be underweighted, not held, or even short-sold.[9]

Fundamental analysts develop estimates of future dividend growth rates and an appropriate discount rate by examining the economic trends and prospects for a company. The way in which this is done is easiest to see from the perspective of a top-down analysis.

Top-Down Analysis. Figure 13-7 presents an overview of the process involved in a top-down fundamental stock analysis. The analysis begins with an examination of both short- and long-run growth in aggregate economic output. This is followed by an examination of the determinants of and potential for future industry growth. For the typical industry, growth of aggregate economic output is the primary force driving industry growth. Finally, a detailed analysis is conducted of the company's recent past and potential future. This culminates in projections of future dividend growth and estimates of fair equity returns (given the risks faced by equity owners) from which estimates of the stock's intrinsic value are calculated.

Determinants of long-run economic growth are examined in Chapter 19 when we discuss asset allocation and the valuation of the aggregate equity market. In summary, most economists believe that long-run economic growth is a function of (1) population growth, (2) work force productivity, and (3) increased competition from less developed countries.

In conducting an analysis of the industry in which a company does business, the analysts should be open-minded about the true nature of the product or service being investigated. For example, commercial banks were historically in the business of raising funds from deposits that were then lent at a higher return than the cost of deposits. In recent years, however, a number of regulations that previously restricted the commercial activities in which banks could engage have been lifted. Today, banks are best thought of as providers of financial services, competing with mutual funds, insurance companies, brokerage firms, and mortgage banks. Similarly, while IBM was historically a manufacturer and distributor of computer hardware and software, the firm today is better thought of as an information processing and communications firm. Be aware of what the product or service really is.

Once the nature of the product or service has been defined, it is often useful to examine historical industry growth in the context of the so-called product life cycle. The concept of a product life cycle, as Figure 13-8 illustrates, can be thought of as consisting of three stages. In the **pioneering stage,** basic research and development of a new product occur. Customer demand tends to be small due to uncertainties about the product's reliability and hoped for technological improvements. Mainframe computers were in this stage in the

---

[9] Overweighting and underweighting are relative to a normal benchmark holding. In the theory of the CAPM, this benchmark is the percentage a stock's capitalization represents of the total capitalization of all traded stocks. In practice, however, the benchmark might be quite different if the portfolio being managed is intended to be a subset of all stocks. Examples would be stocks in the S&P 500 index, stocks with a capitalization of less than $100 million, or technology stocks.

FIGURE 13-7   CONSIDERATIONS IN A TOP-DOWN FUNDAMENTAL SECURITY ANALYSIS

I. Aggregate Economic Analysis
- A. Long-run growth of output
  - 1. Population trends
  - 2. Workforce productivity
    - Education of workforce
    - Technological developments
  - 3. World competition
- B. Stage of business cycle

↓

II. Industry Analysis
- A. Definition of what the industry is
- B. Stage of Life Cycle
- C. Determinants of product demand
- D. Determinants of product supply
- E. Potential affects of
  - 1. Regulation
  - 2. Labor
  - 3. Technology
  - 4. World competition
- F. Projections of sales (real and nominal)
- G. Delineate risks and potentials

↓

III. Company Analysis
- A. Understand product segments & competition
- B. Understand past profitability and growth
  - 1. Risk implications for the future
  - 2. Strength potential for the future
- C. Financial management of
  - 1. Asset investment
  - 2. Expense control
  - 3. Debt use and capacity
- D. Forecasts of future
  - 1. Sales
  - 2. Income
  - 3. Dividends per share
- E. Determine fair return given risks
- F. Estimate ranges of intrinsic value

FIGURE 13-8   THE PRODUCT LIFE CYCLE

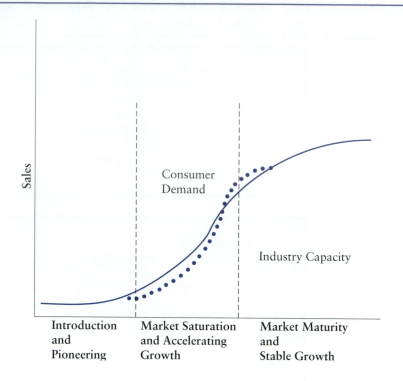

| Introduction and Pioneering | Market Saturation and Accelerating Growth | Market Maturity and Stable Growth |

1950s and early 1960s. In the **market saturation and growth stage,** consumer demand grows more rapidly than producers are able to supply. Mainframe computers were in this stage during the 1960s and early 1970s. During this stage, sales grow rapidly and profit margins are high because there is little price competition. In the **mature and stable growth stage,** a product's potential market is largely saturated, resulting in efforts to reduce production costs and intense price competition. How long the mature and stable growth stage remains depends largely on how long it takes before a new technology supplants the older technology. For example, the growth of the desktop computer industry during the 1980s and 1990s cut severely into the market for mainframe computers.

When analyzing the past and potential future growth of an industry, the analyst should develop clear opinions about the determinants of product demand and supply and how these are likely to change in the future. In some cases, sophisticated statistical models can be developed. In other cases, subjective opinions might be the best that one can develop. The analyst should also consider the potential effects on future growth of industry regulation, labor relations, technological developments, and worldwide competition.

A Review of Financial Statements. An important source of information about the financial condition and profitability of a firm is the annual report that the company provides to shareholders and other interested parties. The more important parts of this report are the following:

- The **management discussion** provides a verbal description by top management of operating results during the past year together with a review of important developments that will affect future operations.

- The **financial statements** present the current investment and financing position of the company (the balance sheet), an analysis of corporate earnings over the past year (the income statement), and a summary of cash flows within the firm during the past year (the statement of cash flows).

- The **footnotes to the financial statements** provide details about important items reported in the financial statements. This includes a description of the accounting principles used in creating the financial statements, minimum payments for the next few years on debt and lease obligations, details about employee pension liabilities, information about employee stock ownership plans (ESOPs), revenues by geographical region and product segment, and so forth. The footnotes are a "must read" for any serious analyst.

- A **summary of financial results** over the most recent five-to ten-year period is commonly shown at the end of the annual report. Information included in the summary includes data such as earnings per share, dividends per share, stockholders' equity, total debt, working capital, return on equity, and so forth.

For the rest of this section we review three of the more important financial statements of a hypothetical firm, General Data Corp.

The 1995 and 1996 balance sheets for General Data are shown in Table 13-1. A balance sheet identifies the sources of capital obtained by management of a firm and how this capital has been invested. For example, by the end of 1996, equity owners of the company had contributed a total of $21.5 million to the company. Of this, $7.0 million had been given to the company in return for the sale of company stock. The remaining $14.5 million had come from the retention of profits within the company. Another $57 million in capital had been lent to the company through various short-term and long-term creditors.

The equity and debt capital obtained by managers ($78.5 million) was invested in various assets. Current assets cost $41.0 million and represented slightly more than one-half the cost of all assets owned. Of the investment in current assets, approximately 25% was invested in cash and marketable securities ($10.5 ÷ $41), more than 50% was invested in accounts receivable ($21.5 ÷ $41), and about 15% was being held in inventories ($6 ÷ $41). In short, the firm's current assets appear to be highly liquid, and the financing of receivables represented a large fraction of the debt and equity capital supplied to the firm. The cost of investments made in net fixed assets was $37.5 million, or 48% of all investment in the firm.

The 1996 income statement for General Data Corp. is shown in Table 13-2. An income statement is intended to show the revenues, expenses, and net profits of a firm during a specified period of time. General Data's 1996 income statement shows the company had net income of $3.0 million on revenues of $64 million.

TABLE 13-1   ILLUSTRATIVE BALANCE SHEETS OF GENERAL DATA CORP. ($ MILLIONS) AT DECEMBER 31

Assets	1996	1995	Liabilities and Equity	1996	1995
Cash	$ 8.0	$ 6.0	Accounts Payable	$ 8.5	$ 8.0
Marketable Securities	2.5	1.0	Wages and Salaries	12.0	13.0
Accounts Receivable	21.5	19.5	Notes Payable	8.5	10.0
Inventory	6.0	7.5	Other	3.0	2.0
Other	3.0	5.0	Total Current	$32.0	$33.0
Total Current Assets	$41.0	$39.0	Long-Term Debt	25.0	27.0
			Total Debt	$57.0	$60.0
Gross Fixed Assets	$77.5	$75.5	Common Equity		
Accumulated					
Depreciation	40.0	34.0	Common Stock	$ 7.0	$ 7.0
Net Fixed Assets	$37.5	$41.5	Retained Earnings	14.5	13.5
			Total Equity	$21.5	$20.5
Total Assets	$78.5	$80.5	Total Financing	$78.5	$80.5

TABLE 13-2   ILLUSTRATIVE INCOME STATEMENT OF GENERAL DATA CORP. ($ MILLIONS) FOR THE YEAR ENDING 1996

Revenues	$64.0
Cost of Goods Sold	38.4
Gross Profit	$25.6
Cash Operating Expenses	13.1
Depreciation Expense	6.0
Net Operating Income before Tax	$ 6.5
Tax @ 40%	2.6
Net Operating Income After Tax	$3.9
Interest Before Tax	$1.5
Tax Reduction due to Interest	0.6
Interest After Tax	$0.9
Net Income After Tax	$3.0
Dividends	$2.0
Increase in Retained Earnings	$1.0

The income statement in Table 13-2 is organized somewhat differently from most published income statements in order to make a number of the points we discuss later easier to understand. First, only two types of operating expenses are shown: (1) operating expenses that require cash outflows, and (2) depreciation that does not require a cash outflow, (in the period covered by the income statement).[10]

Second, a clear distinction is made between net operating income after tax (NOI) versus net income after tax (NI). **Net operating income** refers to the income generated from asset investments prior to any reduction in income due to financing expenses. During 1996, the company's investment in assets generated $3.9 million in net operating income after tax. **Net income** refers to the income earned by equity owners (or net operating income minus the after-tax cost of interest on debt). During 1996, the equity owners of General Data Corp. earned profits of $3.0 million, which consisted of $3.9 million of NOI minus $0.9 million in after-tax interest expense.

Third, the reduction in taxes due to interest expense is shown explicitly. Before tax, General Data had an interest expense in 1996 equal to $1.5 million. But this expense reduces the amount of taxes on operating income by $0.6 million. Thus, the effective after-tax interest expense to General Data during 1996 was $0.9 million.

The statement of cash flows for General Data Corp. is shown in Table 13-3. While corporations have been publishing balance sheets and income statements in their annual reports for many years, the statement of cash flows is a relative newcomer. But since these statements focus on the flow of cash within a firm, they can be quite helpful in understanding important financial trends.

The key to understanding a statement of cash flows is understanding how it is organized. Cash flows are categorized into three basic types:

- **Cash flows from operating activities** include net income adjusted for any noncash expenses such as depreciation. In addition, balance sheet accounts that change due to current operating activities are also included in this section. Balance sheet changes included in operating activities include all current assets and current liabilities (except for short-term notes payable).

- **Cash flows from investing activities** include acquisition or disposal of long-term fixed assets such as plant and equipment.

- **Cash flows from financing activities** include cash inflows and outflows to the firm due to (1) the issuance or retirement of debt obligations, (2) the issuance of new stock, (3) the payment of dividends and repurchase of shares, and so forth.

Let's examine the statement of cash flows for General Data in Table 13-3. During 1996, net income adjusted for the noncash depreciation expense provided an inflow of cash to the firm equal to $9.0 million. After accounting for changes in various current assets and liabilities, operating activities generated a total of $9.5 million of cash inflow to the firm. If there

---

[10] It is assumed that depreciation is the only noncash operating expense. If there are other types of noncash operating expenses such as bad debt expenses or goodwill expenses, they should be added to depreciation in analyses of the type discussed here.

TABLE 13-3 ILLUSTRATIVE STATEMENT OF CASH FLOWS FOR GENERAL DATA CORP. ($ MILLIONS) FOR THE YEAR 1996

Cash Flows from Operating Activities:

Net Income	$3.0
Plus Depreciation Expense	6.0
	$9.0
Additions due to:	
Reduction in Inventory	1.5
Reduction in Other Current Assets	2.0
Increase in Accounts Payable	0.5
Increase in Other Current Liabilities	1.0
Reductions due to:	
Increase in Marketable Securities	−1.5
Increase in Accounts Receivable	−2.0
Reductions in Wages and Salaries Due	−1.0
Net Cash Flows from Operations:	$9.5

Cash Flows from Investing Activities:

Acquisition of Fixed Assets	−$2.0

Cash Flows from Financing Activities:

Reduction in Notes Payable	−$1.5
Reduction in Long-Term Debt	−2.0
Dividends Paid	−2.0
Net Cash Flow from Financing	−$5.5
Net Increase in Cash and Cash Equivalents	$2.0
Beginning Cash and Cash Equivalents	$6.0
Ending Cash and Cash Equivalents	$8.0

---

had been no investment or financing activity during the year, the firm's cash balance would have increased by this $9.5 million. However, $2.0 million was spend on new fixed asset purchases. In addition, $5.5 million was used to reduce debt obligations and pay dividends to equity shareholders. As a result, the cash balance increased $2.0 million.

The cash flows shown in Table 13-3 suggest that General Data Corp. is a financially healthy firm. Operating activities were able to provide cash inflows to the firm sufficient to expand fixed assets, repay debt, and pay a dividend.[11]

---

[11] The data on which Table 13-3 is based is that of IBM in 1994. Prior to then, IBM had suffered a series of yearly cash drains due to operating losses. However, in 1994, the firm earned its first profit in a number of years, allowing IBM management the opportunity to begin to restore financial health to the firm.

Sources of Investment Return. Fundamental analysts typically evaluate two principal types of investment returns: (1) the return on the assets of the firm (ROA), and (2) The return on a firm's equity investment (ROE).

The **return on assets** during a given year is equal to the net operating income (after taxes) divided by total assets.

Return on Assets $$ROA = \frac{\text{Net Operating Income}}{\text{Total Assets}}$$ **(13.2)**

The value used for total assets could be assets at the start of the year, end of the year, or average assets during the year. The most accurate values are obtained using average assets during the year. For simplicity, however, end-of-year assets are commonly used. We follow this convention.

Using the data in Tables 13-1 and 13-2, General Data Corp.'s return on assets in 1996 was 4.97%:

$$0.0497 = \frac{\$3.9}{\$78.5}$$

For each $1.00 invested in assets, $0.0497 in operating profits were generated.

The return on equity during a given year is equal to the net income (after taxes) divided by total equity. Again, we follow the convention of using end-of-year equity.

Return on Equity $$ROE = \frac{\text{Net Income}}{\text{Equity}}$$ **(13.3)**

Using the data in Tables 13-1 and 13-2, General Data Corp.'s return on equity in 1996 was 13.95%:

$$0.1395 = \frac{\$3.0}{\$21.5}$$

Why was the return on equity so much larger than the return on assets during 1996? The answer is that (1) management used $57.0 million in debt financing to support asset investments, and (2) the after-tax interest cost of the debt financing was smaller than the after-tax return generated on assets.

During 1996, the after-tax dollar interest cost (see Table 13-2) was $0.9 million. Dividing this cost by the $57.0 million of debt outstanding results in an after-tax percentage interest cost of 1.58%. Each dollar of debt incurred an after-tax interest expense of $0.0158. But each dollar of debt that was used to purchase assets provided an after-tax asset return of $0.0497. The spread between the after-tax asset return of 4.97% and after-tax interest cost of 1.58% goes to equity holders.

The relationship between ROE, ROA, and debt use is shown in Equation (13.4):

ROE and Financial Leverage

$$ROE = ROA + \frac{\text{Debt}}{\text{Equity}} [ROA - K_d(AT)]$$ **(13.4)**

where $K_d(AT)$ refers to the after-tax cost of debt. In the case of General Data in 1996, the relationship was as follows:

$$ROE = 0.0497 + \frac{\$57.0}{\$21.5} [0.0497 - 0.0158]$$

$$0.1395 = 0.0497 + 2.651 [0.0339]$$

$$= 0.0497 + 0.0898$$

For each dollar of equity invested in the company, a dollar of assets was purchased, which provided a 4.97% return. If the firm had not used any borrowings, this would have been the *ROE* received by equity holders. But the firm did use borrowings to purchase assets. The spread between the *ROA* and the after-tax interest cost was 3.39%. Thus, if the firm had used one dollar of debt for each dollar of equity, the *ROE* would have been 8.36% (4.97% + 3.39%). But the firm actually used $2.651 dollars of debt per dollar of equity. Thus, equity owners earned 4.97% from their equity investment in assets plus 2.651 times 3.39% from the investment of debt in assets.

Two important investment principles can be illustrated with Equation (13-4):

◼ When the after-tax cost of debt financing is less than the after-tax return on assets, then increased debt will increase the return to equity holders.

◼ If there is uncertainty about the after-tax return on assets, then increased debt financing increases the uncertainty of returns to equity owners.

The data shown in Table 13-4 illustrate both principles. The first principle can be seen in the fair and good economic states. In these states, the return on assets is larger than the interest cost, and increased use of debt (for a given level of equity) results in higher returns on equity.[12] The second principle can be seen in the increased variability of *ROE* as the level of debt is increased. For example, the standard deviation of *ROE*

TABLE 13-4   AFFECTS OF LEVERAGE ON RETURN ON EQUITY WITH AFTER-TAX INTEREST COST OF 1.5789%

Economic State	Probability	ROA	Debt-to-Equity Ratio			
			0.000	1.000	2.651	4.000
Poor	0.2	−2.000%	−2.000%	−5.579%	−11.488%	−16.316%
Fair	0.6	4.968%	4.968%	8.357%	13.953%	18.525%
Good	0.2	11.936%	11.936%	22.294%	39.395%	53.366%
Average		4.968%	4.968%	8.357%	13.953%	18.525%
Standard Deviation		4.407%	4.407%	8.814%	16.091%	22.035%

---

[12] Of course, when the return on assets is less than the after-tax cost of interest, increased debt use results in lower *ROE*s.

increases from 4.407%, when no debt is used, to 22.035%, when $4.00 in debt is used for each $1.00 in equity.

An Alternative Analysis of Return on Equity. In Chapter 12, we saw how the return on equity can be separated into three underlying causes: asset efficiency, expense control, and debt utilization as follows:

Return on Equity

$$ROE \quad = \quad \begin{array}{c}\text{Asset} \\ \text{Efficiency}\end{array} \quad \text{times} \quad \begin{array}{c}\text{Expense} \\ \text{Control}\end{array} \quad \text{times} \quad \begin{array}{c}\text{Debt} \\ \text{Utilization}\end{array}$$

$$\frac{\text{Net Income}}{\text{Equity}} \quad = \quad \frac{\text{Sales}}{\text{Assets}} \quad \times \quad \frac{\text{Net Income}}{\text{Sales}} \quad \times \quad \frac{\text{Assets}}{\text{Equity}} \tag{13.5}$$

This analysis is referred to as the **Dupont model,** since the Dupont corporation has used the approach to evaluate the relative performance of its various divisions. The Dupont model is technically not as accurate as Equation (13.4), since it does not properly account for the role of interest in determining *ROE*. Nonetheless, the Dupont model is widely used by analysts because it provides a quick and logical way to analyze financial trends.

In fact, many analysts prefer to use a more detailed Dupont type of analysis that also highlights the effects of interest expense and income tax. Such a model is shown in Equation (13.6):

Extended Dupont Model

$$ROE = \frac{TS}{TA} \times \frac{NOI_{BT}}{TS} \times \frac{NI_{BT} \times (1 - T)}{NOI_{BT}} \times \frac{TA}{E} \tag{13.6}$$

Here *TS* refers to total sales, *TA* to total assets, NOI_{BT} and NI_{BT} to net operating income and net income before tax, *T* to the tax rate, and *E* to total equity. Applied to General Data in 1996, the extended Dupont Model would be:

$$0.1395 = \frac{\$64.0}{\$78.5} \times \frac{\$6.5}{\$64.0} \times \frac{\$5.0}{\$6.5} \times (1 - 0.4) \times \frac{\$78.5}{\$21.5}$$

$$= 0.8153 \times 0.1016 \times 0.769 \times (0.60) \times 3.6511$$

This is interpreted as follows. For each dollar of assets, $0.8153 of sales were generated. For each dollar of sales, $0.1016 in net operating income before taxes were generated. After interest deductions, net income before taxes was 76.9% of net operating income before taxes. After-tax income was 60% of pretax income. Finally, for each dollar of equity, $3.6511 of assets were owned.

Sources of Investment Risk. The risks that equity owners incur originate from the underlying business risk inherent in the firm's asset investments. This business risk is then compounded by the amount of financial leverage used by the firm. This concept is true for both diversifiable and nondiversifiable business risks. However, since most current theory focuses on the importance of nondiversifiable risk, we focus solely on nondiversifiable risk in this section.

The nondiversifiable risk of an investment is commonly measured as the beta of the investment. Although we usually think of beta as the nondiversifiable risk of a common stock (that is, of the equity ownership of a company), it is also correct to speak of the beta of a firm's assets. For example, if a firm uses no debt financing to support asset investments, then the beta of the stock will also be the beta of the assets. However, if the firm uses debt financing, than the beta of the equity will be greater than the asset beta.

As an example, let's say that Firm ABC is initially financed solely with $100 of equity, which is used to buy $100 of assets having a total of 80 units of risk. In this case, the equity owners will bear 80 units of risk or 0.8 units per dollar invested. What would happen if the company were to sell $50 of (risk-free) debt and use the $50 to buy back shares of stock? Now the $100 of asset is supported by $50 of debt and $50 of equity. But since the debt is risk free, all 80 units of asset risk will be borne by the $50 of equity. As such, equity risk per dollar of investment will increase to 1.6 units.

There are two important points in this example. First, the underlying business risk inherent in the assets of a firm is borne by the equity holders of a company. Second, an increase in the use of debt financing also increases the risks borne by equity holders.

The nondiversifiable risk incurred by equity holders can be approximated by the following formula:[13]

Equity Beta as a Function of Asset Beta

$$B_E = B_A + B_A \frac{\text{Debt}(1 - T)}{\text{Equity}} \tag{13.7}$$

where B_E equals the beta of equity investment, B_A is the beta associated with the firm's assets, debt and equity refer to the market value of the firm's debt and equity, and T is the firm's tax rate.

For example, assume the 1996 book values of debt and equity for General Data Corp. are equal to their market values and that the beta of General Data's assets is 0.5; then the firm's equity beta would be 1.295:

$$1.295 = 0.5 + 0.5 \frac{\$57.0(1 - 0.4)}{\$21.5}$$

Equation (13.7) is particularly useful in situations in which a firm is altering its capital structure. For example, if General Data Corp. announced it would soon reduce its ratio of debt to equity from 2.651 times to 1.5 times, then the new equity beta would be estimated as 0.95:

$$0.95 = 0.5 + 0.5 \frac{1.5(1 - 0.4)}{1}$$

Financial Ratio Analysis. Virtually all fundamental analyses include a ratio analysis of the firm's recent financial statements and a comparison with industry averages. Financial

---

[13] Equation (13-7) is an approximation equation, since it is based on a firm with an infinite series of level earnings per share that are fully distributed as dividends. The market value of debt is multiplied by 1 minus the tax rate in order to properly reflect the economic value of the firm's debt obligation. For example, if the debt is worth $100, has a perpetual coupon equal to 10% and a tax rate of 40%, then the after-tax dollar interest cost is $6 each year ($10 times "1 minus 0.4"). Discounting this $6 perpetuity at the risk-free rate of 10% results in the firm's economic liability of $60. This $60 is the same as Debt$(1 - T)$ in Equation (13-7).

analysts use ratios to help them understand important financial relationships within a company. For example, the fact that General Data Corp. had net operating income after tax of $3.9 million in 1996 is not meaningful unless it is related to the $78.5 million in asset investments used to obtain the $3.9 million. Similarly, the fact that accounts receivable were $21.5 million is not meaningful unless this balance is related to the $64.0 million in sales associated with the receivables.

Financial ratios are discussed in most introductory finance textbooks. Thus, we only review some of the more important aspects of ratio analysis.[14] Many of the more widely used ratios are displayed in Table 13-5. Illustrative calculations are based on the 1996 financial statements of General Data Corp.

When conducting a ratio analysis, keep the following points in mind:

- The focus should be on trends in financial ratios.

- Do not try to infer too much into trends of a single ratio. Ideally, the ratios taken as a whole will tell a common story.

- If possible, financial ratios should be compared with those of major competitors or an industry average in order to judge management's relative performance.

- Be careful that the ratios are not unduly affected by accounting principles used by the firm.

Management Evaluation. In the long run, a firm's profit level and risks are determined by the actions of the firm's management. In the short run, however, external forces such as governmental policies, international events, weather, and business cycles can affect profits positively or negatively. Although the historical record is an obvious place to begin an evaluation of management, some care should be taken in how the record is evaluated.

Beyond historical ratio analysis, what can the analyst do? This is a difficult question to answer. In fact, there is no reasonably sure procedure. Instead, the analyst is usually forced to develop a general impression based on a variety of creative observations. Some of these are discussed later.

- **Anticipatory management.** How accurately did management foresee major changes in the industry and position the firm to take full advantage of these changes?

- **Extent and reliability of information provided to the public.** Does management provide a thorough review of the firm' s financial status and prospects, or is minimal information given, and only begrudgingly? How accurately does the information provided to the public seem to reflect the actual situation?

- **Clarity of goals and corporate strengths.** Has management clearly defined the nature of its comparative advantages and then focused only on ventures in which these advantages can be put to best use?

---

[14] References at the end of this chapter provide a number of introductory as well as advanced readings on financial ratio analysis.

TABLE 13-5 GENERAL DATA CORP. SUMMARY OF FINANCIAL RATIOS

Ratio	Formula for Calculation	1996 Example	

I. Liquidity

Ratio	Formula for Calculation	1996 Example	
Current Ratio	Current Assets ÷ Current Liabilities	$41 \div 32$	= 1.28 times
Quick Ratio	(Current Assets − Inventory) ÷ Current Liabilities	$(41 - 6) \div 32$	= 1.09 times

II. Asset Efficiency

Ratio	Formula for Calculation	1996 Example	
Total Asset Turnover	Sales ÷ Assets	$64 \div 78.5$	= 0.815 times
Fixed Asset Turnover	Sales ÷ Net Fixed Assets	$64 \div 37.5$	= 1.707 times
Inventory Turnover			
–on Sales	Sales ÷ Inventory	$64 \div 6$	= 10.666 times
–on CGS	Cost of Goods ÷ Inventory	$38.4 \div 6$	= 6.4 times
Day's Sales in Inventory	360 ÷ Inv. Turn on CGS	$360 \div 6.4$	= 56.25 days
Accts. Receivable Turn	Sales ÷ Accts. Receivable	$64 \div 21.5$	= 2.977 times
Day's Sales in A/R	360 ÷ A/R Turn	$360 \div 2.977$	= 120.9 days

III. Expense Control

Ratio	Formula for Calculation	1996 Example	
Gross Profit Margin	Gross Profit ÷ Sales	$25.6 \div 64$	= 40%
Net Profit Margin	Net Income ÷ Sales	$3 \div 64$	= 4.69%

IV. Debt Levels and Capacity

Ratio	Formula for Calculation	1996 Example	
Debt to Assets	Total Debt ÷ Assets	$57 \div 78.5$	= 72.6%
Debt to Equity	Total Debt ÷ Equity	$57 \div 21.5$	= 2.651 times
Assets to Equity	Total Assets ÷ Equity	$78.5 \div 21.5$	= 3.651 times
Short-term Debt to **Total** Debt	STD ÷ Total Debt	$32 \div 57$	= 56.1%
Times Interest Earned	Net Income before Interest And Taxes ÷ Interest	$6.5 \div 1.5$	= 4.33 times
Times Interest Covered by Cash Flow	Net Income before Interest and Taxes plus Depreciation ÷ Interest	$(6.5 + 6.0) \div 1.5$ = 8.33 times	

V. Dividend Information

Ratio	Formula for Calculation	1996 Example	
Dividend Payout Ratio	Dividends ÷ Earnings	$2 \div 3$	= 66.66%
Dividend Yield	Dividends Per Share ÷ Stock Price	$\$0.5 \div \$10$	= 5% (assuming 4 million shares outstanding and a stock price of $10)

- **Focus of top management.** Does top management spend its time addressing the issues that can lead to increased economic value, such as asset efficiency, expense control, and capital expenditures? Or is a large part of the time devoted to less important factors, such as accounting techniques, expansion of EPS via mergers, engaging in share sales, and repurchases in response to beliefs that share prices are over- or undervalued?

- **Management depth.** Are there a number of top managers who could move into the chief executive officer's position, or is the firm dominated by one or two key managers? Similarly, are all levels of management equally strong, or is just the upper level strong, with weak middle or lower levels?

- **Employee morale.** Even the best management team can do little unless employees are satisfied with their jobs and eager to help the firm.

- **Opinions of competitors.** Usually a good management team will distinguish itself in the industry and gain widespread respect.

Inside Information. An analyst is able to identify an over- or undervalued stock only by having better information than other people. The *sources* of this information can be categorized as follows:

- **Direct information provided by employees** of the firm—for example, the president's projection of EPS or a clerk's statement about unfilled orders.

- **Direct information provided by nonemployees**—for example, a government attorney's private statement that the firm is to be indicted for bribery or a public statement that the Department of Defense has placed a $100 million order with the firm.

- **Inferential information** developed by examining a large amount of data and drawing conclusions about it—for example, concluding that a new law may have dramatic effects on a firm's profits and growth. Or that potential debt structure and foreign competition could seriously increase the firm's default risk.

Under Rule 10-5b of the Securities Exchange Act, *transactions based on direct information provided by employees that has not been made available to the general public are illegal,* and any profits earned must be returned to the original shareholders. An insider trading scandal erupted when the Securities Exchange Commission (SEC) charged Ivan Boesky with a wide variety of insider trades. The common denominator in most of his trades involved privileged information about potential corporate mergers. Boesky obtained tips from individuals who worked for the investment banking firms that were putting the mergers together.

Trading on direct information provided by nonemployees (that is not yet publicly available) may or may not be illegal, depending on the situation. However, trades based on inferential information developed by the analyst as a result of analyzing data in a unique manner are not illegal.

Analysts should be wary of suggesting trades on any material nonpublic information. If such information is offered by employees of the firm, the analyst (or the firm) should make a public announcement before suggesting trades for specific clients.

An Example of Fundamental Analysis: IBM

To illustrate how fundamental security analyses are conducted, we examine the situation of International Business Machines Corporation (IBM) in 1995. IBM is particularly good for this purpose because it has been subject to so many pressures as a result of recent dramatic technological change and increasing global competition.

During the 1980s, revenues of IBM increased in every year and had an average compound annual growth rate of 10%. Earnings per share grew at a lower, but still respectable, rate of 6.5% per year. This period of sales and profit expansion translated into rising stock prices. As Figure 13-9 shows, IBM's stock price rose from about $65 at the end of 1979 to $162 in 1987.

In 1986, however, earnings per share fell by 27%. Naturally, this unexpected decline created a concern about the company's future growth prospects and caused stock prices to decline further. By the end of 1990, share prices were trading for $113. Management responded to the competitive situation it faced in the early 1990s with a significant restructuring of the firm. Various divisions were made into semiautonomous business entities

FIGURE 13-9   IBM HISTORICAL STOCK PRICES

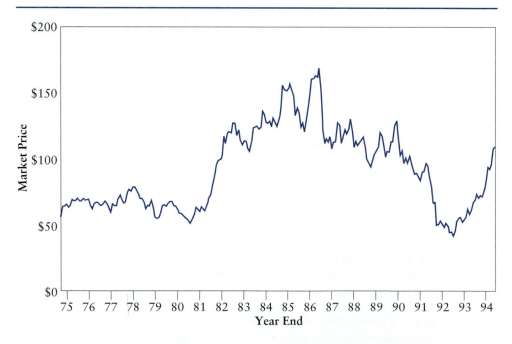

with each enterprise unit operating as an independent firm. The hope was that such a decentralized structure would allow managers in each unit to respond more rapidly to changing market demands. There were even suggestions that these units might sell stock to the public and become totally independent of the parent. Initially, the stock responded favorably to the proposed restructuring, and the stock rose to $130 in early 1992.

But it soon became clear that the problems facing IBM were larger than anticipated. In 1991, for the first time in the corporation's history, revenues declined. And in 1992, the firm's earnings per share fell to a negative $12.03 (compared with a positive $10.51 in 1990). As the stock fell to $50 at the end of 1992, it was clear that dramatic action had to be taken. Among these actions was the resignation of many top officers, including the chairman of the board of directors.

IBM Was Hit by Technological Risk

Firms must be able to forecast changes in technology and react rapidly to such changes. The story of IBM is a perfect example of how changes in technology can hurt firms when they are unexpected. Throughout the three decades before 1986, the computer industry was dominated by large mainframe computers and the software used to run them. Because of its marketing skill in selling mainframes and lead in mainframe research, IBM dominated the computer business prior to the mid-1980s.

Unfortunately, management at IBM did not anticipate the revolution that the introduction of desktop computers would bring to the industry. Although IBM did introduce a line of desktop computers, it lost sales to other firms that competed aggressively on price and performance. In addition, IBM was slow in developing software used to run the new generation of computers. As a result, IBM became a secondary player in this rapidly expanding new industry.

A Review of IBM's Financial Performance

A summary of various financial ratios for IBM from 1977 through 1994 is shown in Table 13-6.[15] In this section, we examine much of this data graphically. Although it is often helpful to compare a firm's ratios with those of an industry average, the product lines of firms in the computer manufacturing business are so different that such a comparison in this case would be meaningless (or even misleading).

Returns on Investment. Figure 13-10 shows trends in IBM's return on assets (*ROA*) and return on equity (*ROE*) over the period 1977 to 1994. Prior to the mid-1980s, IBM had an *ROA* between 15% to 20% per year and an *ROE* between 20% and 25%. During this period, IBM was clearly a very profitable firm. It held a competitive lead in the quality of its mainframe computers (due to extensive research and development), which provided

---

[15] The author obtained this data from a product of Standard & Poor's Corp. known as PC-PLUS. This is a CD-ROM on which financial statement and market price data is provided on virtually all traded firms in the United States. Similar products are available from other firms such as Moody's. Once one becomes familiar with such financial data products, an exhibit such as Table 13-6 can be prepared in less than five minutes.

TABLE 13-6 INTERNATIONAL BUSINESS MACHINES SUMMARY OF HISTORICAL RATIOS

Year	Y77	Y80	Y85	Y90	Y91	Y92	Y93	Y94
I. Liquidity Ratios								
Current Ratio	1.93	1.52	2.28	1.54	1.22	1.08	1.18	1.41
Quick Ratio	1.63	1.07	1.42	1.08	0.88	0.74	0.80	1.10
Working Capital per Share	8.246	5.822	23.784	23.879	12.863	5.171	10.410	20.609
Cash flow per Share	7.999	10.827	15.609	17.916	8.030	4.123	−3.800	12.282
II. Asset Efficiency Ratios								
Inventory Turnover	4.88	3.57	2.38	2.71	2.74	2.84	4.11	4.97
Receivables Turnover	6.33	5.49	5.36	3.22	2.76	2.81	3.06	3.13
Total Assets Turnover	0.99	1.02	1.05	0.84	0.72	0.72	0.75	0.79
Average Collection Period (Days)	57.672	66.477	68.095	113.195	132.275	129.885	119.354	116.662
Days to Sell Inventory	74.849	102.111	153.435	134.751	133.257	128.706	88.773	73.373
Sales/Shareholder Equity	1.437	1.593	1.565	1.611	1.751	2.336	3.177	2.736
III. Expense Control								
Gross Margin	76.290	71.808	63.936	61.596	57.827	59.940	47.717	46.027
EBIT Margin	36.711	32.423	28.530	22.094	14.645	19.570	9.704	14.366
Pretax Margin	28.08	22.50	23.21	14.78	0.19	−13.99	−14.03	8.05
Net Margin	14.997	13.589	13.095	8.722	−0.870	−10.640	−12.735	4.716
IV. Debt Levels and Capacity								
Pretax Interest Coverage	127.21	19.14	22.84	8.06	1.08	−5.18	−5.67	5.13
Debt to Common Equity	2.03	12.76	12.36	27.88	35.75	46.53	81.76	56.19
Debt to Total Equity	2.03	12.76	12.36	27.88	35.75	46.53	77.24	53.59
Total Debt to Invested Capital	3.326	14.500	14.600	35.682	53.640	72.436	78.158	61.506
Total Debt to Total Assets	2.26	10.07	9.97	22.32	29.14	33.82	33.71	27.28
Total Assets to Common Equity	1.504	1.623	1.645	2.044	2.499	3.139	4.350	3.631
V. Profitability Ratios								
Return on Assets	14.3	13.3	12.5	6.9	−0.6	−7.9	−9.8	3.7
Return on Equity	21.6	21.6	20.5	14.1	−1.5	−24.9	−42.8	13.5
Return on Average Assets	14.8	13.9	13.7	7.3	−0.6	−7.7	−9.5	3.7
Return on Average Equity	21.4	22.7	22.4	14.8	−1.4	−21.2	−34.5	14.7
VI. Dividend Information								
Dividend Payout Ratio	70.26	56.37	41.24	46.08	−491.31	−40.28	−11.26	53.59
Dividend Yield	3.66	5.07	2.83	4.28	5.44	9.61	2.80	1.36

FIGURE 13-10   IBM RETURN ON AVERAGE ASSETS AND EQUITY

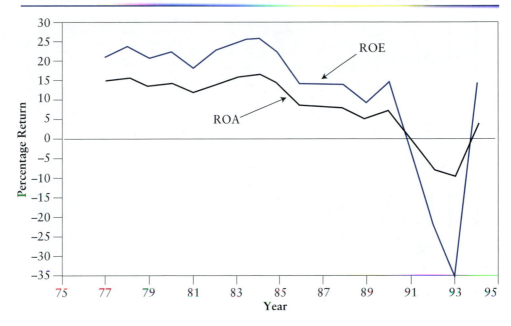

IBM with the opportunity to charge higher selling prices than its competitors. So, in large part, this historical profitability can be traced to high profit margins that the firm was able to obtain from setting high selling prices on its mainframe computer products.

But after the new generation of computers was introduced in the mid-1980s, the firm lost this competitive lead. As a result, returns on assets and returns on equity declined dramatically. The negative returns in 1992 and 1993 were due to onetime restructuring charges incurred as IBM began to change its marketing and product focus.

In 1994, IBM again saw positive investment returns. The level of investment profitability in the future will depend on how successful management is in developing new products and dealing with a highly competitive environment.

Liquidity. Past trends in IBM's current ratio and quick ratio are shown in Panel A of Figure 13-11. Again we see a substantial decline in these ratios after the events of 1986 when the computer industry took a turn to new technology. Yet IBM's ability to meet short-term liabilities has never been in serious jeopardy and began a turnaround in 1993 and 1994. The firm does not appear to have any short-term liquidity difficulties.

Asset Efficiency. Panel B in Figure 13-11 displays trends in two of the more important measures of how efficiently management uses its asset investment: the days of sales in inventory and the average collection period.

Since 1986, management of IBM has significantly improved its management of inventory investment. In the mid-1980s, there were about 150 days of sales in inventory balances. By the end of 1994, this had declined to about 70 days. This is clearly a positive trend for which management deserves credit.

FIGURE 13-11   IBM Ratios

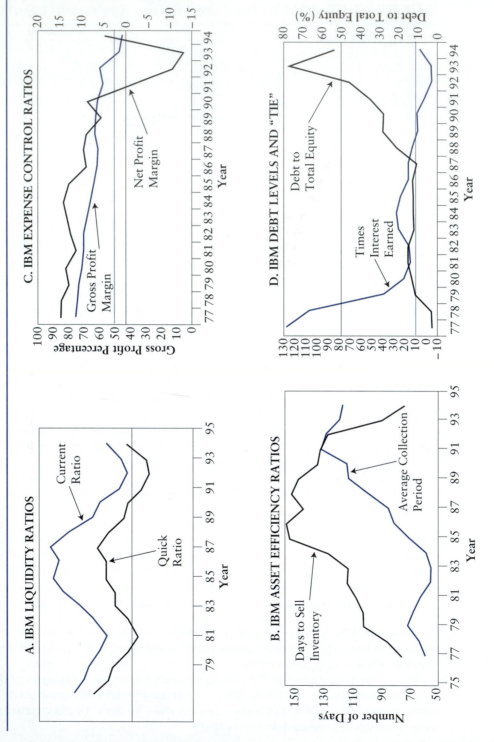

A. IBM LIQUIDITY RATIOS

B. IBM ASSET EFFICIENCY RATIOS

C. IBM EXPENSE CONTROL RATIOS

D. IBM DEBT LEVELS AND "TIE"

In contrast, trends in the average collection period have continued to grow (with a slight decline in recent years). However, this should not be viewed as a negative. The management discussion in IBM's annual reports states that the firm had begun a policy of actively providing financing to customers. They were doing so because this was one area of the business that had not been hit by declining profit margins.

In short, inventory balances exhibited decent control by management, and receivable balances reflected a shift in managerial strategy.

Expense Control. Probably the most serious problem facing IBM has been the decline in profit margins. Trends in the gross profit margin (gross profits divided by total sales) and net profit margin (net income divided by sales) are shown in panel C of Figure 13-11. Gross profit margins are measured against the left Y-axis. Net profit margins are measured against the right Y-axis. Although the negative net profit margins associated with the early 1990s had returned to positive values by 1994, there seems to be a long-run downward trend in both. This decline in profit margins is due, in large part, to a shift in the nature of IBM's product line and increased competition in the industry that had forced a reduction in gross profits in each product line. To illustrate, consider the data presented in Table 13-7. IBM had four major product lines in 1994: hardware, software, services, and financing. With the exception of financing, the gross profit margin had declined in each product line from 1992. The historical strength of IBM had been the sale of hardware. In 1992, the gross profit margin for hardware services had been 41.6%. By 1994 (only two years later), the gross profit margin earned on hardware had declined to 34.1%.

In short, even though IBM had improved its profit margins in 1994 over the prior few years, the company faced a long-term trend toward greater price competition and, thus, lower profit margins.

Debt Levels and Capacity. Ratios reflecting trends in IBM's use of debt financing and debt capacity are shown in panel D of Figure 13-11. The vertical axis on the left of the graph shows the number of times interest was earned before taxes (debt capacity), and the axis on the right shows the ratio of long-term debt to total equity. The times interest earned ratio was in excess of 100 to 1 in the late 1970s. This was a time during which IBM management used virtually no long-term debt financing. However, in 1979, IBM sold its first significant long-term debt issue to support capital expansion. Throughout the early 1980s, IBM was a regular participant in long-term debt markets. But the ratio of long-term debt to equity as well as the times interest earned ratio always remained within acceptable bounds until the late 1980s. During the late 1980s and early 1990s, both ratios deteriorated and created significant concerns about default risk.

Improved profit margins in 1994 provided sufficient cash flow to repay some of the firm's debt and increased the times interest earned ratio to ten times earnings, a moderately acceptable level. Nonetheless, as of early 1995 the firm continued to have too much debt outstanding and needed further improvements in its times interest earned ratio. If future operations remained profitable, a significant portion of operating cash flows would have to go toward further debt reduction.

The Situation in 1995. In early 1995, top management at IBM realized that the market for computer hardware and software had changed forever. During the late 1980s and early

TABLE 13-7   IBM SALES AND GROSS PROFIT MARGINS BY PRODUCT LINE

	1994		1992	
		Hardware		
	$ thousand %	% of Total	$ thousand %	% of Total
Revenues	32,344	50.5%	33,755	52.3%
Gross Profit Margin	34.1%		41.6%	
		Software		
Revenues	11,346	17.7%	11,103	17.2%
Gross Profit Margin	58.8%		64.7%	
		Services		
Revenues	16,937	26.4%	14,987	23.2%
Gross Profit Margin	32.7%		36.7%	
		Financing		
Revenues	3,245	5.3%	4,678	7.3%
Gross Profit Margin	59.6%		58.0%	
		Total		
Revenues	64,052	100.0%	64,523	100.0%
Gross Profit Margin	39.5%		45.6%	

1990s, the battle had been over sales of desktop computers and software that runs desktop computers. And IBM had lost that battle. So instead of continuing to fight a lost war, management began to look for opportunities and trends in new product developments in the computer industry.

Management at IBM believed that the future in computers would come from the development of worldwide computer networks. In an interview, the chairman of IBM told a *Business Week* correspondent, "One of the great things about this industry is that every decade or so, you get a chance to redefine the playing field. We're in that phase of redefinition right now, and winners and losers are going to emerge from it."

IBM management planned to take advantage of industry changes by delivering computer networks that would tie customers to computer resources at IBM. Customers would no longer have to own mainframe computers to perform calculations such as payrolls or inventory management. Rather, they could hire network time on mainframes owned by IBM. Companies would be able to buy computing power and applications software in the same way they buy electricity.

IBM was in a particularly good position to offer such networking services in 1995. The firm was a heavy user of networking within its own offices around the world. Furthermore, the company had just acquired Lotus software (a $3.5 billion purchase), and Lotus had brought Notes, its networking software to IBM. In addition, corporations moving toward large networks would have to purchase mainframe computers to function as "servers" that tie a firm to a network.

In short, by 1995 management at IBM had redefined the major product that they intended to offer in the future, moving away from hardware toward the newly burgeoning industry of business networks. There would be considerable competition from other mainframe computer firms as well as telecommunication firms. But IBM had begun to position itself in a strong competitive posture in a new industry.

Stock Value of IBM in Early 1995. A stock valuation requires two basic estimates: (1) an estimate of a fair rate of return to be earned on the stock, and (2) an estimate of future dividend growth.

To illustrate the estimate of a fair rate of return, we use the capital asset pricing model, which says:

Fair Expected Stock Return = Risk-Free Rate plus Stock Beta times Market Risk Premium

In mid-1995, the yield to maturity on long-term U.S. treasury bonds was about 6.25%. The long-term bond yield is used instead of shorter yields (say on T-bills) because long-term yields include long-term inflation expectations.

Estimates of a stock's beta are more difficult to develop. However, it is certainly worthwhile looking at past beta estimates to gain a feeling for the general level of what might be the stock's beta. In Figure 13-12, beta estimates are presented from late 1965 through mid-1995. Each beta estimate is based on a regression in which 60 months of IBM returns were regressed against 60 months of returns on the S&P 500 index. The average beta estimate was below 1.0, particularly since 1980. The last beta estimate (in June 1995) was 0.66. In our valuation we use a Beta estimate of 0.80.[16]

Estimates of the market risk premium are also difficult to judge. But the real annual return on the S&P 500 (a widely used proxy for the "market" portfolio) has generally been 5% to 7% above returns on U.S. Treasury bonds over periods of 30 years or more. Thus, we will use both 5% and 7% as estimates of the market risk premium. This results in the following range of fair expected returns on IBM stock:

$$10.25\% = 6.25\% + 0.8\ (5\%) \text{ using a 5\% market risk premium}$$

$$11.85\% = 6.25\% + 0.8\ (7\%) \text{ using a 7\% market risk premium}$$

Past dividends per share (DPS) paid by IBM are shown as the bars in Figure 13-13. Between 1961 and 1992, DPS grew from $0.12 to $4.84. This represents a compound annual growth rate of 12.7%. However, in order to conserve cash in the face of declining profits and to help repay debt, IBM cut its DPS to $1.58 in 1993 and $1.00 in 1994.

---

[16] In practice it is often wise to use a number of beta estimates. We do not do so here in order to keep the illustrations as straightforward as possible.

FIGURE 13-12 ESTIMATES OF PAST IBM BETAS

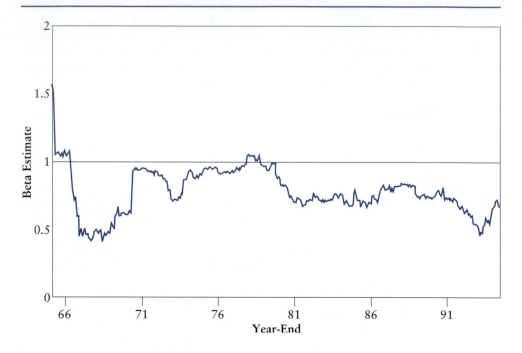

FIGURE 13-13 IBM DIVIDENDS PAST AND PROJECTED

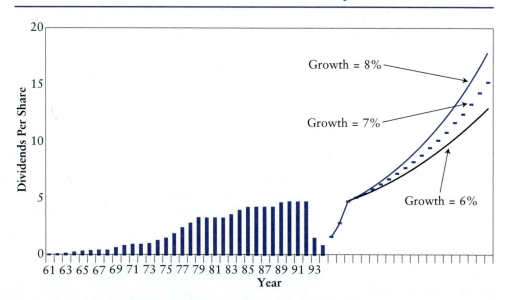

TABLE 13-8 ESTIMATES OF IBM STOCK VALUE AT 1995

Required Return	Long-Term Dividend Growth Rate		
	6.0%	7.0%	8.0%
10.25%	$97.58	$126.41	$180.86
11.85%	$69.93	$ 83.57	$104.29

The following assumptions are used in estimating future dividend growth rates:

■ Faced with increased competition, it is unlikely that IBM's return on equity will return to the 20% to 25% range for any length of time in the future. Instead, long-run returns on equity between 12% and 16% are more likely.

■ Dividends per share will return to their 1992 level of $4.84 by 1997 ($1.69 in 1995 and $2.86 in 1996).

■ After 1997, dividends per share will grow at a constant growth rate consistent with the firm's historical earnings retention rate of 50% and its long-run return on equity.

■ The long-run return on equity after 1997 will be between 12% and 16%. This implies long-run dividend growth rates as follows:

Implied Growth	equals	Return on Equity	times	Retention Rate
6.0%	=	12%	×	0.50
7.0%	=	14%	×	0.50
8.0%	=	16%	×	0.50

The lines shown in Figure 13-12 illustrate the future dividend growth implicit in these assumptions.

Table 13-8 presents the value per share of IBM under the two discount rates (10.25% and 11.85%) and the three dividend growth forecasts. At the time of these forecasts, IBM shares were trading for about $100. Based on the data in Table 13-8, such a price is consistent with (1) a demanded return of 10.25% and a long-run dividend growth rate of 6%, or (2) a demanded return of 11.85% and a long-run dividend growth rate of 8%.

S U M M A R Y

Here are the key concepts:

■ Like all other asset classes, the equity portion of a portfolio may be passively or actively managed. A passively managed portfolio should be well diversified and reflect the liquidity and tax situation of the investor. The common way in which a passive equity portfolio is created is by the purchase of a commingled index fund.

■ Active equity management should be used only if one has special skills and knowledge that can be used to find stocks that are trading at prices other than their intrinsic values.

■ Individual investors can actively manage their equity portfolio by either personally selecting individual stocks or by purchasing mutual funds that are actively managed by a professional manager.

■ Active institutional managers typically have a specific investment style they use in selecting equities. Examples of investment styles include the following:

(1) **Top-down** selection in which the analysis starts with the aggregate economy and moves to the individual stock.

(2) **Bottom-up** selection in which the analysis starts with individual stocks and moves to the aggregate market.

(3) **Quantitative managers** who screen large equity databases for stocks meeting certain criteria or rely on sophisticated statistical modeling to select stocks and control risk.

(4) **Value managers** who focus on low price-to-earnings and low price-to-book stocks.

(5) **Growth managers** who focus on firms with the potential for high earnings growth.

R E V I E W   P R O B L E M

Table 13-A and 13-B present the financial statements of a firm that is similar to IBM Corp., which we call KAL.

  a. Calculate the interest-adjusted return on assets for both years.

  b. If the firm had used no financial leverage in 1996, what would its *ROE* have been?

  c. Calculate various measures of asset efficiency for each year.

  d. Calculate measures of debt level, capacity, and liquidity.

  e. Assume the equity beta of this firm is 0.85. Also assume a risk-free rate of 8.0% and a market risk premium of 5%. What rate of return should you require according to the capital asset pricing model (CAPM)?

  f. If you expect the 1996 return on equity and dividend retention rates to continue into the future, what do you expect the annual sustainable growth rate of dividends per share will be?

  g. Given the answers to parts e and f (i.e., assuming constant dividend growth), what should be the market price of KAL?

  h. KAL shares are selling for $122. Is this a buy, hold, or sell candidate?

TABLE 13-A

KAL, Inc. Balance Sheets (in Thousands)	1992	1996
Cash and Securities	$ 3,300	$ 7,257
Receivable	5,433	10,825
Inventory	3,492	8,039
Other	789	1,628
Total Current Assets	13,014	27,749
Net Fixed Assets	19,527	30,065
Total Assets	$ 32,541	$ 57,814
Current Liabilities	$ 8,209	$ 14,747
Long-Term Debt	2,851	4,169
Deferred Taxes	1,521	4,524
Common Equity	19,960	34,374
Total Liabilities and Equity	$ 32,541	$ 57,814

TABLE 13-B

KAL, Inc. Income Statements (in Thousands)	1992	1996
Revenues	$34,364	$51,250
Cost of Sales	−13,688	−22,706
Gross Profit	20,676	28,544
Operating Expenses	−12,620	−20,685
Operating Income	8,056	7,859
Interest		
Income	328	1,005
Expense	−454	−475
Net Interest	−126	530
Earnings Before Taxes	7,930	8,389
Taxes	−3,521	3,600
Net Income	$4,409	$4,789
Depreciation	$3,143	$3,316
Earnings per Share	$7.39	$ 7.81
Dividends per Share	$3.44	$ 4.40

Solution

	1992	1996
a. Tax Rate	3,521/7,930 = 0.444	3,600/8,389 = 0.429
NOI after tax	4,409 + (1 − 0.444)454 = 4,661	4,789 + (1 − 0.429)475 = 5,060
ROA	4,661/32,541 = 14.32%	5,060/57,814 = 8.75%

b. 8.75%

	1992	1996
c. Total Asset Turn	34,364/32,541 = 1.056	51,250/57,814 = 0.886
Fixed Asset Turn	34,364/19,527 = 1.760	51,250/30,065 = 1.705
Inventory Turn		
(CGS)	13,688/3,492 = 3.92	22,706/8,039 = 2.82
Sales per day	34,364/365 = 94.15	51,250/365 = 140.41
Average Collection		
Period	5,433/94.15 = 57.7 days	10,825/140.4 = 77.1 days
d. Total Debt	8,209 + 2,851 + 1,521	14,747 + 4,169 + 4,524
	= 12,851	= 23,440
Debt to Assets	12,581/32,541 = 0.386%	23,440/57,814 = 0.405
Debt to Equity	= 0.630	= 0.682
STD to Total	= 0.639	= 0.629
Times Interest Earned	(8,056 + 328)/454	(7,859 + 1005)/475
	= 18.5 times	= 18.7 times
Times Interest Covered	(8,384 + 3,143)/454	(8,864 + 3,316)/475
	25.4 times	25.6 times
Current Ratio	13,014/8,209 = 1.58	27,749/14,747 = 1.88
Quick Ratio	9,522/8,209 = 1.16	19,710/14,747 = 1.34

e. Required Return = 8.0% + 0.85(5.0%) = 12.25%

f. $G = ROE \times$ Retention Rate

$= 4,789/34,374 \times (7.81 − 4.40)/7.81$

$= 0.1393 \times 0.4366 = 0.0608$

g. Price $= \$4.40(1.0608)/(0.1225 − 0.0608) = \$75.64$

h. Based on the pricing assumptions, this is a sell candidate.

QUESTIONS   AND   PROBLEMS

1. Evaluate the following two hypothetical statements. Do you agree? Why or why not?
   a. "Most analysts of the office equipment industry are forecasting a substantial increase over prior years in the earnings per share of Amdahl Corporation and Burroughs Corporation. As a result, they are suggesting active purchasing of common shares of both firms."
   b. "Yesterday's announcement by the management of Tech Labs that back orders are continuing to increase is causing many analysts to revise their forecasts of Tech Labs' earnings upward. Yet the market price of the firm's stock doesn't seem to have fully discounted the likely earnings revision. We suggest active buying of these shares at levels below $20."
2. Identify the characteristics of an equity investment portfolio for the following accounts:
   a. A $20.0 million pension fund that will not have to pay large retirement benefits for another 20 years. Employees are factory workers and clerical staff for a young high-technology firm. Most employees own no stocks or bonds of their own.
   b. A 45-year-old lawyer with a successful practice. The lawyer is in a high tax bracket, won't need the funds until retirement, and is willing to accept above-average risk. $200,000 is to be invested. No other investments are held.

c. A 60-year-old machinist with a portfolio worth $80,000, an average tax bracket, and a desire for less-than-average risk. Major retirement income will come from a diversified pension fund.

d. A young family with two children not yet in school. Both parents have promising careers as CPAs and are willing to accept moderate risk. At present they have $10,000 to invest and expect that at least that amount will be available for new investment every year.

3. Using five years of monthly returns, you have estimated the historical equity beta of Marine Products Corporation to be 1.0. During this time span the firm's debt structure was reasonably stable, with the total debt-to-total-asset ratio averaging 0.40. The firm's tax rate was 46%.

a. Estimate the historical asset beta.

b. If the firm's total debt-to-total-asset ratio is expected to increase to 0.70, what is a reasonable estimate of the future beta?

4. A share of stock is expected to pay a dividend of $1.00 one year from now, with a growth at 5% thereafter. In the context of a dividend discount model, the stock is correctly priced today at $10. According to the single-stage constant growth dividend discount model, if the required return is 15%, the value of the stock two years from now should be:

a. $11.03
b. $12.10

c. $13.23
d. $14.40

5. In its latest annual report, a company reported the following:

Net income	= $ 1,000,000
Total equity	= $ 5,000,000
Total assets	= $10,000,000
Dividend payout ratio	= 40%

Based on the sustainable growth model, the most likely forecast of the company's future earnings growth rate is:

a. 4%
b. 6%

c. 8%
d. 12%

6. Mulroney continued her examination of Eastover and Southampton by looking at the five components of return on equity (ROE) for each company. For her analysis, Mulroney elected to define equity as total shareholders' equity, including preferred stock. She also elected to use year-end data rather than averages for the balance sheet items.

a. Based on the data shown in Tables 13-C and 13-D, calculate *each* of the *five ROE* components for Eastover and Southampton in 1990. Using the five components, calculate *ROE* for *both* companies in 1990. Show all calculations.

b. Referring to the components calculated in part a, explain the difference in *ROE* for Eastover and Southampton in 1990.

c. Using 1990 data, calculate an *internal* (i.e., *sustainable*) *growth rate* for both Eastover and Southampton. Discuss the appropriateness of using these calculations as a basis for estimating future growth.

Mulroney recalled from her CFA studies that the constant-growth discounted dividend model (DDM) was one way to arrive at a valuation for a company's common stock. She collected current dividend and stock price data for Eastover and Southampton, shown in Tables 13-E and 13-F.

d. Using 11% as the required rate of return (i.e., discount rate) and a projected growth rate of 8%, compute a constant-growth DDM value for Eastover's stock and compare the computed value for Eastover to its stock price indicated in Table 13-F. Show calculations.

Mulroney's supervisor commented that a two-stage DDM may be more appropriate for companies such as Eastover and Southampton. Mulroney believes that Eastover and Southampton could grow more rapidly over the next three years and then settle in at a lower but sustainable rate of growth beyond 1994. Her estimates are indicated in Table 13-G.

e. Using 11% as the required rate of return, compute the two-stage DDM value of Eastover's stock and compare that value to its stock price indicated in Table 13-G. Show calculations.

TABLE 13-C   EASTOVER COMPANY (EO) ($ MILLIONS, EXCEPT SHARES OUTSTANDING)

Income Statement Summary

	1986	1987	1988	1989	1990
Sales	$5,652	$6,990	$7,863	$8,281	$7,406
Earnings before interest and taxes (EBIT)	$ 568	$ 901	$1,037	$ 708	$ 795
Interest expense (net)	(147)	(188)	(186)	(194)	(195)
Income before taxes	$ 421	$ 713	$ 851	$ 514	$ 600
Income taxes	(144)	(266)	(286)	(173)	(206)
Tax rate	34%	37%	33%	34%	34%
Net income	$ 277	$ 447	$ 565	$ 341	$ 394
Preferred dividends	(28)	(17)	(17)	(17)	(0)
Net income to common	$ 249	$ 430	$ 548	$ 324	$ 394
Common shares outstanding (millions)	196	204	204	205	201

Balance Sheet Summary

	1986	1987	1988	1989	1990
Current assets	$1,235	$1,491	$1,702	$1,585	$1,367
Timberland assets	649	625	621	612	615
Property, plant, and equipment	4,370	4,571	5,056	5,430	5,854
Other assets	360	555	473	472	429
Total assets	$6,614	$7,242	$7,852	$8,099	$8,265
Current liabilities	$1,226	$1,186	$1,206	$1,606	$1,816
Long-term debt	1,120	1,340	1,585	1,346	1,585
Deferred taxes and other	1,000	1,000	1,016	1,000	1,000
Equity—preferred	364	350	350	400	0
Equity—common	2,905	3,366	3,695	3,747	3,864
Total liabilities and equity	$6,614	$7,242	$7,852	$8,099	$8,265

TABLE 13-D   SOUTHAMPTON CORPORATION (SHC) ($ MILLIONS, EXCEPT SHARES OUTSTANDING)

Income Statement Summary

	1986	1987	1988	1989	1990
Sales	$1,306	$1,654	$1,799	$2,010	$1,793
Earnings before interest & taxes (EBIT)	$ 120	$ 230	$ 221	$ 304	$ 145
Interest expense (net)	(13)	(36)	(7)	(12)	(8)
Income before taxes	$ 107	$ 194	$ 214	$ 292	$ 137
Income taxes	(44)	(75)	(79)	(99)	(46)
Tax rate	41%	39%	37%	34%	34%
Net income	$ 63	$ 119	$ 135	$ 193	$ 91
Common shares outstanding (millions)	38	38	38	38	38

Balance Sheet Summary

	1986	1987	1988	1989	1990
Current assets	$ 487	$ 504	$ 536	$ 654	$ 509
Timberland assets	512	513	508	513	518
Property, plant, & equipment	648	681	718	827	1,037
Other assets	141	151	34	38	40
Total assets	$1,788	$1,849	$1,796	$2,032	$2,104
Current liabilities	$ 185	$ 176	$ 162	$ 180	$ 195
Long-term debt	536	493	370	530	589
Deferred taxes & Other	123	136	127	146	153
Equity	944	1,044	1,137	1,176	1,167
Total liabilities & equity	$1,788	$1,849	$1,796	$2,032	$2,104

f. Discuss two advantages and three disadvantages of using a constant-growth DDM. Briefly discuss how the two-stage DDM improves on the constant-growth DDM.

In addition to the discounted dividend model (DDM) approach, Mulroney decided to look at the price to earnings ratio and price to book ratio, relative to the S&P 500, for *both* Eastover and Southampton. Mulroney elected to perform this analysis using 1987 to 1991 and current data.

g. Using the data in Tables 13-E and 13-F, compute both the current and the five-year (1987–1991) average relative P/E ratios and relative P/B ratios for Eastover and Southampton. Discuss each company's current relative P/E ratio as compared to its five-year average relative P/E ratio and *each* company's current relative P/B ratio as compared to its five-year average relative P/B ratio.

TABLE 13-E   EASTOVER COMPANY (EO)

	1986	1987	1988	1989	1990	1991
Earnings per share	$ 1.27	$ 2.12	$ 2.68	$ 1.56	$ 1.87	$ 0.90
Dividends per share	0.87	0.90	1.15	1.20	1.20	1.20
Book value per share	14.82	16.54	18.14	18.55	19.21	17.21
Stock price						
—High	28	40	30	33	28	30
—Low	20	20	23	25	18	20
—Close	25	26	25	28	22	27
Average P/E	18.9x	14.2x	9.9x	18.6x	12.3x	27.8x
Average price/book	1.6x	1.8x	1.5x	1.6x	1.2x	1.5x

Southampton Corporation (SHC)

	1986	1987	1988	1989	1990	1991
Earnings per share	$ 1.66	$ 3.13	$ 3.55	$ 5.08	$ 2.46	$1.75
Dividends per share	0.77	0.79	0.89	0.98	1.04	1.08
Book value per share	24.84	27.47	29.92	30.95	31.54	32.21
Stock price						
—High	34	40	38	43	45	46
—Low	21	22	26	28	20	26
—Close	31	27	28	39	27	44
Average P/E	16.6x	9.9x	9.0x	7.0x	13.2x	20.6x
Average price/book	1.1x	1.1x	1.1x	1.2x	1.0x	1.1x

S&P 500

	1986	1987	1988	1989	1990	1991	5-Year Average (1987-1991)
Average P/E	15.8x	16.0x	11.1x	13.9x	15.6x	19.2x	15.2x
Average price/book	1.8x	2.1x	1.9x	2.2x	2.1x	2.3x	2.1x

h. Mulroney previously calculated a valuation for Southampton for both the constant growth and two-stage DDM as shown here:

	Discounted Dividend Model Using	
	Constant Growth Approach	Two-Stage Approach
Southampton	$29	$35.50

Using *only* the information provided and your answers above, select the stock (EO or SHC) that Mulroney should recommend as the better value, and justify your selection.

TABLE 13-F   CURRENT INFORMATION

	Current Share Price	Current Dividends Per Share	1992 EPS Estimate	Current Book Value Per Share
Eastover (EO)	$ 28	$ 1.20	$ 1.60	$ 17.32
Southampton (SHC)	48	1.08	3.00	32.21
S&P 500	415	12.00	20.54	159.83

TABLE 13-G   PROJECTED GROWTH RATES

	Next 3 Years Growth (1992, 1993, 1994)	Beyond 1994
Eastover (EO)	12%	8%
Southampton (SHC)	13%	7%

D A T A F I L E   A N A L Y S I S

1. **Statement Analysis.** Review the financial statement data in the STCKFINL data file. Select one or more firms and conduct a financial ratio analysis of each. What types of data or other information would you like to have in order to develop an opinion about the stock's intrinsic value?

R E F E R E N C E S

As noted in Chapter 12, a classic text treating fundamental security selection was originally written in 1934 by Benjamin Graham and David Dodd. Its most recent revision is Cottle, Sidney, Roger F. Murray, and Frank E. Block, *Graham and Dodd's Security Analysis,* 5th ed. New York: McGraw-Hill, 1988.

Thorough reviews of financial statement analysis can be found in the following:

Brigham, Eugene F. and Louis C. Gapenski. *Financial Management: Theory and Practice, Eighth Edition,* Fort Worth: Dryden Press, 1996.

Bernstein, Leopold A. *Financial Statement Analysis: Theory, Application, and Interpretation,* 4th ed., Homewood, IL: Richard D. Irwin, 1988.

Helfert, Erich A. *Techniques of Financial Analysis,* 6th ed., Homewood, IL: Richard D. Irwin, 1987.

An interesting security analysis illustration can be found in RANDALL S. BILLINGSLEY, CFA, "Equity Securities Analysis Case Study: Merck & Company," *Equity Securities Analysis and Evaluation,* Association for Investment Management and Research, 1993.

These two articles discuss the determinants of a stock's beta:

Hamada, Robert S. "The Effect of the Firm's Capital Structure on the Systematic Risk of Common Stocks," *Journal of Finance,* May 1972.

Rosenberg, Barr. "Prediction of Common Stock Betas," *Journal of Portfolio Management,* Winter 1985.

14

Commingled Investment Portfolios

After reading this chapter you should have an understanding of the benefits and costs of investing through mutual funds.

One of the more dramatic changes in security markets during the past 25 years has been the movement of investment capital into professionally managed portfolios. At the end of 1970, professional investment management firms were managing about 20% of the value of all actively traded equities in the United States. By 1995, they were managing more than 60% of the value of U.S. equities!

There are many reasons for this growth. But the most important is the growing recognition of both individual and institutional investors that ownership of professionally managed portfolios represents an easy and inexpensive way to create broadly diversified investment portfolios.

Professional investment services are provided by commercial banks, insurance companies, and investment counsel firms. Each of these organizations offers two general types of investment management services: (1) managed commingled funds, and (2) managed separate accounts.

Commingled funds are portfolios owned by a number of investors who pool their resources to purchase a single portfolio. Mutual funds, for example, are commingled funds that can be bought or sold by the general public. However, there are other types of commingled funds not available to the general public because ownership claims to the portfolio are not registered with the Securities and Exchange Commission. Such commingled funds are available only to large private institutional investors such as pensions and endowment funds.

Separate accounts are professionally managed portfolios owned by a single investor; the assets are not commingled with those of other portfolios. For example, a trust account for an individual investor will often be managed by a bank as a separate account. In addition, trustees of pension funds and endowment funds often require the investment management firm to segregate their securities from the other funds managed by the adviser. Investment holdings in a separate account portfolio are often similar to those of a commingled portfolio managed by the invesment adviser. But the assets of a separate account will always be legally segregated from all other assets managed by the adviser.[1]

Our discussion in this chapter focuses primarily on commingled portfolios that are available to the general public. The chapter is organized into the following three sections:

- ◾ **The Professional Investment Industry.** In this section, we review the history of professional investment management, identify the types of firms that provide investment management services, and examine the types of services they provide. These services are provided to two types of investors: (1) trustees of private institutional portfolios, and (2) the general public. Investment management services to the general public are made available mainly through mutual funds and closed-end funds.[2]

- ◾ **Mutual Funds.** In this section, we examine the mutual fund industry. This includes discussions of the industry's growth, investment services that mutual funds provide, costs of fund ownership, and sources of mutual fund information.

- ◾ **Closed-End Funds.** In this section, we discuss differences between mutual funds and closed-end funds (CEFs) and examine why CEFs trade at market prices different from their net asset values.

The Professional Investment Industry

A Brief History of Investment Management

Investors have relied on the services of professional investment counselors for centuries. Prior to the development of active securities markets, well-to-do individuals usually obtained advice from business acquaintances and lawyers about promising ventures. Once active secondary security markets arose, investment advice increasingly came from security brokers and organizations that specialized in investment management. Usually, these investment managers were employees of a financial services firm that could provide the well-to-do client with a full range of services, including demand deposit accounts, personal loans, investment banking advice regarding the client's business, and personal advice about

---

[1] There are a variety of reasons why an investor would choose to invest in a separate account as opposed to a commingled portfolio. The most common reason is that the investor wishes to place constraints on the types of securities to be held that are not suitable for a commingled portfolio. For example, the investor might wish to minimize investments in countries with poor human rights policies.

[2] See Chapter 3 for an introduction to mutual funds and closed-end funds.

investment in financial assets. Prior to World War I, the more important of these "banking houses" were located in Europe (particularly, the United Kingdom) and the United States. Perhaps the most powerful in the United States was The House of Morgan, which was founded by the famous financier John Pierpont Morgan.

At that time, the practice of allowing investment advisers **full discretion** over purchases and sales became common. This meant that the adviser could make security trades without first obtaining approval from the investor. Today, virtually all professional investment managers are given full discretion, allowing them to trade rapidly as prices temporarily depart from intrinsic values.[3] The only constraints currently placed on professional investment managers are legal constraints and any contractual provisions made with the investor.

Prior to the 1920s, virtually all portfolios that an adviser managed for investor clients were held separately from portfolios of other clients. The composition of each portfolio was often different and the holdings of each were physically segregated from other portfolios. This arrangement is still widely used today, and such portfolios are referred to as separate accounts. For example, Florida law requires that securities managed by a professional adviser for police and firefighter pension plans be physically segregated from the assets of other managed portfolios.

As security trading became popular during the 1920s, investment advisory firms began to offer their services to individual investors through a vehicle known as a commingled portfolio. Although a few commingled portfolios had been offered during the late 1800s, they did not become popular until the booming security markets of the 1920s. In a commingled portfolio, investors pool their funds and purchase a single investment portfolio. Each investor owns the same set of assets. Commingled portfolios offered to the general public consist of mutual funds and closed-end funds. In addition, many commingled portfolios are created that are not available to the general public but offered only to large institutional investors.

Between 1920 and 1980, two events occurred that had profound effects on the way security markets look today and the nature of the professional investment-manager community. These were the Glass-Stegall Act and the growth of institutional investment.

The Glass-Stegall Act. In late 1929, stock markets worldwide crashed. In response, broad new security laws were enacted in the United States as an attempt to counterbalance perceived fraudulent practices. In the United States, one of the more far-reaching legislative actions was the **Banking Act of 1933.** Known by the names of its sponsors, the **Glass-Stegall Act** had three critical parts.

First, the act precluded commercial banks from investment banking activities. Banks such as The House of Morgan were split into two organizations—the commercial bank, Morgan Guarantee Trust, and the investment banking firm, Morgan Stanley.

This legislation had dramatic implications. For example, it meant that commercial banks in the United States could not create and offer commingled portfolios in the forms of mutual funds or closed-end investment company shares to the general public. Banks could invest trust accounts maintained at the bank by individuals and institutions in both separate accounts and commingled portfolios created by the bank. But these portfolios

---

[3] Throughout this chapter, security brokers are not considered to be professional investment managers. While many security brokers do provide investment advice, their principal role is to facilitate purchase and sale transactions.

could not be offered outside the trust company to the general public. Revisions are currently before the U.S. Congress to repeal the Glass-Stegall Act.[4]

Because U.S. banks were restricted from the creation and sale of commingled investment portfolios to the general public, other organizations grew to dominate the open and closed-end investment company industry. These included insurance firms, brokerage houses, and firms that specialize solely in investment management services.

The Glass-Stegall Act also prohibited banks from paying interest on demand deposit checking accounts. When interest rates were relatively low, this had only a mild effect on the banking industry; people preferred the convenience and safety offered by their local banks to other alternatives. But as interest rates rose during the 1970s, due to increased inflation, bank depositors looked elsewhere for returns to compensate for inflation losses. The "elsewhere" turned out to be a new form of open-end mutual fund, **money market mutual funds.** Money market mutual funds invest in short-term debt securities with very low risk of default. In fact, most money market funds follow investment strategies that guarantee the net asset value of the fund will never decline. Because of their safety and higher returns, money market mutual funds became serious competition to the banking industry.

Finally, the Glass-Stegall Act created the Federal Deposit Insurance Corporation (FDIC), which insures demand deposits in commercial banks. FDIC insurance and its sister insurance on deposits in savings and loans played an important role in the U.S. economy during the early 1990s.

Institutional Investors. The second major event shaping investment markets since the 1920s has been the increase in institutional security ownership, principally in pension funds. Following World War II, it became common practice for corporations to offer defined benefit pension plans to employees as a part of their total compensation package. To assure employees that promised benefits would be paid, legal escrow accounts were set up to invest yearly employer contributions. Over time, these deposits accumulated with investment earnings to the point that, in 1995, pension fund assets had a claim to about one-third the value of all securities traded in the United States.

During the late 1980s, the popularity of defined benefit pension plans declined in favor of defined contribution plans.[5] Because employees bear the investment risk of defined contribution plans, employers who offer such plans usually allow employees a number of investment options from which to choose. This provides individual employees with the ability to manage the investment risk to which their retirement savings are exposed. But it also requires that employees be given a reasonable number of investment portfolios from which to choose as well as the ability to switch from one set of portfolios to another as their tolerance for risk changes during their working careers.

To provide employees in defined contribution pension plans with a wide array of portfolios from which to choose as well as the ability to switch easily between the funds, in the

---

[4] Recent legislative changes in the United States now allow commercial banks to create and sell mutual funds to the public. Banks are also allowed to engage in many other security brokerage activities.

[5] Defined benefit plans promise a specified benefit payment to employees (typically as a percentage of final salary). If securities do not provide the returns that are expected, the employer must increase contributions to the pension plan to assure that promised benefits will be paid. Thus, employers offering defined benefit plans bear all investment risk. In defined contribution plans, the employer is only obligated to pay a specified contribution to the pension plan each year. Once the contribution has been made to the pension portfolio, the employee bears all investment risk.

late 1980s and early 1990s, many employers turned to mutual funds. This has been a major reason for the recent dramatic growth in mutual fund assets.

Investment Management in the 1990s

Today most investment management firms are organized to service institutional pension funds and individual investors.

Investment management firms refer to their clients as having either tax-exempt portfolios or non-tax-exempt portfolios. **Tax-exempt** clients include institutional investors such as pension funds, foundations, and endowments (these organizations do not pay taxes on profits generated by portfolio assets). **Non-tax-exempt** clients include investors in mutual funds and closed-end funds. Although realized profits of a mutual fund or closed-end fund are not taxed at the fund level, they are taxed when the investor receives the profits.[6] Portfolios managed for tax-exempt and non-tax-exempt clients with a similar investment objective are typically managed in similar fashion. The designation of tax-exempt or non-tax-exempt is used primarily to differentiate between portfolios that are available only to private institutional investors versus portfolios that have been registered with the SEC and are available to the general public.

Investment management services are offered by three types of firms: (1) commercial banks, (2) insurance companies, and (3) investment counsel firms.

Between the 1930s and mid-1970s, the Glass-Stegall Act prevented commercial banks from acting as a security underwriter or from investing directly in corporate equities. Thus, banks were unable to create mutual funds or closed-end funds to sell to the public. In addition, banks could not take a direct ownership position in corporate equities. However, subsidiaries of banks, which were set up as trust companies, were allowed to provide investment management services to clients of the trust. And as investment portfolios of pension funds, endowments, and foundations grew in size after World War II, trust companies used their experience in managing trust assets to run institutional portfolios. By the mid-1980s, the principal clients of bank trust companies had become large institutional investors. In recent years, provisions of the Glass-Stegall Act have been substantially loosened: Bank trust companies are now major issuers of mutual funds to the general public.

Insurance companies were not covered by the Glass-Stegall Act. Thus, they have always been allowed to create investments such as mutual funds. The major legislation faced by insurance firms has come from state laws in which they conduct business. These state laws typically allow insurance firms to provide investment services to clients of the firm, but all client investments must be legally "separated" from investments owned by the insurance firm, hence the widely used name for investments managed for others called "separate accounts." Insurance firms offer all forms of investment management services. Because the major assets held by insurance firms to meet insurance policy claims are fixed income securities, they are most skilled at investment of fixed income investment.

Investment counsel companies represent investment firms that are not affiliated with a bank or insurance company. While some investment counsel firms are subsidiaries of brokerage firms, most are totally independent of any other organization.

---

[6] The term *realized profits* is defined later in the chapter.

Basic information about professional investment management firms is shown in Figure 14-1. The top panel shows that approximately 57% of the value of all actively traded U.S. stocks were managed by professional investment firms at the end of 1994. The remaining 43% of equity values were managed by individual investors. Equity funds managed by professional investors were split about equally between tax-exempt clients (institutional investors) and non-tax-exempt clients (mutual funds and closed-end funds).

FIGURE 14-1   U.S. EQUITY MANAGEMENT AND OWNERSHIP

PERCENTAGE OF U.S. EQUITIES MANAGED BY PROF. INVESTORS VS. INDIVIDUALS (1994)

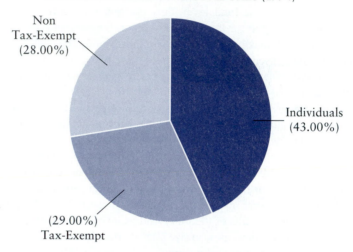

PERCENTAGE OF ASSETS MANAGED BY TYPE OF INVESTMENT MANAGEMENT FIRM

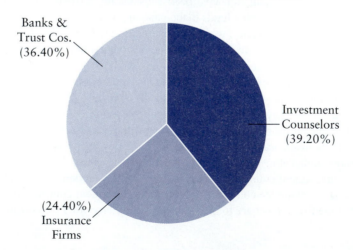

SOURCE: Adapted from *Pension & Investments*, May 15, 1995, published by Craine Communications, Inc.

TABLE 14-1   DATA ON THREE LARGE PROFESSIONAL MANAGEMENT FIRMS

Type of Firm: Firm:	Investment Counsel Firm Fidelity Investments	Commercial Bank Mellon Bank	Insurance Firm Prudential Insurance
	Assets Managed ($ billions)		
Tax-Exempt	$157.04	$134.68	$124.30
Non Tax-Exempt	157.50	68.70	66.20
Total	$314.54	$203.38	$190.50
Equities			
Domestic	156.33	65.64	37.70
Foreign	12.18	NA	3.60
Fixed Income			
Domestic	68.29	54.15	98.30
Foreign	0.90	NA	3.80
Cash Equiv.	76.24	82.29	21.80
Real Estate	0.59	0.17	23.90
Alternative Investments	NA	1.12	1.40

The bottom panel shows the percentage of professionally managed assets run by banks (36.4%), insurance firms (24.4%) and investment counsel firms (39.2%). While investment counsel firms managed the largest portion of assets, no one type of organization dominated the business.

Information on three of the largest investment management firms at the end of 1994 is presented in Table 14-1. The firms were as follows:

■ **Fidelity Investments** is an investment counsel company.[7] At the end of 1994, Fidelity managed about $314 billion in portfolio assets. Approximately half this money was managed for tax-exempt institutional investors and the other half for individuals. Fidelity is the largest provider of mutual funds in the world. In fact, virtually all its investment services are offered through the mutual funds for which it is the investment adviser. When a large institutional investor wishes to have Fidelity manage a portion of the institution's portfolio, Fidelity does so by having the institution buy one or more of the mutual funds that it manages. This policy is somewhat unusual in the investment management business. Usually, institutional investors will invest in a separate acccount or commingled portfolio that may emulate a mutual fund but be legally distinct from the mutual fund.

■ **Mellon Bank** offers investment services through its traditional trust company operations plus a number of subsidiaries. Most of the investments that Mellon Bank

---

[7] Fidelity has a subsidiary that provides brokerages services to clients. It was created, however, as an independent counseling firm, and the largest portion of its revenues come from investment advisory fees.

manages are institutional tax-exempt portfolios, a result of the long time period during which banks could not offer commingled portfolios to the general public. However, during 1994, Mellon purchased Dreyfus Corp., a major creator and adviser to mutual funds. The non-tax-exempt assets of $68.7 billion at the end of 1994 were largely those of Dreyfus Corp.

■ **Prudential Insurance Co.** offers a full range of investment products to both tax-exempt and non-tax-exempt markets. As an insurance company, investment managers at Prudential are experts at managing fixed income products for its insurance operations. The company carries this expertise over to the investment services, which it offers to outside institutional and individual investors. This can be seen in the large dollar amount of fixed income securities that the firm managed ($98.3 billion). A large portion of these fixed income investments were in guaranteed investment contracts issued to tax-exempt institutional investors.[8]

In summary, the assets managed by professional investment advisers come from two sources: individual investors and institutional investors. Advisory services are offered to individual investors through mutual funds and closed-end funds that have been registered with the Securities Exchange Commission (SEC). Advisory services to institutional investors are offered in a variety of ways: (1) through mutual funds available to the general public, (2) through commingled portfolios that are not registered with the SEC, and (3) through separate accounts that are legally separated from all other assets managed by the adviser.

In the following sections, we discuss services available to the general public; mutual funds and closed-end funds.

Mutual Funds

Mutual funds are not a distinct asset class such as stocks and bonds. Instead they represent vehicles that can be used to take positions in various asset classes. For example, if an investor wishes to place a portion of his or her portfolio in large capitalization U.S. equities, the investor could purchase (1) a single mutual fund that maintains an index portfolio of stocks included in the S&P 500 index, or (2) a number of actively managed mutual funds that invest in large capitalization stocks. Similarly, if the investor wishes to have part of his or her portfolio invested in fixed income securities issued in countries other than the United States, there are indexed funds as well as actively managed mutual funds that own foreign bonds. With about 6,000 mutual funds traded in the United States today, there are mutual funds available to meet virtually any investment objective.

Growth and Size of Mutual Fund Assets

Mutual funds generally specialize in a particular asset class or even a segment within an asset class. For purposes of discussion here, we examine U.S. funds that invest in equities, bonds, and money market instruments. These are general designations used by practitioners.[9]

---

[8] Guaranteed investment contracts (or GICs) are discussed in Chapter 3.

[9] The discussions of mutual fund growth relates solely to growth of funds traded in the United States, since accurate long-term data is not available on funds traded in other countries.

Robert C. Puff, Jr., C.F.A.

Executive Vice President; Chief Investment Officer
Twentieth Century Companies, Inc.
Bucknell University, B.S.
University of Pennsylvania, The Wharton School, M.B.A.

Twentieth Century Companies is a family of no-load mutual funds with approximately $45 billion under management in 62 mutual funds. They were founded in 1958 by the current chairman, James Stowers, and are based in Kansas City, Missouri, with offices in California and Denver.

Q: What has been the evolution of the mutual fund industry from Twentieth Century's perspective?

A: It's a dynamic business that has been growing very quickly since the early 1980s and continues to grow pretty substantially today. A lot of that growth is predicated on the fact that mutual funds can be owned by people with relatively small amounts of money. When the IRA legislation was originally introduced in 1981 taxpayers could take up to $2,000 per year and invest it in approved securities. Buying a diversified portfolio with $2,000, which was the yearly IRA ceiling, was relatively difficult. A vehicle that had been around for years, mutual funds, was in a fashion discovered by the general public. A few years prior, people had discovered money market mutual funds as a place where they could invest savings deposit money and earn a much higher rate of return than they had been able to earn in their savings accounts at local banks. People got comfortable with the idea of sending money thousands of miles away to a firm where they'd never met anybody, basically doing financial business by mail.

Now the mutual fund industry is being driven by 401(k) plans, which are probably the fastest growing retirement vehicle in the world. Employers like mutual funds because they are priced every day in the newspaper and employees can easily follow them. Also, baby boomers are thinking about actively saving more money.

Q: How did 401(k) plans become such big business for mutual funds?

A: The corporation used to have ultimate liability for the defined benefit retirement plans. The corporation was in effect putting in its own money and it kept control of all the investment decisions. The whole world of retirement has shifted to defined contribution plans and once it has made its contribution, the company is basically off the hook. While the corporate world liked the transition, so did the working world because they could now control their own destiny. In this kind of situation, mutual funds, which were already available and designed in such a way that they could handle the accounting for thousands of employees, were a natural product set.

Q: Why are Twentieth Century's mutual funds no load?

A: This is how our business has grown up. We've direct-marketed and someone signs up and we've done a good job for them so they tell friends and family. Word of mouth is a big part of what we've done. We use conventional advertising outlets like major magazines and spot advertisements in newspapers. Also, we have a shareholder base of about two million people so we can do a great deal of direct mail advertising based on demographics. We will be doing more of this over time. We do this without any middleman. Just one on one with a customer.

This sales approach helps to keep our expenses down and keeps the expenses down for the shareholder.

Q: From the perspective of chief investment officer, how do you determine what kinds of funds to offer?

A: We try to determine what our customer base wants. We figure that out by talking to our customers and by looking at what investors are doing in other parts of the mutual fund industry. Which product categories are growing rapidly and which aren't? We also do what our firm is good at doing. There are certain product sets we are very good at and we think we can compete at effectively. If we can match up a customer's need or perceived need with our capabilities that's a wonderful opportunity. Then assuming we've matched those two correctly, the likelihood is reasonably high that we can attract enough assets to make it economically viable.

Figure 14-2 and Table 14-2 present information about the historical growth rate of mutual funds in the United States. Between 1940 and 1970, the only mutual funds available to the public were equity funds. A few balanced funds that hold both stocks and bonds were available, but they were so few in number that the industry trade organization, the Investment Company Institute, did not keep track of them. However, during the 1970s and 1980s, two events spurred the introduction and rapid growth of mutual funds that invested in both money market and fixed income securities. These events were a major increase in interest rates and a rapid growth in outstanding bond issues.

Money Market and Bond Funds. During the mid-1970s, interest rates rose dramatically in reaction to increased inflation in the United States. Initially, banks were not able legally to raise the interest rates which they paid on deposits to levels that could compete with the returns available on traded money market instruments such as T-bills and commercial paper. As a result, investment management firms created a new form of mutual fund that invested solely in money market instruments. Individual investors who had neither the capital nor the knowledge to directly purchase money market securities found the high returns and safety of these new money market mutual funds to be an ideal investment. Money

FIGURE 14-2   GROWTH OF U.S. MUTUAL FUNDS

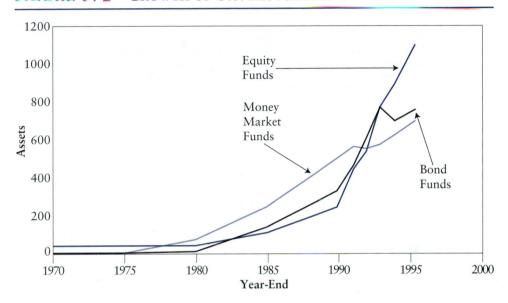

SOURCE: *1995 Mutual Fund Factbook,* Washington, D.C.: Investment Company Institute, Washington, D.C.

market funds were an immediate success and their assets grew throughout the 1970s and 1980s. By 1990, the assets of the money market funds had grown to $500 billion.[10] As interest rates declined during the early 1990s, the growth rate of money market funds declined. But money market funds remain an important investment vehicle for investors who desire stable investment returns. They provide an inexpensive and convenient way for investors to take positions in a diversified portfolio of money market instruments.

Also during the late 1970s and 1980s, the quantity of outstanding bond issues grew dramatically. This was due to rising federal government deficits (which the U.S. Treasury financed by the sale of new Treasury notes and bonds) and by the newly created market of mortgage pass-through obligations. Investment management firms saw this as an opportunity to offer new products to mutual fund buyers in the form of mutual funds that invested in specific types of bonds. New bond mutual funds were sold to the public that managed a wide variety of fixed income obligations. These included U.S. Treasury and agency obligations, collateralized mortgage obligations, and nontaxable municipal bond obligations. In mid-1995, the total market value of bond mutual funds was approximately $750 billion.

Equity Funds. The growth of equity mutual funds has been equally impressive. For example, between 1940 and 1990, the assets of equity funds grew from $0.5 billion to almost $250.0 billion, an annualized growth of about 13%. Yet the most interesting story about equity mutual funds is their recent growth during the 1990s.

---

[10] Initially, commercial banks lost deposits to money market funds. But federal regulations were soon loosened to allow banks to also issue money market funds. This represented the first step towards commercial banks being allowed to offer all forms of mutual funds.

TABLE 14-2   Growth of Mutual Funds Traded in the United States

Total Net Assets ($ billions)

Year End	Equity	Bond & Income	Money Market	Total	Number of Funds
1940	$ 0.5			$ 0.5	68
1945	1.3			1.3	73
1950	2.5			2.5	98
1955	7.8			7.8	125
1960	17.0			17.0	161
1965	35.2			35.2	170
1970	45.1	$ 2.5		47.6	356
1975	37.5	4.7	$ 3.7	45.9	390
1980	44.4	14.0	76.4	134.8	564
1985	116.9	134.8	243.8	495.5	1,528
1990	245.8	322.7	498.3	1,066.8	3,105
1991	411.6	322.7	542.5	1,395.5	3,427
1992	522.8	577.3	546.2	1,646.3	3,850
1993	749.0	761.1	565.3	2,075.4	4,558
1994	866.5	684.0	611.0	2,161.5	5,357
June 1995	1,067.2	741.5	687.0	2,495.8	5,608

SOURCES: Adapted from various issues of *Wiesenberger Investment Companies*, CDA Wiesenberger Financial Services and *Mutual Fund Factbooks*, Investment Company Institute.

At the end of June 1995, equity mutual funds were managing more than $1 trillion of equity assets, an annualized growth from 1990 of 38%. While some of this growth was due to good equity returns during the 1990 to 1995 period, most of the growth was due to large purchases of equity fund shares by the investing public. Many professionals believe three principal forces were at work in creating this demand for equity fund shares in the early 1900s:

- **Decreases in interest rates.** As interest rates fell in the early 1990s, many investors who had previously owned money market funds began to seek out higher investment returns. After owning money market mutual funds for many years, they were used to mutual fund investing and found it natural to switch to equity (and bond) funds.

- **Public recognition of the value of professional equity management.** The returns on equity funds had been relatively good during most years of the 1980s as they participated in the general rise in equity values. As a result, financial magazines and newspapers began to cover equity funds more thoroughly. This resulted in an increased investor knowledge of mutual funds at a time when the so-called baby boom generation was beginning to save actively for retirement.

☒ Growth of defined contribution plans. During the late 1980s and early 1990s, most employers were increasingly using various types of defined contribution pension plans in place of defined benefit plans. A common form of defined contribution plan is referred to as a 401(k) plan after the section of the Internal Revenue Code that allows such plans. Most new 401(k) plans gave employees the choice of a number of mutual funds in which to invest. As a result, a brand-new influx of capital began to flow into equity mutual funds. For example, between 1993 and 1994, assets that Fidelity Investment managed increased about $40.0 billion. About half of this increase was due to funds coming from defined contribution plans.

The growth rate of assets managed by equity mutual funds during the 1990s has been phenomenal, but some people worry that these new funds might leave as fast as they came. If investors in equity mutual funds were to withdraw substantial sums, managers of the funds would be forced to sell fund investments in order to meet fund redemptions. This could create downward pressure on equity prices and a general decline in equity values. While such a scenario is possible, most fund managers believe that large redemptions are unlikely, since a large share of the new money to equity funds represents investments made from defined contribution pension plans. These investments are long-term savings for the investor's future retirement that are unlikely to be removed during temporary declines in stock prices.

Importance of Mutual Fund Assets. At the end of 1994, an estimated 30.2 million U.S. households owned mutual funds either by direct purchase or indirect investment through defined contribution pension plans. This represented 31% of all households in the United States.

Figure 14-3 shows the Investment Company Institute's 1992 estimates of how the financial assets of households (which invest in mutual funds) were distributed. Bank products such as demand deposits and certificates of deposits represented 36% of the financial

---

FIGURE 14-3 DISTRIBUTION OF HOUSEHOLD FINANCIAL ASSETS

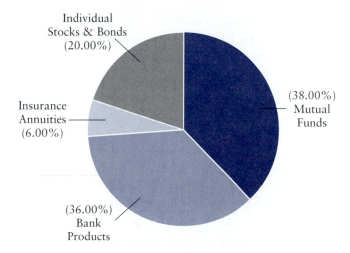

Individual Stocks & Bonds (20.00%)

Insurance Annuities (6.00%)

(38.00%) Mutual Funds

(36.00%) Bank Products

SOURCE: *1995 Mutual Fund Factbook,* Washington, D.C.: Investment Company Institute.

TABLE 14-3 1994 MUTUAL FUND ASSETS AS A PERCENTAGE OF SECONDARY MARKET SECURITY VALUES

Investment Type	Mutual Fund Holdings as a Percentage of Total Security Value
Open Market Paper[1]	43.1%
Corporate Bonds	7.2
Tax-Exempt Municipal Bonds	26.9
Corporate Equity	12.2

[1] Open market paper includes commercial paper, bankers' acceptances, etc. It does not include T-bill holdings.

SOURCE: *Mutual Fund Factbook, 1995,* Investment Company Institute, Washington, D.C.

assets of these households, insurance annuity contracts represented 6%, and individual holdings of stocks and bonds were 20%. But the largest fraction, 38%, was invested in mutual funds. Mutual funds clearly represent a major investment outlet for households that choose to invest in them.

The importance of mutual fund investments in today's security markets is evidenced by the percentage ownership of various securities traded in secondary markets. Table 14-3 shows Investment Company Institute estimates of the fraction that mutual funds own of different securities traded in U.S. security markets. At the end of 1994, mutual funds owned 43% of all open-market paper such as commercial paper and bankers' acceptances. Their smallest ownership position was in corporate debt obligations (7.2%).

World Mutual Fund Markets. Data on the market values of mutual funds traded in various countries around the world is shown in Table 14-4.[11] Mutual fund assets in the United States represented almost 50% of the world total at the end of 1994, funds domiciled in Europe represented 35%, and those in Japan about 10%. Notice the small country of Luxembourg in which about 6% of world mutual fund assets were domiciled. Because Luxembourg does not tax income from securities that are registered in Luxembourg, citizens of other countries transfer financial assets to Luxembourg where they buy Luxembourg mutual funds.[12]

In order for mutual funds created in, say, Country A to have their shares available for purchase to residents of, say, Country B, the Country A fund must register the securities in Country B. Recent regulations within the European Union (EU) permit registered funds in one EU country to be traded without further registration in other EU countries. This will facilitate the growth of mutual funds throughout the EU and should open the European market to many U.S. management firms. In other areas of the world, substantial barriers exist to both the sale of U.S.-based funds to residents of a foreign country and the sale to U.S. residents of a fund registered in the foreign country.

---

[11] Table 14-4 reports on mutual fund assets but excludes closed-end fund assets. In some of these countries, closed-end funds own a large quantity of securities.

[12] There are many other such tax havens around the world including the Bahama Islands and many of the British Isles.

TABLE 14-4   WORLD MUTUAL FUND ASSETS (IN $ BILLIONS)

	1989	1994	1994 Percentage of Total	Five-Year Growth
United States	$981.96	$2,161.50	48.23%	17.09%
Europe				
France	295.75	531.09	11.85%	12.42%
Germany	124.54	253.44	5.65%	15.27%
Luxembourg	NA	289.03	6.45%	NA
United Kingdom	92.85	135.20	3.02%	7.80%
Other	123.32	372.03	8.30%	24.71%
Total	636.46	1,580.78	35.27%	NA
Pacific Rim				
Australia	30.89	44.05	0.98%	7.35%
Japan	408.17	466.89	10.42%	2.72%
Other	33.54	124.16	2.77%	29.92%
Total	472.6	635.10	14.17%	6.09%
Canada	20.27	97.63		
South Africa	NA	6.86		
Total	20.27	104.49	2.33%	NA
World Total	$2,111.29	$4,481.87	100.00%	16.25%

SOURCE: *Mutual Fund Factbook, 1995,* Washington, D.C.: Investment Company Institute.

To help gain access to foreign markets, many funds create joint ventures with investment managers in other countries. For example, a U.S. management company with broad distribution channels in the United States but little international investment experience might enter a joint agreement with a U.K. investment firm that has invested worldwide for many years but has no access to U.S. markets. As security investing became more global in scope during the 1990s, such joint ventures between managers of different countries became quite popular.

Creation and Operation of a Mutual Fund

Creating a New Mutual Fund. Most new mutual funds are originated by a professional investment management firm that becomes the investment adviser to the fund. Conceptually, shareholders of a mutual fund elect a board of directors that is responsible for hiring and monitoring the investment adviser to the fund. Once a fund has been in operation for some period of time, this procedure is used (although it is rare for the investment adviser to be replaced). However, when a new mutual fund company is being formed, the practice is for an investment management firm to develop the investment idea underlying the fund and to select the initial board of directors of the fund.

The investment firm starts by identifying a type of investment portfolio that management believes will be attractive to the investing public. For example, the new fund might use any of the following to make the fund attractive to potential investors:

- ▪ **Unique approaches to selecting investments.** In recent years various quantitative procedures for selecting securities to be bought or sold have become popular with investors. Such quantitative models range from simple rankings of securities using statistics such as earnings growth and price-to-book value ratios, to more statistically sophisticated models based on arbitrage pricing theory.

- ▪ **Invest in asset classes or segments of asset classes that are not available from other funds.** In the 1980s, many new funds were created to invest in tax-exempt municipal bonds and collateralized mortgage obligations. More recently new mutual funds have been created to invest in special areas of international markets such as the emerging markets of Latin America and Pacific Rim countries. Alliance Capital Management, for example, recently offered one of the first money market funds to invest in money market securities domiciled in countries other than the United States. Within a few months after its initial offer to the public, fund assets exceeded $5 billion.

- ▪ **Offer services not provided by other funds.** This was the initial motive for the creation of index mutual funds in the 1970s. Prior to then, all mutual funds were actively managed. More recently, The Vanguard Group offered a broadly diversified equity fund that was to be managed in a manner which would minimize taxes of investors in the fund.

- ▪ **Build on the reputation of existing funds offered by the adviser.** Many investment advisers start with a few mutual funds and, if performance of the funds is satisfactory, offer new funds to round out the offerings of the adviser. For example, a stock management company with good investment results might introduce new fixed income and money market funds to create what is called a **family of funds.** Investors often prefer to purchase shares of funds from a single mutual fund organization in order to simplify record keeping and because costs are often lower if one stays within a given family of funds.

Clearly, there are many ways in which an investment management firm can decide what types of new funds they might offer to the public. All approaches, however, are based on the adviser finding a marketing niche that is not presently filled by other funds. Virtually all new fund offerings are based on a marketing strategy of the investment advisory firm.

Once the investment management firm has decided on the type of fund it intends to offer, a number of knowledgeable individuals are contacted and asked if they would be willing to act as the initial board of directors of the new fund. This board will then work with the investment firm to (1) incorporate the fund, (2) select a custodian who will be responsible for the receipt and disbursement of all cash and securities of the fund, (3) select accountants and legal counsel to the fund, (4) define the investment objectives and constraints of the fund, (5) negotiate the terms under which the investment management firm will be employed as the fund's investment adviser and (6) register the fund with the Securities Exchange Commission (SEC). The registration document that must be filed and approved by the SEC is called the **prospectus.**

The Mutual Fund Prospectus. A fund's prospectus contains information that is important to potential fund investors. Although the prospectus must be approved by staff of the SEC, approval means only that the prospectus provides accurate information about the fund's past history and discloses relevant information about investment policies, constraints, risks, costs, and so forth. Table 14-5 presents the table of contents of a recent prospectus together with comments about the material covered in each heading.

All potential fund investors should read and understand a fund's prospectus. In addition to the prospectus, funds file a "Statement of Additional Information" with the SEC that can be obtained from the fund.

Net Asset Values. After the prospectus has been approved by the SEC, the public may buy shares in the fund. However, whereas most corporations issue a fixed quantity of shares to the public that are then bought and sold in secondary markets, mutual funds are **open-end companies.** This means there is not a fixed number of shares outstanding. Investors who wish to purchase shares, purchase them directly from the company. Investors who wish to sell shares, sell (**redeem**) them directly with the company. As a result, the number of shares outstanding is open-end.

In order to facilitate the trading of shares between the fund and the public, all trades occur at net asset value. Net asset value is simply the per share market value of the shares at a particular point in time. For example, assume that after all securities markets are closed at the end of a day, the total market value of a mutual fund's assets is $150 million and the fund has $2 million in various liabilities. Then the total net asset value of the fund would be $148 million. This, of course, is also the total market value of the equity of the fund. If the fund has 8.0 million shares outstanding at that time, the net asset value per share would be $18.50. That is:

$$\text{Net Asset Value} = \text{NAV} = \frac{\text{Market Value of Assets minus Liabilities}}{\text{Number of Shares Outstanding}}$$

$$\$18.50 = \frac{\$150,000,000 - \$2,000,000}{8,000,000}$$

(14.1)

Any requests to purchase or redeem shares received by the fund during the day would be held until the fund's NAV at the end of the day is known. Then they would be transacted at that NAV. For example, assume that investors had sent $5 million in cash during the day to purchase shares, and requests to redeem 50,000 shares were also received during the day. Then 270,270.27027 new shares would be issued to investors wishing to buy shares:[13]

$$270,270.27027 = \frac{\$5,000,000}{\$18.50}$$

And $925,000 in cash would be delivered to the shareholders who had redeemed their shares:

$$\$925,000 = 50,000 \times \$18.50$$

---

[13] Mutual funds allow transactions in fractional shares so all trades can occur at net asset value.

TABLE 14-5 TABLE OF CONTENTS OF A MUTUAL FUND PROSPECTUS

Topic

Author's Comments

Prospectus Summary

Defines firm as a no-load trust consisting of 19 specific mutual funds. Includes a list of funds and their primary investments. Identifies major risks, investment advisory firm, and how shares can be purchased or redeemed.

Expense Information

States load fees to purchase or redeem shares. Annual operating expenses as percentage of average daily assets are identified for each fund. An example is shown of future expenses assuming a hypothetical annual return and redemption in one to ten years.

Financial Highlights

Yearly details of past changes in each fund's net asset value per share plus yearly returns, operating expense ratios, and investment income as percentage of assets.

Investment Objectives and Policies

Identifies types of investments and investment strategies used in each fund. Precise objectives are not actually specified.

Investment Restrictions

Identifies maximum percentage that can be invested in a given security or securities of a given issuer. Places limits on types and amount of fund borrowing.

Characteristics and Risks of Securities and Investment Techniques

Describes in detail different types of securities and investment techniques used by various funds.

Management of the Trust

Identifies members of the board of directors, the investment advisory firm, and portfolio manager of each fund. States advisory and administrative fees, service fees, other expenses, and expense limitations.

Purchase of Shares

Defines an "Institutional Class" and an "Administrative Class" of shares. Institutional shares are available to institutional investors and high net worth individuals. Administrative shares are offered through broker-dealers, retirement plan administrators, and other financial institutions. Minimum initial purchase and minimum subsequent purchases are stated.

Redemption of Shares

Request to redeem shares can be by mail, telephone, or other wire facility.

Continued

TABLE 14-5   TABLE OF CONTENTS OF A MUTUAL FUND PROSPECTUS

Portfolio Transactions

Transactions will be made in an attempt to seek the best price and execution of trades.

Net Asset Value

Defines how net asset value will be calculated.

Dividends, Distributions, and Taxes

To maintain the fund's tax-free status, the fund will distribute virtually all its income from dividends and interest earned during a year plus any realized capital gains. Such distributions will occur in the year in which the fund receives the gain.

Other Information

State of incorporation, shareholder voting rights, and general information about performance comparisons.

After these transactions, the fund's total net asset value would be $152,075,000, there would be 8,220,270.27027 shares outstanding, and the NAV would still be $18.50:

$$\text{NAV} = \frac{\$148,000,000 + \$5,000,000 - \$925,000}{8,000,000 + 270,270.27027 - 50,000}$$

$$\$18.50 = \frac{\$152,075,000}{8,220,270.27027}$$

Notice that all trades must occur at net asset value. If this were not the case, one party to the trade would win and another would lose. For example, if the fund required that new shares be purchased at NAV plus $X dollars, then new shareholders would be paying more per share than the shares are worth and the NAV of existing shareholders would increase when someone bought at NAV plus $X. Similarly, if new shareholders could purchase shares from the fund at a discount from NAV, then the new shareholder would be able to buy an asset for less than it is worth and existing shareholder's NAV would decline. *The only price at which trades with the fund can occur is the fund's NAV!*

Fund Operations. To understand the investment operations of mutual funds, it is helpful to examine the financial statements of a typical fund. Various financial statements of Vanguard Total Stock Portfolio are shown in Tables 14-6 through 14-9. This is an index mutual fund whose investment objective is to track the returns on a value-weighted portfolio of all actively traded stocks in the United States. It differs from actively managed stock mutual funds in the number of stocks owned and in the size of its yearly operating costs. In all other matters its operations are typical of other mutual funds.

A statement of net assets is shown in Table 14-6. This statement is similar to the balance sheet of other firms. At June 30, 1994, the Vanguard Total Stock Market Portfolio had assets with a market value of $650.8 million of which $630.7 million were invested in

TABLE 14-6   STATEMENT OF NET ASSETS VANGUARD TOTAL STOCK MARKET PORTFOLIO JUNE 30, 1994

ASSET MARKET VALUES:	($ 000)	LIABILITIES & EQUITY:	($000)
U.S. Treasury Bill	$ 594	Liabilities	$11,556
Repurchase Agreement	10,391		
Total	10,985		
		Equity:	
Other Assets	9,096	Paid in Capital	626,401
Common Stocks	630,729	Undistributed Net Investment Income	644
		Accumulated Net Realized Gains	1,440
		Unrealized Appreciation of Investments	10,769
		Total Equity	639,254
Total Assets	$650,810	Total Liabilities & Equity	$650,810
		Total Net Asset Value	$639,254
		Divided by shares outstanding	÷57,903.442
		Net Asset Value Per Share	$11.04

common stocks. Liabilities of the fund were $11.6 million, leaving a total net asset value owned by equity holders of $639.3 million. This equity capital consisted of the following:

Equity Component	($000)
Paid in Capital	$626,401
Funds paid to Vanguard for the purchase of shares.	
Undistributed Net Investment Income	644
Funds received in the form of interest and dividends on securities owned by the fund that have not yet been distributed to shareholders of the fund.	
Accumulated Net Realized Gains	1,440
Gains received on sales of securities that the fund has not yet distributed to shareholders of the fund.	
Unrealized Appreciation of Investments	10,769
Gains on securities purchased that have not yet been sold.	
Total Equity	$639,254

Mutual funds provide details of the fund's equity as shown here because they distribute virtually all **net investment income and accumulated net realized gains** to shareholders of the fund by the end of the fund's fiscal year. These distributions are made in order to avoid the payment of taxes by the fund. Taxes are discussed later. Since June 30 is not the fiscal year-end for Vanguard, the fund had net investment income ($644 million) and net realized gains ($1,440 million) that had not yet been distributed.

TABLE 14-7   STATEMENT OF OPERATIONS VANGUARD TOTAL STOCK MARKET PORTFOLIO SIX MONTHS ENDED JUNE 30, 1994

	($000)
Investment Income:	
Dividends	$7,141
Interest	252
Total Income	7,393
Expenses:	
Investment Advisory Services	45
Management and Administrative	374
Marketing and Distribution	72
Taxes (other than income taxes)	22
Custodian Fees	37
Auditing Fees	5
Shareholder Reports	28
Annual Meeting and Proxy Costs	6
Trustees' Fees and Expenses	1
Total Expenses	590
Net Investment Income	6,803
Realized Net Gains or Losses	
Investment Securities Sold	1,207
Futures Contracts	173
Total	1,380
Change in Unrealized Appreciation	
Investment Securities	(36,994)
Futures Contracts	(392)
Total	(37,386)
Net Increase (Decrease) in Net Assets Resulting from Operations	$(29,203)

Consider now the statement of operations shown in Table 14-7. This is similar to an income statement of other firms. During the first six months of 1994, the portfolio had received $7.393 million in dividends and interest on securities owned by the fund. Mutual funds refer to interest and dividend receipts as investment income. Various expenses of the fund totaled $590 million, leaving a *net investment income* of $6,803 million. To avoid taxes at the fund level, virtually all net investment income is distributed to shareholders by the end of the fund's fiscal year.

Increases or decreases in the market value of securities owned by a mutual fund are identified as being either *realized* or *unrealized*. Realized gains and losses represent changes in the value of a security from its purchase price that the fund has actually realized because the security was sold. Unrealized gains or losses represent price changes on securities not yet sold. For example, if a stock is bought at $50 and increases in value to $70, the fund will record a $20 unrealized gain if the stock is still owned. But if the stock

---

TABLE 14-8   VANGUARD TOTAL STOCK MARKET PORTFOLIO STATEMENT OF CHANGES IN NET ASSETS SIX MONTHS ENDED JUNE 30, 1994

INCREASE (DECREASE) IN NET ASSETS:	($000)
Operations:	
Net Investment Income	$ 6,803
Realized Net Gain (Loss)	1,380
Change in Unrealized Appreciation (Depreciation)	(37,386)
Net Increase (Decrease) Resulting from Operations	(29,203)
Distributions:	
Net Investment Income	(6,447)
Realized Net Gain	—
Total Distributions	(6,447)
Equalization Credits	330
Capital Share Transactions:	
Shares Issued	204,032
Shares Redeemed	(41,740)
Net Increase from Capital Share Transactions	162,292
Total Increase (Decrease)	126,972
Net Assets:	
Beginning of Period	$512,282
End of Period	$639,254

---

is sold, the $20 will be shown as a realized gain. Again, this accounting distinction is made because of tax considerations.

During the first six months of 1994, realized net gains or losses were $1,380 million. Since the equity account in the balance sheet shows accumulated net realized gains of $1,440 at June 30, the difference of $60 million must reflect realized gains from prior years that had not yet been distributed to shareholders. Similarly, the change in unrealized appreciation shown in the statement of operations was a negative $37,386 million. Since the equity account in the balance sheet shows a positive balance of unrealized appreciation equal to $10,769 at June 30, the unrealized appreciation at the start of the year would have been $48,155 ($37,386 plus $10,769).

Table 14-8 shows a statement of changes in net assets (total equity value) during the first six months of 1994. At the start of the year, total net asset value was $512.3 million. By June 30, this had decreased by $29.2 million due to operating losses and by $6.4 million due to the payments of dividends to firm shareholders. However, the sale of new shares brought $162.3 million in assets to the firm. By June 30, total net asset value of equity had increased to $639.3 million.

Finally, Table 14-9 provides details of change in per share NAV during the first six months of 1994. At the start of the year, NAV was $11.29. During the next six months, net investment income of $0.13 per share was received, of which $0.12 was distributed to share-

TABLE 14-9 VANGUARD TOTAL STOCK MARKET PORTFOLIO FINANCIAL HIGHLIGHTS SIX MONTHS ENDED JUNE 30, 1994

For a Share Outstanding Throughout the Period:	
Net Asset Value, Beginning of Period	$11.69
Investment Operations:	
Net Investment Income	0.13
Net Realized and Unrealized Gains (loss)	(0.66)
Total from Investment Operations	(0.53)
Distributions:	
Dividend on Net Investment Income	(0.12)
Distributions from Realized Capital Gains	—
Total Distributions	(0.12)
Net Asset Value, End of Period	$11.04

holders as income dividends. In addition, a general decrease in the market value of equities caused a net realized and unrealized loss on security holdings equal to $0.66 per share.

To summarize, mutual funds receive capital from shareholders who buy or sell fund shares at the fund's current net asset value. Shareholder capital is invested in securities that provide interest and dividends to the fund. Before this investment income is distributed to shareholders, it increases the value of fund assets as well as the fund's NAV. However, virtually all investment income is distributed to shareholders during the fiscal year in which it is received. Changes in the market value of securities that a fund purchases are designated as either realized or unrealized capital gains. Since virtually all realized capital gains are distributed to shareholders during the fund's fiscal year, the main reason for changes in NAV from year to year is unrealized capital gains or losses.

Taxation. Unlike most corporations, the profits of a mutual fund are taxed only when received by investors in the fund. This tax exemption is available if the fund qualifies as a regulated investment company under rules of the Internal Revenue Code. Here are the major requirements of the tax code:

■ The fund must distribute at least 90% of its investment income during its fiscal year as dividends to fund shareholders.

■ The fund must meet certain minimum diversification requirements.

■ The fund must receive more than 70% of its gross income (before operating expenses) from the sale of securities held for more than three months.

Shareholders of a fund pay ordinary income tax rates on fund distributions of investment income (net interest and dividend income received by the fund) as well as any net realized short-term capital gains. Shareholders pay capital gains tax rates on any net realized long-term capital gains. Any tax-exempt income received by a fund (such as interest payments on municipal bond issues) is generally exempt from tax when distributed to shareholders.[14]

For example, assume an investor has an ordinary income tax rate of 30% and a capital gains tax rate of 28%. Also assume that XYX Mutual Fund pays a per share income dividend of $1.00, a realized short-term capital gain dividend of $0.50, and a realized long-term capital gain dividend of $2.00. Then the per share taxes would be as follows:

Type of Dividend	Amount	×	Tax Rate	=	Taxes Due
Income Dividend	$1.00	×	0.30	=	$0.30
Short-Term Capital Gain Dividend	0.50	×	0.30	=	0.15
Long-Term Capital Gain Dividend	2.00	×	0.28	=	0.56
Total	$3.50				$1.01

Many investors unknowingly purchase shares of mutual funds just prior to the fund's distribution of dividends. In such a case, the shareholder will have to pay taxes on the dividends once they are distributed and find that their after-tax value of dividends plus the new share price is worth less than what they recently paid for the shares.

For example, assume you purchase a share of XYZ Fund at its NAV of, say, $13.50 just prior to the fund's payment of the three dividends shown here. Assuming the $3.50 in dividends were paid soon after you bought the shares, the fund's NAV would decline to $10.00 and you would receive the $3.50 in dividends. This looks okay. You paid $13.50 for something now worth $10.00, but you also have $3.50 in cash. Unfortunately, you will have to pay $1.01 in taxes on this cash, leaving you with $2.49 in cash. Thus, you paid $13.50 for something that is now only worth $12.49.

To guard against such events, potential shareholders should be aware of the amount of undistributed profits that a fund will likely pay in the near future.

Dividend Reinvestment. Most mutual funds allow investors to automatically reinvest dividends into new shares. In fact, some funds assume that shareholders wish to automatically reinvest dividends unless the fund is formally notified otherwise. Assume you own 200 shares of XYZ Fund when its NAV is $13.50. If the fund distributes $3.50 in dividends per share, you will receive $700 in dividends. At a new share price of $10, you could reinvest the $700 into 70 new shares ($700 ÷ $10). Thus, your share value would be $2,700 both before ($13.50 × 200) or after ($10 × 270) the dividend payment.

Taxes, however, must be paid on all taxable dividends distributed by mutual funds, even if they are reinvested in new shares of the fund.

Types of Mutual Funds

Mutual funds are vehicles that can be used to invest in various types of marketable securities. Most mutual funds invest in a specific asset class or segment of an asset class. This provides investors with the ability to choose funds that provide broad portfolio asset allocation.

---

[14] Interest on municipal bonds is exempt from federal income taxes. Municipal bond interest is also exempt from state income taxes if the bond is an obligation of a governmental unit within the state. Interest on bonds domiciled in other states is subject to state income taxes.

Mutual funds invest in virtually all types of actively traded securities. There are only three practical limits on the type of securities in which they trade.

1. Mutual funds trade mainly in securities that are actively traded in public markets. This is necessary in order to calculate accurate net asset values at the end of each day and to assure reasonable liquidity in case securities must be sold to meet unexpected share redemptions. For example, mutual funds rarely hold privately placed securities because accurate estimates of the value of these securities are not available. Similarly, shares of small companies in emerging markets are generally not held, since they have poor liquidity.
2. Mutual funds limit ownership of securities in countries that have regulations on withdrawal of capital from the country. Again, this is necessary to maintain liquidity to meet unexpected share redemptions.
3. Some countries limit foreign investment in securities domiciled in the country.

There are many ways of classifying mutual funds. Table 14-10 shows the fund categories presently used in Morningstar Mutual Funds, a widely used source of data on mutual funds. Most mutual funds are part of a family of funds. These are funds offered by a single investment management company. As we noted earlier in the chapter, it is often cheaper to purchase funds from a given family of funds because of reduced fees associated with switching from one member of the family to another.

Investors in Mutual Funds. Although mutual funds were originally created to provide small investors with inexpensive and convenient access to broadly diversified portfolios that are professionally managed, they have also become popular with institutional investors. For example, at the end of 1994, approximately 40% of equity and bond funds in the United States were owned by institutional investors. The largest share of these institutional funds came from retirement plans and insurance companies. Retirement funds consisted of investments made by both defined benefit and defined contribution plans (such as 401(k) plans).

To appeal to both individual and institutional clients, mutual funds have begun to offer different classes of shares on a given commingled portfolio. Institutional investments in a fund are much larger per investor than are individual investments. Thus, institutional share classes are usually charged lower administrative fees. Both classes of shares have a claim to the same commingled portfolio and earn identical rates of return before fund expenses are allocated. But because they incur different fund expenses, they trade at different net asset values.

How Investors Purchase Mutual Funds

Historically, investors purchased mutual funds in one of two ways: through a security broker or directly from the fund. In recent years, due to a gaining popularity of the funds, a variety of new distribution channels have emerged. These include discount brokerage firms, which act as a "supermarket" for many families of funds, organizations that offer funds through their defined contribution plans, the growing profession of financial planners, and a portfolio investment strategy offered by brokers known as a wrap account. Each are discussed here.

When an investor buys a fund through a security broker, the investor is charged a fee called **a load fee.** For example, if the load fee is 6.0% and the investor has $10,000 to invest, then the load commission is $600 (0.06 times $10,000), and the remaining $9,400 is

TABLE 14-10 MORNINGSTAR MUTUAL FUND CATEGORIES

Aggressive Growth: Seek rapid growth of capital, often invest in IPOs and emerging market companies, buy stocks with high price-to-earnings and price-to-book ratios.

Asset Allocation: Income and capital appreciation are dual goals; shift between stocks, bonds, and cash based on analysis of business trends.

Balanced: Mixture of fixed income and stocks; typically do not adjust mix in anticipation of business trends.

Convertible Bond: Invest in bonds and preferred stock that is convertible into common stock.

Corporate Bond—General: Seek income by investing in diversified corporate bonds, primarily investment-grade bonds.

Corporate Bond—High Quality: Invest large percentage in very high-quality (low default risk) corporate bonds.

Corporate Bond—High Yield: Invest major portions in bonds with default ratings of BBB or lower. Prices of bonds are generally affected more by condition of underlying company than by interest rates.

Diversified Emerging Markets: Diversified equity positions of stocks in emerging markets; do not specialize in any single region.

Equity Income: Purchase stocks with high dividend yields.

Europe Stock: Major holdings of European stocks.

Foreign Stock: Primarily in stocks of countries other than the United States.

Government Bond—Adjustable Rate Mortgage: Invest in mortgage-related securities with adjustable coupons, usually backed by U.S. government.

Government Bond—General: Diversified portfolios of Treasuries, agencies, and mortgage-backed securities.

Government Bond—Mortgages: Invest almost exclusively in mortgage-backed securities backed by government agencies.

Government Bond—Treasury: Major portion in U.S. Treasury bonds.

Growth: Pursue stocks with high price growth potential; little concern for current income.

Growth and Income: Stocks with a balance of price growth and dividend income.

Multiasset Global: Various combinations of equities, bonds, and cash instruments of both U.S. and non-U.S. securities.

Multisector Bond: Invest in U.S. government obligations, foreign bonds, and high-yield domestic debt.

Municipal Bond—National: Invest in municipal bonds of any state.

Municipal Bond—Single State: Invest in municipal bonds of a single state.

Pacific Stock: Invest in equities of countries in the Pacific Rim, including Japan, China, Hong Kong, Malaysia, Singapore, New Zealand, and Australia.

Short-Term World Income: Invest in bonds with maturities of three years or less of countries around the world. May engage in substantial currency hedging.

Small Company: Invest in stocks of companies with a capitalization of $1 billion or less; usually no dividend income is paid on such stocks.

Specialty: Funds that invest in defined industries such as health care, financial, natural resources, and real estate.

invested in fund shares at the fund's NAV. Notice that the effective cost is actually 6.38%, since $600 is charged to purchase $9,400 worth of securities. The maximum legal load fee today is 8 1/2%. Most brokers charge much lower fees, however, due to recent competition among load fee funds. Usually about one-half of the load fee goes to the broker who makes the sale. The remainder is split between the firm for which the broker works and other parties involved in distributing the shares of the fund.

Load funds can be identified in the financial press as those that have price quotes for both the fund's NAV and an offering price. For example, if the NAV of a fund is shown as $20 and the offer price is $21.28, the fund is a load fund with a 6% load fee ($1.28 ÷ $21.28). Load fees shown in the financial press are usually the maximum load that would be charged for small transactions. As the value of the transaction increases, the size of the load will decrease and can even be waived for very large trades. As an example, Table 14-11 shows the load fee schedule of a fund published in the fund's prospectus. We discuss load fees more thoroughly later in the chapter when we examine the costs of fund ownership.

Investors can also buy shares directly from many mutual funds without paying a load fee. These are called **no-load** funds. No-load funds are not sold by security brokers, since the brokers do not receive any compensation for their advice to investors. Instead, investors in no-load funds must conduct their own analysis of which fund might be best for them. This is not a difficult task if the investor has a basic understanding of mutual fund investing. Most sources of information on mutual funds provide a wide variety of information on both load and no-load funds.

TABLE 14-11   ILLUSTRATION OF LOAD FEE CHARGES

Size of Investment	Sales Charge(1)	Sales Charge(2)	Reallowed to Dealers (2)
Less than $10,000	6.95%	6.50%	6.00%
$10,000 but less than $25,000	6.38%	6.00%	5.50%
$25,000 but less than $50,000	5.5%	5.25%	4.75%
$50,000 but less than $100,000	4.71%	4.50%	4.25%
$100,000 but less than $250,000	3.90%	3.75%	3.50%
$250,000 but less than $500,000	2.04%	2.00%	1.75%
$500,000 but less than $1,000,000	1.01%	1.00%	0.80%
$1,000,000 and over	0.00(3)	0.00(3)	0.00(4)

(1) As a percentage of net amount invested.
(2) As a percentage of public offering price
(3) No sale charge is payable on investments of $1 million or more. However, a contingent-deferred sales charge of 0.80% on the lessor of purchase or reemption price is imposed if, within one year of purchase, a redemption reduces the account value to less than the original investment. Such contingent deferred sales charge is withheld from redemption proceeds and paid to the distributor.
(4) The distributor may pay a dealer concession for orders of $1 million or more. The terms are negotiated when the order is placed.

Note: The distributor of a fund is the principal underwriter of the fund and oversees all purchases and sales of the fund. Usually, the distributor will be legally associated with the investment management company that is also acting as the investment adviser to the fund.

In recent years, many discount brokerage firms have begun to offer a large number of funds to their clients without any load charges. These include funds which, if not traded through the discount broker, may or may not include a load fee. The discount brokers make arrangements with many families of funds to act as a distributor of their funds and, as a result, are able to offer so many funds that they are often referred to as fund **supermarkets.** The discount brokers, of course, do not provide such services simply as a courtesy to their customers. To get "shelf space" in these supermarkets, the funds usually pay the brokerage firm 0.25% of assets each year. Thus, the costs of buying a load fund are shifted from a onetime commission paid at the date of purchase to an ongoing annual fee. But even though fund purchases through such fund supermarkets do involve a cost, the cost could be much lower than standard front-end load charges.

Another way to purchase mutual funds is through a defined contribution plan sponsored by an employer. Because contributions to retirement savings plans as well as the investment earnings on such plans are not taxed (within legal limits), this is often the best way to invest in mutual funds. In addition, investments made through defined contribution plans typically incur no investment load fees.

Mutual funds are also selected and bought through the services of financial planners. The role of the financial planner is to review all aspects of an individual's financial situation. This includes a long-range financial budget, selection of appropriate investments, tax considerations, and evaluation of insurance needs. Financial planners are paid for their services through commissions received on products that they sell to clients (such as load fees on mutual funds) or through cash payments made by the client. Most independent professionals believe that financial planners can be more objective if they are compensated directly by the client as opposed to through commissions received on products they sell.

In recent years, a new service has been created by brokerage firms called **wrap accounts.** In a wrap account, the broker selects a number of investment management firms that will be responsible for managing the portfolio of a client. Instead of selecting individual stocks and bonds for the client, the client's investment portfolio is allocated to a number of professional managers. The benefits are that the funds are broadly diversified and professionally managed. In addition, costs of the plan are known ahead of time and "wrapped up" into a single yearly charge to the investor. Although many wrap accounts use managers that are not mutual funds, mutual fund wrap accounts are common. The problem with wrap accounts are the costs, currently at about 3% per year. Although 3% might seem like a small amount to pay for all services of investment management, direct ownership of mutual funds that follow active investment strategies generally costs 0.6% to 1.25% a year. And passive index mutual funds can be purchased that cost as little as 0.25% a year.

Costs of Owning Mutual Funds

The two principal costs involved in owning a mutual fund are transaction costs and operating expenses of the fund.

Transaction Costs. Transaction costs refer to fees paid when one buys or sells a fund. They can include the following:

- **Load fees.** As we already noted, these are commissions paid when shares of a fund are purchased (hence the term "front-end" load). Load fees for small investors can be as large as 8 1/2%, although 6.0% is currently a typical load fee. "Low load funds" charge fees of about 3%. Load fees represent compensation to a broker or other adviser for their time spent in identifying the fund(s) that would be appropriate for a given investor.

Some funds also charge load fees on dividends that are reinvested in the fund!

- ✖ **Deferred sales loads.** These are fees charged when shares are sold. Deferred sales charges usually decrease the longer one owns a fund. Often deferred sales charges will be used instead of front-end load fees.

- ✖ **Redemption fees.** These are similar to deferred sales charges but apply to a much shorter time period, usually 30 to 60 days. Redemption fees are imposed to discourage active fund trading. Redemption fees are not paid to a security broker, but are returned to the assets of a fund to compensate remaining shareholders for the costs associated with the share redemption.

How costly is the load fee? Some argue that, when the load fee is spread over a lengthy investment horizon, the annualized fee is well worth the advice of one's broker or financial adviser. Others counter that future wealth can be substantially higher without the load. Consider this example: $10,000 can be invested at date 0 in a no-load fund or a 6% load fund. Assume the compound annualized return over the next ten years is 9% for both funds. The calculations here show the outcomes from these alternatives:

	Load Fund	No-Load Fund
Initial fund investment	($10,000 − $600)	$10,000
Compounded at 9% for Ten Years	1.09^{10}	1.09^{10}
Year 10 Value	$22,253	$23,674
Compound Annual Rate of Return	($22,253 ÷ $10,000)$^{1/10}$ = 1 = 8.33%	= 9.0% by definition

In terms of an annualized 10-year cost, the load fund costs 0.67% per year (9.0% − 8.33%). Notice, however, that the year 10 value is still 6% lower with the load fund.

The decision to select a load or no-load fund depends on whether or not the investor wishes to rely on the advice of a professional security broker. For investors with little knowledge and time, load fees are probably reasonable costs of investing. But investors who have the interest and time to learn about alternative funds should trade only no-load funds.

While there are many load funds that have had much better than average return performance in the past, there have also been about an equal number of no-load funds with similar performance. Load fee status and fund performance are not related.

Operating Costs. Operating costs are costs associated with management of the fund. With the exception of brokerage fees paid in trading securities owned by the fund, all operating costs are summarized in a fund's **operating expense ratio.** The operating expense ratio is calculated as the sum of all yearly operating expenses divided by the average daily

TABLE 14-12   ILLUSTRATIVE MANAGEMENT FEES OF ACTIVELY MANAGED MUTUAL FUNDS

Fund Type	Maximum Management Fee			Minimum Management Fee		
	Average	Minimum	Maximum	Average	Minimum	Maximum
U.S. Treasuries	0.36%	0.20%	0.50%	0.26%	0.12%	0.40%
Municipal Bonds	0.56	0.30	0.75	0.48	0.25	0.75
Short Term World Bond	0.56	0.28	0.75	0.55	0.12	0.75
World Bond	0.65	0.35	0.9	0.55	0.19	0.9
U.S. Corp Bond	0.55	0.30	0.75	0.44	0.18	0.70
Growth Stock	0.73	0.39	2.00	0.52	0.19	1.00
Aggressive Growth Stock	0.91	0.5	2.00	0.78	0.35	2.00
Small Company Stock	0.91	0.35	1.50	0.75	0.35	1.50
World Stock	0.92	0.75	1.00	0.83	0.45	1.00

SOURCE: Developed by the author using a sample of funds presented in Morningstar Mutual Funds.

assets of the fund. Expenses included in the operating expense ratio consist of the following:

■ **Management advisory fees.** These are fees paid to the investment adviser of the fund. Advisory fees are usually based on the total assets being managed. For example, a 1% advisory fee on $100 million of assets would generate a management advisory expense to the fund (which would be a revenue to the investment management firm) of $1 million. Advisory fees are often scaled so that the fee decreases with the dollar amount of assets being managed.

The size of advisory fees depends on (1) the types of assets being managed, (2) the investment strategy used, and (3) past performance of the adviser. Table 14-12 shows typical advisory fees for various types of mutual funds. Since most funds state a maximum and minimum management fee, the table provides information on both maximum and minimum fees. For example, the average maximum and minimum fees charged to manage U.S. Treasuries were 0.36% and 0.26% of net asset value. In contrast, the average maximum and minimum fees charged to manage world stock portfolios were 0.92% and 0.83%. If you look closely at the table, you will notice how variable the management fee charges can be within a given fund type. For example, for the growth stock group, the lowest fee was 0.19% and the largest was 2.00%!

■ **General management expenses.** These consist of the costs associated with accounting, security custody, shareholder reporting, and other general costs of operations.

■ **12b-1 Fees.** The designation "12b-1" refers to a section of the SEC regulations that allows the management of a mutual fund to pay for various advertising expenditures from the assets of the mutual fund. The maximum legal 12b-1 fee is 0.75% of assets. But the typical fee does not exceed 0.25% of assets, and many funds charge no 12b-1 fees. There is considerable controversy over 12b-1 charges. Opponents argue that advertising payments made from assets of the fund reduce the value of existing shareholders' NAVs and are harmful to current shareholders. Proponents argue that the fees are intended to bring new shareholders and assets to the fund, which will increase total fund assets and result in lower per share operating costs due to economies of scale. To date, there have been no rigorous studies showing that proponents are correct.

The definition of advertising costs allowable under the 12b-1 framework is quite broad. In fact, many mutual fund companies use 12b-1 fees to pay yearly fees to brokers whose customers have remained with the fund or to pay discount brokers that include the fund in the brokerage firm's "supermarket" of mutual funds. Payments to brokers of 12b-1 fees are referred to as **trailers.** For many brokers, yearly trailers from 12b-1 fees can be substantial. For example, assume a broker has placed $100 million of the assets of a pension fund invested with mutual funds that pay the broker a 0.25% trailer. This represents an income to the broker of $250,000 per year.[15]

As noted, all operating expenses (except for fund brokerage fees) are shown in a fund's operating expense ratio. These include management advisory fees, general management expenses, and 12b-1 fees. Table 14-13 shows the distribution of recent operating expenses for a variety of fund types. The 50th percentile represents the expense ratio for which one-half of the funds have a lower ratio and one-half have a larger ratio. The 25th percentile represents the point at which one-quarter of the funds have a lower ratio and three-quarters have higher ratios.

Generally, the size of a fund's expense ratio depends on the dollar value of assets managed and the type of assets managed. Due to economies of scale, expense ratios decline as the value of assets being managed increases. And actively managed equity funds generally cost more to manage than actively managed bond funds.

Fund Brokerage Expenses. Mutual fund investors also pay for brokerage fees that the investment adviser incurs in trading fund securities. Brokerage fees paid by mutual funds on a per security basis are usually much lower than an individual investor would pay due to the size of fund trades. For example, a small individual investor might pay $0.20 per share to trade a stock whereas a fund would typically pay $0.01 to $0.06 per share to trade

---

[15] This is not an unusual example. Many pension funds invest in mutual funds (which pay 12b-1 fees to the broker) on the advice of the broker. Unfortunately, many investors are unaware of the existence of 12b-1 trailer fees.

TABLE 14-13   ILLUSTRATIVE MUTUAL FUND EXPENSE RATIOS

Equity Mutual Funds

Percentile	Aggressive Growth	Growth	Growth & Income	Income	Small Company	World Stock
10	1.01%	0.83%	0.58%	0.67%	1.04%	0.97%
25	1.17	0.97	0.78	0.79	1.24	1.49
50	1.55	1.21	1.10	0.98	1.49	1.75
75	1.75	1.64	1.23	1.38	1.70	2.29
90	3.05	2.26	1.53	1.88	2.23	2.58
Minimum	0.83	0.75	0.28	0.42	0.64	0.72
Maximum	4.09	3.50	2.60	2.26	2.95	3.47

Bond Mutual Funds

Percentile	Corporate General	Corporate High Yield	Government General	Government Mortgage
10	0.67%	0.31%	0.70%	0.44%
25	0.81	0.50	0.80	0.52
50	1.00	0.80	1.07	0.82
75	1.20	0.97	1.44	0.98
90	1.50	1.17	1.95	1.16
Minimum	0.49	0.16	0.49	0.25
Maximum	1.94	2.04	2.24	1.93

SOURCE: Developed by the author using data presented in Morningstar Mutual Funds.

the stock. However, if the investment adviser actively trades fund securities, transaction costs can be fairly large.[16]

Fund trading costs are not reported as an explicit cost of fund management. Instead, they are included in the price at which a security is bought or sold. While some funds provide estimates of trading costs in annual reports, trading costs are difficult to measure. For example, many NASDAQ stocks are traded without identifiable brokerage fees. Instead, the fee is included in the security's bid-ask spread. And market impact costs associated with trading large blocks are almost impossible to measure accurately.

The best guide to how large a fund's transaction costs might be is probably the **turnover ratio** of the fund. *Turnover* is defined as the value of securities bought or sold (whichever is the less) during a given period divided by the average total asset value of the fund during the period. For example, if the average assets of a fund are $100 million during a year and the fund bought $60 million of securities during the year and sold $50 million, the turnover ratio would be 50%. Managers would interpret a 50% annual turnover as owning a typical security for two years.

---

[16] Trading costs also include bid-ask spreads and market impact costs.

Index Funds. The operating costs of passively managed mutual funds are, of course, considerably lower than actively managed funds. For example, U.S. equity index funds generally have operating expenses equal to 0.50% of assets or lower. The oldest equity index fund, Vanguard 500 Portfolio, usually has operating expenses of 0.25% or less. There are few purely passive bond mutual funds or international equity mutual funds. However, investment companies do offer such commingled passive portfolios in non-mutual fund form to institutional clients. Since operating ratios of such funds are not public data, we are unable to report them here.

Loss of a Tax-Timing Option. When individuals personally manage their portfolios, they are able to engage in security trades that can reduce their tax payments. The basic tax strategy is to delay realization of taxable capital gains and hasten realization of taxable capital losses. For example, if a security has gone up in value since it was purchased, selling it would create a realized capital gain subject to immediate taxation. However, if the security is not sold, its capital gain remains unrealized for tax purposes and would not be taxed. Similarly, if a security has gone down in value since it was purchased, selling it would create a realized taxable loss that would reduce taxes.

Of course, taxes on capital gains will eventually have to be paid if the investor intends to liquidate the portfolio to meet future consumption needs. And any tax reductions taken today from realized capital losses generally result in higher future taxes. But proper tax management can benefit the investor by the time value of money associated with current tax reductions. The opportunity to manage a portfolio in order to minimize taxes is referred to as the **tax timing option.**

The value of this tax timing option is lost if one invests with a manager who gives no consideration to the investor's tax situation. This is generally the case with mutual funds. The mutual fund manager is running money for a very diverse group of individuals and institutions and simply can not fine-tune investment trades in a manner that minimizes taxes for each fund investor. Although the lost tax timing option is not as easy to identify as load fees and operating expenses, it is a clear expense incurred by investors who pay taxes.

Benefits of Mutual Fund Investing

We listed many of the benefits of owning mutual funds in Chapter 3. It is useful to review them here and introduce a few advantages not previously presented:

■ **Diversification.** Investing in professionally managed portfolios can provide portfolio diversification in two ways. First, investing in a single fund can provide diversification across a large number of securities within a given asset class. For example, the purchase of an international equity fund provides ownership of a large number of stocks domiciled in countries other than the United States. Similarly, purchase of a domestic bond fund provides ownership of a large number of domestic bonds. Second, ownership of funds that invest in different asset classes provides diversification across asset classes. For example, purchasing both an international equity fund and a domestic bond fund provides diversification gains from investing in multiple asset classes. As we noted earlier in the chapter, *mutual funds are not an asset class, they are a vehicle for taking diversified positions in asset classes.*

- **Low portfolio management costs.** While mutual funds incur costs that fund shareholders pay, these costs are usually much lower than investors would incur if they were to personally manage the portfolio. For example, trading costs and cost of security custody are much lower at the fund level due to economies of scale. Even management advisory fees are a good deal when compared with the time and costs that an individual would spend in personally selecting securities to buy and sell.

- **Access to world security markets.** By trading through mutual funds, investors gain access to security markets around the world. For example, an investor with $10,000 to invest would find it difficult to trade in most large denomination money market securities, mortgage-backed securities and securities traded in foreign countries. This is an advantage of using professional managers that is often not fully appreciated. By using mutual funds, the investor has access to virtually any security traded in world markets.

- **Ease of portfolio administration.** The records required to trade mutual funds are much fewer than if one were to personally trade individual stocks and bonds. In addition, all securities are held by the mutual fund's custodian, who assures that all dividends and interest payments are received on time.

- **Continuous accurate return comparisons.** Mutual funds report the returns they earn and compare them with relevant investment benchmarks so the investor can judge the fund's investment performance. If the investor were to manage the portfolio personally, these comparisons would be difficult to develop.

- **Investment liquidity.** The market value of fund shares can be turned into cash within a single day by a simple phone call or fax to the mutual fund. Even shares of funds that invest in inactively traded small stocks or emerging security markets can be quickly redeemed.

- **Professional management.** Although the value of active investment management is hotly debated among investment professionals, the returns that mutual funds provide are probably equal to or better than what most individuals could obtain on their own. At the least, mutual fund managers are less likely to do something rash in reaction to an unexpected market event.

- **Special fund investment programs.** Most fund companies offer a variety of services designed to make mutual fund investing convenient to investors. These include checking accounts, accumulation plans that regularly transfer funds from the investor's bank account to the fund, withdrawal plans that regularly sell fund shares and transfer the funds to the investor's bank account, automatic reinvestment of dividends, and free transfer of funds from one fund in a family of funds to another fund.

Mutual funds also provide a value to society as a whole. By providing the advantages just listed, individuals invest a greater portion of their wealth in securities than they would if the funds did not exist. This increases the supply of capital to financial markets and reduces the cost of capital to security issuers. This increased savings, of course, leads to greater capital expansion and standards of living.

Sources of Mutual Fund Information

Given their growing popularity with investors, it is not surprising that there are a large number of sources of information about mutual funds. Most financial newspapers provide current information about mutual fund prices and carry regular features on mutual fund investing. Financial magazines also provide rankings of past fund performance and interview managers about the strategies they pursue.

One of the best sources of information about mutual funds traded in the United States is presented in Morningstar Mutual Funds. Morningstar provides both hard-copy information and computerized data on CD-ROMs. An illustration of a Morningstar hard-copy report is shown in Figure 14-4. It is worth some time to examine this figure closely, since there is a lot of useful data.

For example, the graph at the top right of the figure provides information about the fund's load status, current NAV, total assets managed, and investment objective. Below this are style boxes that indicate the types of securities in which the fund invests relative to other funds. During the period shown, Neuberger & Berman Partners fund owned medium capitalization stocks with a "value" orientation (low price-to-book and price-to-earnings ratios). Investment performance in the graph is shown for 12 years. The solid line represents the growth of an investment in the S&P 500 index, and the dotted line shows the growth of an investment in the fund. Boxes below the graph show the yearly quartile performance of the fund using growth funds as the objective.

The only serious problem with information services such as Morningstar is that there are so many funds with so much data provided on each that there is an information overload. This is where computerized data sources, such as Morningstar's CD-ROM product, are useful. The value of CD-ROM data is that it can be rapidly screened for funds that meet certain investment criteria. For example, assume you wish to know all funds with an operating expense ratio of less than 0.7% that invest in growth stocks having an average price-to-earnings ratio less than 12. Using Morningstar's CD-ROM program, such a listing can be developed in less than 15 seconds.

A number of other computerized mutual fund services are listed in the references to this chapter.

Closed-End Funds

In contrast to open-end funds, a closed-end fund does not stand ready to buy or sell shares in the fund. Instead, transactions in closed-end shares occur between two market participants trading in the secondary markets, just as for any other common stock. The only time a closed-end fund is directly affected by market transactions is when the shares are initially offered to the public in the primary offering. Brokerage fees identical to those of other common stocks are paid at purchase and sale.

Closed-end funds are widely used in countries such as Germany, France, and the United Kingdom. However, the United States has been dominated by open-end funds since the 1950s.

Recently, closed-end funds have seen a resurgence in the United States with the formation of many "country funds." Country funds invest in securities of non-U.S. countries, usually investing in equities of a single country. Country funds select a closed-end organizational form,

FIGURE 14-4   ILLUSTRATION OF MORNINGSTAR

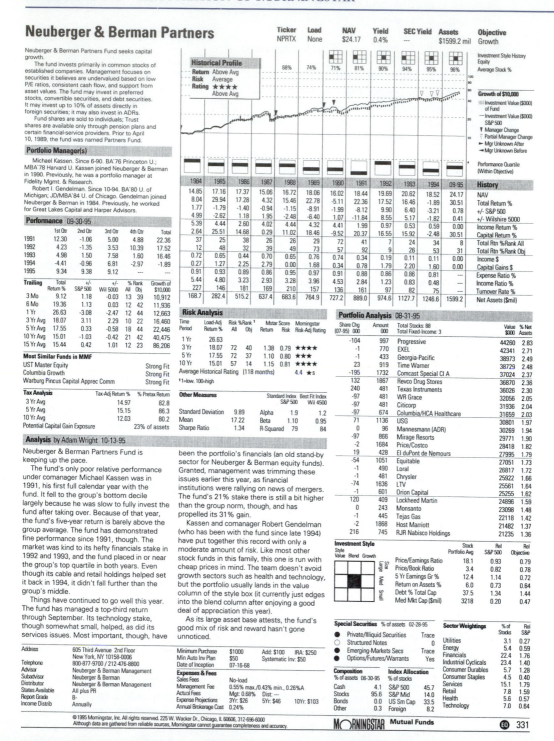

SOURCE: Morningstar Mutual Funds, October 27, 1995, Chicago: Morningstar Inc.

since the assets of the foreign country are often difficult to liquidate and return to the United States. Thus, it might be difficult for fund managers to meet share redemption demands if the fund was open end.

Real estate investment trusts (known as REITs) are similar to standard closed-end investment companies except they are limited to investments in real estate-related assets and make considerable use of borrowing to finance asset holdings. There are three major types of real estate investment trusts. Mortgage trusts invest in packages of mortgages on commercial and residential property as well as in construction and development loans to real estate developers.

During the middle 1970s and late 1980s many of the loans made by mortgage trusts defaulted, resulting in insufficient cash flow to meet their own debt obligations. When their stock prices dropped precipitously, many firms elected to switch their legal status to standard real estate companies, and some went bankrupt. Equity trusts take an equity interest in commercial property, such as shopping centers, office buildings, and so forth. They, too, suffered from many of the problems associated with mortgage trusts, but, on the whole, fared better. Finally, hybrid trusts represent combinations of both equity and mortgage trust assets.

Most real estate investment trusts were initially formed by large banks and insurance companies with a background in real estate lending and investment. Unfortunately, the types of assets in which they invested provided little diversification to protect against shocks within the economy, and many trusts were poorly managed. Real estate investment trusts represent a reasonable way to enter the real estate market, but because of the amount of their inherent diversifiable risk they should represent only a portion of a person's total investment portfolio.

Premiums and Discounts

The major difference between closed-end funds and mutual funds is that closed-end funds trade in secondary markets at prices different from their net asset values (NAVs).[17] Some funds (such as country funds) trade at prices substantially higher than NAV—that is, at premiums. Other funds (such as U.S. equity funds) trade at prices substantially lower than NAV—that is, at discounts. And others (principally bond funds) trade at prices close to NAV. The size of discounts and premiums are illustrated in Figure 14-5.

Although the existence of discounts and premiums has been studied extensively, no definitive explanations have emerged. Potential explanations that have been offered include the following:

◼ **Buying a tax liability.** Many closed-end funds hold securities purchased at prices lower than current market values. If the fund were to "realize" the gain for tax purposes by selling the securities, fund shareholders would be subject to a tax payment. For example, say you are in a 30% tax bracket and purchase a closed-end fund for $50. The fund then sells a security in which it had an unrealized appreciation of $10 per share and distributes the $10 to you as a capital gain dividend. After paying taxes, you have $7 cash-in-pocket and a share worth $40. For a price of $50, you now have wealth worth $47. Proponents of the tax-liability argument state that closed-end funds trade at discounts to reflect the potential tax loss in value.

There are a number of problems with this explanation. For example, it does not explain the existence of premiums. Also, you can eliminate the tax liability above by selling the shares at $40 and realize a $10 offsetting loss. Finally, no

---

[17] When originally issued to the public in a primary offering, the public pays NAV plus a commission to purchase shares.

FIGURE 14-5   ILLUSTRATION OF CLOSED-END FUND DISCOUNTS AND PREMIUMS

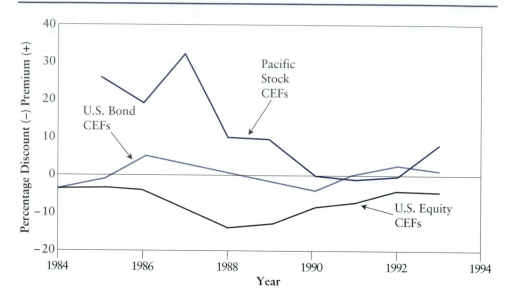

statistical tie has been found between the size of a closed-end fund's unrealized appreciation and its discount.

■ **Performance.** This explanation states that premiums and discounts are caused by investor perceptions of management ability. Fund managers who are believed to be better than average will command premiums and vice versa. While there is some evidence that this might be true, the evidence explains very little variability in discounts and has not yet been tested against country funds.

■ **Operating costs.** This explanation states that discounts reflect the present value of future operating costs. Assume that security markets are efficient such that the market values of shares owned by a fund are "correct". If costs are to be incurred in fund management, then closed-end fund shares will trade at a value lower than NAV equal to the present value of expected future operating costs. The problems with this argument are that open-end funds are not penalized for such operating costs and closed-end fund costs are essentially the same as open-end fund costs. Also, the argument does not explain why premiums exist.

■ **Investor sentiment.** Some recent research claims that discounts change over time due to changes in demand by small, relatively uninformed investors. Larger, more informed investors who might invest in closed-end funds face a price uncertainty associated with unpredictable shifts in future small investor demand. This uncertainty is in addition to the inherent market risk of the closed-end fund security portfolio. To induce larger investors to own closed-end shares, a price inducement in the form of a discount must be offered. Lee, Shleiffer, and Taylor offer empirical tests that they claim validate this explanation. Their evidence, however, is debatable, and the particular investor sentiment theory they develop does not explain why premiums exist.

- **Broker effort.** This explanation is as follows: Premiums and discounts are created by investor demand or lack of it. The level of demand is determined largely by broker advice. Since brokers receive larger commissions on mutual funds, they will push mutual funds and not push closed-end funds, which creates a tendency for a discount to exist.

    Proponents of efficient markets would argue that this explanation would not hold in a rational market and that discounts or premiums from NAV arise due to a rational cause and not simply due to the commission rate schedule of brokers. This hypothesis, however, is difficult to test empirically, since broker efforts cannot be accurately measured.

- **Liquidity.** This explanation states that the market price of traded securities consists of three elements: (1) the present value of future expected cash flows to be paid by the security, plus (2) the value of an option to rebalance (sell) one's holdings in a perfectly frictionless market, less (3) the present value of future expected transaction costs associated with this security, since trading is not costless.

Consider a closed-end fund to be a bottle into which marketable securities are placed. If it is more costly to trade the bottle in secondary markets than it is to trade the individual securities in the bottle, then the closed-end fund (the bottle) will trade at a price less than the NAV of securities held. Similarly, if the bottle is less costly to trade, then a premium over NAV will be paid.

Casual evidence is consistent with this explanation. For example, closed-end funds that invest in U.S. equities are much less actively traded than the securities held by such closed-end funds. Thus, a discount from NAV would be reasonable. In addition, it is much easier for U.S. investors to acquire shares of closed-end fund country funds than to acquire the underlying securities held by the fund. In this case, a premium would be reasonable. To date, only one study has explicitly evaluated this liquidity hypothesis. Interestingly, the results suggested that liquidity could, in fact, be a determinant of closed-end discounts and premia.

S U M M A R Y

In this chapter we examined the professional investment management industry. There are the key concepts:

- Professional investment management services are offered by commercial banks, insurance firms, and investment counsel companies. If a portfolio is physically segregated from other managed funds, it is called a separate account. If the money is pooled with investments of others into a single common fund, it is called a commingled fund.

- Investment management companies offer separate account and commingled portfolios to both institutional and individual investors. In the United States, managed portfolios offered to the general public must be registered with the Securities Exchange Commission. Two types of publicly available investment companies are sold to the general public: mutual funds and closed-end funds.

■ Mutual funds are open-end investment companies in that shares are directly bought from and sold to the fund at net asset value (NAV) per share. When share purchases exceed share redemptions, total outstanding shares of the fund increase. When net share redemptions are incurred, total outstanding shares of the fund decline.

■ After the initial public offering of shares in a closed-end fund, future purchases and sales take place in normal secondary markets between a public buyer and a public seller. Secondary trading prices almost always occur at discounts or premiums from the closed-end fund's net asset value per share. The reason for such discounts and premiums are not well understood.

■ To avoid income taxes at the fund level, virtually all interest and dividends (after operating costs) are distributed to fund shareholders as "income" dividends in the year received. Realized capital gains are also distributed in the form of a capital gain dividend. As a result, net asset values change due to profits or losses associated with unrealized price changes in asset values.

■ Mutual fund investors should read the prospectus of a fund before purchasing it to become familiar with the fund's investment objective, trading strategies, and constraints as well as fund expenses. These expenses consist of transaction fees (such as load charges) and general operating costs. General operating costs are summarized in a fund's operating expense ratio.

R E V I E W   P R O B L E M

Consider the following market value balance sheet of ABC Mutual Fund.

ABC MUTUAL FUND MARKET VALUE BALANCE SHEET (IN $ MILLIONS) CLOSE OF TRADING, SEPTEMBER 8

Assets:		Liabilities:	
Cash Equivalents	$15.0	Accounts payable	$1.0
Bond Investments	10.0	Salaries Payable	0.5
Common Stocks	80.0	Equity (5 million shares)	103.5
Total	$105.0	Total	$105.0

a. What is this fund's net asset value (NAV)?

b. If the fund has a 6% load, how many shares could you purchase with $1,000 and what would be the true percentage cost to you?

c. If the fund were to pay income dividends in an amount of $5 million, what would be the new NAV?

Solution

a. $20.70 = ($105 − $1.5) ÷ 5

b. 45.41 shares = ($1,000 − $60) ÷ $20.70

c. $19.70 = ($100 − $1.5) ÷ 5

QUESTIONS AND PROBLEMS

1. The market value of assets of a mutual fund is $1,230 million, and its liabilities are $15 million. Shares outstanding are 32 million.
   a. What is the fund's NAV?
   b. Why must this be the price at which shares in the fund will trade?
   c. All other things being equal, what would happen to the fund's NAV if security values rose by $19 million?
   d. All other things being equal, what would happen to the fund's NAV if interest is paid on bond holdings (note that the fund uses a full accrual accounting)?
   e. What would happen if the fund pays an income dividend to fund shareholders equal to $0.40 per share? None of the dividend is reinvested in the fund.
   f. Assume that part e occurs, but now one-half of the dividends that shareholders receive are reinvested in new fund shares. What is the effect on the NAV?
2. List and discuss the various benefits of mutual fund investment.
3. What are the costs associated with mutual fund ownership?
4. What is a tax-timing option?
5. What is a 12b-1 fee and a "trailer"?
6. What does it mean when people say that the purchase of a closed-end fund's shares (or a mutual fund's) may involve a tax liability?
7. The equity position of a mutual fund on its Statement of Net Assets shows the following:

Equity at June 30:	($ in millions)
Paid in Capital	$400
Undistributed Net Investment Income	20
Accumulated Net Realized Gains	90
Unrealized Appreciation of Investments	200
Total Equity	$710

   a. If there are 16 million shares outstanding, what is the current NAV per share?
   b. If you own 100 shares and the fund suddenly pays all dividends associated with the undistributed investment income and realized gains, what is your tax liability? (Assume an ordinary tax rate of 30% and a long-term capital gains rate of 28%. Also assume that all realized gains are long-term gains.)
   c. If you were to reinvest all cash dividends (before tax) in shares of the fund, how many new shares would you receive?
   d. Assume that all investors reinvested the dividends they received above. What would the fund's equity position be after the distribution of the $110 million in dividends?
8. Why do some mutual funds have load charges whereas other funds do not? Should investors ever invest in a load mutual fund?
9. How do brokerage firms that allow investors to buy mutual funds from their firm at zero load charges make any money from this service?
10. A friend is considering an investment of $10,000 in one of two mutual funds. One fund charges a front-end load of 8% and the other is a no-load fund. Illustrate the annualized load cost if each fund earns the following annual returns for each of the next five years.
    a. 5% annual return.
    b. 10% annual return.
11. Why does it make sense that mutual funds must trade at net asset values per share?
12. You buy a closed-end fund for $40 when its net asset value is $50. Is this a good deal?
13. Why might closed-end funds trade at discounts and premiums from NAV?

14. Why might an investment advisory firm decide to use a closed-end organizational form, and not an open-end form?

15. If investors in mutual funds believed that security markets are perfectly efficient, what type of U.S. common stock mutual fund would we find being offered to the public?

16. The average U.S. equity mutual fund holds about 60 stocks at any time. Given this, why should the shares of more than one fund be held?

DATAFILE ANALYSIS

1. U.S. Equity Mutual Fund Selection. Review the datafile called OEFUNDS. Juan and Maria Rodriguez are both business professionals with promising careers. They are in their late twenties and just inherited $50,000, which they wish to invest in mutual funds that actively trade domestic U.S. equities. (No index funds are allowed for this exercise even though they are very reasonable alternatives to actively managed portfolios.) They intend to hold the mutual fund shares to supplement their eventual retirement income. Select and justify at least three funds that you would suggest they acquire. (They are expected to own all three funds.)

2. **U.S. Bond Mutual Fund Selection.** Charles and Grace Dee have just begun their retirement. They will receive social security and benefit payments from their respective employers. In addition, they have accumulated savings of $100,000. A portion of this savings will be invested in certificates of deposit in a local bank and a number of equity mutual funds. However, $50,000 will be invested in mutual funds that invest in U.S. government and corporate bonds. Review the datafile called OEFUNDS. Which and how many funds would you suggest they purchase?

REFERENCES

Overview and details about mutual funds can be found in the following references:

Mutual Fund Values, published bimonthly by Morningstar, Inc. Chicago, IL.

Investment Companies, published annually by CDA Wiesenberger Financial Services.

The Individual Investors Guide to No-Load Mutual Funds, American Association of Individual Investors, Chicago, IL, International Publishing Company.

Mutual Fund Fact Book, Investment Company Institute, Washington, D.C.

Interesting current articles about professional money managers and institutional investors are found in these trade journals:

Institutional Investor, published monthly by Institutional Investor Publications, New York.

Pensions & Investments, published biweekly by Crain Communications, Inc. Chicago, IL.

Interesting studies of closed-end fund discounts include the following:

Lee, Charles, Andrei Shleifer, and Richard Thaler. "Investor Sentiment and the Closed-End Fund Puzzle," *Journal of Finance,* March 1991.

Burton, Malkiel. "The Valuation of Closed-End Investment Company Shares," *Journal of Finance,* 1977.

Thompson, Rex. "The Information Content of Discounts and Premiums on Closed-End Fund Shares," *Journal of Financial Economics,* 1978.

Computerized sources of data on mutual funds include:

Business Week Mutual Fund Scorecard, P.O. Box 1597, Fort Lee, NJ.

Morningstar Mutual Funds OnDisc, Morningstar, 225 West Wacker Drive, Chicago, IL.

Mutual Fund Expert Pro Plus, Alexander Steele Systems Technologies, Inc., 12021 Wilshire Blvd., Los Angeles, CA.

15

GLOBAL
INVESTMENT

*After reading this chapter you should
have an understanding of the benefits
and risks of global diversification.*

As you can see in Table 15-1, the value of non-U.S. financial markets has always represented a large fraction of world financial assets. For example, in 1960, the value of stocks and bonds traded in countries other than the United States was about 50% of the world total. By the end of 1995, this value had increased to 68%. Thus, for the sake of broad portfolio diversification alone, it makes sense for both U.S. and non-U.S. investors to invest globally.

International diversification is not without cost, however. Brokerage fees in most countries are larger than in the United States, security markets are less liquid, and financial data on non-U.S. companies is sometimes difficult to obtain. Perhaps the greatest deterrent to international investment is a lack of knowledge—specifically, about exchange rate risks.

Each of these costs has declined substantially during the past 15 years and will continue to decline as global markets become more competitive. Also, as investors continue to learn about the advantages of portfolio diversification and how to deal with exchange rate risk, the fraction of international securities held in portfolios will grow.

In this chapter we look at the issues involved in international investing. We begin by examining historical risks and returns associated with global investment. Next, we look at exchange rate theory, reviewing various economic models of exchange rates, forward exchange rates, and asking why risk-free interest rates vary across countries. Armed with these tools, we move on to looking at ways to control exchange rate risk. We will see that exchange rate risks associated with investing in short-term risk-free securities can be largely eliminated by trading in forward contracts, but that it is difficult to control exchange rate risk when long-term investments are made in securities with uncertain future market values.

TABLE 15-1   MARKET VALUES OF WORLD EQUITY AND BOND MARKETS (IN $U.S. BILLIONS)

	1960	1970	1980	1985	1990	1994
Fixed Income						
U.S.	$ 230.3	$ 322.8	$ 799.1	$3,110.6	$ 5,666.9	$ 8,023.1
Non-U.S.	396.9	390.4	1,906.5	NA	6,358.1	8,052.1
Total	627.2	713.2	2,705.6	NA	12,025.0	16,075.2
Equity						
U.S.	345.0	700.9	1,380.6	2,324.6	3,089.6	5,081.8
Non-U.S.						
Developed Non-U.S.	180.2	309.2	1,049.3	2,172.0	5,700.6	8,174.8
Emerging	NA	NA	NA	168.1	603.5	1,802.0
Total	525.2	1,010.1	2,429.9	4,664.7	9,393.7	15,058.6
Grand Total	1,152.4	1,723.3	5,135.5	NA	21,418.7	31,133.8

SOURCES: Data prior to 1985 from Roger G. Ibbotson and Lawrence Siegel, "The World Market Wealth Portfolio," *The Journal of Portfolio Management,* Winter 1983. Bond data for 1985 and beyond estimated from Salomon Brothers International *Fixed Income Research*. Equity data from 1985 and beyond from *Emerging Stock Markets Factbook 1995*, International Finance Corporation.

Next, we assess important differences between investing in developed versus emerging security markets. Finally, we conclude the chapter with a discussion of how individual investors can actually diversify globally.

Why Invest Globally?

Investment professionals place different meanings on the terms *international investment* and *global investment*. **International investment** refers to investing in securities beyond the borders of one's own country. **Global investment** refers to investing in securities throughout the world. The distinction is important because some investment managers consider themselves to be global managers whereas others are solely international managers. Buying a global portfolio is different from buying an international portfolio. A global investment manager invests in all securities around the world whereas an international manager invests only in securities of countries other than the country of the investor.

The case for global investment is easy to make. In addition to increasing the potential for higher returns by expanding one's portfolio beyond the local country, global investment reduces portfolio risk by expanding diversification opportunities.

If we take the standard capital asset pricing model (CAPM) to its limit, the single optimal portfolio of risky assets that all investors should hold consists of all risky assets in the world. According to the CAPM, to diversify a portfolio properly, investors should consider the biggest possible picture—the aggregate of all equity and bond markets in the world. This, of course, is not actually possible. Political restrictions placed on capital flows into and out of many countries, the lack of liquidity in some markets, differences in the availability of information, and differing tax rates all severely damage the CAPM in a world context.

Nonetheless, an examination of the value of marketable securities in countries around the world suggests that the CAPM principle of broad diversification is valid. Consider Figure 15-1, which shows the proportions of equities and bonds traded in various regions of the world at the end of 1994. Although the figure is a pie chart, think of it as representing the globe. If one were to restrict portfolio holdings—say, to only U.S. markets—then economic shocks that transfer U.S. wealth to other regions of the world would represent a risk that could be eliminated by international diversification.

This theory works in practice. Recall from Chapter 6 that there are two basic ways of diversifying: naive diversification and efficient diversification. Investors employ naive diversification when they are unable to differentiate among the expected returns, return standard deviations, and return correlations of differing securities. In such cases, an equal percentage investment is made in any securities held. Efficient diversification is appropriate when the investor can differentiate among expected returns, return standard deviations, and return correlation coefficients of various securities. Both approaches show that international diversification is valuable in reducing portfolio risk.

Naive International Diversification

One of the classic studies examining the potential for international diversification was performed by Solnik in the mid-1970s. Solnik examined the results of the naive diversification strategy that would result if a U.S. investor had randomly selected securities from two different groups. The first group consisted solely of U.S. stocks. The second group consisted of both U.S. and European stocks. Stock returns were calculated weekly from 1966 through 1971.

FIGURE 15-1 TRADED WORLD BONDS & EQUITIES (1994)

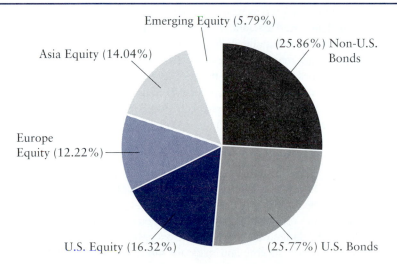

FIGURE 15-2   NAIVE DOMESTIC U.S. DIVERSIFICATION VERSUS NAIVE INTERNATIONAL DIVERSIFICATION

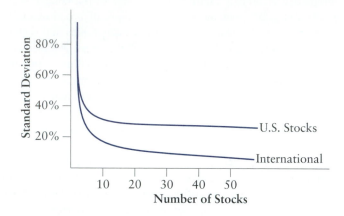

Results are shown in Figure 15-2. As we saw in Chapter 6, naive diversification does reduce portfolio risk up to some limit, referred to as *nondiversifiable market risk.* This happens whether one is dealing with returns on U.S. domestic stocks or returns on both U.S. and international securities. The important implication of Figure 15-2 is that the *nondiversifiable risk of internationally diversified portfolios was considerably lower than that of portfolios restricted to U.S. securities.* Solnik's results have been replicated in numerous other studies.

Efficient International Diversification

The composition of an efficiently diversified portfolio depends, of course, on one's assumptions. If you are sufficiently pessimistic about returns and risks of foreign investments, your efficient portfolio may not call for any international diversification. But consider the past record as well as a little economic logic.

The **Europe, Australia, and Far East (EAFE)** index was created in 1969 as an index of equity returns in economically developed countries other than the United States. As such, it represents the returns that could have been earned on a broadly diversified group of international equities. In Table 15-2 the average returns, standard deviations, and correlation coefficients are shown for three traditional U.S. asset classes as well as for the EAFE index. The data are based on nominal annual U.S. dollar returns. Using this historical data, two historical efficient frontiers, shown in Figure 15-3, were calculated. The frontier shown as a black curve includes only the three U.S. asset classes. The colored curve adds the EAFE index. Clearly, U.S. investors would have been better off since 1969 to have been globally diversified.

To see why this was the case, look again at Table 15-2, particularly the information about the EAFE index. Its average return was clearly the largest, but its standard deviation was also the largest. Both reflect the fact that countries included in the EAFE index experienced rapid reindustrialization as they revived from the World War II economic collapse. It would be dangerous to extrapolate exceptional events of the past to the future. But even if future EAFE returns and risks are more in line with those of the U.S. economy, the

TABLE 15-2   HISTORICAL DATA ON U.S. ASSET CLASSES AND EAFE ANNUAL NOMINAL RETURNS, 1969–1994

Security Class	Average Return	Standard Deviation	Correlation Coefficients			
			TB	GB	SP	EAFE
U.S. T-Bills	7.00%	2.74%	1.000			
U.S. Government Bonds	9.13	11.32	−0.007	1.000		
S&P 500 Index	11.34	15.78	0.009	0.462	1.000	
EAFE	14.15	22.50	−0.222	0.249	0.569	1.000

FIGURE 15-3   HISTORICAL EFFICIENT FRONTIERS (1969–1994)

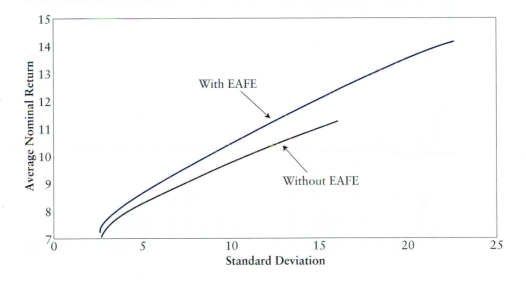

correlation among U.S. securities and international securities suggests that international diversification will reduce portfolio risk in the future.

The historical correlation between EAFE returns and returns on the S&P 500 was 0.57. Remember, these are two very diversified portfolios. The S&P 500 Index is composed of 500 large U.S. stocks. The EAFE index consists of approximately 1,000 stocks spread across 18 countries. A correlation coefficient of 0.57 between two well-diversified portfolios is actually quite low. If portfolios of equivalent size consisting solely of U.S. stocks were to be created, their return correlation would likely be greater than 0.9.

Because security returns are not highly correlated across world markets, international diversification reduces portfolio risk.

As further evidence, consider the information shown in Figure 15-4. This figure displays the correlation coefficients of returns on various countries around the world with returns on the S&P 500 Index. Correlations are shown for returns of both developed countries and many emerging market countries. Again the story is the same. Returns on securities of other countries are not highly correlated with returns of U.S. securities.

These correlation coefficients show that international investment reduces risk because the economies of different countries are based on different industries. As long as this is true, global investment will reduce portfolio risk. Not only would global diversification have worked in the past, logically it will work in the future.

FIGURE 15-4   IFCG PRICE INDEX CORRELATIONS WITH S&P 500 AND LOCAL INDEXES

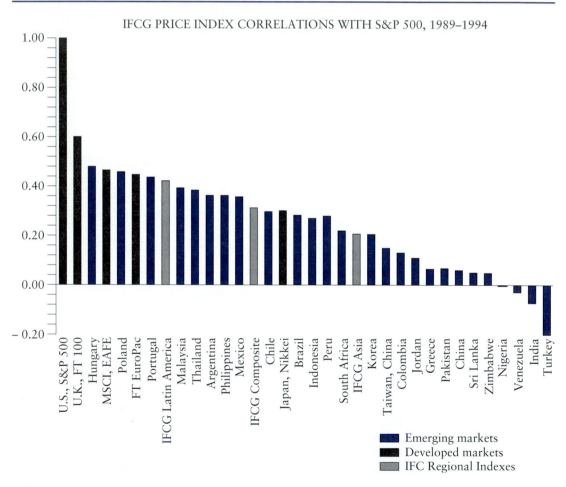

IFCG PRICE INDEX CORRELATIONS WITH S&P 500, 1989–1994

SOURCE: *Emerging Stock Markets Factbook 1995*, International Finance Corporation, Washington, DC.

Domestic Versus International Returns

A **domestic return** is the return people receive in their domestic (local) currency. **International returns** are the returns earned from investing in another country—after conversion to one's local currency.

To illustrate, consider two companies that are similar, except for their country of origin: Tuff Truck, Inc. (TT) is a U.S. firm, and Lloyd's Lorry, Ltd. (LL) a British firm. At the beginning of the year, shares of TT trade on the New York Stock Exchange for $50, and shares of LL trade on the London International Stock Exchange for £50. By the end of the year, TT sells for $60 and has paid a $1 dividend; LL sells for £60 and has paid a £1 dividend. Thus, the return a U.S. resident earns on TT is 22%, and the return a British resident earns on LL is also 22%. However, the return a U.S. resident would have earned on LL (and the return a British resident would have earned on TT) is not necessarily 22%. When an international investment is made, the return on the investment is composed of a return on the underlying security in the foreign country and a currency return. *When you buy a foreign security, you buy both the security and the currency in which the security is denominated.*

To continue with the example, assume that at the start of the year the exchange rate is $1.50 per pound and so it takes $1.50 to buy one British pound. To purchase shares in Lloyd's Lorry at £50, a U.S. resident would have to pay $1.50 per pound, or $75. At the end of the year, the investor would have a claim to £60 in share value and £1 in dividends. But what if the value of the pound has fallen relative to the dollar and the exchange rate is now $1.20 per pound? If the share value and dividends are reclaimed to the United States, the U.S. resident would receive only £61 at $1.20 per pound, or $73.20. As a result, the U.S. investor's return on the British security is a negative 2.4%:

$$-0.024 = \frac{\$73.20}{\$75.00} - 1.0$$

The investment in LL provided a positive return, but this was offset by investment losses on the British pound. This -2.4% return is the U.S. investor's international return.

In order to calculate the international return on an investment in a security, the return on the security must be compounded by the return on the foreign currency. In our example, each $1 U.S. investment in LL resulted in a $+22\%$ return, as $1 grew to $1.22. However, each $1 U.S. investment in the foreign currency resulted in a 20% loss, as the value of £1 fell from $1.50 to $1.20. Compounding the 1.22 by 0.80 results in an end-of-year value of $0.976 for each $1 investment at the beginning of the year:

$$\$0.976 = \$1(1.22)(0.80)$$

This, of course, represents the 2.4% loss.

In general, if R_I represents the international return, R_D represents the domestic security return, and R_x represents the return on the exchange of currency:

Return on International Investment

$$1 + R_I = (1 + R_D)(1 + R_x) \tag{15.1}$$

The international return is equal to a compounding of the domestic security return (in the domestic economy of the foreign country) by the exchange rate return. Applied to the U.S. investor in the preceding example above:

$$1 + R_I = 0.976 = (1.22)(0.80)$$

$$R_I = 0.976 - 1.0 = -0.024$$

And if we apply this equation to the British resident's return on Tuff Truck, a return of +52.50% was earned:

$$0.525 = (1.22)(1.25) - 1.0$$

where

$$R_x = \frac{\$1.50 \text{ per pound}}{\$1.20 \text{ per pound}} - 1$$

$$= 25\%$$

Exchange rate returns can represent a sizable part of the return earned on international investment. For example, consider the data in Table 15-3. Average annual returns and standard deviations are shown for U.S. investments in a variety of countries from 1970 through 1980. Both positive and negative average exchange rate returns were earned. When the average exchange rate return is positive, it means the value of the foreign currency increased relative to the dollar. Thus, U.S. investors who owned the foreign currency profited.

The first three columns of data show average annual domestic returns, exchange rate returns, and total international returns to U.S. residents. For example, consider the data for Germany. The average annual domestic return on an index of German stocks that a resident of Germany would have earned was 4.14%. But U.S. residents wishing to purchase had to purchase German currency to do so. The average annual return on this currency investment was 6.65%. When the domestic return of 4.14% is compounded by the exchange rate return, U.S. investors earned an average 11.07% return per year. In contrast, consider a German resident's investment in U.S. stocks. These stocks provided an average annual domestic return of 6.78%, but the German investor would have suffered a 6.24% exchange rate loss.[1] On net, a German investor in U.S. stocks during the same period would have had a 0.12% average annual return.

The last three columns in Table 15-3 show the annualized standard deviation of domestic returns, exchange rate returns, and total foreign returns to U.S. investors. Note that the standard deviation of total foreign returns is not the sum of domestic and exchange rate standard deviations. This happens because domestic and exchange rate returns are not perfectly correlated.

Two important implications can be drawn from Table 15-3:

1. The **average return** on international investment is often substantially affected by average exchange rate returns.

---

[1] The 6.24% loss is calculated as $(1.0 \div 1.0665)$ minus 1.0. The exchange rate gain to residents of the United States who invested in Germany is not mathematically the exact opposite of the exchange rate loss to German residents who invested in the United States.

TABLE 15-3 EX POST AVERAGE ANNUAL RETURNS AND STANDARD DEVIATIONS FOR U.S. INVESTORS (DECEMBER 1970–DECEMBER 1980)

Stocks of Country	Average Annual Return			Standard Deviation of Returns		
	Domestic	Exchange	Total U.S.	Domestic	Exchange	Total U.S.
Germany	4.14%	6.65%	11.07%	13.87%	11.87%	18.39%
Belgium	7.12	4.97	12.44	13.28	11.02	18.76
Denmark	11.41	2.49	14.18	15.41	10.28	17.65
France	7.79	2.16	10.12	22.00	10.24	25.81
Italy	6.64	−4.22	2.14	24.21	8.58	26.51
Norway	8.05	3.58	11.92	28.61	8.89	29.92
Netherlands	7.02	5.79	13.22	16.37	10.97	18.91
United Kingdom	12.93	−0.12	12.79	28.94	8.84	31.61
Sweden	8.52	1.84	10.52	15.05	8.89	18.06
Switzerland	2.67	9.63	12.56	16.80	14.67	21.40
Spain	0.76	−1.29	−0.54	16.71	9.10	20.26
Australia	10.86	0.53	11.45	24.62	9.15	27.15
Japan	13.80	6.68	21.40	16.39	10.42	19.55
Hong Kong	26.05	−0.41	25.53	47.95	5.63	45.80
Singapore	22.69	−4.69	16.94	35.82	6.52	36.03
Canada	14.85	−1.88	12.69	18.92	4.16	20.29
United States	6.78	0.00	6.78	16.00	0.00	16.00

SOURCE: B. Solnik and B. Noetzlin, "Optimal International Asset Allocation," *Journal of Portfolio Management*, Fall 1982; pp. 11–21.

2. The **volatility of international returns** is also often substantially affected by volatility of exchange rates.

Exchange rates play an important role in the risks and returns on foreign investment. As such, it is useful to have a general understanding of the history of how exchange rates have been determined in the past.

A Brief History of Currency Exchange Rates

From the days of the Egyptian and Roman empires until the early 1900s, gold was used as the international medium of exchange. Each country would declare the units of gold into which its currency could be converted and then attempt to maintain this value over time. The growth in a country's currency was limited to the quantity of gold it could acquire. During World War I, shipping activities were interrupted and most countries suspended the gold standard. Between World War I and World War II, currency exchange rates fluctuated over wide ranges. During that time, a number of countries, including the United States, the United Kingdom, and France, returned to variants of the gold standard. For example, the United States set its nominal price of gold at $35 per ounce of gold but traded gold only with central banks of foreign countries. Individuals were unable to turn in dollars for physical gold.

The **Bretton Woods Agreement of 1944** was adopted by the Allied Powers to aid world economic development in the post–World War II era. This agreement created the International Monetary Fund (IMF) and the International Bank for Reconstruction and Development (World Bank). In addition, all signatory countries fixed the value of their currency in gold but did not have to actually exchange gold for currency. Only the dollar remained convertible, at $35 per ounce. In essence, this meant the U.S. dollar became the world currency standard.

In subsequent years, use of the U.S. dollar as the world standard for fixed exchange rates became a problem due to growing U.S. trade deficits. In 1971, President Nixon suspended all U.S. Treasury purchases or sales of gold when one-third of U.S. gold supplies were sold to non-U.S. central banks during the first half of the year.

In response, the world's leading trading nations (the Group of Ten) signed the Smithsonian Agreement in which currencies were revalued and allowed to depart somewhat from the U.S. dollar. This was the beginning of freely floating exchange rates, exchange rates not tied to a fixed gold exchange rate but to market demand and supply of a currency. In 1976, true flexible exchange rates were allowed in a treaty known as the **Jamaica Agreement.** Nations were not required to make their exchange rates flexible, and many countries continue to maintain fixed rates based on the U.S. dollar.[2]

Figure 15-5 shows the history of U.S. dollar exchange rates versus an index of 15 other countries. Looking at this exhibit, you can see the importance of exchange rate returns to international investors.

Exchange Rate Quotations

Current exchange rates are published daily in most financial newspapers. An example of such exchange rates is displayed in Table 15-4. The values shown in the first column are referred to as *direct quotations*. They represent the number of U.S. dollars required to purchase one unit of the foreign currency. For example, in December 1995, $1.54 would have been needed to purchase one British pound. We refer symbolically to the direct exchange as $S^{d/f}$, where S refers to the spot exchange rate and the superscript d/f stands for domestic per unit of foreign.

Values shown in the second column are *indirect quotations*. They represent the number of foreign currency units that 1.0 U.S. dollars will purchase. For example, one U.S. dollar would have purchased 0.65 British pounds in December 1995. We symbolically refer to indirect spot quotations as $S^{f/d}$.

By convention, most financial newspapers show indirect quotations. Only currencies denominated in pounds are shown as direct quotations. It is also convention on all international currency markets to state exchange rates on a "U.S. dollar basis." For example, to find the exchange rate between Japanese yen and German marks, quotations of the yen per dollar and mark per dollar would have to be examined. This convention reduces confusion when comparing exchange rates on, say, the Frankfurt exchange with those on the Tokyo exchange. Again, the exception is the British pound, in which case a foreign currency quote is shown directly against the pound as opposed to the dollar.

---

[2] Countries whose exchange rates are presently fixed to the U.S. dollar include Angola, Argentina, the Bahamas, Iraq, Liberia, Panama, Syrian Arab Republic, and the Republic of Yemen. With a few exceptions, they are all relatively small countries.

FIGURE 15-5 U.S. Dollar Movement Under Floating Exchange Rates

TABLE 15-4 Illustrative Exchange Rates, December 1995

Currency	Direct Quotation $ Required to Buy One Unit of Foreign Currency	Indirect Quotation Number of Units of Foreign Currency per U.S. Dollar
British Pound	1.5425	0.6483
Canadian Dollar	0.7325	1.3652
French Franc	0.2011	4.9726
German Mark	0.6926	1.4438
Greek Drachma	0.0042	238.0952
Italian Lira	0.00062	1612.9032
Japanese Yen	0.00986	101.4199
Swiss Franc	0.8554	1.16990

ANSWERS TO COMMONLY ASKED QUESTIONS ABOUT CURRENCY TRADING

In early 1992, foreign currency prices moved dramatically in response to uncertainties about the future economic integration of the European Economic Community. This article appeared in the *Wall Street Journal* at that time to explain how currency markets operate and the history of major events in the currency markets. Although a few years have passed since the article was published, it still provides many useful insights.

How Big are the World's Currency Markets?

Huge. According to a 1990 survey by the Bank for International Settlements, $650 billion a day of foreign exchange is traded round the globe. That's more volume than the New York Stock Exchange rings up in two months.

Who Does All This Trading?

A wide range of players. Major banks are most active, accounting for nearly 80% of trading, according to the New York Federal Reserve Bank. But multinational companies account for billions of dollars of trading as well. Global money managers, individual speculators and tourists also are active.

Where Does Trading Occur?

Most trading is done electronically, via bank-to-bank phone links. There isn't any dominant exchange that handles spot trading—the trading of currency for immediate delivery. Instead, activity during any 24-hour period migrates from one time zone to another, moving from Europe to the U.S., Australia, Japan and then back to Europe.

But about $14 billion a day of currency futures are traded at the Chicago Mercantile Exchange. And the Philadelphia Stock Exchange does a sizable business in currency options.

Can Countries Control Their Exchange Rates?

Not very well. World exchange rates have been left to float since 1971, though members of the European Economic Community have tried to loosely link their currencies for most of the past two decades. But as certain European currencies become unusually strong or weak, authorities repeatedly have been forced to change the targeted values of those currencies in what is known as a currency realignment.

How Does a Realignment Work?

Policy makers from European nations agree to boost the targeted values of their strongest currencies, while lowering the targeted values of the weakest currencies. Last weekend, for example, the Italian lira was effectively devalued 7% against other European currencies. By abruptly changing exchange rates, these realignments are meant to bring about a new period of currency stability.

Already this week, though, speculation is mounting that the European Community will need to realign rates again. The betting is that the German mark will strengthen, while the lira once again, the Spanish peseta and the British pound will be devalued.

Aside From Revaluations, Can Countries Do Anything to Control Their Exchange Rates?

Each year, countries' central banks make billions of dollars in currency trades designed to stabilize exchange rates. But such central-bank intervention often proves futile, as even the trading might of the U.S. Federal Reserve, the Bank of England or the German Bundesbank proves insufficient to overcome market forces.

Why Do Currency Values Fluctuate So Much?

Much—but not all of the answer—has to do with economic fundamentals. Traders like to channel money into countries with low inflation rates, trade surpluses and high interest rates. Those currencies, as demonstrated by the mark and the Japanese yen, tend to strengthen over time. By contrast, high inflation rates, big trade or budget deficits and low interest rates often amount to a prescription for a weakening currency.

This week, however, "it would be a mistake to relate what's happening to economic fundamentals," says Will Brown, chief economist at J.P. Morgan & Co.

So What Other Factors Are at Work?

Trader sentiment and political pressures. Within Europe's exchange-rate mechanism, traders have been making money lately by betting that the British pound and Italian lira will weaken, and that the mark will strengthen. As huge buy-and-sell orders course through the market, that view has become a self-fulfilling prophecy.

What's more, European economic unity is up for a crucial French vote this weekend. Although the repercussions of that vote are complex, many traders have decided that it presents one more reason to pile money into favored currencies and bet against weak ones.

In All This Turmoil, Who Is Getting Rich?

If history is any guide, big banks' trading desks should be making a killing. Citicorp, for example, typically earns about $150 million every quarter before taxes and expenses from its currency-trading operation. Bankers Trust New York Corp., Bank-America Corp. and J.P. Morgan each are good for about half that amount every quarter. . . .

Who Are the Losers In This Market?

Central banks, for one. Yesterday, the Bank of England bought pounds aggressively early in the day, in an effort to shore up its currency. But that effort was for naught; the pound kept sinking, and the British central bank was left with trading losses.

Small speculators often end up as losers, too. Of the 1,287 seats on the Chicago Merc's International Monetary Mart, about 25% change hands every year. And market players say that most of the people who sell their seats do so because they have incurred unsustainable losses.

Does Anyone Regulate Currency Trades?

Central banks such as the Fed provide some degree of oversight. And futures trading, in particular, is watched by the Commodities Futures Trading Commission. But in general, the currency markets are much more lightly regulated than stock or bond trading.

Which of the World's Currencies Are the Most Important Ones In Traders' Eyes?

At the top of the list, alongside the dollar, are the mark and the yen. A survey of 300 major traders last year by Greenwich Associates found that 28% of dollar trading in North America is in the mark, 23% in the yen, 13% in the British pound and 9% in the Swiss franc. Rounding out the list of major trading currencies, at 3% to 7% each, are the Canadian dollar, Australian dollar and French franc.

Sometimes, though, less-prominent currencies can take center stage. This week, a lot of attention is turning to the Swedish krone and the Italian lira.

SOURCE: *Wall Street Journal*, September 17, 1992.

Ronald D. Frashure, C.F.A.

Executive Vice President
Acadian Asset Management
Massachusetts Institute of Technology, B.S.
Harvard University, M.B.A. (with high distinction)

Acadian Asset Management, where Mr. Frashure is a senior portfolio manager, is a global and international asset management firm that employs structured and disciplined techniques for portfolio management; they have $2.5 billion under management. Mr. Frashure was an equity analyst before becoming a portfolio manager. He has experience in asset allocation as well and indicates that service in Latin America with the U.S. Navy piqued his interest in economic development issues and international investing.

Q: What is your firm's view on global portfolio diversification?

A: My associate, Gary Bergstrom, prepared one of the first pieces to argue for international portfolio diversification by U.S. investors back in the mid-1970s. Twenty years later we have very clearly seen the benefits—international diversification by U.S. investors has significantly increased portfolio returns *and* reduced aggregate portfolio variability over the last two decades. Looking ahead, we believe that global diversification is *still* a route to higher returns and lower risks—with some new avenues for international diversification having opened up since the middle of the 1970s.

Q: What are the "new avenues" for international portfolios?

A: Emerging or developing markets are a very promising area of international equity diversification. This area has come to prominence as more and more countries have moved to market economies in the last couple of decades. The following exhibit shows the impact on realized risk and return from adding different emerging market allocations to an equity portfolio invested in the developed markets. (Developed markets are represented by the MSCI EAFE; emerging markets are represented by the IFC Global index for 1985–90 and by the IFC Investable index after its inception in 1991.) As can be seen, a significant allocation to emerging markets has shown benefits by adding to portfolio returns as well as reducing aggregate portfolio variability. In addition, differences between the returns to smaller- and larger-capitalization stocks in some of the key international equity markets suggest that small-capitalization

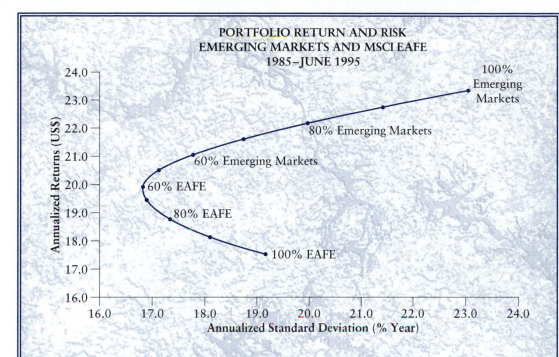

PORTFOLIO RETURN AND RISK
EMERGING MARKETS AND MSCI EAFE
1985–JUNE 1995

portfolio diversification can provide meaningful benefits for global investors going forward.

Q: Just how diversified should a global portfolio be?

A: Evidence from global market performance over the last 20 years indicates that U.S. fund sponsors could have achieved significant risk reduction by investing as much as 40% of their aggregate equity portfolio in foreign equities. Only now are some fund sponsors approaching this level of global diversification. Looking forward, modern portfolio tools such as careful portfolio optimization, using techniques that take into account not only potential future returns from global equities, but also the correlations of international versus domestic stocks and the volatility or variability of returns, can help determine asset allocation. Portfolio optimization must be approached very carefully in such a complex environment. As an example, we have made use of a multi-factor valuation approach for global equity markets and individual stocks that encompasses over 40 individual countries. We have used the most sophisticated risk models available to control portfolio risk in the security selection process. The optimal global portfolio, based on the valuation data, risk measures, and other factors available in September 1995, would have 34.1% in the United States, 39.8% in the developed international markets (those in the EAFE index), 2.9% in Canada, and 23.2% in emerging markets. It is interesting that the recommended allocation to the developed international markets is very close to that which has historically been the risk-minimizing allocation for a portfolio investing in U.S. and developed foreign market equities. The significant allocation to emerging markets is also noteworthy, since the commitment recommended by the optimization is well above the stake that most fund sponsors would have currently in these markets.

Q: Where do you see global diversification going in the future?

A: While global portfolio diversification is no longer a new route to higher returns and lower risk as it was 20 years ago, we believe strongly that the decades ahead are likely to see true globalization of portfolios come to be the accepted norm for investment managers and for investors no matter where they may be located on this small planet!

Exchange Rate Theory

A large body of theory and empirical testing has examined various aspects of currency exchange rates. Although much of it lies beyond the scope of this book, some fundamentals are useful for our basic study of global investment.

We are concerned with four basic questions about exchange rates. First, what causes the existing (or spot) exchange rate between two countries? Second, what causes this exchange rate to change over time? Third, what should be the relationship between expected future spot exchange rates and current forward prices on exchange rates? And, fourth, why are interest rates different across different countries? In attempting to answer these questions, economists have relied on the following four concepts:

1. **Absolute purchasing power parity,** used to explain the current spot exchange rate between two countries,
2. **Relative purchasing power parity,** used to explain why the spot exchange rate between two countries changes over time,
3. **Futures-spot parity,** used to explain the relationship between current spot rates and forward contract prices, and the
4. **International Fisher Equation,** used to explain why interest rates vary across countries.

We will see at the end of this section that all of these theories are closely connected.

Current Spot Exchange Rates

The spot rate of exchange represents the quantity of one currency that can be purchased with one unit of another currency. For example, if one U.S. dollar can be exchanged for 0.6 U.K. pounds, then the spot exchange rate of pounds for dollars is £0.6 to $1.0.

In economic theory, the spot exchange rate between two countries should be determined by the quantity of goods in each country as well as the money circulating in each country. For example, consider two countries that produce only one commodity, say, rice. Country A issues money denominated in units called Azz, and country B issues money denominated in units Bzz. The rice production and money units outstanding for each country are as follows:

	Country A	Country B
Rice Production	100,000 lbs	200,000 lbs
Money Units in Circulation	100,000 Azz	400,000 Bzz
Local Price of Rice	1 Azz/lb	2 Bzz/lb

The equilibrium exchange rate must be 0.5 Azz per 1.0 Bzz (or 2 Bzz per 1.0 Azz). If this were not the case, arbitrage transactions would be possible.

For example, if the current exchange rate were 1.0 Azz per 1.0 Bzz, country B's currency would be overvalued relative to country A for the following reason. A person in country B with 10,000 Bzz of currency could buy 5,000 pounds of rice (10,000 Bzz ÷ 2 Bzz per lb). If the same person wanted to buy rice in the foreign market from country A, the 10,000 Bzz would first be converted to 10,000 Azz (at a 1:1 exchange rate and assuming no transaction costs) and he could then purchase 10,000 pounds of rice in Country A. Knowing this, people in country B would convert their Bzz currency units into units of Azz currency in order to buy rice in country A. As Bzz are used to buy Azz, the exchange rate would change until the exchange rate reached 2 Bzz per 1.0 Azz.

Reality, of course, is considerably more complex. Countries produce a tremendous variety of goods, political restrictions are imposed on the import and export of goods, and so forth. But over long periods of time, the basic variable that determines the level of spot exchange rates is the quantity of money circulating in each country.

To express the determinants of the current exchange ratio symbolically, let:

$S_0^{d/f}$ = the spot exchange rate defined as the number of units of the domestic currency that can be obtained with one unit of the foreign currency at period 0 (e.g., $S_0^{A/B} = 0.5$ and $S_0^{B/A} = 2.0$)

P_0^d = the price per unit of output at period 0 of domestic production (e.g., $P_0^A = 1$ Azz and $P_0^B = 2$ Bzz)

P_0^f = the price per unit of output at period 0 of foreign production (e.g., $P_0^B = 2$ Bzz and $P_0^A = 0.5$ Azz)

Conceptually, the spot exchange rate (domestic units per unit of foreign currency) should be equal to the current spot domestic price divided by the current spot foreign price. This relationship is referred to as **absolute purchasing power parity:**

Absolute Purchasing Power Parity

$$S_0^{d/f} = P_0^d \div P_0^f \qquad (15.2a)$$

This is often written as:

$$P_0^d = P_0^f \times S_0^{d/f} \qquad (15.2b)$$

Equation (15.2b) says the current price level in the domestic market is equal to the current price level in the foreign market times the exchange rate (the number of domestic currency units per one foreign currency unit).

Changes in Spot Exchange Rates

In theory, changes in exchange rates are caused by future relative inflation rates in two countries. To continue with our example, assume that, one year later, rice production in each country is unchanged but there are now 120,000 units of Azz circulating and 420,000 units of Bzz. The unit price of rice in country A will now be 1.20 Azz (120,000 Azz ÷ 100,000 lbs), and the unit price in country B will be 2.10 Bzz (420,000 Bzz ÷ 200,000 lbs). Thus, the new equilibrium exchange rate will be 0.57 Azz per 1.00 Bzz (or 1.75 Bzz per 1.0 Azz).

The exchange rate changed because the countries experienced differing rates of inflation. Inflation in country A was 20%, and in country B it was 5%. Because inflation was more rapid in country A, the value of its currency fell relative to country B's.

The relationship that exists between past and future exchange rates is referred to as the **relative purchasing power parity** model and is written symbolically as:

Relative Purchasing Power Parity

$$S_t^{d/f} = S_0^{d/f} \frac{1 + I_t^d}{1 + I_t^f} \tag{15.3}$$

where

$S_t^{d/f}$ = the number of domestic current units necessary to acquire 1.0 unit of foreign currency at the end of period t

I_t^d = the domestic inflation rate during period t

I_t^f = the foreign inflation rate during period t

According to the relative purchasing power parity model, the spot exchange rate at some future date should be equal to the ratio of spot prices at that date. More importantly, however, *the relative purchasing power parity model says that changes in spot rates are solely a function of relative inflation rates in the two countries.*

Although this model is based on simple logic, in practice, it often does not explain short-term movements in exchange rates. Over short periods of time, exchange rates are also influenced by interest rate levels between countries, monetary policy differences, political stability, and trade imbalances. Over long periods of time, however, there is little doubt that a major force causing shifts in exchange rates is relative inflation rates between countries.

The Price of Big Macs in Various Countries. Since 1986, the *Economist* magazine's Big Mac Index has examined in a very practical manner whether purchase power parity seems to be working.

To test purchasing power parity, staff of the *Economist* surveyed the cost (including sales taxes if appropriate) of McDonald's Big Mac hamburgers in different countries and converted the prices into U.S. dollar costs based on the dollar exchange rates at that time. The idea of purchasing power parity is that the exchange rate of two given currencies should move toward equalizing prices of identical goods or services in each country. By comparing the relative prices of Big Macs, one can gain some sense of whether this is indeed working.

The results are shown in Table 15-5. The average price of a Big Mac in the United States in April 1995 was $2.32. Dollar equivalent prices in other markets varied considerably. On the high side were Big Macs bought in Switzerland ($5.20), Denmark ($4.92), and Japan ($4.65). On the low side were China ($1.05), Hong Kong ($1.23), and Russia ($1.62).

Consider the cost of a Big Mac in Denmark. The local cost was 26.75 Danish Krone (DKr). Translated at the prevailing exchange rate of 5.43 Dkr per U.S. dollar, this represents a cost in the United States of $4.92. Relative to the local U.S. cost of $2.32, the Danish cost of a Big Mac is 112% greater.

The last three columns in Table 15-5 calculate the extent to which the foreign currency appears to be overvalued or undervalued relative to the U.S. dollar. For example, for the cost of Dkr 26.75 in Denmark to be identical to the $2.32 cost, the exchange rate should have been 11.5 Danish Krone per U.S. dollar. Since the actual currency exchange rate was only Dkr 5.43 per U.S. dollar, the Dkr exchange rate appeared to be overvalued relative to U.S. dollars by 112%.

How effective a test is this? The ingredients used to make Big Macs are virtually identical worldwide. Thus, it would seem that the prices should be similar throughout the world if purchasing power parity is working well. However, the hamburger standard does have its flaws. The theory is based on goods and services that are actually traded between countries. (It is hard to imagine how one could engage in arbitrage transactions by trading Big Macs across countries.) In addition, there are other local costs, such as the cost of land rental, which are difficult to quantify. And many countries place significant tariffs on beef.

However, when more sophisticated studies attempt to account for biases such as land costs and trade barriers, they often reach similar conclusions. In the short run, purchasing power parity conditions are often significantly violated. The costs of a similar basket of goods can be substantially larger or smaller in different countries. In summary, purchasing power parity may be useful in explaining trends in exchange rates that arise over lengthy periods of time. But over shorter periods, purchase power parity conditions are often violated.

Forward Exchange Rates

Forward exchange rates are the price agreed to today for the future exchange of one asset for another. In the case of currencies, the forward exchange rate refers to today's agreement to trade one currency for another at a future date. For example, the current spot exchange rate of U.S. dollars for U.K. pounds might be $2.00 per pound. But agreements made today to trade dollars for pounds in one year might occur at $1.90 per pound. The agreement made today to trade in a year from now at $1.90 per pound is called a forward contract.

Consider the following numerical example. Today, one-year nominal risk-free interest rates in the United States are 10% ($RF_{US} = 10\%$) and are 12% in the United Kingdom ($RF_{UK} = 12\%$). The spot exchange rate is $2 per pound or £0.5 per dollar. There is also a forward contract that allows the swap of dollars and pounds in exactly one year at $1.90 per pound or £0.5263 per dollar. We define today's contracted price of this forward as $F_0^{d/f} = \$1.90$.

As a U.S. resident, should you invest in the United States or the United Kingdom? Each $1.00 invested in the United States will provide a payoff of $1.10. An investment of $1.00 in the United Kingdom is a little more complex. When the $1.00 is converted to pounds,

TABLE 15-5 THE HAMBURGER STANDARD

	Big Mac Prices		Implied PPP of Dollar	Actual Exchange Rate (1)	Local currency under (−) over (+) valuation %
	In Local Currency	In Dollars			
United States	$2.32	$2.32	—	—	—
Argentina	Peso3.00	$3.00	1.29	1.00	+29
Australia	A$2.45	1.82	1.06	1.35	−22
Belgium	BFr109	3.84	47.0	28.4	+66
Brazil	Real2.42	2.69	1.04	0.90	+16
Britain	£1.74	2.80	1.33 (2)	1.61 (2)	+21
Canada	C$2.77	1.99	1.19	1.39	−14
China	Yuan9.00	1.05	3.88	8.54	−55
Denmark	DKR 26.75	4.92	11.5	5.43	+112
France	FFr18.5	3.85	7.97	4.80	+66
Germany	DM4.80	3.48	2.07	1.38	+50
Hong Kong	HK$9.50	1.23	4.09	7.73	−47
Hungary	Forint191	1.58	82.3	121	−32
Indonesia	Rupiah3900	1.75	1681	2231	−25
Israel	Shekel8.9	3.01	3.84	2.95	+30
Italy	Lire4500	2.64	1940	1702	+14
Japan	¥391	4.65	169	84.2	+100
Mexico	Peso10.9	1.71	4.70	6.37	−26
Russia	Rouble8100	1.62	3491	4985	−30
South Korea	Won2300	2.99	991	769	+29
Switzerland	SFr5.90	5.20	2.54	1.13	+124
Taiwan	NT$65.0	2.53	28.0	25.7	+9

(1) April 7, 1995.
(2) Against U.S. dollar.
SOURCE: Adapted from "Big MacCurrencies," *The Economist,* April 15, 1995.

you know it will purchase £0.5, which will grow to £0.56 by year-end. To guarantee the exchange rate at which these £0.56 will be returned to the United States, today you would either sell pound futures or buy dollar futures. At the forward exchange rate of $1.90 per pound, the £0.56 will be worth $1.064 ($1.90 × 0.56) at year-end. Since the U.S. investment grows to $1.10 whereas the U.K. investment grows to only $1.064, you should choose to invest in the United States.

In fact, you could engage in an arbitrage in which you purchase U.S. risk-free securities financed by short-selling U.K. risk-free securities. From the perspective of a U.K. resident, investment in the United States is also preferable. Arbitrage trades will continue to occur in the spot currencies and risk-free interest rate markets as well as the currency futures markets until people are indifferent between investing locally or in foreign markets. Symbolically, this will occur when the:

Risk-Free Payoff from Domestic Investment
= Risk-Free Payoff from Foreign Investment

$$1 + RF_D = (1 + RF_F)(F_0^{d/f} \div S_0^{d/f}) \tag{15.4}$$

where RF_D is the risk-free rate in the local domestic economy and RF_F is the risk-free rate in the foreign country. $F_0^{d/f}$ refers to the current price of the futures contract, the number of domestic currency units per unit of foreign currency. The value of $F_0^{d/f}$ divided by $S_0^{d/f}$ is simply the (known) exchange rate return or the price at which you sell pounds divided by the price at which you buy pounds. In this example, you sold pounds at a price of $1.90 per pound, $F_0^{d/f}$, and you bought pounds at the price of $2.00 per pound.

$$(1 + R_x) = F_0^{d/f} \div S_0^{d/f}$$

$$0.95 = (\$1.90 \text{ per pound}) \div (\$2.00 \text{ per pound})$$

Equation (15.4) is often reexpressed in what is called the **futures-spot parity** model:

Futures-Spot Parity $$F_0^{d/f} = S_0^{d/f}[(1 + RF_D) \div (1 + RF_F)] \tag{15.5}$$

In our example, the equilibrium forward rate would be:[3]

$$\$1.96 = \$2.00 [(1.10) \div (1.12)]$$

The nominal risk-free rate (RF) in each country should be equal to a compounding of the real return in each country by the expected rates of inflation in each country.

Expected Inflation, Interest Rates, and Currency Forward Rates

If the current spot rate is $2 per pound and the equilibrium one-year forward rate is $1.96 per pound, the value of the pound is forecast to fall relative to the dollar. This means the ownership of one pound is expected to have a claim to fewer dollars. Why might this be? A similar question could be asked about why the U.K. nominal risk-free rate might be greater than that in the United States. The answer to both questions, of course, could be due to differences in expected inflation in the two countries.

The International Fisher Equation (discussed in Chapter 5) implies that the interest rate which exists in a given country should consist of a real risk-free rate associated with the country compounded by the inflation rate that is expected in the country. Symbolically:

International Fisher Equations

$$(1 + RF_D) = (1 + r_D)[1 + E(I_D)]$$

$$(1 + RF_F) = (1 + r_F)[1 + E(I_F)] \tag{15.6}$$

If the real risk-free return in the local domestic economy (r_D) equals the real risk-free return in the foreign economy (r_F), then the spot futures parity model shown in Equation (15.7) can be reexpressed as follows:

---

[3] This assumes that spot exchange rates and spot interest rates do not change in adjustment to equilibrium.

Spot Futures Parity $$F_0^{d/f} = S_0^{d/f} \frac{1 + E(I_D)}{1 + E(I_F)}$$ (15.7)

The true reason why equilibrium forward rates should differ from current spot rates is due to differences in expected inflation in the local and foreign country. For example, assume the real risk-free return in the United States and United Kingdom is 3%. This implies that expected inflation in the United States is 6.8%, and in the United Kingdom it is 8.7%:

$$1.068 = 1.10 \div 1.03$$

$$1.087 = 1.12 \div 1.03$$

Using Equation (15.7), the equilibrium forward rate is $1.96:

$$\$1.96 = \$2.00(1.068 \div 1.087)$$

Notice that Equation (15.7) states that today's forward rate is simply equal to today's expectation of the future spot rate.

Interest Rate Parity

If capital is allowed to flow between countries at zero cost, if taxes are identical, and currency exchange rates are flexible, then the expected real rate of return for a given risk level should be identical in all countries. If this were not true, then people would borrow in low real-return countries and invest in high real-return countries. This suggests that one should be careful about making an investment decision based solely on quoted nominal returns in foreign countries. Exchange rate gains or losses must also be considered.

For example, assume you are a U.S. resident and are considering investing in risk-free one-year securities available in the United Kingdom or Germany. The following data summarizes the information available to you:

	United Kingdom	Germany
1-year risk-free rate in each country	12%	6%
Spot exchange rate	$2 per £	$0.70 per M (mark)
1-year forward rate	$1.9 per £	$0.74 per M

If you were to neglect the exchange rate information, it would appear the United Kingdom is a good place in which to invest and Germany is a good place to borrow. The opposite, however, is true! When Equation 15.4 is used to calculate the returns net of currency transactions, we find:

Risk-free payoff from Foreign Investment $= \$1(1 + RF_F)(F_0^{d/f} \div S_0^{d/f})$

For an investment in the United Kingdom:

$$\$1.064 = \$1(1.12)(\$1.9 \div \$2.0)$$

For an investment in Germany:

$$\$1.121 = \$1(1.06)(\$0.74 \div \$0.7)$$

As a U.S. resident, a risk-free investment in Germany would provide the greater return after exchange rates are considered. A situation in which German risk-free returns are substantially higher than U.K. risk-free returns (to a U.S. investor) cannot last long if arbitrage is allowed to occur. If such arbitrage is effective in adjusting exchange rates and risk-free rates between countries, the following **interest rate parity** model will result:

Interest Rate Parity
$$\frac{1 + RF_D}{1 + RF_F} = \frac{F_0^{d/f}}{S_0^{d/f}} = \frac{1 + E(I_D)}{1 + E(I_F)}$$
(15.8)

The ratio of forward to spot prices should be equal to the ratio of the risk-free payoff in the domestic economy to the risk-free payoff in the foreign economy. These ratios are all due to differences in expected inflation in the two economies.

This relationship is shown in Figure 15-6. When all markets are in equilibrium, the ratios should plot on a 45-degree line passing through 1.0 on both axes. Recall our first example in this section in which nominal one-year risk-free rates were 10% in the United States and 12% in the United Kingdom. The spot rate was $2.00 per pound and the future was $1.90 per pound. Given this data, the interest rate parity ratios are as follows:

Ratio of Risk-Free Rates   **Ratio of Forward to Spot**

$(1.10) \div (1.12) = 0.982$ $\$1.90 \div \$2.00 = 0.95$

FIGURE 15-6   INTEREST RATE PARITY RELATIONSHIP

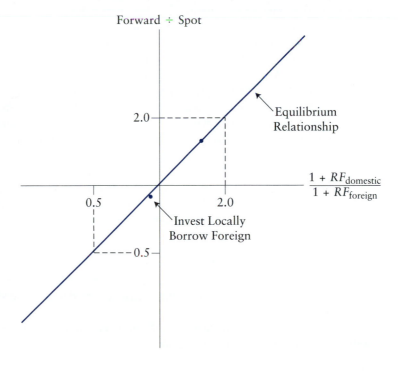

Since the ratios differ, the markets are not in equilibrium and (neglecting transaction costs) an arbitrage trade is possible.

Summary of Parity Models

A summary of the various parity models is displayed in Figure 15-7. The models start with a theory of current exchange rates called **purchasing power parity.** This model implies that the current rate of exchange (in terms of units of the domestic currency per unit of the foreign currency) should be equal to the ratio of domestic prices to foreign prices. A problem in testing this model is that it is difficult to find two identical goods in different countries.

The model explaining future exchange rates is called **relative purchasing power parity.** It implies that changes over time in exchange rates are caused by inflation differences between two countries. For example, if inflation in country D is greater than inflation in country F, then the value of country D's currency will fall relative to country F. One unit of country F's currency will be able to claim a larger quantity of country D's currency. While this model seems quite logical, a variety of economic forces (such as trade imbalances and monetary policies of each country) can cause relative purchasing power to break down over short time intervals.

The basic model explaining levels of nominal risk-free interest rates in any country is the international Fisher equation. This model implies that the nominal risk-free rate of interest in a country should be equal to a real risk-free rate compounded by the inflation expected in the country. When individuals are able to engage in costless arbitrage between countries, the real risk-free rate of interest should be identical in each country. This is the major implication of the interest rate parity model. Again, the application of the model often breaks down in practice due to short-term monetary policies of governmental authorities and restrictions on capital flows between countries (such as trading costs, taxes, or even outright barriers on capital flows).

The final model is referred to as **spot futures parity** and is used to explain current prices of forward contracts. A forward contract is a contract entered into today for the future exchange of two currencies at a price that is agreed to today. There are three ways of explaining the spot futures parity. The first says the forward rate traded today should be the same as today's expectation of the spot exchange rate when the forward contract matures (currencies are deliverable). The second expands on this idea by using the relative purchasing power model and implies that today's forward price should be equal to today's spot exchange rate times a ratio of expected inflation in the domestic economy divided by expected inflation in the foreign economy. The third adds the concept of interest rate parity (in which real risk-free returns are constant worldwide) and implies that the forward price should be equal to the current exchange rate times the ratio of nominal risk-free payoffs in the domestic and foreign economy.

Hedging Exchange Rate Risk

There are three basic ways in which the exchange rate risk associated with international investment can be hedged.

The first involves the maintenance of offsetting positions in both the currency and commodities of a foreign country. For example, assume you are a U.S. investor. You have

FIGURE 15-7   SUMMARY OF PARITY RELATIONSHIPS

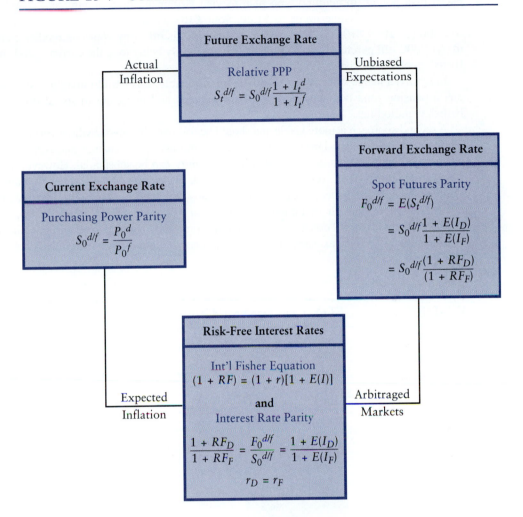

Definitions:

$S_0^{d/f}$ = Spot exchange rate today; number of domestic currency units per unit of foreign currency

P_0^f, P_0^f = Price today of unit good in foreign (f) or domestic (d) economy

$E(I_F), E(I_D)$ = Expected inflation in foreign (F) or domestic (D) economy

I_F, I_D = Actual inflation in foreign (F) or domestic (D) economy

RF_F, RF_D = Risk-free rate in foreign (F) or domestic (D) economy

$F_0^{d/f}$ = Forward rate today for a future exchange of currencies; units of domestic per unit of foreign

purchased shares of a British stock index worth $15,000 when the exchange rate is $1.50 per British pound. In addition, you plan to visit Britain in three months and spend the $15,000. If the exchange drops to $1.20, your £10,000 investment will be worth only $12,000 ($1.20 × £10,000). But this investment loss is offset by your commodity gain— the $12,000 still purchases £10,000 of British goods. By being long the currency and short British goods, your risk is eliminated.

In reality, a hedge such as this is usually unreasonable. It is hard to imagine, for example, a pension fund both investing in British pounds and intending to spend dollars on British commodities.

A second approach is more viable and should be followed by anyone who is serious about international investment: Diversify over many countries. The exchange rate risk incurred when investments are made in a single foreign country can be substantial. However, if exchange rate returns are uncorrelated, much of the risk (depending on the number of countries available) can be eliminated. The economies of many countries are so closely integrated that diversification of foreign investment among them will not reduce exchange rate risk. However, there are many countries for which the correlation is quite small and in which diversification will reduce exchange rate risk. A number of studies have shown that exchange

FIGURE 15-8   USDX COMPONENT CURRENCIES

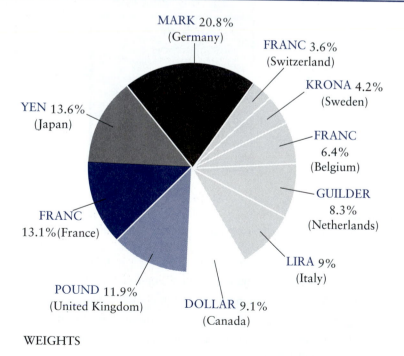

WEIGHTS

SOURCE: Information Literature of FINEX, A Division of the New York Cotton Exchange, 1992.

rate returns are often close to zero. Much, although not all, exchange rate risk can be eliminated by broad diversification among countries.

The third approach to hedging involves positions in derivatives or synthetic derivatives. Options and futures are traded on currencies of most economically developed countries. In addition, derivatives are also traded on currency baskets.

A basket is an index of the currencies of many countries. Examples of two baskets on which options and futures are available are shown in Figures 15-8 and 15-9. The currency weights shown are as of 1992 but they may change over time.

The U.S. Dollar Index (USDX) is a broad index of non-U.S. dollar currencies designed to hedge exchange rate risks that U.S. investors face when a portion of their portfolio is international (non-U.S.). The ECU is a basket of European currencies. It is referred to as the ECU because the new currency of the European community is called the European Currency Unit (or ECU). Currency baskets are often used in place of derivative trades on each currency held in the portfolio to save transaction costs. They are analogous to futures and options on aggregate stock indexes.

As a practical matter, hedging with currency futures and options has its problems. The most obvious is cost. Any option and futures position that is to "overlay" a portfolio of currencies requires active oversight and trading if it is to be successful. For large institutional portfolios with many active international bond and equity managers, costs of oversight and trading can be important.

FIGURE 15-9   ECU COMPONENT CURRENCIES

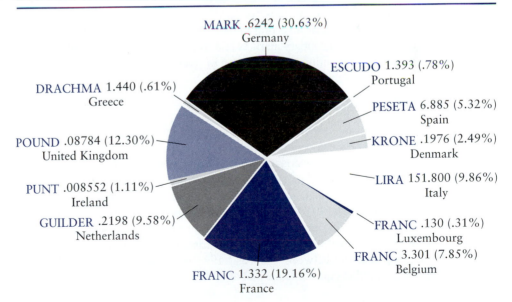

MARK .6242 (30.63%)
Germany

ESCUDO 1.393 (.78%)
Portugal

DRACHMA 1.440 (.61%)
Greece

PESETA 6.885 (5.32%)
Spain

KRONE .1976 (2.49%)
Denmark

POUND .08784 (12.30%)
United Kingdom

LIRA 151.800 (9.86%)
Italy

PUNT .008552 (1.11%)
Ireland

FRANC .130 (.31%)
Luxembourg

GUILDER .2198 (9.58%)
Netherlands

FRANC 3.301 (7.85%)
Belgium

FRANC 1.332 (19.16%)
France

SOURCE: Information Literature of FINEX, A Division of the New York Cotton Exchange, 1992.

There is also the question of how much to hedge. For example, all examples in this chapter have dealt with forward contracts on nominally risk-free securities. Since the security is risk free, the amount of currency to be hedged at year-end is known: That is, you know exactly how many forwards are needed to eliminate exchange rate risk. But if the foreign investment is in risky bonds or equities, the quantity of currency units available at year-end is uncertain. If risky assets are held, hedging with derivatives will reduce but not eliminate currency risk.

Finally, currency derivatives have maturities (delivery dates and expiration dates) that are one year or less. Rolling over a sequence of short-term hedges does not eliminate exchange rate risk to long-term investors. Say, for example, that you purchase a ten-year Japanese (zero-coupon) bond and intend to maintain this investment until year 10 at which time the payoff will be returned to your local currency. To eliminate exchange rate risk in this case, a futures contract with a delivery date of ten years is required. Rolling over one-year contracts may reduce currency risk, but it will not eliminate it.[4] This problem becomes even more complex when there are multiple (probably uncertain) dates at which foreign currency will be returned to one's local economy.

There is no easy answer to how much currency hedging should be used. Because of the costs and complexities of option and futures hedging, many global equity investors rely solely on time and country diversification. In contrast, global investors in fixed income securities (particularly, money market assets) make extensive use of derivatives hedging.

Developed Versus Emerging Equity Markets

Global investment is made in two broad types of security markets, those of economically **developed countries** and those of less developed countries which are called **emerging markets.** When global investing initially became popular in the 1980s, most foreign investment went to secondary markets of developed countries. During the early 1990s, however, increased attention has been given to emerging security markets.

Cross-border Equity Capital Flows

Figure 15-10 shows estimates of net cross-border flows of equity capital (in billions of U.S. dollars) between countries from 1986 through 1993.

The top panel shows countries *into which* investments in equity securities were made. During the late 1980s, most cross-border equity investments were made into European countries. And, although cross-border investment in European equities countries remained strong during the 1990s, there were substantial increases into equity securities of emerging markets. In fact, during 1993, equity investments into emerging markets were about the same as those made into European countries. (Net cross-border investments made into emerging markets between 1986 and 1993 were equal to almost 10% of the value of emerging market equities at the end of 1993.)

---

[4] This is similar to a ten-year U.S. investor rolling over a sequence of one-year T-bills. The return at the start of any year might be known. But the full ten-year return is uncertain.

FIGURE 15-10 TOTAL CROSS-BORDER EQUITY FLOWS (U.S. $ IN BILLIONS)

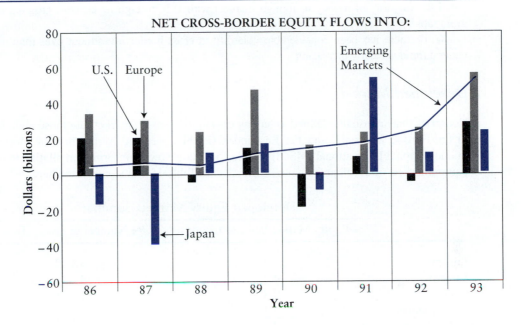

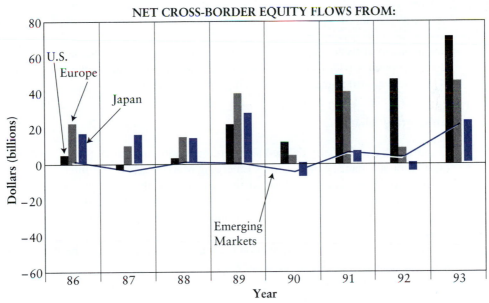

SOURCE: Berta Duran and Stuart Allen, eds., *The Guide to World Equity Markets 1994/1995*, London: *Euromoney Publication PLC* and *G.T. Capital Management PLC*, 1994.

The bottom panel of Figure 15-10 shows *from which* countries new cross-border investments came. Throughout the 1986 to 1993 period, European and U.S. equity investors provided the majority of money to foreign markets with U.S. foreign investment growing the more rapidly.

While there has been considerable volatility in cross-border investment over time, the general trend is clearly increasing.

Developed Markets

Countries that are usually defined as having developed security markets are those included in the Europe, Australia, and Far East index (EAFE) prepared by the firm of Morgan Stanley Capital International (MSCI).[5] Table 15-6 shows recent information relating to the equity markets of developed countries. The data in Table 15-6 is summarized here:

Developed Equity Markets Summary

	1994 Equity Market Value ($ trillions)	1994 Number of Stocks Traded
Europe	$3.4	6,128
Far East	4.3	4,325
Other	0.4	1,871
United States	5.1	7,770
Total	$13.2	20,094

Developed markets are generally characterized by (1) high per capita income, (2) industrialized economies with widespread literacy, (3) strong legal and political institutions, and (4) well-developed primary and secondary financial markets.

Emerging Markets

Countries that are usually defined as emerging equity markets are those included in the International Finance Corporation's Emerging Market Index. The International Finance Corporation (IFC) is a subsidiary of the World Bank that attempts to improve capital flows to countries which the IFC considers to be emerging markets. The IFC is the world's largest multilateral source of financing for private enterprise in emerging markets.

Table 15-7 shows recent information relating to equity markets of these emerging markets. The data in Table 15-7 is summarized on p. 631.

---

[5] Some countries included in the EAFE index are considered by some organizations as emerging markets. For example, the International Finance Corporation includes Malaysia as one of its emerging market countries, whereas MSCI includes Malaysia in its EAFE index.

TABLE 15-6 DEVELOPED EQUITY MARKETS

Country	Dollar U.S. Market Value ($ in Billions) 1994	Dollar U.S. Market Value ($ in Billions) 1985	Number of Listed Firms 1994	U.S. Dollar GNP, 1993 Total ($ billions)	U.S. Dollar GNP, 1993 Per Capita
EUROPE					
Austria	$ 30.2	$ 4.6	1,144	$ 183.5	$23,120
Belgium	84.1	20.8	155	213.4	21,210
Denmark	54.3	15.1	252	137.6	26,510
Finland	38.3	5.8	65	96.2	18,970
France	451.3	79.0	459	1,289.2	22,360
Germany	470.5	183.7	417	1,902.9	23,560
Iceland	0.5	NA	24	6.2	23,620
Ireland	8.4	NA	80	44.9	12,580
Italy	180.1	58.5	223	1,135.0	19,620
Luxembourg	28.5	12.7	60	14.2	35,850
Netherlands	283.3	59.4	317	316.4	20,710
Norway	36.5	10.2	132	113.5	26,340
Spain	154.9	19.0	379	534.0	13,650
Sweden	130.9	37.3	114	216.3	24,830
Switzerland	284.1	90.0	237	254.0	36,410
United Kingdom	1,210.2	328.0	2,070	1,042.7	17,970
Total	3,446.2	924.2	6,128	7,500.0	
FAR EAST					
Australia	219.2	60.1	1,144	310.0	17,510
Hong Kong	269.5	34.5	529	104.7	17,860
Japan	3,719.9	978.7	2,205	3,926.7	31,450
New Zealand	27.2	8.7	207	44.7	12,900
Singapore	134.5	11.1	240	55.4	19,310
Total	4,370.3	1,093.2	4,325	4,441.5	
OTHER					
Canada	315.0	147.0	1,185	574.9	20,670
Israel	32.7	7.6	638	72.7	13,760
Kuwait	10.5	NA	48	34.1	23,350
Total	358.3	154.6	1,871	681.7	
NON-U.S.	8,174.8	2,172.0	12,324	12,623.2	
United States	5,081.8	2,324.6	7,770	6,387.7	24,730
Total Developed Equity Markets	$13,256.6	$4,496.6	20,094	$19,010.9	

SOURCE: Adapted from *Emerging Stock Markets Factbook 1995*, International Finance Corporation, Washington, D.C.

TABLE 15-7 EMERGING EQUITY MARKETS (1994)

Country	Dollar U.S. Market Value ($ in Billions) 1994	1985	Number of Listed Firms 1994	U.S. Dollar GNP 1993 Total ($ billions)	Per Capita
EUROPE/MIDEAST/AFRICA					
Greece	$14.9	$0.7	216	$76.7	7,390
Hungary	1.6	NA	40	34.2	3,300
Jordan	4.6	2.4	95	4.9	1,190
Nigeria	2.7	2.7	177	33.0	310
Poland	3.1	NA	44	87.3	2,270
Portugal	16.2	0.2	195	77.7	7,890
South Africa	225.7	55.4	640	118.1	2,900
Turkey	21.6	NA	176	126.3	2,120
Zimbabwe	1.8	0.4	64	5.7	540
Total	292.3	61.9	1,647	563.9	
FAR EAST					
China	43.5	NA	291	581.1	490
Korea	191.8	7.4	699	338.1	7,670
Philippines	55.5	0.1	189	54.6	830
Taiwan, China	247.3	10.4	313	NA	NA
Total	538.1	17.9	1,492	973.8	
SOUTH ASIA					
India	127.5	14.3	7,000	262.8	290
Indonesia	47.2	0.1	216	137.0	730
Malaysia	199.3	16.2	478	60.1	3,160
Pakistan	12.3	1.4	724	53.2	430
Sri Lanka	2.9	1.4	215	10.7	600
Thailand	131.5	1.8	389	120.2	2,040
Total	520.7	35.3	9,022	644.0	
LATIN AMERICA					
Argentina	36.8	2.0	156	244.0	7,290
Brazil	189.3	42.7	544	472.0	3,020
Chile	68.2	2.0	279	42.5	3,070
Colombia	14.0	0.4	113	50.1	1,400
Mexico	130.2	3.8	208	324.9	3,750
Peru	8.2	0.7	218	34.0	1,490
Venezuela	4.1	1.1	90	58.9	2,840
Total	450.9	52.9	1,606	1,226.4	
Total Emerging Equity Markets	$1,801.9	$168.1	13,767	$3,408.1	

SOURCE: Adapted from *Emerging Stock Markets Factbook 1995*, International Finance Corporation, Washington, D.C.

Emerging Equity Markets Summary

	1994 Equity Market Value ($ trillions)	1994 Number of Stocks Traded
Europe/ Mideast and Africa	$0.3	1,647
Far East	0.5	1,492
South Asia	0.5	9,022
Latin America	0.5	1,606
Total	$1.8	13,767

In contrast to developed markets, emerging markets are generally characterized by the following:

- **Low per capita income.** During 1993, the per capita GNP in the United States was $24,730. In comparison, the highest levels of per capita GNP in emerging markets were between $7,290 and $7,890 (Greece, Portugal, Korea, and Argentina). The lowest were below $500 (Nigeria, China, India, and Pakistan). These are clearly economically poor countries which, if they are able to overcome the forces that have historically caused their economies to be so depressed, could show tremendous growth.

- **Nonindustrialized economies.** Most of these countries are much more dependent on agricultural activities than developed countries. For example, as a percentage of GNP, agriculture typically ranges between 5% to 36% for emerging market economies. In developed economies, agriculture accounts for between zero to 4% of GNP.

- **Significant political risks.** Some of these countries are still ruled by military authorities and in many others the political authorities are closely aligned with the military. Political risks associated with emerging market investing are significant and should not be minimized.

To illustrate the extent of political risks that can be incurred when investing in emerging markets, the following quotes come from a book prepared in 1995 by a major international investment firm. Names of countries as well as the political leaders have been deleted. Each quote refers to a different country.[6]

After many years of instability with frequent interchange of civilian and military government and the resulting lack of continuity in economic policy, . . .

---

[6] The quotes come from Berta Duran and Stuart Allen, eds., *The Guide to World Equity Markets 1994/95*, Euromoney Publications PLC and G.T. Management PLC.

The year was marked by high degree of instability and uncertainty. In 1993, (the country) had three Ministers of Finance, two proposed stabilization programmes and some threats of state intervention.

In March 1990, General (not named here) handed power over to a democratically elected coalition of centre and centre left parties.

(The country) experienced the most stable year of the decade in 1993. The coalition government that sprang from the 1992 elections, held in the wake of the massacre of pro-democracy demonstrators, survived brief challenges in the form of no-confidence motions launched by the opposition.

Also consider the Republic of China (Taiwan) as well as the Korean Republic (South Korea), which are under threat of military invasion. Political risks from international investing are not trivial.

◤ **Significant economic risks.** As you would expect, the economies of emerging markets are often much less stable than those of developed economies. Examples of this can be seen in the panels of Figure 15-11. Each panel shows information for three emerging Latin American countries: Argentina, Brazil, and Mexico. In the first panel, yearly returns (in U.S. dollars) are shown. The highest return was for Argentina in 1991 when a U.S. investor would have earned 396.9%! (The domestic equity return in Argentina during 1991 was 710% and the exchange rate return was a negative 39%!) The lowest return was for Brazil in 1990 when U.S. investors would have lost 65.7%. Underlying these very volatile returns were volatile domestic security returns and currency exchange rates.

    The middle panel in Figure 15-11 shows the currency returns to a U.S. investor in each of the three countries. In virtually every year, these were negative. For example, currency returns from investing in Argentina during this period ranged from a low of negative 78.5% to a high of 0.1%. The exchange rate situation of Brazil was even worse. If a U.S. investor had transferred $1 million to Brazil at the start of 1985 and placed the money in a bank account that earned zero interest (very unlikely) and returned the money to the United States at the end of 1994, it would have been worth $0.14, fourteen cents! As shown in the bottom panel of Figure 15-11, the dramatic decline in each country's exchange rate can be traced to inflation.

◤ **Underdeveloped primary and secondary security markets.** Many emerging market economies are just beginning to develop the primary markets required to bring providers of capital together with those who have productive opportunities for capital. In fact, in many of these economies, secondary markets are better

---

[7] For example, many professionals believe that foreign investment in Mexican securities was a major force behind the recent volatility of Mexican equity values. During the early 1990s, large U.S. mutual funds and other institutional investors were heavy purchasers of Mexican stocks at the same time that Mexican share values were rising. However, when the Mexican equity market fell in 1994, these institutions withdrew their capital from Mexico and, thus, perhaps exacerbated the fundamental decline in the Mexican stock market.

FIGURE 15-11 **EMERGING MARKETS DATA**

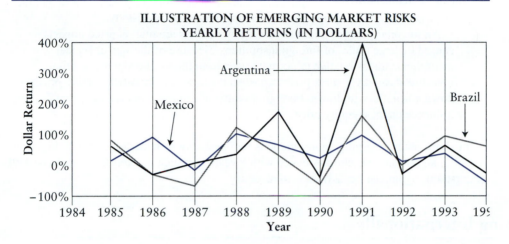

ILLUSTRATION OF EMERGING MARKET RISKS
YEARLY RETURNS (IN DOLLARS)

CURRENCY RETURNS

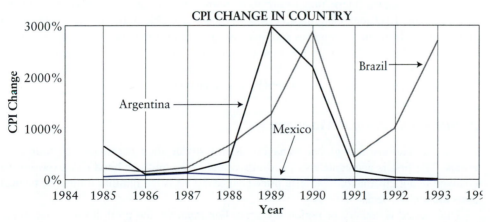

CPI CHANGE IN COUNTRY

developed than primary markets. However, costs of trading on secondary markets can be significantly larger than costs incurred in developed markets. These include costs of researching companies, transacting, and security custody.

An important cost of trading in emerging markets are market price impacts caused by large trades of foreign institutions. Because of the size of typical institutional trades relative to normal trades from the local economy, foreign investment can drive stock prices up when the money is invested or drive prices down when it is withdrawn. Foreign investment can represent an important influence on local equity prices.[7]

In short, many emerging equity markets will probably provide large returns in the future. But significant risks are associated with investing in such markets that should be well understood. Again, the key advice is to diversify.

Investing Internationally

So how can an individual or institutional investor obtain exposure to international securities? The cheapest and easiest way might be to purchase shares in companies that do business worldwide. These are referred to as multinational corporations. Unfortunately, various studies suggest that this might not be an effective approach. Share returns of multinationals are virtually indistinguishable from returns on companies that have no foreign business. However, for investors who wish to take equity positions in many emerging market countries, ownership of multinational companies might be the most effective approach.

A more direct alternative is to purchase American Depository Receipts (ADRs) on shares of foreign stocks. In this case, a U.S. bank purchases shares of a security in the foreign country and places them in safekeeping in its foreign branch. A trust receipt is then issued to the U.S. investor representing a claim to a share held in safekeeping. ADRs are actively traded on the New York Stock Exchange, the American Stock Exchange, and on NASDAQ.

The easiest way to obtain an international position is to purchase shares in a commingled portfolio. Banks, insurance companies, and investment counsel companies offer a variety of commingled international portfolios. Some of these are not registered with the Securities and Exchange Commission (SEC) and are available only to pension funds and endowments. Insurance companies and investment counsel companies also register certain portfolios with the SEC and offer them to the general public as open-end mutual funds and closed-end investment companies. A closed-end form is often chosen when there are restrictions on the sale of securities bought in a given country.

Active International Management

Active international and global managers usually divide their decisions into four categories. The first is aggregate risk exposure. Should the equity or bond risk exposure be changed in anticipation of near-term price changes? This is the familiar timing, or tactical asset allocation, decision.

The second is country or region selection. For example, the portfolio manager might overweight shares of firms in the Pacific Rim and underweight European shares in the belief that the Pacific Rim markets are much less efficiently priced.

Third, the manager must make a currency selection decision. If the country selection is at odds with the currency selection decision, futures and options are used to effect any required changes. Many managers state that they have no ability to forecast currency moves and take no position in derivatives, counting on time and country diversification to wash out exchange rate returns of the portfolio. In contrast, some managers make significant exchange rate bets. Unlike equity portfolios, most international bond portfolios are fully hedged against currency risks. Doing so appears to cut the volatility of international bond portfolio returns in half.

Finally, the manager has to make a security selection decision. Virtually all global managers maintain research staffs in the major financial centers around the world. They are the experts on local economic trends, debt issues, and common stocks.

The performance of active international management is hard to judge. Many have a return history that is too short to develop any statistical confidence. In addition, developing benchmarks to measure their returns against is a complex task, since it must account for both their country selection and currency selection. A recent study by Cumby and Glen suggested that active international management by U.S. equity mutual funds does not beat passively managed international portfolios.

Many of the so-called market anomalies discussed in Chapter 10 also appear to exist in security markets other than the United States. For example, small-firm and price-to-earnings ratio effects have been documented in Japan, the United Kingdom, Germany, and France. Recall that this means small-capitalization firms and firms with low price-to-earnings (P/E) ratios have higher beta adjusted returns than high-capitalization—P/E returns. A January effect also seems to be present in Japan.

Cost of Active Versus Passive Management. The costs of international investing are almost always greater than the costs of investing in one's home country. This is certainly true for U.S. residents, since in this country investment costs in local securities are (generally) among the lowest in the world. Assuming that a professional investment firm such as a mutual fund is hired to manage the international position, these costs consist of (1) custodian fees, (2) management adviser fees, and (3) transaction costs.

Custody fees for a large international commingled fund are generally about 20 basis points per year, or 0.20%. As international trading grows during the 1990s, this fee is likely to fall. Management fees will vary considerably, depending on the investment strategies the adviser uses. An international management fee of 100 basis points is common, although these fees can range between 50 and 150 basis points.

Transaction costs consist of the bid-ask spread, brokerage commissions, taxes, and price pressure effects. Bid-ask spreads are inversely related to the market capitalization and trading volume of the security. Stocks in countries other than the United States, United Kingdom, Germany, and Japan certainly have the largest bid-ask spreads. Commissions and taxes vary widely between countries. For example, commissions in the United States and the United Kingdom are negotiable and quite small if the trade is large. Twelve basis points (0.12%) is typical for a large portfolio. In Japan, equity commissions range between 25 and 125 basis points. Some countries even charge taxes as high as 100 basis points at both purchase and sale. Price pressure costs are hard to measure and there have been no thorough studies of price pressure in non-U.S. markets. Based on U.S. studies, though, smaller capitalization stocks tend to have the greatest price pressure impacts. In short, transaction costs vary between countries but are usually larger for countries other than the United States, United Kingdom, Germany, and Japan.

One way to estimate the summation of these costs is to examine expense ratios for international mutual funds. As we discussed in Chapter 14, the expense ratio is equal to all expenses associated with managing the fund (except transaction costs) divided by the average value of assets during a year. The median expense ratio of actively managed international mutual funds was recently 1.75% compared with a median ratio of 1.10% for domestic U.S. growth and income mutual funds. For actively managed international bond funds, the median was 1.60% versus 1.07% for U.S. government bond funds.

Passively managed portfolios are not as costly to maintain. A total cost of about 50 basis points is reasonable to expect. In short, if active international management is to beat passive management, it must provide pre-expense returns 1.0% to 1.5% more than passive management.

S U M M A R Y

Here are the key concepts:

◢ Given the size of non-U.S. financial markets and improved telecommunications, all investors should give serious consideration to investing globally. The advantage of doing so is the improved diversification that can be gained. Although individual country markets are increasingly interrelated, the economic bases of various countries are sufficiently different that diversification benefits are available.

◢ When a foreign security is purchased, investors actually buy two assets: (1) the security, and (2) the currency of the country in which the security is domiciled. As a result, the return earned on foreign investment comes from both the security return (in its local currency) and an exchange rate return. This creates a new element of risk that investors need to understand and decide how to deal with— exchange rate risk.

◢ Exchange rates between economically developed countries are flexible and free to adjust to market forces. A few less developed countries still retain fixed exchange rates.

◢ The major force underlying changes in exchange rates is differential inflation in two economies. For example, if country 1 has no inflation but country 2 experiences a 10% inflation rate, then the equilibrium value of country 2's currency should decline by 10% relative to country 1. This is referred to as **purchasing power parity.**

◢ Expectations of future inflation are also priced in forward currency contracts. For example, if expected inflation in country 1 is 0% and in country 2 it is 10%, then the forward contract on country 2's currency will be priced 10% lower then its spot exchange rate. This is referred to as **spot futures parity.**

■ If capital is able to move between countries at no cost, then the potential for arbitrage transactions would cause the real rate of return to be equal for all countries. This concept is known as **interest rate parity.**

■ These three equilibrium models are based on costless arbitrage. In real-world situations, arbitrage is impeded by transaction costs, legal restrictions on the free flow of currencies, and economic policies of central governments.

■ The benefits of hedging depend on how long one intends to remain invested internationally and the security risk of the portfolio. Exchange rate risk of a short-term risk-free foreign investment can be eliminated by proper use of forwards, futures, and options. This is because one knows exactly how much currency to hedge and has derivatives with the necessary maturity to engage in a hedge. With risky portfolios, the quantity to be hedged is uncertain. There are currently no long-term derivatives available. Long-term investors in risky securities might best rely on broad country diversification and time.

R E V I E W   P R O B L E M

1. You are a U.S. resident thinking about investing $100,000 in German stocks. The exchange rate is currently $0.30 per mark. You expect that the German stocks will earn 15% for German residents. You also expect that the inflation rate over the next year will be 9% in Germany and 6% in the United States.
    a. If you do not hedge your investment, what is your expected one-year return? What part is due to domestic expected returns and what part is due to exchange rate returns?
    b. Given this information, what do you think the one-year forward rate should be?
    c. Assume the one-year forward rate is exactly what you calculated in part b. What hedge would you make to offset exchange rate risk?
    d. Assume the German stocks do provide a domestic return of 15%, but the exchange rate in a year is $0.40 per mark. If you hedged, what is your return?
    e. Why may this hedge not work?

Solution

a. Dollar and Deutschemark (DM) flows are as follows:

Today		One Year Later
Invest Dollars	$100,000	
Buy DM at $0.30/DM	15%	
Invest DM	333,333 DM ⟶	$383,333 DM Receive DM
	Return	Sell DM at $0.29174
		$111,834 Receive Dollars

$$\text{Expected Spot Rate} = (\$0.30)\,\frac{1.06}{1.09} = \$0.29174$$

$$\text{Expected Return on Dollar Investment} = \frac{\$111,834}{\$100,000} - 1.0 = 11.834\%$$

$$\text{Domestic Return} = 15\%$$

$$\text{Exchange Rate Return} = \frac{0.29174}{0.300} = 0.97248$$

$$\text{Total International Return} = (1.15)\,(0.97248) - 1.0 = 11.834\%$$

Note that by not hedging, your expected return is equal to the compounding of the 15% domestic return and a negative 2.75% exchange rate loss. However, since you are uncertain about the exchange rate one year from now, you are also uncertain about the exchange rate return.

b. The forward rate should be the expected spot rate of $0.29174/DM.

c. Sell futures (or forward) contracts on 383,333 DM at a price of $0.29174/DM. This will lock in the expected return of 11.834%. (This is lower than the 15% domestic German return, but recall that inflation in Germany is expected to be greater by about 3 percentage points. Thus, equilibrium returns on German stocks should be about 3 percentage points higher than the returns on domestic U.S. stocks. Given the lower U.S. inflation rate, the 11.83% might be fair.)

d. You have sold futures contracts on 383,333 DM at $0.29174/DM. If the exchange rate in a year is $0.400/DM, the 383,333 DM received in a year from now can be translated back to $153,333, for a gain of $41,499 more than expected. But this is exactly offset by a $41,499 loss on the futures [(0.29174 − 0.4) × 383,333]. Thus, your return is exactly what was expected—11.83%. Given the hedge there is no uncertainty in your expected return associated with exchange rates.

e. The hedge might not work:
   (1) if contracts in 383,333 DM units are unavailable.
   (2) if the contracts mature on dates other than those on which you intend to translate marks into dollars.
   (3) if the domestic German return is not 15%.

QUESTIONS AND PROBLEMS

1. A $1 million investment is made in Canadian stocks when the exchange rate is $0.70/ Canadian dollars. At that time, the six-month forward exchange rate is $0.72. The expected six-month domestic return is 9%. The U.S. expected inflation rate for the next six months is 5%.
   a. What is the expected inflation rate in Canada?
   b. What is the expected exchange rate for six months ahead?
   c. Is the value of the dollar expected to increase or decrease? Why?
   d. What is the expected foreign return? Without a hedge, what factors create uncertainty about this return?
   e. Assume a hedge is used, the actual exchange rate is $0.68/Canadian dollars in six months, and the domestic Canadian return is 12%. What foreign return is earned and what were its causes?

2. On January 1 the price of a share of a Japanese stock is 10 yen and the exchange rate is $0.40 per yen. The stock pays no dividends during the year. At the end of the year, the stock

is selling for 12 yen and the exchange rate is $0.35 per yen. What was the stock's return to both a Japanese investor and a U.S. investor?

3. The current spot rate between U.S. dollars and British pounds is $1.25/£. The nominal risk-free rate in the U.S. is 8.15%, and the real risk-free rate of interest is 3%.
   a. What is the expected U.S. inflation rate?
   b. If the one-year forward rate is $1.19/£ , what is the expected inflation rate for Britain?
   c. If the real risk-free rate is also 3% in Britain, what should be the nominal risk-free rate in Britain?

4. You are given the following spot quotations:
   $1.9 per 1 British pound
   $0.7 per 1 German mark
   2 German marks per 1 British pound
   a. Are these exchange rates in equilibrium?
   b. What arbitrage might you engage in with $1,000,000?

5. You are given the following information:

Country	One-year Risk-free Rate	Spot Price	One-year Forward Price
United States	8%		
Japan	6%	$0.008 per 1 Yen	$0.008 per Yen
Germany	8%	$0.007 per 1 Mark	$0.007 per Mark
United Kingdom	10%	$1.900 per pound	$1.95 per pound

   a. Use the interest rate parity model to determine which set of prices are inconsistent.
   b. Illustrate any potential arbitrage with $1,000,000.
   c. Assuming that spot currency prices won't change, what should be the exchange rate between marks and pounds?

6. In reading the financial press, you notice that forward prices of U.K. pounds (dollars per 1.0 pound) are lower than spot prices. What should this tell you about current risk-free rates in the United Kingdom relative to the United States?

7. Yearly returns on a portfolio of small capitalization stocks in Japan are shown in both local currency (Yen) and U.S. dollars here. Calculate the yearly exchange rate returns.

	1986	1987	1988	1989	1990
In dollars	60%	87%	32%	38%	−33%
In Yen	26	43	36	58	−37

8. A U.S. mutual fund purchases $1,000,000 worth of a diversified British stock portfolio at an exchange rate of $2 per pound. No futures or forward currency hedge is used. Complete the table here.

Dollar Based on Portfolio Return

Return in Local Currency	Exchange Rate at Year-End		
	$1.75/£	$2/£	$2.25/£
−15%			
10%			
35%			

9. Repeat Question 8, but assume you sell 550,000 one-year pound futures at a price of $2 per pound. _____ _____ _____ _____

10. You are considering an investment in stocks of the United Kingdom and France. Information about your expectations is shown here:

	U.K.	France
Domestic Return		
Expected Return	18%	20%
Standard Deviation	30%	35%
Exchange Rate Return		
Expected Return	5%	−4%
Standard Deviation	10%	10%
Correlation with Domestic Return	0.30	0.00

CFA

a. What is the expected return from a foreign investment in each country?
b. Calculate the standard deviation of the foreign return on each country's stocks. (Hint: Consider this to be a two-asset portfolio in which 100% is invested in each security, the currency, and the stock portfolio.)

CFA 11. The value of the pension portfolio that you manage is $1 billion, and it is all invested in U.S. stocks. Its expected return is 15% and its standard deviation is 25%. Foreign investments are available in other countries; the expected foreign return and the standard deviation of each are 15% and 30%, respectively. The correlation between each foreign return and the U.S. return is 0.30. If you invest the $1 billion equally in the United States and in foreign countries, what are the expected return and standard deviation of your portfolio?

CFA 12. The following chart illustrates the domestic prices of items of similar quality—shoes, watches, and electric motors—in the United States and Israel.

Items	United States (Dollars)	Israel (Pounds)
Shoes	20	80
Watches	40	180
Electric motors	80	600

Assuming that $1 exchanges for 5 Israeli pounds and that transportationcosts are zero, which goods will tend to be imported?
a. Israel will import shoes and watches; the United States will import electric motors.
b. Israel will import shoes; the United States will import watches and electric motors.
c. Israel will import all three goods from the United States.
d. Israel will import electric motors; the United States will import shoes and watches.

CFA 13. If the exchange rate value of the British pound goes from $1.80 (U.S.) to $1.60 (U.S.), then the pound has:
a. Appreciated and the British will find U.S. goods cheaper.
b. Appreciated and the British will find U.S. goods more expensive.
c. Depreciated and the British will find U.S. goods more expensive.
d. Depreciated and the British will find U.S. goods cheaper.

CFA 14. Which one of the following factors is most likely to cause a nation's currency to depreciate on the foreign exchange markets?
a. An increase in the nation's domestic rate of inflation.

b. An increase in the inflation rates of the nation's trading partners.

c. A decrease in the nation's domestic rate of inflation.

d. An increase in domestic real interest rates.

15. Renée Michaels, CFA, plans to invest $1 million in U.S. government cash equivalents for the next 90 days. Michaels's client has authorized her to use non-U.S. government cash equivalents, but only if the currency risk is hedged to U.S. dollars by using forward currency contracts.

    a. Calculate the U.S. dollar value of the hedged investment at the end of 90 days for each of the two cash equivalents in the table provided. Show all calculations.

    b. Briefly explain the theory that best accounts for your results.

Interest Rates
90-Day Cash Equivalents

Japanese Government	7.6%
German Government	8.6%

Exchange Rates
Currency Units per U.S. Dollar

	Spot	90-Day Forward
Japanese Yen	133.05	133.47
German Deutschemark	1.5260	1.5348

16. You are the treasurer of USDS. One USDS board member has suggested that most of FI's cash be invested in one-year U.S. T-bills to reduce exposure to the pont. The suggested hedge is consistent with the firm's comprehensive strategy addressing foreign exchange exposure.

    On January 1, 1990, the YTM on one-year U.S. T-bills was 7.1%, the comparable YTM on one-year Lumbarian T-bills was 14.6%; the exchange rate was 4 ponts per one U.S. dollar. FI's cash position was such that 60 million ponts could be invested for one year without concern that this money would be required for operations.

    a. Assume your economist's exchange rate forecast of a 5% decline in the value of the pont (vs. the U.S. dollar) by year-end 1990 proves to be correct. Calculate the proceeds at maturity, in U.S. dollars, of a 60 million pont investment in U.S. T-bills versus the same investment in Lumbarian T-bills. Assume that the holding period is the 1990 calendar year.

    b. Using the T-bill yield information provided and the four ponts per one U.S. dollar exchange rate at January 1, 1990, calculate the one-year forward exchange rate at the beginning of 1990 that would support the interest rate parity relationship.

    c. Assuming that the one-year forward exchange rate at the beginning of 1990 was 4.1 ponts per one U.S. dollar, describe the transactions that a U.S. arbitrageur could execute to realize riskless profits, and calculate the amount of profits per $100 of exposure a U.S. arbitrageur would realize.

D A T A F I L E   A N A L Y S I S

1. Access the data set called WRLDRTNS and review its contents. In this datafile analysis, use the file that provides yearly returns on developed countries. For developed countries having return data from 1971 and beyond, calculate their correlation with the S&P 500 returns. Interpret the financial significance of the results.

2. Again use the data set called WRLDRTNS but this time identify the data sets related to emerging markets. These include U.S. $ returns, currency returns relative to the dollar, stock

price indexes in each country, and rates of changes in each country's consumer price index (CPI). Using this data to back up your analysis, develop a list of important investment considerations if one were to invest in emerging markets. How could you reduce the risk of emerging market investment?

REFERENCES

Helpful discussions of international investing are presented in the following:

Various issues of *Investing Worldwide,* Association for Investment Management and Research, Charlottesville, VA.

Solnik, Bruno. *International Investing,* 2nd ed., Reading, MA: Addison-Wesley, 1991.

Statistics on international equities traded in developed countries are maintained and published by Morgan Stanley Capital International (MSCI) in their *MSCI Perspective* publications. The data is available at a cost directly from MSCI Geneva Switzerland or in most major libraries.

Statistics on emerging market equities can be found in the yearly *Emerging Stock Market Factbook* published by the International Finance Corporation, Washington, DC. This publication is available at major libraries.

Overviews of the equity markets in most financially developed economies and many emerging markets are provided in the following publications: *The GT Guide to World Equity Markets,* London; *Euromoney Publications PLC* and *G.T. Management PLC,* updated annually.

Interesting articles on international investing include the following:

Agrawal, Anup and Kishore Tandon. "Anomalies or Illusions? Evidence from Stock Markets in Eighteen Countries," *Journal of International Money and Finance, 13,* 1994.

Black, Fischer and Robert Litterman. "Global Portfolio Optimization," *Financial Analysts Journal,* September–October 1992.

Cumby, Robert E. and Jack D. Glen. "Evaluating the Performance of International Mutual Funds," *Journal of Finance,* June 1990.

French, Kenneth R. and James M. Poterba. "Were Japanese Stock Prices Too High?" *Journal of Financial Economics,* October 1991.

Hakkio, Craig S. "Is Purchasing Power Parity a Useful Guide to the Dollar?" *Economic Review,* Federal Reserve Bank of Kansas City, Third Quarter, 1992.

Hunter, John E. and T. Daniel Coggin. "An Analysis of the Diversification Benefit from International Investment," *The Journal of Portfolio Management,* Fall. 1990.

Pringle, John J. "Managing Foreign Exchange Exposure," *Journal of Applied Corporate Finance,* Winter 1991.

Roll, Richard. "The International Crash of 1987," *Financial Analysts Journal,* September-October 1988.

Rudd, Andrew. "Industry versus Country Correlations," *Investing Worldwide,* Association for Investment Management and Research, Charlottesville, VA, 1994.

16

FINANCIAL
FUTURES

*After reading this chapter you should
have an understanding of how contract
prices of financial futures are
determined as well as how financial
futures are used in portfolio hedging
and speculative strategies.*

A revolution in the types of securities traded in financial markets began during the 1970s that continues unabated today: the introduction of derivative securities on financial assets. The use of the term derivative comes from the fact that these securities have a market value which is dependent on (derived from) the value of another asset called the underlying asset. There are two basic types of derivatives: futures contracts and options. We examine futures in this chapter and options in Chapter 17.

Although markets in futures contracts have existed for centuries, they were traded almost exclusively on physical commodities such as grains, precious metals, wood products, and oil. Active trading in financial futures is a more recent phenomena, beginning in the United States during the late 1970s. Although trading of commodity futures remains an active market, the dominant source of trading in today's futures markets is in financial futures.

A futures contract is an agreement between two parties to trade an asset at a stated future date. The contract specifies (1) the asset to be traded, (2) the quantity of the asset to be traded, (3) the date at which the asset and money will be exchanged, and (4) the price to be paid for the asset. The asset to be traded is known as the **underlying** or **spot** asset. The date at which the underlying asset and money are to be exchanged is called the **delivery date.** The price at which the parties agree to trade is known as the **contracted**

futures price, or simply the **futures price.** The party who contracts to buy the asset is the **owner** of the futures contract and is referred to as being **long** the contract. The party who contracts to deliver the good is the **seller** of the futures contract, referred to as being **short** the contract.

Consider the following underlying spot asset: a U.S. Treasury bond with an 8% coupon, a 15-year maturity, and a par value of $100,000. Futures contracts on such Treasury bonds are widely traded. Each contract is an agreement to trade exactly the same underlying Treasury bond. The only difference between one futures contract and another would be the contracted delivery date. Assume that on June 30 a futures contract on such an asset with a delivery date of September 30 is trading at a contracted futures price of $102,000. If one were to buy the futures contract on June 30, he or she would be contractually obligated to pay $102,000 on September 30 and in return would receive the U.S Treasury bond that underlies the contract. If one were to sell the futures contract, he or she would be obligated to deliver the underlying asset on September 30 and would receive $102,000 in return.

There are two motives for any trade in futures contracts: hedging or speculation. **Hedgers** use futures to reduce uncertainties about the price at which they will eventually trade an asset. Consider a corporate treasurer who intends to buy (on September 30) a U.S. Treasury bond similar to the one just described. To guarantee on June 30 the price that will be paid on September 30, the treasurer could purchase the September 30 futures contract. When September 30 arrives, the treasurer would deliver the contracted price of $102,000 and receive the underlying Treasury bond. A portfolio manager owns Treasury bonds and is concerned about a decline in their value due to a probable increase in interest rates. To guarantee a future selling price, the manager could sell the September 30 futures contract. When September 30 arrives, the manager would deliver the Treasury bond that is held in his or her inventory and receive the $102,000. Regardless of the actual market value of such Treasury bonds on September 30, both parties lock in the delivery date price at which they will trade.

Speculators trade futures that they believe are mispriced in an attempt to earn a profit. For example, assume you believe that Treasury bonds underlying the futures contract will trade for less than $102,000 on September 30. You could speculate on this belief by selling the future. If you are correct, you will be able to buy such bonds on September 30 at a price below $102,000 and deliver them to satisfy your short futures position, receiving $102,000 in return. The difference between the contracted futures selling price of $102,000 and your purchase price would represent the profit from the speculation.

We begin our discussion of financial futures with a section examining important principles of futures contracts. In this introductory section, we define more precisely the important features of futures contracts, examine their use in hedging and speculation, and develop a general valuation model of futures pricing. In the four sections that follow, we examine more thoroughly four specific types of financial futures: (1) short-term debt, (2) long-term debt, (3) equity indexes, and (4) currency exchange rates. These are the major types of financial futures traded today.

Before continuing, note this important point: Returns on positions in financial futures are very sensitive to small changes in the value of the underlying security. We will see that ownership of a futures contract is identical to ownership of the asset together with debt borrowings equal to the cost of the asset. Owning a futures contract is ownership of the asset using 100% leverage. Small changes in the value of the underlying asset will have dramatic effects on futures contract returns. This means that people who trade in futures must clearly understand the potential results of their futures trading. *When properly used, futures can provide important hedging devices to portfolio managers. When improperly used, they can result in disaster.*[1]

Principles of Futures Contracts

In this section we examine the fundamentals of financial futures trading. To help in this discussion, we illustrate various concepts with a futures contract on a hypothetical underlying security called the Pacific Rim Fund (PRF). The benefit of using a fictitious under lying financial asset is that it allows us to focus on fundamentals of futures trading as opposed to the specifics of an actual contract.

The Pacific Rim Fund is assumed to be a mutual fund that invests in a specified set of stocks domiciled in various Pacific Rim countries. Stocks held in the mutual fund's portfolio are assumed to be known by investors, the holdings never change, and percentage investments in each security are determined by their relative market capitalizations.[2] These assumptions allow us to analytically develop contract prices at which futures on the fund should trade. In addition, we assume that securities owned by the Pacific Rim Fund will not pay any dividends or interest to the fund and the fund will not pay any dividends to owners. This assumption simplifies calculations of theoretical futures prices. Finally, each futures contract calls for the delivery of exactly one share of PRF at a stated delivery date.

Forwards and Futures

Although this chapter has the title "Financial Futures," much of the discussion also applies to forward contracts on financial assets. Forward and futures contracts are virtually identical. Forward contracts, however, are traded in over-the-counter markets whereas futures are traded on futures exchanges. Both are agreements to trade at a future date. All terms of the trade (the asset, quantity, price, and delivery date) are agreed to today whereas the actual trade occurs later. The buyer of a forward or futures contract is legally obligated to deliver money equal to the contracted price and the seller is legally obligated to deliver the specified good. *A futures contract is simply a forward contract that is traded on a securities exchange.*

For most of this chapter, we assume that forward and futures contracts are identical, although strictly speaking, this is not correct. Differences between them, which we review

---

[1] There have been numerous examples of the improper use of futures during the 1990s that caused many corporations to suffer severe earnings losses. The most notorious example led to a $1 billion loss by Barings Bank and the bank's bankruptcy. Improper futures positions were also a major cause for losses in the investment portfolio of Orange County, California, and the county's bankruptcy. Futures have been compared to a sharp knife. In the hands of a knowledgeable doctor, the instrument can be very beneficial. In the hands of someone without proper knowledge and skill, it can cause significant harm.

[2] Assume the portfolio consists of 100 stocks that have a total market capitalization of $10 billion. Weighting each stock by its market capitalization means that, if the market capitalization of stock A is $1 billion, then 10% of the portfolio is invested in stock A.

later in this section, have relatively minor effects on either their prices or their use as risk management tools.

Forward contracts have been part of commerce for thousands of years. We can trace the first evidence of futures contracts to negotiable *lettres de faire* in twelfth-century Europe. Over time, the center of forward and futures trading moved to London. In the United States, futures trading developed in the mid-nineteenth century in various agricultural commodities. Futures on financial securities, first offered in the United States during the 1970s as a way for investors to hedge financial risk, are currently traded in most economically developed countries. And many less developed countries are in the process of forming commodity futures markets so that local farmers can hedge the price risk of their crops.

Futures Trading

Basic Definitions. We denote the futures price at which buyers and sellers agree to eventually trade as F_{tT}. Date T refers to the date at which the trade is to take place, the delivery date. For a given contract, the delivery date never changes. Date t refers to the date at which a futures with a delivery date of T is priced. When t is equal to zero ($t = 0$) we are referring to the original date at which a futures trade occurred between a buyer and a seller.

As an example, assume that on June 30 a futures contract on one share of PRF with a delivery date of September 30 is trading for $100. That is:

$$F_{0T} = F_{\text{June 30,Sept 30}} = \$100$$

A buyer on June 30 of the PRF futures contract deliverable on September 30 would be legally obligated to pay $100 on September 30 to the seller and the seller would be legally obligated to deliver one share of the Pacific Rim Fund.

On July 1, the September 30 futures contracts will probably trade at contracted prices other than $100. For example, if the closing market price of the September 30 PRF contract is $102 at the close of trading on July 1, then:

$$F_{1T} = F_{\text{July 1,Sept 30}} = \$102$$

Buyers and sellers who trade the September 30 futures on July 1 would be obligated to trade on September 30 at $102. However, the contracted price between buyers and sellers who contracted for $100 on June 30 remains at $100.[3]

Buyers and sellers may hold their contracts open through the delivery date and take actual delivery of the security and cash. However, it is usually more convenient to offset one's position in a futures contract by an opposite trade prior to actual delivery. For example, an initial buyer of a PRF contract with a delivery date of September 30 could offset the trade by selling an identical contract prior to September 30. For example, assume that a June 30 buyer of the September 30 PRF futures decides to sell a September 30 contract on August 31 when the contract is trading at $103. The sale on August 31 will close the fu-

---

[3] For simplicity, we assume that futures trades occur at closing prices of the day. In practice, trading occurs continuously throughout each day. Also, buyers and sellers of futures contracts are affected by daily changes in the contract's price through a mechanism known as mark-to-market. Mark-to-market is discussed later in the chapter.

tures position. The $3 difference in contract prices will represent a profit to the buyer, and cash in the amount of $3 will be delivered after the sale has occurred.

At the delivery date of a futures contract, the contracted futures price must be equal to the value of the underlying asset at that time. If this were not the case, then a profitable arbitrage would be possible. An example of such an arbitrage is presented later in the chapter. If we define S_t as the market price of the underlying spot security on which the futures contract is traded, then:

Futures Value at Delivery Date $\qquad F_{TT} = S_T \qquad\qquad$ **(16.1)**

Financial Futures Traded in World Markets. Today, futures contracts on financial securities are traded in virtually all economically developed countries. Although trading in financial futures was first developed in the United States, their popularity has created a worldwide market.

Table 16-1 shows sample price quotations for the four basic types of financial futures traded during the mid-1990s. The contracts differ in the nature of the underlying security and include (1) short-term interest rate securities, (2) long-term interest rate securities, (3) stock indexes, and (4) currencies. Details about each type are provided in later sections of the chapter.

The first contract shown in Table 16-1 is a *short-term interest rate future*. The deliverable asset is a Eurodollar deposit with a 3-month maturity and a par value of $1 million. The futures has a delivery date in June and is traded on the Chicago Mercantile Exchange (CME). Hedgers would buy this contract if they intend to invest approximately $1 million in 3-month Eurodollars at the end of June. Purchasing the contract would lock in the interest return on such securities, since the price to be paid in June would be known.[4] Hedgers

TABLE 16-1   ILLUSTRATION OF FINANCIAL FUTURES TRADED IN WORLD MARKETS

Type of Asset	Actual Spot Asset	Quantity	Delivery Date	Contract Settle Price	Exchange	Open Interest
Short-term Interest Rate	3-month Eurodollars	$1 million	June	94.86	CME	397,000
Long-term Interest Rate	U.S. Treasury Bond	$100,000	June	118-27	CBT	16,363
Stock Index	Nikkei 225	$5 times Index	March	19,565	CME	26,046
Currency	Deutsche mark	125,000 marks	June	$0.70 per mark	CME	48,751

CBT: Chicago Board of Trade.
CME: Chicago Mercantile Exchange.

---

[4] Details of each futures' price are discussed later in the chapter.

would sell this contract if they intend to borrow approximately $1 million in the 3-month Eurodollar market at the end of June.

The next contract is a *future on long-term interest rates*. The deliverable asset is a U.S. Treasury bond with a par value of $100,000. The futures has a delivery date in June and is traded on the Chicago Board of Trade (CBT). Hedgers would buy this contract if they intend to invest in instruments similar to long-term U.S. Treasury bonds at the end of June. Other hedgers would sell the contract if the intend to borrow in the long-term debt markets at the end of June.

The third contract is a *future on a stock index*. The deliverable asset is the Nikkei 225 (an index of Japanese share values). The contracted futures price is $97,825 ($5 times 19,565) and the delivery date is late March. Hedgers would buy the contract if they intend to buy similar securities in late March. Other hedgers would sell the contract if they currently owned similar securities and wished to reduce their exposure to the security's price risk.

The final contract shown in Table 16-1 is a *future on a currency*. The deliverable asset is 125,000 German deutsche marks with a delivery date in late June. The contracted futures price is $0.7 per deutsche mark. Hedgers would buy the contract if they intend to buy deutsche marks in June or sell the contract if they intend to sell deutsche marks in June.

The data shown as the **contract settle price** represents an average of trading prices during the last few minutes of the day. The settle price is used in calculating daily mark-to-market (discussed later). The data shown as **open interest** represents the number of futures contracts outstanding at the end of a day. For example, if you were to buy one deutsche mark contract from a seller, open interest would increase by 1.0.

The Trading Process. Trading in financial futures is similar in many respects to trades in listed stocks and bonds. An investor places an order with a qualified broker, known as a **futures commission merchant** or **FMC,** to buy or sell a futures with a specified delivery date. Similar to stocks and bonds, the order can be a **market order** (to trade at the next available price), **a limit order** (to trade at a given price or better), or a **stop order** (which becomes a market order if the futures prices hits a specified price—used to protect profits). The trade is transmitted to the floor of the futures exchange where it is taken by a **floor broker** to a location known as the "pit." The **pit** is the place on the exchange where trades in the future are conducted. Each major type of future is traded in a specific pit. For example, futures on short-term debt securities are traded in a pit different from where futures on stock indexes are traded. A picture of a futures pit is shown in Figure 16-1.

Trading in a futures pit, however, is quite different from trading on stock and bond exchanges. For example, there are no specialists through whom trades are transacted and recorded. Instead, all trades take place between **floor brokers** (who manage futures orders for various brokerage firms) and **floor traders** (who trade for their own account—often called **locals** or **scalpers**). Another difference is a technique known as the **open-outcry** system. All orders must be announced by a (very loud) verbal announcement of the futures contract to be traded and the price at which the party is willing to trade. This provides all traders in the pit with information about the trade and the ability to provide a counteroffer to the price.

After a trade has been executed, the futures **clearinghouse** is notified of the terms of the trade. The clearinghouse performs three functions. First, once a buyer and seller have agreed to a trade price, the clearinghouse steps into the trade and acts as the

FIGURE 16-1   PICTURE OF A FUTURES TRADING PIT

"buyer to the seller" and the "seller to the buyer." This is a critical function of the futures exchange, since it eliminates possible default risk between buyers and sellers.[5] Second, the clearinghouse handles all daily accounting and mark-to-market calculations. Finally, the clearinghouse handles any eventual delivery of assets and cash at a futures delivery date.

The Hedging Motive to Trade Futures

Futures contracts are not an asset class such as stocks, bonds, and real estate. Instead, they are indirect future ownership positions in such spot asset classes. Whereas spot assets have a fundamental productivity that generates rates of return to owners of the assets, futures contracts are simply contracts to trade. And, as contracts to trade, they have no inherent productivity.

Futures contracts are not traded for any potential rates of return arising from their productivity; they have no productivity. Instead, *futures contracts exist because they can be used to manage risk more efficiently than other alternatives.* The fundamental rationale for the existence of futures is this risk management, or hedging, motive.

---

[5] To protect the futures exchange from possible default by either party to the futures trade, the futures exchange charges a fee that is placed in an insurance fund to cover losses on trades which default.

Consider futures contracts on the Pacific Rim Fund that have a delivery date of September 30. Earlier in the chapter we assumed that trades in this contract that occur on June 30 are at a contract price of $100 per share of PRF. Buyers of one contract on June 30 are obligated to pay $100 on September 30, and sellers are obligated to deliver one share of PRF. Both parties know the price at which they will trade. Thus, all uncertainty about future trading prices is removed. By trading a futures contract, investors are able to eliminate (or, more generally, reduce) uncertainty about the price at which they will eventually buy or sell. If $F_{0T} = \$100$, both buyer and seller have the obligation to trade at date T at a price of $100.[6]

At the date of the futures trade, both parties to the future know the price at which they can trade at the delivery date and, in this sense, they are able to eliminate uncertainty about future price risk. However, when the delivery date arrives, market prices of the spot good will probably be different from the initial contracted futures price of F_{0T}. If spot prices at date T are higher than the contracted price of F_{0T}, then people who bought the future at date 0 have a futures profit (equal to the seller's loss). If spot prices at date T are lower than F_{0T}, then buyers have a futures loss (equal to the seller's profit). Thus, after the spot good and money are exchanged at date T, an **opportunity profit or loss** equal to the difference between F_{0T} and the spot price on date T is incurred. *But regardless of whether a profit or loss arises from the trade, both buyer and seller have guaranteed the price at which they can trade at the delivery date, thus eliminating price risk.*

The difference between the spot price on the delivery date of a futures (S_T) and the initial trade price of the futures (F_{0T}) is the opportunity profit or loss on the futures position. For the buyer, this value will be $S_T - F_{0T}$. For the seller, it will be $F_{0T} - S_T$. This opportunity gain or loss is known as the futures **investment value** at the delivery date T.

The relationship between delivery date spot prices of the Pacific Rim Fund and the investment values of futures on PRF is displayed in Figure 16-2. Investment values to an owner are shown as the black solid line. Investment values for the futures seller are shown as the colored line. If the value of the underlying PRF asset is $80 at the delivery date, owners of the futures will have a negative investment value equal to $20 per contract. That is, owners must pay $100 for something only worth $80 in the markets at that time. Investment values to sellers of the contract will be the exact opposite of those to owners of the future. For example, if the spot PRF asset is worth $80, a short position in the contract will be worth a positive $20. The seller can buy PRF shares for $80 and deliver them to the futures owner, receiving $100 in return.

Positions in futures contract will lead to profits or losses. *But it is important to understand that, if the futures position is properly managed, futures profits and losses will offset opposite losses and profits in spot positions.* For example, assume that on June 30 you own one share of PRF and you are concerned its value might decline in the near future. One alternative would be to sell the PRF share. But assume this would be costly and time consuming.[7] Another alternative would be to sell a futures contract on one share of PRF.

Figure 16-3 shows the delivery date outcome of selling a September 30 futures on PRF at a contract price of $100. The solid black line represents the investment value associated with owning one share of PRF. The solid colored line represents the investment value being short.

---

[6] Recall that futures traders can reverse their obligation to trade at the delivery date by making an offsetting trade prior to the delivery date.

[7] We discuss why sale (or purchase) of the spot asset might be costly or time consuming later in the chapter.

FIGURE 16-2   DELIVERY DATE INVESTMENT VALUES FOR INITIAL CONTRACT PRICE OF $100

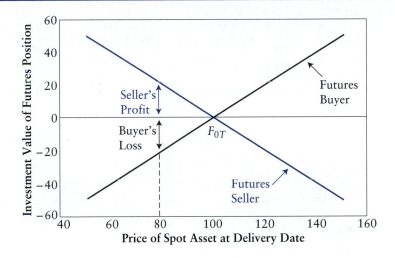

Notice that these two lines exactly offset one another. If the value of the spot PRF share is above $100, you gain on owning the share but lose an equal amount on the short futures position. If the value of the spot PRF share is below $100, you lose on owning the share but gain an equal amount on the short futures position. The net result is a known investment value equal to the contracted futures price, $100. This known payoff is shown as the dotted line.

Principles of Futures Pricing

At the Delivery Date. The prices at which buyers and sellers will agree to trade through a futures contract are always closely related to the underlying spot price at that time. For example, consider the price at which people will agree to trade the Pacific Rim Fund through a PRF futures contract at the delivery date of the future. At the date of delivery, ownership of the spot good and ownership of a futures contract will be identical. They both provide immediate ownership of the spot good. Therefore, the price at which investors will agree to trade via the future should be the same as the underlying spot good's price.

Assume the delivery date of the PRF futures contract is now. What would you do if you observed that shares of PRF are trading at $90 and a futures contract on PRF that is now deliverable is trading for $95? Clearly, you would buy shares in the spot market at $90 and sell in the futures market at $95.

This type of trade, of course, is an arbitrage trade. Recall that an **arbitrage trade** is characterized by the following:

1. No risk is incurred (you both owned the good in the spot market and owed the good in the futures market).
2. No cash investment is required (the $95 delivery price on the future will more than finance the $90 purchase price of the spot).
3. A known profit is earned ($95 − $90).

FIGURE 16-3 HEDGING A LONG SPOT POSITION

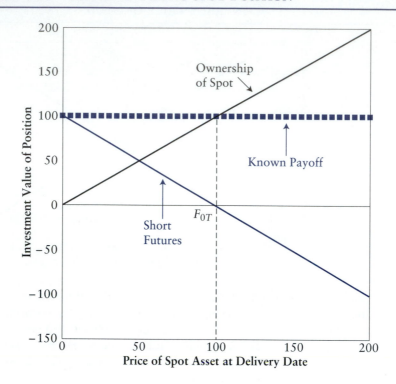

Arbitrage trades such as this are the basis on which futures contracts are priced. In our example, your trading, when added to trades of other arbitragers, would rapidly cause the price of the deliverable futures contract to be identical to the prevailing spot price.

Prior to the Delivery Date. Prior to the delivery date, there is also a relationship between futures prices and the underlying spot good prices that, if violated, creates arbitrage profits. The ownership of a futures contract guarantees you will own the spot asset at date T and guarantees the price you will have to pay. There is another way in which you could accomplish the same outcome (that is, ownership at T at a known price). *This consists of purchasing the spot asset today and fully financing its current cost by borrowing at a risk-free interest rate.*[8] Specifics of the trade are shown here:

Transaction	Cash Flows	
At date 0	Date 0	Date T
Buy Spot Asset	$-S_0$	

---

[8] It is assumed you can borrow at the risk-free rate, since all cash flows are known with certainty.

Borrow at RF Rate		$+S_0$
At date T		
Repay Borrowing		$-S_0(1 + RF)$
Pay Storage Costs		$-SC$
Net	0	$-[S_0(1 + RF) + SC]$

The only net cash flow takes place at date T and is the sum of the borrowing repayment and any storage costs (SC) such as insurance and warehousing fees. For a known cost equal to $S_0(1 + RF) + SC$, you are assured ownership of the spot asset at date T. By engaging in a trade such as this, traders are able to synthetically create payoffs that are identical to those of a futures contract. This is known as a **synthetic futures** contract.

A synthetic future can provide exactly the same outcome as a traded future: ownership of the spot good at the delivery date at a known future cost. Thus, the price at which investors will contract to trade at a futures day using a futures contract must be the same as that available using the synthetic future. *The futures price must be equal to the cost of the synthetic.* If this were not true, then an arbitrage profit would be available by trading in both the synthetic and the future.

The pricing relationship that arbitrage forces between the futures contract and the current price of the underlying spot good is referred to as futures-spot parity. Today's contracted futures price should be equal to the current cost of buying the underlying spot asset compounded by the cost of financing the purchase plus any storage costs associated with keeping the asset until the desired delivery date.

Futures-Spot Parity Model $F_{0T} = S_0(1 + RF) + SC$ **(16.2)**

The prices of all futures contracts are based on this relationship. Minor differences which arise in the price formula for different types of futures are the result of differing types of storage costs.

PRF Example. Consider a futures contract that requires the delivery of one PRF share in three months (bought on June 30 and deliverable on September 30). Assume that share prices of PRF are trading for $98.62 on June 30, the 3-month risk-free rate at that time is 1.4% and no storage costs are associated with ownership of the shares. A synthetic position that exactly replicates a futures contract on PRF shares with a 3 month delivery date could be created in the following way. First, one would buy a share of PRF for $98.62 and immediately borrow $98.62 in order to pay for the spot share. Next the position is left unchanged during the following 3 months. Finally, on September 30, the $98.62 of loan principal together with interest of $1.38 ($98.32 times 0.014) is repaid. This results in full ownership of one PRF share at a total cost of $100, which is paid on September 30.

Because a PRF futures can be synthetically replicated at a cost of $100, the PRF futures must also have a contract price of $100.

The creation of a synthetic futures position is also illustrated in Figure 16-4. The solid colored line represents the investment value associated with owning one share of PRF. The solid black line represents the cash payment made at the delivery date (repayment date of the borrowings). Finally, the dotted line represents the net result, a synthetic futures position.

Each of the examples illustrate long positions in a replicating synthetic. Short replicating positions, of course, can be created by making opposite trades. For example, to effectively sell a futures contract on PRF shares, one would sell a spot PRF share and use the proceeds to buy risk-free debt.

Economic Definition of a Futures Contract. Previously we thought of futures positions in terms of their legal definition. Now that we understand how futures can be replicated by trades in underlying spot assets, it should be clear that a futures position is economically the same as a position in two spot assets. Specifically:

■ Ownership of a futures on asset A with a delivery date of T is identical to buying asset A and issuing risk-free debt to fully finance the purchase. Principal and interest on the debt will be paid on date T.

■ Selling a futures on asset A with a delivery date of T is identical to selling asset A and investing the proceeds in risk-free securities. All principal and interest on the risk-free investment will be collected on date T.

FIGURE 16-4   BUYING A SYNTHETIC FUTURES

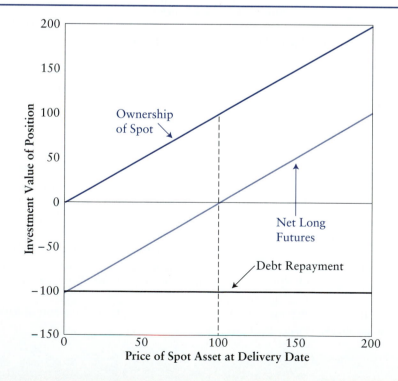

Thinking of futures contracts in this way is useful, since it highlights the leverage associated with a long futures position.

In addition, various hedging strategies are simpler to understand when we think of a future in terms of the underlying spot asset and risk-free debt. For example, assume that on June 30 you have $100,000 invested in a bank account which you intend to invest in a number of actively managed mutual funds that trade in Pacific Rim stocks. But you have not decided on the specific funds in which you will invest and it may take three months before a decision will be made. To obtain immediate exposure to Pacific Rim equities, you could purchase September 30 futures on PRF. Owning the futures is the same as buying the underlying PRF shares with borrowings. But your long position in the bank deposit and short debt position in the futures are offsetting, leaving a net position in the spot PRF shares.[9]

Basis and Basis Risk. The basis of a futures contract is equal to the current futures price minus the current price of the underlying spot good:

$$\text{Basis} = \text{Futures Price} - \text{Spot Price}$$

Typically, futures prices exceed spot prices, resulting in a positive basis. For example, the theoretical futures price of the PRF contract on June 30 was $100 when the spot price was $98.62.

As Equation (16.2) suggests, the basis of a futures contract should consist of interest $(S_0 \times RF)$ and storage costs. Together, these are referred to as **carrying costs.** If market prices are in equilibrium, the carrying costs associated with owning the spot instrument should be equal to the basis on the futures contract. If the two are different, abnormal profits are available by taking opposite positions in the spot and futures.

Now let's examine the relationship between the basis and the risk inherent in a hedged position. The basic motivation of any hedge is to increase the certainty of a future (not futures) trading price. This future trading price can be stated in terms of the initial basis when the hedge is first taken and the cover basis when the hedge is offset (that is, covered):

$$
\begin{array}{ccccccc}
\dfrac{\text{Realized Future}}{\text{Trading Price}} & = & \dfrac{\text{Initial}}{\text{Spot Price}} & + & \dfrac{\text{Initial}}{\text{Basis}} & - & \dfrac{\text{Cover}}{\text{Basis}} \qquad \textbf{(16.3)} \\
P_N & = & S_0 & + & (F_{0T} - S_0) & - & (F_{NT} - S_N)
\end{array}
$$

In Equation (16.3), N refers to the date at which the hedge is lifted (covered) by offsetting trades in the futures and spot markets.

When the hedge is created on day 0, everything is known except for the cover basis. If the spot security and futures contract are on identical instruments and the hedge is covered on the delivery date, then the cover basis will have to be zero and the future trading price to be realized will be known with certainty. A **perfect hedge** is available, meaning all price risk can be eliminated. However, if the cover basis is not known with certainty, a perfect hedge will not be possible. The cover basis will be unknown in two cases: (1) if the cover date is different from the futures contract's delivery date, or (2) if the spot security is different (in type or quantity) from the security underlying the futures contract. *Hedged positions are risky to the extent there is uncertainty about the cover date basis.*

---

[9] Details of the futures trade, such as the optimal quantity of futures to buy, are discussed later in the chapter when we examine each type of financial future.

In Figure 16-5, the relationship between futures and spot prices over a futures life is shown. Prices of the two securities will be very highly correlated. But they will not be perfectly correlated due to changes in carrying costs that affect only the future. The important point in Figure 16-5, however, is the fact that futures basis goes to zero at the delivery date, $F_{TT} = S_T$.

Differences in Futures and Forwards

Generally, we treat futures and forwards as identical instruments throughout this chapter. Doing so allows us to develop simple valuation models and trading strategies. But there are differences between the two types of securities.

Default Risk. The first distinction between futures and forwards is the potential for default under the forward contract. If you are careful in selecting the partner with whom you forward contract, the probability of default may be small, but it does exist. There is no guarantee that the other party will indeed honor the contract. The exchanges on which futures are traded, however, pride themselves on the fact that no customer has lost money through default by the other party to a contract. The exchanges have large insurance reserves to reimburse defaults by buyers or sellers.

FIGURE 16-5   CONVERGANCE OF FUTURES PRICE TO SPOT

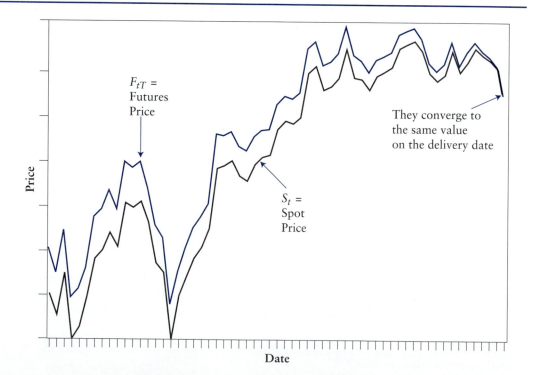

Marketability. A standard forward contract is not marketable. The only way to get out of it would be to renegotiate with the other party to the contract, or, if they are unwilling to renegotiate, to enter into an offsetting contract with still another party. In both cases, you are likely to be in the weaker bargaining position. In addition, there could be substantial time and cost associated with renegotiation. Futures contracts, however, are continuously traded on organized exchanges. You can get out of a futures contract simply by calling your broker.

Transaction Costs. Transaction costs include cash expenses as well as the opportunity cost of time spent in finding a party to trade with. Both of these can be substantial when a standard forward contract is used. In comparison, the transaction costs of entering into or closing out a futures contract or an artificial forward contract are considerably less.

Mark-to-Market. In a forward contract, the only time that cash is paid is at the maturity date. This is not the case for a futures contract. A futures contract requires both an initial cash margin and subsequent cash inflows or outflows associated with a process called mark-to-market. Margin is usually very small, and it can be met by cash, letters of credit, or short-term U.S. Treasury instruments. If letters of credit are used, no cash is actually paid. If U.S. Treasuries are used, the owner still has a claim to the earnings on the securities. Thus, margin does not represent an incremental cash outflow to the person who has bought or sold a futures contract. The process of mark-to-market, however, will usually result in a series of cash inflows and outflows before the contract's maturity. This is a major difference between futures and forward contracts.

Valuation Effects of Mark-to-Market. Because futures are marked-to-market each day, their prices are theoretically different than equivalent forward contracts. To see why this is true, assume you own a futures contract on the Pacific Rim Fund. At the end of each day's trading, you will either receive cash (if the futures price increases) or pay cash (if the future price declines). Also assume that when you receive cash you invest in short-term risk-free securities and when you are required to pay cash you borrow at the short-term risk-free rate. Finally, assume you know that, whenever you receive cash, interest rates are high and, whenever you must borrow, interest rates will be low.

In this case, you expect to earn positive profits from the daily mark-to-market, since you will invest when rates are high and borrow when rates are low. Thus, you would be willing to commit to a higher price with the future than for an equivalent forward contract. In contrast, the futures seller expects to incur losses from daily mark-to-market activities and will require that a higher price be paid on the future than for an equivalent forward.

Our example is clearly extreme, since no one can predict interest rates so precisely. But the example does show that, if futures prices are positively correlated with the level of interest rates, then the price of a future should be greater than the price of an identical forward. The opposite is also true: If futures prices are negatively correlated with interest rates, then the price of a future should be smaller than the price of an identical forward. As a practical matter, however, this correlation is small enough to be neglected, and it is safe to assume that the price of a future should be the same as a forward.

Contract Specifications. Forward contracts may be created on any security or good. Artificial forward contracts may be created on a variety of securities, depending on the spot instruments that exist. Futures contracts, however, can only be traded on futures instruments listed on an exchange. This can be important. For example, assume you are the treasurer of GTE and know you will have to borrow on March 15 in order to pay scheduled quarterly income taxes. To help assure a borrowing rate, you might wish to sell a T-bill future maturing on March 15. Unfortunately, such a futures contract does not exist. There are contracts maturing later in March that can guarantee you a late March trading price. But if you were to sell one of these with the intention of offsetting it on March 15, you would not know the March 15 price and would not be able to eliminate your uncertainty. In contrast, you could enter into a standard forward contract with an investment banker or create an artificial forward contract with the terms you desire. Forward contracts have considerably greater flexibility.

Perfect Versus Imperfect Hedges

A perfect hedge is one in which all price risk has been eliminated. While perfect hedges are possible to create in practice, they are more the exception than the rule. In order to create a perfect hedge, three things must be true:

1. The future's delivery date must be identical to the date at which you wish to trade in the underlying asset. For example, if you intend to invest in shares of the Pacific Rim Fund in late August but the nearest delivery date on a futures contract is September 30, then a perfect hedge is not available. If you use the September 30 contract to provide a partial hedge, the hedge will be covered in August at an unknown cover basis.
2. The quantity of underlying good that you wish to trade must be exactly covered by units of the futures contract. For example, assume each PRF futures contract calls for delivery of 500 shares of PRF stock. Then someone who desires to trade PRF shares in units other than a multiple of 500 would be unable to create a perfect hedge.
3. The asset that underlies the futures contract must be identical to the security you wish to eventually trade. For example, if the Pacific Rim Fund does not invest in Japanese stocks, but you wish to include Japanese equities among your portfolio, then futures on PRF could not be used to create a perfect hedge.

Perfect hedges are rare. However, the closer the futures contract specifications are to a person's needs, the more the hedge can reduce risk.

If a perfect hedge is possible, two rules are helpful in determining how to conduct a hedge. First, *do with the futures what you intend to do with the spot.* If you intend to buy the spot, then buy the future. If you intend to sell the spot, then sell the future. Second, *trade the same quantity of futures as you intend to trade in the spot.* For example, recall our example in which you have $100,000 invested in a bank account and intend to invest the funds in various Pacific Rim mutual funds on September 30. To obtain an immediate exposure to the returns of Pacific Rim stocks, you would buy the PRF futures (since you intend to buy the spot mutual funds). The quantity to trade would be equal to the total dollar value to be traded divided by the current market price of the spot asset.[10]

---

[10] You should not use the market value of the futures contract in determining the number of contracts to trade. Remember, you do with the futures what you intend to do with the spot. To calculate the number of spot units you would trade, you must divide the funds available by the market price of the spot.

Based on the $98.62 market price of PRF shares, you should buy 1,014 futures ($100,000 ÷ $98.62).

Optimal Hedging When Perfect Hedges Are Impossible. When a futures contract's specifications are not identical to the asset being hedged, risk will still remain. However, it can be minimized. Consider a portfolio of two securities: a futures contract and the spot market instrument being hedged. When the hedge is entered into, there is uncertainty about the maturity date futures price (σ_F) plus uncertainty about the value of the spot instrument (σ_S). In addition, there will be a correlation between the delivery date prices of the two securities (r_{FS}). If Q_S refers to the quantity of the spot instrument you wish to hedge, we can use the risk concepts discussed in Chapter 6 to find that amount of the futures contract (Q_F^*) that will lead to a minimum variance portfolio. This value of Q_F^* is:

Optimal Hedge $$Q_F^* = Q_S(\sigma_S r_{FS}) \div \sigma_F \qquad \text{(16.4)}$$

For example, assume you wish to purchase $100,000 worth of PRF shares on August 31, but the nearest futures delivery date is September 30. Most likely, the uncertainty about the August 31 spot price will be close, if not identical, to uncertainty about the futures price on August 31. So assume $\sigma_S = \sigma_F$. But the correlation coefficient between the two will not be 1.0. The correlation will be large, however, say, 0.9. As a result, the optimal value of futures to trade would be $90,000:

$$\$90,000 = \$100,000(1.0)(0.9)$$

If the spot asset is trading at $98.32, 915.38 futures should be bought. Because fractional futures contracts cannot be bought, either 915 or 916 contracts would be traded. Risk would be reduced but not eliminated.

Equation (16.4), as well as simple logic, suggests that the closer the financial future contract specifications are to the spot instrument being hedged, the better the hedge will be. In general, attempt to find contracts that do the following:

1. Provide a security with maturity and risk characteristics similar to those of the spot instrument being hedged.
2. Mature close to the date at which the spot instrument is to be bought or sold.
3. Have a contract value that can closely hedge the total dollar value of spot instruments to be bought or sold.

Short-Term Debt Futures

During the past decade, numerous futures have been offered on short-term, high-grade financial assets. Many of these were unable to develop an active following and are now dormant. The more actively traded contracts (as of the mid-1990s) are shown in Table 16-2. Futures on 90-day U.S. T-bills and Eurodollars are the most active.

TABLE 16-2   ACTIVE SHORT-TERM DEBT FUTURES IN 1995

Contract	Trading Unit	Exchange	December 1995 Open Interest
90-Day U.S. T-bills	$1,000,000	CME	9,900
30-Day Federal Funds Rate	$5,000,000	CBT	21,300
1-month LIBOR	$3,000,000	CME	45,000
3-month Eurodollar	$1,000,000	CME	2,554,000
U.K. Sterling	£500,000	LIFFE	404,200
Euromark	Dm1,000,000	LIFFE	988,500
Euroswiss	Sfr1,000,000	LIFFE	53,700
Eurolira	Itl1,000,000	LIFFE	92,000
Canadian BAN	C$1,000,000	ME	90,300

CBT: Chicago Board of Trade.
CME: Chicago Mercantile Exchange.
LIFFE: London International Financial Futures Exchange.
ME: Montreal Exchange.

T-Bill Futures

To understand various trading strategies available in T-bill futures, it is important to recall a few T-bill pricing relationships. First, T-bills trade at discounts to par value and receive no coupons; they are pure discount bonds. Second, the percentage discount is not the same as the annualized bond equivalent yield. Instead, the quoted discount rate represents the percentage below par at which the bill is bought, not the percentage return on actual money invested. In addition, when calculating the actual dollar discount at which a bill is traded, the Federal Reserve assumes there are 360 days per year.

Assume that at the close of trading on July 30, a T-bill maturing on August 28 could be bought at a quoted discount of 7.13%. Since the bill has a remaining life of 29 days and prices are determined using 360 days per year, the discount would be $0.5744 per $100, giving a purchase price equal to 99.4256% of face value:

Dollar Discount per $100 Face	=	Face Value	×	Quoted Discount	×	Days Remaining / 360
$0.5744	=	$100	×	0.0713	×	$\frac{29}{360}$

Purchase Price $100 Face	=	Face Value	−	Dollar Discount
$99.4256	=	$100	−	$0.5744

For each $99.4256, one could receive $100 29 days hence. This implies a simple interest bond yield of about 7.27%:

$$\text{Simple Interest Yield} = \frac{\text{Face Value}}{\text{Purchase Price}} - 1.0 \times \frac{365}{\text{Days Remaining}}$$

$$= \frac{\$100}{\$99.4256} - 1.0 \times \frac{365}{29}$$

$$7.27\% = 0.5777\% \times \frac{365}{29}$$

Now consider a futures contract on a spot T-bill. All active T-bill futures are traded on T-bills that have a 90-day maturity. Thus, a change in the quoted discount of one basis point represents a $25 change in the value of a $1 million face value futures contract:

$$\$1,000,000 \times 0.01\% \times \frac{90}{360} = \$25$$

For example, if a T-bill contract is purchased at a discount of 5.20%, the delivery price contracted for would be $987,000:

$$\text{Delivery Price} = \frac{\text{Face Value}}{\text{of Contract}} - \left(\frac{\text{Discount in}}{\text{Basis Points}} \times \frac{\text{Amount Change per Basis Point}}{\text{Per \$1 Million Face Value}}\right)$$

$$= \$1,000,000 - (520 \times 25)$$
$$\$987,000 = \$1,000,000 - \$13,000$$

If a person buys a 90-day T-bill future at a 5.20% discount and later sells it at a 5.10% discount, a $250 profit would have been earned:

$$\text{Profit} = \$25 \,[\text{Interest Basis Points at Purchase} - \text{Interest Basis Points at Sale}]$$
$$\$250 = \$25 \quad (520 \quad - \quad 510)$$

or

$$\text{Profit} = \text{Selling Price} - \text{Purchase Price}$$
$$\$250 = [\$1 \text{ million} - (\$25 \times 510)] - [\$1 \text{ million} \times (\$25 \times 520)]$$

Alternatively, if the future had been bought at a 5.20% discount and sold at a 5.30% discount, a $250 loss would have been incurred. This $25 price impact for each 1 basis-point change in a $1 million 90-day T-bill future is quite helpful in quickly pricing T-bill futures contracts and figuring trading gains and losses.

Section A in Table 16-3 shows discounts and market prices for various 90-day T-bill futures at the close of trading on June 30, 19X1. Section B shows discounts and market prices for cash T-bills of various maturities on the same day. We use this information to illustrate a variety of hedging and speculative transactions. While the examples clearly don't exhaust all possible combinations, they do provide a general sense of the types of trades that speculators and hedgers can enter into.

Basic Long Hedge. If an organization's cash flow projections show that in the near future a large sum of excess cash will be temporarily available, T-bill futures can be used to

TABLE 16-3   90-DAY T-BILL FUTURES AND CASH PRICES AS OF JUNE 30, 19X1

A. 90-Day T-bill Futures Prices

| Delivery Date | 6/30/X1 | | |
	Actual Price	Discount	Bond Yield
September 19X1	97.87	8.52%	8.82%
December 19X1	97.84	8.64	8.95

B. Spot T-bill Prices

| Maturity | Days After June 30 | 6/30/X1 | | |
		Actual Price	Discount	Bond Yield
September 23, 19X1	86	97.86	8.97%	9.28%
December 22, 19X1	176	95.78	8.63	9.13

lock in a future interest rate at which the excess cash can be invested. For example, assume it is now June 30, 19X1, and $1 million in cash will be available to invest for a 90-day period as of middle to late September 19X1. As a long hedge, September T-bill futures contracts would be bought on June 30. When the $1 million cash actually becomes available (say, on September 23), the futures contracts would be sold and spot T-bills bought.[11]

Ideally, the $1 million cash would become available and the futures position would be closed exactly on the futures delivery date. This would mean that spot and futures rates on the T-bills would be identical (cover basis = $0), resulting in an actual yield on the cash T-bills equal to the yield at which the initial futures were bought. For example, assume that on June 30, T-bill futures were bought at an 8.52% discount and that by September 23, 90-day spot T-bill rates had fallen to discounts of 8.00%. The net transaction would be as follows:

	Discount Rate	Price per $1 Million T-bills	Bond Yield
Futures			
Bought 90-Day Futures on 6/30/X1	8.52%	−$978,700	8.82%
Sold 90-Day Futures on 9/23/X1	8.00	980,000	8.28
Profit	0.52%	1,300	0.54%
Spot			
Buy 90-Day T-bill on 9/23/X1	8.00	−980,000	8.28%
Net Result	8.52%	−$978,700	8.82%

---

[11] In theory, the futures could be held through delivery and the investment in T-bills made via the futures. In practice, most hedgers close their position in futures by an offsetting trade and buy the spot security in the spot market.

Although discounts available on spot T-bills fell to 8.00%, the futures hedger was actually able to lock in an 8.52% discount because of the profits earned on the futures transactions. This profit of $1,300 was composed of a 52 basis-point change in 90-day futures rates at $25 per basis point ($1,300 = 52 × $25). This allowed the hedger to pay only $978,700 in out-of-pocket cash for T-bills selling for $980,000.

This perfect hedge worked because the cover basis was zero. The 90-day futures sold at the same discount as did the spot T-bill. If the hedge had been placed in futures deliverable at dates different from when cash would become available for spot investment (for example, by buying December futures in the example), the cover basis would most likely be different from zero.

In this example, there is another way to lock in a 90-day rate on June 30 for money that would become available on September 23. Instead of trading in futures, one could create a synthetic forward rate in the cash market. Note that the time difference between the September 23 and December 22 spot T-bills is exactly 90 days. If one was to buy a December 22 T-bill and short-sell some September 23 T-bills, there would be no cash position until September 23. But once the short sale is closed on September 23, a 90-day long position would be held. Details are shown in Table 16-4. On June 30, December 22 spot T-bills are bought for $957,800. To come up with the cash, the 0.9787 September 23 T-bill is sold short. As a result, there is no cash position between June 30 and September 23. However, on September 23 the short position is covered at a cost of $1,000,000 per T-bill or $978,700 in cash outflow, since the 0.9787 September T-bill was short. On December 22 the long position matures and provides $1,000,000. In net, $978,700 is invested on September 23 for a $1 million cash return 90 days later. This represents a return of 2.18% for 90 days: a discount return of 9.52% or a bond equivalent return of 8.82%.

Speculation. According to Table 16-3, a T-bill future now exists that requires the buyer to pay $978,700 in the third week of September 19X1. In return, the buyer will receive 90-day T-bills with a total face value of $1 million. This future is said to sell at a discount of 8.52%, although the effective annual bond yield is actually about 8.82%. If a speculator expected that 90-day cash T-bills would actually be selling at discounts greater than 8.52% toward the end of September 19X1, the futures contract should be sold. The speculator's belief that T-bill rates will rise might rest on any one of a number of reasons, for example, a belief that investors will revise upward their expectations of inflation, unexpectedly tight Federal Reserve policy, or unusually large new Treasury sales in late September. But regardless of the reason, the speculator would sell in anticipation of lower cash T-bill prices in the delivery month than contracted for in the T-bill future.

Assume that on June 30 the speculator sells one September 19X1 T-bill contract. At that time, the normal margin associated with futures trading will have to be posted and a brokerage commission paid. In September the speculator may either hold the contract open for delivery or cover the initial sale by purchasing the same contract just prior to the delivery date. Since the futures contract should sell at the same discount as an equivalent cash T-bill at delivery, the profits or losses from either strategy would be the same. If the speculator had guessed right and 90-day T-bill discounts rise to, say, 9.00%, a profit of $1,200 would have been earned (9.00% − 8.52%, or 48 basis points × $25 per basis point). However, the speculator has gambled that T-bill discounts won't fall. If they do, the speculator would be stuck with having to deliver an 8.52% discount T-bill when the cash

TABLE 16-4   CREATION OF 90-DAY FORWARD RATE AS OF JUNE 30, 19X1

	Cash Flows—In (Out)		
	June 30	September 23	December 12
Buy Dec. 22 Spot T-bill	$957,800		$1,000,000
Short Sell 0.9787 Sept. 23 T-bill*	−957,800	−$978,700	
	$ 0	−$978,700	$1,000,000

Annualized Return:
Discount = 8.52%†
Bond Yield = 8.82%‡

$^{*}\dfrac{\text{Dec. T-bill Price}}{\text{Sept. T-bill Price}} = \dfrac{95.78}{97.86} = 0.9787$

$^{†}\dfrac{\$1,000,000 - \$978,700}{\$1,000,000} \times \dfrac{360}{90} = 8.52\%$

$^{‡}\dfrac{\$1,000,000 - \$978,700}{\$978,700} \times \dfrac{365}{90} = 8.82\%$

T-bill actually available at that time yielded less. For example, if T-bill discounts actually fell by 48 basis points because of a temporary easing of credit by the Fed, a $1,200 loss would have been incurred.

Arbitrage. Arbitrage transactions can be accomplished by going long and short between both spot T-bills and futures. For example, we saw earlier that a 90-day investment return starting on September 23 could be obtained either by buying a 90-day T-bill future deliverable in September or by short-selling some spot T-bills maturing on September 23 and simultaneously buying December 22 spot T-bills. As the example was originally designed, one would have been indifferent between the two approaches, since each was expected to provide the same return. However, if the September future had been selling at 8.30% (with no changes in spot prices), an arbitrage consisting of selling the September future and creating a long September forward position should be entered into. Whenever futures rates are different from implied forward rates in the spot market, a profitable arbitrage opportunity exists (at least before transaction costs).

Consider another potential arbitrage. Suppose 90-day and one-year spot T-bills are selling at 8.80% and 9.00%, respectively. If the following 90-day futures are also available, what sort of arbitrage opportunity exists?

Delivery Month	90-Day T-bill Discount
3 months	8.85%
6 months	8.90%
9 months	8.70%

A one-year investment in T-bills could be obtained either by buying a one-year spot T-bill at 9.00% or by purchasing a three-month spot T-bill plus a strip of each of the 90-day futures at an average discount less than 9.00%. Clearly, the one-year spot T-bill would provide the higher expected return. In fact, an arbitrage consisting of going long the one-year spot T-bill plus short the three-month T-bill and each future would provide a nearly riskless profit.

The Valuation of T-Bill Futures. Consider the spot T-bills shown in Table 16-3. On June 30, a T-bill maturing on December 22 is selling for 95.78% of par. If you were to buy it and hold it until September 23, it would then have a maturity of 90 days. Thus, its price on September 23 should be identical to the price at delivery of the 90-day futures. But the expected price of this December 22 spot T-bill is easily calculated. If you are to invest $95.78 on June 30 in a risk-free security and hold the investment until September 23, you would demand a risk-free rate of return. Since the September 23 spot T-bill is selling for $97.86, the risk-free return associated with the June to September period is:

$$\frac{\$100}{\$97.86} - 1 = 2.187\%$$

Thus the expected price of the December 22 spot T-bill should be $97.87 on September 23:

$$\$95.78 \ (1.02187) = \$97.87$$

It turns out that the September futures are priced correctly. If they had been trading at a value different from the expected value of the spot instrument, arbitrage profits would have been available. In general, if F_{tT}, refers to the price of a T-bill futures contract with a delivery at date T quoted at date t, and S_{T+90} refers to the date t spot price of an instrument that will be a perfect substitute for the futures on date T, then:

T-Bill Futures Contract Price

$$F_{tT} = S_{T+90}(1 + RF_{T-t}) \tag{16.5}$$

The spot instrument chosen must be a perfect substitute for the futures at date T. In addition, the risk-free rate used should apply to the period from t to T.

Eurodollar Deposit Contracts

Recall that a Eurodollar is a deposit in a non-U.S. bank that is reported in a dollar denomination. Because Eurodollar deposits are not subject to U.S. banking reserve requirements or a number of other regulations, the size of this deposit market has increased substantially in recent years. Eurodollar rates are based on the London Interbank Offer Rate, known more commonly as the LIBOR rate. At the end of each day, a number of approved London banks are surveyed for the rate they are willing to pay on Eurodollar deposits. The middle ten interest rates are then averaged and used as the published closing LIBOR rate. This rate is used to settle any Eurodollar futures that are then deliverable. This rate is generally accepted as one of the best indicators of short-term interest rates.

Futures contracts on three-month Eurodollar deposits are the most actively traded short-term debt futures in the world. They are priced on a discount basis similar to T-bill futures. However, settlement occurs in cash based on the spot LIBOR rate; actual security delivery is not allowed.

Intermediate and Long-Term Debt Futures

The most actively traded futures on intermediate and long-term debt issues are shown in Table 16-5. The most active contract is presently the U.S. T-bond futures.

U.S. Treasury Bond Futures

Each contract is on $100,000 of par value U.S. T-bonds having a maturity (or call, if callable) of at least 15 years and an assumed coupon of 8%. Prices are quoted in thirty-seconds of a dollar. Thus, a price of $71-02$ represents a price quote of $71^{2/32}$, or $71,062.50, on a single $100,000 par contract. Each point ($^{1/32}$) represents a value of $31.25 per contract.

Delivery. The price of any futures contract depends on the price at which the deliverable security is expected to sell on the delivery date. For T-bill contracts the deliverable instrument is easily identified. The deliverable instrument on a T-bond contract is not so easy to identify. Because of its critical importance in determining T-bond futures prices, we must look a little closer at T-bond delivery.

Delivery can take place at any time during the maturity month and is initiated by the short side. Once the short has declared an intention to deliver, the clearing corporation matches the short with the oldest outstanding long position, and securities and cash are exchanged two business days later. This uncertainty about the precise date of delivery causes a risk to the futures purchaser that cannot be hedged.

The second aspect of delivery which creates a risk is that the bonds that are deliverable are not precisely defined. Any U.S. T-bond with a maturity in excess of 15 years (or a call date longer than 15 years, if it is callable) will qualify. This means that a wide range of coupons and maturities will qualify for delivery. Recognizing that the value of each bond is affected by its maturity and coupon, the clearing corporation has extensive tables that attempt to adjust for such differences. These tables are used to convert the contractual trade price to an actual invoice price that the purchaser of the future will pay. This adjustment factor is called the delivery factor. Yet the tables are unable to price precisely each of the many alternative bonds available for delivery. There will always be a few bonds that are the cheapest to deliver. As a result, active participants in the market will constantly evaluate the cheapest bonds to deliver and base the futures price on their expected value in the month of delivery.

Potential Use in Portfolio Management. Throughout this chapter most of the examples of how futures might be used have dealt with the hedging of specific cash flow needs or specific security holdings. Implicit in these are speculative and arbitrage profits that could occur if market prices are not in equilibrium. Many of the same techniques also apply to T-bond futures. However, T-bond futures can also be used to manage aggregate bond portfolio risk. It is this potential role that we examine.

Assume you are the manager of a $1 billion pension fund that has a policy of maintaining an asset mix of 50% equities, 40% bonds, and 10% cash. Since the relative performance of each of these security types varies over time, the actual market value mix will often depart from this desired mix. Assume the bonds currently have a market value of $440 million—$40 million more than desired. There are two ways in which the bond position can be restored to $400 million: (1) sell $40 million in spot bonds and allocate it to stocks and cash as appropriate, or (2) sell T-bond futures.

TABLE 16-5   ACTIVE LONG-TERM DEBT FUTURES IN 1995

Contract	Trading Unit	Exchange	December, 1995 Open Interest
U.S. T-Bonds	$100,000	CBT	437,000
U.S. T-Bonds	$ 50,000	MCE	8,200
U.S. T-Notes	$100,000	CBT	257,000
5-year U.S. T-Notes	$100,000	CBT	160,200
2-year U.S T-Notes	$200,000	CBT	20,000
Muni Bond Index	1,000 times BBMBI	CBT	18,700
Long Gilt	£50,000	LIFFE	152,500
German Govt. Bond	Dm250,000	LIFFE	204,000
Italian Govt. Bond	Itl200,000	LIFFE	47,400
10-year Canadian Govt.	C$100,000	ME	21,600
10-year French Govt.	Ffr500,000	MATIF	33,000
3-year Commonwealth Bond	A$100,000	SFE	207,400

BBMBI: Bond Buyer's Municipal Bond Index.
CBT: Chicago Board of Trade.
LIFFE: London International Financial Futures Exchange.
MATIF: Marché à Terme International de France.
MCE: MidAmerica Commodity Exchange.
SFE: Sydney Futures Exchange.

As we saw in Chapter 11, the duration of a bond portfolio (D_p) is a measure of how sensitive the value of the portfolio is to a change in interest rates. Specifically:

$$\% \text{ Change in Bond Prices} = -D_P \times \left[\frac{\% \text{ Change in}}{(1 + YTM)} \right] \quad \textbf{(16.6a)}$$

An alternative way of expressing this relationship is:

$$\% \text{ Change in Bond Prices} = -D_P \left(\frac{YTM_t - YTM_{t-1}}{1 + YTM_{t-1}} \right) \quad \textbf{(16.6b)}$$

Assume the duration of your portfolio is four years. Thus, a 100 basis-point increase in, say, an existing YTM of 10% will cause a 3.64% decrease in your bond portfolio's value, or a dollar loss of $16.0 million:

$$-4 \left(\frac{0.11 - 0.10\%}{1.10} \right) = 3.64\%$$

$$-0.0364 \times \$440 \text{ million} = -\$16.0 \text{ million}$$

This $16.0 million is called the dollar duration of the portfolio. Since the negative sign on D_P is unnecessary, it will be dropped:

$$\text{Dollar Duration} = D_P \left(\frac{YTM_t - YTM_{t-1}}{1 + YTM_{t-1}} \right) \times \frac{\text{Bond}}{\text{Portfolio Value}} \qquad \textbf{(16.7)}$$

Note that if you actually had $400 million invested in bonds, the dollar duration would be $14.55 million (0.0364 × $400). T-bond futures can be sold in an amount that would adjust the actual dollar duration from $16.0 million to $14.55 million—that is, decrease it by $1.45 million.

To calculate the duration of the T-bond future, we must first determine which T-bond is the cheapest to deliver. Assume this cheapest-to-deliver bond has a duration of 6.24 years. Since each contract is a claim on $100,000 worth of an 8% T-bond, the dollar duration of such a T-bond future is:

$$6.24 \left(\frac{0.11 - 0.10}{1.10} \right) \times \$100,000 = \$5,672.73$$

Unfortunately, the bond that is cheapest to deliver does not have an 8% coupon. Thus we must adjust this 8% coupon bond's dollar duration into the actual deliverable bond's dollar duration. Mechanically, this is done by dividing the 8% coupon result by a delivery factor provided in CBT's tables. Assume the delivery factor for this bond is 0.9883. Thus, the dollar duration of the cheapest to deliver T-bond future is:

$$\frac{\text{Dollar Duration}}{\text{T-Bond Future}} = \frac{\begin{array}{c}\text{Duration of}\\ \text{Deliverable Bond}\end{array}}{\text{Delivery Factor}} \left(\frac{YTM_t - YTM_{t-1}}{1 + YTM_{t-1}} \right) \times \$100,000$$

$$\$5,739.88 = \frac{6.24}{0.9883} \left(\frac{0.11 - 0.10}{1.10} \right) \times \$100,000$$

So we finally arrive. To reduce the bond portfolio's dollar duration by $1.45 million, you would sell 253 T-bond futures:

$$\frac{1,450,000}{\$5,739.88} = 253 \text{ T-Bond Futures}$$

There is no doubt this is a tedious calculation. The logic, however, is correct, and the calculations can be easily programmed on any microcomputer and many calculators. The use of T-bonds to alter bond portfolio risk is actually much easier and perhaps cheaper than direct sale or purchase of spot bond instruments.

Equity Index Futures

In 1982, trading in stock index futures began in the United States. By the mid-1990s, futures contracts on stock indexes were among the most actively traded derivatives in the world and markets for them existed in many developed countries. Six of the more active contracts are shown in Table 16-6. These include contracts on two U.S. stock indexes and indexes on shares traded in Japan, France, Britain, and Australia. Contract terms of these contracts are very similar. They differ mainly in the underlying asset. Since the S&P 500 contract is the most actively traded, our discussion will be centered on it.

TABLE 16-6   ACTIVE STOCK INDEX FUTURES 1995

Contract	Trading Unit	Exchange	December 1995 Open Interest
S&P 500 Index	$500 times index	CME	241,800
S&P Midcap 400	$500 times index	CME	14,300
Nikkei 225 Stock Average	$5 times index	CME	24,100
CAC 40 Stock Index	Ffr 200 per index pt	MATIF	52,700
FT-SE100	£25 per point	LIFFE	82,900
All Ordinaries Share	A$ 25 times index	SFE	108,400

CME: Chicago Mercantile Exchange.
LIFFE: London International Financial Futures Exchange.
MATIF: Marché à Terme International de France.
SFE: Sydney Futures Exchange.

The S&P 500 Contract

The S&P 500 Index future is quoted in terms of the value of the S&P 500 Composite Index, but the actual dollar value of each contract is 500 times the quoted value. For example, if the contract's settle price is $600, the contract's value is $300,000. Minimum price moves are 0.05, or $25. If you bought the contract at $600 and later sold at $590, your loss would be $5,000.

As with other futures contracts, no cash payment is made at the date of the trade except for a good faith deposit (margin). The values of daily portfolio positions are marked to market. Contracts are available with settlement dates in March, June, September, and December. Delivery occurs on the third Thursday of the maturity month.

A unique feature of stock index futures is that physical delivery of the underlying asset never occurs. Instead, the contract requires that, at maturity, all profits be paid to the customer by the clearing corporation and all losses be paid to the clearing corporation by the customer. Because of daily mark-to-market, virtually all of the profits and losses will have already been distributed.

Pricing. Refined valuation models that fully take into account daily mark-to-market and other risk features of these contracts are not reviewed here. However, a simple arbitrage valuation model is used in practice and provides prices reasonably close to those observed.

Assume you purchase a stock portfolio at date t that is identical to one "unit" of the S&P 500 Index. The value of this spot portfolio is S_t. You know that you intend to sell the portfolio at date T. Its price at date $T(S_T)$ is, of course, unknown to you today. But the dividends you will receive between t and $T(D_T)$ are reasonably predictable. Let's assume they are known with certainty and will all be paid on date T. Given this information, you could guarantee the price at which you will sell the spot portfolio by selling one futures contract at a price of F_{tT}. The cash inflows and outflows that would result are:

	Date	
	t	T
At Date t:		
Buy Spot Portfolio	$-S_t$	
Sell Future		F_{tT}
At Date T:		
Sell Spot Portfolio		S_T
Buy Future		$-F_{TT}$
Collect Dividends		D_T
Net	$-S_t$	$F_{tT} + D_T$

Two things should be recognized. First, at its maturity, the value of the futures contract must be equal to the spot index value at that time ($S_T = F_{TT}$). That is, after all, how the index contract is legally written. As a result, the S_T and F_{TT} cancel each other out. Second, note that once S_T and F_{TT} cancel, every cash flow is known with certainty. S_t is the current spot index value, D_T is the known dividend, and F_{tT} is the known futures price at which you trade. For an investment of S_t, *a known payoff of $F_{tT} + D_T$ is available*. To eliminate the potential for arbitrage, a risk-free rate must equate the two cash flows. Letting *RF* refer to the risk-free rate available over the period t to T:

Arbitrage Spot and Index Future Relationship

$$S_t = (F_{tT} + D_T) \div (1 + RF) \tag{16.8}$$

Restating this in terms of the futures price:

Arbitrage Stock Index Futures Price

$$F_{tT} = S_t(1 + RF) - D_T \tag{16.9}$$

This arbitrage pricing model says that the contract value of the future is the certainty equivalent value of owning the spot index less the dividends that will be earned on the spot index that are not available on the futures contract.

To illustrate Equation (16.9), assume the following current spot information is known:

Spot Price of the S&P 500 Index	= $600
Annual (discrete) Risk-Free Rate	= 5%
Annual Dividend Yield of the S&P 500 Index	= 4%

Then a three-month contract on the S&P 500 should trade for $601.36:

$$\$601.36 = \$600(1.05)^{0.25} - (0.01 \times \$600)$$

Hedging Strategies

Futures hedging using stock index futures is designed to alter the systematic risk exposure of a portfolio. If index futures are purchased, systematic market risk is increased. If index futures are sold, systematic market risk decreases. Trading in stock index futures has no impact on a portfolio's diversifiable, nonmarket risk. Thus, for the futures contract to be a good hedging vehicle, it should be on a stock index that is similar in makeup to the spot equities owned.

Three of the more common hedging uses of stock index futures are discussed here:

1. Adjusting portfolio betas
2. Creating index portfolios
3. Use in portfolio insurance programs

The examples use the hypothetical data on an S&P 500 future presented earlier. The spot S&P 500 Index is $600, the annual risk-free rate is 5%, and the spot stock index will pay a $6 dividend in exactly three months. We assume a futures contract is available on the S&P 500 that is deliverable in three months and is now trading in the market for $601.36.

Adjusting Portfolio Betas. Assume you are the administrator of a $100 million pension fund. An investment committee that sets investment strategy has a desired T-bill/equity mix of 40/60. The investment committee has also stated that the beta of the equity portfolio should be equal to 1.0 (relative to the S&P 500 Index). A number of professional managers have been employed to run portions of the pension fund in the hopes their unique skills can provide long-run returns in excess of what the fund would earn if it were to fully "index" the portfolio.

Because of recent moves in stock prices and purchases by the managers, the present portfolio differs from the investment committee's stated objectives. At present, the equity portfolio represents $70 million of the $100 million portfolio. And the average beta of stocks held by portfolio managers is 1.0. The situation is summarized here:

| | Actual | | Desired | |
Asset	Dollars	Beta	Dollars	Beta
T-bills	$ 30 million	0.00	$ 40 million	0.00
Equity	70 million	1.0	60 million	1.00
Portfolio	$100 million	0.7	$100 million	0.60

You could achieve the desired position by actually trading in the spot securities—by selling $10 million of stock and using the proceeds to purchase T-bills. But this could be costly, confusing, and time consuming. Alternatively, you could trade in S&P 500 futures to achieve the desired position without disturbing the underlying spot portfolio.

The critical question is not whether stock futures can do the job, but how many contracts should be traded.

Well, consider the present situation. Since the $70 million equity position has a beta of 1.0, it is similar to owning 233 1/3 "units" of the S&P 500 Index:

$$\frac{70,000,000}{\$600 \times 500} = 233 \ 1/3$$

If the beta on the $70 million had been only 0.9, only 210 units of the index would effectively be owned:

$$233\ 1/3 \times 0.9 = 210$$

Stated more formally, the number of effective units of a stock index that is owned can be stated as follows:

$$\text{Actual Units of Stock Index Owned} = \left(\frac{\$ \text{ Value of Actual Equity Portfolio}}{\$ \text{ Value of the Spot Index Unit}} \right)\left(\text{Beta of Actual Portfolio} \right)$$

$$Q_t = \left(\frac{\text{EMV}_t}{S_t \times I} \right)(B_t) \qquad\qquad (16.10)$$

where Q_t equals the effective number of index units owned at date t, EMV_t equals the equity market value at date t, S_t equals the quoted spot index at t, I is an adjustment factor unique to each futures contract (for example, 500 for the S&P 500 futures), and B_t is the equity portfolio beta at date t.

$$Q_t = \frac{\$70,000,000}{\$600 \times 500}(1.0)$$

$$= 233\ 1/3$$

We can use the same logic to calculate the desired units of the index we wish to own. In this case, let's represent desired values with an asterisk:

$$\text{Desired Units of Stock Index} = \left(\frac{\$ \text{ Value of Desired Equity Portfolio}}{\$ \text{ Value of the Spot Index Unit}} \right)\left(\text{Beta of Desired Portfolio} \right)$$

$$Q_t^* = \left(\frac{\text{EMV}_t^*}{S_t \times I} \right)(B_t^*) \qquad\qquad (16.11)$$

In our example, the desired number of units of the spot index is 200:

$$\left(\frac{\$60,000,000}{\$600 \times 500} \right)(1.0) = 200$$

Therefore, the quantity of stock index futures to trade (T_t) is simply the difference between the two:

Optimal Stock Index Futures to Adjust Systematic Risk

$$T_t = Q_t^* - Q_t \qquad\qquad (16.12)$$

Given our illustrative data this would be 33 1/3 contracts.[12]

$$-33\ 1/3 = 200 - 233\ 1/3$$

Thirty-three equity contracts should be traded. The negative sign implies they should be sold.

Would it work? Would the actual portfolio position together with a short position in 50 S&P 500 futures provide exactly the same future payoffs as (costlessly) adjusting the spot portfolio to the desired position? Probably not, since stock index futures transactions can

---

[12] Although fractional futures contracts can not be traded, we assume they can in illustrations.

only adjust systematic risks. Thus, if the spot equity portfolio is not perfectly correlated with the stock index, futures will not provide the same delivery date payoffs. But if the spot portfolio is perfectly correlated with the stock index, trades in futures will provide exactly the desired outcome.

Creating Index Portfolios. An index portfolio is a portfolio of securities that will have a return equal to (or close to) the return on a given security index. The underlying index could be a U.S. common stock index such as the S&P 500 or an international index such as the Nikkei 225 (an index of Japanese stock values). Recall that index portfolios are held in order to obtain broad diversification within a given asset class and in the belief that active investment managers cannot provide greater risk-adjusted performance.

Prior to the introduction of stock index futures, index portfolios were created by actual purchases of the spot securities in weights similar to the index. For example, if an S&P 500 Index portfolio were to be formed, long positions in 500 stocks would ideally be taken with each held in proportions similar to their current weighting in the index. In practice, however, returns on spot index portfolios often do not totally emulate the underlying index. Transaction costs and the inability to maintain identical security weighting both cause return differences.

Stock index futures offer a cheap alternative to creating an indexed position in common stocks. This is done by: (1) purchasing T-bills having a maturity date equal to the stock index futures delivery date and (2) purchasing a proper quantity of index futures. If the stock index future is purchased at a price equal to its theoretical value, the net position will provide a return identical to the underlying index return.

To demonstrate this idea conceptually, let S_t be the quoted value of the spot stock index at day t, RF the risk-free rate over the life of a given futures contract, D the value of known dividends paid on day T, and T the delivery date of the stock index future. The index portfolio transaction is summarized next:

At day 0, T-bills are purchased in a dollar amount equal to the current spot price of the index—S_0. This investment will be worth $S_0(1 + RF)$ at the future delivery date. Also on day 0 a long position in 1.0 future contract is taken. This conceptually obligates you to cash outflow on the delivery date equal to $S_0(1 + RF) - D$, the future's theoretical value. But since the T-bill has a cash inflow at that time equal to $S_0(1 + RF)$, the net of the two cash flows is a positive cash flow equal to the spot index dividend of D. Finally, to obtain a cash inflow equal to the spot index value on day T, you sell the futures contract (initially bought on day 0) at the end of day T. At that time, the value of the future must be identical to the value of the spot index.

		Cash Flows
Today	0	Futures Delivery
Buy T-bills	$-S_0$	$+ S_0(1 + RF)$
Buy 1.0 Futures		$-F_{0T} = -[S_0(1 + RF) - D]$
Net		$+D$
Delivery Date		$+F_{TT} = S_T$
Sell the Future Above	—	
Total	$-S_0$	$S_T + D$

The net effect of this transaction is that you spend S_0 on day 0 and receive $S_T + D$ at the delivery date. Your return is identical to the actual returns on the index!

To illustrate, assume you have $10 million in cash and wish to earn a return identical to that of the S&P 500 Index. It is December 31 and the following spot and futures information is available:

Spot S&P 500 Index	$600
Dividend to Be Paid in Three Months	$ 6
Futures Price (Deliverable in Three Months)	$601.36
Three-Month Risk-Free Rate	1.2272234%

At spot prices of $500 and $700 on the delivery date, the quarterly rate of return on the spot S&P 500 Index would be a negative 15 2/3% and a positive 17 2/3%, respectively:

$$-0.15 \ 2/3 = (500 - 600 + 6) \div 600$$

$$0.17 \ 2/3 = (700 - 600 + 6) \div 600$$

The transactions in Table 16-7 show that a mixed futures and T-bill position would achieve the same results.

Use in Portfolio Insurance Programs. In Chapter 17, we discuss the concept and application of portfolio insurance. A minimum portfolio value can be insured by trading listed put and call options or by using a trading strategy that dynamically replicates the payoffs of the options. Dynamic replication requires that stock be sold when its value declines and bought when its value increases. Because of costs associated with actually trading in the spot stock, stock index futures are commonly used. For example, if the trading strategy calls for the sale of $10,000,000 in spot stock, futures with a claim to $10,000,000 of the stock index are sold instead. Clearly, for this procedure to work, the actual stock held must be reasonably similar to the stock index on which the futures are traded.

TABLE 16-7   CREATING AN INDEXED PORTFOLIO WITH FUTURES

Transaction	Date	Delivery Date	
Today	0	$S_T = \$500$	$S_T = \$700$
Purchase T-bills	−$10,000,000	$10,122,722	$10,122,722
Buy 33 1/3 Futures		−10,022,667	−10,022,667
$10,000,000 ÷ ($600 × 500)			
Delivery Date			
Sell 33 1/3 Futures		8,333,333	11,666,667
Total	−$10,000,000	$ 8,433,388	$11,766,722
Rate of Return		−15 2/3%	17 2/3%

Speculative Strategies

If the futures contract is traded at values different from those implied by Equation (16.9), speculative profits are possible. The most widely known speculation is an index arbitrage.

Index Arbitrage. In the preceding illustration, the S&P 500 futures had a theoretical value equal to $601.36. If the actual futures price is different, an index arbitrage is possible.

Assume the actual futures price is $2 larger, or $603.36. Then an arbitrage consisting of selling the futures would be profitable, since the market price of $603.36 is greater than the theoretical value of $601.36. Details of an illustrative arbitrage are shown in Table 16-8, in which $10 million of futures are sold. At current prices of $603.36, a total of 33.1477 contracts are sold. (We assume fractional contract may be traded to increase precision).

$$33.1477 = \$10,000,000 \div (\$603.36 \times 500)$$

This naked futures position, of course, is quite risky (losing if delivery date spot prices are higher than $603.36 and winning at lower spot prices). To remove this risk, 33.1477

TABLE 16-8   ILLUSTRATION OF INDEX ARBITRAGE

Fair Futures Value = $601.36
Actual Futures Value = $603.36

At Date 0	Date 0	$S_T = \$500$	$S_T = \$700$	Reason
Sell Futures (1)		+$10,000,000	+$10,000,000	Futures Are Overvalued
Buy Spot (2)	−9,944,310			Remove Risk
Sell T-bills	+9,944,310			Provide Financing
At Date T				
Repay T-bills (3)		−10,066,349	−10,066,349	
Receive Dividends (4)		99,443	99,443	
Unwind Arbitrage				
Sell Spot (5)		8,286,925	11,601,695	
Buy Futures (5)		−8,286,925	−11,601,695	
Net Outcome (6)	0	$ 33,094	$ 33,094	

(1) Number of contracts = $10,000,000 ÷ ($603.36 × 500) = 33.1477.
(2) Value of stock = 33.1477 × ($600 × 500).
(3) T-bill payment = $9,944,310(1.05)^{0.25} = $10,066,349.
(4) Dividends = 0.01 × $9,944,310 = $99,443.
(5) Value traded = 33.1477 × ($500 × 500) = $ 8,286,925
        or 33.1477 × ($700 × 500) = $11,601,695.
(6) (603.36 − 601.36) × (33.1477 × 500) = 33,147 off due to rounding.

units of the spot index are bought at a cost of $9,944,310. To finance the cost of the spot index, the same dollar amounts in T-bills are sold short.

At the delivery date, three things happen. First, the short position in T-bills is repaid. At an interest cost of 1.22722%, this requires a payment of $10,066,349:

$$\$10,066,349 = \$9,944,310 \,(1.0122722)$$

Second, dividends are received on ownership of the spot index in the amount of $99,443:

$$\$99,443 = \$9,944,310 \times 0.01$$

Finally, the arbitrage is "unwound" by selling 33.1477 units of the spot and buying the same quantity of futures. Net cash flows of $33,094 are received at the delivery date—*regardless of the spot price at that time.*

A few comments about this index arbitrage are in order. First, although the transaction appears to be complex, it simply involves the purchase of one risk-free security (buy spot and sell an equivalent number of futures) that provided a three-month return of 1.56% and financing it with another risk-free security at a cost of 1.22722%:

$$0.0156 = \frac{\$10,000,000 + \$99,443}{\$9,944,310} - 1$$

$$0.0122722 = (1.05)^{0.25} - 1$$

Second, real-life arbitrages will differ from this example in that fractional contracts cannot be traded and transaction costs are incurred. In practice, there is a low and high price range of index futures for which index arbitrage profits are not available. In the early years of the index contracts, this price range was frequently violated. In recent years, index futures usually lie within this price range, and only low-cost traders are able to take advantage of index arbitrages.

Notice that the arbitrage must be unwound on the delivery date by trading in both the spot and futures market. This is because actual delivery on the futures is not allowed—index futures require cash (profit) delivery. As large arbitrage trades are placed on the delivery date, they can have substantial impacts on market prices. In the example above, shares of the S&P 500 were sold at the delivery date and would depress stock prices. Arbitragers are indifferent to such price pressure impact since they are simultaneously buying in one market and selling in another at the same price. But other investors who happen to trade at the same time are not indifferent and may find they have traded at prices very different from what they expected.

Such price pressure impacts are due to a large influx of arbitrage-related trades that might be requests to either buy or sell stocks in the spot index. If the potential quantity of these arbitrage trades as well as whether they would be buy or sell orders could be predicted, a sufficient number of other investors would place offsetting trades in the hopes of taking advantage of expected price pressures. Unfortunately, such predictions are very imprecise. Thus, starting in 1987, the time of delivery was changed from the close of trading on Thursday afternoon to the opening of trading on Friday morning. This meant that the amount and direction of arbitrage trading would be known to the exchanges, allowing them to both delay opening and publicize the amount of arbitrage trades in order to attract offsetting trades.

Finally, even though index arbitrage did have dramatic effects on delivery date spot prices prior to 1987, the economic function of arbitrage is important. The fundamental reason why futures exist is that they allow the control of price risk—rapidly and cheaply. But this risk management can be effective only if futures are properly priced. If futures prices are allowed to vary from their theoretical values, the true economic benefits of having such markets disappear.

Currency Futures

Currency futures allow one to guarantee today a future rate of exchange between two currencies. The major types of currency futures in the United States are shown in Table 16-9, all of which are traded on the Chicago Mercantile exchange. For example, consider futures contracts on Swiss francs. Assume you buy one of these contracts with a delivery date of late December and a contract price of $0.9 per franc. Then you would be obligated to buy 125,000 francs in late December at a price of $112,500.

Trading in forward contracts on currencies is, by far, a more active market than trading in futures markets. Trading in the forward market occurs on a 24-hour basis and is dominated by major banks around the world. Such banks act as intermediaries for companies engaged in international trade, arranging both spot currency transfers between countries and future transfers.

As an example of a spot currency exchange by a bank, consider an Italian manufacturer who buys goods from a supplier in India. There are many ways in which the Italian manufacturer could pay the Indian supplier. The following conveys the essence of these. The manufacturer provides an Italian bank with the required number of lira to pay for the goods. The Italian bank then enters the spot currency exchange market and arranges with another bank (say a bank in India) to exchange this quantity of lira for the associated number of rupees. Finally, the Italian bank arranges to have the rupees delivered to the Indian supplier's bank. This leaves an Indian bank with the ownership

TABLE 16-9   ACTIVE CURRENCY FUTURES 1995

Contract	Trading Unit	Exchange	December, 1995 Open Interest
Japan Yen	12.5 million yen	CME	79,276
Deutsche Mark	125,000 marks	CME	60,812
Canadian Dollar	100,000 dollars	CME	27,268
British Pound	62,500 pounds	CME	36,899
Swiss Franc	125,000 francs	CME	12,689
Australian Dollar	100,000 dollars	CME	6,127
Mexican Peso	500,000 Mex. peso	CME	14,245

CME: Chicago Mercantile Exchange.

Alex Saitta

Vice President, Technical Analysis Research
Salomon Brothers Incorporated
New York University, B.S.

Salomon Brothers is a trading, brokerage and investment banking firm serving institutional clients. Mr. Saitta analyzes financial and commodities futures prices, volume and open interest in order to publish a daily report which makes speculative trading recommendations. He began his career working on the fixed income trading floor as a futures and options sales liaison. He is now a technical analyst in the fixed income research department.

Q: How are futures utilized by a speculator?

A: The goal of a speculator is to make money without investing a lot of up front capital. Generally only a very small percentage of bond futures contracts go to delivery, meaning the investor may never have to put up the face value of the underlying security. Often the purpose is not to own the underlying security, but to use the futures contract to speculate or as a hedging vehicle. There are three reasons to use futures: (1) they are highly leveraged, (2) they are very liquid, and (3) investors can easily obtain historical price, volume, and open interest data. Additionally, futures are available on many different types of assets making it easier for speculators to invest in a variety of commodities. In the futures market all the trading is done in one room on the exchange making it easy to record data. There are no futures contracts in the OTC market because while cash price and volume data is readily available there is no exchange, per se, to keep the information. For many investors and especially a technical analyst like myself, price, volume, and open interest are extremely important. I analyze the future market in order to make recommendations to clients, salesmen and traders on speculative positions they should take.

Q: Does the position or direction of the futures market provide information to investors other than speculators?

A: Yes, futures contracts are often looked at as a benchmark. For instance, someone trading cash corporates wants to get an idea of which way the treasury bond market is going. He might look at the futures contract because it is a generic benchmark that a lot of people are trading. The treasury bond contract is so liquid that it is used as a benchmark much in the same way the Dow Jones Industrial Average is a benchmark for the equity market. Even equity investors look at the treasury futures market as a proxy for how the bond market fared.

Here is additional information on futures provided by Steve Cusimano, Senior Portfolio Manager at the Florida State Board of Administration. A more detailed interview with Mr. Cusimano appears in Chapter 20.

Q: Rebalancing and trading implications are two of the biggest issues for passively managed portfolios. How is the trading conducted at the State of Florida?

A: Once the buy and/or sell list is determined by the portfolio manager, he/she discusses the characteristics of the trade list with the head trader in order to establish a strategy to minimize transaction costs. They consider the number of exchange listed stocks versus the number of OTC stocks, the industry or sector distribution of the stocks on the list, and the amount of time the portfolio manager is willing to wait to have the positions filled. The strategy includes utilizing a combination of trading venues such as electronic crossing networks that match buyers and sellers of a particular stock at a known price at several points during the day (both during market hours and after the close). Direct access to the floor of the NYSE via DOT is typically used for smaller orders, or for very liquid securities. Finally, institutional block trading desks are utilized to complete larger, more difficult trades, and/or trades that can not be filled on a crossing network. The benefit of electronic trading is that it can be done for lower commissions per share, and in the case of the crossing networks, trades are done at known prices between two anonymous parties which helps to eliminate or minimize impact costs.

Q: What are the benefits of using futures contracts and how are they utilized?

A: We utilize S&P 500 Index futures contracts to minimize trading costs. We equitize the cash balances in each portfolio that occur from dividend flows by purchasing S&P 500 futures. When these futures positions build to a reasonable level, we can do a trade with a broker/dealer called an exchange for physical, or EFP. If I am long futures and cash and want to be long actual stock, I pay a broker to deliver my desired basket of stocks in exchange for my cash and futures position. This type of trade provides the minimum execution costs for index portfolios, and on S&P 500 portfolios may average less than one cent per share (including all commission and market impact costs).

of lira that the bank can exchange into rupees by again trading in the spot currency exchange market.

To illustrate a forward currency exchange by a bank, consider again the Italian manufacturer buying goods from the Indian supplier. Before the supplier would be willing to ship the goods to Italy, he would require that an Italian bank provide a **letter of credit** that guarantees future payment for the goods at a specified date after the goods are received in

Italy. Once an Italian bank issues the letter of credit the bank has an obligation to pay a specified quantity of rupees at a future date. To hedge its exchange rate risk, the bank can prearrange the future exchange rate of rupees for lira by trading with another bank in the forward exchange market. In this example, the Italian bank would purchase forward contracts in rupees.

Due to the important role banks perform in facilitating international trading, they are major players in spot and forward currency markets.

Table 16-10 shows spot and forward exchange rates on many of the actively traded currencies in late 1995. Delivery dates for forward contracts of 30-day, 90-day, and 180-day are common. However, any desired delivery date can be arranged. Forward contracts are contracts between two banks and, unlike futures contracts, a clearinghouse does not guarantee delivery of the underlying currencies. To reverse a forward position, an opposite transaction must be made.

Forward currency contracts can be written on any currency one desires and with any delivery date required. In contrast, liquid futures markets are limited to currencies of economically developed countries and have specified delivery dates. In short, forward trades provide the ability to create better hedges than futures trades.[13]

Hedging Risk-Free Foreign Security Positions

Currency hedges are widely used when investments are made in risk-free securities of a foreign country. Alliance Multi Market Strategy (AMMS) is a U.S. mutual that which invests in low-risk money market instruments traded in countries other than the United States. Assume AMMS has $1 million it wishes to invest in the German equivalent of a 180-day Treasury bill. The following data is known:

TABLE 16-10   ACTIVE CURRENCY FORWARD MARKETS 1995

Currency	Spot Rate ($ per unit)	Forward Exchange Rates (1)		
		30-day	90-day	180-day
British Pound	1.5445	1.5420	1.5399	1.5379
Canadian Dollar	0.7338	0.7324	0.7323	0.7331
French Franc	0.2022	0.2024	0.2026	0.2024
German Mark	0.6942	0.6970	0.6992	0.7007
Japan Yen	0.009542	0.009591	0.009672	0.009650
Switzerland Franc	0.8604	0.8630	0.8713	0.8767

(1) Adapted from the *Wall Street Journal*, January 12, 1996.

---

[13] Because the forward currency market consists of trades between large banks that have considerable capital, there is very little chance of default by either the forward buyer or seller.

- The 180-day mark return on German T-Bills is 3%.

- The current exchange rate is 0.6942 dollars per mark.

- The 180-day forward contract price on German marks is 0.7007 dollars per mark

When AMMS purchases German T-bills, it knows the exact quantity of marks that will be available in 180 days. Thus, it will know the number of forward contracts on marks with a 180-day delivery date which it needs to sell in order to lock in a risk-free return in U.S. dollars. The following transactions would be arranged:

Today

1. Transfer $1,000,000 into 1,440,507Dm.
2. Invest the 1,440,507Dm in 180-day German T-bills. (At a 3% rate of return the payoff at maturity will be 1,483,722.)
3. Arrange to sell 1,483,722Dm in 180-days at a forward rate of $0.7007 per Dm.

At the end of 180 days

4. Collect 1,483,722Dm (1.03 times 1,440,507Dm) as the T-Bills mature.
5. Transfer the 1,483,722Dm into U.S dollars at the contracted forward exchange rate resulting in $1,039,644 (1,483,722 times 0.7007).

The result of these transactions would be a known U.S. dollar return of 3.96% over the next 180 days.

The key point in this example is that forward contracts can be used to create a perfect hedge and a known U.S. dollar return. This is possible because the foreign return (and therefore the number of foreign currency units to hedge) was known. Transactions such as this are widely used by organizations that invest in risk-free foreign securities. But when the return on foreign securities is uncertain, perfect hedges in currency forwards are not possible. This is discussed below.

Hedging Risky Foreign Security Positions

When the foreign currency payoff from an investment is unknown, a perfect currency hedge is not possible. To illustrate, consider the situation facing a mutual fund such as G.T. International Growth (GTI). This is a U.S. mutual fund that invests in non-U.S. equities. Assume GTI has $10 million it wishes to invest in German equities. Management of GTI is unsure what the return on these securities will be during the next 180 days, but they expect a 7% return. Figure 16-6 displays the hedged and unhedged outcomes associated with three possible 180-day returns (the expected return of 7% as well as −10% and 20%).

In the figure, the hedged returns are shown in black. If the actual return on German stocks is equal to the expected return of 7%, then changes in the exchange rate have no effect on the dollar return that GTI earns. However, if the actual return is greater than

FIGURE 16-6   HEDGED AND UNHEDGED RISKY PORTFOLIOS

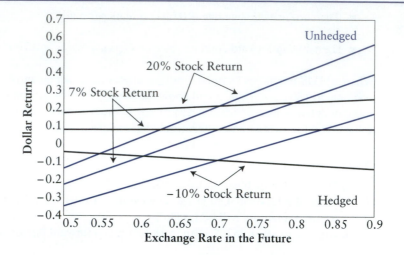

expected, increases in the value of the mark relative to the dollar result in slightly greater returns. This is because GTI receives a larger quantity of marks than expected and these extra unhedged marks can be converted into a larger quantity of dollars than expected. In contrast, if the actual return is negative, increases in the value of the mark relative to the dollar result in slightly lower returns. In this case GTI receives fewer marks than expected. Therefore GTI has to buy marks with dollars (which have decreased in value) in order to be able to deliver marks on its short mark forward contract position.

But even though all currency risk can not be eliminated by means of a currency hedge, exposure to currency risk is much less than if the position were unhedged.

S U M M A R Y

Here are the major concepts:

- ▣ Futures contracts on financial instruments are a phenomenon of the 1980s and 1990s. At present, active markets exist on (1) short-term debt instruments (such as T-bills, CDs, and Eurodollar deposits), (2) long-term debt instruments (such as T-bonds, T-notes, and GNMAs), (3) stock indexes (such as the S&P 500, the Nikkei index, and the FT-SE 100 index), and (4) currencies of many countries.

- ▣ The basic purpose of financial futures is to reduce price risk by hedging one's physical security position with an opposite futures position. A perfect hedge that eliminates all risk is difficult to achieve in practice, but risk can be substantially reduced by selecting futures that (1) mature close to when cash is needed or will be available, (2) have a contract value similar to the amount being hedged, and (3) have a deliverable security similar to the security you intend to buy or sell.

■ Financial futures are one more tool with which the risk and return position of a portfolio can be managed. They open up a variety of new ways to speculate and can easily alter the market risk exposure of a portfolio (the stock/bond mix). However, similar to options, they are complex instruments and should be used only after they are well understood.

R E V I E W   P R O B L E M

Janet Trible is a CFA and works as an equity portfolio manager for Madison Investment Counsel, an investment firm that provides both active and passive management services to corporate and government pension plans. One portfolio for which she has responsibility is a passively managed portfolio that emulates returns on the S&P 500 index. At present, the market value of this portfolio, called the Large Cap Index, is $2 billion. Shares in the Large Cap Index are owned by a variety of Madison's clients. Janet also has responsibility for an actively managed equity portfolio owned by a single client of the firm, The Dogwood Foundation. The market value of the Dogwood portfolio is now $400 million.

To help her in managing both accounts, Janet often trades in S&P 500 futures contracts. Current market information about an S&P 500 contract that is deliverable in 3 months follows:

1.	Current Index value of the S&P 500	$700
2.	Dividends to be paid during the next 3-months on the S&P 500 Index	$7
3.	Risk-free rate over the next 3 months	2%
4.	S&P 500 futures contract price on a contract deliverable in 3 months	$707

a. Due to dividends received on stocks owned in the Large Cap Index portfolio, the portfolio has a cash balance of $10 million. If this is not invested in S&P equities, returns on the portfolio will not track the returns on the actual S&P 500 Index as closely as Janet wishes. How could Janet use the futures contract to more closely track returns on the index?

b. The Dogwood Foundation portfolio presently has a total portfolio beta of 0.62 due in large part to the 60/40 split of the portfolio between equities and T-bills. Trustees of the foundation believe that stock values are more likely to decline than increase during the next 3 months. Therefore they would like to use futures contracts to reduce the portfolio's beta to 0.5. How could Janet use the futures contract to accomplish this objectives. What must be true for this hedge to work?

c. Is the market value of the futures contract correct according to the arbitrage valuation model?

Solution

a. Buy 28.57 futures contracts:
$28.57 = \$10,000,000 \div \$700 \times 500$

b. Actual Units of Stock Index Owned: $\dfrac{\$400,000,000 \times 0.62}{\$700 \times 500} = 708.57$

Desired Units of Stock Index to Own: $\dfrac{\$400,000,000 \times 0.50}{\$700 \times 500} = 571.43$

Difference represents number of contracts to sell $= 137.14$

For this type of hedge to work, the stocks owned in the portfolio must be very similar to the stocks underlying the futures contract.

c. $F_{rT} = S_t (1 + RF) - D_T = \$700 (1.02) - \$7 = \$707$
Yes, the market price is equal to the arbitrage model price.

QUESTIONS AND PROBLEMS

1. What is the difference between a futures contract and a forward contract?
2. It is January 1, and a 90-day T-bill future maturing in June is trading at an 8.85% (360-day) discount. You buy five contracts.
   a. What are you now legally obligated to do under the contract?
   b. If you sell two weeks later at a discount of 8.95%, what is your dollar profit or loss?
   c. If you are considering holding to maturity and selling five contracts at that time (instead of taking delivery), what is your expected profit if the markets are in equilibrium?
3. It is now March 1. You buy a September T-bond future selling at $95.25 to yield 8.57%. On June 1 you cover the long future by selling at $99.25 (8.09% yield) and simultaneously buy spot T-bonds at $99.75. What is your net purchase price?
4. Ninety-day and 180-day spot T-bills are now selling for $99.25 and $98.50, respectively. In addition, you observe that the price of a 90-day T-bill future which matures in 90 days is $99. Create an arbitrage that will take advantage of any price imbalances.
5. Spot and futures prices are shown here for the close of trading on January 1:

Spot T-bill Instruments

Maturity	Quoted Discount
90 days	8.0%
180 days	8.2%
270 days	8.4%
360 days	8.6%

Futures on 90-Day T-bills

Maturity	Quoted Discount
Current	?
90 days	8.0%
180 days	9.0%
270 days	?

   a. What should the discount be on the futures that are currently maturing?
   b. If the markets are now in equilibrium, what should be the discount on the 270-day futures? (Ignore mark-to-market.)
   c. Why did part b require that mark-to-market be ignored?
   d. Again, ignore mark-to-market. Create an arbitrage on the 90- and 180-day futures.
6. Under what conditions would a perfect hedge work?
7. What is the importance of delivery in futures pricing? Contrast the delivery features of futures on T-bills, T-bonds, and stock indexes.
8. On December 30, T-bond futures maturing exactly two years later were quoted at 67–24.
   a. Interpret this price quote.

b. Why is the price so low? These are, after all, default- and call-free U.S. Treasury obligations.

c. In deciding what price is actually paid for any T-bonds actually delivered, the clearing corporation divides the price quotation by a delivery factor that is generally less than 1.0. Why do they do this, and why do you suppose it is less than 1.0?

9. It is now January 1, and you hold $5 million par value of corporate bonds with a market value of $4,893,750. You sell 50 T-bond contracts at $1,025 per bond. By March 15, the basis (between the future and the average corporate bond value) has changed from $46.25 to $51.25. If you simultaneously sell spot and buy futures, what is your net selling price? What is your gain or loss on the initial corporate bond value?

10. People hedge in financial futures to reduce price risk. What must happen to the hedge basis during the life of a hedge in order for the hedge to be perfect, that is, to eliminate all price risk? What features of a financial future should one look at in order to reduce price risks as much as possible?

11. The optimal hedge as shown in Equation 16.4 requires estimates of σ_S, σ_F, and r_{FS}. Assume you are hedging with a contract that has a good history available. How might you estimate each term statistically?

12. Assume you intend to borrow $100 million in mid-February. It is now January 1, and 90-day T-bill futures maturing at the end of March are quoted at an 8.0% discount. Assume you have estimated the following satistically:

- ◼ Standard deviation of futures prices = $2

- ◼ Standard deviation of your borrowing price = $3

- ◼ Correlation between S and F = 0.7

What is the optimal hedge?

13. Outline a basic trading strategy for each of the cases presented next. You may buy or sell any of the financial futures contracts discussed in the chapter. Be sure to specify the contract's maturity month.

a. It is January 1, and the treasurer of a life insurance company maintains large holdings of U.S. T-bills, as follows:

1-month maturity	$1.5 million
3-month maturity	0.7 million
6-month maturity	1.0 million
1-year maturity	2.0 million

The treasurer wishes to hold these T-bills in order to protect the firm from temporary liquidity needs, but wishes to protect against losses in value if interest rates rise.

b. The investment adviser to a college endowment fund has been told that in early June a major contribution of $500,000 will be received. Believing that rates are now at a peak, the adviser will be investing the contribution in T-bonds.

c. In early March a mutual fund manager has a large position in intermediate- and long-term corporate bonds. He is forecasting a rise in interest rates.

d. The situation is the same as in part c, except the manager is forecasting a decline in interest rates.

e. A real estate investment trust buys mortgages from local financial institutions and then packages them for resale to the market. It is February 15, and the package should be ready for sale by middle August.

f. The treasurer of a corporation estimates that on May 15, $10 million in commercial paper will have to be sold to finance seasonal working capital needs. The treasurer believes that by May commercial paper rates will be higher than existing rates on June financial futures.

g. The situation is the same as in part f, except the treasurer believes June futures rates are higher than will exist in May.

14. What does dollar duration measure?

15. It is January 1. The duration of your bond portfolio as measured by D_1 is 6.0 years, its market value is $700 million, and its yield to maturity is 10%. Assume that D_1 for the cheapest-to-deliver T-bond is 6.5 years and has a delivery factor of 0.90.

a. How many futures contracts would you buy or sell to increase the effective value of the portfolio to $800 million with $D_1 = 6.0$ years?

b. How many futures contracts would you buy or sell to leave the market value at $700 million but reduce its duration to four years?

c. In either case, what factors might cause the holding you take on to be wrong?

d. Ignoring part c, what would you do when the futures mature?

16. Hedges of a stock portfolio using stock index futures work best if the portfolio is similar to the underlying futures index. Why is this so?

17. Stock index futures can increase or decrease a portfolio's systematic market risk. They cannot hedge unsystematic risks. Why?

18. You are the administrator of a stock portfolio that is now worth $1 billion and has a beta of 1.1. You would like to reduce the beta to 1.0 and reduce the equity claim to $900 million. Futures prices of the NYSE index contract are 115 and the spot value is 113.

a. How could you accomplish your goal with futures?

b. Actually, you have many maturity dates to choose from. How might you decide which to use?

c. What would you do when the futures mature?

d. Why might this not work out the way you wish?

19. On December 31, six-month T-bills were priced to provide a six-month return of 4.28%. (This is the effective return, not the discount.) At the same time, the S&P 500 Index closed at $400, and the futures contract on the S&P 500 with a June maturity closed at $412. Dividends expected on the S&P 500 between January and June of the next year were $8.00. Was the future priced according to the arbitrage valuation model?

20. A general model for valuing stock index futures is not currently available. However, an arbitrage model is often used to approximate the value of a stock index future.

a. What is the arbitrage that is conducted?

b. Is the current futures price equal to the expected value of the index when the contract matures?

c. What is the role of dividends in this model?

d. What problems does the model assume away?

21. Today is June 30, and you observe the following market data:

Stock Index:	
Current price	$300,00
Dividend to be paid in 3 months	$ 3.00
T-bills:	
Quoted discount on 3-month 90-day T-bill	8.00%
Stock Index Future	
Quoted price of a future with a 3-month (90-day) delivery date	$324.00

a. Is the future properly priced?

b. Illustrate the index arbitrage that could be conducted. (Trade in spot stock now worth $100 million and assume you can trade fractional units.)

c. You manage a $500 million portfolio of equities and T-bills. At present, $250 million of equities with a beta of 1.1 are held. You would prefer that the portfolio effectively have $300 million of equity and the equity beta be 1.0. How many futures could you trade to achieve this outcome without trading the spot equity?

d. Will the futures/spot position taken in part c result in the same portfolio values in three months as an adjustment of the spot portfolio to your desired mix? Illustrate for stock index values of $280 and $320. Explain any difference.

22. The spot exchange rate between U.S. dollars and British pounds is $1.5 per pound. The 180-day forward exchange rate is $1.48 per pound. The 180-day risk-free interest rate in Britain is currently 3%.

a. If a U.S. investor purchases the 180-day British securities and hedges the investment with a trade in forward contracts, what U.S. dollar rate of return will be earned?

b. If the U.S. investor does not hedge the currency position above, what U.S. dollar rate of return will be earned if the exchange rate (1) remains at $1.5 per pound, (2) is $1.4 per pound, and (3) is $1.6 per pound?

 23. On the maturity date, stock index futures contracts require delivery of:

a. common stock

b. common stock plus accrued dividends

c. Treasury bills

d. cash

R E F E R E N C E S

Recent texts with extensive discussion of financial futures are shown below. Each has further detailed listings of references.

Chance, Don M. *An Introduction to Options and Futures,* Orlando, FL: Dryden Press, 1989.

Figlewski, Stephen. *Hedging with Financial Futures for Institutional Investors,* Cambridge, MA: Ballinger, Publishing 1986.

Hull, John. *Options, Futures, and Other Derivative Securities,* 2nd Ed., Englewood Cliffs, NJ: Prentice Hall, 1993.

Marshall, John F. *Futures and Option Contracting: Theory and Practice,* Cincinnati, OH: Southwestern, 1989.

Stoll, Hans R. and Robert E. Whaley, *Futures and Options: Theory and Applications,* Cincinnati, OH: Southwestern, 1993.

Each of the various futures exchanges has extensive literature about their contracts. Write to the following addresses and request a listing of the publications currently available:

Chicago Board of Trade, Literature Services Department, 141 W. Jackson Boulevard, Suite 2210, Chicago, IL 60604–2994.

Chicago Mercantile Exchange, International Monetary Market, 30 South Wacker Drive, Chicago, IL 60606.

Kansas City Board of Trade, Marketing Department, 4800 Main Street, Suite 303, Kansas City, Mis, 64612.

New York Futures Exchange, Inc., 20 Broad Street, New York, NY 10005.

FINEX, Four World Trade Center, New York, NY 10048.

The role of stock index futures in the "Crash of 1987" has been extensively studied. A few of the studies are listed next:

Commodity Futures Trading Commission, *Final Report on Stock Index Futures and Cash Market Activity During October* 1987, 1988.

Harris, Lawrence. "The October 1987 S&P 500 Stock-Futures Basis," *Journal of Finance,* March 1989.

Blume, Marshall E., A. Craig MacKinlay, and Bruce Terker, "Order Imbalances and Stock Price Movements on October 19 and 20, 1987," *Journal of Finance,* September 1989.

Stoll, Hans R. and Robert E. Whaley. "The Dynamics of Stock Index and Stock Index Futures Returns," *Journal of Financial and Quantitative Analysis,* December 1990.

17

OPTIONS

After reading this chapter you should have an understanding of how the market prices of put and call options are determined as well as how options are used in portfolio hedging and speculative strategies.

In 1973, call options on a select number of common stocks began trading on a formal securities exchange for the first time in history. This event marked the start of the revolution created by the trading of derivative securities on financial assets.

When the first listed call options on individual common stocks were introduced, their trading on an exchange was considered by many people to be a risky experiment. Options had been traded for many years in the over-the-counter market. But trading had never been active. The experiment, however, proved to be an outstanding success! Within a decade, call options were available on all actively traded stocks in the United States, put-option trading had begun, option trading had expanded to many U.S. and non-U.S. exchanges, and option contracts had been created on a wide variety of financial securities other than individual common stocks.

By the early 1980s, the extraordinary success of listed option contracts spurred the futures exchanges to offer a competitive product: futures contracts on financial securities. The futures contracts that were offered on common stocks differed from stock option contracts in what turned out to be a key respect. Stock futures were traded on *portfolios* of stocks such as the S&P 500 Index, whereas stock options were traded on individual stock issues. Trading of futures on stock index portfolios soon became the more popular form of derivative trading, since trading in claims to an aggregate portfolio of stocks was a more efficient way to manage a portfolio's total equity risk exposure. As trading in stock index futures grew, trading in options on individual stocks declined.

As expected, the option exchanges countered by offering option contracts on stock portfolio indexes. Two of these option contracts are now the most actively traded options in the world: options on the S&P 100 Index and the S&P 500 Index.

This chapter consists of five major sections. The first two review basic option concepts and option valuation models. The next two sections examine the use of options in hedging and speculative strategies. The final section takes up a variety of specialized option topics.

Basic Option Concepts

Definitions

An option is an agreement to trade at a stated future date and at a stated price, but *only if the buyer wishes to do so;* it is the buyer's option to trade. An option to buy is a **call** option. An option to sell is a **put** option. The stated future date is known as the **expiration date.** The stated price is known as the **exercise price.** Many options provide the right to exercise at any time up to and including the expiration date. These are called **American options.** Options that may be exercised only at the expiration date are called **European options.**

As with futures contracts, options are created by two willing parties. One party purchases the option to trade at a later date and the other sells the option. The seller is called the option **writer.** Buyers of options choose to buy (in the case of a call option) or sell (in the case of a put option) only if it is to their benefit to do so. Call owners buy if the asset's price is greater than the exercise price on the expiration day. Put owners sell if the asset's price is less than the exercise price on the expiration day. Buyers have a potential gain and no loss whereas writers have a corresponding loss but no gain. Therefore, the writer will demand a price to write the option.

Throughout this chapter, we use the following symbols in our discussion:

S_t = Market value of underlying spot good at date t. The trade date is designated as $t = 0$. The expiration date is designated as $t = T$.

X = Exercise price of the option.

C_t = Call value at date t.

P_t = Put value at date t.

For example, assume you are considering the purchase of a call option on a stock index known as the Japan Index that would allow you the right to purchase one unit of the index for $170 on August 25. The spot Japan Index is currently quoted as $175, and the price of the call option is $8. In this case:

$$S_0 = \$175$$

$$X = \$170$$

$$C_0 = \$8$$

$$T = \text{August 25}$$

The option writer is obligated to provide you with one unit of the Japan Index in return for $170 if you decide to trade on August 25. Clearly, you will elect to buy only if the Japan index is worth more than $170 on August 25. For example, if the Japan Index is trading for $177 on August 25, then you will exercise your call and pay $170 for something worth $177. Since your original cost was $8, you would incur a net loss on the transaction. This loss is equal to the option's $7 value on the expiration date less the initial price that you paid of $8. But the net loss of $1 from exercising is better than a net loss of $8 if you do not exercise.

The positive $7 option investment value on the expiration date to the call owner represents a negative $7 option investment value to the call writer. Again, to induce the writer to be placed in such a situation, a reasonable initial cash payment must be given to the writer—the initial option price.

Expiration Date Outcomes

As suggested in the previous discussion, each party to an option trade faces two related but different expiration date outcomes: (1) the option's **investment value,** and (2) the **net profit.** The investment value represents the market value of the option position to either the option buyer or seller. The net profit is the difference between the investment value and the price paid by the buyer or received by the seller. These are shown graphically in Figure 17-1. Outcomes for long (ownership) positions are shown as solid lines. Short position outcomes (those of the option writer) are the dashed lines.

Consider panel A, in which the *investment value* of the option position is shown. At the expiration date, the price at which the option trades in financial markets will be the same as the option's investment value. If the market price is different from the investment value of owning the option, then easy arbitrage profits are possible.[1]

At the expiration date of a call option, the option will have a zero investment value if the underlying spot good is worth less than the exercise price. At spot values greater than the exercise price, the call has an investment value equal to the spot's price minus the exercise price. Symbolically:

Investment Value of Call at Expiration Date

$$C_T = 0 \qquad \text{if } S_T < X$$
$$= S_T - X \qquad \text{if } S_T > X \qquad \textbf{(17.1)}$$

At the expiration date of a put option, the option will have a positive investment value if the underlying spot good is worth less than the exercise price. At spot values greater than the exercise price, the put will have a zero investment value. Symbolically:

Investment Value of Put at Expiration Date

$$P_T = X - S_T \qquad \text{if } S_T < X$$
$$= 0 \qquad \text{if } S_T > X \qquad \textbf{(17.2)}$$

---

[1] For example, suppose the expiration date of the Japan Index call option has arrived. You observe that the spot Japan Index is trading for $175 and the call option is trading for $6 (greater than its investment value of $5). The arbitrage would be for you to purchase the Japan Index for $175 and sell the option for $6. Call option owners would exercise and pay you $170 for the Japan Index that you will deliver to them. The exercise price of $170 that they pay to you plus the $6 of cash inflow from selling the option is more than you paid for the index by $1. Before transaction costs, you will earn a $1 profit on no investment and at no risk.

FIGURE 17-1 EXPIRATION DATE OUTCOMES

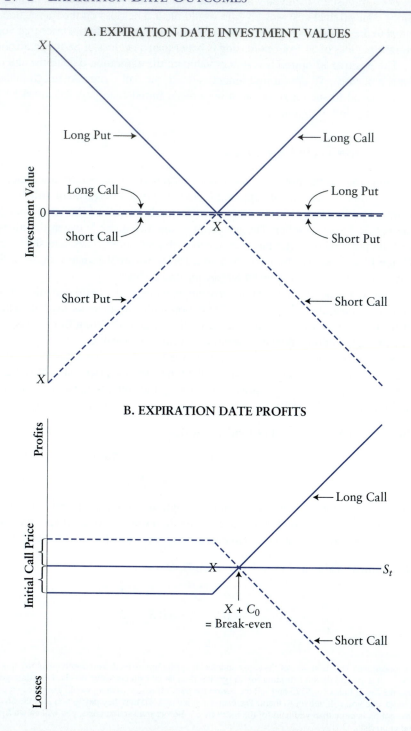

A. EXPIRATION DATE INVESTMENT VALUES

B. EXPIRATION DATE PROFITS

In panel B of Figure 17-1, the *net profits* from a long or short call position are shown for the expiration date. This net profit is simply the investment value of the position minus (for the owner) or plus (for the writer) the initial price paid for the option.

For the call owner to break even, the underlying spot good must have an expiration date value of $S_T = X + C_0$. For example, if $8 had been paid for a call having an exercise price of $170, then the spot asset must sell for more than $178 at expiration for the call owner to profit (or the call writer to lose).

Option Valuation

Two basic models are used to find what the value of an option should be prior to the option's expiration date: the **put-call parity model** and the **Black-Scholes option pricing model.** The put-call parity model focuses on expiration date outcomes whereas the Black-Scholes option pricing model focuses on outcomes during the next instant in time. Both are based on arbitrage profits that could be earned if the respective valuation equation does not explain actual market prices.

In developing these models, we make a number of assumptions. These simplify the analysis and still result in useful valuation equations. The initial assumptions to be used include the following:

- Transaction costs are zero. This causes a precise pricing relationship as opposed to a range of acceptable prices.

- The options are exercisable only at the expiration date; they are European options. This allows us to abstract from problems created by the possibility of early exercise of American options. All future cash flows occur at a known future date. (This assumption is lifted in the last section of this chapter.)

- The underlying securities do not pay dividends. This eliminates the possibility of uncertainty created by unknown dividends and simplifies the analysis. (This assumption is also lifted in the last section of this chapter.)

- Short sales are allowed, and proceeds from the sales may be used to purchase other securities. While this is not true for individual investors, many institutional investors can use the proceeds from short sales.

- A risk-free interest rate exists at which individuals may borrow or lend. While small investors might not be able to borrow at a risk-free rate, there are many ways for large investors to arrange risk-free financing.

The examples of put and call valuation in this section use an hypothetical underlying financial security. This security is a mutual fund called the WIT fund (short for the World Investment Trust fund). Although options are not actually traded on mutual funds, there is no reason why they could not be traded. The benefit of using an underlying asset for which there are no options traded is that we can focus on the general principles involved in option valuation as opposed to institutional characteristics of a specific contract. Assume that shares of the WIT fund are presently worth $95.45.

We develop valuation models for both a call and a put on one WIT share. The put and call have the same exercise price of $100 and the same expiration date T. Following common practice, one unit of time is assumed to be one calendar year. Thus, if the expiration date is 6 months from today, T equals 0.5. Assume the expiration date on the WIT options is 1 year, $T = 1.0$. Also assume the call is presently trading for $6.54 and the put for $2.00.

Finally, we need a zero-coupon risk-free security that can be bought as well as short-sold. This risk-free security must have a maturity identical to the options' expiration date (date T) and a maturity value identical to the options' exercise price of $100. The current market value of this risk-free security is $90.91. This means the risk-free rate available between today and date T when the risk-free security matures is 10%.[2]

Put-Call Parity Model

The put-call parity model is based on expiration date investment values associated with four different securities: (1) a call option, (2) a put option with identical terms, (3) the security on which the options are written (called the underlying or spot asset), and (4) a risk-free security that has a maturity date identical to the options' expiration date and a maturity payment equal to the options' expiration price.

Put-call parity is used for two purposes:

✶ to value a call option relative to a put with identical terms, and

✶ to show how the expiration date payoffs on any one of these four securities can be replicated by taking appropriate positions in the other three securities.

Valuing the Difference in Put and Call Prices. Consider the following portfolio created at $t = 0$. Purchase 1 unit of WIT fund shares, purchase 1 put on the shares, and write 1 call on the shares. The initial cost of the portfolio and the value of the portfolio at the options' expiration date are shown here. Two possible expiration date values of the WIT shares are shown, $50 and $150.

Transaction	Investment At $t = 0$	Investment Value at Expiration Date $S_T = \$50$	Investment Value at Expiration Date $S_T = \$150$
Buy 1.0 WIT share	−$95.45	+$50	+$150
Buy 1.0 put ($X = \$100$)	−2.00	+50	0
Write 1.0 call ($X = \$100$)	+6.54	0	−50
Total Portfolio	−$90.91	+$100	+$100

---

[2] This 10% rate of interest assumes end-of-period compounding. Later we have the need to use continuous compound rates. A discrete compound rate of 10% per period is the same as a continuous compound rate of 9.531% per period.

Notice that *all portfolio cash flows are known*. Today $90.91 is paid and at date T $100 is received, regardless of the value of WIT shares on date T. Since the cash flows are certain, the relationship between them should reflect a 10% risk-free rate of interest. This is true in this example, since $90.91 times 1.1 equals $100.

The generalized outcome of the portfolio position taken here is shown next, using the symbol designating the value of each security.

Transaction	Investment At $t = 0$	Investment Value at Expiration Date	
		$S_T < X$	$S_T > X$
Buy 1.0 WIT share	$-S_0$	$+S_T$	$+S_T$
Buy 1.0 put ($X = \$100$)	$-P_0$	$X - S_T$	0
Write 1.0 call ($X = \$100$)	$+C_0$	0	$-[S_T - X]$
Total Portfolio	$-[S_0 + P_0 - C_0]$	$+X$	$+X$

Again, all cash flows are known with certainty. When the initial trade is made at $t = 0$, cash flows are known, since existing market prices are known. In addition, once the trade is made the net outcome of this portfolio must be the exercise price of the options (which is the same as the maturity value of the risk-free security).

Since all net cash flows are known, the cash outflow at date $t = 0$ should be tied to the known expiration date inflow by the risk-free rate of interest, RF, as shown in Equation (17.3):

Put-Call Parity Model

$$[S_0 + P_0 - C_0](1 + RF)^T = X \qquad (17.3)$$

A portfolio consisting of (1) a long position in one unit of the spot asset, (2) a long position in one unit of the put, and (3) a short position in one unit of the call is a portfolio that has *no investment risk at the option's expiration date*. The cash flows associated with this portfolio are similar to those of buying a risk-free security. Therefore, the net investment in the portfolio should accumulate at a risk-free rate of return. If Equation (17.3) does not reflect actual market prices, then an arbitrage trade can be made.

Equation (17.3) is referred to as the put-call parity model. The model does not value each option individually. Instead, it can be used only to determine the price difference that should exist between the call price and the put price. This difference can be found by rearranging Equation (17.3) as follows:

Put-Call Parity Model

$$C_0 - P_0 = S_0 - [X \div (1 + RF)^T] \qquad (17.4)$$

The call price minus the put price should be equal to the current spot price minus the present value of the exercise price discounted at the risk-free rate of interest.

If we apply Equation (17.4) to the WIT option data, we find that the parity model is working. The model implies that the call should be trading for $4.54 more than the put and this is exactly the price differential observed in the market.

Actual Market Values	Put-Call Parity $C_0 - P_0$ Difference

$$\$6.54 - \$2.00 = \$4.54 = \$95.54 - [\$100 \div (1.10)^1]$$

The actual market price differences and theoretical put-call parity price differences are identical because of the way the example was constructed. We examine an arbitrage that can be conducted if actual market prices violate put-call parity later in the chapter.

Replicating a Security's Date T Payoff. The put-call parity model can be rearranged in a number of ways. But the equations that result are more than mathematical formulas used to find the price of one asset based on the prices of the other three assets. The formulas show how the expiration date outcomes of one asset can be replicated by appropriate positions in the other three assets. For example, four ways of arranging Equation (17.4) are shown next. The left-hand side of each equation represents the asset whose expiration date payoffs are to be replicated. The right-hand side of each equation shows the position that should be taken in the other threes securities in order to conduct the replication. If a variable is preceded by a positive sign, this means the security is held in a long position. If the variable is preceded by a negative sign, the security is held in a short position.

How to replicate investment payoffs on different securities at the option expiration date

Asset to Replicate	The Replicating Portfolio	

Buy risk-free asset: $+X \div (1 + RF)^T = +S_0 + P_0 - C_0$ **(17.5a)**

Buy a call option: $+C_0 = + S_0 - [X \div (1 + RF)^T] + P_0$ **(17.5b)**

Buy a put option: $+P_0 = + C_0 + [X \div (1 + RF)^T] - S_0$ **(17.5c)**

Buy underlying spot: $+S_0 = +C_0 + [X \div (1 + RF)^T] - P_0$ **(17.5d)**

For example, consider Equation (17.5a). The asset being replicated is a long position in a zero-coupon risk-free security with a maturity date of T and a par value of X. Its current market value is $[X \div (1 + RF)^T]$. To replicate the expiration date payoffs of this position by using the other assets, one would buy 1 unit of the stock, buy 1 unit of the put, and sell (or write) 1 unit of the call. (The number of units to trade comes from the fact that each variable is implicitly multiplied by 1.0. For example, S_0 is the same as 1.0 times S_0.) The position associated with Equation (17.5a) should be familiar, since it is the position taken in our example using the WIT fund options.

Equation (17.5b) shows how to replicate the expiration date payoffs of a long position in a call option. In panel A of Figure 17-2, the solid lines show the expiration date investment values of the three individual security positions. The dashed line represents the net outcome of this portfolio, which, of course, is identical to the payoffs of a long position in the call.

The long call payoff is replicated by first buying one unit of the stock and financing the purchase with debt that has a par value of X. If the stock's value at the expiration date is greater than the par value on the debt, the debt is repaid, resulting in a payoff identical to a call option with an exercise price of X. If the stock's expiration date value is less than the

FIGURE 17-2 OPTION SYNTHETICS

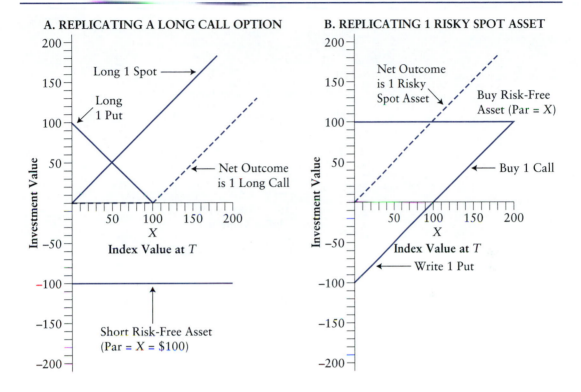

A. REPLICATING A LONG CALL OPTION

Long 1 Spot →

Long 1 Put

← Net Outcome is 1 Long Call

Index Value at T

Short Risk-Free Asset (Par = X = $100)

B. REPLICATING 1 RISKY SPOT ASSET

Net Outcome is 1 Risky Spot Asset

Buy Risk-Free Asset (Par = X)

← Buy 1 Call

Index Value at T

← Write 1 Put

debt's par value, the loss incurred in repaying the debt is exactly offset by the positive payoff on the put. Again, the net payoff is identical to that of a call with an exercise price of X.

Equation (17.5d) shows how to replicate the expiration date payoffs of a long position in the stock. In panel B of Figure 17-2, the solid lines show the expiration date investment values of the three individual security positions. The dashed line represents the net outcome of this portfolio, which, of course, is identical to the payoffs of a long position in the stock.

The important point to be drawn from these examples is that the future payoffs on one security can be synthetically replicated by appropriate positions in other securities. For example, a stock position can be created by positions in risk-free debt, the put option and the call option. This is why many people call options the building blocks from which other securities are created.

Using Options to Create Futures Outcomes. Let's return to the options available on the WIT fund. What would be the expiration date outcome from buying one call and writing one put?

The answer is shown graphically in Figure 17-3. If the WIT fund is selling for more than $100 at date T, you will exercise the call (and the put owner will not exercise the put). You will pay $100 and receive one share of WIT fund. If WIT fund is selling for less than $100, the put owner will exercise the right to sell the fund to you at $100 (and your long call

FIGURE 17-3 LONG CALL PLUS SHORT PUT EQUAL LONG FUTURE

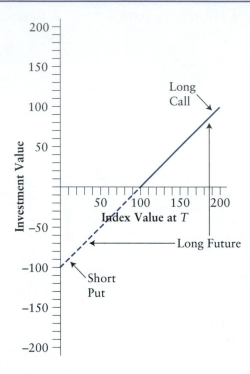

position will not be exercised). In this case, you also buy the fund for $100. The portfolio of one long call and one short put provides the same date T outcomes as a long futures position.

This example reinforces the concept that options can be thought of as the building blocks from which other securities can be made. In addition, the example suggests that prices in the option markets must be interrelated to prices in the futures markets.

The Economic Definition of a Call. So far we have defined what a call option is in legal terms (the right to buy a stated good at a stated price on a future stated date). Now that we understand how one security can be replicated by positions in other securities, we can turn to an economic definition of call options. Consider Equation (17.6), which restates the value of a call option in terms of the put-call Parity model.

Put-Call Parity Value of a Call option

$$+C_0 = S_0 - [X \div (1 + RF)^T] + P_0 \tag{17.6}$$

Equation (17.6) should be read as follows. A long call position is the same as

■ a long position in the underlying spot asset $\{+S_0\}$

■ less the present value of a risk-free debt security that is sold to partially finance the purchase of the asset $\{-[X \div (1 + RF)^T]\}$

◨ plus the cost of a put that acts as insurance to repay the debt issue if the value of the underlying spot is less than the debt par value at the debt's maturity $\{+P_0\}$.

Economically, *a call option is a leveraged ownership position in the underlying spot asset.*[3]

To see the truth in this statement, consider the following example. You would like to buy a 1-year call option on a piece of land. Unfortunately, the landowner is unwilling to sell you a call option but is willing to sell the land for $1,000,000. Assume the 1-year risk-free rate of interest is 10%, and you could borrow as much as $900,000 to purchase the land if you also buy an insurance policy that will pay off the loan if you do not pay the loan's par value. The cost of the insurance is $5,000.

Even though the landowner will not sell you a call option directly, you can replicate the outcomes of a call on the land by taking the following steps. First, buy the insurance policy for $5,000 and arrange a 1-year loan with a par value of $900,000. Based on a 10% interest rate and a 1-year repayment, you will be able to borrow $818,182 ($900,000 ÷ 1.1). Thus, your personal down payment on the land will have to be $181,818. Adding in the insurance cost, the total cost to you will be $186,818.

When the loan is to be repaid in 1 year, you will repay it if the land is worth more than the required $900,000 loan payment. If the land is worth less than $900,000, you will default on the loan and let the insurance policy pay the lender any difference between the land's value and the required loan payment. The outcome is identical to owning a 1-year call option on the land with an exercise price of $900,000! And the cost of this replicated call option is $186,818:

Replicated		Buy		Debt		Insurance
Call	=	Spot Asset	−	Financing	+	Cost
$+C_0$	=	$+S_0$	−	$[X \div (1 + RF)^T]$	+	P_0
$186,818	= $1,000,000		−	[$900,000 ÷ 1.1^1]	+	$5,000

A Put-Call Parity Arbitrage Example. The principal reason for the existence of traded puts and calls is the same as for futures contracts: They can be a cost-effective way to manage portfolio risk. But to be effective in controlling risk, options must trade at theoretically correct values. As with financial futures, it is the process of arbitrage that causes market prices to be close to, or identical to, their fair values.

To illustrate a put-call arbitrage, assume the market price of the WIT fund call is actually $7.00 and the put is trading for $2.00. Given that the call is selling for $5.00 more than the put when put-call parity implies the price difference should be $4.54, the call is clearly overvalued relative to the put. We are unable to tell which security is mispriced. In fact, they both might be mispriced. But we do know that the price differential should be less than $5.00.

Table 17-1 presents the details of an arbitrage on one put and one call given this data. First 1.0 call is sold because it is overvalued relative to the put. Because we do not

---

[3] This insight plays an important role in many areas of finance. For example, it can be used to explain default risk premiums on risky debt and to evaluate the financial conflicts that exist between shareholders and debt holders.

TABLE 17-1 ILLUSTRATION OF A PUT-CALL PARITY ARBITRAGE

Transaction	Investment at $t = 0$	Investment Value at Expiration Date		Why
		$S_T = \$50$	$S_T = \$150$	
Sell 1.0 Call	+$7.00	$0.00	−$50.00	Call is overvalued relative to the put
Buy 1.0 Put	−$2.00	+50.00	0.00	Put is undervalued relative to the call
Buy 1.0 WIT share	−95.45	+50.00	+150.00	To remove risk
Net	−90.45	+100.00	+100.00	
Finance risk-free	+90.45	−99.50	−99.50	90.45(1.1)
Net	$0.00	+$0.50	+$0.50	

know which option is mispriced, the put is bought because it is undervalued relative to the call. This results in a position that would incur losses (profits) if the WIT shares trade for more (less) than the $100 exercise price at the options' expiration date. To offset this risk, 1.0 unit of the WIT shares are bought. At this point, a known cash outflow of $90.45 is made at the date of the arbitrage that will provide a known cash inflow of $100 at the options' expiration date. To make this an arbitrage, $90.45 is borrowed (risk free) so there is no net cash inflow or outflow today. At the 10% interest rate on borrowings, $99.50 will have to be repaid on the borrowings in 1 year. But this repayment will be made from the $100 inflow, which the WIT options and share position provides. The net result of this arbitrage is a zero cash flow today followed by an known inflow of $0.50 in 1 year.

Arbitrage transactions such as this assure that market prices of calls relative to put prices are close to the values implied by the put-call parity model.

Black-Scholes Option Pricing Model

Around the time when the first listed option contracts were traded, Fischer Black and Myron Scholes developed the first option valuation equation in which a call option could be valued independent of the equivalent put option. This was a seminal event in financial research. Today, their model is extensively used (with refinements) by option hedgers and speculators.

The major difference between the option valuation model developed by Black and Scholes and the put-call valuation model is that the Black-Scholes model is able to directly value either option without knowing the market value of the other option. The value of a call option is expressed in terms of the underlying spot asset and a risk-free security. The value of the put is not needed. Similarly, the value of a put can be determined without knowing the value of the call. In contrast, the put-call parity model can only value the relative difference in the prices of the securities. It can not tell whether the price level of either option is correct.

Black and Scholes were able to accomplish this result by showing how the outcomes of either option can be replicated during the next moment in time by a combination of the underlying spot asset and the risk-free security. For example, the outcomes associated with owning one call during the next moment in time might be replicated by buying 0.5 units of the underlying spot asset and short-selling 0.3 units of a risk-free security. If so, the call should trade at a price equal to the cost of the replicating portfolio. If the market price of the call differs from the cost of the replicating portfolio, an arbitrage profit is possible.

Assumptions of the Black-Scholes Option Pricing Model. The put-call parity model is based on outcomes at the options' expiration date. The Black-Scholes option pricing model (BSOPM) is based on outcomes in the next moment in time. It is a continuous-time model. In developing their model, Black and Scholes used all of the assumptions stated earlier in this section plus the following. These additional assumptions were necessary because of the continuous-time nature of their model.

- Stock prices follow a continuous diffusion process.

- Continuously compound rates of return on the underlying spot asset are normally distributed.

- The standard deviation of the spot asset's continuous returns does not change over the life of the option contract.

The assumption of a continuous diffusion process was needed by Black and Scholes because their model was based on the potential for continuous-time replication of the outcomes of either a call or put. A continuous diffusion process is illustrated in Figure 17-4. This assumption simply means that the underlying spot asset is traded continuously in time and that there are no jumps in the spot asset's price. Panel A of Figure 17-4 illustrates a price series in which the spot asset is not traded continuously in time. There are periods during which the security can not be traded. Panel B in the figure illustrates a continuous-time price process with jumps in prices. For example, the price of the spot asset might be $50 one moment and $55 the next, a jump of $5. In a diffusion process, if the spot asset price goes from $50 to $55 it must be tradeable at all prices between $50 and $55. A continuous diffusion process is illustrated in panel C.

In accessing what might happen during the next moment in time, Black and Scholes had to make an assumption about the distribution of instantaneous returns on the underlying spot asset. A convenient, but reasonable, assumption is that continuously compound rates of return on the underlying spot asset are normally distributed.

Finally, the assumption that the standard deviation of the spot asset's continuous returns does not change over the life of the option contract was needed to assure that the outcomes of the replicating portfolio would actually be the same as the option's outcome. For example, a replicating portfolio might be based on a given standard deviation of spot asset returns but, if the standard deviation changes, the option will move to a price level that the replicating portfolio did not predict.

FIGURE 17-4 POTENTIAL STOCK PRICE MOVEMENTS

A. NONCONTINUOUS PROCESS

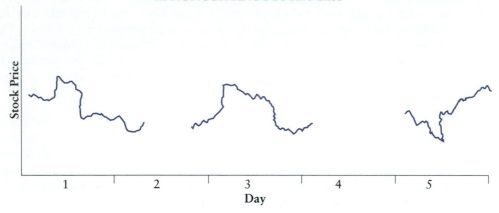

B. CONTINUOUS JUMP PROCESS

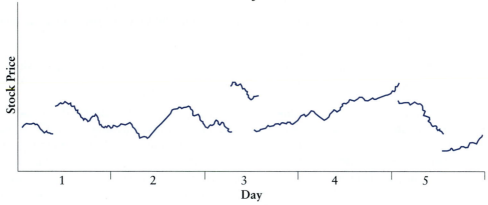

C. CONTINUOUS DIFFUSION PROCESS

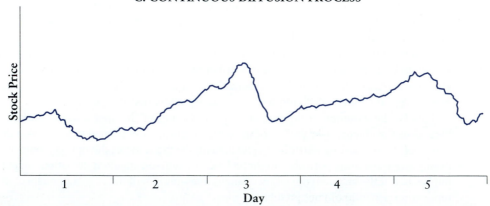

The BSOPM Call Value. Based on these assumptions, Black and Scholes were able to demonstrate that the value of a call option should be as follows:

Black-Scholes Call Valuation Model

$$C_0 = N(d1)S_0 - N(d2)[X \div (e^{(rf)(T)})] \tag{17.7}$$

where e is the transcendental number e (2.7183) and rf is the continuously compound risk-free interest rate.[4] $N(d1)$ and $N(d2)$ play important roles in this model. Statistically, they are the cumulative value of the standard normal density function between $-\infty$ and $d1$ or $d2$. The values of $d1$ and $d2$ are calculated as follows:

$$d1 = \{\ln(S_0 \div X) + T[rf + (\sigma^2 \div 2)]\} \div \sigma\sqrt{T}$$
$$d2 = d1 - \sigma\sqrt{T}$$

Here, σ is the annualized standard deviation of the underlying risky spot assets return (expressed as a continuously compound annual return).

To illustrate calculations involved in the model, assume you have collected the following data on the WIT fund call options:

Known Information	New Information
$X = \$100$	$rf = \ln(1.1) = 0.09531$
$S_0 = \$95.45$	$\sigma = 10\%$
$T = 1.0$ year	

First, $d1$ and $d2$ would be:

$$d1 = \{\ln(\$95.45 \div \$100) + 1.0[0.09531 + (0.10^2 \div 2)]\} \div 0.10\sqrt{1.0}$$
$$= +0.5374$$
$$d2 = 0.5374 - 0.10\sqrt{1.0}$$
$$= +0.4374$$

Second, the value of $N(d1)$ and $N(d2)$ must be found. This is illustrated in Figure 17-5, which represents a standard normal density distribution. The cumulative probability below the zero mean is 50%. The value of $d1$ and $d2$ represent the number of standard deviations away from the zero mean at which a cumulative probability is to be calculated. Positive values of $d1$ and $d2$ represent the number of standard deviations above the mean, and negative values represent the number of standard deviations below the mean. Since $d1$ is a positive 0.5374 in this example, we need to calculate the cumulative probability of the standard normal density distribution between negative infinity and 0.5374 standard deviations above the zero mean. Tables of the standard normal probabilities are provided in Appendix A. Since the standard deviations in the appendix are accurate to two decimal points, we round the $d1$ value of 0.5374 to 0.54. The cumulative probability at a $d1$ value of 0.54 is 0.7054.

---

[4] In the Black-Scholes option pricing model, one must use the continuously compound risk-free rate of interest. In the put-call parity model, either the continuous or discrete risk-free rate may be used. If the discrete risk-free rate is RF, the continuous rate rf is $\ln(1 + RF)$ and the discrete rate is $e^{rf} - 1.0$.

FIGURE 17-5   NORMAL DENSITY FUNCTION, D1 AND D2

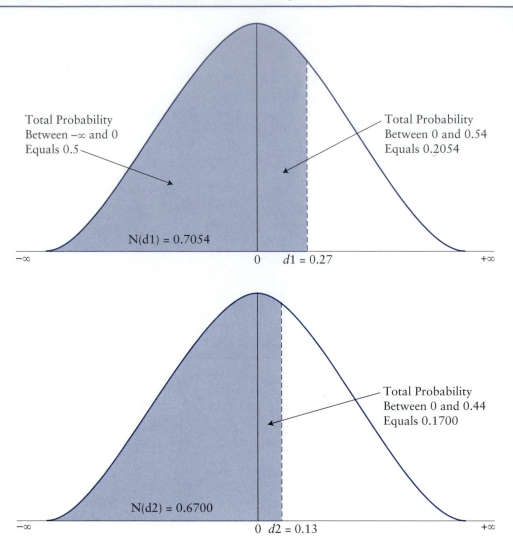

Next, the $d2$ value of 0.4374 is rounded to 0.44 and the appendix is used to find the cumulative probability from negative infinity to 0.44 standard deviations above the mean. This is 0.67.

Finally, these values for $N(d1)$ and $N(d2)$ are placed into Equation (17.7) to find the call's fair value:

$$C_0 = (0.7054)\ \$95.45 - (0.6700)[\$100 \div e^{0.09531(1)}]$$

$$= \$67.33 - \$60.91$$

$$= \$6.42$$

The Black-Scholes value of the call is $6.42. This is very close to the call's market value of $6.54 but suggests the call is slightly overvalued.

What Is $N(d1)$? $N(d1)$ plays an important role in option valuation and option hedging strategies. First, $N(d1)$ can be thought of as *the dollar change in the call option's price for a $1.00 change in the stock's price* (assuming all other variables remain constant).[5] For the calls on WIT shares, a dollar increase in WIT shares will result in a $0.7054 increase in the call price. Second, it can be thought of as *a hedge ratio between the risky spot asset and the call* that will result in an instantaneously risk-free combination. If you purchase 0.7054 shares of stock and write 1.0 call, then this combination is the same thing as instantaneously holding a risk-free security.

Black-Scholes Synthetics. The Black-Scholes option pricing model can be used to synthetically replicate the instantaneous outcomes of any of the three securities. One unit of the risk-free debt security has a current value of $X \div e^{(rf)(T)}$. Define this as TB_0, standing for the price of a T-bill at date 0. Then the following relationships exist. (Positive signs mean purchase; negative signs mean sell.)

Security Being Replicated	Synthetic Replicating Portfolio
Call Option	$= N(d1)S_0 - N(d2)TB_0$
$N(d2)$ T-Bills	$= N(d1)S_0 - 1.0C_0$
Underlying Spot Asset	$= [1 \div N(d1)]C_0 + [N(d2) \div N(d1)]TB_0$

For example, if you wished to replicate instantaneous outcomes of one WIT call, you should purchase 0.7054 shares of WIT and issue 0.67 units of T-bills each worth TB_0. To replicate 0.67 units of T-bills, purchase 0.7054 shares of WIT and sell 1.0 call. Finally, to replicate one share of WIT, purchase $(1 \div 0.7054)$ WIT calls and purchase $(0.67 \div 0.7054)$ units of TB_0.

This all looks complex, but synthetic security portfolios are actively used by sophisticated investors. Consider two actual examples. When investments are made in securities of countries other than one's home country, the investments face exchange rate risk—that is, uncertainty about currency exchange rates when the money is returned. To limit this uncertainty, you could purchase currency puts to guarantee a sale price of the foreign currency. But puts are not available on all currencies, and it may be very costly to insure each currency risk in the portfolio. Alternatively, you could synthetically create a put on the exact "basket" of currencies that you own by appropriate trades in the spot currencies and the domestic risk-free asset. Procedures such as these are also called dynamic strategies. The term *dynamic* refers to the fact that the synthetic is constantly rebalanced as security prices change or time passes.

An *enhanced* portfolio is the term used for another form of synthetic replication. Assume you wish to place $10 million in nominally risk-free securities such as T-bills.

---

[5] Strictly speaking $N(d1)$ should be intepreted only for very small changes in the spot asset price, since its value changes as spot prices change.

Synthetic T-bill returns could also be obtained by mixed futures/risky spot positions and mixed option/risky spot positions. An individual who manages an "enhanced portfolio" chooses the alternative that provides the greatest return.

Call Values Prior to Expiration Date. Figure 17-6 illustrates the relationship between the value of a call prior to the expiration date and the value of the underlying spot asset. When the spot asset's price is less than the exercise price, the option is said to be *out of the money.* When the spot asset's price is greater than the exercise price, the option is said to be *in the money.* The market value of the option can be thought of as consisting of two parts. The **immediate** value is the maximum of zero or the spot asset's price minus the exercise price. This is equal to the extent to which the option is "in the money." The **time value** of the option is the difference between the option's actual value and its immediate value. As shown in Figure 17-6, the time value of the option declines as the price of the underlying spot asset increases.

The Black-Scholes option pricing model can be used in a variety of ways. Most important, perhaps, is its ability to explicitly indicate the various factors that determine call premiums. These are as follows:

- Current underlying spot asset price. The higher the spot asset's price, the greater the call premium.

- Exercise price. The higher the exercise price, the lower the call premium.

FIGURE 17-6   CALL VALUES PRIOR TO EXPIRATION

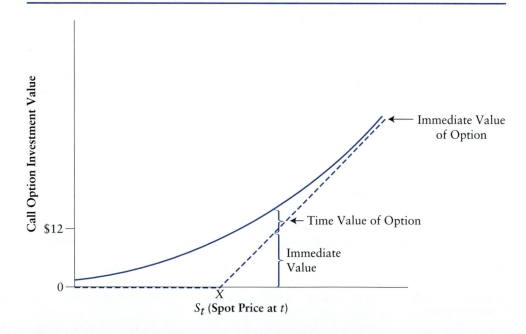

- Time to expiration. The longer the time to expiration, the greater the possibility that the spot asset will eventually sell above the call's exercise price and thus the greater the call premium.

- Variance of spot asset's returns. The more variable the future returns on the spot asset, the greater the possibility the asset will eventually sell above the call's exercise price and thus the greater the call premium.

- Risk-free rate. The greater the risk-free rate, the greater the call's value. This relationship is not as intuitively clear as the others. Recall that a call option is a leveraged position in the underlying asset. The call price is like a down payment on the asset. If all other variables remain the same and the interest rate increases, the size of the down payment will have to increase.[6]

Note that the value of a call is not a "direct" function of expected future stock prices. This point is true for each of the call valuation models developed in this chapter. In none of them is the call price directly affected by possible future stock prices. Only current stock prices are needed to value the call. The reason is simple. Calls are valued based on the fact that they can be mixed with stock positions to create a risk-free portfolio. If the value of the long stock position and short call position is not the same as the value of equivalent risk-free debt, arbitrage profits are possible.

The call price is, of course, affected indirectly by expected future stock prices in that possible future prices determine today's stock price. The important point, however, is that *investors do not need to predict future stock prices in order to value a call.*

Comparison of the Two Models

We now have two call valuation models. They are shown here with a slight modification to the manner in which put-call parity is presented.

	Call Value	=	Value of Long Position in Asset	−	Value of Short Position in Debt	+	Cost of Insurance
Put-Call Parity	C_0	=	$(1.0)S_0$	−	$(1.0)[X \div (1 + RF)^T]$	+	$(1.0)P_0$
Black-Scholes	C_0	=	$N(d1)S_0$	−	$N(d2)[X \div (e^{(rf)(T)})]$	+	0

Notice that each term on the right-hand side of the put-call parity model is multiplied by 1.0. Early in the chapter, we left these terms out. But it was implicit that each is, in fact, multiplied by 1.0.

So how do the models differ? They use different ways of expressing the risk-free rate. But this is a meaningless difference. In fact, the put-call parity model could be expressed in terms of a continuous risk-free rate.

---

[6] The loan repayment of X (the option's exercise price) is assumed to remain unchanged when the risk-free interest rate changes. If the interest rate increases, the present value of the loan decreases. Since the amount that can be borrowed declines, the size of the down payment (the call price) must increase.

Charles W. Smithson

Managing Director, CIBC Wood Gundy

University of Texas at Arlington, B.A.

University of Texas at Arlington, M.A.

Tulane University, Ph.D.

Charles Smithson is the head of the School of Financial Products at CIBC, a Canadian investment and commerce bank. He began his career as a college professor and took a side trip to work for two governmental agencies. In 1984, he switched to the practitioner arena and has been with Chase Manhattan Bank and Continental Bank in addition to CIBC.

Q: There are a variety of reasons for investing in options, including using them as corporate finance tools. Could you give an example of this use?

A: Probably the best example is attributed to Merck Pharmaceuticals. In an article for the *Journal of Applied Corporate Finance,* Merck's CFO and assistant treasurer for international talked about the problem at Merck and how they solved it. It is a nice application of options.

 Merck has a lot of exposure to foreign exchange. If the dollar is weak against the deutsche mark (DM), then the dollar value of any DM-generated revenue is high and Merck's income will be higher. But if the dollar is strong compared to the DM, then a DM coming back to the United States has less dollar value and Merck's income is going to be weaker. There is a volatility in the cash flows. By itself the volatility didn't bother Merck a lot, but they found it was causing them to cut back on the rate of growth in their R&D spending when the dollar was strong.

Q: This was happening even though the overseas arms were profitable in their own currency?

A: The whole firm was profitable, but there was less money in the cigar box. In order to get rid of this R&D spending volatility, Merck used foreign exchange options to insure the firm against DM-dollar, yen-dollar movements. Recently we've seen a lot of firms use options as insurance to make sure they have the cash flow to undertake their businesses.

Q: Is this sort of option "insurance" expensive?

A: The expense is diminished because firms aren't interested in complete protection; they just want to cover catastrophic losses. But options are expensive enough to have caught the eye of corporate boards, especially if exchange rates are favorable enough to make the option purchase unnecessary. One method to contain costs is to reduce the premium paid by purchasing out-of-the-money options. Additionally, the expense and coverage issues have spawned second-generation options like average rate options or Asian-style options.

Q: What are average rate options and why are they attractive?

A: In the example given, Merck is not as concerned about exchange rates on a particular day in the future, like European-style options are traded. They are more interested in what *on average* the exchange rate will be. From a business perspective they would be happier to have an option on an average rather than an option on a spot. With an Asian-style option, the exercise price is compared to the average spot price that has occurred over the time period instead of the spot on that particular day. The reason they are cheaper is because the volatility of the average is less than the volatility of a spot. Since the volatility goes down, so does the premium. The second generation of options has come in response to particular user demands.

Q: Is there backlash from board members who are not sufficiently educated in options who might think the firm has invested in a "risky" security when actually they are trying to moderate risk?

A: Previously, this has been true, but we are seeing less and less of it over the years even with the terrible reports in the press. Ten years ago it was common for me to read board policy statements that excluded options use. Today, I might still hear boards saying we only buy options for protection, we don't sell them. We are moving in the direction of people being more comfortable. When I was in school there wasn't much on this subject, and many of the boards share my problem of these instruments showing up long after we all went to school. True on-the-job training.

Q: What do you do for Wood Gundy?

A: I am managing director of one of the financial products groups. I'm in the business of educating people about a variety of financial products. Generally my client is at the actual point of the transaction—people in the treasury. Periodically, I go visit with boards of directors to answer questions they might feel more comfortable asking me than their treasury.

Q: How does your division generate revenue?

A: When people are asking questions about financial products we expect that they are considering purchasing them. From a business perspective we care about deepening the relationship with the client in order to produce a sale. Because almost all swaps and options look alike and are priced alike, clients are looking for two other things: (1) a creditworthy counterparty—we are AA rated—and, (2) service. We provide excellent education and consultation before, during, and after the decision is made.

They differ in that a put position is needed in the put-call parity model. The put provides a form of insurance to assure that a risk-free rate is available on debt financing. The put is not needed in the BSOPM, since they are able to assure risk-free positions by continuous-time hedging.

In addition, the models differ in the quantity of stock and debt that are held in order to synthetically replicate a call option. In the put-call parity model, the hedge ratios are all 1.0. One share of the spot asset, one unit of debt, and one put option will provide expiration date outcomes identical to a call. In the Black-Scholes model, the hedge ratios, $N(d1)$ and $N(d2)$, are less than 1.0 and change as any of the variables in the model change.

But the striking thing about the two models is not their differences, but their similarities. They are each based on a procedure in which one asset can be synthetically replicated by appropriate positions in the other assets.

Trades Based on Expiration Date Payoffs

Option payoffs can be evaluated at two points in time: on the expiration date of the option or at the next moment in time. In this section we examine various hedging and speculative strategies that focus on an option's expiration date. We discuss continuous-time hedging and speculation in the next section.

Hedging Strategies

To *hedge* usually means to take a position that offsets some type of risk. When applied to options, this risk is the uncertainty about the value (or rate of return) of the underlying security on which the option is written. A hedge is not conducted in the expectation of abnormal profits. Instead, the hedge simply alters the risk inherent in owning the underlying asset.

Portfolio Insurance. An insured portfolio has a minimum floor value if the underlying asset declines beyond some point but increases in value if the asset increases in value. Based on the put-call parity model, an insured portfolio can be created with options in one of two ways:

1. Buy 1.0 put for each 1.0 share owned, or
2. Buy T-bills having a par value equal to the desired minimum portfolio value and calls with any remaining funds.

Although the concept of portfolio insurance could be applied to each of the individual stocks in a portfolio, it is usually cheaper to trade in stock index options that are similar to the hodlings of the aggregate stock portfolio. If a value-weighted portfolio of many large capitalization stocks is owned, index options on the S&P 100, S&P 500, or NYSE might be better. Throughout our examples of portfolio insurance, we use the following price quotes for S&P 100 options:

$$S_0 = \$238.26 \qquad C_0 = \$13.75 \qquad rf = 5.721\%$$

$$X = \$240.00 \qquad P_0 = \$15.00 \qquad T = 3 \text{ months}$$

Portfolio Insurance with Puts. Assume you have $10 million in cash that you wish to invest in equities similar to those included in the S&P 100 Index. You know that in 1½ months the stocks will pay a 0.91% dividend yield, which you intend to reinvest at a risk-free return of 5.721% (continuous annual rate) for another 1½ months. You also believe that the value of the stocks will rise on average during the next three months, but obviously their values could also decline substantially. If you are concerned about possible declines in the value of your portfolio during the next three months, you could either (1) place the majority of the $10 million in stocks but insure a minimum portfolio value by purchasing puts—in effect, buying insurance—or (2) invest more of the $10 million in risk-free securities such as three-month T-bills with the residual in calls.

Consider the insurance available using puts. To guarantee a fixed minimum floor, you should purchase 1.0 put for each 1.0 "unit" of the stock index you own. Since S&P 100 puts with a $240 exercise price are quoted at $15, the cost of one put trade is really $1,500. The actual (or spot) S&P 100 Index doesn't really trade in the market, but, if it did, each unit would be quoted at $238.26. Since each put is on 100 units of the index, the cost of buying a unit of the spot S&P 100 Index would be $23,826 (if it actually traded). Since we need a 1:1 relationship between the long put and long stock position, the number of puts and stock would be identical and equal to 394.85:

$$N(\$1,500 + \$23,826) = \$10 \text{ million}$$

$$N = 394.8511411$$

Here N equals the quantity of stock index units and puts purchased. Although fractional shares and puts cannot actually be traded, we assume they can be in order to see that a truly insured portfolio is conceptually possible. The initial investment consists of:

$$\text{Stock } (N \times \$23,826) = \$9,407,723$$

$$\text{Puts } (N \times \$1,500) = \underline{592,277}$$
$$10,000,000$$

The expiration date value of this portfolio for various S&P 100 Index values is shown in Table 17-2. Dividends will be received in 1½ months and be reinvested at the risk-free rate to provide a known value of $86,255 at the expiration date. The long put position will, of course, have a positive value only if the S&P 100 Index is below $X = \$240$ on the expiration date. Note that, if this does occur, the increased put value exactly offsets the decreased stock value. Below $X = \$240$, the put and stock values move in a 1-for-1 inverse relationship (hence the 1.0-for-1.0 hedge ratio!). The minimum value of this insured portfolio is:

Minimum Portfolio Value

Guaranteed Stock Value	
(394.8511411 units at $24,000/unit)	$9,476,427
Guaranteed Dividend Value	86,225
Total	$9,562,652

TABLE 17-2   PORTFOLIO INSURANCE USING LONG STOCK AND LONG PUTS

S&P 100 Index at Expiration Date	Reinvested Dividends[1]	Put Value[2]	Stock Value[3]	Portfolio Value
$200	$86,225	$1,579,404	$ 7,897,023	$ 9,562,652
$220	$86,225	789,702	8,686,725	9,562,652
$238.26	$86,225	68,704	9,407,723	9,562,652
$240	$86,225	0	9,476,427	9,562,652
$260	$86,225	0	10,266,130	10,352,355
$280	$86,225	0	11,055,832	11,142,056

1. $(0.91\% \times 9,407,723)\, e^{(0.05721\times0.125)} = \$86,225$
2. $(\$240 - S) \times 100 \times 394.8511411$ (or \$0 if $S > \$240$)
3. $(S \times 100) \times 394.8511411$

Any time the S&P 100 Index closes at less than $240, you are guaranteed that the portfolio's value is $9,562,652. But if the stock index increases in value above $240, the insured portfolio also increases in value.

Naturally, there is a cost—one has to pay $592,277 to buy the puts. This represents almost 6% of the portfolio's initial value. To many investors this would represent a rather sizable outlay to insure the portfolio's minimum value three months from now. And if one were to continuously 'roll over' the hedge, there would soon be no portfolio value left to insure! But some investors might be so concerned with short-term losses in the portfolio's worth that they would be willing to pay the cost.

The cost of the portfolio insurance has both direct and opportunity cost components. The direct cost is the $592,277 spent on the puts. The opportunity costs consist of lost dividends and potential lost stock price appreciation on the $592,277. The costs of portfolio insurance can be large, and they increase as the spot index value increases above the put's exercise price.

During the middle to late 1980s, portfolio insurance was the rage-particularly with corporate pension sponsors facing financial distress. In the 1990s, portfolio insurance is not as widely used.

Portfolio Insurance with Calls. Portfolio insurance can also be obtained by buying calls and T-bills. Again, assume you have $10 million in cash to invest. In order to directly compare a "call/T-bill" strategy with the "stock/put" results just described, assume you wish to have a minimum portfolio value identical to that in the stock/put example—$9,562,652. This means you need to purchase 9.562652 T-bills, each having a par value of $1 million. The price of a three-month T-bill (given the continuous annual rate of 5.721%) would be 98.58% of par. Thus, a total of $9,426,861 will have to be spent on the T-bills:

$$0.9858 \times \$9,562,652 = \$9,426,861$$

This would leave $573,139 to purchase calls on the S&P 100 Index, or a total of 416.83 calls:

$$\text{Dollar Investment in S\&P 100 Calls} = \$10,000,000 - \$9,426,861$$

$$= \$573,139$$

$$\text{Number of S\&P 100 Calls} = \$573,139 \div (\$13.75 \times 100)$$

$$= 416.8283636$$

In Table 17-3 the expiration date investment values of this call/T-bill portfolio are shown. The minimum portfolio value is $9,562,652, simply because we bought enough T-bills to achieve this level. And at spot S&P 100 values above $X = \$240$, the portfolio increases in value because of investment value payoffs on the long calls. This is a portfolio with a minimum floor value that also participates with increases in the index above $240.

Similar to portfolio insurance gained with a long put-long stock position, this insurance has both direct costs and opportunity costs. But note that in our example the use of calls instead of puts results in lower opportunity costs. For example, Table 17-2 shows that at an index of $280 the total portfolio is worth $11.142 million if puts and the spot index are bought. However, Table 17-3 indicates that the portfolio would be worth $11.299 million if calls and T-bills are bought.

Why? The answer is due to the fact that (according to put-call parity) the put is slightly overvalued relative to the call. Therefore, strategies that involve purchasing the calls would dominate equivalent strategies using long put positions.

Portfolio Insurance on Other Assets. Minimum portfolio values can be obtained on any security or commodity on which options are traded. For example, assume you own ten T-bonds. You could create a minimum future floor value on the portfolio by purchasing ten puts on T-bonds at the desired exercise price and expiration date. Alternatively, you could emulate the expiration date payoffs of such a portfolio by purchasing calls on T-bonds and T-bills.

TABLE 17-3 PORTFOLIO INSURANCE ILLUSTRATION: LONG CALLS AND LONG T-BILLS

S&P 100 Index at Expiration Date	T-Bill Value[1]	Call Value[2]	Portfolio Value
$200	$9,562,652	0	$ 9,562,652
$220	$9,562,652	0	$ 9,562,652
$238.26	$9,562,652	0	$ 9,562,652
$240	$9,562,652	0	$ 9,562,652
$260	$9,562,652	$ 833,657	$10,396,308
$280	$9,562,652	$1,667,313	$11,229,964

1. $9.562652 \times \$1,000,000 = \$9,562,652$
2. $416.8283636 \times (S - \$240) \times 100$ if $S > \$240$

Portfolio insurance can even be obtained on assets that do not have traded puts or calls by creating synthetic option positions.

Call Overwriting. A common practice among many investors is a technique known as call overwriting. This is simply writing calls on stocks that are owned in the portfolio. The benefit of call overwriting is that it increases the immediate cash inflow to the portfolio. The cost is that it limits portfolio price appreciation.

Assume you own 100 shares of XYZ stock and that the following data currently apply to the calls and XYZ stock:

Stock Price	= $115.625	Call Exercise	= $110.00
Call Price	= $11.25	Call Expiration Date	= 4 months
Stock Dividend	= $1.10 per share paid in 1-month		

The effects of writing 1.0 call for each 100 shares owned are shown in Table 17-4 and Figure 17-7. Note that the immediate value of the portfolio increases by the amount of the call premium—$1,125. Investing this cash inflow in T-bills also tends to increase the expiration date value of the portfolio. But by writing the calls you have stated your willingness to sell the stock to a call buyer at a fixed price of $110 even if the stock is worth more at the expiration date.

TABLE 17-4   CALL OVERWRITING: INITIAL AND EXPIRATION DATE VALUES

At Date of Overwriting Program

Stock Value	+$11,562.50
Call Premium	+ 1,125.00
	$12,687.50

At Expiration Date (in Four Months)

Stock Price	Known Values Premium[1]	Dividend[2]	Calls	Stock	Total
$90	$1,146.66	$111.58	$ 0	$ 9,000	$10,258.24
$100	1,146.66	111.58	0	10,000	11,258.24
$110	1,146.66	111.58	0	11,000	12,258.24
$115.625	1,146.66	111.58	−562.5	11,562.5	12,258.24
$120	1,146.66	111.58	−1,000	12,000	12,258.24
$130	1,146.66	111.58	−2,000	13,000	12,258.24
$140	1,146.66	111.58	−3,000	14,000	12,258.24

1. $1,125 \times e^{0.05721 \times 0.25} = \$1,1146.66$
2. $(100 \times \$1.10)\, e^{0.05721 \times 3/12} = \$111.58$

FIGURE 17-7 CALL OVERWRITING

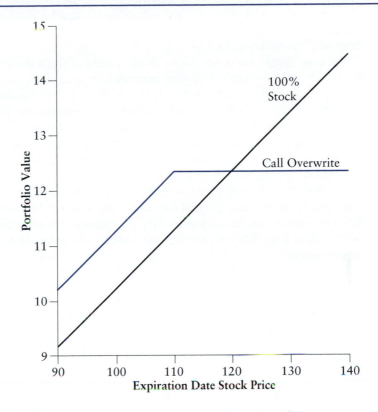

Speculation

Speculative strategies attempt to take advantage of disequilibrium prices (perceived or real). Although a variety of speculations are possible, we focus on index arbitrage.

Index Arbitrage. The term *index arbitrage* is applied to the speculative transaction that can be conducted when the prices of derivative securities are not in line with current prices of a stock index. In a strict arbitrage, there is a zero-risk cash inflow with no required cash outflow.

To illustrate an index arbitrage, we use S&P 100 Index calls and puts. Assume that on December 31, the S&P 100 Index is trading at $238.26, a call (exercisable for $240 in three months) is selling for $13.75, and an equivalent put is selling for $15. Finally, the continuous risk-free interest rate is 5.721% (annualized), and a known dividend of $2.168 will be paid in 1½ months on the index.

Applying the put-call parity model to this data, we would conclude that the put is overvalued relative to the call. Since we cannot be sure which of the two options is mispriced (they both could be), we take offsetting positions in both. Since the put is overvalued relative to the call, the put will be sold and the call purchased.

However, a short put and long call position involves a fair degree of risk. If the stock index falls in value, we lose on the call. If the index rises in value, we win on the put. To offset this risk, a short position in the underlying stock index is taken. We know from put-call parity that if all positions are taken in a 1.0-to-1.0 relationship, the expiration date value of the portfolio is risk free.

But even though we now have a risk-free portfolio, the transaction is not a pure arbitrage, since there is a net cash outflow required at the expiration date. A pure arbitrage will have only one positive and risk-free cash flow. To make the transaction into a true index arbitrage, we must buy T-bills today that have an expiration date payoff sufficient to pay the (risk-free) cash required in the put, call, and stock portfolio.

To illustrate such an arbitrage, assume there are no transaction costs and we can trade in fractional quantities of the assets. Also, all dividends paid on the short sale of the stock are financed initially with the purchase of T-bills.

In Table 17-5, the results of this transaction are shown for an initial trade in 500 puts and calls. Two possible expiration date values are used for the S&P 100 Index ($200 and $250) in order to show that outcomes from the arbitrage are, in fact, insensitive to eventual index values. First, 500 puts are sold and 500 calls bought to take advantage of the price disequilibrium:

1. Sell 500 puts:

$$\text{Net Inflow} = (500 \times 100) \times \$15 = + \$750,000$$

$$\text{Expiration Date Value} = -(500 \times 100) \times (\$240 - \$200) = -\$2,000,000$$

TABLE 17-5   ILLUSTRATION OF A STOCK INDEX ARBITRAGE

	Today	1 1/2	S&P 100 = $200	S&P 100 = $250
1. Sell 500 Puts	+$ 750,000		−$ 2,000,000	$ 0
2. Buy 500 Calls	− 687,500		0	+ 500,000
Risky Option Portfolio	+$ 62,500		−$ 2,000,000	+$ 500,000
3. Sell 500 Units of S&P 100	+ 11,913,000	−$108,400	−$10,000,000	−$12,500,000
	+$11,975,500	−$108,400	−$12,000,000	−$12,000,000
4. Buy T-Bills				
a. Finance Dividends	− 107,627	+$108,400		
b. Finance $12 Million	− 11,829,591		+$12,000,000	+$12,000,000
Net	+$ 32,282	$ 0	$ 0	$ 0

2. Buy 500 calls:

$$\text{Net Outflow} = (500 \times 100) \times \$13.75 = \$687,500$$

$$\text{Expiration Date Value} = (500 \times 100) \times (\$250 - \$240) = +\$500,000$$

Stocks are then added in order to make the portfolio risk free. Note that this will be a short position in stocks requiring the payment of a cash dividend in 1½ months.

3. Sell 500 units of S&P 100 Index:

$$\text{Net Inflow} = (500 \times 100) \times \$238.26 = \$11,913,000$$

$$\text{Dividend} = (500 \times 100) \times \$2.168 = \$108,400$$

$$\text{Expiration Date Value:} = -(500 \times 100) \times \$200 = -\$10,000,000$$

$$= -(500 \times 100) \times \$250 = -\$12,500,000$$

Note that all cash flows are known today. The transactions above provide an immediate cash inflow of $11,975,500. In return, $108,400 must be paid in 1½ months and $12,000,000 at the option's expiration. This is identical to obtaining a risk-free loan! To make it a pure arbitrage, T-bills are used to finance all future cash outflows:

4. a. To finance dividends on the short stock position:

$$\$108,400/e^{(0.05721 \times 0.125)} = \$107,627$$

b. To finance expiration date payment:

$$\$12,000,000/e^{(0.05721 \times 0.25)} = \$11,829,591$$

The arbitrage profit from this transaction is $38,282—received today!

Some comments about such arbitrages are necessary. First, the profit is large simply because the trades were large; index arbitrages are usually conducted only by large institutions. Second, transaction costs and the inability to trade in fractional units of the assets will reduce the profit and increase risk exposure. However, many large institutions pay very small commissions and are able to trade in quantities large enough to minimize risk. In addition, all trades must be executed instantaneously at known asset prices. If the price of an asset changes by the time the trade is expected, all arbitrage profits can disappear. That is why the NYSE's designated order turnaround (DOT) system is critical to successful index arbitrage.

Note that large positions in the stock index must be taken—either long or short. But since the index itself is not traded, how is this done? There are three possibilities. First, one could actually buy or sell all shares in the index in appropriate quantities so the stock position mirrors the index. This is most easily done with options on the Major Market Index, since it consists of only 20 stocks that are equally weighted. Second, one could create a 'basket' of stocks that closely track the index. Finally, one could trade in an index equivalent in the financial futures market.

Trades Based on Continuous Time

In the previous section, we reviewed a variety of hedging and speculative strategies based on an option's value at its expiration date. Such strategies are usually based on applications of the put-call parity model. In this section, we use the Black-Scholes model to illustrate continuous-time option strategies. A continuous-time strategy is constantly rebalanced so the stock/option position has the desired short-term return payoff—usually risk free. In practice, continuous rebalancing can be quite costly, so investors and speculators rebalance daily or weekly.

Hedging Strategies

Continuous-time option strategies can be used to alter the risk exposure of a portfolio. Before examples of such strategies are shown, however, we need to review the importance of the $N(d1)$ term in the Black-Scholes model and see how the (instantaneous) beta of a call can be calculated.

Importance of $N(d1)$. Figure 17-8 plots Black-Scholes call premiums versus stock prices for options exercisable at $50 when the standard deviation of stock returns is 0.5, the risk-free rate is 10%, and three exercise dates are assumed (three, six, and nine months). As

FIGURE 17-8   HEDGING AND OPTION PRICES

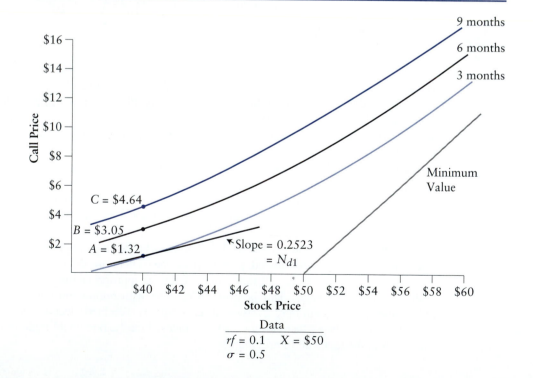

Data

$rf = 0.1$ $X = \$50$

$\sigma = 0.5$

we saw earlier, call premiums increase with the stock's price and expiration date. Assuming the stock is currently selling at $40, the options would be worth $1.32, $3.05, and $4.64, respectively, as illustrated by points A, B, and C in the figure.

Also shown in Figure 17-8 is a line drawn tangent to point A. The slope of this line is important, since it represents the change in the value of the call premium for a very small change in the stock's price. The slope at A is 0.2523, meaning that if the stock price changes from $40 by approximately $0.01, the option premium will move in the same direction by an amount equal to $0.002523.

Another way to view point A is to say that if one share of the stock is bought and one call option is sold, only 74.77% (100% − 25.23%) of the future price variability remains. Alternatively, we could sell 3.96 options (1 ÷ 0.2523) for each share bought and eliminate all price uncertainty. The change in the option's price for a small change in the stock's price is known as the **hedge ratio.** The hedge ratio indicates the *number of shares that should be bought for each call sold in order to eliminate price risk.* $N(d1)$ is this hedge ratio. In the same manner, 1.0 divided by the hedge ratio indicates the number of options that should be sold for each share bought.

The hedge ratio is easily calculated by using the Black-Scholes option model value of $N(d1)$. $N(d1)$ is the hedge ratio that will protect against small price changes. For example, assume you buy one share of the stock in Figure 17-8 for $40 and sell 3.96 of the A options at $1.32 per option. As a result, your investment is $34.77 ($40 − 3.96 × 1.32). If the stock's price immediately falls to $39.50, the option would now sell for approximately $1.19385. Your equity investment remains constant:

Value of Stock	$39.50
Value of 3.96 Calls	−4.73 (3.96 × $1.19385)
Equity Value	$34.77

While the stock decreased $0.50, you gained $0.50 through reduced call values. These hedges are appropriate, however, for only short time intervals and small changes in stock prices. Any time $N(d1)$ changes, the hedge ratio should also be revised. The hedge ratio will change with changes in the stock price, risk-free rate, variance of returns on the underlying spot asset, and time to expiration. Ideally, hedges should be continuously changed. As a practical matter, instantaneous hedges are impossible.

Risk-free positions can also be accomplished using only the options themselves. Assume a stock has two calls available that differ in either expiration date or exercise price. If $N(d1)$ for the first option is 0.4, then 2.5 of this option should be sold for each share bought to create a riskless hedge. If $N(d1)$ for the second option is 0.5, then 2.0 of this option would be sold for each share bought. Alternatively, you could buy 1.25 (0.5/0.4) of the first option for each 1.0 of the second option sold. Or 0.8 of the second should be bought (0.4/0.5) for each 1.0 of the first sold. Options can be combined to yield riskless hedges. But again, such hedges are riskless only for an instant in time.

Call Betas. Continuous time hedges are based on the beta of the underlying portfolio and the beta of the call option. Analytically, if β_c refers to the call option beta and β_s refers to stock beta, then:

Beta of a Call $$\beta_c = N(d1)[S_0 \div C_0]\beta_s \tag{17.8}$$

The economic intuition underlying the beta of a call is relatively straightforward. For a cost of C, you control an asset that is worth S—that is, you have "leveraged up" your investment by effectively borrowing $(S - C)$. Both your investment of C and your borrowing of $(S - C)$ are invested in the stock. Given that the stock has a beta of β_s, the beta of your leveraged position is equal to the "stock price divided by the call price" times the beta of the stock. But the call's price does not move dollar for dollar with the stock. Instead, for each $1 change in the stock price the call price changes by $N(d1)$ dollars (approximately). To reflect this fact, we multiply the leveraged beta position by $N(d1)$.

Adjusting a Portfolio's Systematic Risk. Assume you own $10 million of stock that is very similar to the S&P 100 Index. Since your spot stock portfolio is similar to the index on which the S&P 100 calls are traded, you can use the calls to adjust the (instantaneous) beta risk of your aggregate portfolio.

Assume we have calculated the following values for an S&P 100 call:

<u>S&P 100 Call Information</u>

$T = \frac{1}{4}$ year	$S = \$238.26$
$rf = 5.721\%$	$C = \$\ 13.75$
$\sigma = 17.12\%$	$X = \$240.00$

$$N(d1) = 0.508$$

We assume the beta of the S&P 100 Index is 1.0. Thus, the beta of this call would be 8.8:

$$(\$238.26 \div \$13.75) \times 0.508 = 8.802624$$

As a first example of how calls can be used to adjust systematic risk, assume we wish to continue to own the $10 million in stock but want to trade enough calls so our net portfolio beta is 0.0. This would, of course, mean we would *sell calls* on the S&P 100 Index. When the calls are sold, a call premium will be received. Assume the call premium is invested in T-bills.

We first calculate the dollar value of calls that will result in a portfolio beta of 0.0. Define this dollar call position as $Call:

$$\text{beta}_p = (\% \text{ in stock})(\text{beta}_s) + (\% \text{ in calls})(\text{beta}_c) + (\% \text{ in T-bill})(\text{beta}_{TB})$$

$$0.0 = \frac{\$10,000,000}{\$10,000,000}(1.0) + \frac{\$\text{Call}}{\$10,000,000} \times 8.802624 + \frac{\$\text{Call}}{\$10,000,000} \times 0.0$$

$$\$\text{Call} = -\$1,136,025$$

The negative sign on $Call simply confirms that we should sell calls. A positive sign would have implied call purchases. Thus, if we sell $1,136,025 worth of S&P 100 calls and invest the proceeds in T-bills, the (instantaneous) beta of the total portfolio will be 0.0. Since each call is valued at $1,375 ($13.75 × 100), we need to sell 826.2 calls:

$$\$1,136,025 \div \$1,375 = 826.2$$

The calculations here are based on the relationship between the beta of a call and the beta of the underlying asset. We can also use our understanding of $N(d1)$ to determine the call position that will perfectly offset our stock risk. In this example the value of $N(d1)$ is 0.508, which implies we should sell 1.97 calls for each unit of the S&P 100 Index we own:

$$1.0/0.508 = 1.968504$$

The question then is: *How many units of S&P 100 Index do we own?*

Since the S&P 100 Index has a current spot value of $238.26 and each S&P 100 option is a claim to 100 times the spot value, our $10 million in stock is the equivalent of 419.7 index units:

$$\$10,000,000 \div (\$238.26 \times 100) = 419.70956$$

Thus, we should sell 826.2 calls in order to obtain an instantaneously risk-free position:

$$419.70956 \times 1.968504 = 826.2$$

The answer is the same regardless of the technique used.

Our example was presented for illustrative purposes only. In actual cases, investors would rarely use call options to obtain a completely risk-free position. Instead, options are used to temporarily alter a portfolio's systematic risk by a more moderate amount. For example, assume you have $10 million invested in T-bills and stocks that are similar to those in the S&P 100 Index. Your desired T-bill/stock mix is 20/80, but the actual current mix is 40/60—that is, your desired portfolio beta is 0.8, but the actual current beta is only 0.6. The situation is depicted here:

Asset Class	Beta	Investment	
		Actual	Desired
T-Bills	0.0	$ 4,000,000	$ 2,000,000
S&P 100 Stocks	1.0	6,000,000	8,000,000
		$10,000,000	$10,000,000
Portfolio Beta		0.6	0.8

In this case, we wish to increase the systematic risk of the portfolio with call options. Thus, we should *purchase calls* using part of the T-bill investment to pay for them. Again, letting $Call represent the dollar call position, the quantity of calls to purchase would be:

$$0.8 = \frac{\$6,000,000}{\$10,000,000}(1.0) + \frac{\$Call\,(8.802624)}{\$10,000,000} + \frac{\$4,000,000 - \$Call}{\$10,000,000}(0.0)$$

$$\$Call = +\$227,205$$

$$\text{Number of Calls} = \$227,205/(\$13.75 \times 100)$$

$$= 165.24$$

We should purchase 165.24 calls and pay for them with $227,205 of T-bills.

In our two examples, we used call options on a stock index to adjust the instantaneous systematic risk of the portfolio. Three comments about such trades are appropriate. First, the results apply to only a moment in time. As time passes, as stock prices move, and so forth, the option's beta value will also shift. Therefore, one should select calls that do not experience major changes in their betas with slight changes in other variables. This usually means that options close to expiration (say, one month or less) should not be used. Second, the options can be used to adjust a portfolio's risk level only if the spot stock owned is similar to the index on which the options are written.

Finally, note that each of the stock/option/T-bill positions could have been obtained simply by trading in the spot stock and T-bills. In the first example, we could have obtained a zero beta by selling the $10 million in stock to buy $10 million in T-bills. In the second example, we could have sold $2 million in T-bills and invested the proceeds in stocks. *Whether to trade the options or the spot securities depends on which is cheaper.* Certainly this means the brokerage costs of each should be evaluated. But other, less quantifiable, costs need to be evaluated. For example, a rapid purchase or sale of sizable dollar amounts of stock can affect the stock's spot price or may simply not be possible. A trade in the options might be accomplished more rapidly and at small market price impacts. In addition, large institutions such as pension funds typically employ many investment managers to manage the institution's investments in each security class. For example, a $1 billion pension fund might employ, say, 20 managers to invest the pension's position in equities. 5 managers to invest in bonds, and 2 managers to invest in money market securities such as Treasury bills. If the aggregate portfolio's asset allocation is to be modified, it might be faster and more cheaply accomplished by trading options than by transferring funds from certain managers to other managers.[7]

It is this ability to temporarily adjust a portfolio's risk level without disturbing the underlying spot investments that has caused the rapid growth of trading in stock index options.

Dynamic Replication of Portfolio Insurance

Earlier in the chapter, we reviewed how one could insure a minimum portfolio value by either (1) purchasing stock similar to a stock index and purchasing puts on the stock index, or (2) purchasing calls on a stock index plus T-bills. There are, however, a number of problems with the use of listed options in insuring a portfolio floor. These include the following:

1. The stock portfolio might be quite different in composition from any stock index on which options are traded.
2. The listed options might not have an exercise date identical to the date at which an insured portfolio is desired. For example, a floor value five years hence could not be obtained with listed options.
3. Many listed options in the United States are American options, and thus some degree of risk is incurred from the potential of early exercise.
4. There are maximum position limits for listed puts.

As a result, many portfolio insurance programs do not actually use listed puts or calls. Instead, they rely on the principles of option theory to create synthetic or artificial option positions. This is done by dynamic asset allocation between stocks and T-bills.

---

[7] Investment managers are typically compensated by charging a percentage of the market value of securities managed. For example, an annual fee of 0.75% of asset value would be common for an equity manager. For this reason, managers will fight and delay acting on any requests that the return funds they manage to the portfolio owner.

To understand how this is accomplished, let's review the Black-Scholes model again. Assume the following price relationships exist between market traded calls, risk-free debt, and an underlying stock value:

$$C_t = S_t N(d1) - [(X) \div e^{(rf)(T)}]N(d2)$$

$$= \$100(0.8) - [\$80 \div e^{(0.1)(0.5)}]0.6$$

$$= \$100(0.8) - [\$76.10]0.6$$

$$= \$80 - \$45.66$$

$$= \$34.34$$

The value of the call should be $34.34. This is because the value of the replicated synthetic portfolio costs $34.34. This replicating portfolio consists of purchasing 0.8 shares of stock (for a cost of $100 × .8 = $80) less $45.65 obtained from borrowing via risk-free debt. The par value of this debt is $80, its current value is $76.10, and 0.6 units of the debt are sold. During the next instant, this synthetic portfolio will have the same payoff as the call itself.

Maintaining a synthetic option position by trading in the underlying spot assets is commonly referred to as dynamic replication. Outcomes of positions in puts can also be dynamically replicated.

To see how an insured portfolio can be achieved by dynamic replication of put positions, consider the panels in Figure 17-9. In panel A, the market value of a portfolio is shown on the vertical axis, and the value of a spot stock index is shown on the horizontal axis. In panel B, the percentage invested in equity is shown on the vertical axis. The portfolio's value is now $10.0 million with 80% invested in equities (which are similar to the spot index). The remaining 20% is held in T-bills with a single maturity date of T.

If the portfolio is not insured by dynamic put replication, its value would rise and fall in a manner shown by the line between the points $NI - NI$ (for not insured). However, assume a minimum portfolio value of $8.0 million is desired. To (virtually) guarantee that the portfolio will not fall below $8.0 million, the following dynamic asset allocation strategy is used:

1. If the underlying stock index increases, do not make any alterations to the portfolio's asset allocation.
2. If the underlying stock index falls below its current level, sell some of the stock (at a loss) and invest the proceeds in T-bills having maturity of date T. Continue with such reductions in the stock allocation if the stock index continues to fall. If the stock index falls to a minimum acceptable index or below, all stock should have been sold and reinvested in T-bills.

The results of such a strategy are shown by the solid lines in each panel.

This dynamic replication of owning put options will work only if one is able to trade at stock index prices specified in the strategy. For example, if the strategy requires that 5% of the equity position be sold when the stock index is down by 5 points to $450, then one must be able to sell when the stock index is $450. The strategy clearly would not work if—when the trade is executed—the spot index is down by another 50 points.

Dynamic replication of portfolio insurance in stock portfolios was popular in the years just before the 1987 market crash. Unfortunately, the strategy did not work in a large

FIGURE 17-9   DYNAMIC REPLICATION OF PORTFOLIO INSURANCE

A. PORTFOLIO VALUE

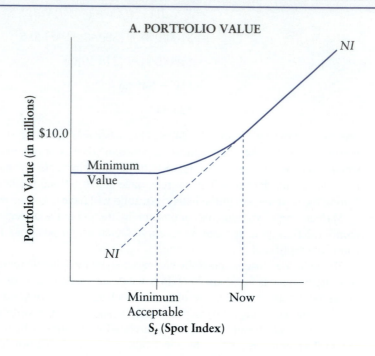

B. PERCENT INVESTED IN EQUITY

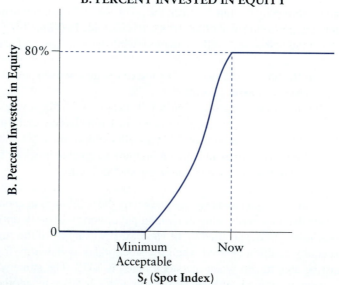

number of cases because stock index prices fell so precipitously that insurance trades in equities could not be accomplished at the prices required by the strategy (if at all). Although dynamic replication of portfolio insurance has been used much less actively on common stocks since 1987, the procedure has been expanded to other asset classes such as debt instruments and currencies.

Speculative Strategies

Continuous-time models can also be used in speculative strategies to take advantage of mispriced options.

Incorrect ISD Values. One speculative strategy is based on the standard deviations that are implied in each option's price. Instead of specifying a standard deviation of the underlying spot asset's returns to calculate the proper option price, the price is used to calculate the standard deviation that results in the option's actual market price. This is referred to as the **implied standard deviation (ISD).**

The ISD should be identical for all calls on a given stock with a given expiration date. If the implied standard deviation is different for two call options that differ only in exercise prices, a speculative profit is possible.

For example, assume you have calculated the following ISD values for two call options on XYZ stock:

XYZ Call Option	ISD	$N(d1)$
Call 1	29.55%	0.6628
Call 2	32.85%	0.4761

Also assume that the options have identical exercise dates and should, therefore, have identical implied standard deviations.

Call 2, however, had a larger implied standard deviation than call 1. Although we cannot say which, if either, implied standard deviation is correct, we can say that call 2 is overvalued relative to call 1, since call 2 has the greater implied standard deviation. To take advantage of this, call 2 should be sold and call 1 purchased. Given their respective $N(d1)$ values, a risk-free position would consist of 1.5088 (1.0/0.6628) of call 1 bought per 2.1004 (1.0/0.4751) of call 2 sold. For each 1.0 of call 1 bought, 1.3920 of call 2 should be sold.

Topics in Option Valuation

In this section, we examine a variety of topics associated with the practical implementation of the Black-Scholes option pricing model. This includes a discussion of the potential for early exercise of American options, adjustments to the model that need to be made when cash dividends are paid, and how various inputs to the model are estimated. The section concludes with an alternative valuation model known as the binomial model.

Early Exercise of American Options

The Black-Scholes equation provides a valuation model for a European option, one that can only be exercised at the stated expiration date. In contrast, American options may be exercised at the expiration date or before. Logically, an American option must be worth at least the same as a European option. If an American option will never be exercised early, then its value will be the same as a European option. If there is a possibility of early exercise, the Black-Scholes option pricing model provides an estimate of the American option's value that is biased downward.

Call Options on Stocks with No Cash Dividend. Consider an American call option that is exercisable at $50 any time during the next three months. The stock is selling for $55 and will not pay any cash dividends during the option's life. The option is trading for $7. This $7 call price can be thought of as consisting of two components, an immediate in-the-money value and a time value:

Immediate Call Value	$5
Time Value	2
Call's Market Price	$7

Assume you own the option but would prefer to own the stock. Should you exercise the option today in order to obtain the stock? No! If you are, in fact, foolish enough to exercise, you would pay the exercise price of $50 to be the owner of the stock. Alternatively, you could sell the option for $7 and use the proceeds together with only $48 to buy the stock in the open market. Clearly, the better alternative is to sell the option, since it results in a smaller out-of-pocket cash flow.

If we exercise any call on a nondividend stock prior to its expiration date, we throw away the time value inherent in the option. The only time that one should exercise a call on a stock that pays no cash dividends is when the call's time value is zero. This will occur only at the call's expiration date.

Since American calls on stocks that will not pay cash dividends should never be prematurely exercised, such American calls will be worth the same as equivalent European calls—that is, the Black-Scholes model can be used to value such American calls.

Call Options on Stocks with Large Cash Dividends. When large cash dividends are to be paid, it is possible that early exercise is optimal. For example, consider the situation of the call option described earlier, but now assume a $15 cash dividend will be paid tomorrow. On the day before the stock goes ex-dividend, the stock is selling for $55 and the call for $7. Assuming the $7 call price is a proper price according to the Black-Scholes model, the call must trade for this amount or arbitrage profits would be available. Tomorrow, however, the stock will go ex-dividend and drop in value to about $40. As a result, the call's value will also fall—to a new Black-Scholes value of, say, $3.

Should you exercise this call? Yes—but only very late on the day prior to the ex-dividend date. By exercising, you capture the call's immediate value of $5 ($55 − $50). If you do not exercise, you will be left with a call that is worth only $3 tomorrow. In short, if the call's immediate value $(S_t - X)$ is greater than the value of the call once the stock goes ex-dividend, you should exercise immediately before the ex-dividend date.

Dividend Adjustments

Listed options are not protected against cash dividends. When such dividends are paid, the value of the underlying stock decreases, which, in turn, causes the call value to fall and the put value to rise. If future dividends are known, there are two ways to incorporate them into current option values. The first treats known discrete future dividends, and the second treats known continuous dividend distributions.

Let D_n represent a known discrete cash dividend to be paid n periods from now. There are N such payments. Define a value of $T = 1$ as representing one year and n as the fraction of one year. In this case, whenever the stock price (S_0) is used in the Black-Scholes model, it should be reduced by the present value of the N discrete dividends.

Discrete Dividend Adjustments to Stock Price

$$S_0 = S_0 - \sum_{n=1}^{N} [D_n \div e^{(rf)(n)}] \tag{17.9}$$

For example, assume the current stock price is $68.125 and known dividends of $2.00 will be paid in exactly one and two months from now. If $rf = 10\%$ per year, then the adjusted stock price would be:

$$S_t = \$68.125 - [\$2.00 \div e^{(0.1)(0.08333)}] - [\$2.00 \div e^{(0.1)(0.1666)}]$$

$$= \$64.17$$

Any Black-Scholes calculation that involves S_t would have $64.17 substituted in place of $68.125.

A similar procedure is used when continuous dividends are paid. This is close to what happens with stock indexes. Although individual stocks in the index distribute discrete payments, when they are summed across all securities in the index the dividend stream is better thought of as continuous. If the continuous dividends rate is defined as d, then the following adjusted stock prices are used in the Black-Scholes equation:

Continuous Dividend Adjustment to Stock Price

$$S_t = S_t \div e^{dT} \tag{17.10}$$

Calculating Black-Scholes Inputs

According to the dividend-adjusted Black-Scholes model, the calls and puts should be a function of six variables:

1. S_t = current stock price
2. X = option exercise price

3. T = time to expiration
4. D_n = cash dividends paid on day n
5. rf = constant, continuously compounded risk-free rate
6. σ = standard deviation of the stock's continuously compounded return

Three of these variables are directly observable: S_t, X, and T. Although T may be expressed in any unit of time you wish, it is commonly thought of as a fraction of one year, since rf and σ are usually expressed as annualized equivalents. The other three variables must be either calculated or estimated.

Cash Dividends. Cash dividends are relatively easy to estimate. In the case of a single stock, one can forecast one or more cash dividends during the option's life based on a historical pattern. In many cases, management will have publicly announced any dividends that will be paid during the option's life. Dividends on stock indexes can also be reasonably predicted for short time horizons based on simple extrapolations of the past. Dividends on stock indexes, however, occur in a continuous fashion instead of at identifiable single dates.

Risk-Free Interest. The best proxy for the risk-free rate is the return on a T-bill with a maturity equal to the option's expiration.[8] We discussed the pricing of T-Bills in Chapter 4. Be sure the risk-free rate is stated in terms of a continuous rate of return as opposed to end-of-period compounding.

Standard Deviation. The standard deviation term in the Black-Scholes equation represents the standard deviation of continuously compound returns on the underlying spot asset, assumed to be constant over the option's life. Since it is not directly observable, it is the toughest variable to estimate. There are two general ways to handle the problem.

In the first approach, we look at the past to estimate what σ might be during the option's life. The choice of the time period chosen will, of course, affect the estimate. If the return-generating process is stationary, statistical theory suggests that the number of return observations should be as large as feasible in order to reduce biases in the results. Unfortunately, there is no reason to believe that the volatility of stocks and stock indexes remains constant over time. The analysis of past standard deviation is, at best, an approximation of what the future holds.

Assume we are examining a sequence of N quarterly returns. For each quarter, we would calculate the continuous compound return as follows:

Discrete Return

$$R_t = \frac{\text{Ending Price} + \text{Dividends}}{\text{Beginning Price}} \qquad (17.11)$$

Continuous Return

$$r_t = \ln(1 + R_t) \qquad (17.12)$$

It is the standard deviation of the r_t series we wish to estimate. First, the average continuous return, m, is found. It is then used to find an unbiased estimate of σ:

---

[8] If the T-bill rate that applies to any intermediate dividend payments is different, then it should be applied to such cash flows.

Mean Continuous Return
$$m = \frac{\left(\sum\limits_{t=1}^{N} r_t\right)}{N}$$
(17.13)

Unbiased Estimate of σ
$$\sigma = \frac{\left[\sum\limits_{t=1}^{N}(r_t - m)^2\right]^{1/2}}{N - 1}$$
(17.14)

Note that $N - 1$ is used in this equation instead of N. In large samples this results in unbiased estimates of σ. Assume this results in:

$$m = 3.54\% \text{ per quarter}$$

$$\sigma = 8.56\% \text{ per quarter}$$

Since rf and T are being expressed as annualized returns, we need to convert the 8.56% quarterly standard deviation to an annualized equivalent. Although we will not show the mathematical proof here, when one is dealing with a series of continuous returns drawn from a stationary distribution and uncorrelated with each other over time, then:

Multiperiod Standard Deviation of Continuous Returns

$$\sigma \text{ for a } T \text{ period outcome} = \sqrt{T} \times \sigma \text{ for 1 period outcome}$$
(17.15)

Therefore, the annualized standard deviation would be 17.12%:

$$\sigma_{annual} = \sqrt{4} \times 8.56\%$$

$$= 17.12\%$$

The second approach to estimating the standard deviation to use in valuing an option uses actual call prices to infer the standard deviation currently being priced in the call—that is, C_t and all other terms are used to calculate the implied standard deviation (ISD) of each option available on a single underlying asset. Once these ISD values are found, a weighted implied standard deviation (WISD) is calculated. The simplest way to calculate the WISD is to treat each ISD equally. If there are N calls outstanding and σ_i is the ISD for call I, then:

Equally Weighted WISD

$$\text{WISD} = \left(\sum\limits_{i=1}^{N} \sigma_i\right) \div N$$
(17.16)

A variety of weighting procedures are used in practice. Some underweight options deep in or out of the money. Others weight by the sensitivity of the option price to changes in the standard deviation. But regardless of the approach taken, WISD values appear to be better predictors of actual future price volatility than estimates based on historical price changes.

A Formula for $N(d1)$ and $N(d2)$. The values of $N(d1)$ and $N(d2)$ are the value of the cumulative normal-density function between minus infinity and either $d1$ or $d2$. They can be found by reference to a table such as that in Appendix A. There is also an approximate formula that can be easily used on hand-held calculators or personal computers. The following equation is usually accurate to four decimal places:

$$N(d) = 1 - N * (d)(a_1 k + a_2 k^2 + a_3 k^3) \qquad \text{for } d \geq 0 \qquad (17.17)$$

$$= 1 - N(d) \qquad \text{for } d < 0$$

where:

$$K = 1 \div (1 + 0.33267d)$$

$$a_1 = 0.4361836 \quad a_2 = -0.1201676 \quad a_3 = 0.937298$$

$$N * (d) = 1 \div \left[\left(\sqrt{2\pi} \right) e^{d^2 \div 2} \right]$$

Put Valuation

The value of a European put option on a stock that pays no dividends can be calculated using a Black-Scholes valuation equation as follows:

European Put Value on a Zero-Dividend Stock

$$P_0 = [X \div e^{(rf)(T)}] N(-d2) - S_0 N(-d1) \qquad (17.18)$$

Note that the values inside the parentheses of $N(\ )$ are evaluated at the negative of $d1$ and $d2$.

   Assume the underlying stock price on which a put is traded is \$40, the put exercise price is \$40, the expiration date is ½ year, the continous risk-free rate is 10%, and the standard deviation of stock returns is 20% per year:

$$d1 = \{\ln (40/40) + 0.5 [0.1 + 0.04 \div 2]\} \div 0.2\sqrt{0.5}$$

$$= 0.4243$$

$$d2 = 0.4243 - 0.2\sqrt{0.5}$$

$$= 0.2828$$

$$N(-0.4243) = 0.3357 \qquad N(-0.2828) = 0.3886$$

$$P_0 = [\$40 \div e^{(0.1 \times 0.5)}](0.3886) - \$40(0.3357)$$

$$= \$1.36$$

The pricing of American puts is more difficult due to the possibility that they might be exercised early.

The Binomial Model

The binomial model is used largely to show the logic underlying option valuation, how one security (say, a call) can be replicated by appropriate positions in two other securities (say, the underlying spot and debt). While the model can be computerized and used to value actual options, it is more commonly used for teaching purposes. It is called the binomial model because it assumes that, during the next period of time, the underlying spot price will go to only one of two possible values.

Although this assumption might seem to be a strange one on which to develop a practical valuation model, it really isn't if we think of a "period of time" as being very short and of the eventual expiration date as being many periods from now.

Single-Period Binomial Model. Suppose one-period call options are available on shares of Unique Corporation. Each option is exercisable at $40, and Unique shares are now selling at $50. The firm owes its name to the fact that at the option's expiration date its shares will be selling at one of only two possible prices—either $62.50 or $37.50. What should the call option sell for?

To answer this, remember that if we could form a portfolio of the stock and option that results in a risk-free expiration date outcome, we could value the option. That is, the stock's price and the price of the risk-free portfolio are observable, so we can infer what the call option value must be.

In the put-call parity model, a risk-free position was obtained by trading in 1.0 units of each asset (for example, buy 1.0 stock, buy 1.0 put, write, 1.0 call). In the current situation this 1 to 1 hedge ratio is no longer valid.

Note that the stock prices could be either $62.50 or $37.50, a price range of $25. In contrast, the call will be worth either $22.50 ($62.50 − $40) or $0, a price range of $22.50. Since the stock price is more variable, the hedge ratio will be less than 1.0. For our stock position to exactly offset a short position in 1.0 call, we should buy less than 1.0 share. It turns out that the risk-free hedge ratio is simply:

Risk-Free Binomial Hedge Ratio

$$= \frac{\text{End-of-Period Range of Option Prices}}{\text{Expiration Date Range of Stock Prices}} \qquad (17.19)$$

In our example, the hedge ratio is 0.90 ($22.50/$25).

The calculations here show that a portfolio of 0.90 shares long and 1.0 call short is indeed risk free. This portfolio replicates a T-bill having a par value of $33.75:

USING A CALL AND STOCK TO REPLICATE A RISK-FREE POSITION

| | | Expiration Date | |
	Today S_T	$= \$37.50$	$S_T = \$62.50$
Buy 0.90 Stock	−45.00	+$33.75	+$56.25
Write 1.0 Call	+C	—	− $22.50
	−$45.00 + C	+$33.75	+$33.75

Assuming the one-period risk-free rate is 10%, the current price of the call should be $14.32:

$$C = 0.90\ (\$50) - \frac{\$33.75}{1.1}$$

$$= \$14.32$$

As we have seen before, you can replicate the outcomes of the call option with a portfolio of stock and cash. In this case, 0.90 shares of stock would initially be purchased and risk-free debt worth $33.75/1.1 would be issued.

The single-period binomial model can be easily extended to many periods by simply following the procedures used here.

SUMMARY

Here are the key concepts:

- An option provides the option owner with the right to trade a specified asset at a future date at a specified price. In contrast, futures contracts are obligations to trade.

- Call options provide the right to buy, and put options provide the right to sell.

- Two basic option valuation models have been developed. The put-call parity model is based on expiration date outcomes and is able to value what the price difference should be between identical puts and calls. The models developed by Black and Scholes are based on continuous time and are able to directly value either type of option. The price of the other option is not needed.

- The put-call parity model as well as the Black-Scholes model are based on the cost of creating a portfolio that will replicate the outcomes of an option. The option must trade at a price equal to the cost of the replicating portfolio or arbitrage profits are possible.

- The basic determinants of an option's value are the current price of the underlying spot asset, the exercise price, the time to the option's expiration, the risk-free interest rate and the standard deviation of returns on the underlying spot asset.

- Economically, a call option is a leveraged ownership position in the underlying spot asset.

- The beta of a call option is equal to the "beta of the underlying spot asset" multiplied by the "ratio of the spot price divided by the call price" multiplied by $N(d1)$.

REVIEW PROBLEM

Consider the following options on a single stock:

	Calls		
	A	B	Put C
Months to Expiration	3	9	3
Continuous Yearly *rf*	10.00%	10.00%	10.00%
Discrete Yearly *RF*	10.52%	10.52%	10.52%
Std. Dev. Stock Returns	40%	40%	40%
Exercise Price	$55	$55	$55
Option Price	$ 2.56	—	$ 6.20
Stock Price	$50	$50	$50
Cash Dividend	$ 0	$ 0	$ 0

a. Why should call B sell for more than call A?

b. Is the put-call parity model working for options A and C?

c. How would you trade call A, the stock, and T-bills in order to replicate the expiration date outcomes of put C?

d. Calculate the Black-Scholes values of call A and call B.

e. Interpret what $N(d1)$ and $N(d2)$ mean.

Solution

a. Call B has the longer time to expiration. There is a greater chance the call will be exercised at a positive value.

b. In theory:

$$C_t - P_t = S_t - X \div (1 + RF)^T$$

$$= \$50 - \$55 \div (1.1052^{0.25}) = -\$3.64$$

$$\text{Actual difference} = \$2.56 - \$6.20 \qquad = -\$3.64$$

Therefore, put-call parity is working.

c. Buy 1.0 call A, sell short 1.0 stock, buy debt now worth $55 \div (1.1052^{0.25})$.

d. <u>Call A Data</u>

$$d_1 = \frac{\ln\left(\frac{50}{55}\right) + 0.25\left(0.10 + \frac{0.4^2}{2}\right)}{0.4\sqrt{0.25}} = -0.25$$

$$d_2 = 0.25 - 0.4\sqrt{0.25} = -0.45$$

$$N(d1) = 0.4013 \quad N(d2) = 0.3264$$

$$C = \$50(0.4013) - \frac{\$55}{e^{(0.1)(0.25)}}(0.3264)$$

$$= \$2.56$$

Call B Data

$$d_1 = \frac{\ln\left(\frac{50}{55}\right) + 0.75\left(0.10 + \frac{0.4^2}{2}\right)}{0.4\sqrt{0.75}} = -0.11$$

$$d_2 = d1 - \sigma\sqrt{T} = -0.23$$

$$N(d1) = 0.5438$$

$$N(d2) = 0.409$$

$$C = \$50(0.5438) - \frac{\$55}{e^{(0.1)(0.75)}}(0.409)$$

$$= \$6.32$$

e. To replicate the instantaneous payoffs of the call, one should buy N(d1) shares and issue N(d2) units of debt that is now worth $X \div e^{rfxt}$.

Q U E S T I O N S   A N D   P R O B L E M S

1. A call and put exist on the same stock. Each is exercisable at $50. They trade now for:

$$S_0 = 45 \qquad C_0 = \$8 \qquad P_0 = \$1$$

Calculate the expiration date investment value, and net profit from:
a. Buy 1.0 call
b. Write 1.0 call
c. Buy 1.0 put
d. Write 1.0 put
   Do this for expiration date stock prices of $40, $45, $50, $55, and $60.
2. Assume that call options on Xerox are to expire today. They have an exercise price of $70, the stock is trading at $65, and the option is selling for $8. What is the arbitrage?
3. Consider the following put and call options:

	Call	Put
Market Price	$ 7	$ 2
Exercise Price	$70	$70
Exercise Date	4 mo.	4 mo.
Risk-Free Rate = 10% annualized (discrete compound)		
Stock Price = $75		

a. Is put-call parity working?
b. What is the arbitrage based on put-call parity?
4. You are given the following information:

$$S_0 = \$74 \qquad P_0 = \$5.09 \qquad X = \$65$$

$$rf = 10\% \qquad \text{Expiration} = 1 \text{ year}$$

Assume the stock pays no dividends and the risk-free rate will remain constant.

a. What should be the price of a call also exercisable at $65 with an expiration date of one year?

b. How could you develop a portfolio of these securities that will have a payoff in one year identical to being long the stock? Short the stock? (You may not buy or sell the stock.)

c. How could you develop a portfolio of these securities that will have a payoff in one year identical to writing one put? (Again, you may not trade the put.)

d. Underlying these calculations is the economic definition of what a call is. What does a call consist of?

5. You wish to purchase a call option on a local warehose having an expiration date of one year and an exercise price of $1 million. The warehouse owner will not sell you such an option but is willing to sell the warehouse for $1.1 million. The current (discrete end-of-period compounding) risk-free interest rate is 9% per year, and insurance on a one-year $1 million loan would be $10,000. How could you create a synthetic call option on the warehouse?

6. An analysis of Hylough Corporation suggests that in one year the price of its common shares will be either $80 or $50. They currently sell for $60. An option that expires in one year with an exercise price of $60 can be bought for $10.23. What is the one-year risk-free rate?

7. Consider the information provided here:

Options on ABC Stock

	Call Options				Put Option
	A	B	C	D	E
Current Market of:					
Option	$16.12	$10.62	$ 8.31	$10.50	$ 7.25
Stock	$80	$80	$80	$80	$80
Option Information:					
Exercise Price	$70	$80	$90	$90	$70
Months to Expiration	3	3	3	6	3
Market Information:					
Continuous Yearly rf	12%	12%	12%	12%	12%
Expected Cash Dividends	0	0	0	0	0
Std. Dev. of Stock Returns	60%	60%	60%	60%	60%

a. Calculate the Black-Scholes value of each option.

b. Note that call A and put E have identical terms. Use the put-call parity model to value the put, given the Black-Scholes value of call A. Comment on why the put's value is the same as found in part a.

c. Interpret what the terms $N(d1)$ and $N(d2)$ mean for call A.

8. What are the underlying assumptions of the Black-Scholes model, and why are they needed?

9. Assume you are given the following information on a stock and its calls:

$$S_t = \$65$$

$$X = \$60$$

$$rf = 12\% \text{ (continuous annual)}$$

$$\sigma = 40\% \text{ (annual)}$$

$$\text{Maturity} = 6 \text{ months}$$

You also know with certainty that the stock will pay a $1 dividend in exactly three months, followed by a $1 dividend just before the option's expiration date in six months.

a. What should be the price of this call?

b Without performing any calculations, if you had neglected to consider the dividend payments, would you have estimated the price to be the same, greater, or less than in part a? Why?

10. All other things being equal, a $1 increase in a call option's exercise price will lead to a $1 decrease in the call option's value. True or false? Why?

11. You have been given the following series of monthly returns on a stock. The returns are discrete returns. Calculate the ex post estimate of the Black-Scholes standard deviation.

1	2	3	4	5	6	7	8	9	10	11	12
5%	15	2	-8	1	−4	20	5	−8	10	8	0

12. You have calculated the implied standard deviations on two call options. They differ only in exercise price. (They are on the same stock and have identical expiration dates.) What is the instantaneous risk-free speculation that is possible?

	Call A	Call B
ISD	40%	50%
N(d1)	0.8	0.6

13. Assume a dividend of D dollars will be paid on the expiration date of a put and call option. Derive the put-call parity model for this case.

14. The market value of a portfolio you manage is $30 million. You have been asked to use either puts or calls in a portfolio insurance program. Since the portfolio is similar to the S&P 100 Index, you intend to use S&P 100 Index options. Relevant data areas follows:

Current Spot Value of S&P 100	= $600
Current Risk-Free Rate (End-of-year compounding)	= 10% per year
Dividend Yield on S&P 100 (Paid in exactly six months from now)	= 2% per year

Option Information:	Call	Put
Current Price	$35	$5
Exercise Price	$580	$580
Expiration Date	6 months	6 months
Option Type	Euro	Euro

a. Is put-call parity working?

b. Illustrate the expiration date values of an insured portfolio using the puts. Do this for S&P 100 values of $500, $550, $600, and $650.

c. Use the calls together with T-bills to create an insured portfolio that has the same minimum floor value as in part b. Calculate its values for S&P 100 values of $500, $550, $600, and $650. Compare the results with those obtained for part b and explain why they are different.

d. Using the puts, at what S&P 100 Index value are you better off with the insured portfolio than with a 100% stock position?

15. Use the data from question 14 to illustrate the outcomes of an index arbitrage. Trade in stock worth $10 million.

16. A local broker has advised the trustees of a charitable organization to sell calls on stocks held in the organization's portfolio in order to increase the portfolio's cash yield. Comment.

17. How does the use of options in a portfolio affect the portfolio's stock/bond mix?

18. You are considering the sale of a call option with an exercise price of $100 and one year to expiration. The underlying stock pays no dividends, its current price is $100, and you believe it has a 50% chance of increasing to $120 and a 50% chance of decreasing to $80. The risk-free rate of interest is 10%.

a. Describe the specific steps involved in applying the binomial option pricing model to calculate the call option's value.

b. Compare the binomial option pricing model to the Black-Scholes option pricing model.

19. Explain the economic intuition underlying what the beta of a call is:

$$\text{Beta}_{Call} = \text{Beta}_{Spot} \times (S \div C) \times N(d1)$$

20. You are the manager of a $100 million portfolio that is now invested as follows: $50 million in stock similar to the S&P 100 and $50 million in T-bills. Relevant data on S&P 100 calls include:

Price of S&P 100 Spot Index = $500

Price of S&P 100 Call   = $30

N(d1) of Call   = 0.75

Beta of S&P 100 Spot Index = 1.0

How many calls would you trade to change the portfolio's instantaneous beta to:

a. 0.0

b. 1.0

c. 0.6

21. EverSafe Insurance Company holds 10,000 shares of Exxon at a cost of $80 per share in the pension account of one of its clients. As portfolio manager for the account you expect the shares to rise gradually over the next six to nine months. The following Exxon call options are quoted on the CBOE:

| | | Expiration | |
Exercise Price	3 months	6 months	9 months
$70	$12	$13	$14½
80	2½	6½	8
90	NA	2½	4½

The current price of Exxon shares is 81. State the rationale for and implications of writing call options that expire in nine months with an exercise price of $80.

22. An at-the-money protective put position (comprised of owning the stock and the put):

a. protects against loss at any stock price below the strike price of the put.

b. has limited profit potential when the stock price rises.

c. returns any increase in the stock's value, dollar for dollar, less the cost of the put.

d. provides a pattern of returns similar to a stop-loss order at the current stock price.

CFA 23. In the Black-Scholes option valuation formula, an increase in a stock's volatility:

a. increases the associated call option value.

b. decreases the associated put option value.

c. increases or decreases the option value, depending on the level of interest rates.

d. does not change either the put or call option value because put-call parity holds.

CFA 24. An American option is more valuable than a European option on the same dividend paying stock with the same terms because the:

a. European option contract is not adjusted for stock splits and stock dividends.

b. American option can be exercised from date of purchase until expiration, but the European option can be exercised only at expiration.

c. European option does not conform to the Black-Scholes model and is often mispriced.

d. American options are traded on U.S. exchanges, which offer much more volume and liquidity.

DATAFILE ANALYSIS

Access the monthly return series for the S&P 500 index. For the most recent 60 monthly returns, calculate the standard deviation (of a sample) of monthly returns. Next, convert this into the equivalent annualized standard deviation.

REFERENCES

Fairly recent published textbooks devoted solely to options include these titles:

Chance, Donald M. *An Introduction to Options and Futures,* Orlando, FL: Dryden Press, 1989.

Hull, John. *Options, Futures and Other Derivative Securities,* Englewood Cliffs, NJ: Prentice Hall, 1989.

Marshall, John F. *Futures and Option Contracting,* Cincinnati, OH: South-Western, 1989. Stoll, Hans R., and Robert E. Whaley, *Futures and Options: Theory and Applications,* Cincinnati, OH: South-Western, 1993.

Some interesting articles treating options are as follows:

Black, Fischer. "Fact and Fantasy in the Use of Options," *Financial Analysts Journal,* July–August 1975.

Chance, Don M. "Option Volume and Stock Market Performance," *The Journal of Portfolio Management,* Summer 1990.

Rendelman, Richard J. and Thomas J. O'Brien, "The Effects of Volatility Misestimation on Option Replication Portfolio Insurance," *Financial Analysts Journal,* May–June 1990.

Classic studies of derivative valuation can be difficult for students who have weak training in mathematics. But the general arguments can usually be followed. You might examine these two articles:

Black, Fischer. "The Pricing of Commodity Contracts," *Journal of Financial Economics,* September 1976.

Black, Fischer and Myron Scholes, "The Pricing of Options and Corporate Liabilities," *Journal of Political Economy,* May–June 1973.

PART 4

Strategy

Prior chapters either focused on specific investment concepts or analyzed individual types of securities. We now put it all together in a discussion of the investment process and investment strategies.

In order to make the basic decisions, all investors must answer these questions: (1) What security classes will be owned? (2) What portion of the portfolio will be held in each asset class? (3) Will the investment within a given asset class be actively or passively managed? (4) If active management is to be used, will the investor decide which securities are to be held or should professional managers be employed? (5) Is the performance of the portfolio reasonable?

In Chapter 18 we look at the process that should be used in making these decisions and how they should be formally documented in a statement of investment policy.

Chapter 19 follows with a discussion of the asset allocation decision. Most professional investors believe the asset allocation decision is the most important one any investor will make, since it determines the risks and expected returns of the portfolio.

In Chapter 20 we discuss various considerations in investment selection. This includes issues associated with the selection of professional managers and tax management.

The concluding chapter, Chapter 21, surveys techniques used to evaluate portfolio performance. This is typically done at the aggregate portfolio level, for each asset class and for each investment manager.

THE PROCESS OF INVESTMENT MANAGEMENT

After reading this chapter you should have an understanding of the process which should be used in managing a security portfolio as well as the contents of the statement of investment policy.

The process of portfolio management is conceptually simple, in that it involves a logical set of steps common to any decision: plan, implement, and monitor. Yet applying this process to actual portfolios can be complex, and opinions are divided on how best to do so. Ideally, investment theory and empirical evidence would provide clear guidelines for each stage of the portfolio management process; but, unfortunately, this isn't the case. Large gaps exist in current theory, and empirical tests often yield contradictory results.

But even though theory and empirical evidence cannot provide definitive answers, they can at least guide the process of portfolio management. Certain basic principles should be applied to all portfolio decisions:

1. *It is the portfolio that matters.* Individual securities are important only to the extent that they affect the aggregate portfolio.
2. *Larger expected portfolio returns come only with larger portfolio risk.* The most important portfolio decision is the amount of risk that is acceptable, which is determined by the asset allocation within the security portfolio.

3. *The risk associated with a security type depends on when the investment will be liquidated.* A person who plans to sell in one year will find future portfolio values to be less risky than a person who plans to sell in 25 years.

4. *Diversification works.* Diversification across various securities will reduce a portfolio's risk. If such broad diversification results in an expected portfolio return or risk level that is lower (or higher) than desired, then borrowing (or lending) can be used to achieve the desired level.

5. *Portfolio decisions should be tailored to the particular needs of its owner.* Contrary to the capital asset pricing model, there is not a single "market portfolio" of risky assets that everyone should own. Investors have differing taxes, knowledge, liquidity needs, regulatory requirements, and so forth, that need to be considered when designing the investment portfolio.

6. *Competition for abnormal returns is extensive.* Investors are constantly searching for information that is not reflected in current security prices so they can profit by being the first to discover the information. As a result, the prices of widely followed securities trade very close to their fundamental intrinsic value. In addition, returns from active speculation appear to be similar to passive investment strategies.

The Portfolio Investment Process

Overview

The process used to manage a security portfolio is conceptually the same as that used in any managerial decision:

- ✖ Plan.

- ✖ Implement the plan.

- ✖ Monitor the results.

This **portfolio investment process** is displayed schematically in Figure 18-1. Each aspect of the process is discussed in some detail later. For now, however, we simply give an overview of the complete process.

The aspect of portfolio management most often overlooked is adequate planning, yet this is perhaps the most important element of proper portfolio investment and speculation. In the planning stage, a careful review should be conducted of the investor's financial situation and current capital market conditions. Taken together, these will suggest a set of investment and speculative policies to be followed. These policies should then be formally documented in a written **statement of investment policy (SIP).** The SIP documents (1) the portfolio objective, (2) strategies that may (or may not) be used, and (3) various investment and speculative constraints. An output of proper planning will be a clearly defined **strategic asset allocation (SAA).** The SAA represents the optimal combination of various asset classes in an efficient market. The SAA is an indexed portfolio

FIGURE 18-1   THE PORTFOLIO INVESTMENT PROCESS

Planning
1. Investor Conditions
2. Market Conditions
3. Investment/Speculative Policies
4. Statement of Investment Policy
5. Strategic Asset Allocation

Implementation
1. Internal-External Management
2. Security-Manager Selection
3. Tactical Asset Allocation

Monitoring
1. Evaluate Statement of Investment Policy
2. Evaluate Investment Performance

that would actually be held if a passive, pure investment strategy is to be employed. The SAA portfolio might never actually be held, since adjustments in line with various speculative strategies may be made, but it represents the basic pure "investment" portfolio against which actual portfolio returns can be compared in order to determine whether speculative strategies are actually "adding value."

In the **implementation stage,** the investor must first decide who will select the individual securities to be held. If the investor wishes to do so personally, it is called internal management. If the investor decides to employ the services of professional investment managers (such as mutual funds), it is referred to as external management. After the internal/external decision is made, individual securities or managers are identified. Investment selection issues are discussed in Chapter 20. In addition, a **tactical asset allocation (TAA)** decision must be made. TAA refers to temporary departures from the SAA in the belief that certain security classes are mispriced. TAA is discussed in Chapter 19.

The last stage in the portfolio investment process consists of monitoring portfolio returns in order to determine which speculative decisions seem to be adding value to the portfolio and to ascertain that the portfolio's objective and constraints are being met and have not changed. Portfolio monitoring is discussed in Chapter 21.

Planning

Aspects of the planning stage are shown in Figure 18-2. Investor and capital market conditions are blended in order to determine a set of investment and speculative policies as well as a long-run strategic asset allocation (SAA). These are formally expressed in the statement of investment policy.

Investor Conditions. The first, and perhaps most important, question that must be answered is this: *What is the purpose of the security portfolio?* While this question might seem obvious, it is too often overlooked, giving way instead to the excitement of selecting the securities that are to be held. Understanding the purpose for trading in financial securities will help to (1) define the expected portfolio liquidation date, (2) aid in determining an acceptable level of risk, and (3) indicate whether future consumption needs are to be paid in nominal or real dollars.

FIGURE 18-2   PORTFOLIO PLANNING STAGE

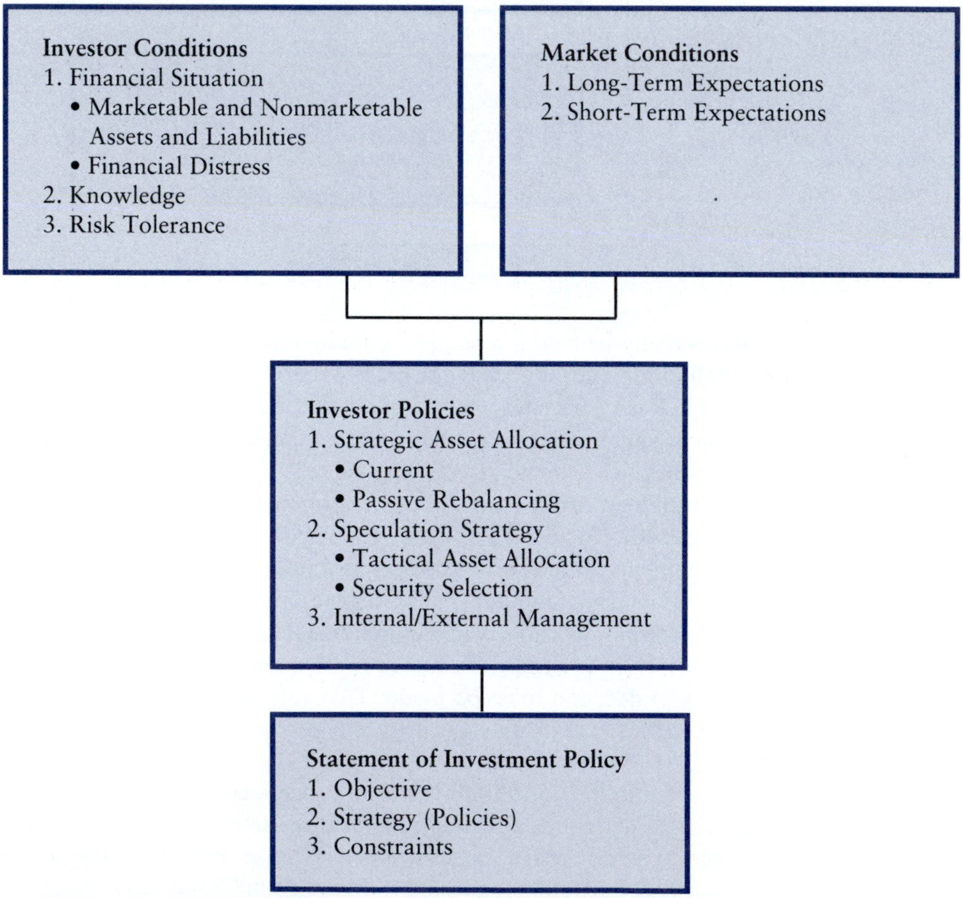

Investor Conditions
1. Financial Situation
   - Marketable and Nonmarketable Assets and Liabilities
   - Financial Distress
2. Knowledge
3. Risk Tolerance

Market Conditions
1. Long-Term Expectations
2. Short-Term Expectations

Investor Policies
1. Strategic Asset Allocation
   - Current
   - Passive Rebalancing
2. Speculation Strategy
   - Tactical Asset Allocation
   - Security Selection
3. Internal/External Management

Statement of Investment Policy
1. Objective
2. Strategy (Policies)
3. Constraints

For example, a 90-year-old woman with small to moderate savings probably (1) has a short investment horizon, (2) can accept little investment risk, and (3) needs protection against short-term inflation. In contrast, a young couple investing for retirement in 40 years have (1) a very long investment horizon, (2) a willingness to accept moderate to large investment risk, and (3) a need for protection against long-term inflation. This suggests that the 90-year-old woman should invest solely in low-default-risk money market securities. The young couple could invest in many other asset classes for diversification and accept greater investment risks. In short, knowing the eventual purpose of the portfolio investment makes it possible to begin sketching out appropriate investment/speculative policies.

Next, the complete financial status of the investor must be understood. For example, consider the augmented balance sheet for a Mr. Paulson, shown in Table 18-1. Two types of assets and liabilities are defined. Marketable assets and liabilities refer to assets that could be sold now and liabilities that could be paid for now. These represent the assets and liabilities that would be reported by standard accounting procedures, only stated at current market value. Mr. Paulson's current marketable net worth is $140.

Nonmarketable assets are of two types. Insurance policies effectively represent long positions in put options that pay off under certain conditions, for example, physical disability or loss of assets through theft or damage. Although they cannot be sold to other individuals, they represent an asset to Mr. Paulson that has a positive (albeit difficult to determine) value. The second type of nonmarketable asset is the present value of expected future pay. This pay comes in three forms: (1) wage income from employment, (2) retirement income from Social Security, and (3) retirement income from employment-based

TABLE 18-1   HYPOTHETICAL PRESENT-VALUE BALANCE SHEET FOR MR. PAULSON

Marketable Assets		Marketable Liabilities	
Security Portfolio	$100	Short-Term Debt	$50
Home	200	Mortgage	140
Personal Possessions	30		$190
	$330		
Nonmarketable Assets		**Nonmarketable Liabilities**	
Insurance Policies	20	Present Value of Minimum Future Consumption	1,500
Present Value of Expected Future Pay:			
Employment	1,000	Net Worth	
Social Security	500	Marketable Equity	140
Pension Benefits	500	Nonmarketable Equity	520
	$2,020		660
Total	$2,350	Total	$2,350

pension benefits. The total risk of each of these nonmarketable assets and the extent to which they can be diversified or hedged differ considerably. For example, the $1,000 asset value arising from future wage income is closely tied to the talents of Mr. Paulson and the future fortunes of his employer. This asset cannot be diversified. The only way in which its risk can be reduced would be by taking offsetting hedges in other asset and liability positions. For example, if Mr. Paulson is employed as a computer salesman by IBM, he could hedge his risk by underweighting IBM shares and the shares of other computer companies in his security portfolio. In contrast, the risk inherent in the $500 present value of future pension benefits can be reduced by making sure the employer has fully funded the pension plan and has invested all pension funds in a well-diversified security portfolio.

How should the $100 marketable security portfolio be invested? This is the critical investment question that Mr. Paulson faces. To answer this question, he should *not* focus on the distribution of returns on the $100 security portfolio itself. Instead, *he should focus on the distribution of his future net worth.*[1]

Portfolio investment and speculation decisions are too often based solely on potential security portfolio payoffs with no attention given to interactions between the security portfolio and other economic assets and liabilities of the individual or investment organization. This is the wrong approach. We saw one example earlier—the underweighting of computer stocks in Mr. Paulson's security portfolio. Consider another example. If the current value of future consumption is directly correlated with unexpected inflation, assets that hedge against this risk should be weighted more heavily than if little inflation risk were present.

The potential for temporary financial distress must also be considered. The economic net worth of Mr. Paulson might always remain positive. But if cash flows from his wage income are variable, he could find himself unable to pay current debts. For example, as a computer salesman, his compensation might be volatile and tied to economic activity. Thus, it is possible his employment income might be low at the same time that the value of his security portfolio has fallen in value as a result of poor economic conditions. This suggests a larger position in low-risk liquid securities should be taken.

In short, the total economic position of the individual must be examined. The unique short- and long-term risks inherent in major assets and liabilities must be understood. Although this is difficult to quantify, the problem is important and deserves careful thought.

The investor's knowledge of various securities also has an important impact on the types of security classes that should be held and the speculative strategies employed. The investor must understand that yearly equity returns are quite variable, short-term returns on bonds are sensitive to the bonds' duration, futures require daily mark-to-market, options are leveraged positions, international investment entails considerable exchange rate risk, and so forth. If the investor does not truly understand the nature and extent of a security's short- and long-term risk, the security should not be held.

Finally, the tolerance of an investor for investment risk must be considered. This is clearly a difficult aspect of developing a proper investment strategy. Investment theories are largely based on a single future date at which the portfolio will be liquidated; theory speaks

---

[1] In previous chapters, we focused on the returns on the underlying asset investments. This implicitly assumed there were no other assets and no liabilities. Thus, the assets and net worth were identical.

to the standard deviation of the security portfolio's value at that date. But this neglects a number of very important practical investment considerations. These include the following:

1. The relationship between investment horizon date payoffs from the marketable security portfolio and payoffs from other assets or liabilities of the investor (both marketable and nonmarketable). Two examples of this were presented earlier.
2. The investor's reaction to portfolio results during periods of time that are shorter than the investor's true investment horizon. For example, even though Mr. Paulson is investing for retirement and should be relatively unconcerned about yearly portfolio returns, a year or two with particularly good or bad returns might cause him to make short-term decisions that are not in his best long-term interest—for example, selling stock after it has fallen in value to buy gold at high prices. Long-term investors must be able to bear up to the despair or euphoria that temporary price swings can cause.
3. Although students of investment theory can interpret what the standard deviation of returns or wealth means, most investors cannot. Thus, the nature and extent of security risk must be communicated to investors in a way they can truly understand.

Market Conditions. An assessment of potential future returns on various classes of marketable securities must also be made. This is discussed in Chapter 19 and not treated here. However, two points need to be made. First, short-term (say, one year) expectations might differ considerably from longer term expectations. If so, the portfolio's tactical asset allocation will differ from the long-term strategic asset allocation. Both short- and long-term market forecasts must be made if one has any intent of engaging in tactical asset allocation (TAA). The forecasts might turn out to be identical. But if TAA is allowed, both forecasts should be explicitly made. Second, forecasts should be stated in real dollars if future consumption and liabilities are tied to inflation. If consumption and liabilities are unaffected by inflation, then nominal return forecasts are appropriate.

Strategic Asset Allocation. The most important investment decision that the owner of a portfolio must make is the portfolio's asset allocation. Asset allocation refers to the percentage invested in various security classes. Security classes are simply the type of securities discussed earlier in the text:

1. Money market investment
2. Fixed income obligations
3. Common stock
4. International securities
5. Real estate investment

Futures and options are not unique asset classes, since they are effectively positions in another asset class such as common stock or bonds. Thus, futures and options do not provide any significant diversification advantages if they are properly priced. They simply alter the nondiversifiable risk position in the underlying asset.

A number of studies have shown that 90% or more of a portfolio's rate of return is determined by the portfolio's asset allocation. Of much less importance are the actual securities held. The simple fact that $X\%$ is invested in stocks as a class or $Y\%$ in bonds as a class is the dominant force that generates portfolio returns.

Strategic asset allocation (SAA) represents the asset allocation that would be optimal for the investor if all security prices trade at their long-term equilibrium values—that is, if the markets are efficiently priced.

Passive Rebalancing. Few investment strategies are static. They require changes as time passes, as the investor's wealth changes, as security prices change, as the investor's knowledge expands, and so on. Thus, the optimal strategic asset allocation will also change. Even if the investor continues to believe that all security prices are fair, the SAA will probably require periodic rebalancing. Such changes are *passive* changes to the portfolio. These are not active changes made in the hopes of earning excess risk-adjusted returns from potential security price disequilibriums. Instead, they represent logical shifts in the investor's strategic asset allocation in response to changes in the investor's condition or (fairly priced) market conditions.

Conceptually, we could think of investors as continually revising their SAA. Thus, there would be no need to plan for a passive rebalancing strategy. At each moment in time, investors would evaluate their personal investment needs and market expectations to develop a current strategic asset allocation. As a practical matter, however, the costs of doing this are too large. For example, pension funds spend large sums of money and months of effort to develop an SAA. They simply cannot afford to engage in a continual analysis of what their SAA should be. Individual investors who have much less capital and knowledge face even larger problems. As a result, it makes sense that part of the SAA decision should be a decision about how the SAA is to be changed as certain important economic variables change.

Thus, the SAA decision should actually contain two elements: (1) definition of a current SAA, and (2) specification of a rebalancing strategy that passively adjusts the current SAA to changes in the investor's situation and security market conditions.

Speculation Strategy. After the investor has determined a current strategic asset allocation and decided how the allocation should be passively rebalanced as time passes, net worth changes, or stock prices vary, a decision must be made as to the types and amounts of security speculation that will be allowed. Speculative strategies can be classified as either tactical asset allocation (timing) decisions or security selection decisions.

Implementation

In Figure 18-3, the implementation stage is shown schematically. This consists of any active timing between asset classes and the selection of individual managers or securities to be held in each asset class.

Tactical Asset Allocation. If one believes that the price levels of certain asset classes, industries, or economic sectors are temporarily too high or too low, actual portfolio holdings should depart from the asset mix called for in the strategic asset allocation. Such a timing decision is referred to as tactical asset allocation (TAA). As noted, TAA decisions could be made across aggregate asset classes (stocks, bonds, and T-bills), industry classifications (steel, airline, food), or various broad economic sectors (basic manufacturing, interest-sensitive, consumer durables).

FIGURE 18-3 PORTFOLIO IMPLEMENTATION STAGE

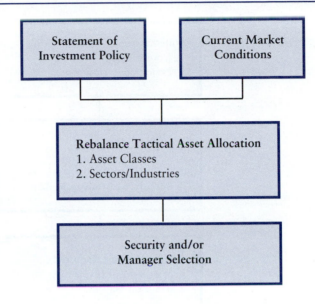

Security or Manager Selection. Investors must decide whether they intend to make individual security selection decisions or whether they intend to employ the services of external professional managers. Large investment pools (pension fund, endowments, etc.) are managed by professionals—either as direct employees of the organization or as contracted service companies. Mutual funds are the logical source of external professional management available to smaller investors.

If one intends to follow a passive investment strategy, then one index fund for each asset class is adequate. Each would be very diversified and designed to track the returns on the aggregate asset class that it emulates. If active external managers are used, then a number of different organizations should be selected in order to obtain reasonable levels of diversification. Active managers tend to specialize and often do not own well-diversified portfolios. Thus, it is important to determine how they differ from each other and invest across managers who are distinctly different.

Portfolio Monitoring

The portfolio monitoring stage is shown schematically in Figure 18-4. There are three aspects to this monitoring. First, the actual portfolio held should be examined to ascertain it is in compliance with the statement of investment policy and to determine whether any passive rebalancing of the asset mix is required. Second, investment performance should be reviewed. This should consist of a review of returns on (1) the aggregate portfolio, (2) each asset class and investment manager, and (3) the returns from any speculative strategies employed. Finally, adjustments to the SIP and investment managers should be made if necessary. Performance monitoring is the subject of Chapter 21.

FIGURE 18-4   Portfolio Monitoring Stage

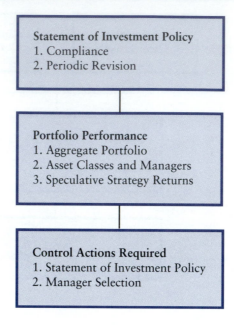

Statement of Investment Policy
1. Compliance
2. Periodic Revision

Portfolio Performance
1. Aggregate Portfolio
2. Asset Classes and Managers
3. Speculative Strategy Returns

Control Actions Required
1. Statement of Investment Policy
2. Manager Selection

The Statement of Investment Policy

The portfolio objective, constraints, and strategy should always be stated explicitly in a written document. This is not a nicety that only large portfolios need—it is a necessity for all portfolios. This statement of investment policy (or whatever one elects to call it) can be amended periodically as economic conditions or the portfolio owner's needs change. In fact, the statement of policy should probably include the requirement that the statement itself be reviewed at least every two to three years.

There are at least four advantages to having a written statement of policy:

1. Requiring a written document forces the investor to make difficult decisions that might otherwise be set aside.
2. A well-thought-out SIP can add discipline and stability to the long-run management of the portfolio, reducing whipsaw reactions to temporary price swings. By acting as documentation and education for why particular decisions were made, it should reduce capricious changes in investment strategies.
3. A well-drafted SIP defines the investor's strategic asset allocation (SAA) and passive rebalancing strategies.
4. Future performance evaluation is simply impossible without a clear benchmark against which a comparison can be made. The strategic asset allocation serves as the benchmark.

In a sense, the statement of investment policy is the constitution under which the investor's assets are to be managed. As such, it should be prepared only after the investor has fully investigated all major aspects of managing an investment portfolio.

The Portfolio Objective

Conceptually, the objective is to maximize expected return for an acceptable risk level. While true in theory, measuring whether the objective is being met in practice is difficult.

Typically, the portfolio objective is a return objective based on the portfolio's SAA. For example, assume the desired SAA is the one shown in Table 18-2. This is certainly a complex asset allocation consisting of a wide variety of security classes. But it is representative of the detail considered by large investment pools such as pension funds and foundations. If a passive strategy is used, then the portfolio objective should be to earn a return equal to the weighted average return on appropriate benchmarks for each asset class. The weights would be the percentage investment in each asset class (w_i), and the benchmarks would be a

TABLE 18-2   HYPOTHETICAL STRATEGIC ASSET ALLOCATION

Asset Class	Strategic Asset Allocation	Total
Short-Term Debt:		10%
U.S.	5%	
Non-U.S.	5%	
Fixed Income:		20
Government and Agency		
U.S. 1–3-Year	1	
U.S. 3–10-Year	3	
U.S. Long Term	1	
Non-U.S.	5	
U.S. Asset Backed	5	
U.S. Corporate		
5–10-Year AAA	3	
High Yield (Junk)	2	
Equities		55
U.S. Large Capitalization	20	
U.S. Mid Capitalization	10	
U.S. Small Capitalization	5	
Europe	5	
Japan	5	
Pacific Rim	5	
Emerging Markets	5	
U.S. Real Estate		15
	100%	100%

good proxy of returns on the asset class in the period examined (b_{it}). For U.S. large capitalization stocks shown in Table 18-2, the weight should be 0.20 and the benchmarks could be an index return such as the S&P 500 or the Russell 1000. Symbolically:

$$\text{Passive Portfolio Return Objective in Period } t = \sum_{i=1}^{N} w_i b_{it} \qquad (18.1)$$

If an active speculative strategy is being used, then the portfolio objective might be 100 to 200 basis points above the passive return.

Notice that the objective is not a specific rate of return. Unless the portfolio is invested relatively risk free, specific return objectives are impractical. Also, the horizon interval over which the objective is measured should be neither too short nor too long. A three- to five-year period is common.

Constraints

Any constraint can, of course, reduce the chances of achieving the portfolio objective. For example, it would be virtually impossible to earn a 4% yearly real return if the portfolio is constrained to holdings of short-term Treasury obligations, since in the past, nominal returns on such securities have barely offset inflation. Common sense dictates that there be a reasonable relationship between the objective and the constraints. Typical constraints included in a statement of policy pertain to the following:

1. **Portfolio risk level.** If the objective is stated in terms of a desired rate of return, the most important constraint should be the acceptable risk of the portfolio. In theory, the risk level could be expressed as a portfolio beta or the standard deviation of portfolio returns.

   In practice, aggregate portfolio risk is usually defined in terms of the percentage of the portfolio allocated to various security types. For example, a 60/40 equity/fixed income asset allocation is a common constraint of many large pension portfolios. Actually, such an approach is a fairly good way to identify allowable portfolio risk as long as the types of securities included in each group are well defined.

2. **Allowed securities.** All parties to the management of the portfolio should have a clear understanding of the types of securities that may be purchased. For example, if 40% of all assets are to be invested in fixed income securities, the intended duration, default risk, callability, tax features, and so forth, should be clearly identified. If an external manager is to be used, such as a mutual fund, the statement of policy should clearly specify the principal investment characteristics of the types of funds that may be purchased—for example, the mutual fund beta, S&P quality, and dividend yield. This is commonly known as a manager assignment statement. (A manager assignment statement is not intended to tell the manager precisely what securities are to be purchased. Instead, it should provide general guidelines as to the types of securities to be purchased. Examples include low dividend yield versus high dividend yield, low beta versus high beta, etc.).

3. **Diversification.** Regardless of whether the portfolio owner, a mutual fund, or some other party will be making purchase and sale decisions, some statement should be made about the extent of diversification desired. This can be done by specifying (1) the minimum number of securities to be held, (2) the maximum percentage of the portfolio that may be held in a given security, (3) the maximum percentage of the portfolio that may be held in a given industry, (4) the R^2 obtained when portfolio returns are regressed against some market index such as the S&P 500, and so on.

   If more than one external manager is to be given money to invest, the diversification restrictions required from each can be less stringent than required for the portfolio as a whole. Nonetheless, the greater the diversification of the aggregate portfolio, the less its risk.

4. **Tax and liquidity.** Consideration should be given to both the tax and liquidity requirements of the portfolio. Investors in a high marginal tax bracket are faced with complex portfolio decisions that only professional financial consultants trained in taxation can address. If taxes are an important factor, however, the principle that it is the total portfolio of all invested assets which matters is particularly critical. Marketable securities and real asset investments must be considered together in order to increase total after-tax portfolio returns. Investors that do not pay taxes, such as pension funds, may wish to exclude the purchase of securities that are priced in large part for their tax advantages. An example would be low-coupon bonds. Investors with average marginal tax rates may wish to include a statement that the portfolio be reviewed periodically during the course of a year in order to identify possible tax swaps.

   Liquidity needs vary considerably among investors. Liquidity can be obtained in two principal ways: (1) by allocating an appropriate percentage of the portfolio to short-term securities or money market managers, or (2) by requiring that the bonds and equities purchased be highly marketable. Which of the two approaches is the more reasonable depends on why liquidity is needed. If quick access to cash is needed in order to make scheduled withdrawals from the portfolio (for bills, vacations, retirement, etc.), the first approach reduces transaction costs. However, if liquidity is desired to enable active speculation, the second approach may be more effective in reducing transaction costs.

5. **Social investing.** A growing concern of the 1980s was the extent to which an investment portfolio should be constrained by social issues. In the mid-1980s, the major issue was investment in U.S. corporations doing business in South Africa. But even prior to that, many portfolios were restricted from purchasing securities of firms engaged in alcohol or tobacco sales. There is no doubt that such restrictions reduce the diversification potential of the portfolio. How much so depends, of course, on the number of securities restricted. In the case of South Africa, the author has seen lists of restricted securities ranging from 30 to more than 200. The elimination of 30 securities probably would have minimal impact on diversification (although some of the 30 were large firms such as IBM). In contrast, the elimination of 200 securities could do severe damage to the ability to diversify.

6. **Strategy.** Finally, the statement of policy should discuss the forms of active speculation that will be allowed. In the broadest sense, speculative transactions can be related to either timing or selection. Based on one's belief in the usefulness of timing and selection speculation, the statement of policy should identify the extent to which they may be used.

Portfolio Types and Their Needs

Security portfolios are owned by individuals and organizations having dramatically different objectives and constraints. To illustrate how the portfolio investment process applies to different situations, we briefly examine two different groups: (1) individuals, and (2) pension funds.

Individuals

The range of portfolio objectives, constraints, and strategies varies more among individual investors than among any other group of portfolio owners. As a result, we can provide only an overview of the major issues that most individual investors face.

Considerations in Setting the Objective. The most likely objective of a person's security portfolio is to provide a supplement to Social Security and pension benefits during the individual's retirement. Other needs, such as saving for a house, vacation, child's education, and so forth, are also common, of course. But the pervasive need is to increase income during retirement. As a result, an individual's age has a significant effect on the perceived riskiness of various types of securities. For example, a person who is 25 years from retirement can ride through the inevitable good and bad years of stock returns, whereas someone in retirement will be immediately affected by such movements, since portions of the portfolio will have to be liquidated to meet current consumption needs. All other things held equal, the amount of equity risk inherent in a portfolio should decrease as an individual draws closer to retirement.

In addition to the individual's age, his or her other assets should be considered. Particular attention should be given to any real estate holdings and the nature of the person's career. In order to ensure the greatest possible diversification, the individual should probably underweight securities whose returns are highly correlated with returns on such existing assets.

Finally, the individual's level of investment knowledge can affect the portfolio's constraints and strategy. Unfortunately, there is often a big difference between what should be done conceptually and what is done in practice. Because most individual investors lack investment expertise, they should attempt to diversify broadly (say, by purchasing a mutual fund), minimize costs (trade little and only in no-load mutual funds), and avoid active speculation and complex securities (such as options and futures). In practice, however, a major portion of the security information that individuals receive comes from brokers, who are paid only if their customers trade.

Consequently, many individuals own security portfolios that are poorly diversified, invest in load mutual funds, trade actively on broker recommendations, and use complex securities such as options and futures to gain speculative profits. Many brokers and brokerage

Donna L. Terry, C.F.A.

President, CEO
Barnett Capital Advisors
Taylor University, B.A.
Boston University, M.B.A.

Donna Terry was a portfolio manager at The Boston Company Asset Management when this interview was conducted. When she started in the business, in 1974, there were few women. Her first boss, Harold Kotler of Gannett, Welch and Kotler, was a willing teacher and a strong leader who expected a high level of achievement and commitment. This early influence profoundly affected Ms. Terry's career, encouraging her to succeed in a challenging environment.

Q: When you are in the office, what is your typical morning like?

A: If I haven't seen the details of what has happened to my accounts the night before, one of the most important things is to review them right away. Fortunately, life has changed over the years and I have more accessibility to see on my computer what is happening to my portfolio on a real-time basis and on an absolute basis rather than having to wait for end-of-day reporting. Even still, I like to review them again in the morning. I look at all the trades that were done the night before, check on the execution, and refresh myself on what happened the day before in the portfolio.

I read the paper and look at the news. I often listen to Bloomberg news on my way into the office so I know how the overseas markets closed or are faring. Basically, I just get myself into the flow of information. I typically get a morning call from brokers. They have spent an hour or more listening to their analysts and strategists and they provide me with the highlights. (Much of this information is now available electronically.) Much of the morning is dependent on individual firm momentum. Here, we have a good group of quant people who provide screens based on criteria that we think is important. We have a chance to review the data; then we meet and talk about the issues surrounding the stocks on the lists. We meet formally two times a week to review the output from the quant group and keep the momentum of the stock selection process going. There is a lot of very good quality electronic information available to professionals now too.

Q: Why do most portfolio managers start out as analysts?

A: Because the best portfolio managers are great analysts. A portfolio manager has to be able to do her own analytical work, make her own decisions on individual companies, and not be solely reliant on other people to give her their interpretation of the information. So if you work your way up through the analytical ranks learning companies, understanding what makes balance sheets and income statements move, and making individual stock decisions, then that helps you when you aggregate those decisions as a portfolio manager.

Q: But portfolio managers can't possibly follow all of the stocks they own if they're running a large number of portfolios or a considerable amount of money.

A: True, but it's a building block process. By the time you're running money with a lot of stocks, you've reduced your analytical methodology to a science, your particular science; it's very individualized. You have the questions and critical variables to ask analysts so you don't have to repeat their work. A lot depends on your environment and the tools you have to work with. If you're in a big investment shop with a full analytical staff, then the analysts perform the majority of the work. In this case, the analysts should be self-starters and initiators of ideas. You also need analysts as a resource to keep you informed of changes in a company or any relevant news. In a smaller shop it's much different; the portfolio manager has greater analytical responsibilities.

Q: After you've picked the stocks you want to have in a portfolio, how do you determine the weightings?

A: I think the marketplace is determining it for you to a large extent. Years ago in order to be a good money manager, you needed to be good at picking stocks and under- or over-weighting sectors. The absolute return was the only thing that was important. The marketplace has gone through a transition and now demands product definition. This phenomenon has created a skeleton on which a portfolio manager has to work and hopefully work successfully. For example, a lot of attention is spent on portfolio construction. Sometimes there's a style constraint; sometimes the portfolio is so large, like in the case of Fidelity Magellan, that you basically are the market with sector tilts. Again, it's highly dependent on what kind of shop you're in and the type of marketing the firm does. Hopefully the investment people have created the proper line of reasoning for the marketing people and not vice versa. Then you have to demonstrate the discipline to stay with it. This can be simplistic measures of valuation and risk or can be complicated by using BARRA or variability studies or dissecting companies for industry exposure. Whatever it is, you need to be able to justify that you've indeed followed through on the concept that was sold.

Additionally, I think some of it has to do with individual personalities. Often portfolio managers are most comfortable in stocks where they once had analytical responsibility. Experience also shapes how you invest. Good managers change with the times. They know which phases have left and have a feel for those that are upon them and those that are coming. Even if your approach is "bottom up" it's important to be flexible with the macro trends.

firms sincerely try to provide general investment counseling. However, as a rule, such efforts are meager in comparison with the efforts devoted to persuading the customer to trade.

In sum, three factors are important in determining the individual investor's portfolio constraints and strategy:

1. A focus on retirement benefits
2. Other assets owned
3. Level of investment knowledge

Constraints. With this as background, various constraints can be considered. Among the most common are the following:

1. **Risk level.** This is a decision the individual should make after reviewing information about the risks and expected returns from various asset mixes. Later in the chapter we examine how this might be done. All other things held equal, the equity portion should decrease as the person approaches retirement.
2. **Strategy.** The investor's knowledge should largely determine what can be held. People with little knowledge should minimize holdings of complex instruments, such as options and futures, and instruments that require close monitoring, such as bonds with above average default risk.
3. **Diversification.** Consideration should be given to the nature of other assets owned so the securities portfolio can underweight similar investments. Mutual funds and bank trust accounts are reasonable ways of achieving a diversified portfolio.
4. **Taxes and liquidity.** Investors in high tax brackets should seek professional advice. In general, they will find that municipal bonds, low-coupon bonds, and low-dividend-yield stocks provide larger after-tax returns. Investors in lower tax brackets should own taxable bonds with high coupons and dividend yields. Liquidity requirements depend on the individual's age and desire to speculate.
5. **Speculation.** In general, individual investors do not have the training and rapid access to new information necessary to successfully engage in speculative trades. They should follow a passive investment approach.

Life Cycle Investment. The major reason why most individuals and families save is to supplement retirement income. In the United States, consumption during retirement is paid from three possible sources: (1) Social Security, (2) pension benefit payments, and (3) personal investment portfolios. The situation varies across other countries with some relying more on Social Security and others relying almost exclusively on personal investment saving. The following discussion focuses on a U.S. investor.

Consider the case of Stuart Chu. Stuart is 35, unmarried, and employed by a food distributor. Stuart intends to retire at age 65 and should expect to live for another 15 years after retiring. Although his current salary is $30,000, it should grow at a real annual rate of 0.5%. Thus, his expected salary at retirement (in current dollars) is $34,840 ($30,000 $\times$ 1.005^{30}). (Throughout this example, we neglect taxes and future inflation.)

In retirement, Social Security benefits should replace about 40% of retirement salary. Pension retirement benefits will provide additional income, say, equal to 30% of final salary. Any remaining income during retirement will have to be provided by Stuart's personal savings plan. Let's assume that Stuart wishes to develop a personal investment strategy that will add $5,000 per year to the income received from Social Security and pension benefits.

The amount that Stuart will have to invest to provide an expected $5,000 annuity between 30 years from now and 45 years depends on two things: (1) when he invests, and (2) the rate of return he expects to earn on his investment (i.e., the risk of the investment).

Let's assume he intends to invest risk free once he reaches retirement and that the best current estimate of what the real risk-free rate will be at that time is 2%. Thus, at the start of his retirement (end of year 35), he will need a portfolio worth $64,246 to provide a 15-year $5,000 annuity at a return of 2%.

$$\$64{,}246 = \sum_{t=1}^{15} [\$5{,}000 \div (1.02)^t)]$$

If Stuart wished to make a one-time investment today that will grow to $64,246, the size of the investment required will depend on the real return he expects to earn between today and retirement. This expected real return will, of course, depend on the risk of the portfolio in which he invests. For example, at a 2% risk-free real rate, he would have to invest $35,469 today. At a moderate risk, he would expect to earn higher returns and, thus, have to invest less today. For example, at a 6% expected return, only $11,186 need be invested today to provide the expected portfolio value of $64,246 in 30 years.

$$\$35{,}469 = \$64{,}246 \div (1.02)^{30}$$

$$\$11{,}186 = \$64{,}246 \div (1.06)^{30}$$

It is unlikely that Stuart would have the resources to make such an investment today. Typically people will save during their working years and spend during retirement years. This is illustrated in Figure 18-5 using the data in this example. Values shown by the dotted lines are associated with a 6% real return. For simplicity, the figure is based on an annuity savings plan. More realistically, people will save a level percentage of income.

In panel A the total value of the portfolio over time is shown. For both assumed preretirement returns, the portfolio is expected to be worth $64,246 at retirement. But since investment earnings on the 2% portfolio are expected to be smaller than for the 6% portfolio, the 2% portfolio requires greater contributions throughout the preretirement period. The differences in these contributions can be easily seen in panel B.

There are good reasons to believe that individuals with many years until retirement will be more risk tolerant about their investment portfolio than the same individuals during retirement. In Chapter 5 we noted the following:

■ **Long-term investors have opportunities not available to short-term investors.** For example, young individuals saving for retirement have the opportunity to work longer hours if their investment portfolio does poorly. Individuals in retirement do not have this opportunity.

■ **The portion of one's wealth that is held in securities is usually smaller for long-term investors.** When people are young, a large fraction of their wealth represents the present value of future income. Wealth held in securities is usually a smaller fraction.

FIGURE 18-5 RETIREMENT SAVINGS AND SPENDING

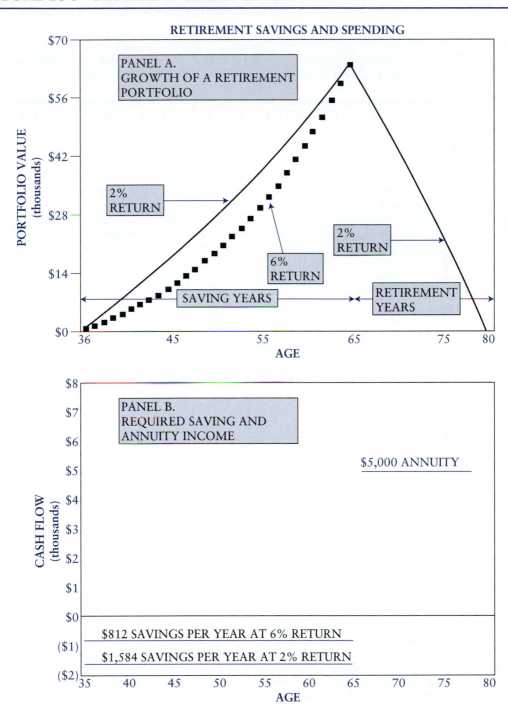

RETIREMENT SAVINGS AND SPENDING

PANEL A.
GROWTH OF A RETIREMENT
PORTFOLIO

2% RETURN

6% RETURN

2% RETURN

SAVING YEARS

RETIREMENT YEARS

PORTFOLIO VALUE (thousands)

AGE

PANEL B.
REQUIRED SAVING AND
ANNUITY INCOME

$5,000 ANNUITY

$812 SAVINGS PER YEAR AT 6% RETURN

$1,584 SAVINGS PER YEAR AT 2% RETURN

CASH FLOW (thousands)

AGE

Assuming the risk inherent in future income is less than the risk of equities, then they might be willing to accept large risk in their security portfolio. However, when people enter retirement, the fraction of wealth held in securities is usually quite large. A security risk that was acceptable when they were younger is no longer appropriate.

The key point here is that there are valid reasons for long-term investors to bear more investment risk than short-term investors.

A STATEMENT OF INVESTMENT POLICY FOR STUART CHU

Asset Allocation

CONSIDERATIONS. The purpose of this investment plan is to supplement my retirement income. Since my retirement will be in the distant future, I am willing to accept greater investment risk today than I will accept as the date of retirement approaches. Also, since one major risk I face is uncertainty about inflation between today and my retirement, the investments that are selected should provide a decent long-term hedge against inflation. A large part of my wealth is presently invested in my home and the land on which it is built. Thus, I need little further investment in real estate other than to provide diversification against the fall in local real estate values. Finally, I am not particularly knowledgeable in security investment selection and wish to minimize my costs of investing. Therefore, I will invest solely in index mutual funds.

CONCLUSIONS. The initial asset allocation of my portfolio will be as follows:

TYPE OF INDEX MUTUAL FUND	PERCENTAGE OF PORTFOLIO
Money Market Funds	10%
Bond Index Funds	15%
Large Capitalization U.S. Stocks	40%
Small Capitalization U.S. Stocks	5%
Foreign Bond Funds	0%
Foreign Stock Funds	20%
Real Estate Investment Trusts	10%
	100%

Objective

Since these funds are to be invested in passive index mutual funds, I expect my return on each to be their index benchmark less 25 basis points per year to cover operating expenses.

Constraints

1. To pay taxes on dividend receipts from the mutual funds, I will retain 30% of all dividends and reinvest the remainder in each fund.
2. At the end of each calendar quarter, I will invest 7% of my net salary in this investment portfolio.
3. Quarterly investments will be made into these funds so that my asset allocation will be approximately the same as stated above.
4. I will engage in no tactical asset allocation (TAA).

Pension Funds

The growth of employee retirement-benefit plans has been one of the dominant forces affecting the security markets since the mid-1900s. Since the early 1960s, of all institutional investors, pension funds have owned the largest amount of common stocks, and their relative importance continues to grow. For example, in 1960, noninsured pension funds owned 5% of the market value of all stocks listed on the NYSE. By 1995, their ownership interest had increased to about 30%.

There are two basic forms of employee benefit plans: (1) defined contribution plans, and (2) defined benefit plans.[2] **Defined contribution** plans specify the amount the employer will contribute to an employee's retirement plan. The contribution could be a flat dollar amount, a percentage of the employee's pay, or a specified share of corporate profits (a profit-sharing plan). Once the contribution has been made, all investment risk is borne by the employee. If the investment portfolio has performed better than expected, when an employee begins to withdraw pension benefits his or her payments will be larger than expected. If investment performance has been lower than expected, the employee's benefits will also be lower than expected. Again, all the investment risk of a defined contribution plan is borne by the employee. Consequently, employees covered by such a plan should be given considerable say in how their funds are invested.

In contrast, **defined benefit** plans specify a contractual benefit that will be paid to the employee after retirement. The size of the retirement benefit is calculated in a variety of ways. Examples of benefit formulas include (1) a percentage of earnings (say, 50% of an employee's average salary during the last three years of employment), (2) an amount per year of service (say, $300 times the number of years of service), and (3) a percentage of earnings per year of service (say, 1% of the sum of all yearly earnings). Regardless of the precise formula used, defined benefit plans provide a contractual retirement benefit to the employee. All investment risk is borne by the employer. As such, the employer should have the strongest say in how plan assets are invested.

Funding a Defined Benefit Plan. Under a defined benefit plan, the employer has a legal obligation to pay employees a contractually agreed upon retirement benefit. The sole purpose of having a pension investment portfolio is to be able to meet these obligations in the future.

To help understand the various forces that determine the objective, constraints, and strategy of a pension portfolio, it is necessary that we understand the general process by which benefit liabilities are "funded." We do not delve too deeply into the details of pension funding here. However, the general process of pension funding is relatively easy to understand. In fact, the pension-funding decision is no more than an application of time-value-of-money concepts.

Assume you are the owner of a business with 100 employees, each of whom now receives compensation of $20,000 a year. You have signed a pension agreement with the employees promising to pay a yearly individual pension benefit equal to 30% of the retiring employee's compensation during his or her last year of employment. This retirement benefit will be paid at year-end during each year of the employee's retirement until the employee dies. A pension investment portfolio has been set up to help pay these future benefits. At present, the portfolio has a market value of $1 million.

---

[2] Keogh plans and individual retirement accounts are discussed in Chapter 20. They are a form of defined contribution plan.

You face two questions:

1. What are the expected benefit payments?
   a. In what years?
   b. In what dollar amounts?
2. What contributions should be made to the pension portfolio to ensure that the expected benefit payments will be met?

In order to calculate the expected benefit payments and required contributions, a number of assumptions need to be made:

1. Salary growth—Merit: 1.0% per year
            Inflation: 5.0% per year
               Total: 6.0% per year
2. Mortality rate—Preretirement: None
            Postretirement: All employees live 15 years after retirement
3. Termination rate: No one leaves employment until retirement in 25 years
4. Years to retirement: Everyone will retire in 25 years
5. Postretirement benefit increases: None (no cost-of-living adjustment)
6. Investment returns—Real: 4% per year
            Inflation: 5% per year
               Total: 9% per year
7. Funding method: Annual annuity sufficient to fully fund by retirement

Estimated retirement benefits and required contributions are calculated in Table 18-3. Consider first the estimated benefits. Current salaries total $2 million. Since no employees are expected to leave employment because of death or termination, and since all employees are expected to retire in 25 years from now, the retirement benefit is based on the expected total salary payout in 25 years. Yearly salary growth consists of a merit increase and an inflation component, which sum to 6% per year. Growing at 6%, the current $2 million salary base will be $8.58 million in 25 years. Since employees have a right to yearly benefits equal to 30% of this total and all are expected to live for 15 years after retirement, the retirement benefits will be a 15-year annuity of $2,575,122 (30% × $8.58 million).

Now let's calculate the contributions required in order to pay these benefits. The yearly contribution will depend on two things: (1) the return we expect to earn on portfolio investments, and (2) the funding method chosen. The expected investment return is 9% per year, consisting of a 4% real return and a 5% inflation component (the same inflation rate used for salary growth). The funding method requires that all benefit liabilities be "fully funded" by the retirement date (end of year 25) and that any contributions necessary to fully fund the portfolio be made in annual annuity installments.[3] The present value at the end of year 25 of the $2.57 million, 15-year-benefit annuity at a 9% investment rate is $20.76 million. Thus, if the pension portfolio has a value of $20.76 million at the end of

---

[3] In practice, contributions are typically not calculated as level-dollar annuities but, instead, as a level percentage of expected future salary.

TABLE 18-3 ESTIMATED PENSION BENEFIT PAYMENTS AND CONTRIBUTIONS

Estimated Benefits	Years of Employment		Years of Retirement			
	0	25	26	...	39	40
Current Salary	$2,000,000	—				
Salary at Retirement:						
$2,000,000 $\times$ 1.06^{25}		$ 8,583,741				
Retirement Benefits:						
$8,583,741 $\times$ 30%		—	$2,575,122	...	$2,575,122	$2,575,122
Estimated Level Contributions						
P.V. of Benefits at Retirement:						
$2,575,122 $\times \sum\limits_{t=1}^{15} (1 \div 1.09^t)$		$20,757,286	—		—	—
Future Value of Current Portfolio:						
$1,000,000 $\times$ 1.09^{25}		$ 8,623,081	—		—	—
Deficiency		$12,134,205				
Level Annuity Contribution						
Required to Meet Deficiency:						
$12,134,205 $\div \sum\limits_{t=1}^{25} 1.09^{t-1}$	$ 143,260	...	$ 143,260			

year 25 and earns 9% each year, it will be able to exactly meet the yearly $2.57 million benefit liability. Unfortunately, the current $1 million portfolio growing at 9% per year will be worth only $8.62 million in 25 years. A deficiency of $12.13 million exists. To meet this deficiency a 25-year contribution annuity of $143,260 is necessary.

Given the assumptions we have made, a level $143,260 yearly contribution to the pension portfolio is required. If any of the assumptions were to change, so would the contribution requirement. For example, what would happen if we increased the assumed inflation rate? Clearly, the yearly benefit liability would rise because the employees' ending salaries would be larger. However, the investment return would also rise and, all other things being equal, cause required contributions to fall. Taking into account both effects, contributions would fall, since the inflation rate increases the investment return for the full 40-year period of the portfolio's accumulation and liquidation, whereas the salary growth is affected for only the 25-year employment period. Increasing the assumed inflation rate without allowing for cost-of-living adjustments to benefits during the employees' retirement harms the employees and provides a gain to the employer in the form of lower contributions.

We do not examine other possible modifications to our assumptions. But two things are clear. First, the analysis can quickly become quite complicated as we move from our simple example to more realistic cases. Second, the assumed investment return is only one of many components that determine a pension fund's contribution requirement.

ERISA. Retirement-benefit plans of corporations are subject to the legal requirements of the **Employee Retirement Income Security Act (ERISA).** Prior to ERISA, pension sponsors were legally responsible for their actions under a somewhat loose common-law principle known as the Prudent Man rule. Historically, the **Prudent Man rule** evaluated the risk of a security in isolation from other securities held in the portfolio and required that professional fiduciaries purchase only securities with low enough risks that a "prudent man" would also own them. In 1974, Congress enacted ERISA, the first nationwide statutory law to regulate the management of corporate pension funds. In many ways, the intent of ERISA was similar to the Prudent Man rule. However, it differs in two important aspects. First, *the risk of a security is now considered in the context of the total portfolio.* Thus, a very risky security may now be purchased (although it may not have been allowed under the Prudent Man rule) if its risk is offset by other securities in the portfolio. Second, *ERISA explicitly requires that sponsors diversify the investments of the plan so as to minimize the risk of large losses, unless under the circumstances it is clearly prudent not to do so.* In short, ERISA is a legislated version of what modern portfolio theory says the Prudent Man rule should be.

Only corporate pension funds must follow ERISA requirements. All other professional fiduciaries are still subject to the common-law Prudent Man rule. However, if logic prevails, legal interpretation of the Prudent Man rule will move more closely toward the risk and diversification concepts inherent in ERISA.

PBGC. At the same time Congress enacted ERISA, it created a governmental agency that guarantees certain minimum benefit payments to employees belonging to defined benefit plans. This agency is the **Pension Benefit Guarantee Corporation (PBGC).** It plays a role analogous to that of the Federal Deposit Insurance Corporation, which guarantees deposits in national banks and savings and loans. PBGC, however, guarantees pension benefits to employees of corporations that default on their pension promises—usually through firm bankruptcy. All firms that fall under ERISA are required to pay a yearly in-surance fee to the PBGC for each member of their defined benefit plans. Since govern-mental pension plans do not fall under ERISA, their future benefits are not guaranteed by the PBGC.

Considerations in Setting Objectives and Constraints. Sponsors of defined bene-fit plans are interested, of course, in the risk/reward characteristics of their investment portfolios. But this is solely because a portfolio's expected return and risk directly affect both expected contributions and uncertainty about such contributions. The objective of a defined benefit plan sponsor is to minimize expected contribution costs without accepting undue risk. Portfolio risk and return must be viewed in this context—as one of a number of factors that influence expected contribution levels and uncertainty.

In view of this, let's examine the constraints we've discussed before:

1. **Risk level.** Again, this depends on the circumstances facing the pension sponsor as well as the sponsor's tolerance for risk. For example, consider a plan that is underfunded, fairly mature, and unable to draw large contributions from the sponsoring corporation or governing body. Such a plan will have to be exposed to larger investment risk in the hopes of greater returns than otherwise. An opposite example would be a plan that is fully funded today.

   Sponsors of this second plan would probably accept less return (and risk) than they would in other circumstances. In short, the risk level a pension plan selects will depend on both the sponsor's risk tolerance and the financial circumstances facing the plan.

2. **Allowable securities.** Because of their large size, most pension funds have the financial ability and investment sophistication to hold a diverse group of different asset classes. For example, direct and indirect investment in real estate equity, international investment, venture capital pools, and so forth, are widely used.

3. **Diversification.** Again, because of their size and investment sophistication, pension plans can purchase a wide variety of asset types in order to increase portfolio diversification. Examples were mentioned earlier and include real estate, foreign investment, and venture capital projects.

4. **Taxes and liquidity.** Pensions do not pay taxes on investment income. As a result, holdings of securities that provide major tax advantages need to be closely evaluated. For example, municipal bonds and preferred stock are rarely purchased. Similarly, much of the return on equity investment in depreciable real estate comes in the form of tax advantages that the pension cannot realize.

   With rare exceptions, the benefit liabilities of pension funds are long term. As a result, there is little need for liquidity and immediate cash flow.

5. **Speculation.** Sponsors of pension plans have access to the best information available through myriad investment consultants. As a result, they are usually aware of the arguments in favor of or against active speculation. Many pension funds have, in fact, concluded that the best approach is to index—to purchase money market, bond, and equity index funds as well as to immunize via dedicated portfolios. Most pension funds, however, have not given up the search for speculative profits. Nonetheless, they maintain close control of the risks that

their managers are able to accept. Managers are usually assigned specific roles. For example, an equity manager might be told to invest only in high-quality, low-beta securities, and a bond manager might be told to guarantee a return via contingent immunization. In short, to the extent speculation is allowed, the sponsor maintains active control over total portfolio risk.

Defined Contribution Plans. In recent years, most newly formed pension plans are defined contribution plans. Their advantages over defined benefit plans include the following:

1. **Administrative costs.** Growing regulation of defined benefit plans and yearly insurance payments to the Pension Benefit Guarantee Corporation have caused many employers who are creating new pension plans to select a defined contribution form.
2. **Investment risk.** Employers bear all investment risk of a defined benefit plan. Recognizing that pension assets are essentially retirement savings plans for employees, many plan sponsors have chosen to pass investment risk to the employee by using the defined contribution plan.
3. **Portability.** Portability refers to employees' ability to take their pension assets from one employer to another when they switch employment. While defined benefit plans are not portable, many (not all) defined contribution plans are portable.

Defined contribution plans are basically tax-sheltered retirement savings plans for employees. Since employees bear all investment risk, they should (in theory) decide the way in which their pension assets should be allocated across various asset classes. But assuring employees make well-informed decisions requires that the employer provide an educational program detailing the expected returns and risks of each asset class available to employees. Typically, the employer will select a number of investment managers who manage various security classes—thus providing employees a wide range of choices. Each employee is allowed to decide the proportion of their pension assets that are allocated to each manager. In some situations, however, the employer, believing the employee is not knowledgeable enough, makes the asset allocation decision of all employees as a pool.

S U M M A R Y

In this chapter we discussed the portfolio investment process. This process consists of three logical stages:

- ◼ Planning. The needs, knowledge, and risk tolerance of the investor are brought together with long-run capital market expectations to define the investor's long-run strategic asset allocation (SAA). The SAA decision should consist of two subdecisions: (1) what the current SAA should be, and (2) how the SAA should be passively rebalanced as time passes, as the investor's wealth changes, or as stock prices change. The portfolio objective, constraints, and all speculative strategies that are to be allowed should be formally documented in a written statement of investment policy.

■ Implementation. Once the strategic asset allocation has been determined, various speculative strategies can be considered. Such strategies fall into two broad approaches: timing and selection. Timing decisions over- and underweight various asset classes, industries, or economic sectors in an attempt to earn excess risk-adjusted returns. Such timing decisions are referred to as tactical asset allocation decisions. Security selection speculation consists of over- or underweighting individual securities within a given asset class. If timing and selection strategies are not used, then the investor's portfolio should consist of index funds that are held in proportions consistent with the SAA. If security prices are efficiently priced, timing and selection decisions will result in a loss of value because of transaction costs.

■ Monitoring. The portfolio should be periodically monitored to ensure that all constraints of the statement of investment policy are being met and to monitor returns from asset allocation and speculative strategies.

R E V I E W   P R O B L E M

You are examining the financial condition and investment policies of two defined benefit pension plans, Yung Technology and Auld Land Signs. Information about each follows:

	Yung	Auld
Current Investment Portfolio Value	$5.0 million	$60.0 million
Employee Information		
Number of employees	1,000	1,000
Average current salary	$20,000	$30,000
Benefit payments as % of final salary	25%	25%
Average years to retirement	30	15
Actuarial Assumptions		
Annual salary growth	4%	4%
Mortality rate prior to retirement	0%	0%
Employee termination preretirement	0%	0%
Retirement cost-of-living increases	0%	0%
Average years of retirement	15 years	15 years
Investment Portfolio Assumptions		
Desired stock/bond mix	70%/30%	30%/70%
Expected nominal stock return (per year)	10%	10%
Expected nominal bond return (per year)	4%	4%
Funding Policy	Year-end annuity to fully fund requirements by end of last employment year	

a. What are the basic differences in the benefit liabilities of each firm?

b. Both Yung and Auld want the value of their investment portfolios to be sufficient to meet the retirement benefits of their employees. Specifically, their goals are to have portfolio values on the last day of an average person's employment equal to the present value of expected future benefit liabilities. What is this desired portfolio value for each firm?

c. Given the asset allocation chosen by each firm, is the current portfolio value sufficient to meet the needs of part b?

d. If Yung wishes to make year-end level-dollar (annuity) contributions to its investment portfolio, what must the contribution be?

Solution

a. The plans differ principally in their maturities. The Yung pension plan has an employee base with an average of 30 years to retirement. In contrast, the Auld pension plan's employees will retire on average in 15 years. All other things being equal, Yung can accept greater investment risk.

b. Present Value of Benefit Liabilities at Average Retirement Date

Benefit Annuity	Yung	Auld
Current Salary Base	$20.000 million	$30.000 million
Compound Rate of Growth to		
Average Retirement	1.04^{30}	1.04^{15}
Retirement Salary Base	$64.868 million	$54.028 million
Benefit Payment Rate	0.25	0.25
15-Year Benefit Annuity	$16.217 million	$13.507 million
Actuarial Investment Return		
Stock Return $(0.7 \times 10\%)$	7.0%	
$(0.3 \times 10\%)$		3.0%
Bond Return $(0.3 \times 4\%)$	1.2%	
$(0.7 \times 4\%)$		2.8%
Expected Portfolio Return	8.2%	5.8%
Present Value Factor of a 15-Year Annuity		

$$\sum_{t=1}^{15} \frac{1}{1.082^t}$$

$$\sum_{t=11}^{15} \frac{1}{1.058^t}$$

= 8.4559   = 9.8404

Present Value of Annuity

    $(8.4559 \times \$16.217)$ $137.129 million

    $(9.8404 \ \$13.507)$ $132.914 million

c.   Growth of Current Portfolio with No Contributions

	Yung	Auld
Current Portfolio Value	$ 5.0 million	$ 60.0 million
Compound Rate of Growth	1.082^{30}	1.058^{15}
Expected Portfolio Value	$53.18 million	$139.78 million

The Auld pension plan has assets that are expected to grow to more than necessary to meet future benefit liabilities. It is overfunded slightly. Management could either reduce the investment risk exposure by investing less in stocks or withdraw some of the assets from the portfolio. Regardless of any such decisions, future contributions are not expected to be needed.

Since the Yung pension plan does not have sufficient current portfolio assets to meet expected benefit liabilities, Yung will have to provide future contributions and may wish to increase its commitments to stocks in order to increase the expected investment returns.

d. Future value annuity factor with interest = 8.2% and period = 30 years is:

$$\sum_{t=0}^{29} 1.082^t = 117.524$$

Value of Liability at Retirement = $137.129 million

Expected Current Portfolio Value = 53.180 million

Deficiency = $83.949 million

Required Annual Contribution = 83.949 ÷ 117.524

= $0.714 million

QUESTIONS   AND   PROBLEMS

1. Consider the data given in the review problem for Yung Technology. Discuss the interrelationship between (a) the expected contribution level and its uncertainty, and (b) the asset allocation decision.

CFA

2. You are being interviewed for a job as a portfolio manager at an investment counseling partnership. As part of the interview, you are asked to demonstrate your ability to develop investment portfolio policy statements for the clients described here:

   a. A pension fund that is described as a mature defined benefit plan, with the work force having an average age of 54. There are no unfunded pension liabilities, and wage-cost increases are forecast at 9% annually.

   b. A university endowment fund that is described as conservative, with investment returns being utilized along with gifts and donations to meet current expenses. The spending rate is 5% per year and inflation in costs is expected at 8% annually.

   c. A life insurance company that is described as specializing in annuities. Policy premium rates are based on a minimum annual accumulation rate of 14% in the first year of the policy and a 10% minimum annual accumulation rate in the next five years.

   List and discuss the objective and constraints that will determine the portfolio policy that you would recommend for each client.

CFA

3. John Smalle, an associate in your firm, has asked you to help him establish a financial plan for his family's future. John is 27 years old and has been with your firm for two years. Anne, his 26-year-old wife, is employed as a psychologist for the local school district. They are childless now but may have children in a few years. John and Anne have accumulated $10,000 in savings and recently inherited $50,000 in cash. They believe they can save at least $5,000 yearly. They are currently in a 25% income tax bracket and both have excellent career opportunities. They are eager to develop a financial plan and

understand it will need to be periodically adjusted as their circumstances change. You tell John you would be happy to meet with Anne and him to discuss their financial plans.

   a. Identify and describe an appropriate investment objective and investment constraints for the Smalles and prepare a comprehensive investment policy statement based on the objective and constraints.

   b. State and explain your asset allocation recommendations for the Smalles based on the policy statement you developed in part a.

4. Jason Robertson is a successful business executive who voluntarily retired at age 63 after 40 years of service with a privately owned firm of which he was a shareholder. He is married and has three adult children who are married and self-supporting. At time of retirement Mr. Robertson owned his own home free and clear of mortgages, held $25,000 in life insurance, and had savings and a miscellaneous list of good-quality bonds and stocks aggregating $50,000 in value. He is also entitled to a yearly pension of $30,000, which is fully funded and has survivor's benefits to his wife of $17,000. Upon retirement, he liquidated the preferred and common shares acquired in his company over a span of 25 years under a stock purchase plan and realized cash of $170,000 (net, after provision for capital gains taxes). As a retirement benefit, Mr. Robertson and his wife are also entitled to the protection of a major medical group health insurance program fully subsidized by his firm.

   As he reviews his financial position at retirement, Mr. Robertson considers himself quite well off, but he believes he should obtain some professional advice about the proper management of his capital resources at this stage of his life. Accordingly, he makes an appointment with you as an investment counselor to discuss his financial affairs. During an initial conversation, you learn that he requires an annual pretax income of $45,000 to $50,000 to maintain his present standard of living, and he would like to leave as large an estate as possible for his three children. He is concerned about the effects that inflation and taxation may have on his desired income and asset objectives.

   a. Discuss the general investment policy Mr. Robertson should follow to attain his financial objectives.

   b. Exhibit A indicates various categories of securities available, assumed yields, and three portfolios that have been constructed for the $220,000 Mr. Robertson has available for investment. Select and justify the portfolio that you think is most appropriate for Mr. Robertson to achieve his investment objectives.

5. You are the chief investment officer for your company's pension fund and are preparing for the next meeting of the Investment Committee. Several committee members are interested in reviewing and updating past discussions relating to the use of index funds for your pension fund, which utilizes both internal management and multiple external managers. Prepare brief answers to the following requests from committee members:

   a. Cite and explain four reasons why consideration should be given to using an index fund.

   b. Cite two decisions that are part of the investment process and should have priority over the decision about whether or not to use an index fund.

   c. Cite and explain four strategies and/or operating features that could cause an index fund portfolio to have a different return from the index itself.

   d. Explain why the following are, or are not, suitable indexes on which to base an index fund:

      (1) The Dow Jones Industrial Average

      (2) Standard & Poor's 500 Stock Index

EXHIBIT A   Three Portfolio Alternatives

Category of Security	Recent Market Yield	Portfolio No. 1	Portfolio No. 2	Portfolio No. 3
Money Market Securities	9.50%	$10,000	$10,000	$10,000
Government Bonds				
Short-Term	8.98			20,000
Intermediate-Term	9.57		10,000	30,000
Long-Term	10.06			50,000
Long-Term Corporate Bonds				
AAA Rated	9.26			50,000
AA Rated	9.46			
A Rated	9.62		30,000	
BBB Rated	10.10		20,000	
Tax-Exempt Municipal Bonds	6.30	80,000	20,000	
Preferred Stocks	8.86			20,000
Transportation Common Stocks	4.95			
Utility Common Stocks	8.95	10,000	30,000	20,000
Financial Common Stocks	5.30	10,000	20,000	
Industrial Common Stocks	5.00	110,000	80,000	20,000
Total		$220,000	$220,000	$220,000

CFA

6. You are a portfolio manager and senior executive vice president of Advisory Securities Selection, Inc. Your firm has been invited to meet with the trustees of the Wood Museum Endowment Fund. Wood Museum is a privately endowed charitable institution that depends on the investment return from a $25 million endowment fund to balance the budget. The treasurer of the museum has recently completed a study that indicates a need for cash flows from the endowment fund of $3.0 million in 1982, $3.2 million in 1983, and $3.5 million in 1984 in order to balance the budget. At the present time, the entire endowment portfolio is invested in T-bills and money market funds because the trustees fear a financial crisis. The trustees do not anticipate any further capital contributions to the fund. The trustees are all successful businesspeople, and they have been critical of the fund's previous investment advisers for not following a logical decision-making process. In fact, several previous managers have been dismissed because of their inability to communicate with the trustees and their preoccupation with the fund's relative performance rather than the cash flow needs.

   Advisory Securities Selection, Inc., has been contacted by the trustees because of its reputation for understanding and relating to its clients' needs. The trustees have specifically asked to meet with you because of your recent article in a professional journal outlining the decision-making process of your firm. In the letter of invitation addressed to you, the trustees have included the flow chart in Exhibit B and the following quotations from a speech by Professor William F. Sharpe that were included in the article:

   It is important to understand that, even if the market were perfectly efficient with every security plotting right on the plane, the investment management process

EXHIBIT B   The Portfolio Managment Process

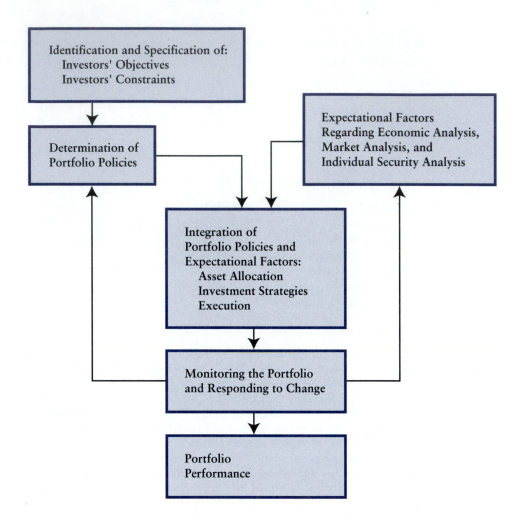

would still require sophisticated procedures. In particular, it would require the tailoring of portfolios to meet clients' attitudes toward risk and clients' attitudes toward yield vis-à-vis gains.

One important part of this exercise [modern portfolio theory] is finding out what the client is all about—where one client differs from another.

The trustees have asked you, as a prospective portfolio manager for the Wood Museum Endowment Fund, to prepare a written report in response to the following questions. Your report will be circulated to the trustees prior to the initial interview on June 15.

a. Explain in detail how each of the following relates to the determination of either investor objectives or investor constraints that can be used to determine the portfolio policies for this three-year period for the Wood Museum Endowment Fund:

- ■ Liquidity requirements
- ■ Return requirements
- ■ Risk tolerance
- ■ Time horizon
- ■ Tax considerations
- ■ Regulatory and legal considerations
- ■ Unique needs and circumstances

b. Interest rate futures, common stock options, immunization, and international diversification are investment strategies that can be used as modifiers of portfolio risk.

    (1) Explain how each of these four investment strategies can be used to modify portfolio risk.
    (2) Identify and explain which one of these four strategies is most suitable for the Wood Museum Endowment Fund.

CFA

7. You have been named as investment adviser to a foundation established by Dr. Walter Jones with an original contribution consisting entirely of the common stock of Jomedco, Inc. Founded by Dr. Jones, Jomedco manufactures and markets medical devices invented by the doctor and collects royalties on other patented innovations.

All of the shares that made up the initial contribution to the foundation were sold at a public offering of Jomedco common stock and the $5 million proceeds will be delivered to the foundation within the next week. At the same time, Mrs. Jones will receive $5 million in proceeds from the sale of her stock in Jomedco.

Dr. Jones's purpose in establishing the Jones Foundation was to offset the effect of inflation on medical school tuition for the maximum number of worthy students.

You are preparing for a meeting with the foundation trustees to discuss investment policy and asset allocation.

a. Define and give examples that show the differences between an investment objective, an investment constraint, and an investment policy.

b. Identify and describe an appropriate investment objective and set of investment constraints for the Jones Foundation.

c. Based on the investment objective and constraints identified in part b, prepare a comprehensive investment policy statement for the Jones Foundation to be recommended for adoption by the trustees.

d. Discuss the issues involved in determining whether or not the investment adviser should make the asset allocation decision for the Jones Foundation investment portfolio.

e. Identify and describe the critical capital market variables required for a two-asset allocation model for the Jones Foundation.

f. Discuss the difficulties associated with using historical information in making estimates of each of the critical variables enumerated in part e.

CFA

8. Jack Quick and Heidi Bronson have been discussing the CFA Level I study materials as they relate to the determination of portfolio policies for different types of investors. Quick remembers reading that behind all investment portfolios are investors, each of whom is unique, and that there is literally a different set of portfolio management opportunities, needs, and circumstances for every investor. Because of this diversity of investor situations, Quick has concluded that it is impossible to generalize about portfolio policy determination—everything must be done on a case-by-case basis. Bronson agrees in terms of specific portfolio construction

but reminds Quick that there is a framework illustrated in the readings through which portfolio policies can be established for even the broadest range of investor types and interests.

a. Outline a broadly applicable framework for establishing portfolio policies, incorporating objectives and constraints, such as the one that Bronson has recalled.

b. Bronson is working on a defined benefit retirement portfolio for a sizable and growing corporation with a young work force. Quick is working on a modest personal portfolio now providing essential income to a 70-year-old widow whose assets pass on her death to her children. Apply your part a framework to each of these investment situations, taking into account all of the relevant framework elements. (You may find it helpful to use a matrix format for this answer.)

D A T A F I L E   A N A L Y S I S

Communication of Investment Risk. Access the annual returns in the INDEXES data set. How might you communicate the historical risks and returns associated with U.S. money market securities, U.S. fixed income securities, U.S. equities, and foreign equities to individuals who have no formal training in finance or statistics?

R E F E R E N C E S

A thorough treatment of the investment process can be found in Maginn, John L., and Donald L. Tuttle, *Managing Investment Portfolios.* Sponsored initially by the Chartered Financial Analysts (now the Association for Investment Management and Research). Boston: Warren, Gorham and Lamont, 1983.

Recent articles related to the process of portfolio management include the following:

Brealey, Richard A. "Portfolio Theory Versus Portfolio Practice," *The Journal of Portfolio Management,* Summer 1990.

Lee, Wayne Y. "Diversification and Time: Do Investment Horizons Matter?" *The Journal of Portfolio Management,* Spring 1990.

Wagner, Wayne H. and Michael Banks, "Increasing Effectiveness via Transaction Cost Management," *The Journal of Portfolio Management,* Fall 1992.

Zeikel, Arthur. "Investment Management in the 1990's," *Financial Analysts Journal,* September–October 1990.

An interesting discussion of the investment policy statement was presented in the *Financial Analysts Journal.* The first article in September–October 1990 presented a mock policy statement about which readers were asked to comment. The follow-up article discussed the reactions to the mock policy statement.

Good, Walter R. and Douglas A. Love, "Investment Policy Statement," *Financial Analysts Journal,* September–October 1990.

Good, Walter R. and Douglas A. Love, "Reactions to the Investment Policy Statement," *Financial Analysts Journal,* March–April 1991.

19

ASSET ALLOCATION

After reading this chapter you should have an understanding of the importance of portfolio asset allocation and how both strategic and tactical asset allocation are conducted.

Choosing the portfolio's asset allocation is clearly the most important investment decision an investor must make. It is the prime force driving future average returns and volatility.

This chapter examines three topics. The first section briefly reviews a study documenting the importance of a portfolio's asset allocation. The following two sections discuss, in turn, strategic asset allocation and tactical asset allocation. Recall from our discussion in Chapter 18 that strategic asset allocation (SAA) represents the asset allocation that investors choose if they believe aggregate security asset classes are efficiently priced. Tactical asset allocation (TAA) represents the asset allocation that investors choose if they believe certain security asset classes are mispriced.

Importance of Asset Allocation

Many studies document the importance of asset allocation in well-diversified portfolios. A recent study by Brinson, Singer, and Beebower (BSB) is an interesting example. They looked at the quarterly returns of 82 pension funds during the ten years ending in 1987. Their study is unusual in that it examined returns of actual aggregate portfolios. Most previous studies examined the returns of single investment managers, usually an equity mutual fund. Since ownership of an individual mutual fund often represents only a part of an investor's total portfolio, prior studies looked at only a piece of the total picture.

The BSB study estimated how a pension fund's actual return could be split into returns arising from the following:

1. The pension fund's strategic asset allocation (SAA).
2. Any tactical asset allocation (TAA) decisions.
3. Security selection decisions of managers employed by the fund.
4. Other effects due to interactions and errors of measurement on their part.

The study's basic findings are shown in Tables 19-1 and 19-2. Table 19-1 shows the rate of returns (annualized) associated with each decision. The average actual fund return was 13.41%. A passive investment based on each fund's SAA would have earned a return of 13.49%. That means the average pension fund in the sample (1) would have earned more if investors had passively invested in their SAA, and (2) a greater part of

TABLE 19-1   DETERMINANTS OF PORTFOLIO PERFORMANCE (82 PENSIONS, 1977–1987)

Return Due to:	Average	Maximum	Minimum
Strategic Asset Allocation	13.49%	14.56	12.43%
Tactical Asset Allocation	−0.26	0.86	−1.81
Security Selection	+0.26	6.12	−3.32
Not Measurable	−0.08	1.33	−3.50
Actual Return	13.41%	NA	NA

NA: Not applicable, since minimum or maximum in each category do not apply to the same pension fund.
SOURCE: Based on results in G. Brinson, B. Singer, and G. Beebower, "Determinants of Portfolio Performance II: An Update," *Financial Analysts Journal,* May–June 1991.

TABLE 19-2   PERCENTAGE OF VARIATION IN RETURNS CAUSED BY PASSIVE AND ACTIVE DECISIONS

Percentage of Return Variation due to:	Average	Maximum	Minimum
Strategic Asset Allocation Plus	91.5%	98.2%	67.7%
Tactical Asset Allocation Plus	93.3	98.3	69.4
Security Selection	96.1	99.8	76.2

SOURCE: Based on results in G. Brinson, B. Singer, and G. Beebower, "Determinants of Portfolio Performance II: An Update," *Financial Analysts Journal,* May–June 1991.

the average pension return was due to the SAA it chose. On average, TAA resulted in a negative 0.26% yearly return. Security selection decisions by investment managers contributed an average yearly return of 0.26%. But the security selection returns ranged from −3.32% to 6.12%.

We should not conclude from Table 19-1 that security selection techniques work and timing techniques do not, since the results are based on a sample of only 82 portfolios. In addition, the extent to which these portfolios actually attempted to time, the effects of management fees, differences in procedures used to calculate return, and so forth, create an uncertainty about the precision of the results. Any one of these items could swamp a 26 basis-point outcome. The data in Table 19-2 confirms the importance of a portfolio's SAA. When a pension fund's actual portfolio returns were regressed against the returns that would have been achieved by passive investment in its SAA, the average R-square was 91.5%. This means that over 90% of all variation in portfolio returns can be traced to the portfolio's SAA. Other decisions are relatively minor.

When regressions were expanded to include returns from TAA, the average R-square increased from 91.5% to 93.3%. And when security selection returns were added, the average R^2 rose to 96.1%. These results imply that TAA and security selection decisions have an effect on portfolio returns but that the dominant factor in diversified portfolios is clearly strategic asset allocation.

Strategic Asset Allocation

A variety of approaches are used in practice to establish the desired strategic asset allocation. Here, we examine four:

* Cash flow requirements.

* Historical risk/return tables.

* Asset pricing models.

* Efficient diversification.

The section concludes with a review of a much misunderstood issue—time diversification.

Cash Flow Requirements

Perhaps the most naive approach attempts to develop an asset mix that will provide interest and dividend cash flow to match the cash needs of the portfolio owner. For example, assume a $10 million endowment fund has anticipated cash outflows of $600,000 for the next year. Current yields on U.S. T-bonds are 11%, and the Standard & Poor's Composite has a dividend yield of 4%. If interest and dividend receipts are to be equal to $600,000, 71.43% of the portfolio should be invested in stocks and 28.57% invested in bonds:

	Dollar Investment	$\times$	*Current Yield*	$=$	*Cash Inflow*
Stocks	$7,143,000	$\times$	4%	$=$	$285,720
Bonds	2,857,000	$\times$	11%	$=$	314,270
	$10,000,000				$599,990

The advantage of this approach is its simplicity. Apart from that, it is wrong. For example, it makes no provision for required future growth in cash outflows. To illustrate, assume the endowment's cash outflows will grow at a 9% annual rate. If the growth rate associated with the common stocks being evaluated is 11% and the growth rate of bonds is 0%, then the 71.43%/28.57% stock/bond allocation will provide a portfolio growth rate of only 7.8% (11% $\times$ 0.7143). The artificial requirement that interest and dividends be the sole source of required cash outflows leads to poor decisions.

But the conceptual fault of this approach is even more fundamental: It ignores the risks associated with portfolios being evaluated. There are numerous stock/bond portfolios that provide expected returns large enough to cover the current and future cash flow needs of this investor. However, they differ considerably in risk. Any asset allocation decision should explicitly consider both the risks and the expected returns associated with the allocation.

Historical Risk/Return Tables

One commonly used way to communicate the risks and returns associated with various asset mixes is to provide tabled values of historical returns. An example is shown in Table 19-3. Two asset classes are evaluated: (1) a GIC (guaranteed investment contract) that is assumed to provide a guaranteed real return (after inflation), and (2) common stocks as proxied by past annual real returns on the S&P 500 Index. Returns are shown for six portfolios ranging from 100% invested in a GIC to 100% in the S&P Composite.

The 50th percentile column shows the portfolio return that should be expected if the future is the same as the past and if the investor holds the portfolio for a one-year period. For

TABLE 19-3   PERCENTILE RETURN DISTRIBUTION ONE-YEAR HOLDING PERIOD

	Asset Mix		Percentile Return				
Portfolio	GIC	S&P 500	10th	25th	50th	75th	90th
A	100%	0%	1.0%	1.0%	1.0%	1.0%	1.0%
B	80	20	−2.8	−0.2	2.6	5.61	8.4
C	60	40	−6.5	−1.5	4.3	8.5	12.6
D	40	60	−10.0	−2.8	5.9	15.4	24.7
E	20	80	−13.5	−4.1	7.6	20.6	33.7
F	0	100	−16.8	−5.3	9.2	26.0	43.4

example, if the future is the same as the past period used in creating the table, the expected return on a stock portfolio that is held for one year and is similar to the S&P 500 is 9.2%.

Columns to the left and right of the expected return show the rate of return for various probabilities. For example, if 100% is held in stock, there is a 10% chance that the annual return will be less than (or equal to) −16.8%. Similarly, there is a 10% chance that the return will be greater than 43.4%. Since many people find it difficult to interpret standard deviations, historical return tables such as this example are used by professional investment counselors to communicate the manner in which asset allocation determines both expected portfolio returns and risks.

Tables can also be used to illustrate how the length of the holding period affects potential annualized returns. For example, Table 19-4 provides similar data to Table 19-3 but for a ten-year investment horizon. The calculations used to develop forecasts such as those in Table 19-4 were discussed in Appendix 5A and are reviewed later in this chapter. The returns shown are not ten-year returns but, instead, are geometric annualized returns. Note that the range of potential realized annualized returns is smaller for the ten-year horizon than for the one-year interval. This observation is important when we discuss the potential for diversification across time later in this chapter.

Tables such as the ones just shown are valuable tools for expressing the returns and risks associated with various asset mixes. They communicate useful information to portfolio owners who are unfamiliar with statistics such as variance and covariance. But they do have weaknesses. Such as the following:

1. The data are very sensitive to the time period chosen. It is not unusual that the inclusion or exclusion of a few years of returns will result in figures that differ by more than 150 basis points. As such, the data should not be interpreted too strictly. Instead, they should be viewed as illustrative of the potential return and risk levels.
2. Many asset classes simply do not have a history of returns that can be trusted. Examples include real estate and international assets.
3. When more than two asset classes are being considered, tabled values become unwieldy to use.

TABLE 19-4 PERCENTILE RETURN DISTRIBUTION ANNUALIZED GEOMETRIC AVERAGE FOR A 10-YEAR HOLDING PERIOD

Portfolio	GIC	S&P 500	10th	25th	50th	75th	90th
A	100	0	1.0%	1.0%	1.0%	1.0%	1.0%
B	80	20	0.9	1.7	2.6	3.6	4.4
C	60	40	0.8	2.4	4.3	6.2	7.9
D	40	60	0.6	3.1	5.9	8.8	11.5
E	20	80	0.4	3.7	7.6	11.5	15.2
F	0	100	0.2	4.4	9.2	14.2	19.0

4. Many people believe that the distribution of past returns is not a good proxy for potential future returns.
5. This approach illustrates risks and average returns on arbitrarily selected portfolio combinations. There is no attempt to isolate efficient portfolios for various risk levels.

Asset Pricing Models

Two major theories exist that attempt to define risk and explain the market value of any asset: the capital asset pricing model and arbitrage pricing theory. Both have implications for an investor's decision on strategic asset allocation.

The Capital Asset Pricing Model. As we discussed in Chapters 7 and 8, the capital asset pricing model (CAPM) has a great deal to say about the optimal portfolio of risky assets for any investor. In particular, the CAPM implies that people should own all risky assets in proportions which depend on the total market values of each asset. For example, if U.S. corporate bonds represent 15% of the value of all risky securities, then 15% of everyone's **risky** security portfolio should consist of U.S. corporate bonds. Once such a risky portfolio has been acquired, there are no further diversification benefits to be gained. If this portfolio is too risky, it can be held in combination with a risk-free security. If it is not risky enough, then the investor should borrow (at the risk-free rate) and invest the borrowings. In short, the CAPM suggests that the optimal risky asset portfolio is the market portfolio of all risky assets.

Although the CAPM is a profound conceptual tool, its practical implications should not be interpreted too strictly. People have differing investment horizons, tax rates, transaction costs, and so forth—each causing different optimal asset mixes. Investment concepts such as the value of diversification and the importance of systematic risk needn't be abandoned. However, the optimal allocation of different classes of assets must consider the unique needs of each portfolio. The CAPM should be used only as a theoretical starting point from which actual portfolios are created that better fulfill the needs of the portfolio owner.

Arbitrage Pricing Theory. In contrast to the CAPM, arbitrage pricing theory (APT) does not give any special importance to the market portfolio of all risky assets. It suggests that a variety of economic risks might be nondiversifiable. As a result, investors will demand a risk premium to accept such risks. Examples of such "priced" risk factors might include inflation, industrial production, default risk, and the slope of the yield curve. If you subscribe to the notion of APT, the first thing you should do is eliminate the non-priced, diversifiable risks by broad diversification. Next, you should specify the priced factors on which you wish to place your bets or to hedge against. For example, if you wish to hold a portfolio that is neutral to all factors, the portfolio sensitivity to each factor should be 1.0. This would result in a risky security portfolio virtually identical to the market portfolio of CAPM. A fully diversified portfolio would have a beta of 1.0 on each non-diversifiable factor risk.

The potential advantage of APT over CAPM lies in the ability to hedge risks in assets and liabilities that the investor incurs outside the marketable security portfolio. For example, assume the investor is the sponsor of a defined benefit pension plan whose business is heavily influenced by unexpected changes in inflation. To partially hedge this risk, securities with large sensitivities to an inflation factor would be underweighted.

As with the CAPM, there are substantial problems in basing a strategic asset allocation (SAA) on the principles of APT. Most important, we don't know what the priced APT factors are! Various consulting firms have assumed a variety of potential return factors, but the empirical evidence that such factors indeed exist is debated by scholars. Yet APT remains an important way to think about problems.

Efficient Asset Allocation

If the investor can develop reasonable estimates of expected returns, standard deviations, and correlation coefficients between security classes, then Markowitz mean-variance efficient portfolios can be found. The process of finding efficient portfolios consists of the following four steps:

1. Segment portfolio needs.
2. Select asset classes.
3. Develop market expectations.
4. Evaluate the efficient frontier for a desired horizon date.

Segment Portfolio Needs. Often the investment portfolio is intended to meet a variety of needs. For example, pension fund portfolios are expected to provide investment returns to help pay benefits to two distinct groups of individuals: (1) past employees who are currently receiving pension benefits, and (2) present employees who will receive benefits at a distant future date. The nature of the liability to each group can be quite different. In the case of "retired lives," the liability is relatively short term, virtually known with certainty, and often in the form of nominal dollars. Thus, the retired-lives portion of the pension plan is ideal for some form of bond immunization. In contrast, the nonretired-lives portion of a pension's liability stream is long term, difficult to predict with precision, and usually varies directly with inflation. As such, it is much less suitable for immunization techniques.

Select Asset Classes. When asset classes are defined, they should be as distinctly different from each other as possible in order to provide the greatest potential for diversification. For example, little is gained by adding a "call option group" to a portfolio that otherwise consists of T-bills and common stock. This is because a call option is essentially a long position in a given stock and a short position in T-bills. In the same fashion, returns on Treasury note financial futures are highly correlated with spot Treasury notes and bonds. In short, little value is associated with including asset classes that are highly correlated.

Many asset classes, however, have returns that are relatively uncorrelated. For example, Table 19-5 presents correlation coefficients on a number of asset classes using annual real returns (after inflation) for the period 1969 through 1994. Returns prior to 1969 were not available for PRISA and the EAFE indexes.[1]

---

[1] PRISA is a commingled equity real estate portfolio managed by Prudential Insurance. It is used here as a proxy for real estate equity investment returns.

TABLE 19-5   CORRELATION COEFFICIENTS, STANDARD DEVIATION, AND AVERAGE RETURNS ON SELECTED ASSET CLASSES (REAL RETURNS, 1969–1994)

Correlation Coefficients

Class	T-bills	Govt. Bonds	S&P 500	Small Company	PRISA	EAFE
T-bills	1.00					
Govt. Bonds	0.64	1.00				
S&P 500	0.41	0.56	1.00			
Small Co.	0.08	0.30	0.78	1.00		
PRISA	0.24	−0.14	0.22	0.26	1.00	
EAFE	0.27	0.37	0.63	0.46	0.30	1.00

Percentage Yearly Real Returns

	T-bills	Govt. Bonds	S&P 500	Small Company	PRISA	EAFE
Average	1.26	3.39	5.60	7.41	1.26	8.41
Standard Deviation	2.82	13.25	16.94	27.06	6.95	23.86

The number of different asset classes that an investor should consider depends in large part on the size of the portfolio and the knowledge of the investor. Once we move from well-known asset classes such as T-bills, government/corporate bonds, and common equities into less known asset classes such as real estate, international equities, and venture capital, there is a greater need for professional expertise. Yet there are no hard and fast rules relating portfolio size to classes of assets selected. The trade-off between potential diversification gains and increased formation costs is a decision unique to each portfolio.

To illustrate the value gained from broad asset allocation, the historical data in Table 19-5 were used in a computer program to find two ex post efficient frontiers. These are displayed in Figure 19-1. The frontier to the right consists of holdings of T-bills, government bonds, the S&P 500 (a proxy for large firms), real estate, and small company stocks. The frontier to the left adds holdings of non-U.S. equities. Notice that the efficient frontier which has the greater number of asset classes provides better risk/reward payoffs. This is the benefit of diversification across asset classes.

Develop Market Expectations. In order to develop Markowitz efficient frontiers, estimates must be made of the expected returns and covariances of returns on each asset class being evaluated. It is at this point that two difficult problems must be faced. First, how can the concept of a single-period efficient frontier be used in the context of a multiperiod decision? Second, how does one develop the expected returns and covariances that are used as inputs to the model?

A reasonable approach to solving the multiperiod problem is to estimate an average date at which there will be net cash outflows. This is done in much the same way that we calculate the duration of the cash inflows for a bond. For example, consider the following simplified example.

FIGURE 19-1   HISTORICAL EFFICIENT FRONTIERS

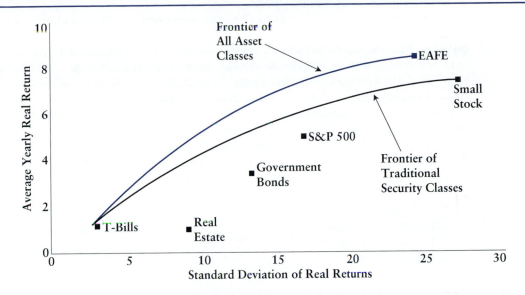

Assume a pension plan will have three equal cash outflows of $100 at the end of years 1, 2, and 3. In addition, the U.S. Treasury yield curve is flat at a yield to maturity of 10%. Note that the cash outflows to the pension plan are, in fact, cash inflows to the pension beneficiaries. In essence, the beneficiaries own a bond that promises to pay $100 at each year-end for three years. The duration of this bond is 1.9 years:

Year-End	Cash Flow	Present Value at 10%	Percentage of Total	Weighted Duration
1	$100	90.91%	36.66%	0.3666
2	100	82.64	33.33	0.6666
3	100	75.13	30.30	0.9090
Total		247.96		1.9422

If beneficiaries are correct in considering their benefits as having a 1.9-year duration, then the pension sponsors are also correct in considering their future liability stream as having the same duration.

By using the notion of duration, a multiperiod pension liability stream can be stated in terms of a single-period cash outflow. And the length of this single-period cash outflow can then be used as the horizon date in the Markowitz model. For example, in our example, the pension sponsor would evaluate expected returns and covariances on various asset groups assuming they are to be held for 1.9 years.

There are difficulties with this technique of reducing a multiperiod problem to a single-period problem. The liability stream is not known with certainty, the covariance between future benefits and security returns isn't considered, and the appropriate interest rate for calculating the duration is unclear. But until investment theory can offer something better, the calculation of benefit duration is a reasonable way to restate a multiperiod problem to fit the single-period asset selection model.

Although the precision of this approach can be questioned, one thing is clear: The risk associated with owning various classes of assets depends on how long one intends to own the assets. Many investors, particularly pension funds, are long-term investors. As such, it is inappropriate for them to evaluate the risk inherent in, say, common stocks by the volatility of one-year common stock returns. *Some attempt must be made to evaluate the risk of a security class over the anticipated holding period.*

Let's move now to the difficulties inherent in estimating expected returns and covariances for each asset class. Ideally, these are informed opinions held by the portfolio owner (pension sponsor) about the likely returns and uncertainty of each asset class. But where do these opinions come from? How can one estimate the required inputs?

In practice, four major approaches are widely used:

1. Historical data
2. Econometric simulations
3. Existing market prices
4. Personal opinion

Historical Data. Historical returns are available on many security classes. A widely used source for such returns is published papers and monographs periodically updated by Ibbotson Associates. They present a series of monthly returns on T-bills, U.S. government and corporate bonds, and the S&P 500 extending back to January 1926. They have also prepared historical estimates of returns on forms of real estate and international investments.

Historical returns are certainly the place to begin. But some care must be taken. Consider the following:

1. Many knowledgeable people believe the future that investors face in the late twentieth century is fundamentally different from the events that shaped the 1920s through 1980s. If this is true, the past will be a poor predictor of the future.
2. Some asset classes, such as international investments, have a very short history of past returns. And during the time periods for which such data are available, only a few major economic events shaped the pattern of returns. For example, the returns to U.S. investors on international securities were swamped by the deterioration of the U.S. foreign exchange rate during the 1970s and 1980s.
3. Some historical return estimates are very imprecise. Estimates of real estate returns, in particular, are usually based on appraised market values instead of actual market trading prices. This tends to smooth out returns and make real estate investment appear to be less risky than it is.

The information obtained from historical data can be sensitive to the time period examined. For example, consider the panels in Figure 19-2. In panel A, average yearly real returns are plotted for various 20-year periods. Each point in the panel represents the average return for the 20 years ended at the date of the point. It is obvious that average yearly returns, even over relatively long time spans, are quite volatile. In panel B, standard

FIGURE 19-2 TRENDS IN AVERAGE RETURNS OF VARIOUS ASSET CLASSES
TRENDS IN STANDARD DEVIATIONS OF VARIOUS ASSET CLASSES

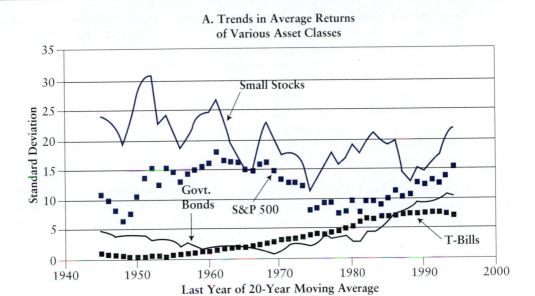

A. Trends in Average Returns
of Various Asset Classes

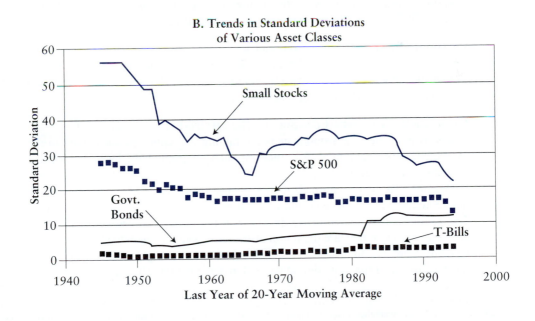

B. Trends in Standard Deviations
of Various Asset Classes

deviations of yearly returns based on a 20-year return series are shown. Although standard deviations are less sensitive to the time period chosen than are average returns, they also depend on the period evaluated. All efficient frontier data estimates based on historical data are sensitive to the historical time period evaluated. This, of course, is simply a result of the basic problem we are trying to deal with—risk.

Econometric Simulations. Econometric simulations are also available from a variety of consulting firms. These simulations are based on empirically tested economic relationships that tie various sectors of the economy together.

Simulations provide at least three principal aids to the analyst. First, developing and understanding the internal structure of the model forces analysts to be explicit in their opinions about the process generating security returns over time. Second, a large variety of alternative strategies can be experimented with to determine the ranges of potential returns during future years. Finally, input variables may be altered in an attempt to determine how sensitive the output is to various input factors. Naturally, the quality of the output is only as good as the quality of the model structure.

Existing Market Prices. Some people use existing market prices to estimate necessary efficient frontier inputs. For example, security analysts at Wells Fargo Bank forecast future dividend growth rates for a large number of stocks and then use these estimates together with each stock's existing market price to estimate expected rates of return. And prevailing yields to maturity (or yields to a given duration) can be used to estimate both current and expected future bond returns. In short, many of the needed inputs can be inferred from prevailing market prices.

Unfortunately, this is a very difficult task for many classes of assets, real estate and international equities in particular. In addition, none of these procedures is able to estimate the correlation coefficient between returns on alternative assets.

Personal Opinion. Certainly one can, and should, examine historical data, econometric simulations, and prevailing market prices. But, in the end, the personal opinion of the portfolio owner should decide the expected returns, standard deviations, and correlation coefficients necessary to determine an efficient frontier.

Evaluate the Efficient Frontier for the Desired Horizon Date. Once the needed inputs are available, it is a simple matter of finding a computer package that can compute a Markowitz efficient frontier. A number of such programs have been developed and are available at moderate cost.

Assume that after a thorough review of historical returns and expected long-run economic conditions, we develop the return distribution assumptions shown in Table 19-6. These represent our beliefs about the one-year return payoffs that we expect to prevail in the long run. Thus, they are the return distribution data on which the SAA decision should be made. They are not necessarily equal to forecasts we might make for the coming year. Such shorter term forecasts should be used in developing the TAA.[2]

---

[2] You might find it useful to compare the ex ante estimates in Table 19-6 with the ex post values in Table 19-5. Do you agree with the differences between the tables? Why or why not? By answering such questions you are beginning to develop ability to make ex ante forecasts.

TABLE 19-6   HYPOTHETICAL EX ANTE RETURN DISTRIBUTION ASSUMPTIONS ABOUT ONE-YEAR RETURNS EXPECTED OVER THE LONG RUN

Correlation Coefficients

Class	T-Bills	Govt. Bonds	Corp. Bonds	S&P 500	Small Company	Real Estate	Int'l. Equity
T-Bills	1.00						
Govt. Bonds	0.60	1.00					
Corp. Bonds	0.60	0.95	1.00				
S&P 500	0.20	0.30	0.30	1.00			
Small Company	0.12	0.20	0.20	0.80	1.00		
PRISA	0.25	0.05	0.05	0.35	0.40	1.00	
EAFE	0.30	0.40	0.40	0.60	0.40	0.30	1.00

Yearly Real Return

	T-Bills	Govt. Bonds	Corp. Bonds	S&P 500	Small Company	Real Estate	Int'l. Equity
Average	1.5%	2.5%	3.5%	8.5%	14.0%	5.0%	11.0%
Standard Deviation	4.0	10.0	11.0	20.0	40.0	15.0	30.0

The efficient frontier that results from these forecasts is shown in Figure 19-3. The composition of five efficient portfolios is shown at the bottom of the figure. Note that portfolio A is dominated by holdings of T-bills. But even such low-risk portfolios include small amounts of other asset classes—in this case, the S&P 500 and real estate—in order to obtain the benefits of diversification.

If an investor has a one-year investment horizon, then the one-year return payoffs shown in Figure 19-3 can be used to determine an appropriate SAA. Rarely, however, will the investment horizon be as short as one year. And, if it were, it is doubtful that forecasts of returns on international equities, corporate bonds, stocks, and so forth, would be necessary, since the SAA would probably be obvious: Invest primarily in one-year, low-default-risk money market instruments. In most cases, we need to determine the return outcomes of various one-year efficient portfolios over longer investment horizons.

In Table 19-7, the payoffs of portfolio C (shown in Figure 19-3) are displayed for various investment horizon dates. We do not review the mathematics underlying the projections, since they are relatively complex and are not needed for the purpose of our discussion.

Table 19-7 has two parts. In the top part, terminal wealth percentiles from initially investing $1 are shown. For example, if $1 is invested in portfolio C, there is a 1% chance the portfolio will be worth less than $0.81 or more than $1.39 after one year. If the investment horizon is one year, there is a significant probability that the portfolio will decline in value! In contrast, consider the 30-year investment horizon. At that point, there is a 1% chance the portfolio will be worth less than $1.30 or more than $25.28. With a 30-year investment horizon, there is little chance the portfolio's value will be less than the initial investment.

FIGURE 19-3 ESTIMATED EFFICIENT FRONTIER BASED ON ANNUAL
REAL RETURNS

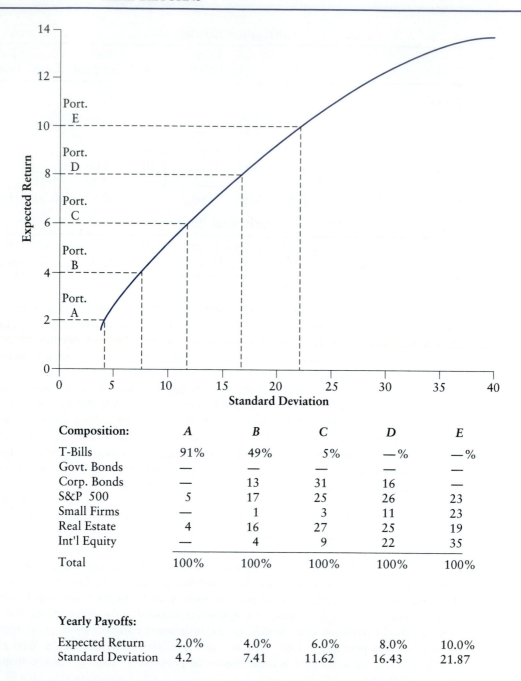

Composition:	A	B	C	D	E
T-Bills	91%	49%	5%	—%	—%
Govt. Bonds	—	—	—	—	—
Corp. Bonds	—	13	31	16	—
S&P 500	5	17	25	26	23
Small Firms	—	1	3	11	23
Real Estate	4	16	27	25	19
Int'l Equity	—	4	9	22	35
Total	100%	100%	100%	100%	100%

Yearly Payoffs:

	A	B	C	D	E
Expected Return	2.0%	4.0%	6.0%	8.0%	10.0%
Standard Deviation	4.2	7.41	11.62	16.43	21.87

TABLE 19-7   INVESTMENT PAYOFFS OF PORTFOLIO C

Investment Horizon Years	Terminal Portfolio Wealth Percentiles								
	.01	.05	.10	.25	.50	.75	.90	.95	.99
1	0.81	0.88	0.91	0.98	1.06	1.15	1.23	1.28	1.39
2	0.77	0.86	0.91	1.01	1.12	1.26	1.39	1.47	1.65
3	0.75	0.86	0.92	1.04	1.19	1.36	1.54	1.66	1.90
4	0.73	0.86	0.94	1.08	1.26	1.48	1.70	1.85	2.17
5	0.73	0.87	0.96	1.12	1.34	1.59	1.87	2.05	2.45
10	0.76	0.98	1.12	1.40	1.79	2.29	2.87	3.28	4.21
15	0.84	1.14	1.35	1.77	2.40	3.24	4.26	5.02	6.83
20	0.95	1.36	1.65	2.26	3.20	4.55	6.24	7.53	10.76
30	1.30	2.01	2.54	3.74	5.74	8.81	12.9	16.34	25.28

	Geometric Return Percentiles								
	.01	.05	.10	.25	.50	.75	.90	.95	.99
1	−19.1	−12.45	−8.67	−1.99	6.00	14.63	23.02	28.32	38.95
2	−12.5	−7.40	−4.60	0.28	6.00	12.03	17.77	21.34	28.36
3	−9.3	−5.08	−2.74	1.31	6.00	10.90	15.51	18.36	23.93
4	−7.4	−3.67	−1.61	1.92	6.00	10.23	14.19	16.63	21.36
5	−6.1	−2.69	−0.83	2.35	6.00	9.78	13.30	15.46	19.64
10	−2.7	−0.2	1.1	3.4	6.00	8.7	11.1	12.6	15.5
15	−1.2	−0.55	0.80	3.26	6.00	8.80	11.39	12.97	16.01
20	−0.2	1.6	2.5	4.2	6.00	7.9	9.6	10.6	12.6
30	0.9	2.4	3.2	4.5	6.00	7.5	8.9	9.8	11.4

Input Assumptions: Portfolio C
Mean Continuous Return: 5.823
Standard Deviation: 11.620
Serial Correlation Assumptions
Serial Correlation: 0.000
Current Return Level: 3.540

Two comments about these terminal wealth forecasts need to be made. First, note that terminal wealth is skewed toward higher wealth levels and this skewness increases as the investment horizon increases. Consider the 30-year horizon. The 50th percentile is $5.74; that is, there is a 50% chance that wealth will be less than $5.74 or greater than $5.74. At the lower end, there is a 1% chance of the portfolio's value being lower than $1.30, a spread of $4.44 from the 50th percentile. But at the upper end, there is a 1% chance of the portfolio's value being greater than $25.28, a spread of $19.54 from the 50th percentile. Clearly, the terminal wealth distribution is skewed "to the right." Second, terminal wealth is displayed in percentile fashion instead of in terms of standard deviations. Because of the skewness of portfolio values, the standard deviation becomes a less meaningful measure of risk. In addition, most investors are able to interpret percentile distributions more easily than statistical measures such as standard deviation and skewness.

In the second part of Table 19-7, percentile distributions are shown for the geometric returns underlying each of the terminal wealth levels just cited. For example, consider the $5.74 terminal wealth at year 30. This translates into a geometric return of 6% per year:

$$\$1.00(1 + G)^{30} = \$5.74$$

$$G = (\$5.74/\$1.00)^{1/30}$$

$$G = 6.00\%$$

Geometric return percentiles are often used in SAA studies because investors are able to interpret them more readily than terminal wealth outcomes.

Short-Sale Constraints. Most investment portfolios have constraints against short-selling any securities. In such cases, the optimal percentage in any asset class is either zero or a positive number. The lowest risk portfolio typically consists of a large investment in T-bills, a small investment in another asset class (due to diversification gains), and zero investment in other assets. The highest return portfolio is a 100% investment in one asset class and a zero investment in all others.

Many asset pricing models, however, assume that one can short-sell and make use of the sale proceeds to purchase other assets. When short sales are allowed, a positive or negative investment is made in every asset class. Roll's critique of empirical tests of the capital asset pricing model (CAPM), for example, requires that one be able to short-sell any asset class and make use of the proceeds.

Because short sales are rarely allowed (particularly for aggregate asset classes), all examples in this chapter have a short sale constraint.

Can Investors Diversify over Many Time Periods?

As we first discussed in Chapter 5, the relationship between the length of one's investment horizon and investment risk is often misunderstood. To see the source of this misunderstanding, look at the geometric mean return outcomes in Table 19-7 for a 1-year holding period and a 30-year holding period. The lowest and highest 1-year returns shown are −19.1% and +38.9%. In contrast, the lowest and highest 30-year geometric annualized returns are 0.9% and 11.4%. It would seem that the longer one's investment horizon, the lower one's investment risk. If true, this would have profound implications on practical portfolio decisions.

This notion that investment risk might decline as the investment horizon increases is shown graphically in Figure 19-4. This figure shows percentile geometric returns (as given in Table 19-7) on the vertical axis and the length of the investment horizon on the horizontal axis. This type of graph is commonly used by financial consultants to suggest that long-term investors face less risk than do short-term investors.

The explanation often given for the narrowing of differences in percentile returns is that good years supposedly offset bad years. Unfortunately, *this conclusion is wrong*. The

FIGURE 19-4 DISPERSION OF GEOMETRIC MEAN DECREASES FOR LONGER INVESTMENT HORIZONS

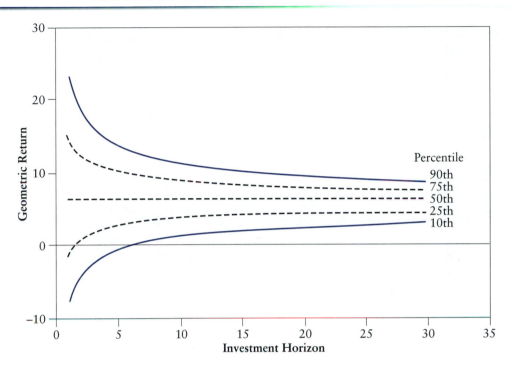

longer one's investment horizon, the greater the investment uncertainty. The narrowing of percentile return differences is simply a mathematical result.

One invests in a portfolio with the intent of future consumption. But one consumes future wealth, not geometric annualized returns. And, the longer one's investment horizon, the greater the uncertainty about future wealth. Time does not reduce uncertainty. Instead, risk compounds over time! This can be easily seen in Figure 19-5, in which various terminal wealth percentiles are shown.

To help understand the intuition of time diversification and see why investing for a longer number of time periods does not reduce risk, let's consider a roulette wheel analogy. If you bet $1.00 and spin the wheel once, there is an uncertainty about the payoff. This is analogous to investing $1.00 in a single stock. Now assume you are allowed to spin the wheel ten times and average the results to determine your payoff. This is analogous to making an equal investment in ten stocks (each with identical risk and zero correlation between their return outcomes). Clearly, averaging ten spins is less risky than taking the payoff from a single spin just as investing in ten stocks is less risky than investing in a single stock. By owning many securities, you spread your risks, and good payoffs on one offset poor payoffs on another.

In contrast, investing for many periods is similar to having a payoff after each spin, accumulating the outcomes of many spins as opposed to averaging the outcomes. In short, investing for many time periods compounds the investment risk of any single period.

FIGURE 19-5   DISPERSION OF TERMINAL WEALTH INCREASES FOR LONGER INVESTMENT HORIZONS

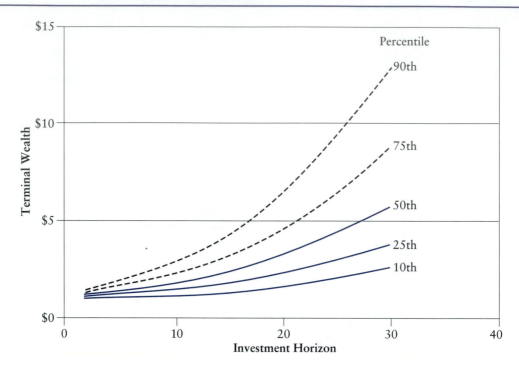

Tactical Asset Allocation

Strategic asset allocation is based on the investor's expectations of long-term risks and returns associated with various asset classes. As such, the SAA will be the portfolio that will, on average, be held. However, short-term investment expectations may occasionally be different from expectations about the long term. If so, the actual portfolio that is held should be different from the SAA. Such temporary changes in the portfolio's composition are commonly referred to as tactical asset allocation (TAA).

The conceptual difference between SAA and TAA is illustrated in Figure 19-6. Two efficient frontiers are shown in the figure. One is based on risks and returns expected on three asset classes over the long run. Together with the investor's risk tolerance, it is used to identify an SAA—in this case, portfolio P, which consists of 40% in T-bills, 10% in bonds, and 50% in stocks. The other efficient frontier is based on short-term expectations. As displayed in the figure, short-term expected returns on high-risk securities are considerably lower than long-run expectations. Thus, the optimal portfolio called for by the tactical asset allocation decision is portfolio P^*, which consists of a temporary underweighting of stocks and overweighting of T-bills.

For TAA strategies to work, one must be able to distinguish between long-term versus short-term risks and expected returns on various asset classes. That is, one must be able to correctly *time* the purchase and sale of aggregate asset classes.

There are many ways of defining an asset class and even more ways to evaluate

FIGURE 19-6   SAA versus TAA

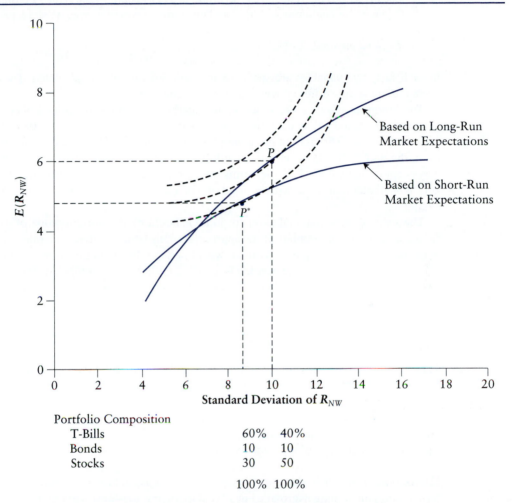

Portfolio Composition

T-Bills	60%	40%
Bonds	10	10
Stocks	30	50
	100%	100%

whether the class should be over- or underweighted relative to the SAA. In the United States, speculators have traditionally timed between stocks and T-bills (known as market timing) or long-term bonds and T-bills (interest rate timing). Recently, however, TAA decisions have been expanded to include real estate, international equities, positions in individual countries, and foreign currency.

In this section, we explore aggregate equity market timing. The techniques discussed are based largely on fundamental analysis.

Equity Market Valuation

The decision to overweight or underweight the portfolio investment in domestic equities can be made by answering any of the following three questions:

1. Given my expectations of long-run dividends and the required rate of return on domestic equities, *is the current level of aggregate stock prices correct?*

2. Given my expectations of long-run dividends and the current level of aggregate stock prices, *is the return from investing in stocks equal to the return I require?*
3. Given my required rate of return and the current level of aggregate stock prices, *is the implied growth rate of dividends equal to my expectations of future dividend growth?*

In each case, two variables are specified and the third variable is calculated. These three questions are simply different ways to view the same issue.

To determine whether aggregate equity markets are currently priced according to long-run return and risk expectations, one has to use a stock index as a proxy of aggregate stock prices. Throughout our examples we use the S&P 500 Index as this proxy. In truth, the S&P 500 reflects the values of large mature U.S. corporations. It might not always capture the value of smaller firms traded on listed exchanges or in the OTC market. Nonetheless, it is a widely used index on which considerable past data are available.

The value of any financial asset (or index) should be the present value of expected future cash flows discounted at an appropriate risk-adjusted discount rate. Thus, we must answer two basic questions if we wish to assess the economic worth of the asset: (1) What do we expect future dividends to be? (2) What is an appropriate discount rate? Since we can never answer either question with absolute certainty, it is wise to use a variety of approaches.

Expected Dividend Growth

Three approaches are commonly used to estimate future dividend growth on stock indexes such as the S&P 500:

1. Historical growth
2. Sustainable internal growth
3. Long-run growth of the total economy

Historical Growth Rates.   In Chapter 12 we discussed how one could estimate historical compound annual growth rates (CAGR) using log-least-squares regression. To do so, the natural log of the variable being measured is regressed against time as follows:

Log Least Squares CAGR $ln(\text{DPS}_t) = a + b(\text{Year}_t)e_t$ (19.1)

Here, DPS_t represents dividends per share in year t, the variable a represents the regression intercept, b is the CAGR estimate, and e_t is an error term in year t. Figure 19-7 and Table 19-8 show various grow rates of $ln(\text{DPS})$ for the S&P 500 Index between 1926 and 1994.

Notice in Figure 19-7 that, except for the Depression and World War II era, dividends per share have not been substantially different than predicted by log-least-squares regression equations (using the full period 1926 to 1994). Also notice that dividend growth has been relatively stable, particularly for nominal dividends. This provides some validity to our use of the constant dividend valuation model letter in this section.

TABLE 19-8   HISTORICAL COMPOUND ANNUAL GROWTH RATES S&P 500 INDEX, 1926–1994

	Nominal		Real	
Period	CAGR	R-Squared	CAGR	R-Squared
1926–1994	4.91%	93.7%	1.25%	66.1%
1946–1994	5.55%	98.3%	1.21%	56.9%
1971–1994	6.68%	98.0%	1.39%	73.7%

FIGURE 19-7   GROWTH OF S&P 500 DIVIDENDS (1926–1994)

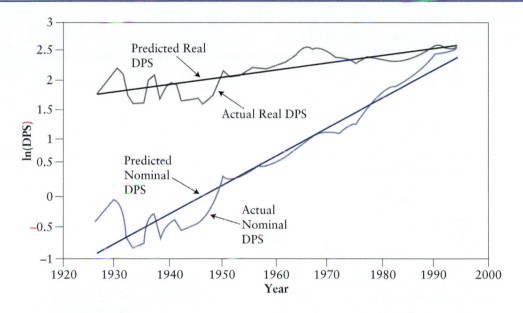

The R-squares reported in Table 19-8 confirm the greater stability of nominal dividend growth. The 20-year period ended in 1994 experienced the greatest rate of nominal dividend growth, but much of this was offset by greater inflation rates.

This data suggests that (1) a constant dividend valuation model might be a reasonable way to value the S&P 500 Index, (2) nominal dividend growth is directly related to future inflation, and (3) nominal growth will exceed inflation by about 125 basis points.

Sustainable Internal Growth. If the return on equity (*ROE*) and dividend retention rates (*B*) are constant in the future, then internal corporate growth can sustain a growth rate in dividends (*G*) equal to:

Sustainable Internal Growth $G = ROE \times B$ **(19.2)**

Robert L. Penter, C.F.A.

Principal
Hewitt Associates LLC
University of Florida, B.S.B.A.
University of Florida, M.B.A.

Robert Penter is the manager of the southeast region investment consulting practice of Hewitt Associates, an international consulting firm specializing in human resource issues. His career in investment consulting for institutional fund sponsors began while he was employed at PI Analytics, Inc. during graduate school. This experience exposed him to the pension fund industry and, specifically, investment consulting.

Q: What is your role in assisting pension plan sponsors with asset allocation decisions for their pension funds?

A: Our role, similar to the role that most investment consultants play with their clients, primarily is oriented toward assisting our clients with *strategic* asset allocation decisions. That is, we assist clients in determining the appropriate *long-term* allocations among major asset classes for their pension funds.

Q: What are some of the key considerations used by pension fund sponsors in determining strategic asset allocation?

A: There are two key factors in determining strategic asset allocation: (1) the plan sponsor's risk posture, and (2) the expected risk and return characteristics of capital market opportunities. Risk posture refers to a plan sponsor's *ability* and *willingness* to accept pension investment risk. We attempt to gauge a plan sponsor's ability to accept pension investment risk through an examination of the demographics of the company's work force, the funded status of the plan, and the business and financial characteristics of the company. A plan sponsor's willingness to accept risk is evaluated through an in-depth discussion of the company's attitudes regarding risk. The determination of risk posture, however, is an inexact science with a fair level of subjectivity. Nonetheless, a reasonable determination of a client's risk posture is a critical element in developing asset allocation strategies, particularly in light of the long time horizons of pension plan sponsors.

Q: How do you develop expected risk and return characteristics in capital markets for purposes of developing strategic asset allocation?

A: Like most other things, we start with historical results. Most major asset classes have data for reasonably long periods of time. Historical data is used to evaluate the returns and risk that have been associated with an asset class, and it is particularly useful for examining how asset classes have behaved in various types of economic environments. While there clearly are limitations in using historical data, such return series can provide insights into the expected returns of asset classes going forward. We recognize, however, that historical data may not be relevant for all asset classes, and recent conditions and fundamental investment theory also should be considered. The best example of this caveat is with fixed income, as historical data before the late 1970s is of little value due to the change in Federal Reserve policy and the elimination of regulation Q (which helped control interest rates).

Q: What is the typical asset mix for pension funds, and what changes in asset allocation are occurring?

A: As you would think, the asset mix of pension plans varies considerably, with equity exposure ranging from 0% to 100%. The current industry averages show total equities to be at about 60%, with about 30% in fixed income and 4% to 5% each in real estate and cash equivalents. The majority of pension plans maintain equity exposure between 40% and 80%. The biggest change occurring is the continued increase in the use of so-called 'alternative' classes such as international stocks and bonds, real estate, timberland, and venture capital.

International stocks now make up more than 10% of pension fund assets, and their use is growing substantially. We expect the growth in the use of alternative assets to continue as plan sponsors seek higher returns and better diversification.

Q: Do you provide clients with assistance in making shorter term asset allocation decisions?

A: Our role with clients primarily is geared toward long-term asset allocation. This focus is consistent with the liability streams (i.e., ultimate funding objective) of most pension funds, which have a very long duration. We do assist clients in evaluating investment management firms that specialize in tactical asset allocation (which is the industry pseudonym for market timing). In most cases, these firms use fairly quantitative, model-driven approaches in their tactical asset allocation decisions.

Q: Have these managers added value through market timing?

A: The data is mixed, and most models have limited histories (less than ten years). Our general conclusion has been that the average model (when used with "real" money) has not added value. As importantly, however, is the pattern of result typically found with market timing models. In almost all cases, the value added has come from avoiding major market downturns, and the value added is very inconsistent. This lack of consistency is a major concern for most clients, particularly given the typical turnover that occurs on investment committees.

For example, if you believe the S&P 500 Index will have a long-run *ROE* of, say, 12% and a dividend retention rate of 55%, this implies that future dividend growth will be 6.6%:

$$12\% \times 0.55 = 6.6\%$$

Although returns on equity and retention rates could be estimated using historical averages, there are at least two related problems in using past data. First, the past is not necessarily a good predictor of the future. Growth estimates vary widely, depending on the time span chosen. Unpredictable events such as unexpected inflation, natural disasters, and wars can have significant effects on any one year's results. Probably more important is the implicit assumption that equity returns and retention rates are related and that growth rates for the average firm are determined by *ROE* × *B*. The assumption is that corporations can increase dividend growth rates simply by retaining larger amounts of profits. Given an *ROE* of 15%, growth will be 10% if two-thirds of profits are retained and 7.5% if one-half of profits are retained. This implies that aggregate dividend growth is determined solely by management—that it is not constrained by economic opportunities.

Over lengthy periods of time this simply isn't true. The growth of corporate profits and dividends is constrained by the growth in aggregate economic activity. It is difficult to envision a situation in which for long periods of time dividends grow more rapidly than the GNP. As a result, a better approach to estimating profit and dividend growth may be to start with a long-run estimate of aggregate economic growth and back into likely dividend growth.

Long-Run Economic Growth. Another approach to forecasting future dividend growth starts by estimating future real growth in economic output.

Figure 19-8 plots real levels of GNP, S&P 500 earnings per share (EPS), and S&P 500 dividends per share (DPS) from 1926 to 1994 (values are reported in constant 1994 dollars). During this time span, real GNP exhibited some volatility caused by various business cycles, but its long-run growth rate was reasonably stable and equal to a compound annual growth rate of about 3.0%.

An alternative to extrapolating past economic growth is summarized in Table 19-9. In this procedure the analyst forecasts growth rates in the various components of aggregate growth. These consist of the following:

- **Labor inputs** such as growth in the number of people employed, growth in the hours they work, and growth in economic output due to changes in the age, gender, and education of the work force

- **Capital inputs** such as investments in plant and research.

- **Changes in productivity** due to advances in knowledge, more efficient resource allocation, and economies of scale.

Table 19-9 shows three estimates for each growth component (pessimistic, expected, and optimistic), together with a brief justification for the forecast.

Once the growth rate of aggregate real economic output has been forecast, an estimate of real dividend growth can be made. If you look closely at Figure 19-8, it will be clear that earnings per share on the S&P 500 index (EPS) have not grown as rapidly in the past

FIGURE 19-8 REAL GNP, EPS, AND DPS

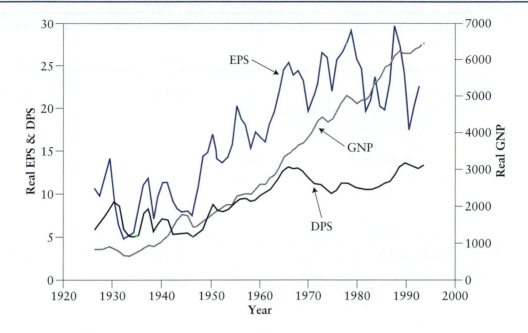

TABLE 19-9 ESTIMATES OF REAL ECONOMIC GROWTH

	Pessimistic	Expected	Optimistic
I. Factor Inputs			
A. Employment. Population growth rates will slow down and proportion of the retired population will increase.	0.95%	1.0%	1.15%
B. Hours Hours worked will continue a slight decline as people continue to move out of the farm sector into the nonfarm sector. Slight changes will be caused by unionization, increased standard of living, smaller families, and leisure alternatives.	−0.22	−0.21	−0.20
C. Age/Sex Composition Historical negative effects were caused mainly by the movement of women into teaching areas. A reversal is forecast as they gain increased responsibility within the business sector.	0.00	0.10	0.13

Continued

TABLE 19-9 ESTIMATES OF REAL ECONOMIC GROWTH (*continued*)

	Pessimistic	Expected	Optimistic
D. Education Major advantages of increased worker education have probably been seen in the past 50 years. However, as better trained women and minorities enter the work force, education will continue to play a positive role.	0.30	0.35	0.40
E. Other	0.09	0.09	0.09
Total Labor	1.12%	1.33%	1.57%
F. Total Capital Major increases in capital will occur as the United States retools to meet international competition and growth in postwar household formations.	0.70	0.90	1.00
Total Factor Input	1.82%	2.23%	2.57%
II. Output per Unit of Input			
A. Advances in Knowledge Not only is this a difficult factor to measure, it seems to be one of the more volatile. There does not seem to be any significant slowdown in scientific knowledge, but, instead, major discoveries in organic chemistry, microcircuitry, power generation, etc.	1.00%	1.20%	1.30%
B. Improved Resource Allocation This is another difficult factor to forecast. A major pro is the development of international human and natural resources, and a major con is the depletion of scarce resources.	0.20	0.25	0.30
C. Economies of Scale	0.35	0.35	0.35
D. Other	−0.05	−0.05	−0.05
Total	1.50%	1.75%	1.90%
Total Annual Growth in GNP	3.32%	3.98%	4.47%

as aggregate economic output. In addition, real dividends per share on the S&P 500 (DPS) have not grown as rapidly as real EPS. Earnings of companies in the stock index have grown less rapidly than aggregate output due, in part, to increased real corporate tax rates. In addition, much of the growth in aggregate output came from companies not included in the S&P 500. Growth in real DPS has lagged growth in real EPS in recent years due to increased profit retention rates.

Thus, it appears that future dividend growth of stocks in the S&P 500 index will be less than future aggregate economic growth. How much less is difficult to judge. But growth of economic output will probably exceed dividend growth of the S&P 500 index.

Finally, a nominal dividend growth rate should be calculated by adding an expected rate of inflation to the real dividend growth forecast.

Selecting an Appropriate Discount Rate

The discount rate reflects the return the investor requires in order to accept the investment risks of the security. We have seen in previous chapters that the standard deviation of yearly returns on the S&P 500 depends on the time period examined, but has generally been between 15% and 20%. The average return earned for bearing risk, however, is much more volatile. For example, 20-year average annual outcomes shown in Figure 19-2 range between 6.5% to 18%. And over the 1926 to 1994 period the following average annual returns were earned on the S&P 500 index and two proxies for the risk-free rate:

Average Annual Return		
S&P 500 Index	12.16%	12.16%
Treasury Bonds	5.25	
Treasury Bills		3.72
Excess S&P 500	6.91%	8.44%

These excess returns are probably larger than the true market risk premium. There are few long horizon periods with stock returns as large as 12.16%. The best strategy is to use a variety of risk premiums that appear to be reasonable in light of past returns and current conditions. In December 1995, the risk-free return on long-term bonds was about 6.0%. Applying risk premiums of 4% to 7% results in discount rates ranging from 10.0% to 13.0%.

Valuation of the S&P 500 at December 1995

The value of any stock or stock index should be the present value of expected future dividends, as shown in Equation (19.3):

Dividend Valuation Model $$P_0 = \sum_{t=1}^{D} D_t \div (1 + K)^t \qquad \textbf{(19.3)}$$

D_t is our expected dividend in year t, K is the required return, and P_0 is the present value of expected future dividends (our estimate of the security's fair value).

If dividends are expected to grow at a constant annual rate of G, Equation (19.3) can be simplified as follows:

Constant Dividend Growth Model

$$P_0 = \frac{D_0(1 + G)}{K - G} \tag{19.4}$$

For individual stocks, the assumption of constant dividend growth is usually too naive. The dividend growth rates of individual firms go through various stages as the firm goes through various stages of its life cycle. However, for an index of large mature firms such as the S&P 500, the assumption of constant growth is often reasonable. Thus, we use the constant growth model of Equation (19.4).

Assume that, after reviewing the various estimates of future S&P 500 dividend growth and required returns, we decide to use $G = 5.5\%$ and $K = 11\%$ as our best estimates. At the end of 1995, the S&P 500 Index closed at $616 and total dividends over the prior 12 months had been $13.79. Using Equation (19.4) with this data implies that the S&P 500 Index should have been trading for $264.5:

$$\$264.5 = \frac{\$13.79(1.055)}{0.11 - 0.055}$$

And by rearranging Equation (19.4), we can also calculate the yearly rate of return one should expect given a price of $616 and the sustainable growth which would justify a price of $616. These are:

Expected Return on S&P 500

$$= \frac{\$13.79(1.055)}{\$616} + 0.055$$

$$= 0.0236 + 0.055 = 0.0786$$

Sustainable Growth Consistent with Existing Price

$$= \frac{\$616(0.11)}{(\$616 + \$13.79)} - \frac{\$13.79}{\$629.79} = 0.08569$$

Clearly, either the constant growth assumption is wrong or the S&P 500 was overvalued at the end of 1995.

Sensitivity Analysis. The estimates just calculated can be quite sensitive to input assumptions. Therefore, it is wise to consider the results of a variety of assumptions ranging from pessimistic to optimistic. An example is shown in Table 19-10. In the left column, various nominal dividend growth rates are shown. The top row shows various desired discount rates.

Entries in the matrix represent intrinsic values of the S&P 500 using Equation (19.4). Note that fair values are in excess of $616 only at low required returns and optimistic

TABLE 19·10 SENSITIVITY ANALYSIS OF S&P 500 INTRINSIC VALUE

G Values	K Values			
	10.00%	11.00%	12.00%	13.00%
0.035	219.58	190.30	167.91	150.24
0.045	262.01	221.70	192.14	169.54
0.055	323.30	264.52	223.82	193.98
0.065	419.61	326.36	267.02	225.94
0.075	592.97	423.55	329.43	269.53
0.085	997.48	598.49	427.49	332.49

D_0 = $13.79.
S&P 500 Actual Value = $615.93 (December 31, 1995).

growth rates. Again, either the S&P 500 Index was overvalued at the end of 1995 or the constant growth model was inappropriate.

Relative Value Measures. Two relative value measures are commonly used by practitioners. These are the price-to-earnings (P/E) and price-to-book-value (P/B) ratios. The P/E ratio is the current market price of a stock (or index) divided by last year's or next year's earnings per share. The P/B ratio is the current market price of a stock (or index) divided by last year's book value per share. (Book value per share is equal to total shareholder equity divided by outstanding shares.)

Both ratios are plotted for the S&P 500 in Figure 19-9.[3] They suggest the U.S. stock market was overvalued in the mid-1990s. However, considerable care must be taken in interpreting P/E and P/B ratios. For example, there is no reason to believe that current levels of each will necessarily return to historical averages. The value of the ratios should and does change in response to changes in market consensus estimates of K and G.

Does Tactical Allocation of Equities Work? Most rigorous studies of market timing suggest that the short-term benefits of equity timing decisions are doubtful. Over periods of approximately ten years or less, the quarterly return series of investment managers who time are, on average, no different from those of managers who do not time. However, no studies have examined equity market timing over longer time periods.

---

[3] The price-to-book ratio shown in panel B is for the S&P Industrial index. Book values for the S&P 500 Index are not available with a sufficiently long enough history to be meaningful.

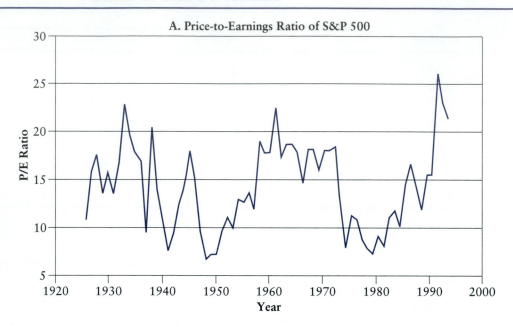

A. Price-to-Earnings Ratio of S&P 500

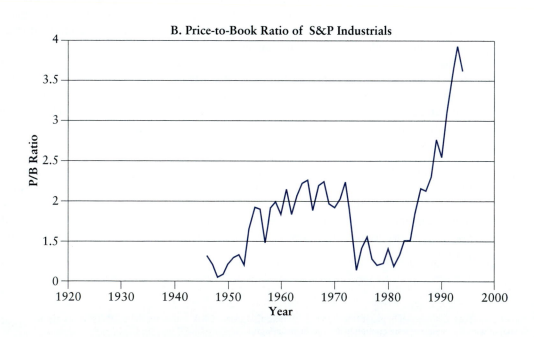

B. Price-to-Book Ratio of S&P Industrials

S U M M A R Y

Here are the key concepts:

◼ The major determinant of a portfolio's returns over time is its asset allocation. A recent study of 82 pension portfolios suggested that more than 90% of return volatility and the major source of average returns was each portfolio's strategic asset allocation (SAA).

◼ The first step in developing an appropriate SAA is to identify an efficient frontier of the asset classes in which the investor is willing to invest. This requires that expected returns, standard deviations, and correlation coefficients be specified for each asset class.

◼ After an efficient frontier has been developed, the statistical results for various portfolios should be recast so they can be better understood by investors who are not comfortable with, say, standard deviation of annual returns.

◼ Typically, this involves two changes: (1) expressing returns and future payoffs in percentile form, instead of expected return standard deviation form, and (2) extrapolating the results to longer time horizons.

◼ Tactical asset allocation (TAA) attempts to profit from short-term swings in relative prices of asset classes. The classic name for this is timing. People attempt to time among a wide variety of asset classes, including aggregate stocks, long-term bonds, country stock markets, and currencies.

R E V I E W   P R O B L E M

You have created your own index of common stock prices, which you call the EMP Index (Equity Market Portfolio Index). At present the economy is in a slump, resulting in depressed dividend levels. Dividends per share on your EMP Index over the past ten years have been as follows:

Year	Dividends	Year	Dividends
1986	$1.39	1991	$2.45
1987	1.39	1992	2.60
1988	1.45	1993	2.65
1989	1.62	1994	2.67
1990	2.00	1995	2.68

You run a log-least-squares regression on the data and get:

$$ln(DPS) = -181.64497 + 0.09161 \text{ (Time)} \quad R^2 = 89.85\%$$

a. What has been the compound annual growth rate in dividends per share?
b. If you use the regression trend line, what is your expected dividend two years from now (1997)? (Assume dividend levels return to their overall trend level by then.)

c. The 1995 dividend was just $2.68. If you believe dividends will increase in 1996 and 1997 by equal dollar increments to the trend line value in part b, what is 1996's dividend expected to be?

d. Beyond 1997 you are unable to identify the impacts of any business cycles. Nonetheless, starting after 1997 you forecast growth rates equal to the historic average in part a. If you require a return of 15% on an investment in the EMP Index, what fair value would you place on the index as of the end of 1995?

e. If the EMP Index is $55.00 at the end of 1995, how would you adjust your stock/bond ratio?

Solution

a. 9.161%—the slope of the log-natural regression.

b. $3.67 = antilog [−181.64497 + 0.09161 (1997)].

c. $\dfrac{\$3.67 - \$2.68}{2} = \$0.495$ per year

1996 dividend = $2.68 + $0.495 per year

d. This requires a nonconstant dividend growth model:

$$P = \frac{D_{96}}{1 + k} + \frac{D_{97}}{(1 + K)^2} + \frac{D_{97}(1 + G)}{K - G} \frac{1}{(1 + k)^2}$$

$$= \frac{\$3.175}{1.15} + \frac{\$3.67}{1.15^2} + \frac{\$3.67(1.09161)}{0.15 - 0.09161}\left[\frac{1}{(1.15^2)}\right]$$

$$= \$57.42$$

e. The estimated intrinsic value of the index is slightly higher than the actual value. Thus, slightly increase the actual equity holding compared with the baseline investment portfolio.

QUESTIONS AND PROBLEMS

1. The capital asset pricing model (CAPM) and arbitrage pricing theory (APT) are two conceptual approaches to defining risk and determining how securities are priced. Discuss the implications each has on the SAA decision.

2. One approach to determining the SAA for an individual (or an organization such as a pension plan) begins by estimating an efficient frontier of expected returns and risks on various classes of securities.

   a. What inputs are needed to do this?

   b. How might you develop such inputs?

   c. Why might such "efficient portfolios" not be the best for an individual or organization such as a pension fund?

3. "Thou shalt diversify!" Explain why.

4. "Thou shalt diversify investments in marketable securities—but not totally!" Explain why.

5. Indexed equity portfolios have been available to pension funds for about 20 years. In recent years, however, specialty index funds have been created that underweight portfolio holdings in economic sectors in which the sponsoring firm does business.

   a. Explain the rationale for such specialty index funds.

   b. What problems do you see in its implementation?

6. As of year-end an equity index is selling at 1,000. To evaluate whether this is a fair value, you have developed the following data:

Equity Index Estimates	Pessimistic	Expected	Optimistic
Long-Run *ROE*	14.50%	15.00%	16.00%
Profit Retention Rate	50.00%	56.67%	60.00%
Current T-Bond YTM	8.00%	8.00%	8.00%
Fair Risk Premium	5.00%	5.50%	6.00%
Year 0 Earnings per Share	$100.00	$106.35	$110.00

a. Develop pessimistic, expected, and optimistic valuations of the equity index.
b. As the investment adviser for a $20.0 million pension fund, you believe a long-run stock/bond ratio of 50/50 should be maintained. However, you are willing to alter the ratio temporarily to take advantage of perceived price imbalances. Based on your answer to part a, would you make such an adjustment now?

7. You have just completed a strategic asset allocation (SAA) study of the following data and identified the following two portfolios as efficient (all data are expressed in annualized real return terms):

Efficient Portfolios		Expected Return	Standard Deviation	Correlations		
A	B			TB	GB	SP
T-Bills	0.7667	0.0235	3.0%	2.0%	1.00		
Govt. Bonds	0.0852	0.2690	5.0%	10.0%	0.10	1.00	
S&P 500	0.1481	0.7075	8.6%	18.0%	0.00	0.50	1.00
Total Investment	1.0000	1.0000					

a. Calculate the expected return and standard deviation of portfolio A and portfolio B.
b. If an international equity class were added as a fourth asset class, what effect should this have on the efficient frontier?
c. This efficient frontier is based on real rates of return (after inflation). As such, is it appropriate for investors facing future nominal liabilities?
d. What is the difference in the efficient frontiers of individuals facing real dollar and nominal dollar liabilities?
e. Use the expected return and standard deviation of portfolio B to calculate the percentile distributions of terminal wealth of $1.00 and geometric return for the end of five years from now. (Assume $E(R)$ and σ are currently expressed as continuous returns. Also, the serial correlation of returns is zero.)
f. Mathematically, any efficient portfolio between portfolio A and portfolio B is a linear combination of them. If X is invested in A and $(1 - X)$ is invested in B, the combination is efficient. Given this, what is the composition of the efficient portfolio providing an expected return of 6%?

8. Dawon Insurance is developing an efficient frontier based on nominal dollar liabilities. The firm can lend risk free by purchasing zero-coupon government bonds or bills. Thus, there is a linear trade-off between risk and return from the risk-free rate to a point of tangency with the efficient frontier of risky assets. Call this point P. Above point P, the firm may not short-sell risk-free governments and use the proceeds to invest in risky assets. How might options and futures be used to create a linear risk-return trade-off above point P?

9. If options and futures are trading at equilibrium prices, should positions in them be considered an additional asset class?

10. Since investment risk compounds over time, then long-term investors will invest in lower risk portfolios than short-term investors. True or false, and why?

11. One of the trustees of the Donner College Endowment Fund is Susan Oliver, the chief financial officer of a local corporation. She is now 55 and plans to take early retirement. Oliver is a Donner College alumna and wants to make some lasting contribution to the college. Upon her retirement, Oliver intends to use the after-tax proceeds from exercising her incentive stock options and nearly all of her rather extensive other liquid assets to establish a charitable remainder trust. Oliver will be the income beneficiary of the approximately $1 million trust and will also have emergency rights of limited access to the principal. Upon her death, the assets of the trust will pass to the Donner College Endowment Fund with no tax liability to Oliver's estate. She will not receive payments from her retirement pension until age 65. Oliver has asked the two investment advisers to meet with her to discuss her investment plans. Their meeting continued in a "debate" format.

Adviser 1: "The life-cycle approach to investment policy and asset allocation is best for the charitable remainder trust. Oliver is no longer young, will have only minimal outside sources of income, and will rely on income from the trust to meet all of her spending needs. The trust's investment policy should emphasize conservatism and the production of high levels of current income. Therefore, the trust should be invested almost entirely in long-term bonds."

Adviser 2: "Oliver's stated desire to make a lasting contribution to the college implies leaving as much in the trust as possible upon her death. Therefore, the trust's goal should be to maximize capital growth. Oliver is entitled to all of its income and to some principal if needed, which should be sufficient to meet her spending needs regardless of how little income the trust might earn. The trust is able to take high risk and should invest almost entirely in small capitalization growth stocks."

Adviser I Rebuttal: "While your approach has a chance to leave a much larger amount to the Donner College Endowment Fund, there is also the unfortunate possibility of leaving very little if stocks do poorly. With my approach, Oliver's income is secure and the trust would be able to preserve its capital."

Evaluate the strengths and weaknesses of each of the two approaches presented.

Recommend and justify an investment policy and an asset allocation (which must add to 100%) that draws from the strengths of each approach and corrects their weaknesses.

D A T A F I L E   A N A L Y S I S

Historical Efficient Frontiers. Review the instructions for the asset allocation (efficient frontier) computer package called ASSETALL. Using historical returns on a variety of asset classes found in the data sets, calculate historical average returns, standard deviations, and correlation coefficients for each. For the ASSETALL program to work without encountering mathematical difficulties, it is best if you select six or fewer asset classes. Among the asset classes include long-term U.S. government bonds. Use the ASSETALL package to find the historical efficient frontier. Do this twice. In the first, you should follow the directions to calculate portfolios that do not allow short sales. In the second, you should allow short sales to occur. Interpret the output. What do these results imply about the validity of using historical averages, standard deviations, and correlation coefficients with no modifications in attempting to find an efficient frontier associated with future security returns'.'

R E F E R E N C E S

The Association for Investment Management and Research has published the proceedings of various seminars on asset allocation. Two of these include the following:

Droms, William G., ed. *Asset Allocation for the Individual Investor,* Homewood, IL: Dow Jones-Irwin, 1987.

Joehnk, Michael D. *Asset Allocation for Institutional Portfolios,* Homewood, IL: Dow Jones-Irwin, 1986.

Interesting articles that investigate the importance of asset allocation in determining portfolio returns include these two:

Brinson, Gary P., Brian D. Singer, and Gilbert L. Beebower. "Determinants of Portfolio Performance II: An Update," *Financial Analysts Journal,* May–June 1991.

Hensel, Chris D., Don Ezra, and John Ilkew. "The Importance of the Asset Allocation Decision," *Financial Analysts Journal,* July–August 1992.

Recent developments in asset allocation models are discussed in the following articles:

Beebower, G.L. and A. P. Varikooty. "Measuring Market Timing Strategies," *Financial Analysts Journal,* November–December 1991.

Ezra, Don D. "Asset Allocation by Surplus Optimization," *Financial Analysts Journal,* January-February 1991.

Garcia, C. B., F. J. Gould, and Douglas C. Mitchell. "The Historical Validity of Short Fall Estimates," *The Journal of Portfolio Management,* Summer 1992.

Haugen, Robert A. and Nardin Baker. "Dedicated Stock Portfolios," *The Journal of Portfolio Management,* Summer 1990.

Leibowitz, Martin L. and Stanley Kogelman. "Asset Allocation Under Short Fall Constraints," *The Journal of Portfolio Management,* Winter 1991.

20

MANAGER SELECTION AND TAXES

After reading this chapter you should have an understanding of the procedures used in a "manager search" as well as various ways to minimize the taxes incurred in managing a security portfolio.

During the past two decades, individuals and institutions have increasingly recognized the benefits of professional investment management. In the individual investor market, this can be seen in the rapid growth of assets managed by mutual funds. In the institutional investor market, virtually all pension and endowment funds rely on external advisers to manage a large portion (if not all) of their portfolios. While many individuals and a few institutions continue to make investment decisions themselves (called internal management), the use of external managers is commonplace in today's security markets.

In the first section of this chapter we turn to three issues associated with the selection of professional investment managers. Should any professional managers be employed or should the portfolio owner make all investment decisions? If managers are to be used, how many different managers are needed? What criteria should be used in manager selection?

We conclude that one of the more important reasons for internal management of a security portfolio as opposed to professional external management is that personal management provides the investor with better control over tax management. Because professionals manage money for a large number of investors and have little knowledge of each investor's current tax situation, they are unable to make investment decisions that maximize each investor's after-tax returns.

Tax management is a major benefit to personal investment management. Thus, in the second section of the chapter, we discuss various tax considerations in investment management. An understanding of these tax considerations should help investors decide whether the benefits of tax management offset the benefits of professional management.

Manager Selection

We discussed the use of professional investment managers earlier in this text. For example, an overview was presented in Chapter 3 and we devoted all of Chapter 14 to a discussion of professional investment management. In this section, we keep a review of issues discussed earlier to the minimum and focus solely on the use and selection of external managers. There is some overlap with the discussions in Chapters 3 and 14. But most of the material is new.

Should External Managers Be Used?

Five principal factors determine whether a portfolio should be managed externally or internally:

1. portfolio size,
2. asset allocation,
3. investor knowledge,
4. fiduciary responsibilities, and
5. tax considerations.

Portfolio Size. Investors with small portfolios might wish to commingle their investment funds with the funds of other investors in order to reduce portfolio management costs and improve the portfolio's diversification. To accomplish this, however, investors must use professional external managers.

Usually, one or more different managers are employed to manage each asset class of the investment portfolio. For example, assume you wish to own some combination of money market securities, domestic bonds, domestic equities, and foreign equities. Then at least four different managers would be employed.

Different managers for each asset class are often required because professional managers tend to specialize in the asset classes in which they choose to invest. In addition, having a manager for each asset class makes it easier to calculate the return performance of the manager in that asset class. Some investment companies do offer managed portfolios that include more than one asset class, typically domestic bonds and domestic equities. Such mixed portfolios are referred to as **balanced portfolios.** The advantage of owning a portion of a balanced portfolio is convenience. The investor does not have to spend the time finding more than one manager. However, if a balanced portfolio is actively managed, it is often difficult to determine how well the manager is performing within each asset class, since only aggregate portfolio returns are calculated.

Institutional investors with very large portfolios would choose to employ multiple external managers for reasons different from those of small investors. Unlike small investors, large institutional investors do not need to pool their funds with other investors in order to reduce portfolio management costs or improve diversification by owning a larger number of securities within a given asset class. Instead, trustees of large portfolios will often decide to use multiple external managers to improve the diversification of ideas. By using multiple managers to actively manage a portfolio, future returns do not depend on the bets of a single person.

Asset Allocation. The decision to use external management is also influenced by the type of asset classes to be held in the portfolio. For example, if the portfolio is to consist solely of investments in U.S. Treasury issues such as T-bills and Treasury bonds, then the investor may not need the services of an external manager. Both securities can be bought directly by the investor with no transaction costs using forms available at most banks. However, if one wishes to invest in equities traded in emerging markets, then a professional who is familiar with such securities should probably be used.

Investor Knowledge. In many respects, the asset allocation of the portfolio and the knowledge of the investor interact when deciding whether external managers should be used. This is clearly the case where one investor wishes to invest in Treasury securities and has the knowledge of how to do so versus another investor who wishes to own emerging market stocks and does not have the personal knowledge of how such investments are made.

Many people believe that individual investors often have unique knowledge which they should exploit by personally managing their portfolios. For example, Peter Lynch, the well-known former manager of the Magellan Fund, argues that small investors are better able to spot companies with great prospects than Wall Street professionals. In his book *Beating the Street,* Lynch provides a list of what he calls his 20 Golden Rules of investing. Many of these are folksy ways of stating various concepts we discussed in earlier chapters of this book. But the overall tone of his rules implies that small investors are able to do as well at stock investing as professional managers. A sampling of his 20 Golden Rules is shown in Table 20-1. Spend some time with them. They are thought provoking.

Fiduciary Responsibilities. Institutional portfolios such as pension funds and endowments typically are placed under the legal control of a board of trustees. Often the trustees have extensive investment knowledge, but there are at least as many cases in which a trustee has little investment background. For example, pension plans that cover employees of a firefighter or police pension plan usually include many firefighters and police officers as trustees of the fund.

To assure that they meet their legal responsibilities as trustees of the portfolio's assets, the trustees hire professionals to manage the portfolio. If the portfolio is large, the trustees might choose to hire managers who become actual employees of the fund and manage assets of the fund full time. However, many institutional portfolios are not large enough to support a full-time investment staff. And, even if the portfolio is large enough to do so, external managers are also used, so a diversity of investment approaches is available.

Tax Considerations. Taxes are not a major investment consideration for most institutional portfolios as well as portfolios of individuals that are tax sheltered (usually IRS-qualified retirement investments). For example, security profits or losses of pension plan portfolios are

Steve Cusimano, C.F.A.

Senior Portfolio Manager
Florida State Board of Administration
University of Florida, B.S.B.A.

After graduating in 1991, Steve Cusimano started at the State of Florida as an assistant portfolio manager. He has been promoted to senior portfolio manager with responsibility for five internally managed domestic equity portfolio strategies as well as quantitative domestic equity research. His portfolio strategies include $1 billion in two actively managed portfolios and $8 billion in three passively managed portfolios.

Q: What surprised you most about the equity markets once you were settled in your first job?

A: My biggest surprise was about the mechanics of the auction market on the floor on the NYSE. It seems elementary to read in a textbook that stocks trade with bid/offer spreads, and that this marketplace is highly liquid and efficient. All of that is true.

However, being able to trade with minimal market impact is an integral component of portfolio management, which unfortunately, is often not discussed in college investment classes. By market impact I mean the price change between the last sale of stock and the price at which you execute your trade. Knowing how and when to trade specific stocks or how to trade a large block of stock in a particular name can really help and add value to an investment strategy. If you have a good investment idea but can't implement it at the price you desire, it becomes a missed opportunity.

Q: When constructing passive equity portfolios, what indices do you emulate and how do you develop the emulating portfolio?

A: We emulate three different indices, or benchmarks: the S&P 500, the Wilshire 2500, and a customized medium capitalization high-yield benchmark. All three passively managed portfolios are constructed through quadratic optimization that utilizes the BARRA E2 Risk Model. This risk model is similar to an APT model, but the factors in the BARRA models are all prespecified. There are 13 risk factors and 55 industry classifications. The risk factors are intuitive characteristics about equity securities that help explain their behavior and performance. They include items such as P/E and P/B ratios, relative price variability (akin to beta), stock size (market capitalization), dividend yield, measures of balance sheet leverage, and historic earnings variability. Each month BARRA estimates the exposure of the stocks in a large capitalization universe to each of the factors in the risk model using regression analysis. These exposures are standardized (made into Z-scores); an exposure of 0.00 to a particular factor means the stock has the average exposure. Likewise, a factor of +1.00 means the stock exhibits one standard deviation greater exposure to that factor than the universe of stocks.

For a passive portfolio, the optimizer seeks to minimize the managed portfolio's departures from its benchmark index with respect to the 13 risk factors and the 55 industry classifications, all subject to the constraints imposed. With no constraints, the optimizer will select all of the securities in the benchmark index in their exact weights. When certain liquidity and turnover constraints are imposed, a subset of the benchmark index is selected that mimics its characteristics. For example, in the S&P 500 portfolio we own 320 of the 500 stocks in the index, but the portfolio exhibits only minimal departures from the index with respect to the risk factors and industry weightings. This is possible because the S&P 500 is capitalization weighted, and the largest stocks by market capitalization account for the vast majority of the weight of the index. Therefore, owning most of the large companies and only some of the smaller ones will make the portfolio look very much like the index.

Q: Does the State of Florida run all of its defined benefit plan money internally?

A: No, we employ a number of external equity managers who use a variety of approaches to active management. We obtain fairly good diversification by owning a large number of securities in our internally managed portfolios. Even so, it makes sense to obtain the "diversity of ideas" that comes from the use of multiple external managers.

Q: How do you think changes in technology are affecting institutional equity money management?

A: Advanced computer technology has made it possible to do tens of millions of calculations in shorter periods of time. This has provided researchers with the ability to apply more advanced statistical techniques such as neural networks and genetic algorithms to problems in finance. As technology continues to improve, the only limitation on researchers is the length of data that is available. There is only one set of historical data to perform research on, and the number of statistically independent periods within this data set is limited.

Technology also enables those who know how to use it to do more with less. The impact of this on the investment business will be consolidation. There has already been a shift in private corporate pension fund management away from internally managed funds toward outsourcing most investment management and record keeping tasks. The typical beneficiaries are very large multiproduct investment management operations that are able to realize economies of scale. This has helped to create an environment that is increasingly characterized by two types of investment organizations: smaller niche participants and the very large investment operations.

TABLE 20-1   A SAMPLING OF PETER LYNCH'S "20 GOLDEN RULES"

■ Your investor's edge is not something you get from Wall Street experts. It's something you already have. You can outperform the experts if you use your edge by investing in companies or industries you already understand.

■ Over the past three decades, the stock market has come to be dominated by a herd of professional investors. Contrary to popular belief, this makes it easier for the amateur investor. You can beat the market by ignoring the herd.

■ Often, there is no correlation between the success of a company's operations and the success of its stock over a few months. In the long term, there is 100 percent correlation between the success of the company and the success of its stock. This disparity is the key to making money; it pays to be patient, and to own successful companies.

■ You have to know what you own and why you own it. "This baby is a cinch to go up!" doesn't count.

■ Owning stocks is like having children—don't get involved with more than you can handle. The part-time stock picker probably has time to follow 8–12 companies, and to buy and sell shares as conditions warrant. There don't have to be more than 5 companies in the portfolio at any one time.

■ If you can't find any companies that you think are attractive, put your money in the bank until you discover some.

■ Avoid hot stocks in hot industries. Great companies in cold, nongrowth industries are consistent big winners.

■ In every industry and in every region of the country, the observant amateur can find great growth companies long before the professionals have discovered them.

■ If you study 10 companies, you'll find 1 for which the story is better than expected. If you study 50, you'll find 5. There are always pleasant surprises to be found in the stock market—companies whose achievements are being overlooked on Wall Street.

SOURCE: Adapted from Peter Lynch, *Beating the Street* (New York: Simon & Schuster, 1993).

not subject to income taxes; neither are the profits or losses of individual investments held in an Individual Retirement Account (known commonly as an IRA). However, individual investors often have substantial investments that are subject to federal and state income taxes.

Unfortunately, unless the size of an individual investor's portfolio is quite large, professional investment managers are usually unwilling to consider the effects of income taxes in their security trading decisions. It is simply not cost effective for them to do so. Additionally, in the case of commingled portfolios, there are many different portfolio owners, each facing a different tax situation. Effectively, the only way in which an individual investor who does not have a sizable portfolio can manage the tax consequences of trading decisions is to manage the portfolio personally. *Tax management is a major economic motive for personal portfolio management.*

How Many Managers Are Needed?

Volatility Risk vs. Uncertain Mean Return Risk. Early studies of naive diversification across U.S. equities, U.S. bonds, and global equities suggested that relatively few securities are needed to virtually eliminate any risk which is diversifiable. For example, in a 1968 article published in the *Journal of Finance*, Evans and Archer concluded that their results "raise doubts concerning the economic justification of increasing portfolio sizes beyond 10 or more securities." If this is true, then shouldn't the employment of a single active manager who owns 30 or more securities provide sufficient diversification? The answer is no!

Individual managers tend to specialize in two possible ways: (1) the types of securities they trade, and (2) the methodologies they use to select securities. The employment, for example, of a manager who owns 60 stocks provides little diversification if all 60 are related to medical technology and are selected by a particular computer scoring system. Given that managers specialize, more than one manager is usually needed to effectively reduce diversifiable risk.

In addition, early diversification studies used a risk proxy that understates the true risk of an investment strategy, specifically the standard deviation of a time series of portfolio returns. We refer to this as the time-series standard deviation (TSSD).

Unfortunately, the TSSD focuses only on the volatility of returns around an average periodic rate of return. TSSDs do not directly capture uncertainty associated with the average (or expected) rate of return. Thus, when studies of diversification focus solely on decreases that occur in a portfolio's TSSD as the number of securities held in the portfolio are increased, not all portfolio risk is being considered. Uncertain mean return risk is missed.[1]

To see the problem intuitively, consider the situation depicted in Figure 20-1. You are evaluating a potential investment in manager A, manager B, or both managers. The managers invest in similar types of securities. Thus, the time series of future returns of the managers will be quite similar. Figure 20-1 displays one possible sequence of their future returns. As displayed in Figure 20-1, the TSSD of each manager is assumed to be the

---

[1] If the process that generates single-period rates of return is stationary, the time-series standard deviation can be used to estimate the uncertainty about the mean rate of return. Specifically, the standard deviation of the mean return is equal to the standard deviation of the time series divided by the square root of the number of time-series observations. However, adjusting the TSSD for uncertainty about the mean return does not sufficiently reflect the mean return risk that multiperiod investors face. The standard statistical adjustment for uncertain means simply restates the risk associated with a single period of time. We discuss the risks faced by multiperiod investors later in the chapter.

FIGURE 20-1   ILLUSTRATION OF INVESTMENT RISK USING THE TIME SERIES STANDARD DEVIATION

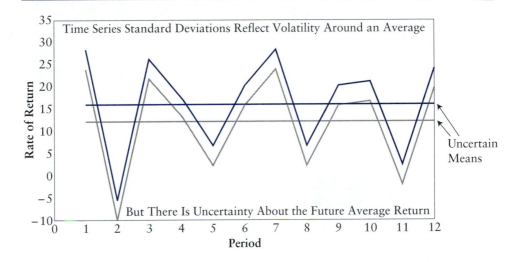

same. In addition, it is assumed their future time-series returns will be perfectly positively correlated. In practice, no two managers will have TSSDs that are identical and, while the returns on two managers might be highly correlated, the correlation will not be 1.0. However, these assumptions allow us to focus on uncertainty you have about each manager's expected return. You probably have an estimate of each manager's expected return but *you have an uncertainty about each expected return estimate*. Aside from the periodic volatility in returns around each manager's future average periodic return, *you do not know which manager will have the higher periodic average return*.

To summarize, manager A and manager B have identical future TSSDs and a time-series return correlation coefficient of +1.0. But there is an uncertainty as to which manager will have the higher average return. For simplicity, assume one manager will have an average periodic return of 12% and the other manager will have a 16% average return. But, again, you do not know which manager will have which average return. Are there any benefits to diversifying across the two managers?

If we examined only how the TSSD would be affected, there would not seem to be any benefits to owning both. Any combination of the two would result in the same calculated TSSD. But the TSSD does not account for the uncertainty you have about their expected returns. If you are lucky and select the higher return manager, then you will compound returns at 16% per period. If unlucky, you will compound returns at 12%. It is this risk that the TSSD does not capture and that can be reduced by diversifying across both managers.

Investment Risk and the Need for Diversification.   The amount of risk inherent in an asset class and the need for diversification are directly tied. This concept is depicted in Figure 20-2. For example, if one intends to invest in money market securities, there is little risk other than minor default risk. Thus, if default risk is controlled by purchasing only high-grade instruments, then the returns on each instrument would be virtually identical. In such investments there is little need for diversification.

FIGURE 20-2   NEED FOR DIVERSIFICATION AND INVESTMENT RISK

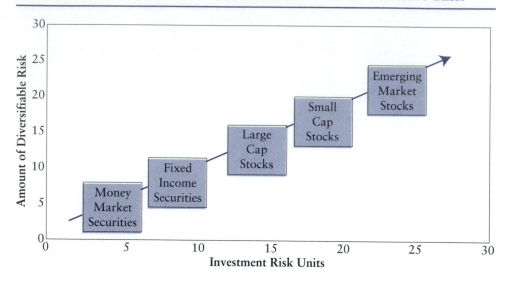

However, as the amount of investment risk is increased, the amount of diversifiable risk also increases. For example, if one intends to invest in stocks traded in emerging stock markets, there would be considerable currency risk, political risk, and country-unique economic risk. As a result, investments in stocks of emerging markets require considerable diversification.

Random Diversification Revisited. We first discussed the concept of random, or naive, diversification in Chapter 6. There are two different ways in which one can examine the reduction in risk that comes from random diversification:

- **Relating TSSDs to the number of securities held.** In this approach, one randomly selects N securities, assumes that $1/N$ is invested in each security at the start of each period, and calculates the time-series standard deviation of this portfolio. This procedure is then simulated, say, 1,000 times. Finally, the average TSSD for a portfolio of N securities is plotted with TSSD on the vertical axis and N on the horizontal axis. The number of securities N is increased from 1 to some large number.[2]

- **Relating the standard deviation of terminal wealth to N.** In this approach, a portfolio of N securities is selected as above and rebalanced so $1/N$ is invested in each security at the start of each period. But in this approach the uncertain variable of interest is the terminal wealth obtained from an initial investment of $1 in the portfolio. Terminal wealth is calculated by compounding the $1 investment by the

---

[2] Notice that this procedure assumes the mean return on each randomly selected security portfolio is known once the N securities are known.

portfolio's returns in each period. This procedure is then simulated, say, 1,000 times. Finally, the standard deviation of the terminal wealth values is calculated. We refer to this as the cross-sectional standard deviation of terminal wealth (CSSD). This CSSD is then plotted with CSSD on the vertical axis and N on the horizontal. The number of securities N is increased from 1 to some large number.[3]

Virtually all tests of random diversification have used the first approach.[4] As a result, these tests have suggested that relatively few securities are necessary to reduce diversifiable volatility risk. Yet, as already discussed, this approach does not account for uncertainty that investors have about average returns.

To contrast the results of both approaches when applied to investment manager selection, the author used each procedure on two databases. The simulation procedures are summarized in Table 20-2. The first database represented all U.S. mutual funds that invested in bonds during the ten years ended December 31, 1995. The second database represented all U.S. mutual funds that invested in U.S. equities during the same ten-year period.

Results when the time-series standard deviation approach is used on the equity mutual fund database are shown in Figure 20-3. Results on the bond mutual fund database were similar, varying only in scale. During this ten-year period, the average TSSD for a single equity mutual fund was 8.42%. When portfolios of four mutual funds were randomly created, the average TSSD fell to 7.96%, not a major reduction in risk. In fact, when a portfolio consisting of all funds in the sample was created, the TSSD was 7.68%. These results imply that diversification over equity mutual funds does not have a significant reduction in portfolio risk. But remember that this approach to evaluating the benefits of diversification focuses solely on diversifiable volatility risk, variability around a given mean rate of return. It does not capture uncertainty about the mean future portfolio return.

Results for the approach that focuses on the variability in the year-10 terminal wealth from an initial investment of $1 are shown in Figures 20-4 and 20-5. Figure 20-4 displays outcomes for random selection of bond managers and Figure 20-5 displays outcomes for equity managers.

Consider the bond manager outcomes in Figure 20-4. During the ten-year period ending December 31, 1995, an investment of $1 would have had an average terminal wealth of $2.47. However, most managers would have provided a terminal wealth either greater or smaller than $2.47. In fact, the cross-sectional standard deviation of the terminal wealth generated by the bond manager database was $0.29. This means that approximately one-third of all investors who invested $1 with a single bond manager would have had a terminal wealth either less than $2.18 or more than $2.76. If this difference seems small, translate the value to millions. The difference between $2.76 million and $2.18 million is certainly not trivial. Investment in a single bond manager has considerable risk. The more important implication of the data plotted in Figure 20-4, however, is that broad diversification across many bond managers is needed to reduce uncertainty that exists in future

---

[3] Notice that this procedure focuses on the uncertain mean portfolio returns and diversifiable volatility risk. It does not estimate nondiversifiable market risk.

[4] Elton and Gruber were the first to discuss uncertain mean risk. However, they did not recognize the importance of this form of risk to investors with multiperiod horizons. Instead, they focused on single-period reductions in volatility risk and uncertain mean return risk.

TABLE 20-2   METHODOLOGY OF MUTUAL FUND SIMULATIONS

For an investment in a single mutual fund:

1. For a given mutual fund, find the terminal value at December 31, 1995, from investing $1 at January 1, 1986.
2. Find the time-series standard deviation of quarterly returns for the manager.
3. Repeat for all managers.
4. Calculate the cross-sectional standard deviation of terminal wealth across all managers.
5. Calculate the average time-series standard deviation of quarterly returns.

For a portfolio of N mutual funds:

1. Select N funds at random.
2. Calculate the quarterly returns from a portfolio in which 1/N is invested in each fund at the start of each quarter.
3. Calculate the time-series standard deviation of this portfolio as well as the terminal wealth from investing $1.
4. Repeat steps 1 through 3 300 times.
5. Calculate the average time-series standard deviation over the 300 simulations.
6. Calculate the cross-sectional standard deviation of the year-10 terminal wealth obtained from the 300 simulations.
7. Iterate N from 2 to 16.

FIGURE 20-3   MUTUAL FUND DIVERSIFICATION AND THE TIME SERIES STANDARD DEVIATION

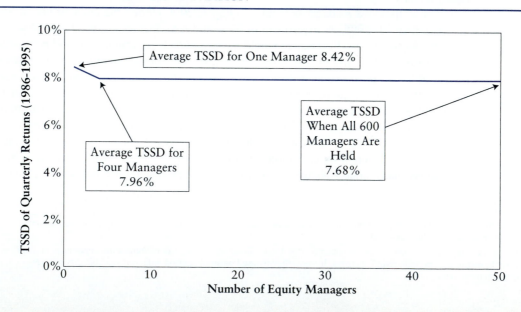

FIGURE 20-4 **DIVERSIFICATION ACROSS ACTIVE PROFESSIONAL BOND MANAGERS**

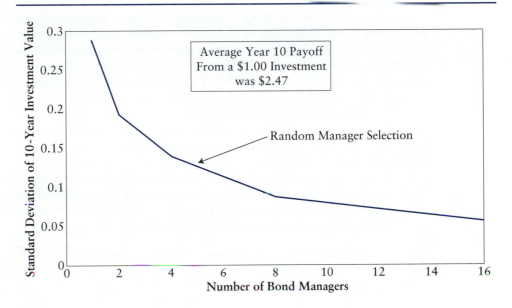

FIGURE 20-5 **DIVERSIFICATION ACROSS ACTIVE PROFESSIONAL EQUITY MANAGERS**

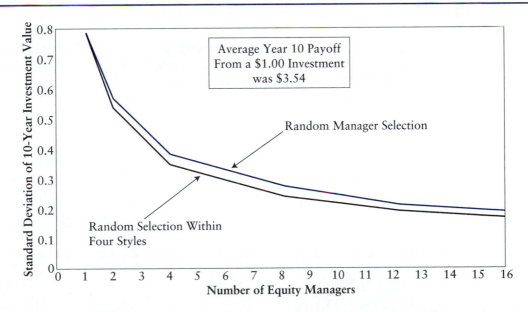

average returns. Unless you are able to distinguish between bond managers who will have large future average returns from managers who will have low future average returns, broad diversification is needed to reduce uncertainty associated with future mean returns.

The story is even more striking for the sample of equity mutual funds. During the ten-year period tested, an investment of $1 in the average equity mutual fund would have grown to $3.54. But the cross-sectional standard deviation of equity manager terminal wealth outcomes was about $0.80. Thus, one-third of all investors who invested in a single equity manager would have had a terminal wealth of less than $2.74 or more than $4.34!

Again, the mean return risk associated with owning a single active investment manager is sizable. And considerable diversification across equity managers is needed to reduce this risk. Unless you are able to distinguish between equity managers who will have large future average returns from managers who will have low future average returns, broad diversification is needed to reduce uncertainty associated with future mean returns.

In summary, diversifiable volatility risk can be eliminated rapidly by holding a relatively small number of securities or investment managers. But uncertainty about future average returns requires considerable diversification. To eliminate this form of risk, a number of active investment managers should be employed.[5]

Diversification and Manager Styles. A widely used approach to diversifying across active investment managers is called **styling,** which consists of defining groups of managers that differ in certain characteristics.[6] The belief is that, if funds are owned which have differing security characteristics, then the portfolio will be sufficiently diversified.

An example of manager styling is the approach followed by Morningstar Mutual Funds. They define two dimensions on which an equity manager is styled: size of the companies the mutual fund buys, and the "value" versus "growth" characteristics of the stocks bought.

Size represents the average market capitalization of companies owned by the equity fund. If the average market capitalization is less than one billion, the fund is classified as a small cap fund. If the average market capitalization is between one and five billion, the fund is classified as a medium cap fund. Funds with an average capitalization above five billion are classified as large cap funds.

Value funds own stocks with low price-to-earnings and price-to-book ratios. Growth funds own stocks with high price-to-earnings and price-to-book ratios. Finally, blend funds own stocks with price-to-earnings and price-to-book ratios that are in the middle.

The usefulness of style diversification depends, of course, on how the styles are defined. However, even simpleminded styling does work. For example, consider Figure 20-5 again. The dark curve below the colored curve represents the cross-sectional standard deviation results associated with diversification and the methodology described in Table 20-2. This is a very simple methodology that could probably be refined to lead to better diversification results than displayed in Figure 20-5. But these naive styling results show that diversification across manager styles does work.

---

[5] This discussion relates only to the employment of managers who actively manage their portfolios. If passive management is used, a single index fund is sufficient to reduce all forms of diversifiable risk (within that asset class).

[6] Style definitions are also discussed in Chapter 21.

Diversification and the Investment Horizon. The longer the investment horizon, the greater the need for diversification, whether across individual securities or investment managers. To understand why this is the case, think of investing in equity mutual funds. If you select one manager at random, you face two types of uncertainties associated with the value of the investment in one year. The first source of risk is uncertainty associated with the future mean return of the manager. In this section, we have referred to this as **uncertain mean return risk.** The second source of risk are random yearly returns that are generated around the true future mean return. We have referred to this as **volatility risk.**

Both sources of risk can be thought of as consisting of a diversifiable risk, which can be eliminated if one holds all securities (or mutual funds in our example), and a nondiversifiable risk. Based on post–World War II equity returns and the 10-year sample of equity mutual funds discussed earlier, the size of these risks are approximated in Table 20-3.

Table 20-3 suggests that the standard deviation of annual volatility risk for a single security is about 30% and the standard deviation of the uncertain mean return is about 8.7%. If the portfolio is well diversified, the volatility standard deviation would be about 15% and the standard deviation of the uncertain mean would be about 3.4%. Based on these estimates, *the dominant risk for an investor with a one-year time horizon is volatility risk,* whether the portfolio is diversified or not diversified.

TABLE 20-3   ILLUSTRATIVE ESTIMATES OF YEARLY INVESTMENT RISKS

Yearly Volatility Risks	Variance	Standard Deviation	Comments
Total Annual	0.0900	0.3	Approximation of annual single stock standard deviation post World War II.
Nondiversifiable	0.0225	0.15	Approximation of annual S&P 500 standard deviation post War World II.
Diversifiable	0.0675	0.2598	Difference
Yearly Uncertain Mean Risks			
Total Annual	0.007556	0.087	Addition of nondiversifiable and diversifiable risks estimated below
Nondiversifiable	0.001156	0.034	$0.15 \div 20^{1/2}$ using formula for standard deviation of uncertain mean with a stationary series
Diversifiable	0.0064	0.08	Implied from a 10-year standard deviation of mutual fund terminal wealth of $0.80

NOTE: All values are stated in decimal form. For example, 0.08 represents 8%.

Both forms of risk increase with the time horizon. That means that investors with, say, a 10-year investment horizon face more uncertainty today about the ending value of their portfolio than do 1-year investors.

But these two risks increase with time at different rates. Using reasonable assumptions, the variance of volatility risk N periods in the future is equal to the variance of one period multiplied by N. For example, if the volatility variance of one-year returns for a nondiversified portfolio is 0.09 (a standard deviation of 30%), then the variance of portfolio value for a 10-year investor caused by volatility risk is 0.90 (0.09 times 10). In contrast, the variance associated with an uncertain mean N periods in the future is equal to the variance of one period multiplied by N squared. For example, if the uncertain mean variance of one-year returns for a nondiversified portfolio is 0.007556 (a standard deviation of 8.7%), then the variance of portfolio values for a 10-year investor caused by an uncertain mean is 0.7556 (0.007556 times 100).

The reason for the different growth rates of these variances is caused by the fact that volatility returns are uncorrelated from period to period whereas uncertain mean returns are perfectly positively correlated. For example, if returns in a given period caused by volatility risk are much larger than expected, this has no effect on any future returns. Volatility returns are serially uncorrelated. In contrast, if you believe the expected long-run return on a manager will be 8% but the true mean return for the manager is 6%, then your two percentage point error applies to all future periods over which risk is being extrapolated. Uncertain mean return risk has a serial correlation of +1.0.

Three important conclusions emerge. First, not only does investment risk increase with the investment horizon, it increases at an increasing rate. Second, the longer one's investment horizon, the greater the importance of mean return risk. Short-term investors' major source of risk is volatility risk. But very long-term investors should also focus on mean return risk. Finally, the longer one's investment horizon, the greater the investor's need for diversification. Studies such as those cited earlier in the chapter which concluded that 10 to 30 securities are sufficient to virtually eliminate diversifiable risk are true for short-term investors. But long-term investors need considerably more diversification!

Figure 20-6 displays the concepts just discussed. Data used to construct the figure are shown in Table 20-3. The data is based on a single period as being one year. Thus, the horizontal scale can be interpreted as years. The vertical scale represents variance of ending portfolio values (based on a $1 investment).

Criteria Used in Selecting Managers

Passive Managers. If the investor chooses to use passively managed index funds, the selection criteria is relatively straightforward. Choose a fund that has had a small return tracking error when compared to the actual index returns and a fund which requires a low cost of ownership. Index funds are created for clearly defined portions of an asset class. For example, Vanguard has a fund that emulates the S&P 500 Index and another fund which emulates the aggregate of all traded stocks in the United States. When buying an index fund, be sure you know what the index is. In addition, one index fund will have to be purchased for each asset class in which an investment is made.

Active Managers. Ideally, investors would like to select active managers who will have good future performance and improve portfolio diversification. Although investors

FIGURE 20-6   DIVERSIFICATION AND THE INVESTMENT HORIZON

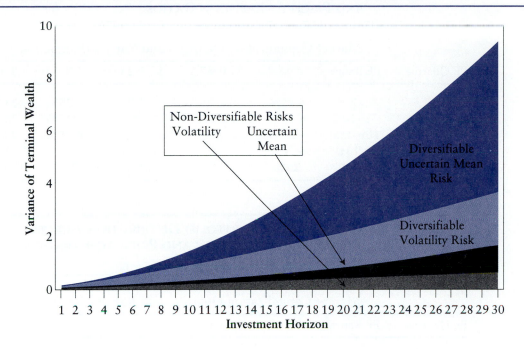

have little control over a manager's future performance, they can have total control over portfolio diversification. Thus, while opinions about future performance will play an important role in selecting managers, the first criteria should be to select a group of managers who provide broad portfolio diversification. In practice, people obtain this diversification by investing in managers who have different investment styles.

We noted earlier that there are many ways to define investment styles. For illustrative purposes, assume the styles of equity managers are defined according to the size of companies in which they invest (measured by the average market capitalization of stocks held) and by the average price-to-earnings ratio of the fund. Also assume the current market capitalization and price-to-earnings ratios of individual stocks are distributed as shown in Table 20-4.

One way to seek broad diversification would be to select equity managers so that, in aggregate, they have a price-to-earnings (P/E) and market capitalization (Cap) distribution similar to the actual distribution of traded stocks. For example, assume the investor's current portfolio consists of three mutual funds that, in aggregate, have the distribution of P/E and Cap as shown in Table 20-5.

A quick look at Table 20-5 indicates that the portfolio has a larger proportion of holdings in large cap and high P/E ratio companies than are present in the security markets. To more fully diversify the portfolio, investment managers who invest in low cap and low P/E ratio stocks should be acquired.

Another way to analyze the extent to which the portfolio is properly balanced is to compare the industry sector weightings against the weightings in a specified stock index. For example, Figure 20-7 shows the sector weightings of a domestic U.S. equity manager

TABLE 20-4   STOCK DISTRIBUTION ACROSS MARKET CAPITALIZATION AND PRICE-TO-EARNINGS RATIOS

PE Quartile	PE Range	Market Capitalization Quartiles and Ranges ($ in billions)				
		< $1.0	$1.0–$7.5	$7.5–25.0	> $25.0	Total
1	<7x	6.25%	6.25%	6.25%	6.25%	25%
2	7x–10x	6.25%	6.25%	6.25%	6.25%	25%
3	10x–13x	6.25%	6.25%	6.25%	6.25%	25%
4	> 13x	6.25%	6.25%	6.25%	6.25%	25%
	Total	25%	25%	25%	25%	100%

TABLE 20-5   HYPOTHETICAL PORTFOLIO DISTRIBUTION ACROSS MARKET CAPITALIZATION AND PRICE-TO-EARNINGS RATIOS

PE Quartile	PE Range	Market Capitalization Quartiles and Ranges ($ in billions)				
		< $1.0	$1.0–$7.5	$7.5–25.0	> $25.0	Total
1	< 7x	0%	0%	5%	0%	5%
2	7x–10x	0%	0%	5%	5%	10%
3	10x–13x	0%	5%	5%	20%	30%
4	> 13x	0%	10%	10%	35%	55%
	Total	0%	15%	25%	60%	100%

versus those of the S&P 500 Index. Notice that the manager has overweighted holdings in the technology sector and underweighted stocks in the basic industry and finance sectors.

To summarize, the first objective when selecting investment managers should be to achieve broad diversification. Unless a passive index manager is used to diversify within an asset class, multiple managers will probably have to be employed in order to obtain the necessary diversification.

In addition, the following criteria should be considered in manager selection:

- The manager should use a consistent investment approach so the investor can count on the manager to provide a consistent role in diversifying the portfolio.

- The manager should be experienced and knowledgeable (as evidenced by a CFA certification).

- The professional staff of the management firm should be stable and provide strong backup to the manager.

FIGURE 20-7 HYPOTHETICAL SECTOR ALLOCATIONS SECTOR WEIGHTING FOR PORTFOLIO VS. S&P 500

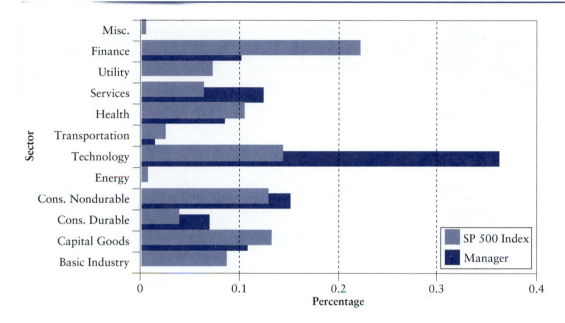

- ✺ The manager should use a logical investment approach that is consistently adhered to and used for a number of years.

- ✺ The management firm should have strong internal research capabilities.

- ✺ The management firm should show gradual growth in assets under management and not rely on a few major investors for the majority of assets managed.

- ✺ Management and operating fees should be competitive.

Persistence of Manager Performance. Even though broad portfolio diversification should be the first goal when selecting investment managers, most investors look primarily at a manager's past performance. Performance can be measured in many ways. The simplest measure is simply an average return for some past time interval. More sophisticated measures that consider both average returns and return volatility are discussed in Chapter 21. A performance measure that individual investors use extensively is the star rating system prepared by Morningstar Mutual Funds. Morningstar gives each mutual fund it follows a rating ranging from one star (the worst) to five stars (the best). These star ratings are based on (1) the manager's average return versus average returns for other managers who have the same investment objective, and (2) a measure of the risk inherent in the manager's past returns.

Regardless of how performance is measured, most studies indicate that past relative performance is unrelated to future relative performance. The data displayed in Figure 20-8

Ann Rubin Dominic, C.F.A.

Senior Manager, Capital Management
MCI Communications Corporation
Smith College, B.A.
Vanderbilt University, M.B.A.
Owen Graduate School of Management

MCI is a telecommunications service provider. Ann Dominic worked in public accounting after graduating from business school and was then involved in corporate financial analysis for about ten years before moving to her current position at MCI. She has made a point to follow her interests and seek challenging positions.

Q: Does MCI manage its retirement assets internally, externally, or both?

A: MCI has made the decision to manage all funds externally. Funds management is not a core business for MCI nor is it indirectly related to a core business. For this reason, MCI has not had a reason to develop this expertise internally.

Q: How does MCI choose external money managers, and how is a pension consultant incorporated into the process?

A: MCI uses a well-developed process to choose its money managers. First, a preliminary list of candidates is developed, working in conjunction with the pension consultant. MCI's pension consultant provides in-depth knowledge of the investment managers to Treasury. The consultant maintains an extensive database of investment managers' quantitative and qualitative information, including performance data, firm history, and principals' background. In addition to providing statistical information, the consultant also meets in person with the investment manager at the manager's office to review the investment process. Next, MCI and the consultant develop criteria for the selection of the manager based on performance, investment process, fit to the pension plan's needs, fit with the other investment managers, and other specific requirements. MCI's consultant will then extensively review each manager on the list, in order to recommend the top candidates. Treasury reviews the information presented by the consultant, including quantitative and qualitative characteristics, selecting a small number to interview in person. The final selection is made based on the further information obtained from the managers' presentations and a review of their fit with the selection criteria.

Q: How does MCI determine how many asset managers it will employ and what type of assets they will manage?

A: The number of asset managers is primarily determined based on the investment style and the need for diversification. With a small cap investment or a more volatile investment, more diversification and a large number of investment managers may be desirable. Because fees are based on the size of the assets under management, pension plans generally limit the number of managers in order to pay the lowest total fees.

Q: How is the performance of money managers evaluated?

A: Performance of the money managers is evaluated primarily quantitatively but also qualitatively. A performance benchmark is established for each of the managers depending on the approach or style of the manager. The benchmark is generally a replicable index specific to the investment style. For example, the benchmark for the large capitalization manager is the Russell Large Cap Growth Index. The performance for a manager is judged relative to the performance of the benchmark index. The qualitative aspects of performance measurement are more diverse and focus on the investment process, personnel, and the firm: Is there stability in the investment personnel who have previously created the fund's results? Do the investment professionals stay with their stated investment style, even when results are lagging?

The combination of the quantitative and qualitative assessments completes the evaluation. Action will be taken as necessary depending on the results of the evaluation.

Q: Are MCI employees involved in deciding who will manage their retirement funds?

A: MCI has both a defined benefit plan and a defined contribution plan. In the defined benefit plan, the employee is not involved in deciding who will manage the funds. But in the defined contribution plan the employee does decide who will manage his or her retirement funds. The selection of money managers offered the employee is a decision made by the Pension Investment Committee, which is composed of internal and external board members.

Q: How is your statement of investment policy developed and used?

A: MCI has had an investment policy since the inception of the pension plan in the early 1980s. It is continually refined, primarily as a result of changes in investment practices and MCI's asset allocation. The investment policy frames the investment classes for the plan as well as the target allocation to each class. This asset allocation is developed from studies of the expected return and risk for each asset class combined with the expected liability of the plan. The policy also stipulates specific guidelines for investing the pension funds that the pension managers must follow. There are guidelines specific to the asset classes and to the manager.

FIGURE 20-8

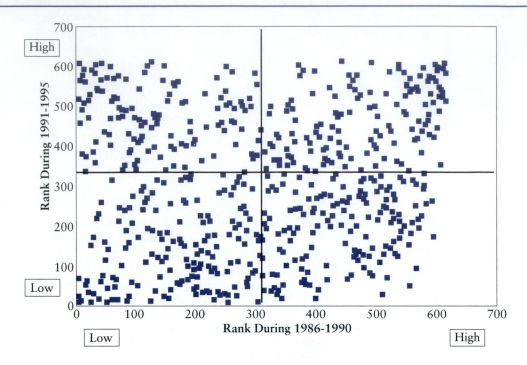

illustrates this point. The author selected all mutual funds that invested in U.S. common stocks during the ten-year period ending December 31, 1995. This resulted in 614 funds. The average quarterly return for each fund was calculated and ranked for two periods. The first period consisted of the years 1986 to 1990 and the second consisted of 1991 to 1995.

Each point in Figure 20-8 represents a given mutual fund and where its average quarterly return ranked in the two periods. Funds that ranked below average in both periods are plotted in the bottom left quadrant. Funds that ranked above average in both periods are plotted in the upper right quadrant.

The data suggest there are no patterns present. Performance rankings in the first period are unrelated to performance rankings in the second period. Some funds did rank high in both periods and others ranked low in both periods. But it is impossible to tell from this data whether such rankings were due to skill or chance!

In recent years a number of studies have suggested there might be some persistence in performance when rankings are based on shorter time intervals than used in Figure 20-8. For example, a study by Goetzmann and Ibbotson (1994) seemed to find evidence that good performance during periods ranging from a single month to two years is related to subsequent performance over the same time interval.

Using a sample of U.S. equity mutual funds, the researchers calculated the adjacent two-year returns for each fund over the period 1976 to 1987. For each two-year period, each manager was classified as a "winner" or "loser" depending on whether the manager's two-year return was in the top half or bottom half of the sample. Finally, a table was prepared showing

TABLE 20-6   PERSISTENCE IN EQUITY MUTUAL FUND RANKINGS

	Subsequent Two-Year Winners	Subsequent Two-Year Losers
Initial Two-Year Winners	486 (59.9%)	325 (40.1%)
Initial Two-Year Losers	327 (40.3%)	484 (59.7%)

how winners and losers fared in an initial and subsequent two-year period. Table 20-6 summarizes the findings.

If there was no relationship between initial and subsequent performance, one would expect one-half of the winners in the initial period to be winners in the subsequent period. The same would be true for initial losers. However, Table 20-6 shows that about 60% of initial winners remain winners in the subsequent period.

The researchers performed a variety of other tests examining performance across two independent time intervals (of three years or less). With few exceptions they found that winners tended to remain winners and losers tended to remain losers. The implication of these results is clear. Past short-term performance appears to be mildly related to future short-term performance.

Results such as these have not gone unchallenged. In fact, the authors of the study raise serious questions about drawing implications about the predictability of short-term relative rankings. Probably the most important practical problem is the difficulty in identifying those managers who will continue to win during the subsequent period. Remember that 40% of the winners became losers and 40% of the losers became winners. In addition, the costs of trying to take advantage of such small persistence that might exist would probably offset possible gains.

In addition, the following are possible explanations for the apparent persistence in rankings:

■ Survivorship bias could cause such results. A number of studies suggest that results such as those shown in Table 20-6 could be caused by the disappearance of managers with historically poor performance. If one uses a sample that consists of managers who have historically had higher returns than managers who disappear, there would be a bias in such studies for winners to repeat.

■ The winners could be high-risk funds. If the winners are high-risk funds and the losers are low-risk funds, then volatility risk could explain the tendency for one group to consistently have higher returns than the other group. In fact, if managers are ranked on their average return divided by their standard deviation of return, the persistence in relative ranking disappears.

■ Securities held by the manager could show persistence in the short term. An implication in studies such as these is that the good and poor relative performance is due to manager skill (or lack of it). However, it is possible that the results are simply caused by the types of securities held. For example, managers who own low price-to-earnings stocks will have similar returns regardless of whether they are above or below average. It is possible that returns on securities with similar fundamental characteristics will have returns that rank above or below average for periods of four or more years. This explanation has not been tested to date.

Tax Management

A major reason to manage a security portfolio personally as opposed to employing professional investment managers is the ability to manage the tax consequences of investment decisions. In this section we review the basics of investment tax management. Regulations underlying how security transactions are taxed are very complex, and changes in the regulations occur frequently. Thus, our discussion must be general in nature, covering the most important concepts of security taxation.

We begin with a short overview of how federal income taxes are calculated on security transactions. This is followed by a discussion of ways to defer tax payments and a section on tax avoidance.

Basics of Security Taxation

Institutional investors such as pension funds, endowment funds, and mutual funds do not pay taxes on profits earned on security investments as long as they comply with requirements of the Internal Revenue Code.

Individual investors pay taxes on two types of income: ordinary income and capital gain (or loss) income. **Ordinary income** includes salaries and wages from employment as well as interest and dividends on security investment. **Capital gains and losses** represent profits or losses that are realized when a security is sold. Typically, the maximum tax rate on capital gains is less than the maximum tax rate on ordinary income. Ordinary and capital gains tax rates change considerably over time. However, the basic structure of rates is shown in Table 20-7. In 1995, the maximum capital gains rate was 28%. Capital gains are identified as short-term gains when the security has been held for less than one year. Long-term capital gains arise when the security is held for more than one year. At some times, the long-term capital gains rate will be lower than the short-term capital gains rate. They were equal in 1995.

Securities are bought or sold for tax purposes on the trade date, not the settlement date. The **basis** represents the purchase price for tax purposes and is equal to the full amount paid for the security including brokerage commissions. When you sell the security, any commissions paid are used to reduce the realized selling price. For example, assume you buy 100 shares of Steel Corp. at a price of 40 3/8 on December 31, 1997, and sell them for 45 1/2 on December 16, 1998. Both transactions incur a commission of 2%. Then the cost basis of the purchase will be $4,118.25 ($4,037.50 plus 0.02 times $4,037.50) and the realized selling price will be $4,459 ($4,550 minus 0.02 times $4,550). This results in a short-term capital gain equal to $340.75 ($4,459.00 minus $4,118.25).

TABLE 20-7   FEDERAL INCOME TAX RATES (1995)

Ordinary Tax Rate	15%	28%	31%	36%	39.6%
Capital Gains Tax Rate	15%	28%	28%	28%	28%

Filing Status	Taxable Income Ranges				
Single	<$23,350	$23,350–$56,550	$56,550–$117,950	$117,950–$256,500	>$256,500
Head of Household	<$31,250	$31,250–$$80,750	$80,750–$130,800	$130,800–$256,500	>$256,500
Married Filing Jointly	<$39,000	$39,000–$94,250	$94,250-$143,600	$143,600–$256,500	>$256,500
Married Filing Separately	<$19,500	$19,500–$47,125	$47,125–$71,800	$71,800–$128,250	$128,250

We do not discuss tax details associated with the various types of securities that are available. However, a summary of general tax rules is provided in Table 20-8.

Delaying Tax Payments. Stock investments have a possible tax advantage that is not as sizable with most bond issues: the ability to time the date at which capital gains will be recognized. For example, consider a stock that has a total pretax expected return equal to 12%. Assume this 12% consists of a dividend yield of 4% and an expected annual growth in the stock's price of 8%. Also consider a bond that is selling at par value with a yield to maturity of 8%. The stock has two possible tax advantages relative to the bond. First, the 8% price growth will be taxed at a capital gains rate that is likely to be smaller than the ordinary tax rate for many investors. In contrast, the full 8% pretax return on the bond will be taxed at the ordinary tax rate. Second, the stock investor can delay payment of taxes on the stock's future price growth for many years by simply not selling it. Taxes will not be paid on capital gains until the gain is actually realized for tax purposes by a sale of the security. Although taxes will eventually have to be paid on any price gains, one saves by delaying the realization of gains due to the time value of money created by delaying tax payments.

The ability to delay capital gains tax payments is a major reason why many people choose to manage their portfolio personally. This ability to delay capital gains payments is referred to as the **tax timing option.** While tax timing options are greater for stocks than bonds (and greatest for stocks that pay no taxes), tax timing can also be used on bond holdings if the bonds are bought at a discount.[7] If the investments are turned over to professional managers who actively manage the account, taxable gains will be realized continuously over time as the manager trades the account and the value of the tax timing option will be zero.[8]

---

[7] Over time, all bonds tend to move toward par value at that bond's maturity date. Thus, delaying sale of bonds bought at par or at a premium will usually result in lower future selling prices.

[8] Passive managers usually create fewer realized capital gains than do active investment managers. This is because passive managers attempt to trade securities as seldom as possible.

TABLE 20-8 TAXATION OF SECURITY TYPES TO INDIVIDUAL INVESTORS

U.S. Savings Bonds. Income taxes may be deferred until the bond is cashed.

Treasury Bills. Federal income taxes are paid at the ordinary rate in the year the securities are either sold or mature. Profits on T-bills are not subject to state or local income taxes.

Treasury Bonds Notes. Interest received is subject to federal income tax in the year received but not subject to state or local income taxes. Realized gains or losses from the sale of these securities are taxed in the year in which the profit or loss is realized. Interest income and realized gains or losses are not subject to state or local income tax.

Treasury STRIPS and Other Zeros. The discount at which the security is bought is amortized over the investment's life and treated as ordinary income. Such income of Treasury STRIPS is not taxable at state and local levels. The income recorded increases the cost basis of the security. If the security is sold prior to maturity, a capital gain or loss is incurred (equal to the sale price minus the current cost basis of the security).

Agency Issues. Ginnie Mae, Fannie Mae, and Freddie Mac issues are taxable at federal, state, and local levels. All other agency issues are taxable only at the federal level. Interest is taxed as ordinary income. Realized gains or losses are taxed in the year of sale.

Corporate Bonds. Interest received is subject to federal, state, and local income tax in the year received. Realized gains or losses from the sale of these securities are taxed in the year in which the profit or loss is realized.

If the securities are bought at a discount when the securities are first issued, the security is referred to as an original issue discount (OID) bond. The discount on an OID bond must be amortized over the bond's life and treated as taxable interest income. As the discount is amortized, the cost basis of the bonds is increased. If the securities are bought at a discount after original issue, one may either amortize the discount and treat the amortization as interest (similar to OID bonds) or pay ordinary taxes at the bond's sale on the portion of the discount that represents accumulated interest.

If the securities are bought at a premium, the premium may be amortized and used to reduce yearly interest income. The amortization reduces the bond's basis. It is usually advantageous to follow this procedure. Alternatively, if the premium is not amortized, a capital loss is incurred when the bond is redeemed or sold for less than what was initially paid. If sold for more than the initial price, a capital gain is incurred.

Municipal Bonds. Interest income is not subject to federal tax and is not taxed in the state in which the security was issued. Realized gains or losses are taxed in the year of sale.

Preferred Stock. Individuals pay ordinary tax rates on dividend receipts and capital gains rates on realized gains or losses.

Common Stock. Individuals pay ordinary tax rates on dividend receipts and capital gains rates on realized gains or losses.

Mutual Funds. Dividends paid to shareholders from net interest and dividend income received by the fund are taxed at the ordinary rate. These are referred to as income dividends. Dividends paid to shareholders from realized gains or losses of the fund are taxed at the capital gains rate. These are referred as capital gain dividends. The mutual fund specifies the dollar amount of each type paid. Taxes must be paid on all mutual fund dividends even if reinvested in the mutual fund. In a switch from one fund into shares of another fund within the same "family" of funds, the exchange is treated as a sale.

Municipal Bond Mutual Funds. Interest received on investments of the fund in municipal bonds is not subject to federal income taxes and may be excluded from state and local taxes if the bonds owned were issued in the taxing state.

Variable Annuities. All profits of investment made in a variable annuity are not taxed until the annuity is redeemed. At redemption, profits are taxed at the ordinary income tax rate.

What If You Must Sell? Situations arise in which the delay of taxes on capital gains is offset by a desire to sell the security, either in the belief that it is overvalued or because cash is needed. In this case, there are a number of ways to reduce the tax burden.

One way is to sell another security in which you have a capital loss and replace it with a substantially similar security. For example, assume you bought 100 shares of two different stocks, both at a price of $50 per share. Stock A has increased in value to $70 and you wish to sell it because you are concerned it is presently overvalued. In contrast, stock B has fallen in value to $30 per share, but you would prefer to continue holding it because you believe its value will soon increase.

To minimize the taxes from a sale of stock A you could proceed as follows. Sell both stock A and stock B. The capital gain of $2,000 on stock A will be offset by the $2,000 capital loss on stock B. In addition, to maintain a long position similar to that of stock B you would buy a similar stock. Although it would be nice if you could have repurchased stock B, regulations of the Internal Revenue Code declare the sale of a security followed by a purchase of the same security or a "substantially similar" security within 30 days to be a **wash sale,** which means the capital loss on the sale would not be allowed as a tax deduction. The definition of "substantially similar" would clearly be violated if you bought shares of stock B. But if you buy shares of another stock in the same industry, the rule would not be violated.[9]

Another way to minimize capital gains is to specify the batch of stocks being sold. For example, assume you bought 100 shares of stock A at two different dates, one at a price of $50 and one at $60. If you intend to sell 100 shares of stock A at $70, you could earmark the shares bought at $60 as those being sold. Good accounting records must be kept if this is to be done. And when the order to sell is made the order must specify the batch of stocks being sold.

Tax Deferral

The best way to defer taxes is to make the investments under the framework of special retirement programs created by the U.S. Congress. These include Individual Retirement Accounts (IRAs), Keogh plans, and other vehicles discussed here.

These retirement savings plans allow two levels of tax deferral:

- In one type of retirement savings plan, an *after-tax* contribution is made into a retirement portfolio. Profits earned by the portfolio are not taxed until withdrawn in retirement. When withdrawals are made during retirement years, any withdrawals that represent profits generated by the portfolio over its life are taxed as ordinary income. Some IRA investments are examples of this type of retirement program.

- In the other type of retirement savings plan, a *pre-tax* contribution is made into a retirement portfolio. This simply means the employee elects to assign a portion of his or her job income to a qualified retirement savings plan. As above, profits earned by the portfolio are not taxed until withdrawn in retirement. When withdrawals are made

---

[9] After 30 days, stock B could be repurchased and the temporary holding sold.

during retirement, all withdrawals are taxed as ordinary income. Defined contribution plans, Keogh plans, and some IRAs are examples of this type of investment plan.

The better of the two approaches is clearly the second, since it provides for investment income to be earned on a pretax contribution. However, there are legal limits to the amount of pretax contributions that can be made during a year. We discuss these limits later. After-tax retirement savings plans should be used only after the legal limit on pretax contribution plans has been reached.

Importance of Tax Deferral Benefits. To illustrate the importance of the benefits generated by the deferral of taxes under both types of retirement savings plans, consider the following three investment scenarios:

1. **Scenario 1.** In this scenario, a contribution is made to a portfolio from after-tax wages and salary into a savings plan in which all profits that are made during a given year are taxed as ordinary income during the year. This scenario represents an investment plan created by the investor without the tax benefits available from qualified retirement savings plans or a tax timing option created by personal tax management.
2. **Scenario 2.** In this scenario, a contribution is made to the portfolio from after-tax wages and salary into a savings plan in which profits are not taxed until withdrawal during retirement. This scenario represents a qualified retirement savings plan created with after-tax contributions or a tax timing option created by personal tax management.
3. **Scenario 3.** In this scenario, a contribution is made from pretax wages and salary. All future profits are not taxed while the retirement funds are invested. At retirement, all withdrawals (representing both the initial contribution and investment earnings) are taxed as ordinary income.

We assume a pretax income of $1,000, an ordinary tax rate of 30%, and a yearly investment return (pretax) of 6%. For simplicity, we also assume the portfolio is completely liquidated at a single retirement date. This is called a **lump sum** withdrawal. Typically, withdrawals are made over a number of years during retirement.

The results of these three scenarios are displayed in Figure 20-9. The horizontal axis represents retirement dates ranging from 1 year to 40 years. The vertical axis shows the lump sum amount of money available after the payment of all taxes. Notice that payoffs from scenario 3 (where the most taxes are deferred) are approximately double the payoffs from scenario 1 (where no taxes are deferred). Scenario 2 lies between the other two. When retirement occurs in 40 years, the after-tax portfolio values are as follows:

	Scenario 1	Scenario 2	Scenario 3
After-Tax Portfolio Value in 40 Years	$3,629.17	$5,250.00	$7,200.00

In scenario 1, the investor starts with $1,000 on which $300 in taxes are paid. This leaves $700 for investment. Each year an after-tax return of 4.2% is earned (6% less the taxes on 6%). This results in a year-40 portfolio value of $3,629.17:

FIGURE 20-9 GROWTH OF $1,000 IN INCOME INVESTED AT 6% UNDER DIFFERENT TAX SITUATIONS

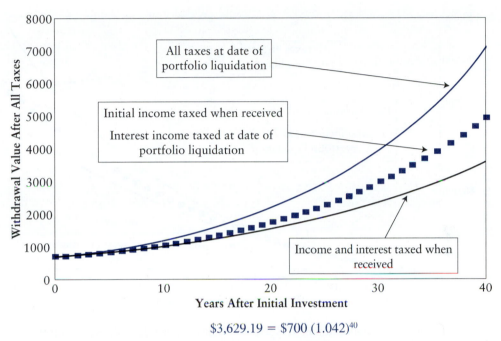

$$\$3,629.19 = \$700 (1.042)^{40}$$

In scenario 2, $700 of after-tax income is again invested but grows by 6% each year, since portfolio profits are not taxed. This results in a pretax portfolio value of $7,200:

$$\$7,200.00 = \$700 (1.06)^{40}$$

However, to withdraw money from the portfolio, taxes must be paid on the difference between its value at withdrawal and the initial $700 investment. These taxes would equal $1,950:

$$\$1,950.00 = (\$7,200 - \$700) \times 0.3$$

Subtracting these taxes results in the final value of scenario 3 of $5,250:

$$\$5,250.00 = \$7,250 - \$1,950$$

Finally, in scenario 3 the full $1,000 of pretax income is invested for 40 years at a pretax return of 6%. After 40 years, the value of this investment will be $10,285.72. This full amount will be subject to ordinary income taxes equal to $3,085.72. After taxes the value of scenario 3 will be $7,200:

$$\$7,200.00 = \$10,285.72 - (\$10,285.72 \times 0.3)$$

As further proof that tax deferral savings plans should be used if they are available to the investor, consider the information shown in Figure 20-10. This figure uses the same scenarios and assumptions as in Figure 20-9 except that Figure 20-10 is based on an annual contribution of $1,000 pretax ($700 after tax).

FIGURE 20-10   GROWTH OF $1,000 ANNUITY INVESTED AT 6% UNDER DIFFERENT TAX SITUATIONS

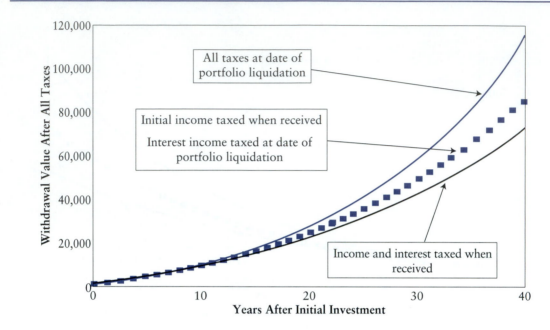

When retirement occurs in 40 years, the after-tax portfolio values are as follows:

	Yearly Pretax Investment of $1,000		
	Scenario 1	Scenario 2	Scenario 3
After-Tax Portfolio Value in 40 Years	$73,731	$89,483	$115,533

Clearly, there are significant tax benefits to retirement savings plans that allow for the deferral of taxes.

Types of Retirement Tax-Deferred Savings Plans. Many employers provide retirement benefits to employees through defined benefit plans. Under these plans the employer contracts with the employee for a specified retirement benefit. Often the employees make no contributions to these retirement portfolios. The employer makes any contributions necessary to provide the specified retirement benefit to the employee. However, in many defined benefit plans, employees agree to forgo a portion of their wage or salary in order to improve promised retirement benefits. The employer contributions are tax deductible to the employer and any contributions made by the employee are not taxed until withdrawn. Portfolio investment income is nontaxed until withdrawn during retirement. The total payment made to employees during a given year of retirement is treated as ordinary income to the employee during that year. While these represent a form of deferred tax savings, employees do not bear any investment risk since they are provided with a promised retirement benefit. In addition, employees have little discretion over the amount they invest in such plans.

Retirement savings plans that allow employees discretion over the amount they will invest as well as the types of securities in which they invest are called defined contribution (DC) plans. The following summarize the major types of DC plans and their investment limits:

- **401(k) Plans.** The label 401(k) refers to the section of the Internal Revenue Code that provides for defined contribution plans offered by profit-seeking corporations. Other sections of the 401 code provide for nonprofit organizations. Under the 401(k) provisions, employers may set up DC plans that allow employees to invest up to $9,240 (in 1995) each year. All employee contributions are pretax, meaning they are not taxed in the year in which the contribution is made but, instead, at the time of withdrawal during retirement. All investment earnings also accumulate tax free until withdrawn during retirement. Withdrawals may not be made until the employee is 59 1/2 years of age. Early withdrawals are subject to ordinary taxes plus a 10% excise tax. Withdrawals during retirement are treated as ordinary income.

- **Keogh Plans.** These are retirement savings plans for individuals who are self-employed. The maximum contribution in a given year is $30,000 or 15% of self-employed income. As with 401(k) plans, contributions and investment earnings are not taxed until withdrawn during retirement.

- **SEP.** This stands for Simplified Employee Pension. It is similar to a Keogh plan but is designed for small firms and the self-employed. Its advantage relative to a Keogh plan is simplicity. A small firm can create a SEP in 30 minutes with minimal documentation. Most of the larger mutual fund companies provide investment products and administration for SEP accounts. Contributions are limited to 15% of self-employment income. As with 401(k) plans, contributions and investment earnings are not taxed until withdrawn during retirement.

- **IRAs.** Individual Retirement Accounts are not created through one's employer. They are personal savings plans. Tax deductible contributions to IRAs are currently limited to individuals who are not covered by a retirement savings plan of their employer. The annual limit is $2,000 per person or $2,250 with a spouse. If the employer offers a retirement plan, individuals with small income are allowed to make a nontaxable contribution to an IRA somewhat less than the $2,000 and $2,250 limits. However, even if the individual is covered by an employer retirement savings plan, the after-tax contribution of $2,000 or $2,250 may be made annually. While the contribution is made with after-tax dollars, all investment income will not be taxed until withdrawn during retirement.

    When an employee leaves a firm in which he or she had a defined contribution plan (or the employer goes bankrupt or is bought by another company), the market value of the employee's defined contribution portfolio is given to the employee as a lump sum. This money must be invested into another tax-deferred retirement savings plan within 60 days or it will be taxed. If the new employer offers a defined contribution plan, the moneys can be transferred to this new plan. However, if the new employer does not have a DC plan, the moneys should be rolled over into an IRA account.

▸ **Variable Annuities.** A variable annuity is an investment made into an investment product of an insurance firm. Employees of certain nonprofit organizations may make contributions to the variable annuity from pretax dollars. As with other retirement savings plans, any income generated by the investment product is not taxed until withdrawn.

Tax Avoidance

In the United States, the only type of security on which interest income is not taxed at the federal level are bonds of state and local governmental authorities, called municipal bonds. If the municipal bond was issued in the state of the bond owner, interest income will not be subject to any income taxes of the state either. Capital gains or losses from trading in municipal bonds are subject to income taxes.

Because of this tax advantage, municipal bonds trade at lower yields to maturity (YTM) than equivalent maturity and default risk corporate bonds. To determine whether one should buy a municipal bond or equivalent taxable bonds, the municipal bond's after-tax YTM should be converted to an equivalent before-tax YTM.

This is a fairly simple process. The after-tax YTM on a taxable bond is equal to the before-tax YTM times "one minus the tax rate":

After-Tax YTM on a Taxable Bond

$$AT = BT\,(1 - TR) \tag{20.1}$$

Here AT represents the after-tax YTM, BT represents the before-tax YTM, and TR represents the marginal tax rate. Equation (20.1) can be rearranged to find the before-tax YTM associated with a given after-tax YTM and marginal tax rate as follows:

Before-Tax YTM Equivalent on a Municipal Bond

$$BT = AT \div (1 - TR) \tag{20.2}$$

For example, if a municipal bond has a yield to maturity of 5.0% and the investor's marginal tax rate is 28%, then the before-tax equivalent yield to maturity is 6.94%:

$$0.0694 = 0.05 \div (1 - 0.28)$$

If yields to maturity are greater than 6.94% on taxable bonds, then an investor who has a marginal tax rate of 28% should purchase the taxable bonds.

Table 20-9 provides a sample of before-tax yield to maturity associated with various after-tax yields and marginal tax rates. If the before-tax yield to maturity on a taxable bond

TABLE 20-9   MINIMUM TAXABLE YIELDS TO MATURITY FOR VARIOUS
NON-TAXABLE YIELDS AND MARGINAL TAX RATES

Marginal Tax Rate	Current Municipal Bond YTM			
	4.0%	5.0%	6.0%	7.0%
15%	4.71%	5.88%	7.06%	8.24%
28%	5.56%	6.94%	8.33%	9.72%
31%	5.80%	7.25%	8.70%	10.14%
36%	6.25%	7.81%	9.38%	10.94%
39.6%	6.62%	8.28%	9.93%	11.59%

is greater than the tabled values, then the taxable bond will provide the greater after-tax return. Otherwise, the municipal bond provides the better after-tax return.

SUMMARY

Here are the key concepts:

- The decision whether to manage an investment portfolio personally versus employing external managers is determined principally by the size of the portfolio, the asset allocation of the portfolio, investor knowledge, fiduciary responsibilities, and tax considerations.

- If external managers are used, at least one manager is usually employed for each asset class to be held in the portfolio.

- The traditional measure of investment risk (the time-series standard deviation, or TSSD) measures only the volatility around a mean rate of return. Unless you have no uncertainty about your estimate of the future expected return, the TSSD does not capture all risk. It misses uncertain mean return risk.

- The major risk faced by short-term investors is volatility risk as measured by the TSSD. The diversifiable risk inherent in the TSSD can be virtually eliminated by the random selection of 30 or less securities in a given asset class.

- The longer one's investment horizon, the more important diversifiable mean return risk becomes. As a result, the longer one's investment horizon, the greater the need for diversification.

- If the investor decides to use a passive investment strategy, then one passive index fund should be selected for each asset class held. The passive manager should have a small return tracking error when compared with the index the fund emulates.

- ✖ If the investor decides to use an active investment strategy, then multiple managers should be held in each asset class who differ in investment style.

- ✖ There is little evidence that long-term past relative performance of investment managers is a good predictor of future relative performance.

- ✖ An important motive for personally managing one's security portfolio is to take advantage of a tax timing option, the value that can be created by minimizing the present value of future tax payments.

- ✖ Significant tax savings can be obtained by investing through various retirement savings programs. These programs delay taxation of profits until withdrawn during retirement and often allow pretax contributions from wage and salary income that are then taxed in retirement.

R E V I E W   P R O B L E M

Anne has just received a $1,000 bonus from her employer that she wishes to invest in long-term bonds which will provide a yearly pretax rate of return of about 7%. Her tax rate is 30%. Yields to maturity on similar municipal bonds are 4.8%. There are two ways in which she could invest the money. Using the first alternative, she could take the bonus as income, pay taxes on the income, and invest the remainder. Under this alternative, the full 7% would be taxed each year if she buys the taxable bonds. Using the second alternative, she could invest the full $1,000 in a qualified savings plan that her employer offers. The $1,000 contribution and future profits would not be taxed until she withdraws the funds at retirement. Her expected retirement date is 30 years from now.

a. If she elects the first alternative, should she buy the taxable bond or the municipal bond?
b. If she elects the second alternative, should she buy the taxable bond or the municipal bond?
c. What is the expected after-tax value of the portfolio under both alternatives in 30 years? Assume that all funds would be withdrawn from the retirement program alternative as a lump sum.
d. What, if any, advantages are there in the first alternative?

Solution

a. The after-tax return on the taxable bond is 4.9%, which is greater than the after-tax return on the municipal bond. Buy the taxable issue.

$$0.049 = 0.07(0.7)$$

Alternatively, given an after-tax return of 4.8% on the municipal, the equivalent before-tax return equivalent is 6.86%. Again, select the taxable bond.

$$0.0686 = 0.048 \div (1 - 0.3)$$

b. The second alternative is a tax-sheltered retirement program. She should not place tax shelter securities in such a program because she would not be able to take advantage of the security's tax shelter. It would be better to accumulate money in the retirement program at 7% yearly than at 4.8%.

c.

	Alternative 1		Alternative 2	
	Initial Contribution	Yearly Return	Initial Contribution	Yearly Return
Before taxes	$1,000	7.0%	$1,000	7.0%
minus taxes	300	2.1	0	0.0
After taxes	$ 700	4.9%	$1,000	7.0%
Year-30 values Before tax	$700(1.049)^{30} = \$2,940.10		$1,000(1.07)^{30} = \$7,612.26	
minus tax	0		2,283.68	
After taxes	$2,940.10		$5,328.58	

d. The only advantage of using the first alternative is that it allows her to sell the securities before retirement if she needs the money. Under the retirement program alternative, she would have to pay a 10% excise tax if she withdrew the money before legal retirement.

The retirement program will still beat the first alternative if she intends to keep the money in the program a minimum number of years. You can easily calculate this date using a spreadsheet program. Up through year 7, early withdrawal of funds from the retirement program will result in lower cash value after the 10% penalty tax is paid. Beyond year 7, the retirement program would provide greater cash value, even after the extra 10% tax.

QUESTIONS AND PROBLEMS

1. Discuss how the following factors influence whether the investor will decide to use external managers to run some, or all, of the investor's portfolio.
   a. Size of the portfolio.
   b. The asset allocation of the portfolio.
   c. The decision to use a passive versus an active investment management approach.
   d. The investor's knowledge.
   e. Fiduciary responsibilities.
   f. Tax considerations.
2. Assume the trustees of a defined benefit pension plan with $1 billion in assets decides to invest passively in the following asset classes: domestic fixed income, foreign fixed income, domestic equity, and foreign equity. How many passive index managers would the fund employ, and what criteria should the trustees use in selecting the managers?
3. You are considering an investment in two mutual funds. Their past yearly returns and other information are shown here.

Year:	1	2	3	4	5
Manager 1	18%	−5%	12%	−7%	22%
Manager 2	22%	−1%	16%	−3%	26%

	Average Return	Standard Deviation	Correlation Coefficient
Manager 1	8.0%	11.88%	
Manager 2	12.0%	11.88%	1.0

    a. In terms of volatility risk and average annual past return, manager 1 has done better than manager 2. Does this mean manager 1 will do better than manager 2 in the future? What does the evidence presented in this chapter imply about past and future performance?

    b. The standard deviation number shown for each manager is the time-series standard deviation of past returns. Since they are equal and the correlation between past returns is +1.0, would there be any benefit to diversifying across both managers?

    c. If you used the data shown here as estimates of future expected returns, risk, and correlation in an efficient frontier program (as discussed in Chapter 6), what would the efficient frontier look like?

    d. Given your answers above, comment on the use of time-series standard deviations (which measure volatility risk) as a measure of an investment's risk.

4. What is meant by the idea of an uncertain expected return? Provide a couple of examples that illustrate this concept (try to develop examples using issues other than manager selection).

5. If investors decide to employ professional investment managers who use active investment strategies, why might they wish to use more than a single manager in a given asset class?

6. The longer the investment time horizon, the greater the need for diversification. Explain.

7. The more risky the asset class, the greater the need for diversification. Explain.

8. Are past investment manager returns predictable? Discuss.

9. What is meant by the term *tax timing option?*

10. What is the difference between tax deferral and tax avoidance?

11. William has just received a $1,000 bonus from his employer that he wishes to invest in long-term bonds which will provide a yearly pretax rate of return of 6.4%. His tax rate is 31%. Yields to maturity on similar municipal bonds are 4.5%. There are two ways in which he could invest the money. Using the first alternative, he could take the bonus as income, pay taxes on the income, and invest the remainder. Under this alternative, yearly interest income would be taxed if he chooses to invest in the 6.4% taxable bonds but not taxed if he chooses the 4.5% municipal bonds. Using the second alternative, he could invest the full $1,000 in a qualified savings plan that his employer offers. The investment could be made in either bond issue. The $1,000 contribution and future profits would not be taxed until he withdraws the funds at retirement. His expected retirement date is 40 years from now.

    a. If he elects the first alternative, should he buy the taxable bond or the municipal bond?

    b. If he elects the second alternative, should he buy the taxable bond or the municipal bond?

    c. What is the expected after-tax value of the portfolio under both alternatives in 40 years? Assume that all funds would be withdrawn from the retirement program alternative as a lump sum.

DATAFILE ANALYSIS

Access the data set called OEFUNDS to see mutual funds that invest primarily in U.S. equities. Information about each fund's load fees, operating expense ratios, net assets, 12b-1 fees, and historical rates of return are provided. Review the data set for its contents.

    Mary and Jerry Tompkins are both young professionals with promising careers. They are in their late 20s and have just inherited $50,000, which they wish to invest in equity mutual funds. They intend to hold the mutual funds to help pay for the college education of their children. They are presently expecting their first child, so it will be almost 20 years before the portfolio will be liquidated. Select and justify (at least) three funds that you would suggest to them. Should they invest in all three funds, two of the funds, or only a single fund?

R EFERENCES

Recent articles that investigate the issue of short-term persistence in investment manager performance include the following:

Brown, S., W. Goetzmann, R. Ibbotson, and S. Ross. "Survivorship Bias in Performance Studies," *Review of Financial Studies,* December 1992.

Goetzmann, W. and R. Ibbotson. "Do Winners Repeat?" *Journal of Portfolio Management,* Winter 1994.

Hendricks, D., J. Patel, and R. Zeckhauser. "Hot Hands in Mutual Funds: Short-Run Persistence of Performance, 1974–88," *Journal of Finance*, March 1993.

There are many tax guides that can aid in answering basic tax issues involved with investment management. The first two listings here are basic overviews. The next two represent broad tax guides.

Schmedel, S., K. Morris, and A. Siegel. *The Wall Street Journal Guide to Understanding Your Taxes,* New York: Lightbulb Press and Dow Jones, 1995.

1995 Personal Tax & Financial Planning Guide. Prepared for the American Association of Individual Investors by Deloitte & Touche LLP. Waterford, CT: Prentice Hall, 1995.

Garner, R., R. Coplan, B. Raasch, and C. Ratner. *Ernst & Young's Personal Financial Planning Guide,* New York: Wiley, 1995.

J.K. Lasser's Your Income Tax 1996. Prepared by the Lasser Institute. New York: Simon & Schuster, 1995.

Classic studies of naive diversification include:

Elton, E. and M. Gruber. "Risk Reduction and Portfolio Size: An Analytical Solution," *Journal of Business*, October, 1977.

Evans, J. and S. Archer. "Diversification and the Reduction of Dispersion,"*Journal of Financial and Quantitative Analysis*, December, 1968.

Fisher, L. and J. Lorie. "Some Studies of Variability of Returns on Investment in Common Stock," *Journal of Business*, April, 1970.

PERFORMANCE MONITORING

After reading this chapter you should have an understanding of AIMR Performance Presentation Standards as well as how the equity performance of a portfolio can be evaluated.

The last step in the process of portfolio management is to monitor the portfolio over time and make any changes that appear appropriate in light of these occurrences:

1. Changes in expected future asset returns and risks.
2. Changes in the financial needs of the portfolio owner.
3. Unacceptable portfolio performance.

Changes in expected asset returns and risks could require modifying the portfolio's strategic asset allocation (SAA). For example, if the risk of equity ownership increases, the portfolio commitment to equities would probably be reduced. Changes in the financial needs of the portfolio owner would probably require a change in the statement of investment policy as well as the definition of the SAA. For example, the pension plan of a corporation that is currently facing unexpected competition and declining profits may have to redefine its portfolio objectives and constraints as well as its strategic asset allocation. Both events, however, can be handled by simply repeating the planning stage of the portfolio process, which we discussed in Chapter 18. In this chapter, we focus solely on the third reason for portfolio monitoring—to detect unacceptable performance.

We chose the title for this chapter, Performance *Monitoring,* carefully to use in place of the commonly used phrase, performance *measurement.* The term *measurement* has a connotation of precision to it that is simply not possible in evaluating investment performance. Throughout this chapter, we encounter the problems that arise whenever we attempt to evaluate the past risk/return performance of a portfolio. For example, there are many (quite valid) ways of measuring returns, there is no truly acceptable way to measure investment risk, and all performance analyses examine relatively short historical time periods when it is usually long-term future performance that matters. We are simply unable to accurately *measure* performance.

But a number of reasonable approaches exist that allow us to *monitor* the level of historical performance compared to other investments of similar risk. Precise evaluation of portfolio performance is impossible, but broad yardsticks are available that can detect clearly superior or inferior performance. Regardless of the techniques used to monitor performance, remember these three factors:

1. *It is the total portfolio that is most important.* If multiple managers are used, their individual performances are secondary to the performance of the aggregate portfolio. While data on individual managers have to be accumulated in order to determine aggregate portfolio performance, the actual performance analysis should proceed in a top-down fashion. The aggregate portfolio should be evaluated first, followed by an evaluation of each individual manager. As obvious as this point might seem to be, many performance services provide little or no information about aggregate portfolio performance. Instead, they concentrate solely on individual managers.

2. *Any performance analysis must examine both returns and risk.* An examination of past returns provides little information about performance unless the returns are related to the risk level incurred. Again the point is obvious but often not followed in practice. For example, some performance services compare the returns on a governmental pension fund with other government pensions. Unfortunately, such pension funds have substantially different asset holdings and risk exposure.

3. *An attempt should be made to determine why a particular performance level occurred.* If an understanding of why the performance was bad (or good) can be gained, proper steps to improve (or continue) can be taken. Knowing *why* performance was poor is much more important than knowing simply that performance was poor.

AIMR Performance Presentation Standards

In the early 1990s, the Association for Investment Management and Research (AIMR) developed standards that all members of the association are required to follow when presenting information about their returns to the public. These standards are called the AIMR Performance Presentation Standards.

The **AIMR Performance Presentation Standards** consist of both *requirements* that must be followed if return calculations are to be in compliance with the standards as well as *recommendations* that the AIMR encourages but does not require (at present). For example, the standards require that accrued interest income on bond investments be recognized as part of the market value of a portfolio but only recommends that accrued dividend income be included in the value of the portfolio. The differences between requirements and recommendations is usually not because a requirement is deemed to be more important than a recommendation. Instead, many items are recommended as opposed to being required due to difficulties that many investment managers would have in fulfilling the item if it were required. For example, many investment managers use accounting systems that provide information about accruals of interest income but do not provide dividend accrual information. Many present recommendations are likely to become requirements in the future.

Table 21-1 presents a summary of various **requirements** of the Performance Presentation Standards. Table 21-2 presents a summary of various **recommendations.** The information in both tables is important for students who wish to pursue an investment management career.

The AIMR standards are designed for professional investment managers who offer their management expertise to individuals and institutions. Usually these managers provide information about past rates of return that they earned in managing investments for other people. The standards are designed to provide an accurate and common standard on which investment returns are calculated. Since investment managers have investment discretion over a large number of portfolios, the AIMR requires that portfolio composites be calculated and shown to people who might employ the management firm to manage their investments.[1]

Calculating Portfolio Returns

We saw in Chapter 5 that the return the investor receives can be different from the return actually earned on the underlying securities owned. For example, assume Investor A employs Manager B to manage her investment portfolio. It is possible that, during a given period of time, the return Investor A receives could be 3% when the return on the securities managed by Manager B is 5%. Such differences arise when the investor either invests additional cash into the portfolio or withdraws cash from the portfolio.

The return the investor actually receives is called a **dollar-weighted return (DWR).** DWRs are affected by any cash investments or withdrawals to the portfolio during the period over which the return is calculated. In our example, Investor A's DWR was 3%.

The return on the underlying securities owned by the investor is called a **time-weighted return (TWR).** TWRs are not affected by any cash investments or withdrawals to the portfolio during the period over which the return is calculated. In our example, Investor A's TWR was 5%.

Both TWR and DWR measures are valid measures of return. They simply measure two different things. The DWR measure is appropriate when asking *what return the investor received.* The TWR measure is appropriate when asking *what return the securities provided.*

When our goal is to evaluate the return performance of an investment manager, time-weighted returns should be used. It would be inappropriate to attribute gains or losses that investors who employ the manager receive from the timing of cash transfers to or from the investment manager. Thus, the Performance Presentation Standards focus on calculations of TWRs. Unfortunately, the data necessary to make precise calculations of TWRs are often not

---

[1] Much of this section is based on the *Performance Presentation Standards* document. The symbology is consistent with that used in the document.

TABLE 21-1   SUMMARY OF AIMR PERFORMANCE PRESENTATION STANDARDS: REQUIREMENTS

To comply with AIMR standards, managers must calculate and present historical rates of returns according to the following practices:

1. **Total returns.** Figures must include dividend and interest income plus any capital gains or losses, whether realized or not.
2. **Accrual accounting.** Returns on fixed income securities must include accrued interest income. Accrual accounting for dividends as of their ex-dividend date is recommended but not required. But cash accounting is acceptable only if it does not distort performance. Accrual accounting is recommended but not required for returns calculated prior to January 1993.
3. **Time-weighted returns.** Returns must be time weighted using a minimum of quarterly portfolio valuations. For periods exceeding one quarter, returns must be calculated by a geometric linking of quarterly time-weighted returns.
4. **Cash and cash equivalents.** Portfolio returns must include holdings of cash and cash equivalents. This requirement applies to returns on portfolios or a composite of portfolios and to periods after 1992.
5. **All portfolios managed.** At least one composite must include all portfolios over which adviser had discretionary control.
6. **Separation of model from actual portfolio.** Actual returns must be separated from presentations of returns on "simulated" or "modeled" portfolios.
7. **Market-weighted returns.** For composites of more than one portfolio, returns must be based on market weighting of composite portfolio returns. Equally weighted composite returns must be supplemented with market value-weighted returns.
8. **All portfolio results.** Newly managed portfolios must be included in a composite after the start of the next reporting period. Terminated portfolios must be excluded from future composite performance but included for periods during which the portfolio was managed.
9. **No restatements.** Returns must not include restatements of portfolio returns if a management firm reorganizes.
10. **No portability.** Performance is a record of the firm, not of an individual. Records of a new affiliation may not include performance results from an affiliation with a previous management firm.
11. **Unbundled costs.** Trading costs and embedded costs (such as wrap fees) cannot be unbundled must be deducted from performance results.
12. **Long-term record.** Annual returns must be for at least a ten-year period or since inception.

Note: Additional requirements for international and real estate portfolios are not shown here.

SOURCE: Adapted from the *Report of the Performance Presentation Standards Implementation Committee,* Association for Investment Management and Research, December 1993.

TABLE 21-2   SUMMARY OF AIMR PERFORMANCE PRESENTATION STANDARDS: RECOMMENDATIONS

The AIMR encourages the following practices:

1. **Accrual accounting.** Accrual accounting applied to all investments and for periods prior to 1993.
2. **Time-weighted returns.** To calculate precise time-weighted returns, the portfolio should be valued whenever cash is placed into the portfolio or withdrawn from the portfolio. Revaluation of portfolios is recommended whenever cash flows and market action combine to cause a material distortion of performance. AIMR suggests that a cash flow equal to 10% or more of the portfolio value should require a revaluation.
3. **Trade Date accounting.** Trade date accounting should be use to value the portfolio as opposed to settlement date accounting. Settlement date accounting must be disclosed if used.
4. **Before fees and taxes.** Returns should be presented before the subtraction of management fees or taxes unless net-of-fee calculations are required by the Securities Exchange Commission.
5. **Convertibles.** Convertibles or other hybrid securities should be treated consistently within and across composites.
6. **Additional information.** The following information is recommended for disclosure:

   ▪ External risk measures such as the standard deviation of composite returns across time.

   ▪ Benchmark returns that have similar risks or investment styles the client portfolio is expected to track.

   ▪ Internal risk measures such as the dispersion of returns across portfolios in a composite.

   ▪ Cumulative returns for all periods.

   ▪ If leverage has been used, results on an unleveraged basis where possible.

   ▪ Equal-weighted composite returns in addition to asset-weighted composites.

Note: Additional recommendations for international and real estate portfolios are not shown here.

SOURCE: Adapted from the *Report of the Performance Presentation Standards Implementation Committee,* Association for Investment Management and Research, December 1993.

available, particularly for time periods of a calendar quarter or less. In such cases, short-term dollar-weighted returns may be calculated and used as a proxy for the more accurate TWR.

No Cash Flows to Portfolio. Think of the portfolio as a box. In this box are a variety of securities. Over time the value of these securities change, interest and dividends are collected and reinvested, and various securities are bought and sold. But as long as the investor who owns this box of securities does not withdraw cash from the box or invest cash into the box, both TWR and DWR will be the same. This, of course, is the simplest possible return calculation and is shown here:

Portfolio Return with No Cash Flows

$$TWR = DWR = (MVE - MVB) \div MVB \qquad (21.1)$$

where MVB is the market value of the portfolio at the beginning of the period, and MVE is the market value at the end of the period.

For example, assume the composition of a portfolio at the end of December 31 and the following January 31 is as follows:

	Market Value of Portfolio on:	
Asset Listing	December 31	January 31
Cash Equivalents	$ 5,000	$ 7,000
Bonds	10,000	8,000
Stocks	120,000	130,000
Total	$135,000	$145,000

MVB	MVE
Dec. 31 ———————————— Jan. 31	
$135,000	$145,000

If no contributions or withdrawals were made to the portfolio during the month of January, then the January TWR and DWR would be 7.41%:

$$0.0741 = (\$145,000 - \$135,000) \div \$135,000$$

With Cash Flows to Portfolio. When cash investments or withdrawals are made to the portfolio during a given period of time, DWRs and TWRs for that period will differ. To help illustrate various calculations, we use the preceding data but add the assumption that an additional $50,000 cash investment was made to the portfolio on January 5 with the following outcome:

	Market Value of Portfolio on:			
		January 5 Investment		
Asset Listing	December 31	Before	After	January 31
Cash Equivalents	$ 5,000	$ 4,000	$ 54,000	$ 7,000
Bonds	10,000	11,000	11,000	60,650
Stocks	120,000	122,700	122,700	130,000
Total	$135,000	$137,700	$187,700	$197,650

Time-weighted returns are calculated by compounding the subperiod returns between each date at which a cash inflow or outflow to the portfolio is made. In this example, there are two subperiods with the following subperiod returns:

Subperiod	Subperiod Return
Dec. 31–Jan. 5	($137,700 − $135,000) ÷ $135,000 = 2.0%
Jan. 5–Jan. 31	($197,650 − $187,700) ÷ $187,700 = 5.30%

Compounding these two subperiod returns results in the following TWR for the month of January:[2]

$$0.0741 = (1.02)(1.053) - 1.0$$

MVB		Cash Inflow	MVE
	└——————————$50,000———————		┘
Dec. 31		Jan. 5	Jan. 31
Before Inflow $135,000		$137,700	
After Inflow		$187,700	$197,650
1 + Return	——1.02——→	——1.053———→	

To calculate a TWR for a given period, the period is divided into subperiods. Each subperiod ends when a cash flow occurs, and the return during the subperiod is calculated using Equation 21.1. The various subperiod returns are then compounded in order to calculate the total period return. The procedure used is shown here:

Time Weighted Returns

$$\text{TWR} = (1.0 + S_1)(1.0 + S_2) \dots (1.0 + S_N) - 1.0 \tag{21.2}$$

Each subperiod return, S, represents the return earned from the date of the last cash flow to the date of the next cash flow using Equation (21.1). *This procedure focuses solely on returns on securities held in the portfolio, eliminating any effects of cash contributions and withdrawals to the portfolio.*

Dollar-weighted returns are calculated using one of two methodologies. The first methodology is widely used elsewhere in finance and is called the internal rate of return (IRR). The second methodology is an approximation to the IRR and is called the Dietz methodology.

The dollar-weighted return DWR using the internal rate of return methodology is found by solving the following equation for DWR:

DWR IRR Method

$$\text{MVE} = \text{MVB}(1 + \text{DWR}) + \sum F_i (1 + \text{DWR})^{w(i)} \tag{21.3}$$

Here MVE equals the portfolio's market value at the end of the period, MVB is the portfolio's market value at the beginning of the period, the F values are cash flows into (F is positive) or out of (F is negative) of the portfolio, and $w(i)$ is the fraction of the period that a given cash flow was in or out of the portfolio.

Applying Equation (21.3) to our example results in the following:

---

[2] This 7.41% TWR is the same as in the preceding example in order to maintain a consistency in the examples.

$$\$197,650 = \$135,000(1 + DWR) + \$50,000(1 + DWR)^{26 \div 31}$$

Solving for DWR results a January dollar-weighted return of 0.0716, or 7.16%. Notice this is slightly lower than the TWR found earlier. The explanation for this lower return is that, while the initial $135,000 earns 7.41% over the full month, the $50,000 investment on January 5 earns only 5.3% (the period from January 5 through January 31). Thus, the average of the two investments results in a DWR that is smaller than the TWR.

The internal rate of return approach to finding a dollar-weighted return suffers from the fact that there can be multiple IRRs if multiple cash investments and withdrawals are made. Each IRR is mathematically correct. But the analyst is left trying to decide which of these IRRs should be reported. To eliminate the problem, the Dietz methodology can be used. In this case the DWR is found by solving the following equation:

DWR Dietz Method

$$DWR = \frac{MVE - MVB - \sum F}{MVB + \sum FW(i)} \qquad (21.4)$$

where $\sum F$ represents the sum of all cash investments (positive numbers) and withdrawals (negative numbers) and $\sum FW(i)$ represents the sum of each cash transaction times the fraction of the period which the transaction was in the portfolio.

Applying Equation (21.4) to our example results in the following:

$$DWR = \frac{\$197,650 - \$135,000 - \$50,000}{\$135,000 + \$50,000(26/31)}$$

$$= \frac{\$12,650}{\$176,935}$$

$$= 0.0715$$

The numerator in Equation (21.4) represents the period profit or loss. The denominator represents the average investment in the portfolio during the period.

In our example, the IRR and Dietz methods result in very similar values. This will usually be the case. But they are clearly different from the portfolio's time-weighted return.

Which Should Be Used: TWR or DWR? Both types of returns are equally valid. TWR returns measure returns on the securities held in a portfolio (or the performance of an investment manager). DWR returns measure the returns to the owner of the portfolio allowing for the benefits or losses associated with cash contributions and withdrawals during the measurement period. Thus, when evaluating the returns to the owner of a portfolio, both types of returns provide useful information.

However, to evaluate the performance of an investment manager, TWR returns should be used. But the calculation of time-weighted returns requires that one know the market value of the portfolio at each date at which a cash investment or withdrawal is made to the portfolio. In some cases this information is known, particularly with mutual fund transactions. However, many investment managers obtain accurate market values of their portfolios only at the end of a month and in some cases only at the end of a calendar quarter.

When this is the case, the AIMR standards allow investment managers to use DWRs as proxies for TWRs during the month or quarter.

Manager Fees. As compensation for their advisory services, investment management firms charge the owner of a portfolio a yearly fee. This is usually a stated percentage of the average market value of the portfolio. Yearly fees of 0.5% to 1.0% are common for managed equity portfolios.

Owners of a mutual fund all pay the same annual management fee. However, owners of professionally managed portfolios that are not registered with the Securities Exchange Commission (SEC) as mutual funds (or closed-end funds) pay a fee which is negotiated with the investment adviser. For example, GT Capital Management might have a commingled international portfolio that is not registered with the SEC and thus not available to the general public. But private pension funds could purchase ownership interests in the portfolio. In such cases, the management fee charged to each owner is negotiated between the adviser and individual owners.

AIMR standards require disclosure of whether a portfolio's returns are stated gross or net of management fees. Returns that are stated gross of fees represent returns before the deduction of management fees. Returns that are net of fees represent returns after fees have been paid. In addition to requiring disclosure of the method used, the AIMR recommends that returns be presented gross of fees. The AIMR's rationale is that, except for mutual funds and closed-end funds, each investor pays a slightly different management fee. Thus, net-of-fee calculations would be very difficult to develop and meaningful only to investors who paid the average management fee.[3] When performance is presented gross of investment management fees, fee schedules should be provided.

Cash Versus Accrual Accounting. Under cash accounting, interest and dividends are included in return calculations during the period in which they are received. Under accrual accounting, interest and dividends are included in return calculations during the period in which they are earned.

For example, assume we are evaluating a portfolio at the end of June 30. At that time, the portfolio includes a bond on which a $30 coupon is due but that has not yet been received and a stock on which a $4 dividend payment is due but not yet received. Both payments will be received during July. Cash accounting would include both payments as increases in the value of the portfolio during July when the cash is actually received. Thus, under cash accounting, interest and dividends affect a portfolio's returns during the period in which they are received. However, under accrual accounting, both payments would be treated as receivables due the portfolio at the end of June. By considering them as receivables at June 30, they increase the June 30 portfolio value and thus the portfolio's return during June.

The AIMR standards require accrual accounting for interest on fixed income securities. The standards recommend that dividends also be calculated on an accrual basis.

---

[3] The SEC has ruled that performance results be stated net of management fees. For mutual funds and closed-end funds this is easy to do, since all investors pay the same fee. For other managed portfolios, the SEC requirement presents significant calculation problems. The AIMR has taken the position that net-of-fee returns be presented only when required by SEC regulations.

Trade Versus Settlement Date Accounting. As we discussed in Chapter 4, there is a difference (typically three business days) between the date at which a trade is made and the date at which securities and cash are actually swapped (settled). This time delay allows buyers and sellers time to deliver funds and securities to their broker in order to accomplish the transfer of cash and securities.

Trade date accounting records the purchase and sale of securities as occurring on the actual trade date. For example, if 100 shares of ATT are sold on June 29, they will not be included in the inventory of the portfolio on June 30. Settlement date accounting records the purchase and sale of securities on the day of settlement. A sale of 100 shares of ATT on June 29 would be shown as a reduction in ATT shares on July 2; they would remain a part of reported inventory on June 30.

AIMR standards recommend that trade date accounting be used. The logic underlying the standard is straightforward. Trade date accounting properly reflects the true economic position of the portfolio. For example, assume you sold 100 shares of ATT on June 29 at $40 just prior to a decline in ATT share values to $38 on June 30. Under trade date accounting, you would show the sales price of the trade as a receivable to the portfolio of $4,000. Under settlement date accounting, you would show an inventory position in ATT shares equal to $3,800.

Although trade date accounting is clearly better than settlement date accounting, a large number of brokerage firms and security custodians continue to use settlement date accounting. This will certainly change in the future, in part due to recommendations of the AIMR standards.

Reporting Composite Portfolio Time-Weighted Returns

Virtually all investment advisers manage more than one portfolio. For example, Alliance Capital Management manages a large number of mutual funds as well as numerous other portfolios for individuals and institutions. These portfolios are invested in a wide variety of asset classes and are managed by a large number of different portfolio managers. Instead of reporting returns on every portfolio that the company manages, composites are created. A **composite** is made up of a number of individual portfolios or asset classes. The **composite return** is intended to reflect the average performance of the portfolios included in the composite. To properly reflect the composite return it should be close to the return that would have been earned if all portfolios in the composite had actually been combined and managed as a single portfolio.

The following methods might be used to obtain a composite return:

■ The **equal-weighted return** (simple average). Under this procedure, one simply adds the returns of all portfolios included in the composite and divides by the total number included. For example, if three portfolios are included during a given month with returns of 5%, 8%, and 9%, then the equal-weighted composite return would be 7.33%:

$$7.33\% = (5\% + 8\% + 9\%) \div 3$$

The AIMR allows managers to present equal-weighted composites but prefers one of the following methods.

R. Charles Tschampion, C.F.A

Managing Director
General Motors Investment Management Corporation
Lehigh University, B.S. Industrial Engineering
Lehigh University, M.B.A.

In addition to his responsibilities for the investment strategies and asset allocation of General Motors' worldwide employee benefit assets and other investable assets, Charles Tschampion has volunteered a considerable amount of time to the Association for Investment Management and Research. One of the many projects in which he is currently involved is as Co-Chair of the Performance Presentation Standards Implementation Committee.

Q: How did the Association for Investment Management and Research (AIMR) become involved in helping shape the presentation of performance numbers?

A: It all started back in 1986 when Ted Mueller was president of the Financial Analysts Federation (FAF). The organization felt there were no performance presentation standards and that some practices were less than adequate in terms of full and fair disclosure. Basically, some shops were giving in to the temptation of putting their best foot forward in ways that might be considered a breach of ethics. There are a lot of very competitive pressures, and firms wanted to be able to display that as active managers they were able to beat benchmarks. In addition, there was a lot of pressure from passive management. A performance presentations committee was put together, and they came up with standards that basically tried to accomplish full disclosure, primarily meaning that the firm should present results for all real accounts they have, over all time periods they've managed that money. The standards also attempt to provide full disclosure of the type of account to ensure measurement against an appropriate benchmark. Additionally, there are calculation standards in order to achieve some sort of comparability among managers. For example, there is a requirement of time-weighted rates of return using total rates of return and accruing income in bond portfolios.

Q: Are there now a large number of disclosure statements attached to performance figures as a result of the committees' actions?

A: One of the remedies is that firms are disclosing what may be a little different. Built into the standards by the implementation committee is an attempt to deal with individual problems. There are many subissues like transportability, verification, asset class definitions, international and currency issues, private placements, and venture capital. Often solving one of these issues creates another. It grows in complexity. As a result, the standards themselves start to appear confusing to people. So now we have a continuing education challenge. But as I view it, for the bulk of the money being run, we really just want to make sure that investment shops are displaying their results for all of their accounts and all of the time periods they have been in existence.

Q: Have the standards been successful?

A: I think so. But because we didn't have someone like the SEC issuing a mandate, it has been sort of a gradual adoption of the standards by the industry. There are two forces operating. One is whether the portfolio management firm perceives that they need to comply for competitive reasons and the other is whether the plan sponsors know enough to determine if a firm is in compliance or not. We need to keep making people on the user side more aware that there is a standard out there. The process has been slower than we would have liked but probably not any slower than we should have expected.

Q: Is part of the delay that firms are incapable of complying because of systems that are either not in place or antiquated?

A: Except in some very specialized areas, like dealing with disclosure requirements as opposed to calculation methodologies or composite construction, the issue in terms of the application of technology is more

that people don't want to undertake the cost and there is little enforcement. I think there are a number of very adequate software products and firms that will undertake the calculations for you that get at 95% to 99% of the issues. While it may be a matter of cost for smaller firms, mostly it has to do with the education of the end user. We really have at AIMR no enforcement teeth to go to an investment firm and say you are in violation of the AIMR performance standards.

Q: Does the competition help exert peer pressure on a firm to comply?

A: We're hopeful for peer pressure and for pressure from the client or end user. Again, one problem is a lack of understanding of the standards. An investment firm may say they are in compliance when they're not, and the end-user can't tell. The education issue is magnified in the institutional, plan sponsor area; because of the pressures of their jobs, many of these people really can't devote the time to fully understanding the standards. One avenue to dealing with this problem is to hire a consultant or tell the manager that they want the performance results verified by an independent party. While we've promulgated a verification procedure and recommend that it be used, we don't require performance to be verified. Often the mistakes are in the more subtle things like equal- instead of asset-weighted composites. It may not even be done in a purposeful manner; instead they might have an education gap. It's an ongoing challenge to keep the ball rolling.

■ The **asset-weighted return** (market-value-weighted average). Under this procedure, the return on each portfolio in the composite is weighted by the beginning market value of each portfolio. For example, if each of the first two portfolios earlier represented 25% of the composite's beginning market value and the third represented the remaining 50%, then the asset-weighted composite return would be 7.75%:

$$7.75\% = 0.25(5\%) + 0.25(8\%) + 0.50(9\%)$$

The AIMR prefers this procedure.

■ The asset-weighted and cash-flow-weighted return. The asset-weighted methodology can lead to biased composite return estimates if large cash additions or withdrawals are made to portfolios during the period over which the return is estimated. To handle this, the asset-weighted and cash-flow-weighted method includes the effects of each cash flow. Under this approach, the aggregate market value of all portfolios in the composite as well as the aggregate cash inflows and outflows are used in either Equations (21.2), (21.3), or (21.4).

All portfolios managed by a firm must be included in at least one composite. New portfolios should be included in a composite during the first full reporting period after the portfolio is formed. The return history of old portfolios that are no longer managed must be included in at least one composite.

Composites should include cash and cash equivalents associated with managing the account. For example, if the portfolio is intended to be invested in common stock, some cash will also be held. This cash should be considered as part of the portfolio in calculating returns.

Finally, when an investment manager leaves employment at firm 1 to accept employment at firm 2, his or her return record at firm 1 remains with firm 1. The manager's return record may not be advertised or displayed by firm 2. Return records are not portable. They belong to the firm and not the manager.

Monitoring Equity Performance

Performance Within Investment Style

Performance monitoring consists of a comparison of historical returns against the risks associated with such returns. A number of methods can be used to evaluate risk. Perhaps the most common approach to dealing with risk is to assign managers to various styles of investing and then compare one manager's returns against those of other managers having a similar style.

The investment styles used vary considerably. Table 21-3 provides a listing of the types of styles commonly used. Often sophisticated statistical procedures are used to categorize managers into groups with similar characteristics and evaluate the probability of a manager's belonging to one or another of various investment styles. An example of such an analysis is shown in Figure 21-1 for Putnam Voyager mutual fund. In the figure, four

TABLE 21-3   ILLUSTRATIVE STYLE DEFINITIONS

Style Name	
Income	Primary purpose in security selection is to achieve a current yield significantly higher than the S&P 500.
Growth	Primary purpose in security selection is to achieve long-run price growth significantly higher than the S&P 500.
Value	Selection of stocks that are believed to be undervalued relative to fundamental intrinsic value. Selection is often based on low price-to-earnings and price-to-book ratios.
Aggressive Growth	Purchase high-growth stocks with above average risk. Often these portfolios will own substantial amounts of small capitalization stocks.
Micro Cap	Purchase very small firms.
Timers	Securities held in each asset class are similar to an indexed portfolio of that asset class. However, percentages held of stocks, bonds, and other asset classes are actively timed using various methods of tactical asset allocation.
Contrarians	Purchase securities that are temporarily out of favor with other investors and minimize holdings of securities which are being actively bought by other investors.

styles are used and a statistical procedure known as discriminant analysis is used to evaluate the probability of the fund's being in each style for various quarter-ends.

One widely used procedure for styling investment managers consists of regressing a manager's past returns against various security indexes. For example the following regression might be used:

$$R_{M,t} = a + b(R_{\text{T-bills},t}) + c(R_{\text{S\&P},t}) + d(R_{\text{EAFE},t}) + e_t$$

where the R variables refer to returns during period t, M represents the manager, T-bills represents Treasury bills, S&P represents the S&P 500, EAFE represents the EAFE index, and e is a residual error term.

This approach was initially suggested by William Sharpe as a simple method of styling managers. To help in interpreting the results, the regression parameters (b, c, and d) are constrained to be positive and to sum to 1.0. For example, assume the following results are obtained for Manager ABC:

$$R_{M,t} = 2.0\% + 0.10(R_{\text{T-bills},t}) + 0.70(R_{\text{S\&P},t}) + 0.20(R_{\text{EAFE},t}) + e_t$$

The results would be interpreted as follows: During the period examined, the manager had a constant 2% return per period. In addition, the manager's returns reflected the returns on various asset classes. Specifically, the manager's returns were similar to investing 10% of the portfolio in T-bills, 70% in the S&P 500 Index, and 20% in the EAFE index.

FIGURE 21-1 ANALYSIS OF HISTORICAL STYLE PROBABILITIES, PUTNAM VOYAGER

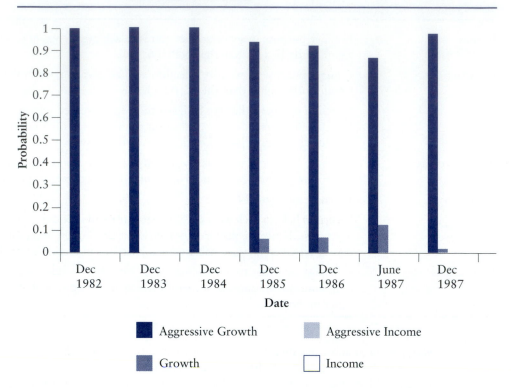

Although this styling methodology is relatively simple to compute, there are a number of drawbacks to the procedure. The two most important concerns are as follows:

- There is an uncertainty about the indexes that should be used to style a manager. A reasonable case can be made for many different indexes.

- The regression parameters capture the average style during the period evaluated. The current style position could be quite different.

Monitoring Based on the Capital Asset Pricing Model

Comparing a manager's past returns against returns of managers with equivalent investment styles is a reasonable way to begin an evaluation of the returns earned for the risks incurred. Such comparisons, however, are often not as precise as could be desired and certainly don't address why a particular risk/return performance level occurred. In order to obtain more precise risk/return calculations and to examine why a specific performance level occurred, more precise estimates of risk are needed. To date, the most widely used approaches are based on the capital asset pricing model (CAPM).

Illustrative Data. To help demonstrate how the CAPM is used in evaluating investment performance, we use the data shown in Table 21-4. This data represents actual rates of return on U.S. T-bills, the S&P 500, and AMF for a recent five-year period. Two return series are shown. The "raw return" series represent actual quarterly rates of return earned on each security. The "excess return" series are calculated by subtracting T-bill returns in any period from a security's actual raw return. Under particular interpretations of the CAPM, these excess returns reflect the return earned for bearing risk. The original version of the CAPM was a one-period model, meaning that investors invest today and liquidate at a single future date. If the investor's time horizon is three months, then the risk-free return available is a three-month T-bill (neglecting inflation). To examine whether an active manager is able to provide risk-adjusted returns in excess of passive combinations of the risk-free security and the market portfolio of risky securities, we could take sample drawings of the manager's excess returns and compare them with excess market portfolio returns. This interpretation of the CAPM of course is difficult to accept, since it requires an extremely short investment horizon. Thus, researchers invoke multiperiod CAPM models that allow investors to make "myopic decisions."[4] That is, even though they might have a long investment horizon, investors will make investment decisions based on expected returns and risks over much shorter horizons. This is the logical justification for analyzing a series of excess returns calculated over short time intervals (say, quarterly or monthly).

The Sharpe Performance Index. Using the concepts of the capital market line, Sharpe suggested that historical performance be calculated as *the return earned for bearing risk per unit of total risk*. Symbolically, the Sharpe index (referred to as S_p) is calculated as follows:

Sharpe Performance Index

$$S_p = \frac{\overline{R}_p - \overline{RF}}{\sigma_p} \tag{21.5}$$

where $\overline{R}_p$ is the average portfolio return and $\overline{RF}$ is the average risk-free return.

The return for bearing risk is shown in the numerator as the average portfolio return minus the average risk-free rate. Total risk (both diversifiable and nondiversifiable) is measured in the denominator by the standard deviation of past portfolio returns (σ_p).

Using data in Table 21-4, the Sharpe performance index for the S&P 500 and American Mutual Fund would be:

$$S_{\text{S\&P 500}} = (2.296\% - 1.182\%) \div 5.742\%$$

$$= 0.194$$

$$S_{\text{AMF}} = (2.037\% - 1.182\%) \div 3.947\%$$

$$= 0.217$$

Although the average quarterly excess return on AMF was smaller than the excess return of the S&P 500, AMF's standard deviation of quarterly return was also smaller. In terms of

---

[4] Such multiperiod models assume the investment opportunity set (efficient frontiers) never changes and the investor's utility of consumption never changes.

TABLE 21-4 RETURN PERFORMANCE DATA

Quarter	T-Bills	Raw Returns on		Excess Returns on	
		S&P 500	AMF	S&P 500	AMF
Q901	1.79	−3.02	−1.44	−4.81	−3.23
Q902	1.99	6.29	2.26	4.30	0.27
Q903	2.30	−13.78	−8.68	−16.08	−10.98
Q904	1.86	8.95	6.91	7.09	5.05
Q911	1.45	14.56	8.09	13.11	6.64
Q912	1.43	0.21	1.64	−1.22	0.21
Q913	1.42	5.38	4.16	3.96	2.74
Q914	1.19	8.36	5.98	7.17	4.79
Q921	0.97	−2.50	−1.43	−3.47	−2.40
Q922	1.03	1.97	3.46	0.94	2.43
Q923	0.91	3.10	2.90	2.19	1.99
Q924	0.71	5.10	2.76	4.39	2.05
Q931	0.73	4.40	6.49	3.67	5.76
Q932	0.72	0.51	2.88	−0.21	2.16
Q933	0.76	2.56	4.21	1.80	3.45
Q934	0.71	2.32	0.09	1.61	−0.62
Q941	0.72	−3.79	−3.21	−4.51	−3.93
Q942	0.83	0.42	1.19	−0.41	0.36
Q943	1.00	4.89	3.35	3.89	2.35
Q944	1.12	−0.02	−0.87	−1.14	−1.99
Average	1.182%	2.296%	2.037%	1.114%	0.855%
Standard Deviation	0.474%	5.656%	3.810%	5.742%	3.947%

Performance Measures

Sharpe				0.194	0.217
Treynor				1.114%	1.340%
Jensen				0.0000	0.144%

Regression Output

Constant		0.144	
Std Err of Y Est		1.544	Correlation
R Squared		0.862	Coefficient 0.93
No. of Observations		20	
Degrees of Freedom		18	
x Coefficient(s)	0.638		
Std Err of Coef.	0.060		

excess return per unit of standard deviation, AMF did slightly better than a passive invest-ment in T-bills and the S&P 500 would have yielded. That is, during this time period, the management of AMF slightly outperformed a passive strategy.

The Treynor Performance Index. Treynor chose to treat only the nondiversifiable market risk of an investment and developed the following performance index (referred to as T_p):

Treynor Performance Index $$T_p = \frac{\overline{R}_p - \overline{RF}}{\beta_p}$$ (21.6)

where β_p represents the beta of the portfolio.

The Treynor index treats only that portion of a portfolio's (or a security's) historical risk that is important to investors as estimated by β_p and neglects any diversifiable risk. As such, it is a general performance measure that can be used regardless of any other securities an investor migh own or the extent of diversification in the portfolio being evaluated. This nondiversifiable past risk is measured as β_p, the historical beta of the investment's returns. Like S_p, T_p is a relative measure and must be compared with the values of other funds as well as the aggregate market in order to determine how well an investmen t actually fared. Using Table 21-4 data, The Treynor measure for the S&P 500 and AMF would be:

$$T_{\text{S\&P 500}} = (2.296\% - 1.182\%) \div 1.00$$

$$= 1.114\%$$

$$T_{\text{AMF}} = (2.037\% - 1.182\%) \div 0.638$$

$$= 1.340\%$$

By assumption, the beta of the market proxy is 1.0. The beta for AMF can be estimated in either of two ways: (1) by regressing the fund's raw returns against raw market proxy returns, or (2) by regressing excess fund returns against excess market proxy returns. The second approach is theoretically better and is the approach used in our example. The re-gression results are shown in Table 21-4 with the x coefficient being the beta estimate.

Per unit of beta, AMF provided an excess return of 1.340% versus 1.114% for the S&P 500. Again, AMF slightly outperformed a passive strategy of investing in T-bills and the S&P 500.

Performance rankings obtained by the Sharpe and Treynor indexes are usually very similar. When they differ, it is because some funds are not perfectly diversified. To see this, recall that beta is measured as:

$$\beta_p = (\sigma_p r_{pm}) \div \sigma_M$$

where r_{pm} is the historical correlation coefficient between the portfolio and market returns. Thus we could restate the Treynor index as:

$$T_p = \left(\frac{\overline{R}_p - \overline{RF}}{\sigma_p}\right)\left(\frac{\sigma_m}{r_{pm}}\right)$$

$$= \left(\frac{\text{Sharpe}}{\text{index}}\right)\left(\frac{\sigma_m}{r_{pm}}\right)$$

The Treynor index is equal to the Sharpe index multiplied by the standard deviation of market returns and divided by the correlation coefficient. If investments being evaluated are perfectly diversified ($r_{pm} = 1.0$), the Treynor index is equal to the Sharpe index multiplied by the market's standard deviation (a constant), and rankings obtained using either approach will be identical. If investments being evaluated aren't perfectly diversified ($r_{pm} < 1.0$), performance rankings using S_p might be different from those using T_p.

Which of the two measures is the better? This depends on the nature of the investments being evaluated. If the investments being evaluated represent all of an individual's security portfolio, the Sharpe measure is probably more meaningful. In this case, the total risk (both systematic and unsystematic) of the investments is the same as the risk being borne by the individual. However, if the investments being evaluated represent only a fraction of the individual's security portfolio, the Treynor measure might be more appropriate. In this case, only the nondiversifiable, systematic risks of the investments represent risk to the owner.

The Jensen Performance Index. Like Treynor, Jensen relied directly on the CAPM to develop an estimate of investment performance. However, unlike Treynor's relative measure of performance, Jensen's alpha is an absolute measure that estimates the constant periodic return an investment was able to earn above (or below) a buy-hold strategy with equal systematic risk.

Jensen begins with the one-period security market line, which states that the expected return on an investment during period t is equal to the prevailing risk-free rate plus a risk premium (equal to the portfolio's beta multiplied by the market risk premium). That is:

SML for a Portfolio $$E(R_{pt}) = RF_t + \beta_p[E(R_{mt}) - RF_t] \qquad \textbf{(21.7)}$$

As long as investors aren't fooled into consistently over- or underestimating realized returns, the historical counterpart to this expectational model would be:

Market Model for a Portfolio

$$\tilde{R}_{pt} = \tilde{R}F_t + \beta_p(\tilde{R}_{mt} - \tilde{R}F_t) + \tilde{E}_{pt} \qquad \textbf{(21.8)}$$

Each of the returns in Equation (21-4) is an actual realized return during some time interval—say, a month, a quarter, or a year. The value of β_p is the historical estimate of beta, assumed to remain constant during the time period being examined. The term $(R_{mt} - RF_t)$ represents the earned risk premium on the market portfolio during period t and can, of course, be negative. Finally, the E_{pt} term reflects portfolio returns that are unrelatd to market returns. The more completely diversified a portfoli0, the smaller the non-market-related returns in any period.

Jensen then expresses Equation (21-8) in excess-return form by subtracting RF_t from both sides. This allows him to concentrate returns earned solely for bearing risks and results in Equation (21-9):

Excess Return Regression in Equilibrium

$$(\tilde{R}_{pt} - \tilde{R}F_t) = \beta_p[\tilde{R}_{mt} - \tilde{R}F_t] + \tilde{E}_{pt} \qquad \textbf{(21.9)}$$

If the CAPM is correct and speculators neither win nor lose in their efforts to find mispriced securities and call market turns, then Equation (21.9) will describe the return series on all security holdings. However, if some speculators consistently win and others consistently lose, portfolio returns would be better described as follows:

Jensen's Alpha $(\tilde{R}_{pt} - \tilde{RF}_t) = \alpha_p + \beta_p[\tilde{R}_{mt} - \tilde{RF}_t] + \tilde{E}_{pt}$ **(21.10)**

In this model, the portfolio alpha, α_p, represents the constant periodic return that the portfolio manager is able to earn above (or below, if negative) an unmanaged portfolio having identical market risk. Jensen suggested that statistical regression procedures could be used to estimate α_p and β_p values in Equation (21.10). If the estimated alpha values were positive and statistically significant, the fund would have outperformed a passive buy-hold strategy. If the alpha values were negative and statistically significant, the fund would have underperformed a buy-hold strategy.

When Equation (21.10) is applied to the excess returns in Table 21-4, the following results are obtained:

$$(R_{AMF,t} - RF_t) = 0.144 + 0.638 \, (R_{SP,t} - RF_t)$$

$$\text{Standard Error of Estimates} = 1.544$$

$$R - \text{Square} = 86.00\%$$

These results are visually displayed in Figure 21-2.

The estimated beta for AMF is 0.638. This could be passively duplicated by investing 63.8% of one's portfolio in the S&P 500 and the remainder in T-bills. And the excess return on such a passive portfolio would be exactly equal to 0.638 times the excess S&P 500 return. But notice that AMF had an average quarterly return slightly greater than 0.638 times the excess S&P 500 return. Jensen's alpha for AMF was 0.144% per quarter.

Statistical Significance of Alpha. One advantage to using the approach suggested by Jensen is that we can determine whether the performance is statistically significant. This is done by calculating the following t-statistic and determining whether the t-statistic is significant at the desired level of confidence by consulting a "t-statistic table." (For a large number of observations, t-statistics are distributed very close to z-statistics. In such cases, Appendix A can be used.)

$$t = (\text{alpha} - 0) \div \sigma_a$$ **(21.11)**

Here σ_a is the standard deviation of alpha and we are testing the hypothesis that alpha is zero.

The only difficulty in applying Equation (21.11) is that σ_a must be calculated. While most computer packages aimed at statistical analyses will provide σ_a estimates, common spreadsheet packages do not. If you are using a spreadsheet package, then σ_a can be calculated as:

$$\sigma_a = \text{Standard Error of } Y \text{ Estimates} \left[\frac{1}{n} + \frac{\bar{x}^2}{\Sigma \, (x_t - \bar{x})^2} \right]$$ **(21.12)**

FIGURE 21-2   ILLUSTRATION OF CHARACTERISTIC LINE

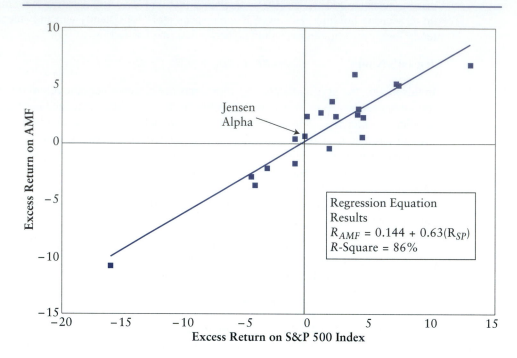

where x_t refers to the excess return on the portfolio in period t, x is the average excess portfolio return, and n is the number of observations.

When applied to the AMF example, the σ_a is:

$$\sigma_a = 1.544[(1 \div 20) + ((1.114)^2 \div 659.39)]$$

$$= 0.0811$$

Thus, the t-statistic for AMF is $1.77(0.144 \div 0.0811)$. At typical confidence levels, the alpha is not statistically different from zero. *Although AMF supposedly beat a passive investment in T-bills and the S&P 500 according to the Sharpe, Treynor, and (calculated) Jensen alpha, this performance was not statistically significant.*

Difficulties in Finding Statistical Significance. Due to the variability of security returns, it is difficult to find portfolios that will actually exhibit statistically significant returns that beat passive investment. This does not mean that a portfolio manager has no active management skills. It may be solely due to the lack of statistical power of the tests.

For example, let's assume we are examining a manager whose quarterly excess returns have a standard deviation equal to that of our passive market proxy, say 9.0% per quarter. And the hypothesis that we intend to test is whether the active manager has a mean quarterly return different from the mean quarterly return on the passive benchmark. To obtain a

FIGURE 21-3   REQUIRED QUARTERLY RETURN DIFFERENCE

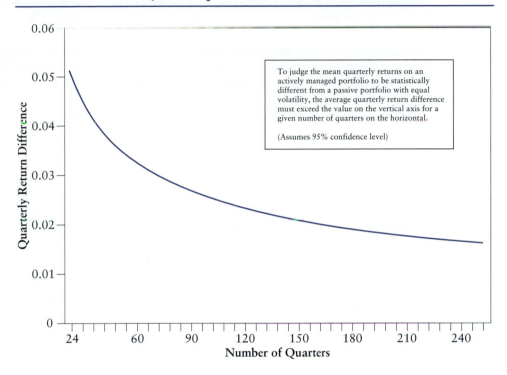

To judge the mean quarterly returns on an actively managed portfolio to be statistically different from a passive portfolio with equal volatility, the average quarterly return difference must exceed the value on the vertical axis for a given number of quarters on the horizontal.

(Assumes 95% confidence level)

z-statistic equal to 1.96 using 20 quarterly observations (as in Table 21-4), the difference in the two means would have to be 5.58%.[5]

In Figure 21-3, such required return differences are plotted against the number of quarterly return observations available. Clearly, either a large number of observations are required to claim statistical significance, or a very large return difference is needed for a small sample size. This is a simple result of the large volatility of security returns.

Problems with Capital Asset Pricing Model Performance Measures

During the years in which the capital asset pricing model (CAPM) was being developed and refined, performance measures such as those suggested by Sharpe, Treynor, and Jensen were used extensively by researchers to examine historical mutual fund performance. In more recent years, practitioners have used these approaches to evaluate investment manager performance. Yet serious questions have arisen about the validity of such CAPM-based performance statistics.

---

[5] This uses the following equation:

$$z = (R_{port} - R_{proxy}) \div (\sigma \sqrt{(1 \div n_1) + (1 \div n_2)}) \text{ where } n_1 \text{ and } n_2 \text{ are 20.}$$

First, there is a growing belief that the CAPM is a (seriously) inadequate description of real-world security pricing. No empirical test to date has been able to show that expected and realized security returns are closely tied to beta estimates employed in the tests. This could be due to inadequate beta estimates or inadequacy of the model. A growing number of people believe it is the latter. In probably the best known recent study, Fama and French found no relationship between future security returns and prior beta estimates. In contrast, they found the stock's price-to-earnings ratio, total market capitalization, and price-to-book value ratios are inversely related to future stock returns.

There is also a serious problem with the proxy one uses to estimate aggregate stock returns. For example, the level of Jensen's alpha can differ substantially if one uses the S&P 500 Index, the CRSP Index, the Russell 3000 Index, and so forth.

Finally, we need to recall the conclusions of Roll's critique of the CAPM discussed in Chapter 8. In short, his thought about performance monitoring goes like this. The CAPM is an equilibrium model stating that the lowest level of risk for any level of return is obtained by passive portfolios that combine holdings of risk-free securities and the risky market portfolio. No other portfolio can beat the risk/return combination of such passive positions. If one then uses a performance measure based on this theory and finds active managers who do, in fact, beat the passive combination, then one of two things is the case. Either the CAPM itself has been proved wrong, or the market proxy index that was used is wrong. Regardless, if a CAPM-based performance measure is used and a manager "beats" the market, then the performance measure is logically incorrect!

Nonetheless, since the procedures remain widely used, it is important that they be understood.

Analysis of Timing and Selection

Many performance analysts attempt to attribute unexpected portfolio returns to timing and selection returns. The **timing return** represents gains or losses due to temporary departures from the long-run target beta that is called for in the portfolio's strategic asset allocation. **Selection returns** are gains or losses within each asset class that differ from a passive holding of the asset class. The model most widely used to calculate timing and selection returns is the security market line of the CAPM. In Chapter 8, we defined the SML as follows:

Security Market Line $E(R_i) = RF + B_i[E(R_M) - RF]$ **(21.13)**

where: $E(R_i)$ = the expected return on portfolio (or security) i
B_i = the beta of portfolio (security) i
$E(R_M)$ = the expected return on the market portfolio of all risky assets

Its ex post form can be written as:

Ex Post SML $E(R_{it}) = RF_t + B_{it}(R_{Mt} - RF_t)$ **(21.14)**

where: $E(R_{it})$ = the expected return on portfolio i during period t
RF_t = the risk-free rate associated with period t

B_{it} = the estimated beta of portfolio i during period t

R_{Mt} = the actual return on the market portfolio during period t

For example, assume that during a quarter ended September 30, the return on the S&P 500 (our proxy for the market portfolio) was 9.68% and the return on T-bills (our proxy for the risk-free rate) was 2.50%. Thus, the relationship between the expected return on an investment portfolio and its estimated beta for the quarter would be:

September 30 Ex Post SML

$$E(R_{it}) = 2.50\% + B_{it} (9.68\% - 2.50\%)$$

$$= 2.50\% + B_{it} (7.18\%) \qquad \textbf{(21.15)}$$

Now assume that during that quarter Twentieth Century Growth mutual fund had an estimated beta of 0.94. Thus, the return we would have expected it to earn was 9.25%:

$$9.25\% = 2.50\% + 0.94(7.18\%)$$

If Twentieth Century Growth's actual return during the quarter was 5.45%, its return was 3.8% lower than we would have expected given its estimated beta. These results are shown graphically in Figure 21-4. The difference between the return that was expected given a portfolio's current beta risk and the actual return is referred to as the return from stock selection. Given the portfolio's current beta risk, Twentieth Century Growth would be expected to earn 9.25%. Since it earned only 5.45%, the difference is attributed to poor stock selection.

Now let's consider timing returns. Many investment managers attempt to time equity market returns by adjusting their stock/nonstock mix and by adjusting the beta level of the stocks held. Their goal, of course, is to reduce (or increase) equity holdings and betas prior to poor (or good) stock market returns.

FIGURE 21-4 TWENTIETH CENTURY GROWTH, ANALYSIS OF RETURN

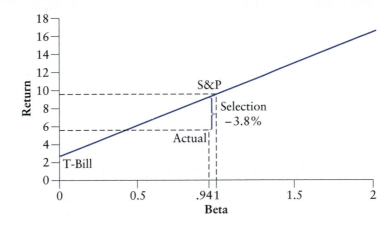

Assume that over the past five years, Twentieth Century Growth fund had an average beta estimate of 1.30. We refer to the fund's intended long-run beta as its **target beta** and use the historical average as a proxy for the target beta.

If the fund had been at its target beta of 1.3 during the September 30 quarter, we would have expected it to earn 11.83%:

$$2.50\% + 1.3(7.18\%) = 11.83\%$$

This expected return given its target beta is referred to as its benchmark return. However, the fund had actually reduced its estimated beta to 0.94, a level at which we would expect a 9.25% return. The difference between the return expected given its current beta and the return expected at its target beta (the benchmark return) represents the measure of timing return. For Twentieth Century Growth, this timing return was a negative 2.58%.

Figure 21-5 summarizes the analysis. Given the estimated target beta (b_{iT}), the benchmark return was 11.83.

CAPM Benchmark Return

$$RF_t + b_{iT}(R_{Mt} - RF_t) \tag{21.16}$$

$$11.83\% = 2.50\% + 1.30(9.68\% - 2.50\%)$$

The timing return represents the difference between the current fund beta and the target beta multiplied by the excess return on the market portfolio. For Twentieth Century Growth, this was −2.58%:

CAPM Timing Return

$$(B_{it} - b_{iT})(R_{Mt} - RF_t) \tag{21.17}$$

$$-2.58\% = (0.94 - 1.30)(9.68\% - 2.50\%)$$

Finally, the selection return represents the difference between the actual return (R_{it}) and the re-

FIGURE 21-5   TWENTIETH CENTURY GROWTH, ANALYSIS OF RETURN

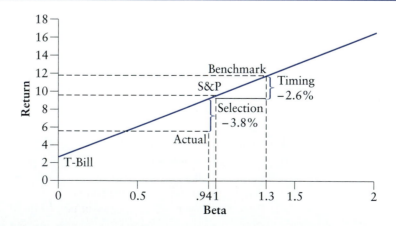

turn expected given the current beta estimate. For Twentieth Century Growth, this was -3.8%:

CAPM Selection Return

$$R_{it} \quad [RF_t \ | \ b_{it}(R_{mt} - RF_t)] \tag{21.18}$$

$$-3.8\% = 5.45\% - [2.50\% + 0.94(9.68\% - 2.50\%)]$$

To summarize these relationships:

Actual Return =	Benchmark Return +	Timing Return +	Selection Return
5.45%	11.83% +	(−2.58%) +	(−3.80%)

Problems in Application. Calculation of these performance statistics requires access to considerable data. In particular, a realistic estimate of the manager's current beta is needed to determine both timing and selection returns. This can be accomplished only if the analyst knows the current portfolio holdings and has an estimate of the beta for each holding. If, for example, 30 stocks are held, the beta on each is first estimated using the market model, and the market-value-weighted average of these is used as an estimate of b_{it}. Such b_{it} values are constantly updated as stocks are sold and replaced by new stocks. Note that this procedure differs from the approach commonly used to estimate a portfolio beta that applies the market model to total portfolio returns over some past time interval. This second approach is certainly easier to calculate, but it cannot be used to evaluate a quarter-by-quarter portfolio beta. In fact, this approach is at best an estimate of the average beta position of a manager over many time periods in the past.

If a sequence of b_{it} values cannot be obtained from portfolio inventory listings, a detailed period-by-period analysis of timing and selection cannot be conducted. Some methods are discussed in the next section that allow estimates of average timing and selection abilities over a large number of periods. But these techniques do not allow for a period-by-period analysis and thus cannot investigate why timing or selection was particularly good (or bad) in a given period.

Average Estimates of Timing and Selection. Usually a sequence of past total portfolio returns is all that's available for measuring portfolio performance. In this case, two variants of the traditional characteristic line can be used to evaluate a manager's average timing and selection abilities.

Consider the characteristic line shown in panel A of Figure 21-6. The vertical axis is used to plot excess returns on the portfolio (portfolio returns in period t minus the risk-free rate in period t). The horizontal axis is used to plot excess returns on the market portfolio. The traditional characteristic line is shown as the best-fit linear relationship and is found by the following regression equation:

$$E\tilde{R}_{it} = a_i + b_i(E\tilde{R}_{Mt}) + \tilde{e}_{it} \tag{21.19}$$

where: $E\tilde{R}_{it}$ = the excess return on portfolio i in period t
$E\tilde{R}_{Mt}$ = the excess return on the market portfolio in period t
$\tilde{e}_{it}$ = the residual excess return on portfolio i in period t
a_i = the constant excess return on portfolio i
b_i = the systematic risk (estimated beta) of portfolio i

FIGURE 21-6   TIMING AND SELECTION ANALYSIS USING CHARACTERISTIC LINE ANALYSIS

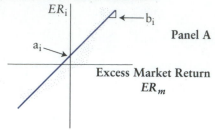

EXCESS PORTFOLIO RETURN

Panel A

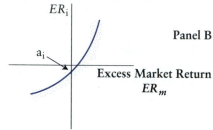

EXCESS PORTFOLIO RETURN

Panel B

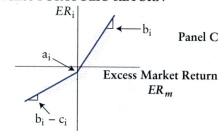

EXCESS PORTFOLIO RETURN

Panel C

As shown in panel A, the positive a_i suggests that the portfolio manager had a constant excess return. This, of course, is Jensen's alpha, which we discussed in previous chapters. In this chapter we interpret it as the average level of security selection return earned by the portfolio manager. But this linear characteristic line is unable to tell us anything about the timing ability of the manager—even if there appears to be some evidence of timing from the pattern of the points around the line.

Two approaches have been suggested that attempt to capture both timing and selection ability. The first approach is attributed to Treynor and Mazuy. They suggested that a quadratic regression be examined as follows:

$$E\tilde{R}_{it} = a_i + b_i(E\tilde{R}_{Mt}) + c_i(E\tilde{R}_{Mt})^2 + \tilde{e}_{it} \tag{21.20}$$

Such a quadratic curve is displayed in panel B. A positive value of c would suggest that portfolio returns are more sensitive to large positive market returns than to large negative market returns. This, of course, would be indicative of good market timing. The intercept term, a_i, would still represent an estimate of security-selection ability. Panel B suggests a positive market-timing ability and a zero (or perhaps negative) selection ability.

A second approach for examining market timing has been suggested by Henriksson and Merton. They suggest that two straight lines be fit to the excess returns as shown in panel C and in the regression equation here:

$$\tilde{ER}_{it} = a_i + b_i\,(\tilde{ER}_{Mt}) + c_i(\tilde{Z}_t)^2 + \tilde{e}_{it} \tag{21.21}$$

The new term reflects whether the market is rising or falling and takes on the following values with the resulting regression equations:

If	Then	Implied Regression Relationship
$ER_{Mt} > 0$	$Z_t = 0$	$ER_i = a_i + b_i(ER_{mt})$
$ER_{mt} = 0$	$Z_t = 0$	$ER_i = a_i$
$ER_{mt} < 0$	$Z_t = ER_{mt}$	$ER_i = a_i + (b_i - c_i)(ER_{mt})$

Clearly b_i is the slope of the characteristic line when the market is rising and $(b_i - c_i)$ is the slope when the market is falling. The value of c_i reflects the extent of market timing ability. If c_i is statistically greater (or less) than 0.0, there is evidence of positive (or negative) market-timing ability. If c_i is not statistically different from zero, no evidence of market timing is present. As before, a_i represents the average security-selection ability.

Performance Attribution

Some performance-monitoring firms attribute portfolio returns to (1) over- or under weighting of various economic sectors within the portfolio, and (2) above- or below-average returns within the sectors. The first is similar to previous measures of timing, and the second is similar to the approach used in security selection.

To illustrate, assume the market portfolio consists of three economic sectors with the following average stock returns in each sector during the past quarter:

THE MARKET PORTFOLIO

Sector	Percentage of Total	Quarter's Return	Product
A	20%	−10%	−2.0%
B	50%	5%	2.5%
C	30%	10%	3.0%
	100%	Average Return	3.5%

Now consider portfolio XYZ, which had the following weighting and returns during the same quarter:

PORTFOLIO XYZ

Sector	Percentage of Total	Quarter's Return	Product
A	10%	-10%	-1.0%
B	60%	8%	4.8%
C	30%	12%	3.6%
	100%	Average Return	7.4%

The 7.4% return of portfolio XYZ is explained as a function of (1) the 3.5% market return, (2) a return associated with over- or under weighting various market sectors, and (3) a return associated with performance within the market sectors.

The return associated with over- or underweighting sectors is equal to 1.5% and is calculated next. The difference between the percentage that each sector represents of the total market and the portfolio weighting given to a sector is multiplied by the market return of the sector. When summed across all sectors, we have a measure of the portfolio's return that is attributable to over- or underweighting sectors. In concept this is similar to the measures of timing that we discussed earlier:

Sector	Sector Weighting Portfolio	−	Market	=	Difference	Market Sector Return	Product
A	0.10	−	0.20	=	-0.10	-10%	1.0%
B	0.60	−	0.50	=	0.10	5%	0.5%
C	0.30	−	0.30	=	0.00	10%	0.0%
					Sector-Weighting Return		1.5%

The performance within sectors is calculated by multiplying the portfolio's percentage weight in a sector by the difference between the portfolio's return within the sector and the market's sector return. In our example, this within-sector return is 2.4%:

RETURN DURING QUARTER

Sector	Portfolio Weighting	Portfolio	−	Market	=	Difference	Product
A	0.10	-10%	−	(-10%)		0.0%	0.0%
B	0.60	8%	−	5%		3.0%	1.8%
C	0.30	12%	−	10%		2.0%	0.6%
	1.00			Within-Sector Return			2.4%

In sum, the portfolio's return is composed as follows:

Portfolio Return = Market Return + Sector Weighting + Within Sector

7.4%   3.5%   1.5%   2.4%

As we noted earlier, such an analysis results in measures similar to those used in timing and selection returns. The difficulties with the procedure are basically pragmatic: A great deal of data is needed. At the least, the analyst needs end-of-period inventory figures in order to determine sector weightings and returns. But if the analysis is to be truly accurate, the date of every security trade within a period is also needed. Only then can a correct sector-return attribution be conducted.

Empirical Evidence of Timing and Selection

There have been few rigorous empirical studies of whether investment managers consistently earn market-timing and selection returns. The reasons are probably twofold: (1) a lack of precise estimates of beta targets and temporary beta departures from the targets, and (2) a conceptual concern with the use of CAPM-based measurement techniques. In this section, we review two important studies of stock timing and selection.

Selection

Recall that stock-selection returns represent the difference between the actual portfolio return in a given time period and the return that would be expected given the portfolio's actual beta during the period. From Equation (21.18):

$$\text{Selection Return} = R_{pt} - [RF_t + b_{pt}(R_{Mt} - RF_t)] \qquad \textbf{(21.22)}$$

In order to estimate selection returns, beta estimates for each time period (b_{pt}) are necessary. In practice, such an estimate is difficult to determine. It requires that the manager hold only common stocks (no cash equivalents or bonds) and that the analyst have the end-of-period inventory listing of these stocks for all time periods for which performance is being evaluated. Kon and Jen have suggested a statistical procedure that simplifies the data requirements.[6] They provide a way to use only total portfolio returns to derive one, two, and so forth, beta estimates. When Kon applied this "switching regression" methodology to the returns on 37 mutual funds, he concluded that 25 of the funds could be said to have used two distinct beta levels and that the remaining 12 used three beta levels. Based on such changing beta estimates, he evaluated both selection and timing returns.

---

[6] See S. Kon and F. Jen., "The Investment Performance of Mutual Funds: An Empirical Investigation of Timing, Selectivity and Market Efficiency," *Journal of Business* 52 (1979): 263–289, and S. Kon, "The Market-Timing Performance of Mutual Fund Managers," *Journal of Business* 56 (1983): 323–347.

Of the 37 funds examined, 25 had positive estimated selectivity, of which 5 were statistically significant at a 95% confidence level. In addition, across the total sample, there was evidence that the funds as a group exhibited an ability to generate positive selection performance.[7] Both findings are, of course, contrary to the strong-form version of efficient market theory.

Timing

Kon also evaluated the timing ability of the mutual funds. Of the 37 funds, 14 had overall timing performance estimates that were positive, but none was statistically significant (at 95% confidence). He concluded that mutual fund managers should stress their skills of stock selection and not try to time the market.

Another study of timing, conducted by Henriksson, was based on the regression model in Equation (21.20):[8]

$$\tilde{ER}_{pt} = a_i + b_p(\tilde{ER}_{Mt}) - c_p(Z)_t + e_{pt} \tag{21.23}$$

where: $\tilde{ER}_{pt}$ = the excess return (above the risk-free rate) on fund p during period t
$\tilde{ER}_{mt}$ = the excess return on the market portfolio in period t
e_{pt} = residual return in period t
$Z_t = \begin{cases} 0 & \text{if } ER_{mt} \geq 0 \\ ER_{mt} & \text{if } ER_{mt} < 0 \end{cases}$

The parameter a_i measures net selectivity over the time period examined. The parameter b_p is the slope of the regression in rising markets, and c_p reflects the extent of market-timing ability. If c_p is statistically greater than zero, there is evidence of market timing ability.

Results of Henriksson's tests are shown in Table 21-5. Monthly returns on 116 mutual funds were used for the period February 1968 through May 1980. Looking first at the measure of timing (c_p), the study simply did not find any evidence of a consistent timing ability. Of the 116 funds over the full time interval tested, only 3 had statistically significant positive estimates of timing ability. In contrast, 9 funds had negative timing estimates that were statistically significant.

Kon also conducted a nonparametric test of the funds' timing abilities with similar results. Mutual funds did not exhibit any ability to consistently time equity market moves.

Is Performance Predictable?

When investors select investment managers, they commonly examine the relative past performance of a group of managers and select those with better-than-average results. But can one rely on past performance as a reasonable predictor of future performance?

---

[7] Because of the lack of normality in the data, Kon expressed some concern about the true statistical significance of the results.

[8] See R. Henrikson, "Market Timing and Mutual Fund Performance: An Empirical Investigation," *Journal of Business* 54 (1984): 73–96

TABLE 21-5   Market-Timing Test Results

$$\tilde{ER}_{pt}= a_p + b_p\,(\tilde{ER}_{pt}) + c_p\,(Z_t) + \tilde{e}_{pt}$$

Period	Feb. 1968–June 1980	May 1974–June 1980
Average Estimate of		
a_p	0.0007	0.0022
b_p	0.92	0.86
c_p	−0.07	−0.08
Number of Funds with*		
$a_p > 0$	11	21
$a_p < 0$	8	5
$c_p > 0$	3	2
$c_p < 0$	9	3

*At 95% confidence.

TABLE 21-6   Correlation Between Past and Future Performance 190 U.S. Equity Mutual Funds, 1973–1990

Correlation between average quarterly return:

1973–1981 vs. 1982–1990	−0.078

Correlation for adjacent 5-year periods:

	Jensen Alpha	Sharpe	Treynor	Average Return
1973–1977 vs. 1978–1982	0.23	0.17	0.19	0.14
1978–1982 vs. 1984–1988	−0.23	−0.19	−0.20	0.16

Unfortunately, the correlation between past and future performance is weak. The data in Table 21-6 reports on the correlation coefficients for a variety of performance measures. The sample consisted of 190 U.S. equity mutual funds for which quarterly returns were available from March 1973 through December 1990. The first correlation coefficient shown is the correlation between average quarterly returns during the first nine years of the time period and average quarterly returns in the second nine years. The value of −0.078 suggests that past relative raw return performance is not predictive of future performance.

The other correlations shown are based on performance in one five-year period versus a subsequent five-year period. Although the correlations are somewhat different from zero, the sign of the correlation depends on the periods selected.

Numerous academic studies confirm these results. In short, there is no discernible tie between past relative performance and future performance.

SUMMARY

Here are the key concepts:

- Investment performance should be actively monitored for two principal reasons: (1) to determine whether the objective of the baseline investment portfolio is being achieved, and (2) if the objective is not being achieved, to understand why this is the case so that proper action can be taken.

- Performance of individual managers should be based on the manager's time-weighted Return (TWR) in compliance with the Association for Investment Management and Research Standards. But the analyst should never forget it is the aggregate portfolio that is most important and should receive the most attention. After all calculations have been completed, the actual analysis of returns should proceed in a logical, top-down manner, starting with the aggregate portfolio, then the aggregate equity and fixed income portfolios, and, last, the individual managers within the equity and fixed income portfolios.

- Considerable care should also be given to risk adjustments. The returns on an actual portfolio should be compared only against those on a benchmark portfolio with equivalent risk. The security market line is a widely used tool for equity performance monitoring. When it is used, the benchmark portfolio consists of an estimated beta-adjusted stock market index such as the S&P 500. When fixed income performance is monitored, benchmarks are often specifically designed that have similar duration, call risk, and default risk to those called for in the baseline bond investment portfolio. The accuracy of a portfolio's risk-adjusted performance depends heavily on the benchmark used. Therefore, a great deal of thought should go into its determination.

- Finally, an examination of why particular performance was obtained should be conducted, if possible. This usually involves the calculation of timing and selection returns.

REVIEW PROBLEM

Peter Nielson's only investment holdings for the past five years have been shares of ABC Mutual Fund. The management of ABC Mutual Fund has stated that they intend to maintain virtually a 100% equity position in stocks with prospects of above-average price growth. The purpose of this problem is to review the historical performance of ABC Mutual Fund and Nielson's investment in the fund.

a. As of November 30, 1997, Nielson owned 1,000 shares having a net asset value (NAV) of $40 per share. On December 15, he bought 120 additional shares at an NAV of $42 per share. On December 31, the fund's NAV was $39. What were the dollar- and time-weighted December returns?

b. Why do these two returns vary?

c. During the months of October and November 1997, ABC Mutual Fund had time-weighted returns of 10.0% and 0.50%. What was the total quarterly return ended December 31, 1997?

d. ABC's estimated beta during this quarter was 1.3. In the past they have had an average beta of 1.0. The return on a market portfolio proxy was 12.0% and the return on T-bills was 2.5%. Estimate the fund's benchmark return and returns from timing and selection.

Solution

a. Dollar-weighted return:

IRR Method

$$MVE = MVB(1 + DWR) + \sum F_i(1 + DWR)^{w(I)}$$

$$\$43,680 = \$40,000(1 + DWR) + 5,040(1 + DWR)^{16/31}$$

$$DWR = -0.0319$$

Dietz Method

$$DWR = \frac{MVE - MVB - \sum F}{MVB + \sum FW}$$

$$-0.0319 = \frac{\$43,680 - \$40,000 - \$5,040}{\$40,000 + (16/31)\$5,040}$$

Time-weighted return:

	11/31	Precontribution	Postcontribution	12/31
Shares	1,000	1,000	1,120	1,120
NAV	$ 40	$ 42	$ 42	$ 39
Value	$40,000	$42,000	$47,040	$43,680
Return		5%	−7.14%	

$$TWR = (1.0 + S_1)(1.0 + S_2) \ldots (1.0 + S_N) - 1.0$$

$$\text{December TWR} = (1.0 + 0.05)(1.0 - 0.0714) - 1.0 = -0.025$$

b. The dollar-weighted return includes the positive or negative results for the portfolio owner due to timing of contributions and withdrawals, whereas the time-weighted return represents solely the performance of the investment manager. In this case, the dollar-weighted return is smaller, since Nielson made a contribution just before ABC declined in value.

c. $(1.1)(1.005)(0.975) - 1.0 = 7.79\%$

d. Benchmark = $2.5\% + 1.0(12.0\% - 2.5\%) = 12.0\%$
Timing = $(1.3 - 1.0)(12.0\% - 2.5\%) = 2.85\%$
Selection = $7.79\% - [2.5\% + 1.3(12.0\% - 2.5\%)] = -7.06\%$

Benchmark	+	Timing	+	Selection	=	Actual
12.0%	+	2.85%	+	(−7.06%)	=	7.79%

QUESTIONS AND PROBLEMS

1. In the chapter, three important points were mentioned that any performance-monitoring system should include. What were these?

2. Mr. Curphey has experienced the following annual return on his portfolio during the past four years. You are asked to calculate an estimate of the average yearly return. Do so and justify your answer.

Year	1	2	3	4
Return	20%	−12%	15%	3%

3. Ms. Jane Tear invested $10,000 in a mutual fund two years ago. Since then she has regularly made an additional investment of $1,000 at each quarter-end. Today, just after her eighth and last contribution, her portfolio is worth $25,000. What was her annualized rate of return? The mutual fund reported an annualized return for this two-year period of 20%. Why is there a difference?

4. Mr. Morgan's only security investment is in the shares of a mutual fund called Hightech Fund. During the month of June, the following transpired:

Date	Transaction	Net Asset Value	Total Shares	Portfolio Value
May 30	Beginning-of-Month Balance	$15.00	1,000	$15,000.00
June 15	Invested an Additional $10,000	$10.00	2,000	$20,000.00
June 30	Dividends Worth $360 Received and Reinvested	$18.00	2,020	$36,360.00

   a. Calculate the time-weighted rate of return for June.

   b. Will the dollar-weighted rate of return be higher or lower than the time-weighted return in this case? Why?

5. Performance analyses are often made on the basis of investment styles. State what you believe to be the pros and cons of evaluating performance by categorizing investment managers according to their various styles.

6. Mr. Hope has just reviewed a report on the returns of an endowment fund for which he is a trustee. The report compared his endowment portfolio returns with a large number of other endowment funds. Can you suggest what critical analysis may be missing from this report?

7. Ms. A. Davis is an investment performance analyst for a major investment advisory firm. She has before her the following information about the performance of Investech Advisers for the past quarter:

$$\text{Benchmark Return} = 8.5\%$$
$$\text{Timing Return} = 1.0\%$$
$$\text{Selection Return} = -1.5\%$$
$$\text{Actual Return} = 8.0\%$$

Market Return = 8%, Risk-Free Rate = 3%

What were the actual and target betas of Investech Advisers during this quarter?

8. The performance of two mutual funds is shown here. *WS* represents the Wilshire 5000 Index. (Standard deviations of the regression parameters are shown in brackets below each estimate.)

	AMF	Putnam Investors
Average Excess Quarterly Return	2.58%	1.64%
Standard Deviation of Excess Quarterly Returns	6.96%	9.36%

$$\tilde{ER}_{AME,t} = 0.96\% + 0.75[\tilde{ER}_{WS,t}] + \tilde{E}_{AME,t} \qquad R^2 = 92.7\%$$
$$\phantom{\tilde{ER}_{AME,t} = }(0.31) \quad (0.03)$$

$$\tilde{ER}_{PI,t} = -0.49\% + 1.00 [\tilde{ER}_{WS,t}] + \tilde{E}_{PI,t} \qquad R^2 = 88.9\%$$
$$\phantom{\tilde{ER}_{PI,t} = }(0.51) \quad (0.06)$$

a. Calculate the Sharpe, Treynor, and Jensen performance measures for each fund.
b. Did either of these funds statistically outperform the market? (Use 95% confidence levels.)
c. Which of the funds was more diversified?
d. Which of the funds had a greater systematic risk?

9. To evaluate the historical performance of McMaster Fund, you collect the following data:

Percentage Return in Year

	1	2	3	4	5	6	7	8
McMaster Fund	17.2	2.6	−33.9	−32.5	19.7	31.0	14.5	17.3
S&P 500	14.3	19.0	−14.8	−26.5	37.3	24.1	−7.2	6.6
DJIA	9.8	18.5	−13.5	−23.7	44.9	22.9	−12.9	2.8
One-Year T-Bills	7.0	6.0	7.5	8.0	8.5	8.5	9.0	8.5

a. Calculate S_p and T_p using both the DJIA and the S&P 500 as the market proxy.
b. Plot McMaster returns against the S&P 500 and visually estimate alpha.
c. Using this plot, estimate McMaster Fund's beta.
d. Use a computer-based spreadsheet program to repeat parts b and c.

10. Suppose you have gathered quarterly data on the net returns of four funds and related them to equivalent market returns (S&P 500) and 90-day T-bill returns via the following regression model:

$$\tilde{ER}_{pt} = a_p + b_p(\tilde{ER}_{mt}) + \tilde{E}_{pt}$$

Fund	a_p Coefficient	a_p Std. Dev.	b_p Coefficient	b_p Std. Dev.	R^2
1	0.98%	1.00%	0.80	0.05	95%
2	2.18%	1.50%	1.30	0.15	80%
3	2.18%	0.75%	1.20	0.12	90%
4	−0.04%	0.50%	1.02	0.08	97%

a. Which funds' returns were most closely related to market returns?
b. Which fund had the most market risk?
c. Which fund had the most total risk?
d. Rank these funds in terms of the Jensen performance measure.

e. Which funds statistically outperformed or underperformed the market? (Use 95% confidence levels.)

f. Restate the alpha values in terms of their annualized equivalents.

11. Which one of the following is not consistent with AIMR's Performance Presentation Standards?

a. Composites must include all portfolios, size weighted.

b. Composites may exclude cash and cash equivalents.

c. Performance must be presented on a total return basis using accrual basis accounting (except for stock dividends and retroactive compliance).

d. Presentation of performance may be either gross or net of investment management fees, as long as the method and fees schedules are disclosed.

The following data apply to the next two CFA questions. The administrator of a large pension fund wants to evaluate the performance of four portfolio managers. Each portfolio manager invests only in U.S. common stock. Assume that during the most recent 5-year period, the average annual total rate of return including dividends on the S&P 500 was 14%, and the average nominal rate of return on government treasury bills was 8%. The following table shows risk and return measures for each portfolio.

RISK AND RETURN DATA

Portfolio	Average Annual Rate of Return	Standard Deviation	Beta
P	0.17	0.20	1.1
Q	0.24	0.18	2.1
R	0.11	0.10	0.5
S	0.16	0.14	1.5
S&P 500	0.14	0.12	1.0

12. The Treynor portfolio performance measure for portfolio P is:

a. 0.082

b. 0.099

c. 0.155

d. 0.450

13. The Sharpe portfolio performance measure for portfolio Q is:

a. 0.076

b. 0.126

c. 0.336

d. 0.880

14. An analyst wants to evaluate portfolio X, consisting entirely of U.S. common stocks, using both the Treynor and Sharpe measures of portfolio performance. The following table provides the average annual rate of return for portfolio X, the market portfolio (as measured by the Standard & Poors 500 Index), and U.S. Treasury Bills (T-bills) during the past eight years.

	Average Annual Rate of Return	Standard Deviation of Return	Beta
Portfolio X	10%	18%	0.60
S&P 500	12	13	1.00
T-Bills	6	n/a	n/a

n/a = not applicable

a. Calculate both the Treynor measure and the Sharpe measure for both portfolio X and the S&P 500. Briefly explain whether portfolio X underperformed, equaled, or outperformed the S&P 500 on a risk-adjusted basis using both the Treynor measure and the Sharpe measure.

b. Based on the performance of portfolio X relative to the S&P 500 calculated in part A, briefly explain the reason for the conflicting results when using the Treynor measure versus the Sharpe measure.

15. What are the problems associated with using CAPM-based measures of investment performance?

D A T A F I L E   A N A L Y S I S

Equity Mutual Fund Performance. The purpose of this datafile analysis is to examine the historical performance of mutual funds that invest primarily in domestic U.S. equities. Access the data set that provides quarterly returns on U.S. stock mutual funds.

a. Select one fund and calculate excess quarterly returns for the S&P 500 and the Wilshire 5000. Use the regression option to calculate the Jensen alpha. Do this twice, once for each market proxy.

b. Use the fund's beta calculated in part a to calculate the Treynor performance measure for the fund.

c. For all funds in your data set as well as the three market proxies, calculate the Sharpe performance measure. What portion of the funds had performance in excess of the S&P 500? What portion of the funds had performance worse than the S&P 500?

d. Calculate two Sharpe measures for all funds using the S&P 500 as the market proxy. The first should be based on the first one-half of the period for which returns are available. The second should be for the second one-half of the period. Plot first period performance on a vertical axis versus second period performance on the horizontal. Comment on the results.

R E F E R E N C E S

Classic studies of mutual fund performance based on the CAPM include the following:

Jensen, Michael. "Risk, the Pricing of Capital Assets, and the Evaluation of Investment Portfolios," *Journal of Finance,* April 1969.

Sharpe, William F. "Mutual Fund Performance," *Journal of Business,* January 1966.

Treynor, Jack L. "How to Rate Management Investment Funds," *Harvard Business Review,* January–February 1965.

The arbitrage pricing model (APM) has also been used to evaluate active manager performance in Chang, Eric, and William Lewellen, "An Arbitrage Pricing Approach to Evaluating Mutual Fund Performance," *Journal of Financial Research,* Spring 1985.

An interesting study of the use of benchmark portfolios and the apparent success of value line ratings is Copeland, Thomas, and David Mayers, "The Value Line Enigma (1965–1978): A Case Study of Performance Evaluation Issues," *Journal of Financial Economics, 10,* 1982.

A recent study that examines the consistency of investment manager performance is Goetzmann, William, and Roger Ibbotson, "Do Winners Repeat?" *The Journal of Portfolio Management,* Winter 1994.

Studies of managers' ability to actively time movements in asset classes include the following:

Henrickson, Richard and Robert Merton. "On Market Timing and Investment Performance II, Statistical Procedures for Evaluating Forecasting Skills," *Journal of Business, 54,* (4), 1981.

Kon, Stanley, and Frank Jen. "Estimation of Time-Varying Systematic Risk and Performance for Mutual Fund Portfolios: An Application of Switching Regression," *Journal of Finance,* May 1978.

Lee, C. F., and S. Rahman. "Market Timing, Selectivity and Mutual Fund Performance: An Empirical Investigation," *Journal of Business,* April 1990.

Procedures that investment managers are expected to follow in calculating and reporting their portfolio return performance should comply with the *Performance Presentation Standards,* Association for Investment Management and Research, Charlottesville, VA, December 1993.

Appendix A-1

AREA OF THE NORMAL DISTRIBUTION: ABOVE THE DISTRIBUTION MEAN

d1, d2 or Z-score	0	0.01	0.02	0.03	0.04	0.05	0.06	0.07	0.08	0.09
0.00	0.5000	0.5040	0.5080	0.5120	0.5160	0.5199	0.5239	0.5279	0.5319	0.5359
0.10	0.5398	0.54381	0.5478	0.5517	0.5557	0.5596	0.5636	0.5675	0.5714	0.5754
0.20	0.5793	0.58317	0.5871	0.5910	0.5948	0.5987	0.6026	0.6064	0.6103	0.6141
0.30	0.6179	0.62172	0.6255	0.6293	0.6331	0.6368	0.6406	0.6443	0.6480	0.6517
0.40	0.6554	0.65909	0.6627	0.6664	0.6700	0.6736	0.6772	0.6808	0.6844	0.6879
0.50	0.6915	0.69496	0.6985	0.7019	0.7054	0.7088	0.7122	0.7156	0.7190	0.7224
0.60	0.7257	0.72906	0.7324	0.7356	0.7389	0.7421	0.7454	0.7486	0.7517	0.7549
0.70	0.7580	0.76114	0.7642	0.7673	0.7703	0.7734	0.7764	0.7793	0.7823	0.7852
0.80	0.7881	0.79103	0.7939	0.7967	0.7995	0.8023	0.8051	0.8079	0.8106	0.8133
0.90	0.8159	0.81859	0.8212	0.8238	0.8264	0.8289	0.8315	0.8340	0.8365	0.8389
1.00	0.8414	0.84376	0.8461	0.8485	0.8508	0.8531	0.8554	0.8577	0.8599	0.8622
1.10	0.8643	0.86651	0.8687	0.8708	0.8729	0.8749	0.8770	0.8790	0.8810	0.8830
1.20	0.8849	0.88687	0.8888	0.8907	0.8925	0.8944	0.8962	0.8980	0.8997	0.9015
1.30	0.9032	0.90491	0.9066	0.9083	0.9099	0.9115	0.9131	0.9147	0.9162	0.9177
1.40	0.9193	0.92074	0.9222	0.9236	0.9251	0.9265	0.9279	0.9292	0.9306	0.9319
1.50	0.9332	0.93448	0.9357	0.9370	0.9382	0.9394	0.9406	0.9418	0.9429	0.9441
1.60	0.9452	0.94630	0.9474	0.9485	0.9495	0.9505	0.9515	0.9525	0.9535	0.9545
1.70	0.9554	0.95637	0.9573	0.9582	0.9591	0.9599	0.9608	0.9616	0.9625	0.9633
1.80	0.9641	0.96485	0.9656	0.9664	0.9671	0.9678	0.9686	0.9693	0.9699	0.9706
1.90	0.9713	0.97193	0.9726	0.9732	0.9738	0.9744	0.9750	0.9756	0.9761	0.9767
2.00	0.9772	0.97778	0.9783	0.9788	0.9793	0.9798	0.9803	0.9808	0.9812	0.9817
2.10	0.9821	0.98256	0.9830	0.9834	0.9838	0.9842	0.9846	0.9850	0.9854	0.9857
2.20	0.9861	0.98644	0.9868	0.9871	0.9874	0.9878	0.9881	0.9884	0.9887	0.9890
2.30	0.9893	0.98954	0.9898	0.9901	0.9903	0.9906	0.9909	0.9911	0.9913	0.9916
2.40	0.9918	0.99201	0.9922	0.9924	0.9926	0.9928	0.9930	0.9932	0.9934	0.9936
2.50	0.9938	0.99395	0.9941	0.9943	0.9944	0.9946	0.9948	0.9949	0.9951	0.9952

(Continued)

d1, d2 or Z-score	0	0.01	0.02	0.03	0.04	0.05	0.06	0.07	0.08	0.09
2.60	0.9953	0.99546	0.9956	0.9957	0.9958	0.9960	0.9961	0.9962	0.9963	0.9964
2.70	0.9965	0.99663	0.9967	0.9968	0.9969	0.9970	0.9971	0.9972	0.9973	0.9974
2.80	0.9974	0.99752	0.9976	0.9977	0.9977	0.9978	0.9979	0.9979	0.9980	0.9981
2.90	0.9981	0.99819	0.9982	0.9983	0.9984	0.9984	0.9985	0.9985	0.9986	0.9986
3.00	0.9986	0.99869	0.9987	0.9988	0.9988	0.9989	0.9989	0.9989	0.9990	0.9990

The data above represent the area between negative infinity and a certain number of standard deviations above the mean of a "normal" distribution. For example, if the number of standard deviations is 0.67 above the mean (or expected value), then the cumulative probability from minus infinity to 0.67 is   0.7486.

This table can be used in the Black-Scholes Option Model for positive values of "d1" or "d2." See Chapter 17 for a discussion of this application.

The data can also be used to find the number of standard deviations associated with a given return percentile. See Chapter 5 for a discussion of this application.

Appendix A-2

AREA OF THE NORMAL DISTRIBUTION: BELOW THE DISTRIBUTION MEAN

df, d2 or Z-score	0.00	−0.01	−0.02	−0.03	−0.04	−0.05	−0.06	−0.07	−0.08	−0.09
0.00	0.5000	0.4960	0.4920	0.4880	0.4840	0.4801	0.4761	0.4721	0.4681	0.4641
−0.10	0.4602	0.4562	0.4522	0.4483	0.4443	0.4404	0.4364	0.4325	0.4286	0.4246
−0.20	0.4207	0.4168	0.4129	0.4090	0.4052	0.4013	0.3974	0.3936	0.3897	0.3859
−0.30	0.3821	0.3783	0.3745	0.3707	0.3669	0.3632	0.3594	0.3557	0.3520	0.3483
−0.40	0.3446	0.3409	0.3373	0.3336	0.3300	0.3264	0.3228	0.3192	0.3156	0.3121
−0.50	0.3085	0.3050	0.3015	0.2981	0.2946	0.2912	0.2878	0.2844	0.2810	0.2776
−0.60	0.2743	0.2709	0.2676	0.2644	0.2611	0.2579	0.2546	0.2514	0.2483	0.2451
−0.70	0.2420	0.2389	0.2358	0.2327	0.2297	0.2266	0.2236	0.2207	0.2177	0.2148
−0.80	0.2119	0.2090	0.2061	0.2033	0.2005	0.1977	0.1949	0.1921	0.1894	0.1867
−0.90	0.1841	0.1814	0.1788	0.1762	0.1736	0.1711	0.1685	0.1660	0.1635	0.1611
−1.00	0.1586	0.1562	0.1539	0.1515	0.1492	0.1469	0.1446	0.1423	0.1401	0.1378
−1.10	0.1357	0.1335	0.1313	0.1292	0.1271	0.1251	0.1230	0.1210	0.1190	0.1170
−1.20	0.1151	0.1131	0.1112	0.1093	0.1075	0.1056	0.1038	0.1020	0.1003	0.0985
−1.30	0.0968	0.0951	0.0934	0.0917	0.0901	0.0885	0.0869	0.0853	0.0838	0.0823
−1.40	0.0807	0.0793	0.0778	0.0764	0.0749	0.0735	0.0721	0.0708	0.0694	0.0681
−1.50	0.0668	0.0655	0.0643	0.0630	0.0618	0.0606	0.0594	0.0582	0.0571	0.0559
−1.60	0.0548	0.0537	0.0526	0.0515	0.0505	0.0495	0.0485	0.0475	0.0465	0.0455
−1.70	0.0446	0.0436	0.0427	0.0418	0.0409	0.0401	0.0392	0.0384	0.0375	0.0367
−1.80	0.0359	0.0352	0.0344	0.0336	0.0329	0.0322	0.0314	0.0307	0.0301	0.0294
−1.90	0.0287	0.0281	0.0274	0.0268	0.0262	0.0256	0.0250	0.0244	0.0239	0.0233
−2.00	0.0228	0.0222	0.0217	0.0212	0.0207	0.0202	0.0197	0.0192	0.0188	0.0183
−2.10	0.0179	0.0174	0.0170	0.0166	0.0162	0.0158	0.0154	0.0150	0.0146	0.0143
−2.20	0.0139	0.0136	0.0132	0.0129	0.0126	0.0122	0.0119	0.0116	0.0113	0.0110
−2.30	0.0107	0.0105	0.0102	0.0099	0.0097	0.0094	0.0091	0.0089	0.0087	0.0084
−2.40	0.0082	0.0080	0.0078	0.0076	0.0074	0.0072	0.0070	0.0068	0.0066	0.0064
−2.50	0.0062	0.0060	0.0059	0.0057	0.0056	0.0054	0.0052	0.0051	0.0049	0.0048

(Continued)

df, d2 or Z-score	0.00	−0.01	−0.02	−0.03	−0.04	−0.05	−0.06	−0.07	−0.08	−0.09
−2.60	0.0047	0.0045	0.0044	0.0043	0.0042	0.0040	0.0039	0.0038	0.0037	0.0036
−2.70	0.0035	0.0034	0.0033	0.0032	0.0031	0.0030	0.0029	0.0028	0.0027	0.0026
−2.80	0.0026	0.0025	0.0024	0.0023	0.0023	0.0022	0.0021	0.0021	0.0020	0.0019
−2.90	0.0019	0.0018	0.0018	0.0017	0.0016	0.0016	0.0015	0.0015	0.0014	0.0014
−3.00	0.0014	0.0013	0.0013	0.0012	0.0012	0.0011	0.0011	0.0011	0.0010	0.0010

The data above represent the area between negative infinity and a certain number of standard deviations below the mean of a "normal" distribution. For example, if the number of standard deviations is 0.67 below the mean (or expected value), then the cumulative probability from minus infinity to negative 0.67 is   0.2514.

This table can be used in the Black-Scholes Option Model for negative values of "d1" or "d2." See Chapter 17 for a discussion of this application.

The data can also be used to find the number of standard deviations associated with a given return percentile. See Chapter 5 for a discussion of this application.

Appendix B

ASSOCIATION FOR
INVESTMENT MANAGEMENT
AND RESEARCH CODE OF
ETHICS AND STANDARDS
OF PROFESSIONAL CONDUCT

Effective January 1, 1990
As amended May 2, 1992

Code of Ethics

A financial analyst should conduct himself with integrity and dignity and act in an ethical manner in his dealings with the public, clients, customers, employers, employees, and fellow analysts.

A financial analyst should conduct himself and should encourage others to practice financial analysis in a professional and ethical manner that will reflect credit on himself and his profession.

A financial analyst should act with competence and should strive to maintain and improve his competence and that of others in the profession.

A financial analyst should use proper care and exercise independent professional judgement.

The Standards of Professional Conduct

I. Obligation to Inform Employer of Code and Standards

The financial analyst shall inform his employer through his direct supervisor that the analyst is obligated to comply with the Code of Ethics and Standards of Professional Conduct and is subject to disciplinary sanctions for violations thereof. He shall deliver a copy of the Code and Standards to his employer if the employer does not have a copy.

II. Compliance with Governing Laws and Regulations and the Code and Standards

A. Required Knowledge and Compliance

The financial analyst shall maintain knowledge of and shall comply with all applicable laws, rules, and regulations of any government, governmental agency, and regulatory organization governing his professional, financial, or business activities, as well as these Standards of Professional Conduct and the accompanying Code of Ethics.

B. Prohibition Against Assisting Legal and Ethical Violations

The financial analyst shall not knowingly participate in or assist any acts in violation of any applicable law, rule, or regulation of any government, governmental agency, or regulatory organization governing his profession, financial, or business activities, nor any act which would violate any provision of these Standards of Professional Conduct or the accompanying Code of Ethics.

C. Prohibition Against Use of Material Nonpublic Information

The financial analyst shall comply with all laws and regulations relating to the use and communication of material nonpublic information. The financial analyst's duty is generally defined as to not trade while in possession of, nor communicate material nonpublic information in breach of a duty, or if the information is misappropriated.

Duties under the Standard include the following: (1) if the analyst acquires such information as a result of a special or confidential relationship with the issuer or others, he shall not communicate the information (other than with the relationship) or take investment action on the basis of such information if it violates that relationship. (2) if the analyst is not in a special or confidential relationship with the issuer or others, he shall not communicate or act on material nonpublic information if he knows, or should have known, that such information (a) was disclosed to him, or would result in a breach of a duty or (b) was misappropriated.

If such a breach of duty exists, the analyst shall make reasonable efforts to achieve public dissemination of such information.

D. Responsibilities of Supervisors

A financial analyst with supervisory responsibility shall exercise reasonable supervision over those subordinate employees subject to his control to prevent any violation by such persons of applicable statutes, regulations, or provisions of the Code of Ethics or Standards of Professional Conduct. In so doing, the analyst is entitled to rely upon reasonable procedures established by his employer.

III. Research Reports, Investment Recommendations, and Actions

A. Reasonable Basis and Representations

1. The financial analyst shall exercise diligence and thoroughness in making an investment recommendation to others or in taking an investment action for others.

2. The financial analyst shall have a reasonable and accurate basis for such recommendations and actions, supported by appropriate research and investigation.

3. The financial analyst shall make reasonable and diligent efforts to avoid any material misrepresentation in any research report or investment recommendation.

4. The financial analyst shall maintain appropriate records to support the reasonableness of such recommendations and actions.

B. Research Reports

1. The financial analyst shall use reasonable judgement as to the inclusion of relevant factors in research reports.

2. The financial analyst shall distinguish between facts and opinions in research reports.

3. The financial analyst shall indicate the basic characteristics of the investment involved when preparing for general public distribution a research report that is not directly related to a specific portfolio or client.

C. Portfolio Investment Recommendations and Actions

1. The financial analyst shall when making an investment recommendation or taking an investment action for a specific portfolio or client, consider its appropriateness and suitability for such portfolio or client. In considering such matters, the financial analyst shall take into account (a) the needs and circumstances of the client, (b) the basic characteristics of the investment involved, and (c) the basic characteristics of the total portfolio. The financial analyst shall use reasonable judgement to determine the applicable relevant factors.

2. The financial analyst shall distinguish between facts and opinions in the presentation of investment recommendations.

3. The financial analyst shall disclose to clients and prospective clients the basic format and general principles of the investment process by which securities are selected and portfolios are constructed and shall promptly disclose to clients any changes that might significantly affect those processes.

D. Prohibition Against Plagiarism

The financial analyst shall not when presenting material to his employer, associates, customers, clients, or the general public, copy or use in substantially the same form material prepared by other persons without acknowledging its use and identifying the name of the author or publisher of such material. The analyst may, however, use without acknowledgment factual information published by recognized financial and statistical reporting services or similar sources.

E. Prohibition Against Misrepresentation of Services

The financial analyst shall not make any statements, orally or in writing, which misrepresent (1) the services that the analyst or his firm is capable of performing for the client, (2) the qualifications of such analyst or his firm, or (3) the expected performance of any investment.

The financial analyst shall not make orally or in writing, explicitly or implicitly, any assurances about or guarantees of any investment or its return except communication of accurate information as to the terms of the investment and the issuer's obligations under the instrument.

F. Performance Presentation Standards

1. The financial analyst shall not make any statements, oral or written, which misrepresent the investment performance that the analyst or his firm has accomplished or can reasonably be expected to achieve.

2. If the analyst communicates directly or indirectly individual or firm performance information to a client or prospective client, or in a manner intended to be received by a client or prospective client ("Performance Information"), the analyst shall make every reasonable effort to assure that such performance information is a fair, accurate, and complete presentation of such performance.

3. The financial analyst shall inform his employer about the existence and content of the Association for Investment Management and Research's Performance Presentation Standards, and this Standard II F, and shall encourage his employer to adopt and use the Performance Presentation Standards.

4. If performance information complies with the Performance Presentation Standards, the analyst shall be assumed to be in compliance with III. F. 2 above.

5. An analyst presenting performance information may use the following legend on the Performance information presentation, but only if the analyst has made every reasonable effort to assure that such presentation is in compliance with the Performance Presentation Standards in all material respects:

This report has been prepared and presented in compliance with the Performance Presentation Standards of the Association for Investment Management and Research.

This Standard shall take effect January 1, 1993.

G. Fair Dealing with Customers and Clients

The financial analyst shall act in a manner consistent with his obligation to deal fairly with all customers and clients when (1) disseminating investment recommendations, (2) disseminating material changes in prior investment advice, and (3) taking investment action.

IV. Priority of Transactions

The financial analyst shall conduct himself in such a manner that transactions for his customers, clients, and employer have priority over transactions in securities or other investments of which he is the beneficial owner, and so that the transactions in securities or other investments in which he has such beneficial ownership do not operate adversely to their interests. If an analyst decides to make a recommendation about the purchase or sale of a security or other investment, he shall give his customers, clients, and employer adequate opportunity to act on his recommendation before acting in his own behalf.

For purposes of these standards of Professional Conduct, a financial analyst is a "beneficial owner" if he directly or indirectly, through any contract, arrangement, understanding, relationship, or otherwise, has or shares a direct or indirect pecuniary interest in the securities or the investment.

V. Disclosure of Conflicts

The financial analyst, when making investment recommendations, or taking investment actions, shall disclose to his customers and clients any material conflict of interest relating to him and any material beneficial ownership of the securities or other investments involved that could reasonably be expected to impair his ability to render unbiased and objective advice.

The financial analyst shall disclose to his employer all matters that could reasonably be expected to interfere with his duty to the employer, or with his ability to render unbiased and objective advice.

The financial analyst shall also comply with all requirements as to disclosure of conflicts of interest imposed by law and by rules and regulations of organizations governing his activities and shall comply with any prohibitions on his activities if a conflict of interest exists.

VI. Compensation

A. Disclosure of Additional Compensation Arrangements

The financial analyst shall inform his customers, clients, and employer of compensation or other benefit arrangements in connection with his services to them which are in addition to compensation from them for such services.

B. Disclosure of Referral Fees

The financial analyst shall make appropriate disclosure to a prospective client or customer of any consideration paid or other benefit delivered to others for recommending his services to that prospective client or customer.

C. Duty to Employer

The financial analyst shall not undertake independent practice which could result in compensation or other benefit in competition with his employer unless he has received written consent from both his employer and the person for whom he undertakes independent employment.

VII. Relationships with Others

A. Preservation of Confidentiality

The financial analyst shall preserve the confidentiality of information communicated by the client concerning matters within the scope of the confidential relationship unless the financial analyst receives information concerning illegal activities on the part of the client.

B. Maintenance of Independence and Objectivity

The financial analyst, in relationships and contacts with an issuer of securities, whether individually or as a member of a group, shall use particular care and judgement to achieve and maintain independence and objectivity.

C. Fiduciary Duties

The financial analyst, in relationships with clients, shall use particular care in determining applicable fiduciary duty and shall comply with such duty as to those persons and interests to whom it is owed.

VIII. Use of Professional Designation

The qualified financial analyst may use as applicable, the professional designation "Member of the Association for Investment Management and Research," "Member of the Financial Analyst Federation," and "Member of the Institute of Chartered Financial analysts," and is encouraged to do so, but only in a dignified and judicious manner. The use of the designations may be accompanied by an accurate explanation (1) of the requirements that have been met to obtain the designation, and (2) of the Association for Investment Management and Research, the Financial Analysts Federation, and the Institute of Chartered Financial Analysts, as applicable.

The Chartered Financial Analyst may use the professional designation "Chartered Financial Analyst," or the abbreviation "CFA," and is encouraged to do so, but only in a dignified and judicious manner. The use of the designation may be accompanied by an accurate explanation (1) of the requirements that have been met to obtain the designation, and (2) of the Association for Investment Management and Research, and the Institute of Chartered Financial analysts.

IX. Professional Misconduct

The financial analyst shall not (1) commit a criminal act that upon conviction materially reflects adversely on his honesty, trustworthiness, or fitness as a financial analyst in other respects, or (2) engage in conduct involving dishonesty, fraud, deceit, or misrepresentation.

Amended May 2, 1992. Standard III. C, E, G, IV, and VI C revised.
Amended May 2, 1992. Standard III. F added.

Masculine personal pronouns used throughout the Code and Standards to simplify sentence structure shall apply to all persons regardless of sex.

Correspondence with the AIMR:

5 Boars Head Lane

P.O. Box 3668

Charlottesville, VA 22903-0668

(804) 980-3668

Fax (804) 980-3670

ANSWERS TO SELECTED END-OF-CHAPTER PROBLEMS

Chapter 1

6. Assume the price of Treasury bills having maturities in 1 year varies at two banks as follows:

   Price if traded in New York: $943,000
   Price if traded in Chicago: $944,000

   Then an arbitrage such as shown here could be conducted.

Transaction	Cash Today	Cash in 1-Year
Today:		
Sell the Chicago issue	+$944,000	
Buy the New York issue	− 943,000	
In 1 Year:		
Repay the Chicago issue		−$1,000,000
Redeem the New York issue		+ 1,000,000
Net	+$ 1,000	$ 0

   The instruments must have the same maturity in order to know with certainty all cash flows.

7. a. If the coin is a "fair coin" (meaning the chance of a head or tail of the coin appearing in a toss is 50%), then 500 students are expected to have a correct prediction after one toss.

   b. 250 students = 1,000 (0.5 × 0.5)

   c. 0.97656 students = 1,000 × 0.5^{10}

   d. You would expect that about one student would have ten correct predictions. Thus, observing that one student did successfully predict ten outcomes is consistent with chance.

Chapter 2

13. a. To create a passive portfolio that invests in these 14 countries, the percentage invested in each should be equal to the percentage which a country's market capitalization represents of the total capitalization. For example:

   % to invest in
   Austria: $30 ÷ $3,270 = 0.917%

   % to invest in
   United Kingdom: $1,145 ÷ $3,270 = 35.015%

The $100 million should be invested as follows:

($ million)		($ millions)	
Austria	0.917	Italy	5.413
Belgium	2.569	Netherlands	6.850
Denmark	1.407	Norway	1.101
Finland	1.101	Spain	4.618
France	13.578	Sweden	3.608
Germany	14.556	Switzerland	8.685
		United	
Ireland	0.581	Kingdom	35.015

(Note: These proportions represent the relative market capitalizations of these countries in 1994.)

Chapter 3

1. a. Buy price = 100 − 100(0.087)(14 ÷ 360) = 99.6617% par
   Sell price = 100 − 9(14 ÷ 360)   = 99.65% par

   b. Days to maturity = 30(Jan) + 28(Feb) + 15(March) = 73
   Buy price = 98.2176%; Sell price = 98.1507%

   c. $r = 9.074\%$

   d. Profit = $9,854,958 − $9,821,758 = $33,200

2. Price of 1 BP = $1,000,000 × 0.0001 × (91 ÷ 360)
                  = $25.28

3. a. $992,911.11 = $1,000,000 − $1,000,000 (0.088) (29 ÷ 360)

   b. Bid = 91.00 Asked = 91.20

   c. Simple interest annualized:
   r = [(100 − 99.291111) ÷ 99.291111](365 ÷ 29)
      = 8.986%
   Compound interest annualized:
   $r' = 1.0071395^{365/29} − 1.0$
        = 9.367%

   d. r = [(99.47222 − 99.291111) ÷ 99.291111](365 ÷ 9)
        = 7.397%
   $r' = 1.00182^{365/9} − 1.0 = 7.671\%$

4.
(A) Discount	(B) Dollars	(C) % of Total	(A) × (C)
8.50%	$ 200	13 1/3	1.13333%
8.55	400	26 2/3	2.80000
8.56	600	40	3.42400
8.58	300	20	1.71600
	$1,500	100.00	8.55333%

Noncompetitive bidders receive the weighted average discount of 8.55 1/3%:

$r = 8.864\%$ $\qquad$ $r' = 9.163\%$

6. a. FM shares = $\$1,000 - 0.03(\$1,000) = \$970$
$\$970 \div \$33.37 = 29.068$ shares
PNH shares = $\$1,000 \div \$12.88 = 77.6398$ shares

b. NAV is the per share market value of portfolio assets minus the per share value of any debt that the mutual fund has outstanding.

7. a. $(\$500 - \$10) \div 7 = \$70$ NAV

b. $\$10,000 \div \$70 = 142.857$ shares

8. a. & b. No change in NAV

c. NAV increases $\$2.86$ to $\$72.86$

d. Nav falls by $\$5$ to $\$65$

9.a. Corporate bond = $8\%(1 - 0.3) = 5.6\%$
This is better than 5% on the municipal bond.

b. $8\%(1 - X) = 5\%$; $X = 0.375$

Chapter 4

5. a.

	Per Share
Underwriter spread	$\$2.50$
Out-of-pocket ($\$37,500 \div 50,000$)	0.75
Price concession	2.00
Total	$\$5.25$

7. a. Equity = $0.60 \times (\$40 \times 500) = \$12,000$

Debt = $\$20,000 - \$12,000 = \$8,000$

b. $0.40 = \dfrac{\text{Price} \times 500 - \$8,000}{\text{Price} \times 500}$

Price = $\$26.67$

c. Assuming the new cash is used to repay some of the loan balance:

$0.40 = [(500 \times \$20) - (\$8,000 - \text{Cash})]$
$\div (500 \times \$20)$

Cash = $\$2,000$ (new loan will be $\$6,000$)

d. $0.4 = \$20(500 - N) - (\$8,000 - \$20N)$
$\div \$20(500 - N)$

$N = 250$ shares

9. a. $R_{\text{Jennifer}} = \dfrac{\$6,900 - \$5,000 + \$100}{\$5,000} = 40\%$

$R_{\text{Jason}} = \dfrac{100(\$69 - \$50 + \$1) - \$2,500(0.08)}{\$2,500} = 72\%$

b. $R_{\text{Jennifer}} = \dfrac{\$3,900 - \$5,000 + \$100}{\$5,000} = -20\%$

$R_{\text{Jason}} = \dfrac{100(\$39 - \$50 + \$1) - \$200}{\$2,500} = -48\%$

c. The use of margin acts as "leverage" in that it magnifies any percentage profits or losses.

Chapter 5

2. a. Expected 1.0 + Geometric

Year	Inflation	Average Inflation
1	4%	1.04
2	6%	$[(1.04)(1.06)]^{1/2} = 1.05$
3	8%	$[(1.04)(1.06)(1.08)]^{1/3} = 1.06$
4	5%	$[1.2501]^{1/4} = 1.0574$

From Fisher equation:

Year	Nominal RF	Calculation
1	7.12%	$(1.03)(1.04) - 1$
2	8.15%	$(1.03)(1.05) - 1$
3	9.18%	$(1.03)(1.06) - 1$
4	8.91%	$(1.03)(1.0574) - 1$

b. From approximate Fisher equation:

Year	RF	Calculation
1	7.00%	$0.03 + 0.04$
2	8.00%	$0.03 + 0.05$
3	9.00%	$0.03 + 0.06$
4	8.74%	$0.03 + 0.0574$

c.

Year	Value	Calculation
1	$\$93.35$	$\$100 \div (1.0712)$
2	$\$85.49$	$\$100 \div (1.0815)^2$
3	$\$76.84$	$\$100 \div (1.0918)^3$
4	$\$71.08$	$\$100 \div (1.0891)^4$

4. Nominal return = $(100/90) - 1 = 11.11\%$

Real return = $(1.1111/1.05) - 1 = 5.82\%$

or = $11.11\% - 5\% = 6.11\%$
(using approximate Fisher equation)

5. a. Using the approximate Fisher equation, expected inflation would be:

Italy $\quad 11.2\% - 2.0\% = 9.2\%$

Japan $\quad 3.07\% - 2.0\% = 1.07\%$

b. Using approximate Fisher equation, expected real returns would be:

U.S.   6.93% − 4.83% = 2.10%

U.K.   8.00% − 3.85% = 4.15%

The higher real return is available in the U.K.

7. a. Time Weighted Return Calculations:

Subperiod	1.0 + Subperiod return
June 1–June 10	(25+1) ÷ 20 = 1.30
June 10–June 30	22 ÷ 25 = 0.88

Month of June TWR: (1.30 × 0.88)−1.0 = 14.4%

b. Dollar Weighted Return Calculations:

$$\text{MVE} = \text{MVB}(1 + \text{DWR}) + \sum F(1 + \text{DWR})^{w(i)}$$

$$\$4,488 = \$2,000(1 + \text{DWR}) + \$2,700(1 + \text{DWR})^{10 \div 30}$$

The DWR is approximately −7.25%

c. DWR are affected by the timing of cash inflows or cash outflows to the portfolio. In this example, the DWR is lower than the TWR because a deposit was made to the portfolio just before the value of securities held in the portfolio declined.

d. Both are correct return measures. But they represent returns from two different perspectives.

8. a. (−20 + 30 + 5 + 15 −4) ÷ 5 = 5.2%

b. $[(0.8)(1.3)(1.05)(1.15)(0.96)]^{1/5} - 1.0 = 3.81\%$

d.

0	1	2	3	4	5
1.0000	0.8000	1.0400	1.0920	1.2558	1.2056

e. Geometric mean from 2 through 5
$[1.2056 \div 1.04]^{1/3} - 1.0 = 5.05\%$

f.

Period	1	2	3	4	5
Return	−20	30	5	15	−4
Squared Difference from Average	635.04	615.04	0.04	96.04	84.64

Sum of Squared Differences = 1430.8

Variance = 1430.8 ÷ (5 − 1) = 357.7

Standard Deviation = $(357.7)^{1/2}$ = 18.91

11. Expected return on T-bills:
3.0% = 0.2(5.0%) + 0.6(3.0%) + 0.2(1.0%)
Expected return on bonds: 4.6%
Expected return on stocks: 10.0%

Variance of returns on T-bills:
$1.6\% = 0.2(5.00 − 3.0)^2 + 0.6(3.0 − 3.0)^2$
$+ 0.2(1.0 − 3.0)^2$
Variance of returns on bonds: 6.64%
Variance of returns on stocks: 250%
Standard Deviation of returns on T-bills:
$(1.6\%)^{1\div2} = 1.26\%$
Standard Deviation of returns on bonds: 2.57%
Standard Deviation of returns on stocks: 15.81%

12.

Percentile	0.05	0.10	0.25	0.50	0.75	0.90	0.95
Associated z-score	−1.64	−1.28	−0.67	0.00	0.67	1.28	1.64
Value of 1.0 Standard Deviation	40%	40%	40%	40%	40%	40%	40%
Total Difference from Mean Return	−65.6%	−51.2%	−26.8%	0.0%	26.8%	51.2%	65.6%
Plus Means Return	20%	20%	20%	20%	20%	20%	20%
Percentile Return	−45.6%	−31.2%	−6.8%	20%	46.8%	71.2%	85.6%

Chapter 6

5. From the equation for minimum portfolio risk:

$$X_A = [\sigma_B^2 - \sigma_A\sigma_B r_{AB}] \div [\sigma_A^2 + \sigma_B^2 - 2(\sigma_A\sigma_B r_{AB})]$$

letting X_A represent X_1, then:

$X_1 = [0.5^2 - 0] \div [0.4^2 + 0.5^2] = 0.60976,$

$X_2 = 0.39024$

6. a. For the S&P 500:

Average return
$= (−3.17 + 30.55 + 7.67 + 9.99 + 1.32) \div 5 = 9.272$

Standard deviation of a sample (uses $N − 1$):

$= [(−3.17 − 9.272)^2 + (30.55 − 9.272)^2$
$+ \cdots + (1.32 − 9.272)^2] \div (5 − 1) = 12.97953$

Standard deviation of a population (uses N):

$= [(−3.17 − 9.272)^2 + (30.55−9.272)^2$
$+ \cdots + (1.32−9.272)^2] \div (5) = 11.60925$

For other security classes:

	Average	Sample Std. Dev	Pop. Std. Dev
Small U.S. Stocks	14.086	24.77861	22.16267
EAFE	3.636	21.87493	19.56554

b. Correlation using population standard deviations:
For S&P 500 and small U.S. stocks:

r = covariance (S&P 500, Small stocks) ÷ $(\sigma_{S\&P} \times \sigma_{small})$

$$= \frac{[(-3.17 - 9.272)(-21.56 - 14.086) + \cdots + (1.32 - 9.272)(3.11 - 14.086)] \div 5}{11.60925 \times 22.16267}$$

$$= \frac{234.1882}{257.29198} = 0.9102$$

Full correlation matrix

	S&P 500	Small Stocks	EAFE
S&P 500	1.0000		
Small Stocks	0.9102	1.0000	
EAFE	0.4712	0.5725	1.0000

c. Using the standard deviation of a sample $(N - 1)$:
17.43126

d. This is lower than the average of 19.87769 because the returns are not perfectly correlated.

8. If you only know the market cap of each country, invest proportionately in each:

Country	1	2	3	4	5	Total
Invest	9.1%	18.2%	27.3%	22.7%	22.7%	100.0%
						(off by rounding)

9. a. Expected return in Hong Kong: $0.25(-25) + 0.25(-5)$
   $+ 0.25(0) + 0.25(30) = 0.0\%$
   Std. Dev. in Hong Kong: $[0.25(-25-0)^2$
   $+ \cdots + 0.25(30-0)^2]^{1\div 2} = 19.685\%$

   b. Expected return in Tokyo: 7.5%
   Standard deviation in Tokyo: 17.5%

   c. Returns from equal investment in each: $-17.5\%, -7.5\%,$
   $12.5\%, 27.5\%$
   Expected return from equal investment: 3.75%
   Standard deviation from equal investment: 17.4553%

10. a.

	U.S. Govt.	U.S. Stock	Non-U.S. Stock
Average return	1.77%	8.05%	6.107%
Variance (of population)	2.4494%	34.4326%	104.2579%
Std. Dev. (of population)	1.5651%	5.8679%	10.2239%
Std. Dev. (of sample)	1.6497%	6.1853%	10.7769%
Correlations:			
U.S. Govt.	1.0000		
U.S. Stock	−0.4197	1.0000	
Non-U.S. Stock	0.1596	−0.12169	1.0000

d.

	05 Govt., 0.5 U.S. Stock	0.5 U.S. Stock, 0.5 Non U.S.	One-third in Each
Std. Dev. (of population)	2.7006%	5.5758%	3.7149%
Std. Dev. (of sample)	2.8467%	5.8774%	3.9159%

11. An equal investment in security A and security B results in a risk-free portfolio. This portfolio held in combinations with security C represents the efficient frontier.

12. $E(R_C) = RF + \sigma_C [E(R_P) - RF] \div \sigma_P$

   $= 6.0 + \sigma_C [11.0 - 6.0] \div 20$

   $= 6.0 + \sigma_C [0.25]$

   and $\sigma_C = X_P(\sigma_P) = X_P\,20$

   Here σ_C is the standard deviation on the combination and X_P is the percentage invested in the risky portfilio.

   a. $8.5\% = 6.0\% + 0.25\,\sigma_C$

   $\sigma_C = 10$

   so X_P must be equal to 0.5.

   Invest one-half in risky security P and the remaining one-half in the risk-free security.

   b. $10 = X_P\,20$; so X_P equals 0.5. As in part a, invest one-half in risky security P and the remaining one-half in the risk-free security.

   c. $16.0\% = 6.0\% + 0.25\,\sigma_C$

   $\sigma_C = 40$

   $40 = X_P\,20$; so X_P must be 2.0

   Invest all of your money in P plus borrow an equal dollar amount risk free that is then invested in P. This represents a 200% investment in P.

   d. Invest 150% of your equity in P by borrowing $0.50 for each $1.00 of equity invested.

16. Relative risk of security: $[30 \times 0.5] \div 10 = 1.5$

Chapter 7

1. True. The only portfolios that can be perfectly correlated with the market portfolio must be some combination of the market portfolio and the risk-free security.

5. There are a number of ways to address this question. The easiest is to estimate the beta of XYZ and the calculate whether XYZ provides a fair expected return given this beta.

The following data result from this problem:

	Expected Return	Std. Dev.	Correlation
Market			
Portfolio	11.8%	4.74974	
XYZ	12.2%	9.15205	1.0 (rounded)

Beta of XYZ = [9.15205 (1.0)] ÷ 4.74974 = 1.9268

Required XYZ return = 7.0% + 1.9268 (11.8% − 7.0%)

$\quad$ = 16.248%

Since the expected return on XYZ (12.2%) is less than the required return (16.2%), do not buy shares of XYZ.

6.

Portfolio	σ
1	7% = 0.7(10%)
2	15% = 1.5(10%)

Notice that beta is the same thing as the percentage invested in the market portfolio

7. a.

Portfolio	$[E(R) - RF]/\sigma$
1	0.667
2	0.667
3	0.875 optimal
4	0.846
5	0.778

b. $E(R) = 6.0\% + 4.0\%[0.875] = 9.5\%$; No

c. $16.5\% = 6.0\% + 12.0\%[0.875]$

Borrow 50% and invest 150% of IDC capital in portfolio 3.

9.   Beta = [40(−0.3)] ÷ 20 = −0.6

$E(R) = 5.0\% + (-0.6)(5.0\%) = 2.0\%$

$P_0 = (70 + 4) \div 1.02 = 72.549$

10.   a., b., and c.

Security	Beta	Beta Next Period	$E(R)$
Mesa	1.6409	lower	16.4863%
Anheuser Busch	0.3663	higher	7.5641%
Teledyne	1.3402	lower	14.3814%
XYZ	1.1488	lower	13.0416%
Index	1.0000	same	12.0000%

d. Beta = (1.6409 + 0.3663 + 1.3402) ÷ 3 = 1.1158

11.   a., b., c.

Security	$E(R)$	$E(R)$ Given Market	Residual
1	14.0%	5.0% + 1.5(5.0%) = 12.5%	15% − 12.5% = 2.5%
2	11.0%	5.0% + 1.0(5.0%) = 10.0%	11.0% − 10.0% = 1.0%

e. $\sigma^2 = B_p^2 \, \sigma_M^2 + \sigma_e^2$

$400 = 2.25(\sigma_M^2) + 100$

$\quad \sigma_M^2 = 133.33$ and $\sigma_M = 11.55\%$

12. a. Plan 1 is the most risky, since it consists solely of stocks.

b. 7.0%.

c. Pursue the low-risk plan 3.

13. a. Fund 4 is most correlated with market (highest R^2).

b. Fund 2 (highest beta).

c. Fund 2 (highest beta and residual risk).

d. For Fund 1; $(1.0098)^4 - 1.0 = 3.98\%$.

Chapter 8

2. a. $E(R) = 0.5 + 1.0(10) + (-0.35)(3)$

$\sigma^2 = (1.0)^2(225) + (-0.35)^2(100)$

$\quad + (0.5)^2(19.4)^2 + (0.5)^2(27.5)^2$

$\quad = 520.4025$

$\sigma = 22.81$

8. a. Factors 2 and 3 are best thought of as firm-unique factors in this example. In a broadly diversified portfolio the positive and negative values net to zero.

b. Per APT the expected returns should be:

$E(R_1) = 6.0(3) = 18.0\%$

$E(R_2) = 1.5(3) = 4.5\%$

Per actual market conditions, expected returns are:

$E(R_1) = (45 \div 40) - 1.0 = 12.5\%$

$E(R_2) = (10.7 \div 10) - 1.0 = 7.0\%$

Stock 1 is overvalued and stock 2 is undervalued.

Transaction	$	Factor Score
Sell 1.0 Stock 1	$ 40	(6)
Buy 4.0 Stock 2	$(40)	6
Net	$ 0	0

Chapter 10

2. a. $YTM_A = 8.9975\%$ $YTM_B = 7.0038\%$ $YTM_C = 7.0055\%$

b. Bond C has the lower coupon and thus the lower effective tax rate if ordinary rates are higher than capital gains rates. In that case, equilibrium would occur only when the (before-tax) yield to maturity on bond C is lower than on bond B.

c. Bond C; it has the longest maturity and lowest coupon.

d. Bond C; lower coupon.

e. $P_A = 960.17$; $P_B = 1,294.07$; $P_C = 852.43$

6. $f_{Mt} = f_{1,5} = [(1.09)^6/(1.087)^5] - 1.0 = 10.51\%$

7. a. $f_{1,6} = [(1.09)^6/(1.08)^5] - 1.0 = 14.14\%$

   b. $f_{2,6} = [(1.095)^7/(1.08)^5]^{1/2} - 1.0 = 13.34\%$

8. $f_{15,5} = [(1.08)^{20}/(1.085)^5]^{1/15} - 1.0 = 7.83\%$

Transaction	Date		
	0	5	20
Buy 1.0 20-Year	(214.548)	—	1,000.00
Short-Sell			
0.3226 5-Year	214.548	(322.60)	—
Net	—	(322.68)	1,000.00

9. a.

Transaction	Date		
	0	1	2
Buy 1.0 2-Year	(873.00)		1,000.00
Sell 0.94 1-Year	873.00	(942.76)	
873/926 = 0.94276			
Net	—	(942.76)	1,000.00

b. Return = $(1,000.00 \div 942.76) - 1.0 = 6.07\%$

c. No. Do the opposite.

10. a. IRR = 9.3%

$$\$1,120 = \frac{\$120}{1.093} + \frac{\$120}{1.093^2} + \frac{\$120}{1.093^3}$$
$$+ \frac{\$120}{1.093^4} + \frac{\$120}{1.093^5} + \frac{\$1,120}{1.093^6}$$

b. Yes, issue bonds at 8% and save 9%.

c. For years 1–4 you earn 12% on your investment of $1,000. In years 5–10 you earn 8%. In addition, you receive $120 in call premium, which earns 8% in years 5–10. Thus, your end-of-year: 10 portfolio value would be:

$1,000 (1.12)^4(1.08)^6$ = $2,496.97

$120 (1.08)^6$ = 190.42

Total end of year 10   = $2,687.39

Return = $2.68739^{1/10} - 1.0$ = 10.39%

Chapter 11

1. a. $P_A = 1,000$ $P_B = 1,013.76$

   b. Short-sell bond B and buy equal dollar amount of bond A.

2.

Period	$	PV	%	× Period	= Product
1	40	38.10	4.07%	1	= 0.0407
2	40	36.28	3.88	2	= 0.0776
3	40	34.55	3.69	3	= 0.1107
4	40	32.91	3.52	4	= 0.1408
5	40	31.34	3.35	5	= 0.1675
6	40	29.85	3.19	6	= 0.1914
7	40	28.43	3.04	7	= 0.2128
8	1,040	703.91	75.25	8	= 6.0200
Total		935.37	100.0		6.9615

Duration in years = 6.9615/2 = 3.481 years

3. a. $D^* = 7.3 \div 1.12 = 6.51786$

   b. $R = -6.51786(0.11 - 0.12) = 0.06518$

4. a. $D = 0.1(1) + 0.2(3) + 0.1(5) + 0.2(7)$
$$+ 0.4(12)$$
$$= 7.4 \text{ years}$$

   $D^* = 7.4 \div 1.09 = 6.78899$

   b. $-6.78899(0.10 - 0.09) = -0.06789$

5. First, find the purchase price:

$$\text{Price} = \sum_{t=1}^{10} \frac{90}{1.1^t} + \frac{1,000}{1.1^{10}} = 938.55$$

Next, find end of year-3 value:

End-of-Year Coupon	1	2	3	End-of-Year 3 Value
3			90 =	90.000
2		90 × 1.08	=	97.200
1	90 × 1.08^2		=	104.976
Price at end of year 3			=	1,052.060
Total value end of year 3				1,344.236

Annualized return = $(1,344.236/938.55)^{1/3} - 1.0$
$$= 12.72\%$$

Price risk was most important here, since the bond was sold prior to maturity.

6. Annualized return $= [(1.1)(1.08)(1.08)]^{1/3} - 1.0$

$\qquad = 8.66\%$

The risk in this case is reinvestment risk. Your return was lower than 10% because reinvestment rates declined.

Chapter 12

4. a. Annual dividend growth $= (\$5.00 \div \$2.54)^{1/10} = 1.0$

$\qquad = 7.00\%$

$K = 6\% + 1.5(4\%) = 12\%$

Fair value price $= [\$5.00(1.07)] \div (0.12 - 0.07)$

$\qquad = \$107.00$

b. Dividend yield $= \$5.35 \div \$107.00 = 5.0\%$

Capital appreciation $=$ Growth rate $= 7.0\%$

5. $G = 0.60[(10\%)(1.25)] = 0.6[12.5\%] = 7.5\%$

$K = 8\% + 1.3(5\%) = 14.5\%$

Price $= [\$2.50(1.075)] \div (0.145 - 0.075) = \$38.39$

Since the stock is trading for \$45, short-sell it.

6. a. $ROE = 4(2\%)(2.0) = 16\%$

b. $G = 16\%(0.25) = 4.0\%$

c. $K = 8\% + 1.5(6\%) = 17\%$

Fair value price $= [\$3.00(1.04)] \div (0.17 - 0.04)$
$\qquad = \$24.00$

7. Growth rate implied in today's price $= 7.5\%$

8. Required return implied in today's price $= 12.06\%$

9. a. $P = \dfrac{\$3.60}{1.18} + \dfrac{\$4.32}{1.18^2} + \dfrac{\$5.184}{1.18^3}$

$\qquad + \dfrac{\$5.184(0.95)}{0.18 - (-0.05)} \times \dfrac{1}{1.18^3} = \$22.34$

b. $P_3 = \dfrac{\$5.184(0.95)}{0.18 - (-0.05)} = \$21.41$

$P_4 = \dfrac{\$5.184(0.95)(0.95)}{0.18 - (-0.05)} = \$20.34$

Chapter 14

1. a. $\$37.96875 = (\$1,230 - \$15) \div 32$

c. $\$38.5625 = (\$1,249 - \$15) \div 32$

d. Remain the same

e. NAV would fall by \$0.40 per share

f. No effect

7. a. $\$44.375 = \$710 \div 16$

b.

	Before Tax	Taxes
Income DPS:	$\$20 \div 16 = \$1.25$	$\$0.375 = 0.3(\$1.25)$
Capital Gains DPS	$\$90 \div 16 = \$5.625$	$\$1.575 = 0.28(\$5.625)$
Total	$\underline{\$6.875}$	$\underline{\$1.950}$

c. NAV after dividend distribution: $\$37.50 = (\$600 \div 16)$
$\qquad = \$44.375 - (\$1.25 + \$5.625)$

d. Paid in Capital $\qquad$ \$510
$\quad$ Unreal Appreciation $\qquad \underline{200}$
$\qquad\qquad\qquad\qquad\qquad \underline{\$710}$

10. Value of load fund in 5 years:

$(1.05)^5 \; \$9,200 = \$11,741.79$

$(1.10)^5 \; \$9,200 = \$14,816.69$

Annualized return and cost:

$0.03260 = (\$11,741.79 \div \$10,000) - 1.0;$
$\quad \text{cost} = 0.01740 = 0.05 - 0.0326$
$0.08181 = (\$14,816.69 \div \$10,000) - 1.0;$
$\quad \text{cost} = 0.01819 = 0.10 - 0.08181$

Chapter 15

1. a. Inflation in Canada $= I_C$

$0.72 = 0.70(1.05 \div 1 + I_C)$

$I_C = 2.08 \; 1/3\%$

b. 0.72—the current 6-month forward rate

c. decrease; higher expected inflation in the United States than in Canada

2. $R_{Japan} = 20\%; \quad R_{U.S.} = 5\%$

3. a. $E(I_{U.S.}) = 5.0\%$

b. 10.29%

c. 13.6%

4. a. no

b.

Dollars	\$1,000,000
times M/\$	\underline{1.4286}
Marks	1,428,571M
times £/M	\underline{0.5000}
Pounds	714,286
times \$/£	\underline{1.9000}
Dollars	\$1,357,143

7.

Year	86	87	88	89	90
R_X	26.98%	30.77%	-2.84%	-12.66%	6.35%

8.

	Exchange Rate Return		
Local Return	-12.50%	0.00%	$+12.50\%$
-15.00%	-25.63	-15.00	-4.38
10.00%	-3.75	10.00	23.75
35.00%	18.13	35.00	51.88

10. a. $E(R_{UK}) = 23.9\%$ $E(R_F) = 15.2\%$

b. $\sigma^2_{UK} = 1.0(30^2) + 1.0(10^2) + 2(30)(10)(0.30) = 1,180$

$\sigma_{UK} = 34.35$ $\sigma_F = 36.40$

11. $E(R_P) = 15\%$ $\sigma_P = 22.22\%$

Chapter 16

2. a. Pay $977,875 per contract or $4,889,375 for five contracts in late June.

b. Selling price at an 8.95% discount = $977,625. Your loss will be $250 per contract ($977,625 − $977,875) or 10 basis points times $25 per basis point.

3.   Net spot price = spot price − futures profit

$95.75 = $99.75 − $4.00

4.   90-day forward rate available in the spot market is:

$1 + R_{180} = 100 \div 98.50 = 1.015228$

$1 + R_{90} = 100 \div 99.25 = 1.007557$

forward rate $= (1.015228 \div 1.007557) - 1.0$
$= 0.7613\%$

future's return $= (100 \div 99) - 1.0 = 1.0101\%$

Arbitrage: Buy future, sell 180-day T-bill, and buy 90-day T-bill. Do this in quantities so the initial cash flow is zero and the amount received on the spot T-bills at day 90 is equal to the value of futures purchased.

5. a. 8.00%. Since they are maturing, they should sell at a price identical to spot T-bills.

b. Forward rate in spot market between day 270 and 360:

$P_{270} = 100 - 100(0.084)(270 \div 360) = 93.70$

$P_{360} = 91.40$

$1 + R_{270} = 100 \div 93.70 = 1.06724$

$1 + R_{360} = 100 \div 91.40 = 1.09409$

$\text{Forward}_{270-360} = (1.09409 \div 1.06724) - 1.0 = 0.02516$

Price of futures due in 270 days:

$100 \div 1.02516 = 97.5457$

Discount on futures due in 270 days:

Dollar discount $= 100 - 97.5457 = 2.4543$

Discount percentage quotation $= 2.4543 \,(360 \div 90) = 9.817\%$

9.

Realized Future Trading Price	=	Initial Spot	+	Initial Basis	− Cover Basis
973.75	=	978.75	+	(1,025 − 978.75) −	51.25

Gain or loss:

Sell spot	973.75
Buy spot	-978.75
Loss	-5.00 per $1,000 par

or $-\$5.00$ times 5,000 ($1,000) par bonds $= -\$25,000$

12. $\$105 = \$100 \,(3 \div 2)0.7$

15. a. Dollar duration of portfolio addition:

$6.0[(0.11 - 0.10) \div 1.10] \$100 \text{ million} = \$5.4545 \text{ million}$

Dollar duration of cheapest to deliver:

$(6.5 \div 0.9)[(0.11 - 0.10) \div 1.1] \$100,000 = \$6,565.66$

Number of T-bond futures to buy:

$\$5,454,545 \div \$6,565.66 = 830.77 \text{ contracts}$

18. a. Number of spot units now owned:

$1 billion ÷ ($113 × 500)	= 19,469

Number of spot units desired to own:

$0.9 billion ÷ ($113 × 500)	= 15,929
Number of contracts to <u>sell</u>	3,540

19. $F = \$400(1.0428) - \$8 = \$409.12$

Futures are overvalued.

21. a. Price of T-bill $= 100 - 100(0.08)(90 \div 360) = 98$

$1 + 90\text{-day T-bill Return} = 100 \div 98 = 1.02041$

$F = 300(1.02041) - 3 = 303.12$

Market price is too high.

b.

	Today	$0	$ at Delivery
Sell 666 2/3 Futures (1)		−	$108.000 million
Buy 666 2/3 Spot		(100 million)	
Sell T-bills (2)		100 million	($102.041 million)
At Delivery			
Receive dividends (3)			1.000 million
Buy futures and sell spot			a wash
Net		0.0	6.959 million

(1) 100 million ÷ (300 × 500) = 666 2/3 contracts

(2) 100 million (1.02041) = 102.041 million

(3) (666 2/3 × 500)3.00 = 1.000 million

c. Number of stock units held:

(250 million × 1.1) ÷ (300 × 500) = 1,833 1/3

Number of stock units desired:

(300 million × 1.0) ÷ (300 × 500) = <u>2,000.00</u>

Number of contracts to buy = <u>166 2/3</u>

Chapter 17

1. a. through d.

	$40	$45	$50	$55	$60
			Expiration date cash flows		
Buy 1.0 call	0	0	0	−50	−50
Write 1.0 call	0	0	0	50	50
Buy 1.0 put	50	50	0	0	0
Write 1.0 put	−50	−50	0	0	0

	$40	$45	$50	$55	$60
			Expiration date investment values		
Buy 1.0 call	0	0	0	5	10
Write 1.0 call	0	0	0	−5	−10
Buy 1.0 put	10	5	0	0	0
Write 1.0 put	−10	−5	0	0	0

	$40	$45	$50	$55	$60
			Expiration date net profits		
Buy 1.0 call	−8	−8	−8	−3	2
Write 1.0 call	8	8	8	3	−2
Buy 1.0 put	9	4	−1	−1	−1
Write 1.0 put	−9	−4	1	1	1

2.
Sell call option	$8
Buy stock	(70)
Receive cash when exercised	65
Net cash to you	$3

3. a. $C - P = \$75 - \$70 \div 1.1^{4/12} = \$7.19$ in theory
$C - P = \$7 - \$2 = \$5$ in market
Thus, the call is undervalued relative to the put.

b. Illustration for spot at expiration of $60 and $80:

		Expiration Day	
	Today	$60	$80
Buy 1.0 Call	(7)	—	10.00
Sell 1.0 Put	2	(10.00)	—
Sell 1.0 Stock	75	(60.00)	(80.00)
Net	70	(70.00)	(70.00)

Buy T-bills	(70)	72.26	72.26
Total	0	2.26	2.26

4. a. $C = \$74 - (\$65 \div 1.1) + \$5.09 = \$20$

b.
Long Stock	Short Stock
Buy 1.0 call at C	Sell 1.0 call at C
Buy debt worth $X \div (1 + RF)$	Sell debt
Sell 1.0 put at P	Buy 1.0 put at P

c.
Write Put
Buy 1.0 call
Short sell 1.0 stock
Buy debt worth $X \div (1 + RF)$

5.
Buy warehouse	$1.0000 million
Borrow 1-year debt	0.9174 (1.0 ÷ 1.09)
Buy insurance	0.0100
Call cost	0.1926 million

6.
	Value at Expiration		
	High = 80 Low = 50 Range		
1.0 share	$80	$50	$30
1.0 call	20	0	20

For each 1.0 call traded, trade two-thirds share of stock.

Buy two-third share	53.33	33.33
Write 1.0 call	(20.00)	—
Net	33.33	33.33

So: $2/3(\$60) - \$10.23 = \$33.33 \div (1 + RF)$
and RF = 11.96%

7. a.
	Call A	Call B	Call C	Call D
$d1$	0.70	0.25	−0.14	0.08
$d2$	0.40	−0.05	−0.44	−0.35
$N(d1)$	0.7580	0.5987	0.4443	0.5319
$N(d2)$	0.6554	0.4800	0.3300	0.3632
Call	16.12	10.62	6.72	11.77

$P = 0.3446[70 \div (e^{0.12 \times 0.25})] - 0.242(80) = 4.05$

b. $P = -80 + [70 \div (e^{0.12 \times 0.25})] + 16.12 = 4.05$

9. a. PV of Div = $[1 \div (e^{0.12 \times 0.25})] + [1 \div (e^{0.12 \times 0.5})] = 1.91$
Stock value to use in call option model:

$= 65 - 1.91 = 63.09$

Call value = 10.45

$$= \$63.09\,(0.7019) - [60 \div e^{0.5}]\,(0.5987)$$

9.   Standard deviation of continuous returns = 8.22%.

10.   The calls should have identical ISD values. Since call A has the smaller ISD, its price is undervalued relative to call B. Buy 1.0 call A and write 0.8 call B (0.4 ÷ 0.5).

Chapter 19

6. a.

	Pess.	Expected	Opt.
G	7.25%	8.50%	9.60%
K	13.00%	13.50%	14.00%
D_0	50.00	46.08	44.00
D_1	53.63	50.00	48.22
Price	932	1,000	1,095

Chapter 20

11. a. After-tax on taxable issue: 0.04416 = 0.064
    (1 − 0.31)
    After-tax on muni issue: 0.045
    Thus, the muni wins on an after-tax basis in this situation.

    b. If savings are made into a tax-sheltered savings plan, tax-sheltered securities should not be held.

    c. After-tax value of municipal bond investment:

    $40,132.92 = (1.045)^{40}\ \$6,900$

    After-tax value of tax-sheltered investment:

    $82,511.45 = (1.064)^{40}\ \$10,000$
    $\qquad\qquad -031[(1.064)^{40}\ \$10,000]$

Chapter 21

2.   Arithmetic Average Return =

      $(20 - 12 + 15 + 3) \div 4 = 6.5\%$

      Geometric Average Return =

      $(1.2 \times 0.88 \times 1.15 \times 1.03)^{1/4} - 1 = 5.75\%$

3.   Find R in:

      $$10,000 = \sum_{t=1}^{8} - \frac{1,000}{(1+R)^t} + \frac{25,000}{(1+R)^8}$$

      R = 5.455% per quarter

      or 23.67% per year: $1.05455^4 - 1.0 = 0.2367$

The 23.67% return is a dollar weighted return. The 20% return reported by the investment manager is probably a time weighted return.

4. a.

Period	(1 + R)
May 30–June 15	10 ÷ 15 = 0.6666
June 15–June 30	36,360 ÷ 20,000 = 1.818

Full month = (0.6666)(1.818) − 1.0 = 21.19%

   b. Find R in:

   $$15,000 = \frac{-10,000}{(1+R)} + \frac{36,360}{(1+R)^2}$$

   $$= 25.89\% \text{ per 15-day interval}$$

   or $1.2589^2 - 1.0 = 58.48\%$ monthly

7. $8.5\% = 3.0\% + B_T\,(8.0\% - 3.0\%)$; so $B_T = 1.1$

      $(B_a - 1.1)(8.0\% - 3.0\%) = 1.0\%$; so $B_a = 1.3$

8. a.

	AMF	Putnam
Sharpe	2.58 ÷ 6.96 = 0.3707	1.64 ÷ 9.36 = 0.1752
Treynor	2.58 ÷ 0.75 = 3.44	1.64 ÷ 1.00 = 1.64
Jensen	0.96	−0.49

   c. AMF was more diversified as evidenced by the larger R^2.

   d. Putnam has the greater systematic (beta) risk.

9. a.

	McMaster	SP 500	DJIA
Average	−3.39	−1.28	−1.78
Beta:			
SP 500	0.89	1.00	NA
DJIA	0.73	NA	1.00
Standard Deviation	24.25	21.5	22.77
Sharpe Treynor:	−0.1397	−0.059	−0.078
SP 500	−3.80	−1.27	NA
DJIA	−4.64	NA	−1.78

These values are based on excess returns and using (N − 1) in standard deviation calculations.

Acknowledgments

Rosario Benavides, "Market Value of Publicly Traded Fixed Income Securities" from *International Bond Market Analysis,* August 1995. Copyright © 1995 Salomon Brothers Inc. Reprinted by permission. Although the information in this chart had been obtained from sources that Salomon Brothers believes to be reliable, Salomon does not guarantee its accuracy, and such information may be incomplete or condensed. All figures included in this chart constitute Salomon's judgment as of the original publication date.

"Percentage Bid-Ask Spreads" excerpted from T. J. George, G. Kaul and M. Nimalendran, "Estimation of Bid-Ask Spread and Its Components: A New Approach" in *The Review of Financial Studies, Volume 4* by Oxford University Press. Copyright © 1991. Reprinted by permission of Oxford University Press, Inc.

"Typical Full-Service and Discount Broker Commissions" adapted from "Spot the Bargains Using the 1994 Discount Broker Survey" in *American Association of Independent Investors Journal,* January 1994. Reprinted by permission of American Association of Independent Investors, 625 N. Michigan Ave., Ste. 1900, Chicago, IL 60611.

"Beta Estimates Move to 1.0" from M. Blume, "On the Assessment of Risk" in *Journal of Finance,* Vol. 6, no. 1 (March 1971), pp. 1–10. New York University. Reprinted by permission.

"Predictability of Beta Values" from M. Blume, "Betas and Their Regression Tendencies" in *Journal of Finance,* Vol. 10, no.3 (June 1975), pp. 758–796. New York University. Reprinted by permission.

"Results of the King Study" adapted from B. King, "Market and Industry Factors in Stock Price Behavior" in *Journal of Business,* Vol. 39 (January 1966).pp. 139–140. Reprinted by permission of the University of Chicago Press.

"Determinants of Portfolio Returns" from "Common Stock Management in the 1960s" in *Journal of Portfolio Management,* Winter 1990. This copyrighted material is reprinted with permission from Journal of Portfolio Management, a publication of Institutional Investor Inc., 488 Madison Avenue, New York, NY 10022.

"Douglas Test of CAPM" from G. Douglas, "Risk in the Equity Markets: An Empirical Appraisal of Market Efficiency" in *Yale Economic Essays,* Vol. 9, no. 1 (1969).

"Fama-French Cross-Sectional Regression Results" adapted from Fama & French, "The Cross-Section of Expected Stock Returns" in *Journal of Finance,* Vol. 47 (June 1992). New York University. Reprinted by permission.

"The Performance of Past Winner and Loser Portfolios" from W. DeBont and R. Thaler, "Does the Stock Market Overreact?" in *Journal of Finance,* Vol. 11, no. 3 (July 1985). New York University. Reprinted by permission.

"Position Duration Management (Page 1)" from The Bloomberg terminal. Copyright © 1995 Bloomberg Financial Markets. All rights reserved. Reprinted by permission of Bloomberg Financial Markets.

"Stock Price Movement Around Stock Splits Incurring Dividend Policy Changes" from E. Fama, L. Fisher, M. Jensen and R. Roll, "The Adjustment of Stock Prices to New Information" in *International Economic Review,* February 1969. Copyright © 1969 International Economic Review. Reprinted by permission of the publisher and E. Fama.

"Evidence on Unexpected Earnings" from Rendleman et al., "Empirical Anomalies Based on Unexpected Earnings and Importance of the Risk Adjustments" in *Journal of Financial Economics,* November 1982, Vol. 3, p. 285. Reprinted by permission of *Journal of Financial Economics.*

"Position Duration Management (Page 3)" from The Bloomberg terminal. Copyright © 1995 Bloomberg Financial Markets. All rights reserved. Reprinted by permission of Bloomberg Financial Markets.

"Naive Bond Diversification" from R. McEnally and C. Boardman, "Aspects of Corporate Bond Portfolio Diversification" in *The Journal of Financial Research,* Spring 1979. Reprinted by permission of *Journal of Financial Research*, Arizona State University.

"Yield Curve—US Treasury" from The Bloomberg terminal. Copyright © 1995 Bloomberg Financial Markets. All rights reserved. Reprinted by permission of Bloomberg Financial Markets.

Illustration from *S&P Stock Guide,* reprinted by permission of Standard & Poor's, a division of the McGraw-Hill Companies.

Illustration from *Moody's Handbook of Common Stock,* Summer 1995. Preprinted by permission of Moody's Investor Service, NY.

Illustration from *Value Line Investment Survey.* Reprinted by permission of Value Line Publishing, Inc., NY.

"US Equity Management and Ownership" adapted from *Pensions & Investments,* May 15, 1995. Copyright © 1995 Crain Communications, Inc. Reprinted with permission.

"Growth of US Mutual Funds" from *1995 Mutual Fund Factbook.* Reprinted by permission of Investment Company Institute, Washington, DC.

"Distribution of Household Financial Assets" from *1995 Mutual Fund Factbook.* Reprinted by permission of Investment Company Institute, Washington, DC.

"1994 Mutual Fund Asset as a Percentage of Secondary Market Security Values" from *1995 Mutual Fund Factbook.* Reprinted by permission of Investment Company Institute, Washington, DC.

"World Mutual Fund Assets" from *1995 Mutual Fund Factbook.* Reprinted by permission of Investment Company Institute,

Illustration from *Morningstar Mutual Funds,* October 27, 1995. Reprinted by permission of Morningstar, Inc.

"IFCG Price Index: Correlations With S&P 500 and Local Indexes" from *Emerging Stock Markets Factbook 1995.* Copyright © 1995 The World Bank. Reprinted by permission.

"Ex Post Average Annual Returns and Standard Deviations for US Investors" from "Optimal International Asset Allocation" in *Journal of Portfolio Management,* Fall 1982. This copyrighted material is reprinted with permission from *Journal of Portfolio Management,* a publication of Institutional Investor, Inc., 488 Madison Avenue, New York, NY 10022.

"Answers to Commonly Asked Questions about Currency Trading" by George Anders, from *Wall Street Journal,* September 17, 1992. Reprinted by permission of *Wall Street Journal,* © 1992 Dow Jones & Company, Inc. All rights reserved.

"Net Cross-border Equity Flows Into:" and "Net Cross-border Equity Flows From:" reprinted from *The Guide to World Equity Markets 1994/95.* Reprinted by permission of Euromoney Publications PLC. For more information, please call (London) 0–11–44–171–779–8562.

"USDX Component Currencies" from informational literature by FINEX. Reprinted by permission.

"ECU Component Currencies" from informational literature by FINEX. Reprinted by permission.

"The Hamburger Standard," adapted from "Big MacCurrencies" in *The Economist,* April 15, 1995. Copyright © 1995 The Economist Newspaper Group, Inc. Reprinted with permission. Further reproduction prohibited.

"Developed Equity Markets" adapted from *Emerging Stock Markets Factbook 1995.* Copyright © 1995 The World Bank. Reprinted by permission.

"Emerging Equity Markets (1994)" adapted from *Emerging Stock Markets Factbook 1995.* Copyright © 1995 The World Bank. Reprinted by permission.CFA ® Exam Questions are reprinted by permission from *The CFA Study Guide, 1992.* Copyright © 1992, Association for Investment Management and Research, Charlottesville, VA. All rights reserved.

"Summary of AIMR Performance Presentation Standards: Requirements" from *The Report of the Performance Presentation Standards Implementation Committee.* Copyright © 1993 Association for Investment Management and Research, Charlottesville, VA. All rights reserved. Reprinted by permission.

"Summary of AIMR Performance Presentation Standards: Recommendations" from *The Report of the Performance Presentation Standards Implementation Committee.* Copyright © 1993 Association for Investment Management and Research, Charlottesville, VA. All rights reserved. Reprinted by permission.

Association for Investment Management and Research Code of Ethics and Standards of Professional Conduct. Copyright © 1990 Association for Investment Management and Research, Charlottesville, VA. All rights reserved. Reprinted by permission.

CFA ® Exam Questions are reprinted by permission from *The CFA Study Guide, 1992.* Copyright © 1992, Association for Investment Management and Research, Charlottesville, VA. All rights reserved.

Index

Investors, individual (*continued*)
  sources of information for, 6,
    114–117
  use of professional management,
    561–564, 595, 810–816
Investors, institutional. *See* Institutional
  investors
Isabella, C.F.A., Warren J., 94–95
Israel, 93t
Italy, 93t

J

J. P. Morgan, 611
Jamaica Agreement, 608, 609f
January effect, 350, 352–353, 366, 370
Japan, 92, 93t
Jensen's alpha (Jensen performance
  index), 273, 864–866, 868, 872
Jobber, 154
Johnson & Johnson, 278t
Johnson, C.F.A., Dennis A., 515–517
Junk bonds, 394, 498, 757

K

Keogh plan, 835, 839
Kidder, Peabody and Company, 88
Kotler, Harold, 755
Kritzman, C.F.A., Mark, 236–238
Kushner, C.F.A., David, 491–492

L

Large-block trades. *See under* Trades
Law of one price, 293, 304
Lead underwriter, 121
Lehman Brothers Bond Indices, 73f
Lehman Brothers Government/Corporate
  Bond Index, 439
Lender of shares, 145–146, 147
Lenders, maturity preferences of, 390
Lending portfolio, 264, 239–241,
  259–260, 261, 273, 742
Letter of credit, 79, 679–680
Leverage, 291, 533, 850t
  with derivative securities, 655, 678,
    699, 720, 732, 746
Leveraged buyouts, 399
Liability duration, 426–427, 428,
  433–436
Limit book, 128, 128n8, 130, 131, 136,
  156
Limit order, 128, 128n8, 131, 136, 156,
  648
Limit trader, 128
Line of credit, 77
Liquidation, of firm, 85, 86, 90, 91
Liquidation value, 474, 523
Liquidity, 149, 541. *See also*
  Marketability
  of bonds, 85, 372, 396, 407, 409, 444
  of closed-end funds, 103, 595
  of commercial paper, 77, 171
  of derivatives, 511
  of futures, 678
  in global market, 96, 599
  of mutual funds, 581, 590

as portfolio constraint, 60, 62t, 64,
  547, 742, 753, 757, 765, 814
provided by mortgage-backed
  securities, 442–443
in secondary markets, 20–21, 21n10,
  25, 127, 491
of STRIPS, 84
of swaps, 107
of U.S. agency issues, 84
Liquidity preference theory, 390–392,
  408
Liquidity premium, 382, 390–392, 408
Liquidity trader, 130
Load fees, 101, 581–585
Locals, 648
London Interbank Offer Rate (LIBOR),
  86–87, 106, 107
London Stock Exchange (LSE), 153–154
Long position, 104, 105, 145, 147, 745,
  781, 835
  of equity vs. debt claims, 393–394,
    408, 497–498
  on futures, 644, 654, 655, 661–665,
    666
  in options, 691–693, 695–698, 707,
    711–713, 716–717
Lotus software, 545
Lump sum distribution, 28, 836
Lutz, Friedrich, 387
Lynch, Peter, 517, 812, 815t

M

Macaulay, Frederick, 423
Macaulay duration, 423–424, 430
Magellan Fund, 812
Maintenance margin, 140, 143, 144, 145
Major Market Index, 717
Management
  of firm, and fundamental analysis,
    527, 535–537
  of investments. *See* Portfolio
    management; Professional
    management
Management forecasts, effect on stock
  prices, 343, 362
Manager assignment statement, 752
Managing underwriter, 121
Margin, 140–145, 147, 240, 273
  on futures contracts, 657, 663, 669
Marginal call, 143–145
Marginal utility, 214–215
Mark-to-market, 143, 646n3, 648, 649,
  657, 669, 746
Markese, Ph.D., John, 8–9
Marketability, 365, 753. *See also*
  Liquidity
  and SEC registration, 123, 128
  of various security types, 78, 81, 83,
    84, 85, 155, 444, 450, 452, 657
Market conditions, 747, 748, 749f
Market effects, on stock return
  variability, 305t
Market equilibrium, 259, 261–262
Market maker, 134–135, 149, 147, 149,
  153, 154, 156, 407

Market model, 274–277, 283, 289–291,
  349, 354, 355–357, 360, 364, 508,
  864, 871
Market order, 136, 648
Market portfolio, 164, 272
  and APT, 303, 324
  in CAPM, 259–268, 269, 282, 283,
    306t, 307t, 310, 313–316, 470,
    742, 780, 861, 868
  definition of, 257, 259, 264
  expected returns, 306t, 307t
  market model of, 274–276, 283
  in performance evaluation, 870, 871,
    872t, 873, 876
  returns on, 279, 302, 304, 306t, 307t,
    308, 356
  tests of, 314–316
Market risk. *See* Systematic risk
Markets. See *also* Efficient market;
  specific market
  benefits of, 19–22, 25
  emerging, 626, 627–632, 812, 818
  frictionless, 282, 340, 595
  global, 10, 12–14, 22–23, 25, 79, 81,
    82t, 90, 91f, 93–96, 106, 152–154,
    264, 265t, 600t, 601f. *See also*
    Global investment
  growth in, 14, 25
  over-the-counter. *See* Over-the-
    counter market
  primary, 7, 19, 20, 23, 24, 25
  regulation of, 151–152. *See also*
    Securities and Exchange
    Commission
  secondary, 7–10, 19–21, 21n10, 23,
    24, 25, 76, 97, 102, 107
  securitization of, 23, 87, 88, 442
  structure of, 6–10
Market saturation and growth stage, of
  product life cycle, 526
Market segmentation theory, 382–384,
  390, 408
Market timing. *See* Tactical asset
  allocation; Timing
Market-to-book ratio, 489
Market-to-value
  of bond at horizon date, 419–420,
    423, 430
  of convertible bond, 403–406
  of tranche, 463
Market value added (MVA), 487–489
Market value weighting, 282, 508, 511,
  575, 710
  in performance evaluation, 849t,
    858, 871
Markowitz, Harry, 161, 230, 231
Marzol, Adolfo, 442–443
Mature and stable growth stage, of
  product life cycle, 526
Maturity
  of bankers' acceptances, 79
  of bonds, 71, 81, 372–375, 378, 401,
    403, 408, 439n9, 833
  of bonds, and duration, 421,
    423–424, 429–430, 448–449

KEY EQUATIONS

Basic Security Valuation

Basic Valuation Model

$$P_0 = \frac{CF_1}{(1+K)} + \frac{CF_2}{(1+K)^2} \cdots \frac{CF_N}{(1+K)^N}$$

Constant Dividend Growth

$$P_0 = D_0(1+G) \div (K-G)$$

Sustainable Dividend Growth

$$G = ROE * b$$

Return Measurement

Single Period Return

$$R_t = \frac{P_t - P_{t-1}}{P_{t-1}} + \frac{C_t}{P_{t-1}}$$

Unit Value at Period T

$$UV_T = \prod_{t=1}^{T} (1 + R_t)$$

Arithmetic Average Return

$$\overline{R} = \left(\sum_{t=1}^{T} R_t \right) \div T$$

Geometric Average Return

$$\overline{G} = [UV_T]^{1/T} - 1.0$$

Expected Security Returns

Fisher Equation

$$RF = (1 + pr)(1 + E(I)) - 1.0$$

Capital Market Line

$$E(R_p) = RF + \sigma_P(RP_M \div \sigma_M)$$

Security Market Line

$$E(R_i) = RF + \beta_i(RP_M)$$

Expected Portfolio Return

$$E(R_p) = \sum_{i=1}^{N} X_i E(R_i)$$